The
Columbia
Guide to
STANDARD
AMERICAN
ENGLISH

The Columbia Guide to STANDARD AMERICAN ENGLISH

Kenneth G. Wilson

Columbia University Press

NEW YORK

Columbia University Press
New York   Chichester, West Sussex

Copyright © 1993 Columbia University Press
All rights reserved

Library of Congress Cataloging-in-Publication Data
Wilson, Kenneth G. (Kenneth George)
    The Columbia guide to standard American English / by Kenneth G.
  Wilson.
        p.   cm.
      ISBN 0–231–06988–X
      1. English language—United States—Usage—Dictionaries.
    2. English language—Usage—Dictionaries.   3. Americanisms—
  Dictionaries.   I. Title.
  PE2835.W55   1993
  428′.00973—dc20   92–37887
                                                          CIP

Casebound editions of Columbia University Press books
are Smyth-sewn and printed on permanent
and durable acid-free paper.

Printed in the United States of America
c 10 9 8 7 6 5 4 3 2 1

To Marilyn

ACKNOWLEDGMENTS

For their help—whether in useful lore, fruitful suggestions, generous service, steady encouragement, wise counsel, great patience, or in all of these—I'm grateful to family, friends, colleagues, former students, readers, lexicographical acquaintances, libraries and their staff members, and my publishers. I'm especially grateful to my editors, Anne McCoy, James Raimes, and Sarah St. Onge, and I also want to express my gratitude to the Homer Babbidge Library of The University of Connecticut, the Mansfield (Connecticut) Town Library, Irving Allen, Raymond Anselment, Robert Baker, Eve Bayrock, Frederick Biggs, Bill Bramlette, Lois Brandt, Joseph Cary, Irving Cummings, Jack Davis, Yakira Frank, Brinley Franklin, John Gatta, Stephanie Haas, Joan Hall, David Hankins, Robert Hasenfratz, Thomas Jambeck, David Kapp, Frances Kim, Nancy Kline, Julia Kocich, John Manning, John McDonald, Casey Miller, William Moynihan, Robert Pearson, Sam Pickering, Donald O'Hara, Arnold Orza, Richard Reynolds, Thomas Roberts, Barbara Rosen, William Rosen, Kim Schleicher, Helen Smith, Suzanne Staubach, Milton Stern, Norman Stevens, Kate Swift, Katherine Tardif, Dennis Thornton, Marilyn Waniek, Thomas Wilcox, Roger Wilkenfeld, Rebecca Wilson, and Marilyn Wilson.

Many, many thanks to all.

INTRODUCTION

Standard American Usage

Standard American English usage is linguistic good manners, sensitively and accurately matched to context—to listeners or readers, to situation, and to purpose. But because our language is constantly changing, mastering its appropriate usage is not a one-time task like learning the multiplication tables. Instead, we are constantly obliged to adjust, adapt, and revise what we have learned. Our language can always serve us effectively if we use its resources wisely; to keep itself ready to serve us it continually changes and varies to meet our needs. If we are a practical and hard-headed people, it will come to reflect that fact; if we become technologically and scientifically venturesome, our language will change to meet that need; if we become poets, it will change to accommodate the demands of our poetry; and if we are filled with prejudice or hatred, our language will reflect that too.

Failing to keep our usage—our words, meanings, pronunciations, spellings, grammatical structures, and idiomatic expressions—abreast of changing and varying standards may earn us moderate disapproval if a usage is doubtful, vigorous disapproval or outright rejection if it is wholly inappropriate, substandard, or taboo. Nor is there just one immutable standard, one unvarying code of manners. Influential people fully in command of the standard language speak and write it at different levels to meet the demands of different contexts. A great many of us use American English, and we differ a good deal in what we wish to communicate to one another. Furthermore, we use this language in a wide range of situations and for many different purposes. Pillow talk between couples differs from the ways each talks to children, neighbors, colleagues, friends, acquaintances, complete strangers, or to groups of all kinds and sizes. Our vocabulary, our syntax, and every other aspect of our usage vary with the person or persons we are addressing, with the purpose of our utterance, with the situation, and indeed with the entire context: an address from the podium of a convention hall filled with political partisans demands language very different from that required for a relaxed discussion among a few close friends. Our speech can vary considerably between the social chatter before the meeting and the business discussion in the meeting itself.

What is true of contextual variation in our speech is just as true of contextual variation in our writing: to whom, when, where, under what circumstances, and for what purpose we write can make many differences in what we write and how the reader understands it. The note to the package delivery driver, the love letter or the letter of condolence, the letter to the editor, and the committee report require different language. Writing for publication has its variations too: because we rarely ever meet our readers, we must try to imagine accurately what they are like and try to anticipate and meet their expectations.

Most of the words, meanings, and grammatical structures we use belong to everybody's English usage. All English—British, Canadian, or American; Standard, Common, or Vulgar—has *dogs* and *cats,* verbs and direct objects. But the differences, although relatively few when measured against the size of the whole language, stand out clearly and sometimes even leap out at us. Most of us know a few of the "funny" expressions the British and the Australians use; many of us are aware of the "funny" way many Canadians say *schedule.* But perhaps because relative to the whole they are so few, these differences can be fiercely significant. It is not just dialectal variations such as those between American *trucks* and *molasses* and British *lorries* and *treacle;* even more important to us are the everyday variations within American English itself: What makes southerners sound so different from the rest of us? (The Southern and South Midland regional dialects differ importantly from each other as well as from other American dialects.) How should we view *ain't?* (Standard English can use it, but only in strictly limited contexts.) And is *irregardless* a word or not? (It is, but its inadvertent use in Standard English can mean real trouble for the user.)

Hence our need to know which locutions must be limited to casual contexts in the spoken language only, which ones should be limited mainly to pulpit or platform, which ones are appropriate in all spoken and written contexts, and which ones should be restricted to use at, say, formal written levels only: *Mr. and Mrs. John Robert Smith request the pleasure of your company at a reception in honor of their daughter, Mary Jane Smith* is no more the appropriate way to write an informal invitation than is *the party of the first part* suitable for reaching oral agreement on the stakes in a friendly card game. We must match the level of our language to the context in which we use it. When we blunder in our choices or misread the tastes and expectations of those we are addressing, we can raise eyebrows, cause misunderstandings, or even shock our listeners or readers to a point where they truly cannot hear whatever it is we intend to convey. Any small inappropriateness in usage may hamper effectiveness, and a single big blunder can destroy it. And remember: when we assess the experience, temper, tastes, and expectations of our listeners or readers, their receptivity will vary just as our own can; some of them will be linguistically conservative, some linguistically liberal, and some in between. Best advice on this score is still Alexander Pope's, expressed in his famous comparison of fashions in dress and other manners with fashions in language:

In words as fashions the same rule will hold,
Alike fantastic if too new or old:
Be not the first by whom the new are tried,
Nor yet the last to lay the old aside.
An Essay on Criticism, II.133–136.

The Columbia Guide

This guide to Standard American usage tries to help you keep up with the new and keep track of the old, so that you can make your language fit all the contexts you encounter whenever you speak or write. It seeks to help you make some of the choices Standard users must make if their usage is to be what they want it to be and what their listeners and readers expect it to be. There are many variables at work, and answers can only infrequently be both simple and accurate. Much more often, the accurate answer to a usage question begins, "It depends." And what it depends on most often is where you are, who you are, who your listeners or readers are, and what your purpose in speaking or writing is.

Most usage guides address themselves primarily or even exclusively to writers and problems of writing and thus may inadvertently lead us to infer that we should try to speak the language exactly as our best writers write it. But neither our best writers nor most of the rest of us really talk like books; some of our language must of course be suitable for use in books, but usage problems are by no means limited to those we encounter in writing for publication. Most of us do most of our communicating orally—face to face or over the telephone—and much of the rest of it in informally written notes, letters, and memos. Being able to match our spoken levels of usage to these differing contexts is every bit as important as is being able to match our formal written English to the demands of its contexts.

Commentators have long argued the virtues and defects of prescriptive and descriptive methods of treating Standard usage. This guide prescribes whenever real rules make prescription a sensible way of proceeding. But for most grammatical and usage questions description-based generalizations, not rules, provide better answers (see the entry RULES AND GENERALIZATIONS), because they take into account both the changes and the variations that are always in progress in a living language. For further discussion of how best to interpret the advice this guide offers, see the entry PRESCRIPTIVE AND DESCRIPTIVE GRAMMAR AND USAGE and the entries CONSERVATIVE USAGE and LIBERAL USAGE.

The Columbia Guide to Standard American English is unique in showing systematically how today's language is appropriately used in five levels of Standard American speech, ranging from the most relaxed conversation to the most elevated public address, and in three levels of Standard American writing, ranging from the most informal of personal notes to the most formal of printed publications. The figure schematically displays these levels of speech and writing and indicates the relative relationships among them and the cluster labels under which some of them fall. It is based on the work of two linguists. Martin Joos, in a very influential little book, *The Five Clocks* (1962, 1967), described

The Levels of Standard American English

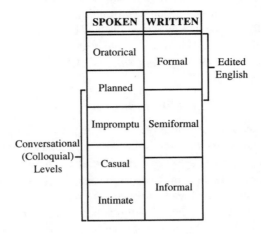

five distinctive context-related "styles" that we employ when we use our language. H. A. Gleason, Jr., in his *Linguistics and English Grammar* (1965), expanded and revised Joos's scheme, describing these contexts as five "keys" (rather than "styles") particularly applicable to the usage variations in our spoken language. He also described three somewhat broader categories against which to measure variations in the standard written language.

My system owes much to Joos's scheme and even more to Gleason's elaboration and refinement of it. I have substituted the term *levels* for Gleason's "keys," because *levels* seems to have embedded itself in the national consciousness when we talk of usage, and I have applied it to both spoken and written usage in order to suggest some of the connections between them. I have used the labels *Impromptu* and *Planned* for Gleason's "consultative" and "deliberative," seeking to make them readily accessible to general reader and language professional alike. I have also added the cluster labels *Conversational* and *Edited English*.

Many words, idiomatic expressions, meanings, pronunciations, spellings, and grammatical and rhetorical structures are found at every level of speech and writing and are appropriate in every context. The verb *goes* in *The family goes to Maine in August* is one such. Other uses of that word, however, may be appropriate only in limited Standard contexts, as is the noun *go* in *We'll have a go at it,* which is Standard only at Conversational levels or in the Informal or Semiformal writing that imitates them. And still other uses of *go* are inappropriate anywhere in Standard spoken or written English: for example, the uninflected dialectal third person singular verb *go* in *She go to school at Central High* is Substandard.

In this guide, any entry containing no explicit label describes a Standard usage. Some entries, on the other hand, may cover sets of words or phrases, variously labeled Standard, Nonstandard (marked by usages found in and characteristic of Common English and some regional dialects), and Substandard

English (marked by and characteristic primarily of Vulgar English). Some items may be described as being in divided usage. Words and meanings may be further identified with labels such as *slang* (normally restricted to Impromptu speech or Informal writing), *jargon* (appropriate usually only in special speech communities), *profanity* (limited to severely restricted contexts), and *obscenity* (usually taboo), or with labels indicating the current status of the locution (*archaic, obsolescent,* and *obsolete*). Words and locutions may also be defined in terms of their acceptability to conservatives or purists, whose attitudes to the language contrast so strongly with those of liberals, for whom permissiveness, with all its implications for good and ill, is often the mode.

Each of the labels just mentioned, as well as those in the figure, has its own full entry in this guide, as do *level, context,* and nearly all other language-related terms that appear in the advice given in the guide's roughly sixty-five hundred usage entries. Whenever you encounter a language-related term of which you are unsure, seek the entry for it.

The entry words are of two sorts: those in all capital letters define, explain, and illustrate most of the grammatical and other linguistic terminology used throughout this guide. The entry words printed in lowercase letters are the usage items themselves—the words, phrases, spellings, pronunciations, combined forms, meanings, and idioms about which there are questions or division of opinion among Standard users, expressions about which problems of appropriateness frequently arise. Cross-references—of which there are many—appear in all small capital letters, most often at the end of entries. Cross-references generally consist of entry words up to the first mark of punctuation, coded with numbers for clarity where necessary. Variant pronunciations and variant spellings are presented with the version judged most frequent in Standard American English given first, the least frequent last. (See the section on pronunciation at the end of this introduction.) The sample entries on page xv illustrate the way the entries in this guide—in a single alphabetical list—typically present their information and advice.

Guide to Pronunciations

Where clear rhyme words will guide, they are provided: *snood* rhymes with *food*. Pronunciations are printed in italics: *ahead* is pronounced *uh-HED*. Hyphens separate syllables: *implicit* (*im-PLIS-it*) has three syllables, separated by the two hyphens. A syllable in all capital letters has a heavy, usually primary, stress: *knitted* is pronounced *NIT-id*. When a word has both primary and secondary or tertiary stresses, the syllable that receives primary stress is in boldface italic capital letters: *boldfaced* is pronounced ***BOLD-FAIST;*** *commander in chief* is pronounced *kuh-MAND-uhr-in-CHEEF;* secondary and tertiary stressed syllables in such words are in italic capital letters. So-called weak or unstressed syllables are in italic lowercase letters: *sofa* is pronounced *SO-fuh*.

Transcription of Stressed Vowel Sounds [1]

KAT = cat	*FAIT* = fate	*FAH-thur* = father
FAWN = fawn	*FRET* = fret	*FEET* = feet
FEIT = fight	*FIT* = fit	*FO* = foe
FOOD = food	*FOUND* = found	*FOIL* = foil
FUL = full	*FUHJ* = fudge	

Transcription of Unstressed Vowel Sounds [1]

HAP-en = happen   *LIV-id* = livid   *SO-fuh* = sofa

Transcription of Certain Vowels plus R [1]

PAHR = par	*PER* = pair[2]	*PIR* = peer
POR = pour	*POOR* = poor	*PUHR* = purr

Transcription of Consonant Sounds [1]

BED = bed	*DET* = debt	*FED* = fed
GET = get	*HED* = head	*JUHG* = jug
KAD = cad	*LAIM* = lame	*MAT* = mat
NET = net	*SING-uhr* = singer	*FING-guhr* = finger
PET = pet	*RED* = red	*SET* = set
TEN = ten	*VET* = vet	*YET* = yet
WICH = witch[3]	*HWICH* = which[3]	*CHUHRCH* = church
SHEEP = sheep	*THEI* = thigh[4]	*THEI* = thy[4]
A-zhuhr = azure	*VI-zhuhn* = vision	*mi-RAHZH* = mirage

---

1. The sounds under discussion here are in boldface for clarity; in the guide proper, boldface type in pronunciations generally denotes primary stress, except in certain instances where it highlights a particular sound under discussion.

2. See the entry for MERRY, MARY, MARRY for comment on certain regional variations.

3. Some Standard dialects pronounce *which* as a homophone of *witch*.

4. Note that the voiced *th* sound in *thy* is printed with a ligature, to distinguish it from the voiceless *th* sound in *thigh*, which is printed without a ligature.

Entry words are in boldface type.

Meanings appear within quotation marks, with amplifications or variations within parentheses.

Sounds within parentheses in a pronunciation are optional.

Entries that would otherwise be identical in abbreviated cross-references are differentiated with numbers.

Subsequent occurrences of the entry word within its own entry are in italics.

Entry words in capital letters are language-related terms.

Most language-related terms are discussed in entries of their own.

Pronunciations are in italics, with hyphens between syllables. See the Guide to Pronunciation for a description of the transcription system.

Parts of speech are in italics and may be abbreviated.

Words cited as words are in italics.

Cross-references are in small capital letters, usually at the ends of entries. Two or more are separated by semicolons.

Examples are in italics. Alternatives or asides in examples appear within square brackets.

Boldface type is sometimes used to emphasize an example within an illustrating phrase or sentence.

Syllables receiving primary stress are in boldface italic capital letters; syllables receiving secondary stress are in italic capital letters; unstressed syllables are in italic lowercase letters.

adieu (*interj., n.*) This phrase, borrowed from the French, is a shortened farewell, "[I leave you] to God." Like *goodbye* ("God be with you"), *adieu* has become a noun. The plural, spelled either *adieus* or *adieux,* is pronounced *uh-D(Y)OOZ,* although some Americans may retain a nearly French pronunciation of *adieux: ah-DYU.* See FOREIGN PLURALS.

advance 1, advanced (*adjs.*) These mean very different things: *advance* means "ahead of the others, earlier than others": *Please give me advance notice. The advance team will prepare the ground for the candidate's visit.* *Advanced* means "beyond the elementary level" or "far out front in concept and development": *I took an advanced course in French. Their ideas on child care are thought to be advanced. Her symptoms suggest that her case is quite far advanced.*

advance 2, advancement (*nn.*) When these are synonymous, *advance* is the more common: *We're in favor of the advance [advancement] of science. Advance* means "the course forward," while *advancement* can refer to "the policy designed to foster a course forward." In some specialized senses, however, an *advance* is "money given before it is earned or due, in order to assist writers or salesmen to meet their expenses," and in institutional life, an *advancement* is often "a promotion to higher rank."

ADVERB (*n.*), **ADVERBIAL** (*adj., n.*) An *adverb* is a part of speech that modifies either a verb (*He ran **swiftly***), an adjective (***enormously** large*), or another *adverb* (***extremely** badly built*). *Very* is the *adverb* most frequently used, particularly because it is also an intensifier.

The adjective *adverbial* refers to words, phrases, or clauses that function as adverbs; the noun *adverbial* applies to any locution—a word, a phrase, or a clause—that behaves *adverbially.* In *She cried **as though her heart would break,*** the last clause is *adverbial,* modifying the verb *cried.*

aerate (*v.*) is pronounced as either a two-syllable word (*ER-ate*) or a three (*AI-uhr-AIT*); it has no medial letter -*i*- in its spelling, and it is never pronounced *ER-ee-AIT.*

The
Columbia
Guide to
STANDARD
AMERICAN
ENGLISH

A

a, an (*determiner, art., adj.*) Choose *a* or *an* according to what sounds right, and you will almost certainly be correct: most variations are Standard English. Americans usually use *a* (pronounced *uh* when unstressed) before words beginning with consonant sounds, as in *a dog,* and *an* (pronounced *uhn* or occasionally *an,* especially at higher levels of speech) before words beginning with vowel sounds, as in *an apple.* But when *a* and *an* receive heavier stress than the nouns they precede, as in *a boy, not **two** boys,* and *an army, not **several** armies,* they rhyme with *day* and *can,* respectively. Atypical and Nonstandard is any use of *a* with words beginning with a vowel sound. Using *an* before words spelled with initial vowels but pronounced beginning with consonant sounds, as in *an union,* is rare and may seem affected.

Use of *a* and *an* varies before words beginning with *h-.* When the *h* is silent as in *honor,* use *an;* when it is always sounded, as in *horror,* use *a.* When a spoken *h* is sounded in one context but not in another, as with *hysterical,* use either *a* (*uh his-TER-i-kuhl WIT-nes*) or *an* (*an is-TER-i-kuhl WIT-nes*); Edited English requires *a* rather than *an,* regardless of which way readers might pronounce it aloud. When the sound of initial *h-* is in divided usage, as in *herb,* use either *an UHRB* or *uh HUHRB,* depending on your pronunciation of the noun.

a-, an- (*prefixes*) In some applications, these prefixes derive from the Old English prepositions *an* and *on,* meaning "in," as in *asleep, afoot.* The Old English prefix *a-,* meaning "out," "out of," or "up," gives us *arise,* and from still another Old English prefix, *of-,* meaning "of" or "off," we get words like *akin.* Nautical terms alone made from Old English prefixes are impressively numerous: consider *aback, abaft, abeam, adrift, ahead, alee, astern,* and *awash.* The Greek prefix *a-/an-,* meaning "not," yields another larger group of words, as in *anemic, amoral, atypical,* and *anesthetic.* If the word to which one of these prefixes is to attach itself begins with a consonant, the prefix will be spelled *a-* as in *apolitical;* if with a vowel, the prefix will be spelled *an-* as in *anarchy.* See AFFIX.

aback, abaft See A-; TAKE ABACK.

ABBREVIATIONS are variously shortened forms of words: *AC* for *alternating current, CT* for *Connecticut, no.* for *number, D.D.S.* for *Doctor of Dental Surgery, ZIP* for *zone improvement plan* and *ZIP code, pro* for *professional, vet* for *veteran* or *veterinarian, Fannie Mae* for *Federal National Mortgage Association, E.R.A.* for *Earned Run Average,* and *sonar* for *sound navigation ranging* illustrate several types. All are pronounced either letter name by letter name (*E.R.A.,* for example, is pronounced *EE-AHR-AI*) or as spelling pronunciations of what thus become new words: *sonar* is pronounced *SO-NAHR.* For the several sorts of *abbreviations,* see ACRONYMS; APHERESIS; APHESIS; CLIPPING; INITIALISMS. For comment on punctuation, see PERIOD (1). On pronunciation, see SPELLING PRONUNCIATIONS.

abdicate, abrogate, arrogate (*vv.*) To *abdicate* is "to give up a high position such as a kingship," as in *Edward VIII abdicated the British throne,* or "to give up a right or fail to exercise a responsibility," as in *He abdicated his responsibility and let his family fend for itself.* To *abrogate* is "to repeal, cancel, or annul an agreement or treaty," as in *The dictator abrogated agreements that no longer suited his purposes.* To *arrogate* is "to seize or appropriate wrongly to yourself," as in *The general arrogated all civilian authority to himself,* or "to attribute without reason" or "to ascribe as to a source," as in *He arrogated to the prince several inflammatory statements, each suitable as a basis for opening hostilities.*

abdomen (*n.*) The pronunciation *AB-duh-min* is more frequent than *ab-DO-min,* but both are Standard. See BELLY.

abeam See A-.

abettor, abetter (*n.*), meaning "someone who helps or incites others," occasionally takes on some of the pejorative senses attached to the verb *abet,* which is often used disparagingly. It has two Standard spellings, but *abettor* is the more frequent.

abhorrent (*adj.*), **abhorrence** (*n.*) The *h* is sounded. When *abhorrence* combines with a preposition, it nearly always takes *of* or *for: I have a great abhorrence of* [*for*] *funerals. Against* is rare but possible too. *Abhorrent* works in the other direction: the thing *abhorred* is the subject, and the adjective usually takes *to: Funerals are abhorrent to me.*

abide (*v.*) The past tense and past participle both take either of two forms: *abode* or *abided.* As past participle, *abidden* is now obsolete, and *abode* is usually limited to the sense of "resided in or at" and has an old-fashioned or literary ring. For all other uses the verb now follows the weak pattern, with *abided.* Currently the present tense appears most often, especially in the negative, as in *I can't abide his conceit* (which may have a regional ring), and in the combined form, *abide by,* meaning "follow, adhere to, obey": *She will abide by her mother's decision.*

ability, capacity (*nn.*) *Capacity* is applied to inanimate as well as animate things; *ability* refers mostly to people and animals. In combined use, *ability* takes *to* plus an infinitive, *capacity* takes *for,* in a prepositional phrase: *She has the ability to beat the current champion. He has a remarkable capacity for hard work. Capacity* with *for* is also used literally for what either persons or things can contain: *Teenaged stomachs* [*Teenagers*] *have an astonishing capacity for food.*

-ability See -IBILITY.

a bit See KIND OF.

abject (*adj.*) *Abject poverty* is a cliché, and in that use *abject* may be only an intensifier. In other uses it seems to retain its full meanings, "miserable, degraded, without self-respect, of the lowest kind": *He cowered at home, sunk in abject despair.*

abjure, adjure (*vv.*) Although they are both based on the Latin verb *jurare,* meaning "to swear," these two are rarely confused, probably because they mainly occur in Formal and Oratorical uses: *abjure* means "to give up, swear off, renounce, recant"; *adjure* means "to command, advise earnestly, entreat." See also AFFIX.

ablative 1 (*adj.*), **ablation** (*n.*), **ablate** (*v.*) The adjective *ablative* that is related to the verb *ablate,* "to wear away," and to the noun *ablation,* "a wearing away," is pronounced *uh-BLAI-tiv.*

ABLATIVE 2 (*adj., n.*), **ABLATIVE ABSOLUTE, ABLATIVE CASE** Latin has an *ablative case.* Latin's *ablative absolute* is a syntactically separate phrase, usually made up of a noun and a modifier, both in the *ablative case*; it works like a sentence modifier. English has no *ablative case,* but it has structures that grammarians have compared to *ablative absolutes: The homework completed, we hurried to the stadium.* The grammatical term *ablative* is stressed on the first syllable, *AB-luh-tiv,* as noun or adjective. See also ABSOLUTE CONSTRUCTIONS.

able (*adj.*) takes *to* plus an active infinitive, whether or not the subject is human: *She is able to hit high C. This review will be able to persuade anyone.* But if the infinitive is passive, the sentence is at least clumsy, and some Standard users strongly object to it: *He is able to be persuaded. My old car is able to be sold now.* Logically, neither *to be persuaded* nor *to be sold* is an ability possessed by the subject, which is what *being able* suggests, whereas *to hit high C* and *to persuade* are indeed abilities possessed by the subject. The Conversational levels may not always insist on such rigorous logic, but Edited English usually does. *To be able to* is a bit more constrained than the more frequent and more concise *can,* but either can suggest "has the strength to": *She is able to* [*she can*] *play the oboe.*

-able, -ible (*suffixes*) The only difficulty involves the spelling of the two unstressed vowels: because they're usually pronounced *uh,* it is impossible to tell from the sound which of these variant suffixes to tack on in writing. Both are derived from the Latin *habilis,* meaning "able." We got the *-able* ending chiefly from the many words we borrowed from French, especially during the Middle English period, and then used it to turn English words (mainly verbs) into adjectives, as in *lovable,* "easy to love" or "inspiring love," or *drinkable,* "fit for drinking." But we also borrowed many Latin words with the suffix already attached, and these typically were spelled *-ible.* As a result, we have many *-able* words and many *-ible* words, plus a few with variant spellings (e.g., *collectable/collectible, extendable/extendible, gullable/gullible, includable/includible, processable/processible*). But in *passible* (a rare word meaning "able to feel or suffer") and *passable* ("can be traveled or crossed" or "tolerable") and *impassible/impassable,* the spelling of the suffix marks a semantic difference: these are not variant spellings, but different words with different meanings. In the end, a dictionary is your only sure guide.

abnormal See SUBNORMAL.

abode (*n.*), meaning "place of residence," is bookish but Standard. See also ABIDE.

aborigine, Aborigine, Aboriginal (*nn.*) The lowercase noun refers to one of the original inhabitants of a region. Most Americans are probably aware that capitalized it specifically means one of the aboriginal inhabitants of Australia. Some may know that the preferred term is now *Aboriginal.* Pronounce the first two *AB-uhr-IJ-uh-nee;* the third *AB-uhr-IJ-uh-nuhl.*

aborning (*adv.*) This word appears almost solely with the verb *die* in a cliché meaning "It died just as it was being born, just as it was getting under way": *The new firm died aborning.*

abortive (*adj.*) in its general and figurative use means "to come to a fruitless end, to fail, to end imperfectly, usually prematurely."

abound (*v.*) takes the prepositions *in* and sometimes *with: The countryside abounds in [with] quaint villages.*

about 1 (*adv., prep.*) serves frequently as a qualifier: *The train was very crowded, but somewhere about Cleveland we were able to get dinner. They were about ready to call the police.* When numbers are involved, *about* serves similarly: *There were about a thousand spectators at the game. It was about 6:45 when we reached home.* All these uses are Standard, even those (as in the last example) that soften very specific numbers. At the higher levels of speech and in Formal writing, especially in expository writing, avoid the redundancy of qualification when you've already suggested a range, as in *Anthropologists estimated that the queen was [about] forty to forty-five years old.* But in Conversational levels or Informal and Semiformal writing, *about* sometimes effectively emphasizes an important uncertainty: *I'd say she was about forty to forty-five years old.*

Another indefiniteness appears in some sportswriters' old-fashioned use of *about* to mean "around" or "somewhere in the vicinity of," as in *The thug punched him about the face and ears.* Use such archaic clichés only to sound quaint.

about 2, (that's) what it's all *What it's all about* has been a cliché since about 1960. *This is what we're [all] about* is an idiomatic way of saying "This is what we believe in" or "This is what the situation means." It does not mean "This is what we are on the point of doing" or "This is what we are trying to accomplish." Now tiresomely familiar, *What it's all about* should be limited to Conversational and Informal or Semiformal use, and even then only when you're sure its brevity will cause your readers or listeners to forgive the cliché.

about to, not about to *About to* (*She was about to lock up for the night*) means "on the point of, just ready to" and poses no usage problem. *Not about to,* however, has only very recently become Standard at all levels. While this negative phrase can function as the negative of *about to,* usually it means "to have no intention whatsoever of," as in *The islanders are not about to be intimidated by threats of blockade.* For more, see NOT ABOUT TO.

above (*adj., n.*) There's nothing wrong with *the above address, the statement above,* and the like, except perhaps for a bit of stiffness, especially when repeated as formulas. But make sure that both adjectival and noun uses are appropriate to the context, and be aware that Edited English dislikes them for their imprecision. You need not avoid *above* meaning "more than" or "over," although some uses may have a slightly elderly ring, as in *She had been to their cottage above ten times that summer.*

abridge (*v.*), **abridged, unabridged** (*adjs.*), **abridgment/abridgement** (*n.*) *To abridge something* is "to reduce, shorten, or condense it." Among reference books (especially dictionaries) an *abridgment* is a shortened version of a longer original work. *Abridgment* is the object of two frequent lay misunderstandings. First, it is not necessarily a bad thing: it can be well done and for good reason. And, second, an *unabridged* dictionary is not necessarily a complete record of all the words in the language: it is simply the biggest and most nearly complete dictionary published by a particular publisher. Several *abridged* editions of various sizes and purposes may be based on it, from *collegiate* and *desk* dictionaries to tiny pocket-size spelling aids that may do little or nothing with meanings. *Abridgment's* spelling is in divided usage: Americans today slightly prefer the variant without the medial *-e-.* See SPELLING (1). Compare ACKNOWLEDGMENT; JUDGMENT. See also ABSTRACT (1); ABSTRACT (2).

abrogate See ABDICATE.

absence of, in the; conspicuous by its (*his, her, their*) absence *In the absence of* is padded prose. *Conspicuous by its* [*his, her, their,* etc.] *absence* is a cliché, also well padded.

absent (*adj., prep.*) The adjective means "not present." The preposition means "lacking, in the absence of, without." It was once limited mainly to rather Formal legal writing but now has much wider and more general use, especially in introductory (albeit somewhat formal) clauses: *Absent better news from the Middle East, the market will almost certainly continue its decline.*

absent, absently See ABSTRACTED; DISTRAIT.

absent-minded, absent-mindedly See AB-STRACTED; DISTRAIT.

absolute (*adj.*), **absolutely** (*adv.*) Both are often used as intensifiers, and both are sometimes criticized as overkill in Formal prose. *What you say is absolute nonsense* and *I think you are absolutely right* are examples of hyperbole, which has its place, albeit usually at the Conversational levels or in the writing that imitates them. See also ABSOLUTE CONSTRUCTIONS.

ABSOLUTE ADJECTIVES (sometimes called *incomparables,* with stress on either the second or the third syllable) are those adjectives that cannot be or ought not to be compared because they stand for qualities that are not matters of degree; adjectives such as *unique* (meaning "one of a kind," "the only one"), *perfect, square, complete,* and the like, as opposed to *tall, dirty,* and *poor,* which are relative qualities. The statement *This object is more round than that one* will usually evoke the conservative correction, "You mean *more nearly round* than that one." Nevertheless, in all but the most Formal contexts our natural love for hyperbole and intensifiers often leads us to compare some adjectives that conservatives consider *absolutes* and would never put into comparative or superlative degree. Moreover, in one or another of their meanings nearly all adjectives, including some *absolutes,* can accept *more* or *most* in periphrastic comparative or periphrastic superlative use: *Charlie Brown's head is rounder* [or *more round*] *than anybody else's.* But *uniquer/ uniquest* and *more/most unique* are shibboleths best avoided in other than humorous use. See ADJECTIVES (1).

ABSOLUTE COMPARATIVES We seldom notice these incomplete or "understood" comparisons, and they are quite acceptable in most speech and in some writing: *This bulb will give brighter light.* Occasionally, though, the incompleteness can blind us to concealed meanings. In advertising, the comparison may be with an unstated and therefore untestable something else. Some uses of the comparative form of the adjective occur in positions where we intend a relative meaning: *She prefers older* [not *old*] *men.*

ABSOLUTE CONSTRUCTIONS, ABSOLUTE PHRASES The *absolute constructions* that cause most concern are participial phrases not directly connected to the rest of their sentences. The "subject" of the participial phrase (*train*) in the following sentence is not the same as the subject of the main clause (*he*): *The train moving away, he had to run to catch it.* If the "subject" of the participial phrase is unexpressed and differs from that of the main clause, the construction is a dangling modifier: *Running to catch the train, it pulled away from him. Absolute constructions* that don't dangle are usually Standard (*Its whistle blowing, the train began to move*). See also ABLATIVE (2); DANGLING MODIFIERS.

ABSOLUTE POSSESSIVE PRONOUNS Some grammars give this name (others prefer the name *independent genitives*) to the pronoun forms *mine, yours, his, hers, its, ours, yours,* and *theirs,* as in *This book is mine. Her* is possessive; *hers, absolute possessive. His* and *its* are both possessive and *absolute possessive* forms. *Yourn, hisn, hern, ourn,* and *theirn* are all Substandard Vulgar forms, and Substandard too are the Standard forms when they're misspelled with an apostrophe inserted before the *s* (*her's, their's*). Compare ATTRIBUTIVE ADJECTIVES.

ABSOLUTISTS See PURISTS.

absolve (*v.*) regularly combines with the prepositions *of* and *from,* and less often with *for,* in the meanings "to forgive" or "to free from an obligation": *Following their confessions, the priest absolved the sinners of their sins. The bank officers absolved him from having to make further restitution. He was absolved for his misdemeanor once the judge heard his explanation.*

absorb, adsorb (*vv.*) *Absorb* is a widely used word meaning "to drink in, to soak up," both literally and figuratively. *Adsorb* is a specialized technical term, meaning only "to collect a condensed gas or liquid on a surface."

abstain (*v.*) Unless used alone, as in *I shall abstain, abstain* nearly always takes *from: She has abstained from* [rarely *in*] *voting on these issues for several years.*

abstemious, abstinent (*adjs.*), **abstinence** (*n.*)
To be *abstemious* means "to eat and drink very sparingly," but *to be abstinent* is "to abstain entirely." Thus *total abstinence* is redundant.

abstract 1 (*v.*) usually combines with *from* to mean "took" or "quoted," as in *I abstracted these statements from the longer essay,* and sometimes with *into* meaning "condensed" or "abridged," as in *We abstracted pages of notes into three short paragraphs.* The verb is also used jocularly or euphemistically to mean "steal," as in *She abstracted some money from her mother's purse.* The adjective is pronounced with heavy stress on either syllable; the noun is stressed on the first syllable. The verb is stressed on the second syllable except when it means "to summarize," when it is stressed on the first syllable. See ABSTRACTED.

abstract 2, abridgment, abridgement, condensation, précis (*nn.*) Although *condensation* has other senses as well, these four words are synonyms in the sense of "a brief restatement of the argument or substance of a proposal, an essay, or other longer statement." See ABRIDGE.

abstracted, absent, absent-minded, agitated, distracted (*adjs.*), **abstractedly, absently, absent-mindedly, agitatedly, distractedly** (*advs.*) Someone *abstracted* or figuratively *absent* is wrapped up in thought; someone *distracted* is shaken, clearly unable to concentrate; someone *agitated* is excited, upset; someone *absent-minded* is forgetful and inattentive. The adverbs are similarly distinctive. See also DISTRAIT.

ABSTRACTITIS The clearest prose is usually the most specific. Consider this verse from *Ecclesiastes:*

I returned, and saw under the sun, that the race is not to the swift, nor the battle to the strong, neither yet bread to the wise, nor yet riches to men of understanding, nor yet favor to men of skill; but time and chance happeneth to them all. (Eccles. 9:11)

and George Orwell's parody of it, a splendid example of *abstractitis:*

Objective consideration of contemporary phenomena compels the conclusion that success or failure in competitive activities exhibits no tendency to be commensurate with innate capacity, but that a considerable element of the unpredictable must invariably be taken into account.
(in Dean, Gibson, and Wilson 1971:307)

Fowler's (1965) term for the overuse of abstract language quite properly made a disease of it (by means of the suffix *-itis*). Polysyllabic, low-frequency words, ponderous, convoluted syntax, and circumlocutions contribute to *abstractitis,* and too much passive voice often makes it worse. See also ABSTRACT NOUNS; SCIENTIFIC ENGLISH; VOICE (2).

abstractly, abstractedly (*advs.*) *Abstractly* means "not concretely, not specifically": *He described his idea abstractly, without any illustrative examples. Abstractedly* means "preoccupied, not paying attention," as in *She replied abstractedly, her mind on other things.* See ABSTRACTED.

ABSTRACT NOUNS are frequently nouns made from verbs by the addition of word-forming suffixes such as *-ation* and *-ance* (*solicitation* from *solicit; governance* from *govern,* for example); overusing them can make long-winded, hard-to-follow prose. If you think your idea will be more impressive when expressed in *abstract* language, you probably deceive yourself. Such words cannot make an idea more important than it really is; they usually just express it less clearly: *enhancement and improvement of the domiciling arrangements* is not as clear as *fixing up the house.* See also ABSTRACTITIS; SCIENTIFIC ENGLISH; VOICE (2).

abstruse See OBTUSE.

ABUSAGE is an old noun, put back into service by Partridge in 1947 (1963b), where its meaning was and continues to be only "the misuse or abuse of English." All other *abuses* are just *abuses,* not *abusages: child abuse, abuse of privilege.*

abuse, substance See SUBSTANCE ABUSE.

abut (*v.*) The transitive verb needs no preposition but occasionally takes *on* following the direct object: *Our property abuts the Moynihan land on the east.* The intransitive verb can take any of several prepositions, but primarily *on* and *upon: The rear of the parsonage abutted on* [*upon*] *the churchyard wall.* See also CONSONANTS (2).

abysm, abyss (*nn.*) These are two old synonyms for "the pit," the fearsome void that medieval and later Christians envisioned below the earth. We now use *abyss* fairly frequently, meaning either "hell" or "any great hole," such as the seemingly bottomless cracks in the ice that Antarctic explorers had to avoid. *Abysm* (from which the adjective *abysmal* comes) is much less common these days and seems to be reserved almost wholly for a figurative sense dealing with time.

abysmal, abyssal (*adjs.*) *Abysmal* means "very deep," but mostly in figurative senses: Consider the cliché *abysmal ignorance,* or *Her concentration was abysmal.* It means "deeply awful," "incredibly bad," and is pejorative in all senses, as is the much-used intensifying adverb, *abysmally* (*She was abysmally gloomy*). *Abyssal* is a technical term in oceanography, referring to the greatest depths (*the abyssal zone*).

-ac See SPELLING OF *-ING* AND *-ED* FORMS OF VERBS ENDING IN *-IC, -AC.*

academe, academia, academy, Academy (*nn.*) All four of these words are in Standard use today: *academe* (pronounced **AK**-*uh-DEEM* or *AK-uh-DEEM*) and *academia* initially referred to the grove where Plato taught (*The Academy was Plato's*). But both they and *academy* have come today to apply to a variety of metaphoric aspects of formal education. Typical uses distinguish the world of scholarship and formal, especially higher, education from the world of practical existence. *Academy* is frequently incorporated into the titles of secondary educational institutions, as well as into the names of the four American military service institutions.

academic (*adj., n.*), **academicals, academician** (*nn.*) An *academic* is someone engaged in the *academic* profession; the noun is Standard but probably not usual in Oratorical or Formal uses. The plural, *academics,* means both "teachers and scholars" and "academic subjects, programs, or courses," especially as distinguished from athletics or other collegiate activities: *She was obliged to devote more time to her academics than to basketball.* The adjective *academic* has much wider use, meaning "anything associated with formal learning and its practitioners" but later picking up its most common use, in the pejorative sense of "impractical, useless": *The question is academic, because events have answered it.* When you use the adjective in its other senses, especially "pertaining to the academy," be wary that derogation doesn't creep in with it. *Academicals* are academic regalia—caps, gowns, and hoods. An *academician* is a member of an academy, teacher or scholar. See also *-IC.*

Acadian, Cajun (*adjs., nn.*) *Acadians* were the French colonists who during the seventeenth century settled what later became the Canadian Maritime (now Atlantic) Provinces and part of Quebec. The colony probably was named after the mythical Arcadia. *Acadia* is sometimes used as another name for French Canada, as *Acadians* is for French-Canadians. *Cajun* (sometimes *Cajan*) is the Louisiana pronunciation of *Acadian* applied to *Acadians* resettled there (see Longfellow's *Evangeline*), to their descendants in the *Cajun* parishes of Louisiana, to their language, and most recently to their style of cooking (lately in vogue across the continent) and to their music. See ZYDECO.

a cappella, a capella, from the Latin for "to the chapel," is an Italian phrase that means "choral singing done without instrumental accompaniment" (as would be likely in a small chapel lacking organ or other musical instrument). Pronounce it *AH kuh-PEL-uh,* and spell it either way.

accede, exceed (*vv.*) *Accede* means "to agree" and combines usually with *to* (*She acceded to the request*). It can be a near-homophone of *exceed,* but context should prevent confusion. See *-CEDE.*

accelerate, exhilarate (*vv.*), **accelerator** (*n.*) The verbs are not homophones (*ak-SEL-uhr-AIT* vs. *eg-ZIL-uhr-AIT*), but Vulgar English sometimes confuses *exhilarate,* meaning "to excite," and *accelerate,* meaning "to speed up or cause to speed up" and specifically "to press a foot throttle and increase a vehicle's speed." An *accelerator* is generically "any agent used to speed up a chemical reaction or some other activity," and it has a common specialized meaning, "the foot throttle of a motor vehicle." See AGENTIVE ENDINGS.

ACCENT 1 (*n.*) *He speaks with a slight foreign accent* means that his speech has some foreign-sounding consonants, vowels, or intonations, even though his speech may in all other respects be impeccable Standard English. Don't use *dialect* as though it were interchangeable with this sense of *accent; accent* is a characteristic of speech; only in eye dialect does *accent* (1) appear in writing. See DIALECT.

ACCENT 2, ACCENT MARK (*nn.*) English sometimes retains *accent marks* in words borrowed from languages that regularly employ them in writing but sometimes drops them, particularly in words felt to have become fully naturalized by long or heavy use. British English typically retains more *accent marks* than does American English. For example, British

English generally retains both French acute accents in *résumé*, but American English now has in divided usage *resume* and *résumé*, which means that sometimes context must prevent confusion between the noun and the verb *resume*. Note that in indicating pronunciation American English sometimes uses a symbol very similar to the acute accent (´) to indicate a syllable more heavily stressed than those around it, as in *décanal* and *decánal*. Other *accent marks* sometimes encountered in printed or written English are the French grave (*vis-à-vis*) and circumflex (*tête-à-tête*) accents; the German umlaut (as in *Köln*—pronounced a bit like *KULN*—for *Cologne*) and the dieresis (which indicates two syllables where contiguous vowels might mistakenly be read as a single syllable, e.g., *naïve* and *coöperate* for *naive* and *cooperate*), both of which use the same symbol in English writing and printing; the cedilla used by French, Spanish, and Portuguese (*garçon, curaçao*) to make a medial letter -*c*- sound like an *s*; the Spanish tilde (*cañon, señor*), which indicates that a *y* sound should follow a nasal; and the haček, which occurs mainly in Czech names and words (*haček, pronounced HAH-CHEK*). See also ACUTE ACCENT; BREVE; CEDILLA; DIACRITICS; GRAVE ACCENT; HAČEK; MACRON.

accent 3, accentuate (*vv.*) Although *accent* has some generic use (*Adding mustard will accent the flavors of the salad dressing*), many of its uses are technical, especially in language matters: *Germanic languages tend to accent* [*i.e.,* stress] *the first syllable. Accentuate* has many more figurative uses than *accent* and is much more widely used in the sense of "to increase through contrast": *That blue scarf accentuates the blue in your eyes.* In some uses the words may be nearly interchangeable, especially in the sense of "to stress," but only *accentuate* has the additional figurative meaning "to increase," as in *Their woeful lack of leadership only accentuates their general air of disarray.*

accept, except (*vv.*) Because these verbs are often homophones, they are sometimes inadvertently written or printed for each other, but confusion in speech is unlikely and usually undetectable: *accept* means "to grant, to receive, to submit to, to answer yes, to agree to be a member or to take a position" and has several other specialized senses: *Oberlin accepted her as a transfer student. Except* as a verb means "to take out, to leave out, to take exception to": *I except from my anger anyone who has already paid.* (*Except* is also a conjunction, usually followed by *that*,

and a preposition, but it seems not to pose any particular usage problems in these functions.)

acceptable, agreeable (*adjs.*) *Acceptable* means "worth accepting, satisfactory (sometimes just passably so), allowable": *The guests found the meal to be quite acceptable.* But *acceptable* does not mean "receptive." *I'm acceptable to your suggestion* is wrong; *I'm agreeable to it, I'm open to it,* or *I'm receptive to it* would be better.

acceptance, acceptation (*nn.*) *Acceptance* is the word in far more general use; it means "the act of accepting" in all the senses of the word. *Acceptation* is mostly a much more specialized *linguistic* term, meaning "the usual or accepted version of an idea or meaning of a word," and it has been labeled archaic when used to mean "acceptance."

access 1, accession (*nn.*) The main sense of *access* is "the means or opportunity to get to something," as in *She gained access to the attic. Accession* means "an acquiring" or "an increase" and has two specialized senses: "assuming some high office or title," as in *Her accession to the throne followed her father's lingering death;* and librarians' specialized sense, "the entering of books in the library's records in the order of their being acquired," as in *The order of accession is always chronological.* It also means such books: *Shelve the new accessions here.*

access 2, excess (*nn.*) These words are not normally confused, despite their possible overlap in certain pronunciations (*access* is always stressed on the first syllable; *excess* may be stressed on either). In combined forms, *access* frequently uses *to*, as in *We gained access to his papers; excess* does not. But in speech confusion can occur in combined forms with *of*, especially when these uses deal with emotions: *In an excess* ("an overabundance") *of anger, he shouted things he would later regret* could be confused with *In an access* ("a sudden flow or burst") *of anger, he shouted things he would later regret.*

accessorize (*v.*) There is nothing wrong with *accessorize* when it is used in the right place, as in *The ensemble was accessorized to the point of gaudiness.* It's relatively new and an Americanism, however, and both those things can put some people off (as can mispronunciation: many people say *uh-SES-uhr-EIZ,* but only *ak-SES-uhr-EIZ* is Standard). Some conservatives strongly dislike new coinages like this one, made of a noun plus the verb-making *-ize* suffix. At present, *accessorize* is mainly an argot word applied only to clothing, interior decorating, and the like, but it could easily take on figurative or transferred senses for use with more general topics, even in Edited English. See AFFIX.

accessory, accessary (*adj., n.*) *Accessary* is a little-used variant spelling of the noun *accessory,* and Americans are often surprised to learn that it is not a misspelling. The adjective is nearly always *accessory.* See SPELLING (1).

accident See MISHAP.

accidentally, accidently (*adv.*) Stick with *accidentally*; it is by far the preferred spelling. (Indeed, many conservative people consider *accidently* a misspelling, and some conservative dictionaries do not even record it as a variant, though it has been accepted off and on for many years.) Pronounce the word with either four or five syllables.

acclamation, acclimation (*nn.*) *Acclamation* is related to *acclaim* and means "being accorded applause, approval, or cheers"; *He was elected by acclamation. Acclimation* is a noun made from the verb *acclimate,* meaning "to get adjusted to a climate or an environment" or "adapt to new circumstances"; *acclimation* means "such an adjustment or adaptation," as in *After weeks of feeling chilled, they finally achieved acclimation to the cold.* It is not a commonly used word. See ACCLIMATE.

acclimate, acclimatize (*vv.*), **acclimatization, acclimation** (*nn.*) All these words have to do with adapting to a different climate or environment. American English uses both verbs, putting primary stress in *acclimate* on either the first or second syllable, in *acclimatize* on the second only. Of the nouns, only *acclimatization,* with primary stress on the fifth syllable and a lesser stress on the second, is much used by Americans.

accommodate (*v.*) and the related words *accommodation, accommodating,* and the like are frequently misspelled, and such errors are often considered shibboleths. In combined use, *to* is the most frequent preposition: *I can accommodate to your schedule. Her eyes accommodated quickly to the lack of light.* But it can also take several other prepositions: *Most of the guests were accommodated on the first two floors. I expected to be accommodated by my aunt and uncle [at a hotel, in their guest room].*

accompanist See PIANIST.

accompany (*v.*) combines most frequently with *by* (especially for people) but also with *with* (only for things): *He was accompanied by his father. The potato salad was accompanied with [by] a limp dill pickle.*

accord, of one's own; on one's own account These idioms differ slightly but significantly: *She enrolled in the class of her own accord,* means "she did it voluntarily; nobody else influenced her action." *She spoke up on her own account,* means "she did it for herself, not relying on others; she represented only herself."

according (*adj.*), **according as** (*subord. conj.*), **according to** (*prep.*) *According* means "agreeing," although it is in infrequent use: *The according splinter parties had some temporary strength. According as* means "depending on whether, precisely as, to the degree that": *Each of us will give according as we're able. According to* means "in agreement with": *Everything was arranged according to the rules,* or "as stated or reported in or by": *According to the* Times, *the enemy broke the truce last night.*

account (*n., v.*) *To give an account of something* is to narrate it: *She gave us an account of her day in the city.* The noun also has several idiomatic combined forms. *To call to account [for]* means "to challenge or to hold responsible for": *His superiors called him to account for the missing funds. To give a good account of yourself* is "to perform well": *She gave a good account of herself in the meeting. On account of* means "because": *The umpire called the game on account of poor visibility. On no account* means "under no circumstances": *On no account am I going to accept the offer. On your own account* means "on your own, for yourself": *They were interested in the case on their own account, not just because they were acquainted with the accused. To take into account* means "to consider, to allow for": *Even when she took into account his intentions, she couldn't forgive his mistakes.* Combinations with the verb are almost always with *for: We can account for most of what happened that night* means "explain, give reasons for." *The hero accounted for all three of the villains* means "killed or captured them." It can also combine with *to,* meaning "explain or justify myself, as in *I don't have to account to you for my actions.* See ACCORD; JUSTIFY.

accountable (*adj.*) You are *accountable to* someone *for* something if you must justify yourself to someone: *I consider myself accountable* to the voters for the actions of everyone on my staff. See also JUSTIFY.

accrete, accrue, accumulate, cumulate (*vv.*), **accretion, accrual, accumulation, cumulation** (*nn.*) The verbs are synonyms, and so are the nouns. *Accrete* is relatively low frequency and means "to stick or grow together, to *accumulate*," as in *Over time lichen accretes on tree trunks and rocks. Accrue, accumulate,* and *cumulate* all mean "to pile up over time, incrementally," as in *Let these funds accumulate (cumulate, accrue) until you return.* The nouns all refer to the results of these actions.

accrue (*v.*) is both transitive (*In thirty years with the firm, he had accrued a reputation for honesty*) and intransitive (*This season's rainfall continues to accrue in the streams and rivers*). It has a considerable figurative use, and it need not be limited to legal, financial or other numerical issues.

accumulate, accumulation See ACCRETE.

accumulative, cumulative (*adjs.*) These two are partly synonymous, but generally, *accumulative* has an overtone of acquisitiveness, as in *He has accumulative drives you might not suspect; he craves money and the things it will buy,* or it suggests a characteristic of a person or thing that simply collects, as in *Her accumulative energies are unflagging; she is one of the great collectors. Cumulative* usually lacks any pejorative edge, as in *Most periodical indexes are cumulative.*

accursed, accurst (*adj.*) *Accursed* may be pronounced with either three syllables (*uh-KUHRS-id*) or two (*uh-KUHRST*), and the latter pronunciation is sometimes spelled *accurst*.

ACCUSATIVE CASE, OBJECTIVE CASE

These are two names for the same grammatical case in English. *Accusative* is the older term, but because there is no longer any morphological distinction between dative and *accusative* cases in English, some grammarians concluded that one catchall case name, *objective*, would serve. Today this case's forms are morphologically distinguished from other cases only in the personal pronouns (*me, him, her, us, them,* and *whom*), but syntactically many grammars still label as *accusative* or *objective case* any nouns and other nominals found in any of these functions: direct object (*I hit the pitch*); indirect object (*We fed the baby lunch*); object complement (*I tagged him it*); object of a preposition (*through the window*). See CASE (1); DIRECT OBJECT; INDIRECT OBJECT; MORPHOLOGY; OBJECT COMPLEMENT; OBJECT OF A PREPOSITION.

accuse (*v.*) You *accuse* someone *of* doing something wrong, *of* wrongdoing, and that person is *accused by* you. These are Standard. Occasionally you may hear *accuse* someone *with* doing something wrong, *with* wrongdoing, but that use is dialectal at best; avoid it.

accused (*adj., n.*) Journalism and those who imitate it have problems with the adjective, which may properly modify any identification of *the accused* except one that appears to assume guilt prior to conviction. *The accused rapist, accused burglar,* and *accused arsonist,* may be deemed actionable when they appear in print before conviction; responsible journalism prefers *alleged.* Note too that *Dr. Brown, the alleged murderer,* may be taken as more damaging than *Dr. Brown, who is alleged to have committed the murder,* because *the alleged murderer* is an appositive of *Dr. Brown* and may seem therefore to assert more strongly. See also ALLEGE; SUSPECTED.

ace (*adj., n., v.*) Most of its figurative uses are Conversational. Tennis's use, meaning "the unreturnable service," is Standard, unlike golf's, meaning "a hole in one," *to ace* someone or something, meaning "to win decisively (usually with one stroke or shot)," or the student's *She aced the final exam,* meaning "She got an A on it"; all these are slang. The military flying designation *ace* is Standard now for the pilot who has shot down five or more enemy planes, as is the use meaning someone highly expert in a skill or occupation (*an ace designer*). *To come* [or *be*] *within an ace of,* meaning "to be very close to doing something," is an idiom Standard in all but the most Formal use.

acerbic See ACID.

Achilles' heel, meaning "a fatal weakness or vulnerability," is so much used as a metaphor that it now sometimes appears in Edited English without the apostrophe.

acid, acerbic, acidulous, acrid (*adjs.*) All have literal sensory referents: *acid* usually refers to taste, as in *I have an acid taste in my mouth,* but is often used figuratively, especially to describe what someone says, as in *She made several acid remarks; acerbic* also means "acid" but is almost always used figuratively, again, mostly about what someone says, as in *His acerbic comments about the book did not please the aspiring novelist; acidulous* means "sour, biting" and is usually figurative, as in *Her acidulous observations spoiled the evening; acrid* usually deals with smells, as in *Acrid fumes rose from the furnace,* but it too can be used figuratively of sharp and unpleasant comments, as in

The reviewer's acrid observations on the quality of the work outraged the artist. And of course all four can also be applied to glances that speak volumes (which is a cliché).

acid test, litmus test (*nn.*) *Acid test* is a cliché and a dead metaphor, at least for those unaware that it originated with the testing of gold by putting acid on it. The *litmus test* is a similar metaphor, and probably not many people can remember which way the colors go (litmus paper turns red when dipped in an acid, blue when dipped in a base). Both tests have proved to be useful figurative language for more general use, and they are good examples of the quantities of language we've borrowed from the sciences for general figurative use, perhaps for the air of exactness they lend. See CATALYST; CHEMISTRY.

acknowledgment, acknowledgement (*n.*) These are variant spellings, *acknowledgment* being the usual American one, the other frequently being British. See SPELLING (1). Compare ABRIDGE; JUDGMENT.

acoustics (*n.*) The name of the science itself is singular: *Acoustics has been his main interest for many years.* When *acoustics* refers to the sound qualities of a room or hall, however, it is plural: *The theater's acoustics are warm and alive.*

acquaint (*v.*) usually takes *with: Let me acquaint you with the situation.* Archaic combinations with *of* are still to be encountered, as are constructions with *that* clauses, but neither use is really current today in Standard English.

acquaintance, acquaintanceship (*nn.*) Both are Standard, but for most purposes *acquaintance* is the only noun you'll need. Either word will do in this sentence: *Our acquaintance [acquaintanceship] began many years ago.* Best advice: use *acquaintanceship* only to communicate an abstraction when there is possible confusion from context with the meaning of *acquaintance* as "a person whom you know."

acquiesce (*v.*) most frequently takes *in,* as in *She acquiesced in their taking over the company,* although you will encounter occasional American uses of *acquiesce to* and *acquiesce with,* mostly from earlier in the century. Use *in.*

acquire (*v.*) Just as *purchase* is somewhat more formal and self-conscious than *buy,* so *acquire* is stiffer than *get.* But both *acquire* and *purchase* are fine in their proper places.

acquired, innate (*adjs.*) These words mark the two sides of the classic nature/nurture problem in human development. The question persists: How much of this or that characteristic is *innate* (that is, how much of it were we born with) and how much of it is *acquired* (that is, learned after birth)? Use the two precisely: *innate* in particular is inexactly used to describe general qualities or attributes. See GENETIC; INNATE.

acquit (*v.*) takes *of: The court acquitted him of the charge of forgery.* It also takes a reflexive pronoun as a direct object, often followed by *in: She acquitted herself well in class.*

acrid See ACID.

ACRONYMS are pronounceable abbreviations made up of initial letters or initial parts of words in a phrase, as with *NASA,* for *National Aeronautics and Space Administration.* Some *acronyms* are slang or are at least relatively Informal (*PhysEd,* for **physical education,** for example), but many, such as *sonar,* the *Delmarva* peninsula, and *OPEC,* are now Standard English. The *CAT* in *CAT scan* stands for *computerized axial tomography* and is a convenient abbreviation of a long, low-frequency technological term. These days we seldom establish a new organization without creating for it a phrasal name that yields an easily recognizable and perhaps additionally instructive *acronym:* for example, *MADD* for *Mothers against Drunk Driving* or *NOW* for the *National Organization for Women.* One problem: those who use an *acronym* may forget what its letters stand for. Probably few of us recall the exact phrase that gave us *radar:* **radio detecting and ranging.** See ABBREVIATIONS; APHERESIS; CLIPPING; INITIALISMS.

acrophobia, agoraphobia (*nn.*) *Acrophobia* (*ak-ruh-FO-bee-yuh*) is "fear of heights," and *agoraphobia* (*AG-uhr-uh-FO-bee-yuh*) is "fear of open or public places."

across (*adv., prep.*) is Substandard when pronounced with a final *-t,* to rhyme with *lost.* That pronunciation is sometimes spelled *acrost* in eye dialect. Only *across* (rhymes with *moss*) is Standard.

act, action (*nn.*) These two have both overlapping and distinctive meanings. *His generous action* [*act*] *was much appreciated* illustrates synonymous use. An *act* may also be "the thing done, viewed as a whole and static," whereas an *action* may be considered "a continuous process and may include several *acts.*" *Her action suggested that she might be ill. These apparently unfriendly acts made it appear that he had changed his allegiance.* The idiomatic phrases *to go* [or *be*] *where the action is,* meaning "to be where the important and interesting things are happening,'' and *to get a piece of the action,* meaning ''to share in or to make an investment in whatever is going forward,'' are Conversational or Informal at best.

action (*v.*) is commercial and administrative jargon: *Action this report* means ''Act on it, or take action on it.'' Avoid *action* as a verb.

activate, actuate (*vv.*) The overlap between these two verbs lies in the sense ''to put into motion,'' ''to set working,'' ''to stimulate or prod into action'': *We activated the third regiment as soon as we heard the news. It was fear that actuated our efforts. Activate* also means ''to make radioactive,'' ''to accelerate a chemical reaction,'' and the like, and most of its senses connote real *activity*; *actuate* carries only the more general sense of ''to get something started.''

ACTIVE VOICE See VOICE (2).

actual (*adj.*), **actually** (*adv.*), **actuality** (*n.*) All three have frequent (and often semantically half-empty) use as intensifiers or hyperbolic helpers. *In actual truth* means ''In real truth'' and underscores the truth of this truth, as contrasted with the untruth of the ''truth'' you've heard before. *Actually,* like *really,* seems to try to dispel doubts as yet unexpressed. *In actuality* means ''Here's what really happened.'' All three words have useful literal senses too, but care is required to evoke them. See REAL. Compare FACT.

actuate See ACTIVATE.

acuity, acumen, acuteness (*nn.*) *Acuity* is ''keenness of thought or senses'': *His visual acuity was remarkable. Acumen* (stress it on either the first or second syllable) means ''keenness and sharpness, particularly of mind and understanding; shrewd judgment'': *Her financial acumen will be a great help. Acuteness* is the most general of the three terms, meaning ''possessed of a general shrewdness, sharpness, quickness of mind, and sensitivity'': *Those three judges combine a range of acuteness of perception and mind that should make their decisions very wise indeed. Acuteness* is also the choice when a pain is literal and physical: *The acuteness of the toothache drove all thought from my mind.*

ACUTE ACCENT This accent mark (´) occurs in English mainly in words of French origin, such as *étude, épée,* and *soigné,* although in high-frequency words American English sometimes drops the accent mark, where British English continues to retain it. *Soiree,* for example, is in divided usage in the United States, appearing usually without the *accent,* but some-

times with it. An *acute accent* also indicates that the quality of the vowel letter *e* is fairly close to that of the American English vowel *a* in *hate,* and at the ends of words, a final *-e* with an *acute accent* means that the *e* is syllabic and must be pronounced, as in *passé,* unlike the usually silent final *-e* in English. See also ACCENT (2); DIACRITICS.

acuteness See ACUITY.

A.D., B.C., (A.)C.E., B.C.E. *A.D.* (or *AD*) is an abbreviation for *anno Domini,* ''[in] the year of our Lord,'' for dates after the year conventionally numbered 1, and *B.C.* (or *BC*) stands for ''before Christ,'' for dates before that year. *A.D.* appears either before or after the number of the year (*A.D. 1066* or *1066 A.D.*), although conservative use has long preferred before only; *B.C.* always follows the number of the year (55 *B.C.*). The use of the periods is a matter of style.

Recently *B.C.E.,* meaning either ''before the Christian era'' or more frequently ''before the common era,'' has had some champions, but Edited English seems only rarely to have adopted it thus far. *(A.)C.E.,* ''(after the) common (or Christian) era,'' seems to have prospered even less, perhaps because some regard it as slighting Christianity (which is ironic, given that both alternatives were proposed to avoid the possible disrespect implied by the more popular terms). Common era (*C.E.*) itself needs a good deal of further justification, in view of its clearly Christian numbering. Most conservatives still prefer *A.D.* and *B.C.* Best advice: don't use *B.C.E., C.E.,* or *A.C.E.* to replace *B.C.* and *A.D.* without translating the new terms for the very large number of readers who will not understand them. Note too that if we do end by casting aside the *A.D./B.C.* convention, almost certainly some will argue that we ought to cast aside as well the conventional numbering system itself, given its Christian basis. At present the familiar Latin/English convention has the considerable advantage of being the one most of the world's written languages use in communicating with cultures other than their own. See DATES.

ad, advert, advertisement (*nn.*) The clipped form *ad* is Informal and Conversational. The full word has at least four acceptable pronunciations in American English: *AD-vuhr-TEIZ-mint, AD-vuhr-TEIZ-mint, ad-VUHR-tiz-mint,* or *ad-VUHR-tis-mint.* The clipped form *advert* is British only and Informal.

adage, old *Old adage* is certainly a cliché, which perhaps takes some of the sting from charges that it is also a tautology. *Adage* used by itself is not a cliché. See APHORISM.

adagio See PLURALS OF NOUNS ENDING IN -*O*.

adapt, adopt (*vv.*), **adept** (*adj., n.*) Only *adapt* and *adopt* are likely to be confused in use. *Adapt* means "to change or adjust something to fit a different purpose or circumstance" or simply "to change or adjust": *We adapted the old stove to fit the new countertop. She adapted easily to her new surroundings. Adopt* means "to choose, to accept" or "to take a child into your family and rear it as your own": *We'll adopt some new rules. Paul's family had adopted him when he was a baby.* The adjective *adept* means "expert or highly proficient," and the noun means "someone who is adept": *She was adept at repairing small appliances. Everyone recognized her as a real expert—an adept.*

adaptation, adaption (*nn.*) *Adaptation* is far more common; *adaption* is a much less frequent synonym.

adapter, adaptor (*nn.*) *Adaptor* is an infrequent variant spelling of *adapter*. Neither spelling is attached exclusively to persons or to things. See also AGENTIVE ENDINGS.

addendum (*n.*) is singular; *addenda* is the usual plural, although *addendums* can be found occasionally. *Addenda* occurs as a singular but is not Standard. See AGENDA; FOREIGN PLURALS.

addict, addiction (*nn.*), **addicted** (*adj., n.*) All three are nearly always pejorative, not only because the most frequently mentioned *addictions* are to tobacco, alcohol, or drugs, but also because *addiction* implies excess or loss of self-control. More neutral uses of these words are often criticized by those who believe that the pejorative senses are too strong to permit the neutral to work. Proceed with caution in neutral uses. *Addicted* plus *to* must be followed by a noun or a gerund, not by an infinitive: *She is addicted to jogging [exercise]*, not *She is addicted to jog.*

additional See ANOTHER.

additionally (*adv.*) is Standard as a sentence adverb, although it sometimes seems pretentious and occurs less often than *in addition, besides,* or *also.* Some conservatives object to it as they do to *hopefully,* which see.

address (*n., v.*) The noun is pronounced either *uh-DRES* or *A-dres* in Standard English; the verb is always *uh-DRES.* See ORATION.

ADDRESS, DIRECT AND INDIRECT See DIRECT ADDRESS.

adduce, deduce (*vv.*) The prefix *ad-* means "to or toward," *de-* means "from or away." Thus, *adduce* means "to cite something as proof," "to lead in some evidence": *The detective adduced a series of timetables in support of his theory. Deduce* means "to trace the origin of," "to infer, to conclude on the basis of reason": *The crumbs on the counter, the open jar of jelly, and the knife with traces of peanut butter led me to deduce that he'd been snacking.* See also DEDUCE.

adept See ADAPT.

adequate (*adj.*) has been called an absolute adjective, but such uses are rare; *adequate* seems often to cover a general *area* of satisfactoriness rather than a precise *threshold* or other *point* of satisfactoriness. We hear *This one is more adequate* more often than *This one is more nearly adequate. Adequate* can take *for* or *to* plus either an infinitive or a gerund: *This contribution will be adequate to meet [for meeting] our needs. Enough* and *sufficient* may serve as good substitutes. When used to describe a performance or the qualities of an artifact, *adequate* is almost always faint praise: a reviewer's *"Her performance last night was adequate"* will not elate the performer.

adhere, cohere (*vv.*), **adherence, adhesion, coherence, cohesion** (*nn.*), **adhesive, cohesive** (*adjs.*) *Adhere* is Standard when used either literally or figuratively with the preposition *to: That masking tape adheres firmly to the wall. We'll try to adhere to the original scheme. Cohere* is a synonym, differing only in its suggestion that the entities in contact stick together.

Adherence and *adhesion* are synonyms meaning "a sticking together," but they are not used identically in all circumstances. Both are Standard, but *adhesion* is usually literal, *adherence* usually figurative. Both often take of and *to: The adherence [or adhesion] of X to Y [or to Y of X] is expected in all cases.* The plural *adhesions* often refers to a pathological condition in which two types of tissue become stuck together, typically as a postsurgical difficulty.

Coherence and *cohesion* are partial synonyms, but *coherence* is used chiefly in a figurative sense meaning "logically consistent, understandable," whereas *cohesion* is again simply "a sticking together."

The adjectives *adhesive* and *cohesive* both mean "sticking," but *adhesive* suggests one entity does the sticking, as in *adhesive tape*, whereas *cohesive* means that entities "stick together," as in *The team was finally a cohesive unit.*

ad hoc Englished as either *AHD HOK, AHD HAHK, AD HOK,* or *AD HAHK,* this Latin tag means "in this instance only," "only for this purpose.'' An *ad hoc* committee is automatically discharged when its single purpose has been accomplished. See FOREIGN PHRASES.

ad hominem This Latin tag (pronounced *AD HAHM-i-nem*) means literally ''to the man'' and applies to an argument that attacks the character of the opponent rather than reasonably addressing the issues. See also FOREIGN PHRASES.

adieu (*interj., n.*) This phrase, borrowed from the French, is a shortened farewell, ''[I leave you] to God.'' Like *goodbye* (''God be with you''), *adieu* has become a noun. The plural, spelled either *adieus* or *adieux,* is pronounced *uh-D(Y)OOZ,* although some Americans may retain a nearly French pronunciation of *adieux: ah-DYU.* See FOREIGN PLURALS.

ad infinitum is a Latin tag meaning ''to infinity'' or ''endlessly''; it is usually pronounced *AD in-fi-NEIT-uhm.* See FOREIGN PHRASES.

ad interim is a Latin tag pronounced *AD IN-tuhr-im* and meaning ''temporarily'' or ''in the meantime.'' See FOREIGN PHRASES.

adjacent (*adj.*) means either ''close to'' or ''next to and touching'': *We were in adjacent seats in the third row.* In combined use *adjacent* is always followed by *to: Their cottage was adjacent to ours.*

ADJECTIVE (*n.*), **ADJECTIVAL** (*adj., n.*), **ADJECTIVALLY** (*adv.*) An *adjective* is a part of speech that modifies nouns or other nominals: in *clear water, forest primeval, happier days,* and *easy listening, clear, primeval, happier,* and *easy* are *adjectives,* modifying the nouns *water, forest,* and *days* and the nominal *listening,* respectively.

Adjectival and *adjectivally* (not *adjectively*) are grammatical terms that have to do with the functions of *adjectives:* an *adjectival* (pronounced *a-jek-TEI-vuhl*) *modifier* is ''a word, phrase, or clause that works like an adjective'': *people in the car* has an adjectival phrase (in construction it is a prepositional phrase), *in the car,* modifying the noun *people.* Similarly, *The man who bought the car* has an adjectival clause, *who bought the car,* modifying *man.* See MODIFIERS.

ADJECTIVES, ABSOLUTE See ABSOLUTE ADJECTIVES.

ADJECTIVES 1, COMPARISON OF There are two patterns for *comparison of adjectives,* the inflected and the periphrastic. The inflected pattern adds *-er* to the positive degree of the adjective to form the comparative degree: *small* becomes *smaller, happy* becomes *happier.* To form the superlative degree, it adds *-est: smallest, happiest.* The periphrastic pattern uses the adverbial intensifiers *more* and *most:* the comparatives of *beautiful* and *ostentatious* are *more beautiful* and *more ostentatious*; the superlatives are *most beautiful* and *most ostentatious.* The generalizations that seem to account for whether we choose the inflected pattern or the periphrastic are these: (1) most one- and two-syllable adjectives use the inflected pattern; (2) adjectives of three and more syllables almost always use the periphrastic; (3) the higher the frequency of two-syllable adjectives, the more likely they are to inflect for *comparison*; (4) the periphrastic *more* and *most* may on occasion be used with any one-syllable or high-frequency two-syllable *adjective,* e.g., *more dear, most happy.*

ADJECTIVES 2, IDIOMATIC PLACEMENT OF Ideally, modifiers should be placed as close as possible to the words they modify; the best place for an attributive adjective is usually directly before the noun it modifies. But often, especially in speech, we use more relaxed idiomatic patterns: *a hot bowl of soup* [instead of *a bowl of hot soup*], *an old pair of overshoes* [instead of *a pair of old overshoes*]. *A large doorman's umbrella* is ambiguous in writing, but in speech, context and intonation tell us that the umbrella is what's large. Most Americans accept these locutions at almost all levels of speech and in all but the most Formal writing. Indeed, many Standard users accept them in all situations. See also ADJECTIVES (3).

ADJECTIVES, PARTICIPIAL, WITH VERY See VERY.

ADJECTIVES 3, PLACEMENT BEFORE AND AFTER NOUNS The normal position of English adjectives is before the nouns they modify—*white cats, long hair*—but certain adjectives, particularly some borrowed from French, especially in stereotypical phrases, appear after the noun, in what grammarians sometimes call the post-positive position: *chaise longue, moment supreme, attorney general, fudge royale.* Adjectivals can also occupy either position, although phrase and clause modifiers tend to follow the nouns they modify: *the house* **with the red roof,** *the man* **who came to dinner,** but *his* **put-up-or-shut-up** *glare.*

ADJECTIVES, PREDICATE See PREDICATE ADJECTIVE.

ADJECTIVES USED AS NOUNS Making nouns of adjectives is easy in English: *sick persons* become *the sick; homeless persons* become *the homeless; flighty persons* become *the flighty.*

Some nouns made on this pattern are mass nouns that normally do not inflect for the plural, even though they are treated as plural for purposes of agreement: *The poor* (not *the poors*) are always with us. Others are count nouns: *quarterly journals* become *quarterlies,* and *collectible objects* become *collectibles*; like other count nouns, these inflect for the plural and when so inflected agree with plural verbs: *Collectibles are all the rage today.* See MASS NOUNS.

adjoin, adjourn (*vv.*) These two are homophones only in certain regional dialects (notably Metropolitan New York City, Southern, and some Eastern New England) that have lost their *r* coloration before consonants and have slightly modified the vowels in those now *r*-less syllables. *Adjoin* means "to be next to, to touch or be in contact with": *The shed adjoins the house.* *Adjourn* means "to close a meeting or move to another place and time": *The committee decided to adjourn until Saturday morning.*

adjudicate See ARBITRATE.

ADJUNCT See NOUN ADJUNCT.

adjure See ABJURE.

adjust (*v.*), **adjusted** (*adj.*) Combinations include *adjust to,* as in *We adjusted easily to the time change,* and *adjust for,* as in *These figures have been adjusted for inflation.* Some have observed that *adjusted prices* and *We have adjusted our prices* almost always are euphemisms meaning "*higher* prices" and "We have *raised* our prices." The adjective has been much used in the sense "adjusted to the realities of life," as in *This child is well-adjusted.*

administer (*v.*) is both transitive, as in *She administers a large law office,* and, very rarely, intransitive, as in *The physician administered to all the injured* (*ministered to* is more usual in this sense).

administrate, administer (*vv.*) *Administrate* is somewhat less frequently used than *administer,* perhaps because it is longer and sounds stuffier, but they are synonyms, and each is Standard in every respect. Some have faulted *administrate* as a back-formation (which would be no crime), but in fact it isn't a back-formation at all; it just looks like one. Whereas *administer* was formed in the fourteenth century from the Latin infinitive *administrare,* *administrate* was formed in the seventeenth century from *administratus,* the past participle of *administrare.* Like *administer,* *administrate* is both transitive and intransitive.

admissible (*adj.*) The unstressed vowel of the third syllable of this word is spelled *i,* not *a.* See -ABLE.

admission, admittance (*nn.*) Synonymous in most senses, although *admission* is much more widely used, these two can be semantically different in one or two uses. For example, *to be granted admittance* is "to be allowed to go inside," whereas *to be granted admission* is "to be allowed to join the group or body." Many Standard users, however, tend to use the terms interchangeably, except in the negatives *No admittance,* meaning "No one can go in," and *No admission,* usually meaning "No money will be charged." *Admission* also has a clearly specialized meaning not shared with *admittance,* "confession or acknowledgement": *He made no admission of guilt.*

admit (*v.*) regularly takes *to,* as in *She admits to having avoided us for weeks,* and most but not all these uses can be replaced by *admit* alone, as in *She admits having avoided them. Admit* also combines with *to* (or *into*) in the transitive sense of *She admitted him to* [*into*] *the house* or *They admitted him into* [*to*] *law practice. Admits of* is another combined use, in the sense of "to allow or permit": *This plan admits of no variation.* See also CONSONANTS (2); PERMIT.

admittance See ADMISSION.

admonishment, admonition (*nn.*) There is almost no semantic difference between these two; they are almost completely synonymous. Both mean "a mild reproof or reprimand, a warning or caution, a reminder," but *admonition* is far more frequently used.

ad nauseam is a Latin tag meaning "to the point of making someone sick," "disgustingly, sickeningly." *He carried on ad nauseam* means he caused nausea in his listeners, not in himself. Pronounce it *AHD* or *AD NAW-zee-uhm, NAW-zee-am,* or *NAW-zee-ahm.* See FOREIGN PHRASES.

adolescent See TEEN.

adopt See ADAPT.

adopted, adoptive (*adjs.*) Regarding the *adoption* of children, Standard English usually still distinguishes: customarily the child is *adopted* (*an adopted child*), and the new parents are *adoptive* (*her adoptive parents,* as opposed to *her natural* [or *biological*] *parents*). Your new country, however, may be either *your adoptive country* or *your adopted country.*

adrift See A-.

adsorb See ABSORB.

adult (*adj., n.*) There are two pronunciations, *A-duhlt* and the more frequently heard *uh-DUHLT*, and each occurs in both noun and adjective. More recently the adjective has added a specialized meaning, "containing explicit sexual or pornographic materials" and hence "not for children": *adult movies, an adult bookstore.*

adumbrate (*v.*) means "to prefigure or foreshadow," "to sketch in vaguely," and hence possibly "to obscure or put in shadow." Only the learned will know the word; for others it may impress the impressionable and befuddle or irritate the rest. *To suggest, to imply,* or *to sketch in briefly* may work better.

advance 1, advanced (*adjs.*) These mean very different things: *advance* means "ahead of the others, earlier than others": *Please give me advance notice. The advance team will prepare the ground for the candidate's visit. Advanced* means "beyond the elementary level" or "far out front in concept and development": *I took an advanced course in French. Their ideas on child care are thought to be advanced. Her symptoms suggest that her case is quite far advanced.*

advance 2, advancement (*nn.*) When these are synonymous, *advance* is the more common: *We're in favor of the advance [advancement] of science. Advance* means "the course forward," while *advancement* can refer to "the policy designed to foster a course forward." In some specialized senses, however, an *advance* is "money given before it is earned or due, in order to assist writers or salespeople to meet their expenses," and in institutional life, an *advancement* is often "a promotion to higher rank."

advantage, vantage (*vv.*) An *advantage,* literal or figurative, is "anything that gives you a better opportunity than another might have." A *vantage* is "a position with more good points than other positions might offer," a *vantage* point, "a high point from which you might overlook all and perhaps dominate." In combined uses, *advantage* can take *over—Our team has several advantages over theirs*—and *of—We'll take advantage of our opportunity. Take advantage of* can also have a pejorative meaning, "unfairly to triumph over or deceive someone," as in *When she isn't looking, they'll take advantage of her.* In some contexts this use can have sexual reference, as in *He took advantage of her inexperience,* which could even be a euphemism for rape.

adventure (*n.*), **venture** (*n., v.*) These two overlap in several meanings, such as "a dangerous or risky undertaking." The differences are primarily in *adventure*'s sense of romance and *venture*'s senses of chance and of application to business or commercial undertakings. As a verb *venture* means "try" or "offer," as in *I venture to say that's untrue.* The adjectives *adventurous, venturous, adventuresome,* and *venturesome* show much the same overlappings and the same specializations, but with this semantic difference: the suffix *-ous* means "characterized by," and the suffix *-some* means "tending toward" *adventure.*

ADVERB (*n.*), **ADVERBIAL** (*adj., n.*) An *adverb* is a part of speech that modifies either a verb (*He ran **swiftly***), an adjective (***enormously** large*), or another *adverb* (***extremely** badly built*). *Very* is the *adverb* most frequently used, particularly because it is also an intensifier.

The adjective *adverbial* refers to words, phrases, or clauses that function as adverbs; the noun *adverbial* applies to any locution—a word, a phrase, or a clause—that behaves *adverbially.* In *She cried **as though her heart would break***, the final clause is *adverbial,* modifying the verb *cried.*

ADVERBIAL DISJUNCTS See SENTENCE ADVERB.

ADVERBIAL GENITIVE Standard and apparently a relic of Old English, the *adverbial genitive* appears in idioms such as *He goes to school days and works as a watchman nights.* In earlier English, the *adverbial genitives days* and *nights* meant something like "of day," "by day," "of days," or "in the daytime" and "of night," "by night," etc. Compare *He studied physics* and *He studied nights.*

ADVERBIAL INTENSIFIERS are the most frequently used intensifiers, employed to emphasize or strengthen other words or constructions, as in ***very** sick, a **really** bad storm, **awfully** loud music. So,* as in *I'm **so** sick of her complaining,* is also an *intensifier,* but it is limited to Conversational and Informal use. Many such *adverbs* are formed by adding *-ly* to an adjective. Overuse of *adverbial intensifiers* fairly frequently drains them of their usual force and turns them into simple hyperboles, as in *a frightfully bad night, a terribly slow train,* or *a horribly boring speech.* See INTENSIFIERS.

ADVERBS 1, COMPARISON OF Like adjectives, *adverbs* may be compared: they have positive, comparative, and superlative degrees. Flat adverbs, such as *slow, quick,* and *soon,* usually inflect for *comparison: My watch runs slowest of all our clocks. Come quicker if you* *can.* Most other *adverbs,* including *quickly,* use *more* and *most* or *less* and *least* in periphrastic comparatives and superlatives: *more reasonably, less smoothly; most pleasantly, least harshly, more quickly, least quickly.*

ADVERBS 2, POSITION OF *Adverbs* are syntactically very flexible; they can appear in nearly all positions in the sentence, and native speakers can usually let their ears guide them on placement. Consider these locations for *usually: Usually, he stayed at the office. He usually stayed at the office. He stayed at the office usually.* Context will dictate which makes the most effective sentence. Only putting *usually* within the prepositional phrase *at the office* is not English syntax. See ONLY.

adverse, averse *(adjs.) Adverse,* means "contrary, opposed, or unfavorable," as in *Adverse winds kept them in harbor* and *The circumstances were adverse. Adverse* combines frequently with *to: He expressed himself as adverse to a public debate. Averse* also combines with *to* and also suggests "opposition to," but mainly in the sense of "not wanting to," of "not being inclined to," and of "disliking to": *He's averse to sailing in any form.* The synonymous use of these two words occurs mainly with *to* and refers to persons—rare *for adverse,* which is normally used of impersonal things. Synonymous uses are more likely to occur in the negative, as in *I'm not adverse to lawyers* (I'm not opposed to them) and *I'm not averse to lawyers* (I don't dislike them); otherwise we're most often *adverse to* actions, events, and things (which we most frequently describe as *adverse* or designate as *adverse forms* or *adversities*). We're *averse to* (rarely *from*) things and people we dislike, but we almost never speak of an *averse* thing or person.

advert See AD.

advert, avert, avoid, prevent *(vv.) To advert to something* is "to refer or call attention to it": *Early in his remarks he adverted to his own criminal history. To avert* is "to turn away from or to ward off": *His quick response averted disaster.* The cliché is *to avert one's gaze* or *glance. To avoid* is "to shun, to keep away from, or to keep from happening": *By responding quickly, she avoided disaster. To prevent* is "to anticipate and so keep from happening": *She prevented his departure by hiding the car keys. Advert* is a very Formal word—even stuffy in some contexts. *Avert, avoid,* and *prevent* are near-synonyms in the sense of "to keep from happening." All four verbs are Standard.

advertise See SPELLING (1).

advise *(v.),* **advice** *(n.)* Spell the verb with an *s* (pronounced *z*), the noun with a *c* (pronounced *s*); misspellings of these are much-cited shibboleths.

advisedly *(adv.)* means "after careful consideration, thoughtfully, with deliberation": *When I say he lied, I use the verb advisedly.*

advisement, take it under This locution is flatulent; *consider it* or *think about it* instead. See PADDED PROSE.

adviser, advisor *(nn.)* Both spellings are Standard. See AGENTIVE ENDINGS.

advocate *(n., v.)* The verb means "to recommend, to speak in favor of": *Do you advocate capital punishment?* The noun combines with *of, for,* and *with: An advocate of something has a favorite cause,* and *for* sometimes works similarly: *Her grandparents were advocates of [for] women's suffrage.* But more often an *advocate for* represents an organization or a person: *He's an advocate for the Central Committee of the Party. With* and *before* are used to show where or with or before whom the advocacy will be undertaken: *She'll be your advocate with [before] her parents.*

ae-, æ-, oe-, œ- See DIGRAPHS; LIGATURES.

aegis, egis *(n.)* Originally a cloak, shield, breastplate, or some other part of Zeus's apparel, the *aegis* (pronounced *EE-jis*) has continued to generalize in Standard English. The metaphoric phrase *under the aegis of* currently means "under the protection of, under the sponsorship of, under the auspices of, or under the direction or control of." All such figurative uses are Standard. (The *egis* spelling is a Standard variant but is not widely used.) See DIGRAPHS; LIGATURES.

aeon See EON.

aer-, aero-, air- *(prefixes)* All three of these prefixes having to do with the air are still in use, but *air-* has replaced *aer-* and *aero-* in some of the most common aviation nouns, especially in American English: *airport, aircraft, airplane, airlift, airspeed, airmail,* and the like. But the other two are regularly used as well: see *aer-* in *aerial, aerial photography,* and *aerialist,* and *aero-* in *aerobatics, aerobic,* and *aeronautics.*

aerate *(v.)* is pronounced as either a two-syllable word (*ER-ate*) or a three (*AI-uhr-AIT*); it has no medial letter *-i-* in its spelling, and it is never pronounced *ER-ee-AIT.*

aerie, aery, eyrie, eyry (*n.*) All these are variant spellings of the word for an eagle's nest (and figuratively any other high habitation). Pronunciations are just as numerous, and include *AI-uhr-ee, EE-ree, UHR-ee,* and *ER-ee.* Say it firmly in a loud voice while looking your listeners straight in the eye: most of them will be every bit as unsure as you are. See DIGRAPHS.

aesthete, esthete (*n.*), **aesthetic, esthetic** (*adj.*) American English uses both variant spellings of each word, but the *ae* spellings predominate slightly in Edited English. See SPELLING (1).

affadavit See AFFIDAVIT.

affair See PROPOSITION.

affect, effect (*nn., vv.*) Nearly all the *effect* and *affect* words are or can be pronounced alike. Only the low-frequency noun *affect,* meaning "a state of mind, an emotion attached to an idea or thing," regularly has the stress on the first syllable: *Psychologists continue to study the strong affects* (pronounced *A-fekts*) *often associated with weapons.* But the *affect/effect* spellings crucially differentiate on paper many of the other senses that in speech only context can differentiate, and many misspellings reflect conscious wrong choices of meanings that even the user couldn't spot in speech. Among the verbs: *She affects* [pretends] *to be deaf. He affects* [wears, probably self-consciously] *red velvet vests. Their tears affected* [moved] *everyone in the room. We effected* [brought about] *several changes.* (See also INFLICT.) The noun *effect* means "result, influence, change"—*Our desperate measures had little effect*—and, especially in the plural, *effects* are "possessions": *The officers put the injured man's personal effects in the ambulance.*

affection, affectation (*nn.*), **affected, affectionate** (*adjs.*) *Affection* is "a tender feeling toward someone" (*I have a lot of affection for my aunt*), which in the plural often means "feelings of love" (*My affections have long centered on her*). An infrequent technical sense also exists, meaning "a pathological or otherwise abnormal mental or emotional state": *She has been diagnosed as having an unspecified affection of the speech centers of the brain. Affectation* is quite another matter—"a fake, a pretense, something done consciously to impress": *He has all sorts of affectations of speech, dress, and manners.*
Affectionate means "openly demonstrative of affection or love": *They're an affectionate cou-*

ple. Affected means "unnatural, insincere, deliberately deceptive": *His affected manners are painful to endure.*

affidavit (*n.*) is the correct spelling. See SPELLING OF UNSTRESSED VOWELS.

affiliate (*n., v.*) The verb combines most frequently with *with: Our organization is affiliated with the international group.* British English also uses *to,* perhaps somewhat more frequently than *with.* The verb can also be intransitive: *We've decided to affiliate in the spring.* The verb has a secondary stress on the last syllable (*uh-FIL-ee-AIT*), but the noun's final syllable is usually unstressed (*uh-FIL-ee-it*).

affinity (*n.*) combines with *for, with, between, among, to,* and some other prepositions. Its meanings range from "blood relationships" to "tendencies" and "cravings": *There is a close affinity among Queen Victoria's many grandchildren. I have an affinity for almost anything Norwegian. Baseball has affinities with hot dogs and peanuts.*

affirmative, negative (*adjs., nn.*) *We were answered in the affirmative. His reply was negative* [or *in the negative*]: these uses are often criticized for being stuffy circumlocutions, but they have a long tradition in English, particularly in the law. In other uses where they are not too ponderous, they sometimes do quite well.

affirmative action is a standard idiom. It means "an action that will support or carry out a policy designed to undo the effects of discrimination on the basis of race, sex, or ethnic origin," and it has come to mean that policy itself, as well. But the term has had such heavy use, both technical and loose, that users must be careful that its precise meaning is clear from context. The difference between a policy, an intention, and an emotional set can be crucial.

AFFIX is the generic name for an addition to the beginning, middle, or end of a word: a prefix precedes a base word: the prefix *pre-* + *fix* becomes *prefix*; an infix fits into the middle of a base word, as in Latin the infix *-ab-* added to *amo* gives us *amabo*; a suffix follows a base word, as when the suffix *-ence* attached to the verb *differ* yields *difference*.

afflict See INFLICT.

affluent (*adj.*), **affluence** (*n.*), **effluent** (*adj., n.*) These words derive from Latin *fluere,* meaning "to flow." *Affluent's* literal meaning is "flowing toward or to" and hence "abundant, wealthy." *Effluent* means "to flow out, to flow from" and as an adjective is relatively rare;

as a noun, it is more commonly used, especially to refer to the result of various processes from which contaminated liquids come. The word commonly has a pejorative quality: most *effluents* are undesirable, but if you carefully control context you can use it without permitting that inference to be drawn. *Effluent* is usually stressed on the first syllable; *affluent* (and the noun *affluence*) are nearly always stressed there too. Some speakers of Standard English do say *af-FLOO-int* and *af-FLOO-ins,* but the pronunciation grates on many ears. Best advice: stress all on their first syllables.

affray (*n.*), a fairly fancy Standard English name for "a brawl, a fight," is not likely to occur Conversationally or Informally, except as whimsy. Stress it on the second syllable.

affront (*n., v.*), **effrontery** (*n.*) The verb *affront* means "to insult, to offend deliberately"; the noun means "insult" and takes *to* or, less frequently, *of: I couldn't forgive his affront to* [*of*] *his mother. Effrontery* is "impudence, boldness, audacity, presumption": *She then had the effrontery to ask a favor.*

aficionado (*n.*) (plural: *aficionados*) is variously pronounced in American English, but the most frequent Standard pronunciation is *af-FI-shuh-NAH-do.* The word means a "devotee of a sport, hobby, or other activity; a fan." Spell it with one *f.* See PLURALS OF NOUNS ENDING IN *-O.*

à fond See AU FOND.

aforementioned, aforesaid (*adjs.*) Like *the above,* these are both common in legal documents. Perhaps because of those associations, both are sometimes used whimsically in Informal and Conversational situations.

afraid (*adj.*) combines with *of,* as in *We were afraid of causing more trouble,* with *for,* as in *I was afraid for my life,* or with *to* plus an infinitive, as in *She was afraid to ask.* It is Standard in all. *Afraid* is almost always a predicate adjective. Even when no symptoms of *fear* are involved, *afraid* is perfectly proper in "regrettable, unfortunate" circumstances, as in *I'm afraid I must disappoint you,* even as it continues to involve real fear in other uses: *In the dark and creaky house that night, he was afraid.*

African(-)American, Afro-American, Black, Colored, Negro (*adjs., nn.*) *African-American,* with or without a hyphen, is the most recently adopted and now the most widely accepted—in Edited English, at least—of a long succession of group names, although *people of color, persons of color,* and other phrases using *of color*

as modifier are also in regular Standard use today. Most of these names began as descriptive terms but then pejorated, sometimes to the extent of being almost as offensive as the hated slang and dialectal *nigger.* From the 1960s until the late 1980s, *Black* was the preferred Standard term, replacing the earlier *Negro* and *Colored* (capitalization of all three varied from time to time and with grammatical function) as acceptable both to members of the group and to those outside it. *Afro-American* developed during the same period. Be alert to the fact that as long as racial matters continue to be sensitive, terminology may suddenly change as events give sanction or take it away.

Afrikaans, Africander, Afrikander, Africaner, Afrikaner (*adjs., nn.*) *Africander, Afrikander, Africaner,* and *Afrikaner* are variant spellings (the last of which is preferred) of the name given white South Africans of Dutch ancestry (also called Boers); it was once generally (but is now infrequently) applied to white South Africans of any European ancestry. *Afrikaans,* which developed from seventeenth-century Dutch, is the language of the *Afrikaners.*

after (*adv.*) Some purists have argued that *after,* meaning "afterward," should never be used except with a modifying adverb: *My ankle got better quickly, but my shoulder pained me long after.* (*Long after* is Standard.) The Irish dialectal *I was after going to the store* means "I had gone to the store" or "I was about to go to the store."

aftermath (*n.*) Originally, "a second crop, grown after the first one had been cut," an *aftermath* came to mean "something that not only follows something else, but somehow results directly from it." Like *subsequent,* it has now generalized in many uses, so that often an *aftermath* only follows another event, without necessarily being caused by it. Most *aftermaths* are bad or unpleasant; to avoid pejorative overtones you must control context carefully.

afterward, afterwards (*adv.*) Both variants are Standard in American English: *Afterward*[*s*] *we went out for supper.*

against (*subord. conj.*), as in *We'll camp right here in the valley against their party comes back,* is Nonstandard and dialectal. In that use, *against* is often pronounced *uh-GIN* and sometimes even spelled *agin.* Use *until.* See also WITHOUT.

***-AGE,* PRONUNCIATION OF WORDS ENDING IN** Pronunciation often tells us something of the frequency of use and length of time in English of originally French words ending in *-age*. *Triage, mirage,* and *barrage* are relatively low frequency words not long in English; the stress remains on their last syllables, and they are pronounced with the French-sounding *-AHZH*. But in Modern English the primary stresses of *marriage* and *advantage* (in Middle English pronounced *mah-ri-AHZH* and *ah-vahn-TAHZH*) have moved forward, and the final syllable in each is anglicized to the pronunciation *-ij*. *Garage,* on the other hand, is in divided usage in today's American English, pronounced acceptably either *guh-RAHZH* or *guh-RAHJ*, with the stress remaining on the last syllable. (In British English there is a third pronunciation: *GER-ij*.)

aged (*adj., n., v.*) The past tense of the verb *age,* as in *During the war, Mother aged perceptibly,* is a one-syllable word. The noun is almost always a two-syllable word: *The care of the aged is becoming a major social problem.* The adjective can have either one or two syllables: *my aged grandmother* has two syllables; *an aged red wine* has only one. See SENIOR CITIZEN.

ageing See AGING.

ageism (*n.*) is a relatively new word, meaning "prejudice against the elderly." It was created on analogy with words like *racism* and *sexism,* but it has not had the vogue of those and is much criticized by language conservatives who object to the proliferation of such *-isms* and consider this one jargon at best.

agenda (*n.*) is now both singular and plural: *These agenda have [this agenda has] been recirculated for the postponed session.* The Latin plural, *agenda,* has been largely overwhelmed in Standard use by the English plural, *agendas.* Most Standard speakers would consider the Latin singular, *agendum,* archaic. See also FOREIGN PLURALS; HIDDEN AGENDA.

AGENTIVE ENDINGS, -ER, -OR The suffixes *-er* and *-or* are called *agentive endings* and usually are added to verbs to make new nouns meaning "someone who performs whatever action the verb stem describes" (*driver; conductor*). American English has many such words, for which the suffixes seem almost randomly chosen. In certain instances, however (see SAILER), each word preserves a semantic distinction; in still others the meaning is the same, but the spelling is in divided usage (See ADVISER). Other *agentive endings* added to other parts of speech include *-ist* (*physicist*) and *-ian* (*grammarian*). See also *-ESS*.

aggravate (*v.*), **aggravating** (*adj.*), **aggravation** (*n.*) Most purists from the nineteenth century on have insisted that *aggravate* means only "to make worse," as in *The climate here aggravates all my symptoms,* considering the "annoy" meaning (*If that boy aggravates me much more, I'm going to spank him*) at best colloquial and more probably Vulgar. However, both senses seem to have been Standard all along, although Edited English uses the "make worse" sense almost exclusively, and you may appropriately use *aggravate* to mean either "make worse" or "annoy" in all but Formal contexts.

aggregate (*adj., n., v.*) Functional shift permits these homographs to serve as adjective (*We deal in aggregate figures here*), as verb (*The full list aggregates more than a hundred members*), and noun (*In the aggregate there is sand, gravel, cement, and water; In the aggregate, their troops outnumbered ours*). The final syllable of the verb is pronounced *-GAIT,* secondarily stressed; for the noun and adjective, it's *-git,* unstressed.

aggress (*v.*) has been around since the eighteenth century, although it may be an independently re-created word, this time as a back-formation from *aggression,* meaning "to perform the first act of aggression" as in *The rebels aggressed [upon] the helpless villagers.* At any rate, whether in politics, geopolitics, zoology, or psychology, it seems to be a Standard but very low frequency word.

aggressive (*adj.*) has increasingly been a pejorative word: *to be aggressive* usually is not admirable. But one sense of *aggressive* has an elevated aura: Good salespeople are *aggressive* and go after the business, rather than waiting for it to find and claim them. Be careful that the pejorative senses do not color an intended elevated or neutral use.

aggressor See AGENTIVE ENDINGS.

aging, ageing Americans spell the word either way.

agitated See ABSTRACTED; DISTRAIT.

agitator See AGENTIVE ENDINGS.

agnostic (*adj., n.*), **atheist** (*n.*), **atheistic** (*adj.*) An *agnostic* believes that we can't know God or prove the existence of a god or any ultimate reality; an *atheist* denies the existence of God.

ago (*adv., adj.*) *Ago* is both adjective, as in *The murder took place many years ago,* and adverb, as in *The murder took place long ago.* It is Standard in both uses. See SINCE.

agoraphobia See ACROPHOBIA.

agree (*v.*) combines with several prepositions in Standard English: *about,* as in *We agreed about the site*; *as to,* as in *They agreed as to the next step*; *in,* as in *We agreed in all details*; *on,* as in *I trust we can agree on a suitable date*; *to,* as in *I think he'll agree to the compromise*; *upon,* as in *The president and I must agree upon an agenda*; and *with,* as in *I agree with you. Agree* also can take *that* plus a clause, as in *We agreed that we'd call on them next week,* and *to* plus an infinitive, as in *She agreed to marry him.*

agreeable See ACCEPTABLE.

AGREEMENT, CONCORD Grammars often use these terms interchangeably. *Agreement* or *concord* is required in Standard English mainly in two situations. (1) Subjects and verbs must agree in number. For most verbs this agreement (or concord) is a problem only with a singular subject and a third person singular present tense verb: *he/she/it goes,* but *I, you, we* and *they go.* In the past tense, both *she* and *they went.* Failure of *agreement,* particularly when subject and verb are close together, is a serious blunder, Substandard in both speech and writing. (2) Pronouns must agree with antecedent nouns in number, gender, and sometimes case, and failures in these agreements are also Substandard. Only the genitive case is distinctive in English nouns these days: *Spot is Mary's dog, her dog, hers; these are the children's bikes, their bikes, theirs.* In addition, the adjectives *this* and *that* must agree in number with the nouns they modify: *this hat, these hats; that belief, those beliefs.* See AGREEMENT OF INDEFINITE PRONOUNS AND OTHER SINGULAR NOMINALS WITH VERBS AND OTHER PRONOUNS.

AGREEMENT, NOTIONAL See NOTIONAL AGREEMENT.

AGREEMENT OF COLLECTIVE NOUNS WITH VERBS AND PRONOUNS See COLLECTIVE NOUNS.

AGREEMENT OF COMPOUND SUBJECTS WITH THEIR VERBS AND SUBSEQUENT PRONOUNS Two generalizations are simple and clear: (1) *Compound subjects* joined by *and* always require plural verbs: *A horse and a cow were in the field.* (2) *Compound subjects,* when composed of singular nouns connected by *or* (or *nor*), take a singular verb: *A dog or a cat is good company.* Then the complications begin. If one part of the *compound* is plural, then the verb will agree with the number of the part closer to it: *Either a companion or several pets are necessary.* And

if the compound seems notionally plural, even if grammatically singular, it will frequently take a plural verb, especially at Conversational and Informal levels: *We concluded that the cause for all these robberies, killings, and other crimes are not known.* Finally, in compound like constructions with *with, together with,* and the like, and those in which the second element is set off with dashes or parentheses *(The husband, with his wife and baby, comes in every morning; Fred—and Mary when she has time—jogs every morning),* usually, if the first element of a near-compound subject is singular, the verb will be singular, and if plural, the verb will be plural, as in *The parents—and their large dog—are waiting for the school bus.* But because of the so-called principle of proximity, no matter how singular the first element, enough intervening plural material will cause the verb to be plural too, unless the sentence is carefully edited. Hence most problematic instances occur at the Conversational levels of speech and Informal writing, not at Oratorical levels or in Edited English.

Similarly, when a pronoun refers to a *compound subject,* the grammatical plurality of *Dick and Jane* will call for a plural pronoun such as *they: Dick and Jane are punctual, and they will arrive on time.* But with the compound *Dick or Jane,* particularly if the pronoun is some distance away, the notion of plurality is very likely to call forth a plural *they,* despite the grammatical call for a singular to match the singular in gender: *Jane or Dick is likely to do the job well, and they can be counted on.* And frequently we anticipate the problem and avoid it thus: *The piano music of Schubert or the piano music of Schumann—both are romantic, but in different ways.* See AGREEMENT OF SUBJECTS AND VERBS (4); COORDINATING CONJUNCTIONS; HE; INCLUSIVE LANGUAGE; SEXIST LANGUAGE; S/HE.

AGREEMENT OF INDEFINITE PRONOUNS AND OTHER SINGULAR NOMINALS WITH VERBS AND OTHER PRONOUNS Indefinite pronouns often cause problems because they are not gender-specific. Traditionally, Edited English has demanded a generic masculine singular pronoun for subsequent reference: *Everybody may put on his coat.* Increasingly, however, all levels of speech except Oratorical and all written English except the most Formal employ a plural pronoun in order to avoid making the gender-specific choice among *his, her,* or *its* in this situation: *Everybody may put on their coat[s].* The same problem arises with the relative and interrogative pronoun, *who,* which is neither gender- nor number-specific: *Who has time these days to do their homework before dinner?* A similar problem arises with singular nouns that can apply to either or both sexes, as in *The individual in every instance will have to make up their own mind[s].* Use either singular or plural pronouns in all these instances, depending on which sound more natural or more precise, except in most Oratorical or Edited English, where you should use *he or she* or *she or he,* or use the masculine and feminine pronouns alternately, or shift the entire construction to the plural, using *they* or *people.* See also AGREEMENT; ANYBODY; HE; INCLUSIVE LANGUAGE; NOTIONAL AGREEMENT; SEXIST LANGUAGE; S/HE; THEY.

Note too that other singular nouns sometimes seem notionally to suggest more than one such thing; in this situation too Standard English frequently uses a plural pronoun for reference to a singular noun: *The bow tie seems to be coming back; I see them almost everywhere I go.*

AGREEMENT OF SUBJECTS AND VERBS 1: CLAUSES BEGINNING WITH *WHAT* USED AS SUBJECTS Notional agreement seems to govern the number of the verb following a *what* clause. Consider these Standard examples: *What is her name? What are their names?* Here *name* and *names* govern whether *what* is to be singular or plural. But when the *what* is direct object, the *what* clause can agree with either a singular or plural verb: *What I need is names and addresses* and *What I need are names and addresses* are both Standard, although the notional attraction from the plural predicate nominatives will tend to make the plural *are* the choice. Nearly every other use of the *what* clause requires a singular verb, as in *What we need to know today is how much time is left [how many hours are left].* See NOTIONAL AGREEMENT.

AGREEMENT OF SUBJECTS AND VERBS 2: COLLECTIVE NOUN PHRASES FOLLOWED BY PLURAL NOUNS Proximity (attraction), notional agreement, and logic conspire here to make the verb choice plural: *A number of us are going to attend. A flock of starlings were making loud conversation.* But at Conversational levels the doubts of the speaker and in Edited English the stylebook's unwavering rule that subjects and verbs must agree in number can sometimes produce the singular: *A pair of hits in the bottom of the ninth usually turns the trick.* Either singular or plural is Standard in such constructions, although the plural usually seems more natural and comfortable. See AGREEMENT OF SUBJECTS AND VERBS (4); ATTRACTION; NOTIONAL AGREEMENT.

AGREEMENT OF SUBJECTS AND VERBS 3: COLLECTIVE NOUNS AS SUBJECTS Athletic teams and governments are usually treated as plural by the British, both for pronoun reference and *subject-verb agreement: Manchester United are expecting great things from their new forward. The government are not yet willing to change their earlier stand.* Americans generally use the singular for the verb, but the subsequent pronouns will often be plural: *Boston is expecting great things from their [its] new pitcher. The administration is not yet willing to change its [their] earlier stand.* But note too that many nouns can be either collective nouns or mass or count nouns: *Drama is my favorite study. Dramas are my favorite reading.* All these are Standard. Note also that verbs following titles can sometimes be affected by notional agreement: *Eliot's* Four Quartets *were [was] immensely popular in the 1950s.* Bach's Goldberg Variations *is [are] a matchless achievement.* See COLLECTIVE NOUNS; MASS NOUNS.

AGREEMENT OF SUBJECTS AND VERBS 4: THE PRINCIPLE OF PROXIMITY If a subject is widely separated from its verb by intervening modifiers, and if the intervening material differs in number from the subject, it is quite likely in speech that *proximity* (or attraction) will govern, and agreement between subject and verb will be notional rather than grammatical: *Everything I've heard about their appeals and interventions suggest that they're going to delay us.* Edited English does not permit this sort of lapse, although the lower levels of speech and Informal writing often overlook it. See NOTIONAL AGREEMENT.

AGREEMENT OF SUBJECTS *ONE OR MORE, ONE IN THREE, ONE OUT OF FOUR,* AND THE LIKE WITH THEIR VERBS *One or more* is a compound subject, the second element of which is plural, and it always takes a plural verb: *One or more of them are coming tomorrow.* (See AGREEMENT OF COMPOUND SUBJECTS WITH THEIR VERBS AND SUBSEQUENT PRONOUNS.) But *one out of* any plural number is still *one* and requires a singular verb: *One out of ten students was late.*

a half, a half a See HALF.

ahead See A-.

ahold is limited to Conversational levels and the Informal writing that imitates them. The Standard idiom for all levels is [*get, take, lay, grab,* etc.] *hold of,* as in *Try to get hold of his teacher.*

aid 1, aide (*nn.*) Both mean "helper or assistant," but *aide* is a clipped form of *aide-de-camp,* the military title, and is always the spelling for military contexts. Americans use both spellings in titles for assistants, although *aide* may be slightly more frequent. *Visual aids, hearing aids,* and other helpful objects are always spelled *aid.*

aid 2, help (*nn., vv.*) In most senses these words are synonyms, but *help* is more common. Some conservatives consider *aid* to be journalese, but sometimes its formality and impersonality are what's wanted. See also SUCCOR.

aim (*v.*) *Aim* combines regularly both with *to* followed by an infinitive and with *at* followed by a gerund: *We aim to please* [*at pleasing*] *as many as possible.* Although *aim to* has much Conversational use in Southern and South Midland dialects, it is current Standard spoken English and can appropriately appear in all levels of written English as well.

ain't, amn't, an't, a'n't, aren't (*contrs.*) *Am I not* is the usually preferred Standard way of negating *I am* and *I'm,* although the expression often seems uncomfortably stiff and formal in Conversational use. Long a shibboleth for twentieth-century Americans, the negative contraction *ain't* continues to be Substandard when used unconsciously or unintentionally. It is a word, though, and in Vulgar and some Common use, it replaces *are not, is not, am not, has not,* and *have not* in statements. Standard English replaces *I ain't* with *I'm not* and the interrogative *ain't I* (which is often added to statements, e.g., *I'm safe, ain't I?*) with a choice of somewhat clumsy locutions: *am I not? aren't I?* or an even more roundabout *Isn't that so? Ain't* probably developed out of the differently pronounced, now rare, and Nonstandard *an't* and *a'n't;* but it may also have developed from other contractions as well (e.g., *amn't,* from *am not,* or *IN-it,* a pronunciation of *isn't it?*). The firm rejection of *ain't* in Standard use is hard to explain, but clearly Americans have come down hardest on it, and they have made the rejection stick in Standard American English. Consciously jocular uses are acceptable, but using *ain't* in circumstances that do not suggest deliberate choice may brand you as a speaker of Vulgar English. See HAIN'T.

air (*v.*) has long been Standard, meaning "to make public," so it is not surprising that the more recent sense, "to broadcast, to put on the air through radio or television," became Standard almost at once. Most dictionaries report this sense today with no restrictive labels.

air- See AER-.

aka, AKA is an initialism meaning "also known as," or "alias," as in *Clark Kent, aka Superman.* Pronounce it *AI-KAI-AI.* See ALIAS; NOM DE PLUME; PSEUDONYM.

akin (*adj.*) combines with *to: Its appearance suggests that the house finch is closely akin to the purple finch.*

à la, a la This French phrase means "in the manner or style of," and American English frequently drops the grave accent. In French the noun following it would be feminine, because *la* is feminine, but in English the *la* works universally, irrespective of gender. See FOREIGN PHRASES.

Alabamian, Alabaman (*adjs., nn.*) Both adjectives and both nouns (referring to someone from Alabama) are Standard.

à la carte is a French phrase pronounced *ah lah KAHRT* and meaning "as set forth on the bill of fare," "with each item on the menu priced separately." Compare PRIX FIXE and TABLE D'HOTE. See FOREIGN PHRASES.

albeit (*conj.*) means "although, but": *He was still a handsome man, albeit a bit past his prime. Albeit* (pronounced *awl-BEE-it*) may seem slightly stiff in some Informal contexts.

albino (*n.*) The second syllable rhymes with *buy,* and the plural is *albinos.* See PLURALS OF NOUNS ENDING IN -O.

albumen, albumin (*nn.*) *Albumen* is "the white of an egg," and *albumin,* and its variant *albumen,* is "any of several proteins found in egg white, milk, various animal tissues, and some plant juices and tissues." Both words are pronounced *al-BYOO-min.*

alee See A-.

alias (*adv., n.*) The noun means "an assumed name": *She had a new alias this time.* The adverb means "otherwise known as": *Smith, alias Smythe, is not a very imaginative person.* See AKA; NOM DE PLUME; PSEUDONYM.

alibi (*n., v.*) The noun originally referred to a legal proof of the physical impossibility that an accused person could have been at the scene of the crime, but Americans have extended it to mean "any excuse used to explain away a mistake or to account for an unfortunate action, however trivial and noncriminal.'' Americans use it a great deal, but the British don't like the extended sense, and some Edited English still rejects it in favor of *excuse, explanation,* or the like.

Functional shift created a verb, *to alibi,* meaning "to offer an excuse for," the status of which has so rapidly improved that it is now at least Conversational.

alien (*adj.*) combines mostly with *to: His views are alien to my conception of how things ought to be. Alien from* also occurs but appears to be fading. See also FOREIGN; INTERNATIONAL.

all (*pron.*) is singular or plural, and the choice is notionally decided: *The food is cooked, the gifts are wrapped, and all is ready for the party. The bands have arrived, and all are ready for the parade.* See also ALL OF.

all-around, all-round (*adj.*) The British use *all-round* exclusively, but Americans consider both terms Standard: *He's an all-around athlete, able to play any sport. She's an all-round musician, able to play in any style.*

allege (*v.*), **alleged** (*adj.*), **allegedly** (*adv.*) There are two *l*'s in *allege* and no medial *-dg-* cluster (a frequent misspelling). *Allege* has just two syllables, *alleged* two or sometimes three (*uh-LEJD* or *uh-LEJ-id*), and *allegedly* has four. The adjective has drawn most of the usage discussion: an *alleged criminal* has been accused but not yet convicted of a crime. Some also question whether a crime can be *alleged* (we're not sure a crime has been committed) or whether only persons can have the adjective fastened on them: *the alleged murderer,* but not the *alleged murder.* The media have so often applied the adjective both ways in order to avoid the legal penalties that might be imposed on them for prejudging a matter not yet decided that both uses have become Standard today. *Suspected* is applied to someone about whom neither allegations nor formal charges have yet been made. Compare ACCUSED; SUSPECTED.

allegory, fable, myth, parable (*nn.*) An *allegory* is a narrative, drama, or device in which characters and events symbolize ideas or abstractions. A *fable* is a story with a moral or lesson to impart, often through the actions of animals that speak and act like people; one extended sense is pejorative: *fables* never really happen, so they're lies. A *parable* is a brief story told to illustrate a moral or religious idea. A *myth* is a narrative that explains the prehistory of a people, often dealing with their origins and their gods; by extension it is a modern effort to represent the origins and values of a race or nation, and, by the very nature of its imaginative qualities, it has acquired pejorative senses.

alleluia, hallelujah (*interj.*) These are accepted variant spellings of the same anglicized word, ultimately from Hebrew via Greek and Latin.

allergy, allergen (*nn.*), **allergenic, allergic** (*adjs.*) An *allergy* is "a hypersensitivity to a food, dust, pollen, or other element." Someone *with an allergy* (or *who has an allergy*) is said to be *allergic.* An *allergen* is a substance that causes an *allergy* or an *allergic reaction* in people. *Allergenic* is the adjectival form of *allergen: The allergenic substance is unidentified.*

Purists have objected to the transferred and figurative senses of *allergic,* meaning "to have an aversion to or dislike for" and applied to all sorts of nonmedical matters: *She says she's allergic to Wagner; she can't stand his operas.* Despite their arguments, it and the other three words are Standard in their figurative uses, just as they continue to be in their older, technical senses. Still, you would be well-advised to limit some of the figurative uses to Semiformal and Informal writing and to the Conversational levels of speech.

all in, meaning "worn out, tired out" (*I was all in after that long practice session*) is Conversational and Informal.

ALLITERATION is the repetition of the initial sounds or sound clusters of two or more words, as in *pretty Polly, invisible ink,* or *the splendid splinter. Alliterated* words are usually placed very close together, but they need not be immediately contiguous. *Alliteration* may often be catchy in advertisements and in certain kinds of oratory, but its overuse in expository prose can strike some readers as sophomoric. See RHYME.

all . . . not See NOT ALL.

all of With nouns, the syntax of both *all of the children* and *all the children* is Standard, although some conservatives argue strongly for dropping the *of.* With pronouns *all of us, you,* or *them* is Standard, but *us, you,* or *them all* is the Standard order when *of* is omitted: *She invited all of us* [*you, them*]. *She invited us* [*you, them*] *all.* (In *All* [*of*] *you people must leave, you* becomes adjectival.) Compare BOTH; SOME OF.

ALLOPHONE An *allophone* is any of the variant forms of a single phoneme. The exploded *t* sound of *top* and the unexploded one in the middle of *later* are *allophones* of the phoneme /t/. They are different sounds, but English speakers hear them both as *t* and can usually ignore the differences between them. (In English /t/ and /d/ are different phonemes.)

allow, allow as how, allow of Some commentators still occasionally insist that *permit,* not *allow,* is the only Standard verb to use when authorization is required, as in *They will not permit nonmembers to attend.* Actually, both words are Standard in such sentences. *Allow of* is a combined use, Standard with either a person or something impersonal as subject: *The leaders [The situation] would not allow of any deviation from the agreement.* See also PERMIT.

He allowed he'd come back in the morning is dialectal and archaic; *She allowed that he had done well* and other uses with a *that* clause are Standard. *To allow as how* is idiomatic and may have some regional dialectal coloration. Compare AS HOW.

all ready (*adj.*), **already** (*adv.*) *All ready* is an adjectival, meaning "completely prepared" (*She's all ready to begin*); *already* is an adverb, meaning "by or even before the time specified" (*She's here already*), "even now" (*He's already an hour late*), and in a Nonstandard dialectal use, it's an expression of irritation (*Stop, already!*). When you mean *all ready,* be careful not to spell it *already;* that blunder may be harshly judged.

all right, alright (*adv., adj.*) *All right* is the only spelling Standard English recognizes.

all-round See ALL-AROUND.

all that, as in *She's not all that busy,* has a Conversational, Informal ring. Note that it is usually adverbial: *I'm not all that interested. It's not all that cold today.* Note too that it is usually used in negative statements, but, as in the adjectival *Stop all that noise!* and the pronominal *I'm interested in classical art—music and dance and all that,* it does occur in other contexts. All these uses of *all that* are now Standard in most Edited English and in Oratorical contexts, although the expression is much more frequent at the Conversational levels and in the writing that imitates them.

all the, all the farther *All the* is mainly an intensifier, used frequently with a comparative: *All the better to see you with, my dear.* Such uses are Standard, but *All the* plus a comparative is often challenged as being a Nonstandard dialectal substitute for *as* plus adjective or adverb plus *as:* Many prefer *That's as far as I can go* to *That's all the farther I can go.* At any rate, Edited English does not admit *all the farther, all the easier,* and others on that model,

although they are quite common in Inland Northern and North Midland Impromptu and Casual speech.

all-time (*adj.*) is an intensifier and a cliché, meaning "as compared with examples from all of history," as in *He's the all-time career leader in stolen bases.* The use is heaviest in the Conversational and Informal contexts of sports, but there is much wider application of the term, which some publishers print as one word, *alltime.*

all together (*adv.*), **altogether** (*adv., n.*) *All together* means "with all members of the group functioning as one": *We went to the concert all together.* If you can separate the two words with intervening words without changing the meaning, as in *We all went to the concert together,* then separated or not, spell them *all together.* If you can't separate them without changing the sense, then the word—and spelling—you want is *altogether,* meaning "completely or wholly," as in *We were altogether disappointed,* "all told," as in *There were five cars in the accident altogether,* and "on the whole, or everything considered," as in *Altogether, I thought it was a fine performance.* There is also a slang, Informal, or Conversational noun in the idiom *in the altogether,* a euphemism for "naked": *There were several people in the pond, bathing in the altogether.*

all told is a Standard idiom meaning "all counted"; *told* in this sense is related to the bank *teller's* job, i.e., counting.

allude, elude, mention, refer (*vv.*) *Allude* and *elude* look different enough, but in speech they are very close to being homophones, varying only in their unstressed first syllables: *allude* (*uh-LOOD*) and *elude* (*ee-LOOD* or *i-LOOD*); *allude* means "to refer to indirectly," *elude* means "to evade or escape from." *Allude* is a synonym for *mention* and *refer,* but it is more indirect than they: *The judge alluded to the prisoner's alleged accomplices, but without mentioning their names. Refer* is very explicit: had he *referred* to them, the judge might well have read off their names. *Mention* is less explicit and perhaps less rhetorically stressed: had the judge *mentioned* them, he might have tossed off their names hurriedly, in an aside or a parenthetical remark. All four words are Standard.

allusion, elusion, illusion (*nn.*) These three sound surprisingly alike, because their first syllables, the only places they differ, are all unstressed. An *allusion* (*uh-LOO-zhuhn* or *a-LOO-zhuhn*) is "an indirect reference," an *illusion* (*uh-LOO-zhuhn* or *i-LOO-zhuhn*) is "a false perception or appearance," and an *elusion* (*ee-LOO-zhuhn*) is "an evasion, an escape." The words most often confused are *allusion* and *illusion*. *Elusion* is a very low frequency word; the gerund, *eluding,* is much more common. See also ALLUDE; DELUSION.

allusive See ELUSIVE.

ally (*v.*) combines with either *to* or *with* and sometimes with *against:* *We've allied ourselves to [with, against] several Western countries.*

-ally See -LY.

almond (*adj., n.*) is pronounced *AH-muhnd, A-muhnd, AL-muhnd, AHL-muhnd*; but most Standard English speakers keep the *l* silent.

almost (*adv., adj.*) *Almost* is a Standard adverb meaning "nearly," as in *I was almost ready to retire.* The adjective *almost* is rare in such uses as *She's distantly related to me—an almost cousin of sorts;* today we are more likely to find *near-* in that use, as in *It was a near[-]disaster. Almost* occurs much more frequently in such uses as *He had almost nothing to say.*

alms (*n.*) is pronounced *AHMZ,* with no *l* sound, and is most often treated as plural: *The bishop's alms were* [rarely *was*] *welcome.*

-alogy See OLOGY.

alone (*adv., adj.*) The adjective, meaning "only," as in *I alone am left to tell the tale,* is Standard and has a somewhat Formal air. The adverb, meaning "by myself, without company," as in *I work alone,* is also Standard and is in more general use.

along (*prep.*) combines with *with* in Standard English and means "beside, together with" (*I was raking leaves along with Joe*); some purists consider it redundant or at least wasteful, but it is simply a rambling Conversational style. *Along with* also is Standard in the meaning "as well as," as in *We had roast beef, along with all the trimmings. Along of,* however, is Nonstandard and means either "because [of]" or "with": *They left shortly, along of they hadn't had supper. I went to the movies along of my mother.*

alongside of, alongside (*adv., prep.*) The *of* is Standard but unnecessary. The choice between *I pulled up alongside the truck* and *I pulled up alongside of the truck* is a matter of style and level. In expository prose, where economy and rigor are often required, dispense with the *of.*

aloof (*adj.*) normally combines with *from,* as in *She holds herself aloof from daily frictions,* al-though *to,* as in *She is aloof to all the noise and dust of the neighborhood* also occurs.

alot is a Substandard spelling of *a lot,* as in *She sees a lot of him these days. Alot* is increasingly found in Informal correspondence and student writing, but it has as yet received no sanction in print except on the op-ed and sports pages. See also LOTS OF.

a lot of See LOTS OF.

aloud See OUT LOUD.

already See ALL READY.

alright See ALL RIGHT.

also (*adv., coord. conj.*) As an adverb in close proximity to the verb or late in a sentence, *also* is Standard and poses no usage problems: *We were also invited. We were invited also.* But beginning a sentence with the conjunctive adverb *also* has frequently been criticized, usually on grounds that it is not a coordinating conjunction (some commentators also decry beginning a sentence with *any* coordinating conjunction): *None of us had eaten. Also, we were very weary.* Nevertheless, like *besides, also* is Standard as a *conjunctive adverb.* A more prudent course may be to limit that use to Conversational levels only, but even in Formal writing, *also* is Standard in inverted sentences: *Also running for the office were three total unknowns.* See CONJUNCTIVE ADVERBS; COORDINATING CONJUNCTIONS.

altar (*n.*), **alter** (*v.*) Confusing these homophones occurs only when the unstressed vowel each word has in its second syllable is misspelled; the meanings and functions are distinctly different: an *altar* is a piece of religious furniture, and *to alter* means "to change, to modify," or "to neuter an animal, especially a dog or cat" (this sense is an American euphemism).

alternate 1 (*v.*) The verb is pronounced *AWL-tuhr-NAIT,* and it combines with *with* and occasionally with *between: Manning alternates with Rosen at tackle. Her emotions alternated between delight and anxiety.*

alternate 2, alternative (*adjs., nn.*) Today's Standard American English pronounces the adjective and noun *alternate, AWL-tuhr-nit.* The adjective means "every other (one)," as in *This summer our foursome played golf on alternate Mondays.* The noun means "a substitute or replacement," as in *She was appointed an alternate, not a full delegate.* The adjective *alternative* (pronounced *awl-TUHR-nuh-tiv*) means "substitute," or "another": *They gave us an* *alternative proposal.* Recently, however, *alternate* seems more and more to be replacing *alternative* in that sense: *They sent us an alternate [alternative] selection.* Both are Standard. *Alternative* is also Standard meaning "nontraditional or unconventional": *He goes to an alternative school. She listens to alternative music.* The adverbs *alternately* and *alternatively* echo similar patterns of meanings and pronunciations. The noun *alternative* is pronounced like the adjective, of which it is a functional shift.

Etymologically, *alternatives* come only in twos, but today *alternatives* may occur in any numbers, and Standard English readily accepts such sentences as *She offered me several alternatives, not one of them really pleasant.* Conservatives prefer (and some Edited English still requires) *options* when there are more than two choices: *There were originally two alternatives, but this latest offer now gives us three options.* See also CHOICE; OPTION.

alternately, alternatively See ALTERNATE (2).

altho (*conj.*) is a Nonstandard variant spelling of *although* employed by many Standard users to save space in personal correspondence. Edited English will have none of it; *altho* occurs in print almost solely in the comics.

although (*subord. conj.*), **though** (*adv., subord. conj.*) As subordinating conjunctions, *although* and *though* are interchangeable and Standard: *I agreed to attend, although [though] I did so reluctantly.* The choice of one or the other can be made on the basis of the rhythm of the prose. *Though* also lives a separate life as a conjunctive adverb with a Conversational flavor and a meaning of "however": *His house is in the village, though.*

alto (*adj., n.*) The plural of the noun is *altos.* See PLURALS OF NOUNS ENDING IN *-O.*

altogether See ALL TOGETHER.

aluminum, aluminium (*adj., n.*) Americans call the metal *uh-LOOM-i-nuhm*; the British call it *AL-yoo-MIN-i-yuhm.* The respective spellings reflect these pronunciations. See also SPELLING (1).

alumnus, alum, alumna (*nn.*) *Alumni* (pronounced *uh-LUHM-nei* or *uh-LUM-nei*) is the Latin masculine gender plural of *alumnus,* borrowed by English to refer to men and boys who have graduated from an educational institution. Its use as the generic plural for mixed groups of male and female graduates is considered exclusive language by many but continues in general and conservative use. *Alumnae* (pronounced *uh-LUHM-nee* or *uh-LUM-nee*) is the feminine gender plural of *alumna,* used for women and girls. *Alums* is the plural of the clipped form *alum,* used Conversationally and Informally, irrespective of sex. The popularity of the clipped forms has no doubt increased because *alum* and *alums* are inclusive language and because some Standard speakers are unsure of the spellings, pronunciations, and genders of the four unclipped Latin forms. See also FOREIGN PLURALS; GRADUATE.

A.M., P.M. These abbreviations (for Latin *ante meridiem,* meaning "before noon," and *post meridiem,* meaning "after noon") are unexceptionably Standard except when used redundantly, as in *It was 3* A.M. *in the morning when we got to bed.* Both abbreviations are occasionally used as nouns at Conversational and Informal levels to indicate the general part of the day: *We didn't arrive until the wee hours of the* A.M. In the United States, A.M and P.M. are usually printed as small capital letters with no spaces between the letters and sometimes without the periods. In Britain, the abbreviation is usually printed lowercase.

amalgam (*n.*), **amalgamate** (*v.*) *Amalgam* combines with the preposition *of: That smile is an amalgam of insincerity and expert dentistry.* The verb *amalgamate* combines with *with* (*Our group amalgamated with the other cooperative*) and, much less frequently, with *in* or *into* (*My fiscal policy proposals were amalgamated in [into] the final party platform*).

amateur (*adj., n.*) AM-*uh-chuhr,* AM-*uh-tuhr,* AM-*uh-CHYOOR,* and AM-*uh-TOOR* are all Standard pronunciations. As a noun *amateur* usually takes the preposition *of:* you are an *amateur of something,* although *in* and *at* sometimes occur: *He's an amateur of [in, at] astronomy.*

amatory, amorous (*adjs.*) *Amorous* means "filled with, driven by, or expressive of love," as in *Each had amorous play in mind. Amatory,* a slightly more restrained or intellectual word, while it can be a synonym for *amorous* in all those senses, usually means a more reserved "related to or connected with love," as in *Petrarch's amatory sonnets* or *her several amatory adventures.* There's more heavy breathing in *amorous.*

ambidextrous, ambidextrously, ambidexterity See DEXTEROUS.

ambience, ambiance (*n.*) American English spells it *ambience,* but you may occasionally encounter the original French *ambiance,* without italics to indicate its foreign nature. Americans say *AM-bee-yens,* but *ambiance* can *also* be pronounced *AHM-bee-YAHNS,* although some listeners may consider that precious.

ambiguous See EQUIVOCAL.

AMBIGUOUS (*adj.*),   **AMBIGUITY** (*n.*) *Ambiguity*—being *ambiguous*—is saying something in such a way as to obscure meaning, to suggest more than one meaning, or otherwise to make meaning uncertain. Inadvertent *ambiguity* can hamper or prevent clear communication. In expository prose and most speech we ordinarily try to avoid it, although both it and double meaning (*double entendre*) are often deliberate in literature and sometimes in speech. Some *ambiguities* of the written language disappear when we speak the words aloud. On paper *a Spanish teacher* may be "a teacher of Spanish" or "a Spanish person who teaches," but stress in speech usually clears up any *ambiguity:* stress on *Spanish* makes *Spanish teacher* a compound, meaning "a teacher of Spanish"; stress on *teacher* makes *Spanish teacher* "a Spanish person who is a teacher." Newspaper headlines often contain inadvertent *ambiguities* (in *Teacher Strikes Idle Students,* is the verb *strikes* or *idle?*), and speech can too: without spelling and apostrophes as guides, *boyz BEIKS* is *ambiguous* (is it *boy's bikes,* or *boys' bikes?*). Pronoun reference can also be *ambiguous* if the antecedent is too far back for clear recall or if it is unclear: *John and then George came to the meeting. Later he said he'd be willing to serve.* (Which one said it?) Avoid inadvertent *ambiguity.*

ambition (*n.*) combines most commonly with *to* plus an infinitive, as in *She had an ambition to become an airline pilot,* but can also combine with *of* or *for* plus a gerund or other noun: *His ambition of winning the lottery would not die. Their ambition for their children was unbounded.*

ambivalent means "undecided, of two minds about it," and is used to describe a person's mental state, combining with *about* or *concerning: I'm ambivalent about [concerning] our next move.* See also EQUIVOCAL.

ameba See AMOEBA.

ameliorate, counteract, mitigate, relieve (*vv.*) All four words have to do, at least in part, with how to improve unsatisfactory conditions or situations. *Ameliorate* means "to make better, to improve": *The agency did what it could to ameliorate housing conditions. Counteract* means "to use an equal and opposite force to prevent another force from dominating a situation": *These pills should counteract your indi-*

gestion. *Mitigate* and *relieve* both mean "to make less, to make easier, to reduce": *His kind words mitigated [relieved] her embarrassment somewhat.* An important distinction is that you can *counteract suffering,* and you can *mitigate* or *relieve it,* but you cannot *ameliorate suffering:* that would "improve it," which might well mean "increase it." Compare MILITATE.

AMELIORATION See ELEVATION.

amen (*n., interj.*) Standard English pronounces it either *AI-MEN* or *AH-MEN.*

amenable (*adj.*) means "responsive, receptive" and combines regularly with *to: He is even-tempered and amenable to correction.* Pronounce it either *uh-MEN-uh-bul* or *uh-MEEN-uh-bul.*

amend, emend (*vv.*) The only meaning these two have in common is "to correct and improve a text or document." *Amend* is the verb most generally used: *I move to amend the motion.* The use of *emend* is limited almost exclusively to repairing errors in written texts: *Professor Skeat emended freely whenever the manuscript's text didn't make sense.* Unless you're a literary or historical scholar and must deal often with *emendations* (the noun), the chances are you'll need only *amend* (whose noun is *amendment,* although one can also *make amends*).

amenity (*n.*) is pronounced either *uh-MEN-i-tee* or *uh-MEEN-i-tee.* It is most commonly used in the plural, meaning "manners, comforts, conveniences": *Our suite offered all the amenities.*

American (*adj.*), **America** (*n.*) We of the United States of *America,* citizens of only one of many nations in the Americas, North, Central, and South, have preempted the informal name of our country, *America,* and our title, *Americans.* It may be arrogant and inaccurate that we do so, but the fact is that no other citizens of the Americas seem to want to be confused with the *Americans* of the USA. Nor have others coined any other universally recognized names for us. *Yankees* and *Yanks* sometimes applies to all of us but often only to Northeasterners (particularly New Englanders) and twentieth-century soldiers. Our flag is almost always "the American flag." Only the precision of *The United States of America* and of *a citizen thereof* can be official and usefully substituted, and the rest is language history: we speak American English, we live in the United States, the U.S. (or USA), or America (the beautiful), and we're *Americans,* even if we only adapted and adopted the language and the lands. It is not likely that these usages will change soon, so overwhelming is their use both by others and by us.

AMERICAN AND BRITISH DIFFERENCES IN MEANING, PRONUNCIATION, SPELLING, AND VOCABULARY
See MEANING; PRONUNCIATION (2); SPELLING (1); VOCABULARY (2).

AMERICAN ENGLISH is that very important variety or dialect of the English language spoken by most people in the United States of America as their first or native language and as a second or third language by millions of others over much of the world. *American English* differs in aspects of its phonology, its orthography, its morphology, its syntax, and its vocabulary from other major dialects of English, such as Australian English, British English, Canadian English, Irish English, and South African English, to say nothing of the English of other large populations of the globe who use various forms of it, usually as a second language, a lingua franca. See AMERICAN.

AMERICAN ENGLISH CONSONANTS
See CONSONANTS (1).

AMERICAN ENGLISH VOWELS
See VOWELS.

American Indian See INDIAN; NATIVE AMERICAN.

AMERICANISMS are locutions of several sorts: words or meanings invented in the United States, often from native American materials (*woodchuck*), words or meanings brought here from Britain, often from British seventeenth- and eighteenth-century rural dialects (the verb *loan*, for example), words that then became Standard here while dying out or remaining dialectal in Britain (the noun *scallion*), words that mean one thing in Britain but have new American meanings here (a British *vest* is an American *undershirt*; an American *vest* is a British *waistcoat*). These and many other classes of words and syntactic practices that are American in origin or influence are often called *Americanisms*. Mencken (1945a) claimed a good deal more influence in Britain for American varieties of English than perhaps was warranted in his day, but now even the most reluctant Briton recognizes the deluge of American words and expressions that have invaded and conquered some of Britain's English, including some aspects of Received Standard Southern British and the language of the BBC: the Americanism *fan*, for example, is now used everywhere in Britain, where once only *supporter* might have meant the partisan of an athletic team. *Americanisms*

from the beginnings to World War II are well documented in two excellent scholarly dictionaries (Craigie and Hulbert 1938–1944; Mathews 1951) and in some commercial dictionaries. *Webster's New World Dictionary* (1988) marks with a marginal star each entry it considers an *Americanism*.

amicable (*adj.*) is pronounced *AM-ik-uh-bul*.

amid, amidst (*preps.*) These Standard prepositions are synonyms, although *amid* is of a slightly higher frequency. They may have either singular or plural nouns as objects, and these nouns may be either mass or count nouns: *amid [amidst] the noise; amid [amidst] the cries of birds and insects.* See also AMONG.

am I not, amn't I See AIN'T.

amoeba, ameba (*n.*) has two acceptable spellings: the general public regularly prefers the spelling with the ligature *æ* or the digraph *oe*, as in *amoeba*; biology and medicine now often use *ameba* in their journals.

amok, amuck (*n.*) Both spellings are acceptable, but *amok* occurs more often today; the word usually appears in the idiom *to run amok*, meaning "to go on a wild, demented killing spree" or, figuratively, "to behave violently and uncontrollably."

among, amongst (*preps.*) These two prepositions are interchangeable in meaning, but *among* is far more frequent in American English; for some, *amongst* has a rather dusty-genteel quality. It occurs far more often in British English. Three other usage issues involve *among* (and *amongst*). (1) The *Oxford English Dictionary* observes that *among* is often followed by a singular collective noun, especially if the noun is the name of a substance: *among the straw; some lean among the fat.* Plural objects of the preposition are of course very common: *among the dozens of people; among the causes.* (2) Although *among* does occur occasionally with *each other* and *one another*, the far more usual (and better) choice is a plural -*self* pronoun: *They agreed among [amongst] themselves;* or, use *with* and *each other*, as in *They agreed with each other.* (3) See BETWEEN.

amoral, immoral (*adjs.*) *Amoral* (the first syllable rhymes with *day*), means "above, beyond, or apart from moral consideration," and "neither moral nor immoral." *Immoral* means "not in conformity with the moral code of behavior, not moral."

amorous See AMATORY.

amount, number (*nn.*) Use *amount* with singular mass nouns (*an amount of money; the amount of love*), and use *number* with plural count nouns (*the number of castles; a number of sophomores*). Common and Vulgar English frequently use *amount* with plural count nouns (*a huge amount of children on the playground*), and repeated exposures to that usage often blur the Standard models for us. There are also instances where plural count nouns are treated as representing those items in mass and hence usable with *amount* (*He contracted for an enormous amount of apples*). In speech such a use might go almost unnoticed, but Edited English would most likely change it to *number* or find an entirely different way to say it. See also NUMBER (2).

The noun *amount* combines with *of* plus object: *The attic was filled with a large amount of junk.* The verb combines with *to* plus object: *He'll never amount to much.*

AMPERSAND This character (&) stands for *and.* Its name is an altered form of the phrase *and per se and,* meaning "& by itself means *and.*"

amphitheater, amphitheatre (*nn.*) Americans prefer the *-er* spelling, the British, the *-re.* See SPELLING (1).

ample enough One of *ample*'s meanings is "enough." Hence the phrase *ample enough* is a tautology. Use *ample* or *enough,* not both. See SUFFICIENT.

amuck See AMOK.

amuse 1 (*v.*), **amused** (*adj.*) The verb *amuse* combines with *by* and *with: He amused her by doing card tricks. She was amusing the crowd with her antics.* The participial adjective combines with *at: We were both amused at his tantrum.* The verb also takes *to* plus an infinitive: *You will be amused to hear this.* It can also take a reflexive pronoun as direct object: *We amused ourselves for an hour.*

amuse 2, bemuse (*vv.*) "To divert" is the only meaning these words have in common, and even there they are not quite synonyms. With *amuse* the sense is "to entertain, to occupy with pleasant things," whereas with *bemuse* the sense is "to confuse, baffle, or preoccupy." If you are *amused,* your attention is turned to cheerful things; if you are *bemused,* your attention is so blocked that you cannot respond to other stimuli.

an See A.

an- See A-.

ANACOLUTHON Etymologically the term describes a grammatical structure that "does not march together" and hence "does not follow." In rhetoric and in grammar it describes a sentence that interrupts itself in midflight and then resumes in a wholly unrelated syntactic way: "*I want to speak today about—can you all hear me in the back?*" Or it may be a pushmi-pullyu sort of syntax, as in *We have to face the problem is that we can't win.* It is characteristic of some inexperienced Planned speaking, where its unfinished syntax can sound disarmingly unstudied and sincere, but *anacolutha* (also *anacoluthons*) should *not* appear in Formal and Semiformal prose.

anaemic, anaemia See ANEMIC.

anaesthetic See ANESTHETIC.

analogous (*adj.*) means "like, similar to, resembling" and combines often with the preposition *to: This election shows some trends analogous to those of elections a generation ago.* With also occurs: *Our congressional situation is analogous with that faced by the British parliament in 1939.*

ANALOGY 1 In language matters, *analogy* is a process whereby the force of similarities common to a large group of locutions causes an originally different locution to conform to the larger pattern. For example, most English noun plurals end in *-s,* so the word *pease* (as in *pease porridge hot*) was thought to be plural too, although it actually was a singular whose stem simply ended in *-s. Analogy* then made us construct a new singular, *pea,* to go with what we thought was the plural, *pease* (pronounced *PEEZ* and now spelled *peas*). *Analogy* with the word *hamburger* works in folk etymology to bring about words such as *cheeseburger, nutburger,* and *fishburger;* these analogies are false, but they work nonetheless.

analogy 2 (*n.*) can take various prepositions: *among,* as in *We saw several analogies among these results; between,* as in *There was an obvious analogy between this situation and that of Europe in the thirties; of,* as in *This example can serve as an analogy of our actual problem* (although here *an analogue of* would be better); *to,* as in *This analogy to your own observations may help persuade you;* and *with,* as in *Here's an obvious analogy with the difficulty they're facing.*

analysand See ANALYST.

analyse, analyze See -ISE; SPELLING (1).

analysis 1, in the final (*last*) This idiom means "in the end," "after all," "when everything is known and taken into account," as in *In the final [last] analysis, we turn out to have been right.* It's also a cliché.

analysis 2, synthesis (*nn.*) These two represent diametrically different processes: *analysis* results when you separate something into its component parts; *synthesis* occurs when you assemble some parts into a new whole.

analyst, annalist, analysand (*nn.*) *Analyst* and *annalist* are homophones with very different meanings: an *analyst* is "someone who analyzes" (it is also short for "a psychoanalyst"); an *annalist* is "someone who writes *annals* (chronologically recorded annual reports of events)." An *analysand* is a person undergoing psychoanalysis; the *analyst* does the psychoanalysis of the *analysand*.

analyzation (*n.*) is a rare and probably seldom-needed synonym of *analysis*.

ANAPHORA is repetition of initial words or phrases in successive clauses or sentences, done for rhetorical or poetic effect, as in Psalm 150, with its nine successive clauses each beginning "Praise him. . . ." Martin Luther King, Jr.'s "I have a dream . . ." speech, in which each repetition of that clause introduced a fresh elaboration of his message, is a familiar example of *anaphora* from recent American oratory. See also PLEONASMS; TAUTOLOGY.

anchorperson (*n.*) is a fairly recent coinage, one of many that substitute *-person* for *-man* or *-woman* in the effort to replace gender-distinctive words with an inclusive word. Since the generic clipped noun *anchor*, with the same meaning, seems to be widely used for the same purpose, there is no certainty that *anchorperson* will prevail: both words are Standard at present. Compare CHAIR; CHAIRMAN.

ancient, antiquated, antique (*adjs.*) All these synonyms mean "old," but their full definitions partly distinguish each from the others: *ancient* means "very old, even classically old"; *ancient history* is the history of Greece and Rome and even earlier civilizations. *Antique* also means "ancient," but particularly it has come to mean "old-fashioned, in an older style." Anything *antique* or *ancient* may be either revered or scorned; *antiquated*, however, is pejorative, meaning "out-of-date, not useful, obsolete." All these words are used widely in hyperbolic figurative senses too: something scornfully called *ancient*, *antique*, or *antiquated* may be no more than a few years old.

ancillary (*adj.*) is pronounced either *AN-sil-ER-ee* or *an-SIL-uhr-ee* and means "auxiliary or subordinate"; it combines with *to*: *Alas, her studies were always ancillary to her partying.*

and (*coord. conj.*) Avoid frequently beginning sentences with the coordinating conjunctions *and* or *but*. Such sentences can be stylistically appropriate at any Standard level, but as a habitual beginning, especially in writing, the initial conjunction can seem unpleasantly garrulous and mechanical. See also BUT.

and etc. See ETC.

and/or (*coord. conj.*) *And/or* is a coordinating conjunction that developed first in legal writing and has gradually generalized to such frequent use at many levels that it has become a cliché. Often it affects a precision it cannot provide. Usually we use it to mean "either this one or that one or both of them." Sometimes, fully spelling out all three possibilities or using *either or both* may be clearer than *and/or*. It may be useful in Informal correspondence, note taking, and the like, but elsewhere you should avoid this graceless phrase.

and so (*coord. conj.*) is much used at the lower levels of speech. It should not become a habit or a formula in your writing, however. See AND; ETC.; VOCALIZED PAUSES.

and which, and who, and that serve frequently to begin the second of what should be two paired, parallel clauses functioning as modifiers. Frequently, however, in speech and in careless prose these introductory structures will be out of parallel and therefore inappropriate in Edited English and at the higher levels of speech (see FAULTY PARALLELISM; PARALLELISM), as in *Games thought to be in hand and which were unexpectedly lost came back to haunt them.* One parallel version might be *Games which [that] were thought to be in hand, and which [that] were unexpectedly lost, came back to haunt them.* The sentence would also be parallel with two participial phrase modifiers (*Games thought to be in hand and unexpectedly lost . . .*). Otherwise rearrange the syntax completely to eliminate any need for parallelism.

anecdote, antidote (*nn.*) The initial and final syllables are identical, but only the inexperienced would be likely to confuse these words. An *anecdote* (*AN-ek-dot*) is "a short narrative," and an *antidote* (*AN-ti-dot*) is "a remedy that counteracts a poison or anything else injurious." *Antidote* combines with *to*, *against*, and *for*: *Music can be an antidote to [for, against] gloom.*

anemic, anaemic (*adj., n.*), **anemia, anaemia** (*n.*) Both spellings of each word are Standard, but *anemic* and *anemia* are more frequent in the United States, *anaemic* and *anaemia* in Britain. See DIACRITICS; LIGATURES; SPELLING (1).

anent (*prep.*), stressed on the second syllable (*uh-NENT*), is a formerly archaic word that has staged a modest comeback. It means "concerning, about" and, though a useful word, it has a stuffy, impersonal quality, inappropriate in many contexts: *We wish to consult you anent [about, concerning] your business in Asia.*

anesthetic, anaesthetic (*adj., n.*) Both spellings are Standard, but *anesthetic* has become a bit more frequent in American English. See DIACRITICS; LIGATURES; SPELLING (1).

anesthesiologist, anesthetist (*nn.*) An *anesthesiologist* is "a physician specializing in *anesthesiology,* which is the study of *anesthetics* and their application." *Anesthetist* is a more general term, meaning "a nurse or anyone else trained to give anesthetics."

angle 1 (*n., v.*) *Angle*'s usage issues involve the noun's figurative senses: in the meaning "point of view, standpoint," as in *From your angle, what's the situation?*, *angle* is Standard, although some conservatives may still consider it slang. In the meaning "a personal motive, or a tricky way of doing something," as in *I don't know what his angle is, angle* should clearly be limited to Conversational or Informal use. The verb, which means "presented with a particular or slanted point of view," as in *We heard the story, but it was angled from the victim's vantage point,* is also Conversational and Informal. The related verb, meaning "to go fishing, to fish for," has long been Standard, however; in Old English *angul* meant "fishhook," and all *angles* derive from the Greek *ankylos,* meaning "crooked or bent." See also STANDPOINT.

Angle 2, Anglia (*nn.*), **Anglian, Anglican** (*adjs., nn.*) The *Angles* were the Germanic people whose tribal name gives us the first component of the name Anglo-Saxon, as well as dozens of other words: *Anglia* was named after them and later was modified to *England* (*Angleland*); *East Anglia* of today is an area in eastern Britain once an Anglo-Saxon kingdom and now comprising mainly the counties of Norfolk and Suffolk.

The adjective *Anglian* describes the tribe, their language, or their culture; the adjective *Anglican* has two meanings: a rarely encountered sense, "English," and the more familiar sense having to do with the established Church of England. Functional change permits both words to serve as nouns identifying persons as *Anglians* or *Anglicans.*

ANGLE BRACKETS See BRACKETS.

Anglican See ANGLE (2); EPISCOPAL.

anglicized, Anglicized, anglicised (*adj.*) Americans spell it (and the verb from which it is made) with a *z* and capitalize it or not. *Anglicised* is the British spelling. See SPELLING (1).

Anglo (*n.*) is the Mexican-Americans' name for any white American not of Mexican derivation. It began as a dialect word and has been used by Spanish-Americans as a racial epithet for whites, but now it has been increasingly adopted by most other Americans for nonpejorative use in discussing the ethnic and other demographic patterns of the Southwest.

ANGLO-ENGLISH is a term adopted by some British commentators as a name for British English, the English spoken in the United Kingdom.

ANGLO-INDIAN is what some dialectologists call the dialects of British English spoken as second languages by many people of India, Pakistan, Bangladesh, Sri Lanka, and Nepal—all former British possessions. Prodigious diversities of race, language, and religion among the enormous populations of the Indian subcontinent (in 1990 some 988 million people) made the need for a lingua franca overwhelming: British English, having had a head start, has become that language.

ANGLO-SAXON See OLD ENGLISH.

angry (*adj.*) combines in Standard English with the prepositions *with* (*She's angry with her dog*), *about* (*She's angry about his having chewed up her dictionary*), and *at* (*She'll probably stay angry at him a bit longer*). One can also be angry *toward* (or *towards*) someone or be angry *for some* (or *a good,* or *no*) *reason.* See also MAD (1).

angst, Angst (*n.*) This German word, which we acquired through Danish, means "a feeling of anxiety and gloom" and can be heard with a German pronunciation (*AHNGST*) or an American one (*ANGST*). Most dictionaries now consider it a Standard anglicized noun that need be neither capitalized in the German fashion nor put into the italics that would indicate its still-foreign status.

animadversion, aversion (*nn.*), **animadvert** (*v.*) *Animadversion* (meaning "adverse comment or criticism") combines with *on* or *upon*: *Her animadversions on [upon] his clothes seem* *unnecessarily brutal. Aversion* (meaning "an intense dislike") combines with *to, from,* and *for,* and rarely *toward* (or *towards*) and *against: I have an aversion to spinach, an aversion from asparagus,* and *an aversion for broccoli too.* A confusion of *aversion* and *animadversion* may lead to combining the latter with *to,* but *Her animadversions to his clothes* is Nonstandard. Like the noun *animadversion,* the verb *animadvert* combines with *on* or *upon: The reviewer animadverted at length on the failings of the author's prose.*

annalist See ANALYST.

annex (*n., v.*), **annexe** (*n.*) The verb *annex* is pronounced either *uh-NEKS* or *AN-eks*; the noun is pronounced *AN-eks. Annexe* is the British variant spelling of the noun. See SPELLING (1).

anniversary (*n.*) An *anniversary* is the same date exactly one or more years later. The usage problem has arisen because *anniversary* is sometimes used Informally to mark other occasions, as in *our first week's "anniversary"* or *our three-month "anniversary."* There is no harm in this extended sense, as long as it stays in the Conversational levels and Informal writing. Note that even in this written use, the word is placed within quotation marks to indicate its special status.

anno Domini See A.D.; FOREIGN PHRASES.

annoint See ANOINT.

annoyed (*adj.*) combines regularly with the prepositions *with, by, at,* and *about: She was annoyed with [by, at] her father. He felt annoyed about her sulky behavior. Annoyed* can also take *to* plus an infinitive (*I was annoyed to learn that she'd resigned*) or be followed by a *that* clause (*They were annoyed that I hadn't waited for them*).

annual, perennial (*adjs., nn.*) An *annual* event happens every year; *annuals* are plants that grow and bloom for only one season. *Perennials* are plants that grow and bloom year after year; *a perennial loser* loses over and over again. See BI-; BIANNUAL.

annunciate, enunciate (*vv.*), **annunciation, enunciation** (*nn.*) *Annunciate* is a very rare verb meaning "to announce, to proclaim." *Enunciate* overlaps the "announce" meaning but also means "to state positively or definitely, to pronounce clearly, and to speak distinctly." The possibility of inadvertent misspelling also exists for the two nouns (*The Annunciation* refers to Gabriel's telling Mary she would bear Jesus— from *Luke* 1:26–38—and to the Christian festi-

val commemorating that event.) In most connected speech, they're homophones.

anodyne (*adj., n.*) The adjective means "soothing, pain-relieving," and the noun is "a soothing medicine, anything that relieves pain." But the important thing to remember is that *anodyne* also has pejorative senses: "bland, dull, weak" for the adjective, and "something that represents or displays one or more of those qualities" for the noun.

anoint, annoint (*v.*) The Standard spelling is *anoint,* but *annoint* is sometimes listed as a variant. Stick with *anoint.*

anorexia, anorexia nervosa (*nn.*), **anorexic, anorectic** (*adjs., nn.*) All are Standard. *Anorexia nervosa* is a psychological and physiological disorder primarily of teenaged females: irrational fears of obesity lead them to reduce their food intake radically, causing malnutrition, severe loss of weight, and even death (compare BULIMIA). It is frequently abbreviated *anorexia* in the media and in nontechnical use. The noun *anorectic* means "anyone suffering from loss of appetite or from *anorexia nervosa*" or "a drug or other agent causing loss of appetite." The noun *anorexic* usually means "a person suffering from *anorexia nervosa.*" It almost never is used for a drug or other agent inducing loss of appetite.

The adjectives are synonyms in nearly all respects. *Anorectic* is the more general, used most often to mean "marked by or causing loss of appetite" but sometimes also referring to someone suffering from *anorexia nervosa.* The adjective *anorexic* usually means "suffering from *anorexia nervosa*" or, less often, "loss of appetite, or producing loss of appetite." It is the more frequently used and has begun to take on figurative senses, as in *Your music is anorexic, nothing but skin and bones.*

another, additional, more (*adjs.*) All three can modify count nouns, as in *another drink, additional drinks,* and *more drinks.* For a mass noun such as *water,* however, both *additional water* and *more water* will work, but *another water* usually will not. Some purists have argued that since *another* means "one more," you ought not to say or write *There were another ten entrants that year,* when what you really mean is "There were ten *more* (or *additional*) entrants that year," but usually only Edited English respects this distinction. Please your own ear.

an't, a'n't See AIN'T.

antagonist, protagonist (*nn.*) An *antagonist* is "an opponent, an adversary"; a *protagonist* is "the main character in a narrative or drama, the person on whom the action centers."

Antarctic (*adj., n.*), **Antarctica** (*n.*) The Antarctic is another name for the ice-covered southernmost continent, *Antarctica,* and for the area in which it lies. Many Standard speakers object to the pronunciation *ant-AHR-tik* instead of *ant-AHRK-tik,* but it appears to be acceptable to other Standard speakers. See also ARCTIC.

ante-, anti- (*prefixes*) The prefix *ante-* (pronounced *AN-tee*) means "prior to" (*antebellum, antedate*) or "in front of" (*anteroom, antecedent*). *Anti-* (pronounced *AN-tee, AN-ti, AN-tei,* or *AN-TEI*) means "against, opposed to" (*antidrugs, antiwar*), "something that works against something else" (*antitrust, antibiotic*), "something that neutralizes something else" (*antitoxin, antidote*), and the like. In conversation we also create a good many nonce words with *anti-: She's been anti-computers for years; He's an anti-everything grouch.* Standard words with *ante-* or *anti-* are only rarely hyphenated, unlike nonce words, which usually are.

ANTECEDENT 1 The *antecedent* of a pronoun is its referent, the word it replaces: *My* **brother** *is over there; he is the one in the red sweater.* In Standard English, pronouns nearly always agree in number and gender with their *antecedents.*

antecedent 2 (*adj.*) means "something that went or goes before," and it often takes the preposition *to: These demonstrations were all antecedent to the riots themselves.*

antelope See ZERO PLURALS.

antenna (*n.*) has two semantically differentiated plurals: "the feelers of insects and crustaceans" are either *antennae* or *antennas.* In radio and television applications, the plural is always *antennas.* See FOREIGN PLURALS.

anterior (*adj.*) is a technical adjective in medicine, biology, and the like: *the anterior blood vessel* is "the one before or in front" (*the posterior vessel* is "the one in back or behind"). When it combines elsewhere, *anterior* uses the preposition *to* and is usually limited to pretentious Formal or Oratorical contexts.

anthropomorphism (*n.*) is "the attribution of human characteristics and interests to gods, animals, or objects." See also PERSONIFICATION.

anti- See ANTE-.

anticipate (*v.*) Some purists try to limit the uses of *anticipate* to mean "to use in advance" (*He anticipated his allowance and had it all spent before he had even received it*), "to forestall or

prevent" (*She anticipated trouble and prepared for it*), and "to expect or foresee" (*Everybody anticipated a heavy snowstorm, but it never came*), but these efforts are doomed. It also means "to look forward to" (*He eagerly anticipated her return*), "to plan on or for" (*I anticipated several more guests than actually stayed for dinner*). Nor is there anything wrong with *anticipate* followed by a *that* clause. All these uses are Standard, and you must control the precise meaning contextually.

ANTICIPATORY SUBJECTS See DUMMY SUBJECTS.

antidote See ANECDOTE.

antipathy (*n.*) combines with several prepositions, but *to* and *toward* are the most common (*Her antipathy to [toward] her sisters was embarrassingly clear*). We can also *feel antipathy for* or *between* (*You can feel their antipathy for each other. There is great antipathy between those women*).

antique See ANCIENT.

anti-Semitic See SEMITIC.

antiseptic (*adj., n.*), **aseptic** (*adj.*) The adjectives are partly synonymous, but something that is *antiseptic* kills bacteria, while something *aseptic* is "surgically clean or sterile." *Antiseptic* has the primary stress on the third syllable; *aseptic* has it on the second, with the first syllable rhyming with *day.*

antisocial, asocial, nonsocial, unsociable, unsocial (*adjs.*) An *antisocial* person is "one opposed to the established society, one who shuns company and defies or breaks society's rules." An *asocial* person simply "doesn't get on in society and avoids mixing with others." An *unsociable* person is "not congenial and neither seeks nor tolerates the company of others." An *unsocial* person is either "one who does not seek society or one who actively avoids or hates it." In short *unsocial* overlaps nearly all these others. *Nonsocial* is often used with *behavior* to indicate "having no social quality or character," and so "uninterested in society or in socializing." All these words are Standard.

ANTONYM An *antonym* is a word that means the opposite of another word; thus *antonym* is the *antonym* of *synonym.* The related adjectives are *antonymous* and *antonymic*; they occur infrequently and mean much the same thing, "like or characteristic of an *antonym.*" *Antonymy* is a relatively rare noun meaning "a pair of such opposed terms."

anxious, eager (*adjs.*) *Anxious* meaning "eager" is unquestionably Standard English, even though some purists have long urged that we use *anxious* to mean only "nervous, apprehensive, or fearful" and let the word *eager* replace *anxious* in sentences such as *She was anxious to meet her new teacher.* If you say "I'm *anxious* to get started," everyone will understand your eagerness, some may understand that you are nervous at having failed to get started sooner, and others may not recognize any nervousness in the statement at all. Both "eagerness" and "nervousness" are Standard senses. See also EAGER. Compare SANCTION.

any (*adv., pron.*) The pronoun *any* is either singular or plural: *Any of those titles sounds* [*sound*] *better than this one.* The choice is based on notional agreement. One usage argument favors changing the Standard but idiomatic *any* in *the largest of any tomatoes I've seen* to read *the largest of all tomatoes . . .* ; similarly, the argument would change the *than any* in *taller than any giraffe I've seen* to read *taller than any other giraffe I've seen, taller than all other giraffes I've seen,* or *the tallest giraffe I've ever seen.* Edited English usually defers to this argument, especially for Formal use, but the other is idiomatic in other contexts.

The adverb *any* is also Standard: *The price of gas hasn't changed any this week.* Its frequency is much greater at Conversational levels than in Edited English.

any and all is a cliché from the law, designed to close all loopholes. Unless you are writing contracts or laws, don't use it; instead, choose either a crisp *any* or a precise *all,* nailing your idea once, exactly, rather than raining blows all around it.

anybody, anyone (*prons.*) These indefinite pronouns are unusual in that they take singular verbs, but subsequent pronouns are frequently plural in most levels: *Anybody* [*anyone*] *who hasn't done so is welcome to telephone their parents now.* Edited English is the exception, usually insisting that subsequent pronouns also be singular (*Anyone* [*anybody*] *who believes differently is welcome to his or her opinion*). Each of these indefinite pronouns is spelled as one word, but the parts of the compounds can also serve as adjective plus noun: *Did they find any body in the wrecked car? Use any one of the three entrances.* See AGREEMENT; AGREEMENT OF INDEFINITE PRONOUNS AND OTHER SINGULAR NOMINALS WITH VERBS AND OTHER PRONOUNS; HE; INCLUSIVE LANGUAGE; NOTIONAL AGREEMENT; SEXIST LANGUAGE; S/HE; THEY.

anymore, any more (*adv.*) These spellings are both acceptable, although *anymore* is more frequent: *We don't go there anymore. Anymore* [*any more*] poses no usage issues except when it occurs in non-negative contexts: *All he does anymore is complain.* Such uses are dialectal in origin but are now found at Conversational levels nearly everywhere. Edited English usually won't tolerate them, however, still preferring *lately, of late, now, nowadays,* or the like and reserving *any more* for use in such sentences as *Do you want any more to eat?,* in which *any* is an adjective modifying the noun *more.*

any number of This Conversational and Informal idiom may be construed as singular or plural but is usually a notionally plural subject meaning "a large number of" or "many," as in *Any number of people were* [*was*] *milling about in the hall.*

anyone See ANYBODY.

any other See ANY.

anyplace, everyplace, noplace, someplace (*advs.*) Most of these relatively young compounds are Americanisms. They are usually labeled Informal or Colloquial and should be limited to the Conversational levels and the writing that imitates them, although they do occasionally occur in Edited English, as in *They said to put our coats anyplace we like.* Some commentators have insisted that because *place* is a noun, adjectives such as *any* ought to modify it only in two-word phrases, e.g., *Any place we can park will serve* and *Sit in any place you choose.* But the compound has now clearly become an adverb.

anytime (*adv.*) is an Americanism usually spelled as one word (*The meeting can be scheduled anytime*), although it can still be two words when it is an adjective modifying a noun (*I will not have any time until Thursday*).

anyway, anyways (*adv.*) *Anyways* is dialectal, primarily Southern and South Midland; it raises Standard users' eyebrows nearly everywhere else in all speech and is unacceptable in Edited English. Use *anyway* instead, which American English spells as one word (*I think I'll stay home anyway*) and stresses like other compounds. The two-word phrase (adjective modifying noun) is not a compound: *You can use this gadget* [*in*] *any way you like.* See COMPOUNDS.

anywhere, anywheres (*adv.*) Outside its dialectal constituency, *anywheres* is unwelcome. Standard English requires *anywhere* at all levels, spoken and written: *He can sleep anywhere.*

apart from (*prep.*) This two-word preposition is Standard in both American and British English, meaning both "except for" and "besides," depending on context: *Apart from the new freshmen, all the students were there. Apart from the members of the chorus, we also had to accommodate a full orchestra on the stage.* See ASIDE FROM; BESIDES.

apathy (*n.*), **apathetic** (*adj.*) *Apathy* means "a lack of concern, interest, or emotion," as in *Her apathy was apparent; she dozed off.* When it combines, *apathy* does so most often with the prepositions *toward* and *towards: They showed an apathy toward[s] any kind of intellectual activity.* You can also show *apathy about, regarding,* or *to* something, although these prepositions occur infrequently. *Apathetic* means "emotionless, spiritless, impassive": *His apathetic manner discouraged us.* See also EMPATHETIC.

ape, to go is an already fading slang idiom meaning "to be wildly enthusiastic."

apex (*n.*) has two plurals: *apexes* (pronounced *AI-peks-iz*) is far more common in Standard American English than *apices* (pronounced either *AP-uh-seez* or *AIP-uh-seez*). See also FOREIGN PLURALS.

APHERESIS (*uh-FER-uh-sis*) is the dropping or clipping from a word of a first (frequently unstressed) syllable or syllables. (*Aphaeresis* is a variant spelling.) It is the process of abbreviation that gives us *phone* from *telephone, bus* from *omnibus, drawing room* from *withdrawing room,* and the like. We usually begin by spelling the new version of the word with an apostrophe in place of the front syllable(s) missing in some spoken uses: *'cept* for *except,* and *'til* for *until,* for example, and then later on the apostrophe too may be dropped: *cello* and *cellist* are Standard, and we rarely ever encounter *'cello* or *'cellist* today (much less *violoncello and violoncellist*). See also APHESIS; APOSTROPHE (2); ELLIPSIS (2); EYE DIALECT; TILL.

APHESIS (*n.*), **APHETIC** (*adj.*) These two refer to one kind of apheresis, in which an unstressed vowel is dropped from the beginning of a word: *'bout* for *about, squire* for *esquire.* Pronounce the noun *AF-uh-sis,* the adjective *uh-FET-ik* or *a-FET-ik.* See ABBREVIATIONS; APHERESIS; CLIPPING; SLANG.

aphorism, (old) adage, apothegm, maxim, proverb, (old) saw, saying (*nn.*) All these overlap with one another, sometimes a little, sometimes a lot, sometimes completely. An *aphorism* is a short statement expressing a piece of wisdom, often wittily put. An *adage* is an old *saying* that has become accepted as a truth. An *apothegm* (pronounced *AP-uh-THEM* and also spelled *apophthegm*) is a terse, witty *saying*. A *maxim* is a concise statement of a principle, a truth, or a rule of conduct. A *proverb* is a short pithy *saying,* expressing a folksy truth that is widely accepted. An (*old*) *saw* is a familiar *saying,* much worn and sometimes distorted through long use. And a *saying* is almost any of these. See ADAGE; SAW (2).

apiary, aviary (*nn.*) An *apiary* is a place for housing bees; an *aviary* is one for the birds.

apiece (*adv.*) is Standard and in frequent use; *each* can replace it but is no better: *Give them a dollar apiece* [*each*].

aplomb (*n.*), meaning "poise, self-assurance," is pronounced either *uh-PLAHM* or *uh-PLUHM.*

APOCOPE (pronounced *uh-PAHK-uh-pee*) is the process of dropping a final letter, a final syllable, or an even longer final part of a word, leaving an abbreviation such as *vet* for *veteran* or *mike* for *microphone.* Common examples in American English are *singin', dancin',* and *raisin'* cain, and the student names for the academic subjects *psych, home ec, math,* and *chem.* See APOSTROPHE (2).

apologize, apologise See -ISE; SPELLING (1).

apophthegm See APHORISM.

a posteriori, a priori To reason *a posteriori* means to reason "from effect back to cause, from particulars to generalizations, inductively, empirically." To reason *a priori* is exactly the opposite process: to reason "from cause forward to effect, from generalizations to particulars, deductively." *A priori* reasoning is theoretical, based on logic; *a posteriori* reasoning is practical, based on experience and experimentation.

APOSTROPHE 1, literally "a turning away," is the rhetorical figure in which the speaker or writer addresses someone not present or an imaginary listener. "*O grave, where is thy victory?*" is an *apostrophe.*

APOSTROPHE 2 is the mark of punctuation (') used (1) to indicate a missing letter or letters, as in contractions such as *isn't, they're,* and *it's,* (2) to distinguish genitives of nouns from noun plurals not in the genitive (*boy's, boys',* but plural *boys*), and (3) sometimes to mark plural numbers and letters (*three 6's, two A's*). Never use an *apostrophe* in front of the *-s* ending that forms a plural noun (*The sign says Fine Meal's*), in front of the *-s* that forms a third-person singular present tense verb (*Accused Plead's Insanity*), or before the *-s* in an absolute possessive pronoun (*This hat is her's*). *Apostrophes* appearing where they ought not to be or missing from where they ought to be are devastating shibboleths in the view of many Standard users, who will penalize the perpetrators mercilessly for them regardless of whether haste, inadvertence, or ignorance caused the outrage against convention. Be warned. See ITS.

apothegm See APHORISM.

apparatus (*n.*) has the Latin plural *apparatus* and the English plural *apparatuses* in divided usage. (The third syllable is stressed and rhymes with either *rat* or *rate*.) See FOREIGN PLURALS.

apparently, evidently (*advs.*) *Apparently* means "this statement appears to be true, although it might not be," and *evidently* means "the evidence suggests the statement is true, and I know of nothing to contradict it." *Apparently she's a good student, but I haven't seen her transcript. Evidently she's a good student: her transcript is full of high grades in demanding courses.*

append (*v.*) combines with *to: I appended a bibliography to my report.* The verb is fairly Formal; *add* would be much less stiff and more appropriate in Conversational uses and Informal writing.

appendix (*n.*) has two plurals in divided usage: the regular English *appendixes* is probably more common, but the Latin *appendices* gets a good deal of use in academic and other cultivated circles. See also FOREIGN PLURALS.

applicable (*adj.*) Most dictionaries give two Standard pronunciations, but conservatives universally prefer *A-plik-uh-bul* to *uh-PLIK-uh-bul*, and some still consider the second pronunciation Substandard. Compare INEXPLICABLE.

apportion (*v.*) combines with the prepositions *among, between,* and *to: The captain apportioned the unpleasant jobs among [to] the junior officers. We will apportion responsibility between the two of you.*

APPOSITIVE, APPOSITION A word, phrase, or clause that has the same referent and the same or a similar grammatical function as a preceding word or phrase is said to be an *appositive, in apposition with* that preceding word or phrase: in *My father, that tall man over there, always votes Republican,* the words *that tall man over there* form a *phrasal appositive* for *father. Her name, Arabella, was also her mother's name,* illustrates a single-word *appositive.* In *This news, that my brother is getting mar-*

ried, astonished me, the words enclosed in commas are a *clausal appositive.*

APPOSITIVE GENITIVE This is a kind of periphrastic genitive, such as *the state of Alabama, the town of Windham,* or *the art of cooking.* See GENITIVE CASE; PERIPHRASTIC.

appraise, apprise (*vv.*) Though these are seldom confused in Edited English, the inexperienced confuse them frequently in speech and writing. *Appraise* means "to evaluate": *The audience openly appraised the champion's physique. Apprise* means "to notify, to inform," and it combines regularly with *of,* as in *I want to apprise you of the latest developments,* or occasionally occurs in the passive voice, *apprised* followed by a *that* clause: *We were apprised that there would be no deliveries this week.*

appreciate (*v.*) The third syllable is pronounced like either the pronoun *she* or the noun *sea. I don't appreciate her interference* means "I don't like it; I resent it." *I have learned to appreciate Mozart* means "I have learned to understand or enjoy or admire Mozart." Both uses are Standard, but the negative is usually appropriate only in Conversational contexts.

apprehend See COMPREHEND.

apprehensive (*adj.*) Whether the objects of the prepositions are persons or things, *apprehensive* combines with *about, of, concerning, regarding,* as in *Her parents were apprehensive about [of, concerning, regarding] her safety.* When the object of the preposition is a person only, it can combine with *for* (*He was apprehensive for his wife and family*). *Apprehensive* can also introduce a *that* clause (*I am apprehensive that our deception won't fool him*). See also COMPREHEND.

apprise See APPRAISE.

APPROPRIATENESS, THE DOCTRINE OF See CORRECTNESS.

approve (*v.*) is both transitive and intransitive (*His family approved his decision to marry. His whole family approves*). But American English in particular also favors the high-frequency Standard idiom with *of* (*We all approve of Sally, the young woman he hopes to marry*).

approximate (*adj., v.*) The adjective's final syllable is unstressed and pronounced *-mit* or *-muht*; the verb's final syllable has a tertiary stress and rhymes with *mate.* The verb is both transitive (*His ideas sometimes approximate common sense*) and intransitive, when it can combine with *to* (*His behavior only vaguely approximates to good manners*).

approximately (*adv.*) is applied usually as a qualifier for numbers for which exactness cannot be claimed: *There were approximately thirty people present.* The word is somewhat more Formal than *about, nearly, almost,* and the like, which can perform a similar qualifying task.

approximation (*n.*) combines with *of* in most general use, as in *This sketch is an approximation of the floor plan,* and with *to, for,* and *of* in some technical uses, as in *This explanation is based on a first approximation to* [*for, of*] *the data available.*

a priori See A POSTERIORI.

apropos (*prep.*) The French original was two words, *à propos,* but it is now one word in English (pronounced *a-pruh-PO*), and it has dropped the grave accent as well. It is Standard both when used as a single-word preposition, meaning "about, concerning," and when used in the clusters *apropos of* and *apropos to: I've been meaning to speak to you apropos your latest proposal. I doubt that these discussions will be considered apropos of* [*to*] *our main purpose.* See FOREIGN PHRASES.

apt, calculated, liable, likely, prone (*adjs.*) These are synonymous only in the meaning "inclining or tending." (All have other meanings as well, for which see your dictionary and elsewhere in this guide.) *She is apt to get into arguments* means "She has a tendency toward these things." *She is liable to get into arguments* means much the same thing, but *liable* in this sense is pejorative and deals usually with potentially unpleasant results. Joan may be *apt either to win* or *to lose poker games,* but she's *liable to lose them.* If she's *likely to win,* then the odds are in her favor, and she probably will. If she is *prone to* something, it's probably not desirable, but she is inclined to it by nature: she's *prone to losing,* never *prone to winning.* If she's *calculated to win,* then we're back to figuring the odds, and they favor her. As the examples illustrate, all these words can combine with *to* plus an infinitive or another nominal.

aqueduct, aqualung, aquamarine, aquarium, aquatic, aquatint, aqueous All these words come from the Latin *aqua,* meaning "water," but two are spelled with a medial *-e-* instead of the expected *-a-* (*aqueduct* and *aqueous*); the rest (there are a few more than are listed here) are spelled with a medial *-a-*. The first syllable of *aqueous* rhymes with either *cake*

or *back*; the other words all begin with either *sack* or *sock* rhymes.

Arab, Arabian, Arabic (*adjs., nn.*) None of these terms has any racial or nationalistic opprobrium attached to it, except the once-jocular pronunciation, now considered an ethnic slur, of *Arab* as *AI-RAB* (sometimes spelled *A-rab* in eye dialect) instead of *ER-uhb. Arabian* is the regular adjective applied to people, customs, horses, and artifacts, and it is also a noun meaning "a person from Arabia" or the horse; *Arabic* is both noun and adjective when used of the language(s). See also ETHNIC SLURS AND TERMS OF ETHNIC OPPROBRIUM.

Arabic numerals are *1, 2, 3, 4, 5, 6, 7, 8, 9,* and *0,* and larger numbers made up of them (*23, 685*). A year (*1995*) is written without a comma, but other numbers may have commas setting off their thousands (*5,999; 1,200,000*). See ROMAN NUMERALS.

arbiter, arbitrator (*nn.*) These words are partly interchangeable, although *arbiter* is usually generalized, meaning "someone empowered to make judgments," whereas *arbitrator* has specialized meanings, "an official appointed under labor contracts and the like to hear and decide grievances" and "an official appointed to decide between the claims of rival persons or organizations."

arbitrate, adjudicate, mediate (*vv.*) To *arbitrate* is "to have a third party, chosen by the disputants, decide a dispute"; to *mediate* is "to serve as mediator, a third party who will attempt to conciliate the disputants, to find some compromise agreement," and to *adjudicate* is "to serve as a judge, to hear and decide a case." *Adjudicate* suggests that neither conciliation nor compromise is a goal.

arbitrator See ARBITER.

arbor, arbour (*nn.*) American English spells the *arbor* that is the axle of a circular saw and the *arbor* that is the leafy bower in the garden alike; British English spells the axle as we do but the bower as *arbour.* See SPELLING (1).

arch-, arche-, archi- (*prefixes*) *Arch-, archi-,* and *arche-* are variants of the same prefix, which came to Old English via Old French, from Latin, and ultimately from Greek. They mean "chief, first, main, most important, most primitive"; *arch-* has two pronunciations, *AHRCH-* and *AHRK-,* but *archi-* and *arche-* have only one, *AHRK-i.* We can therefore have trouble with words beginning with *arch-* that we rarely have to say, such as *archangel* (*AHRK-AIN-jel*), *archduke* (*AHRCH-dook* or *AHRCH-dyook*), *archbishop* (*AHRCH-bish-uhp*), *archpriest* (*AHRCH-PREEST*), and *archenemy* (*AHRCH-EN-uh-mee*). When a vowel follows *arch-* the *ch* is usually pronounced as a *k*, as in *archipelago* (*AHRK-i-PEL-uh-go*), *archetype* (*AHRK-uh-TEIP*), and *archiepiscopal* (*AHRK-i-ee-PIS-kuh-puhl*). *Archenemy* is the exception; its first syllable rhymes with *march*.

archaeology, archeology (*nn.*) The more frequent spelling is with *ae*, but both are Standard spellings.

ARCHAIC, ARCHAISM In language contexts, these terms refer to words or expressions once widely used but no longer current, dated but still usable in certain old-fashioned contexts. *Spake* is an *archaic* form of the past tense of the verb *speak*. Compare OBSOLETE (1).

archipelago (*n.*) is pronounced *AHRK-i-PEL-uh-go,* and it has two plural spellings: *archipelagoes* and *archipelagos.* See PLURALS OF NOUNS ENDING IN *-O*.

archive (*n.*) The singular and the plural can be applied alike to a collection of documents large or small, although the singular generally names a collection devoted to one topic, and the plural a collection of many papers on many topics: *The library's archives include, among other things, the archive of the annual short story contests.* Sometimes the name of the building housing *archives* will be plural but will be treated as a singular: *The National Archives is an impressive building containing even more impressive exhibits.*

Arctic (*adj., n.*), **arctics** (*n.*) Both the *Arctic* (the Far North) and *arctics* (the overshoes or galoshes) have two pronunciations: *AHRK-tik* is preferred for the North, both adjective and noun, but *AHR-tik* is widely used, even though many Standard speakers object to it. The overshoes are more often called *AHR-tiks,* although *AHRK-tiks* is also Standard for that sense. See ANT-ARCTIC.

ardor, ardour (*n.*) Americans spell it *ardor,* the British, *ardour.* See SPELLING (1).

area, field, province, realm, sphere (*nn.*) These have other meanings that are distinctive but are synonyms in the much-used generalized sense of "an area or division of an activity, a subject matter, or a realm or sphere of inquiry." Commentators sometimes criticize their use as wasteful, claiming that *He was well-known in the field of neurosurgery* would be briefer and better as *He was well-known in neurosurgery.* Others have argued that generalized uses of these words have become clichés or jargon in some

constituencies, such as education, the law, and the social sciences: *We're both in economics, but she's not working in my area nowadays.* However, when used specifically and literally for space or figuratively when delineating the bounds of an idea or a concept, these are useful words for which there are few really helpful synonyms. Make certain, though, that some space really is involved and not just a point; all should refer to true expanses, like *back* or *belly, region* or *district.* See also ASPECT (2).

aren't I See AIN'T.

ARGOT is a highly specialized vocabulary of terms peculiar to a constituency, a group of users. We speak of the *argot* of the underworld, of jazz musicians, or of baseball players. To label a word or a sense of a word *argot* is to suggest its strictly limited world of use. You may know what the American baseball pitcher means by a *slurve* (a combination *slider* and *curve*), but what is the British cricketer's *googly*? Both are *argot,* and only the initiated can understand. See also JARGON; SECRET LANGUAGES; SLANG.

arguably (*adv.*), **arguable** (*adj.*) Some have objected to the use of *arguably* as a sentence adverb instead of *It can be argued* or *It might be argued,* an objection that *hopefully* has encountered and seems now to be overcoming. Another objection is that *arguably* is always positive, whereas *arguable,* the adjective, can be either positive or negative. But this is merely one of the many ways semantic change works; such matters are neither logical nor predictable. *Arguably*'s main problem now is overuse, especially as an adverbial modifier of comparative and superlative adjectives: *He is arguably the best hitter in either league. She is arguably the more skilled of these two young singers. Arguably* appears at all levels these days, and its use is especially heavy in journalese. For now, therefore, be sparing. Try *perhaps, possibly,* or even *probably,* instead.

arise See RISE.

aristocratic (*adj.*), **aristocrat** (*n.*) Most Americans say *uh-RIS-tuh-KRAT*; some others (and most Britons) say *ER-is-tuh-KRAT,* with the primary stress on the first syllable. For the adjective, most Americans (and some Britons) say *uh-RIS-tuh-KRAT-ik.* Other British people (and a few Americans) say *ER-is-tuh-KRAT-ik.* See PRONUNCIATION (2).

armada (*n.*) may be pronounced either *ahr-MAH-duh* or *ahr-MAI-duh.*

armor, armour (*n.*) *Armor* is American; *armour*, British. See SPELLING (1).

aroma See ODOR.

around 1, about (*advs., adjs., preps.*) In almost all instances these words are interchangeable in Standard English: *He is around [about] fifty years old. I looked around [about] for help.*

around 2, round (*advs.*) It is widely believed that Americans say *around* and Britons *round*, but actually speakers of both dialects use both words these days. The use of an apostrophe (*'round midnight*) to replace the *a* in *around* is rare today and probably archaic.

arouse, rouse (*vv.*) These verbs are each transitive and intransitive: *We aroused [roused] the neighbors. Once roused [aroused], nobody could get back to sleep.* Some suggest that *rouse* is more often used literally ("to wake from sleep") and *arouse* more often figuratively ("to stir up, to move to action"), but both words have both literal and figurative senses and are Standard either way. Compare AWAKE.

arpeggio (*n.*) The plural is *arpeggios.* See PLURALS OF NOUNS ENDING IN *-O*.

arrant See ERRANT.

array (*v.*) combines with several prepositions, usually with a modification of the meaning: *The general arrayed his forces **against** attack from the east. He arrayed the first squad **at** the edge of the woods. She arrayed her pupils **before** her in a semicircle. The admiral arrayed his huge fleet **in** battle order. The troops were arrayed **on** the parade ground, ready to pass in review.* All these have to do with arranging and placing people or objects *in, on, before, within, around, in front of, in back of,* or *behind* something. Another major cluster of meanings also uses *in* and sometimes *with,* and has meanings such as "to dress or decorate or equip oneself or someone else with": *She was arrayed **in** her judicial robes. He arrayed himself **with** [**in**] every conventional sign of wealth and taste.*

arithmetic progression See PROGRESSION.

arrive 1 (*v.*) can take *at,* as in *She arrived at four*; *in,* as in *When he arrived in Chicago, he was exhausted*; *on,* as in *They arrived on Thursday*; *upon,* as in *They arrived upon his parents' anniversary* and *He arrived upon an elderly, sway-backed horse*; *from,* as in *She arrived from Detroit*; and *by,* as in *We arrived by taxi.* Also common are uses with the function word *to* plus infinitive, as in *She arrived to find him asleep.* The regular preposition *to* is rare, however, in either literal or figurative use after *arrive.* All the others are in current Standard use, as is the formerly slang and now Informal and Semiformal sense meaning "to have made it, to have made good, to have become a success," as in *After years of only modest achievement, he finally had arrived: he was rich and famous at last.*

arrive 2, depart (*vv.*) used without following prepositions may be travel bureau jargon, as in *You are scheduled to arrive Chicago at five* and *You will depart Dulles at noon,* but they are appropriate in travel situations, although most commonly in Informal and Conversational use. Edited English seems not ordinarily to permit the omission of the prepositions after *arrive* and *depart* in any other circumstance. Note the restoration of the preposition in journalese when the reporter turns from the airplane to the traveler: *Air Force One departed Los Angeles at six* A.M. *The President arrived in Washington at three* P.M. *but is scheduled to depart from the White House shortly after six tonight. Leave* instead of *depart [from]* and *get to* instead of *arrive [in* or *at]* are admirably unpretentious alternatives. See also DEPART.

arrogate See ABDICATE.

arse See BUTTOCKS.

art 1, arts, fine arts, liberal arts *Art,* if the reference is broad, is the realm of creative, imaginative skill (*the art of letter writing, the art of playing the harp, the art of love*), but when we speak more concretely, *art* includes painting, photography, sculpture, drawing, music, drama, dance, and literature; these are *art,* and they are also *the arts*; people who create or perform any of them are artists. A narrower use, when the reference is only to the *visual arts* or the *plastic arts,* includes such pursuits as drawing, painting, sculpture, and the like, the things you expect *art teachers* to teach in *art departments.* The broad categories, taken as a whole, are what we also call *the fine arts,* to distinguish them from the mechanic arts or crafts (see CRAFT [1])—a very clear distinction, sometimes, when you compare what the blacksmith usually makes with what the sculptor in metal creates, but a very blurred line indeed when you try to decide which clay pots are art and which are craft works. The term *liberal arts* used most generically (see ARTS AND SCIENCES) can include the *fine arts,* the humanities, and some of the social sciences, but often we speak of two separate clusters, *the fine arts and the liberal arts* (with or without some social sciences). See ARTISAN; ARTIST.

art 2, state of the In a new scientific, techno-logical, or developmental enterprise of any sort, *state of the art* is a cliché meaning "the latest, most nearly current, and therefore most advanced and modern level."

artefact See ARTIFACT.

artful, artistic, artsy-craftsy, arty, arty-crafty (*adjs.*) Of these, only *artistic* refers positively to those arts we think of as the fine arts: *The performance was an artistic triumph.* The pejorative edge appears if the praise seems faint or snide: *She's very artistic* may be sincere praise, or it may invite the inference that she is modish and self-consciously interested in displaying her taste, which some consider trivial and derivative. *Artful* means "skillful, inventive, clever," as in *She's an artful weaver,* but much more common are its pejorative senses that mean "scheming, crafty, or cunning," as in *He's an artful deceiver, not to be trusted.* Be very careful of context here: make sure you don't transmit an insult when you intend a compliment. *Arty* means "pretentiously artistic" and is unrelentingly, unquestionably pejorative: *His apartment is arty, just as he is—flashy but dull.* *Artsy* means "even more trivial and silly than arty,"* and *artsy-craftsy* (sometimes *arty-crafty*) is scornfully applied to pretensions that real artists and all people of taste consider beneath serious consideration.

arthritis (*n.*) The word has three syllables only: *ahrth-REI-tis.* Mispronunciation of *arthritis* as *ahr-thuh-REI-tis* (in eye dialect spelled *Arthur-itis*) is sometimes deliberately jocular, but it occurs quite often as inadvertent error among Vulgar and Common speakers; it is a shibboleth that can trip up the unwary speaker.

ARTICLES Words used to identify nouns are called *determiners,* and the *articles a/an* (the *indefinite articles*) and *the* (the *definite article*) are perhaps the most frequent of the determiners in English. In some grammars *articles* are considered a single part of speech; in others they are classed as adjectives.

artifact, artefact (*n.*) Both spellings are Standard; *artifact* is more frequent in the United States, *artefact* in Britain.

artificial, counterfeit, ersatz, fake, false, imitation, sham, spurious, substitute, synthetic (*adjs.*) The number of these synonyms in English is very great. *Artificial* is the antonym of *natural* and *real* and usually indicates something man-made, in imitation of something found in life or nature. The term can be ameliorative: there is nothing innately bad about *an artificial lake.* But it can also be pejorative: *The flower I had admired so much turned out to be artificial. Counterfeit* is clearly pejorative, as in *counterfeit money;* a *counterfeit* is an imitation deliberately intended to deceive, and dishonestly at that. *Ersatz,* a word borrowed from German, applies only to things clearly inferior to those they are intended to replace. Thus, *ersatz coffee* usually tastes terrible. *Fake* and *sham* things are patently *false: fake eyelashes* or *false eyelashes* will usually deceive no one, even if, like *false teeth,* they may be better for their purposes than nothing. *Spurious* also makes clear the deliberate deception: *a spurious police officer* is someone pretending to be a police officer, probably for no honorable purpose. A *substitute police officer,* like a *substitute teacher,* may not always be inferior to the original, but our experience leads us to expect that to be the case; hence *substitute* is frequently pejorative. *Synthetic* is not necessarily pejorative but rather suggests something made chemically to approximate as nearly as possible something natural: *synthetic rubber.*

ARTIFICIAL LANGUAGE See NATURAL LANGUAGE.

artisan, artist (*nn.*) An *artisan* is a person skilled in a craft or a trade, such as a *carpenter* or a *housepainter.* An *artist* is someone skilled in work in the fine or performing arts, or, by extension, anyone who does anything with professional polish, imagination, and sensitivity.

artist, artiste (*nn.*) To call someone an *artist* is perhaps simply to indicate a vocation or an avocation, but it can also be to give a fine compliment. To describe someone as an *artiste* (pronounced *ahr-TEEST*) may once have been a compliment, but applied today to man or woman, it is facetious, deliberately overblown, and uncomplimentary. Its conventional use as a French feminine form for artist is obsolescent in English today, enduring only in the obviously sexist uses in advertising of strippers. Compare -ESS.

artistic See ARTFUL.

artless (*adj.*) is a two-edged word: it can mean "naive, without guile, innocent, and natural"— all words of an ameliorative character: *He was a simple, artless young man, with no harm in him.* Or it can mean "clumsy, ignorant, uncultured, and crude"—all pejorative words: *The young man was artless and rough, an unmannerly boor.* Control its meaning carefully through context.

art object See OBJET D'ART.

arts and sciences This term refers to the basic parts of the liberal curriculum. The fine and liberal arts are included under the term *arts*; *sciences* comprises the natural, the physical, and the social sciences. *Arts and sciences* is shorthand, handy but not entirely explicit. See also ART (1).

artsy-craftsy, arty, arty-crafty See ARTFUL.

ary (not), nary These two are American dialectal (Southern and Midland) expressions, *e'er a* and *ne'er a,* very old contractions of *ever a* and *never a,* meaning "a single (one) or any (one)," and "not a single (one)," as in *We haven't had ary* [or *we've had nary*] *a rainy day this summer.* *Ary* and *nary* are of course Nonstandard today and appear only in writing that imitates the speech of an older time or that of a limited dialectal region.

as 1 (*subord. conj.*), meaning "because," is Standard but not as high frequency as *because* and *since* in causal use: *As I still had my homework to do, I didn't wait for dessert.* Like *since,* causal *as* can sometimes be ambiguous: *As I was voting, I took my coffee with me.* The question is, Did I take my coffee with me *because* I was voting or *while* I was voting? But in fact it is difficult to construct examples of causal *as* that are always ambiguous, even in writing (intonation in speech usually avoids the problem). Nevertheless, causal *as* will receive close scrutiny from those who expect it to lead to ambiguity, so be braced when you write it. Even suspected but undemonstrated ambiguities can cost you readers, however unfairly.

Another use of *as* as a *subordinating conjunction* is in functions where American English more commonly uses *if, that,* or *whether,* as in *I don't know as I want any more to eat.* It is limited almost entirely today to the Conversational levels, usually introducing subordinate clauses following main clauses whose verbs are *know, say, see, wonder,* and possibly a few others of that sort, but always in the negative: *Her letter doesn't actually say as she's decided to accept him.* Most Standard speakers never use *as* in this way; even in the most likely possibility, *I don't know as I believe it,* most would use *if, as if, as though, that,* or *whether.* Some would reserve *that,* as in *I don't know that I believe it,* for Oratorical or other higher-level use. See AS HOW.

as 2 (*prep.*) *As* as a preposition is unquestionably Standard English in such sentences as *As a novice at the game, I try to keep out of the limelight* and *George served as secretary.* A slightly more formal prepositional use has the force of *like: His enthusiasm was as a breath of fresh air to the organization.* The choice between *like* and *as* causes the most anxiety: what we frequently get as a result of the furor over *like* as a conjunction is silly use of *as* where only *like* makes sense. *Fred appeared as a fool when he missed his cue* doesn't mean quite the same thing as *Fred appeared like a fool when he missed his cue.* In object complement structures *as* is often omitted—*We elected Stanley chairman*—but with some verbs the *as* is necessary: *We initiated them as new members. They installed him as warden.* With most other verbs, the *as* is optional and certainly not wrong: *They appointed her* [*as*] *interim president.* See LIKE (2).

as 3 (*pron.*) occurs in Standard English at all levels in constructions with *such* and *same: It was a crash such as I'd never heard before. This dish is the same as one I was served many years ago in Spain.* To use *as* by itself as a relative pronoun is dialectal or archaic: *Those as wish*[*es*] *to inherit must change their ways.* Use it in this way only "in quotes," even in speaking.

Such as, however, as in *such uses as these* or *uses such as these* is Standard. See LIKE (3).

as . . . as, so . . . as Today these pairs are interchangeable in negative contexts: *This fall has not been as* [*so*] *wet and rainy as last fall was.* In positive contexts, usually (although not always) only *as* makes sense: *It's as bad a case as I've seen.* It is Standard in Conversational, Informal, and Semiformal contexts to drop the first *as* in such constructions as *She's* [*as*] *nice as can be,* although Standard Formal and Oratorical contexts almost always retain it.

The most vexed longstanding usage issue involves the choice of case for the pronoun following the second *as:* Is it *She's as young as I* or *as young as me?* The grammatical question is, is that second *as* a preposition, requiring an objective case pronoun as its object (*as young as me*), or is it a coordinating conjunction, requiring a nominative case pronoun as the subject of the subordinate clause it introduces (*as young as I* [*am*])? You'll no doubt recall being taught that the bracketed verb was "understood." Best advice: in Formal and most Edited English, use the nominative and "understand" that verb; in Semiformal and Informal writing, use either nominative or objective case. Follow the same practice in speech: do as you wish in Casual, Impromptu, and some Planned uses, but elsewhere use the nominatives in these structures.

as bad or worse than See AS GOOD OR BETTER THAN.

as best, as in *We must all try to do as best we can,* is Standard; *the best we can* is slightly more Formal.

ascendancy, ascendency (*nn.*), **ascendant, ascendent** (*adjs., nn.*) These variant spellings are all Standard; recent dictionaries indicate the *-ancy, -ant* spellings occur rather more frequently than the *-ency, -ent* ones.

ascent (*n.*), **assent** (*n., v.*) These homophones are wholly unlike in meaning, and only *assent* functions as both verb and noun. The noun *ascent* means "a rise, a climb, an upward slope"; *ascend* is the verb form. The verb *assent* means "to agree, to concur" and, as a noun, "an agreement, a concurrence." Stress both words on their second syllables.

ascertain (*v.*) apparently began by meaning "to establish as accurate, to fix, to decide"; eighteenth-century lexicographers set out to *ascertain* the language, that is, "to decide and then freeze the meaning of each word." But the verb *ascertain* has also long meant "to find out for sure, to learn with certainty." Dictionaries report that the first definition is now archaic, but it seems equally likely that the two have coalesced for many users. Use *ascertain* in either sense, but if you promise *to ascertain that politician's position on the issue,* almost everyone will conclude you mean "to find out where he stands," and only a few will sense that you mean "to decide or determine what his position really is or should be." In any event, *ascertain* is a Formal, almost stuffy term.

aseptic See ANTISEPTIC.

as far as, so far as (*prep., conj.*) Using *as far as* and *so far as* in prepositional phrases wherein *far* is a literal distance (*We're going only as* [*so*] *far as Chicago*) is Standard (but *so* may be regional). Using these two as subordinating conjunctions in what appear to be elliptical clauses from which the verbs have been omitted (*As far as preparation for the game, we think we're ready; I'm ready for the exams, as far as doing all the assigned reading*) has created a good deal of adverse comment, because the *as far as* looks like a preposition, not a conjunction. Many linguistic conservatives consider this use Substandard even in speech, and Edited English won't admit it. Even so, the prepositional phrase turns up quite frequently in Semiformal writing, particularly in journalese, where it might best be punctuated with a dash, to indicate the anacoluthon that is coming: *As regards our preparation—we think we're ready.* Best advice, though: fill out the ellipsis. And when you do, be wary that you don't exchange frying pan for fire: watch agreement of the verb you add: *The coach was satisfied, as far as the need for better players was* [not *were*] *concerned.* Many listeners will be more put off by failure of agreement than by ellipses. See AGREEMENT OF SUBJECTS AND VERBS (4).

as follows Whether the preceding matter is plural or not, *as follows* is always singular: *The reasons for these decisions are as follows.* To use *as follow* instead is sufficiently precious sounding to make your reader break stride: don't do it. You can use *the following* instead, but you needn't. Less stiff would be *The reasons for these decisions are these,* or *Here are my reasons,* or *My reasons are, first, . . . ,* and the like.

as for, as to (*preps.*) Both are Standard: *As for your tuition, I'll pay it. As to how to repay me, you can work something out. She said we should decide as to the time and place of the meeting.* See also AS TO WHETHER.

as good as, meaning "practically" (*The contest is as good as over*), is Standard, and you need not limit it to Semiformal, Informal, or Conversational uses.

as good or better than, as great or greater than This structure, called dual comparison, is idiomatic, at least at Conversational levels and in their written representations, but Edited English avoids it because it is often criticized for its faulty parallelism. In *His second novel is as good or better than his first, good* needs *as,* not *than,* for both parts of this dual comparison to be parallel: *as good as or better than.* Or you may change it to *His second novel is as good as his first or better.* Particularly in longer sentences, punctuation gets more complicated when you restore the *as: He is as handsome and well-mannered as, or even handsomer and better-mannered than, his older brother.* See PARALLELISM.

as how is a Nonstandard dialectal (especially Midland and Southern) locution meaning "that," especially when combined with the verbs *say* and *allow* or the present participles *seeing* and *being: She allowed* [*said*] *as how she might be interested. Seeing* [*being*] *as how we were ready, we went off without waiting for her.*

Asian, Asiatic, Oriental (*adjs., nn.*) *Asian* is the most acceptable of the words applied to those peoples native to the continent of Asia and its neighboring islands. Applied to things, both

Asian and *Asiatic* are acceptable as adjectives, but *Asiatic* is usually considered offensive when it refers to a person, and particularly when it is a noun meaning "a person from Asia." *Oriental* as an adjective is acceptable when applied to things, but that noun too is sometimes considered offensive when used for people. You should be alert for the possible development over the next few years of further taboos against these and related terms. Most Americans pronounce *Asian* and its relatives with the first consonant sound *zh*, as in *AI-zhuhn*, but a few (and many of the British) pronounce it *sh*, as in *AI-shuhn*.

aside from (*prep.*) is Standard in two senses, each of which must be controlled contextually: "in addition to" or "besides," as in *Aside from being exhausted by the trip, I had had nothing to eat for nearly twenty hours*, and "apart from" or "except for," as in *Aside from a few limes, there was nothing to eat in the refrigerator*. The second meaning is probably more frequently encountered. See APART FROM; BESIDES.

as if, as though (*conjs.*) These two are currently interchangeable in meaning in Standard English, and the verbs in the clauses they introduce may now be either indicative, as in *He looked as if* [*as though*] *he was going to cry*, or subjunctive, as in *He looked as if* [*as though*] *he were going to cry*, apparently without effect on level. See also LIKE (2).

as is (*adv., adj.*) is always singular, even when as an adjective it modifies a plural noun: *In the sale all china sets will be offered under "as is" principles*. In *They're to be offered "as is," as is* serves as an adverb. It's a Standard idiom, but it's usually put in quotation marks to prevent confusion.

ask (*v.*) is another high-frequency verb used in many combinations: You *ask for* people either on their behalf or when you want to talk with them; you also *ask for* something when you want to obtain it, and there is in addition a slang idiom, *to ask for trouble* [*a fat lip*, or other retribution], meaning that your behavior almost guarantees that you will be hurt by those you are affronting; you *ask about* (or *after* or *concerning*) others in order to get information about them; you *ask of* someone or something in order to get him, her, or it to do or provide something; *you ask from* someone or something whatever it is you want to obtain; you may *be asked to* a party or *for* a date, or you may be invited by *being asked out*. And *ask* is also followed regularly by either *to* plus an infinitive, as in *I asked*

her to come to see us, or a *that* clause as direct object, as in *I asked that she come to see us*. With the one slang exception noted, all these combinations are Standard.

as long as, so long as (*subord. conjs.*) These two are interchangeable and Standard; they mean "since," "during the time that," "if," and the like: *As* [*So*] *long as you're satisfied, I am too.*

as much or more than See AS GOOD OR BETTER THAN.

asocial See ANTISOCIAL.

as of (*prep.*) is a Standard Americanism in uses that fix a date or time: *These are the total sales figures as of month's end*. Limit the idiom *as of now* (*What we have as of now suggests that there has been no progress*) primarily to Informal and Conversational levels. For more elevated levels, consider these: *What we have learned* [*so far*] *suggests . . .* or *What we have learned up to now suggests. . . .*

ASPECT 1 is a grammatical term categorizing verbs according to some of their relationships to time, not as in tense, but as in matters such as duration, repetition or iteration, or completion. Some grammarians would say that *He runs in the afternoons* illustrates either *durative aspect* (lasting) or *iterative aspect* (repeated).

aspect 2 (*n.*) is a useful term in its many specialized meanings (see your dictionary), but it has also become a half-empty generalization in much current speech and writing. Be careful not to overuse it: *Another aspect of the matter* is simply "a different view of it." See also AREA.

as per (*prep.*) is from the jargon of stuffy commercial correspondence: *The shipment will arrive prior to December first, as per our agreement*. (*As we agreed* or *as agreed* would be better.) Used in other writing or in speech, *as per* may be either jocular or deliberately impersonal. See PER; PREVIOUS TO.

aspirant (*adj.*) has two Standard pronunciations: *AS-puhr-int* is the more frequently heard, but *uh-SPEI-ruhnt* also occurs.

aspiration (*n.*) combines mainly with the prepositions *of* (plus a gerund), as in *He has aspirations of winning the chairmanship*; *for*, as in *Her aspiration is for the post of general secretary*; *to*, as in *His aspiration is to stardom*; *toward*, as in *Her aspirations are all toward financial independence*. *Aspiration* can also be followed by *to* plus an infinitive, as in *Their aspirations are to win fame and fortune*, and by *that* clauses, as in *The president's aspiration that the company's profits grow has proved vain*.

Aspiration is stiff and formal; *hope* would be simpler and more natural in many contexts.

aspire (*v.*) combines most frequently with *to* and *toward(s)*, very infrequently with *for*, and even more rarely with *at: He aspires to* [*toward(s)*] *international recognition. To* plus an infinitive is also frequent: *She aspires to win accolades from the critics.* In all these uses *aspire* is stiff; *hope* would be more natural in most contexts.

as regards See REGARDING.

ass See BUTTOCKS.

assassin, murderer (*nn.*) A *murderer* kills another person, usually deliberately; an *assassin* murders a prominent person, usually for political or religious reasons, and sometimes for hire. *Assassin* is much used in less specific contexts, however, for almost anyone who kills in cold blood. See also EXECUTE.

assassinate See EXECUTE.

assay, essay (*vv.*) *Assay* and *essay* derive from the same word, but their meanings have largely diverged. *Assay* means "to assess, evaluate, or test," as in *We had the ore samples assayed*; the archaic meaning "to attempt" also makes a rare reappearance (as in *to assay a run for office*). *Essay* also means "to try, attempt," as in *The climbers had never essayed such a tall peak.* Pronounced with their first syllables unstressed, they are homophones; when the first syllables are given secondary or tertiary stress (*A-SAI*), they are not.

assemble See FORMULATE.

ASSEMBLY OR ASSEMBLAGE, NOUNS OF Many of the terms coined to name groups of individuals are familiar to the point of cliché. A few examples (drawn from Lipton 1968 and 1991) from this rich lode are:

a host of angels	a leap of leopards
a herd of antelope(s)	a pride of lions
a sheaf of arrows	a troupe of minstrels
a cete of badgers	a troop of monkeys
a swarm of bees	a rope of onions
a flock of birds	a litter of pups
a pack (deck) of cards	a covey of quail
a brood of chickens	a bundle of rags
a draggle of deans	a clamour of rooks (Br.)
a clutch of eggs	a field of runners
a gang of elk	a suit of sails
a school of fish	a flight of steps
a bunch of flowers	a bevy of swans
a gaggle of geese	a clump of trees
a troop of kangaroos	a pod of whales (seals)
an exaltation of larks	a pack of wolves

assent (*v.*), when it combines with a preposition, takes *to,* with a noun as object (*She reluctantly assented to the transfer*) or with a following infinitive or gerund (*She assented to transfer* [*transferring*] *there*). See ASCENT.

assertive (*adj.*), meaning "confident, outspoken," and even sometimes "aggressive," has both positive and negative overtones; use it carefully. Where to be confident is a virtue, being *assertive* rather than diffident will be thought a good thing; where to be aggressive is a defect, being *assertive* will be thought a bad thing, unless a distinction is made between *assertive* and *aggressive.*

assignment, assignation (*nn.*) Confusion of these two is unlikely, except as a malapropism. An *assignment* is "a designation" or "a duty to be performed"; an *assignation* is "an appointment, especially a lovers' clandestine tryst."

assimilate (*v.*) In combined use *assimilate* can take any of several prepositions; *to, in,* and *into* occur most often: *The new ideas were quickly assimilated in* [*into, to*] *the party platform. By* suggests an agent (or means or time) of completion: *Within a few generations the immigrants were assimilated by the urban masses.* All these are Standard.

ASSIMILATION In language, *assimilation* is the process that causes one speech sound to be modified or changed by its proximity to an adjacent sound: the negative prefix *in-*, as in *interminable*, is *assimilated* to *im-* in *imperfect* because of the following *p*, which is bilabial like *m. Pancake* can be either *PAN-KAIK* or *PANG-KAIK*; *cupboard* reduces the medial cluster to a simple *-b-*, and *bookcase* reduces it to a single medial *-k-. Izzatcher hat?* (for *Is that your hat?*) is a written rendition of what we are very likely to say in Standard Casual English because of *assimilation.*

assist (*v.*), meaning "to help," is often combined with a direct object plus *in* plus a gerund, as in *We have assisted them in finding work,* or with a direct object plus *to* plus an infinitive, as in *We have assisted them to find work.* It also occurs with *with* or *in* before a noun or a gerund, as in *The audience assisted with* [*in*] *the cleaning.* But *help* would be much more natural and less stiff in both instances. *Assist* can also mean "to be present" or "to take part in" and in that sense combines with *at* or *in,* as in *Her friends assisted at* [*in*] *the ceremony.* Again, *help* is the simpler verb.

associate (*adj., n., v.*) The verb is pronounced either *uh-SO-shee-AIT* or *uh-SO-see-AIT,* with the second syllable getting the primary stress. The adjective and noun are both usually *uh-SO-shuht* or *uh-SO-shee-it* but are sometimes pronounced as is the verb.

ASSONANCE See RHYME.

as such This phrase is Standard English, used mainly for emphasis: *The story lines of Wagner's operas display surprisingly little narrative skill as such.* Formal English often tends (sensibly) to omit it. See also QUA.

assume, presume (*vv.*) are synonymous only in the meaning "to accept as true, but without proof," as in *I assume [presume] you know what you're doing?* In all other senses their meanings are quite different, *assume* being the more general word. In its specialized meanings, especially "to take upon oneself" and "to act presumptuously," *presume* cannot ordinarily be replaced by *assume*.

assurance See INSURANCE.

assure (*v.*) usually takes both an indirect object and a direct object: *This poll will assure the candidate the support of the independent voters.* Sometimes the direct object is a clause: *I assure you [that] they will turn out.* Or *assure* will take the preposition *of* plus an object: *These letters will assure him of our devotion to the cause.* All these are Standard. See also INSURE.

ASTERISK is the name of the superscript character or printer's mark (*) often used to make a reference (typically, it appears after a word or sentence in the text and then introduces a note preceded by an *asterisk* at the bottom of the page); before a word it indicates an undocumented form or a hypothetical locution (**florp*); and it can indicate the omission of letters (*b**t**d*). Pronounce it *AS-tuhr-isk*, never *AS-tuhr-ik*. Its plural is *asterisks*, and it can also be a verb, meaning "to provide or print an *asterisk.*"

astern See A-.

as the saying goes See SAYING GOES.

asthma (*n.*), **asthmatic** (*adj., n.*) *Asthma* is pronounced with a single consonant sound at the end of the first syllable: *AZ-muh* (British *AS-muh*); the adjective is *az-MAT-ik* (British *as-MAT-ik*). See also PRONUNCIATION (2).

as though See AS IF.

as to See AS FOR.

astonished (*adj.*) can take the prepositions *at* and *by*: *We were astonished at [by] his remark.*

as to whether, as to how, as to which, as to who(m), as to why (*subord. conjs.*) All these

are Standard, introducing subordinate clauses, although some commentators urge the omission of the *as to* in each: *We inquired [as to] whether Fred had called back.* [*As to*] *why he had not done so, she could not say.*

astronaut, cosmonaut (*nn.*) An *astronaut* is a person trained for work in outer space; the Russians call their astronauts *cosmonauts,* and therefore we usually do too.

astronomical (*adj.*) applies literally to matters of *astronomy,* but its figurative uses are frequent and Standard too: *The budget was being discussed in astronomical numbers.* Don't overdo the hyperbole.

as well as (*subord. conj., prep.*) As a subordinating conjunction, *as well as* is Standard: *You know as well as I that he's a fool. Do your homework as well as you can.* As a preposition, it governs prepositional phrase modifiers: *He received a new car, as well as several smaller gifts.* But many uses that appear at first to be prepositional are really Standard coordinating conjunctions: *Visitors came from Canada and the United States, as well as from Europe and the Near East.* The main usage problems arise when *as well as* makes a subject compound, so that it calls for a plural verb, or when *as well as* and its object are set off by intonation or commas, thus making the second element a parenthetical expression that does not affect the agreement of subject with verb: *Their seven-foot center as well as their huge forwards were simply too tall for our average-sized players. Their seven-foot center, as well as their huge forwards, was simply too tall for our average-sized players.* Both these agreements are Standard, but the second example is clumsy. Probably better than either example would be to drop *as well as* in favor of a different approach: *Their center was too tall, and so were [as were] their forwards.* Make sure that your punctuation reflects the way you would speak the sentence, and treat the subject as either singular or compound (and plural) accordingly.

at (*prep.*) For idiomatic uses of *at* following the adverb *where*, see WHERE . . . AT.

at about Because *about* lives a double life as a preposition (*The puppy ran about the room*) some have incorrectly called its combination as an adverb with the preposition *at* redundant. It's not: in its sense of "approximately," it is Standard, although *at* may be omitted: *I expect to arrive [at] about noon.*

ate is the past tense of the verb *eat.* Most Americans pronounce it to rhyme with *mate,* but some dialectal pronunciations still rhyme it with *met,* as does the usual British pronunciation. See PRONUNCIATION (2).

at hand See HAND.

atheist, atheistic See AGNOSTIC.

athlete, athletics (*nn.*), **athletic** (*adj.*) Pronounce them *ATH-leet* and *ath-LET-ik(s).* Never add an extra unstressed medial syllable, as in *ATH-uh-leet* and *ath-uh-LET-ik(s)*; these mispronunciations are Vulgar and are shibboleths to speakers of Standard English.

at home See HOME (1).

at long last is a hyperbolic idiom, meaning "finally, after much time (and effort)," and although it may also be a cliché, its simple emphasis makes it a useful one.

atop (*prep.*) is Standard, meaning "on (the) top of," as in *We built the lookout tower atop a good-sized hill.* As an adverb, *atop* is much less frequently encountered: *His huge head and the silly hat he wore atop added to his odd appearance.*

attain (*v.*) is Standard in both transitive use (*She attained a victory*) and intransitive use, where it combines with *to* (*He attained to a sort of reputation*), and you may *attain* not just desirable things, but (rarely) undesirable ones too (*After many tries, he attained only another defeat*).

attempt (*n., v.*) The noun combines with several prepositions: *at,* as in *We made another attempt at getting through*; *against,* as in *She feared another attempt against the offices of the station*; *on* and *upon,* as in *They feared another attempt on [upon] the prince's life.* The noun also combines with *to* plus an infinitive: *We made an attempt to telephone the police.* All these are Standard, as is the verb, meaning "to try, to undertake." Some commentators have called it a long word where a short one (*try*) would do, but brevity isn't the only virtue good prose may display. See also ENDEAVOR.

attend (*v.*), in its meaning of "listen," combines usually with *to: Please attend carefully to my instructions.* It also means "take care of" when combined with *to: I'll attend to the supplies and transportation.* It also can mean "wait upon," "serve," and "be present"; here it combines with *on, upon,* and rarely *at: Peter attends faithfully upon [on] his ailing father. We attended at every lecture the series offered.* Here *at* is more often omitted or used with the noun *attendance* plus the preposition *in,* as in *We were in attendance at every lecture.*

at this point in time See POINT IN TIME.

attitude (*n.*) combines usually with *toward* or (mainly in British English) *towards: American attitudes toward[s] the rebels remain unfriendly.* (See TOWARD.) It also combines with *to,* as in *What is the general's attitude to the press?* and with *about,* as in *He has a good attitude about the long hours required of him. Attitude* can also take *in respect of, with* or *in regard to, regarding,* or *as regards: Their attitude in respect of [with or in regard to, regarding, as regards] extending the deadline is quite negative.* All these are Standard.

attorney, attorney-at-law See LAWYER.

attorney general (*n.*) *Attorneys general* is still the most frequently encountered Standard plural, recognizing as it does the borrowed French word order of noun followed by modifier. *Attorney generals* is now Standard too, but some older or more conservative people may not yet be used to it and some Edited English isn't, either. See also PLURALS OF COMPOUND NOUNS. Compare MOTHER-IN-LAW.

ATTRACTION See AGREEMENT OF SUBJECTS AND VERBS (4); NOTIONAL AGREEMENT; other entries beginning with AGREEMENT.

ATTRIBUTIVE ADJECTIVES Adjectives are called *attributive* when they are adjacent to the *noun* they modify (*red hair, chocolate candy*); *adjectives* are said to be predicate adjectives rather than *attributive adjectives* when they appear following linking verbs (*Her hair is red; the candy was chocolate*). Many Standard users object strongly to appositives or predicate nominatives such as *president of the largest republic on the Asian rim* being turned into *attributive modifiers,* as in *President of the largest republic on the Asian rim General Park arrived in . . . ,* as can often be found in journalese. The pronouns *my, your, his, her, its,* and *their* can be *attributives* too, as in *my pencil, their car,* etc. See also ADJECTIVES (3); NOUN ADJUNCT.

ATTRIBUTIVE GENITIVES See ABSOLUTE POSSESSIVE PRONOUNS.

attrit, attrite (*vv.*) *Attrit,* pronounced *uh-TRIT,* is apparently a slang back-formation from *attrition.* It is military and journalese jargon, meaning "to win by attrition," "to defeat by reducing the enemy's numbers and means." *Attrite,* on the other hand, is pronounced *uh-TREIT* and is a relatively infrequent but old (seventeenth-century) verb. It occurs most frequently in its participial adjective form, pronounced *uh-TREIT-id,* and it means "worn or rubbed or reduced by friction": *Constant deskwork had attrited the elbows of his jackets.*

at variance See VARIANCE.

au contraire is a borrowed French phrase meaning "on the contrary." It may seem to add class but it is more likely to sound precious, as foreign phrases often can. *On the contrary* is clear and unpretentious and therefore better for nearly all purposes. See also FOREIGN PHRASES.

au courant is a borrowed French phrase meaning "up to date," "fully informed on the latest information," and unlike *au contraire* it may on occasion permit you to say more succinctly what might take several English words to express. But be certain your reader or listener will understand the phrase. See also FOREIGN PHRASES.

audible See PERCEPTIBLE.

audience, hearers, listeners, readers, spectators, viewers (*nn.*) *Audience* and the list of plural nouns all have explicit meanings that refer to one or more of the human senses: technically an *audience* listens, as do *listeners* and *hearers*; but some *audiences* can both hear and see. Those who can see are *spectators, readers,* or *viewers.* But *spectators* at a theatrical or musical event can also hear, and today's television *viewers* can both see and hear. The result is that in all but the most technically precise uses, we tend to use these terms more or less interchangeably, understanding that a book can have an *audience,* just as a motion picture can. Be precise when you can, but don't be finical at the expense of efficiency and pace.

au fait is a borrowed French phrase meaning "in fact," "to the point," "well-informed," and hence "competent, expert, or socially correct." Someone *not quite au fait* is "not quite on top of the subject, not quite what the situation requires." (Compare the British cliché, *not quite the thing.*) Unless your audience knows French well, some of them are quite likely to miss the exact import of *au fait.* And some may see it as pretentious anyway. Use English. See also FOREIGN PHRASES.

au fond, à fond These two French idioms have been overused in English: *au fond* means "basically, at bottom, fundamentally," and *à fond* means "to the bottom," and hence "completely, exhaustively." Almost the only thing these expressions add to your speech or writing today is pretentiousness. See FOREIGN PHRASES; GRAVE ACCENT.

auger, augur (*nn.*) These homophones are likely to be confused only in spelling: an *auger* is a tool for boring holes, and an *augur* is a person who predicts events by reading omens (or it may

be the omen itself). The verb *augur* therefore means "to foretell or to give promise of."

aught (*pron., n., adv.*) The pronoun is archaic except in the idiomatic *for aught I know* and similar uses; as a noun, it still means "zero" and stems from the faulty division of the words *a naught* into *an aught*; as an adverb *aught* is archaic (if in fact it isn't a noun in this use): *I don't care aught for her now.* Don't confuse it with its homophone, the auxiliary *ought.* See NAUGHT; OUGHT; ZERO.

augment (*v.*) combines with *by* and *with: We augmented the water supply by drilling a new well. She augmented the brass section with three additional trumpets.*

augur See AUGER.

augury See AUSPICE.

au naturel is a borrowed French phrase (pronounced *O NA-chuhr-EL*) meaning "in a natural state," and it is also an overused euphemism for "naked." In cooking it means that a dish has been made "very simply" or "without sauces." It's a cliché in almost any use. Except in cooking, limit it to jocular use. See FOREIGN PHRASES.

aunt (*n.*) Most Americans make it a homophone of *ant,* but in Eastern New England Regional Dialect it sounds like *AHNT.* Both are Standard. For an adjective, see AVUNCULAR.

au pair, au pair girl (*nn.*) are the names widely used in the United States for the young woman who agrees to accept room and board in exchange for doing housework and helping care for the children of the household. The term *au pair* means literally that she will be treated "as an equal" and so will live as a member of the family. This locution is also used as an adjective, as in *au pair girl,* and as an adverb, as in *She's working au pair this year.* Typically *au pairs* want to live abroad for a time in order to master a new language and culture. Pronounce it *o-PER.* This foreign phrase has no exact English synonym, and not every American knows what it means.

aural, oral (*adjs.*) These homophones mean different things but often occur in contexts that could be confusing, since they both can deal with sounds—*oral* (having to do with the mouth) with *making* speech sounds, and *aural* (having to do with the ears) with *hearing* them. See also VERBAL.

auspice, augury (*nn.*) An *auspice* (*AW-spis*) is "an omen or the watching for omens"; an *augury* is essentially the same thing—either "an omen" or "the process of divination to seek one." *Auspices* (*AW-spi-seez*) is the plural of *auspice*, and in the plural usually means "the sponsorship, patronage, blessing, or support of some agency or person": *The contest was held under the auspices of the Olympic Committee.* *Auguries* is the plural of *augury*, and it usually means "indications, omens, portents, or prospects": *All the auguries for the tournament were excellent.*

auspicious (*adj.*) Purists have sometimes tried to limit the use of the adjective to meaning "of good omen," but the meaning has long since generalized to mean "favorable, successful": *This has been an auspicious organizational meeting, one that gets the company off to a good start.*

AUSTRALIAN ENGLISH Americans have become much more familiar with the sounds of this regional dialect or variety of English during the past generation or so, thanks in part to the sounds of Australian tennis and golf stars' voices on our radio and television and, more recently, to the wide distribution and acclaim given some Australian films. The "Strine" dialect (*Strine*, a near-rhyme with *dine*, is their own jocular term) sounds to Americans somewhat but not wholly British. It developed mainly from the provincial and lower-class dialects of Australia's first settlers (mainly convicts and soldiers). Because Australia has become increasingly independent of British influences since the late eighteenth century, it has developed many of its own sounds and locutions, just as has the United States.

aut- See AUTO-.

authentic, genuine (*adjs.*) These synonyms differ only slightly: *authentic* means "trustworthy, reliable, officially or legally attested," whereas *genuine* means "not artificial or fake," "trustworthy," or "sincere." Hence they overlap in *These documents appear to be authentic* [*genuine*]. But only *genuine* fits the sense of *His manner seemed genuine and warm.* See GENUINE.

author (*v.*) Some Standard users strongly dislike *author* as a transitive verb (*He authored ten books*), but it has a long if somewhat mixed history. At present it is seriously threatened with the status of cliché. Perhaps for now you would be wise to reserve it (in the combined form with *co-*) for occasions when you wish to describe collaborative authorship, as in *coauthored by A. and B. To author*, as a synonym for *to write*, serves little purpose other than to distinguish between writing for a living and simply writing letters or producing penmanship.

authoress (*n.*) was once the usual term for a female writer (along with poetess). It had become old-fashioned and archaic long before the recent efforts to find inclusive language for the names of vocations and professions and is now obsolete: *author* is today's noun for a writer of either sex. See also -ESS; SEXIST LANGUAGE; TABOO.

authoritarian, authoritative (*adjs.*) These words are markedly different: *authoritarian* means "requiring unquestioned obedience to authority, dictatorial," as in *His approach to discipline was authoritarian; he would brook no disagreement or discussion whatsoever. Authoritative* has no pejorative overtones where it means "reliable, official, well-qualified," as in *She has written the authoritative biography of the poet.* The only overlap is in the sense of "being fond of exerting authority," but *authoritarian* is much the stronger in that meaning and suggests a less admirable quality.

authority (*n.*) combines with *on* (*an authority on Keats*), *upon* (*an authority upon almost any topic you raise*), *in* (*an authority in trade and tariffs*), *of* and *among* (*the authority of* [*among*] *all authorities*), *about* (*the greatest authority about jazz*), *over* (*authority over the entire county*). *Authority* also combines with *to* plus an infinitive—*She has the authority to make decisions*—and with *that* introducing an adjectival clause—*He exhibits an authority that is easy to accept.* All are Standard.

auto-, aut- (*prefixes*), **auto** (*n.*) Except for *auto*, which is an increasingly old-fashioned clipped form of *automobile* (the plural is *autos*), these are prefixes that are nearly always parts of full words. They mean "self," "of, by, or for oneself or itself," and "self-acting or automatic," as in *automobile, autobiography, autograph, autodidact*, and the like. The *aut-* form goes before words beginning with vowels (*autism, autarchy*).

automaton (*n.*) is pronounced *aw-TAHM-uh-TAHN* and has two Standard plurals in divided usage, *automatons* and *automata*. See also FOREIGN PLURALS.

autumn, fall (*nn.*), **autumnal, fall** (*adjs.*) The *n* is silent in the noun *autumn* but pronounced in the adjective: *AW-tuhm* and *aw-TUHM-nuhl. Autumn* and the names of the other seasons are almost never capitalized as proper nouns these days, except as personifications. Americans use both *fall* and *autumn*, but *fall* occurs more often, as both noun and adjective. The British seem to prefer *autumn*.

AUXILIARIES, AUXILIARY VERBS

These are the parts of speech sometimes called *helping verbs*. They are a finite list of words (we rarely create new ones) that English uses with certain forms of verbs to help form tenses, moods, voices, and aspects of those verbs. The chief *auxiliaries* are *shall, will, should, would, may, might, can, could, ought, have, had, be,* and *do*. Some, such as *have, be,* and *do,* come in various forms; others, like *ought,* are monoforms. Many grammars assert that *auxiliaries* are not verbs at all, since they behave differently from verbs: most of them have no past participles such as verbs have. See BE; CAN (1); COULD; DO (1); HAD; HAVE; MAY; OUGHT; SHALL; SHOULD.

avail (*v.*) can be transitive, as in *His efforts availed him nothing,* with an indirect object (*him*) followed by a direct object (*nothing*); but its most frequent use is with reflexive pronouns and *of,* as in *We availed ourselves of such coaching as could be had*. *Avail* is Nonstandard in the passive voice: *It was a break to be availed of if at all possible*.

avant-garde, cutting edge, leading edge, van, vanguard (*nn.*) These synonyms are actually the same French phrase borrowed twice into English. The French means "advance guard," and we took it into Middle English, where it evolved into the anglicized *vanguard* (with the stress moving forward to the new first syllable, *van*), with first a military reference and then a figurative one, referring to anyone "out front" in a venture: to be *in the van* is to be ahead of the main body of troops. Then we borrowed *avant-garde* again in the early twentieth century, this time primarily for the figurative sense of "those in the forefront of an artistic, political, or intellectual movement." For *avant-garde* (which can also be an adjective), Americans use two pronunciations, an anglicized *uh-vahn(t)-GAHRD* and an approximation of the French, *uh-VAHN-GAHR*, usually with the middle syllable nasalized. *Leading edge* and the cliché *cutting edge* are now high-frequency replacements for many uses of *avant-garde* and nearly all uses of *in the van*. See also STATE OF THE ART; VAN (1).

avenge (*v.*), **revenge** (*n., v.*), **vengeance** (*n.*) All three refer to "getting even, to punishing someone for having injured you or yours." *To avenge* is "to get revenge" or "to take vengeance"; it suggests the administration of just punishment for a criminal or immoral act. *Revenge* seems to stress the idea of retaliation a bit more strongly and implies real hatred as its motivation. The verb *revenge* is usually used with a reflexive pronoun: *He revenged himself on those who had killed his parents*; *He revenged his parents* sounds very odd and is rare in Standard use; *He avenged them* would be more likely. *Vengeance* is "retribution or the hot desire for retribution"; hence to do something *with a vengeance* is to do it fiercely, thoroughly, or excessively.

aver (*v.*) is a very low frequency, stiff-sounding synonym for *say*. It may mean "declare positively," as some commentators suggest, but it may also be a synonym for the verb *opine*, meaning "to offer an opinion": *Her friend averred that she knew nothing of the crime*.

average (*adj., n., v.*) Despite a good deal of comment to the contrary, *average* is Standard in the sense of "normal, ordinary, or typical." See MEDIAN; SUBNORMAL.

The verb can take *out*: *It averages out at about an even dozen*; it can also be transitive: *We averaged four hundred miles a day*.

averse See ADVERSE.

aversion (*n.*) combines regularly with the prepositions *to, for,* and *from,* although *to* is most usual today: *I have an almost overpowering aversion to* [*for, from*] *asparagus in any form*. *Toward(s)* also may combine in Standard use. See ANIMADVERSION.

avert See ADVERT.

aviary See APIARY.

avid (*adj.*) You may be *avid to do* something (that is, "eager to do" it) or *avid of* or *for* something (that is, "desirous of having" it or "desirous for" it); or you may simply be *an avid person,* (that is, one "full of zeal, enthusiasm, desire, or eagerness").

avocation, vocation (*nn.*) An *avocation* is something you do primarily for pleasure, apart from your *vocation,* what you do to make a living: *Her vocation is practicing law, but her avocation is playing jazz piano*.

avoid See ADVERT.

avuncular (*adj.*) means "typical of or suitable to an uncle"; it also has figurative senses meaning "kind, indulgent, undemanding, sexless": *His treatment of her was more avuncular than amorous*. It's perhaps a cliché in its most frequent company, *avuncular advice*. A curiosity: English has no similar adjective to deal with matters or qualities typical of an aunt: *auntish* and *auntlike* are about as close as we can come.

await See WAIT.

awake, awaken (*vv.*) Both verbs are Standard. *Awake*'s principal parts are in divided usage: its past tense is either *awoke* or *awaked,* and the past participle is either *awaked* or *awoken. Awake* is both transitive, as in *She awoke me at six,* and intransitive, as in *I awoke at six. Awaken* is a regular weak verb (*awaken, awakened, awakened*) with essentially the same meaning as *awake; awaken* too is both transitive (*He awakened her at six*) and intransitive (*She awakened at six*). See also AROUSE; WAKE.

aware (*adj.*) means "alert," as in *She was wide awake and fully aware of the night noises,* and "knowing, informed," as in *He was well aware of their interest in the project. Aware* can be used in either adjunct or predicate adjective positions (*He's an aware sort of person. He is always aware of his surroundings*), and it combines regularly with *of* (*She's aware of the difference*) and with *that* clauses (*They became aware that something was wrong*).

awash See A-.

away (*adv., adj., n., intensifier*), **way** (*adv., adj., intensifiers*) *Way* (it is sometimes spelled 'way) is a clipped or aphetic form of *away;* it has some of the adverbial and intensifier meanings that *away* has, but its use in these senses is restricted mainly to dialectal, Conversational, and Informal uses: *Go away* ['*way*]; *I thought he was way off in his estimates.* In other adverbial uses, *away* is never clipped: *I went away for the day. And away we go!* As a noun, *away* appears when natives of places where we vacation observe that we're *from away.* As an adjective, *away* is often idiomatic, with special senses in (for example) sports: *You're away* (in golf), means "your ball is farther from the hole, and therefore you must play first"; *They're playing three away games in a row* (in team sports of all kinds, where *home games* are on the team's own field or court, and *away games* are played on the other team's); *His home run came with two away in the ninth* (in baseball, this means that "two were out"). Limit such uses to relevant contexts. See WAY (2).

awesome (*adj., intensifier*), **awesomely** (*adv., intensifier*) *Awesome* has long meant "awe inspiring," or "awe expressing," but in the eighties it was suddenly taken up as a hyperbolic adjective to describe anything better than average: *My roommates thought my new car was really awesome.* The student world often pioneers such

uses and then drops them and moves on to the next vogue word for the next brief season, leaving its elders (who should know better) to carry on with the old vogue words for up to a decade or two longer. Consider the recent and similar histories of *super, gross, outstanding, wicked,* and many others. Similarly hyperbolic is the use of *awesome* and *awesomely* as intensifiers, now running wild: *He had an awesome great motorcycle. She gets awesomely high grades. Awesome* and *awesomely* will no doubt one day be perfectly useful words again, but just now they are shopworn and weary. Compare AWFUL; SLANG.

awful (*adv., adj., intensifier*), **awfully** (*adv., intensifier*) The basic long-term meanings of these words have been and continue to be "awe inspiring, full of things to cause awe and fear" and, by extension, "terrible and wonderful." But today it takes careful contextual control to make *awful* exceed the horrors of a hangnail. At the Conversational level and even in some of the higher levels of written English we encounter *awful* almost everywhere, meaning (as an adjective) anything from "slightly below average or mildly unpleasant" to "terrible, monstrous, and horrible." *Traffic was awful, and we were almost half an hour late. It was an awful hurricane; hundreds were killed.* Any cold short of pneumonia can be described as *awful bad,* illustrating the Nonstandard intensifier, just as for somewhat more consciously Standard-speaking Americans, that chest cold may instead be *awfully bad.* Like *real* and *really, awful* and *awfully* are (and have for a good while been) much overused in these hyperbolic ways, particularly in speech.

awhile (*adv.*), **a while** (*determiner plus noun*) *Lie down awhile, and get some sleep* illustrates the adverb, which is spelled as one word. *Take a while to get oriented* and *Lie down for a while, and get some sleep* illustrate the determiner *a* plus the noun it modifies. For many uses, only writing it will distinguish which syntactic structure you use.

ax, axe (*n.*) These are variant spellings of the wood-cutting tool's name; Americans generally use *ax,* the British *axe,* and both use a plural *axes,* pronounced AKS-*iz.* See SPELLING (1).

axis (*n.*) Use the borrowed foreign *axes* (pronounced AK-*seez*) for the plural, but never for the singular (pronounced AK-*sis*). At the lower Conversational levels, Standard speakers may rarely (and perhaps jocularly) use *axises* as the plural, but Standard English neither speaks nor writes it at the higher levels.

aye, ay (*adv., n.*) These are variant spellings of the affirmative reply "yes" and also of the noun for such replies (*The ayes have it.*) By far the most frequent spelling is *aye,* which is also used in the sailor's double response to an order (*Aye-aye, sir.*) The cry of anguish, sorrow, or bereavement is usually spelled *ay,* as in *Ay, ay, ay! or Ay me!*

B

-b-, -bb- See CONSONANTS (2).

babe (*n.*) is an old-fashioned, literary-sounding version of *baby,* meaning "infant," but it is also used figuratively to mean "someone ignorant, inexperienced, helpless, or naive," as in the cliché *a babe in the woods. Babe* is also Standard English slang, meaning "a sexually attractive and possibly promiscuous woman." And it is still a frequently used nickname, either as a term of endearment (echoing the Standard senses of the word) or as an echo of the undying reputation of George Herman "Babe" Ruth, the baseball hero.

BABY TALK is language typical of very young children first learning to speak. It is characterized by truncated syntax, modified phonemes, and a special vocabulary. *Baby talk* is also the special speech adults use when addressing very young children, an Intimate level intended to imitate and exaggerate childish sounds, syntax, and vocabulary.

bachelor, bachelor girl, bachelor's degree A *bachelor* is an unmarried man, a young unmated fur seal, a medieval knight attached to another knight's entourage, or a person who has a baccalaureate degree (also called a bachelor's degree). *Bachelor girl* was once a Conversational and Informal name for a young, employed, unmarried woman living on her own. Probably the only reason it has not come under attack for its use of *girl* to mean "an adult female" is that it has nearly fallen out of use.

bacillus (*n.*) The plural is *bacilli. See also* BACTERIA; FOREIGN PLURALS.

back See REFER BACK.

BACK-FORMATION is the name of a process (and of a word formed by that process) whereby a new and usually shorter word, often another part of speech, is formed from an old and longer one by lopping off a suffix. Often the purpose of the back-formation is functional shift, and the new word looks as though it were the source of the old one: *burgle* looks like the source of *burglar,* but it is the other way round. *Back-formations* have given English the verbs *enthuse* from *enthusiasm, donate* from *donation,* and *execute* from *execution* and the new noun *statistic* from *statistics.* There is nothing intrinsically wrong with this word-forming process, but frequently a particular *back-formation* will irritate some purists, who will argue that English has no need for the new word. Occasionally, at least for a time, their opposition will keep the word out of Standard English, as was the case with *enthuse* for many years. But for every *back-formation* that encounters resistance, dozens of others fill real needs and become part of the Standard language with scarcely any fuss at all.

background (*n., v.*) The noun in its literal visual sense as the antonym of *foreground* is Standard, but some people have objected to its use in the senses of "origin, history, training and experience, preparation" and "the series of events leading up to something," as in *She has a good background for this sort of work* and *Fill us in on the background of this speech; what led to its delivery?* These uses, however, are unquestionably Standard today. The verb, as in *The press secretary will background the media people at three,* is Conversational, and its use in Edited English is limited to the Semiformal.

backgrounder (*n.*) A *backgrounder* is a briefing providing background information to the media, or it is an essay, article, or editorial designed to summarize such information for the public. The term is journalese; limit it to Semiformal and Informal writing and to the Conversational levels.

backlash (*n.*) is much in vogue these days as a graphic synonym for *reaction,* especially a loud or violent negative one: *No one expected the public backlash stirred up by the candidate's*

TV commercial. The word is Standard, and it has become a cliché in the media.

backlog (*n., v.*) The noun has two senses, a literal original, "the large log at the back of a fireplace fire that may keep the fire going overnight," and a figurative sense, "an accumulation (and arrearage) of tasks left undone, paperwork unprocessed, duties unperformed." Both senses are Standard. The verb, a functional shift of the figurative sense, means "to accumulate"; some consider it jargon, but it has probably earned a Standard label by now: *Ungraded term papers were backlogged on his desk.*

back of, in back of (*preps.*), **in back** (*adv.*) *Back of* and *in back of* are compound prepositions that seem to have originated and become Standard in American English: *We kept the boat trailer in back of [back of] the garage.* Curiously, commentators have labeled both locutions Colloquial or Vulgar off and on for most of this century, although with no accuracy and little effect. The objection usually was that *behind* was preferable because briefer and more succinct. *In back* is an idiom that functions as an adverbial phrase, and it also is Standard: *She ran a small candy store, and she lived in back.*

backpack (*n., v.*), **rucksack** (*n.*) *Backpack* is an Americanism for what the British (and other Germanic languages) call a *rucksack.* Functional shift created the American verb, *to backpack,* meaning "to hike and camp, carrying all food, clothing, and shelter in and on a *backpack.*" Both noun and verb are Standard.

backside See BUTTOCKS.

back slash, backslash See VIRGULE.

backward (*adj., adv.*), **backwards** (*adv.*) The adjective is always *backward: He's a backward child.* Americans use both *backward* and *backwards* as adverbs, interchangeably: *She moved backward[s] as fast as she could.* For the adverb British English uses *backwards* only.

back yard (*n.*), **backyard** (*adj.*) Spell the noun as two words and put the primary stress on *yard*; spell the compound adjective as one word, and pronounce it either with primary stress on *back* or with the two parts relatively equally stressed: *They took her into the back yard to show her their backyard barbecue pit.*

bacteria (*n.*) is the plural, which has much higher frequency of use than the singular, *bacterium. Bacteria* occurs occasionally as a singular in Nonstandard use, and insecurity over its correct singular form may well have given *bug* its popularity as a slang or Conversational substitute,

meaning "an infection and its cause." See BUG; GERM; FOREIGN PLURALS.

bad (*adv., adj.*), **badly** (*adv.*), **bad(ly) off** (*adv.*) *Bad* as adjective is Standard in both attributive and predicate adjective use: *This puts us in a bad light. The light is bad in here. Bad* as adverb works Conversationally and Informally almost exactly as does the older *badly: We all did bad [badly] on the exam. My arm was hurting bad [badly] after the game.* But *bad* as adverb in other levels is Common English at best and is clearly not acceptable in Edited English. As an intensifier, only *badly* is Standard: *She was badly injured in the accident. Bad* and *badly* with linking verbs, such as *look, seem, appear,* and the like are discussed in the entry for FEEL BAD. See also FLAT ADVERBS.

BAD GRAMMAR See GRAMMAR.

bade See BID.

badmouth (*v.*) is a slang word meaning "to criticize harshly, with or without justification" as in *She was always badmouthing her landlady.*

bag 1 (*n., v.*) A *bag* is a container made of paper, cloth, plastic, or leather, or an amount that a *bag* might contain, but in addition to those and other related Standard meanings, it has several that require usage labels. It is slang in the sense of "what one enjoys and does best," as in *Selling is my bag; I was meant to be a salesman.* A *bag* in baseball is a slang term for a base, and it is a Standard name for a woman's purse or pocketbook or for a piece of luggage. An ugly or unattractive woman is insultingly referred to as a *bag* (this is a clipping of *baggage* and is slang).

At best, the phrase uses are Conversational: anything that's *in the bag* is assured of success; a person *in the bag* is drunk, and to be *left holding the bag* is to be left to take the blame and consequences for some sort of failure.

The verb *bag* is Standard, meaning "to capture or kill, as in hunting": *He bagged his buck the first day out.* A related slang sense means "to collect or win something": *She bagged three new customers yesterday. Bag* is Standard in the sense "to hang loosely in a kind of bag shape," as in *The knees of his unpressed trousers bagged badly.*

bag 2, poke, sack (*nn.*) *Sack* and *poke* were both originally regional terms for *bag. Sack* has since become a Standard term like *bag,* but *poke* remains regional, mainly in South Midland Regional dialect.

baggage, luggage (*nn.*) *Baggage* has several Standard senses, including "suitcases, trunks, and other things carried by a traveler" and "an army's equipment and supplies"; *a baggage* (once slang but now just old-fashioned) is "a woman no better than she ought to be, a prostitute" or simply "a lively and attractive young woman." Finally, *baggage* is also a pejorative in the sense "outmoded, worthless ideas, procedures, and the like; useless stuff still being carried about." *Luggage* is simply Standard for "suitcases, trunks, and other things carried by a traveler." If *luggage* has any air of superiority about it (and it may), this is probably due to its British origins.

bail, bale (*nn., vv.*) The verb *bail,* often used with *out,* has three main meanings: (1) "to set or provide *bail,* a sum of money put up as a guarantee against a prisoner's appearance in court, so that he or she can be released pending trial," (2) to use a "*bail* (a noun meaning can, scoop, or bucket) to bail water from a boat," and (3) "to jump from an aircraft, using a parachute" (the British sometimes spell this *bale*). A *bail* is also the curved handle of a kettle or bucket or a part of a typewriter—the *paper bail*—used to hold the paper flat against the platen. The verb *bale* means "to bundle hay, cotton, etc., into a tightly compressed cube, called a *bale,* for ease of handling and storing." And another noun *bale* is an old, rather literary word meaning "woe, sorrow, or disaster." All these are Standard. See BALEFUL.

bait (*n., v.*), **bate** (*v.*) Of these homophones, the verb *bait* has a long string of specialized senses, most of them pejorative: *to bait people or animals* is "to harass or torment them," "to set dogs on them," "to tease," "to entice or entrap them with food or other *bait* (noun)," as in *I'm using worms as bait the next time I go fishing.* There are also two related archaic senses of the verb, "to feed animals during a break in a trip" and "to stop for food while traveling." To *bate* is an apheitic form of *abate* or of the Middle English *abaten,* meaning "to hold back, reduce, slow down, or lower," as in the participial adjective in *with bated breath.* There are also specialized senses of the verb *bate* from falconry and the tanning of leather, for which see an unabridged dictionary.

balance 1 (*n.*) *Balance* meaning "the money left in the account," or "the rest of the money owed," and the like has long been Standard (and can be either singular or plural), but some conservative comment has tried unsuccessfully to restrict this Americanism to such uses and to insist that a sentence such as the following be considered slang or Conversational at best: *Many*

of the choir members rode on the bus; the balance went in two cars. Best advice: avoid it in most Oratorical or Formal contexts.

balance 2, on The phrase *on balance* combines most frequently with the prepositions *among, between,* and *with: On balance among [between] these contenders, I prefer Smith. The advantages are on balance with the disadvantages.*

BALANCE, BALANCED are rhetorical terms applied particularly to syntactic structures. A typical *balanced* sentence might be compound, with two mirrored clauses, one on either side of a coordinating conjunction, or it might contain other sets of parallel constructions. Not least of the virtues of *balanced* syntax is its clarity, whether it is Thomas Huxley's description of the intellect of the liberally educated person, which can "spin the gossamers as well as forge the anchors of the mind"; or Abraham Lincoln's "government of the people, by the people, for the people."

bald, balding (*adjs.*) Some argue that *bald* is the only word we need. The objection may have begun with *balding*'s overuse, but there may also be a semantic difference: just as there is a difference between being *aged* (having already achieved that state) and *aging* (approaching or coming to it), so *balding* seems to mean "becoming *bald,* but not yet completely naked on top"—a significant difference at least to those who are losing their hair. Both words are Standard.

bale See BAIL.

baleful, baneful (*adjs.*) Anything *baleful* is "harmful, threatening, or sinister," whereas anything *baneful* is "ruinous, woeful, or deadly." The overlap in meaning is considerable, but *baleful* is perhaps only ominous and threatening, whereas *baneful,* unchecked, promises death.

balk (*n.*), **balk, balk at** (*vv.*), **balky** (*adj.*) The British frequently spell these *baulk* and *baulky.* Rhyme them with *talk;* the *l* is silent. The noun means "a ridge of land left unplowed, either deliberately as a boundary [hence figuratively the territory behind the *balkline* on a billiard table] or carelessly [hence figuratively the error in baseball, wherein the pitcher moves illegally while his foot is on the rubber; runners are given the next base as penalty for the unfair hindrance this poses to their advancing]." A *balk* is also a rough-hewn piece of timber, probably an analogy with the rough, unplowed strip of land. The verb *balk* means "to stop or impede as with an obstacle," as in *The horse balked when I tried* *to lead it across the bridge,* and also to commit a *balk* in baseball. To *balk at* is intransitive, and means "to shy away from, to refuse to cooperate," as in *He balked at going to the concert.* The adjective *balky* means "uncooperative, resistant, stubborn": *Balky horses are dangerous nuisances.* All these senses are Standard, even the use in baseball jargon. See also BUCK.

ballad, ballade (*nn.*) The word *ballad* means either "a popular short stanzaic verse narrative" or "a sentimental song, usually about love." Many are anonymous, set to music, and essentially of the people, rather than of the court or upper classes. There are also what might be called literary *ballads*—deliberate imitations of the *ballad* form and content.

A *ballade* is a sophisticated verse type of Old French and Provençal origin: usually three stanzas of eight to ten lines each, often with an interlocking rhyme scheme, with the final line in each stanza a refrain, and frequently ending with a summarizing or dedicatory stanza (called an *envoy*) four or five lines long, also with a final refrain. Many were written in Middle English and Middle Scots, but the form is considered harder to work with in today's English, thanks in part to changes in the stress patterns of the many Modern English words borrowed from French during the Middle English period.

ball game, a whole new See WHOLE NEW BALL GAME.

ball's in your court, the This is a tennis expression whose figurative meaning is that what happens next is the other's responsibility, as in the expression *Your move,* from chess, checkers, and other board games. Most editors will limit both these Standard Conversational expressions to Informal or Semiformal use.

balmy, barmy (*adjs.*) *Balmy* began with a Standard meaning, "mild, soothing, balmlike," as in *The night air was warm and balmy.* It then developed a second meaning, "crazy, silly, unbalanced, deranged," as in *Her chatter drove us balmy.* This slang use appears to be a variant of *barmy,* a British slang word meaning "frothheaded, crazy," from *barm*—"yeast." In some British dialects, *balmy* and *barmy* are both pronounced *BAH-mee.*

baloney See BOLOGNA.

baluster, balustrade, banister, bannister, railing (*nn.*) A *baluster* is an upright post or support for a railing (or a similar part of a chairback, etc.); a *balustrade* (pronounced **BAL**-uh-STRAID or BAL-uh-**STRAID**) is a railing and the posts that support it on a stair or along a balcony; a *banister* (variant spelling *bannister*) is the railing on a flight of stairs, held up usually by *balusters;* a *railing* is a generic term for either the handrail or the rail and the posts that support it, as along stairs or the edge of a balcony, deck, or bridge. All are Standard terms; the *bannister* spelling is relatively less frequent than *banister.*

banal (*adj.*), **banality** (*n.*) *Banal,* meaning "trite, foolish, commonplace," is pronounced *BAI-nuhl, buh-NAL,* or *buh-NAHL.* The noun *banality* is pronounced either *buh-NAL-i-tee* or *bai-NAL-i-tee.*

band, combo, ensemble, group, orchestra (*nn.*) These are names for various sorts of musical organizations. *Band* and *orchestra* are the generics, the *band,* as in the *military band,* being composed usually of the brass, reed, and percussion instruments only, and the orchestra, especially the *symphony orchestra,* having all these plus stringed instruments as well. Both terms are used loosely, however, and *bands* and *orchestras* can be made up of three or four or more players and instruments of almost any types. An *ensemble* (pronounced *ahn-SAHM-bul*) is any group of musicians or singers or their instruments; it is simply a group consisting of a collection of these, again of varying sorts. *Combo* is a slang clipped form of *combination,* meaning "a group of musicians, usually playing and singing popular, jazz, or folk music"; *group* is a term almost interchangeable with the older *combo* for such a popular *band* or *ensemble,* frequently with an entourage of fans and followers. This sense of the noun *group* is probably Conversational at best, although most other meanings of these words are Standard. See GROUPIE.

bandit (*n.*) The plural in English is usually *bandits,* but *banditti* occurs occasionally. See FOREIGN PLURALS.

bandwagon (*n.*) The *bandwagon,* full of musicians playing loud, catchy tunes, was used in the circus parade before the show to attract crowds to the circus ground, was adopted for political parades, and became an American Colloquial cliché. *To climb, jump, or get on the bandwagon* is to join the popular party, support its candidate(s) or proposals, and be on the winning side.

bane (*n.*) has two obsolete senses: "a cause of death, ruin, or irreversible harm" and "a deadly poison" (now Standard only in compounds such as *ratsbane*). Nowadays *bane* is used primarily to mean "a curse" or "a source of harm," as

in *She is the bane of my existence.* But see also
BALEFUL.

baneful See BALEFUL.

banger (*n.*) is British slang for a kind of sausage: *His favorite supper was bangers and mash.*

banister, bannister See BALUSTER.

banjo (*n.*) The plural is *banjos* or *banjoes.* See
PLURALS OF NOUNS ENDING IN *-O.*

bank of a river, the left, the right *The left
bank of a river* is the one on the left when the
viewer is looking downstream. The *right bank*
is on the right-hand side.

banquet (*n.*) has been from time to time declared pretentious when applied to dinners of
ordinary menu and presentation, but the term is
still much used and Standard both for truly fancy
occasions and for more mundane ones that are
celebratory in some sense.

banshee (*n.*) is a Celtic name for a female spirit
who wailed a warning outside a house where a
death would soon occur. It is sometimes spelled
banshie. To wail like a banshee—that is, loudly
and scarily—is now a cliché, used to describe
any loud wailing sound. The term *banshee* is
Standard in Celtic folklore.

Bantu (*adj., n.*) The noun is the name of a group
of languages from the Niger-Congo family and
also the name applied until recently to members
of Bantu-speaking tribes. Among linguists and
anthropologists it is still in carefully controlled
use but is otherwise taboo in most uses because
of South African whites' use of it as an offensive name for black Africans. Most African versions of English and the American English of
international relations and thoughtful journalism
now reject *Bantu* as a racist term unacceptable
to black Africans. Ideally one should use the
more particularized names of the individual languages and dialects and tribal names within that
larger group. See AFRICAN(-)AMERICAN.

baptismal name See FIRST NAME.

bar See SALON.

barbarian (*n.*), **barbaric, barbarous** (*adjs.*),
barbarism, barbarity, barbarousness (*nn.*)
A *barbarian* is someone from a nation or people
considered uncultivated or primitive by other
nations claiming to be civilized. A *barbarian* is
also anyone fierce, cruel, brutal, and, by extension, anyone crude, boorish, or uncultivated.
Barbaric and *barbarous* are synonymous adjectives; they stress savagery, coarseness, primi-
tively uncivilized qualities. *Barbarous* is ap-

plied to manners, and hence to language use,
more often than is *barbaric. Barbarousness,
barbarity,* and *barbarism* represent all the qualities associated with *barbarians,* with *barbarity*
in particular stressing inhuman, brutal, cruel acts.
All these terms are Standard.

BARBARISMS Perhaps because moral recti-
tude and cultivated sensibilities appear to some
defenders of the language to be inseparable from
ability to use Standard English, commentators
have long used the term *barbarism* to describe
any locution or other language practice that seems
to them clearly below the standard of language
use they themselves accept. If I believe that
what I say is acceptable, yet your practice differs, there is a good chance I will label your
practice a *barbarism.* Since standards vary, so
do our several lists of *barbarisms*; we will agree
on the Substandard status of certain grammatical
usages, however, such as gross failure of subject-verb agreement or use of a Vulgar pronoun
form such as *hisn* or a Vulgar past tense such as
drownded.

barbecue (*n., v.*) Spell it *barbecue* (not *bar-
beque*). As a modifier use either the participial
adjective (*barbecued ribs*) or the noun adjunct
(*barbecue ribs*); conservative usage and most
Edited English prefer the participial adjective,
but both forms are Standard.

barber See COIFFEUR.

barbiturate (*n.*) The Standard pronunciations are
bahr-BICH-uh-rit, bahr-BICH-uh-RAIT, and
BAHR-bi-CHOO-rit. Commonly heard is a
mispronunciation omitting the second *r* (*bahr-
BI-choo-it*), which is reflected in an equally
common misspelling that omits it.

bare (*adj., v.*), **bear** (*n., v.*) These homophones
are so common, and their spelling so clearly
different, that confusion of meanings should be
nearly impossible, and misspelling should be
rare and the result only of mechanical stumble,
not ignorance. The principal parts of the verbs
are *bare, bared, bared,* and *bear, bore, borne*
or *born.* The adjective *bare* means "uncovered,
without adornment," as in *The cupboard was
bare* or *She was bare-headed.* The verb *bare*
means "to expose, to uncover," as in *She bared
her very soul to her sister.* The verb *bear* means
"to carry, to bring forth, to take along," and
the like, as in *He bore the bad news bravely* and
She had borne two sons. See especially BORN.
The noun *bear* refers to the wild animal.

barely (*adv.*) Commentators frequently lump
barely with *hardly* and *scarcely* as one of those
adverbs that must not be combined with the

auxiliaries *can* or *could* in the negative because the combination makes a double negative, as in *You couldn't hardly see ten feet in the fog.* But the fact is that *barely* seems not to behave exactly like *hardly* and *scarcely* and is rarely found used with *can* plus a negative: *You can barely see the streetlights* is Standard, but *You can't barely see the streetlights,* unlike *You can't hardly see the streetlights,* simply doesn't mean the same thing at all and seems never to occur with the negative anyway. See HARDLY.

bargain (*v.*) can combine with several prepositions and adverbs: (1) *We bargained **with** their lawyer. He bargains **with** great skill.* (2) *We bargained **for** [**on**, **over**, **about**] improved working conditions.* (3) *Don't bargain **away** what you've already won.* (4) *They promised to bargain **in** good faith* (a cliché). (5) *We'll bargain **down** [**up**] the cost-of-living clause.* (6) *We bargain **to** impasse* or *bargain **out** a settlement.* All are Standard except *bargain out,* which is jargon and at best Conversational.

bark, barque (*nn.*) These homophones overlap. The noun *bark* means (1) "the covering of stems of plants, especially the trunks of trees," (2) "the sound made by a dog or fox" (a functional shift from the verb *bark*), and (3) "a small ship or boat, technically a sailing vessel with three masts, the front and middle masts square-rigged, the rear mast rigged fore-and-aft." *Barque* is a variant spelling for meaning (3). Both spellings are Standard, but *barque* is old-fashioned.

barmy See BALMY.

barque See BARK.

barrage (*n.*) has a little-known technical meaning, "a dam or barrier put in a river or other channel to increase depth or divert the flow of water"; this use is unexpectedly pronounced in the English way, *BAHR-ij.* The more familiar meanings of *barrage* are the literal "screen of artillery fire" and the figurative "heavy and prolonged burst of words, ideas, or other overwhelming matters." These senses are both pronounced in the French way, *bah-RAHZH,* or in an American approximation, *buh-RAHZH.* See also PRONUNCIATION OF NOUNS ENDING IN -AGE.

barring, meaning "except for," is usually a dangling participle, but it is idiomatic and therefore Standard: *Barring unforeseen emergencies, our funds should last for another month.*

barrio (*n.*) is a Spanish word applied in Spanish countries to a suburb or smaller area or district of a city. A *barrio* in the United States (pronounced *BAH-ree-o;* plural *barrios*) is a Spanish-speaking neighborhood in a city, especially one in the Southwest. *Barrio* seems so far not to have taken on, for most of those who live there at least, pejorative overtones of the sort that the word *ghetto* has acquired over the years, perhaps because none of those living in *barrios* have been legally required to live there, as the Jews once were in ghettos. However, the status of Hispanic words in American English environments is particularly subject to change today, and if the term becomes synonymous with poverty or ethnic issues, its semantics could change suddenly.

barrister See LAWYER.

bar sinister, bend sinister Since the invention (apparently by Sir Walter Scott) of the heraldic term *bar sinister* as a symbol of bastardy, there has been a good deal of objection to it by people full of heraldic lore. In the arcane world of heraldry there is no *bar sinister*; it is illegitimate and unrecognized there. (Heraldry does have a *bend sinister,* but that carries no information about bastardy at all.) Nevertheless, for the world today the term *bar sinister* is a Standard figurative term symbolic of illegitimate birth, and that's that.

basal See BASIC (1).

base See BASS.

baseball, the language of The vocabulary of baseball, probably more than that of any other sport, is as popular in figurative use throughout the society as is the argot of the theater and other entertainments or the cant of the underworld. *To strike out, to be a bush leaguer* [or just *to be bush*], *to balk, to bat three hundred* [or, hyperbolically, *a thousand*], *to give* [or] *get an assist, to pinch hit, to score, to shut out, to begin a whole new ball game,* or *to be off base, to be in left field,* or *to be a screwball, to have somebody throw you a curve,* and many, many more words and phrases have come into the general vocabulary from baseball's slang and argot, to a point where many people use them who may not really be very sure about the nuances of the game itself. Indeed, many people who have never even seen a major or minor league or college game, even on television, use baseball terms, probably some without even being aware of the origins of the expressions they employ. Some of these baseball terms have become Informal or Semiformal and Conversational in the general vocabulary (*to throw someone a curve, to drop the ball*), others remain slang (*to whiff, to throw a slurve*), and a few indeed may have reached full Standard status (*to make a hit, to swing and miss*). Use only the language your audience will understand.

based (*past participle*) combines with *on* or *in* when the combination means "founded or resting on": *Her novels are based on [in] her own youthful experiences*. When combined with *at, in,* or *on* plus a place-name, the combination means "located at," "assigned to": *The unit was based at Manila [in San Diego, on Guam]. Across* and sometimes *over* can also combine with *based,* to mean another sort of location: *The advanced headquarters was based across [over] the river*.

based on, based upon These combined uses as participial phrases, when they begin a sentence, often turn out to be dangling modifiers, although it is not necessary that they be so: *Based upon the facts we have, my conclusion should stand up under scrutiny*. But the fact is that *based on* and *based upon,* even when they dangle, are idiomatic in all but the most careful Edited English: *Based upon [on] what we've heard, the police probably are ready to make an arrest*. Most listeners will not notice such danglers at Conversational levels or in Semiformal and Informal writing.

bases (*n. pl.*) *Bases* is the plural of two nouns: the noun *base,* the plural of which is pronounced BAI-siz, and the noun *basis,* the plural of which is pronounced BAI-seez. See FOREIGN PLURALS.

basic 1, basal (*adjs.*) These two are Standard synonyms in the senses meaning "fundamental," "a starting point," "forming a base." *Basic* also has a specialized use in chemistry, meaning "containing a base" or "alkaline."

BASIC 2, BASIC ENGLISH *Basic English* lives a double life (the adjective by itself a triple one, because *BASIC* is also the acronym for a computer language: *Beginners All-Purpose Symbolic Instruction Code*). As common nouns *basic(s)* and *basic English* frequently stand for the fundamentals of good language use, especially in the oversimple opinions of some purists. But *Basic English* and *Basic* as proper nouns refer to C. K. Ogden's 850-word vocabulary (1934) of his proposed simplified English, designed as an international language. It made a great splash just before World War II, and analysis of its strengths and defects can show us much about how language works. Review of the reasons for its failure as an international language will also reveal some of the flawed logic of more recent champions of a (lowercase) *basic*

English. To be able to function, a natural language must be allowed to change. See also NATURAL LANGUAGE.

basically, basicly (*adv.*) *Basically* is the Standard spelling; *basicly* also occurs, but very rarely. Edited English accepts only *basically*. Some people object to *basically* as a sentence adverb, but there is nothing specifically wrong with it except that overuse has tended to geld it and so limit its effectiveness. It is Conversational and Semiformal in tone, and in such uses it is Standard.

basinet See BASSINET.

basis (*n.*), **on the basis of, on a basis of** (*compound preps.*), **on a . . . basis** (*idiom*) When combined with a preposition, the noun *basis* (plural *bases,* pronounced BAI-seez) usually takes *of* or *for,* as in *The basis of [for] our suggestion is our experience of last year*. Since *basis* has a great deal of general use, frequently in compound prepositions such as *on the basis of* and *on a basis of,* it has acquired a bad name for vagueness and wordiness; many editors urge the use of simpler, shorter words such as *on, after, because, by,* or *because of*. Sometimes such substitutions will work, preserving the same meaning in fewer and clearer words: in *On the basis of what we've just heard, I think we ought to cancel the performance, in view of* would be a bit shorter, *because of* shorter still, and *after* shortest of all (although *after* may slightly change the meaning). But, particularly at the Conversational levels, brevity is not necessarily the only virtue. You need not avoid *on the basis of* except where Edited English requires the greatest conciseness you can muster.

The idiom *on a [blank] basis* is admittedly clumsy, especially when the blank is filled with phrases like *cash flow, accrual accounting,* or *pay-as-you-go,* but it also gets the job done. In the end, especially for Informal and Semiformal writing and for Conversational use, you may find it both clearer and—in the end—shorter than the circumlocutions required to say it another way: *Harvard describes its funding of programs as being done on an each-tub-on-its-own-bottom basis*.

basketball, the language of *Basketball* has yet to furnish the general language as many new words and meanings as baseball has supplied, although the jargon (*dribble, free throw, foul trouble, traveling*) and the slang (*slam dunk, full-court press, in the paint, low post*) are widely known among the game's fans and players. Perhaps the sport is still too young and special to have accomplished what baseball has done with its long history and great popularity. See BASE-BALL.

bass, base (*nn.*) *Bass,* pronounced *BAIS* and meaning "a male singer with a low voice," "a large stringed instrument with a very low register," and "the musical part they sing or play," is a homophone of *base* meaning "foundation," "any of the bases in baseball," and a whole range of other specialized senses besides. *Bass,* pronounced *BAS,* is the name of a fish. In speaking, make certain that context distinguishes the musical terms from the identically pronounced "foundation" or "third base," and in writing make certain that context distinguishes the musical term from the fish spelled just like it.

bassinet, basinet (*nn.*) A *bassinet* is a kind of cradle; a *basinet* is a light helmet, a piece of armor. They both come from the French *basin* ("basin") plus the diminutive *-et* and can be homonyms: each can be stressed on either the first or last syllable, but *bassinet* is usually stressed on the last, *basinet* on the first.

bastard (*adj., n.*), **bastardize** (*v.*) The basic meaning of *bastard* is "an illegitimate child, one born out of wedlock," and the term, like the social plight of the unlucky child, was taboo in polite mixed company in the United States during most of the nineteenth and early twentieth centuries; today this sense is Standard and now applied almost equally to males and females. Extended senses include "something fake, imitation, or inferior," which is Standard, and the slang uses—reserved almost exclusively for males—meaning "anyone regarded with contempt, hatred, or scorn" or "anyone so termed out of playfulness." Both these slang uses are considered obscene and even continue to be taboo in some Conversational and Informal situations. As adjective the term is Standard meaning "something illegitimate," "something not like others of its kind," and "something that looks like the original but is not genuine." *To bastardize* is "to make a bastard of," in the literal sense, but is more frequently used to mean "to cheapen, to debase."

bastille, bastile, Bastille (*nn.*) The common noun *bastille,* spelled with either two *l*'s or one, is the name for a small military tower or fortress, frequently one used as a prison. Today the word is sometimes still used as a jocular name for a prison. The proper noun was the famous fortress and prison in Paris that fell at the beginning of the French Revolution, on July 14, 1789, on the anniversary of which the French now celebrate *Bastille Day.*

bastion (*n.*) means "a fortified place" and hence, by extension, "a stronghold," "a center of strength." *He and his friends have created a bastion of conservative thought.*

bate See BAIT.

bathos, pathos (*nn.*), **bathetic, pathetic** (*adj.*) In style, *bathos* (pronounced *BAI-thahs*) is the sudden intrusion of the commonplace, the trite, or the trivial into the midst of elevated, high-toned matter. Specifically *bathos* is fake, hypocritical, or overdone imitation of *pathos* (first syllable pronounced *PAI-* or *PA-*; second syllable pronounced *-thahs* or *-thos*), which is an emotion evoking pity and compassion. The adjectives *bathetic* and *pathetic* rhyme. All four words are Standard.

bathroom (*n.*), **go to the bathroom** *Bathroom* may indeed refer to a room for taking a bath or shower only, but Standard American English uses the word mostly to refer to a room containing a bathtub or a shower or both (or neither), a toilet, and a washbasin. (A *lavatory,* a room containing a washbasin and, usually, a toilet, is often loosely called a *bathroom.*) *Bathroom* is therefore a euphemism, and *go to the bathroom* is another, this one an idiom adopted in order to avoid having to be explicit about the acts of urinating or defecating, one or both of which may be the reason for *going to the bathroom.* See also WASH UP.

baton (*n.*), **batten** (*n., v.*) A *baton* (pronounced *buh-TAHN*) is an orchestra conductor's stick, a staff, a nightstick, or a drum major or majorette's stick. A *batten* (pronounced *BAT-in*) is a narrow piece of lumber, such as is often put over the joints between siding boards to make what is called *board-and-batten* siding for a building. *Batten* is actually two verbs, one meaning "to apply battens," as in *Batten down the hatches,* the other "to grow fat or to fatten," as in *The landlord battened on the rents of his poor tenants.* The first *batten* combines almost always with *down,* and the second with *on* or *upon.*

bay window, bow window (*nn.*) A *bay window* protrudes outside the wall of the house, often leaving a window seat available within. A *bow window* is a curved *bay window.*

bazaar (*n.*), **bizarre** (*adj.*) These are homophones. A *bazaar* is a market, especially in the Near East, but more recently it has come to refer to a money-raising affair—a combined sale and carnival—at an English or American church.

Anything *bizarre* is peculiar, unusual, strange, or extravagantly odd.

-bb- See CONSONANTS (2).

B.C., B.C.E. See A.D.

be (*v., aux.*) The form *be* itself is the infinitive of the verb (*To be, or not to be*) and also the present subjunctive, as in *If you be the man we need, then welcome.* The subjunctive *be* is Formal, and in most Conversational and Informal uses that last sentence would begin *If you are the man we need.* We preserve the form, however, in some stereotyped phrases, such as *So be it* and *Be that as it may. Be* is most commonly used in Standard English as the second person singular and plural verb or auxiliary in imperative sentences: *Be there on time, please. Please be seated.*

Be is used also in Black English as a Substandard auxiliary meaning continuing actions, things being done over and over again, continually: *She be studying Spanish.* The use of forms of *be* and *have* as auxiliaries can give us either a perfect tense, as in *He has completed his work,* a predicate adjective, as in *Her work is completed,* or a passive voice, as in *Her work has been completed.* See also INDICATIVE; REGIONAL DIALECT.

bear See BARE.

bear, bull (*nn.*), **bearish, bullish** (*adjs.*) These words are, among other things, terms used in the stock market: a *bear* is a person who believes stock prices will fall and who therefore advises you to sell your stocks; a *bull* is a person who believes stock prices will rise and who therefore urges you to buy stocks. *Bearish* and *bullish* are used to describe people, their opinions about the market, and the market itself and its tendencies.

beastly (*adj., intensifier*) The Standard adjective means "brutal, savage, or bestial," but it has a Conversational and Informal use that is much milder, meaning simply "nasty or unpleasant." The British also use the word Colloquially as an adverbial intensifier, as in *She was beastly rotten to him.* There has been some recent American use of the intensifier, perhaps in conscious imitation of the British expression.

beat (*v.*) The principal parts are *beat, beat,* and either *beaten* or *beat,* as in *They had beaten [had beat] us in the last four games. Beaten* is Standard as past participle in almost all uses, but *beat* is also widely used, especially in Semiformal, Informal, and Conversational contexts. The verb has a number of slang or Conversational senses: "to puzzle, confuse, or baffle (*That*

beats me!); "to trick, cheat, swindle (*He beat the landlord out of the last week's rent*); "to escape punishment," a slang use (*They both have beat the rap again*); and the intransitive Casual use, in the past tense, meaning "won" (*I beat!*). Both *beat* and *beaten* also serve as participial adjectives, but *beaten* is always Standard in uses such as *beaten gold* and *the beaten white of an egg,* whereas *beat* has a slang meaning, "worn out," "exhausted," as in *I've worked for ten hours straight, and I'm beat.* The *beat generation* of the 1950s opposed conventional manners, dress, and behavior. There are also two Conversational uses of the participial adjective *beat* meaning "defeated," as in *It just can't be beat,* and with *get* as auxiliary, as in *Their free safety got beat on that long pass.*

beau (*n.*) *Beau,* meaning "a woman's regular escort," "her boyfriend," rhymes with *go* and has two plurals, the French *beaux* and the regular English *beaus,* both pronounced to rhyme with *goes.* Today *beau* is old-fashioned at best, and probably could be labeled archaic or even obsolescent. See FOREIGN PLURALS.

beauteous, beautiful (*adjs.*) These are synonyms, of course, but *beautiful* is by far the more frequently used in current speech and writing; *beauteous* has an old-fashioned air about it.

beauty (*adj., n.*) The noun is Standard as an abstraction, as in *The beauty of the landscape was breathtaking,* as a word meaning "a beautiful thing, animal, or person (especially a woman)," as in *The new foal promised to be a beauty,* and as a desirable feature or quality, as in *The beauty of the proposal was its simplicity.* The slang use as adjective is Substandard and dialectal, and that use may already be disappearing: *The beauty part was that we won.*

because (*subord. conj.*) Edited English insists on *The reason is [that],* but *The reason is because* continues to be used at the Conversational levels of the Standard language. *Is because* (*without reason*) is standard at all levels to introduce noun and adverbial clauses: *It is because I love you that I constantly try to improve you* (noun clause); *Because I love you, I constantly try to improve you* (adverbial clause).

Because introducing a clause that is the subject of a sentence has also been proscribed, but in fact such constructions are Standard, although limited to Conversational and Informal use: *Just because I've missed a few classes doesn't mean I'm not interested in the course.* Some commentators have said that *because* ought not to begin a sentence, but it occurs there regularly in the Semiformal Edited English of our magazines and newspapers, as well as almost everywhere in our conversation: *Because the rent was overdue, the landlord evicted our family.*

Finally, *because* following a negative verb has been pointed out as a possibly grammatically ambiguous use, as in *They didn't accept because her invitation seemed insincere.* Of course a comma after *accept* ends the ambiguity; in speech, intonation does the same thing. It's not *because* that causes the trouble in writing, but lack of punctuation. Just as with any other phrasal or clausal modifier in this position, we must know whether it is restrictive (no comma) or nonrestrictive (with a comma); it can't be both at once. See also AS (1); RESTRICTIVE AND NONRESTRICTIVE CLAUSES; RESTRICTIVE AND NONRESTRICTIVE MODIFIERS; SINCE.

because of See DUE TO.

beck See STREAM.

become (*v.*) is a linking verb, and it can take either a predicate adjective (*She became ill*) or a predicate nominative (*He became an officer*). As a transitive verb (*His suit and tie became him beautifully*), it means "is suitable to or for" and takes a direct object. All are Standard.

become of is a Standard idiom meaning "happen to, be the outcome of": *What has become of your former teacher? What will become of our proposal?*

been is the past participle of the verb and auxiliary *be*. Americans almost always pronounce it *BIN*, but the British and Canadians usually pronounce it *BEEN*.

before See PREVIOUS TO.

beg (*v.*) is used in a number of idiomatic formulas that can either lend a desirable and rather courtly formality to discourse or correspondence or coat them with an unfortunate and unnatural stuffiness. Only *I beg your pardon* and its variants are universally right for nearly every occasion. All the others in the following list are rather stiff: *I beg to differ (with you), I beg your forgiveness, I beg your indulgence, I beg to acknowledge, I beg to remain,* and so on.

begin (*v.*) The Standard principal parts are *begin, began, begun*. In writing from the eighteenth and nineteenth centuries, you can find *begun* as past tense as well, but today that use is dialectal and Substandard. *Began* as past par-

ticiple is Vulgar English. See STRONG VERBS (1); STRONG VERBS (2).

beg the question is an idiomatic expression meaning "to assume the truth of the conclusion of one's argument without bothering to prove it" and then, by extension, "to evade or dodge the question and argue another matter instead": *Her argument for a second chance was eloquent, but it begged the question: she never explained why she had failed to appear for the original examination.*

behalf, behoof (*nn.*), **in behalf of, in behoof of, on behalf of** (*preps.*) The noun *behalf* means "part, side, interest." *Behoof* means "benefit, interest, sake, profit, advantage, or need." In American English *in [on] behalf of* are interchangeable, meaning "as the representative of" or "for the benefit of." *In behoof of* means only "for the benefit of" and occurs infrequently.

behavior, behaviour (*n.*) Americans spell it *behavior*, the British, *behaviour*. See SPELLING (1).

behest, request (*nn.*) A *behest* is a command, an urging, or a very strong request: *At the president's behest, we made an appointment with the foreign minister.* A request is anything asked for, petitioned for. *Behest* is a more formal and old-fashioned, but it is still in regular use.

beholden to means "indebted to, obliged to be grateful to," and it is usually used in situations where someone is reluctantly obliged to feel grateful to someone else: *I'd rather not ask for favors—I hate to be beholden to anybody.* It may sound a trifle old-fashioned, but it is Standard and not really archaic.

behoof See BEHALF.

behoove, behove (*v.*) Most Americans spell it with two *o*'s, the British spell it with only one; most Americans pronounce it *bi-HOOV*, the British *bi-HOV*, but the British spelling and pronunciation are also considered infrequent American variants. The transitive verb is in full use today: *It behooves you to study hard for the final,* meaning "it is necessary for you, incumbent upon you, or advantageous to you." The intransitive verb is rare in American use: *She was modest, as it behooved,* meaning "as was right and proper."

beige (*adj., n.*) is pronounced *BAIZH*.

being, being as, being as how, being that All these locutions, as in *Being [being as, being as how, being that] you're in town, why don't we have dinner?* are dialectal, from Eastern New

England, South Midland, or Southern regions. Standard English, especially written, requires that you avoid them except in Conversational and Informal use within one of those areas. *Because, since,* and *inasmuch as* are Standard and will serve instead.

belabor, belabour, labor, labour (*vv.*) *Belabor,* when it means "to treat or discuss in tiresomely great detail," is a pejorative and is also a synonym for and interchangeable with the verb *labor* in a sentence such as *He belabored [labored] the point until we were quite sick of it. Belabor* can also mean literally "to beat as with a stick, to pound on," as in *The watchmen belabored him with nightsticks until they had subdued him,* or figuratively "to chastise or ridicule," as in *The boss belabored his staff with many harsh words. Belabor* is Standard in all three senses. British English spells both *belabor* and *labor* with an *-our* ending. See SPELLING (1).

belie (*v.*) means "contradict, misrepresent, or disguise," as in *His humble words belie his fierce pride. Belie* never means "betray."

believe, feel, think (*vv.*) are almost interchangeable when used to express opinions, ideas, or feelings: *I believe [think, feel] I'm coming down with a cold.* In most uses none of the three is very explicit, and any precision you hope to gain by choosing one over the others is likely to be blurred or lost in transmission, at least in all but the most Formal or Oratorical uses. See also SENSE.

belittle (*v.*) *Belittle* is a Standard verb, meaning "to make something seem small or unimportant," "to depreciate," as in *He was always belittling his brother's abilities as a golfer.*

bells (*n.*) *Bells* are used in nautical time telling, being rung each half hour of the twenty-four as follows:

BELLS	TIME (A.M. AND P.M.)		
1	12:30	4:30	8:30
2	1:00	5:00	9:00
3	1:30	5:30	9:30
4	2:00	6:00	10:00
5	2:30	6:30	10:30
6	3:00	7:00	11:00
7	3:30	7:30	11:30
8	4:00	8:00	12:00

First watch runs from 4:00 to 8:00 A.M., second from 8:00 to 12:00 noon, third from 12:00 noon to 4:00 P.M., first dog watch from 4:00 to 6:00 P.M., second dog watch from 6:00 to 8:00 P.M., fourth watch from 8:00 P.M. to 12:00 midnight, and the fifth watch from 12:00 midnight to 4:00 A.M., when the cycle begins again.

bellwether (*adj., n.*) is literally a male sheep (a *wether*) that wears a bell and is followed by the rest of the flock. Figuratively a *bellwether* is a leader (*He is bellwether for the entire class; wherever he goes, they follow*) or anything suggesting leadership (*She seems to have some bellwether qualities, despite her youth*) or the direction events may take (*The bellwether indicators I watch are interest rates and the price of gold*). All these uses are Standard.

belly (*n., v.*) Victorian American manners made the word *belly,* like *leg, cock, bull,* and many others taboo in most mixed company. *Abdomen, stomach, midriff,* and the cute *tummy* and jocular *breadbasket* were used as euphemisms instead. Today *belly* is Standard (although conservatives may prefer *abdomen*) in a range of literal and figurative meanings, the most central of which are the literal "the front lower part of the human body," "the stomach," "the abdominal cavity," and "the underside of an animal's body." As a name for the womb, *belly* is partly archaic, partly Conversational: *Where do babies come from? From Mommy's belly.*

The figurative meanings of the noun generally have to do with the shape of something—of a sail or the hull of a ship—or the vulnerable part of something—such as a continent, as in Winston Churchill's famous "the soft underbelly" of Europe. The verb is also mainly figurative, usually meaning "to curve or swell, to bulge." And there are two widely used slang senses combined with *up: Belly up,* meaning "step right up close," and *to go belly up,* an expression that graphically evokes the picture of a dead animal or fish and is frequently applied to enterprises or other ventures that fail.

beloved (*adj., n.*) is usually pronounced with two syllables (*bee-LUHVD*) when used alone as a predicate adjective (*She was beloved by all*) but with three syllables (*bee-LUHV-id*) when used as a noun or as an adjective in front of a noun (*She is my beloved, the woman I hope to marry. He was the beloved patriarch of the family*). The two-syllable version usually combines with either *of* or *by: The queen was beloved of [by] all her subjects.*

below (*adj., n.*) Using *below* as a reference to matters appearing lower on a page or later in an essay is a Standard practice (although Edited English prefers more precision), and it is also a convention of scholarly writing: *See the argu-*

ment below and *See below* are idiomatic for this purpose. But be wary of overuse. See ABOVE.

BELT AND SUSPENDERS CONSTRUCTION See REDUNDANT.

bemuse See AMUSE (2).

bend sinister See BAR SINISTER.

benedict (*n.*) should be used ideally of a long-confirmed bachelor who has just married. The word comes from the name of just such a character (Benedick) in Shakespeare's *Much Ado About Nothing*. Be certain that your audience understands the meaning.

benefactor, beneficiary (*nn.*) A *benefactor* is someone who gives help, a patron, especially one who gives money; a *beneficiary* is the receiver of help, especially someone who is left money or property. Originally a *beneficiary* was a person in holy orders who held a *benefice*, an ecclesiastical office with an endowment attached.

benign, benignant, malign, malignant (*adj.*) These pairs are antonyms. *Benign* means "kindly, pleasant, beneficial," and in medicine specifically "not malignant," as in *a benign tumor*. *Malign* means "evil, injurious, very harmful," and "malignant," as in *His look was malign and full of hate*. *Malignant* means much the same as *malign*, "malevolent, highly injurious, evil," and in medicine specifically it describes an abnormal growth, one likely to grow and therefore likely to kill, as in *a malignant tumor*. *Benignant* is built on analogy with *malignant* and means "kindly, pleasant, beneficial," and in medicine specifically "not malignant." *Benign* and *malignant* are the higher-frequency adjectives, especially in the medical senses, but all four are Standard.

benny (*n.*) is a fading slang term for an amphetamine pill; it is a clipped form of the trade name *Benzedrine*, which is an amphetamine. See DRUG(S).

benzine, benzene (*nn.*) *Benzine* is the generic term for any of several volatile hydrocarbons that can be used as motor fuels or solvents; gasoline is a *benzine*. *Benzene* is one of these hydrocarbons, C_6H_6, used in chemical synthesis and also as a motor fuel or a solvent.

bereave (*v.*) The past tense and past participle are *bereaved* or *bereft*. The verb means "to take away, to rob (of)," and most uses are archaic and stiffly formal: *He was bereaved of all reason. Her tragedy bereaved her of all interest in life.* Far more frequent are the two participial adjectives and the noun formed by one of them.

Bereft has the more generalized meaning, "stripped of, robbed of, deprived of": *He was bereft of friends, money, and purpose. Bereaved*, as adjective, is more specialized, referring to those who have lost a relative or friend to death: *The bereaved parents were bearing up well.* Functional shift has made *bereaved* a noun that is both singular and plural: *The clergyman spoke privately to the bereaved, and she [they] seemed helped by his words.*

Berkeley (*n.*) Americans pronounce the name of the California city and campus to rhyme its stressed first syllable with *lurk*; the British pronounce the name of the London square to rhyme the first syllable with *dark*. See PRONUNCIATION (2).

beseech (*v.*) The past tense and past participle, *besought* or *beseeched*, are in evenly divided usage, and both are Standard, though perhaps somewhat literary: *He beseeched [besought] her to trust him. Beseeched* may occur somewhat less frequently with a nonhuman direct object than does *besought*, which in turn seems to be giving way to *sought*. Compare SEEK.

beside (*prep.*), **besides** (*adv., prep.*) *Beside* is Standard as a preposition (*She sat beside her brother*), and two Standard idiomatic uses occur in the sentences *He was beside himself* and *That's beside the point*. Standard English now uses *besides* as adverb almost exclusively, instead of *beside: She hasn't got time, and she simply doesn't want to meet him, besides. Besides* is both an adverb, meaning "in addition to, except, else, and moreover," as in *Besides, she's not going to be home then*, and a preposition, usually meaning "except" or "in addition to," as in *Besides the two of us, there was only the driver* and *Besides her arthritis, she has few complaints.* See APART FROM; ASIDE FROM.

bespeak (*v.*) has these principal parts: *bespeak, bespoke*, and *bespoken* and *bespoke*. The verb has three current Standard meanings: (1) "to reserve beforehand," as in *Our cottage is bespoken*, (2) "to show or indicate," as in *His calluses bespeak manual labor*, and (3) "to point to, suggest, or promise," as in *Her smile bespeaks real warmth and friendliness.*

bespoke (*adj.*) *Bespoke* is one of two Standard past participles of *bespeak*, and it is regularly used in British English as an adjective meaning "custom-made, made to order," used particularly of clothing: *His dinner jacket fitted him well, as a bespoke dinner jacket should.* See also READY-MADE.

best, had best See HAD BETTER.

best foot forward, put your is an old cliché, meaning "present yourself at your very best, making the most of your virtues and minimizing your defects," and it is unquestionably Standard, even though it contains a superlative degree used of two.

bestir (*v.*), meaning "to rouse, to get moving," is always used with a reflexive pronoun: *Bestir yourself; get going!*

bestow (*v.*) combines with the prepositions *upon* and *on: The old man bestowed most of his property on [upon] his children.* With echoes of *stow* perhaps helping to influence it, sometimes *bestow* combines with *in,* when the idea is "to put something in a particular place": *She bestowed her confidence in him.*

be sure and See TRY AND.

bet (*v.*) *Bet* has two forms each for past tense and past participle, *bet* and *betted,* but in Standard American and British English *betted* is becoming rare. Use *bet* as all three principal parts.

betake oneself (*v.*) This reflexive use, meaning "to cause oneself to go," is the only sense of the verb still Standard; other senses are archaic at best. What's left is now an idiom and a cliché, arch but respectable: *She betook herself to her aunt's house to pay her respects.*

bête noire is a French phrase meaning literally "black beast," and it is used in English figuratively to mean "any person or thing that is to be feared, hated, and if possible avoided," as in *Algebra was always his bête noire.* Pronounce it *bet-NWAHR.* It seems to keep its accent mark in English, and in the plural each word gets a silent final -*s, bêtes noires.* See FOREIGN PHRASES.

betray See BELIE.

better (*adj.*) is an absolute comparative in phrases such as *at better department stores* and in the names of the departments in them where you can buy *better dresses.* It is Standard but probably limited to other-than-Formal contexts.

better See BETTOR.

better, had better See HAD BETTER.

better part of, the This phrase is idiomatic and Standard and appears in any context that deals with time or groups. It means, roughly, "more than half": *The formal address took the better part of an hour.* It is also a Standard idiom and cliché in statements involving whatever quality or action turns out to be *the better part of valor.*

better than, in place of *more than* (*It's better than [more than] an hour's drive from here*), is

frequently criticized when it appears in writing, but it is nonetheless a Standard idiom, although limited mainly to the Conversational levels and to Informal and Semiformal written imitations of them.

better than I, better than me Edited English and most Standard levels of speech above Casual, plus all written levels above Informal, insist on *He is better [at basketball] than I [am].* *Than* is a subordinating conjunction introducing a clause whose subject should be in the nominative case; the clause serves as adverbial modifier of *better,* in many instances with the full clause suppressed and only the conjunction and pronoun actually spoken or written. In Casual, Impromptu, and some Informal use, however, you will also find *He is better [at basketball] than me,* where *than* is construed as a preposition, with its object properly accusative. The prepositional phrase then is an adverbial modifier of *better. My sister is better at math than me* is Casual and Impromptu, and appropriate only at those levels and in their written imitations.

bettor, better (*nn.*) *Bettor* is the usual spelling of the noun meaning "one who bets," but *better* is a variant, as well as a noun meaning "one who is better than someone in some respect," as in *You should heed your betters.* See AGENTIVE ENDINGS.

between, among (*preps.*) It is often argued that *between* should be used to express a relationship involving two of something, and *among* should express relationships involving three or more, but in fact that generalization does not describe the way English has long used these prepositions. *Between* can be used of as many items as you like if the relationship is one-to-one, however much it may be repeated with different partners: *Economic relations between Great Britain, France, and Italy [or between some members of the EEC] are tense at present. Among* works with any plural number above two: *Among the milling ballplayers, fans, and reporters were the four umpires.* Best advice: use *between* of two and *among* of three or more in Edited English, but elsewhere, and especially at lower levels, feel free to use *between* of two, three, or more. But see also AMONG.

between a rock and a hard place is a cliché meaning "in an impossible situation between equally unpleasant, unyielding threats."

between each, between every *Between* can be followed by a singular noun (*He changed his shirt between every inning*), but this use is idiomatic, appropriate at the Conversational and Informal levels, rather than at the Oratorical and the Formal, which always prefer the full logic of *between* with plural nouns (*between innings*) or the more explicit *after each inning.*

between-maid, tweeny (*nn.*) was a servant who assisted the cook in the kitchen and the housemaids in the rest of the house. The rank of a *tweeny* was low, her portfolio neither the one thing nor the other, but *between.*

between you and I, between he and his mother *Between* is a preposition, and Standard English requires that its objects be in the accusative case, so these phrases should be *between you and me, between him and his mother.* Mistakes in the cases of pronouns occur most frequently in compound subject and compound object phrases like these; *between us* would almost never be confused with *between we,* unless the pronoun were part of a compound nominal, such as *between the boys and we* [should be *us*]. Standard English users enforce these case choices rigorously in both speech and writing; failures are shibboleths.

betwixt, betwixt and between *Betwixt* is an archaic or obsolescent preposition, except in the idiom and cliché *betwixt and between,* which means "neither the one thing nor the other," "halfway between," "in the middle," "on the fence": *She simply couldn't make up her mind, and so she hesitated there, caught betwixt and between.*

bi-, semi- (*prefixes*) When prefixed to nouns meaning periods of time, *bi-* means "every two," so that *bimonthly* means "every two months," *biweekly* "every two weeks." *Semi-,* when prefixed to words meaning periods of time, means "half," or "halfway through," so that *semimonthly* means "every half month," or "twice a month," and *semiweekly* means "every half week," or "twice a week." Unfortunately, when you *bisect* a line you divide it into two equal parts, and a good many other words begin with a *bi-* that means "into two," rather than "every two." So a rare but naggingly recurrent meaning of *bimonthly* is also, alas, "twice a month." Best advice: when you use *bi-* and *semi-* words, let context help define them, even at the cost of some redundancy. See BIANNUAL.

biannual, biennial, semiannual The *bi-* prefix on *biannual* "divides into two," so that *biannual* usually means "twice a year." *Biennial* comes from a Latin word whose prefix *bi-* meant "two," so *biennial* means "every two years," as in a *biennium,* "a two-year period." *Semian-*

nual also means "every half year," or "twice a year." *Biannual* is almost a hopeless case, conveying only the idea of two, but not specifying when; *semiannual* is a little more helpful, suggesting as it does "half-yearly." Make certain that context makes your meaning clear, no matter which word you use; in fact, given the potential for confusion, *half-yearly* and *two-yearly* may be better than any of these. See also BI-.

bias (*n., v.*) The plural of the noun is *biases.* Spell the past tense and past participle of the verb either *biased* or *biassed,* the present participle either *biasing* or *biassing*; Americans slightly prefer the first spellings. See CONSONANTS (2).

Bible, bible (*nn.*), **biblical** (*adj.*) Capitalize *Bible* as the name of the Christian sacred book, as a name for the Jewish Old Testament, or for any other sacred book, such as the *Koran,* the Muslim *Bible.* Lowercase the word when it refers to an official book of some sort, such as in *The Infantry Drill Manual is the infantryman's bible.* The adjective *biblical* is never capitalized except as the first word in a sentence.

bicentenary, bicentennial See CENTENNIAL.

biceps, triceps (*nn.*) Each has two Standard plurals—an unchanging one of fairly high frequency (*biceps, triceps*) and one of much lower frequency made on the regular pattern for English plurals (*bicepses, tricepses*).

bid (*n., v.*) The principal parts of the verb are *bid, bade* (pronounced *BAD* or *BAID*) or *bid*; and *bidden, bid,* or *bade.* Present tenses are identical for both clusters of meaning in *She bids four spades* and *She bids you welcome.* In the cards and auction cluster, however, only *bid* is past tense, as in *Last night she bid her hands badly,* while in the command and instruction cluster, the past tense can be either *bade* or *bid,* as in *She bade [bid] us all good night.* In the past perfect tense, *bid* is the only form for the cards and auction cluster, as in *They had bid against each other at the auction,* but for the other senses, three past participle forms are Standard: *They had bidden [bid, bade] us gather around the piano.*

The noun has a number of senses resulting from functional shift, but the sense meaning "an invitation to be a member" (*He got a bid to join the country club*) is limited to Conversational and Informal or Semiformal use.

bide (*v.*) is archaic, obsolete, or dialectal in the senses "stay, dwell, and wait," except in the idiom *to bide one's time,* which is Standard and means "to be patient until the right moment to act,'' and in the cloying cliché that still turns up as the name of summer cottages, *Bide-a-Wee.*

biennial See BIANNUAL.

bight, bite, byte (*nn.*) A *bight* is a loop or curve in a piece of rope, the course of a river, or the curve of a bay; a *bite* is a chunk or piece or mouthful, such as might be cut out with the teeth. *Byte* is a computer term meaning ''a string of eight bits,'' a basic unit of information in digital computing. They are homophones.

bigness See ENORMITY; SYNONYM.

big of a deal, (not) that See OF A.

bilateral, multilateral, unilateral (*adjs.*) *Bilateral* means ''two-sided, probably symmetrically so,'' as in *His hearing loss was bilateral; it involved both ears. Unilateral* means ''one-sided, involving only one party, independent,'' as in *She took unilateral action, not waiting to see whether her neighbors would decide to join her. Multilateral* means ''many-sided, involving many parties,'' as in *They finally all agreed to sign a very complex multilateral commercial treaty.* All these words are Standard.

bilk (*n., v.*) To *bilk* someone (of something) is ''to cheat, swindle, escape from, or specifically to get away without paying,'' as in *He managed to bilk all his creditors when he fled the country.* The noun means either ''an instance of *bilking,*'' as in *His sales pitch was nothing but a bilk,* or ''one who *bilks,*'' as in *The police knew him as an experienced bilk.* All are Standard, but the noun senses are rare.

billet doux (*n.*) This French phrase (pronounce it *BIL-ee-DOO*) literally means ''sweet letter'' and hence ''love letter.'' The plural is *billets doux,* pronounced just like the singular. See FOREIGN PHRASES.

BILLINGSGATE was the London fishmarket of the seventeenth century, where, it was said, the fishwives used the foulest, most colorful, and most profane English of all. Many Americans no longer know the term, but to those speakers of English who do, *billingsgate* still means profanity or obscenity—the foulest and most abusive imaginable.

billion (*n.*) A *billion* is a thousand millions (1,000,000,000), but the British once used the term to mean what we mean by a trillion. See MILLIARD; TRILLION.

bimonthly See BI-.

biodegradable (*adj.*) means that materials so described are capable of being broken down by the action of bacteria or other microorganisms, as is the case with some detergents. The word is much in vogue these days as concern grows for our environment, whose landfills overflow with things that are not *biodegradable* or are insufficiently so and therefore threaten to outlast and ultimately bury us.

bipartisan (*adj.*) means anything representing the work of or involving two parties, such as *a bipartisan proposal.*

birth (*v.*), **birthing** (*n.*) These are found mainly in Southern and South Midland regional dialects. The verb, meaning to bear young, is still dialectal, but the noun appears to have become Standard, although some people may consider it still too special and will argue that it should continue to be labeled dialectal or as some of the jargon of modern midwifery and natural childbirth.

birthday suit, in one's This old chestnut means ''naked.'' The cliché is still slang after many generations of use.

bisect, dissect (*vv.*) To *bisect* (pronounced *BEI-sekt* or *bei-SEKT*) is ''to divide into two usually equal parts''; to *dissect* (pronounced *di-SEKT, DEI-sekt,* or *dei-SEKT*) is ''to take apart, to separate into pieces'' and figuratively ''to analyze in minute detail by breaking down into component parts.''

bison See BUFFALO.

bit (*nn.*) *Bit* is three different nouns, two of them related, the other wholly unrelated. The oldest was originally an Old English noun and means ''something bitten or held in the teeth'': among its meanings are ''the *bit* put in the horse's mouth and attached to the bridle,'' ''the *bit* of a tobacco pipe or cigarette holder,'' ''the drill *bit,*'' ''the jaws of pliers, tongs, and the like,'' and ''the working shaft end of a key.'' All belong to this first noun, and all are Standard.

The second is related to an Old English verb meaning ''to bite,'' and this *bit* is ''a bite or bite-sized morsel'': a *bit* of food or a small quantity of anything; an eighth of a dollar, more familiar to us in the slang term for a quarter, *two bits;* anything unimportant or brief, as in *wait a bit, a bit of a nuisance, every bit as bad;* and in the theater a small part—a *bit,* a *bit part,* or a *bit role*—and some sort of brief routine—*a comedy bit.* All these are Standard. The idiom *the whole bit,* meaning a collection of all the pieces of an idea or a situation, is slang, as in *I couldn't stand their modishness—the precious conversation, the finical manners, the contrived humor—the whole bit bored me.*

This same *bit,* meaning "bite or morsel," is also used as a qualifier, meaning "somewhat" or "rather," as in *This movie is a bit dull.* The idioms *a bit much* (*She's a bit much; I can't stand her*), *bit by bit* (meaning "little by little"), *to do one's bit* (meaning "to do one's share"), and *every bit as* (meaning "wholly, entirely, altogether," as in *She is every bit as unpleasant as I feared*) are clichés but Standard. See also KIND OF.

The third noun is an acronym, made from the first two letters of *binary* and the last letter of *digit* (or the first letter of *binary* and the last two letters of *digit*); in computerese it means "one digit in a binary number system" and hence "a yes or no choice and the electrical or other physical representation of such a choice on tape, punch card, or in a computer memory." This *bit* is a single basic unit of information used in computing and in information theory. See BIGHT.

bitch (*n., v.*), **bitchy** (*adj.*) *Bitch* is Standard as a noun meaning "a female dog, wolf, or other canid." Meaning "a promiscuous woman" the term is old-fashioned, perhaps archaic, and has certainly been overwhelmed in all but veterinary uses by the meaning "a bad-tempered, vicious, spiteful, domineering woman," a use that is Standard but taboo in circles where polite manners rule it out. It is slang when used to mean "a complaint," as in *What's the bitch?* or to describe a task or situation as difficult or unpleasant, as in *This assignment is a bitch.*

As a verb *bitch* has two slang meanings, "to complain" and "to botch a task," as in *That mechanic bitched* [*up*] *the valve job on my engine*; in the second sense it is probably related to *botch.*

Bitchy, the adjective, means "irritable, nasty, and unpleasant" when applied to people and their behavior and "difficult or unpleasant" when applied to tasks or situations.

bitch goddess The *bitch goddess* is a cliché of unknown origin, a personification of Success or Luck, the worldly kind; she is a tricky lady to serve, fickle, ungrateful, and cruel. The term is Standard.

bite (*n., v.*) The verb has a past tense, *bit,* and two past participles, *bitten* and *bit. Bitten* is much more frequently used in Standard English, but *bit* continues to occur as past participle, especially in idioms such as these: *The other cowboy had already bit the dust. We have bit the bullet. He's been bit by mosquitoes.* All these are Standard, although Edited English would more often use *bitten* in other than these idiomatic instances. Predicate adjectives such as

snake-bit and *dog-bit* are Substandard and dialectal. The idioms *bite the hand that feeds you,* meaning "to harm someone who is helping you," and *bite off more than you can chew,* meaning "to try to do more than you can accomplish," are both Conversational and Informal.

The noun *bite* is Conversational in the graphic figurative use *take a bite out of,* as in *Taxes took a large bite out of my paycheck.* See also BIGHT.

bitter cold, bitterly cold In these phrases, *bitter* and *bitterly* are both adverbs used as intensifiers; *bitter* in this use is a flat adverb. It can also be an adjective, in constructions such as *It was a bitter day* and *She seems bitter.*

bitter end is a sailor's term. The *bitter end* of a rope on shipboard is the inboard end, the end wound around the *bitts.* Hence *bitt-er.* Since it is the very end, and it is tied to the ship, when you reach the *bitter end,* you have no slack to play with. Figuratively, at the *bitter end* you have no room to maneuver, and overtones of *bitterness* (rather than the *bitts*) come through: the *bitter end* then becomes the very end and the unpleasant end, hard to take.

bivalve (*n.*) is a generic name for mussels, clams, oysters, and other two-shelled, hinged mollusks. Some commentators think it is pretentious when used nontechnically, as in *We lunched on some succulent bivalves, an excellent salad, and a good wine,* but it is Standard.

bivouac (*v.*) Spell its past tense and past participle *bivouacked* and the present participle *bivouacking.* See SPELLING OF -*ING* AND -*ED* FORMS OF VERBS ENDING IN -*IC,* -*AC.*

biweekly See BI-.

bizarre See BAZAAR.

black 1 (*adj., n.*) As the color name, *black* can be noun or adjective, and in each function the word has a fair number of specialized meanings. Current usage is particularly interested in the word *black,* or *Black,* because until recently it was the only acceptable Standard name for members of the Negro race. See AFRICAN(-) AMERICAN.

The idioms *in the black,* meaning "with our finances recorded in black rather than red ink—that is, with a profit" or "without debt," and *into the black,* meaning "getting into a profitable or debt-free situation," are both Standard, although perhaps not wholly suitable for the most Formal writing.

black 2, blacken *Black* as a verb means "to make black," as in *She blacked the stove* and *In the fight he blacked both my eyes. Blacken* means "to become black," "to make black," "to darken," and figuratively "to slander or sully": *The night blackened and the stars came out. He tried to blacken her reputation.* The combination *to black out* means "to cover writing with black so as to make it illegible," "to shutter or curtain the windows of a house at night so that no interior light can be seen from outside," and "to cause or experience a literal or figurative *blackout*—a loss of consciousness or of memory." The past participle of *blacken* has become famed too for its use in Cajun cuisine: *They serve a good blackened catfish.*

BLACK ENGLISH is one of several names for the dialect or group of dialects spoken by many North American Blacks. Afro-American and African-American are other names for these versions of American English, the most fully studied dialect of which is usually called Northern Urban American Black English. Like other complex regional and social dialects with large numbers of speakers, *Black English* differs from Standard American English in some of its phonology, morphology, syntax, and vocabulary. Although it exhibits many regional variants, *Black English* is most frequently characterized by its use of multiple and double negatives, by its own special pattern for the use of the several forms of the verb and auxiliary *be,* by its having no inflected possessive case for nouns, by its usually lacking the third-person singular present tense *-s* ending on verbs, by its considerably different vocabulary, and by a number of pronunciations distinct from those of other American regional and social dialects.

black humor, often called "gallows humor" or "sick humor," is humor that is perceived as morbid, nasty, psychopathic, twisted, and often very funny. See SICK HUMOR.

blackout See BROWNOUT.

blame 1 (*n.*), when it combines with prepositions, takes *for* and *on: She accepts the blame for the mistake. They laid the blame squarely on the reporter. Of* is sometimes encountered, but not usually in Edited English, where you're more likely to find *of* following the gerund *blaming* than the noun *blame: He won't allow the blaming [blame] of his mother*; even more frequent is *to* plus a passive infinitive: *He won't allow his mother to be blamed.*

blame 2 (*v.*) frequently combines with *on* followed by the cause of the problem or with *for* followed by the name of the problem: *We blamed the leak on faulty flashing around the chimney. We blamed the leak on the builder. We blamed*

the builder for the leak. We blamed the faulty flashing for the leak. Blame* is also sometimes combined with *with,* as in *She was blamed with all the troubles they'd had,* and *on* or *onto,* as in *That's right, blame everything on [onto] me! Onto* is clearly Conversational and Informal only.

blanch, blench (*vv.*) To *blanch* is "to turn white," "to bleach," or, in cooking, "to scald or parboil," as in *She blanched at the thought of meeting him again. They blanched the linen in the sun. Only furiously boiling water should be used to blanch vegetables. Blench* is a variant spelling of *blanch,* but it is also another verb entirely, this one meaning "to flinch," "to turn away," "to draw back in fear." Best advice: use only *blanch* for "turning white," and reserve *blench* for "turning back from lack of courage," even though it can also mean turning pale.

blasé (*adj.*) always retains the acute accent that reminds us that the word has two syllables, pronounced *blah-ZAI.* When it takes a preposition, it is usually *about: She was quite blasé about her achievements.*

blatant, flagrant (*adjs.*) Anything *blatant* stands out because it is loud and boisterous. Anything *flagrant* stands out because it is glaringly, flamingly, blazingly visible, and hence calls attention to itself. *Blatant misdeeds announce themselves loudly; flagrant wrongs are easily seen.*

blaze, blazon (*vv.*) *To blaze the news abroad* is to make it public, to announce it loudly. *To blazon the news abroad* is also to publish it, to proclaim it. (*Blazon* comes from the armorial *blazon,* the heraldic coat of arms, which announces who you are.) Both are old words, infrequently used today, and both sound rather poetic, if not pretentious.

bleeding See BLOODY.

blench See BLANCH.

blend (*n., v.*) The past tense and past participle are *blended* or (sometimes) *blent. Blend* combines with *into, with, in with,* and *in: The spies blended into [with, in with] the general population. Blend in the vanilla.* The noun *blend* means "combination" or "mixture" and combines with *of,* as in *This sherry is a blend of fino and amontillado.* The noun also has two specialized senses, one in language (see BLENDS) and one meaning a kind of whiskey in which neutral grain spirits predominate.

BLENDS *Blends* are words made up of parts of two other words: *brunch* combines **breakfast** and **lunch,** *smog* starts with the front of **smoke**

and ends with the end of *fog.* Lewis Carroll—
who named his *blends portmanteau words,* after
the two-compartment suitcase of his day—said
that his *slithy* combined *lithe* and *slimy,* and our
current *guesstimate* (or *guestimate*) is both noun
and verb, a *blend* of *guess* and *estimate.* Although many *blends* start and end as nonce words,
some become slang or Informal, and still others
achieve full Standard status: for example, *simul-
cast* (**simul**taneous plus broad**cast**), *splatter*
(probably **spl**ash and s**patter**), and *travelogue*
(*travel* plus probably either *monologue* or *dialogue*) are all Standard.

BLENDS, SYNTACTIC See SYNTACTIC
BLENDS.

blessed (*adj.*) is pronounced either *BLEST* or
BLES-id, and the monosyllabic pronunciation
may also be spelled *blest.* The monosyllable
predominates in predicate adjective uses such as
He was blessed with excellent coordination and
I'll be blessed [in this use probably a euphemism for *damned*] *if I know where they came
from.* The two-syllable pronunciation predominates in adjunct uses such as *The blessed St.
Mary will protect us* and *The blessed lawnmower won't start* (another example of the euphemism). Compare BELOVED.

blind See SHADE.

BLIND AGREEMENT, like attraction, is still
another name for the agreement of a verb with
an intervening noun, rather than with the subject
of the sentence, as in *The noise of these groups
of children shouting and screaming were simply
deafening.* See also AGREEMENT; AGREEMENT
OF SUBJECTS AND VERBS (4).

blink (*v.*) As an intransitive verb *blink* means
literally "to close and open the eye(s) quickly,"
as in *She blinked in the sunlight;* it is currently
used figuratively to mean "flinch" or "back
down," as in *They stared belligerently at each
other, waiting to see who would blink first.* Also
intransitive is *blink* in combination with *at,* which
means "evade, avoid" or "shut the eyes to,
refuse to recognize": *She usually blinks at the
cheating in order to avoid unpleasantness.*
Transitive verb *blink* can have the same figurative meaning ("evade, avoid, or shut one's eyes
to"), as in *We can't blink the truth of his charges.*

blithe, blithesome (*adjs.*) These are synonyms,
meaning "cheerful, happy, carefree." Neither
is widely used, and *blithesome* may seem a bit
literary to some ears, but each is Standard and
worth using occasionally.

blizzard (*n.*) is a term for a long-lasting storm
with dry blowing snow, especially one with very
high winds and very cold temperatures. Technically the winds must be at least thirty-five miles
per hour, and blowing snow should make visibility near zero. But our love of hyperbole makes
us exaggerate, and serious meteorologists cringe
as we and the media whip ordinary snowstorms
into blizzards. Note too the frequent and graphic
figurative uses of the term: *a blizzard of appeals
for money, a blizzard of fan mail.*

bloc, block (*nn.*) A *bloc* is a political combination of some sort (*the farm bloc, the Middle
Eastern oil bloc*); *block* is generic, with many
general and special senses.

blond, blonde (*adj., n.*) *Blonde* is the usual adjective and noun applied to females, *blond* to
males, although the noun *blond* is occasionally
applied to women too. For wood finishes and
other nonhuman things, use either *blond* or *blonde*
as either part of speech. See BRUNET.

blood (*n.*) used in certain extended and figurative senses (the literal senses are of course Standard) gives us several clichés. Some are old-
fashioned, such as *There's bad blood between
them* (that is, "anger, dislike"), *Blood will tell*
(that is, "heredity"), *Her blood is up* ("she's
angry"), and *He's all duded up like a young
blood* ("a dandy"). *We need new blood in the
department* ("younger, newer people") is
Standard.

blood money (*n.*) is a compound noun meaning
either (1) "money collected at the cost of lives,"
(2) "money paid to a hired killer," or (3)
"compensation paid to the family of the victim
by the killer or the killer's family or tribe." All
three are Standard and require careful contextual
help to prevent readers from going astray.

bloody (*adj., intensifier*) was, in Britain, once
considered profanity in one sense, but some
Americans have taken it up, usually self-consciously, as slang. The word in this use means
"very," "very much," and you should limit it
to Conversational and Informal use: *It's a bloody
awful night.* It is also used as a slang adjective,
again to intensify (usually) an already loaded
noun: *She's a bloody fool. Bleeding, ruddy,* and
blooming are euphemistic substitutes, also Conversational and Informal. Compare FRIGHT-
FULLY.

blooming See BLOODY; FRIGHTFULLY.

blow (*v.*) Standard principal parts are *blow, blew,
blown,* but Nonstandard *blowed* is dialectal as
both past and past participle. One Conversa-

tional cliché use remains a Standard idiom: *I'll be blowed,* meaning "I'll be damned," or some such, an echo of an older time and use.

Blow has several senses usually labeled Informal or Conversational: "to spend money wildly" (*He blew his winnings on a three-day spree*); "to treat someone to something" (*She blew me to dinner after the meeting*); "to brag" (*He is always blowing about his famous friends*); "to forget or misspeak lines in a play" (*They both blew their lines in the last act*). There are also many slang uses: "to go away" (*Let's blow this joint*); "to overstress and break an engine" (*He blew his engine in the final lap of the race*); "to make errors and so fail in a task" (*We blew it*). And there are several idiomatic phrases, some of them slang: *to blow away,* meaning "to shoot and kill someone" or "to be emotionally overcome"; *to blow hot and cold,* meaning "to vacillate between being eager and doubtful"; *to blow in,* meaning "to arrive suddenly" (*He just blew in from Miami*); *to blow off,* meaning "to boast, or to give vent to rage or other emotion" (*Ignore him—he's just blowing off steam [a lot of hot air]*) or "to skip, to forgo" (*It was a nice day so I blew off the class—I already knew all the material anyway*); *to blow up* or *to blow one's stack,* meaning "to explode emotionally"; *to blow someone's mind,* meaning "to shock or surprise," "to upset or amaze"; and *to blow one's own horn,* meaning "to boast about one's own accomplishments." These are slang, although some of them may achieve Conversational status shortly. Others—*to blow out, to blow over, to blow up,* as in *to blow out a candle, to have a storm blow over,* or *to blow up* (that is, *inflate*) *a balloon*—are Standard idiomatic combinations. Vulgar, obscene, taboo, and usually slang are the labels attached to the transitive sense of the verb, meaning "to perform fellatio," and to the compound noun *blow job,* meaning "the act of fellatio."

blue book, bluebook (*n.*) Usually printed as one word, a *bluebook* has three Standard meanings: "a government document bound with a blue cover, often a directory of officers and agencies," "a real or imaginary social register of prominent people," and "one of the blank booklets with blue covers in which American college students usually write their tests and examinations." Compare WHITE PAPER.

blue-collar, white-collar (*adjs.*) These are Standard adjectives applied to people who work for a living: *blue-collar workers* work with their hands and with machines and are thought of as wearing blue workshirts that don't show dirt; *white-collar workers* do desk work, and they typically wear white dress shirts because they don't get dirty at what they do, in this figurative labeling at least.

blue law (*n.*) means (1) one of the highly restrictive laws, published bound in blue paper, adopted by the Puritans to regulate virtue in colonial New England or (2) any laws then or now that restrict or prohibit dancing, drinking, swearing, cardplaying, fornication, contraception, working on Sundays, or other behavior considered unseemly by those in power.

blush, flush (*nn., vv.*) Both of these describe red faces or the turning of faces red, usually from emotion. *To blush* is to turn red from shyness, embarrassment, or modesty. *To flush* is to grow red-faced with anger or to glow red with pride or menopause.

boast (*v.*) is used transitively to mean that "you have something and wish to call attention to it": *She boasts a head of remarkably bright red hair.* Intransitively, *boast* means "immodestly to announce your virtues to the world": *He boasts constantly.* Intransitive *boast* frequently combines with prepositions *of* and *about: He has been boasting of [about] his new wardrobe.*

boat See SHIP (2).

boater (*n.*) has two meanings: it is a hard, stiff straw hat or a person who goes boating. Both senses are Standard. See AGENTIVE ENDINGS.

boatswain, bosun (*nn.*) *Boatswain* is the conventional spelling of the full title of the petty officer in charge of a ship's hull and its maintenance. *Bosun* is an alternate spelling of *boatswain,* reflecting its usual pronunciation, *BO-suhn.* But *BOT-SWAIN* is also heard (see SPELLING PRONUNCIATIONS).

bobby See COP.

bobby pin (*n.*) is the Standard compound name for a flat metal hairpin, so named for its use with *bobbed* hair.

bodacious (*adj.*) is a Nonstandard term from Southern and South Midland regional dialect, meaning "extremely remarkable," or "audacious, unceremonious," probably a blend of *bold* and *audacious.*

bodega See SHOP (2).

body, dead See DEAD BODY.

BODY ENGLISH When we "put English on" a thrown or struck ball (as in billiards), we apply a twist or sideways motion that causes the ball to curve. *Body English* occurs when the player further mimics that twist with his body after the ball is on its way: the golfer leans the way she wishes her ball would curve; the bowler twists his torso the way he intended his ball to go. In instances where the movement is unconscious, it may also be said to be a kind of body language.

BODY LANGUAGE is made of gestures, facial contortions, or other mostly unconscious taking of postures, of squirming, twisting, or moving of the arms and legs, or of positioning the whole body, that·convey meanings without—or in conjunction with, or even in contradiction of—words: *She said she was glad to meet him, but her body language belied the words.*

boffin (*n.*) is British slang, meaning "a research scientist, someone full of arcane knowledge."

bogey (*n., v.*), **bogy, bogie** (*nn.*) *Bogey* (pronounced *BO-gee*) is the golf term; in Great Britain it is said to be named after the imaginary *Colonel Bogey,* a golfing partner who played a splendid game. *To play to bogey* was at first to score what would be considered par for an average golfer. Today, however, *bogey* is one over par for each hole, both here and in Britain. *To bogey* [*a hole*] means to score one over par for the hole. *Bogey,* pronounced *BO-gee* or, more commonly, *BOO-gee* or *BU-gee,* means "an evil spirit," "a goblin, a bogle" (also *boggle,* related to the verb, which see). In the singular this occurs in the compound *boogieman, bogyman,* or *bogeyman. Bogies* (always pronounced *BO-geez*) are also the low swiveling assemblies of wheels under the ends of a railroad car, as well as the various wheel-and-axle combinations used on tracked vehicles and other military cars, trucks, and tanks designed for off-the-road operation. All the meanings and all the spellings (interchangeable for all but the golf terms, which are usually *bogey* and *bogeys*) are Standard, except for the *BOO-gee* pronunciation and *boogie* spelling where these are applied to an African-American; this is a racial epithet and taboo as racist language. See BOOGIE-WOOGIE; BUG.

boggle (*v.*), **mind-boggling** (*adj.*) *Boggle* is Standard as both a transitive verb with a direct object, as in *What she heard simply boggled her mind,* or an intransitive verb, as in *Having heard the news, I have to admit that my mind boggles.* The intransitive verb also combines regularly with *at* (*I boggle at the thought of paying so much*). The adjective *mind-boggling* (*The new numbers were mind-boggling*) is also Standard.

bogie, bogy See BOGEY.

bogus titles See FALSE TITLES.

Bohemian, bohemian (*adj., n.*) Capitalize the word when the referent is someone or something from *Bohemia,* the area around Prague in the modern Czech Republic. When the reference is to an unconventional or gypsylike person or style, spell it *bohemian,* without the initial capital letter.

Bologna, bologna, baloney, boloney (*n.*) *Bologna* (pronounced *buh-LON-yuh*) is the Italian city; *bologna* (or *bologna sausage*) is the large sausage named for the city and pronounced *buh-LON-ee, buh-LON-yuh,* or *buh-LON-uh. Baloney* and *boloney* are Americanized variant spellings of the name of the sausage and widely used in the relatively long-standing slang noun and retort meaning "nonsense, foolishness."

bomb (*n., v.*) In U.S. theatrical slang, *bomb,* noun and verb, means that a play is a failure, a disaster, as in *We bombed in Boston* and *The new play is a bomb!* In Britain, however, the noun means just the opposite: if the new play in London is said to be a *bomb,* it is a hit, a tremendous success. See VOCABULARY (1).

bona fide(s) is a Latin tag (pronounced *BON-uh FEID, BON-uh FEI-dee,* or *BAWN-uh FEI-dee*) that literally means "in good faith." In Standard English, it functions as an adjectival meaning "real, genuine, without deceit," as in *The letters of recommendation made it clear he was a bona fide expert.* The noun *bona fides* (pronounced *BO-nuh FEIDZ*) is singular in Latin but looks like an English plural, and so it has developed another sense in English: "credentials or other written evidence of authenticity and good faith," as in *Then she asked to see my bona fides.* So far the back-formation of the singular *bona fide,* meaning "one evidence of authenticity," occurs only at Conversational levels of speech. See FOREIGN PHRASES.

bonkers (*adj.*) is slang, meaning "crazy": *The noise in here is driving me bonkers!*

bonk (on the head) (*n., v.*) The noun means "a blow," the verb "to strike," and both usually combine with the phrase "on the head." They are slang.

bonnyclabber (*n.*) is a dialectal term for thick sour milk, the stuff of which cottage cheese is made. The word is found in Northern and North Midland regional dialects.

bonus See SALARY INCREMENT.

boob (*n.*) is a rather elderly slang term meaning "a fool, a dolt, an ignorant bumpkin" and a coarse slang term, usually in the plural, meaning "a woman's breasts." The word in that sense is taboo in polite discourse. See BOURGEOIS.

booboisie See BOURGEOIS.

boob(s) See BREAST(S).

boogie-woogie (*n., v.*) The noun refers to a kind of jazz music, especially and originally for the piano, with constantly repeated "walking" figures in the bass. The verb means "to play or dance to such music." Pronounce both these rhyming compounds either *BUG-ee-WUG-ee* or *BOO-gee-WOO-gee*. The noun is specialized but Standard; the verb is probably slang and Conversational or Informal at best, perhaps with extended uses meaning simply "to go" or "to get going."

boon (*adj., n.*) One craves or is granted a *boon*, "the favorable response to a petition or prayer." A *boon companion* is something else, a cliché that is the only use left of *boon* as adjective, meaning "favorable, pleasant, convivial." All other senses of the adjective are obsolete or archaic.

boondocks, boondockers, boonies (*nn.*) *Boondocks* is an American adaptation of a Tagalog word for "mountain," made by American servicemen in the Philippines in the 1920s. It has become a humorous and pejorative word for the wilderness, the backcountry, or "the sticks" (as earlier slang had it). *The boonies* is a clipped form of the word, still slang, but in such wide use that it may well become Conversational. *Boondockers* is a slang term for the heavy hiking shoes soldiers and backpackers wear.

boondoggle (*n., v.*) A *boondoggle* is one of those braided leather, plastic, or straw handicraft objects that summer campers bring home as gifts for their parents. By extension, a *boondoggle* means "any waste of time and effort, particularly any waste of public money," and to *boondoggle* is to engage in such wasteful activities.

boonies See BOONDOCKS.

boost (*n., v.*), **booster** (*n.*) To *boost* is "to push, especially to push up, to assist, and to promote, and hence to increase": *He boosted his son up to the window ledge. She always boosts local charities.* The noun is a literal or figurative push up: *He'll give new employees a boost whenever he can.* A *booster* is any person or device that assists, promotes, or increases the power or influence of something: *He's a staunch booster of community endeavors. The second stage is a*

booster rocket of considerable power. All these uses are Standard.

boot (*nn., v.*) There are two nouns, one based on the Old English word meaning "remedy," the other from a medieval French word for "a leather covering for the foot." From the "remedy" sense comes the phrase [*something*] *to boot*, which is something "in addition, besides," as in *If you'll agree to make the trade, I'll give you an extra widget to boot.* The verb that comes from that source, in the idiom *What boots it?* means "What does it matter? Of what worth or value is it?" It is archaic and a cliché *to boot*.

From the footcovering we get the British name for the trunk of a car (the *boot*), the Conversational "kick of excitement" (*I get a real boot out of her singing*), the slang name for Marine and Navy recruits, *boots* (probably from the leather collars Marines once wore—it is reported that Marines were once called *bootnecks*), and the *boot camp* where they get their basic training, as well as the specialized *Denver boot*, a large locking clamp police departments place on one wheel to immobilize the cars of scofflaws who don't pay their parking tickets.

Among verb uses that require explanation are the Conversational *to boot out* [*of office*], meaning "to dismiss, to fire"; the specialized baseball jargon, probably also slang, *to boot* [*a play or a ball*], meaning "to commit an error"; the horseracing slang use *to boot home a winner*, meaning "to ride the winning horse"; and the computer jargon term meaning "to load onto a disk a program or other information," usually with *up: After she had booted up the new program, she was ready to work.* There are also the Conversational cliché *you* [*can*] *bet your boots*, meaning "you can rely on this," and the slang cliché, *to get* or *be given the boot*, meaning "to be fired."

borax (*n.*) is a slang term for "cheap, gaudy, shoddy merchandise, especially furniture." Its Standard meaning is of course the name of the cleaning agent, a white powder called *sodium borate*.

border (*v.*) in figurative uses meaning "is nearly like" combines with *on: Her demeanor borders on the zany.* Literal use showing physical relationships can be in the passive, with *by: Connecticut is bordered on the east by Rhode Island.*

born, borne (*past participle, adj.*) The verb *bear* has two past participle forms, *born* and *borne*. *Born* is used in the passive voice and as a participial adjective whenever the topic is birth: *She* *was born in Ohio. We are New England-born, all of us.* When the topic is *birth,* use *borne* as the past participle, as in *She has borne three sons*—but only in the active voice (i.e., do not say *The baby was borne to a very young woman*). In the senses of *bear* that involve carrying, enduring, proving, and the like, the past participle is always *borne,* whether the verb is active or passive: *He had borne his guilt for many years. It was an insult not to be borne even by a placid person.* Spelling errors are frequent, particularly *borne* for *born* when the topic is birth but the use is passive or adjectival. See BARE.

born-again (*adj.*) means "to have taken on a revived or renewed, changed faith in personal evangelical Christianity": *She describes herself as a born-again Christian. He says he's been born again.* (Note that the adjective is hyphenated, but the auxiliary and verb are not.) When applied to renewed and improved dedication to other enterprises and in other contexts, *born-again* threatens to become a cliché: *I'm a born-again jazz fan.*

borrow (*v.*) combines with several prepositions: *from* indicates the source from which the borrowing is done (*She borrowed ten dollars from her roommate*); *of* suggests either the source or what was borrowed (*He had borrowed of his brother almost everything that would fit; She borrowed freely of the canned goods in the pantry*); *on* and *against* put the emphasis on security and how the loan will be repaid (*She borrowed on some of her jewelry; He borrowed against the next royalty check*). *Off* is Conversational only: *He borrowed a buck off me this morning. Off of* in that same sentence would be Substandard. *Borrow* meaning "to lend" and the noun *borrow* meaning "a loan" are Nonstandard, found chiefly in Northern dialect, in the western Great Lakes states.

bosom See BREAST(S).

boss (*adj., n., v.*) The noun is Standard and means "the person in charge of the workers"; the verb is Conversational and Informal and describes what the *boss* does—directs others in their work. By extension, the verb has some added pejorative qualities, meaning "to give unnecessary and arbitrary orders, to overplay the role of the person in charge." This has led to the wholly pejorative adjective *bossy.* The noun also means "an unofficial political leader, one who, usually without holding elected office, controls party and patronage." The adjective, meaning "the chief or the very best," is slang, or at best Conversational (*He's a boss guitarist*).

bosun See BOATSWAIN.

both (*adj., pron., coord. conj.*) (1) *Both* as adjective (*both bicycles*) and pronoun (*both of our parents*) is used with two and is Nonstandard when used with three or more. When used as coordinating conjunction, much like *either, both* can be used with three or more, as in *We needed both food and rest and protection from our pursuers,* but most Edited English will insist on limiting reference to two. (2) *Both* has often been charged with redundancy, better omitted where its presence contributes nothing to meaning. Specifically, *You and I are both in agreement* is indeed too wordy and redundant, whereas *We are both in agreement* supplies information (that two people are involved) not available without *both.* Moreover, sometimes redundancy adds emphasis, and such deliberate use is a matter of style. (3) *Both of them* is Standard, but note that you can't have *both them*—pronouns require the *of,* except when order is reversed: *We nominated both of them. We nominated them both.* (4) Constructions with *both . . . and . . .* are grammatically clearer and stylistically more balanced when they introduce structures exactly parallel: *I take my pills both when I get up and when I go to bed.* (5) *The both,* as in *I like the both of them,* is sometimes objected to and seldom used at other than Conversational levels of speech. (6) The possessive with *both* is usually with *of* (*It's both of our problem*) rather than inflected (*It's both's problem*). A better alternative that avoids the awkwardness altogether is *It's a problem for both of us.*

bottleneck (*n.*) This graphic metaphor for an unwanted constriction in the flow of work or something else can occasionally become absurd if logic goes awry, as in *He created a huge bottleneck.* Which is worse—a bigger or a smaller *bottleneck?*

bottom See BUTTOCKS.

bottom line is a bookkeeper's image and a weary cliché meaning "the final total," "the end result." Seek a fresher figure when you can.

boughten (*adj.*) is a curious word, made up of a past participle of *buy* with an extra *-en* suffix, a sign of the participle in some strong verbs such as *write* and *speak,* tautologically tacked on. *Boughten* is Nonstandard and dialectal and has two meanings: (1) "paid-for, or hired," as in describing an army of mercenaries as *a boughten army*; and (2) "bought at a store," in contrast to *homemade,* as in *They served boughten bread* (sometimes *store-boughten* to make even clearer the contrast to *homemade* bread: *store-bought* is better). Whether *boughten* occurs in print or speech (it is mainly Conversational), it is almost always self-consciously dialectal, and writers and speakers frequently accompany it with quotation marks or use intonation or other nonverbal signals to underscore the whimsy of the choice.

bouillabaisse (*n.*) is the name of the fish stew or soup for which Mediterranean France is famous. Pronounce it either *BOO-yuh-BES*, *BOO-yuh-BAIS*, *BOOL-yuh-BES*, or *BOOL-yuh-BAIS*.

bound and determined is a tautological cliché (*bound* in this use means "constrained, forced") often usefully employed for emphasis in Standard contexts.

boundary (*adj., n.*) Because it is frequently pronounced with only two syllables instead of three (Standard pronunciation is either *BOUND-ree* or *BOUND-uh-ree*), *boundary* is sometimes misspelled without the *a*.

bounden (*adj.*) is an archaic variant form of the past participle of the verb *bind* (the regular participle is *bound*). *Bounden* is used only in the idiom and redundant cliché *bounden duty*, meaning "an obligatory matter."

bourgeois (*adj., n.*), **bourgeoisie** (*n.*) The adjective means "of the urban middle class," "materialistic and determinedly respectable," and hence sometimes "mediocre, dull, and tasteless," or "commercial-minded and money-grubbing." These last senses are of course strongly pejorative, and they affect the use of the noun *bourgeois*, "a citizen of the middle class," as well. The plural is also *bourgeois*, and the feminine form of the word, applied to a woman of the middle class, is spelled *bourgeoise*. The noun is not so strongly degraded as the adjective is, but make certain that context controls whether the reader should take it as a pejorative. *Bourgeoisie* is the name of the middle class itself; a *bourgeois* or *bourgeoise* is a member of the *bourgeoisie*. Pronounce the adjective and the masculine noun *BOOR-ZHWAH*, the feminine form of the noun *BOOR-ZHWAHZ*, and the collective noun *BOOR-zhwah-ZEE*. H. L. Mencken coined the slang blend *booboisie* (*boob* plus *bourgeoisie*), and the dated American slang *bushwa* (or *bushwah*), meaning "nonsense," may be a result of an Americanized mispronunciation of the adjective, *BOOZH-WAH*.

boutique See SHOP (2).

bow window See BAY WINDOW.

boy (*n.*) One important caveat: use of this term in direct address to a nonwhite adult by a white person is taboo. One minor observation: adult males regularly use it of themselves Conversationally in expressions such as *I'm going to play poker with the boys*.

boyfriend See GIRLFRIEND.

boyish, girlish (*adjs.*) When applied to children and very young adults, these are generally flattering terms suggesting the attractive qualities of youth of the relevant sex. When we apply these words to adults, however, *boyish* suggests only youthful qualities generally, usually not to excess, while *girlish* seems to stress immaturity and some of the giggly awkwardness that adult women are expected to replace with poise. Moreover, *boyish*, unlike *mannish*, can be a compliment to a young woman.

bracero (*n.*) is a Mexican migrant farm worker. The name (pronounced *bruh-SAIR-o* in American English) comes from the Spanish word *brazo*, "arm" and is best known to speakers of the Southwestern regional dialect.

BRACES are signs ({ }) used to group and link together items on a page. They may be of any size, and they may be used in pairs or singly. In text, they are used to set off material already enclosed within square brackets, which in turn are inside parentheses. In mathematics, the signs are used in the reverse order: {[()]}. See BRACKETS; PARENTHESES.

braces See SUSPENDERS.

bracket (*n.*) is, among other meanings, a jargon term used by sociologists and governments in classifying salaries, jobs, and people in various groups. Salaries, for example, may be grouped in classes from highest to lowest, and someone whose salary falls within a particular group is said to be in that *bracket*.

BRACKETS (SQUARE, ANGLE) Brackets ([ ]), also called *square brackets*, are marks of punctuation that have three main purposes. (1) In quotations they distinguish material added to a quotation, such as disclaimers of responsibility for a misspelling in the original text ("*it was a seperate* [sic] *meeting*") or to further explain quoted matter (*He said, "I read my favorite novel* [War and Peace] *every year"*). (2) *Brackets* also serve as parentheses within parentheses in text (or as parentheses around parentheses in complex mathematical equations). (3) Conventionally, *square brackets* set off phonetic symbols (*Phone begins with an* [f] *sound*). *Angle brackets* (⟨ ⟩) are sometimes used for these same

purposes, but much less often. See BRACES; PA-
RENTHESES; PUNCTUATION.

brae See STREAM.

brag (*n., v.*) The verb *brag* combines with *about,*
as in *He brags about his batting average.* It also
occasionally combines with *of,* although *boast*
is more commonly found with that preposition,
as in *She'll brag [boast] of her rich friends.*
Brag on is dialectal: *He's always bragging on
his children.* The noun *brag* is not fully synonymous with the noun *boast:* a *boast* is a single
statement, but a *brag* may be more general,
synonymous with *bragging: He was all brag
and bluster.*

brain 1 (*v.*) *She brained him with a rolling pin*
is a slang use of *brain,* meaning "to strike on
the head."

brain 2, brains (*n.*) The plural is used frequently to mean "intelligence," as in *She has
the brains in the family,* meaning "She is the
smartest member of the family." The usage is
Standard. In *He's a real brain,* meaning "He's
very intelligent," and *She's the brain[s] of the
company,* meaning "She's the one with the most
intelligence, the one who does its thinking,"
brain and *brains* are chiefly Conversational and
Informal.

branch See STREAM.

brand (*n.*), meaning "a kind or sort or variety
of something," as in *Her brand of humor is
pretty cruel,* is Standard.

brand-new (*adj.*) is hyphenated and means
"new, unused, and fresh from the fire, as in
something newly minted or newly forged; newly
made, unused." (The *brand* is "a brand from
the fire.")

brass See BUREAUCRAT; HIERARCHY.

brass (*n.*) *Brass* meaning "impudence, self-assurance, brazen effrontery," as in *He had the
brass to ask me to recommend him,* is Conversational and Informal. *The [top] brass,* meaning
"the high officers, the top management, the
important people," is a clipped form of *brass
hat[s],* the military slang term for officers of
ranks that wear gold braid on their caps. Today
the term is slang for all sorts of leaders, not just
military ones. It usually takes plural verbs and
pronouns: *The brass are just coming in now;
they'll meet in the board room. Brass* meaning
"money" is now dated slang in the United States.

brass tacks means "fundamentals, basic details
or facts" and appears usually in the idiom *Let's
get down to brass tacks.* It is very probably
rhyming slang for *facts.* Limit it to Conversational and Informal use.

bravado, bravery, bravura (*nn.*) *Bravado* is
"blustery pretended courage": *His bravado didn't
really mask his terror. Bravery* is "the showing
of courage in the face of danger, a display of
nerve": *His bravery in the face of frightening
odds was truly splendid. Bravery* is also "a fine,
showy appearance": *The bravery of their uniforms made the troop sparkle. Bravura* is "brilliant style, daring boldness" and, in music, "a
display of technique, the showy brilliance of the
performer's skill"; it may be used as a noun
adjunct: *His horsemanship was brilliant, a bravura demonstration. The "Carnival of Venice"
is a bravura showpiece for the cornetist.*

brave (*adj., v.*) means "courageous" (*a brave
soldier*), "showy and colorful" (*a brave show
of flags and uniforms*), and "splendid, grand"
(*a brave new concept of world peace*). All are
Standard, although *brave* in the "showy, colorful, splendid, grand" senses has a slightly archaic flavor today. The verb, meaning "to defy,
to withstand," is Standard: *They braved all critical comment.*

bravery, bravura See BRAVADO.

breach, breech (*nn., vv.*) A *breach* (pronounced *BREECH*) is "a break, a failure, a
hole or tear": *We fear a breach in the dike. The
charge is breach of the peace.* The verb means
"to make such a break" or "to fail to comply,"
as in *The union claims that management has
breached the contract,* or "to break through,"
as in *to breach a wall.* When a whale leaps clear
of the water, it is said to *breach. Breech* is a
homophone of *breach,* but the noun means "the
buttocks," "the rear of the barrel of a gun,"
and "the bottom of a pulley block." In addition, either as a homophone of *breaches* or more
commonly pronounced *BRICH-iz* (and sometimes spelled *britches* to reflect that pronunciation), the plural *breeches* means "short trousers
or knickerbockers" and also occurs as a jocular
term for any trousers or pants, as in the idiom
too big for one's breeches.

bread (*n.*), in addition to its Standard senses, is
also somewhat dated slang for "money."

breakdown (*n.*), **break down** (*v.*) The noun is
a one-word compound, the verb two words. The
noun means "a collapse, a disintegration, or an
analysis into component parts, a classification";
it also means "a rapid, shuffling country dance
and the music for it." The verb means "to
collapse, to come apart, to disintegrate, to analyze into component parts, to classify components." All these senses are Standard.

breakthrough (n.), **break through** (v.) The noun (a one-word compound like *breakdown*) has two meanings: (1) "the act of breaking through a barrier or a defensive line, as in warfare" and (2) "a scientific discovery of great importance or a technological advance of great significance." The verb (two words) means "to make a breakthrough." All these uses are Standard.

breakup (n.), **break up** (v.) The noun is one word and means "a disruption," "a shattering," "an interruption or ending." A frequent specialized use refers to the end of an emotional relationship: *Their breakup had been long anticipated by their friends. Break up* is a combined verb and preposition with several Standard meanings, including "to disrupt," "to break into pieces," "to bring to an end," and the like. All these are Standard, as are three specialized meanings: "to end a romance or an emotional attachment," "to cause someone to laugh," and "to laugh uncontrollably." The transitive and intransitive verbs having to do with laughter, as in *Her remarks always break me up* or *When he appeared in that awful outfit, I broke up,* appear in Edited English but are probably better limited to Semiformal use there and to Conversational levels of speech.

breast(s), boob(s), bosom(s), bust, chest, tit(s) (nn.) The nouns *breast, chest, bosom,* and *bust* all have Standard meanings: *breast* (singular) is a general word with an old-fashioned air, meaning literally "the front of the torso between waist and neck, the part containing heart and lungs, the part where the *breasts* are located." The heart's being there seems to explain the literary sense of the *breast* as "the seat of emotions and feelings." *Chest* is generic too, a physiological term for the same part of the front of the torso, and it is applied in general use somewhat more frequently to males than to females. *Bosom,* like *breast* once frequently used to describe the figurative seat of the emotions in both women and men, is now applied particularly in a literal sense to females, referring to the neck and breast area. The *bosom* of a shirt (especially a stiff, formal shirt) and the *bosom* of the family are self-defining, the one literal, the other figurative. *Bosom* is also used as a term for one of a woman's *breasts, bosoms* for both. A *bust* is of course a sculpture of the head and shoulders of a person, but it also refers specifically to a woman's *breasts,* shoulders, and neck, and the emphasis is frequently on the *breasts.* And then there is the range of slang and Vulgar terms for a woman's *breasts,* such as *tits, titties* (which are both developments of *teats*), *boob(s),* and others, nearly all of them taboo in polite contexts.

breech, breeches See BREACH.

brethren, brothers (nn.) *Brethren* is a relic, a variant plural of the noun *brother, brothers* being regularly formed. It is used mainly in religious and fraternal societies or in jocular contexts imitative of Oratorical or Formal religious use. *Brothers* is the plural for general use.

BREVE The mark (˘) used in printing to indicate the pronunciation of a short vowel, as in *brĕve* (BREV). The *breve* is also used in scanning poetry, where it marks an unstressed syllable. See also DIACRITICS.

BREVITY, CONCISENESS, CONCISION, TERSENESS (nn.) In stylistic use, as applied particularly to speaking and writing, *brevity* is "being brief and saying things in short time or short space"; the synonyms *conciseness* and *concision* are in some ways also synonyms of *brevity,* but their shortness is achieved by spareness, lack of ornament or decoration, and clarity. *Terseness* also describes prose or speech devoid of excess but differs from *conciseness* and *concision* in that the latter two use polish and fine finish to remove excess, whereas *terseness* may involve even more severe excision of superfluity. All these except sometimes *terseness* are frequently said to be qualities of the best expository prose, because they can ensure accuracy, clarity, coherence, and completeness, and certainly they are welcomed as well by those who must listen to spoken exposition. Ornament, variation, and even repetition can serve useful ends too, but for many readers and listeners, *brevity* et al. may well be the most important virtues of all exposition, spoken or written.

briar, brier (n.) *Brier* is a variant spelling of *briar,* which is much the more common, both for the specific plant, the general name for such prickly plants, and the plants' thorns themselves. *Briar* is also the only spelling American English uses for "a tobacco pipe made of the root of the briarwood plant."

brickbat (n.) is literally a brick or other hard object, especially one intended as a missile. Figuratively it is an uncomplimentary or harshly critical remark. The word is Standard in all uses.

bridegroom See GROOM.

brier See BRIAR.

bright (*adj.*), meaning "intelligent, quick," is sometimes pejorative when applied to grown-ups. Be careful to avoid sounding patronizing if that is not what you intend.

bring 1 (*v.*) has as its Standard principal parts *bring, brought,* and *brought. Brang* or *brung* as past tense and *brung* as past participle are dialectal and Substandard, so much so that Standard users sometimes use them jocularly in Conversational or Informal situations in full confidence that their listeners will not think their use inadvertent.

bring 2, fetch (*vv.*) These are interchangeable Informally and at Conversational levels of speech, but there is a distinction that purists like to enforce and that Edited English prefers: you *bring* something from where you now are, as in *Since you're in the kitchen, could you bring me a glass of water when you come back?* but you *fetch* something that is elsewhere, as in *Would you fetch me my glasses when you're upstairs?* Both are Standard in this use. *Fetch* is also Standard in *to fetch a good price. To fetch someone a blow,* meaning "to hit him or her," is old-fashioned, Informal, and Conversational, as is the meaning "to attract," as in *That outfit really fetches me.* The adjective *fetching* and the adverb *fetchingly,* however, are both Standard in their senses of "attractive" and "attractively."

bring 3, take (*vv.*) *Bring* implies movement toward the speaker, *take,* movement away from the speaker, so long as these directions are clear: *Please bring me my coat. Will you take some cookies to your sister?* Where the directions are unspecified, unimportant, or equivocal, the words are frequently interchangeable: *Let's bring [take] our raincoats with us to the game. He took [brought] her to a movie, and after they'd had something to eat, he brought [took] her home again.* All these are Standard, although purists are usually quick to attack when they feel they see clear movement toward or away that is not reflected in your choice.

bring up See RAISE (1).

Brit See BRITISH.

Britain, British Isles, England, Great Britain, (the) U.K., (the) United Kingdom (*nn.*) These are Standard names for that island realm or for parts of it. Technically, *Great Britain* (plus some of the small offshore islands such as Wight and Skye) is the main island, containing *England,* Scotland, and Wales, although jurisdictionally the term is also used for the main island plus Northern Ireland. *Britain* is simply a convenient and familiar Informal clipped form of *Great Britain.* The *"United Kingdom* of Great Britain and Northern Ireland" is the full official title of this European country, often shortened to *(the) United Kingdom,* or to *(the) U.K.,* pronounced as the names of the two letters. *(The) British Isles* is the term used for the geographical area itself, including the main island, Ireland (containing Northern Ireland and the independent country Eire), and numerous small offshore islands.

britches See BREACH.

BRITISH AND AMERICAN DIFFERENCES IN MEANING, PRONUNCIATION, SPELLING, AND VOCABULARY See MEANING; PRONUNCIATION (2); SPELLING (1); VOCABULARY (2).

BRITISH ENGLISH is the dialect of the English language spoken in the United Kingdom; the prestige dialect of *British English* is usually designated Received Standard Southern British, and there are also modified Standard British dialects reflecting regional variation, including overseas dialects.

British (the), Brit, Britisher, Briton, (the) English (*nn.*) *The British* is the name for the people who live in the United Kingdom. *The English* is used generically too, but people of Irish, Scottish, and Welsh origins sometimes prefer not to be put under that umbrella; in that case, then, the *English* live in England. *Britons* is the name given the ancient Celtic residents whom the Anglo-Saxons harried. Some of today's *British* dislike the term *Briton* for present-day citizens, although it is used by a number of current British writers. *Britisher* is an Americanism, not much admired by some in Britain; *Brit* is slang, a clipping of *British* or a related term; it is much used in journalese, especially in Great Britain. Americans should stick to *the British, the English* (and *the Scots, the Irish,* and *the Welsh* when necessary) in Edited English and in any writing or speaking to people with British passports. For American eyes and ears only, *Briton* is quite acceptable, and *Britisher* and *Brit* are useful Conversationally and Informally. The best rule, however, is to call people what they wish to be called.

Briton See BRITISH.

broach, brooch (*nn.*) A *broach* is a pointed tool, a skewer, a spit, or the like, used for piercing. A *brooch* is a piece of jewelry, worn at or near the neck, and so named because it has a pointed pin and lock as a clasp. Both come from the same root, the Middle English *broche*, "pointed tool." *Broach* is always pronounced *BROCH*, *brooch* either *BROCH* or *BROOCH*.

broad (*n.*) is an insulting term for a woman; it is a coarse term and generally suggests that the woman to whom it is applied is coarse too. See SEXIST LANGUAGE.

broadcast (*v.*) The past tense and past participle are either *broadcast* or *broadcasted*, whether you are sowing seed, spreading the word, or doing radio or television programs; all three forms are Standard.

broke, broken (*adjs.*) *Broke* is past tense, *broken*, past participle of the verb *break*. *Broken* is Standard as participial adjective: *She has a broken arm*. In the sense "out of order," *broke* as participial adjective is Substandard, Vulgar, and a shibboleth, as in *My watch is broke*. *Broke* as participial adjective meaning "without funds," however, is Standard Conversational language, and it occurs in some Semiformal Edited English as well: *She was broke and hungry until her father's check arrived*.

brolly (*n.*) is a British English Conversational or slang term for "umbrella."

brooch See BROACH.

brook See STREAM.

brother-in-law See -IN-LAW; PLURALS OF COMPOUND NOUNS.

brothers See BRETHREN.

brown bag, brown bagging, brown bagger (*nn.*), **brown-bag** (*adj., v.*) These useful words are all Standard. They refer literally to the small brown paper bag used for carrying a lunch to school or work. The first two nouns mean "the bag itself" and "the process of carrying a lunch." If you do it, you are a *brown bagger* (even if you carry a lunchbox instead of the bag). The adjective describes anything characteristic, including *a brown-bag lunch* or *a brown-bag attitude* toward work, saving money, and the like, and the verb means you do it.

brownnose (*n., v.*), **brownnoser** (*n.*) The verb means to curry favor by obsequious behavior, and both nouns (the doer) and the verb are based on an extension of the Vulgar slang locution, "to kiss (someone's) ass." The terms were taboo until fairly recently in any mixed group, but like some other terms based on excretory acts and products they now seem to retain their figurative meanings while losing or at least suppressing their origins. All are slang in any use; choose your audience with care.

brownout, blackout (*nn.*) A *brownout* means "a loss or reduction in electric power and the resultant reduction in night illumination." A *blackout* is a total loss of power and light. Both terms are Standard.

browse, graze (*nn., vv.*) To *browse* is literally "to eat leaves and twigs and such during much of the day," as giraffes do, and a *browse* is what that food consists of. To *graze* is literally "to eat grass and weeds," as cattle and horses do during much of the day, and one meaning of the noun is what that food consists of. But the figurative senses of the two verbs are also interesting: to *browse* is also "to read here and there in a book or to pull books at random off shelves and dip into them here and there." *Grazing*, figuratively, is applied to people who snack through the day, sampling foods at random exactly as the *browser* samples books. *Grazing* in this sense may still be Informal and Conversational, but all the other senses of *browse* and *graze* are Standard.

brunch (*n., v.*) *Brunch* is a blend of **br**eakfast and **l**unch, and although some dictionaries still label it Colloquial or Informal, the noun at least is clearly Standard, meaning "a substantial late-morning or early-afternoon meal, often served buffet style, combining foods that might be found at either breakfast or lunch, often with wine and other alcoholic drinks."

brunet, brunette (*adj., n.*) The adjective describes someone of relatively dark coloring, of hair especially (compare BLOND), with the *brunet* spelling supposed to be applied to males, *brunette* to females. In fact both spellings refer usually to females (a man more often will be called "dark-haired"), although *brunette* is the usual generic spelling, especially for the noun. Edited English tries to keep the masculine-feminine spelling distinction, but in lower levels practice is less rigid.

brusque, brusk (*adj.*) means "abrupt, harsh, blunt, especially in speech." It is usually spelled *brusque*, but *brusk* does occur; Americans pronounce it *BRUHSK*, but the British say it with either the vowel of *boot* or the vowel of *foot*.

buck (*nn., v.*) *Buck* is actually several different nouns: (1) a male deer, goat, etc., although extended use of this sense as either noun or adjunct is now considered a slur, especially when applied to any man of color; (2) a sawhorse or gymnastic "horse"; (3) a marker (probably a knife with a buckhorn handle) to identify the dealer in a poker game, and hence an indicator of final responsibility, as in *The buck stops here* and *She's just passing the buck* (an extension of this word is the Conversational or Informal slang word for *dollar*). The verb describes the horse's leaping and jumping, often in the effort to unseat its rider; it's probably from *balk* (which see), and there are many figurative uses from this sense, many of them Standard.

buckaroo, buckeroo (*n.*) is the result of folk etymology, an Americanization of the Spanish *vaquero*, also meaning "cowboy," and our southwestern version was no doubt influenced by the verb *buck*. It is slang and cowboy argot but widely used and understood over the whole country today.

buff (*n.*), **in the buff** *Buff* was originally the yellowish leather of the American buffalo or bison, and it came to refer to both the leather, its color, and the leather-covered block of wood used to polish or shine. *Buff* then came to mean "skin-colored," and "skin": hence the Conversational idiom *in the buff*, meaning "naked." The word *buff* meaning "fan" is Informal and Conversational, as in *I'm an opera buff*, and comes apparently from the nineteenth-century enthusiasts who rooted for their favorite New York fire companies (the firemen wore *buff*-colored coats).

buffalo, bison (*nn.*) As every schoolchild should know, the American *bison* is not a *buffalo* at all. *Buffaloes* (or *buffalos* or *buffalo*; see PLURALS OF NOUNS ENDING IN -*O*) can be any of several wild oxen that live in Africa and elsewhere, but not in North America. Nonetheless, *buffalo* persists as the popular name for the American *bison*, especially in the Wild West of history and imagination, and both words are Standard English, except in biologically precise use, where *bison* must prevail.

buffet (*nn.*, *v.*) A *buffet*, pronounced *BUHF-it*, is a blow, usually by hand or fist. *Buffet* is also another name for a dining room sideboard, a lunch or refreshment counter, or a meal where you serve yourself from a table covered with various dishes. This *buffet* is pronounced either *buh-FAI* or *boo-FAI* in the United States and *BUHF-it* in Britain. Both nouns are French in origin, the first from the Middle Ages, the second from the eighteenth century. The verb, which is related to the older *buffet*, means "to strike a blow" and is much used figuratively of wind and wave.

bug (*n.*, *v.*) has a variety of senses. The noun means "an insect," especially pests (in Britain, specifically "a bedbug"), and the term is Standard but usually nontechnical. Another sense, which is Conversational and Informal, means "a bacterium or other unspecified causer of disease, a microscopic organism, or, loosely, the disease itself" (related to that use is the slang use meaning "some general flaw in any system": *There's some sort of bug in this computer program; we'll have to debug it*). There are also the slang meanings "a hidden microphone, used for surveillance and eavesdropping," "an enthusiast, especially a hobbyist," "a very small car, specifically one of the post-World-War-II Volkswagens," and "the apprentice jockey's weight allowance for the first year," apparently so called because of the asterisk (which looks vaguely like an insect) next to the jockey's name in the racing program. As a verb, *bug* is slang in these senses: "to install or use a hidden microphone," "to annoy, bother, or irritate someone," "to pop the eyes open wide, to make them protrude" (this sense often combines with *out*), presumably like some insects' goggle eyes, and two combined idiomatic forms, *bug off*, meaning "go away," as in *Bug off and leave me alone!* and *bug out*, meaning "to run away," as in *I was afraid, so I bugged out and went home.* One other use of the noun is sometimes labeled obsolete but is only archaic slang, meaning "bugbear, monster, or simply someone important and powerful": *Her father is a really big bug in the banking business.* Compare BOGEY.

bugger (*n.*, *v.*) The problem with all senses and uses of *bugger* was always *buggery*, a noun meaning "sodomy." Hence *to bugger* is "to commit sodomy," and for many Americans that sense put all others under taboo. (In any serious context, most Americans would use the term *sodomy* rather than the term *buggery*, just to avoid being judged to use Vulgar or obscene slang.) *Bugger* also can mean something quite inoffensive, however: "a rascal, a little scamp" or "an uncooperative object or apparatus," and these slang senses are quite without sexual referents. And of course a *bugger* is also someone who installs electronic *bugs*. When the British say *Bugger all!* they mean only something like "Damn!" or "Nothing!"

bulimia (*n.*), **bulimic** (*adj.*) Pronounced *b(y)oo-LIM-ee-uh* or *b(y)oo-LEEM-ee-uh*, *bulimia*, along with other dietary disorders found especially in young women, has received considerable media attention in recent years. Also called *bulimia nervosa* and *bulimarexia*, it means "an insatiable appetite" and especially "a syndrome involving binge eating and vomiting,'' usually exhibiting cycles of severe dieting or other guilt-driven efforts to undo the effects of enormous eating binges. Note the spelling: There is only one *l* and the medial vowel is *-i-*. The infrequent adjective is *bulimic*. Compare ANOREXIA.

bulk (*n., v.*) *Bulk of* is Standard with both mass and count nouns, as in *the bulk of the criticism* and *the bulk of the potatoes*. The idiomatic use of the verb in *These experiences bulk large in my mind* is also Standard. See also LARGE.

bull, bullish See BEAR.

bum (*adj., n., v.*) The noun is an Americanism, meaning ''a hobo or vagrant,'' and in that use it is Standard. In compounds such as *ski bum*, meaning ''someone who spends all his or her time skiing and hanging around ski lodges,'' it is Conversational. As an adjective, it means ''incompetent,'' as in *She's a bum skater*, or ''poor quality,'' as in *We had a bum meal at that place*, or ''damaged or injured,'' as in *I've got a bum shoulder*; all these senses are slang. Among idioms the noun provides *to get or give the bum's rush*, meaning ''to be thrown out,'' or ''to throw someone out,'' and *to be on the bum*, meaning ''to be wandering, living off the land''; these are slang. The idioms *to bum around*, meaning ''to wander aimlessly,'' and *to bum out*, especially reflexively, as in *That really bums me out*, meaning ''That really irritates me,'' are also slang. In British English, the noun *bum* means ''buttocks'' (see BUTTOCKS).

bumble-bee, humble-bee (*nn.*) They are *bumble-bees* both here and in Britain, but the British also call them *humble-bees*, and that term has had some older poetic use in the United States.

bummer (*n., interj.*) The noun is slang, meaning ''something unsatisfactory, unpleasant,'' as in *That party was a bummer*. The interjection is simply a cry of disappointment, and it too is slang.

bunch (*n.*), meaning ''our group,'' as in *She's not a member of our bunch*, is archaic today. All other uses of *bunch* meaning ''group,'' as in *a bunch of the boys*, or ''a lot,'' as in *We had a whole bunch of problems*, or ''a good deal of,'' with a mass noun, as in *a bunch of trouble*, are Standard at all Conversational levels and in Informal and Semiformal writing as well. Most count nouns, as in *a bunch of flowers* or *bunches of daisies*, are Standard with *bunch(es)*.

bungalow (*n.*) India gave us this word, originally a one-story house with a wide veranda; early in the twentieth century in the United States an imitation of that *bungalow* became very popular and bore the same name; it was low, with dormer-windowed attic and a full front porch under the full front-to-rear gabled roof.

bunk into, meaning ''bump into,'' is dialectal in New York City. See METROPOLITAN NEW YORK CITY REGIONAL DIALECT.

buns See BUTTOCKS.

bureau (*n.*) has two plurals: the regular *bureaus* and the French *bureaux*. See FOREIGN PLURALS.

bureaucrat, bureaucracy (*nn.*), **bureaucratic** (*adj.*) All three of these words have pejorative overtones, suggestive of inefficiency, inflexibility, waste, and lethargy. All these *bureau-* words are based on the idea of divisions and subdivisions such as are found in bureaus and in other places for storing paper. See also HIERARCHY.

burgeon (*v.*), **burgeoning** (*adj.*) *Burgeon* began by meaning ''to send forth buds and sprouts,'' but it has long since generalized to mean ''to grow, to expand, and simply to flourish.'' *Bourgeoning* too has generalized, although some commentators have discouraged the semantic change. Both words are Standard in the original and expanded senses.

burger See HAMBURG.

-burgh, -burg (*suffix*) The suffixes on the names of these American cities, *Pittsburg*, California, and *Pittsburg*, Kansas, are all pronounced like that in *Pittsburgh*, Pennsylvania, *-BUHRG*, whereas Scotland's *Edinburgh* ends in the pronunciation *-BUHR-uh*. But *burgher* is always pronounced *BUHRG-uhr*.

burglarize, burgle (*vv.*) Both these verbs are only a bit over a century old, and both are Standard today, although *burglarize* seems to have more widespread acceptance, perhaps because *burgle* is a back-formation (see also -ISE). Your house can be *burglarized* whether you are at home or not, whereas—theoretically, at least—someone can rob you only by taking your possessions when you are present; and to rob your house someone would have to take the whole structure, again, in your presence; to rob you, the thief would have to make off only with only something of yours, not with you yourself. But see ROB. See also BACK-FORMATION.

burglary, robbery (*nn.*) The technical difference (in law, at least) is that a *burglary* is "breaking and entering with the intent to steal something," whereas *robbery* is "stealing something from someone by violence or threat of violence." See also BURGLARIZE; ROB.

burgle See BACK-FORMATION; BURGLARIZE.

buried See BURY.

burlesque, caricature, farce, lampoon, parody, travesty (*nn.*) A *burlesque* is a play or other literary piece that elevates the mundane or reduces and ridicules the noble for purposes of making people laugh. The American *burlesque* show presented bawdy comedy, skits, and striptease acts, making gross fun of human behavior. *Caricature* is the humorous exaggeration in pictures or words of people, places, or events, as in political cartoons. A *farce* is a comedy filled with wit, lively and unlikely social situations, and exaggerated language. A *lampoon* is a harsh satire, designed to ridicule someone or something. A *parody* is a piece of music or literature in which another work is imitated for humorous purpose or ridiculed through exaggeration or distorted imitation. A *travesty* is a gross distortion of an original work, exaggerated for comic purposes or with intent to ridicule.

burn (*v.*) The principal parts are *burn, burned* or *burnt, burned* or *burnt. Burned* is much more common in both transitive and intransitive use in American English: *We burned the rubbish. The last bridge had burned.* British English uses *burnt* more frequently, especially in intransitive use. The participial adjectives in the United States are both *burned* and *burnt.* Both *burned* and *burnt* are used in compounds too, and all these uses are Standard. Compare CREEP.

burn out (*v.*), **burnout, burn-out** (*n.*), **burned-out, burnt-out** (*adj.*) *To burn out* is an idiom meaning "to stop burning because of lack of fuel": *The fire had burned out sometime during the night. Burnout* is the usual spelling of the noun, *burn-out* an infrequent variant: it is the point at which a booster rocket has consumed all its fuel and is dropped away from the next stage, or the point at which a jet engine stops after burning all its fuel. *Burnout* is also a figurative term for emotional exhaustion stemming from overwork or other on-the-job strain, as in *A newly recognized educational problem is teacher burnout,* and *burned-out* or *burnt-out* is the adjective of this sense.

burst (*v.*) The Standard principal parts are *burst, burst, burst. Bursted* for past tense or past participle is dialectal and Substandard. See also BUST.

bury (*v.*), **buried** (*adj.*), **-bury** (*suffix*) The verb, meaning "to inter," "to hide away," and the like, rhymes with *ferry,* not with *furry.* The adjective rhymes with *harried* or *ferried; hurried* as a rhyme for it is Nonstandard and probably dialectal. The suffix *-bury* (in place names it is a variant of *-burgh*) sometimes rhymes with *berry,* especially in the United States, but in British English and occasionally in the United States the usual pronunciation either rhymes with *curry* or assimilates the suffix's first syllable entirely, as in *Sudbury* (*SUHD-buhr-ee* or *SUHD-bree*). The idiom with the verb, *bury the hatchet,* meaning "agree to stop fighting," is Standard and a cliché.

bus, buss (*nn., vv.*), **bus boy, busboy** (*n.*), **bus** (*v.*) The motor vehicle for carrying passengers is spelled *bus;* its plural is either *buses* or *busses,* both Standard. The verb *bus,* meaning "to transport by bus," developed quite regularly through functional shift. It met some opposition at first, primarily because it was new, but the movement toward racial equality in education in the sixties brought it into widespread use, and it is now Standard: *The board decided to bus the children to the suburban schools.* Its participles are both spelled either way: *bused, bussed; busing, bussing.* The other noun, meaning "kiss," is always spelled *buss,* and the plural and the third person singular of that verb are spelled *busses.* This word, both noun and verb, is Standard but perhaps now either arch or old-fashioned.

A *bus boy* or *busboy* assists the waiter or waitress in a restaurant; he clears dishes (he *buses* or *busses* them), and all of his duties come under the heading of *busing* or *bussing.* The origin of this Americanism is uncertain. It is almost certainly from a clipping of *omnibus,* but whether because *busing* involves pushing a cart (a *bus*) full of dirty dishes or clearing everything (food, dishes, silver, glassware, and crumbs—a regular *omnibus* of items) from the table is unknown. There is no *bus girl,* but some speakers are beginning to use *bus person.* See CONSONANTS (2).

bush, bush league (*adjs., nn.*) *Bush* in this sense is actually a clipped form of the compound *bush league,* meaning "second rate," "cheap," from its use as a jargon name for the minor leagues in baseball, especially in the first half of the twentieth century. The terms suggest the unpolished manners, the ignorance, and the lack of "class" thought by those who had made it to the major leagues to be characteristic of life in the boondocks. Both terms are slang, having grown beyond the jargon of baseball: *The way he behaved to his colleagues was strictly bush [league].*

bushwa, bushwah See BOURGEOIS.

business (*adj., n.*) has a wide range of meanings, nearly all of them Standard. Its specialized senses include the commercial, such as *I'm in business for myself, His business is making widgets for export* and *Our company really wants your business.* There is also an important specialized theatrical use: *During the pause in the dialogue, the director had him do some business involving lighting a cigarette and pouring a drink.* These senses pose no problems. The generalized senses, as in *This is a messy business you've gotten us into, What business is it of yours?* and *I hate the business of cleaning up after a party,* are a bit more troublesome. Sometimes they work at Conversational levels of speech, but they usually seem weak and flabby in expository prose. There are also some useful idioms, including the Conversational *to mean business,* "to be serious, intent," as in *The glint in her eye showed she meant business,* and *to get down to business,* meaning "to turn to serious discussion or action," as in *We chatted for a minute or two, but then we got right down to business*; and the slang *to give someone (or to get) the business,* meaning "to treat someone (or to be treated) harshly," as in *When she finally arrived, he really gave her the business for being late.* See also BUSYNESS; PROPOSAL.

buss See BUS.

bust (*n., v.*) The verb was once a Substandard slang form of *burst,* and in some uses *bust* is still more nearly slang than it is Conversational. But many uses of both the verb and the noun made from it are now Standard, though limited mainly to the lower Conversational levels and the Informal writing that imitates them.

The verb *bust* (past tense and past participle are both either *busted* or *bust*) is Conversational in these senses: "break or burst" (*The dam has busted*); "to make or to become penniless" (*I busted the bank at the casino; The poker game busted me*); "to reduce or be reduced in rank," especially in the military (*He busted me to private again*); "to tame a horse" (*He busts horses for a living*); "to break up, to bring to an end," especially with *up* (*The cops busted up the crap game*); "to hit with the fist" (*He busted me right in the eye*); "to place or be placed under arrest" (*She got busted for speeding*).

Conversational or slang are these noun senses: "a raid by police"; "a drunken party"; "a punch"; "an arrest"; "a financial crash." Note too that *trustbusting* is Standard gerund and participle, even though usually limited to Informal and Semiformal written use. And *busted* is a Standard Informal and Conversational adjective: *She's got a busted arm.* The noun *bust* also means simply "a failure": *the new play was an absolute bust.* it is Conversational, or perhaps slang.

bust See BREAST(S).

busyness, business (*nn.*) *Busyness* stresses the vigorous, nonstop activity indicated by the adjective *busy: Her busyness as she hurried about the office exhausted me. Business,* however, has a long list of specialized and generalized meanings, none of them overlapping with *busyness.* See BUSINESS.

but (*coord. conj., prep.*) To start a sentence with *but* is Standard English, and it is often very effective if used sparingly and if not set off with a comma when it simply introduces an independent clause, as in *But this reasoning will not stand up.* You may also begin a sentence with *but* followed by a comma or a dash, so long as it is to set off a parenthesis, as in *But, objections or not, we plan to bring suit on Monday.* And you may occasionally want to use a dash to imitate a pause in a spoken version: *But—we never saw him again.*

But is a function word that serves as both preposition (*all but Fred*) and coordinating conjunction (*I was there, but I left early*), and sentences such as these are Standard: *Everyone was satisfied but me* (with the accusative case pronoun as the object of the preposition *but*) and *Everyone was satisfied but whoever threw the rotten egg* (with *but* serving as a preposition with a clause, of which *whoever* is subject, serving as the object of the preposition).

But meaning "only" is Standard, as in *I regret that I have but one life to give for my country,* but when a negative precedes it the construction is rare in Edited English; it occurs primarily at Casual and Impromptu levels of speech: *There aren't but three people left in line.* But expect objection from conservatives, even for Informal use.

But that (*I don't know but that I'll take up knitting again*) and *but what* (*There's no doubt but what we'll see some changes*) are both Standard, although *but what* is limited mainly to Conversational and Informal contexts, while *but that* does occur in some Edited English as well.

buttle (*v.*) is a back-formation from *butler* (past tense and past participle are *buttled*) describing what this functionary does: at best it is Conversational and Informal; at worst it is slang.

buttocks, arse, ass, backside, bottom, bum, buns, butt, can, cheeks, rear (end), rump (*nn.*) *Buttocks* is the Standard term meaning "the two rounded fleshy parts of the backside on which humans rest when they sit." *Buttock* is the singular. There are almost endless terms for this part of our anatomy, some of them euphemisms because of scatological connections, more of them slang, often graphic. The list here is not exhaustive: *backside, bottom, rear,* and *rear end,* are Standard but euphemistic. British *arse* and American *ass* are both Vulgar slang, although the taboo is much diminished. *Bum* is also British, and Vulgar slang. *Can, cheeks,* and *buns* are figurative, graphic, and slang. So also are the terms borrowed from the butcher shop, *rump* and *butt,* two cuts from analogous parts of meat animals; these are Standard, but in these senses best limited to Conversational and Informal contexts. Clearly, Americans are somewhat uncomfortable naming this as well as other parts of their bodies, so be careful to suit the term you choose to your context.

but which, but who See AND WHICH.

buy (*n., v.*) The verb meaning "accept, believe," as in *I didn't buy his explanation,* is still considered slang by some commentators, but probably a more accurate assessment is that it is now quite at home at all Conversational levels of speech and in Informal and Semiformal writing. The noun, meaning "bargain, a good investment," was also long considered slang, but seems now to be Standard in all but the most Formal uses.

BUZZWORD is a noun, itself an impressive-sounding vogue word that is a label for vogue words. *Buzzwords* mean little but suggest much, including great technical sophistication and importance, as well as other up-to-the-minute qualities. *Buzzwords* are used mainly by the knowing and modish to impress each other and the uninitiated.

by- (*prefix*) means "separate(d) from," "near," or "secondary," as in *by-election* (the British term used to designate a vacancy-filling election held between general elections), *bypass* (as a noun, "a way around," and as a verb, "to circumvent or circumnavigate"), *byplay* ("action going on separately from the main action, as in a drama"), and *byproduct* ("something turned out as a secondary result of producing

the main product"). All these are Standard. See PREFIXES.

by (*prep.*) is a word easily made ambiguous in some contexts. *The statue was located by the tour guide* can mean either "the guide found it," or "others found it beside the guide." Ambiguity usually can be avoided by choice of a different preposition or syntactic pattern: *The statue was standing near the tour guide. The tour guide found the statue.*

by all means See MEANS.

by and by, by and large, by the by, by the way, bye-bye, bye (*n.*) The first four locutions are idioms: *by and by* means "sooner or later," and there is also a cliché from a song, *in the sweet by and by,* meaning "some time far off, perhaps in the afterlife"; *by the by* and *by the way* mean "incidentally" or "please note"; *by and large* means "on the whole, taking everything into consideration," and it has another meaning in sailing argot: *to sail by and large* means "to sail on the wind, but off sufficiently to make certain that one need not fear being taken aback" (see TAKE ABACK). All these are Standard, although the sailing argot needs careful contextual support. *Bye-bye* is baby talk for "goodbye," and there is a cliché using it as a noun: *to go bye-bye* is baby talk for "to go for a walk, to leave, to go away." Today *bye-bye* is Casual for saying goodbye, stressed on either syllable. The noun *bye* is the status of a contestant who has no match in the first round of a tournament: *She draws a bye.* The term is limited mainly to sports argot, but it appears regularly in Edited English on sports subjects.

by heart, by rote These idioms are synonyms. *To know something by rote* is to have memorized it as if to sing or chant it to the accompaniment of a sort of harp (*rote*). *To know something by heart* is also to have it—words or tune—memorized perfectly.

byte See BIGHT.

by the by See BY AND BY.

by the same token See TOKEN.

by the way See BY AND BY.

by way of being is an idiom and cliché meaning "almost," "on the way to becoming," or similar rather vague and padded ideas, as in *She is by way of being a pretty good tennis player.* It is chatty language, better limited to Conversational and Informal use.

Byzantine, byzantine (*adj.*), **Byzantium** (*n.*) The adjectives refer to the Greek city of *Byzan-*

tium, now *Istanbul* and once called *Constantinople,* and to its culture and government. The word *byzantine* or *Byzantine* has come to mean "complex, devious, and unfathomable," all of which describe the political and religious history of the place. Americans pronounce the adjectives *BIZ-in-teen,* the British either *bei-ZAN-tein* or *bi-ZAN-tein.* The noun *Byzantium* is either *bi-ZAN-chee-uhm* or *bi-ZAN-ti-uhm.*

C

cabaña (*n.*), meaning usually "a bathhouse or shelter at a beach or pool," is a Spanish word. Americans pronounce it *kuh-BAN-yuh, kuh-BAHN-yuh, kuh-BAN-uh,* and *kuh-BAHN-uh* and usually spell it without the tilde: *cabana.*

cabaret (*n.*), "a nightspot for dancing, dining, and drinking" or "the entertainment offered there," is usually pronounced *KAB-uh-RAI,* but it sometimes is further anglicized to *KAB-uh-RAI.*

cabernet sauvignon The popularity in America of this grape and particularly of the wines made from it, together with the prestige attached to knowing about wines and the pronunciations of their names, has led Americans to do their best with the French, which usually comes out *KAB-uhr-NAI SO-vee-NYAWNG* (or, where the French nasal is unheard, *-NYAWN*), with the primary stress on the final syllable.

cablecast (*n., v.*) A recent coinage modeled on *broadcast* and *telecast* (both now Standard), *cablecast* is still communications jargon; depending upon how useful the distinction between *telecast* and *cablecast* ultimately becomes to the rest of us, it could become Standard.

cacao, coca, coco, cocoa (*nn.*) *Cacao* (pronounced *kuh-KAI-o* or *kuh-KAH-o*) is the seed or bean of which *cocoa* (*KO-ko*)—both the powder and the drink made from it—is made; *coca* (*KO-kuh*) is the plant from whose dried leaves the drug cocaine comes, and *coco* (*KO-ko*) is the name of both the palm tree that bears coconuts and the fiber that comes from their husks.

cache (*n., v.*) Pronounce both like *cash,* not *catch.*

cactus (*n.*) The plural is either *cactuses* or *cacti.* See FOREIGN PLURALS.

caddie, caddy (*nn.*) *Caddie* (from French *cadet;* variant *caddy*) is the term for the person or cart that carries a golfer's bag; a *caddy* (from a Malay word for a small unit of measure) is "a container for loose tea or for carrying other small items"; *caddy* is also a slang clipping of the trade name of an American automobile, the *Cadillac.*

cadre (*n.*) Pronounce it *KAD-ree, KAD-rai, KAHD-ree,* or *KAHD-rai.*

caesarean, caesarian See CESAREAN.

cagey (*adj.*) means "sly, tricky, shrewd" or simply "cautious"; most Standard users believe it should be limited to Conversational or Informal use, although a few consider it appropriate in all contexts.

Cajun See ACADIAN; ZYDECO.

calculate (*v.*), **calculated, calculating** (*adjs.*) When *calculate* means "to figure out, to determine by mathematics, to estimate," the verb is Standard. When it means "to intend" or "to think," it is dialectal and sounds rural and unpolished, like certain uses of *reckon* and *figure: I calculate [on] going to town tomorrow.* The past participle is the participial adjective *calculated,* as in *a calculated risk,* meaning "an anticipated, expected, or likely risk" (see also APT); the present participle, *calculating,* is a participial adjective meaning "making calculations," as in the compound *calculating machine,* but its figurative sense of "shrewd or foresighted" has also developed a pejorative sense, "scheming, crafty, conniving." Unless you control the context, calling someone *calculating* will usually denigrate.

calculus (*n.*) is both the "hard matter that grows in the human body, as in gallstones or on teeth" and "the branch of mathematics conventionally referred to by mathematicians as *the calculus.*" See also FOREIGN PLURALS.

caldron, cauldron (*n.*) Both spellings are Standard American English; *caldron* is slightly more frequent. See VARIANT SPELLINGS.

calendar (*n.*), **calender** (*n., v.*) The *calendar* (originally "an account book" in Latin) is our familiar way of keeping track of the time of week, month, and year; a *calender* (in Latin it was "a cylinder or roller") is a machine that makes paper and other fabrics by flattening materials between rollers; rubber is *calendered* to form the plies of which tires are made.

caliber, calibre (*n.*) Americans usually spell it *caliber*. See SPELLING (1).

calk, caulk (*nn., vv.*) A *calk* is "a spike or plate on a shoe, designed to prevent slipping"; horseshoes always have *calks,* and "to provide a shoe with calks" is *to calk it.* (*Corked soles* is a dialectal variant of *calked soles.*) *To caulk the seams of a boat's deck or the fittings of pipes* is "to make them watertight by filling all gaps with a *caulk* or *caulking* material." Alas, each of these words, in each of its functional shifts, has a variant spelling like the other.

calligraphy (*n.*) Its generalized sense is "any and all sorts of handwriting," but it also has a specialized meaning, "handwriting as an art form," which is much more faithful to its Greek original, meaning "beautiful handwriting."

callous (*adj., v.*), **callus** (*n., v.*), **calloused, callused** (*adjs.*) These words have the same etymon, the Latin *callum,* meaning "hard skin." The usual adjective, meaning "hard-skinned," is always spelled *callous* (*He has a callous disposition*). But the participial adjective is more frequent, in either spelling: *callused* [*calloused*] *hands; callused* [*calloused*] *disposition.* The noun, meaning "thickened skin," is always spelled *callus: I have calluses on my hands from rowing.* The most usual spelling of the verb is *callous,* but *callus* also occurs in that use (*My hiking boots calloused* [*callused*] *my feet*).

Calvary See CAVALRY; METATHESIS.

camp (*adj., n.*), **campy** (*adj.*) This slang word of unknown etymology seems to be fading, after a decade or two of very heavy use. The adjective means "banal, ostentatious, pedestrian, or artificial," and overtones of "effeminate" and "homosexual" have been attached to it since the early 1930s. During the sixties and seventies it became a vogue word, along with an adjective *campy,* and its noun form meant the manners or artifacts called *high* or *low camp.* Should you use *camp* today, however, some of the young may require definitions.

can See BUTTOCKS.

can 1, may (*aux.*) These auxiliaries are said by tradition to have been distinguished from each other semantically: *You **can** go if you have the strength. You **may** go if you have permission.* In actual practice they are nearly interchangeable in most uses, and *can* is used much more than *may,* especially at all Conversational levels and in Informal writing. In the negative, *can't* is frequently used at nearly all levels; *mayn't* is quite rare in American English, although it does occur in relatively Formal uses, and *cannot* has a much, much greater frequency than *may not.* In speech we frequently use *may* only when we want to express a possibility—*I may go with you, or I may not; I haven't decided*—and frequently we will then heavily stress *may.* But note too the likely further comment: *If I can, I will.*

In polite requests, especially written ones, *may* is always the preferred word: *May I have your attention, please?*

can 2, tin (*nn.*), **canned, tinned** (*adjs.*) Americans put *canned* things in *cans*; the British put *tinned* things in *tins.* See VOCABULARY (1).

canard (*n.*) is now English enough that we often pronounce the final *-d,* but it remains French enough to require a primary stress on the final syllable. A *canard* in American English is "a false story, a swindle." A *vile canard* is a cliché; there is almost no other kind.

can but See CANNOT HELP BUT.

cancel out is a combined form of the verb *cancel* ("to call off") that is a Standard idiom meaning "to offset, to reduce two opposing forces equally": *Her inexperience usually cancels out her determination.*

candelabrum, chandelier (*nn.*) Both words have multibranched candle-holding lighting fixtures as their original referents: a *candelabrum* is freestanding (on floor or table), a *chandelier* hangs down from the ceiling (and today is usually electrified). *Chandelier* still reflects its French origins in the American pronunciation of its initial consonant cluster and its primary stress on the final syllable: *SHAN-duh-LEER;* its plural is *chandeliers. Candelabrum* has three Standard plurals: *candelabrums, candelabra,* and the sometimes questioned *candelabras,* which occurs because for many years the Latin plural *candelabra* has also been construed as an English singular, even in Edited English. See also FOREIGN PLURALS.

canine (*n.*) is sometimes objected to as pretentious, when just plain *dog* would be simpler (you don't say "nice canine, good canine"), but sometimes you really do need a more general word than *dog:* The world's *canines,* after all, include both wolves and dogs, as the world's *dogs* do not. And *canine loyalty* has a different tone from *doggy loyalty* or *doglike loyalty.*

cannibalize (*v.*) The figurative sense, meaning "to steal parts from one thing to repair another," is now unquestionably Standard.

cannon, canon (*nn.*) Of these homophones, a *cannon* is an artillery piece, a big gun, whereas a *canon* is a law, a principle, a kind of clergyman, or the list of genuine works by a single author, or an accepted group of standard literary or other artistic works, among many specialized senses.

cannot, can not, can't The negative of the auxiliary *can, cannot* occurs less frequently than the contraction *can't* but much more frequently than *can not*, which is sometimes used for emphasis and to reflect the fact that this locution may be stressed on the *not* as well as on the *can. Cannot* is Formal, *can't* relatively Informal in writing, and *can't* is the more frequent in Conversational contexts, but it is often appropriate as well even in some Oratorical uses. All three forms are Standard. *Cannot*, like *can't*, is a very frequent replacement for *may not*. See also CAN (1).

cannot help but, can but, cannot but, cannot help, cannot choose but, can't but, can't help, can't help but These locutions all mean something like "to be able to do no other than." Some of them (but not *can but* and *can't help*) have been called double negatives, but they are all Standard idioms, those with *cannot* simply being more formal than those with the contraction *can't*. *Cannot but* is both very formal and old-fashioned too.

canon See CANNON.

cañon See CANYON.

CANT See JARGON.

can't See CANNOT.

can't but See CANNOT HELP BUT.

can't hardly See DOUBLE NEGATIVE; HARDLY.

can't help, can't help but See CANNOT HELP BUT.

can't seem See DON'T THINK; RAISING.

Canuck (*n.*) To some the noun means simply "a Canadian, a citizen of Canada," about on par with *Yankee* as a name for a U.S. citizen—slang or Conversational at worst, and certainly nondisparaging. To others it means "a French-Canadian," and some people consider it an ethnic slur and therefore taboo. The Separatist movement in Quebec embroils the word in quarrels of language, religion, and nationalistic politics; it can be explosive. And some think it ironic that the western provinces are proud of the Vancouver *Canucks*, a National Hockey League team, while Quebec's Montreal NHL team bears the all-Canadian name of *Maple Leafs*. Be wary of using *Canuck* in other than hockey contexts; many Canadians find it offensive when applied to them by outsiders, even though they may use it of themselves. See OFFENSIVE EPITHETS AND DISPARAGING LABELS.

canvas (*n.*), **canvass** (*n., v.*) *Canvas*, the heavy cotton cloth, has several figurative meanings, including "the sails of ships" and "the floor-covering of a boxing ring." *Canvass* is a verb meaning "to examine closely, especially to seek and to survey for votes"; through functional shift, it has become the noun *canvass*, "the process of such surveying, electioneering, and estimating." To confuse the issue, both words occasionally show up with alternate spellings involving one more or one less *s*. Stick to the distinctions given.

canyon, cañon (*n.*) The current English spelling of this Southwestern narrow river valley between high cliffs is *canyon*, but older writings and placenames often preserve the Spanish spelling with the tilde over the *n*. Either way, it is pronounced *KAN-yuhn*.

capable (*adj.*), **capability** (*n.*) *Capable*, when combined with a preposition, almost always takes *of*, regardless of the construction that follows: *He is capable of murder and of getting away with it, too.* When *capability* is followed by a preposition, it is either *of*, as in *We have the capability of fielding a good team*, or *for*, as in *His capability for causing trouble is well known*; *to* also occurs when an infinitive is to follow: *This young woman has the capability to hold an audience's attention* (but *capable of* plus a gerund sounds much less stiff to American ears: *She is capable of holding . . .*).

capacity (*n.*) You may combine this noun idiomatically with the prepositions *for, of*, and *to*: *She has an admirable capacity for hard work; The room has a capacity of fifty; He has the capacity to talk an idea to death. As* can occur after *capacity* in constructions with *in*: *In his capacity as leader, he has served for ten years.* See also ABILITY.

capital (*adj., n.*), **capitol** (*n.*) These are homophones, but failure to distinguish their spellings is a shibboleth for meticulous readers of Standard English. *Capital* is the term for the city that serves as the seat of government of a state or country, for an uppercase letter, and for the entrepreneurial wealth and power in *capital and labor*. It means "principal" and "most important" when used as adjunct: *the capital city.* It's from *caput,* the Latin for "head." *Capitol,* almost always *capitalized,* is from Capitolium, the name of a specific Roman temple; it refers to a building—a state or the national *Capitol.* The *Capitol* (building) is in the *capital* (city). As an adjective *capital* is archaic or at least old-fashioned slang meaning "splendid, first-rate": *She has a capital idea.* But see CAPITAL PUNISHMENT.

CAPITAL LETTERS, CAPITALIZATION See CAPITALS.

capital punishment, corporal punishment *Capital punishment* is the penalty of death (*caput* is Latin for *head,* which in early methods of *capital punishment* was chopped off). *Corporal punishment* is punishment inflicted on the body (*corpus* is Latin for *body,* and such punishments as whipping, confining to stocks, maiming, or spanking are *corporal*). A *capital crime* is one that carries the death penalty.

CAPITALS, CAPITAL LETTERS, CAPITALIZATION *Capital letters* are an important part of English spelling. Generally speaking, English *capitalizes* the first letter of the first word in a sentence, as in *Summer is my favorite season,* the pronoun *I* and usually the pronouns whose referent is the Deity, as in *Praise Him,* and all proper nouns, such as the names of people, places, events, titles of literary and other artistic works, and the like (as in *Frederick S. Smith, Akron, Ohio, the Fourth of July, Pride and Prejudice,* etc.), and the adjectives and nouns in proper names that are in phrase form as in *International Ladies Garment Workers' Union.* But note that in titles of literary and other artistic works, usually articles, conjunctions, and prepositions are not capitalized unless they are the first words in those titles: *Pride and Prejudice, Of Human Bondage, The Mill on the Floss.* Since the details of *capitalization* required to meet the style of a given press or publication may sometimes be idiosyncratic, you should consult a desk dictionary or your publisher's manual of style. See UP STYLE.

capitol See CAPITAL.

carat, caret, carrot, karat (*nn.*) A *carat* is a unit of measure (two hundred milligrams) used in weighing precious stones. A *karat* is a unit of measure for specifying the pure gold content of an artifact: something that is *one karat gold* is one-twenty-fourth pure gold and otherwise an alloy of other metals. A *caret* is a proofreading symbol, an inverted *v* put into a line to show where something was omitted (in Latin *caret*

means "it is lacking"). Above the *caret* you then write the correction. (*Caret* is also a variant spelling of *karat,* as *karat* is of *carat.*) The last of these four homophones, *carrot,* is of course the common orange-yellow root vegetable, the alternative to the stick.

carbon monoxide, carbon dioxide *Carbon monoxide* (CO) is the odorless, colorless, and very poisonous gas given off by internal combustion engines and other carbon-burning devices; *carbon dioxide* (CO_2) is the odorless and colorless nontoxic gas we give off when we breathe; we also use it in fire extinguishers and in our carbonated drinks. See GREENHOUSE EFFECT.

carburetor, carburettor (*n.*) *Carburetor* is the American spelling, pronounced *KAHR-buhr-ai-tuhr* or *KAHR-byuh-rai-tuhr; carburettor,* pronounced *KAH(R)-byuh-ret-uh(r),* is British. See CONSONANTS (2); SPELLING (1).

cardinal number See ORDINAL NUMBER.

care (*n., v.*) The verb combines with *about* (*I care a lot about family*), with *for* (*I don't care for cauliflower; She cares for her bedfast mother*), and with *to* followed by an infinitive (*I don't care to swim today*). The noun combines with *of* (*I have the care of an abandoned puppy*) and with *for* (*We have to provide care for our aged parents*).

careen, career (*vv.*) *To careen a ship* is "to beach it for repairs in such a way that it will lean far over onto the curve of its bottom and side"; a generalized sense then, for ship or other vehicle, is "to tip or tilt to one side." A figurative sense of *careen* is "to lurch and tip from side to side, as though out of control." *To career* is "to race madly, at full speed, and possibly out of control." This verb comes from the French noun for "a race course, especially a carriageway so used." Both terms are Standard when applied to persons or vehicles proceeding rapidly and erratically: *The wagon careened [careered] wildly down the hill.*

careful, carefree, careless (*adjs.*) *Careful* means "full of care" and hence "meticulous, cautious, and painstaking"; it combines chiefly with prepositional phrases introduced by *of* or *about,* as in *She's careful of [about] her clothes,* a gerund introduced by *in* or *about,* as in *She's careful in [about] choosing her friends,* or an infinitive introduced by *to,* as in *She's careful to hang up her clothes at night. Careless* means "unworried, untroubled," but its pejorative senses, "inattentive, heedless, sloppy, or inconsiderate" are much stronger. It combines usually with prepositional phrases introduced by *of* or *about*, as in *He's careless of [about] time*, or sometimes by *in*, as in *He's careless in his dress*. *Carefree* means "free of worry, untroubled," and when it combines, it usually takes *in*, occasionally *about*, as in *She's carefree [about] in everything she does*.

CAREFUL WRITER, GOOD WRITER, THOUGHTFUL WRITER, and other similar labels often describe the writer who follows the gospel according to that particular usage commentator. The terms suggest quite clearly both our insecurities in many matters of usage and the approval we hope to win if we can make our language convey the information that we are *careful, good,* and *thoughtful* whenever we write.

A better way to look at the matter might be to consider the *careful writer* one who consciously considers his or her choices in matters of usage and style. It is also important to remember that a *careful writer* need not be a timorous one, nor must a *good writer* mean only one who is obedient, conventional, and not venturesome. See also CONSERVATIVES IN LANGUAGE MATTERS.

A final word: most readers will never meet you; they'll base their judgments solely on your writing. Results count the most, therefore.

care less See COULD CARE LESS.

careless See CAREFUL.

caret See CARAT.

caricature See BURLESQUE.

carillon (*n., v.*) The noun is the tuned set of bells in a tower or the tower containing them; the verb means "to play them." Both are almost always pronounced *KER-uh-LAHN*, rarely *kuh-RIL-yuhn*. The past tense and present participle double the final consonants before adding *-ed* or *-ing*, and the player of the bells is a *carillonneur* (*KER-uh-lahn-NUHR*).

caring (*adj.*) is a vogue word, a present participle meaning "feeling concern, responsibility, interest, showing kindness." We speak of *caring parents, caring teachers, caring judges;* truly, one must be a pretty poor specimen of humanity these days not to merit the ascription. Indeed, the adjective may already be a cliché; the gerund, on the other hand, as in *Caring for a sick child can be strenuous*, is unexceptionably Standard.

carousal, carousel, carrousel (*nn.*) The noun *carousal*, like *carouse*, is based on the verb *to carouse* and means "a loud, drunken party." It is pronounced *kuh-ROUZ-il*. A *carousel* (some-

times spelled *carrousel*) is "a merry-go-round in an amusement park" or a device that imitates it, such as "a baggage *carousel* at an airport" or "a slide *carousel* for holding photographic slides to be projected on a screen." It is pronounced *KER-uh-sel* or *-zel*, and sometimes its final syllable receives secondary or even primary stress.

carrot See CARAT.

carrousel See CAROUSAL.

CASE 1 In English grammar, *case* is displayed in the distinctive inflectional form of a noun, pronoun, or adjective that indicates that word's grammatical relationship to other words or parts of a locution. In Old English, all three parts of speech were inflected for the nominative, genitive, dative, accusative, and (early in the period) instrumental *cases*. Today, only the personal pronouns show a fairly full range of distinctive *case* forms: nominative (*I, you, he, she, it, we, you, they, who*); genitive (*my/mine, your/yours, his/his, her/hers, its/its, our/ours, your/yours, their/theirs, whose/whose*); accusative (or objective) (*me, you, him, her, it, us, you, them, whom*). Gone are the distinctive inflections for the dative and instrumental, all covered instead today by the multipurpose objective *case* forms. In nouns, only the nearly all-purpose (e.g., *dog/dogs*) and the genitive (e.g., *dog's/dogs'*) *case* forms still exist. In adjectives, *case* no longer appears in any inflections. Nevertheless, some grammars continue to refer to *case*, even where no formal, morphological indication of it appears, making *case* stand only for the grammatical function once indicated by form.

Where case inflections still exist today, and especially in the pronouns, they remain grammatically very powerful, and errors in their use are often serious blunders against Standard usage. Obvious inadvertent failures to meet Standard users' expectations can have the force of shibboleths. But complicating the situation is the fact that in some instances *case* is currently in divided usage; see IT'S ME; WHO.

case 2 (*n.*) is one of those filler words, like *event, business, instance, thing, matter, concern,* and the like, that we use as syntactic counters while we are giving speaker or writer and listener or reader time to pull information together, get organized, and begin to comprehend: *In case you haven't heard . . .* is a temporary substitute for *If you haven't heard. . . .*

casket, coffin (*nn.*) *Coffin* is the generic term in English, but *casket* has been an American euphemism for *coffin* for more than a century credited usually to undertakers' efforts to prettify death. There is frequent objection to *casket,* but it seems well established, with some evidence of a semantic distinction: a *coffin* (the regular British term) is usually *coffin*-shaped, tapered roughly like a flat-faceted mummy case; a *casket* is essentially a regular rectangular box. (People used to keep jewels and other valuables in small *caskets,* but today these are *jewel boxes,* perhaps in part because *casket* has become so funereal.)

cast (*n., v.*), **caste** (*n.*) These are homophones whose different spellings distinguish them: a *cast* is "a throw," "a mold," or "the people who act in a play," and it has other specialized and figurative senses functionally shifted from the verb whose base meaning is "to throw," as in *to throw a pot,* and hence also "to make a (plaster) cast." (Note that you can *cast* actors in or for their parts in a play, or you can *cast* the play, i.e., assign actors to its parts, thus making them the *cast* of the play.) *Caste* is from a Portuguese word for "race," based in its turn on a Latin word meaning "pure." Specifically, *caste* refers to the hereditary Hindu class structure, and in its generalized senses, to any social class or to any system based on social class.

caster, castor (*nn.*) You get little help from spelling in distinguishing these two homophones: *caster* is distinctive, but only in its agentive sense, "one who casts." The two other senses of that word are "a bottle or rack of bottles for condiments" (hence *castor sugar,* the mainly British name for a sugar fine enough to be sprinkled from a *castor)* and "the swiveling wheel or ball fitted to a piece of furniture so that it can be rolled about," and both these senses may be spelled either *caster* or *castor.* The other word, whose usual spelling is *castor,* refers (1) to beavers and beaver-related things, such as "the perfume fixative obtained from one of the beaver's glands," "a beaver hat," and "a heavy cloth made of wool," and (2) to the *castor bean* (from the *castor-oil plant*) and to the lubricating oil and cathartic that can be pressed from it. But *caster* is a rare variant spelling of these senses, too.

CASUAL SPEECH is the level immediately above Intimate speech. It is the level we use for relaxed talk, one on one or with small numbers of close friends and acquaintances, on familiar subjects, in familiar circumstances. Speaker and listener(s) have a great deal in common, and they expect to understand each other. Hence they freely use slang and other words peculiar to their particular constituency. Their language frequently omits conjunctions, relative pronouns, and other unstressed words and phrases; *Borrow your pencil?* is as likely in Casual as *May I borrow your pencil?* As long as such truncations and omissions are limited to situations where *Casual* speech is appropriate, they are Standard. See LEVELS OF USAGE.

casualty (*n.*) Etymologically *casual* had to do with accident or chance; earthquakes and storms claim *casualties,* chosen as it were by chance to suffer injury or death. Hence, in its most general sense, a *casualty* is "anyone or anything injured, killed, or destroyed in an accident or incident" (however, referring to those killed, wounded, and missing in battle or war as *casualties* is probably a euphemism). Fire and *casualty* insurance is written to cover losses from fires, accidents, or other disasters.

CATACHRESIS (*n.*),   **CATACHRESTIC, CATACHRESTICAL** (*adjs.*) This noun (pronounced *KAT-uh-KREE-sis*) and its adjectives (pronounced *KAT-uh-KRES-tik-[uhl]*) describe either the misuse of a word or a mistaken form of a word, as in a mixed metaphor such as *He kept a tight rein on his boiling temper,* a paradox such as *a tall dwarf,* or an explanation of a word that leads to a folk etymology, such as *sparrow grass* for *asparagus.* These examples are *catachrestic(al),* and each such locution is itself a *catachresis.* See also FOREIGN PLURALS.

cataclysm, catastrophe (*nn.*) These two are partial synonyms, but only in their generalized senses: *cataclysm* began by meaning "a huge flood" and then generalized to mean "any great disaster or upheaval, such as a hurricane, an earthquake, or a battle." A *catastrophe* is etymologically "an overturning," and so in theater it signified "the tragic downturn." From that, it generalized to mean "any violent or sudden overthrow or any great disaster or great failure or collapse." The singular is never spelled *catastrophy,* and the plural is *catastrophes,* not *catastrophies.* See FOREIGN PLURALS.

catacomb, catafalque, cenotaph (*nn.*) A *catacomb* (pronounced *KAT-uh-KOM*) is an underground burial vault; *catacombs* are a series of these; *The Catacombs* are those tunnels underneath Rome where the bones of early Christians have been found. A *catafalque* (pronounced *KAT-uh-FALK* or *-FAWLK*) is the platform on which the body of a ruler or other public person lies in state for viewing prior to burial. A *cenotaph* (pronounced *SEN-uh-TAF*) is a monument erected, usually in a prominent public place, to the memory of one or more persons buried somewhere else.

catalog, catalogue (*n., v.*) Both noun and verb occur in both spellings. *Catalogue* is more conservative, *catalog* probably slightly more prevalent today.

catalyst (*n.*) The figurative use of *catalyst,* applied to any person or thing that gets things moving or that causes change or stimulates action, has made some purists object; they argue that the term ought to be restricted to its chemical field, *catalysis,* wherein a *catalyst* speeds or otherwise influences the pace of a chemical reaction. Both uses are Standard, however, and the only real danger is that *catalyst*'s figurative use may become a vogue word and a cliché.

catastrophe See CATACLYSM.

catch (*adj., n., v.*) There are two pronunciations, *KACH* and *KECH,* the latter limited to the lower Conversational levels. The verb, noun, and adjective are Standard in most uses and combinations, but a few uses are limited to the Conversational levels and to Informal and Semiformal writing. Among these are: for the verb, *I got to the theater in time to catch the last act*; for the noun, *I knew there was a catch in it* ("a trick or a hidden penalty"); and for the adjective: *She put several catch questions on the exam.*

catchup See KETCHUP.

categorical (*adj.*), **categorically** (*adv.*) To make *a categorical statement* or *denial, to deny* [*something*] *categorically,* and *to deny categorically that . . .* are clichés. They mean "to deny step by step in every category and particular." That sense has generalized to mean to deny "completely, absolutely" and now often means simply "emphatically."

category (*n.*) means "class" in any of its general senses, and it is not restricted, as some would have it, to use in philosophical discussions or scientific classifications.

cater (*v.*) Americans *cater* mostly *to* their customers and only occasionally do they *cater for* a public. The British more frequently *cater for.* Both *to* and *for* are Standard combined forms, and *cater* can also be transitive, as in *This firm caters parties and banquets.*

cater-corner(ed) See KITTY-CORNER(ED).

catholic, Catholic Use *catholic* to mean "generally widespread, universally held or practiced, broadly understood or accepted": *He has catholic interests in music; he likes all kinds.* Use *Catholic* with a capital *C* to refer to the Roman Catholic Church or, with careful distinctions, to some other Christian churches.

catsup See KETCHUP.

catty-corner(ed) See KITTY-CORNER(ED).

Caucasian, Caucasoid (*adjs., nn.*) *Caucasians* come from the Caucasus, a mountain range between the Caspian and Black seas, and both the adjective and noun *Caucasian* accurately refer to those people, their cultures, and their languages. Anthropologists also use the term *Caucasoid* to apply in a technical sense to a very widely distributed ethnic group characterized by relatively light-colored hair and skin. Unfortunately, *Caucasian* has come to have one sense essentially meaning "Caucasoid," yet obviously the Caucasus can't hold all the world's *Caucasoids,* nor is it probable that all *Caucasoids* originated there. The better course for most of us is to keep both terms in use in their specific senses, and when we mean to designate "the white race or white ethnic groups," to say just that.

cauldron See CALDRON.

caulk See CALK.

CAUSAL *AS* See AS (1).

cause (*n.*) In combination cause appears in Standard English with either *for, of,* or *to: There is no cause for worry. She is the cause of my anxiety. You have no cause to doubt him.* See REASON.

caution (*v.*) combines in Standard English with the prepositions *against, about,* and *concerning,* as in *They cautioned us against* [*about, concerning*] *talking to strangers.* It also occurs with *to* and an infinitive, as in *We cautioned the children to avoid strange dogs,* and occasionally with *of,* as in *I cautioned them of the loud noise there would be.*

cavalry, Calvary (*nn.*) Soldiers mounted on horses are called *cavalry; Calvary* is the hill on which Jesus was crucified. The words are sometimes confused in spelling or pronunciation, because of metathesis.

cay See QUAY.

C.E. See A.D.

-ce, -cy (*suffixes*) We replace with these suffixes the final *-t* in adjectives ending in *-ant* or *-ent* to turn them into nouns: *brilliant* becomes *brilliance* or *brilliancy; virulent* becomes *virulence* or *virulency.* These pairs of nouns are synonyms, but those ending in *-cy* are of lower frequency and may even sound pretentious or archaic. Other, similar pairs are not fully synonymous: see DEPENDENCE.

-cede, -ceed, -sede (*word-forming roots*) All these are pronounced like *seed,* but the three different spellings cause problems. Most English words are spelled with *-cede,* as in *accede, concede, precede, recede,* and the like. But *proceed, exceed,* and *succeed* differ, and *supersede* is one of a kind.

CEDILLA This is the mark (¸) printed or written under the letter *c* in certain Romance languages to indicate that it is to have the sound of *s,* as in French *façade* and *garçon.* See also ACCENT (2); DIACRITICS.

-ceed See -CEDE.

ceiling, floor (*nn.*) These two graphic clichés have long served economists and legislators as metaphors for limits above which (*ceiling*) debt and below which (*floor*) revenues must not slip.

celebrant, celebrator (*nn.*) Historically (and still in most British English) *celebrant* was used only for "the priest at a religious ceremony"; "people with funny hats and noisemakers" were called *celebrators.* But Americans have generalized the meaning of *celebrant* to include secular occasions, and today we make only minimal use of *celebrator,* preferring *celebrant* for all occasions and purposes, where it is now Standard.

cello (*n.*) The plural is usually *cellos* (the initial consonant sound is always pronounced *CH-*), with *celli* occasionally turning up in technical writing about music and especially in rubrics on musical scores. Rarely the word is spelled with an initial apostrophe ('*cello*) to remind us that it is short for *violoncello* (plural *violoncellos*). And note that it is not *violincello.* See PLURALS OF NOUNS ENDING IN -*O*.

Celsius, centigrade Anders Celsius (1701–1744), a Swedish astronomer, invented the thermometer with a scale of 100 degrees from freezing to boiling of water, but English called it a *centigrade* thermometer until in 1948 an international convention decided to honor Celsius by giving it his name. Conventional notation for such temperatures remained unchanged: it is still *10°C* or *22°C* for *centigrade* or *Celsius*; both are Standard.

Celt (*n.*), **Celtic** (*adj., n.*) Scholars of *Celtic* language and literature usually call the people *KELTS* and pronounce the adjective and the language *KEL-tik* (indeed, they were once regularly spelled with a *k*), but Boston basketball fans know that the American kind are *SELTS* or *SEL-tiks*; gradually the popular pronunciations seem to be overtaking the scholarly ones for both words.

cement, concrete, mortar (*nn.*) *Concrete* is the modern technical name (since the mid-nineteenth century) for the building and paving material made of cement, sand and aggregate, and water, and some purists object when lay persons call it *cement* instead of *concrete.* But *cement* has been used from as early as 1300 to designate hard surfaces containing rocks, sand, stone chips, and lime, poured soft to dry hard. Today, *cement* is any of many substances used for sticking things together, and in particular it is the burned lime and clay mixed with water and sand to make *mortar* for laying bricks and stone, or mixed with water, sand, and an aggregate of pebbles to make *concrete* for roads, walks, and buildings.

cenotaph See CATACOMB.

censure (*n., v.*), **censor** (*n., v.*), **censer** (*n.*) Only the last two are homophones, but still some people confuse all three: to censure (*SEN-shoor* or *SEN-shuhr*) is "to disapprove strongly," and *a censure* is such a disapproval; to censor (*SEN-suhr*) is "to remove or prevent circulation of anything thought objectionable, harmful, or impermissible," and *a censor* is "the person who does the censoring"; a *censer* is "an incense-burner used in religious services."

centennial, centenary (*adjs., nn.*) Americans use *centennial* as both parts of speech, whereas the British are said to use *centenary* more as a noun. The same general patterns of use appear to obtain with *bicentennial* and *bicentenary,* *tercentennial* and *tercentenary,* etc. Pronounce *centennial* with primary stress on the second syllable, *centenary* with it on the first *or* second.

center 1 (*v.*) Purists insist that matters can *center* only *on* or *in something,* since a *center* is a single point. Logic notwithstanding, today's American English usage increasingly permits *center around* and *center about* at nearly all levels except Oratorical and Formal and Edited English, where they are Substandard or at least Nonstandard usages. But see also CENTRIFUGAL.

center 2, centre (*adjs., nn.*) Americans spell it *center,* the British, *centre.* See SPELLING (1).

centigrade See CELSIUS.

centimeter (*n.*) Pronounce it *SEN-ti-MEET-uhr.*

centre See CENTER (2).

centrifugal, centripetal (*adjs.*) A *centrifugal* force tends to hurl objects out and away from the center around (on) which they are revolving; a *centripetal* force throws them in toward the center they are revolving about (on).

centrist See ORTHODOX.

century (*n.*) *During this century* usually means "since 1900 or 1901" or "within the twentieth century," usually not "within the last hundred years"; *a century ago* would mean that. And the numbered centuries always encompass the preceding hundred years: the eighteenth century ran from 1700 or 1701 to 1800, the twelfth from 1100 or 1101 to 1200, and so on. As was argued at the turn of the last century and will no doubt be argued again in 2000 and 2001, *the turn of the century* may be the point when the first two numbers increase by one, from 1899 to 1900, or 1999 to 2000. But more logically, given the way in most numerical systems the decades begin with one and end with ten, the new century ought to begin at the point when the last two numbers in the year change from 00 to 01, making 2001 the first year of the twenty-first century.

cereal, serial (*adjs., nn.*) Distinguishing these homophones should cause no trouble: *cereal* is "food made from grain" or "the grain plant itself," and a *serial* is "a row of ordered numbers or parts, as in a *serial* story or television drama, disseminated sequentially."

cerebral (*adj.*) Pronounce it either *SER-uh-bruhl* or *suh-REE-bruhl*.

ceremonial (*adj., n.*), **ceremonious** (*adj.*) If an event is a *ceremonial* or a *ceremonial occasion,* it relies on ritual and accepted form; if a person is *ceremonious,* he or she will be unusually formal and meticulously correct in manner. Only occasions and things can be *ceremonial*; only people can be *ceremonious.*

certain (*adj.*) *He has a certain method for restoring old furniture,* is ambiguous: either the method is *certain* and cannot fail, or it is just one among many methods and not necessarily any good at all. Control meaning with context. See also ABSOLUTE ADJECTIVES.

certainly (*adv., intensifier*) Purists frequently object to *certainly* as an intensifier, arguing that if a thing is *certain,* it is absolute, and if it is *certainly likely,* then it is "absolutely so." But such mild hyperbole is frequent in all levels of language, and *certainly* as adverb and intensifier is Standard; the only danger is overuse.

certificated, certified, licensed (*adjs.*) *Certificated* is a Standard word; the occasional purist objection must be based on unfamiliarity. The verb *license* (that is, "to provide someone or something with a license") has given us the Standard participial adjective *licensed* (*He's a licensed driver*). To assert formally in writing that someone or something meets a standard or test you administer or enforce is to say that that person or thing is *licensed* or *certified*. Precisely the same conditions have long obtained with *to certificate* and hence with *certificated*. The Scarecrow was wise, and Dorothy, the Lion, and the Tin Man *certified* it, but he insisted on being *certificated* as well, so the Wizard of Oz gave him a diploma. Either word will serve: *certified* stresses status; *certificated* reports its literal documentation.

cesarean, caesarean, caesarian (*adj.*) This word offers two minor variant spellings: the digraph *ae* is frequently replaced with *e* in American publications, and the *-ean* ending is also infrequently but acceptably spelled *-ian*. See DIGRAPHS; LIGATURES.

cession, session (*nn.*) These homophones have different meanings: a *cession* is "the ceding or granting of territory or rights," and a *session* is "a meeting or series of meetings or simply an occasion on which people meet to discuss or act on something."

chaff, chafe (*vv.*) *Chaff* (rhymes usually with *graph*) means "to josh or tease mildly"; *chafe* (rhymes with *safe*) means "to annoy, to rub against, to vex, or to become irritated." Now and then you may also see *chafe* spelled *chaff,* as in *Dad was chaffing at the delay.* The *Oxford English Dictionary* reports examples of this spelling from the sixteenth to the nineteenth centuries, but when inexperienced persons use this spelling today, it's usually because they are mispronouncing *chafe* to rhyme with *graph.*

chain reaction (*n.*) A *chain reaction* is "a series of events, each of which is caused by the one that precedes it," and some commentators argue that the term should not be used figuratively to refer to a group of sequential but unrelated events. Such figurative uses are of course not dangerous, and this one is Standard English, but in writing you would do well to remember that some of your readers may prefer and still others may demand precision.

chair (*n., v.*) Both the verb, meaning "to preside over (a meeting)," and the noun, meaning "the person presiding," are Standard, but the noun, the clipped and once Colloquial form of *chairman,* has undergone a great increase in use and an amelioration to full Standard status in recent years, thanks to our search for inclusive language. See INCLUSIVE LANGUAGE; SEXIST LANGUAGE.

chairman, chairlady, chairperson, chairwoman (*nn.*) The last three terms in this list represent efforts to find nonmasculine names for the one who chairs the meeting or the committee. *Chairwoman* and *chairlady* had been in use for some time prior to recent attempts to eliminate exclusive language—examples of which both certainly are. *Chairlady,* however, never had much real support and may always have evoked fewer ideas of equality than could be really helpful. *Chairperson,* on the other hand, has been widely accepted and has been the term of choice until recently, when *chairman* has recovered some status, thanks to its being preferred by many female occupants of the chair themselves, particularly in legislatures. But see also CHAIR; -ESS; FEMININE OCCUPATIONAL FORMS; INCLUSIVE LANGUAGE; SEXIST LANGUAGE.

chaise longue, chaise lounge (*n.*) *Chaise longue* (pronounced in the French way, *shez LAWNG*) is the borrowed name for that curious combination of chair and daybed, but at a quick glance *longue* looked much like the English *lounge,* and given the posture of the person reclining, *lounge* became folk etymology's contribution to the name of the artifact, so that some Americans now both spell and pronounce it as an American hybrid, *chaise lounge* (*shez LOUNJ*). Both terms are Standard today, but those who know French still take exception to *chaise lounge.*

champagne, champaign (*nn.*) These French homophones still retain their French stress and initial consonants: both are pronounced *sham-PAIN. Champagne* is the sparkling wine, named after a French department or province, and *champaign* is the French term for flat, open country, e.g., the topography of Champaign County, Illinois.

chance (*n., v.*) The noun combines with the prepositions *at, for, of,* and *on*—*Mary has a chance at winning; There's no chance for me now; There's a chance of his cooperating; I'll take a chance on entering*—and with *to* plus an infinitive—*They'll offer him the chance to go.* The verb combines with several prepositions, including *on* and *upon* (*I chanced on* [*upon*] *a fine new song*), *by* (*I just chanced by after work*), *into* (*He chanced into the office on Sunday to get the mail*), and with *to* plus an infinitive (*I chanced to meet him yesterday*). All are Standard.

chancel, chantry, choir (*nn.*) The *chancel* is the area of a church where the altar is located; it is usually set off behind a rail or screen. A *chantry* is an endowment used to pay for the saying of masses and prayers on behalf of someone, usually the maker of the endowment; a *chantry* is also a small chapel or an altar funded by and used for such an endowment. A *choir* is the chorus of singers in a church, and architecturally the *choir* is the part of the church, usually behind the *chancel,* where the *choir* sits.

chancery, chancellery, chancellory (*nn.*) *Chancery* is a court of equity or of record; *chanceries* in both church and state keep archives; in Britain *Chancery* is a division of the High Court of Justice. A *chancellery* (pronounced *CHAN-sel-uh-ree* or *CHAN-suhl-ree*; also spelled *chancellory,* especially in British English) is the office of *chancellor,* the building that houses the *chancellor,* and often the name given an embassy building or consulate.

chandelier See CANDELABRUM.

CHANGE, LINGUISTIC See LINGUISTIC CHANGE.

CHANGE, SEMANTIC See SEMANTIC CHANGE.

CHANGE AND VARIATION IN LANGUAGE Most linguists distinguish between *linguistic change* and *linguistic variation* as follows: *Linguistic change* occurs over time; for example, the differences in spelling and pronunciation between Middle English *niht* and Modern English *night* represent *linguistic changes* that developed between (roughly) the fourteenth and the sixteenth or seventeenth centuries. In contrast, *linguistic variation* exists at one given time. One variety is represented by the different pronunciations of a word like *barn* by an Eastern New Englander and by a speaker of the Great Lakes Northern dialect; another is illustrated in the difference between the chief British and American meanings of the noun *vest.*

chantry See CHANCEL.

chaperon, chaperone (*n.*) *Chaperon* is the more commonly encountered spelling, but both are Standard. Since *chaperones* were traditionally women, some people prefer the second spelling, because the word is French and a final *-e* is a typical French feminine ending for a noun.

character, nature (*nn.*) Sometimes these words lead us to pad our speech or prose: *He presented opinions of a character not likely to reassure us* means *He intended his opinions to frighten us. She sang songs of a suggestive nature* means *She sang suggestive songs.* Sometimes a slower, more deliberate pace is useful, but don't be windy.

characteristic (*adj.*) In combined use, *characteristic* is usually followed by the preposition *of*, as in *Pontification is characteristic of emeritus professors*, but *in*, *for*, and *about* also occur in Standard English: *Severe pain is characteristic in cases of gout. Insomnia is characteristic for people your age. What's characteristic about her is her energy.*

charged with (by) When *charged* is used in idiomatic combinations, these are Standard: *The man was charged with vagrancy. She was charged by the storekeeper.*

charisma (*n.*), **charismatic** (*adj.*) In its meaning of "a special charm, attractiveness, or magnetism," the noun *charisma* and its adjective *charismatic*, meaning "having those qualities," have sometimes become vogue words. Used precisely they are most useful; overused, they can become hyperbolic.

chary (*adj.*), meaning "careful, cautious, sparing" and pronounced *CHER-ee*, regularly combines with *of*, as in *I'm chary of door-to-door salesmen*, and occasionally with *about*, *as to*, *in*, and *with*, as in *She is chary about [as to] the people she is seen with. Fred is very chary in giving opinions. I'm chary with praise.*

chastened (*adj.*) is used with *by* or *for*, depending on the meaning: *He was chastened by his experience* indicates what restrained or subdued him; *She was chastened for her unpleasant behavior* indicates why she was criticized or chastised.

chastise (*v.*) is Standard, meaning either "to punish by beating" or "to punish by scolding and criticizing."

château, chateau (*n.*) has two plurals: the French *châteaux* and the regular English *châteaus*. The circumflex accent is increasingly omitted in Edited English. See also FOREIGN PLURALS.

chauvinism, chauvinist (*nn.*), **chauvinistic** (*adj.*) *Chauvinism* is "fanatical, boastful, unreasoning patriotism" and by extension "prejudiced belief or unreasoning pride in any group to which you belong." Lately, though, the compounds *male chauvinism* and *male chauvinist* have gained so much popularity that some users may no longer recall the patriotic and other more generalized meanings of the words. Use them sparingly and explicitly with their *male* referents, and be sure to have context make clear any other referent you might intend.

cheap (*adv.*, *adj.*, *n.*), **cheaply** (*adv.*) The adjective means either "inexpensive" or "shoddy"; only context can control what your reader or listener thinks you intend: *This wine was excellent and cheap besides* talks only of its being inexpensive. *We had a cheap dinner* is open to differing but usually pejorative interpretations. The adverb comes in two forms, an old flat adverb, as in *I can get you that house cheap*, and a conventionally inflected adverb, as in *She furnished the house cheaply but comfortably*. Both adverbs are Standard, but *cheaply* often has the same ambiguity as the adjective. The noun occurs in a British idiom that dates from around 1800: *He does everything on the cheap* (that is, "as cheaply as possible"). *On the cheap* is still slang, albeit *literary-sounding* slang, and it is pejorative.

check 1 (*v.*) is used in many combinations with prepositions alone and in clusters, and although some of these combinations may seem to tend toward the Informal and the Conversational, in fact almost all are Standard idioms: *check on* (*Be sure to check on his luggage*), *check over* (*Just check over that menu, will you please?*), *check in* (*What time will you check in at your hotel?*), *check into* (*Do check into his references*), *check up* (*Check up to see if we'll have time to eat first*), *check up on* (*I'll check up on her performance*), *check out* (*His testimony checks out*), *check out of* (*When are you going to check out of your room?*), *check over* (*I've checked over the lists, and they are correct*), *check around* (*Will you check around and see whether you can find a sitter?*).

check 2, cheque (*n.*) Americans call the draft on a bank a *check*; *cheque* is the British spelling. See SPELLING (1).

checkers (*nn.*) This familiar board game is *checkers* in the United States, *draughts* in Britain. See VOCABULARY (1).

cheeks See BUTTOCKS.

cheerful, cheery (*adjs.*) *Cheerful* means "being in or displaying good spirits," *cheery* means only "displaying good spirits": *He is a cheerful young man, always first with a cheery [cheerful] greeting.*

cheeseburger See HAMBURG.

chemistry (*n.*) is of course Standard in its uses referring to that physical science, but it is also Standard in figurative uses referring to relationships among members of groups or sexual attractions between individuals. In addition, many of *chemistry*'s technical terms have taken on figurative meanings in the general vocabulary (see, e.g., ACID TEST; CATALYST).

cheque See CHECK (2).

cherub, cherubim, cherubs (*n.*) For most Americans, the singular *cherub* calls to mind an infant of endearingly plump appeal or the winged representation of one as a lower-order or decorative angel, particularly as developed in Italian art. But the plurals may be semantically distinctive: *cherubs* calls to mind the babies and the angelic little Italian figures, but *cherubim,* the Hebrew plural, may also or instead evoke a taller, sterner order of angelic figures. All are Standard uses, although the figurative sense of *cherubs* as applied to infants is by far the most widely used, perhaps because of its hyperbole. Note too that since many English speakers are unaware that *cherubim* is a Hebrew plural, the English plural *cherubims* is also Standard today. See FOREIGN PLURALS.

chest See BREAST(S).

chesterfield (*n.*) is both a kind of sofa and a fitted overcoat or topcoat with a velvet collar. See also SOFA.

Chicano (*adj., n.*) This word, first printed in the 1950s, is a form of *Mexicano,* as pronounced and apparently first used by Mexican-Americans of themselves. It may for a time have been used derisively by others as well, but it now appears to be a widely accepted nonpejorative Standard name for members of this ethnic group. The plural is *Chicanos,* and the female form is *Chicana* (plural: *Chicanas*).

chide (*v.*) The principal parts are in divided usage: the past tense is either *chided* or *chid,* and the past participle is *chided, chid,* or *chidden,* with the weak verb form, *chided,* more frequently encountered in American English, *chid* and *chidden* in British. When combined with a preposition, *chide* most frequently takes *for,* as in *We'll chide him for his behavior,* but others also occur—you can be *chided on, about,* or *concerning* your sloppy dress or *chided with* or *about* being late.

chief justice (*n.*) The official title of this officer is the "Chief Justice of the United States," but you may also see and hear "Chief Justice of the United States Supreme Court," or the "Chief Justice of the Supreme Court of the United States of America." In Semiformal and Informal contexts, however, and in speech as well, the reference is often simply to *the Chief Justice,* although context must also make clear whether it is of a state or the nation.

childish, childlike (*adjs.*) *Childlike* is usually used of adults, meaning they are "innocent, trusting, or uncomplicated," like children at their best. *Childish,* when used of children, under-scores their immaturity and other youthful qualities; when used of adults, *childish* is pejorative, meaning "immature, unreasonable, foolish, or fretful." *Childishness* is frequently cited as an unfortunate symptom of senility.

chili, chile, chilli (*n.*) The first two spellings are American variants of the name of the pepper and of the familiar dish made with it; *chilli* is a preferred British spelling.

Chinaman, chinaman (*n.*) *Chinaman* is an ethnic slur, taboo in American English; the accepted term, noun (singular and plural) or adjective, is *Chinese.* An echo of the taboo word is in the idiom (now much suppressed as well) *a Chinaman's chance,* which means "no chance at all." In British English *chinaman* (lowercase) is an accepted term in cricket argot, meaning "a lefthanded bowler's off-break to a right-handed batsman."

chintzy (*adj.*) From its literal sense, meaning "characteristic of the fabric *chintz* or looking like it or covered with it," the adjective has undergone what may well turn out to be a permanent figurative pejorative semantic change to a slang or at best a Conversational cluster of meanings, "cheap, penny-pinching, gaudy, trashy."

choice (*n.*) The excessively literal-minded sometimes insist that logically there may be two or three things from which to choose but only one is the *choice.* Not so. *Choice* can indeed mean "the one I choose," but it can also mean "the range of things from which I will choose, the *choices* offered me." In other words, it can mean what the compound adjective *multiple-choice* means. Both meanings are Standard today. See also ALTERNATE (2); OPTION.

Choice as adjective or noun can be tricky, as comparison with federal meat-grading terms will remind you: at one time *prime* was best, *choice* only second-best, and *standard* (or another term) meant something like "the lowest grade acceptable for human consumption."

CHOICE ENGLISH is another name for good, appropriate English, but it is not very exact: it may mean Standard English, Formal English, Oratorical English, or Edited English, or it may mean merely "the language *I* (or *we*) like best—*our* choice."

choir, quire (*nn.*) A *choir* is a group of singers, and its homophone *quire* is a measure for writing paper—"one-twentieth of a ream (480, 500, or 516 sheets)." *Quire* is also a now-obsolete variant spelling of *choir.* See also CHANCEL.

chord, cord (*nn.*) There are really two words spelled *chord*. The musical *chord* is composed of three or more usually concordant notes sounded at the same time, and in mathematics, geometry, and engineering, a *chord* is a line that joins two points on a curve. The musical *chord* comes from *accord*; the math *chord* comes from Greek *chorda,* meaning "string or gut." A *cord* is also a string, and some strings make music. So is it *vocal chords* or *vocal cords, spinal cord* or *spinal chord?* Both spellings are historically accurate, but today's American English pretty much insists on *vocal cord* and *spinal cord.* Still, it is no wonder questions arise.

A *cord* of wood is a measure: a stack four by four by five feet; it was originally the amount that could be tied with a *cord. Cord* is also a fabric—*corduroy* is one such—in which the ribbed texture looks like *cords.*

Christian name See FIRST NAME.

chronic (*adj.*) means "long-lasting, recurrent, constant, or habitual," and in American English it should not be used as an intensifier meaning "bad or severe." *Chronic* headaches recur, but they may or may not be *severe* headaches as well. The *Oxford English Dictionary* has evidence suggesting that *chronic* may be a British slang intensifier, but in American English such use would be Substandard.

chukker See STANZA.

chutzpah, chutzpa (*n.*) means "brashness, audacity, brass." Conversational or Informal in most circumstances, this word is also labeled slang in some dictionaries, but in jocular use it seems to be gaining status. Pronounce it either *HUTS-pah* or *KHOOTS-pah.* See YIDDISH WORDS IN AMERICAN ENGLISH.

-ciate, -ciation, -tiate, -tiation Pronunciation of the medial consonant clusters *-ci-* and *-ti-* differs in different words, especially when the *-tion* ending (sounds like *shun*) follows. Compare these pronunciations:

appreciate: -ci- sounds like either *she* or *see*
appreciation: -ci- sounds like either *she* or *see*
associate: -ci- sounds like either *she* or *see*
association: -ci- sounds like either *she* or *see*
depreciate: -ci- sounds like *she*
depreciation: -ci- sounds like *she*
emaciate: -ci- sounds like *she*
emaciation: -ci- sounds like either *she* or *see*
enunciate: -ci- sounds like *see*
enunciation: -ci- sounds like *see*
negotiate: -ti- sound like *she*
negotiation: -ti- sounds like either *see* or *she*
pronunciation: -ci- sounds like *see*

propitiate: -ti- sounds like *she*
propitiation: -ti- sounds like either *see* or *she*
vitiate: -ti- sounds like *she*
vitiation: -ti- sounds like *she*

cipher, cypher (*n., v.*) Americans use *cipher,* the British, *cypher.* See SPELLING (1).

circle (*v.*) The verb is Standard by itself, as in *We circled the city at about five thousand feet,* and it is idiomatic, not redundant, in combination with *around, round,* and *about,* as in *They circled around the ballroom in a breathless waltz.*

CIRCUMFLEX This mark (ˆ) is printed or written over a vowel in certain foreign languages to suggest the quality of that vowel. After adopting such words, English frequently spells them with or without the *circumflex,* as in the case of the French *fête* (*fete*). See also ACCENT (2); DIACRITICS.

CIRCUMLOCUTION is a matter of style—sometimes a good thing, sometimes not. English offers an almost infinite number of ways of saying things, and users of Standard English do well to avail themselves of as many of those resources as will help them achieve precisely what they want their words to do for them. Some commentators argue that briefer is always better in speech or in prose, and often they're right: *at this point in time, in close proximity to, in view of the fact that,* and *until such time as* are all wordy clichés better replaced by more succinct synonyms. But sometimes *circumlocutions* are useful and pleasant: *Get me a drink,* even with *please* tacked on, is to the point but not very mannerly; *Will you please get me a drink?* is better, and in a formal atmosphere *Would you be good enough to get me a drink?* sounds very fitting indeed. See also PERIPHRASTIC.

circumstances (*n. pl.*) Some purists have been vexed that *under the circumstances* often replaces *in the circumstances,* arguing that *circum* means "round," and that we can be *in* circles, but not *under* them. This is an etymological fallacy: both *in* and *under* have long been Standard when used with *circumstances.* Nor do we insist that people *in difficult circumstances* must have troubles while standing around; they may suffer seated in straight rows if they wish.

cite, site, sight (*nn., vv.*) These homophones are each both noun and verb: *cite,* verb, means "to summon, to quote, or to refer to," and as a noun a *cite* is the clipped form of *citation,* "a reference or quotation." *Site,* noun, is "the place or location of something," and the verb means "to place or locate something at a *site.*" The verb *sight* means "to see something," and the noun *sight* is "the thing seen," as well as "the sense of *sight* itself." All are Standard except *cite* as noun, which is lexicographers' jargon.

citizen (*n.*) has three current Standard meanings: (1) someone born in a particular place or nation; (2) a voting member of a republican city, nation, or state, who has various rights and responsibilities because of that status; and (3) a civilian, as contrasted with a soldier or other official. This last sense occurs in the common phrase *an ordinary citizen,* meaning one with only the powers and status conferred by that citizenship.

civilian (*n.*) means "a lay person or an ordinary citizen, not a uniformed soldier or a member of another uniformed group." It is Standard in that sense, as it is also when used to distinguish a person or persons from a group of others not necessarily uniformed: *The zoning board is composed entirely of civilians; town officers and other officials many not serve on it.* Compare CITIZEN.

clad (*adj.*) is a variant past participle of the verb *clothe* (the regular past participle is *clothed*). It is sometimes thought to be old-fashioned but in fact is still in common use in current Standard English (*warmly clad skiers*; *stainless-clad copper pans*; *She was clad top to toe in fur*).

claim (*v.*) means "to ask for, to demand, to state as a fact, and to assert." All these meanings are Standard, although Fowler and others once claimed that *claim* should be used primarily to mean "to demand recognition of a right" and that it ought not to be used to mean "to assert." But it is, frequently and appropriately.

clandestine (*adj.*) means "secret, furtive, or concealed," sometimes because what is concealed is illegal, sometimes simply because it is to be kept unknown. Stress the second syllable.

clang See CLING.

CLASS DIALECT See SOCIAL DIALECT.

classic (*adj., n.*), **classical** (*adj.*) In some of their senses these are synonymous, but in others they are distinctive: A *classical profile* means much the same as a *classic* profile, one based on the norms of ancient Greek and Roman statuary. Artifacts whose reputations stay bright over the centuries, are *classic*—as in *cars*—and *classical*—as in *music*. Sometimes, though, *classical music* simply means "serious music," as contrasted with popular music; in that sense, a piece of *classical music* could be only a few hours old. *The Iliad* and *The Aeneid* are *classical lit-*

erature, and they are also *classics*. Indeed, all the art and literature of the Greeks and Romans is *classical* (because that is the period of origin), but as individual pieces only the best among them are *classics* "for all time." The *classical languages* are still Greek and Latin.

CLASSIFYING GENITIVE See DESCRIPTIVE GENITIVE.

CLAUSE For most grammatical purposes a *clause* is a syntactic structure containing both a subject and a predicate. An independent clause, or main clause, can stand alone; it is a sentence. A dependent clause cannot stand alone but must hang from (in Latin *dependere* means "hang down from") an independent clause or some part of one. In *That's the car that I hope to own,* the dependent clause is *that I hope to own.* See also SITUATION UTTERANCE.

CLAUSE MODIFIERS See PHRASE AND CLAUSE MODIFIERS.

clean 1 (*adv., adj.*), **cleanly** (*adv.*) The adjective is quite regular, as in *a clean break,* but *clean* is also a Standard flat adverb, as in *The robbers got clean away.* For other adverbial uses, *cleanly* is more frequent: *The kitchen floor had been cleanly mopped. He fought all his fights cleanly.* But *He always fought clean* is also Standard.

clean 2, cleanse (*vv.*), **cleaner, cleanser** (*nn.*) These pairs are synonyms, but for some to *cleanse* something is somehow to make it more nearly spotless, more nearly unblemished, a bit more figuratively and ideally *clean* than just to *clean* it. Perhaps this explains why some advertisers seem to believe a *cleaner* (a soap or other cleaning agent, or the name of the person who does the cleaning) sounds somehow less effective than a *cleanser. Cleanser* is also a dialectal name for a dry-cleaning shop in parts of southern New England.

The verb *clean* also combines into several phrasal idioms: *to clean up* is "to settle, to clear up" (*The judge cleaned up a big backlog of cases*) or "to make a large profit" (*Investors who sold off the stock on Thursday really cleaned up*). This latter sense is slang, as is *to clean up on,* meaning "to beat badly" (*The champ really cleaned up on the challenger*). *To clean out* means "to take away everything," "to drive out or expel," and especially "to strip of all financial resources"; *to clean house* is "to get rid of everything and everyone undesirable"; and *to come clean* is slang meaning "to confess, to tell all."

cleanly (*adj.*), **cleanliness** (*n.*) *Cleanly* (pronounced *KLEN-lee*) is fairly rare these days, but the noun (pronounced *KLEN-lee-nes*), a result of functional shift from the adjective, is very commonly encountered and is "next to godliness" in the cliché.

clean room (*n.*) This compound (pronounced *KLEEN-ROOM*) is a contaminant-free room devoted to medical procedures, scientific laboratory work, or manufacturing processes requiring an absolutely clean and sterile atmosphere for the assembling of precision parts.

cleanse, cleanser See CLEAN (2).

clear 1 (*v.*) has several combined forms: *to clear away* is "to remove clutter from a space" (*We cleared away all the downed trees and branches*); *to clear off* is "to go away, to leave" (*The owner ordered us to clear off*) or "for the bad weather to go away"; *to clear up* means "to remove all irrelevant matters or unnecessary things" (*His testimony cleared up the problem*), "for symptoms to disappear" (*His headaches cleared up after the change in diet*), or "for the weather to brighten" (*The clouds cleared up, and the sun came out*). *To clear the air* is also idiomatic in a figurative sense, meaning "to rid the atmosphere of unpleasantness, emotional stresses, and the like," and *to be in the clear* means "to be free of suspicion, physical danger, or other threats."

clear 2, clearly (*advs.*) *Clearly* is the regular adverbial form; *clear* is a flat adverb: *He was clearly their best outfielder. You could see clear to the horizon.* Both are Standard.

cleave (*vv.*) This curious pair of Standard verbs has diametrically opposed meanings. *Cleave* (1) is a transitive verb, from Old English *cleofan*; its principal parts are *cleave, cleft, clove,* or *cleaved,* and *cleft, cleaved,* or *cloven,* and it means "to divide or split": *His ax clove* [*cleaved* or *cleft*] *the oak logs easily.* As the divided usages indicate, this *cleave* is a strong verb beginning to adopt weak verb forms as well, and all its uses seem to have a rather literary or perhaps even an archaic flavor. For the participial adjective of this verb, American English uses either *cloven* (*a cloven hoof*) or *cleft* (*a cleft palate*).

Cleave (2) is an intransitive verb, from Old English *cleofian*; its principal parts are those of a regular weak verb, *cleave, cleaved, cleaved,* and it means "to stick to, to cling to": *The marriage ceremony advises husbands and wives to cleave to each other for the rest of their lives*—almost precisely the opposite of *cleave* (1).

clench, clinch (*vv.*) *Clinch* is a variant of *clench,* and both mean "to close or grip tightly," as in *He clenched his fist,* and "to bend nails over to make them hold firmly," as in *He pounded the nails flat, clinching them into the plywood.* But *clinch* also means "to settle a deal," as in *His agreement to our terms clinched the deal,* and "to make a victory secure," as in *His ninth-inning home run clinched the win for our side.* In boxing, *clinch* is both verb, describing two boxers trapping each other's arms in such a way that neither can strike the other, and noun, meaning the act itself. There are also familiar slang meanings, taken figuratively from the boxing senses, meaning "to embrace" and "an embrace," respectively.

clergyman See PRIEST.

clever (*adj.*) *Clever* began by meaning "skillful with the hands" (*She's a clever potter*), and then it came also to mean "quick-witted, intelligent" (*She's a clever lawyer*). The second meaning, however, has become ambiguous: *a clever lawyer* may be "quick, witty, ingenious, and resourceful" or "superficial, not substantial, perhaps not quite ethical." Control ambiguity with context.

clew See CLUE.

CLICHE is spelled with or without an acute accent over the final *-e,* and is a usage label meaning that an expression, figure, or word is shopworn, predictable, and possibly ineffective. *Clichés* seldom have any juice left in them and hence add little fresh flavor to your prose, although they are sometimes less dull in conversation than in writing. *Pretty as a picture* no longer conjures up a very clear image.

client, customer, patron (*nn.*) Preserve for each of these its unique sense, even if they overlap in other uses. A *patron* is of course "a benefactor," as in *a patron of the arts,* but the word also means "a regular customer." A *customer* is someone who is buying goods, or sometimes services (there is also a Conversational use, as in *She's a tough customer,* beginning presumably as an extended sense involving a *customer* hard to satisfy, but coming ultimately to mean little more than "anyone hard to please or persuade"), and we also have many other names for the person who hopes to be served in one way or another: *shopper, diner, consumer, buyer,* and the like. A *client* is someone for whom a professional such as a lawyer or physician renders professional services. All these terms, however, have generalized, *client* in particular, as more and more vocations come to consider themselves professions. As H. L. Mencken and Sinclair Lewis pointed out, apparently people don't want to be known as *real estate agents* when they can be called *realtors* or, better still, *professional realtors*. As a result, grocers and gardeners have both *customers* and *clients* these days—but then so do social workers and prostitutes.

climactic (*adj., n.*), **climatic** (*adj.*), **climacteric** (*n.*) The first two of these get confused only because of misspelling or mispronunciation: *climactic* refers to *climax, climatic* to *climate,* but sometimes *climactic* will be pronounced or spelled without the full medial consonant cluster as *klei-MAT-ik* instead of *klei-MAK-tik.* These errors can not only mislead your listeners or readers; they can also serve as shibboleths to judge you by. Compare ANT-ARCTIC; ARCTIC.

Climacteric (pronounced *klei-MAK-tuhr-ik*) is closely related to *climax,* as *climate* is not, and its meaning is "a point or period in life when major physiological change takes place"; the usual example is menopause, but puberty is another. There is also a generalized sense, "any very important or critical period in life."

climb (*v.*) The principal parts today are *climb, climbed,* and *climbed*; all other forms, such as *clim* or *clum,* are dialectal and Substandard today. Some commentators have thought that *climb up* is redundant and *climb down* impossible because *climbing* goes only up. But the differences between *climb* and *climb up* are mostly stylistic variants (*Climb [up] the stairs*), although *climb up on* is idiomatic (*Climb up on grandpa's lap*). As for *climbing down,* in most contexts *climb* means "to go up," and to reverse the direction you must say *climb down.* Moreover, the figurative use is very important and requires *down: When he realized we had the evidence, he climbed down from his denial very quickly.*

clinch See CLENCH.

cling, clang (*vv.*) *Cling*'s principal parts once were *cling, clang, clung,* but today they are *cling, clung* (not *clang*), *clung* (not *clinged* or *clanged*), which only very young children and some speakers of Vulgar English employ today).

Clang is another verb entirely (*clang, clanged, clanged*), an echoic word meaning "to make a loud ringing sound": *The warning bell clanged urgently.*

CLIPPING, CLIPPED FORMS, CLIPPED WORDS These are respectively the process of cutting off the ends of words and the shortened words that result. Philologists usually distinguish between *clipped forms,* which have lost the rearmost parts of the original words, and aphetic forms, which have lost their fronts. In that distinction, *fan* is a *clipped form* of *fanatic, pike* an aphetic form of *turnpike.* But the terms *clipping* and *clipped form* are also used generically for the cutting off of either end of the original word. Usually these abbreviations begin as slang (*deli* from *delicatessen,* and *psych, math, soc,* and *chem* on nearly every college campus), but lasting *clipped forms* frequently become Informal (*flu,* from *influenza*) or even Standard (*bus,* from *omnibus*). See ABBREVIATIONS; APHERESIS; APHESIS; JARGON; SLANG.

clique (*n.*) The French pronunciation, *KLEEK,* is more frequently heard than the anglicized *KLIK,* but both are Standard.

clone (*n., v.*) The original biological meaning was "genetically identical cells or organisms descended from a single ancestor and so identical in all respects." The word is now Standard as a noun with a generalized meaning of "a duplicate," as in *an IBM-PC clone,* and as a verb meaning "to make a duplicate," as in *I wish they could clone our best teachers.* In recent criticism of art, books, motion pictures, and the like, as well as in discussing topics such as teenagers or cult types, to be a *clone* or to create *clones* is frequently used in a pejorative sense: *Her recent pictures are clones of the first one, and they're even less worth seeing.*

close proximity is a redundancy, since *proximity* means "closeness," but it is probably more important to note that *close proximity* is hyperbolic. And it is only sensible to note too that this locution occurs frequently enough to be considered by some a cliché.

closure See CLOTURE.

clothes (*n. pl.*) This word almost always rhymes with *chose,* and rarely (usually only affectedly) is it made to rhyme with *loathes. KLOZ* is the Standard way to say it.

cloture, closure (*nn.*) *Cloture* (pronounced *KLO-chuhr*) is a technical term in parliamentary procedure: a vote of *cloture* "closes debate and puts the matter before the body to an immediate vote without further discussion." *Closure* is the general term for "a closing, an end." Both are Standard.

club soda See SODA.

clue, clew (*n., v.*) *Clue* is the spelling for almost all uses today except the nautical, wherein a *clew* is "a lower corner of a square sail or the aft lower corner of a triangular mainsail"; wherein hammocks are suspended by lines called *clews*; and wherein *to clew up* is "to roll cord into a coil or ball or to raise the lower corners of a square sail by means of *clew lines.*" *Clew* is also an older spelling of *clue*, rarely used today. *Clue*, noun, is anything, information or object, that leads toward the solution of a mystery. *To clue* is a verb meaning "to indicate or provide with *clues*," and *to clue people in* is a Conversational or Informal idiom, a combined form meaning "to provide them with needed information, to bring them up to date."

co- (*prefix*) Three usage questions frequently arise: (1) Does *co-* mean "equal to" or "subordinate to" when it occurs with words such as *coworker* and *copilot?* Answer: it means either and both, and the referents and context will control. A *coworker* usually is neither subordinate nor superior to a fellow *worker*, but the *copilot* is always subordinate to the *pilot*. (2) Do newly created words using the prefix always begin as slang, or are words such as *cohost* and *co-agent* Standard from the start? Answer: such words, and nonce words using the *co-* prefix as well, are usually Standard almost at once, so long as the concept is clear: for example, *sled-dog drivers* and their *codrivers* are probably in the same relationship to their enterprise as *pilot* and *copilot* are to theirs: one is *captain* and in overall charge, and the other is the *mate*; and only one can actually be at the controls at any given time. (3) How should the *co-* prefix be attached to the base word, with a hyphen or without? Answer: usually without a space or hyphen (*coincidence, coordinate*), but occasionally when the base word begins with *o* (*co-opt, co-own*—but see also DIERESIS) or when a word is so new as to look odd and risk misreading without a hyphen (*co-anchor* or *co-belligerent*), a hyphen will help. The prefix *co-* means "together, joint," as in *co-owner*; "equally, mutually," as in *coextensive, cooperative*; "partner with, associate to," as in *coauthor, coproducer*, or *to cosign* [*a note*]; and "assistant or subordinate to," as in *coadjutor*. And sometimes the "equal or subordinate" issue is ambiguous, as in *cohost, co-anchor*. (There are also mathematical senses meaning "complement," as in *cosine, cotan-*

gent.) Three other forms occur: *col-* (before *l*, as in *collaborate*); *com-* (before *b, p,* and *m,* as in *combine, companion,* and *commiserate*); and *con-* (before other sounds, as in *contaminate*).

coalesce (*v.*) combines with the prepositions *in* or *into* (*My separate worries finally coalesced in [into] one nightmarish problem*), with *on* (*Our only hope is that our several plans will coalesce on a single venture*), with *with* (*Our small programs coalesced nicely with their two large ones*), and with *around* (*Our membership coalesced around the one leader we had left*).

coal oil See KEROSENE.

coarse (*adj.*), **course** (*n., v.*) The spelling of these homophones is the only problem; the adjective, in all its senses, is *coarse: His language was inexcusably coarse.* The noun and verb in all their senses are spelled *course: Our course is clear. The sweat coursed down his face in rivulets.* The academic term *course description* is a compound noun; in it *course* is a noun adjunct.

COASTAL NEW ENGLAND DIALECT See EASTERN NEW ENGLAND REGIONAL DIALECT.

coca See CACAO.

cockamamie (*adj.*) is a slang word, possibly American in origin but of uncertain etymology, meaning "confused, uncertain, worthless."

cock a snook (at) *To cock a snook at* is "to thumb your nose at." It was probably slang at the outset, but now it is Standard and a euphemism.

coco, cocoa See CACAO.

coed, co-ed (*adj., n.*) The noun, meaning "a female college or university student," is a once-slang, once-Informal term now rare in that sense. The noun is not yet archaic, perhaps, but it is headed that way, not least because it suggests that female students are the exception instead of the norm they are. *Coed* (or *co-ed*) as an adjective, however, is still in regular use; a clipped form of the adjective *coeducational*, it is most frequently used to distinguish single-sex colleges from colleges that enroll students of both sexes; a *coed dormitory* houses students of both sexes. Both spellings are Standard, *coed* the more frequent.

coequal (*adj., n.*) The word is Standard in both functions, and it is Formal but not redundant. See CO-.

coffin See CASKET.

cognate (*adj.*, *n.*) The adjective means "related, as by blood" and hence refers to words from different languages that come from the same common root (*corpse* and *corps,* for example, from the Latin *corpus*). The noun *cognate* means "a word that has such a relationship with another word," as English *hound* is a *cognate* of German *Hund*.

cohere, coherence See ADHERE.

COHERENCE Speech or writing that has *coherence* is logical, consistent, and clear. It hangs together. See ADHERE.

cohesion, cohesive See ADHERE.

cohort (*n.*) was originally the name for one-tenth of a Roman legion, but it has generalized, especially in American English, in ways not every commentator likes. It came first to mean "any group or gathering of soldiers" and then "a group of any sort." Later it came to mean "supporters" in the political sense, and then it took on in this country the meaning "a group of individuals," rather than "a unit of troops." And so it came to mean "friends" or even "stalwarts, companions, partners, or buddies." And all these senses are now Standard, the earlier, more specialized ones needing careful contextual control to prevent ambiguity.

coiffeur, coiffeuse, coiffure, barber, hairdresser (*nn.*) A *coiffeur* is a male hairdresser, a *coiffeuse,* a female hairdresser, and a *coiffure* a hairdo. The two French terms for *hairdressers* occur now primarily only in tony hairdressing establishments if at all: *hairdresser* is now a more commonly used word, since it is both inclusive as regards the sex of the practitioner and unambiguous as regards the sex of the customers the practitioner serves. (Many of today's *hairdressers* and *barbers* regularly cut the hair of both females and males.) Stress *coiffeur* and *coiffure* on the final syllable—*KWAH-FYOOR*.

coined titles See FALSE TITLES.

col- See CO-.

cola, COLA (*nn.*) *Cola* is the name of the tree whose seeds are the base for the flavoring of certain soft drinks, which are also called *colas*. *Cola* is also the second element in several trade names for such soft drinks. *COLA* is an acronym from wage and other financial matters: it stands for *Cost of Living Adjustment*. Both words are pronounced *KO-luh*. See SALARY INCREMENT.

cold slaw, coleslaw, cole slaw (*n.*) The Dutch word *koolsla* ("sliced or chopped cabbage") ended up in American English more or less as it sounded, as *coleslaw* or *cole slaw* (both spellings are Standard, although the one-word version is apparently gaining ground), but folk etymology has led many Common and Vulgar spellers to make it *cold slaw,* no doubt reflecting their pronunciation as well, and that spelling still occurs occasionally in Nonstandard menu prose.

coliseum, Colosseum (*nn.*) The generic English spelling for a large stadium or building containing an amphitheater or sports arena is *coliseum,* but the name of the original Roman amphitheater is the *Colosseum*.

collaborate (*v.*) In its combined uses, *collaborate* is usually followed by the prepositions *in, on, about,* and *concerning,* as in *We collaborated in [on, about, concerning] our public relations efforts,* each phrase indicating the topic or effort in which there was cooperation. *With* also occurs when we want to indicate with whom we *collaborated: We collaborated with them on our public relations efforts.* See also COOPERATE.

collaborator, collaborationist (*nn.*) *Collaborator* is both an unexceptional, semantically neutral term for anyone who works cooperatively with others on a project or in an enterprise and, in a specialized and pejorative sense particularly stressed during and since World War II, a person who treasonably cooperates with a foreign invader. The other pejorative name for that sort of traitor is *collaborationist,* which has no other meaning. See QUISLING.

collectable, collectible (*adj.*, *n.*) These Standard spellings are interchangeable regardless of part of speech: *The collectable [collectible] bills were piled on the desk. She has cabinets full of china collectibles [collectables]*.

COLLECTIVE NOUNS are nouns designating a class or group of individual persons or things, all of them members of that class or group (such as *class, flock, group, herd, team, committee, bunch,* and *cluster*). These nouns are distinctive as subjects because they can take either singular or plural verbs and subsequent pronouns: *The committee votes on its procedures tomorrow* or *The committee vote on their procedures tomorrow.* These *collectives* are interesting too in that they can also be inflected for the plural to designate more than one such group of similar individuals or things; then they always take plural verbs. See AGREEMENT OF SUBJECTS AND VERBS (3).

collide (*v.*), **collision** (*n.*) It has often been argued that these words can properly be used, literally or figuratively, only of two bodies in motion, not of one at rest and one in motion. Not true. People may *collide with* brick walls, and innovative reforms may be *in collision with* entrenched privilege. Such uses are Standard, although when the corner of the dresser *collides with* your bare foot, that usage is jocular and wry.

COLLOQUIAL, COLLOQUIALISM is the label many dictionaries put on words and meanings that are not suitable for use at the highest levels of the spoken language or in Formal and some Semiformal writing. *Persnickety,* for example, is a *colloquialism* in its meaning "fussy, overparticular," and most contractions—i.e., *isn't, shouldn't, it's, they're*—are *Colloquial.* Some dictionary users incorrectly understand *Colloquial* to be a pejorative label, but it is actually no more pejorative than a field-restrictive label (such as *mathematics* or *music*) would be: a *Colloquial* usage is Standard English, but only in a *Colloquial* situation. In this book any locution labeled Conversational or *Colloquial* is acceptable at the Conversational or *Colloquial* levels of speech (mainly Intimate, Casual, and Impromptu) and in the written levels that imitate them (Informal and Semiformal). See LEVELS OF USAGE.

collude (*v.*), **collusion** (*n.*) These words are always pejorative: they involve cooperation for dishonest, illegal, unethical, or immoral purposes. *To collude* is "to connive."

COLON This punctuation mark (:) can (1) signal a forthcoming list, as in *He sold sundries: needles, thread, pins, buttons, and thimbles*; (2) introduce a further amplification or a summary of what has just been said, as in *After years of work, he finally had it: the championship*; (3) let one clause explain another, as in *He was late: his car had broken down*; (4) lead into a long quotation, as in *Jefferson wrote: When in the course of human events, . . .*; and (5) do such separating tasks as these: *Henry IV, Pt. I, II:iv:122; Dear Sir:; New York: Longman, 1987; and 11:15* A.M.

colored, of color See AFRICAN(-)AMERICAN.

Colosseum See COLISEUM.

com- See CO-.

coma, comma (*nn.*) Inadvertent confusion of these spellings can be disastrous: a *coma* to the layperson is "a state of unconsciousness," and a *comma* is a punctuation mark. (*Coma* is also the spelling of another word that has several very technical meanings: in astronomy it is the technical name for "a part of the head of a comet," in botany it is "a tuft of hairs on certain seeds," and in optics it is an "aberrant image of a point of light, one that looks like the 'hair' on a comet.") Write *coma* for *comma* or *comma* for *coma,* and laughter will drown out your message.

comatose (*n.*) The first syllable is appropriately pronounced like either *comb* or *calm.*

combine (*n.*) (stressed on the first syllable) can sometimes be unexceptionable as the name for a political or commercial group: British English seems almost always to have considered it an unprejudicial term, although American English used to use it only as a pejorative. Today American English uses the word either as a pejorative or as a noncommittal term, carefully controlling it by context. The other American use of *combine,* the name of that huge harvesting machine that cuts, threshes, separates the grain, and ties up the straw, all in one *combined (kuhm-BEIND)* operation, poses no usage difficulties.

COMBINED FORMS: PREPOSITIONS AND ADVERBS COMBINED WITH VERBS English makes much use of *combined forms* (sometimes called phrasal verbs) to create idioms such as these with the verb *to run: to run over* (a curb or a new song); *to run through,* meaning "to pierce with a rapier" or "to rehearse"; *to run down* (a reputation or a pedestrian); *to run up* (a bill or the hill); and dozens more. *Combined forms* are still another way English has of expanding its vocabulary.

combo See BAND.

come (*v.*) in idiomatic phrases such as *Come Sunday* is Standard: *Come Sunday we'll be finished* grammatically is a reversal of subject and verb, with the verb in the subjunctive.

come and See TRY AND.

comfort, comforter See QUILT.

comic, comical (*adj.*) These two are interchangeable in many uses; where there is a distinction it may involve the planned (*a comic situation*) versus the inadvertent (*a comical situation*).

COMMA 1 This punctuation mark (,) usually separates one element of a locution from another without actually setting them completely apart. It separates independent clauses joined by coordinating conjunctions such as *and* (*He ordered them, and he paid for them*) and sets off nonrestrictive modifiers, appositives, and other parenthetical elements (*Fred, who teaches Spanish, is being promoted; George Smith, my uncle, has died; His humor is, I think, bizarre*).

The *comma* also separates sentence adverbs and adverbial clauses and phrases from the main clause they precede, and if the adverbial clause interrupts the main clause, *commas* surround it (*Furthermore, I don't believe that she's guilty; I don't believe, furthermore, that she's guilty*). *Commas* separate words in series (*a horse, a dog, and a cow*; note that American English prefers and many editors require the *comma* after *dog*, but the British rarely use it, and some Americans don't use it either) and in a string of adjectives modifying a noun (*a dark, windy, unpleasant day*). The *comma* can introduce, enclose, and end direct quotations (*I said, "Go home"; I said, "Go home," and I threw him out; "Go home," I said*). It also separates contradictory locutions (*It's green, not blue*), sets off direct address (*Yes, Fred, I'll be there*), and marks off certain rhetorical questions (*He's a fool, isn't he?*). And the *comma* can make clear that a word or words have been omitted in an otherwise repetitive locution, as in *Some like it hot; others, cold*, and serves (see COMMA FOR CLARITY) to prevent ambiguity, as in *For John, Henry was a model*.

The comma also performs a range of stylistic chores (see STYLE), which sometimes differ slightly from publisher to publisher and stylebook to stylebook. It may separate date and year (*July 4, 1776*), city from state (*Chicago, Illinois*), day from date (*Monday, April 10*), a name from a title in apposition (*David Hankins, Building Monitor*), and the last name from the first, when they are presented in reverse order (*O'Hara, James D.*). In each of these cases, a comma may (and sometimes must) follow the second element as well. Commas also mark the thousands in a long number (*$10,000,000*) and often signal the end of salutation and complimentary close in personal letters (*Dear Milton, Love, Harriet*).

See also COMA.

COMMA 2, INVERTED *Inverted commas* are quotation marks, double or single, in British English.

COMMA FAULT, COMMA BLUNDER, COMMA ERROR, COMMA SPLICE

When teachers of composition discover that students have tacked two independent clauses together with only a comma to join them, they fall on that flaw and mark it with one of these terms. Edited English almost never lets comma splices through, so we seldom see them in print, although they are common problems for the inexperienced. There are three Standard ways to punctuate sequential independent clauses: join them with a *comma* plus a coordinating conjunction such as *and*, separate them completely with a period and use a capital letter to begin the second clause (now a new sentence), or link them loosely with a semicolon, which will suggest a logical linkage of some sort between them but only minimal grammatical connection.

In fiction, poetry, and other imaginative literary forms you may occasionally encounter *comma faults* used deliberately to create special effects such as informality or another mood, as in *I'm sick, I'm tired* or *Maybe she'll call, maybe she won't*. Some American authors use a British style of punctuating linked independent clauses, distinguishing between short clauses and long ones, and using *commas* between short ones, where most American stylebooks and editors would insist on semicolons, regardless of length of clauses.

COMMA FOR CLARITY *As he climbed, the stairs got steeper.* Without the *comma*, you might read *As he climbed the stairs* and then have to begin again to find a subject for *got steeper*. In speech, intonation would make the syntax clear; in writing, use a *comma for clarity*.

COMMA SPLICE See COMMA FAULT.

COMMAND This rhetorically defined sentence type (also called an imperative sentence) usually contains only a predicate, as in *Eat your broccoli*, although it may also have a noun in direct address, as in *Spot, go home!* But it lacks a subject: *Leave the room at once. Send me your address.* (Some school grammars teach that the command has a subject, *you*, "understood": *[You] Stop!*) The other two sentence types are the question and the statement.

commander, commandant, commando (*nn.*) A *commander* in the word's generalized sense is, like a *commandant*, simply "the officer in charge, the commanding officer of the unit, large or small (the abbreviation is *the C.O.*)." The specialized sense of *commander* is "the Navy and Coast Guard rank below captain and above lieutenant commander (equivalent of the Army lieutenant colonel)." A *commando* was originally a Boer Afrikaans name for a military unit; the British adopted the term as a name for special group of raiding troops, and Americans now use the term as well, both for that type of unit and for its members. *Commander* and *commando* are stressed on the second syllable, but *commandant* displays its French origins in its pronunciation, with the primary stress on the third syllable: *KAHM-en-DAHNT*.

commence (*v.*) Some people insist that *to commence* instead of *to begin* or *start* is inflated diction that ought to be suppressed in favor of a simpler word. But *to embark on, to commence, to set* or *venture forth,* and a range of other words are perfectly good in their place, for variety if not for elegance. See ELEGANT VARIATION.

commend (*v.*) means "to praise someone for something," as in *She commended him for his thoughtfulness,* and "to recommend or to entrust something to someone," as in *He commended the defense of his reputation to his friends.*

commensurate (*adj.*) can take either *with* or *to: Her wit is commensurate with* [*to*] *her good looks.*

commentate (*v.*) is a back-formation (probably from the noun *commentator*) that some conservatives want to suppress in favor of *comment. Commentate* has been around for a good while, however, and it does have a specialized sense that reflects what commentators do that isn't quite the same as what *comment* means: "to give a continuous running comment on an event taking place just then," "to do a commentary." Still, remember that a good many purists still don't like this word, particularly in Edited English. Compare ORIENTATE.

commiserate (*v.*) is used mainly as an intransitive verb these days, followed by either *with* or *over* or both these prepositions: *We commiserated with each other over our consistently bad luck.*

commitment (*n.*) is spelled with only one medial *-t-,* even though *committing, committed, committal,* and *committee* have two. See CONSONANTS (2).

committee See COLLECTIVE NOUNS.

common See MUTUAL.

commonality, commonalty (*nn.*) *Commonality* means "the common people as a group," as opposed to "the nobility" or "the wealthy" or "the few," and it has another sense, "those characteristics held in common within a group," as in *Hiking, camping, and canoeing were big parts of their commonality of interests. Commonalty* is easily confused with *commonality* both in speech and writing, and it overlaps the base sense of *commonality,* "the common people." But *commonalty* also means "a group or corporate body and its membership." It is a relatively low frequency word.

COMMON ENGLISH is the English used by that portion of the population that has not mastered Standard English but avoids the obvious marks of Vulgar English usage in syntax, morphology, and vocabulary. For example, *He does* is Standard and Common, *He do* is Vulgar, and *He don't* occurs in both Vulgar and Common English, but not in Standard. *A very bad cold* is Standard, *an awful* [*a real*] *bad cold* is typical of Common. See STANDARD.

COMMON NOUNS See PROPER NOUNS.

common sense (*n.*), **common-sense, commonsense** (*adj.*) The noun is spelled as two words, the adjective either with a hyphen or as one word.

commune (*n., v.*) The verb is pronounced *kuh-MYOON,* but the noun in all its senses puts a primary stress on the first syllable and a tertiary on the second: *KAH-MYOON.*

communicate (*v.*), **communication** (*n.*) These words have become much higher frequency words in recent years, and some purists have complained that they've even become vogue words. Nevertheless, they are both Standard. In combined uses, *communicate* usually takes *with,* but sometimes *to: I'll communicate with my friends; I'll communicate my views to them.*

commute (*n., v.*), **commuter, commutation** (*nn.*) *To commute* sometimes means "to exchange one thing for another," often "to substitute a less severe penalty for another," as in *to commute a sentence of death to life imprisonment.* That use is Standard. *To commute to work* is also Standard, as are *commuters* themselves, whether the referents are the travelers or the buses, vans, or short-flight airlines and their planes on which these people travel. *Commutation,* as the trip itself, the process of commuting, or *the commutation of a death sentence to life imprisonment,* is also Standard. Some dictionaries, however, still label the noun *commute,* meaning the trip itself, either Colloquial or Informal.

comparable See INCOMPARABLE.

COMPARATIVE, COMPARATIVE DEGREE The name of the second or middle degree of comparison in adjectives and adverbs, the *comparative* (as in *faster*) is a degree greater or more than the positive (*fast*), but not the greatest or best, the superlative (*fastest*). See also ABSOLUTE COMPARATIVES; ADJECTIVES (1); ADVERBS (1); DOUBLE COMPARATIVE; IMPLICIT COMPARISON; POSITIVE DEGREE; SUPERLATIVE DEGREE USED OF TWO.

comparatively (*adv.*) Some argue that *comparatively* should be used only when a literal comparison is stated and never used to mean "fairly." But it is, because it does, and it has for a long time been Standard in that sense: *We've had comparatively good weather this year.* The meaning has generalized.

compare (*v.*), **contrast** (*n., v.*) *Compare* usually implies that a discussion will emphasize similarities; *contrast* usually implies that it will emphasize differences. Hence the teacher's frequent directive: *compare and contrast.* The noun *contrast* is pronounced **KAHN-TRAST**, the verb either *kuhn-TRAST* or **KAHN-TRAST**.

compare to, compare with These are in most instances interchangeable: *I'll compare Mary to other dancers I've known* and *I'll compare Mary with other dancers I've known* mean much the same thing. After the past participle *compared,* *with* and *to* again can occur interchangeably: *Compared with [to] mine, your car looks new.*

COMPARISON See COMPARATIVE and all references therein; FALSE COMPARISON.

COMPARISON, ILLOGICAL See FALSE COMPARISON.

COMPARISON OF ADJECTIVES See ADJECTIVES (1).

COMPARISON OF ADVERBS See ADVERBS (1).

compass, a pair of compasses (*nn.*) The two instruments, each called a *compass,* are the magnetic one for finding direction and the pair of dividers used for measuring or drawing circles. The latter is also called *a pair of compasses* and in that construction is usually construed as singular: *This pair of compasses is broken.*

compatible (*adj.*) In combination with prepositions, *compatible* usually is followed by *with* and sometimes by *to: A transformer will make your hair dryer compatible with [to] European voltages.*

compel, impel (*vv.*) *Compel* means "to force": *The principal compelled me to stay after school.* *Impel* means "to force forward, to push ahead," but it is frequently used figuratively, and it often suggests a moral force at work: *My sense of guilt impelled me to confess.*

compendious (*adj.*) was borrowed from the Latin meaning "small," and its predominant sense once was "concise." But today many people seem to understand it to mean "comprehensive, fully detailed." This rather striking semantic change is still in progress, and you should not assume that all your readers and listeners will be aware of the "concise" sense.

compendium (*n.*) has, like *compendious,* undergone considerable semantic change from the meaning some dictionaries give it: "a concise but comprehensive summary or abstract." Today it frequently means simply "a collection," often "a comprehensive collection," and not necessarily "an abridgement of a collection." Its plurals are either *compendiums* or *compendia.* See FOREIGN PLURALS.

competence, competency (*nn.*) *Competence* means both "a sufficient amount to live on, to meet one's needs" and "having legal or practical ability to perform." *Competency* means the same things but is less frequently used, except in educational argot, where *competencies* are the various skills pupils are to be taught and teachers are to be prepared to teach. The plural *competences* occurs infrequently.

complacence, complacency (*nn.*) Both mean "quiet satisfaction, contentment, or smug self-satisfaction." Use either, but be aware that the pejorative sense is strong and will likely override the idea of "guiltless contentment" unless you control it in context.

complacent, complaisant, compliant (*adjs.*) These three afford several chances for confusion. *Complacent* is the adjective that belongs with the nouns *complacence* and *complacency.* *Complaisant* means "obliging, willing to please." *Compliant* means "willing to obey, submissive." Also similar are the pronunciations of *complacent* (*kuhm-PLAIS-ent* or *kuhm-PLAIZ-ent*) and *complaisant* (*kuhm-PLAIZ-ent, kuhm-PLAIS-ent,* or *KAHM-pluh-zent*). The quite differently pronounced *compliant* is stressed on the second syllable: *kuhm-PLEI-ent.*

complaint See PLAINTIFF.

complaisant See COMPLACENT.

compleat (*adj.*) This obsolete spelling of the adjective *complete* suggests an air of antiquity that seems to please some of those who name things, usually books for which they wish to claim *compleat* authority, as in Izaak Walton's *The Compleat Angler* (1653), where this form of the adjective got its start. Use such quaintnesses only with great restraint.

complected, complexioned (*adjs.*) *Complected* is an Americanism in wide use despite outcry against it as provincial, dialectal, or otherwise Nonstandard. In fact, it is every bit as Standard as *complexioned,* but you should be aware that many conservatives still consider it a shibboleth.

complement, compliment (*nn., vv.*) These homophones are spelled differently. The mnemonic reminds you that *to complete* is "to provide the *complement,* that is, to fill out the *complete* set" and *complete* and *complement* are both spelled with *-ple-. Compliment,* verb and noun, meaning "praise or flattery" and "to give it," is spelled with a medial *-pli-.* See SUPPLEMENT.

complementary, complimentary (*adjs.*) These homophones, like *complement* and *compliment,* differ in meaning and spelling, and it is therefore only in writing and spelling or in ambiguous oral contexts that they can be confused. Something *complementary* "completes, supplies what is missing"; something *complimentary* "praises, expresses courtesy or admiration," as in *The reviews were all highly complimentary,* or "is given free of charge," as in *The menu said we could have complimentary second cups of coffee.* See SUPPLEMENTARY.

COMPLEMENTS are grammatical structures that regularly follow verbs and with them make up full predicates. Chief among them are (following transitive verbs) indirect and direct objects and object complements and (following linking verbs) predicate nominatives and predicate adjectives (all of which please see).

complete (*adj.*), **completely, wholly** (*advs.*) The usage issue with these three is whether they are absolutes (See ABSOLUTE ADJECTIVES) or not. It seems clear that in Edited English and at the Oratorical level, Standard users usually prefer to consider them absolutes and hence not modifiable by qualifiers such as *more* or *most.* But the fact is that in most uses *complete, completely,* and *wholly* are frequently used with qualifiers in all Conversational and Semiformal circumstances: *I've never made a more complete fool of myself. She was the most completely obnoxious of all those students. They were almost wholly persuaded.* This is not a grievous problem; it is merely hyperbole. See COMPREHENSIVE.

complex (*n.*) The transfer of this word's psychological and psychiatric meanings to general Conversational and Informal lay use, as in *getting a complex about homework* or *having a complex about driving in traffic,* has brought objection from conservative quarters, but the fact is that this word is now Standard in such uses in all but the most Formal contexts.

complexioned See COMPLECTED.

COMPLEX SENTENCE This is the grammatically classified sentence type made up of one independent clause and one or more dependent clauses: *When it rains, it pours. After he's had enough sleep, if you can believe this, he becomes absolutely cheery, although he still won't talk much.*

compliance (*n.*) Standard combined uses are *in compliance with* (*We're in compliance with the present regulations*) and *the compliance of* (*We're seeking the compliance of all retailers in the community*).

compliant See COMPLACENT.

compliment See COMPLEMENT.

complimentary See COMPLEMENTARY.

comply (*v.*) in combined use takes *with* in most instances and occasionally *to: They refuse to comply with* [rarely *to*] *the laws of the land.*

compose See COMPRISE; FORMULATE.

COMPOUND-COMPLEX SENTENCE This is the grammatically classified sentence type composed of two or more independent clauses and one or more dependent clauses: *My parents are coming tomorrow, but I hope they won't stay very long, because I have a date tomorrow night.*

COMPOUND PREPOSITIONS (sometimes called *phrasal prepositions*) are made up of two or more words. They function exactly the way one-word prepositions do (*before, after, in, on, of,* etc.) Among *compound prepositions* are *previous to, in addition to, in spite of, in advance of, instead of,* and the like. Advocates of brevity often urge their replacement with single-word synonyms, but on occasion they provide variety or improve precision. They are simply additional resources to be used appropriately.

COMPOUNDS, COMPOUNDING English makes many new words by forming *compounds,* particularly *compound nouns, compound verbs,* and *compound adjectives.* Typically a *compound* begins as a kind of cliché, two words that are frequently found together, as are *air cargo* or *light colored.* If the association persists, the two words often turn into a *compound,* sometimes with a meaning that is simply the sum of the parts (*light switch*), sometimes with some sort of figurative new sense (*moonshine*). The semantic relationships of the parts can be of all kinds: a *window cleaner* cleans windows, but a *vacuum cleaner* does not clean vacuums. We can be sure we have a *compound* when the primary stress moves forward: normally a modifier will be less heavily stressed than the word it modifies, but in *compounds* the first element is always more heavily stressed.

English spells *compounds* as two words (*junior college,* n.), as hyphenates (*low-grade,* adj.), and as single words (*bluebird,* n.), and it compounds all sorts of part-of-speech combinations: *high school* is a noun made of adjective plus noun, *high-priced* is an adjective made of an adverb and a participial adjective, and *lookout* is a noun made of verb and adverb. Indeed, almost any two words can be compounded:

NOUNS	VERBS	ADJECTIVES
headache	to backspace	three-day
butcher shop	to sweet-talk	(weekend)
swindle-sheet	to plea bargain	newborn (baby)
		hard won
		(victory)

See also PLURALS OF COMPOUND NOUNS; SPELLING OF COMPOUND WORDS.

COMPOUND SENTENCE This is the grammatically classified sentence type that contains two or more independent clauses linked in one of three ways: with a comma followed by a coordinating conjunction, as in *He got a new bicycle, but he didn't like its color*; with a semicolon, as in *We didn't arrive until seven; they served us breakfast at once*; or with a colon, as in *She was incredibly excited: today she was going to ride in a balloon!*

COMPOUND SUBJECTS, AGREEMENT WITH VERBS See AGREEMENT OF COMPOUND SUBJECTS WITH THEIR VERBS AND SUBSEQUENT PRONOUNS. See also AGREEMENT.

comprehend, apprehend (*vv.*) *Apprehend* means "to capture, to grasp (literally or figuratively), to understand, or to fear"; in practice, however, American English seems to use *to be apprehensive (about)* for "to fear." *Comprehend* too means "to understand, to grasp with the mind," but also means "to include, to comprise." Only in the "understand" sense are these words synonyms, although *apprehend* seems to stress understanding in the sense of "recognizing" (*He seems to have apprehended, finally, that he has no standing in the case*), whereas *comprehend* seems to stress understanding as "the intellectual process required to achieve comprehension" (*After studying the various proposals, we finally comprehended what all the fuss was about*). See also APPREHENSIVE.

comprehensive, complete, comprehensible (*adjs.*) *Comprehensive* means "large in scope, all-inclusive, fully detailed, containing all or much of something"; *complete* means "lacking nothing"; *comprehensible* means "understandable, intelligible." *Comprehensive* also has two widely used specialized senses, extensions of "all-inclusive": the *comprehensive insurance policy,* which covers a specified variety of risks in a single policy; and *comprehensive examinations* (also called *comprehensives*), which are examinations given at the end of undergraduate study or during or at the end of graduate study that cover an entire field of knowledge and typically are the final examinations for a degree program.

comprise, compose, consist, constitute, include (*vv.*) Of these, *comprise* offers the only truly vexed usage issue: commentators have strongly objected to both the *X is comprised of Y and Z* and *Y and Z comprise X* constructions, insisting that only *X comprises Y and Z* is acceptable. The active voice use, as in *Many items comprise a single whole,* and the passive, as in *This list is comprised of sixty items* or *These dishes are comprised of many ingredients,* are thoroughly established in Standard English, but there are still some party lines drawn about their acceptability. Best advice: if using *comprise* makes you nervous and unsure, why not use one of the synonyms—*constitute* or *compose* for the active use (which receives the most criticism) and *include(s)* or *consist(s) of* for the passive? The truth is that no matter how you use this word, someone can almost always be found to object. None of the many neat schemes purporting to describe its correct use seems accurately to describe the way Standard English users actually employ *comprise.*

One other point: be careful to use *include* only of incomplete lists: A baseball team is made up of nine players. It *includes* a pitcher, a catcher, and four infielders. It *is composed of* these, plus three outfielders. (And the team *comprises* these nine players; they *compose* the team.)

comptroller, controller (*nn.*) This officer (*comptroller* is simply a variant spelling of *controller*) is the chief accountant of an enterprise or organization. *Comptroller* seems to be used chiefly of governments, *controller* chiefly in private businesses and corporations. The pronunciation of both words is most frequently *kuhn-TRO-luhr,* but spelling pronunciations that pronounce the medial *-mp-* or *-m-* in *comptroller* or that sometimes stress the first syllable (*KAHM(P)-*) rather than the second are also Standard.

compulsive, compulsory (*adjs.*) *Compulsive* behavior is driven by irresistible, nonrational internal urges; *compulsory* behavior is that required by regulation or law.

COMPUTERESE is the special vocabulary of computer technology. It includes *bits, bytes,* and a great list of acronyms like *RAM* (*random-access memory*) and *ROM* (*read-only memory*), plus *mouse, floppy disks* and *hard disks, drives,* and *ports,* all parts of this arcane and growing lexicon. It is a jargon initiates must learn, and a surprising number of its terms are beginning to drift into extended or figurative use in the general vocabulary, as in computers being ''down'' or ''crashing'' and the like.

con- See CO-.

concave, convex (*adjs.*) The circumference, or outer edge, of a *concave* object is closer to the viewer, and its center curves farther away; *convex* objects bulge the opposite way, with the center close to the viewer and the edge or circumference curved farther away. One-half of a hollow rubber ball illustrates both forms: viewed from inside, it's *concave;* from the outside, it's *convex.* (Mnemonic: a cave—as in *concave*—is hollow too.)

concensus See CONSENSUS.

concept, conception (*nn.*) A *concept* is ''a fairly general abstract idea,'' and a *conception* is ''a mental picture or grasp of a *concept*'': *I have heard Fred's proposed new concept of feudal law, but I have no real conception of what it implies.* The two words are sometimes used as synonyms, but the distinction is worth keeping when possible. From their very natures both are always under pressure to generalize, and both are currently suffering a bit from overuse—indeed some people think them clichés. (*Conception* of course has another meaning in mammalian reproduction.)

concern (*n.*) is used in combinations with *about, for, over,* and *with,* to mean ''worry, uncertainty, interest, or fear'': *My concern is about meeting my deadline. His concern was for* [*over*] *his mother's safety. Our study's concerns were with injuries resulting from industrial accidents.* It combines with *in* to mean ''interest or involvement'': *Our concern is in budgetary matters.* See PROPOSAL.

concerned (*adj.*) A full range of prepositions appears with *concerned: about,* meaning ''worried over'' (*She was concerned about her children*); *at,* meaning ''wondering at or nervous about'' (*I was concerned at the level of noise in the hall*); *by,* meaning ''upset about'' (*Everyone was concerned by the screams coming from the basement*); *for,* meaning ''worried or anxious about'' (*We were concerned for those who were left on the dock*); *in,* meaning ''involved in''

(*George was concerned in the deliberations and couldn't leave*); *over,* meaning ''bothered or worried about'' (*The director was concerned over how late we were*); and *with,* meaning ''interested in'' (*We were concerned with winning the election*). All are Standard, and *concerned* is threatening to become a vogue word. Compare CARING.

concert, recital (*nn.*) *Concert* is generic, but when a distinction is made, it is usually that orchestras, bands, choruses, and other good-sized groups give *concerts,* and soloists or very small groups give *recitals.*

concerto (*n.*) The plural is *concertos* or *concerti* (pronounce them *kuhn-CHER-toz* and *kuhn-CHER-tee*). See PLURALS OF NOUNS ENDING IN -O.

CONCISENESS 1, CONCISION ''Be concise,'' say schoolteachers and editors, and that's good advice for writers of expository prose. ''Speak your piece simply and briefly, and then sit down,'' say the speech coaches, and that's sound advice too. But don't let your *concision* make your prose laconic, difficult, or unclear, or your speech dark or mysterious. *Conciseness* is not the only virtue. ''Eighty-seven years ago our ancestors began this country . . .'' is not the only way to say it. But neither is ''That nice gentleman has leaned too far over the rail and tumbled over it into the water'' the most appropriate thing to shout in the shipboard emergency; ''man overboard!'' would be more *concise*—and more helpful.

conciseness 2, concision (*nn.*) *Conciseness* means ''brevity and clarity together, a quality of things put succinctly.'' *Concision* means essentially the same thing (although it also has an obsolete or archaic meaning ''a cutting-off''), but it is a very low frequency word today.

conclave (*n.*) simply means ''a meeting or gathering of people,'' and although it sometimes seems to be a stab at elegant variation or whimsy, it is a Standard, somewhat ceremonious word.

conclude (*v.*) has two meanings, both now Standard: ''to decide,'' as in *She concluded that she ought to go to Paris,* and ''to bring to an end, to stop, or to close,'' as in *We concluded the meeting without setting a date for reconvening.*

concoct See FORMULATE.

CONCORD See AGREEMENT.

CONCORD, NOTIONAL See NOTIONAL AGREEMENT.

concrete See CEMENT.

concretize (*v.*), although it has been in print at least since 1884, had its most recent vogue beginning in the 1940s, and it appears to have been caught up in the furor over *maximize* and *finalize* and other bureaucratic coinages using the *-ize* suffix. It means "to make concrete" or "to turn into substance what before was nebulous and insubstantial." In those senses it's useful and Standard. See -ISE.

concur (*v.*) can combine with several prepositions: with *in* it means "agree with and join in on" (*I concur in your decision to hire them*); with *on* it means "agree on" (*We all concur on your choice*); with *with* it means "agree with" (*Management concurs with the union on this issue*). *To* plus an infinitive can also follow *concur*, as in *It seemed that all our problems concurred to make life miserable.*

condemn, contemn (*vv.*) *Condemn* means "to judge harshly, to bring judgment against, to convict." *Contemn* means "to treat with contempt, to scorn or despise." It is infrequent and often considered a "literary" word, and it is sometimes mistaken for a misspelling of *condemn*. Let context help your readers recognize *contemn*: *The neighbors contemned our failure to maintain our property.* See POETIC.

condensation See ABSTRACT (2).

condition (*n.*) is an accurate nonspecific word for use in medical discussions wherein specific information is unavailable (*He's got a heart condition*), and in such uses it is Standard. *She's in an interesting condition,* however, is a euphemism for *She's pregnant;* today it sounds whimsical or faintly Victorian in tone. See also PRECONDITION.

CONDITIONALS See INDICATIVE.

conducive (*adj.*), when combined with a preposition, always combines with *to* and means "leading to, contributing to," as in *This unbearably hot weather is not conducive to sleeping well.*

conductor See PRODUCER.

conduit (*n.*) has two Standard pronunciations, *KAHN-doo-it* and *KAHN-d(w)it.*

conferencing (*n.*) is relatively recent jargon or argot, turning up first in the field of education and now in computers. In the former, *conferencing* and *conferencing techniques* were names for holding educational conferences; their use outside the bounds of educationese might have withered with other slang had not *computer conferencing* suddenly become a jargon term used by a still-larger constituency. Like *conference*

calls on the telephone, *computer conferencing* permits computers to communicate among themselves. Thus in neither use does *conferencing* mean the same thing as *conferring*, but in its two specialized senses it appears to be approaching Standard status.

confess (*v.*) In Standard English intransitive *confess* can combine either with *to* plus a gerund, as in *He confessed to worrying about the legality of the purchase,* or with *to* plus a noun, as in *The mayor confessed to the embezzlement. Confess* is also Standard with a direct object only, as in *He confessed the theft.*

confidant, confidante (*nn.*), **confident** (*adj.*) *Confidant* is generic, meaning either a male or a female in whom one confides; *confidante* is used only of females. The nouns are pronounced either *KAHN-fi-DAHNT* or *KAHN-fi-DAHNT.* *Confident* (*KAHN-fi-dent*) is the adjective, and its unstressed final syllable is spelled *-ent*, not *-ant*.

confide (*v.*) In Standard English you *confide in* someone, *confide **that** something is true,* or *confide* something *to* someone.

confident (*adj.*) may be followed in Standard English by a *that* clause, as in *I'm confident that we'll persuade the voters,* and may be combined with *about*, as in *He's confident about making the climb,* with *as to*, as in *I'm confident as to my ability in this sport,* with *of*, as in *Roger is confident of his success,* and with *on*, as in *I'm confident on the issue of a tax increase.* See also CONFIDANT.

conform (*v.*) combines in Standard English with the prepositions *to*, *in*, and *with*: *They must conform to the new regulations. I try to conform in dress and manners. This news conforms with what I heard this morning.*

conformity (*n.*) The noun combines most frequently with the prepositions *to* and *with*: *The need for conformity to [with] his boss's whims irked him greatly.* We also speak of *conformity **among** several things, conformity **between** two of them, and conformity **of** some things **in** or **with** certain qualities.* All these are Standard.

CONFUSION OF SIMILAR OR APPARENTLY SIMILAR WORDS See HOMOGRAPH; MALAPROPISM; METATHESIS; SPOONERISMS.

confute, refute (*vv.*) Both mean "to deny something or prove its falsity"; perhaps because of its archaic sense "to confound," *confute* may be a bit stronger than *refute*, but it is also less frequently seen or heard, especially in Informal writing and at Conversational levels.

congenial, genial (*adjs.*) If you meet someone *genial*, you may find him or her *congenial* too, but usually when used of people *genial* is personal and *congenial* is characteristic of groups and of an individual's relationships to them. *Genial* means "warm, friendly, kindly, and (of climate or surroundings) welcoming, pleasant, and conducive to growth." *Congenial* means "of similar and sympathetic tastes, pleasant and sociable, and (of climate and surroundings and people as well) suitable, and agreeable."

congenital See GENETIC.

congratulate (*v.*), **congratulation(s)** (*n.*) Unfortunately, a good many Americans pronounce these words with a medial *j* sound where Standard English has a *ch* sound. Some Standard speakers will consider your rhyming the second syllable with *badge* instead of *batch* a shibboleth.

congruence (*n.*), **congruent** (*adj.*) Each has two Standard pronunciations, either *KAHN(G)-groo-ins*[-*int*] or *kahn*(*g*)-*GROO-ins*[-*int*].

conjugal, connubial (*adjs.*) *Conjugal* has two pronunciations, *KAHN-juh-guhl* and *kuhn-JOO-guhl*. *Connubial*'s primary stress is always on the second syllable. These synonyms mean "marital, of the married state, between husband and wife," and although some commentators suggest that *conjugal* tends to stress the legal side of the relationship and *connubial* the emotional, it is difficult to prove that the distinction exists and therefore hard to be confident that your audience will always perceive it. *Conjugal fidelity* and *connubial bliss* are clichés that may help you with such distinction as there may be.

CONJUNCTION This part of speech is actually two groups of function words, each with a different grammatical function: coordinating conjunctions and subordinating conjunctions. *Coordinating conjunctions* connect two equal grammatical structures, as in *I wanted a bath, **and** I needed food; man **and** wife;* and *weary **but** happy. Subordinating conjunctions* connect dependent clauses to or include them in independent clauses: *I've had no sleep **since** they arrived. **Until** she spoke, we didn't recognize her. We were unaware **that** she had left.* See COORDINATING CONJUNCTIONS; SUBORDINATING CONJUNCTIONS.

CONJUNCTIVE ADVERBS See SUBORDINATING CONJUNCTIONS.

connect (*v.*) combines with the prepositions *to* and *with: The pipeline connects the wellhead to [with] the storage tanks. By* is used when one thing is connected to another *by* something. Sports

and general use give us other meanings: *The batter connected for a home run* is sports argot, labeled Colloquial or Informal in most dictionaries. Either similarly labeled or slang is the intransitive use meaning "to succeed, to achieve whatever you were after," as in *I knocked on a hundred doors with no luck, but I finally connected; I found the right one.*

connection, connexion (*n.*) *Connection* is the American spelling, *connexion,* the usual British one. See SPELLING (1).

connote, denote (*vv.*) *To denote* is "to mean or to indicate the explicit" or "to signify directly"; *to connote* is "to convey indirectly" or "to mean or indicate the inexplicit." The word *money denotes* wealth, and to most of us it *connotes* travel, clothes, cars, and good times.

connubial See CONJUGAL.

consciousness, conscience (*nn.*), **consciousness raising** (*n.*), **consciousness-raising** (*adj.*) *Consciousness* is what people are aware of, what they deliberately think about, the state of being aware. *Consciousness raising* is therefore the bringing to the surface of perceptions, feelings, or intuitions perhaps latent or unrecognized before: specifically, it is making others aware—perhaps during a *consciousness-raising session* (which is a cliché)—of the problems of groups you consider to be insufficiently recognized or served. *Conscience* is the sense of right and wrong.

consensus (of opinion) There are two usage problems: (1) *Concensus* is an obsolete variant spelling of *consensus* and is now considered a misspelling; avoid it. (2) *Consensus,* many commentators insist, already means "an agreement among holders of opinion," so *consensus of opinion* must be redundant. Not entirely so: there are many kinds of *consensus* that do not involve opinion—*consensus* of political forces, of military tactics, of ordinances, of evidence, and the like. Actually, *consensus (of opinion)* is in divided usage; its chief flaw is a matter of style: it is not as concise as some would wish. Use it if you will, but if you do, be aware that some people will judge you ignorant on what they are sure is a blunder in usage. *General consensus,* however, is almost always redundant; avoid it. Compare COURSE OF.

consequent (*adj.*) is combined usually with the prepositions *on* and *upon* and occasionally with *to: The weariness consequent on [upon] his long swim felled him as soon as he got ashore. Consequent to your call, the general assembled his staff.* Note that these uses have a Formal air.

From would make the first example less stiff, as *after* would for the second.

consequential, inconsequential (*adjs.*) *Consequential* means "of consequence" and hence "important," whether applied to people, as in *She's a good actress and a consequential one*, actions, as in *His speech was not a consequential one, and the press scarcely reported it at all*, or things, as in *That white limousine looks consequential, just the thing to carry an aspiring candidate*. In the case of people, it may also mean "self-important," as in *She kept casting consequential glances at those around her, but nobody seemed curious about what they meant*. *Inconsequential* is an antonym of *consequential* and means "unimportant, trivial"; it is a much higher frequency word: *Both she and her ideas are inconsequential, so nobody pays any attention to either*.

conservative (*adj.*) continues to mean (among other things) "moderate, cautious, numerically on the low side": *One thousand was a conservative figure for the deaths the earthquake caused*. This sense is Standard. See ORTHODOX.

CONSERVATIVES IN LANGUAGE MATTERS favor conservative usage. They usually seem mature, are middle-aged or older, and typically have considerable social, political, and economic power. They often hold key editorial and publishing positions (or they have held them), and they are frequently authors, speakers, and editors of reputation. See CONSERVATIVE USAGE, and compare LIBERALS IN LANGUAGE MATTERS.

CONSERVATIVE USAGE prefers and defends the older, the tried and tested, and the widely accepted. It prefers not to pioneer, and it usually rejects the new whenever it has the choice. It comes very close to accepting the standards of Edited English for all writing other than Informal, and in speech it rarely drops into Casual even when the situation might invite it. At its worst, *conservative usage* can seem unbending and stuffy; at its best, it may sometimes seem slightly more Formal than the situation requires, but it will frequently make up for its reserved air with its precision, clarity, and good manners. Because it conserves many of the longest-lived traditions of the language, it is the kind of language least likely to age into incoherence, even as it is also the kind of language least likely to sound modish, up tempo, or flexible. Compare LIBERAL USAGE.

consider (*v.*), when used with *of*, as in *to consider of something*, is either archaic or no longer

idiomatic. *Consider what you say*; don't *consider of it*. *Consider* is also one of those rare doubly transitive verbs that take both a direct object and an object complement introduced by a particle: *He considers her a problem*.

considerable (*adv., adj., n.*) All adjectival uses of *considerable* are Standard: *Considerable* [or *a considerable*] *rain fell during the night*. The flat adverb *considerable* still exists but seems to be limited to Common and Vulgar English today; most Standard English insists on *considerably* as the adverb: *She felt considerably* [not *considerable*] *better this morning*. Most uses of *considerable* as a noun are Conversational or Informal; editors would almost certainly change *considerable* to an adjective rather than a noun in each of these uses: *The fans raised considerable of an outcry* [*a considerable outcry*] *over the decision. He's written considerable* [*a considerable amount*] *about his family*.

considerateness, consideration (*nn.*) These two both mean "to have regard for others, to be careful of others' feelings, and to be thoughtful of others," but *consideration* has several other senses not shared by *considerateness:* "the act of thinking," "a thing to be taken into account," "something thought of," "a fee or kind of compensation," and a legal sense, "something of value given in return for making a contract or agreement binding." All these additional senses of *consideration* are Standard.

consist See COMPRISE.

consistent (*adj.*), when it combines with *with*, is Standard: *His conclusions are consistent with ours*.

consistently, persistently (*advs.*) Things done *consistently* are done regularly and uniformly; things done *persistently* are done repeatedly, with unflagging patience or monotonous regularity. *Persistently* has pejorative overtones.

consist in, consist of *Consist in* means "is inherent in or lies within": *His social success consists in being able to persuade everyone of his amiability*. It usually occurs in sentences with singular subjects that *consist in* either singular or plural nominals. *Consist of* means "is composed or made up of": *His fleet consists of a day sailer, a canoe, and a small skiff*. It usually appears in a sentence with a singular subject that *consists of* a plural group of nominals.

CONSONANCE See RHYME.

consonant (*adj.*) combines with only one preposition: *with*, as in *Her actions are consonant with her opinions.*

CONSONANTS 1, THE AMERICAN ENGLISH

The *consonants* technically are both sounds and letters of the alphabet, and we use the term in both senses. The following table illustrates the *American English consonant sounds* initially, medially, and finally (note that not every *consonant* occurs in all three locations in the word, and note too that there can be several conventionally spelled representations of a given *consonant sound,* as for the *f* sound in *fit, staff, laugh, cipher,* and *half).*

	INITIAL	MEDIAL	FINAL
b	bad	cabin	nib
d	dad	bedding	bed
f	fad	awful	staff
g	gas	haggard	bag
h	hat	ahold	far (as in *r*-less dialects, or as semivowel only)
j	jib	midget	badge
k	king	baker	sack
l	less	mellow	mill
m	meat	demur	dam
n	now	menace	tin
p	par	taper	nape
r	reed	teary	far (in dialects with final *r*)
s	sat	thistle	lass
t	tile	bitten	hat
v	voice	sliver	brave
w	will	awash	how (as semivowel only)
y	yacht	union	bay (as semivowel only)
z	zebra	dazzle	raise
ch	chin	catcher	pitch
sh	shin	mission	fish
th	thin	nothing	bath (voiceless)
tħ	this	bother	lathe
zh	Jean (French only)	leisure	beige
ng	Ngaio (Maori only)	singer	long

Note that *zh-* does not occur initially in English words, although it does in French *gendarme* and the like. Note also that *ng-* does not occur initially in English words.

The English *letter consonants* are *b, c, d, f, g, h, j, k, l, m, n, p, q, r, s, t, v, w, x, y,* and *z.* Compare VOWELS.

CONSONANTS 2, DOUBLING OF

Here are some useful generalizations about this spelling issue:

1. Words that end in a single vowel plus a single *consonant* usually double the final *consonant* before adding a suffix that begins with a vowel: *stop* becomes *stopped, stopping, stopper,* and *unstoppable.* Thus *snip* becomes *snipper,* but *snipe* becomes *sniper.*

2. Most words that end in two *consonants* do not ordinarily double the final *consonant* before a suffix: *print* becomes *printed, printing,* and *printer.*

3. If the suffix begins with a *consonant* instead of a vowel, the final *consonant* of the base word stays single: *ship* becomes *shipment* and *clap* becomes *claptrap.*

4. Words of two and more syllables that are stressed on the final syllable normally double the final *consonant* before adding a suffix: *infer* becomes *inferred* and *inferring.*

5. But two-syllable words stressed on the final syllable do not double the final *consonant* when the suffix begins with a *consonant: regret* becomes *regretting* but *regretful.*

6. And words stressed on the final syllable but ending with two *consonants* or with a vowel do not double the *consonant: predict* becomes *predicting* and *predicted; reduce* becomes *reducer* and *reduced.*

7. Words that end in *-c* usually add a *k* before the suffix: *panic* becomes *panicking; picnic, picnicked.* And see also SPELLING OF *-ING* and *-ED* FORMS OF VERBS ENDING IN *-IC, -AC* for curious problems that arise when we add the suffix.

8. In words of more than one syllable ending in a consonant, especially *-l*, the English generally (but not always) double the final *consonant,* and Americans generally do not, although American dictionaries frequently report divided usage. Here are some examples:

AMERICAN ENGLISH	BRITISH ENGLISH
canceled, cancelled	cancelled
crueler, crueller	crueller
dueled, duelled	duelled
jeweler, jeweller	jeweller
kidnaped, kidnapped	kidnapped
labeled, labelled	labelled
quarreled, quarrelled	quarrelled
traveled, travelled	travelled
transshiped, transshipped	transshipped

See SPELLING (1) for other differences.

The best guide is always a good current desk dictionary; its currency is important, because over time, spelling too can change.

conspicuous by its See ABSENCE OF.

CONSTITUENCY

The *constituencies* to which you belong (and everyone belongs to more than a few) help set limits and add variety to your usage. They include the members of your family, your closest friends, your colleagues at work, people who share your religious preference, your political interests and loyalties, your racial and ethnic roots, your age, and your sex, and all the other groups large and small to which you may belong. Your dedication to particular hobbies and fandoms links you to still other *constituencies.*

The *constituencies* to which you belong set the standards for your language practice within each. Obviously they overlap, but obviously too you are unconsciously skillful at saving the jargon of philately for your talking and writing to other stamp collectors and restricting the private diction and syntax of your Intimate level to use with those at home. Children, with their lack of experience, make frequent errors in adapting to new *constituencies,* and adults of limited experience also sometimes suffer when faced with new *constituencies.* Being able to adjust accurately and quickly to each new *constituency* and context you encounter is a mark of the mature, widely experienced person; this book tries to help you do so.

constitute See COMPRISE.

constrain, restrain (*vv.*) *To constrain* means "to hold onto, to confine within bounds" and, combined with *to,* "to compel or oblige," as in *They were constrained to comply with the government's request. To restrain* means "to control, to hold back, to deprive of liberty, and to restrict." In some senses *constrain* tends to force the person or thing *constrained* to do something, whereas *restrain* in some senses tends to immobilize or prevent the person or thing *restrained* from doing something. In other senses, the two words' meanings are nearly identical.

consul See COUNCIL.

consummate (*v., adj.*) The adjective has two pronunciations: *kuhn-SUH-mit* or *KAHN-suh-mit*; the verb is pronounced *KAHN-suh-MAIT.* Each has two Standard meanings: the adjective means either "perfect, the best or worst there is, complete," as in *The room was decorated in consummate ugliness,* or "superbly accomplished or skilled," as in *She is a consummate public speaker.* The verb has a general meaning of "to finish, complete, or accomplish," as in *With all the signatures on the document, we could finally report the negotiations consummated in a treaty,* and "to carry out the full meaning of a marriage by having the first post-ceremony sexual intercourse," as in *That night*

at the beachhouse they consummated their marriage.

contact (*v.*) Through functional shift from the noun, American English added this verb, meaning "to get in touch with by calling, visiting, or writing, or by any other means." Economy of expression made it a success, even though for more than thirty years a partially successful but now failed rearguard action against it persuaded schools and editors to consider it Nonstandard or Colloquial at best. It is Standard, but you should be aware that a few mainly elderly readers and listeners out there may still object to *contact* as a verb.

CONTACT CLAUSES See OMITTED RELATIVE.

contagious, infectious (*adjs.*) Medicine distinguishes between these two, a *contagious* disease being caught as a result of contact, an *infectious* one being spread by some sort of *infectious* agent, but the figurative uses of these words are almost fully synonymous. There is some indication that both pleasant and unpleasant things can be figuratively *contagious* (*contagious laughter* or *contagious fear*), whereas only pleasant things are usually figuratively *infectious* (*infectious hilarity*).

contemn See CONDEMN.

contemporaneous, contemporary (*adjs.*) Although they once were nearly exact synonyms, these are now usually distinguished from each other in almost all uses. You will rarely be misunderstood if you use *contemporaneous* to mean "at the same time" (*Myles Standish and Peter Stuyvesant were contemporaneous residents of North America*) and *contemporary* to mean "right now, of today, or at the present time" (*I find the contemporary "country" style of interior decoration silly*).

contemptible, contemptuous (*adjs.*) Once interchangeable, those older senses are now obsolete, and these two now mean different things: *contemptible* means "worthy of scorn, despicable" (*Her behavior marks her as contemptible in every way*); *contemptuous* means "scornful, full of contempt" (*Her contemptuous smirks make clear her scorn for us*). *Contemptuous* as predicate adjective frequently takes the preposition *of: She's contemptuous of her roommate's pretensions to culture.*

contend (*v.*), when used in its sense of "to assert, to affirm, or to state," always suggests that contrary assertions, affirmations, or statements have been made or are expected; *I contend that* *she would make a good representative* implies that others *contend* otherwise.

CONTEXT, CONTEXTUAL, CONTEXTUALLY

The noun *context* (*contextual* is the adjective, *contextually* the adverb) is crucial to any discussion of usage. At its broadest and most generic, *context* controls both what you say or write and how you say or write it, because it is made up of the situation, the circumstances for the language, the purpose to which it is being put, and the audience or readers for whom it is being created. Every speech act involves a *context:* the speaker and his or her purpose, the audience—whether one person or many—and the occasion. And language—grammar, vocabulary, usage, and the rest—varies to fit each new *context.*

Context also means another group of conditions or circumstances, the explicit linguistic surroundings—the nearby grammar, the other words in the sentence, the information already given, and the semantic content of the paragraph and of the discourse. If you are alert to their nuances, you can use these aspects of *context* to minimize the chances that your language will confuse or mislead and thus make your speech and writing more appropriate and thus more effective. (Consider these sentences: *The puppy growls and bares his teeth. The woman bears her many burdens lightly. Two bears broke into our food supplies last night.* Even if the words were spoken, you would know from *context* what sort of *bears*/*bares* each sentence intends.) Make certain therefore that the *grammatical* and other *linguistic context* of your speech and writing helps and does not hinder their transmission. For example, the more complex or abstract your idea, the simpler and more concrete your linguistic *context*—words and syntax and style—should be. And make certain that your words meet the needs of the larger *context* as well: the situation, the purpose, the occasion, and the audience.

continual, continuous (*adjs.*) A *continual* annoyance is one that goes on repeatedly, as in *Continual bursts of gunfire kept us awake all night.* Presumably it was intermittent, with silences between bursts. *Continuous* works in either time or space and means "unending, without interruption." *Continuous* gunfire would not cease for even a moment.

continually, continuously (*advs.*) Unlike the adjectives, these two are frequently interchangeable, although they preserve some distinctions in much of Standard English. *Continuously* is used to treat of space: *These filaments come continuously from the machine.* It is also used of time: *It rained continuously for nearly a week; it never ceased.* In *It rained continually for nearly a week,* we usually understand that the rain stopped briefly from time to time.

continuance, continuation, continuity (*nn.*) These nouns have slightly different senses: A *continuance* is "the act of continuing, a duration" and, in the courts, "a postponement to a future time." Interchangeable with it in most senses is *continuation,* but *continuation* is distinctive in its use meaning "to extend and carry on further," as in *His second novel is a continuation of the first. Continuity* means "consistency through time," as in *Continuity of publication is much debated by candidates for the title of the state's oldest newspaper. Continuity* also has a specialized sense in motion pictures, radio, and television dramas, where it means "the linkage of one episode to the next." In that sense it is a kind of outline of the script.

continue on This combined verb form is an idiom rather than a redundancy (as it has sometimes been labeled), and it means "to resume traveling or another activity": *We paused for lunch and then continued on with our work.* It can also mean "did not stop an activity," as in *The others went to lunch, but I continued on at my computer.*

continuity See CONTINUANCE.

continuous See CONTINUAL.

continuously See CONTINUALLY.

CONTRACTIONS

A *contraction* is the result of compressing a word or phrase by omitting certain sounds (or letters) and closing up the string that is left: *He is* becomes *He's; I am* becomes *I'm; they are* becomes *they're.* The most common *contractions* in American English are those between subject and auxiliaries, such as *have, do, shall,* and *will,* and the verb *be,* and in negative combinations with these auxiliaries (*John won't* [*will not*]; *Mary shouldn't* [*should not*]; *I can't* [*cannot*]). *Contractions* are above all Conversational. They sound like talk, and indeed they are characteristic of all but the most elevated levels of American English speech. Standard English employs them as well in writing, although conservative use limits them to Informal writing, and most other Standard use employs them sparingly in Semiformal and rarely or never in Formal writing. But there is nothing wrong with *contractions* in the right context, and there can sometimes be a good deal wrong without them.

contrast (*n., v.*) Always pronounce the noun with primary stress on the first syllable; pronounce the verb with primary stress on either the second or, less frequently, the first syllable. The noun is followed most commonly by the prepositions *to* and *with* (*Our welcome was a startling contrast to [with] previous ones*), but combinations with *among* and *between* also occur (*The contrasts among their playing styles were many*; *The contrast between mother's and daughter's dispositions was startling*). See also COMPARE.

controlled substance See SUBSTANCE ABUSE.

controller See COMPTROLLER.

convenience store, convenience food (*nn.*) These compounds are Americanisms of recent vintage. Both are Standard, and both reflect the current reverence for the consumer's wish to save time. *Convenience stores* sell a little of nearly everything from gasoline to milk, from aspirin to zwieback, but their main reason for being is not their stock but their hours; they are open almost always—many of them twenty-four hours a day, every day, Sundays and holidays included. *Convenience foods* are packaged to require little effort to serve; typical examples are frozen dinners and prepared mixes, all claiming to require minimal time and effort for preparation.

convenient (*adj.*) As a predicate adjective *convenient* often takes the prepositions *for* and *to*: *Our house is convenient for those of us who like to sleep late and still get to school on time. It is also convenient to grocery store and bank.* *Convenient* also takes *to* plus an infinitive: *It will be convenient to have lunch a bit later.*

conventional See ORTHODOX.

conversant (*adj.*) is most often followed by the preposition *with*, as in *She's conversant with a great deal of sports lore*, and sometimes with *in*, especially when the topic is the ability to use language or languages, as in *The twins are conversant in Estonian: their whole family spoke it at home in order that the children might not lose it.*

CONVERSATIONAL is a synonym for *Colloquial.*

CONVERSATIONAL LEVELS These include the Intimate, Casual, and Impromptu levels of speech, and part of the Planned level; all sound like someone talking directly to another or to a small group of others. Only the Oratorical level and some speech at the more formal Planned level sound like one person addressing a large, impersonal group. See LEVELS OF USAGE.

converse See OBVERSE.

convex See CONCAVE.

convict (*v.*) combines regularly with the prepositions *of* and *on*: *They convicted him of shoplifting. She was convicted on charges of breaking and entering.*

convince, persuade (*vv.*) Some conservatives still cling to what was once thought to be a semantic and grammatical distinction between these two: semantically you were to *persuade somebody to act* but *convince somebody that something was true*, and grammatically you were to use *persuade* plus *to* and an infinitive and *convince* plus *that* and a clause. But although both conventions were strongly if confusingly and unevenly defended until quite recently, neither describes the practices, then or now, of Standard users, most of whom continue to use the two words interchangeably with *of*, as in *Let me persuade [convince] you of the need to act [the truth of my remarks]*.

cool (*adj., nn., v.*), **coolth** (*n.*) Overuse in slang and Conversational senses has made most figurative uses of *cool* problematic in other than the Conversational levels and the Informal writing that imitates them. Exceptions are *We received a cool reception* and *He was cool toward our new proposal.* These, plus all the literal senses, are Standard.

Coolth, once a nonce word made on analogy with *warmth*, is now tiresomely jocular: *The coolth of the water in the early morning is too much for me.*

cooperate, collaborate (*vv.*) *Cooperate* means "to work together, to be helpful," but it has lately also come in certain contexts to mean "go along with, submit, or obey," as in *If you don't cooperate, we'll sell out.* *Collaborate* means "to work together, usually on some project involving mental rather than physical work": you *cooperate* in building a house, but you *collaborate* in writing a musical. You and someone else *cooperate* or *collaborate*, or you *cooperate* or *collaborate with* someone else. *Collaborate together* and *cooperate together* are redundant, but they may sometimes be useful for special emphasis. See also COLLABORATE.

COORDINATING CONJUNCTIONS connect in parallel all sorts of grammatical structures—words, phrases, or clauses—and give them equivalent rank and function: *Fred and Mary; run and play; tired but happy; swiftly but carefully; if and when; now or never; He left, yet she stayed.* The list of *coordinating conjunctions* is brief and finite; these are most of them:

and, but, for, nor, not, or, yet, and *so* (some of them can also be prepositions, and *so* and *yet* are also adverbs), plus *both/and, either/or, neither/nor, not only/but also, rather than,* and *not (this)/but (that).*

cop (*n., v.*), **bobby** (*n.*) Most uses of *cop* are still slang, but the noun, meaning "police officer," is widely used in journalism and is quite appropriate in much Informal writing and at all but the Oratorical and higher Planned levels of speech. It has pejorative overtones in some contexts, and some police officers who use it of themselves might prefer that others not use it of or to them. *To cop a plea* is "to plead guilty to a lesser crime in order to avoid the risk of standing trial for a more serious one," and *to cop out* is "to quit, to confess and implicate others, or to back out of an agreement." Both these uses of the verb are slang. The term *bobby* (after Robert Peel, who created the London police force) is reportedly fading in Britain. See OFFICER.

cope (*v.*) is Standard both in its long-established combination with *with,* as in *She learned to cope with many inconveniences,* and in the absolute use to which some commentators objected when it began to appear in American English after some decades of acceptable use in British English, as in *I'm so tired I don't think I can cope.* A few still insist that this use is Casual or Informal at best, but they are overreacting; the only reasonable limitation might be to avoid using it in Formal and Oratorical contexts.

cop out, cop a plea See COP.

COPULATIVE VERBS See LINKING OR COPULATIVE VERBS.

copy See REPLICA; REPLICATE.

cord See CHORD.

core, corps (*nn.*) Of these homophones (pronounced *KOR*), the *core* is "the heart of something, the center, both literal and figurative"; a *corps* is "any organized group of people, such as a drum and bugle corps, or the Marine Corps." See also CORPSE.

coronate (*v.*) is a Nonstandard back-formation from the noun *coronation,* perhaps coined first as a jocular nonce word. The Standard verb is *to crown* or *to be crowned,* and the usual idiom is *to have a coronation.*

corporal, corporeal (*adjs.*) When *corporal* modifies a noun, the noun usually means something unpleasant that is being done to the body or otherwise affects it, as in *corporal punishment* or *corporal misery* (compare CAPITAL PUNISHMENT). *Corporeal* also refers to the body but simply stresses the idea that there *is* one, usually in contrast to something *without* body, that is, spiritual, nonmaterial, evanescent—or *incorporeal.*

corps See CORE.

corpse, corpus, corpus delicti (*nn.*) A *corpse* is a dead body (pronounce the full final consonant cluster); a *corpus* is also a body, but this time it is the full body of an author's work, a large collection of written works, or, in the Latin tag *corpus delicti* (note the spelling of *delicti*), "the body involved in the offense." *Core* and *corps* are cognates and homonyms, pronounced *KOR*.

correct (*adj.*) is frequently considered an absolute adjective, one that can't be qualified or improved. When it is absolute, something can be *correct, more nearly correct than something else,* or *incorrect;* it cannot be *the most correct* or *more correct.* But some uses of *correct* are clearly not absolutes: *His deportment was quite correct* illustrates an acceptable use with a qualifier or intensifier, as does *Her manner toward her mother was very correct.*

CORRECTNESS, THE DOCTRINE OF, AND THE DOCTRINE OF APPROPRIATENESS Through years of arguing over correct grammar, correct usage, correct spelling, and correct language of all sorts, many laypeople have come to the rigid conclusion that there must always be just one right answer, one right form, and one right usage. It is this *doctrine of correctness* that makes people say that *judgment* is the correct spelling, so that *judgement* must be incorrect (it's not), that *I shall see you tomorrow* is correct, and so *I will see you tomorrow* or *I'll see you tomorrow* must be incorrect (they're not). The truth is that in many language matters *appropriateness,* not *correctness,* is the doctrine to be heeded. Years ago Charles C. Fries pointed out that the dominant characteristics of the language of those who used only Vulgar English were not double negatives or mistakes in case or failures of agreement but a consistent poverty of expression, an inability to avail themselves of the myriad resources English has to offer, not just in vocabulary, but in syntax and other grammatical and stylistic matters as well. You have many choices before you, rich possibilities from among which you may select language appropriate to every context you encounter. That, and not *correctness,* should be your goal. And since the language is in a constant state of change and variation, *ap-*

propriateness is a particularly sensible doctrine; there is a good chance that a usage deemed correct and mastered by ten-year-old schoolchildren today will turn out to be inappropriate in a similar context a generation hence.

correspond (*v.*) When the verb means "to be in agreement, to match, and to conform," it is followed by either *with* or *to,* in these senses: *The city statute corresponds with [to] the federal regulation.* When *correspond* means to exchange letters regularly, it always uses *with: We've corresponded with each other for years.*

corrode See ERODE.

cosmetic (*adj., n.*), **cosmetic, cosmeticize, cosmetize** (*vv.*) Anything *cosmetic* is intended "to improve the appearance, beautify, or hide the blemishes," and the adjective often has a pejorative coloration: *The changes are merely cosmetic; they don't address the deeper ugliness.* From either the adjective or the noun *cosmetic* ("a substance used to beautify, etc."), we now have three verbs, none of them overwhelmingly popular: *cosmeticize* seems usually to be figurative, meaning "to prettify"; *cosmetize* seems usually to be used literally, particularly in the undertaking business, where the undertaker *cosmetizes* the corpse to improve its appearance. *To cosmetic,* the verb made by functional shift, also occurs: *The prostitutes cosmeticked themselves garishly.* Of these, only *cosmeticized* is in most dictionaries at the moment, but it is perfectly possible that all three verbs will last, the first two because of the difference in their main meanings and the last probably mainly as a convenient past participle and participial adjective. The two *-ize* forms, however, may be ostracized by some who object on principle to new polysyllables ending in *-ise* or *-ize.*

cosmonaut See ASTRONAUT.

cost (*vv.*), **cost out** (*v.*) The principal parts of the transitive and intransitive verb *cost,* as in *Yesterday gas cost twenty cents less a gallon* and *That mistake is going to cost,* are *cost, cost, cost.* The second sentence means "it will be expensive," and this sense is best limited to Conversational use. But there is still another set of meanings, "to set a price on, to estimate the cost of making or doing," with different principal parts: *cost, costed, costed.* This *cost* is frequently used with *out,* with the same meaning: *Our financial people costed [costed out] the machines at about twelve hundred dollars apiece.* Keep these two *cost* verbs separate—both principal parts and meanings. Both are Standard.

couch See SOFA.

could, might (*auxs.*) These auxiliaries can both suggest a possible outcome: *She might [could] change her mind,* and in many such uses they are interchangeable. *Might,* however, works with the negative, as in *She might come, but then again she might not,* whereas, in its "able to" sense, *could* means something different in the negative: *She could resign, but then again she could not* makes no sense. Ambiguity can also arise: *He might be badly injured* and *He could be badly injured* can both mean either "He may now be injured" or "He may be in danger of being injured in the future." See also MAY, MIGHT.

coulda See OF (2); SHOULDA.

could care less, couldn't care less Although many have tried, no one has yet satisfactorily explained how the negative fell out of the older and accepted *couldn't care less,* although logic of course says that *could care less* makes no sense. Both forms are clichés, and both are certainly best restricted to the lower Conversational levels and the most Informal of writing. But *could care less* could also earn you the scorn of logic lovers and cliché haters alike. Avoid it as Nonstandard.

couldn't hardly See HARDLY.

could of See OF (2); SHOULDA.

council (*n.*), **counsel** (*n., v.*), **consul** (*n.*) *Council* and *counsel* are homophones (the stressed first syllable rhymes with *town*), but a *council* is "a committee or group of advisers," and the noun *counsel* is "advice," or "another name for a lawyer." The verb *counsel* means "to advise." *Consul* is pronounced differently (*KAHN-suhl*) and means "the commercial representative of a national government who is based in a foreign city," or "an old Roman or French chief magistrate." See LAWYER.

councilor, councillor, counselor(-at-law), counsellor(-at-law) (*nn.*) Americans generally prefer the single-*l* spellings, but accept the double *ll* as well. A *council(l)or* serves on a council; a *counsel(l)or* gives advice and counsel (or is a lawyer). See LAWYER.

counsel See COUNCIL; LAWYER.

counteract See AMELIORATE.

counterfeit See ARTIFICIAL.

counterproductive (*adj.*) Some have called this a vogue word, and others term it a cliché, but it's still useful in the right places. Its primary sense, "bringing about a result the very opposite of the one intended," is explicit and appears to have no exact synonym. But if you mean only "unfortunate," "bad," "self-defeating," or "troublesome," use one of those terms, and save *counterproductive* for its explicit niche.

COUNTERWORDS Most dictionaries define *counterwords* as "words overused as terms of approval or disapproval"—words such as *great, outstanding, terrific, neat, swell,* and *super,* or *lousy, terrible, gross,* and *awful*—to such an extent that they no longer carry their full meanings; they are simply *counters,* carrying a generalized plus or minus charge but no particular semantic load beyond it. *Nice* is the classic example of the *counterword,* and high school and college students create and cast off dozens of new *counterwords* every year, often to the bafflement of their parents and teachers.

COUNT NOUNS See MASS NOUNS.

coup de grace is a French phrase meaning "the death blow," "the shot that puts the victim out of his misery." Either pronounce it right (*KOO duh GRAHS*), or don't use it. If you rhyme *grace* with *bra,* the knowing may snicker at your ignorance.

couple (*adj., n.*) For agreement with verbs, the noun *couple* can be either singular, as in *The couple by the window has just bought a new condominium,* or plural, as in *The couple over there are being divorced. Couple* always takes a singular demonstrative (*that couple,* not *those couple*), but with pronouns, agreement is more complex. *Couple* as a unit can be referred to as *it,* or, when considered as individuals, as *they: That couple is now living in their new apartment. Let's invite the new couple; you phone them. Each couple must bring its own beverage and dessert.*

couple of, a Commentators have sometimes argued that *a couple of,* meaning "two" or, loosely, "a few," as in *A couple of nights ago it rained heavily,* is an Informal or Conversational locution. It's not; it's Standard at all levels, although it may be rare in Oratorical and Formal use.

The omission of the *of* between *couple* and the number or the plural noun that follows, as in *a couple hundred dollars* or *a couple weeks later,* occurs more and more often at the Casual and Impromptu levels—perhaps even in some Planned speech—and in Informal and Semiformal writing. But Edited English and any consciously polished Planned or Oratorical speech will retain the *of* or use an entirely different, more precise locution.

course See COARSE.

course of, in the; during the course of Both these locutions have been called wordy and even redundant, and they are certainly not notably brief or crisp. But there is nothing wrong with either of them in the right place, so long as they're not overused.

courtesy, curtsy (*nn.*) *Courtesy* is, among other things, an obsolete form of *curtsy,* the female dip that is the equivalent of the male bow or genuflection. But *courtesy*'s primary senses today are "gracious behavior, a kindness, an honor," and the like.

court martial (*n.*) now has two Standard plurals: *courts martial* is generally required in Edited English, but *court martials* is now also considered Standard in some print media and at the Conversational levels.

cover (*n., v.*) The verb *cover* is Standard in most of its senses, many of which generalized from the jargon of particular activities (*to cover a loss or a bet, to cover a mare, to cover a sales region or a distance or a topic*). But a few uses may need comment: *To cover someone with a gun* is now Standard, but *to cover someone's king with an ace* is cardplayers' jargon still, especially when used intransitively. *To cover a story* is now Standard but was media jargon, and in many sports *to cover a player, an area, or a base* is the jargon of sports defense. *To cover up (for someone)* is "to provide an alibi" and is Standard in all but the most Oratorical and Formal use, but the related noun, a *coverup,* is journalese, mainly Conversational and Semiformal or Informal. *To break or blow one's cover* is "to give up one's disguise or other concealment or shelter," spy jargon now Standard in all but Oratorical and Formal uses. Related are the Standard idioms *to seek* or *take cover. Under cover* is Standard now as both phrasal idiom ("in shelter or hiding") and adjective (*an undercover agent*).

The noun *cover* is slang when it means "a recording of a popular song by someone other than the person or group that made it famous," and the verb *cover,* meaning "to make or issue such a recording," is also slang.

craft 1 (*n., v.*) A *craft* is a vocation, usually one involving skilled manual work with tools; it typically involves making things. When applied as it is today to the construction of everything from sideboards to credit card schemes, from wine decanters to con games, the verb, a product itself *crafted* by means of functional shift, has become a vogue word in the field of marketing.

But repetition can make vogue words a bore, and you would do well to reserve the verb *craft* for the literal making of things that really do require the painstakingly acquired handwork skills only apprenticeship and experience can provide. For now, *form* your sentences carefully instead of *crafting* them; leave *crafting* to real craftspeople who *have* crafts or trades and don't need the verb to prove it. See SKILLFUL.

craft 2 (*n.*), meaning "an airplane, a ship or boat, a spacecraft, or any other vehicle for sailing the air or the water," is both singular and plural, as in *This craft is seaworthy* and *Those craft are called trimarans.* (*These crafts* suggests skills or trades, not boats.) Generally compounds ending in *-craft* also have unchanged plural forms, although an *-s* plural for compounds might rarely occur, as in *All three spacecrafts were in need of repair.*

craft paper See KRAFT PAPER.

crape, crepe (*nn.*) These were originally only variant spellings, but *crape* now seems to refer particularly to the black material used for mourning armbands and funeral drapery of various sorts, whereas *crêpe* (in the original French spelling, but in American English usually without the circumflex accent) is the crinkly cloth or paper, the crinkly rubber sole, and the French pancake. *Crape* and *crepe* rhyme with *tape*, except that the pancake sometimes may keep the French pronunciation but sound the *s* in the plural, rhyming more or less with *steps*.

crass (*adj.*) is a pejorative word meaning a range of unpleasant, gross, affrontive, tasteless, stupid, egregious, insensitive things, and it is often used, especially in the adverb *crassly,* as an intensifier with no very explicit meaning. It is Standard in these senses and uses.

crayfish, crawdad (*nn.*), **crawfish** (*n., v.*) All these are variant names for various freshwater crustaceans a bit like small lobsters. *Crayfish* seems to be the most common spelling (first syllable rhymes with *ray*), *crawfish* is a variant (possibly American in origin, whose first syllable rhymes with *saw*), and *crawdad* is a dialectal Americanism from west of the Appalachians (first syllable also rhymes with *saw*). *To crawfish* is a slang or dialectal expression meaning "to back off, to retreat."

crazy, like See MAD (2).

create havoc See WREAK.

credence, credibility, credulity (*nn.*), **credit** (*n., v.*), **credible, creditable, credulous** (*adjs.*) The first syllable of *credence* rhymes with *freed*;

the other words in this entry rhyme their first syllables with *bed*. All seven have a common root in the Latin verb *credere* ("to believe") in one or another of its forms, but they differ among themselves in ways often confusing to speakers and writers of Standard English. *Credence* means "belief": *I gave no credence to his stories* means "I didn't believe his stories." *Credibility* means "believability": *His stories—and in the end, he himself—had no credibility* means "Neither he nor his stories were believable." *Credulity* (pronounced *kre-DYOO-li-tee*) is "the gullibility of listener or reader": *His credulity made him the butt of every practical joker.* To give people *credit for something* is to say that "you believe they did it, that they were the inventors or authors of it." That use of *credit* is usually a favorable thing, an ameliorative sense. *I take credit for our victory* means "I claim responsibility for our winning." But the verb *to credit someone with something* may be either ameliorative or pejorative, depending on whether the act is judged good or bad: *The papers credited the lifeguard with saving the child's life. An anonymous phone call credited a new rebel group with the bombing.*

Among the adjectives *credible* means "believable" (*The dean thought her story credible and signed the permission slip*), *creditable* means "favorable, praiseworthy" (*His performance, although not his best, was still creditable*), and *credulous* means "gullible, naive" (*His mother's credulous acceptance of his explanation stunned us*). See also INCREDIBLE.

creek See STREAM.

creep (*v.*) Past tenses and past participles of *creep, dream, leap, kneel,* and *sleep* have the strong verb's change of internal vowel, and these forms are Standard: *creep, crept, crept; sleep, slept, slept; dream, dreamt, dreamt; leap, leapt, leapt; and kneel, knelt, knelt.* All but *sleep* and *creep* have long had the weak verb pattern as well, so that *dream, dreamed, dreamed; leap, leaped, leaped;* and *kneel, kneeled, kneeled* are also Standard forms. Now *creep* has begun to develop *creeped* as past tense and past participle, in divided usage with *crept,* although thus far *creeped* seems to be restricted to the lower Conversational levels and rarely occurs even in Informal writing. It will be interesting to monitor *creep*'s development, since it could follow at least two different analogical models—that of *sleep* or that of *leap.*

cremains (*n. pl.*) is a euphemism from undertakers' jargon, an unctuous blend of *cremate* or *cremation* and *remains* that means "the ashes left after a corpse has been cremated.'' Best advice: use *ashes*.

crème de menthe (*n.*) means "cream of mint," and American pronunciations vary. *KREM-duh-MAHNT* is quite close to the French way of saying it, but *KREEM-duh-MINT* and other anglicized variants often irritate some Standard users. *Mint liqueur* is a good way around the pronunciation problem. But see LIQUEUR.

crepe See CRAPE.

crescendo (*n.*) has long meant "a gradual rise in intensity of sound," but lately it has begun as well to mean "the peak point, the apex of such a rise," and some editors and commentators object to the change. Clearly the more commonly used sense will continue to be the Standard primary sense, but normal semantic change seems to be winning acceptance for the new one from many users of Standard English.

crevice, crevasse (*nn.*) A *crevice* is smaller by far than a *crevasse*, whether in literal application to cracks and fissures in rocks and glaciers or in figurative senses, such as references to the tiny *crevices* between our teeth and the yawning *crevasses* in our knowledge of the universe.

crew (*n., v.*) The noun names those who work the ship or boat and also names the sport of rowing in two-, four-, and eight-oared racing shells. There are also extended senses: television's *camera crews*, racing's *pit crews*. The verb (principal parts *crew, crewed, crewed*) means "to serve as a member of a crew": *I crewed for her in the sailboat races last summer. Crew* is also a past tense of *crow* (see CROW).

crick See STREAM.

cripple (*n.*), **crippled** (*adj.*) Applied to people with physical impairments, these terms are rare these days, having been deemed cruel and unfeeling. They have been replaced by euphemisms (*handicapped, disabled, disadvantaged,* and the strained, most recent one, *differently abled;* see POLITICALLY CORRECT), except when they are used figuratively and modified by an adjective suggesting a new and different look at a figurative disability: *He's such a sentimental cripple that he can't even visit sick friends.* Or the noun is used of other than living things: *The pitcher threw a curve that didn't break, a cripple the batter hit into the stands.*

criterion (*n.*) The Standard singular is *criterion,* and the plural is *criteria.* But this word of increasingly higher frequency of use was borrowed in a now unfamiliar Greek pattern, and

so *criteria* as singular is often heard and seen (although not usually in Edited prose) where Standard *criterion* is expected. There is a fair possibility that, like *agenda* and *data, criteria* will begin one day to be Standard as both singular and plural at other levels than the Conversational and Informal, where it now has considerable use. *Criterions* is now also a Standard variant plural form, although many conservative users are reluctant to approve it, but *criterias* (the old Greek plural with the English *-s* plural added on) is usually limited to Common English. See FOREIGN PLURALS.

criticize (*v.*), **criticism** (*n.*) These words retain their primary senses having to do with even-handed evaluation and judging. But far more prevalent are the pejorative senses of "judging unfavorably" and of "finding fault." See also CRITIQUE.

critique (*n., v.*) The noun, meaning "an analysis, discussion, or evaluation of a situation or a work of literature or art," is Standard, particularly as a technical term for the work of literary and art critics. The verb has met some resistance in the past forty years or so, probably because it represents a functional shift, but it appears to have become modish at least partly because it seems not to be loaded pejoratively as *criticize* is. *The jurors criticized her playing of the concerto* suggests their response was entirely negative; *the jurors critiqued her playing of the concerto* suggests only that they evaluated it.

crochet (*n., v.*), **crotchet** (*n.*), **crotchety** (*adj.*) The needlework called *crochet* (pronounced *kro-SHAI*) was once spelled both *crotchet* (now obsolete) and its present *crochet,* and the intricate stitches of *crochet* were once called *crotchets* too. Now *crotchet* (pronounced *KRAH-chit*) means "a quirk or idiosyncrasy, an eccentricity," and the adjective simply describes someone full of such eccentricities and therefore peevish and difficult to get on with. Apparently most of the problems involve misspelling the eccentricity as *crochet.*

crow (*v.*) has five principal parts: *crow, crowed* or *crew, crowed* or *crew,* with both weak and strong verb patterns in divided usage. For most Americans, the *crew* forms are reserved for literary and poetic *cocks: The cock crew thrice, and the day dawned.* But we describe ordinary American roosters as having *crowed,* and all figurative senses seem to use *crowed* for both past tense and past participle: *"I win!" she crowed.*

crunch (*n.*) The *crunch* is an Informal or Conversational term for "a critical confrontation, a time of decision": *If it comes to the crunch, he'll help.* This phrase, *comes to the crunch,* is also something of a cliché, as *crunch* is in the slang "*It's crunch time!*"

cry See WEEP.

cryptic See EQUIVOCAL.

-ction, -xion See -ECTION.

culminate (*adv.*) appears intransitively with *in* and, much less often, with other common prepositions: *Our efforts culminated in victory. The opening ceremonies culminated with the singing of the national anthem.* It also occurs transitively: *This ceremony culminates several days of celebration.* It means both "to rise to the highest point, to climax" and simply "to end (in)," and most current uses are figurative, often stressing simply the end of a string of events or other entities, rather than its highest point.

cultivated, cultured (*adjs.*) Both words are Standard in meaning "well-read, well-mannered, polished," but *cultivated* seems to have somewhat greater use in these senses; some reserve *cultured* for the pearls that are sown and harvested rather than found in nature. Perhaps *cultivated* as applied to persons suggests more effort by the *cultivated* than would have been required simply to acquire a patina of *culture.*

cum is a Latin preposition long adopted by Standard English as a preposition meaning something like "combined with, together with" or even "plus": *She served us a sort of brunner— a brunch cum dinner.* Its other considerable use in American English is in hyphenated series: *His latest book is a novel-cum-sermon that I found quite dull.* Pronounce it *KUM* or *KOOM*.

cumulate, cumulation See ACCRETE.

cumulative See ACCUMULATIVE.

cupful The plural is *cupfuls.* See PLURALS OF COMPOUND NOUNS.

curate See PRIEST.

curb, kerb (*n.*) Americans spell it *curb,* the British, *kerb.* See SPELLING (1).

cured (*adj.*) combines with the preposition *of*: *I'm cured of my craving for chocolate.*

current, currant (*nn.*) The flow in tide, stream, or electric wiring is spelled *current,* as are the figurative *current events*; the seedless raisin is spelled *currant.* They are homophones in most American regional dialects.

currently See FORMERLY.

curriculum (*n.*) The plural is either the Latin *curricula* or the English *curriculums,* the latter form being much more common outside the halls of formal education. See FOREIGN PLURALS.

curtains See DRAPES.

curtsy See COURTESY.

customer See CLIENT.

custom-made See BESPOKE; OFF-THE-RACK.

cute (*adj.*), in its ameliorated senses, has repeatedly fallen victim to overuse and the resultant hatred of many, but it continues to be used in nearly all senses, old and new: it means "pretty and diminutively attractive" (*What a cute baby!*), "artificial or contrived" (*The little house, with all its gingham and bows, was so cute it made me want to gag*), "sharp, shrewd, or clever" (*His last manipulations of the company stock were pretty cute*). This last sense is usually labeled Colloquial, even though it is the oldest meaning, from the clipped form of *acute,* '*cute*. Best advice: limit *cute* to Conversational and Informal contexts.

cut in half From time to time the literal minded become concerned over whether this idiom should not be *cut in halves.* Worry is needless: *cut in half* is Standard. In fact, *to cut something in* [or *into*] *halves* is simply a description of the result of an action; to describe the action itself, we need the idiom.

cutting edge See AVANT-GARDE; STATE OF THE ART.

-cy See -CE.

cymbal, symbol (*nn.*) These homophones are not likely to be confused, because the spellings and meanings are both distinctive: a *cymbal* is the percussionist's brass instrument, either struck or crashed onto its twin to make a loud noise, and a *symbol* is something that stands for something else and therefore suggests it.

cynosure, sinecure (*nn.*) These two differ in meaning, pronunciation, and spelling, but they are sometimes confused even so. A *cynosure* is "a focal point, a guiding light, a center of attention": *Resplendent in uniform, the general was the cynosure of all eyes that night.* A *sinecure* is "a post that brings rewards without requiring much service in return": *His assignment as bartender for a houseful of teetotalers was a sinecure.* One possible cause of confusion is the pronunciations, which are identical even in their variants, except for the consonants that begin their final syllables. *Cynosure* is pronounced either *SEIN-uh-SHYOOR* or *SIN-uh-SHYOOR,* and *sinecure* is pronounced either *SEIN-uh-KYOOR* or *SIN-uh-KYOOR*.

cypher See CIPHER.

cypress, Cyprus (*nn.*) These homophones are rarely confused: *cypress* is the tree, *Cyprus*, the Mediterranean island.

D

-d-, -dd- See CONSONANTS (2).

d', de, di, du In proper names, the three spellings of the Romance language word meaning "of" are sometimes capitalized, sometimes not, usually according to convention or the wishes of the bearer of that name: *Hernando de Soto, Roger Martin Du Gard, Walter De la Mare, Gabriele D'Annunzio, Charles de Gaulle, Giuseppe di Stefano.* Lowercase particles of this sort (the *de* in *de Gaulle*) are capitalized when they begin a new sentence. See also VAN (3).

dab, darb (*nn.*) These slang words have somewhat similar meanings, but their etymologies are unclear, and they are apparently unrelated. A *dab* or a *dab hand* is British slang for someone who is an expert; *darb* is an Americanism probably nearly obsolete today, a slang word from the 1920s meaning "something or someone very handsome, valuable, attractive, or otherwise excellent."

daemon See DEMON.

dago (*adj., n.*) (plural: *dagos* or *dagoes*), an ethnic or racial insult that English speakers once applied to people of Italian or Spanish (or, loosely, any other Mediterranean) ancestry, has become a taboo word. Today its use is limited mainly to fiction and drama set in the early twentieth century. Some recent college desk dictionaries omit it.

dairy, diary (*nn.*) A *dairy* processes and sells milk, and a *diary* is a daily personal journal or engagement calendar. Only spelling error can explain anyone's confusing these nouns.

dais (*n.*) is a raised platform: its accepted pronunciation is *DAI-is*, but it is frequently pronounced *DEI-is* as well and then sometimes misspelled *dias.* See also PODIUM.

Dame, dame is Standard but old-fashioned or archaic in the senses meaning "an elderly woman" or a "woman of authority"; the meaning "a woman, a girl" is slang and taboo in nearly all Standard contexts. The British capitalize the honorific title given to a woman: *Dame Agatha Christie.* See also SIR.

damn, dam('), damfool, dammit, damnable, damnation, damned, damnedest, damning, etc. The final *-n* is frequently dropped in eye dialect forms, such as *dammit* and *damfool*, because it isn't pronounced (consider *DAM, DAMD*, and *DAM-ing*), but otherwise it is retained in spelling and pronounced in some compounds wherein the suffix would otherwise begin with a vowel, as in *damnable* (*DAM-nuh-bul*) and *damnation* (*DAM-NAI-shuhn*). Verb, noun, adjective, adverb, and interjection, *damn* in all its forms and compounds began as a very strong word meaning "to condemn or doom," but its very high frequency of use has tamed it so that it is now a mild curse as an interjection and a weak intensifier as an adverb (*a damned good golfer*). As a noun (*I don't give a damn*) it's not very powerful these days, and in most circumstances as a verb it is no longer much stronger than the *darn* or *darned* sometimes used as a euphemism for it. Most free use of *damn* and its compounds and combinations is limited to Conversational English, but it does occur in its curse-related senses in Informal and Semiformal writing as well. And it is still fully Standard as a verb at all levels in its old, literal religious sense, "to condemn to eternal punishment."

dance (*n.*) is usually used without an article when it refers to dancing as an art: compare *She's been interested in dance nearly all her life* with *We went to the dance at the club on Saturday.* One other (rarer) distinction: *She studies dance* means she's a dancer; *She studies the dance* suggests she's a historian or an observer of it.

DANGLING ADVERB See SENTENCE ADVERB.

DANGLING MODIFIERS, which include *dangling phrases* of various kinds—*dangling gerunds, dangling infinitives, dangling participles,* and just plain *danglers*—as well as misplaced or misrelated modifiers, are much criticized but much used and frequently unnoticed too. The most typical is the *dangling participial modifier,* as in *Opening the front door, the clock struck midnight.* The participial modifier is a saver of time and space, in that it replaces a full clause of some sort—*When I opened the front door,* for example, in the preceding sentence—but in making the transformation to a participial phrase, the speaker or the writer of unrevised or unedited prose may shift ground on reaching the second clause. In the example, *clock* became the subject, instead of *I,* and our grammatical expectation is that the implied subject of the modifier must be *clock* too. With *dangling infinitives, dangling gerunds,* and the like, the problem is essentially the same: the grammar of the sentence is at least technically ambiguous. This sort of usage gaffe is most likely to be noticed in Formal writing, less so in speech, and particularly less so at the lower levels of speech. *Dangling modifiers* of all sorts have long managed to get by in the best English and American literary company without being noticed. If meaning is clear from context, often no one notices the ambiguity, but if there is anything possibly ludicrous in one of the grammatical alternatives, the reader may very well discover it, even though a listener might miss it. It's the funny ones that cause trouble. Best advice: when writing Formally, make certain that the implied subject of the phrase modifier has the same referent as the stated subject of the main clause it modifies: not *Hurrying up the stairs, the door was locked,* but *Hurrying up the stairs, I found that the door was locked.* You will continue to create many technically dangling modifiers in your speech and Informal writing, and most of them will pass unnoticed. Just don't get caught: the traffic sign Stop When Flashing and the manufacturer's instruction Shake Before Using are both danglers and when noticed cause unintended amusement.

darb See DAB.

dare (*v., aux.*) *Dare* as a full verb can be followed by *to* plus an infinitive, and it is inflected in the third person present singular: *I dare him to jump in. She dares to hope they'll accept.* As a modal auxiliary, *dare* is followed by an infinitive phrase, but without *to,* and the third person present singular is uninflected as a subjunctive: *She dare not think about tomorrow. Roger daren't phone his mother.* When you use *dare* with other auxiliaries, it is often difficult to say whether you have used the modal or the verb: *I didn't dare ask him. I didn't dare to ask him.* The old past tense form *durst,* as in *They durst not challenge him,* is archaic or obsolete in Standard English, although it may continue still in some regional dialects. Today most Americans would say *They dared not challenge him.* See also DASSENT.

daresay, dare say The one-word spelling is a verb in itself, used only in the first person: *I [we] daresay we'll wish we'd stayed.* But it can also be spelled as two words: *I dare [to] say [that] he will be sorry to have missed the meeting.* *Daresay* can be followed by a clause, either with or without *that: I daresay [that] there will be no objection.* Note that the two-word spelling can appear as a subjunctive or an indicative in the third person singular: *If he dare[s] say anything unpleasant, I'll leave.*

darkling (*adv., adj.*) is an obsolete literary word, meaning "in the dark, dim, only faintly visible."

DASH The *dash* (—) is a mark of punctuation similar to but physically longer than a hyphen and used for other purposes. Typed, a *dash* is usually rendered with two hyphens; in printed matter, it is usually a mark one em long, whereas a hyphen is only one-quarter em long (an *em* being a typographical measure, the square space needed to contain the letter *M*). It signals an interruption in syntax and in the idea of a sentence: *When the governor understood how—did you hear the phone?* It also can be used as a colon might be used, to introduce a summarizing phrase following a list of details: *We had studied math, English, chemistry, philosophy, history—the whole liberal arts curriculum.* It can replace commas or parentheses that enclose grammatically parenthetical clauses or phrases: *They took every precaution—it seemed to take forever—to ensure our safe arrival.* It can also be used to set off an interjected question or exclamation: *The need now—urgent, is it not?—is for more funding.* The *dash* also appears in attributions of quotations: *Water, water, every where, nor any drop to drink. —Coleridge.* Finally, the *dash* is frequently used in Informal writing—especially in personal letters—to suggest the spontaneity, breeziness, and relaxed structure we usually find in conversation. It can be effective when so used, but its overuse to avoid other punctuation and to evade the requirements of more conventional syntax can be trying for the reader, even in a personal letter. In more Formal writing overuse can suggest that the writer is hasty, careless, and imprecise. See also DATES.

dassent, dassn't These are variant spellings of the contraction of *dare(s) not,* a regional dialectal locution now archaic and reflective of our literary past. See also DARE.

dastard (*n.*), **dastardly** (*adj.*) A *dastard* was once a coward, but today the noun is rare and means simply "an unprincipled, treacherous villain." The adjective means "sneaky, underhanded, and treacherous," and in those meanings still echoes the original sense. Today it's a word rather hard to take seriously.

data, datum (*n.*) *Data* is now both singular and plural: *This data is* [*these data are*] *enough to make our case.* When *data* is singular, it is always a mass noun and takes a singular verb and determiner: *The data has all been checked. Datum,* the old Latin singular, is still in use, particularly as a count noun taking a singular determiner and verb, as in *This datum is the missing one,* and it has its own plural, the regular English *datums,* although this form occurs rarely. But *a datum* is a frequent locution in science and elsewhere, mainly because *a data* simply doesn't occur very often, even though it is Standard. Other more general uses of *datum* may seem rather precious "corrections" from use of *data* as singular. The first syllable can rhyme with *late, cat,* or *blot.* See also FOREIGN PLURALS.

date (*n., v.*) *I made a date* ["an appointment"] *for lunch with John and his assistant* says nothing of any male-female arrangement, unlike *My date* ("the person I'm escorting or being escorted by") *is the dark-haired one by the piano* or *George dated* ("escorted," "went about with," perhaps "went 'steady' with," or even "lived with") *Mary Ann off and on for two years.* Yet another sense of the verb occurs in *Your ancient jokes and the cut of your jacket date you* ("reveal that you're outmoded," "show your age") *irretrievably.* All these meanings of *date* are now Standard, although some conservatives would insist that the "the person I'm escorting or seeing" sense is only for Conversational levels.

dates The day, month, and year are variously styled in the United States and Britain. *April 15, 1950,* is the most common American style, but these are also widely used: *15 April 1950, 4–15–50,* and *4/15/50.* (Computers often require a zero to fill in a space when the month has only a single digit, as in *04–15–50.*) The British way of expressing the numbers-only styles can be confusing for Americans. It gives the same date as *15–4–50, 15.4.50,* or *15/4/50,* and whether month or day is being given first is unclear when the day of the month is a number smaller than 13. Another overseas style is occasionally used in North America: *15.iv.50.* To show dates *from*

and *to,* use either a hyphen (printing uses something called an *en dash,* a mark about twice as long as a hyphen and half the size of an *em dash;* see DASH)—*June–October, 1978; January 1–15, 1990*—or the prepositions. Some stylebooks omit the comma between month and year: *January*[,] *1968; June*[,] *1970.* For an academic or fiscal year that takes in parts of two calendar years, use a virgule: *1991/92.* When you want to refer to a decade or a century, use no apostrophe: *the 1800s, the 1930s.* You will often abbreviate certain months of the year in correspondence but rarely in other Formal situations: *Jan., Feb., Aug., Sept., Oct., Nov.,* and *Dec.* The four- and five-letter-named months rarely need abbreviating, but when they do (chiefly in lists and the like, rather than in connected discourse), they may be written *Mar., Apr., Jun., Jul.,* and rarely, *Sep. May* is almost never abbreviated. Occasionally you'll need to indicate whether a date is B.C. or A.D. (See A.D. for an account of the newly ventured B.C.E. and C.E. substitutes.) Convention orders these this way: *The Roman fabulist Phaedrus lived from about 15* B.C. *to about* A.D. *50* (or more briefly: *ca. 15* B.C.—*ca.* A.D. *50).* A doubtful date uses a question mark: *Pericles, 495?–429* B.C. One final caveat: when giving beginning and ending dates, never mix dashes with words—it's either *1946–1948* or *from 1946 to 1948,* never *from 1946–1948.*

DATIVE CASE is the grammatical case that marked Old English (and Latin) nouns and pronouns functioning as indirect objects or the objects of certain prepositions. Today the preposition *to* accomplishes periphrastically the *dative* function as indirect object, as in *I gave the keys to him,* or syntax does the job alone by putting indirect object before direct object: *I gave him the keys.* In today's English, only the pronouns inflect for the *dative,* but that case is now an all-purpose *dative*-accusative, often called the objective case. Its forms are *me, you, him, her, it, us, you,* and *them.*

datum See DATA.

daughter-in-law See PLURALS OF COMPOUND NOUNS.

davenport See SOFA.

day and age, in this is a cliché. For variety, try *nowadays,* or *today.*

day bed See SOFA.

daylight saving(s) time See SAVING.

days See ADVERBIAL GENITIVE.

de See D'.

de-, dis-, dys- (*prefixes*) These three affixes have essentially negative meanings involving stopping, separating, contracting, and the like. *Decontaminate* means "to take away or remove a contaminant"; *deduce* means literally "to lead away from"; *depend,* literally "to hang down"; *decipher,* literally "to reverse or undo"; *deplane,* "to get off a plane"; *denominate,* literally "to derive from a nominal." *De-* can also combine to mean "completely," "wholly," as in *defunct. Dis-* can combine to mean "to stop" (*discontinue*), "to undo" (*disprove*), "to deprive of" (*disarm*), "an absence of" (*disagreement*), "not" (*disappear*), and the like. *Dys-* in combination can mean "bad" (*dysphoric*), "abnormal" (*dysgenic*), "nonfunctional" (*dysfunctional*), "impaired" (*dyslexic*), and the like.

dead (*adj.*) is usually considered an absolute adjective. When it is, most editors would replace a cliché such as *more dead than alive* by *more nearly dead than alive.* But this hyperbolic cliché poses no serious problem, limited as it usually is to Conversational levels of speech and to levels of writing other than Formal.

dead body is a locution sometimes criticized as being a journalese tautology. *Body* is in this sense "a corpse," and hence it is already *dead. Dead corpse* is clearly tautological, *dead body* possibly is too, but *dead person* clearly is not.

deadly, deathly (*adjs.*) *Deadly* things are killers; they threaten or cause death (*The wine contained a deadly poison*). *Deathly* things are deathlike; they have the appearance of death, and so they remind us of it (*She was deathly pale*).

DEAD METAPHORS See FROZEN FIGURES.

dead reckoning, dead center, dead right, and many other phrases with *dead* as the modifier or intensifier have in common either the certainty of death or its precision, exactness, or finality (with no room for adjustment or argument). *Dead reckoning* locates your ship's position by using the speed recorded by the log, the time spent on the course, and the compass reading of that course, all adjusted for winds, currents, or tides; all these are numbers, and they permit little guessing or estimating. *Dead center* is the precise center of something, and if you're *dead right,* you are as right as death is certain and irreversible.

DEADWOOD *Pruning deadwood* is an editorial metaphor. If your editors object to the *deadwood* in your prose, they object to parts of your prose that contribute nothing to its life and effectiveness. See also WORDINESS.

deaf, deafened (*adjs.*) If your hearing is permanently impaired, you are *deaf,* or at least your hearing is imperfect; if something has impaired it temporarily, you've been *deafened* by that something, as with the loud noise of jet engines, which can *deafen* anyone within earshot. See DUMB.

deal (*n., v.*) The principal parts of the verb are *deal, dealt, dealt.* The past tense and past participle end with the dental suffix, but they also display a shift in the vowel, from long to short, *DEEL* to *DELT. Dealed* is Substandard as past and past participle, occurring both as a child's error and as a Vulgar dialectal form. The verb (intransitive) combines with *with* to mean "to do something with, to get involved with," as in *She'll deal with the financial mess later.* If *deal* means "to sell something," it usually combines with *in* (*He deals in rare porcelains*); the exception is the slang *to deal drugs. Deal* also occurs uncombined in the Standard idiom *to deal [the] cards.* The noun, meaning "a business or other transaction or agreement," was once slang and then became Conversational, but it is now Standard (and sometimes pejorative) in all but the most resolutely Formal prose and Oratorical speech: *The party leaders offered a deal the opposition simply could not refuse.* The Conversational and slang limitations still apply to the clichés *big deal, no deal, done deal,* and the like, however.

deal, (not that) big of a See OF A.

dean, doyen, doyenne (*nn.*) In addition to its specific ecclesiastical and educational senses, *dean* also means "the senior and most eminent member of the group," as in *He is the dean of American political columnists. Doyen* and *doyenne* are exact synonyms of that meaning of *dean,* except that *doyen* is masculine, *doyenne* feminine; all three words derive from the Latin *decanus. Doyen(ne)* may stress age and seniority as reasons for eminence, but *doyenne* seems to be fading out because it is exclusive language, and *doyen* too is fading in its "senior and eminent" sense: *dean* seems to be replacing both, although it is too early to say that *doyen* will not become inclusive in English. It is, however, a very old-fashioned-sounding word. All three words are Standard, although all are now clichés in some contexts, as on some sports pages. Stress *doyen* on either syllable, *doyenne* on the second syllable.

dear (*adj.*, *n.*) is the Standard salutation used in American correspondence, Formal or Informal—*Dear Mr. President, Dear Senator Smith, Dear Jonathan A. Smart, Dear Janie, Dear Mother, Dear Roomie*—its degree of formality or intimacy being controlled by the form used for the name that follows. The noun is appropriately used as a term of address among intimates or close friends, but used in direct address by a man to a woman in circumstances wherein a man would be called *sir,* as in *Sir, is this your umbrella? dear* or *my dear* is considered offensive. See MADAM.

dear (*adv.*, *adj.*), **dearly** (*adv.*) When they mean "at a high price or cost," these two are interchangeable adverbs: *These strawberries are priced too dear* [*dearly*] *for me*; in all other contexts, only *dearly* is an adverb: *I'd dearly love to be present when they meet. Dear* is also an adjective meaning "expensive": *Medical insurance is becoming too dear for many Americans.* The sense is more frequent among the British; more commonly Americans use *expensive* or *costly,* favoring *dear* instead in the sense "beloved, treasured," as in *my dear friend.* All these uses are Standard, however.

dearth (*n.*) rhymes with *earth* and means "scarcity or lack," as in *There is a dearth of good plays this season.*

deathly See DEADLY.

debacle (*n.*) means "a great defeat, a disaster, a breakup or collapse," as in *Their last loss was such a debacle that it cost the coach his job.* The main problem with this word borrowed from French is how to say it: *di-BAHK-uhl* is perhaps most common, but various combinations of *dee-, di-,* and *duh-* for the first syllable, with *BAHK* or *BAK* for the second, plus a reasonable approximation of the original syllabic French *l,* such as *dai-BAHK-l,* are all appropriate.

debar, disbar (*vv.*) To *debar* people from doing something is "to prevent them from doing it"; it is a fairly general term. *Disbar* is specialized: it means "to strip lawyers of the privilege of practicing law, to take away their credentials as trial lawyers." In combination, *debar from* is most frequently encountered, as in *The committee debarred him from his professional practice by voting to disbar him.* See CONSONANTS (2).

debark, disembark (*vv.*) These verbs are synonyms, and both can be either transitive or intransitive, meaning "to take or assist people off a ship or plane" or "to get off a ship or plane": *The captain debarked* [*disembarked*] *several unruly passengers; at the next port the rest of the passengers disembarked* [*debarked*]. Both are Standard. Compare DE-.

debatable (*adj.*) drops the final *-e* of *debate.*

debate (*v.*) All Standard users approve the use of *debate* plus direct object: you may *debate* an issue or an opponent. Some Standard users also assert that you may *debate about* or *on* a subject as well and that you may *debate in* or *within* your own mind *on, about, over,* or *concerning* a question. Certain conservatives object to this use, however, so assess your audience carefully.

debouch, debauch (*vv.*) Except for a superficial similarity in the spellings, these Standard words differ greatly. *Debouch* is a French word (pronounced either *dee-BOOSH* or *di-BOOSH*) meaning "to come out into the open," as troops might from a narrow declivity into an open field or as a river does at its mouth into an ocean or bay. *Debauch* (pronounced *di-BAWCH* or *di-BAHCH*) means "to seduce," "to corrupt or to lead away from virtue." *Debouch* is a very low frequency word, and there is little likelihood of its being confused with the much more frequently encountered *debauch.*

debrief (*v.*) means "to interrogate, receive the report of, to instruct a returning pilot, emissary, or negotiator," "to find out what he or she learned." Typically such agents are *briefed* (that is, given instructions, provided with necessary letters, etc.) just before they depart, and on their return the process is reversed, and those who dispatched them *debrief* them. The word is Standard, but it has recently picked up some pejorative overtones, which suggest that those being *debriefed* are also being instructed on what they may say publicly and to the media.

debris, débris (*n.*) We spell this word today both with and without the acute accent, but more frequently without. Several pronunciations are in divided usage: *di-BREE, DAI-BREE,* and (rarely) *DAI-bree.* The British use the last and one other, *DAI-BREE.* The word means "the bits and pieces left from destruction," "rubble."

debug See BUG.

debut (*v.*) Many commentators and conservatives still strongly dislike *debut* as a verb, as in *She debuted in* Manon *at a small opera house in Germany,* but it is Standard in most Edited English and at most levels of speech, apparently because it is more economical to let a verb carry the full load, than to use an idiomatic phrase with the noun (*to have* or *to make one's debut*).

Pronounce the present tense as you would the noun (*di-BYOO* or *DAI-BYOO*) and the past tense and past participle either *di-BYOOD* or *DAI-BYOOD*.

debutant, debutante (*nn.*) The pronunciations reflect stages in the anglicization of a word originally French: Americans now say it either *DEB-yoo-TAHNT* or *DEB-yoo-TANT*, although the primary stress in each pronunciation may also fall instead on the first syllable. A *debutant* is technically a person of either sex making a debut, but almost no one applies that term to a man these days; a *debutante* is a female making a debut, either her introduction to society on her reaching a suitable age or her first appearance as a performer, but today the term has been labeled exclusive language, and that spelling is now generally being avoided. Indeed both nouns seem to be falling into disuse, in favor of the verb *debut* and the noun *debut*, and most uses of any of these today deal with performers, not with those entering society.

deca-, dec-, deci- (*prefixes*) All three prefixes involve the number *ten*. Pronounce the first two *DEK-uh-* and *DEK-*, respectively; they both mean "ten times." *Deca-* combines with bases beginning with consonants, as in *decagon*, "a polygon that has ten sides and ten angles"; *dec-* combines with bases beginning with vowels, as in *decathlon* (only three syllables), "an athletic event in which performers each compete in ten different events." *Deci-* is pronounced *DES-i-* or *DES-uh-* and means "one-tenth"—A *deciliter* is "one tenth of a liter."

decade (*n.*) A *decade* is technically a ten-year period covering years numbered 1 through 10, such as *1951–1960,* but in general use it is more often the ten-year period from 0 through 9, as in *1950–1959.* In that use a *decade* is referred to as *the '50s* or *the 1950s,* sometimes written out as *the (')fifties.* See also DATES.

decadence (*n.*), **decadent** (*adj.*) Each has two standard pronunciations: *DEK-uh-dens* or *di-KAI-dens* and *DEK-uh-dent* or *di-KAI-dent.* The first in each pair is the more frequent.

decease (*n., v.*), **deceased** (*adj., n.*), **decedent** (*n.*) These words are usually found in the jargon of undertakers, lawyers, and the clergy. People's *decease* is their death, when they may be said (stiffly) *to decease.* A *deceased* relative is one who has died or is dead, and at funerals and will readings, we hear frequent references to *the deceased* or to the *decedent,* "the person who has died" (*decedent* is standard legal jargon). Unless your context calls for distance and ritual

impersonality, use *die, dead,* and *death,* much simpler words that are not so impersonal, euphemistic, or solemn.

deceitful, deceptive (*adjs.*) These synonyms both mean "dishonest, intended to deceive." *Deceitful* has a stronger suggestion of deliberate lying, whereas *deceptive* suggests the deliberately misleading more than the flatly false. *Deceptive* advertising misleads, most likely with half truths; *deceitful* advertising probably lies.

decent See DECOROUS.

deceptive See DECEITFUL.

deci- See DECA-.

decide (*v.*) is both transitive, as in *They will decide the question this week,* and intransitive. The intransitive verb can combine with several prepositions: *against,* as in *I decided against calling him*; *for,* as in *The judge decided for the prosecution*; *on* and *upon,* as in *I haven't been able to decide on [upon] a moderator*; *between* and *among,* as in *She'll have to decide between [among] us*; *about,* as in *Only yesterday did she decide about going*; and *in favor of,* as in *The jury decided in favor of the defendant.* All these are Standard.

decided, decisive (*adjs.*) *Decided* means "unquestionable, clear, unwavering, determined," as in *She has some decided views on this year's candidates. Decisive* is a near-synonym, meaning "clear, determined, unmistakable, critically important," but adds the idea of "bringing to decision," "conclusive," as in *Because the other members are evenly divided on the issue, his vote will be decisive; that is, it will decide the contest. Decided* opinions are strong; *decisive* opinions carry the day.

decimate (*v.*) Today, *decimate* means "to destroy or kill or otherwise wipe out a lot of any group or thing": *Disease and hunger have decimated the population of the Horn of Africa.* When we first acquired this word from Latin, its meaning was "to execute one of every ten"; it was the way the Romans punished mutiny in the ranks. Some commentators have insisted on that as the only allowable meaning, but in fact it has long been obsolete, and the extended sense meaning "to take away or destroy a tenth part of anything" is at least archaic and perhaps obsolescent. Even if you use *decimate* intending it to mean "to destroy one tenth," your audience will not understand it that way. See ETYMOLOGICAL FALLACY.

decisive See DECIDED.

DECLARATIVE SENTENCE See STATE-MENT.

declare (*v.*) is a much more emphatic word than *say*; it means "state positively or for the record," as in *He declared his undying devotion to country and western music.* It also has specialized meanings, such as in the idiom *to declare war* and its customs use, *to declare all dutiable purchases on reentering the country.*

déclassé (*adj.*), **declass** (*v.*) The adjective is a borrowed French word, one in which we retain the two acute accent marks when we write it and also attempt something like the French sounds when we pronounce it: *DAI-klah-SAI.* It means "having lost social status, of inferior class or rank." A related but in English an older word is the verb *declass,* meaning "to reduce in class status." This one is fully anglicized, with no acute accents and with only two syllables: *dee-KLAS.*

decline (*v.*) If someone offers you something, you may *decline it,* or if you are asked to do something, you may *decline to do it.* But you never *decline the loan* [or *the lending* or *borrowing*] *of your car;* instead, you *decline to loan* [or *lend it*] or *decline to permit someone to borrow it.* The specialized grammatical sense, "to *decline* (a pronoun)," means "to give the *declension* of that pronoun."

décolletage (*n.*), **décolleté** (*adj.*) These borrowed French terms retain their acute accent marks in written English, and they are pronounced in something approximating the French sounds: *dai-kuhl-(uh)-TAHZH* and *dai-kuhl-(uh)-TAI.* Both refer to a style of woman's dress displaying a good deal of bare neck, bosom, and shoulders.

decor, décor (*n.*) is a French word meaning "the scheme of decoration (of a room)." It's in divided usage in both spelling (either with or without the acute accent mark) and pronunciation (either with the main stress on the second syllable, approximating the French sound, *dai-KOR,* or with the stress anglicized to fall on the first syllable: *DAI-kor*).

decorous, decent (*adjs.*) Pronounced *DEK-uhr-uhs* (or, rarely, *di-KOR-uhs*) and *DEE-sint,* both words mean "respectable, with propriety," but *decorous* also means "showing good taste, fitting, well-mannered," while *decent* also means "acceptable, sufficient, or adequate," as in *a decent salary* or *a decent room;* "proper, appropriate, fitting," as in *a decent black dress;* "morally sound," as in *a decent home* or *a decent burial;* or "wearing enough clothes or sufficient to meet standards of moral decency." This specialized sense (*Are you decent? May I come in?*) should be limited to Conversational and Informal use; the other senses are fully Standard.

decoy (*n., v.*) Stress on the first syllable is more frequent in the noun (*DEE-koy*), on the second in the verb (*dee-KOY*), but each part of speech also has the other stress pattern as a divided usage.

decriminalize (*v.*) is now Standard, although it is not much more than twenty years old. By no means every Standard user likes it, partly because it is new, having been made up to express the view that possession or use of drugs such as marijuana ought not to be a crime, and partly because it avails itself of the much-criticized *-ize* suffix. *Decriminalize* may seem clumsy, but because it has met a specific need in our discussion of a pressing social problem, it will no doubt continue to serve, because *to make no longer a crime* seems even clumsier.

decry, descry (*vv.*) *Decry* means "to speak out strongly against, to disapprove publicly and emphatically": *The school board decried students' using their Walkmans in school buildings.* *Descry* is also Standard but relatively rare; it means "to see, to catch sight of, to discover or discern": *Through the fog we could vaguely descry the drifting barge.*

dedicated (*adj.*) has long meant "faithful and devoted," but now a new and specialized extension of that "devoted" sense is Standard among computer-using constituencies: a *dedicated* computer or other piece of such electronic gear is one devoted exclusively to one task. Similarly, *dedicated funds* are reserved for a particular purpose: *Driver's license fees are put in a dedicated fund for roads and bridges.*

deduce, deduct (*vv.*), **deduction** (*n.*) To *deduce* is "to reason deductively, identifying the unknown by reasoning from the known": *From the fact that the coffeepot was still warm, we deduced that someone had been in the kitchen not long before.* To *deduct* something is almost always "to subtract it": *I deducted the interest and escrow charges from the total payment.* But *deduct(ed)* is now beginning to appear in some instances where most Standard users still expect *deduced: From that one thing we deducted the presence of someone else in the room.* That the noun *deduction* represents a functional shift from either verb may contribute: *Our deductions were correct: we had the answer* and *We are entitled to an extra deduction for having paid cash.*

Although a change may be in progress, best advice today is still to limit *deduct* to subtraction, *deduce* to reason. See also ADDUCE.

deductive, inductive (*adjs.*) These two words describe two kinds of reasoning: that from the general to the specific is called *deductive:* All mice like cheese; this is a mouse; therefore this mouse likes cheese. That from the specific to the general is called *inductive:* The mice I know like cheese; these mice are typical; therefore all mice must like cheese.

deem (*v.*) is a Standard verb regularly used to mean "think, consider, conclude," and the like, and commentators who *deem* it always pretentious are wrong; it is merely more formal than *think* and some others.

deep, deeply (*advs.*) *Deeply* is regularly encountered as an adverb, as in *She was deeply miserable at the loss* and *We drank deeply of the new cider,* but *deep* is both an adjective and a flat adverb, meaning "far down," "to a deep extent," as in *Probe deep in the subconscious for the answer* and *You have to plant tulip bulbs deep in the ground.*

deer (*n.*) The plural of *deer* is always *deer,* never *deers.* See RELIC PLURALS OF NOUNS.

de-escalate (*v.*) is always hyphenated. Its transitive meaning is "to turn back something that has been going up," so that it decreases or goes down instead, as in *We hope to de-escalate interest rates this spring.* Its intransitive meaning is "to cause something once on its way up to start going down," as in *Oil prices de-escalated last spring.*

de facto See DE JURE.

defect, deficiency (*nn.*) Both nouns can combine with either *in* or *of,* interchangeably: *The proposal had a serious defect in [of] design. The chief deficiency was of [in] her ability to delegate.*

defective, deficient (*adjs.*) These are synonyms, but they are slightly different in that a thing that is *defective* is flawed, whereas a thing that is *deficient* lacks something: *The driver's side windshield washer was defective; it wouldn't work. The car's instrumentation was deficient in that there was no oil pressure gauge.*

defence See DEFENSE.

defend (*v.*) can combine with *from* and *against: He defended her reputation from [against] all criticism.*

defenestrate (*v.*) is a back-formation from the seventeenth-century noun *defenestration,* "the

throwing (of something) out (through) a window." The verb is recent, Standard, and whimsical: *The canon and the barber defenestrated most of Don Quixote's library.*

defense, defence (*n.*), **defense** (*v.*) The noun *defense* (*defence* is the British spelling; see SPELLING [1]) is usually pronounced *di-FENS,* but in the jargon of football and certain other team sports where it means "the defensive unit, or the team currently on the defense, playing against the team with the ball," it is pronounced *DEE-fens.* The verb *defense* is also restricted to sports argot: it means "to design and execute a defense, to defend against," and it too may be stressed on either syllable. See DEFEND.

defensible, defensive (*adjs.*) A *defensible* position can be defended successfully, literally or figuratively; a *defensive* position is only passive and protective—one does not attack from it.

deficiency See DEFECT.

deficient See DEFECTIVE.

deficit (*n.*) was originally a Latin verb used in inventories, meaning "there is lacking," but we have used it almost solely of financial matters, meaning "a shortage of funding to meet scheduled needs." But recently Standard English has begun to use it figuratively, especially in matters such as nutrition, where a dietary *deficit* in certain minerals might contribute to a person's health problems.

defile (*v.*), meaning "to make dirty or unclean, to pollute, to corrupt," combines with either *by* or *with: Don't defile your reputation by [with] disreputable associations.*

definite, definitive (*adjs.*), **definitely, definitively** (*advs.*) The adjectives differ markedly: *definite* means "clear, precise, positive," as in *Let's set a definite date,* but *definitive* means "conclusive," "the most nearly complete and accurate, authoritative," "the one that defines," as in *After some thought, he gave us a definitive answer.* The adverbs are similarly distinctive: *definitely* means "clearly, precisely, positively," as in *The matter is definitely settled now,* while *definitively* means "completely, once and for all, authoritatively," as in *The Supreme Court's decision answered the questions definitively.*

The final unstressed vowel in *definite* and its relatives is frequently misspelled: the final syllable is always spelled *-ite,* never *-ate.*

deflection, deflexion (*n.*) *Deflection* is the American spelling, *deflexion,* the British. See SPELLING (1).

defuse, diffuse (*vv.*) These near-homophones (pronounced *dee-FYOOZ* and *di-FYOOZ,* with only the unstressed syllables differing) are usually distinguished by context, but to choose the wrong spelling can be inadvertently funny, because the usual meanings when context is not definitive are almost directly contradictory: to *defuse* a tense argument is to render it less explosive and hence harmless, whereas to *diffuse* such an argument is to spread it around even further and thus perhaps make it worse. (The adjective *diffuse* is not homophonous with these verbs: it is pronounced *di-FYOOS.*)

dégagé (*adj.*), meaning "uncommitted, relaxed, unconstrained," is a French import for which we retain both the acute accent marks and an approximation of the French sounds and stress: *dai-gah-ZHAI.*

DEGRADATION, DEGRADED, DEGRADING See PEJORATION.

DEGREE See POSITIVE DEGREE.

degree, to a; to the nth degree Once *to a degree* meant what we now mean when we say *to the nth degree,* meaning "as much as possible, to the outermost limit": *She scrubbed and polished everything to the nth degree.* Today it means "somewhat, a little bit, not very much," as in *To a degree we're prepared, but we're not ready for any unusual proposals,* although modifiers such as *largest* or *greatest* can restore some of its original force.

degreed (*adj.*) is widely used in the jargon of employment and the help-wanted ads: *We seek a degreed laboratory technician.* Some Standard users would prefer *degree-holding, with degree,* or another circumlocution in which *degree* remains a noun, and *degreed* is not yet fully Standard, but this kind of functional shift has long been an acceptable English word-making process—consider *booted, gloved,* and *hatted,* meaning "provided or equipped with these things." See ANALOGY (1).

déjà vu is a French expression meaning "already seen," and in psychology it means "a feeling that something now being experienced for the first time, so far as one knows, has in fact been experienced before." We borrowed the term, but we have generalized its meaning to stress simply the idea that "whatever is now before us is familiar, something we've seen before," although the idea that the "remembered" experience is illusory is retained in some uses. Recent overuse has made the phrase a cliché, even to the point of being adopted in a tautological joke attributed to (among others) Yogi Berra:

"It's déjà vu all over again!" *Déjà vu* is usually italicized in Edited English as a foreign phrase and keeps its accent marks. Use it sparingly; it's very tired. And if you mean it in the illusory sense, you must make that clear in context. See FOREIGN PHRASES.

de jure, de facto *De jure* is a Latin phrase meaning "by right" or "legally" that English has taken over first in legal jargon and then adopted into the general language. It usually contrasts with *de facto,* which means "in fact but not in law." A *de jure government* is one legally in place; a *de facto government* is one effectively in power and operating, but without legal authority. Spell both locutions as two words, and pronounce *de* either *dee, dai,* or *di,* stressing the first syllable of the second word in each phrase, *JOOR-ee* (or *JOOR-uh*) and *FAK-to.* See FOREIGN PHRASES.

delectable (*adj.*) means "wonderfully pleasing, delightful, of good taste (both literally and figuratively)": *The main dish was a delectable but hearty salad.* It's not ironic unless you make it so.

deleterious (*adj.*) means "harmful, injurious." Be certain that your audience knows it before you throw it about, however. Pronounce it *del-uh-TIR-ee-uhs.*

deli (*adj., n.*) This clipped form of *delicatessen* is used everywhere at Conversational levels and in Informal and Semiformal writing as the name of the food store itself, as in *We bought these pickles at the corner deli,* and as an adjective identifying products likely to be sold especially at such places, as in *This deli corned beef sandwich is the best in town.*

deliberate, deliberative (*adjs.*) *Deliberate* has two meanings: "slow, steady, unhurried, careful, measured," as in *He walked with heavy, deliberate steps,* and "intentional, premeditated," as in *The charge was deliberate murder.* *Deliberative* means "considering and discussing before deciding; deliberating before acting": *The deliberative bodies on the campus are the several faculties.*

DELIBERATIVE LEVEL See PLANNED LEVEL.

delible See LOST POSITIVES.

delimit, delimitate See LIMIT.

deliver (*v.*) One transitive and one intransitive sense of this verb should be limited to Conversational and Semiformal or Informal use: "to cause political support to go where promised" (*We delivered to our candidate a majority of the* *independent voters*) and "to make good on a promise of any sort" (*I said I'd arrange an enthusiastic reception for them, and I delivered*).

deliverance, delivery (*nn.*) *Deliverance* is specialized; it means "a rescue, a liberation," as in *The cavalry were usually the means for deliverance of the settlers threatened by rustlers*. *Delivery* is the more general term, its meanings ranging from "the distribution of mail," "speech making," "child bearing," and "pitching a ball." It also means "the keeping of promises," "the surrender or liberation of prisoners," "the sending of something to its destination," "the producing of promised votes or any other promised result," and "anything delivered."

delusion, illusion (*nn.*) These overlap in meaning and can therefore sometimes be confused. A *delusion* is a belief that something is true or real that isn't, and the belief is usually strong and of long duration, even to the point of being irrational or psychotic: *She has always had the delusion that she is a great singer*. An *illusion* is also an impression that something not true or real is true or real, but it is usually a fleeting impression: *Optical illusions make things appear to be other than they really are*. See also ALLUSION.

deluxe, de luxe (*adj.*) Americans spell it as one word, the British as two. Pronounce the second, stressed syllable *-LUHKS* or *-LUKS*. See SPELLING (1).

demand (*n., v.*) The noun combines with the prepositions *for*, as in *The demand for oil keeps prices high; on*, and *upon*, as in *His mother's demands on* [*upon*] *his time are excessive; by*, as in *Demands by labor are higher this year;* and *of*, which can lead to ambiguity. Consider the two possibilities in *The demands of the taxpayer:* are *the demands on* or *by the taxpayer?* Make context prevent ambiguity, or choose a clearer preposition. The verb *demand* can also take a direct object plus *of, from*, or *by* and an object of the preposition: *This work demands concentration of* [*from, by*] *every employee*.

demean 1 (*v.*) This verb *demean* developed from the noun *demeanor*, meaning "deportment, behavior." Today it is literary and perhaps archaic, a low-frequency reflexive verb meaning "to behave, comport, or conduct oneself," as in *We shall strive so to demean ourselves as to win their approval*.

demean 2 (*v.*) By far the more commonly encountered verb *demean* means "to lower, degrade, or debase." It was formed from the ad-

jective and noun *mean*, meaning "humble, dull, inferior, contemptible, base, or stingy," on analogy with the verb *debase*. It can be used reflexively or not, as you choose: *He groveled before the professor, demeaning himself most disgustingly. They made him do all the dirty work and then demeaned him for being dirty*.

demeanor, demeanour (*n.*) *Demeanor* is the American spelling, *demeanour*, the British. See DEMEAN (1); SPELLING (1).

demesne, domain (*nn.*) These nouns come from the same Latin word, *dominium*, but the word we borrowed from French, *demesne* (pronounced *di-MAIN* or *di-MEEN*), is more specialized, meaning "the lands around a manor house, an estate," while *domain* has many more meanings, both general and special, including "the area under one's control or governance." Both words are Standard, but *demesne* is rare.

demi- (*prefix*), means "half," "smaller," or "partly," as in *demitasse, demigod*, and *demimonde*. Words with *demi-* are usually not hyphenated. See SEMI-.

demise (*n.*) means "death, the end of someone's or something's existence." Commentators have frequently considered it pretentious, but although it is a rather self-conscious synonym for *death*, perhaps a euphemism for it, it has a good deal of figurative use when applied to agencies, organizations, proposals, and movements: *The demise of X's candidacy* means he is dead only as a candidate.

demo (*n.*) (plural: *demos*) is a clipped slang form of *demonstrator*. It is applied especially to sound recordings and tapes designed to showcase the work of the artists who made them or to automobiles or appliances used as *demonstrators* that potential purchasers may try out. The word is also infrequently used as a clipped and slang form of *democrat*. See PLURALS OF NOUNS ENDING IN *-O*.

Democrat (*adj., n.*), **Democratic** (*adj.*) The proper noun is the name of a member of a major American political party; the adjective *Democratic* is used in its official name, *the Democratic party*. *Democrat* as an adjective is still sometimes used by some twentieth-century Republicans as a campaign tool but was used with particular virulence by the late senator Joseph R. McCarthy of Wisconsin, a Republican who sought by repeatedly calling it *the Democrat party* to deny it any possible benefit of the suggestion that it might also be *democratic*. Other nations also have political parties with the words *Democrat* and *Democratic* in their names. The uncapitalized words *democrat* and *democratic* have to do with believers in and supporters of government based on majority rule, the principles of equal rights, and the representative procedures developed to permit these principles to operate. Capitalize only the proper noun and the adjective when it refers to the Democratic party.

demon, daemon (*n.*) Americans spell it *demon;* the British often use *daemon.* Some Americans use *daemon* to refer not to an evil spirit, but to a lesser classical god or a familiar spirit. See DIGRAPHS; LIGATURES; SPELLING (1).

DEMONSTRATIVE PRONOUNS, DEMONSTRATIVES

The *demonstrative pronouns* are *this* and *that* and their plurals, *these* and *those.* Some grammars describe them as members of the class of function words called determiners, since they identify nouns and other nominals. The *demonstratives* agree in number with the nouns they modify (*this boy, that cucumber, these interruptions, those computers*), and when serving as *demonstrative pronouns* and subjects, they agree in number with their following verbs (*This is it; These are the ones I want; That seems best of the bunch; Those seem the strongest*). For other uses of *that,* see the several THAT entries.

demur (*n., v.*), **demurral, demurrer, demurrage** (*nn.*) *To demur* (pronounced *di-MUHR;* to pronounce the second syllable *-MYOOR* is Substandard) means "to delay, to hesitate because of doubts," as in *Tom's concerns over finances caused him to demur.* What he registered is called a *demur* or a *demurral,* each of which is an objection, or—if it's a matter of law—a *demurrer,* which he may file when he believes that whether the evidence is true or not, it will not support the allegations before the court. Confusingly, a *demurrer* can also be "one who demurs," tacking the agentive ending onto the verb *demur. Demurrage* is another sort of delay, a technical term from the shipping business, meaning "the amount charged the shipper for delay of the ship beyond the agreed-upon time for loading and unloading the cargo"; it can be expressed in money or time.

denominator, numerator (*nn.*) A *denominator* (as in a *common denominator*) is a figurative use from mathematics, which means simply "a shared characteristic": *Their [common] denominator is their dislike of all football.* In mathematics, the *denominator* is the bottom or right-hand figure in a fraction, and the *numerator* is the number above or to the left of the line separating the numbers. In the fraction *3/4, 4* is the *denominator, 3* the *numerator.*

denote See CONNOTE.

denouement, dénouement (*n.*) is "the final outcome, the unwinding of a complex series of events or actions, specifically in a literary narrative or drama, and generally in life itself." American English spells it both with and without the acute accent over the first *e* and pronounces it either *dai-noo-MAWN* or *dai-NOO-mawn;* some will nasalize the final syllable.

dent, dint (*nn., vv.*) *Dent,* meaning "to make or put a dent in" and, as a noun, "the *dent* or hollow made in the thing struck," is by far the more common of the two. *Dint* as a noun means "a blow" but is now chiefly found in the cliché *by dint of,* meaning "by force of": *They won by dint of trying harder.* Other uses of the noun *dint* are archaic, but the verb, though of low frequency, is still Standard, meaning "to strike, to deliver a blow."

DENTAL SUFFIX is the conventional name for the regular weak verb inflections for the past tense and past participle, so named because the sounds *d, t,* and *id* in their endings (as in *pan/panned/panned, slap/slapped/slapped,* and *pat/patted/patted*) all involve *dental* consonants, made with the tip of the tongue tapping the backs of the upper front teeth or the alveolar ridge behind them. Choice of one of these suffixes is conditioned by the final sound in the word stem: these verbs add a *t* sound after voiceless consonants except *t,* a *d* sound after any voiced sound except *d,* and an *id* sound after *t* or *d.*

depart (*v.*) *Depart* is Standard in transitive and intransitive use and can combine with several prepositions: *We can depart from Chicago for Salt Lake City in half an hour, or on Tuesday at five-thirty, or before nine, or after midnight.* Figuratively the most common use is with *from: She departed from the text of her speech only twice.* Although some commentators used to say that it should only be intransitive, except in the cliché *depart this life,* both transitive and intransitive uses are Standard: *Our flight departs New York at 8:30 P.M.; After dinner we departed.* See also ARRIVE (2).

depend (*v.*) can be an absolute construction: *Will I be here tomorrow night? Well, that depends. It all depends.* That idiom can be used in full sentences without a combining preposition, but its use is usually limited to the Conversational levels and to Semiformal and Informal writing: *It depends if she calls back in time.* A higher level would require something such as *It de-*

pends on whether she calls back in time. It depends on if she calls back in time is more likely to be Conversational and Semiformal or Informal. *Depend* regularly combines with *on* and *upon: Our going depends upon [on] his being able to drive.*

dependant See DEPENDENT.

dependence, dependency (*nn.*) *Dependency* has one specialized sense that it does not share with *dependence:* "a territory that is under the jurisdiction of another state," as in *Those three small islands are dependencies of Japan. Dependence* means "the state of being dependent on," as in *His mother's dependence on him for full support was well documented,* or "addiction to," as in phrases such as *dependence on drugs or alcohol.* But *dependency* is used in these senses too, as in *drug dependency,* although perhaps somewhat less frequently. In such uses the two words are synonyms, and Standard. See -CE.

dependent (*adj., n.*), **dependant** (*n.*) The adjective is always spelled *dependent* and means "hanging from, contingent on, relying on or supported by, or addicted to": *The necklace has a large diamond with several smaller ones dependent from its setting. I am wholly dependent on my father's monthly check. He is said to be drug-dependent.* In American English the noun is nearly always spelled *dependent* too, as in *He declared three dependents on his tax form,* although occasionally you will see the noun spelled the British way, *dependant.*

DEPENDENT CLAUSES are clauses that are included in an independent clause or that modify one or some element in one. They are frequently introduced by interrogative or relative pronouns or by subordinating conjunctions: *The woman **who arrived late** is over there. I know **what you mean.** We'll come **when we can.***

depository, depositary, repository (*nn.*) *Depository* and *depositary* are synonyms: *That library is the depository [depositary] for all printed books on that subject. The director of the museum is designated the depositary [depository] for those drawings.* You'll make more Standard users comfortable, however, if you use *depository* for places and *depositary* for persons. A *repository* is a room or container where things are stored, or, figuratively, a person or place full of information or ideas: *She's a repository for [of] literary gossip.*

depot, station (*nn.*) A *depot* (pronounced *DEP-o* by the U.S. military and by the British) is a warehouse or storage place for materiel, and in the military it is also an assembly place for troops. A *depot* (pronounced *DEE-po*) is an old-fashioned American term for a railroad station, particularly a small one not in a large city. It started out referring to a freight station only, but in small communities the same building often served both freight and passengers.

deprecate, depreciate (*vv.*) Semantic change has caused some overlap between these words today, and spelling too may contribute to confusion (*depreciate* has an *i*; *deprecate* has none). Today, *depreciate* deals mostly with money and property: "to reduce in price or value, to diminish in worth": *Automobiles depreciate [or are depreciated] greatly during the first year of ownership, and a bit more slowly thereafter.* But figuratively *depreciate* sometimes is used to mean "to make something seem of less worth" and hence "to disparage, belittle, or put down." *Deprecate* also but primarily means "to disparage, belittle, or put down," as well as "to express mild disapproval," particularly when it is self-criticism: *She deprecated her own role in the victory.* Best advice: keep *depreciate* (*di-PREE-shee-AIT*) for financial comments, and use *deprecate* (*DEP-ruh-KAIT*) for negative criticism of any sort. See also DEPRECATING; SELF-CONFESSED.

deprecating, deprecatory, depreciatory (*adjs.*) *Deprecating* is the present participle of the verb *deprecate,* and as a participial adjective it closely follows its parent verb's meaning: a *deprecating* remark is "a disparaging remark." The other two adjectives are a bit trickier: *deprecate* and its relatives derive from the Latin *deprecari,* "to avert by prayer"; hence *deprecatory* began in English meaning "prayerfully, apologetically." A *deprecatory* remark then was "one calculated to win forgiveness, to ingratiate." But it is not far from that sense to the present meaning, "belittling, putting down," especially oneself. *Depreciatory* has long meant "disparaging," "devaluing, devalued"; a *depreciatory* remark makes something seem of less or little importance or value. See also DEPRECATE.

depreciate See DEPRECATE.

depreciatory See DEPRECATING.

depression, recession (*nn.*) In economics, a *depression* is a time of rising unemployment, falling prices and financial failure: *No one who lived through it can forget the Great Depression of the 1930s.* Sometimes a euphemism for *depression, a recession* is somehow smaller, briefer, and less intense—"a temporary downturn in the midst of a general upward-trending economy, but with all the indicators in depressed condition'': *Most economists would not yet admit that we were already in a major recession, let alone even whisper the word* depression.

deprive (*v.*) combines primarily with *of* in the sequence *to deprive X of Y: Her sprained ankle deprived her of mobility. Deprived from* also occurs, most frequently with a gerund: *His night shift assignment deprived him from [of] seeing much of his children.* But most Standard users would prefer *of* in that instance as well.

derby, Derby (*nn.*) Americans pronounce the man's hat, the Connecticut city, and the Kentucky horse race *DUHR-bee;* the British pronounce their city and the horse race named for it *DAH(R)-bee;* the Englishman's hat most like our *derby* is called a *bowler.*

derelict (*adj., n.*), **dereliction** (*n.*) *DER-uh-likt* and *DER-uh-LIK-shuhn* are the Standard pronunciations, and the third syllable is always spelled *-lict,* not *-lect.*

de rigueur is a borrowed French phrase meaning ''required by the code of fashion, etiquette, or good taste''; Americans frequently misspell it and sometimes pronounce it awkwardly. Attend carefully to the number of *u*'s, and pronounce the phrase *duh ree-GUHR,* managing the vowel and final consonant of the last syllable in your best near-approximation of the French sounds. And don't pronounce the *de* to rhyme with *day!* See also FOREIGN PHRASES.

derisive, derisory (*adj.*) Pronounce them *di-REI-siv* (*-REI-ziv, -RIZ-iv,* or *-RIS-iv*) and *di-REI-suhr-ee* (*-zuhr-ee*). These are synonyms, meaning ''worthy of, causing, or expressing derision,'' but *derisive* seems to be used more often for ''expressing or causing derision,'' as in *She had a derisive smirk on her face,* and *derisory* seems to be used more often for ''worthy of derision,'' as in *He was trapped in what was a most derisory situation.*

derive (*v.*) combines regularly with the preposition *from: She derives her stamina from her father, who taught her to share his interest in rigorous conditioning. Of* is also Standard, but it may sometimes sound somewhat old-fashioned: *Their riding horses were derived of Arabian stock.* The passive voice *is derived from* and the active voice *derives from* are both Standard.

derogate (*v.*), **derogation** (*n.*) *Derogate* means ''to detract, to take away,'' and as a transitive verb, it means ''disparage'': *He constantly derogated her intellectual abilities.* When *derogate* is intransitive, it combines with *from: This new*

claim *need not derogate from such agreements as have already been achieved.* The noun *derogation* can combine with either *of* or *from: To point out her reluctance to speak is no derogation of [from] her abilities as a speaker.*

DEROGATORY TERMS See ETHNIC SLURS AND TERMS OF ETHNIC OPPROBRIUM; PROFANITY; RACIST LANGUAGE; SEXIST LANGUAGE; TABOO WORDS.

derrière See BUTTOCKS.

desalinate, desalinize, desalt (*vv.*) These verbs are synonyms, *desalt* being the first (1909) to appear in American dictionaries, *desalinate* (1949) and *desalinize* (1963) presumably reflecting renewed interest around the world in removing the salt from sea water to make it drinkable. *Desalinate* and *desalinize* may make your language sound more technical and chemically sophisticated; *desalt* even a child will understand. All mean exactly the same thing, so match your audience and purpose. The related nouns are *desalination, desalinization,* and the gerund *desalting* (which is again the least technical); the chemical and manufacturing processes seem mainly to use one or both of the *-ation* nouns.

descendant, descendent (*adj., n.*) Americans spell both adjective and noun either way, although *-ant* seems somewhat the more frequent.

description (*n.*) combines with *of: We gave the police a description of the car. About* occurs too, but is Nonstandard.

DESCRIPTIVE GENITIVE is one of several overlapping terms for some functions of the English genitive case different from those of the *possessive genitive* (as in *Mary's hat*). *The mountain's top* and *a day's pay* are *descriptive genitives.* A few of the crustiest purists continue to argue that inanimate objects cannot use the genitive because they often cannot be said actually to *possess* the quality named, as in *a day's pay.* In fact, the genitive case—in English as in Latin before it—has always had many more purposes than simply indicating possession, and *descriptive* (and other nonpossessive) *genitives* are and long have been Standard English. See PERIPHRASTIC.

DESCRIPTIVE GRAMMAR AND USAGE See PRESCRIPTIVE AND DESCRIPTIVE GRAMMAR AND USAGE.

descry See DECRY.

desegregate, integrate, segregate (*vv.*) *Segregate* and *integrate* have been in the language for centuries, and they have long had generic meanings: "to put like or similar things into separate groups or collections (to *segregate* them)" or "to put pieces or parts together to form functionally working wholes (to *integrate* them)." Both *segregate* and *integrate* still have those generic meanings. But *desegregate*, whose only meaning is "to end the sequestering of racial minorities," and the social change that the idea of *desegregation* represents, are relatively young (1952 is an early citation), and that much-used word has added specialized meanings as well to the other two words, which now can be used generically only if context controls them carefully.

desegregation, integration, segregation (*nn.*) Like its related verb, *desegregation* is a word from the 1950s with a single specialized sense, "the removal of racial or other minorities from isolation or sequestration in society." *Segregation* and *integration* are sixteenth-century words with broad generic meanings, but like the related verbs they too have added specialized meanings, such that when you intend a generic sense, you must carefully control context—for example, when the topic is public health, and the effort is *to segregate those exposed to a disease from those not exposed*.

desert (*nn., v.*), **dessert** (*n.*) The verb *desert* (1), meaning transitively "to leave or forsake" or intransitively "to run away from duty" (*He promised never to desert us*; *After two years of service, he deserted*), is pronounced *di-ZUHRT*. *Desert* (2) is a noun meaning "what is deserved" and is usually used in the plural (*They got their just deserts: they were fired*). It is homophonous with *desert* (1). *Desert* (3) is a noun meaning "a wilderness, a dry, barren sandy area" and is pronounced *DEZ-uhrt*. *Dessert* is also homophonous with *desert* (1) and *desert* (2), but it means "the sweet course served at the end of the meal" (it comes from the French verb *deservir*, meaning "clear the table").

deshabille See DISHABILLE.

desideratum (*n.*), meaning "something needed or desirable," is pronounced either *di-ZID-uhr-AI-tuhm* or *di-ZID-uhr-AH-tuhm* (the first syllable may also be pronounced *dee-*), and its usual plural is the Latin *desiderata*, although *desideratums* also occurs as a Standard variant. See FOREIGN PLURALS.

design, destine, intend (*vv.*) The passive voice for each of these verbs affords some opportunity for confusion. *Design* and *intend* are sometimes interchangeable: *His speech was designed* [*intended*] *to sweep away all objections*. *Destined,*

intended, meant, and even *fated* also seem to overlap, although there clearly is a distinction between what people plan and what the gods or fortune design: *She had long been destined* [*intended, meant, fated*] *to be his bride*. Choose carefully among these senses.

(-)designate (*adj.*), as part of a title such as *ambassador designate,* is sometimes but not always hyphenated, and the plural inflection goes on the first element: *ambassadors designate*. See HYPHEN; PLURALS OF COMPOUND NOUNS.

designed See DESIGN.

desirable, desirous (*adjs.*) Something *desirable* displays qualities that make it worth desiring (*a highly desirable piece of land*). Someone *desirous* is someone motivated by a desire to have something (*desirous of admiration*). *Desirous* usually combines with *of* followed by a noun (*desirous of attention*) or another nominal, such as a gerund (*desirous of winning*). Less often it combines with *to* plus an infinitive (*desirous to win the world's praise*).

desire (*v.*) Some call *desire* a pretentious word better replaced by *wish, wish for, long for, need, want, seek, crave, request,* and others. These are indeed synonyms, but each has its own specific characteristics as well. In a sentence such as *I desire that you telephone your parents,* *desire* helps to create a formal, unbending quality; *I want you to telephone your parents* is simpler and less consciously elevated. Note too that one of *desire's* special senses has to do with sexual drives, and in this sense it is neither stiffer nor stuffier than the suggested synonyms: all can suggest similarly heavy breathing.

despair (*v.*) combines most frequently with *of* (*I despair of ever housebreaking that puppy*), less often with *at* (*I despair at her unwillingness to hear my side of it*). Apparently we usually *despair of* success, but *despair at* failure, especially repeated failure.

despatch See DISPATCH.

desperado (*n.*) has two Standard pronunciations, either *DES-puhr-AH-do* or *DES-puhr-AI-do*, and variant plural spellings too: *desperados* or *desperadoes*. See PLURALS OF NOUNS ENDING IN -O.

despicable (*adj.*) may be pronounced either *DES-pik-uh-bul* or *des-PIK-uh-bul*.

despite (*prep., n.*) As a preposition, *despite* is used alone to head a prepositional phrase (*despite his concern; despite their intervention*) and should not be combined with *of* (*despite of this; despite of that,* both of which are Nonstandard) except in the archaic *in despite of,* which is really a compound preposition with the noun *despite* in the middle: *In despite of everyone's urging, he chose not to comply.* The more usual (and more widely appropriate) phrase (also a compound preposition) is *in spite of,* which can replace the preposition *despite* in all situations. But see IN SPITE OF.

despoil (*v.*) is a rather formal word that combines regularly with *of* to mean "to rob, to take by force, to plunder," as in *The marauders despoiled the travelers of all their possessions.*

despondent (*adj.*) can be applied to people, animals, or figuratively to inanimate things. Just as a lost dog or a decaying barn can look *forlorn,* so can either appear—or even *be*—figuratively *despondent.*

dessert See DESERT.

destine (*v.*), **destined** (*adj.*) These combine with *to* and *for. Destined to* can be followed by either an infinitive, as in *He was destined to become a judge,* or, less commonly, a noun, as in *She was destined to success. Destined for* is followed by a noun or another nominal, as in *She is destined for the stage* and *He is destined for singing and dancing his way to stardom.* See also DESIGN.

destroyed (*adj.*) Like *dead, destroyed* can be an absolute adjective. But equally important is our penchant for hyperbole: there are instances wherein *completely destroyed* is on the mark, tautology and all. Style is the key.

destruct, self-destruct (*vv.*) *Destruct* is a backformation from *destruction,* apparently reinvented (the *Oxford English Dictionary* has a 1639 citation for an obsolete participial adjective) by the aerospace industry to describe what a rocket or a satellite does when it automatically or on command destroys itself, presumably to avoid some greater calamity. From this beginning developed the verb *self-destruct: If its lock were tampered with, the briefcase would immediately self-destruct.* Both verbs are Standard, *destruct* mainly within its limited aerospace constituency, *self-destruct* almost everywhere. See SELF-CONFESSED.

destructible, indestructible (*adjs.*) Both spell the final suffix *-ible,* not *-able.* See -ABLE; SPELLING OF UNSTRESSED VOWELS.

destructive (*adj.*) combines with the prepositions *of* and *to: Salt air is destructive of [to] automobile finishes.*

detail (*n., v.*) Both noun and verb are pronounced in two different ways in Standard En-

glish: *di-TAIL* is more frequent, but *DEE-TAIL* is quite acceptable in either function. In the sense "to assign to a particular duty," as used in the military services in *The sergeant detailed him to a week as latrine orderly,* the verb is always *DEE-TAIL.*

detente, détente (*n.*) in American English is acceptably spelled either with or without the acute accent over the first *e* and is pronounced either *dai-TAHNT* or *DAI-TAHNT.*

deter, deterring, deterrent See CONSONANTS (2).

deteriorate (*v.*), meaning "to go down in value, to become inferior, to cause to depreciate," is sometimes ineptly pronounced with only four syllables (omitting the *-or-*); Standard English insists on five: *dee-TIR-ee-uhr-AIT* or *di-TIR-ee-uhr-AIT.* It is either intransitive or transitive: *Wooden buildings deteriorate in the weather. Weather deteriorates wooden buildings.*

determinately, determinedly (*advs.*) *Determinately* (pronounced *di-TUHR-min-it-lee*) is much rarer than its negative *indeterminately.* It means "decidedly, conclusively, precisely, with proof and limits demonstrated" (*If these reports could be proved determinately accurate, we would carry the day*) but also can mean "resolutely, determinedly," hence the problem of overlap with *determinedly* itself, which means "resolutely, unwaveringly, and with the mind made up": *She maintained her ground determinedly. Determinedly* (pronounced *di-TUHR-mind-lee*) is the more frequently encountered word today, and you would do well to limit *determinately* to meanings involving precision and accuracy, letting *determinedly* handle determination.

DETERMINERS are a type of function word, such as *the, a/an, this, that, each, some, either, my, any, every,* and the like. They specify (or *determine*) a following noun and can make other parts of speech and grammatical structures function like nouns; for example, the *determiner the* permits you to talk about a preposition as a word, as in *the of at the end of the first line.* See also ARTICLES; DEMONSTRATIVE PRONOUNS; PARTICLE.

deterrent (*adj., n.*), **deterrence** (*n.*) Both these words today have new prominence and a specialized set of meanings having to do with nuclear armaments and the efforts to prevent nuclear war. Generically, anything *deterrent* "deters, delays, or temporarily prevents": *Proper rest may be a deterrent force in preventing some minor illnesses.* We now use the adjective regularly as a noun too, especially when we speak of *a nuclear deterrent,* "a policy or device that might reduce the possibilities for nuclear conflict." The plural *deterrents* may be mistaken in speech for the singular abstract noun, *deterrence,* the referent for which is overwhelmingly nuclear these days: *Deterrence [of nuclear war] is the diplomatic concern of nearly every major power.*

detour (*n., v.*) has two pronunciations in divided usage: the noun is either *DEE-TOOR* or *dee-TOOR,* the verb mainly *DEE-TOOR* (although it too may sometimes be encountered with primary stress on the final syllable).

detract, distract (*vv.*) Some would prefer *detract* to mean only "to take away something," as in *His manners detract from the impression of sophistication he hopes to give,* and *distract* to mean only "to divert attention," as in *The doorbell distracted me so that I missed seeing the home run.* But *detract* is also used to mean "to divert attention," as in *The Middle East crisis detracted media attention from the trouble with the domestic economy,* and some dictionaries now consider that use Standard. Even so, best advice: don't let this new confusion *distract* your reader and *detract* from your efforts at clarity.

develop (*v.*), **development** (*n.*) There is no *e* after the *p* in either word.

DEVERBAL OR DEVERBATIVE NOUNS
English makes many nouns from verbs through the process of functional shift that adds a *deverbative* suffix, such as *-er* or *-ation* to a verb: *drive* plus *-er* becomes *driver; preserve* plus *-er* becomes *preserver* and plus *-ation* becomes *preservation; fix* becomes *fixation.* See AGENTIVE ENDINGS.

deviate (*n., v.*), **deviant** (*adj., n.*) The verb combines almost always with *from* and only rarely with *into: We will not deviate from our plan. An orderly demonstration began to deviate into a pushing and shoving match.* The verb is pronounced *DEE-vee-AIT;* the adjective and noun *deviate* are usually *DEE-vee-uht* or *DEE-vee-it.* Both adjective and noun are synonymous with *deviant,* which like them has specialized reference to sexual behavior.

device (*n.*), **devise** (*n., v.*) *Device,* the noun, is spelled with a *c* and pronounced *di-VEIS* or *dee-VEIS; devise,* mainly a verb, is spelled with an *s* and pronounced *di-VEIZ* or *dee-VEIZ.* Lay persons rarely encounter the noun *devise,* a le-

gal term referring to the willing of real property and to such property itself.

devil's advocate is the title given the Roman Catholic officer who puts forward all possible arguments against the canonization of a candidate for sainthood, this to make certain that all doubts have been met. By extension, *to play [the] devil's advocate* is to argue against whatever seems to be the more-likely-to-be-approved course, simply for the sake of argument or to test all favorable arguments.

devise See DEVICE.

deviser, devisor, divisor (*nn.*) When they occur in connected speech, these three are virtual homophones, but each has its own distinctive spelling and meaning: a *deviser* is "one who devises, composes, creates, or makes up something"; a *devisor* (a legal term) is "someone who in a will leaves property"; a *divisor* (in arithmetic) is "the term by which the dividend is divided, thus producing the quotient." See also AGENTIVE ENDINGS.

devoid (*adj.*), meaning "without" or "entirely lacking (in)," combines with *of: He is devoid of any instinctive kindness.*

devolve (*v.*) combines usually with the prepositions *on* and *upon: All the financial responsibility will now devolve upon [on] their children. To* and *from* also occur occasionally: *Direction of the program now devolves to her in her role as vice chair. Her shrill behavior appears to devolve from the militancy of her early training.* But this last combination is rare.

dexterous, dextrous (*adj.*), **dexterously** (*adv.*), **dexterity, dexterousness** (*nn.*), **ambidextrous** (*adj.*), **ambidextrously** (*adv.*), **ambidexterity** (*n.*) *Dexterous* (pronounced either *DEK-stuhr-uhs* or *DEKS-truhs*) is the more usual American spelling of the adjective; *dextrous* is a variant. The related adverb and both related nouns, however, have no variants and are spelled *dexterously, dexterity,* and *dexterousness,* respectively. Curiously enough, *ambidextrous* and *ambidextrously* are the only Standard spellings of the adjective and adverb, and *ambidexterity* is the only related noun.

di See D'.

diabolic, diabolical (*adjs.*) Most dictionaries cite these as variants, two forms of the same adjective. Some commentators say that *diabolic* is more literally devilish in its referent, whereas *diabolical* is mainly figurative, meaning "awful, dreadful, fearful,'' but in fact context can shift either adjective either way.

DIACRITICS, DIACRITICAL MARKS

Spelling, punctuation, and context cannot always give us all we need to pronounce and in other ways distinguish one word from another. Sometimes we need the help of *diacritical marks* or *diacritics*. Dictionary entries use *diacritical marks* and other special symbols to indicate how to pronounce words. For example, *Webster's New World Dictionary of American English* (1988) uses *diacritics* to help distinguish the verb *resume* (ri zōōm', -zyōōm') from the noun *résumé* ('rez'-ə-mā', ra'z -; rā'z mā'); the macrons, single and double, indicate vowel length (ōō), ā) and in the entry word *résumé* (noun, meaning "summary"), that dictionary retains two acute accents, again indicating the quality of the vowels so marked. Other *diacritical marks* include the breve (as in [pĕt], indicating that the vowel of *pet* is short), the cedilla (French *garçon*), the circumflex (*raison d'être*), the haček (Czech *haček*), the macron (as in [bōt], indicating that the vowel of *boat* is long), the umlaut (German *Göring*), the dieresis (French *naïve*), the grave (French *à la carte*), and the tilde (Spanish *señor*), plus primary and secondary stress marks in words like *dictionary* ('dik-shə-ˌner-ē). In dictionaries that do not avail themselves of certain symbols of the International Phonetic Alphabet (IPA), e.g., the schwa (ə), other special marks serve a *diacritical* function, such as the ligatures frequently used to tie together the spelling of the š sound in *ship*, the spelling of the ž sound in the middle of *vision*, the spelling of the voiceless θ in *theme*, and the spelling of the voiced ð sound in *these*. See also ACCENT (2).

diagnose (*v.*) is usually considered Standard with either a malady or a person as direct object: *Physicians had diagnosed measles in the schools. Dr. Smith diagnosed Fred as having chicken pox.* But some conservatives object to the use of a person as either direct object or subject of a passive *diagnose*, as in *Fred's sister was diagnosed as having measles too*, except in Conversational or Informal use, and some editors will not permit either use in Edited English.

diagnosis, prognosis (*nn.*) The noun *diagnosis* retains its foreign plural, *diagnoses*, pronounced *dei-ig-NO-seez*. It is "the process of identifying or describing an illness"; *prognosis* (plural: *prognoses*) is the prediction of the likely course the disease may take and of whether and how soon the patient may recover. Today Standard

English makes increasing figurative use of both words.

DIAGONAL See VIRGULE.

diagram (*v.*) In adding grammatical suffixes, some forms can use only one *m*, but two *m*'s seem more frequent: both *diagrammed* and *diagramed*, *diagramming* and *diagraming* are Standard. *Diagrammatic(al)* and *diagrammatically*, however, are spelled only with two *m*'s. See CONSONANTS (2).

dial (*v.*) spells its past tense, past participle, and present participle either *dialed* or *dialled*, *dialing* or *dialling*. See CONSONANTS (2).

DIALECT Our language practices vary regionally and socially. The dominant community, the chief constituency of speakers to which we belong, provides us with our regional *dialect* (or with a mixture of regional *dialects*) and with the features of our social *dialect* (or a mixture of social or class *dialects*). We learn these *dialects* from parents, siblings, playmates, and a great many others who influence us during our most formative years, and we further modify our personal idiolects as we later encounter new influences. Like our clothes and our other manners, our *dialects* tell others where we are from and give strong evidence of our formal education or lack of it, of our economic status, and of our social class.

Dialects differ from languages, generally speaking, in that different *dialects* of a given language are usually mutually intelligible, albeit occasionally with some difficulty at first. For example, Americans and Australians each speak a *dialect* of the English language and usually have little trouble understanding one another. An accent—whether an American Southern accent or a German or other foreign accent in English—is often just another label for a *dialect* different from one's own. In a technical sense, however, accent involves only sound, whereas *dialect* can involve sound, spelling, grammar, and vocabulary.

DIALECTAL, dialectical (*adj.*), **dialectic(s)** (*n.*) Although *dialect* and *dialectics* sprang from the same root, their modern English meanings are very different. To refer to dialect, both *dialectal* and *dialectical* are used as adjectives in Standard English, but language experts usually try to reserve *dialectal* for language matters and to use *dialectical* only for referring to *dialectics*, the practice in philosophy of using argument to dismantle an opponent's position and so win a contest of ideas.

DIALECTOLOGY, DIALECTOLOGIST
(*nn.*) A *dialectologist* studies *dialectology*, the study of dialects.

dialogue, dialog (*n., v.*) The more commonly used spelling is *dialogue*, but *dialog* is a Standard variant for both noun and verb. The intransitive verb has been a recent vogue word, meaning "to converse," but it strikes some conservatives as slangy and graceless: *We dialogued for half an hour, but we got nowhere. Dialogued* also smacks of the jargon of labor relations: *spoke, talked, discussed, conversed,* and the like would be better. The transitive verb, meaning "to put into dialogue," is very rare. See also DUO; MONOLOGUE.

diamond, diaper (*nn.*) Each has two Standard pronunciations, one without and one with a middle unstressed syllable: *DEI-muhnd* and *DEI-puhr* are more commonly heard than *DEI-uh-muhnd* and *DEI-uh-puhr.* The loss of the middle syllable resulted from anglicizing words originally French: putting a heavy stress on the initial syllable in the English way led to the fading-out of the middle unstressed vowel. Some purists still argue for the three-syllable pronunciations, but their cause with *diamond* seems to be nearly lost, and that for *diaper* to be losing ground rapidly. The Oratorical level exhibits more three-syllable pronunciations of these words than does any other.

diarrhea, diarrhoea (*n.*) Both spellings are Standard. See also DIGRAPHS; LIGATURES.

diary See DAIRY.

diatribe (*n.*) A *diatribe* is a bitter, vindictive, denunciatory speech or piece of writing, often heavily sarcastic.

dice (*n., v.*) *Dice* is the plural, *die* is one singular, and *dice* is also a Standard singular form. *A pair of dice* usually takes a singular verb. We keep the singular *die* primarily in the cliché "The die is cast," and in tool and *die* (the plural of which is *dies*) work. The verb *dice* means "to play gambling games with *dice,*" and it also has a figurative use meaning "to cut up (vegetables) into small cubes shaped like *dice.*" Those cubes are sometimes referred to by a curious noun plural, limited mainly to cookbooks: *dices* (*Dice the carrots, and simmer the dices in a cup of stock*). See DIE; FOREIGN PLURALS.

dicey (*adj.*), meaning "risky, hazardous," was once only British, but Americans now use it occasionally; it is limited to Conversational levels: *The road was slippery, and it was dicey going.*

dichotomy (*n.*) means "something that has two parts" but not just any two-part thing; there should be great opposition or contrast between the two parts, as when opposing arguments offer little possibility of compromise.

dictate (*n., v.*) Stress the noun on the first syllable. The verb is usually pronounced that way too (*DIK-TAIT*), but it has a second, less common Standard pronunciation—*dik-TAIT.*

DICTION means "choice of words or vocabulary employed," as in *The poet's diction was varied and colorful*, and "precision or clarity of enunciation or pronunciation of words," as in *Her diction was so clear you could understand every word she sang.*

DICTIONARIES are of several kinds, and American English is well served in each classification. The most universally useful of dictionaries is the *desk* or *collegiate dictionary*, a peculiarly American contribution to lexicography. Desk *dictionaries* are inexpensive and portable, and they are usually the most nearly current of our *dictionaries*, because revisions and new editions appear frequently. A good desk *dictionary* is one of the greatest book bargains available anywhere—some fourteen to fifteen hundred pages of up-to-the-minute information about the spelling, pronunciation, forms, meanings, origins, and usage of the most-used words in the vocabulary, plus a mine of encyclopedic information, such as biographical and gazetteer lists, guides to punctuation, and lists of signs, symbols, and abbreviations. College students are urged to have their own, and every literate household should have one too—a recent one. The huge market makes competition among publishers fierce, and Americans can choose from several excellent desk or collegiate *dictionaries.* Among the current best are *Webster's Ninth New Collegiate Dictionary* (1983), *The American Heritage Dictionary*, second college edition (1982; a third edition was published in 1992), *Random House Webster's College Dictionary* (1991), and *Webster's New World Dictionary*, third college edition (1988).

Of *historical dictionaries*, which record not just the present state but the full history of each word, *The Oxford English Dictionary* (1886–1928) remains the foundation, and its supplements (1972–1986) made it helpful in documenting some of American English's recent history as well. The second edition (1989) now incorporates the *dictionary* and all its supplements in a single alphabet. Craigie and Hulbert (1938–1944) and Mathews (1951) are useful for Americanisms prior to World War II. Whitney

(1899–1910) was for its time an excellent American historical *dictionary,* and it remains in many ways the finest (although now outdated) of our *encyclopedic dictionaries,* a peculiarly American phenomenon, that give full information about people and places and ideas, do not treat only the "lowercase" words in the language, and go well beyond conventional lexicographical information.

The current best of our general *unabridged dictionaries* is still Merriam's *Third New International* (1961), with a strong but different (and slightly smaller) unabridged work being *The Random House Dictionary of the English Language,* second edition (1987). American English also has a good new *dictionary* of slang (Chapman 1986), which is profitably used in conjunction with Partridge (1984), and now at last the long-awaited *Dictionary of American Regional English* has begun to appear (Cassidy 1985; Cassidy and Hall 1991). All this says nothing of the dozens of *specialized dictionaries* of nearly every possible description, size, special purpose, and quality that American publishers keep in print for the remarkably large American *dictionary*-buying (if not always *dictionary*-using) audience. See the bibliography for the names of all the *dictionaries* consulted in the course of preparing this book.

dictum (*n.*), "an authoritative saying or statement of a principle or opinion," has two Standard plurals: *dicta* and *dictums.* See FOREIGN PLURALS.

didn't ought See HAD OUGHT.

didn't use to is the negative of the idiom *used to* (pronounced *YOOS-too* or *YOOS-tuh*) and means "was not (were not) accustomed to" or "was not (were not) in the habit of": *I* [*we*] *didn't use to wear jeans to school.* The negative idiom has long been Standard but is still limited to the Casual and Impromptu levels. See USED TO.

die, dye (*nn., vv.*) *Die* and *dye* are homophones, but the spellings reflect their very different meanings. The verb *die* means "to expire, to cease to exist" (*Annual flowers die in the fall*). The noun *die* is either "a device for cutting out or stamping out objects from metal or other material," as in *He made the dies for forming the gears,* or "one of a pair of dice," as in *The die is cast.* (See DICE.) The noun *dye* is "a coloring agent used on cloth or other material," as in *This dye won't fade when it's washed,* and the verb *dye* means "to apply *dye* to something in order to color it," as in *She dyed her hair a*

remarkable red. Similarly, *dying* has to do with the ending of life (*Her dying wish was that they let her die in peace*), and *dyeing* has to do with coloring textiles, hair, and the like (*She insisted on dyeing her hair*). Both forms can be gerunds: *Her dyeing of linen makes a mess of the kitchen. His dying was a great release for his family.* The participial adjective *dyed* forms part of a frozen metaphor or cliché, *deep-dyed,* which seems always to go with *villain* or *villainy.*

The verb *die* is used with several prepositions and adverbs. *Of* and *from* indicate the cause, as in *He died of malnutrition* and *She died from overexertion. For* and *in* explain a purpose for the dying, as in *The soldiers died for their country* and *They died in the effort to save their country.* Those are Standard. *With,* also indicating a cause of *dying,* as in *The baby died with pneumonia,* is an old-fashioned idiom at best and is now dialectal or Nonstandard. *To die off, to die away,* and *to die down* are a few of the Standard combinations with adverbs, each used both literally and figuratively.

DIERESIS, DIAERESIS A *dieresis* (the plural is *diereses*; *diaeresis*/*diaereses* are the usual British variants) is the diacritical mark (¨) placed over the second of two consecutive vowel letters to indicate that it is to be given full syllabic force; thus each of the two contiguous vowels in *naïve* is to have a syllable to itself: *nei-EEV.* Today American editors frequently specify a hyphen rather than a *dieresis* in some words (*co-opt* instead of *coöpt*) that might otherwise confuse; in others, they often drop the *dieresis* and let context distinguish (*naivete* or *naïvete*; *reënlist, re-enlist,* or *reenlist*). See ACCENT (2); DIGRAPHS; LIGATURES; SPELLING (1).

diesel (*n., v.*) The *i* precedes the *e,* and the two Standard pronunciations are *DEE-zul* and *DEE-sul.* A specialized intransitive sense of the verb applies to an internal combustion engine that continues to run even after it has been turned off; the engine is said *to diesel,* and the phenomenon is called *dieseling.*

dietetics, dietician, dietitian (*nn.*) *Dietetics* is the study of diet and nutrition, and a *dietitian* (by far the preferred spelling; the variant *dietician* is becoming rare) is a professional practitioner.

differ (*v.*) combines most commonly with the prepositions *with,* meaning "to disagree," as in *The author and the editor differ with each other over what constitutes sexual stereotyping,* and *from,* meaning "is unlike," as in *Their diet differs markedly from ours.* Other prepositions occurring with *differ* also mean "to disagree": *on* and *over* (*Tom and I differ on* [*over*] *nearly every political issue*); *as to* and *about* (*She and her husband differed as to* [*about*] *what time to set the alarm*). The preposition *among* used with *differ* means "have opposing opinions": *The professors differed among themselves on the proper way to phrase the resolution*. All these are Standard idioms.

different, separate (*adjs.*) *Different* means "not alike in some or all characteristics; dissimilar, distinctive." It appears in American English as a predicate adjective especially with *from* and *than* (see DIFFERENT FROM), but it also occurs frequently without a following preposition or subordinating conjunction: *She has a different hairdo today* (meaning "it is different from her former hairdo"); *I always have chocolate; today I want something different* (meaning "I want a flavor other than chocolate"). It also occurs at Conversational levels and in Informal writing in sentences such as *I don't know what it is about her; she's just different* (meaning, "she's unlike anyone I've encountered before"). These are all Standard. Some will object, however, to the use of *different* to mean "distinct," as in *I worked in three different restaurants* (meaning "in three restaurants, each in a distinct location, but not necessarily different from each other unless context insists on it"). They argue that *different* carries no semantic load here and merely contributes to wordiness. At worst it's a Standard cliché, but limit it to Casual or other Conversational use. The adjective *separate* is similarly used: *We saw them on three separate* [that is, *distinct, specific,* or *particular*] *occasions*. In this use it should be limited much as *different* should be. See also SEPARATE; VARIOUS.

different from, different than, different to These three have been usage items for many years. All are Standard and have long been so (*different to* is limited to British English, however), but only *different from* seems never to meet objections: *She is different from her mother in many ways. He feels different from the way he did yesterday. You look different from him. Different than* has been much criticized by commentators but is nonetheless Standard at most levels except for some Edited English. Consider *She looks different than* [*she did*] *yesterday. He's different than me* (some additional purist discomfort may arise here). *You look different than he* [*him*]. The problem lies in the assumption that *than* should be only a subordinating conjunction (requiring the pronouns that follow to be the nominative case subjects of their clauses), and not a preposition (requiring the pronouns that follow to be the objective case objects of the preposition). But Standard English does use *than* as both preposition and conjunction: *She looks different than me* is Standard and so is *She looks different than I* [*do*]. And with comparative forms of adjectives, *than* occurs with great frequency: *She looks taller* [*older, better, thinner,* etc.] *than me* [*than I do*]. Still, best advice for Formal and Oratorical levels: stick with *different from*.

differentiate, distinguish (*vv.*) These are synonyms, and each can be transitive: *She can differentiate* [*distinguish*] *colors now*. Both can combine with *from*, as in *I could never differentiate* [*distinguish*] *the first theory from the second*, with *between*, as in *My color blindness prevents me from distinguishing* [*differentiating*] *between red and green*, and with *among*, as in *It is impossible for me to differentiate* [*distinguish*] *among all these tiny brown warblers*. See DISTINGUISHED.

differently abled is one of many euphemisms recently put into use to avoid suggesting that people with physical or other disabilities or limitations are unable to participate fully in all aspects of human affairs. Alas, changing the name does not change the referent itself, as the quick casting aside of older euphemisms such as *disabled* and *disadvantaged* demonstrates. It is unclear whether more is gained or lost by these continuing efforts at making language lead the way in reforming situations that ultimately must first themselves be changed, but we seem determined to try. Quite possibly, *differently abled* will yield to another euphemism eventually. Some usage matters have a special poignance. Compare CRIPPLE; EUPHEMISMS; POLITICALLY CORRECT; UNDERPRIVILEGED.

different than, different to See DIFFERENT FROM.

diffuse See DEFUSE.

dig (*n., v.*) The verb combines with prepositions *up* and *out* in meanings such as "to uncover, to discover, to find out": *The reporters dug up* [*out*] *a good deal of shocking information*. Such uses are Standard. *Dig*, meaning "to notice, to admire, to understand," and the like, also figures in several slang uses: *Dig that car across the street! I really dig* [*on*] *his kind of basketball. Do you dig my idea?* And there are a number of other Conversational senses of the verb as well, sometimes with *in: I dug hard at my studies. Dig in to that pizza. We always dug* *in* [dug foxholes] *for the night before we dared to eat.* The noun also has some figurative senses: *He gave me several digs in the ribs* [he poked me] *to get my attention. She made a really nasty dig* [sarcastic comment] *at him.* And *a dig,* or *the site of the dig,* is an archaeological excavation in progress. The "poke" and "sarcastic comment" senses are Conversational, as is the British sense—always in the plural—meaning "living quarters." The "excavations" sense is jargon.

digest (*n., vv.*) The noun, meaning "a condensation of information or an abridgment of a longer work containing such things," is pronounced *DEI-jest.* The verb meaning "to make such a condensation" is also *DEI-jest,* but the verb meaning "to assimilate food in a digestive system" or, figuratively, "to understand" is pronounced *di-JEST* or *dei-JEST.*

DIGRAPHS are two-letter combinations that represent a single sound; English has a great many: *oa* as in *coat, oo* as in *blood* or *root* or *good, au* as in *jaunt, ea* as in *steak, ck* as in *sick,* and dozens more. Frequently when people use the word *digraphs* they refer specifically to the ligatures, those two-letter symbols that are either tied together by overlapping or by having a line (or thread or *ligature*) tie them together: *œ* (as in *onomatopoeia*) and *æ* (as in *mediaeval*) are the ligatures most frequently encountered in English, usually conventionally spelled *oe* and *ae.* See also DIPHTHONG.

dike, dyke (*n., v.*) A *dike* is an embankment designed to retain water or keep it out, and it is also used as the name of several other related or analogous structures. *To dike* is to make a *dike.* These words are Standard. But *dike* also is a variant spelling of the taboo word *dyke,* an offensive slang name for "a female homosexual, a lesbian, particularly one with masculine qualities."

dilapidated (*adj.*), **dilapidate** (*v.*) These two mean, respectively, "fallen into disrepair, ruined, shabby," and "to get or be put into such a state." They are both Standard, although the verb is somewhat rare. See ETYMOLOGICAL FALLACY.

dilemma (*n.*) Since it begins with the Greek *di-,* meaning "two," a *dilemma* is often said to have two horns (like an aggressive animal of some sort), and it still can mean (1) "in argument, a choice between two equally likely alternatives to be used against your opponent," (2) "any choice between two equally unpleasant alternative actions," (3) "a choice between one pleasant and one unpleasant option," and (4) "the choice between any two alternatives." Thanks to generalization, however, it is also Standard meaning "any serious problem." Pronounce it *di-LEM-uh* or *dei-LEM-uh.*

diminuendo (*n.*) The plural is *diminuendos.* See PLURALS OF NOUNS ENDING IN -O.

diminution (*n.*) is often mispronounced with an extra syllable *di-MIN-yoo-ISH-uhn* (perhaps by analogy with words like *fruition*) rather than in the Standard ways, *di-mi-NOO-shuhn* or *di-min-YOO-shuhn.*

dine (*v.*) In some contexts this verb may sound a bit pretentious; it is often used somewhat whimsically too. It is quite acceptable in Formal and Oratorical use; *Where shall we dine tonight?* may seem stuffy or perfectly natural, depending on context.

dinghy (*n.*), **dingy** (*adj.*) A *dinghy* (pronounced *DING-ee* or *DING-gee*) is a small boat; anything *dingy* (pronounced *DIN-jee*) is dirty, shabby, or squalid.

dinner, supper (*nn.*) A *dinner* is the main meal of the day, whether served at noon or later in the day; it is also a ceremonial banquet or any full-course meal. A *supper* is the evening meal, especially if *dinner* is the midday meal, or a fund-raising or communal meal such as *a church supper,* or a light repast, especially after the theater or in the late evening, as in *a midnight supper.*

dint See DENT.

diphtheria, diphthong, naphtha, ophthalmology (*nn.*) The Standard pronunciations of these four words are usually *dif-THIR-ee-uh, DIF-thawng, ahf-thal-MAHL-uh-jee,* and *NAF-thuh.* But many speakers of Standard English begin these words with the sounds *dip-, dip-, ahp-,* and *nap-,* respectively, and these speakers include physicians, phoneticians, eye doctors, and chemists. Widespread it may be, but some conservatives object to this Standard variant pronunciation. See -PHTH-.

DIPHTHONG A *diphthong* (pronounced *DIF-thawng* or, frequently, *DIP-thawng*) is a two-part vowel sound beginning with the sound of one vowel and moving to or toward another vowel or semivowel sound within the same syllable: the words *cow* and *joy* can be described as containing *diphthongs* made up of vowel and semivowel (*aw* and *oy*). English borrowed two ligatures from Greek and Latin, *æ* and *œ,* and sometimes preserves them in some spellings, but American English has tended to change many of those spellings to reflect the simple vowels that have replaced the *diphthongal* sounds of the ligatures in their original languages. We now usually spell *mediaeval, oeconomics,* and *oestrogen* to reflect their modern English pronunciations, *medieval, economics,* and *estrogen,* although we sometimes retain the ligatures, at least in modern digraph form, in spelling the names of *OEdipus (Oedipus)* and *AEsop (Aesop).* See also DIGRAPHS.

diplomat, diplomatist, diplomate (*nn.*) A *diplomat* (pronounced *DIP-luh-MAT*) is either a representative of a government who deals with representatives of foreign governments, negotiates treaties, and the like, or anyone who has the skill in negotiation, good manners, and tact typical of the best of such public representatives. A *diplomatist* (a somewhat formal word, pronounced *di-PLO-muh-tist*) is anyone skilled in diplomacy. A *diplomate* (pronounced *DIP-lo-MAIT*) is a physician who has been certified as a specialist by that specialty's board; he or she then holds the diploma for that specialty (and probably displays it on an office wall).

direct (*adv., adj.*), **directly** (*adv.*) *Direct* can, of course, serve as an adjective before a noun: *They began to use direct mail.* The flat adverb *direct* and the *-ly* form *directly* are interchangeable in some uses: *I went direct [directly] to the station.* But *direct* cannot interchange with *directly* as a modifier immediately preceding the adjective or phrase it modifies: *I sat directly in front of the speaker; She was more directly outspoken than her sister. Directly* will also modify a preceding verb, if a prepositional phrase follows (*The tree fell directly on the parked car*), and it has some other uses that the flat adverb *direct* cannot perform: meaning "at once," as in *I'll be there directly*; meaning "sometime soon, after a while," as in *We expect to reach home directly, as long as the horses give no trouble*; and meaning "as soon as," as in *Directly we get our visas we'll be on our way.* All three of these uses are in one sense or another dialectal. The first is predominantly British, the second predominantly old-fashioned American, perhaps mainly South Midland and Southern, and the third predominantly British (in the United States it is frequently labeled Nonstandard, and in Britain some commentators consider it suitable only for Informal use). See also IMMEDIATELY.

DIRECT ADDRESS, DIRECT QUOTATION, INDIRECT ADDRESS, INDIRECT DISCOURSE, INDIRECT QUOTATION *Direct address* is a term used to describe the use of a name or a personal pronoun to gain the attention of one or more persons being spoken to face to face, over the telephone, or in an apostrophe (see APOSTROPHE [1]), as well as in writing (*Now, dear reader, . . .*). Intonation in speech and punctuation in writing distinguish *direct address* from another structure: compare *Can you hear, John?* (which is *direct address*) and *Can you hear John?* (which is not). *Direct address* is also the exact words used by a speaker or writer, and this sort of *direct address* is always put within quotation marks. *Indirect address* and *indirect discourse* are paraphrases of a person's words (hence no quotation marks), as in *I said that I couldn't go.*

These are the conventions for handling *direct* and *indirect quotations* in writing: when you quote someone directly, you give the exact words uttered, and you enclose them in quotation marks: *He said, "Go home."* An *indirect quotation* paraphrases those exact words, usually with *that,* and no quotation marks are needed. *He said [that] I should go home.*

DIRECT OBJECT A noun or nominal in a predicate containing a transitive verb is called a *direct object*; the action specified in the verb is worked on it: *Tom saw **Fred**. We ate **pizza**. I love **playing golf**.*

director See PRODUCER.

dirigible (*adj., n.*) Both parts of speech have two pronunciations in divided usage, *DIR-ij-i-bul* and *di-RIJ-i-bul.* The adjective has long meant "steerable," and the noun is a clipped form of the phrase *dirigible balloon,* a "steerable balloon."

DIRTY WORDS are usually words with referents that are sexual, scatological, or ethnically or racially insulting. Many of them are taboo, at least in certain constituencies and contexts. See also ETHNIC SLURS AND TERMS OF ETHNIC OPPROBRIUM; OBSCENE (1); PROFANITY; RACIST LANGUAGE; VULGAR.

dis- See DE-.

disability, disabled, disadvantaged See CRIPPLE; DIFFERENTLY ABLED; UNDERPRIVILEGED.

disagree (*v.*) combines with the preposition *with,* as in *I disagree with you on this matter,* and also with the prepositions *about, on, concerning,* and *over,* as in *We disagreed about [on, concerning, over] the disciplining of the children.*

disappointed (*adj.*), **disappoint** (*v.*), **disappointment** (*n.*) Spell each with one *s,* two *p*'s. The adjective *disappointed* combines with several prepositions: *about, over, concerning, with,* and *at (She was much disappointed about [over, concerning, with, at] the outcome)*; *in (I was particularly disappointed in him)*; and *of (She was disappointed of her hopes)*. The combination with *of* is sometimes considered a bit old-fashioned, but it is Standard.

disapprove (*v.*) can be used with a direct object, as in *They disapproved my application* (meaning "They turned it down"), or combined with the preposition *of* in nearly the same sense, as in *She disapproved of the restaurant I chose* (meaning "She didn't like it"), or with *by,* as in *My choice of restaurant was disapproved by the entire party* (meaning that "The entire party disliked my choice"—i.e., the object of the preposition did the disapproving).

disassemble See DISSEMBLE.

disassociate See DISSOCIATE.

disastrous (*adj.*) has just three syllables (*diz-AS-truhs* or *dis-AS-truhs*); a frequent misspelling (*disasterous*) by the inexperienced gives it four, probably reflecting a mispronunciation (*diz-AS-tuhr-uhs* or *dis-AS-tuhr-uhs*). Both misspelling and mispronunciation are shibboleths.

disbar See DEBAR.

disburse, disperse (*vv.*) These are not exact homophones, although they might easily be confused if heard without helpful context. The medial consonant clusters differ (*-sb-* and *-sp-*), and the second element of the first is voiced, whereas the second element of the second is voiceless. *Disburse* means to "to pay out, to distribute money or other assets," as in *The treasurer had disbursed all available funds. Disperse* means "to scatter, to break up, to spread out," as in *The members quickly dispersed and fled the city.*

disc See DISK.

discernible, discernable (*adj.*) These two spellings are in divided usage, but Americans seem to prefer *-ible* here, just as they prefer *-able* on certain other words. See SPELLING OF UNSTRESSED VOWELS.

disciplinary (*adj.*) The American pronunciation is *DIS-i-plin-ER-ee,* the British, *DIS-i-PLIN-uhr-ee.*

disco (*adj., n., v.*), **discotheque, discothèque** (*n.*) The noun *disco* is a clipped form of *discotheque* (sometimes still spelled with the grave accent), meaning "a night spot where dancing is done to the music of phonograph records or discs." To enlarge its lexicon, this once-modish entertainment quickly availed itself of func-

tional shift: a *disco club* and *disco dancing* display the adjective; *to disco,* that is "to go to such a place to dance," is the verb. The noun *disco* is Standard, but the other parts of speech may be Semiformal or Conversational—as the phenomenon has faded, so too have these words. See PLURALS OF NOUNS ENDING IN *-O.*

discombobulate (*v.*) is an Americanism, a humorous word meaning "to upset, to disconcert, to confuse thoroughly." It is used mainly at Conversational levels or in Semiformal or Informal writing, and it contains its own hyperbole, suggesting that the disarrangement so caused is complete: *Our trick so discombobulated our opponents that they forgot to retaliate.*

discomfit (*v.*), **discomfiture** (*n.*), **discomfort** (*n., v.*), **uncomfortable** (*adj.*), **uncomfortably** (*adv.*) The verb *discomfit* once meant "to defeat or to frustrate completely," but because of their similarity in sound and spelling *discomfit* and *discomfort* have become synonyms in the sense "to make uncomfortable." *Discomfiture* is the noun made from *discomfit,* although it is getting to be rare; there is no such Standard word as *discomforture,* although it occasionally turns up in conversation or correspondence, apparently as still one more confusion of *discomfit* and *discomfort.* The noun of choice seems to be *discomfort,* and it is in increasingly wide Standard use; *discomfit* may be turning into the verb of choice. The adjective has long been *uncomfortable,* and the adverb *uncomfortably.*

discontent (*n.*) combines primarily with *with* and *over: Students usually display discontent with [over] the quality of dining hall meals.*

discotheque See DISCO.

discourage (*v.*), when combined with a preposition, is usually followed by *from (The noise in the hall discouraged them from their studies [from studying, from the completion of their assignments]),* although combinations with *by* and *into* are also Standard (*She was discouraged by their weak support; The negative reports from his staff discouraged him into declining the nomination after all*). The following combinations, however, are best limited to Conversational and Informal contexts: *The low returns discouraged him **with** the idea of running again. The complaints discouraged me **about** trying again.*

discourse See ORATION.

DISCOURSE, INDIRECT See DIRECT ADDRESS.

discover, invent (*vv.*) It used to be argued that these two words were mutually exclusive in meaning: you could *discover* what was unknown but there all along; you could *invent* only what had not existed heretofore. Today the two words are sometimes interchangeable. *Invent* can be followed only by a noun as direct object: *They invented a biodegradable plastic*. *Discover* can also be used in such structures, but it can be followed as well by a phrase with *how to* or a clause: *During their research they discovered* [*invented*] *a biodegradable plastic. They discovered that the stream was not polluted. Charles Goodyear discovered how to vulcanize rubber.*

discreet, discrete (*adjs.*) *Discreet* means "prudent, able to keep confidences, having good judgment": *She has always been discreet about her father's business affairs*. *Discrete* means "separate, distinct, noncontinuous": *These are discrete elements that share no basic characteristics*. These homophones come ultimately from the same Latin word, although by slightly different routes, and their spellings were once in confused divided usage. A fair number of what may be either spelling errors or confusions of the meanings of the two words continue to turn up in print, plus many more in correspondence and other Informal writing. Of course only context can clarify which word a speaker is using.

discrepancy, disparity (*nn.*) There is a good deal of overlap, but usually a *disparity* is a much greater difference than is a *discrepancy*. A *discrepancy* is "an inconsistency, a lack of agreement, a difference": *There was a discrepancy between the two accounts of what happened, but it didn't seem particularly significant*. A *disparity* is usually "an important difference, an inequality, something incongruous, markedly distinct, or fundamentally different": *The disparity between their proposals made compromise unlikely.*

discrete See DISCREET.

discriminate (*v.*), **discrimination** (*n.*) Both verb and noun have developed two very different senses, one—the older—describing a useful skill or ability: *His discrimination of colors is remarkably good. She discriminates colors poorly*. It gives us an elevated participial adjective: *Her tastes are refined and discriminating*. *Discrimination* has in recent years taken on a specialized sense, wherein public policy has been avowedly to end *discrimination* (the uneven or unfair application of laws and standards) against members of minority groups: *Discrimination*

(*racial, ethnic, or sexual*) *is a bad thing. That firm appears to discriminate illegally in its hiring*. The intransitive verb *discriminate* can combine with the prepositions *between* and *among* (*I can discriminate between whole milk and skim milk. Experienced cooks can discriminate by name among many forms of pasta*), and in a specialized sense meaning "to avoid racial discrimination," usually in the negative, intransitive *discriminate* appears without a following preposition: *I've been taught that in racial matters, you ought never to discriminate*. Transitive *discriminate* takes a direct object followed by a prepositional phrase, usually with *from*: *You must learn to discriminate the good kind of cholesterol from the bad kind*. The transitive uses are rarely pejorative; intransitive ones may be either pejorative or ameliorative.

discus (*n.*) has two Standard plurals, but *discuses* is used much more often than *disci*. See FOREIGN PLURALS.

discuss (*v.*) is followed by a direct object, not by a preposition; *We discussed his plans for the future* is Standard; *We discussed about his plans for the future* is not.

discussable, discussible (*adj.*) The Standard spelling of this suffix is in divided usage in this word. See SPELLING OF UNSTRESSED VOWELS.

disembark See DEBARK.

disenfranchise See DISFRANCHISE.

disfavor, disfavour (*n.*) The American spelling is *disfavor*. See SPELLING (1).

disfranchise, disenfranchise (*vv.*) The two verbs are exact synonyms meaning "to remove, cancel, or take away the franchise." *Disfranchise* is older and more frequent than *disenfranchise*. The noun *franchise* is the key: it means "the right to vote," "a privilege granted by an authority," or "an exclusive right to sell a product in a particular area" or "the area itself," plus some other figurative uses. To *enfranchise* and to *franchise* are also synonyms, meaning "to grant a franchise." The prefix *dis-* reverses the meanings of *franchise* and *enfranchise* alike.

disgruntle, disgruntled See GRUNTLE.

disgusted (*adj.*) can combine with prepositions *at, by,* or *with: We were all disgusted at* [*by, with*] *the way things turned out.*

dishabille, deshabille (*n.*) *Dishabille*, an English noun meaning "casually, carelessly, or only partly dressed," is the more commonly encountered spelling of what was once a French past participle, *déshabillé,* "undressed." The usual English pronunciation is *dis-ah-BEEL,* although there are variant pronunciations that echo the French a trifle more. *Deshabille*, without the acute accents, is a variant spelling.

disinformation, misinformation, propaganda (*nn.*) *Disinformation* is a relatively new word, meaning "deliberately false or distorted information given out in order to mislead or deceive." *Misinformation*, a much older word, means "inaccurate or erroneous information, provided usually without conscious effort at misleading, deceiving, or persuading one way or another." *Propaganda* is "information, ideas, and the like spread in order to advance or injure a cause." Presumably *propaganda* could contain a mixture of truth, *misinformation*, and *disinformation*; the main point is that whatever information there is will be so arranged, edited, and displayed that it will assist the cause the *propagandist* supports or injure the cause the *propagandist* hopes to damage. The suppression of information can of course play a part in all three.

disinterest, disinterestedness, uninterest (*nn.*) The noun *disinterest* regularly stirs up defenders of the language who are dead certain but dead wrong in asserting that it should be used to mean *only* "impartiality." In fact, it has two current meanings, "lack or absence of interest," as in *His disinterest in sports baffles his father*, and "impartiality," as in *Her disinterest makes her ideal as an arbitrator. Disinterestedness*, on the other hand, means only "impartiality": *The storied judicial temperament has its foundation in disinterestedness. Uninterest* occurs less frequently but seems always to mean "lack or absence of interest": *Her uninterest in his devotion to her was embarrassingly clear.*

disinterested, uninterested (*adjs.*) *Uninterested* is not very much used these days, whereas *disinterested* is frequently used to mean "indifferent, not interested, unconcerned" and "having just lost interest or concern," in addition to its older meaning of "without bias, impartial." All these are Standard today, even though many commentators would prefer *uninterested* to handle all need for an "indifferent" sense and reserve *disinterested* for the "impartial" sense alone. At present, even though Edited English and Formal and Oratorical contexts try to prevent the use of *disinterested* to mean "indifferent or having just lost interest," all these examples are Standard: *Her disinterested intervention in the quarrel helped to restore calm. His disinterested expression suggested that his thoughts were far away. After listening to her drone on for an hour, I became disinterested.*

Uninterested will also work nicely in the latter two examples, and some purists insist that only it is appropriate in them. In any event, whenever you use *disinterested*, context must make clear the sense you're using. See also INTEREST.

DISJUNCTS, ADVERBIAL See HOPEFULLY; IRONICALLY; SENTENCE ADVERBS.

disk, disc (*nn.*) These were once variant spellings, but American English seems now to have made *disk* the generic word (the British prefer *disc* for this purpose), meaning "a flat round object, whether literally a *disk*, such as a coin, or something that appears disk-shaped, such as the image of the sun." The bits of cartilage between the vertebrae in the human spine are also *disks. Disc* then has specialized in American use, meaning particularly "a phonograph record or a compact *disc*," but it seems now to be being replaced by *disk* in most computer-related senses and to be in fading but divided usage as the name of the farmer's *disk* [*disc*] *harrow.*

dislike (*n., v.*) The noun combines mainly with *of* and *for*, as in *I have a dislike of [for] formality*, though it occasionally combines with *to* as well, as in *She took a sudden dislike to his parents* (*take a dislike to* is idiomatic). The verb combines with gerund and infinitive phrases (*She dislikes seeing him so upset; He dislikes to be seen in that state*), although the infinitive phrase is relatively rare in Standard English.

dismayed (*adj.*) combines with the prepositions *at*, *by*, and occasionally *with*, as in *Peter was dismayed at [by, with] her lack of concern*. It can also combine with an infinitive phrase, as in *He was dismayed to find no one at home.*

disorient, disorientate (*vv.*) These two are exact synonyms, but some commentators who seek conciseness and dislike polysyllables prefer *disorient* and argue that *disorientate* is both ugly and unnecessary. Such pronouncements are based strictly on opinion—both words are Standard. See ORIENTATE.

DISPARAGING LABELS See OFFENSIVE EPITHETS AND DISPARAGING LABELS.

disparate (*adj.*) means "different, unequal, dissimilar," as in *Their disparate ways of preparing food puzzled us*. Its pronunciation is in divided usage, either *DIS-puhr-it* or *dis-PER-it*. Some objections have been raised to using intensifiers with this already powerful adjective, but both comparisons and intensifying with *more* and *most* here are matters of taste and style.

disparity See DISCREPANCY.

dispassionate, impassioned (*adjs.*) These two are antonyms. *Dispassionate* means "not influenced by emotion or strong feelings," "calm, detached": *His appraisal of their chances for escape was cool and dispassionate. Impassioned* means "filled with intense emotion, moved by strong feelings," "warm": *Her plea for their cooperation was impassioned and persuasive.*

dispatch, despatch (*n., v.*) *Dispatch* is the usual spelling, *despatch* an infrequent Standard variant.

dispel (*v.*) means "to drive away or scatter," as in *The wind and sun eventually dispelled the clouds.* See CONSONANTS (2).

dispense, dispose (*vv.*) These two may be confused in their one shared sense, "to distribute," as in *She dispensed [disposed of] her personal possessions to her children. Dispense* means both "to deal out, distribute," as in *He dispensed apples and candy bars to the children,* and "to prepare and give out," as in *The pharmacist dispenses prescription drugs.* It also means "to administer," as in *The squire dispensed rough justice from his front stoop.* When used in the passive with *from,* it also means "to excuse," as in *She was dispensed from having to attend chapel. Dispense* in combination with *with* is an idiom meaning "to suspend operations," "to do away with," or "to get along without": *We'll dispense with introductions and go right to work. We can dispense with observers and staff people. Dispense* also combines with *to,* as in *We dispensed coffee to all the guests.*

Dispose of means "to transfer or distribute things in an orderly fashion," as in *In the will he disposed of his estate very sensibly,* "to do away with," as in *We have to dispose of all those old tires somehow,* and "to complete, bring to conclusion," as in *We finally disposed of all the business before the committee. To be disposed* means "to have an inclination or tendency to" as in *She's disposed toward colds and sniffles all winter long*; *to dispose* means "to set in order, arrange," as in *The general disposed his troops on the high ground.* All these uses are Standard.

dispersal, dispersion (*nn.*) These are synonyms in the sense "a breaking up, a scattering about, a dispelling," but *dispersion* also has several specialized senses (as *dispersal* does not), most of them scientific and technical. See your dictionary.

disperse See DISBURSE.

dispersion See DISPERSAL.

displace, replace (*vv.*) To *displace* something is "to move it, to put something in its place, to remove from office or to fire": *The new robot displaces nearly twenty workers. The hulls of a catamaran displace surprisingly little water.* To *replace* something is either "to put it back where it was" or "to supplant it with something new": *I replaced the broken window pane. The new robot replaces nearly twenty workers.* See also REPLACE.

disposal, disposition (*nn.*) These are synonyms in certain senses, quite different in others. Both nouns mean "the arrangement or settlement of items, affairs, or issues" (*The disposition [disposal] of his personal effects was left to his widow*), "the getting rid of something" (*The disposal [disposition] of toxic wastes has become a serious national issue*), and "the power and authority to dispose" (*She has his entire estate at her disposal [disposition]*). But a *disposal* (sometimes a trade name usually pronounced with a *secondary* stress on the final syllable, rhyming with *fall*) is also a garbage grinder built into a kitchen sink. Your *disposition* is quite another matter: it may be either an inclination or a tendency (*a disposition to evade responsibility*) or your temperament (*a sunny disposition*).

dispose, dispose of See DISPENSE.

disposition See DISPOSAL.

dispossess (*v.*), when it combines with a preposition, uses *of* most of the time: *The judge's ruling dispossessed the defendant of her house, her car, and much of her jewelry.* Occasionally but rarely it combines with *from: Dispossessed from all his property, he left the country.*

disputable (*adj.*) has three pronunciations in divided usage: *dis-PYOOT-uh-bul, DIS-pyuht-uh-bul,* and *DIS-pyoot-uh-bul.*

dispute (*n., v.*) The verb is pronounced *dis-PYOOT,* and this is also one of two Standard pronunciations of the noun; the other for the noun is *DIS-pyoot,* although many Standard speakers consider that pronunciation Nonstandard.

disqualified See UNQUALIFIED.

disqualify (*v.*), when it combines with a preposition, does so with either *from* or *for: She was disqualified from further competition. He was disqualified for failing to sign up before the deadline. Disqualify* can also take a direct object: *Failure to sign up before the deadline disqualified him.*

disregard (*n.*) When it combines with a preposition, the noun *disregard* is followed by either *of* or *for*: *Your disregard of the regulations will prevent your competing. Your disregard for the safety of your passengers could cause you to lose your license.*

disremember (*v.*), meaning "forget" or "do not remember," as in *I've seen her before, but just now I disremember her name,* is dialectal and Nonstandard.

dissatisfied, unsatisfied (*adjs.*) These two are synonyms in the sense "not satisfied," but they differ in other ways. *Dissatisfied* means "displeased, discontented, or not satisfied" and usually describes people or other animals: *We were dissatisfied with our rooms. The dog seemed dissatisfied when confined to the tiny run. Unsatisfied* means "not satisfied, not fulfilled, or left undone" and modifies conditions, needs, and other inanimate matters, as in *The appetites of the hungry hikers were left unsatisfied* and *An unsatisfied requirement in science prevented her graduation,* and also modifies persons, where it suggests that their needs are not fully met. Both *dissatisfied* and *unsatisfied* combine regularly with the prepositions *at, by, with,* and *after,* as in *Dissatisfied at [by, with] the filthy state of his room, he complained to the clerk at the desk* or *She was unsatisfied [dissatisfied] after her meal. Dissatisfied* can also combine with *about* and *concerning: My parents were dissatisfied about [concerning] the teacher's apparent laxity in discipline.*

dissect See BISECT.

dissemble, disassemble (*vv.*) As a transitive verb *dissemble* means "to disguise or to conceal, especially a feeling or an emotion": *She dissembled her feelings of fear so well that no one suspected how frightened she was.* As an intransitive verb, it means "to pretend, to conceal, to be hypocritical": *The only way to fool his captors was to dissemble, to pretend to be cowed. Disassemble* is quite unrelated; it means "to take apart": *The child disassembled the alarm clock in record time.*

dissension (*n.*) is sometimes, but rarely, spelled *dissention.*

dissent (*n., v.*) Both parts of speech combine mainly with the prepositions *from* and *against: She insisted on dissenting from [against] the majority's proposal. Our dissent from [against] the resolution was unpopular.* The verb sometimes combines with *to* (*We were dissenting to the list of solutions they had suggested*), but some Standard users don't like it, and therefore you should avoid it. Say *We opposed the list . . . instead.*

dissertation, thesis (*nn.*) Each of these words has a specialized academic sense, plus another more general sense. In academic circles, a *thesis* is the name usually given the long research paper submitted as one of the requirements for a master's degree: *a master's thesis.* For the doctor of philosophy degree, the long, written "original contribution to knowledge" is usually called the *dissertation,* or *the doctoral* [or *Ph.D.*] *dissertation,* although it is sometimes the custom at some universities to call it *a doctoral thesis.* To call the *master's thesis* a *master's dissertation* is much rarer, but not unheard of. The more general senses of these words are also Standard: a *dissertation* is a term applied, sometimes jocularly, to a long, perhaps boring monologue by an earnest speaker, as in *He then delivered us a long dissertation on the importance of interstate banking regulations*; a *thesis* is simply the main point or thread of an argument, oral or written, as in *Her thesis is that day-care centers for the elderly are an economic necessity today.*

dissimilar (*adj.*) can combine with either *from* or *to*: *Arguments dissimilar from [to] these are harder to find than once they were.* Both combined uses are Standard, although objections have occasionally been raised over the use of *to.*

DISSIMILATION is a process in speech whereby one of two similar sounds gets changed or dropped as we actually say the word in context. In English, *l*'s and *r*'s are the sounds most often affected: *thermometer* gets pronounced *thuh-MAHM-i-tuhr, governor GUHV-uh-nuhr,* and *colonel KUHR-nuhl.* The first two examples are acceptable at all levels except the Oratorical; *colonel* is pronounced in the *dissimilated* fashion at all Standard English levels.

dissimulate See SIMULATE.

dissociate, disassociate (*vv.*) Both mean "to cut ties with or break off relationships with," but *dissociate* is much more frequently used and has a greater variety of meanings, such as "to separate," "to cause to dissociate," and the idiomatic *to dissociate oneself from,* which means "to deny that one has any connection or affiliation with or interest in": *He had long since dissociated himself from the supply-side economists.*

distaff (*adj., n.*) A *distaff* is the staff for holding flax or wool when you spin thread in the timeless classical method; as the man's staff or spear was the symbol of his activities and person in the classical world, so the *distaff* was the woman's, and so *distaff* remains, mainly in adjectival use, a synonym for *female* or *woman* or *women*. Reference to *the distaff side* is a cliché of some stature and tradition in subjects ranging from literature and politics to horseracing and the family, and thus far the term appears not to have been challenged as sexist language, although it is clearly exclusive. It continues in full Standard use, although some may consider it old-fashioned.

distaste (*n.*) combines most frequently with the preposition *for,* as in *His distaste for anything mathematical baffled his parents.* But occasionally *distaste* will combine with *at* or *over,* as in *Her distaste at [over] being obliged to attend children's recitals was painfully obvious,* and rarely *toward* or *towards* will occur, as in *She makes clear to everyone her distaste toward [towards] popular music of every description.*

distasteful, tasteless (*adjs.*) Anything *distasteful* is "unpleasant or disagreeable," but the *taste/distaste* part of it is all figurative: *When his family was away, he found most distasteful the silence. Tasteless,* however, has both literal and figurative meanings; it means "without literal flavor" and "offensive to any of the other tastes we have developed," as in the literal *Her soups were somehow always almost tasteless and watery* and the figurative *She thought his comments rude and tasteless. The furnishing of the house was almost uniformly tasteless and uninteresting.*

distil, distil (*v.*) American English has largely settled on *distill* for the infinitive, though *distil* is a variant spelling. Even in the variant, however, the inflected forms *distilled* and *distilling* double the *l.* The verb combines with several prepositions but most commonly with *from, out of,* and *of* when referring to raw materials, with *through* for the midpoint of the process, and with *to* and *into* for the resultant *distillate* itself: *They distilled the whiskey from [out of, of] corn and some other grains. They distilled the first liquids through a homemade copper apparatus. They distilled the new whiskey once again into [to] something that would after aging ultimately be drinkable.*

distinct, distinctive (*adjs.*) Anything that is *distinct* is clearly distinguishable from everything else; something *distinctive* is a quality or characteristic that makes it possible for us to distinguish one thing from another. *Distinct* speech is clear; *distinctive* speech is special or

unusual. So a pileated woodpecker is a woodpecker *distinct* from most other woodpeckers, *distinguishable* from other woodpeckers; its large size is *distinctive,* helping us *distinguish* it from most other woodpeckers.

distinguish See DIFFERENTIATE.

distinguished, distinguishing (*adjs.*) *Distinguished* means "renowned, eminent, marked by excellence, dignified in appearance or manner," as in *She was a distinguished novelist and literary critic* or *He is a distinguished-looking man. Distinguishing* is applied to "those characteristics or qualities that make a person, an idea, or an artifact outstanding, observably different from others of the same general sort," as in *The distinguishing characteristics of the bird's appearance are its very large size, its very long, strong beak, and its strikingly contrasting red, white, and black feathers.* See DIFFERENTIATE.

distract See DETRACT.

distrait, distracted, distraught (*adjs.*) These words are at least partly synonymous. *Distrait* is a word of French origin, still pronounced in the French way, (*dis-TRAI*); it also has a French feminine form, *distraite* (pronounced *dis-TRAIT*), now rare in English; *distrait*'s meanings in English are variously "upset, confused, inattentive, distracted, abstracted." It is a very low frequency word, perhaps even precious-sounding, limited to relatively Formal and literary uses or to consciously cultivated speech: *She was flushed and nervous, so distrait that she did not notice that her purse was open. Distraught* means "extremely confused, maddened, wild with anxiety": *The parents were hysterical, distraught with fear for their missing child. Distracted* has two related senses: "having the attention drawn away, diverted to something else" (*The squeal of tires distracted her from her writing*) and "being confused, drawn in all sorts of conflicting directions, not able to be fully rational" (*The noise finally drove me distracted; I could neither think nor talk sensibly*). See also ABSTRACTED.

distressed (*adj.*) has some specialized figurative senses, beyond the general "full of distress, troubled" meaning, that are not always obvious out of context: (1) a *distressed area* is "a district, area, or other place known to be full of the poor, the unemployed, the have-nots"; (2) *distressed goods* are "repossessed or reclaimed furniture and other goods," to be sold at *a distressed sale* or *a sale of distressed household goods,* etc.; and (3) a *distressed finish* is "an artificial finish put on furniture to make it look antique.'' All are Standard.

distrust See MISTRUST.

distrustful (*adj.*) combines with the preposition *of: The old woman is distrustful of her children's intentions.*

dive 1 (*n.*) is Standard in most literal and some figurative senses having to do with the act of diving but is best limited to Conversational and Informal use in the sense "an unsavory, cheap, tough place of entertainment, a disreputable tavern.'' From football comes the jargon sense "a dive play, when the ball carrier dives into the line, seeking short yardage.'' The idiom *to take a dive,* meaning "to pretend to be knocked out in boxing'' or, more generally, "deliberately to lose a contest of any sort,'' is slang.

dive 2 (*v.*) has long been a weak verb, with past tense and past participle *dived,* as in *We dived for cover.* Today *dived* in the past tense is in divided usage with *dove* (rhymes with *cove*), perhaps developed in an analogy with *drive/drove* or *strive/strove: We dove from the pier.* Both *dived* and *dove* are Standard, although some conservatives still dislike *dove,* and some speakers of Northern and some other dialects think *dived* sounds a bit odd. *Dove* is thought to be gaining ground on *dived* these days. Use whichever sounds right to you.

divergent (*adj.*) Pronounce it either *di-VUHR-jint* or *dei-VUHR-jint.*

diverse, divers (*adjs.*) *Diverse* (pronounced *di-VUHRS, dei-VURHS,* or—rarely—*DEI-vuhrs*) means "dissimilar, different, varied, diversified,'' as in *The foods on the menu were diverse enough to meet almost any taste. Divers* (pronounced *DEI-vuhrz*) means "varied or several,'' as in *The candies were in divers colors, shapes, and flavors.*

diversion See INVERSION (1).

divest (*v.*) (pronounced either *di-VEST* or *dei-VEST*) means "to strip of, to take away, to get rid of.'' It has until recently been followed by a reflexive pronoun in most uses: *You will need to divest yourself of all stocks that might suggest any conflict of interest.* This structure, in which the verb regularly combines with *of,* continues to be the one accepted as fully Standard English at all levels. Lately, however, *divest* has also begun to take a direct object other than a reflexive pronoun: *The foundation decided to divest all its South African stocks.* This use has been controversial in much of Edited English and appears to be limited mainly to journalese, to

Semiformal and Informal writing, and to the Conversational levels. But it seems to gain ground daily, and it may well be fully Standard soon, particularly if *divestiture of* (a much more frequent Standard combined form) investments in controversial environmental, human rights, commercial, and other vexed areas continues to attract attention. *Divest* can also be heard with a personal pronoun as direct object: *They divested him of his coat and hat.*

divide, divide up (*vv.*) *Divide* frequently combines with the prepositions *into* and *in* (*We divided into discussion groups; The moderator divided the group in half*) and with *among* and *between* (*Party members were badly divided among themselves; The chamber was nearly equally divided between conservative and liberal deputies*). It also combines with *from,* as in *Our views of economics seem always to divide me from my father,* and *over, on,* and *upon* can appear in a similar set of senses dealing with the nature of the division: *Our family councils divided on* [*upon, over*] *almost every political issue. Divide with* also occurs, as in *We divided most of the prizes with their team. Divide by* is both a mathematical formula, as in *Divide your elapsed time by the number of miles you've driven* and a more generalized meaning, as in *We are divided by our nationalities, our languages, and our religions.* Finally, *divide up,* like *break up, think up,* and other combinations with *up,* has caused concern in some quarters, where the *up* has been declared superfluous. Both *Divide the spoils* and *Divide up the spoils,* however, are Standard. The difference in these *up* combinations is either idiomatic (*break* and *break up* are not the same actions, for example) or else a matter of relative emphasis and style. Conservative editors will usually prefer whenever possible to omit *up* for the sake of economy of style.

DIVIDED USAGE We say that a *usage* is *divided* when the constituency under study considers acceptable either of two or any of three or more forms, senses, constructions, spellings, or pronunciations. The spellings *judgment* and *judgement* are both acceptable American English; the word's spelling is *in divided usage.* The plural of *curriculum* is either *curricula* or *curriculums*; these plurals are *in divided usage*; both are Standard. But *curriculas* is not acceptable as a plural and hence is not in *divided usage* within the constituency that embraces Standard English. Most people have their favorites: some prefer *judgment,* for example, and some, especially those with a bit of Latin stored away, dislike *curriculums* and prefer *curricula.* You must keep in mind, though, that publishers may specify their house preferences for one *divided usage* over another (this author, for example, prefers *rime* to the *rhyme* spelling required by his publisher). And since *divided usages* may be evidences of change in progress, make every effort to keep track of the way such usages fare: society may make a single choice from options in *divided usage* and then begin to enforce that choice as the only Standard, sometimes within a surprisingly short time.

dividend, divisor, quotient (*nn.*) In mathematics the *dividend* is "the quantity to be divided: in *6 ÷ 2 = 3*, the *divisor* is *2*, the *dividend* is *6*, and the *quotient* is *3*. A *dividend* is also a periodic share of profits declared by a company to be paid to its shareholders. Both these senses are Standard. *Dividend,* meaning "a bit extra," as in *There's a bit more in the pitcher; care for a dividend?* is Informal and Conversational.

divide up See DIVIDE.

divisive (*adj.*), meaning "causing disagreement or division," has pronunciations in divided usage: *di-VEIS-iv, di-VIS-iv, di-VEIZ-iv,* and *di-VIZ-iv.* The first two are much more commonly heard.

divisor See DIVIDEND.

divorce (*v.*), when combined with a preposition, almost always does so with *by* or *from,* depending at least in part on who initiated the action: *Last year he was divorced by his wife* (she initiated it). *Last year he was divorced from his wife* (the usual inference would be that he initiated it: *Last year he divorced his wife* would remove any doubt).

divorcé, divorcée (*nn.*) are, respectively, the terms used to specify "a divorced man" and "a divorced woman." These French words almost always keep their acute accent marks and masculine or feminine endings to distinguish them from the verb and noun *divorce* and to remind us of their three-syllable French-styled English pronunciation, *di-vor-SAI* (for each). See FEMININE OCCUPATIONAL FORMS.

djin, djinn See GENIE.

do 1 (*v., aux.*) *Do* is one of the highest-frequency verbs/auxiliaries in English. It is first of all a verb, both transitive (*He did his best*) and intransitive (*He'll do,* meaning "he'll meet our needs and serve us satisfactorily"). The transitive uses are legion, particularly in the many idioms, such as *do the dishes, do your homework, do the tax return, do my nails, do the*

cleaning, and the like. People also *do a play,* meaning "they put it on," *do something for a living,* meaning "have a job of some sort, work at a profession or vocation," and report that *the chicken is done,* meaning "it's finished baking or cooking." There are many, many more such idioms, some of them fully Standard, and many more of them slang or Conversational and Informal. Among the rapidly shifting slang idiomatic uses of *do: He's been doing time,* meaning "He's been in prison," *She doesn't do drugs,* meaning "She doesn't take drugs," *You've been done,* meaning "You've been cheated," *That's already been done,* meaning "Your idea has already been treated in a book, play, novel, etc.," and the now almost passé *Shall we do lunch?* meaning "Shall we have lunch together?" Other idioms involve combinations with prepositions: *do up* means "to wrap or assemble" (*Will you do up a package of these?*); *do up right* means "to complete the job carefully," often used sarcastically (*When he smashed the car, he really did it up right*); *do in* means "to destroy literally or figuratively" (*Her pride did her in*); *do with* means "would like or need" (*I could do with a haircut*); *do over* means "to remodel, to redesign" (*She's done over the kitchen*); and the like. The list could be much longer were there space. And some of these slang idioms may eventually become Standard (as have those at the head of the list).

Do is also an auxiliary, used to intensify or to emphasize in contradistinction to some claim to the contrary: *He does believe her story. I do do windows. She does do nice work.* (In these latter two examples, as well as in *What did you do then?* both the full verb and the auxiliary appear.) And we also use the auxiliary as a substitute word in conversation: "Please call home." "I already *did.*" (Note the frequent use of *do* as an auxiliary to replace *have,* in perfect tenses.) At all the Conversational levels and in the Informal and Semiformal writing that imitates them, *do* lives a rich and varied life.

do 2, doings (*nn.*) *A big do* is slang for "an impressive party or other social occasion"; *big doings* are "important activities," as in *There are big doings in the Capitol tonight.* The no *un do* is also a slang clipping of *hairdo,* "an arrangement of (usually) a woman's hair."

dock, dry dock, graving dock, pier, wharf (*nn.*), **dry-dock** (*v.*) An American *dock* has come to mean a *pier* or *wharf,* a structure alongside which ships tie up for loading and unloading, although there may be a *dock,* tiny by comparison, for a rowboat at a summer cottage too. A British *dock* is a walled-in basin in which ships shelter behind gates while they load, unload, or get repairs. Americans still use a version of that sense in the terms *dry dock* and *graving dock*. The latter is a permanent structure made of stone or concrete that can be pumped dry so that work can be done on a ship's hull. A *dry dock* has a similar purpose but is frequently a floating affair that is sunk to admit the ship to be repaired and then floated again to get the ship high and dry. To put a ship in (into) *dry dock* is to *dry-dock* it, spelled as one hyphenated word. *Piers* are columns and hence are also shore structures that thrust out into the water, supported by *piers*. An American *wharf* is usually large and may be built along the shore, rather than thrust far out into the water like a *pier*. The important usage observation is that American landlubbers (and others too) use all three terms almost interchangeably.

doctor (*n.*), **Dr.** (*abbrev.*) Americans are said to have long been enamored of titles. Certainly many Americans love to be called *Doctor*, a fancy that is amusing and harmless except to those duped by it. Generally, our punctilio goes something like this: licensed medical people in this country usually refer to themselves as physicians or surgeons and use the *Doctor* title only as a term of direct address. Dentists, veterinarians, and other licensed practitioners also use the title, many of them primarily as a matter of courtesy. In academe, the larger and more prestigious the institution, the more likely its faculty are to possess earned doctorates in other than medical fields and to use by preference the title of *Mr., Ms., Mrs., Miss,* or *Professor, not Doctor*. In smaller, less prestigious institutions, the fewer the earned doctorates, the more those who have them are likely to prefer the title. More than most other nations—more even than the Germans—Americans invite and permit all sorts of people in all sorts of vocations to earn or be given or even give themselves the title of *Doctor*. It is, of course, quite frequently simply a matter of euphemism, but it is also said to enhance the fortunes of persons who can successfully claim or pretend to the title. Our universities are generous with honorary doctorates, and few people of any distinction or longevity in public life have failed to snare at least one or two of them. We also have a long history of having used the title for quacks and pretenders, from purveyors of snake oil to piano players in wild western saloons. Now of course things are much improved.

doctrinal (*adj.*) Most Americans say it *DAHK-tri-nuhl,* but some of us also use the British pronunciation, *dahk-TREI-nuhl,* which is in divided usage in the United States.

dodo (*n.*) was the name of a flightless bird, now extinct. When using it figuratively, consider it Conversational at best, but more probably slang, and use it figuratively only of old fools and of younger folk who behave stupidly. The cliché *dead as a dodo* probably also deserves extinction. See PLURALS OF NOUNS ENDING IN -O.

doesn't See DON'T.

doff, don (*vv.*) These two were originally Middle English verbs, combined forms made up of *do off* and *do on*; hence *doff* means "take off, remove" as with a hat or coat or other clothing, and *don* means "put on, wrap yourself in," again as with a hat or coat or other clothing. These are somewhat bookish or ceremonious words today, often used jocularly as well, and they are Standard.

dogged (*adj.*), **dog** (*v.*) The adjective is pronounced with two syllables, *DAW-ged,* and means "unflagging, stubborn," as in *He worked with untiring, dogged determination*. The past tense of the verb, *dogged,* is pronounced as a single syllable, *DAWGD,* meaning "followed closely, as by a faithful dog," as in *The youngsters dogged their scoutmaster's footsteps through the woods*.

dog watch See BELLS.

doings See DO (2).

dolor, dolour (*n.*), **dolorous** (*adj.*) The American spelling of the noun is *dolor,* the British is *dolour,* and both dialects spell the adjective *dolorous. Dolor* is a literary word for "suffering, grief, anguish." See SPELLING (1).

dolphin, porpoise (*nn.*) The *dolphin* and *porpoise* are related to each other, both being small, toothed whales. Furthermore, each is often called by the other's name, even though they look a bit different in that the *dolphin* has a beaked nose unlike the *porpoise's*.

domain See DEMESNE.

Domesday, doomsday (*nn.*) *Doomsday* was a day in Old English times when judicial decisions were pronounced, and it also became the name Christians gave to the day of the Last Judgment. *The Domesday Book* is the huge survey of landholdings in England done for William the Conqueror in the eleventh century, so named because it was a legal undertaking, and it aimed to be as fair and relentless as Judgment Day itself. *Doom* and *doomsday* are pronounced

DOOM and *DOOMZ-DAI,* but the name of William's famous 1086 survey tome is pronounced either the *DOMZ-DAI* or *DOOMZ-DAI* book.

domicile *(n., v.)* has four pronunciations, *DAHM-i-sil, DAHM-i-seil, DOM-i-sil,* or *DOM-i-seil.* The noun is a dwelling or residence, and the verb means "to establish one of these" or "to live there."

dominate, domineer *(vv.),* **domineering** *(adj.)* To dominate is "to control, to rule, to tower over, to have first place," as in *The Russians have dominated pairs skating for the last several Olympics. To domineer* is even tougher, harsher; it means "to bully, to play the tyrant over, to rule harshly," as in *He domineered in every possible way.* Both *dominate* and *domineer* can combine intransitively with *over: Some teachers dominate [domineer] over every thought their pupils entertain.* More common than *domineer* today is its present participle, which is now a participial adjective, *domineering,* meaning "overbearing, tyrannical": *A domineering supervisor can be an employee's torment.*

dominie See PRIEST.

domino *(n.)* The plural is either *dominoes* or *dominos.* See PLURALS OF NOUNS ENDING IN *-O.*

don See DOFF.

donate *(v.),* meaning "to give money, goods, or services to a fund or cause," is a back-formation from the noun *donation,* and it is a verb to which commentators once took exception. Now, however, it is Standard English. Stress it on either syllable.

done *(past participle, adj.)* Some commentators apparently thought *finished* would be a more explicit and genteel word than *done,* meaning "finished or completed" *(The chicken is done; We're all done with our work),* and for a time they tried to restrict *done* in this sense to Conversational use. But today both *done* and *finished* are Standard, and you may use whichever one meets the style requirements of your speech or writing. The adjective *done,* in the slang expression, "a done deal," is commercial jargon meaning "the agreement is final." *Done* as past tense, as in *He done it,* is considered Vulgar and dialectal. *Done* as an auxiliary, as in *She done got her a new dress,* is dialectal and Nonstandard, was earlier limited to Southern and South Midland dialects, and is probably most active today in Northern Urban Black English. Its use in Standard English is a shibboleth. See also DO (1).

donnybrook *(n.)* A *donnybrook* (sometimes capitalized, after the name of the nineteenth-century Irish fair so renowned for its drunken brawling) is a free-for-all rough-and-tumble fight, often alcohol-aided. The word is considered Standard by most people, although some would limit it to Conversational and Semiformal or Informal use: *What began as a shouting match between pickets and bystanders turned quickly into a regular donnybrook.*

don't, doesn't The present tense negative contraction of the verb *do* is *don't* for all persons except the third person singular, which has a Standard negative contraction, *doesn't,* one probably not heard before 1800. Indeed, well into the twentieth century many Standard speakers used *don't* instead of *doesn't.* The usage continues strong in some Conversational use in certain regional dialects and in Common and Vulgar English and remains Standard among some older speakers at the Casual and Intimate levels: *He don't have the money for it. It don't seem to matter now.* Inadvertent use of *it don't* or *she don't* outside those limits is Nonstandard, although no great fuss is made about their Casual use. In Formal and Semiformal writing and at the Oratorical and most Planned and Impromptu levels, *it don't* is Substandard. It is an odd form to begin with, its pronunciation being very different from what we might consider a normal contraction of *do* plus *not.* It seems to have come about through analogy with *won't,* which is just as oddly pronounced and even more oddly formed. Both *do* and *will,* however, are auxiliaries—high-frequency words that are in many ways idiomatic laws unto themselves. And *do* is a very high frequency verb as well, so anomalies in its forms and uses should not surprise. See also CONTRACTIONS; DO (1).

don't let's See LET.

don't seem See DON'T THINK.

don't think, as in *I don't think it's raining,* is fine in conversation, although purists often criticize it for being illogical. You *did* think, the objector notes; the negative belongs with the *raining,* not with the *thinking;* that is, *I think it is not raining.* But idioms don't have to be logical, and *(I) don't think* is a Standard Conversational idiom, widely accepted in all but the most Formal writing as well. See CONTRACTIONS; RAISING.

donut See DOUGHNUT.

doomsday See DOMESDAY.

dope *(n., v.)* As a Standard noun, *dope* is a generic term for any thickish liquid, any varnish-like substance used as a finish, especially the *dope* used to coat and tighten the fabric on early airplane wings. *Dope* is also Informal or Conversational as a general term for a narcotic, although some would argue that it is in most uses outdated and possibly archaic in that sense. (It is currently revived as slang for marijuana only.) *Dope* also has other slang uses, in the transferred sense "a stupid, dull person" and (from the inside information gamblers consulted about whether a horse had been *doped* or not) a further transferred sense meaning "information, especially inside information." But this use too is dated. The verb is Standard meaning "to apply dope to a surface"; Informal or Colloquial meaning "to administer a narcotic"; archaic slang meaning "to take drugs"; and slang too, though dated, in the combined use with *out,* meaning "to figure out what something means," as in *I think I've doped out what they're after.* The main thing about *dope* in its senses concerned with drugs is that it has mostly faded; in the world of drug dealing and drug using, today we have many more Standard terms to describe the national problem now that it is out in the open, and many, many more Slang terms, argot terms, and the like that keep bubbling up from beneath the problem's surface.

dote (*v.*) means "to be old, weak-minded, and foolish" and, in combination with the preposition *on,* "to be fond or affectionate to the point of foolishness," as in *She simply dotes on her grandson, showering him with gifts and endearments.*

dotty (*adj.*) has a Standard literal meaning, "covered with dots," but its Informal and Conversational sense is more commonly encountered, although the young may consider it dated: "feeble-minded, daft, unbalanced, crazy," as in *They've gone dotty in their old age, taking up one silly hobby after another.*

DOUBLE COMPARATIVE, DOUBLE COMPARISON *Double comparison* is taboo in Standard English except for fun: *Your cooking is more tastier than my mother's. I can see more better with my new glasses.* These illustrate the classic *double comparative* construction, with the periphrastic *more* or *most* used to intensify an adjective or adverb already inflected for the comparative or superlative. A belt-and-suspenders usage, this is a once-Standard but now unacceptable construction (like the double negative) that illustrates yet again our penchant for hyperbole. Shakespeare (*the most unkindest cut of all*) and other Renaissance writers used *double comparison* to add vigor, enthusiasm, and emphasis, and so do young children and other unwary speakers of Nonstandard English today, but the eighteenth-century grammarians seem to have prevailed, and one comparison per adjective is all today's Standard English will allow. The power of this usage decision shows clearly in the ease with which most Standard speakers use *double comparisons* jocularly; they can do so confidently only because they know their readers and hearers know that they know better. See ADJECTIVES (1).

DOUBLE ENTENDRE See DOUBLE MEANING.

DOUBLE GENITIVE Although English has long and happily employed the *double genitive,* as in *That lawnmower of Eleanor's works fine,* this construction, which wraps both the periphrastic genitive with *of* and the inflected genitive with the apostrophe plus *s* around *Eleanor* to make possession double, is now limited to our Informal and Semiformal writing and to the lowest levels of our speech, if we use it at all. Once again eighteenth-century argument (that one genitive is enough, and two are improper) has at least partly won out over exuberance, hyperbole, and redundancy. But only partly. A good many of us do use some *double genitives* and do not notice that they are double. Some language liberals argue that in Informal and Casual contexts the *double genitive* is idiomatic and not overkill, but few editors of Standard English will be likely to let it stand in Formal writing. It's either *friends of my sister* or *my sister's friends*; even in conversation, *friends of my sister's* may grate harshly on some purists' ears.

DOUBLE HYPHEN This punctuation mark (=) is called for in some stylebooks to separate parts of a word at the end of a line and the beginning of the next when the word would ordinarily already be hyphenated at that point anyway; if the break came at the hyphen in *high-energy,* for example, the line would end *high* = , and the next line would begin *energy.*

double in brass This frozen figure means "to be able to do one's own job and another one too." It is said to have arisen in vaudeville or the circus, where many performers could do their own acts and play in the band or orchestra as well. We use it figuratively now for almost any demonstration of versatility: *She was the weekly paper's only reporter, but she also doubled in brass when necessary and helped sell advertising.* See FROZEN FIGURES.

DOUBLE MEANING, DOUBLE EN-TENDRE

The French term, pronounced either the English way (*DUH-bul ahn-TAHN-druh*) or something like the French way (*DOOB-lahn-TAHN-druh*), and its English translation describe a word or expression that can have two different meanings, one of which is frequently suggestive or off-color. In speaking or writing you may use *double entendre* to amuse, but be sure that your audiences will both understand and enjoy it, or it would be better not to attempt it at all. Inadvertent *double meanings* can embarrass writers or speakers.

DOUBLE MODAL AUXILIARIES

I might could be able to visit later on. George had ought to pay you back for the loan. She shouldn't ought to be here. Nearly all these *double modals* are from the spoken language only, and most of them have some regional limitations, too: *might can* and *might could* have usually been limited to Southern and South Midland dialects, and *hadn't ought* is probably mainly Northern. Only the combinations with *ought* and especially the negative combinations such as *shouldn't ought* and *hadn't ought* are much heard these days. They are Nonstandard, and you *should not* or *shouldn't* or *ought not to* or *oughtn't to* use them except in the most Casual circumstances wherein your hearers regularly use them too. See MODAL AUXILIARIES.

DOUBLE NEGATIVE

Most kinds of *double negative* are inappropriate in spoken and written Standard English, except in jocular use: *Don't never say that again. I can't do nothing about it.* Eighteenth-century grammarians decided that since two negatives made a positive in mathematics and logic, they must do so in spoken and written English too. This was not always so, however, and the *double negative* remains one of the best illustrations of what was once a perfectly acceptable locution being driven by the decisions of grammarians, not out of the language, but out of Standard use. Chaucer used *double* and even *triple negatives,* and so did Shakespeare: these were simply powerful, heavily stressed, multiple negatives. And many speakers still use these constructions today, even though they are now shibboleths that mark speakers of Vulgar English.

Can't hardly is usually also classed as a *double negative. You can't hardly expect her to be grateful,* when analyzed, is doubly negative, in that *You can't expect her to be grateful* is renegated by the overlay of *You can hardly expect her to be grateful.* Other adverbs of a negative quality, such as *scarcely,* are also considered *double negatives* when used with a negative auxiliary such as *can't* or *cannot.*

Another kind of *double negative* occurs mostly in relatively Formal writing and at the higher levels of speech: *Let me give you my address now, in the not unlikely event that the train is late. I was not uncomfortable on the terrace.* The *not un-* construction can be the mark of the careful qualifier, the thoughtful speaker or writer trying to achieve an accuracy that may be, in fact, not inappropriate, but is, not improbably, hard to achieve; after all, if an act is described as *not unwitting,* it must be deliberate. Avoid pussyfooting unless you really must be that precise. Someone, somewhere, will dislike this sort of *double negative* because it is needlessly opaque and sounds stuffy. If it obtrudes, even when you think you are being amusing, it will not amuse. See LITOTES.

DOUBLE PASSIVE

This topic was claimed to have been studied to death. That sentence has two verbs in the passive voice, *was claimed* and *to have been studied,* and one is all that the single subject, *topic,* can bear. Such sentences occur occasionally in a Casual remark or a first draft, but they should not live longer than that. Better would be *She claimed that this topic has been studied to death*; best, *She claimed that we have studied this topic to death.* Now, at last, we know who *claimed* and who *studied.* This is a matter of effectiveness, efficiency, and style. See also VOICE (2).

DOUBLE POSSESSIVE

See DOUBLE GENITIVE.

DOUBLE QUOTATION MARKS

See QUOTATION MARKS.

DOUBLESPEAK, DOUBLE TALK

Both terms describe language practices intended to deceive. *Doublespeak* frequently renames the world with euphemisms—especially the political, the economic, and the social world—so that what is ugly or cruel or inexcusable may be made to appear plausible or kind or acceptable. *Revenue enhancement* is thought by some to be a term more acceptable to the citizen than *tax increase* would be; our Vietnam *pacification programs* were soothingly named, even though they resulted in the death and suffering of civilian populations.

Double talk is even more directly meant to deceive, in that it uses big nonce words, nonsensical polysyllables that sound as though they *ought* to be words, and fuddling syntax to baffle the brains of listeners or readers. A NASA comment illustrates:

The normal process during the countdown is that the countdown proceeds, assuming we are in a go posture, and at various points during the countdown we tag up on the operational loops and face to face in the firing room to ascertain the facts that project elements that are monitoring the data and that are understanding the situation as we proceed are still in the go condition.   (Quoted in Lutz 1989, 223)

The words seem to say something important, yet we don't really know what that something is. *Double talk* is a trap of the sort set by those tailors who made the emperor's new clothes. It *sounds* much like English, and the insecure worry that everyone but them must understand it. Avoid using either doublespeak or double talk even inadvertently, unless your intent is to deceive. And be constantly on guard against their use on you by others, and don't let others' jargon befuddle you; used to overwhelm the uninitiated, it too is meant to deceive or give a false impression of competence. See also JARGON; NEWSPEAK.

DOUBLE SUBJECTS *My brother he's a good student.* Schoolteachers have long worked to drive the *double subject* from student prose and student speech; nevertheless, it can be helpful when a long, complex subject and its modifiers need to be pulled together before the verb arrives: *That splendid leader, with his spellbinding voice and the calm poise that courage gives, and with the support of nearly everyone in the government—he was truly worth serving.* Save such repetition for when you need it to clear up syntactic confusion; better yet, especially in Oratorical and Formal contexts, put all the modifiers and qualifiers first, and then use the subject just once: *With his spellbinding voice and the calm poise that courage gives, and with the support of nearly everyone in the government, that splendid leader was truly worth serving.* Repetition for emphasis, however, is quite appropriate: *Ann is here, Fred is coming, but George—George, I'm afraid, is too ill to travel.*

DOUBLE SUPERLATIVE See DOUBLE COMPARATIVE.

DOUBLE TALK See DOUBLESPEAK.

DOUBLING See CONSONANTS (2).

doubt (*n., v.*) The verb can combine with a following clause introduced by *that, if,* or *whether,* or by a contact clause introduced by no conjunction at all: *He doubts that we will be able to find a time to meet. She doubted if there would be enough people interested. They doubt whether* she'll agree to serve. I doubt any of these things will really work out. The noun can similarly combine with any of these conjunctions plus a clause or with a contact clause alone: *He had doubts that any of this would work out. Our gravest doubt was if we should wait any longer. His chief doubt was whether he ought even to try. I have no doubt we'll win.* The noun can also combine with *but* and *but that: There is little doubt [but, but that] he'll win the election.* The noun *doubt* also combines with several prepositions, such as *about, as to, of, over,* and *concerning: There's no real doubt about [as to, of, over, concerning] his interest in our cause.*

doubtful (*adj.*) frequently combines with prepositions, such as *about, of, concerning,* and the like: *Her mother was doubtful about [of, concerning] her willingness to cooperate.* It can also combine with the conjunctions *that, if,* and *whether* introducing following clauses or with contact clauses introduced by no conjunction at all: *He was doubtful [that, if, whether] we would arrive in time for dinner.* See DUBIOUS.

doubtless (*adv., adj.*), **doubtlessly, indubitably, no doubt, undoubtedly, unquestionably, without doubt** (*advs.*) *Doubtless* can be an adjective meaning "free of doubt," but it is relatively rare: *He is doubtless and fearless when he begins his performance. Doubtless* is also an adverb, as are all the other locutions in this entry; all mean "probably," "certainly," or "absolutely." *Doubtless* and *doubtlessly* (which is rare and often considered clumsy since the flat adverb *doubtless* is available too) may not always sound very certain; they usually express the sense of "probably, very likely." *No doubt* is perhaps a bit stronger, but not quite certain in some contexts; in others it shares the force of *undoubtedly. Undoubtedly* and *without doubt* are stronger; they express certainty. *Indubitably* and *unquestionably* are the most forceful of all. They express dead certainty, leaving not the shadow of a doubt. Try each of them in place of *doubtless* in this sentence for an idea of the gradations: *It will doubtless rain this afternoon.*

doughnut, donut (*n.*) *Doughnut* is the conventional spelling, *donut* a variant used in advertising or signs and as eye dialect. But see SPELLING (2).

dour (*adj.*) It means "hard, unyielding, gloomy, or sullen," and it is pronounced to rhyme with either *poor* or *sour. Romances usually picture crabbed old Scotsmen, taciturn of speech and dour of outlook.*

douse, dowse (*vv.*) *Douse* rhymes with *mouse* and means "to immerse in liquid or to drench." With fire, its figurative meaning is "to put out, extinguish by pouring on water": *Douse your campfire [with water] before you leave it. Dowse* rhymes with *browse* and means "to use a divining rod to find underground water": *We agreed that he should dowse to locate the best site for our well.* A slight complication: *douse* is also a rare variant spelling of *dowse,* as *dowse* is of *douse.* Avoid the variants.

dove See DIVE (2).

dower (*n., v.*), **dowry** (*n.*) There are two legal definitions of the noun *dower:* an archaic sense, "the part of a dead man's real estate left to his widow through agreement made when he was alive," and the current sense, which is also the main meaning of *dowry,* "the money or property a bride brings to her husband at their marriage": *Her family's farm was part of her dower [dowry] when she married.* The verb *dower* means "to provide with a *dower* (or *dowry*)": *Their father dowered both daughters generously. Dowry* also has two other meanings of note: a specialized sense is "the name of the payment made by her family at the time a woman enters some orders of nuns"; a more general figurative sense is "a talent or natural gift," as in *One valuable part of her dowry was her good common sense.* In this last sense it is occasionally also used of a man.

down (*adv., adj., v.*) *To pay money down* and *to make a down payment* are Standard adverbial and adjectival uses, respectively, of *down: These down payments are the first and confirming installments, paid down at the time of agreement.* As a verb, *down* combines with *with* to be "an exhortation to overthrow, to destroy something": *Down with greed, vice, and unpleasantness!* Another adjectival combined form is the cliché *down to earth,* meaning "sensible, realistic, practical," as in *She's a down-to-earth politician with no idealistic illusions.* Also adjectival is the Conversational use of *down* meaning "depressed, discouraged": *He's been down ever since he learned we'd lost the contract.* Also adjectival and primarily Conversational is the expression *down on,* meaning "angry with, opposed to, impatient with," but it may occur as well in some Planned or Edited English contexts, as in *She's been down on all teachers since she failed her first course.* The idiom *to come down (hard) on* (someone or something) means "to discipline or criticize sharply," "to proscribe some act or behavior firmly." These are Standard.

down and out is a cliché borrowed from the prize ring: when a boxer is *down and out* ("unconscious"), the contest is over, and he's the loser. The cliché has wide figurative use in economic contexts: Anyone *down and out* is destitute of funds and hope.

downer, upper (*nn.*) These two are slang and may already be somewhat faded. A *downer* is a drug or other depressant and refers particularly to a barbiturate or similar drug. The figurative use is also slang and is widely encountered; it means "any experience or news that depresses": *Last night's meeting was a real downer.* An *upper* is also slang, with exactly the opposite meaning: drugs or other stimulants that exhilarate, such as amphetamines, are *uppers,* and the figurative sense could be applied to any cheering experience. There is also an older, Standard sense of *upper,* meaning "an upper berth in a Pullman railroad car or other travel sleeping accommodation": *We each had an upper on the trip to Cleveland.* (The lower berth is called a *lower,* not a *downer.*) The idiom *on one's uppers* means that the soles of one's shoes are worn through, so that what's left is just the upper parts of them, the *uppers;* hence, *He's on his uppers* means "he's down and out."

downplay (*v.*) is Standard today, despite its youth. It means "to underemphasize": *Representatives will downplay the idea that taxes may be increased.*

downsize (*v.*) The verb appeared in the late 1970s, an explicit reference to American automakers' reducing the size and weight, and hence the gasoline consumption, of their cars. It began as argot but became Standard in the media. Today it has added another meaning: to *downsize* is "to cut back manufacturing and commercial work forces and operations in the face of economic bad times." This sense of *downsizing* is a euphemism for layoffs and firings. It's a variation on the old *belt-tightening* metaphor and appears to be Standard too.

DOWN STYLE See UP STYLE.

down the drain, down the pipe, down the tube(s) These expressions are slang, and all mean figuratively that whatever is *down the drain, pipe,* or *tube* is "wasted, lost, and irretrievable": *There go six weeks of work down the tube. We sent a couple of weeks' pay down the pipe.* See also UP THE PIPE.

down the pike is a cliché, a Conversational figure meaning "in the future, ahead," wherein *pike* is another word for *road: We're ready to cope with whatever comes down the pike.*

down the pipe, down the tube See DOWN THE DRAIN.

downward (*adv., adj.*), **downwards** (*adv.*) *A downward spiral, a downward trend:* these are Standard uses of *downward* as adjective. The adverb is either *downward* or *downwards,* both Standard: *The plane glided downward [downwards] through the clouds.*

dowry See DOWER.

dowse See DOUSE.

doyen, doyenne See DEAN.

dozen (*adj., n.*) The noun *dozen* has two plurals: *dozen* and *dozens.* The inflected plural is used by itself and also modified by a prepositional phrase: *Complaints came the next morning by the dozens. Dozens of people came to see us.* When *dozen* is modified by a number, it takes the *s*-less form of the plural noun: *Send me three dozen eggs.* Normally the *s*-less plural is not followed by a prepositional phrase with *of: Three dozen of linen napkins* was once acceptable, but today Standard English says *Three dozen linen napkins.* Note, however, that with pronouns as objects of the preposition *of,* the construction is Standard (*three dozen of these*; *two dozen of them*), as it also is when *these* or *those* are determiners (*three dozen of these cups*; *two dozen of those apples*). After *dozens,* the *of* is Standard when there is no modifying number: *dozens of linen napkins.* See also PLURALS OF NOUNS.

Dr. See DOCTOR.

draft, draught (*adj., n., v.*) *Draft beer, a draft on your neck, to draft a letter, to draft young men for service, the draft of a ship, a draft resolution,* and all other senses and functions of the word are spelled *draft* in the United States. British English still uses *draught* for most of these uses and senses. One distinction further: the British play *draughts*; Americans call the game *checkers.*

drag (*v.*) is a weak verb, with past tense and past participle *dragged. Drug* as a past tense or past participle is Vulgar and Substandard. *To drag on* and *to drag out* mean "to be too prolonged or to prolong," as in *The meeting dragged on interminably* and *She dragged out her report until we were all asleep. To drag the feet or heels* is "to delay, to be uncooperative," as in *The senator continues to drag his feet, determined not to let the bill reach the floor.* These figures are Standard and may strike some as clichés, but they are sometimes very effective.

drank See DRINK.

drapes, draperies, curtains (*nn.*) For some time during the middle of the twentieth century, purists argued that *drape* was a verb only. But of course it could also be a noun if we wished it to be, and we did, so it now is Standard (frequently in the plural, *drapes*), along with *draperies* and *curtains. Drapery* can also be a mass noun: *Greek sculptors excelled in their rendering of drapery. Draperies* (thought to be somewhat less common-sounding) has been grudgingly accepted among interior decorators, but *curtains,* they point out, sounds much less pretentious. Note too that many dictionaries make a distinction between the translucence of *curtains* and the opacity of *drapes.*

draught(s) See DRAFT.

drave See DRIVE.

drawer, drawers (*nn.*) A *drawer* is someone who draws—pictures, beer, or money from an account. It is pronounced *DRAW-uhr.* A *drawer* is also a boxlike container that fits into a table or desk; it is pronounced either *DRAW-uhr* or *DROR* and is so named because when you open it, you draw it toward you. The plural, *drawers,* is pronounced *DRORZ,* as in *a chest of drawers,* but it is also another name for underpants, undershorts, or underdrawers—rather a pretentious or jocular and archaic name for them these days, particularly when they themselves are fading terms.

drawing room See LIVING ROOM.

dream (*n., v.*) *Dream* has long had two sets of Standard past tense and past participle forms, *dreamed* and *dreamt: She dreamed [dreamt] she won the lottery. I had dreamed [dreamt] that I was being pursued.* Americans may slightly prefer *dreamed* and the British *dreamt,* but both occur frequently in American English. To *dream a dream* or to *dream dreams* is Standard and not considered redundant; you can also *have dreams.* Both verb and noun can combine with either *of* or *about: He dreamed of [about] chocolate bars. She had a dream about [of] falling through space.* For more on the verb's principal parts, see CREEP.

dreck, drek (*n.*) These are variant spellings of one of a large number of Yiddish words in American English. It is slang, meaning "dung" or "trash." See YIDDISH; YIDDISH WORDS IN AMERICAN ENGLISH.

drench (*v.*) is often followed by *with* or *in: We were drenched with cheap champagne. The children had drenched themselves in some awful* *perfume.* In the passive, *drench* may combine with *by: We were drenched by the sudden rainstorm.*

drier (*adj., n.*), **dryer** (*n.*) The comparative of the adjective *dry* is spelled *drier,* and that spelling is also used for a substance put into paint to make it dry quickly. The appliances for drying clothes or hair or hands are all usually spelled *dryer,* although Americans occasionally use *drier.*

drily See DRYLY.

drink (*v.*) The principal parts are *drink, drank, drunk* (or the older *drank*), and today all are unquestionably Standard except *drank* as past participle: *They have drank their coffee already* is only rarely accepted in Casual use, and most Standard users consider it Substandard, with many enforcing it as a shibboleth. Certainly it is not acceptable in Edited or other written English. In eighteenth- and nineteenth-century Standard English you will frequently find *drunk* also as a Standard past tense, as in *We drunk tea for an hour,* but it is no longer appropriate in place of *drank* in that use: *We drank tea for an hour* is Standard now. See STRONG VERBS (1).

drive (*v.*) *Drive, drove, driven* are the principal parts of this verb, and Standard usage accepts no variation. *She drove to school yesterday. She has driven for nearly a year. Drave* is an archaic or obsolete past tense form from Early Modern English. See STRONG VERBS (1).

drivel (*n., v.*) The literal sense predominates in the verb, meaning "to drool," as in *The baby driveled on my necktie,* but the figurative sense predominates in the noun, "nonsensical talk," as in *I've never heard such drivel.* Americans normally don't double the *l* in *driveled* and *driveling;* the English normally do. See CONSONANTS (2).

driven See DRIVE.

drop 1 (*v.*) combines with a number of prepositions to form idioms: *to drop behind* means "to fall back, to fail to keep up" (*I dropped behind the rest of the class*); *to drop by, in,* or *over* means "to make a brief, unannounced visit" (*I just decided to drop in [by, over] to see you*); *to drop off* has three meanings, "to fall asleep" (*I dropped off after dinner*), "to decrease in number" (*Attendance dropped off this month*), and "to leave something or someone somewhere" (*I dropped them off at school*). *To drop out* means "to leave the group, to disappear" and especially "to cease to attend school (high school or college)," as in *He dropped out at the end of his junior year.* All but the "to fall asleep"

sense (which is Conversational) are fully Standard.

drop 2 (*n.*) combines to make several important idioms: *a drop in the bucket* is a cliché for "the infinitesimal," "the trivial." *At the drop of a hat* means "at the slightest provocation," as in *He'll fight at the drop of a hat,* also a cliché. *To get the drop on* is slang, originally gunslingers' or duelists' jargon meaning literally "to get one's gun aimed at the enemy before the enemy can take aim at you" and figuratively "to get an advantage over someone," as in *I got the drop on him by turning in my request first.* The expression probably stems from the duelists' practice of awaiting the drop of a handkerchief by a third party as the signal to aim and fire; *to get the drop* was to be the first to respond to the signal.

dropout (*n.*) is a functional shift, a noun made from the verb *drop out;* a *dropout* is someone who leaves the group, but more particularly someone who leaves school without finishing or getting a diploma or certificate. It is now Standard.

drought, drouth (*n.*) *Drought* rhymes with *lout* in Standard English; it means "dry weather," "lack of rain"; *drouth* is an archaic spelling reflecting an older pronunciation.

drove See DRIVE.

drown (*v.*) The verb is a regular weak verb, with principal parts *drown, drowned, drowned* (both past tense and past participle rhyme with *sound*), but *drown* has long had a Substandard *drownded* form. The error is clearly one of inexperience when encountered in children, but it is a serious shibboleth when it occurs in adult speech.

Most people will understand these three examples as meaning the same thing: *He drowned in his pool. He was drowned in his pool. He became drowned in his pool.* But the passive voice of the idiom in the second example could also suggest that he was drowned *by someone,* especially if there is no context to suggest otherwise.

drug See DRAG.

druggist, pharmacist (*nn.*) *Druggist* is still in use, but *pharmacist* is replacing it, especially when it refers to the person licensed to fill prescriptions. *Druggist* is sometimes used loosely to refer to the owner of a drugstore, whether a *pharmacist* or not.

drug(s) (*n.*) Unless context automatically removes any doubt, make very sure that your reader knows whether you mean *prescription* *drugs, over-the-counter drugs, illegal drugs,* or whatever. And note that *prescription drugs* can sometimes be obtained illegally. Note too that we have several compounds with the word *drug: drugstore* has been with us for generations, but *drug culture* and *drug paraphernalia* and the like have jumped up like weeds in the past three decades, bringing into the media and the entertainment world parts of an argot once limited to the underground world of *drug users, drug addicts, drug sellers, drug pushers,* and the like. Meantime the worlds of medicine and pharmacology are equally industrious at providing us with new words and meanings as they seek, through new drugs, to defeat disease and to make life better or longer or both.

drunk (*n., past particip.*), **drunken** (*adj.*) The noun *drunk* has two Standard uses: to refer to a person overcome by drink (*His mother is a drunk, a real alcoholic*), and to refer to a bout of drinking, a spree (*She keeps going off on three-day drunks*). The latter sense is for Conversational, Informal, or Semiformal use only.

Drunk is also the Standard past participle of *drink* (*She had drunk her coffee*) and is sometimes seen as a past tense in eighteenth- and nineteenth-century writing. In all but one situation, *drunk* appears only as a predicate adjective (*She is drunk*; *He looks drunk*), and *drunken* is used as an attributive adjective (*He walked with a drunken weave; A drunken stupor gripped her*). The exception: anything having to do with *drivers* and *driving* will take *drunk* as well as *drunken* as an attributive: *He was arrested for drunk* [*drunken*] *driving. Her car was wrecked by a drunk* [*drunken*] *driver.* Headline writers seeking shorter words, plus the recent deluge of slogans used in campaigns against *drunk drivers* and *drunk driving* and the legal definitions of *driving while drunk* or *drunk driving,* seem to have caused this exception. All the examples above are Standard, although some purists claim to see a semantic distinction between a *drunken driver* (one who has been drinking excessively) and a *drunk driver* (one who is guilty of breaking a law). Both *drunk* and *drunken* appear in the adjunct position (*a drunk person, a drunken person*), but *drunk,* not *drunken,* is the usual predicate adjective.

The idea of *drunkenness* appears to have fascinated us always: we have more slang, Conversational, cant, and argot terms for *drinking,* for the symptoms of *being drunk,* for *drunkenness,* and for *drunks* themselves than for almost any other condition we can get ourselves into. Among Standard synonyms are *intoxicated* (a rather upright, technical, or even pretentious word, one that preaches etymologically about poison), *inebriated* (another euphemism, and a pompous one at that), plus a wide range of adjectives of all sorts, descriptive of the various symptoms of *drunkenness.*

druthers (*n.*) *If I'd had my druthers, I wouldn't have gone. Druthers,* probably a contraction of either *would rather* or *had rather,* very likely from a Southern pronunciation of the phrase, means "preferences, wishes"; it is Informal and Conversational.

dry dock, dry-dock See DOCK.

dryer See DRIER.

dryly, drily (*adv.*) These are Standard variant spellings.

du See D'.

dual (*adj., n.*), **duel** (*n.*) The adjective *dual* means "double, having two parts," as in *a dual exhaust system, under dual sponsorship.* The noun *dual* is the name of a grammatical number: early Old English had a three-part declension of the personal pronouns, which had singular forms to refer to one, *dual* forms to refer to two, and plural forms to refer to three or more. In late Old English the *dual* disappeared, leaving us with the present two numbers, singular for one, and plural for two or more. Only the comparative degree and a few pairs like *between/among* and *either/both* are left to remind us of that special interest our grammar once had in viewing things by twos and distinguishing between two and more than two.

The noun *duel,* a homophone of *dual,* refers to a formally arranged fight between two persons or, figuratively, between two teams or other forces.

DUAL COMPARISON is the name some commentators apply to constructions such as *It was as fine if not finer than any cloth they'd ever sold,* wherein the parallel structure on which the sentence embarks is not completed: *It was as fine . . . than any cloth . . .* simply does not work. *It was as fine as, or finer than, any cloth . . .* would put the parallelism right, stiff though it sounds. Since your finished prose may be closely inspected for logic and parallelism, avoid the *dual comparison* when you write. In Informal writing and at the lower levels of speech, it should not often be a problem, but with some audiences it could be, even there. See AS GOOD OR BETTER THAN.

DUAL PRONOUN DECLENSION See DUAL.

dub (*n., v.*) has two long-established meanings, both Standard: "to confer a title on," especially "to confer a knighthood on," as in *I, King Arthur, dub thee knight*; and "to add a soundtrack to a film" or "to insert new things into a soundtrack, especially a translation of the spoken dialogue into another language," as in *The film shown in this country had English dubbed in to replace the original Italian*. From the expanding world of sound recording come a new Standard verb meaning "to rerecord the sound of an existing recording" and the new Standard noun *dub* as the name of such a rerecording. See CONSONANTS (2).

dubious (*adj.*), when it combines with prepositions, usually takes *of, about, over*, and *concerning*, as in *We were dubious of [about, over, concerning] their sincerity*. See also EQUIVOCAL.

duct tape, duck tape (*n.*) *Duct tape* is the fabric tape, sticky on one side, used by plumbers and furnace installers to seal pipe joints and repair leaks in ductwork of many types. As with *bookcase, duct tape*'s repeated medial consonants have coalesced into one in rapid speech, giving us the curious folk etymology *duck tape*—first spoken and now occurring in print on occasion. See HANDICAP PARKING; ICE CREAM.

duel See DUAL.

due to, because of, owing to *Due to* and *owing to* mean just what *because of* means. All three are prepositions. *Owing to* fought and won its way to respectability a good while ago, and now *due to* has almost won its battle, although there is a residue of conservative unhappiness over it when it does not follow a linking verb, as in *He arrived late, due to a flat tire*. Some Edited English and Oratorical speech will still avoid such uses, but at all other levels all three locutions are Standard: *Because of [owing to, due to] his having sprained his ankle, he walked with a cane. Because of [owing to, due to] his sprained ankle, he walked with a cane.*

due to the fact that This locution permits the preposition *due to* to serve as a subordinating conjunction, just as *because* and *since* do: *Due to the fact that [because, since] the traffic was so snarled, we missed our plane*. (*Owing to* and *because of* can also be combined with *the fact that*.) Many object to *due to the fact that* on grounds of wordiness, and it is true that where economy is the primary concern, *because* or *since* will usually do the job better. But sometimes neither will meet the semantic need exactly, and sometimes economy is not the pri-

mary concern. However, *due to the fact that*, like any other cliché, can be tiresome when overused—save it for the places where only it seems right. And be sure *the fact that* refers to a *fact*, not just to a *wish*, a *guess*, or a *hope*.

dully, duly (*advs.*) These are not likely to be confused except by inexperienced spellers. *Dully*, pronounced *DUHL-lee*, means "without spirit or edge or luster, stupidly," as in *He sat there dully, thinking of nothing. Duly*, pronounced *DOO-lee* or *DYOO-lee*, means "as required, on time, necessarily," as in *After she had served for a year, she was duly promoted to corporal.*

dumb, mute (*adjs., nn.*) These synonyms mean "speechless, unspeaking" and are Standard in that use: *We were struck dumb [mute] with surprise. Dumb* also has a longtime Conversational sense, "stupid," which may be either a cruel extension of the "speechless" sense or an adoption of the Pennsylvania German *dumm*. There are also other extended senses of *dumb*—a *dumb barge* is a barge with no engine, for example. In recent years some *mutes* have found *dumb* offensive as a description of their disability. *Deaf-mute* seems to be an acceptable term at present to replace *deaf-and-dumb* both as noun and adjective.

dumbfound, dumfound (*v.*) *dumbfound* (*dumfound* is a standard variant spelling) means "to strike speechless," "to shock into silence": *What I have to tell you will dumbfound you. I was dumbfounded when I heard the news*. Lexicographers agree about its etymology, but that etymology is curious. *Confound*, or the *-found* part of *confound*, is universally cited as the etymon of the second part of the word, usually in the sense "to throw into confusion, to surprise." The *Oxford English Dictionary* then points out that the Colloquial sense of this use of *confound* is expressed in *dumbfound* and *flabbergast*. (Both are now standard in that meaning of "surprised and confused.") See SURPRISE.

DUMMY SUBJECTS In sentences such as the following, *there* and *it* are variously called *expletives, empty subjects, anticipatory subjects*, or *dummy subjects: There is a high wind tonight. There are several latecomers in the lobby. It's easy to see she's worn out*. In speech and Informal writing these *dummy subjects* are handy entries into sentences whose real subjects you have not yet chosen. And sometimes, even in finished writing, the formulaic beginning can be a welcome, pace-changing inversion. To replace *A high wind is blowing tonight; Several latecomers are in the lobby; You can easily see* *she's worn out,* the formulaic beginning sometimes serves well, particularly to suggest a Conversational tone. The only caution is against overuse. See also EXPLETIVES (2); THERE.

duo (*n.*), **duo-** (*prefix*) *Duo,* the noun, has two plurals: the regular *duos* and the almost never-used *dui.* A *duo* is two, a pair, a couple: *They made a duo around town for the better part of the year.* The word has an Informal or Conversational air in some uses, probably because it looks as though it were the result of clipping or another process of abbreviation (it's not), but it is Formal in music when it refers to two performers or to a piece of music for two performers or two instruments (*a duo for violin and viola*). The prefix *duo-* occurs in words such as *duodecimal* (two plus ten), *duologue* (conversation for two; we've usually preferred *dialogue* instead), and *duopoly* (a rare term for a ruling political combination of two powers).

duodecimo, folio, octavo, quarto, twelvemo, 12mo (*nn.*) *Duodecimo* is a Latin tag meaning "in twelve," and English applies it to a page size for books (the sheet is folded and cut to create twelve pages about five by seven-and-a-half inches in dimension); it also means a book of that page size. The plural is *duodecimos.* *Twelvemo* is an English variant, and *12mo* is its abbreviation. All three are Standard. Other common page and book sizes are *folio, quarto,* and *octavo*; a *folio* has the sheet folded once, a *quarto* is folded to make four leaves, and an *octavo* has eight leaves. See PLURALS OF NOUNS ENDING IN -O; PAGE; RECTO.

duologue See DIALOGUE; DUO; MONOLOGUE.

duopoly See DUO; MONOPOLY.

duplicate (*adj., n., v.*), **duplication, duplicity** (*nn.*), **duplicitous** (*adj.*) *Duplicate* (pronounced *DOO-pli-kit* or *DYOO-pli-kit*) is an adjective meaning "identical to, one of two similar things," as in *These neckties are duplicates.* The verb is spelled like the adjective but pronounced *D(Y)OO-pli-KAIT,* with a lesser stress on the final syllable. It means "to reproduce another exact copy": *Please duplicate this door key for me.* The nouns are *duplicate* (pronounced like the adjective, as in *This key is a duplicate of mine*) and *duplication* (pronounced *d(y)oo-pli-KAI-shuhn*), which refers to the process of making an exact copy: *The duplication of these keys is illegal.* See REPLICA; REPLICATE.

The adjective *duplicitous* and the noun *duplicity* also begin with *dupli-,* meaning "double, or two alike," but there the similarities end.

Duplicity means "double dealing, deliberately deceiving or misleading"; *being two-faced* is a kind of *duplicitous* behavior. The noun is pronounced *d(y)oo-PLIS-i-tee,* the adjective *d(y)oo-PLIS-i-tuhs*: *He was a master of duplicity; he always promised something quite other than what he intended. He was duplicitous through and through.*

durance, duress (*nn.*) Their Latin roots are different but related, *durance* coming from a word meaning "to last a long time," and *duress* from a word meaning "hard." *Durance* (related to *endurance* and stressed on the first syllable) is "restraint by force, or long imprisonment," as in the cliché *to be in durance vile.* It is a rather self-conscious, bookish term. *Duress* is "forcible restraint, compulsion, or imprisonment" and is stressed on the second syllable. The idiom is *to be under duress,* meaning "to be compelled or forced to do something," as in *She agreed only under duress to go with them. Duress* is a much more frequently used word than *durance.*

during the course of See COURSE OF.

Dutch, Pennsylvania Dutch (*adjs., nn.*) The *Dutch* are the people of The Netherlands, and they were old enemies of the English even before the two nationalities were at odds in the lower Hudson Valley, which probably accounts for some usage items. Some phrases with a *Dutch* element are ethnic slurs, although many people who use them are unaware of this; some are of English origin, some of American, and it is not always easy to be certain in some instances which is which: *Dutch courage* (an insult, since it is achieved only by drinking alcohol); *to go Dutch* (meaning you each pay your own way); a *Dutch treat* (no treat at all, since you pay your own bill); and to be *in Dutch* (to be "in trouble," as in *I don't know what I've done, but I'm in Dutch with her*). A *Dutch uncle* (as in *He talked to me like a Dutch uncle*) is "someone who never stops reproving, correcting, chastising, and giving advice." Other combinations are not at all pejorative: a *Dutch door* has an upper and lower part that can be opened separately; a *Dutch oven* is a brick wall oven or a kind of cooking pot. There are various *Pennsylvania Dutch* foods and phrases as well. Keep in mind, however, that the *Pennsylvania Dutch* are not *Dutch* but *Deutsch*—that is, *Pennsylvania Germans.* It is not always easy to distinguish which locutions containing the word *Dutch* mean *Dutch* and which mean *Deutsch.*

duvet See QUILT.

dwarf (*n.*) has two plurals: *dwarfs* (pronounced *DWORFS*) and *dwarves* (pronounced *DWORVZ*). *Dwarfs* is the more frequent, but both are Standard. See NOUNS ENDING IN -*F*.

dwell (*v.*) has two past tense and past participle forms: *dwelled* and *dwelt*. *Dwelt* is far more commonly encountered, and it is usually pronounced *DWELT*. *Dwell* is a rather literary or even pretentious term, like *reside*; *live* is the high-frequency, commonly used verb. *Dwell* combines with at least a dozen prepositions, mostly those showing spatial relationships and associations, as in *They dwelt in* [*near, outside,* etc.] *the county seat* and *They dwelt among* [*beside, with*] *the Indians*. Other prepositions used with *dwell* include *behind, beneath, on, over,* and *under*.

dyeing See DIE.

dyke See DIKE.

dynamo (*n.*) The plural is *dynamos*. See PLURALS OF NOUNS ENDING IN -*O*.

dynasty (*n.*) means "the successive generations of rulers from the same family" and "the period of such a family's reign." Americans pronounce it either *DEI-nuh-stee* or *DEI-nas-tee*; the British say it *DIN-uh-stee*.

dys- See DE-.

dyslexia (*n.*), **dyslexic** (*adj, n.*) *Dyslexia* is "any impairment of the ability to read"; it is a general term, describing the effect of the disability, not its causes, which may be many and varied. *Dyslexic* is the adjective, as in *He has some sort of dyslexic problem not yet really diagnosed*, and it also serves as the noun meaning "one who has symptoms of *dyslexia*," as in *His teachers think he's a dyslexic*.

DYSPHEMISM The process and the result of substituting an ugly or otherwise unpleasant locution for one more attractive in sound or meaning are both called *dysphemism*, of which the World War I sailors' name for tapioca pudding, *fisheye soup*, is a graphic and printable example. *Dysphemism* is an antonym of euphemism.

E

each (*adj., pron.*) Usage problems concern agreement of *each* with verbs, antecedents, and subsequent pronouns. As pronoun and subject, *each* takes a singular verb and can take a singular subsequent pronoun: *Each is housed in its* [*his, her*] *own space*. But notional agreement takes over frequently with the subsequent pronoun, and sometimes with the verb as well, especially if there is intervening plural material or if the intent is to use inclusive language: *Each of them do their own laundry*. Such plural subsequent pronouns are far more common in today's Standard English than they used to be; only Edited English consistently tries to avoid them.

Despite some purists' objections, Standard English does have a genitive case pronoun, *each's*, as well as *each one's*: *Each boy's hat has a feather, each's jacket has a tall collar, and each one's raincoat is yellow*.

At all levels of Standard English the adjective *each* modifying a singular noun is always followed by a singular verb: *Each student is to provide his or her own calculator*. But again, except in careful Edited English, that sentence frequently may go on to read *Each student is to provide their own calculator*. When the adjective *each* follows and modifies a plural subject, the verb is always plural: *We each have personal file drawers*. See AGREEMENT.

each and every, each and all are Standard locutions used for emphasis: *I want each and every one of you to straighten up your room*[*s*]. These phrases can be helpful when hyperbole is appropriate; overused, they have the effect of clichés.

each other, one another These phrases are synonymous and interchangeable, although *one another*, which is also Standard for reference to more than two, may seem more formal: *Be nice to each other* [*one another*]. Both phrases can be used in the genitive: *They were wearing each other's* [*one another's*] *raincoat*[*s*].

eager (*adj.*) frequently takes the preposition *to* plus an infinitive, as in *She was eager to please her parents*, and also can take *for* and *in*, as in *He was eager for a chance to play* and *They were eager in manner and alert to everything that was said*. See also ANXIOUS.

EARLY MODERN ENGLISH is the language of the Renaissance, roughly from the invention of printing with movable type to the middle of the eighteenth century. Scholars sometimes date it from the end of the Middle English period, around 1550, to 1700 or 1750. *Early Modern English* was Shakespeare's English and the English of the King James Bible (1611), and it was from this English that American English developed.

early on (*adv.*) is relatively new (1928 is the *Oxford English Dictionary*'s earliest citation) but Standard, a compound adverb, not always precisely interchangeable with *early*, that means usually "at a stage early in the development of something": *We joined the group early on, before belonging had become the thing to do.*

Earth, the earth (*n.*) The name of this planet is sometimes capitalized but often not when *the* is used with it. See CAPITALS.

earthly, earthy, earthen (*adjs.*) have different meanings, and occasionally the inexperienced may confuse the first two. *Earthly* means "related to or characteristic of this world," as in *The ashes, his earthly remains, were scattered as he had requested. Earthy* means "down-to-earth, crude, or coarse," as in *Her repeated earthy observations about life did not amuse them. Earthen* means "made of earth," as in *They kept the kindling by the fireplace in a huge earthen pot.* Compare WORLDLY.

easily See EASY.

east, East, easterly, Eastern (*adjs., nn.*), **eastern** (*adj.*) Capitalize the compass directions when they are truly proper nouns, as in *She took the next plane back to the East this morning,* meaning to the East Coast or to the eastern states. When *east* is the direction or the general area, not the destination, don't capitalize it. One distinction among *east* as adverb and *eastern* and *easterly* as adjectives is simply that they are decreasingly specific, in that order: *We sailed east* is very specific, *We sailed on an eastern course* is a bit less so, and *We sailed in an easterly direction* is vaguer still. *Eastern* can also be part of a proper noun, often serving as one by itself when clipped, as with *Eastern Airlines,* which was often called simply *Eastern. Easterly* as a noun is the name of a wind or a current coming from that direction: *There were strong easterlies assisting our flight to Seattle.* The problem is that *easterlies* may also be winds or currents blowing in that direction, not coming from it. Context must make clear which you mean.

The other compass directions—*north, northern, northerly, south, southern, southerly,* and *west, western, westerly*—behave similarly in Standard English.

EASTERN NEW ENGLAND REGIONAL DIALECT This subdialect of the Northern Regional dialect of American English is spoken primarily in eastern Massachusetts, Rhode Island, eastern Connecticut, New Hampshire, much of Maine, and a bit of eastern Vermont. It has its own regional subgroups as well, but the rest of the United States notices the speech of eastern New England particularly for its dropping of the *r* sound before some consonants, adding an *r* sound at the ends of some words that end in vowels, as in *law and order* (pronounced *LAHR uhn AW-duh*), as well as its different pronunciation of the vowel *a* in words like *barn* and *plant* (*BAHN, PLAHNT*). It is also sometimes called *Coastal New England Dialect.*

eastward (*adv., adj.*), **eastwards** (*adv.*) *Eastward* is the only adjective (*The window looked out on an eastward prospect*), but *eastward* and *eastwards* are both Standard as adverbs (*We flew eastward [eastwards] for several hours*). British English tends to use only *eastwards* as adverb; Americans more often use *eastward. Westward(s), northward(s),* and *southward(s)* behave similarly.

easy, easily (*advs.*) Both *easy* and *easily* are Standard as adverbs, but they are not usually interchangeable. The flat adverb *easy* is used in Conversational utterances such as *take it easy* or *she can earn several hundred a week, easy.* The regular adverb *easily* is Standard almost everywhere else: *This is easily the best game she's played. We easily defeated them.* There are also a few Conversational or Informal instances wherein either form will work, as in *Mathematics comes easy [easily] to me* and *We'll get there in time, easily [easy].*

eatable, edible (*adjs., nn.*) If the food is *eatable,* then it is both safe and reasonably tasty. Sometimes *edible* food is *eatable* too, but more commonly *edible* only means "useful as food and not harmful if eaten." Both words are also used, especially in the plural, as nouns meaning "things to eat," as in *We brought the edibles [eatables] in from the car.*

echelon (*n.*) was once primarily a military word, first for a kind of stair- or steplike military or aircraft formation and later for the levels of command in a military hierarchy: *The higher echelons were unaware of what was happening at company and battalion.* Today, the general vocabulary has appropriated the word, and it most frequently means "the levels of any sort of governmental or other institutional organization": *In the lower echelons of party government no one knows what will happen next.*

ECHOIC WORDS are words that sound or try to sound something like the actual noises they imitate; *zip, thump,* and *screech* are *echoic*. See also ONOMATOPOEIA.

ecology, environment (*nn.*) *Ecology* (pronounced *ee-KAHL-uh-jee*) is "the system of relationships between biological organisms and their environment"; it also means "the study of such matters." The *ecology* of a particular plant or animal is an account of its relationships with the physical environment in which it occurs. The *environment* is "the full range of conditions and circumstances in which biological organisms live." So, ideally at least, *ecology* is both the system itself (*ecosystem*—pronounced *EE-ko-sis-tem*—is the blend coined to make explicit this meaning) and the study of it, and *environment* is the detailed locus in which such a system operates. Lately, however, the vogue of these subjects increasingly has caused the two words to be used interchangeably to mean "the full range of circumstances in which organisms, especially human beings, exist." Such uses are now Standard, but much Edited English still tries to preserve the distinction between *ecology* and *environment,* particularly in technical contexts; you would do well to try to preserve it too. See also GOVERNMENT.

economic, economical (*adjs.*) In most uses, these two are not synonyms. The adjective *economic* means "dealing with finances, money matters, or wealth" and "having to do with meeting material needs": *We spent money only on economic necessities that year. Economical* means "saving, thrifty, not wasteful": *This new car has a much smaller, more economical engine.* See -IC.

ecstasy, ecstacy (*n.*) *Ecstasy* is the most frequent spelling; *ecstacy* is an increasingly rare variant. It is "overpowering emotion, especially of joy or delight or pleasure."

ect. See ETC.

-ection, -exion (*suffixes*) These suffixes are often the ends of nouns made from verbs ending in *-ect,* such as *connect, elect,* and *dissect.* Generally British English makes a bit more use of the *-exion* spelling than does American English, but see the partial list in SPELLING (1).

edible See EATABLE.

edifice (*n.*) is often criticized for being pretentious, but it is the building to which the word is applied that must live up to the word. Use it only for deliberately imposing buildings, unless you are exaggerating for effect. Cathedrals and castles, not capes and cottages, are *edifices.*

EDITED ENGLISH is a hypothetical printed level of the language, essentially Formal in character, the written dialect, so to speak, as edited and printed by this country's leading commercial publishers and most reputable journals and university presses. It is conservative in usage matters of all sorts, and thanks to its stylebooks and editors, its standards tend to be fairly self-perpetuating, at least over the short range. Even the most stylistically liberal of newspapers and journals will rarely find *Edited English* too constrained or stuffy for their pages, even though they may not require that their writers always meet all the standards *Edited English* itself would insist on. The main reason not to try to imitate *Edited English* in all your language use, however, is that it is a written, not a spoken, form of English. It rarely imitates the lower levels of American English speech, therefore, and when your writing calls for such imitation, you should look to other versions of Standard English for your models, rather than to *Edited English* alone: compare, for example, *We were working at top speed* (*Edited English*) to *We were working flat out* (Casual or Impromptu level). But for your Formal and Semiformal writing, Edited English will do pretty well for nearly all written occasions. See LEVELS OF USAGE; STANDARD USAGE.

EDITORIAL *WE* See WE.

EDUCATIONESE is the name sometimes given to the jargon too frequently employed by some of those who train our schoolteachers. It is characterized typically by its humorlessly abstract, Latinate, and polysyllabic diction and its involuted, rambling, and frequently passive syntax. Its fights are never fights and rarely even quarrels; they're *conflict situations.* At its worst, instead of correcting imprecision and ignorance, it tries to conceal them, frequently even from itself.

educationist, educator (*nn.*) *Educator* is the generic noun applied to teachers, school administrators, and others professionally engaged in formal education at any level. Some consider the term pretentious, although the media use it frequently, especially for administrators who do little or no teaching. An *educationist* is a theorist in educational matters, particularly one connected with a school of education. *Educationist* is unexceptionable in Britain, but it is frequently used disparagingly in the United States, as, indeed, *educator* sometimes is as well. These pejorative overtones are by no means unrelated to educationese and its implications.

-ee (*suffix*) The *-ee* suffix added to a verb creates a noun meaning "one who does, undergoes, or is an exemplar of the action indicated by that verb": *retire/retiree; escape/escapee; trust/ trustee; stand/standee; employ/employee*. The suffix is frequently used in humorous nonce word coinages built on this pattern: if the person who *cheats* is a *cheater*, for example, the person *cheated* must be the *cheatee*.

e'er, e're, ere (*adv.*), **ere** (*prep., subord. conj.*) Both these words are pronounced like the word *air*. *E'er, e're*, and *ere* are archaic and poetic forms of the adverb *ever*, as in *Where e'er [e're, ere] she is, there would I be also*; the apostrophe indicates the omission of the *v*. (This word is a versifier's delight: choose the two-syllabled *ever* or the more literary one-syllabled *e're/ere/e'er*, as your meter requires.) *Ere* is an archaic or at least old-fashioned and poetic preposition and subordinating conjunction meaning "before," as in the palindrome *Able was I ere I saw Elba*.

effect See AFFECT.

effective, effectual, efficacious, efficient (*adjs.*) *Effective* means "useful, impressive, producing a satisfactory result," as in *an effective legislator*; used of soldiers, it means "equipped and ready to fight," as in *Only half our troops are trained and effective*. *Effectual* overlaps somewhat with *effective*, especially in the sense "producing the desired effect," but it also means "valid, legal," as in *The law offers no effectual remedy in this case*. *Efficient* means "causative," as in *the efficient or actual cause*, and, again, "producing a desired result," but this time with the additional sense of "economically, without waste or loss of effort," as in *an efficient engine*. *Efficacious* means much the same as *effective* in the sense of "useful, able to produce the result sought," as in *an old-fashioned but efficacious remedy*. All these are Standard.

EFFECTIVENESS, when used of prose, is its ability to accomplish its purpose, to achieve its aims. *Effective expository writing explains effectively*.

effectual See EFFECTIVE.

effectuate (*v.*) means "to put into effect, to bring about." It is a rather Formal word, but it's likely to be considered pretentious only in relaxed Conversational and Informal use.

effeminate, female, feminine, womanly (*adj.*) *Effeminate* applies to males certain behavioral qualities usually associated with or attributed to females, and in that use it is frequently derogatory: a man labeled *effeminate* is usually thought to be weak and unmanly. *Feminine* is the adjective indicative of qualities usually thought to be typical of women, including some qualities traditionally considered desirable—*gentleness, modesty, dependence,* and the like—but now viewed less positively by many. *Womanly*, which has primarily favorable associations when applied to females, differs from *feminine* in suggesting qualities particularly or solely associated with maturity, especially in contrast with girlishness. *Female* is the sexually explicit adjective; its basic information is biological. See GENDER (1); GENDER (2); MANNISH.

effete (*adj.*) long meant "exhausted, unfruitful, or worn out," but those meanings have been largely replaced in this century. *Effete* now usually means "decadent, overrefined and precious, snobbish, or even sterile." It still signifies weakness and lack of utility, but now it is the weakness of triviality, superficiality; applied to men it can be synonymous with *effeminate*. It is always pejorative.

efficacious, efficient See EFFECTIVE.

effluent See AFFLUENT.

effluvium (*n.*) is a bad smell, such as might be given off by a factory or such as might result from the wastes in various processes. Piggeries and paper mills are often noted for their *effluviums* or *effluvia* (both plurals are Standard). See FOREIGN PLURALS.

effrontery See AFFRONT.

e.g., i.e. (*abbrevs.*) Properly used, each of these is Standard. *I.e.* abbreviates Latin *id est*, "that is"; use it when you wish to repeat in different words what you've just finished saying: *I'm strongly opposed; i.e., I'm determined not to cooperate*. *E.g.* abbreviates the Latin tag *exempli gratia*, "for the sake of example, for example." People sometimes say the names of the letters *i* and *e* or *e* and *g* instead of saying the English *that is* or *for example*, but the abbreviations aren't much shorter, and most of us would prefer the English words in speech, no matter how familiar the Latin abbreviations are in writing. Note carefully the punctuation and typeface (roman or italic) requirements of use; these may vary with the publisher. Most editors put them in italics; all require a comma after the second period. See FOREIGN PHRASES; VIZ.

egis See AEGIS.

egoist, egotist (*nn.*) *Egoist* is much the less frequently used term. Its technical sense is "someone who believes in *egoism* (which argues that self-interest is a proper end for all human action; *egoism* is an antonym of *altruism*)." But *egoist* has also come to be a synonym for *egotist*, "a person who talks only of self and is full of selfishness and conceit." *Egotist* and the noun *egotism* meaning "excessive attention to and interest in self," are always pejorative; *egoist* and *egoism*, at least in their ethical senses, need not be. For most Americans, *egoist* is an unfamiliar term, so if you use it in its reference to *egoism*, control its context carefully.

egregious (*adj.*), **egregiously** (*adv.*) The adjective *egregious* means "outstanding or distinguished for bad qualities, flagrant, noticeably undistinguished," as in *He's an egregious ass* or *She committed an egregious blunder*. The adverb is similarly pejorative in all current uses: *His comments were in egregiously bad taste.* Compare GRATUITOUS; SUPERFLUOUS.

either (*adj., pron.*), **either . . . or** (*coord. conj.*) *Either* (pronounced *EE-thuhr* or *EI-thuhr*) as adjective or pronoun) is Standard as a substitute for *each*, usually used for one of two persons or things: *You know my parents; either* [*either one*] *would make an excellent director.* As a conjunction (in the *either/or* construction), *either* is Standard when used of more than two, as in *She is a good athlete, working either golf, tennis, or swimming into her daily routine*, although Edited English prefers its use with two only.

Generally, and especially in Edited English, the *either/or* construction is most effective when syntactic parallelism is exact, although clarity is rarely destroyed when it is not. Compare the following: *I expect to meet them in either New York or Boston or Philadelphia this winter. I expect to meet them either in New York or in Boston or in Philadelphia this winter. I expect to meet them either in New York or Boston or Philadelphia this winter.* Edited English would prefer the first or second version, because both are meticulously parallel; the third version is not, but it is perfectly clear and is probably typical of both Informal writing and most Conversational levels. Above all, however, Edited English would prefer *either/or* with just two rather than three or more options.

When the paired *either/or* conjunctions introduce subjects, the verbs that follow usually agree with the second element: *Either her cats or my dog is to be sold. Either my dog or her cats are to be sold.* But with intervening plural materials, as in *Either her cats or one of my dogs are to be sold*, notional agreement may appropriately take over everywhere in Standard except in Edited English. See INDEFINITE PRONOUNS; NEITHER.

eke, eke out (*vv.*), **eke** (*adv., coord. conj.*) The old verb *eke* is obsolete or dialectal today, but in the combined *eke out* it still forms a Standard locution, meaning "to supplement or stretch out a supply" (*We eked out our little bit of hamburger with lots of beans and rice*) or "to manage with difficulty to make a living" (*For several years they managed to eke out a bare existence on the little land they owned*). The other *eke*, which is archaic and turns up mainly in old literature, means "also": *Supposing the wax good and eke the thimble* (from Laurence Sterne, *The Life and Opinions of Tristram Shandy*, 1759).

An *ekename* was "an alternate or added name," and in Middle English it became *a nekename* and ultimately *a nickname*.

elder (*adj., n.*), **eldest, older, oldest** (*adjs.*) Usually *elder* and *eldest* are used only of people, as in *She's my elder sister*, whereas *older* and *oldest* can be used of either persons or things, as in *She's my older sister* and *These are my oldest clothes*. When used with *than*, *older* is almost always the choice: *She is two years older than I*. With *of*, either *older* or *elder*, *oldest* or *eldest* will do: *She's the oldest* [*eldest, older, elder*] *of my children*. Functional shift has given us *elder* and *eldest* as nouns as well: *Be respectful to your elders. He is an elder in his church. She is our eldest.* See THAN.

elderly See SENIOR CITIZEN.

eldest See ELDER.

electric, electrical, electronic (*adjs.*), **electronics** (*n.*) *Electric* and *electrical* are synonymous in the sense "run by electricity," as in *These are all electric* [*electrical*] *appliances*. *Electric* can mean in addition "highly charged, as with electricity," in a figurative sense, as in *The atmosphere in the courtroom was electric*. *Electronic* means that a device so labeled is run by tubes or transistors that emit streams of electrons, as is the case with the vacuum tubes and transistors that make possible computers and much modern wireless communications equipment. *Electronics* is the science (and its related technology) that deals with these matters; it is construed as either a mass noun, as in *Electronics is a complicated study*, or a count noun, as in *All these electronics—computers, electric eyes, televisions, and the like—are already outmoded by new, better designs*.

elegant (*adj.*), **elegance** (*n.*) If the thing be rich, full of grace, luxury, and good taste, if the person be refined in manner and tasteful of dress and speech, or if the solution to the problem be concise and artfully or ingeniously contrived yet simple and handsome in effect, then the thing, the person, and the solution all merit the adjective *elegant*. *Elegant* is pretentious only when used of inelegant things: *It was an elegant restaurant: they gave us real cloth napkins.*

ELEGANT VARIATION is Fowler's (1926, 1965) term for the inept writer's overstrained efforts at freshness or vividness of expression. Prose guilty of *elegant variation* calls attention to itself and doesn't permit its ideas to seem naturally clear. It typically seeks fancy new words for familiar things, and it scrambles for synonyms in order to avoid at all costs repeating a word, even though repetition might be the natural, normal thing to do: *The audience had a certain bovine placidity,* instead of *The audience was as placid as cows. Elegant variation* is often the rock, and a stereotype, a cliché, or a tired metaphor the hard place between which inexperienced or foolish writers come to grief. The familiar middle ground in treating these homely topics is almost always the safest. In untrained or unrestrained hands, a thesaurus can be dangerous.

elegy, eulogy (*nn.*) An *elegy* is a poem, typically one memorializing and praising the dead or (loosely) one with a mournful and gloomy contemplative tone; it may also be a piece of music of similar topic and tone. A *eulogy* is a speech, formal and elegant in form, in praise of someone recently dead.

elephantine See PACHYDERM.

ELEVATION, ELEVATED Also called *amelioration, elevation* is a process of semantic change in which improvement in the status of the referent of a word causes the word itself to become "better," "more important," or "elevated in status." A *steward* was once "the guardian of the pigs, a sty ward" but today is a much more important officer. A *governor* was once simply "the steersman of a vessel" but now steers whole organizations, states, and commonwealths. *Minister* has elevated from "servant" to "the leader of a congregation or the holder of an important governmental portfolio." All these words have *elevated,* or *ameliorated*. See also PEJORATION, the opposite process, also known as *degradation*.

elicit (*v.*), **illicit** (*adj.*) The verb *elicit* means "to draw forth, evoke, or bring out by means of

inquiry," as in *Her speech elicited a good deal of favorable comment. Illicit* is an adjective meaning "unlawful, illegal, or impermissible," as in *They were running an illicit still back in the hills.* The only basis for confusion is that their pronunciations in continuous speech are likely to be identical, *uh-LIS-it*. Careful enunciation will make them respectively *ee-LIS-it* and *il-LIS-it*.

eligible, ineligible (*adjs.*) *Eligible,* when combined with a preposition, usually takes *to* or *for. To* is usually followed by an infinitive, as in *This time she is eligible to run, for* by a noun or some other nominal, as in *she is eligible for nomination. Eligible*'s antonym is *ineligible,* meaning "unqualified or unsuitable," as in *His grades have made him ineligible to play.* Stress *eligible* on its first syllable, *ineligible* on its second. See ILLEGIBLE.

ELLIPSIS 1 is the omission of words from a locution when the context can make clear what is meant: *He runs much faster than I* [*can*]. *That is the book* [*that*] *I wish I had written. I think Mozart's music is the best of all, and I'll bet you do too.* In the last example, the *ellipsis* is accomplished by means of that all-purpose auxiliary, *do. So* can also substitute for other words in this way: *I think she's a winner; I hope the judges think so too.*

ELLIPSIS 2 is the process whereby some sounds are lost in speech because they are unstressed. Contractions are a very common kind of *ellipsis*. Apheresis (which includes aphesis) is the *ellipsis* wherein one or more unstressed syllables drop off the front of a word ('*Most all the time*). Apocope is the disappearance of sounds, especially a final member of a consonant cluster, from the ends of words (*Give me your han'; Where are you goin'?*). Syncope is the omission of midword sounds and syllables, as in the usual pronunciations of many polysyllables in connected speech: for example, *business* (*BIZ-nis*), *family* (*FAM-lee*), and *Wednesday* (*WENZ-dee* or *WENZ-DAI*), which are all Standard pronunciations. The lower the level, the more likely are various sorts of *ellipsis: Are you going to sneeze?* is, in Casual use, quite often said as *Gonna sneeze?* See APHERESIS; APHESIS; APOCOPE; CLIPPING; CONTRACTIONS; SYNCOPE.

ELLIPSIS 3 is the use of periods or other marks to indicate the omission of words in a quotation: "*Better late than never, but. . . .*" Conventionally, use three periods within a sentence. When your *ellipsis* ends with the end of a phrase, clause, or sentence in the original, use four periods or three plus whatever mark ended the original.

elope (v.), **elopement** (n.) The verb means "to run away or to abscond, particularly in order to get married" or, occasionally, "in lieu of getting married." Obviously context must make clear which is meant; some readers will understand that marriage is intended unless it is specifically excluded. The noun offers similar possibility for ambiguity.

else (adj.) When else is combined with the pronouns anybody, somebody, anyone, someone, or who, Standard English adds the genitive inflection to else, not to the pronoun: This hat must be somebody else's. Did they find anyone else's keys? Who else's could it be? See also APOSTROPHE (2).

elude See ALLUDE.

elusion See ALLUSION.

elusive, allusive, illusive, illusory (adjs.) Elusive means "evasive," "hard to grasp or catch," "baffling," as in Bill collectors found him elusive: he never seemed to be at home. Illusive and illusory are synonyms, but illusory is the much higher frequency word. Both words mean "not real," "resulting from illusion," "deceptive," as in All her plans were illusory [illusive] and without any foundation. Allusive has to do with allusions or indirect references, as in His comments were allusive, especially to the many important people he claimed to know. See also ALLUSION.

emanate (v.) When combined with a preposition, emanate usually takes from and means "flows or issues forth from," as in His columns now emanate from a different world capital every week. Only rarely does emanate combine with in, and such uses usually have to do with the language or the publication in which something is circulated: Although he writes in English in this country, his work in Europe usually emanates in one or another French-language journal. Even in that example, from would be more likely.

embark (v.) In combination, embark usually takes the prepositions on or upon, as in We embarked on [upon] an entirely new venture this month. In its literal senses of boarding and sailing on a ship, it can also combine with for to indicate destination, from to indicate point of departure, or in to give the vessel's name or other information about it: He embarked last Friday for London. She embarked from Montreal. They embarked with some trepidation in a bulk carrier that took only a few passengers.

These days embark has much more use in figurative settings-forth than in the literal boarding of ships or planes.

embellish (v.), meaning "to ornament, decorate, or improve," when combined with a preposition, almost always takes with: He embellished his tales with some macabre line drawings. To embellish the truth means "to exaggerate, to lie, to add spurious detail" and is pejorative, as the verb alone is not.

emend See AMEND.

emerge (v.) can combine with a good many prepositions, but from and as occur most frequently: She emerged from relative obscurity. He emerged as our new leader. Other prepositions that can occur with emerge include about, at, and toward (She emerged about [at, toward] five o'clock), in, into, near, on, onto, upon, and through (He emerged in [into, near, on, onto, upon, through] Market Street), between (We emerged between two parked cars), and with (They emerged with no harm done).

emigrant, emigration, immigrant, immigration, in-migration, migrant, migration, out-migration (nn.), **emigrate, immigrate, migrate** (vv.) All these refer to moving considerable distances (usually), especially from one country to another. To migrate is "to move (one's home) from one place to another." To emigrate and to immigrate are also "to move from one place or country to another," but emigrate stresses leaving the old place (combined form is emigrate from the old place to the new place), and immigrate stresses going to the new place (combined form is immigrate to the new place from the old one). Of course confusion between emigrate and immigrate can result from the similarities in their pronunciations in connected speech (IM-i-GRAIT and EM-i-GRAIT).

The nouns migrant, emigrant, and immigrant are similarly distinctive: a migrant moves from one place to another, an emigrant leaves an old place, and an immigrant arrives at a new place. And so it is too with the abstract nouns migration, emigration, and immigration.

Creation of in-migration and out-migration (and in-migrant, out-migrant, in-migrate, and out-migrate) may in part have been an effort to avoid possible confusion, but these words also have an advantage if you intend to concentrate solely on the effects of migrations on a single place, keeping track of who enters and who leaves but paying no immediate attention to where the in-migrants come from or where the out-

migrants go. All these terms are Standard, although *in-migrate* and *out-migrate* and their other forms are only about fifty years old.

eminent, immanent, imminent (*adj.*) *Imminent* and *immanent* are frequently homophones (both pronounced *IM-uh-nent*), and *eminent* usually differs only in its first vowel (*EM-uh-nent*), so at least in speech it is possible to confuse these words. *Eminent* means "prominent, standing out above others, distinguished": *He is an eminent composer and conductor. Imminent* means "impending, threatening, likely to occur at any moment," as in *It appears that a real downpour is imminent. Immanent* is a relatively low frequency word, meaning "inherent, residing within, self-contained," as in *These ideas are immanent in most Christian belief.*

emote (*v.*) is a back-formation from the noun *emotion,* and it is usually used humorously or at least lightly, or else somewhat pejoratively, although critics of actors and acting sometimes seem to use it in technical discussions of the range of someone's acting abilities: *For a person to weep convincingly while facing the camera or the audience is a difficult thing, but this actor can emote in that fashion most convincingly.* Limit your use of the verb to the Conversational levels and Informal or Semiformal writing; elsewhere use *display, show,* or *reveal emotion,* instead.

emotional, emotive (*adjs.*) Each adjective refers to the emotions, but differently. *Emotional* has a general sense of "having to do with the emotions," but it has unique specialized senses as well, including "displaying emotions strongly or easily, stimulating emotional displays, and appealing directly to people's emotions," as in *The witness was very emotional, weeping one minute, giggling the next* and *The first speaker spoke quietly and matter-of-factly, but the second was emotional throughout. Emotive* is a more abstract term, referring generally to anything having to do with emotion or the emotions: *The emotive use of language is the attempt to use words to appeal to people's emotions.* The terms overlap only in their generic senses.

empanel See IMPANEL.

empathetic, sympathetic (*adjs.*), **empathize, sympathize** (*vv.*), **empathy, sympathy** (*nn.*) These related pairs make essentially similar distinctions: *empathy* is the imaginative putting of yourself in others' shoes, being able to identify with their feelings; *sympathy* involves supporting or at least understanding the plight of others.

You can be *sympathetic* without necessarily being *empathetic*; *sympathy* may require only pity, whereas *empathy* would require first your imagined identification with the sufferer and might not require *sympathy* as well. You are *empathetic* [*sympathetic*] *with* [not *for*] *someone*; you *show* or *feel* or *have empathy* [*sympathy*] *for* [not *with*] *someone;* you *are in sympathy* [not *empathy*] *with* [not *for*] *someone*; and you *empathize* [*sympathize*] *with* [not *for*] *someone.* All these are idiomatic and Standard. See also APATHY.

EMPHASIS is added force, impetus, or strength given to something. In language increased stress or loudness can give *emphasis,* as can choice of words, length of sentence, use of figures, and choice of syntax. Putting important words in positions in a sentence that normally get relatively heavy stress can help provide *emphasis*; so sometimes can repetition and redundancy. See also EMPHATIC PRONOUNS.

EMPHATIC PRONOUNS are the *-self* forms (see REFLEXIVE PRONOUNS) used for emphasis, as in *I myself hate spinach.*

employ (*v.*) is appropriate as a substitute for the verb *use,* particularly when you want to stress purpose: *We decided we had to employ many more specific examples if we were to persuade our readers. Employ* is a longer, lower-frequency word, but it is not necessarily pretentious; it may serve well to provide variety or explicitness. *Employ* also has a specialized sense meaning "to hire or to pay for services rendered": *She employed three secretaries in her office.*

employee, employe (*n.*) *Employee* is the usual American English spelling, but *employe* is a Standard variant used especially by some corporate house organs and business publications.

emporium (*n.*) means "a marketplace," and nineteenth-century and early twentieth-century small towns applied it to any general or dry goods store. We still use it today, even though jocularly or hyperbolically more often than not. It has two plurals: *emporiums* (the usual one) and *emporia* (the Latin one we borrowed with the word). See FOREIGN PLURALS.

empowerment (*n.*) is a current vogue word of mixed and rather vague meaning. It usually means "possession of the right to exercise authority, to make choices, and the like," and it is used chiefly in connection with the *empowering* or granting of *empowerment* to people or groups who have heretofore lacked them. A jargon word from the world of social and political reform, it is frequently used as a counter in discussions of liberal political correctness. Compare ENTITLEMENT.

EMPTY SUBJECTS See DUMMY SUBJECTS.

enamor (*v.*) is usually used in the passive voice or as a participial adjective, in either case followed by *of: He became enamored of at least one of his teachers every year.* Sometimes it is followed by *with,* as in *I've never been enamored with her acting,* and it can occasionally be heard or seen with *by,* as in *I'm not enamored by the jazz he likes to play,* but many consider that combination Nonstandard or Casual at best: you would do well to avoid it.

enclave (*n.*) Pronounce it either *EN-KLAIV* or *AHN-KLAIV.* It means "a group or political entity surrounded by a larger country or another entity": *Little Norway is an enclave in southern Brooklyn.*

enclose, inclose (*v.*), **enclosure, inclosure** (*n.*) The usual spellings are *enclose* and *enclosure*; *inclose* and *inclosure* are rare variant spellings.

encomium (*n.*) means "high and glowing praise, formally expressed." Two plurals are Standard: *encomiums* and *encomia.* See FOREIGN PLURALS.

encounter (*v.*) meaning "meet with" is Standard and is not necessarily pretentious in such uses as *I hope to encounter more of her paintings some day.*

encroach (*v.*), when it combines with prepositions, usually takes *on* or *upon,* as in *They were clearly encroaching on [upon] our land. Into* and *onto* also occur in Standard use: *The junkyard gradually encroached into [onto] the neighboring property.*

end (*v.*), when it combines intransitively, can take *as, at, by,* or *on,* as in *He'll end as a winner; The road ends at the water; She will surely end by taking the prize; Their disagreement ended on a note of real rancor.* See also END UP.

end, rear See BUTTOCKS.

endeavor, attempt, try (*vv.*) These are synonyms. *Endeavor* is the most formal verb, *attempt* somewhat less so, and *try* the least formal. Each can serve you well in the right place: *Try to get some sleep. We urged them to attempt to find time to rest. Patients should endeavor to get at least eight hours sleep each night.*

ended, ending (*adjs.*) Use *the period ending* [or *that ends*] *July 1* for future time, *the period ended July 1* for time past. Both uses are Standard idioms.

endemic, epidemic, pandemic (*adjs.*) Something *endemic* is native to a particular place or always to be found in a particular region, as are some plants or trees or certain pathological conditions that neither increase nor decrease but are simply always present there. Something *epidemic* is prevalent and spreading rapidly in a particular region or community, as might a contagious disease; something *pandemic* is omnipresent, spread over a huge area, to be found everywhere: *Malnutrition is pandemic in the Horn of Africa, but this season starvation is epidemic there as well.*

ending See ENDED.

ENDING A SENTENCE WITH A PREPOSITION See PREPOSITION (1).

endite See INDICT.

endless (*adj.*), meaning "innumerable, neverending, continual, and (literally) without end," represents hyperbole, probably in all senses but its literal one: *The perimeter of a circle is an endless line.* On occasion, such exaggeration can be rhetorically useful, and in all hyperbolic uses, *endless* is Standard, as in *There was an endless wait at the ticket office,* but conservatives often insist that *endless* needs a qualifier, as in *a seemingly endless wait.* See ABSOLUTE ADJECTIVES.

endorse, indorse (*v.*) A few commentators have fallen for the etymological fallacy here and argued that *endorse* can mean only "to sign on the back." This is no longer true, however: *endorse* does stem ultimately from the Latin *dorsum,* meaning "back" (compare the fish's *dorsal fin*), but today has generalized to mean "any signature, on the back of a check or anywhere else on a document." It also has figurative senses meaning simply "to approve or support," as in *She endorsed the platform in a speech that very evening.* All these current senses are Standard, as are both spellings, although *endorse* is by far the more frequent.

endow (*v.*) combines most frequently with the prepositions *with,* indicating the nature of the endowment, and *by,* indicating who did the endowing: *Their grandfather endowed the library with nearly a million dollars. The museum was generously endowed by a famous collector of Renaissance paintings.*

end product, end result These phrases sometimes can be considered redundant, but each has justifiable Standard uses too: other *products* and *by-products* of a process may precede an *end product,* and although *result* may suitably replace *end result* in many situations, the full phrase may sometimes help differentiate preliminary results from the final one. These phrases can be considered clichés, but they have the force of idioms as well. Don't routinely avoid them if they can serve you, but use *product* or *result* alone if either will serve your purpose.

end up (*v.*) is Standard and need not be limited to Conversational or Informal use. It means "to reach a final state or position," and the verb *end* by itself cannot always satisfactorily replace it: *The game's increasingly effective publicity caused it to end up on national television.* (Were it to *end on national television,* the sentence would be ambiguous.) *End up* can be followed by any of several prepositions, such as *in, with, at, near,* and the like: *The game ended up in a tie. I ended up with a black eye. We ended up at the police station.*

enervate, innervate, innerve (*vv.*) Here the prefix *e-* means the same as the prefix *un-*, and to *enervate* is to "unnerve or to weaken." If you're *enervated,* you have no verve, zeal, or nervous energy. The word is sometimes mistakenly used to mean the opposite, however, which is essentially what the much rarer *innerve* and *innervate* mean, "to provide with nerve(s), or to give courage or strength to." To use *enervate* to mean *innervate* is Substandard and a shibboleth.

enfranchise See DISFRANCHISE.

engage (*v.*), when it combines with a preposition, does so frequently with *in* followed by a gerund or another nominal: *I try not to engage in criticizing others. Don't get engaged in his quarrels. Engage* also combines with *to* plus an infinitive, as in *Our trio was engaged to play during the dinner hour.* Other prepositions that are Standard in combination with *engage* include *as, by, for, on, upon,* and *with: She was engaged as [or by] the head gardener. They were engaged for a two-week run of the play. We were engaged on [upon] a very dubious enterprise with several others from the college.*

England See BRITAIN.

ENGLISH AND AMERICAN DIFFERENCES IN MEANING, PRONUNCIATION, SPELLING, AND VOCABULARY See MEANING; PRONUNCIATION (2); SPELLING (1); VOCABULARY (2).

English (the) See BRITISH.

enhance (*v.*) Today's Standard use employs *enhance* to make better or to improve our perception of some quality or characteristic already good or favorably viewed: *Her ready smile much enhanced her already engaging manner.* Also

note that you *enhance* things, not people: the smile does not *enhance* the woman herself.

enigma, mystery, puzzle, riddle (*nn.*) All these mean "something difficult to explain or resolve," "something baffling." *Enigma* began as a problem posed in language, a tale or riddle that was hard or impossible to fathom; then figuratively it came to be applied to anything difficult to explain or resolve, anything baffling, including a person who may be described as an *enigma,* a *mystery,* a *puzzle,* or a *riddle.*

enigmatic (*adj.*) means "mysterious, baffling, secret, or puzzling" but not "questionable or doubtful." See also EQUIVOCAL.

enjoin (*v.*) can take a direct object followed by an infinitive, where it means "ordered, directed," "urged," or "admonished," as in *His father enjoined him to consider carefully what he was about to undertake. Enjoin* can also combine with the preposition *from,* where the combination means "to forbid," "to order," or "to prevent," as in *The court order enjoined him from using [from use of] credit cards for two years.* These are Standard, as are the less frequent combinations with *on* and *upon,* as in *We enjoined on [upon] the committee the necessity for speed.*

enjoy (*v.*) is a transitive verb meaning "take pleasure in, like": *I enjoy reading.* It is also Standard with a reflexive pronoun: *She always seems to enjoy herself. Enjoy* is deliberately ambiguous in an expression such as *He has enjoyed poor health for the past year,* wherein a sense of *enjoy* meaning "has undergone or had the advantage or use of" suggests that the man takes pleasure in complaining about his health. *Enjoy* is sometimes labeled pretentious when it means simply "to undergo" and either the experience cannot really be felt as pleasurable, as in *The building will enjoy considerable renovation this year,* or, as with poor health, the experience promises to be quite the reverse of pleasant, as in *She has already enjoyed her eighty-seventh birthday, which was her tenth in the nursing home.* At the Casual and Impromptu levels, *enjoy* is also used in an elliptical transitive sense: *Enjoy!* meaning "Enjoy yourself; Have a good time."

enormity, enormousness (*nn.*) *Enormousness* means "extremely large size" and has no pejorative overtones, but *enormity* is in the midst of a major semantic change, and you must use it with great care. It has long meant "monstrousness, great wickedness," and the like, as in *The enormity of his crimes shocked everyone,* in addition to its senses of hugeness, great size, and scale. But today the word is used more and more often, in speech and in print, to indicate only something of great size not in any way unpleasant, criminal, outrageous, or unnatural. Some editors still won't accept it in this new, elevated sense, but the use is growing, as all dictionaries now attest. Best advice: control the reader's response by means of context, and be aware that older or conservative audiences consider *enormity* pejorative. See SYNONYM.

enough See SUFFICIENT.

enquire, enquirer, enquiry See INQUIRE.

en route (*adv., adj.*) is a French phrase, meaning "on the way (to)" or "along the way," that is now fully anglicized. We usually print it as two words, although one-word versions do occur, and we pronounce it *en ROOT, ahn ROOT,* or in the nasalized French way, *awng ROOT.* Its usage problems include the careless spelling of the *en* as *on,* to match one of its English pronunciations, and the spelling of the phrase as one word: Edited English approves neither of these. Also to be avoided as Substandard is the pronunciation of this use of *route* to rhyme with *out.* See FOREIGN PHRASES.

ensemble See BAND.

ensure See INSURE.

en't, in't These contractions are eye dialect representations of *isn't* as Vulgar speech frequently utters it. *Isn't it?* often is similarly represented in eye dialect as *innit?* Compare AIN'T.

enter (*v.*) may be combined with a long list of prepositions, including *as* (*He entered the contest as a candidate for the council*), *at* (*She entered at the last minute*), *by* (*The thief entered by the back door*), *for* (*She entered for a joke*), *from* (*They entered from the garage*), *in* (*She entered her turtle in the second race*), *into* (*They entered into the spirit of the occasion*), *on* (*I entered my name on Friday*), *onto* and *upon* (*The door entered directly onto* [*upon*] *the stage*), *under* (*He entered under an assumed name*), and *with* (*She entered with the other dancers*). All are Standard.

enthrall, enthral (*v.*) Americans spell it either way, but usually *enthrall*; the British spell it *enthral.* Both dialects spell *enthralling* and *enthralled* with two *l*'s (see CONSONANTS 2). When combined with prepositions, *enthrall* takes either *by* or *with: The children were enthralled by* [*with*] *her storytelling.*

enthuse (*v.*) is a back-formation (from *enthusiasm*) that even after more than a century of slow climb toward full Standard status has not yet achieved it, at least in the view of some lexicographers and some commentators on usage. Col-

ceives, and in fact the word today is Standard in all but the most Formal and Oratorical uses. Nonetheless, some Edited English is still reluctant to accept it, so assess your audience's taste carefully: when in doubt, don't *enthuse; show enthusiasm* or *be enthusiastic.*

entitle (*v.*) is Standard in both these senses: "to be named or titled," as in *Her book is entitled* ***The Great American Novel***; and "to give a legal right or title to," as in *Her authorship of the book entitled her to ten free copies.*

entitlement (*n.*) has come to be widely used in the sense of "something to which you are entitled," particularly to mean "any of various governmental programs for which people qualify because of poverty, illness, age, or another condition toward which government directs financial or other assistance." All such programs are called *entitlements,* and the term is now Standard. See EMPOWERMENT.

entomology, etymology (*nn.*) These words are frequently confused: *entomology* is the branch of zoology that deals with insects, and *etymology* is the branch of language study that deals with word history and word origins. See ETYMOLOGY.

entrust, intrust, trust (*vv.*) *Entrust* is the usual spelling, *intrust* a relatively rare variant spelling. You *entrust* someone *with* something, or *entrust* something *to* someone. *Trust* and *entrust* are not entirely interchangeable: *I will trust you* and intransitive uses, as in *She just naturally trusts,* are Standard, as are structures such as *He is too trusting* that use the present participle as a predicate adjective. *Entrust,* however, can only be transitive: *I will entrust you with my car* is Standard, but *I will entrust you* is unidiomatic, as is *She is entrusting.*

enunciate, enunciation See ANNUNCIATE.

enure See INURE.

envelop (*v.*), **envelope** (*n.*) The verb is pronounced *en-VEL-uhp* and is now spelled without a final -*e*; it means "to wrap or cover up, to surround, or to conceal": *Whenever the power goes off, the darkness envelops us.* The noun is spelled with a final -*e* and is pronounced either *EN-vuh-LOP* or *AHN-vuh-LOP* (for a time some commentators thought the *AHN-* pronunciation affected, but it is a Standard variant today). It means "a flattish rectangular paper container for a letter or papers" or "the gas-holding fabric bag of a balloon or blimp" and has several other similar figurative but specialized meanings.

envious, enviable (*adjs.*) *Envious* means "feeling or showing envy," as in *He was rich and handsome, but we tried not to be envious,* while *enviable* means "worthy or desirable enough to be envied or to cause envy," as in *She had an enviable ease of manner. Envious* sometimes combines with the preposition *of,* as in *We were all envious of her new car.*

environment See ECOLOGY.

ENVIRONMENT IN PRONUNCIATION

Speech sounds often change when they accommodate to preceding or following sounds. Consider the surname *Cronkite,* which Walter Cronkite himself pronounces *KRAHN-KEIT.* In others' speech, the clear *n* in his pronunciation is often assimilated to the following *k,* yielding the pronunciation *KRAHNG-KEIT.* For other processes that can cause change in pronunciation as a result of the phonetic *environment,* see APHERESIS; APHESIS; APOCOPE; DISSIMILATION; ELLIPSIS (2); INTRUSION; METATHESIS; SYNCOPE.

envisage, envision (*vv.*) These two are synonyms, interchangeable in all uses, meaning "to create a mental picture, to picture to oneself," or simply "to imagine," as in *We don't envision* [*envisage*] *his causing any further difficulty.* Both words are somewhat elevated in tone, perhaps, but are unquestionably Standard today.

envoy 1, envoi (*n.*) *Envoy* has a variant spelling, *envoi,* reflecting its medieval French origin; it means "the concluding, often dedicatory, remarks at the end of a book or other literary work," and it is also the technical name for the brief (usually four-line) summary or dedicatory stanza at the end of a French poem called a *ballade.* See BALLAD; FOREIGN PHRASES.

envoy 2 (*n.*) is the title given a minister or other representative of one government sent on a mission to a foreign government, as in *He was the Spanish envoy to the British court.* See FOREIGN PHRASES.

eon, aeon (*n.*) Both spellings are Standard. Pronounce it either *EE-uhn* or *EE-AHN.* It means "a great length of time," "thousands of years."

epic (*adj., n.*) The word's basic meaning is "a kind of long narrative heroic poem, such as *The Iliad, The Aeneid,* or *Beowulf,*" but our penchant for hyperbole has made us apply it today to novels and motion pictures with any sort of claim to gigantic scale, historical importance, or simply monumentalism, however defined. Then by functional shift we create the corresponding adjective, *epic.* Most use of *epic* is cliché nowadays—and so hyperbolic as to be nearly meaningless—but in its original senses it still can serve us well.

EPICENE PRONOUNS

Etymologically, *epicene* has had overtones of effeminacy, even decadence, but language commentators nowadays use the term principally to refer to nouns that have only one form for both sexes (*chicken,* for example, as compared with the feminine *hen* and the masculine *rooster*) and to pronouns that lack characteristics applying to only one sex. (The Greek root meant "common to many.") Thus all the plural pronouns, the first and second person singular pronouns, the relative pronouns *who* and *that,* and the indefinite pronouns, such as *everyone* and *somebody,* are said to be *epicene.* See GENERIC PRONOUNS; INCLUSIVE LANGUAGE; SEXIST LANGUAGE; THEY.

epicure (*n.*), **epicurean, Epicurean** (*adj.*), **epicureanism, Epicureanism** (*nn.*) An *epicure* (named after *Epicurus* [341–240 B.C.], whose philosophy embraced luxury and the pleasures of eating and drinking) is a person who has a well-developed taste for and an enjoyment of good food and drink; anyone *epicurean* (lowercase *e*) is said to be fond of luxury and especially of eating and drinking well, just as anything *epicurean* assists or suggests such tastes. Capitalize the adjective when it refers to the philosopher or his philosophy, *Epicureanism.* And distinguish *epicureanism* from both gluttony and drunkenness: it refers to glorious sensory experiences, not to gobbling and swilling.

epidemic See ENDEMIC.

epigram, epigraph, epilogue, epitaph (*nn.*) An *epigram* is a short poem or a short, witty, and memorable statement, such as Ogden Nash's *Candy/Is dandy,/But liquor/Is quicker.* An *epigraph* is either an inscription on a building or a monument, or a short quotation at the head of an essay, or of a chapter in a book, that is related in some way to what is intended or what is to follow. An *epitaph* is a memorial inscription on a gravestone or something written in honor of someone recently dead. An *epilogue* (sometimes spelled *epilog*) is a closing speech or set of remarks at the end of a play or other literary piece; it frequently rounds off or comments further on the meaning of the work just ended.

episcopal, Episcopal (*adjs.*), **Anglican, Episcopalian** (*adjs., nn.*) The adjective *episcopal* means "governed by bishops" and applies to Protestant churches so governed, including particularly the Protestant *Episcopal* Church in the United States and the *Anglican* Church in Britain. These two churches, plus the Canadian and other churches of this group, are referred to as the *Anglican* Communion. The congregations of these churches—all *Anglicans*—are also called *Episcopalians* in the United States, and the related adjectives are used to describe attributes of the churches and their constituents.

epistle, missive (*nn.*) Both are elegant, often pretentious names for letters or other written messages. See also MISSILE.

epitaph See EPIGRAM.

epithet (*n.*) An *epithet* is a descriptive adjective, noun, or phrase intended to label or characterize someone. Originally, such a label could either praise or derogate, but some commentators argue these days that an *epithet* always derides or criticizes. Others insist that an *epithet* can still be either pejorative or ameliorative. What is clear is that you must make sure that context removes all doubt on this point, even if this means calling the *epithet* itself a *flattering* or *disparaging epithet* when you introduce it. Because not everyone believes *epithets* always disparage, the possible accusations of redundancy seem worth the risk.

epitome (*n.*), pronounced *ee-PIT-uh-mee*, means "a summary or a brief statement covering a longer topic," as in *His brief statement is an epitome of the full manifesto,* or "a typical or an ideal example of something," as in *She is the epitome of good manners.* There is a difference of opinion over whether an *epitome* is only typical or whether it must be ideal. At the moment Standard English uses it in both meanings. An *epitome* that is ideal, however, may also *epitomize* either the best or the worst: *His comments were the epitome of bad taste.* Make certain that context clarifies these points when you use the word.

epoch (*n.*) means both "the start of a new period of time" and simply "a period of time," and the second and newer sense is by far the more frequently used today, as in *The eighties were an epoch marked by huge increases in consumer debt.* To convey the older sense, you must almost always specify the idea of beginning.

EPONYM (*n.*), **EPONYMOUS** (*adj.*) is the real or legendary person whose name has become the name of a place, an event, an artifact, or a characteristic: *diesel, quisling,* and *Cleveland* are all *eponymous* names.

equable, equitable (*adjs.*) have clearly different meanings. The first means "unvarying, steady, moderate, tranquil": *She has an easy,* equable disposition. *Equitable* means "fair-dealing, just, even-handed": *His decisions are always equitable; he never shows favoritism.*

equal (*adj.*) means "the same in size or quality" and is often considered an absolute adjective. (That limitation makes possible the Orwellian *Animal Farm* [1946] dictum "All animals are equal, but some animals are more equal than others," a seeming impossibility that makes clear the totalitarian abuse of the principle of equality.) But as a general adjective, *equal* has long been subject to comparison in some Standard uses.

When it combines with prepositions, *equal* usually takes *to,* as in *Her raise is equal to the average received by the rest of us,* but can also take *with,* as in *Infant mortality rates are equal with drug-related crime as critical urban problems today.*

equally as (*adv.*), meaning "just as" or "every bit as," has long been called redundant because either *equally* or *as* will replace it in most uses: *She is equally as bad [equally bad, as bad] a bridge player as he is.* Despite all criticism, it is usually considered Standard, although many editors won't accept it in Edited English.

equilibrium (*n.*) has two plurals: *equilibriums* and *equilibria.* See FOREIGN PLURALS.

equine (*adj., n.*) The adjective means "like, concerning, or characteristic of a horse," and the noun is simply another (Latinate) word for "horse." The noun in particular is frequently considered pretentious, an elegant variation designed to elevate a *horsy* matter. The adjective is not usually so judged, perhaps because *equine* is used almost universally as the generic adjective and in veterinary and other specialized terminology, whereas *horsy* and *horsey* sound rather whimsical or childish. But compare CANINE; FELINE.

equitable See EQUABLE.

equivalent (*adj., n.*) The adjective can combine with the prepositions *to,* as in *The payment is equivalent to a week's wages,* and less frequently with *with,* as in *It's equivalent with the one we got a year ago.* The noun can combine with *of, to,* and *for,* as in *His award was intended to be an equivalent of [to, for] hers.*

equivocal, ambiguous, ambivalent, cryptic, dubious, enigmatic, mysterious (*adjs.*) All these are somewhat synonymous. *Ambivalent* is perhaps the most explicit; it means "experiencing conflicting or contradictory feelings or views" or "being unable to make up one's mind." *Equivocal* means "undecided," "in doubt," or "capable of more than one interpretation," and it may also mean "deliberately deceptive." Something *ambiguous, enigmatic,* or *cryptic* may also be deliberately deceptive. *Ambiguous* means "with two or more meanings," or "unclear." *Cryptic* and *enigmatic* stress the idea of bafflement and an inability to penetrate a mystery; *mysterious* does the same. *Dubious* stresses the doubtful and untrustworthy characteristics of whatever is so called.

Equivocal combines with *toward(s)* and *about: He's equivocal toward(s) [about] her candidacy.* See also AMBIVALENT; DUBIOUS; ENIGMA; ENIGMATIC.

-er, -est (*suffixes*) The suffix *-er* is added to some adjectives and adverbs to form the comparative degree, as in *slow/slower; -est* is the suffix added to form the superlative degree, as in *slow/slowest.* See POSITIVE DEGREE; see also ADJECTIVES (1); ADVERBS (1).

-er, -or See AGENTIVE ENDINGS.

-er, -re See SPELLING (1).

e're, ere See E'ER.

erode, corrode (*vv.*) Both mean "to wear away" or "to eat into," and they are therefore synonyms, but *erode* stresses the wearing away of something as by the action of wind or water, whereas *corrode* stresses the eating away of something as by rust or another chemical action: *The river eroded the canyon walls. The acid corroded the battery terminals.* Both verbs can be used figuratively too: *Age erodes muscular flexibility; lack of exercise can corrode it.*

erotic (*adj.*) The word means "of or arousing sexual love or sexual desire," "amatory," "susceptible to sexual stimulus." In the "amatory" sense its referent is simply "sexual love," but in its other senses it has come to refer more and more explicitly to sexual desire and stimulation, with less and less reference to the love or sentiment that might accompany it.

erotica (*n.*), meaning "works of art or literature on erotic subjects, or of an erotic character," was originally a Greek plural, but in English today it is sometimes construed as a mass noun taking a singular verb, as in *This erotica is now legally publishable.* It also regularly takes a plural verb when *erotica* is clearly construed as plural, as in *These ancient erotica were long considered modern forgeries.* Both patterns are Standard today, but Edited English usually insists on a plural verb. See FOREIGN PLURALS.

err (*v.*) is pronounced to rhyme either with *stir* or *stare,* but those speakers of Standard English

who regularly rhyme it with *stir* usually consider the *stare* rhyme a blunder. See also ERRANT.

errant, arrant (*adjs.*) *Errant* means "wandering, off course, lost," and so "mistaken," as in *The errant child needed direction, not punishment. Arrant* comes from the same root, but in this case the wandering leads away from and never returns to the right path; today *arrant* means only "very bad," "notorious," "incorrigible," as in *He's an arrant criminal; he makes no pretense about it.* They can be homophones, pronounced *ER-int,* but *arrant* is more frequently pronounced *A-rint.*

errata (*n.*) is the Latin plural of *erratum.* We use it mostly in the plural as the heading of a list of typographical and similar errors not caught before a new publication was released. We say usually *The **list** of errata is . . .* or *The errata **are.** . . .* See FOREIGN PLURALS.

ersatz See ARTIFICIAL.

erstwhile (*adv., adj.*), **erstwhiles** (*adv.*) The adverbs, which mean "formerly, long ago," are archaic, as in *We lived there erstwhile[s], when our ancestors were young.* The adjective, meaning "former, once-upon-a-time," is still in use, although it has an old-fashioned quality about it, as in *When we returned we saw a few of our erstwhile acquaintances. Former* would have a less literary air, perhaps. Compare QUONDAM; SOME TIME; WHILOM.

erupt, irrupt (*vv.*), **eruptive, irruptive** (*adjs.*) *Erupt* means "to burst out or break out," as in *When I was fourteen, my acne erupted; Lava erupted from the side of the volcano. Irrupt* means "to burst into" or, of populations, "to burst into vigorous growth": *The floods overran the dike and irrupted into the city streets. When the years of drought ended, the prairie grasses of the area simply irrupted. Eruptive* and *irruptive* are similarly differentiated: essentially something *eruptive* bursts out, something *irruptive* bursts in.

-es See -S.

escalate (*v.*) *Escalate* is a Standard back-formation from *escalator* and means "to increase or rise," as in *The rate of unemployment has escalated rapidly this spring.* Compare DE-ESCALATE.

escalator (*n.*) and related words are frequently mispronounced *ES-kyuh-LAI-tuhr,* rather than the Standard *ES-kuh-LAI-tuhr;* the intrusion of the *-yuh-* is variously explained, but it probably is a false analogy with words like *granular* and *singular.* Such pronunciations are Substandard and may well be considered shibboleths. Compare NUCLEAR.

escape (*v.*) To pronounce it *eks-KAIP* instead of *es-KAIP* is Substandard. When combined with a preposition, *escape* usually takes *from*, as in *We escaped from the party eventually*, but it can also take a direct object and not use a preposition, as in *He escaped custody and fled the country*. Both constructions are Standard.

escapee (*n.*), meaning "one who escapes," is pronounced *es-KAIP-EE, es-KAIP-EE,* or *ES-kuh-PEE*. It means the same as the older word *escaper*, which it has largely replaced in general use. See -EE.

esophagus, oesophagus (*n.*) *Esophagus* is the usual American spelling, *oesophagus* the British.

especial, especially See SPECIAL.

espresso, expresso (*n.*) *Espresso* (pronounced *es-PRES-so*) is the beverage produced by forcing live steam through finely ground dark-roasted coffee beans. The variant *expresso* is frequently considered Nonstandard—it is both a mistaken spelling and a mistaken pronunciation (*ek-SPRES-so*)—but some dictionaries now accept both pronunciation and spelling as Standard. Be aware, though, that some conservative users of Standard English accept only *espresso* (plural: *espressos*). See PLURALS OF NOUNS ENDING IN -O.

Esq. See ESQUIRE.

-esque (*suffix*) means "in the manner of," "in the style of," or "in imitation of," as in *Romanesque* (like the Roman), *grotesque* (like a grotto, and hence fanciful), and *statuesque* (large, imposing, unmoving). In some uses it may have slightly pejorative overtones, suggesting only "an imitation of" rather than "very much like." See -ISTIC.

Esquire, Esq. (*n.*) In the United States, where there are no knights or other titled gentry, *Esq.* (the abbreviation) is an honorific title (see HONORABLE 2), used primarily in writing instead of the *Mr.* to which all males are presumably entitled. Lawyers make use of *Esquire* in corresponding with each other, but since no one seems to know what to use as an equivalent honorific for the increasing numbers of women who are lawyers, the term *Esquire* may fade away, at least among lawyers. Usage requires that you use either *Mr.* or *Esq.*, never both. Best advice is probably not to use *Esq.*; today it is increasingly jocular or playful, not seriously meant.

-ess, -ette, -euse, -ienne, -ine, -ix These are some of the feminine endings or suffixes that English can add to nouns to make feminine versions of occupational names: *aviator/aviatrix; chorus boy/chorus girl/chorine; dancer/danseuse; masseur/masseuse; hero/heroine; priest/priestess; steward/stewardess; usher/usherette*; and so on. Most of these except *priestess* (which now has a referent limited almost entirely to ancient and pagan religious matters) and *hero/heroine* and *masseur/masseuse* (which maintain distinctions we apparently still insist on) have fallen into disuse, usually in favor of all-purpose use of the word once reserved for males or another inclusive term now used for either sex: *pilot* or *flier* and *flight attendant*, for example. In some instances semantic distinctions still retain the feminine ending: *governor* and *governess* are not simply gender- or sex-distinctive forms with the same referent. *Actress* and *comedienne* seem still to be in use, but in divided usage with *actor* and *comedian*. Still other terms continue in use much as before: *waitress, goddess, princess, countess, duchess, lioness*, and the like. But a good many more, including *poetess* and *authoress*, are archaic and rapidly becoming obsolescent or obsolete, primarily of historical interest today. See also FEMININE OCCUPATIONAL FORMS; INCLUSIVE LANGUAGE; -IST; SEXIST LANGUAGE.

essay See ASSAY.

essential (*adj., n.*) Although the point has sometimes been argued, Standard English clearly does not consider *essential* an absolute adjective: *This program is much more essential to our purposes than that one*. The adjective, when combined with a preposition, usually takes *to, in,* or *for,* as in *Her contributions are essential to [in, for] our success*. The noun can combine with *of, for, in,* or *to,* as in *Persistence is one of the essentials of [for, in] successful salesmanship* and *Eight hours of sleep are an essential to my well-being*.

-est See -ER.

Establishment, the (*n.*) is a term meaning "the (usually conservative, often stodgy or even reactionary) group of people and their institutions currently in power in government, finance, and society." *The Establishment* is what innovators feel they must overcome if anything new or different is to succeed. The term became a vogue word among liberals and other advocates for change in the United States during the 1960s, and it has continued in Standard use since then, now perhaps having become less of a cliché.

esthete, esthetic See AESTHETE; LIGATURES.

estimate (*n., v.*) The verb (pronounced *ES-ti-MAIT*) can combine with the prepositions *at, as, for, by,* and *from,* as in *She estimated its weight at [as] four hundred pounds; Three hundred dollars was the profit he estimated for the week; We estimated by using the averages of the last three years; He estimated from his previous experience with costs.* The noun (pronounced *ES-tim-it*) usually combines with *of: I made an estimate of how long the job would take.*

Estimate and *estimation* already suggest approximation, so *to estimate at about* and *an estimate [estimation] of about* are both redundant, but they occur frequently at Conversational and Informal levels.

estimation (*n.*), meaning "opinion, view, or judgment," as in *She has risen greatly in my estimation,* is Standard English, in spite of some earlier objections to it.

estrange (*v.*), when combined with a preposition, almost always takes *from: Her recent behavior is almost certain to estrange her husband [her from her husband].* *Estrange* is most commonly used in the passive voice, combined with *from: He is estranged from his wife.*

estrogen, oestrogen (*n.*) Americans usually spell it *estrogen*; the British prefer *oestrogen.*

et al. is a Latin tag, an abbreviation of *et alii* (masculine), *et aliae* (feminine), or *et alia* (neuter), meaning "and [the] others." The period after *al.* is sometimes omitted in English, and the phrase is so much used that it often is not printed in italics. It is regularly used in footnotes to save space, and it also occurs in expository prose, even in some Edited English, despite some conservative objections. See FOREIGN PHRASES.

etc., et cetera *Etc.* is an abbreviation of the Latin tag *et cetera,* which means "and the rest," "and the like, "and so on," or "and so forth." Conservative practice often objects to its being used in expository prose, but it is Standard at nearly all levels, always either pronounced in full (*ET SET-uhr-uh* or *ET SET-ruh*) or freely translated as "and so forth" or "and (the) others" but usually abbreviated in writing. Don't use it after *e.g.,* since that "for example" has already selected from the crowd. Avoid the frequent Substandard blunder of saying or writing *and etc.—et* means "and." Retain the period after the abbreviation, and never, never misspell it *ect* or mispronounce it *ek SET-uhr-uh.* See FOREIGN PHRASES.

eth See OLD ENGLISH.

-eth (*suffix*), is the obsolete (except in King James Bible language, for which the proper label today is archaic) third person singular present tense ending of English verbs, as in *He liveth and reigneth.* It is frequently adopted for imitative jocular use and is often inappropriately attached to plurals or to tenses and persons where it historically never belonged. Use it accurately or not at all.

Ethiopian (*adj., n.*) is useless today as an objective racial designation and in such use is now taboo in American English. Its appropriate use now designates citizens of the country of Ethiopia.

ethnic (*adj., n.*), **ethnicity** (*n.*) The adjective means "of or concerning groups of people with a common national, racial, or other background": *The neighborhood's population comprises several distinct ethnic groups.* The noun means "a member of an ethnically distinctive group" and is used frequently in the plural, as in *Ethnics in general are in favor of the proposal,* though this use has an Informal ring that some Edited English considers inappropriate. *Ethnicity* is a noun meaning "possessing the qualities of an *ethnic* person or group or an *ethnic* affiliation": *Ethnicity is of increasing political importance in many of our large cities.* Sometimes we speak of *ethnic* and racial divisions in the inner city, and sometimes we use *ethnic* to cover both, plus religious, linguistic, and similar divisions as well. But reference to a group of similar national origin is its most specific sense.

ETHNIC SLURS AND TERMS OF ETHNIC OPPROBRIUM, ETHNIC DESIGNATIONS The slurs and terms of opprobrium are the words that this often unmelted melting-pot, the U.S.A., has learned and unlearned as it has dealt with its ethnic mix. Like many terms now considered racist language, many of these ethnic names have become taboo only after unexceptionable beginnings. Scotch, for example was (and in some uses still is) perfectly acceptable as a name for the Scottish people and people of Scottish descent, but once the term picked up its stingy overtones, many Scots (especially American Scots) decided that they didn't like it and preferred *Scots* instead. Some slang designations were always intended to be cruel or to mock: *Polack, Bohunk, Kraut, Spic, Dago, Wop, Frog, Chink, Jap, Squarehead,* and dozens of others were the result of hatred or scorn, whether caused by war, as were *Hun, Kraut,*

Jap, Gook, and the like, or by the social strife that waves of immigration, competition, and poverty (and religious or racial differences too) have so often caused, which gave us *Mick* for the Irish, *Wop* and *Dago* for the Italian, and the term *wetback* for illegal immigrants from Mexico. One of the sure signs that such terms are being tabooed and shoved underground is the development in this century of a large number of hyphenated designations to replace them: *Mexican-American, Spanish-American, Polish-American, Japanese-American,* and the like. Once tolerated in the mouths of otherwise decent Americans, the older terms of ethnic opprobrium are now almost all taboo in Standard English, and ignorance or absence of malice never justify their use. Always use yourself and teach your children to use the designations preferred by the groups in question.

Two points seem especially worth stressing. First, many of these terms, once fully reported in dictionaries because of their wide slang use, are now being dropped from all but the unabridged and historical dictionaries because they have almost ceased to have Standard or Common use. And second, so rapid can be the rise and fall of some of these slang terms, and so volatile and sudden the change of status of such words, that you must use great care if you are not to offer insult where you intend none. This book advises on terms common at the moment, and desk and collegiate dictionaries try to keep up, but the best guide will be your own sensitivity to this very vexed issue. If you suspect the term expresses scorn, derision, or hatred, don't use it. Note too that sometimes an acceptable designation, objectionably pronounced can become an *ethnic slur,* as with *Italian* pronounced *EI-TAL-yuhn* and *Arab* pronounced *AI-RAB.* Again, the best advice is to call ethnic groups and their members whatever they prefer to be called. And this advice is good for members of both minorities and majorities: not every American wants to be called a *Yank* or *Yankee.* See also RACIST LANGUAGE.

-ette See -ESS.

ETYMOLOGICAL FALLACY This is the name of a much-practiced folly that insists that what a word "really means" is whatever it once meant long ago, perhaps even in another language. A classic example is the argument that the adjective *dilapidated* should be applied only to deteriorating structures made of stone, because its ultimate source was the Latin *lapis,* meaning "stone." Actually, the Latin *dilapidare* meant "to throw away, to scatter, as if scattering stones," and the infinitive *lapidare* meant "to throw stones." And in any case *dilapidated* no longer has anything to do with stones in American English; today it means "broken down, fallen into decay or disrepair," and it can be applied to any object, garment, or structure, whatever it is made of.

ETYMOLOGY is word history. The *etymology* of a word is its history from its beginnings, including its forms and its meanings as far back as these can be documented and its record of being borrowed and adapted into other languages. As *etymologists* bring the record forward or trace it backward, they try where they can to explain whatever linguistic and semantic change they encounter. Although science is a necessary part of it, *etymology* is finally as much art as science, and many of today's dictionaries have been obliged to substitute the more accurate comment "origin unknown" for what were once thought to be good guesses at the *etymology* of many words. Likely possibilities are simply not the same as proofs. See ENTOMOLOGY; ETYMOLOGICAL FALLACY.

ETYMON An *etymon* is an earlier form of a present-day word in this or another language. It is the original word from which the present-day word has evolved. See also ETYMOLOGY.

eulogy See ELEGY.

euphemism, euphuism (*nn.*) Although they both have to do with diction and therefore with style, there is little reason for confusion of these words. Euphemisms are words substituted for others because they are thought to be less offensive, distasteful, crude, or ugly than the originals. *Euphuism* was the extremely artificial, pretentious, and high-flown style espoused in sixteenth-century Britain by the novelist John Lyly and his imitators. It was full of elaborate similes, extreme balance and antithesis in syntax, and a generally self-conscious elegance in every aspect of its language. Today a *euphuistic* style can also refer to any such artificial, consciously ornate, decorative style of prose.

EUPHEMISMS, GENTEELISMS *Euphemisms* (Fowler's term was *genteelisms*) are words with meanings or sounds thought somehow to be nicer, cleaner, or more elevated and so used as substitutes for words deemed unpleasant, crude, or ugly in sound or sense. It can be argued, perhaps cynically, that whatever we dislike but conclude that we cannot make better, we rename *euphemistically* instead. But renaming a *slum* an *inner city* does not improve living conditions there. Certainly renaming the world in order to make it seem less unpleasant need not be considered a base activity unless our purpose is deliberately to conceal ugliness that we might be able to amend were we to face up to it. Perhaps therefore, since we cannot stop death, it is not so cowardly of us to refer to someone's recent *passing*. But none should countenance the impersonal disguises that *euphemisms* often seek to provide for killing and other horrors, such as the Persian Gulf War's *collateral losses* for deaths and injuries to civilians. And all should be able to penetrate the flimsiness of *revenue enhancement* as a disguise for *tax increases* or *urban renewal* for what used to be called *slum clearance*. *Euphemisms* are sugarcoatings, and sometimes they try to hide things that ought not to be hidden. See DOUBLESPEAK; NEWSPEAK; WEASEL WORDS.

euphuism See EUPHEMISM.

-euse See -ESS.

evacuate (*v.*) All these are Standard: *The population evacuated the city. The population was evacuated [from the city]. The city can be evacuated of [by] its population.* Be careful of context here lest your use stumble into reference to *evacuate* as used of the bowels.

even (*adv.*) Its location in the sentence can sometimes change the grammatical function and also the meaning of this adverb, just as can happen with *only*, particularly in writing. Compare *Even I don't like the teacher, I don't even like the teacher,* and *I don't like even the teacher.* And those of course are not the only placements possible. In speech, intonation can control what *even* modifies, almost irrespective of its placement, but in writing *even* will normally modify the element that follows it.

event (that), in the This phrase means "if," with or without the *that,* and its slower pace and elevated formality can sometimes make it appropriate, especially at the higher levels of use: *In the event [that] the attacks continue, we will retaliate.* In other contexts it may seem too wordy.

eventuate (*v.*), **eventuality** (*n.*) *Eventuate* is an elevated (some say pretentious) verb meaning "to result ultimately," and it combines frequently with *in,* occasionally with *by: Their efforts are likely to eventuate in [by] causing an even worse impasse.* The word has a somewhat dry, academic flavor. The noun *eventuality* is by no means so positive as the verb: it means "possibility, contingency," "a possible occurrence or a possible outcome," as in *Please be*

prepared to leave quickly, in the eventuality of some change in plan.

ever (*adv.*), **ever so (often)**, **ever such** (*intensifiers*) The adverb *ever* is Standard in uses such as *I doubt that she'll ever change her mind;* it is also Standard as an intensifier in uses such as *This is an ever-increasing problem.* The uses of *ever* as intensifier in phrases with *so* and *such* are Standard only at the Conversational levels and in the Informal writing that imitates them: *Mother was ever so upset. We had ever such a wonderful time.* The phrase *ever so often,* as in *I've been to their house ever so often,* means "a great many times" and is also Conversational only. Compare EVERY SO OFTEN.

every (*adj.*) The adjective always modifies a singular noun or pronoun, as in *Every dog has its day* and *Make certain that every one of those toys gets picked up,* and the structure always takes a singular verb. Compound subjects, as in *Every Tom, Dick, and Harry knows that joke,* usually take a singular verb too, although occasionally a plural may slip in at the Conversational or Informal level: *Every jockey, trainer, horse, and exercise boy were closely watched by the police.* But such uses do not occur in Edited English.

Reference of subsequent pronouns, however, shows two different patterns. In much Edited English the pronoun too will be singular, as in *Every boxer must take his physical exam first,* especially when as here we know that the referent is masculine. If the referent can be of either sex, or if it could notionally include both, as in *Every student needs his or her [or their] own notebook,* Edited English will either insist on the two singular pronouns or accept a plural. But much Edited English will avoid the issue by putting the whole sentence in the plural: *All students need their own notebooks.* The plural pronoun following the singular *everybody* is of course very widespread at other levels of Standard English, both because of notional agreement and because of conscious efforts to use inclusive language whenever possible. When both sexes are mentioned, the plural is nearly always used: *I want every boy and girl to take their seats.* See also GENERIC PRONOUNS.

everybody, everyone (*prons.*) These indefinite pronouns are grammatically singular but notionally plural. Both *everybody* and *everyone* as subjects agree regularly with their singular verbs: *Everybody is expected for dinner.* But with subsequent pronouns they may take either the singular *his or her* or the notionally plural *their: Everyone is to bring his or her [their] calcula-*

tors. See AGREEMENT OF INDEFINITE PRO-
NOUNS AND OTHER SINGULAR NOMINALS WITH
VERBS AND OTHER PRONOUNS; NOTIONAL
AGREEMENT; THEY.

everyday (*adj.*), **every day** (*adv.*) Spelled as one
word, *everyday* is Standard as an adjective: *These
are my everyday clothes.* The adjective-noun
combination *every day,* as in *Every day is a new
opportunity,* can also serve as an adverb, as in *I
have lunch with them every day.* Spelling the
adverb as one word is Nonstandard.

everyone See EVERYBODY.

everyplace See ANYPLACE.

every so often (*adv.*) The adverbial phrase *every
so often* is an idiom meaning "now and then,
once in a while" as in *We visited their cottage
every so often, but not very frequently.* Compare
EVER.

every time (*adv.*), as in *I forget to call home
every time* or *Every time I need help, I consult
her,* is never spelled as one word. The phrase—
adjective *every* modifying noun *time*—can function idiomatically as an adverb. Although it may
occasionally turn up in print as a single word,
that spelling is still Nonstandard.

every which way (*adv.*) is a delightfully graphic
Standard idiom, still usually limited to Conversational and Informal use and meaning "scattered, in no recognizable order, in every direction."

evidence (*v.*), meaning "to show or display,"
is Standard, both as a transitive verb, as in *His
garden evidences his hard work and good taste,*
and in the passive voice with *in* or *by: All the
careful planning is evidenced by* [*in*] *the
smoothness of the actual presentation.* The word
is rather formal.

evidently See APPARENTLY.

evoke, invoke (*vv.*) These two both derive from
the Latin *vocare,* "to call," but the prefixes
made these verbs differ both in Latin and in
English. Today *to evoke* is "to call forth, to
summon, to elicit," as in *Just the mention of
his name evoked smiles from all who knew him.*
To invoke means "to call upon and hence to
appeal to, to resort to, to beg or ask for," as in
*She invoked the wrath of the gods upon the
traitor* and *Their argument invoked the First
Amendment.* Both are Standard in these senses.

evolute, evolve (*vv.*) are synonyms, but *evolute,* a back-formation from *evolution,* is very
rare and looks and sounds strange to most people. Some commentators oppose it, and most
desk dictionaries omit it. So should you, in

favor of *evolve,* as in *These birds are thought to
have evolved from reptiles.*

ex- (*prefix*), **former, late** (*adjs.*) Add *ex-* to a
noun to suggest someone or something formerly
entitled to that name or classification: *my ex-
wife, an ex-baseball player, an ex-racing grey-
hound.* Be sure to prefix the *ex-* to the right
element in phrases and compounds (*an ex-land
grant college president, an elderly ex-jazz trumpet player*), and don't use this prefix in Formal
or Oratorical contexts; there, *former,* which
means the same thing but is considerably less
breezy, would probably be a better choice. It
normally suggests not that the person is dead,
but that he or she no longer is playing that role
or is engaged in that activity. Note too that some
commentators maintain that only the most recent holder of an office can be *ex*; all previous
living holders of it are *former.* But most Standard users are likely to miss this distinction,
although there is no harm done if you try to
use it.

Late used to modify an occupational or similar classification indicates that the person is
dead—*my late mother* and *the late Supreme Court
justice* are both dead. *The late* seems to be
appropriate if the person was alive at any time
during the speaker's lifetime or if the death
occurred relatively recently. In a slightly different structure—e.g., so-and-so, *late of the Yankees*—the adjective suggests simply a change of
job. Here we might also say *formerly* [or *lately*
or *until recently*] *with the Yankees. Late* can
also apply to other than persons: *our late allies*
are "former"—not necessarily dead, though the
alliance is. See also ERSTWHILE.

Using *ex* by itself to refer to a former spouse
is slang for Conversational and Informal use
only: *My ex is still trying to get custody of the
kids.*

exact same (*adj.*) This expression has been called
a redundancy and a cliché, and technically it
may be both, but it really is simply an emphatic
idiom regularly encountered in speech and frequently used in writing. It is Standard in all but
the most Formal and Oratorical contexts, as in
*She arrived every morning at the exact same
time.* Formal use would prefer *at exactly the
same time* or *at the very same time.*

exceed See ACCEDE.

exceedingly, excessively (*advs., intensifiers*)
Exceedingly means "extremely, exceptionally,
especially in size or degree," as in *He was
exceedingly fat. Excessively* means "immoderately, overly, inordinately, much too," as in

Her sister seemed to me excessively thin. As intensifiers both are sometimes used to mean "very," (as Jane Austen sometimes used *excessively* in her novels) but be careful not to overlook the "much too" sense of *excessively: He was exceedingly nervous* and *He was excessively nervous* mean different things today.

except See ACCEPT.

exception (*n.*) combines chiefly with the prepositions *of* or *to: With the exception of her sister, the whole family was there. I took exception to some of his remarks.* Take exception to means "object to." *With the exception of* is a rather formal but not necessarily pretentious way of saying *except, excepting,* or *except for.* In the right context it's not padded prose, and using it can stress the rarity of the occurrence: *Everyone was in favor, with the sole exception of the governor.*

exceptionable, exceptional (*adjs.*) *Exceptionable,* which means "objectionable," "likely to be questioned or objected to," is a relatively low frequency word, and its meanings are all of a piece: *One of his proposals seems to me exceptionable: I believe it is unconstitutional.* (Compare UNEXCEPTIONABLE, which is much more frequently used.) *Exceptional,* which means "not like most, different from the average," usually is elevated in meaning, "better than average or normal": *An exceptional runner* is thought to be better than most. But Americans in education have turned to euphemism and stretched the term's meaning in that context: at one time an *exceptional child* was brighter and better equipped for learning than most; today, however, the *exceptional child* may be either unusually bright or unusually dull, and a frequent use of *exceptional* as applied to children in today's educational world means "handicapped or impaired." Anticipate how your readers will take the word, and use context carefully to assist them.

exception proves the rule, the The older meaning of *prove* is "to test, or to establish by trial or experience"; hence a trial impression made of a print or engraving or of type is called a *proof,* we *proofread* text to correct any flaws, and the original meaning of the idiom is "the exception *tests* the rule." (The British still call a "test flight," a *proving flight.*) But many Standard users and their listeners and readers understand it to mean "the exception *establishes* the rule." Generally the confusion of the one sense for the other may not be very great, since both suggest the power and accuracy of

the rule. In any event, the idiom is a cliché, a very weary one that needs a rest.

excess See ACCESS (2); IN EXCESS OF.

excessively See EXCEEDINGLY.

excise (*n., vv.*) The noun *excise* means "a tax, especially on a commodity," and the word is commonly used in a compound, *excise tax.* Stress the first syllable of both noun and compound. One verb, pronounced also with stress on the first syllable, means "to impose an excise on." These two words came through Dutch from a French root probably meaning "assessment" or "sitting to make such assessments." The other verb *excise* (pronounced with stress on the second syllable) derives from a Latin verb meaning "to cut" or "to remove by cutting": *The surgeon attempted to excise the tumor.* All three uses are Standard, although the first verb is relatively rare, and the second perhaps fairly formal.

excitement, excitation (*nn.*) *Excitement* is the more general term, meaning "something that excites" or "the state or process of exciting": *There was great excitement abroad when the news came out.* In science and technology, *excitation* is the technical or specialized term for "the process of applying a stimulus to something": *The excitation of the nerve is accomplished by tiny electrical charges.* Excitation is a low-frequency term, probably pretentious in general contexts.

EXCLAMATION POINT, EXCLAMATION MARK The *exclamation point* (!) is the punctuation mark used to give the sort of emphasis to a word, phrase, or sentence that suggests loud, vigorous, forthright delivery. *Never! Free at last! Never darken my door again!* In English it always goes at the end of the locution to be emphasized. But stridency is seldom approved in speech, and so in writing too be sparing of the *exclamation point.* Rely on your words, not your punctuation, to make your passion ring forth.

exclude (*v.*), when it combines with a preposition, almost always takes *from: They've excluded him from their meetings.*

exclusive (*adj.*) Combine *exclusive* with *of* followed by the thing excluded: *She works a full shift most days, exclusive of Sundays and holidays.*

EXCLUSIVE LANGUAGE See INCLUSIVE LANGUAGE.

excuse (*n., v.*) The verb *excuse,* pronounced ek-SKYOOZ, is followed mainly by *from,* as in

The judge excused her from jury duty, but sometimes by *for,* as in *He was excused for reasons of health.* The noun is pronounced *ek-SKYOOS;* compare ALIBI.

execrable See INEXECRABLE.

execute, assassinate, kill, murder, slay (*vv.*) all mean "to deprive someone or something of life," but they differ in important ways. *Execute* has long meant "to perform, to carry out an action or a duty, to enforce a law," and a number of other senses not necessarily involving taking life, and for some time in the nineteenth century, commentators deplored the use of *execute* in the sense of "put to death." (Their unhappiness may also have been caused in part by the fact that *execute* is a back-formation from *execution.*) But today, *execute* clearly also means "to put to death," usually under order of a court: *The judge sentenced the convicted murderer to be executed by means of lethal injection.* (Ironically, gangsters, mobsters, and terrorists often claim to be *executing* victims judged guilty in their own informal tribunals.)

To *murder* is usually "to kill with malice aforethought and unlawfully": *He murdered the bank guard who had tried to stop him.* To *assassinate* is "to kill a public or political figure," and it often is a crime performed for hire or at least on assignment by an organization: *The terrorists assassinated the governor of the province.* To *slay* is a literary word—a bit old-fashioned (*David slew Goliath*) but beloved of the press because it fits headlines (*Dissidents Slay Rebel Leader*). *Slay* gives a change from the more common *kill,* which is, of course the generic term, meaning simply "to take the life of": *We killed hundreds of mosquitoes.* All these verbs except *execute* have considerable figurative use in Standard English, mainly in Informal and Conversational contexts: *That pianist is murdering Chopin. The press is assassinating her reputation. My feet are killing me. That comedian simply slays me.*

executor, executioner, executrix (*nn.*) An *executor* (pronounced *eg-ZEK-yoo-tuhr* or, rarely, *eg-SEK-yoo-tuhr*) is the person appointed to administer and carry out the provisions of a will. *Executrix,* the feminine form, is still in official use in some jurisdictions, but it is archaic and is rapidly being replaced by *executor,* the referent of which is now inclusive (see -ESS). An *executioner* (pronounced *eks-i-KYOO-shuhn-uhr*) is a person whose job is the carrying out of sentences of capital punishment prescribed by the courts. See AGENTIVE ENDINGS.

exemplar (*n.*), **exemplary** (*adj.*) An *exemplar* is a model or a pattern, an example suitable for imitation. The noun therefore frequently means "a good example." *Exemplary* is the adjective describing that quality, but it may be an even more elevated word: a revered leader may be considered *exemplary,* but criminals are seldom so labeled.

exhaustive, exhausting (*adjs.*) *Exhaustive* means "thorough," "omitting nothing," as in *We undertook an exhaustive search of the house.* *Exhausting* means "tiring out," "weakening," "wearying," as in *I found the eight hours of steady hiking exhausting.*

exhibitor, exhibitioner, exhibitionist (*nn.*) An *exhibitor* is any person or organization that enters an exhibit in an exhibition: *The exhibitors were all assembled in the main gallery just before the exhibition opened its doors to the public.* An *exhibitionist* in the generalized sense is someone who likes to show off, to parade his or her talents: *Modesty is not characteristic of exhibitionists.* In psychology *exhibitionist* has a specialized meaning, "a person with the sexual perversion of exposing the genitals in public": *Another exhibitionist was arrested in the stacks of the library.* In British education *exhibitioners* are students who are being supported in school on awards called *exhibitions: All the exhibitioners were remarkably bright and hardworking.* See AGENTIVE ENDINGS; -IST.

exhilarate (*v.*), **exhilaration** (*n.*) To avoid misspelling these words and their related adjectives, note the unpronounced *h* and the two *a*'s. See ACCELERATE.

exhorbitant See EXORBITANT.

exhuberance, exhuberant See EXUBERANCE.

-exion See -ECTION.

exist See SUBSIST.

existence (*n.*), **existent** (*adj.*) Very frequent spelling errors are to spell the final syllables *-ance* and *-ant,* respectively (see SPELLING OF UNSTRESSED VOWELS). These Substandard misspellings do turn up in print, but very rarely in Edited English.

exonerate (*v.*), when it combines with prepositions, does so most frequently with *from* or *of,* as in *He was exonerated of [from] all allegations of wrongdoing. As to* also occurs in Standard use: *The panel exonerated her as to the several accusations of misconduct.*

exorbitant (*adj.*) Spell it without an *h* before the *o,* and pronounce it that way too: *eks-OR-bit-ant.*

expatriate (*adj., n., v.*), **expatriot** (*n.*) *Expatriate* (pronounced either *eks-PAI-tree-AIT* or *eks-PAI-tree-uht*) is the Standard spelling of the noun meaning "someone either excluded from or self-exiled from the native land," and the adjective is spelled and pronounced the same way. The verb *expatriate* is pronounced only *eks-PAI-tree-AIT* and means "to be exiled or to withdraw from one's own country," "to leave it permanently." *Expatriot* is either a misspelling (on analogy with *patriot*, no doubt) or a nonce word meaning "former patriot," which might better be spelled *ex-patriot*; presumably it would refer to one's loyalties but not one's location.

expect (*v.*) is now Standard in the meaning "suppose," as in *I expect you'll be wanting something to eat;* in that sense it is probably still best limited to Semiformal and Conversational uses. In the meaning "anticipate, look forward to," as in *We have long expected his appointment,* it is Standard at all levels. *Expect* is often followed by the preposition *to* plus an infinitive: *She expected him to call her yesterday,* and it also combines with *from* and *of,* as in *We never expected such vehemence from* [*of*] *him.*

expectant, expecting (*adjs.*) *Expectant* and *expecting* have a generalized meaning, "awaiting, anticipating something," as in *We stayed close to the depot all afternoon, expectant* [*expecting*] *that a train would appear. Expectant* and *expecting* also have a specialized sense, "pregnant, "expecting the birth of a child," as in *She is an expectant mother* or *She's been expectant* [*expecting*] *for some months now.* Both these senses are Standard English, but *expecting* in the "pregnant" sense is more likely to be encountered in Conversational and Informal or Semiformal contexts than in Oratorical or Formal uses: *The women concluded from her comments that their hostess was expecting.* Such uses are almost elephantinely whimsical today, given our usually frank reporting of such matters.

expectorate (*v.*), **expectoration** (*n.*) Today these two are limited to medical matters (the raising of mucus from the lungs and the like) and to jocular use as heavily self-conscious euphemisms for *spit* and *spitting.* Other uses in the general vocabulary are archaic today, if not obsolete.

expediate See EXPEDITE.

expedience, expediency, expedition, expeditiousness (*nn.*) *Expedience* and *expediency* are synonyms; each means "the doing of what is necessary, sufficient, appropriate, or of interest to self"': *His only motive was expedience* [*expediency*]—*whatever would work to his advantage.* But *expedience* can also be pejorative, as in *His expedience did nothing to enhance his reputation for low integrity. Expedition* has two main meanings: "a journey or a group of people undertaking such a journey" and "speed, efficiency, dispatch": *The expedition included seven men and more than a hundred dogs. Proceed cautiously, but with as much expedition as you can muster.* In this last sense, *expedition* and *expeditiousness* are synonyms.

expedient, expeditious (*adjs.*), **expediently, expeditiously** (*advs.*) That which is *expedient* has an elevated sense, meaning "whatever will be most easily useful to achieve the purpose": *The use of a special messenger seems expedient just now.* But it can also have pejorative overtones, meaning "whatever will serve one's own purposes, regardless of its ethical or moral defects": *She never operated on principle but instead always took the expedient course. Expeditious* simply means "done with speed, promptly and efficiently": *Send the package by the most expeditious means available.* The adverbs match their adjectives in that *expediently* is usually pejorative and *expeditiously* never is.

expedite, expediate (*vv.*) *Expedite,* meaning "to speed, hasten, or assist," is the usual Standard verb; *expediate* is either a nonce word or an exceedingly rare synonym for *expedite,* substituting one verb-making suffix for another.

expedition See EXPEDIENCE.

expeditious, expeditiously See EXPEDIENT.

expeditiousness See EXPEDIENCE.

expel (*v.*) *Expel* means "to drive or put out, to dismiss," as in *They were expelled from school.* It doubles its final consonant before adding suffixes (*expelling, expellable, expeller,* etc.). When combined with a preposition, *expel* always takes *from.*

expensive (*adj.*) means "costly, high-priced" or "too high in price," as in *Single-malt whiskey is expensive—but worth every penny.* Note that usually the commodities themselves are or seem *expensive;* their prices generally are or seem *high* or *low,* not *expensive* or *cheap.*

experience (*v.*) represents a functional shift from the noun. The verb, which has been in the language for centuries and has been fully accepted in Standard English for many years, means "to have experience," "to learn by experience," or "to undergo experience," as in *She experienced* *real doubt on hearing the report.* The participial adjective, *experienced,* combines usually with the prepositions *in* or *at,* or sometimes *with,* as in *He is experienced in [at, with] all sorts of water sports.*

expert (*adj., n.*), **expertly** (*adv.*) The adjective means "well-trained, extremely skilled, and knowledgeable," as in *She has long been considered an expert skier.* The noun means "a person who has great skill, experience, and knowledge in a particular field or endeavor," as in *He's an expert in botanical illustration.* When combined with prepositions, both adjective and noun take *in* and occasionally *at: They're expert in [at] making and repairing furniture. I'm getting to be an expert in [at] identifying birds.* The adjective and the adverb can be stressed on either the first or second syllable.

expertise (*n.*) came into the language in the nineteenth century meaning "expert opinion, expert commentary," but although that sense is still sometimes encountered, today it usually means "expert knowledge" or "the expert's skill," as in *She has the expertise to handle any problem in her field.* Pronounce it with heavy stress on the final syllable, either *-TEEZ* or *-TEES.*

expertize (*v.*), meaning "to give or pronounce an expert opinion," is a very low frequency word whose final syllable has a secondary stress and rhymes with *size.*

explain, explanation See EXPLICATE.

EXPLETIVE 1 is related to expletive (2) in that each refers to something essentially empty of meaning inserted into an utterance. In *Expletive (1)* that "empty" addition is a profanity or an obscenity—an oath: *That dog is no **damned** good. **Hell,** I didn't know she was there.* Most swearwords are also called *expletives.* Because they mean so little, you do not need to use them often, if at all, and the more use they get, the emptier they become; note how debased the currency of words like *hell* and *damn* has become these days. See SWEAR.

EXPLETIVE 2, like expletive (1), is an essentially empty word or phrase inserted into a sentence. It too adds little or nothing to meaning but sometimes fills a useful structural or stylistic purpose. Hence a dummy subject such as *there* in *There is another sailboat* is an *expletive (2).* The adverb *there* is always readily distinguished from the expletive *there;* the adverb comes either first or at the very end of the clause (the adverbs are in boldfaced type): ***There** there is another*

*sailboat. There is another sailboat **there.*** See DUMMY SUBJECTS.

explicable See INEXPLICABLE.

explicate, explain (*vv.*), **explication, explanation** (*nn.*) The simple, everyday verb is *explain,* meaning "to make understandable or clear, to give reasons, to make something plain," as in *He explained how to get there from here.* To *explicate* is to do much the same thing, but more eruditely, more elegantly; it means "to explain in the fullest, most scholarly detail," as in *She proposes to explicate several poems to her students.* The nouns *explanation* and *explication* differ much as the verbs do. In the wrong setting, *explicate* can be pretentious; generally, you should reserve it for its specialized academic uses (but don't bother to *explicate* even there when an *explanation* of a single point will do the trick as well). For all other *explanations,* *explain* is just right; it can also add the sense of "account for," as in *I can explain my mistake.* See also JUSTIFY.

exposé (*n.*), pronounced *eks-PO-ZAI* to reflect its French origin, is a commonly encountered word meaning "a public disclosure of a crime or scandal or something else discreditable," as in *Last fall the papers had a big exposé of bribery in high places within the government.* *Exposé* usually (but not invariably) keeps its acute accent in Standard English, probably because of the possible confusion with the verb *expose.*

EXPOSITORY WRITING, EXPOSITION *Exposition* is explanation. *Expository writing* is nonfiction prose that sets forth ideas, facts, values, arguments, and the like. The essay and much journalism are *expository* in nature. *Expository writing* is a term used frequently to distinguish that sort of prose from the writing we often call *creative,* a term that technically refers primarily to fiction, although the line of demarcation is certainly not always clear—the familiar essay and the narrative sketch often overlap, for example.

ex post facto is a Latin tag meaning "from after the fact" and refers to something done after the triggering fact became known. *To lock the stable door after the horses are stolen* is an *ex post facto* action. This foreign phrase is perhaps most commonly used by Americans in connection with legislative acts: a law passed in an effort to prevent certain actions cannot be used to try or convict someone for such an action if it took place before the new law took effect; that is, *ex post facto* application of a law is not legal.

expressive (*adj.*), when it combines with a preposition, takes *of*: *Everything she said that day was expressive of her contempt for the proceedings.*

expresso See ESPRESSO.

expressway See THRUWAY.

exquisite (*adj.*) Today Standard English has two pronunciations, either *EKS-kwiz-it* or *eks-KWIZ-it*, although purists sometimes consider the second pronunciation odd.

extant See EXTENT.

extemporaneous, impromptu (*adjs.*), **extempore** (*adv., adj.*) *Extemporaneous* and *extempore* as adjectives are synonyms: they refer particularly to speeches and mean either "given on the spur of the moment, without preparation" or "given with preparation, but without being memorized and usually without notes." Both these meanings are Standard, although the second is more specialized and is sometimes limited to contexts involving the teaching and learning of public speaking. In such contexts *impromptu* is often used synonymously with the first sense meaning "done without any previous preparation, on the spur of the moment," to distinguish this sort of speaking from that described by the second sense. *Impromptu* is frequently applied to other performances, not just to public speaking. *Extempore* functions as either adjective, as in *She gave an extempore speech,* or adverb, as in *She spoke extempore.*

extemporize, temporize (*vv.*) To *extemporize* is "to improvise," "to speak or act on your feet, without any preparation," as in *The rest of the company being late, she was obliged to extemporize and to put on an impromptu show for the audience until her colleagues arrived.* To *temporize* is "to stall, to beat about the bush and waste or fill time until you can move directly," as in *The orchestra temporized, playing several unscheduled numbers, until the soprano finally appeared onstage.* See -ISE.

extended, extensive (*adjs.*) *Extended* means "long," "prolonged," "lengthy"; *extensive* means "widely spread, covering a wide area, far-reaching, in great detail." In *They took an extended trip through Europe* and *They took an extensive trip through Europe,* the difference is that the *extended* one took a long time but may not have covered many places, while the *extensive* trip covered a great deal of ground and probably didn't skip many countries.

extension (*n.*) ends in *-sion*. *Extention* is now considered a spelling error.

extent (*n.*), **extant** (*adj.*) *Extent* means "the range, scope, or limits of something," as in *I had no idea of the extent of their holdings. Extant* means "in existence at present," as in *It's the largest white oak tree extant.*

extenuate (*v.*), **extenuating** (*adj.*) The verb today means "to weaken," "to explain away," "to excuse," but it applies only to circumstances and other nonhuman entities, not to people: *All his supporters tried to extenuate the seriousness of the charges against him.* The adjective means "mitigating, lessening, tending to excuse," as in *There were extenuating circumstances that could account for her odd behavior.*

exterior, external, extraneous, extrinsic (*adjs.*) *Exterior* means "on the outside" or "the part outside," as in *We painted the exterior walls. External* means essentially the same thing but in addition stresses "the outwardly visible," as in *External appearances offered no clue to what they were feeling. External* also can suggest "not germane," as in *The external factors seemed not to be of any real force.* Anything *extraneous* is "inessential, not really a part of, foreign, or not relevant," as in *She gave us a lot of extraneous information, but nothing very helpful. Extrinsic* is nearly synonymous with *extraneous,* meaning "not connected to," as in *Extrinsic forces seem not to have had much effect.* But it also has a distinctive sense, meaning "coming from or acting from outside and in that sense foreign," as in *Political considerations all seemed extrinsic to the grim economic matters confronting us.*

extract, extricate (*vv.*) *Extract* means "to pull out, to remove with some difficulty from something," as in *She extracted my remaining wisdom tooth. Extricate* means "to disentangle" and "to remove from an entanglement," as in *We extricated ourselves from their welcome with great difficulty.*

When *extract* combines with a preposition, it usually does so with *from,* as in *Extract your letters from the pile,* although occasionally a redundant *out of* also occurs: *We extracted some information out of the waiters.*

extraneous See EXTERIOR.

extraordinary (*adj.*) has at least four Standard English pronunciations: *eks-**TROR**-din-ER-ee, eks-TROR-din-uhr-ee* (or *-din-ree*), *eks-truh-**ORD**-in-ER-ee,* and *eks-truh-ORD-in-uhr-ee* (or *-in-ree*).

extricate See EXTRACT.

extrinsic See EXTERIOR.

exuberance (*n.*), **exuberant** (*adj.*) Neither has an *h* at the beginning of the second syllable.

exude (*v.*), meaning "to ooze, to give off from the pores," combines with the preposition *from* to stipulate the source of what is being *exuded: She exuded from every pore an air of prosperity.* With only a direct object, *exude* stresses what is being *exuded: He exuded pomposity.*

EYE DIALECT is created by deliberately misspelling words to suggest in writing a Nonstandard or dialectal pronunciation: *wimmin* for *women* and *gonna* for *going to* are examples of *eye dialect.* Both these spellings reflect the actual sounds of Standard speech, *gonna* of course rather literally transcribing speech at a lower level, whereas *wimmin* suggests by its spelling that the speaker is too uncultivated to be able to spell it correctly anyway. In fiction, drama, and dramatic poetry, *eye dialect* is frequently used to suggest the actual sounds of a particular person's speech, flaws and all. Use it sparingly: such renderings can be very hard to read, and they can therefore cause some readers to give up.

eye to eye See SEE EYE TO EYE.

eyrie, eyry See AERIE.

F

-f, -fe See NOUNS ENDING IN *-F*

fable See ALLEGORY.

fabulous, fabled (*adjs.*) *Fabled* still means "as described in stories or fables" and also "fictitious and maybe not true." But the most frequent meaning is "celebrated, renowned," as in *Helen's fabled beauty caused the Trojan War. Fabulous* is synonymous with *fabled* in the sense of "storied," but hyperbole has caused it to be weakened through overuse, until today it frequently means nothing more than "remarkable or wonderful," as in *She had a fabulous new outfit for the party.* This use is Conversational and Informal and occurs in Edited English only in gushy quotations. When you want to stress the "legendary" sense today, stick with *fabled.*

façade, facade (*n.*) Spell it either with or without the cedilla. Pronounce it *fuh-SAHD.*

faced (*adj.*), when combined with a preposition, takes *with* or *by* to designate what confronts you: *We were faced with two unattractive choices. We were faced by about fifty angry demonstrators.* To mean "covered or surfaced with," *in* or *with* is usual: *Faced in [with] red brick, the house front was quite conventional.*

face down (*v.*) This phrasal verb is a Standard idiom meaning "to overcome or resist successfully by either literally or figuratively outstaring someone, by letting the unwavering determination of your gaze force the other person to look away or back down": *She steadfastly faced down the opposition and made them back off.*

face up to (*v.*) This phrasal verb is a Standard idiom, meaning "to confront and unflinchingly deal with": *She was threatened with bankruptcy, but she simply would not face up to it.*

facilitate (*v.*) is a self-consciously impressive sort of word meaning much the same thing as *help, assist,* or *make easier.* In Edited English you can *facilitate* things or actions but not people: You can *facilitate Mary's arrival* or *her trip to the embassy,* but you do not *facilitate Mary.*

facilitator (*n.*), which means "someone who makes matters go better, more smoothly, more easily," has become jargon, a euphemism intended to boost the dignity of the person who coordinates or directs meetings while trying to appear to do neither.

facility, faculty (*nn.*) When these are applied to a person, the distinction is close but important: *She has a facility for making friends* means "She makes friends easily"; *She has a faculty for making friends* simply means "She is able to make friends." The ease of *facility* is the distinction. *Facility* is also a noun meaning "a building, an installation, a place": *They're building new facilities for the emergency room.* And *facilities,* usually in the plural, is a euphemism for *toilet(s). Faculty* too has other meaning clusters, notably "any power or ability, especially the senses and the thought processes" (*Her faculties seem unimpaired following the stroke*), and "the teaching staff of a college or other educational institution, distinct from the nonteaching support personnel" (*Each faculty walked behind its own banner*). It is Nonstandard when used to mean "a *faculty* member," as in *She's a faculty in the History Department,* but Standard in *She's faculty, not administration.* In the plural, as in *There were several biology faculty present,* it is at least Conversational in academic contexts; perhaps it should be labeled jargon in that use.

facsimile (*n.*) Pronounce it *fak-SIM-uh-lee,* and avoid if you can the cliché *a reasonable facsimile,* so overworked these days in merchandising's coupon offers.

fact (*n.*), **in fact, in point of fact, the fact is, the fact of the matter is, the fact that** The noun *fact* functions often as an inexact name for an idea, a hope, a wish, or some other vaguely conceived "thing" and often simply as a grammatical placeholder stuck into the sentence until the speaker or writer can figure out a destination and a way to approach it. *In fact* and *in point of fact* are also used to attempt to focus a scattered argument or discussion. In all these locutions *fact* is also frequently used presumptuously, and even more often unconsciously, to give *factual* status to something actually far from *factual.* In the prosecutor's "*Do you deny the fact that . . . ?*" the first thing the witness needs to consider before answering is whether it is in *fact* a *fact.* Best advice: omit *the fact* in honest exposition and argument, in favor of a direct question or statement, unless you are deliberately distinguishing between *facts* and *nonfacts.* See POINT IS; TRUE FACTS.

factious, factitious, fictitious, fractious, frangible (*adjs.*) These adjectives have little in common but their vaguely similar sounds and spellings: someone or something *factious* is "causing dissension," "causing people to break into factions," as in *Factious people always cause arguments. Fractious* means "rebellious, unmanageable, irritable, hard to get along with," as in *At the end of a long day, a fractious child is especially hard to take. Factitious* means "artificial, not natural," as in *The sudden demand for the toy was entirely factitious; once children had one, it bored them. Fictitious* means "imaginary, false, made up," as in *She registered under a fictitious name.* Both *factitious* and *fictitious* have an overtone of spuriousness. *Frangible* is a low-frequency word meaning "breakable." All five adjectives are Standard.

fact is, the; the fact of the matter is See FACT.

factitious See FACTIOUS.

factor (*n.*) is often criticized for overuse and frequently functions as a filler or counterword.

Literally, a *factor* is anything that contributes to a result: *The rain-slicked street was a factor in the accident.* Other more general substitutes tend to be longer (*consideration, circumstance, characteristic, constituent, component,* and the like), and of course each has a slightly different meaning. Best advice: use *factor* when its literal sense is called for; limit its figurative and extended uses (such as when *thing* will fit almost as well) to Casual and other Conversational contexts, and when you write, try to do without *factor* and the cliché *contributing factor* unless you really intend to be vague and imprecise. Instead of *The restaurant's popularity among celebrities was a contributing factor in its success,* try *The restaurant's popularity among celebrities contributed something to its success,* or, even better, *The restaurant's popularity among celebrities helped it succeed.*

factotum (*n.*) is "a person with many duties, a handyman, a jack-of-all-trades" (its etymological meaning was "to do all things"), and its plural is *factotums. General factotum* is a redundant cliché.

facts, true See TRUE FACTS.

fact that, the See FACT.

faculty See FACILITY.

faerie, faery See FAIRY.

fag, faggot, fagot (*nn., vv.*), **fagoting, faggotting** (*n.*) The verb *fag* means "to work hard" and especially in the participial adjective, "to work to exhaustion," as in *I'm all fagged out.* In British public schoolboy jargon, underclassmen had to *fag* for, that is "be servants for," upperclassmen; those who had to do those chores were called *fags. Fag* is also a rather old-fashioned slang word for "cigarette" in both Britain and America. *Faggot* is a taboo slang term for a male homosexual, and *fag* is a clipped noun form of it, also taboo. A *fagot* or *faggot* is a small bundle, usually of sticks to be used for firewood, and a verb meaning "to make such a bundle." *Faggoting* (spelled with one *g* or two) is an openwork embroidery stitch and the embroidery it produces. The embroidery senses and variant spellings of these words are Standard; the homosexual senses are taboo, and the rest are either slang or at best Conversational.

fag end is a cliché, a frozen figure whose origins are almost forgotten: the *fag end* of a piece of cloth or rope is frayed, worn, and worth little. Hence *the fag end of a difficult day.* It is thought to come from a Middle English word meaning "flap," but it may in some way be related to the verb meaning "to exhaust, to wear out." In British slang, a *fag end* is "a cigarette butt."

faggot, faggotting, fagot, fagoting See FAG.

fail (*v.*) in its transitive use (*She failed Spanish; The teacher failed three students in that section*) has received criticism in the past, but it is clearly Standard today. When it takes a preposition, *fail* frequently takes *to* plus an infinitive: *She failed to notice the time. In, at, by,* and *from* are also fairly common: *He failed in three successive attempts. We failed at getting them to sign up. We failed by not planning carefully enough. Our company failed from lack of capital. On* can also be found in Standard English: *The proposal failed on every count.*

failing (*prep.*) is idiomatic in uses meaning "lacking" or sometimes "instead of, in place of" or "without," as in *Failing any other advice, consult your member's manual.* See also DANGLING MODIFIERS.

fair (*adj., n.*), **fare** (*n., v.*) These homophones have many meanings and should rarely be confused. As adjective *fair* means "lovely, of light coloring (as of hair or complexion), clear and bright (as of the weather), impartial, just, nondiscriminatory, according to the rules, favorable (as in *a fair wind*)," etc. As a noun, *a fair* is a carnival or other such event, but representing people *the fair* can also mean "those who are possessed of one or more of these qualities, especially beautiful women," and "those who are just and impartial." The verb *fare* means "to travel, to get along, to succeed, and to eat"; the noun means "the price of a ticket for travel, a paying passenger, food and other things to be consumed." All these senses of each word are Standard.

fairy, faerie, faery, fay (*adjs., nn.*) *Fairy* is the Standard word for the magical mythical being, both as noun and adjective. Also as noun it is the usually taboo and always disparaging slang term for a male homosexual; context must make clear which sense you intend. *Faerie* and *faery* are variant spellings of a poetic noun that means both "fairyland" and "a fairy," again, the mythical creature; both can also be used as adjectives. *Fay* is also a literary word, meaning "fairy" or "elf" or, as an adjective, "fairylike" or "elfin." See also FEY.

fait accompli, pronounced either *FET* or *FAIT uh-kahm-PLEE* or *a-kahm-PLEE,* means in French "an accomplished fact" and in English "something already accomplished or completed, presumably not to be undone." Its plural is spelled *faits accomplis,* with the last syllable

pronounced either *-PLEE* or *-PLEEZ* and the rest unchanged. See FOREIGN PHRASES; FOREIGN PLURALS.

faithfully See SINCERELY.

fake See ARTIFICIAL.

faker, fakir (*nn.*) A *faker* (pronounced *FAIK-uhr*) is "one who deceives by faking and hence a cheat or confidence man," and a *fakir* (pronounced *fuh-KEER* or *FAI-KEER;* variant spelling *fakeer*) is "a Muslim beggar or dervish" or "a Hindu ascetic or magician."

fake titles See FALSE TITLES.

fakir See FAKER.

fall See AUTUMN.

fallacy (*n.*) means a type of false argument in logic, but Standard English by no means limits it to that sense. It also has a general sense of "any false or mistaken idea," "any failure in argument," as in *It's a widely held fallacy that women can't do science.*

fallible, fallacious (*adjs.*) *Fallible* means "capable of making or likely to make a mistake, mistake-prone," as in *He means well, but he's fallible like the rest of us. Fallacious* means "misleading," "mistaken," "containing a fallacy," as in *Your argument is obviously fallacious.*

false See ARTIFICIAL.

FALSE COMPARISON, ILLOGICAL COMPARISON, INCOMPLETE COMPARISON These are all names for the omission of one word or several in statements of comparison: *Grades for this semester were much lower than last semester. Those for* before *last semester* was omitted, and the ellipsis thus slightly mars the parallelism. Omitting such small words is common in Casual and Impromptu speech, and ordinarily no one becomes confused, but in all but the most Informal writing, clarity and reader comfort will be improved if you omit no words whose absence mars the parallelism. See AS GOOD OR BETTER THAN; ELLIPSIS (1).

falsehood, falseness, falsity (*nn.*) A *falsehood* is "a lie," and the quality that makes it *false* is its *falseness* or *falsity* (these two are synonyms). All are Standard.

false titles, bogus titles, coined titles, fake titles, and similar terms have been applied by commentators to the journalese practice (probably made popular by, if not invented by, *Time Magazine*), of using a string of descriptive terms in front of a person's name to identify him or her: *mother-of-the-bride Mary Jones, school-board-member Sam Pickering; bearded actor, flower-salesman, and erstwhile end Merlin Olson.* Such appositives, placed before instead of after their referents, can be tiresome.

falsity See FALSEHOOD.

familiar (*adj.*), when combined with a preposition, is usually followed by *to* or *with,* as in *The children are familiar to her* and *She is familiar with them,* and occasionally by *from,* as in *He looks familiar from his many years on television.*

fantastic (*adj.*), **fantastically** (*adv., intensifier*) *Fantastic* in its literal sense means "based on fancy" and hence "not real," "greater or more extravagant than life." *His paintings were fantastic renderings of nightmarish scenes.* But like so many adjectives, *fantastic* has been taken over by hyperbole and now also means "extreme," "wonderful," and "great or large," as in *We had a fantastic time at your party.* And that in turn has led the adverb *fantastically—He was made up fantastically as a dinosaur of some sort—*to drift on to become an intensifier: *Her new dress looked fantastically expensive.*

fantasy, phantasy (*n.*) *Fantasy* is the usual spelling; *phantasy* is a rare variant.

farce See BURLESQUE.

fare See FAIR.

farther, all the See ALL THE.

farther, fartherest, farthest, further, furtherest, furthest (*advs., adjs.*) Use either *farther* or *further* as an adjective for literal distance (*The airport is farther [further] than I had figured*), but also use *further* to mean "additional," as in *She gave a further opinion that evening.* (The adjective *further* used to be limited to such figurative uses, just as *farther* continues to be applied only to literal distance.) As adverbs, *farther* and *further* are nearly interchangeable today, although *further* is much more frequently used: *We walked further [occasionally farther] today than ever before. He expanded further [rarely farther] on his original proposal.* But use only *further* as a sentence adverb: *Further, he insisted that we stay overnight.* (Some commentators predict that *further* will one day overwhelm *farther* in all uses except the adjective meaning "literal physical distance.") See also ALL THE.

Farther and *further* are comparatives, both based ultimately on the adjective *far. Farthest* and *furthest* are the superlatives: *This is the farthest [furthest] point reached by the paved road. Quitting was the thought furthest [farthest] from my mind.* These uses are Standard; the forms *fartherest* and *furtherest* are Vulgar English and Substandard.

fascinated (*adj.*), **fascination** (*n.*) When *fascinated* combines with a preposition, it most frequently takes *by,* whether the object of the preposition is human or nonhuman: *She has long been fascinated by stamp collecting. He has long been fascinated by her.* Other Standard combinations include *with, about, at,* and *over,* usually with nonhuman objects of the prepositions: *They were fascinated with [at, about, over] his stories. Fascinated* also takes *to* plus an infinitive, as in *She was fascinated to hear about their experiences in Africa.*

The noun *fascination* can cause ambiguity in sentences such as *She has a fascination for me,* which could mean either that "I am fascinating to her" or that "She is fascinating to me." Let context help you avoid such ambiguity, or, better, let syntax do it: choose the verb instead of the noun, as in either *She fascinates me* or *I fascinate her.* Note that *fascination* can be considered hyperbole; some also consider it gushy.

fascinator (*n.*), in addition to its generalized meaning "someone who fascinates," is also a filmy or openwork woman's scarf, often worn over the hair with evening dress.

fatal, fateful (*adjs.*) If an accident is *fatal,* someone dies in it; *fatal* can also be used figuratively to suggest any disastrous consequences, as in *Their procedures had a fatal flaw, and it caused the bill to be defeated.* If an incident is *fateful,* a life or lives are changed importantly by it, but for either good or ill: *He made the fateful decision to join the Air Force* could be followed either by *and ultimately he rose through the ranks to become a successful general* or *and two years later he was killed* [or *severely injured*] *in a training accident.*

fated See DESIGN.

fateful See FATAL.

father (*n., v.*) As a transitive verb *father* is Standard: *He had fathered three children by the time he was twenty-five.* The intransitive verb, usually as a gerund, *fathering,* is apparently fairly recent, perhaps an imitation of *parenting* and certainly on analogy with *mothering.* It is a low-frequency word of uncertain future, but it appears at present to be acceptable in all but the most conservative uses.

father-in-law See -IN-LAW.

fault (*v.*), in transitive use, as in *They couldn't fault his performance,* has sometimes been objected to, but it is clearly Standard English today.

FAULTY PARALLELISM English teachers have long tried to root out *faulty parallelisms,* wherein, usually on either side of an *and* or a *but,* the writer places functionally different rather than functionally similar structures: *He likes to swim and diving too.* Only crude *faulty parallelisms* usually bother us; we speak and write a good many more that go unnoticed. One of the most noticeable, however, is the *and who* clause out of parallel with a preceding phrasal modifier: *My father is a teacher very knowledgeable about his subject and who shows great enthusiasm as well.* Say or write either *My father is a teacher who is . . . and who shows . . .* or *My father is a teacher very knowledgeable . . . and very enthusiastic as well.* See also PARALLELISM.

faun, fawn (*nn.*) These homophones differ in both meaning and spelling: a *faun* is a figure in Roman myth, half man, half goat, something like a *satyr* (see SATIRE); a *fawn* is a very young deer, usually less than a year old.

fauna, flora (*nn.*) These are singular, not plural, meaning, respectively, "all the animals of a place or a period of time" and "all the plants of a place or period." *Fauna* has two plurals—*faunas* and *faunae*—and so does *flora—floras* and *florae.* The phrase *flora and fauna* nicely includes all the living things in a region or an environment and hence is a convenient cliché. See FOREIGN PLURALS.

faux pas is a French phrase meaning "false step," which English has borrowed to mean "a social blunder." Pronounce it *FO-PAH* or *FO-PAH,* with plural *faux pas* pronounced either like the singular or *FO-PAHZ* or *FO-PAHZ.* See FOREIGN PHRASES; FOREIGN PLURALS.

favor, favour (*n.*) *Favor* is the American spelling, *favour,* the British. See SPELLING (1).

favorable (*adj.*), when it combines, usually takes the prepositions *to, for,* or *toward.* When you intend to support something, you are *favorable to* or *toward* it; when conditions are *favorable to* or *for* something, they will assist or at least not hinder it.

favorite (*adj.*) In *My favorite dessert, favorite* is an absolute adjective; no modifier can be added, so *My most favorite dessert* is Nonstandard, an objectionable hyperbole. In *A favorite dessert,* however, *favorite* can take a modifier, as in *a*

very favorite dessert, one among many favorites, perhaps. See ABSOLUTE ADJECTIVES.

favour See FAVOR.

fawn See FAUN.

fay See FAIRY; FEY.

faze, fease, feeze (*vv.*), **phase** (*n., v.*) *Faze, fease,* and *feeze* are variant spellings and represent variant pronunciations of the same verb, which means "disturb, upset, embarrass." *Faze* is the most commonly used spelling today, and the verb is most frequently used in the negative: *Her outburst didn't seem to faze him at all.* *Phase* is a quite separate noun, whose most frequent meaning is "a stage or form in a series of cyclic changes in something": *Two-year-old children are in a difficult phase.* The related verb means "to do things by stages" or "to put things in *phase* order," and it combines with *in* or *out: We phased the plan in [out] gradually.*

-fe See NOUNS ENDING IN -F.

fearful, fearsome (*adjs.*), **fearfully** (*adv., intensifier*), **fearsomely** (*adv.*) *Fearful* means "terrifying, awful," and it also means "afraid, full of fear" and "timorous." *We saw a fearful animal* is ambiguous, since you can't tell from the sentence whether *the animal* fears us or causes us to fear it. Making *fearful* even more elusive is its latest and increasingly frequent use to mean "huge, great," usually applied to things thought unpleasant or bad, as in *a fearful crash* or *a fearful cold.*

Fearsome means "dreadful, frightening, causing fear" but also has an opposite sense, "frightened, timorous," which causes confusion just as do the contradictory senses of *fearful.* Good advice: when you use either *fearful* or *fearsome* to mean "frightened," state the cause of the fear, too (*She's fearful [fearsome] of the dark*). Better still: don't use *fearsome* in that sense at all; use it for the horrible, not the timorous.

Fearfully, the adverb, has meanings similar to the adjective *fearful,* but it has gone on to develop into an intensifier as well: *I have a fearfully bad cold. Fearsomely* is an adverb meaning "horribly, frighteningly," and it seems not to have developed beyond nonce word use as an intensifier.

fease See FAZE.

feasible (*adj.*) means both "doable" and "reasonable, likely," or even "practical." *A feasible plan* can be any of these things, and *a feasible proposal* may be just "possible," but its success could also be "probable." The "reasonable" sense has been challenged by some commentators, but it is clearly Standard.

feature (*n., v.*) The noun, meaning "a characteristic or a part, especially a prominent part," is Standard, even though it has occasionally been faulted, perhaps for its associations with the world of entertainment: *One noteworthy feature of the performance was his drum solo.* As verb, meaning "give prominence to," *feature* is also Standard: *The concert will feature a piano concerto.* Only the use of the verb meaning "to conceive of, to imagine," as in *Can you feature her having the nerve to ask him?* is slang and mainly Casual slang at that.

feaze See FAZE.

February (*n.*) Unusually careful speakers may say it *FEB-roo-ER-ee* or *FEB-roo-uhr-ee*, but the most widely heard American Standard pronunciations are *FEB-yoo-ER-ee* and *FEB-yoo-uhr-ee*. See DISSIMILATION.

fee See SALARY.

feed (*v.*), when combined with prepositions, usually takes *on, upon,* or *off,* as in *Llamas can feed on [upon, off] pastureland that is very dry.*

feedback (*n.*) has some Standard specialized meanings in electronics and electricity and in processes of various kinds, but it also has a more generalized sense, "response to a process that in turn helps to modify the process," as in *We got good feedback from the first graduates of the program, and that helped us make the second version a good deal stronger.* This sense is now Standard too.

feel (*v.*), meaning "think" or "believe," was once objected to, apparently because feeling was considered more of an emotional or intuitive activity than thinking. But the objections have faded: *She feels she understands the system better* is Standard. See also BELIEVE; SENSE.

feel bad, feel badly Whatever line you take—to use both, differentiating on some semantic basis or other, to use only *feel bad* and proscribe *feel badly,* or to follow some other line—you will find some Standard users who agree with you and others who do not. Some differentiate their choices on the basis of part of speech and conclude that since *feel* is a linking verb that takes a predicate adjective, *bad,* not *badly,* is called for, regardless of whether the cause is poor health or guilt feelings. Others point out that *bad* is a flat adverb and that therefore the *-ly* adverb form is wholly unnecessary and overcorrective. Still others say that *badly* goes with emotion, *bad* with physical health; and the

converse is also occasionally argued too. Still others insist that the best thing to do is avoid *badly* entirely, and still others return to the old argument that *to feel badly* is to describe a flawed sense of touch. There may be some truth in each of these, but none of them is a satisfactory explanation for this pattern of Standard divided usage. Best advice: if you say and write *feels bad,* you may irritate fewer people than you will with *feel badly,* but you should be aware that this usage problem continues alive and vigorous, and neither the explanations nor the solutions being offered are likely to satisfy everyone. See also BAD; GOOD.

feel good, feel well See FEEL BAD; GOOD.

feet See FOOT.

feeze See FAZE.

feisty (*adj.*) was once a dialectal word (mainly Midland and Southern) but seems to have passed through a period of growing Conversational and Informal use to a point where it is now Standard, although there is still some conservative objection to its use in the most Formal of Edited English. It means "spunky, quarrelsome, exuberant, belligerent, aggressive," and it is faintly humorous but approving too: *That young woman is feisty, full of spirit and ready to challenge anyone.*

feline (*adj., n.*) Like *canine* and *equine* the noun *feline* is first of all a generic term for any and all members of the cat family, from sabertooths to housecats. The usage problem arises when the noun is used as an elegant variation for the word *cat.* The adjective is Standard meaning "characteristic of members of the cat family," and since *catty* and *catlike* have other meanings ("spiteful, malicious" and "with a cat's speed, grace, and silence of movement," respectively), *feline* is often the least likely to mislead. But *feline* also has both a pejorative sense ("crafty, devious") and an elevated sense ("sleek and sinuously graceful") that you must control by context. See CANINE; EQUINE.

fell swoop, one This is an idiom and a cliché, Macduff's graphic figure on finding his wife and children killed by Macbeth. *Fell* is archaic but not obsolete and means "cruel, deadly, terrible," with *swoop* suggesting the hawk diving on defenseless little birds.

felony, misdemeanor, violation (*nn.*) In statutory schemes, each of these terms has its definition peculiar to the jurisdiction in which it exists. In general, a *violation* is the breaking of any law, and statutes then may class such *violations* as either *misdemeanors* or *felonies.* A *felony* is a major crime, for which the punishment is more severe (usually ranging from imprisonment to death) than for *misdemeanors,* which are minor crimes. *Misdemeanor* can also be a generic term for any sort of misdeed. In its specialized senses, often as specified in law, *violation* may refer to rape, sexual assault, or desecration of sacred or other protected places.

female (*n.*), used for a woman (and the plural for groups of women unsorted as to age), has remained in use through a good deal of worry about whether it is degrading or insulting or facetious. The quaintness of the term's sound to modern readers of Jane Austen and James Fenimore Cooper should not surprise us, nor should the Victorian furor over its denying women their humanity. Today's use of the word is largely biological and generic and has the advantage of including all ages and sorts of females; for full-grown human *females* the term *woman/women* seems to have preference in most contexts. Compare EFFEMINATE; GENDER (1); MANNISH.

feminine See EFFEMINATE.

FEMININE GENDER was once solely a grammatical term, having to do with declensions that were (in Old English, for example) generally unrelated to the sex or absence of sex of the referent. Today, however, the term is frequently used as a synonym for *female sex,* biologically rather than grammatically determined. But see GENDER (2), for a fuller discussion.

FEMININE OCCUPATIONAL FORMS, FEMININE GENDER FORMS In recent years many Standard English users and most publishers have decided that along with other exclusive language, most specifically feminine suffixes and other forms that have peculiar and particular reference to females, and especially to women, should be phased out in favor of generic terms that include both men and women as referents (i.e., inclusive language). In some instances it is clear that exclusive terms are much diminished in use, archaic or even obsolescent—among them, *aviatrix, authoress, chorine, danseuse, poetess,* and *usherette.* Some others are still in use, even though many object to them: *stewardess* (now more often *flight* or *cabin attendant* of either sex), *hostess, waitress,* and *seamstress.* The *doyen/doyenne* pair seems to be settling for *doyen* for both male and female referents (but see DEAN). In entertainment the *comedian/comedienne* pair is still in flux: female comics are indeed now called *comedians,* but

their publicity releases still sometimes use *comedienne,* particularly to refer to women who specialize in comic theatrical parts. Alternatives suitable for generic use have not yet been proposed for some other words, such as *governess.* Society's attitude toward women, not lists of new taboos, will continue to do the most to set the pace of change, just as it has until now; where we still feel the need for a distinction, we will retain words that distinguish; otherwise, we will find inclusive synonyms or invent them. When the referent ceases to be single-sex, then whatever term we choose will be inclusive, as is already the case with *cabin attendant, physician, priest,* and *actor* today. Whether we let words such as *priestess* and *actress* continue with a different role to play or in the same one or instead we let them become obsolete will work out on a word-by-word basis only, and we cannot safely predict what will become of all words of this sort. See CHAIRMAN; -ESS; INCLUSIVE LANGUAGE; PEOPLE; SEXIST LANGUAGE.

feminism (*n.*), **feminist** (*adj., n.*) The literal meaning of *feminism* is "a theoretical concept urging the social, economic, and political equality of the sexes," and *feminist* is both the related adjective and an agentive noun, meaning "a holder or supporter of such views." Used in that sense, these words are nearly neutral in semantic overtones, but their specialized uses assume that such equality does not in some ways yet exist and that therefore equality of the sexes inevitably involves struggle—whether to achieve it, to prevent it, or to make women "more equal than men" (to paraphrase George Orwell). Even though the majority of Standard users appear to believe in the desirability of equality of the sexes, by no means all who support the position agree on what it may entail or are willing to be called *feminists.* So widely varied are the programs proposed under the banner of *feminism,* so intemperate some of their champions and adversaries, that both terms have pejorated to a point where they are no longer useful in most rational discussion.

In this guide we observe occasionally that "some feminists" agree or disagree on a given usage's fairness or utility, but such uses almost invariably bring editorial objection from one or another editor. No one, clearly, dares define what anyone else means by *feminism,* which is not surprising, given the intensity of the emotions the issue currently attracts. Best advice: because these terms are unusable in many contexts, including some Edited English, either find euphemistic substitutes for them or use circumlocution. The oft-heard "I favor the equality of the sexes on all issues, but I'm no feminist" makes clear the precarious usage items *feminism* and *feminist* are today. Compare SEXISM.

FEMINIST VIEWS OF ENGLISH See -ESS; FEMININE OCCUPATIONAL FORMS; FEMINISM; INCLUSIVE LANGUAGE; SEXISM; SEXIST LANGUAGE.

ferment, foment (*nn., vv.*) Intransitive *ferment* means "to be in a state of fermentation," and transitive *ferment* means "to cause to *ferment*," "to work into a state of agitation, to agitate or excite." This figurative sense overlaps with the verb *foment*, the most central literal sense of which is "to promote the growth or development of," but which also means figuratively "to instigate, to stir up, to incite": *One of my chief pleasures in high school was to ferment [foment] rebellion in the classroom.* The noun *ferment* refers to the process of *fermentation* and figuratively to "a state of agitation or excitement." *Foment* as a noun is rare and synonymous with *fomentation*, the more commonly encountered noun; its literal senses refer to the application of hot substances and moist heat to reduce pain and the figurative sense is again "the act of fomenting" or "instigation."

ferrule, ferule (*nn.*), **feral** (*adj.*) A *ferrule* is the circular metal ring or casing that is placed over the wooden tip of an umbrella or cane to prevent it from splitting on repeated contact with the ground. A *ferule* is a flat strip of wood, often marked off to serve as a ruler, used to punish schoolchildren; figuratively, it stands for schoolroom discipline. Both are pronounced *FER-uhl*, as is the adjective *feral* meaning "wild, untamed," which is used particularly of domesticated animals that have reverted to the wild state.

fervent, fervid (*adjs.*) *Fervent* means "glowing with intense feeling," as in *He made a fervent promise to love and serve her.* To be *fervid* is to be "extremely or excessively *fervent*": *His protestations at first seemed fervent and charming, but in the end she found them fervid and overdone.*

fever See TEMPERATURE.

fewer See LESS.

fey, fay (*adjs.*) These homophones (pronounced *FAI*) in different ways mean "not of this world" but are in all other respects dissimilar. *Fey* has a general meaning of "able to see the future," "otherworldly," and so by extension, "demented," "touched in the head": *Mediums often behave in peculiarly fey ways.* There is also an older and mainly Scottish sense of *fey* meaning "with second sight, especially of deaths and disasters," and sometimes this sense occurs in literary contexts today: *The old vagrant claimed to be fey, and he regularly predicted the end of the world. Fay* means "elfin," "elflike," as in *The little children were dressed like elves and fairies and danced about in a mode their teacher apparently considered fay.* See FAIRY.

fiancé, fiancée (*nn.*) A man engaged to be married is a *fiancé*, the woman, a *fiancée*. Both words retain their acute accents in American English, and three variant pronunciations suggest that the word is becoming Americanized but has not yet lost some of its French pattern: *FEE-ahn-SAI, fee-AHN-SAI,* or *FEE-ahn-SAI.* See FOREIGN PLURALS; GENDER (2).

fiber, fibre (*n.*) These variant spellings are homophones: *fiber* is American, *fibre,* British. See SPELLING (1).

fictitious, fictional (*adjs.*) *Fictitious* means "false," "fake," as in *He gave out a mostly fictitious résumé that included a fictitious address. Fictional* means "having to do with fiction, with characters or events from that sort of narrative": *Her fictional characters seem more lifelike than her historical ones.* See also FACTIOUS.

fiddle (*n., v.*) *Fiddle* is of course an Informal and Conversational name for a violin, but it also has Standard use as noun and verb, distinguishing a style of playing and a musical literature different from that of the classical violin; *fiddling* in this sense is often the rural or "country" style of violin playing. A *fiddle* is also the low edging fastened onto shipboard dining tables to keep plates and food from tumbling off as the ship rolls. The noun also has a slang sense, "a petty confidence game or swindle," and there is a slang verb to go with it: *to fiddle someone* is to cheat him or her. More important general Conversational and Informal uses are the verbal senses meaning "to play with or handle aimlessly," as in *He was constantly fiddling with the silverware,* and the idioms *to fiddle away,* meaning "to waste time," as in *He fiddled away the morning doing nothing,* and *to fiddle around,* meaning "to get nothing done," as in *She fiddled around with several different opening paragraphs but had nothing to show after two hours.*

field See AREA.

FIELD LABELS are labels such as *Music, Mathematics, Architecture, Arms and Armor,* and the like, attached by dictionary editors to word meanings (or to words themselves) whose use is peculiar to particular fields or areas of study or use. Such terms or meanings are Standard unless otherwise labeled, but their frequency may be low except within the specified field.

figurative See LITERAL.

figuratively See LITERALLY.

figure (*v.*), in the meaning "to think, decide, or conclude," has sometimes been criticized as slang, but this Americanism is clearly Standard, although sometimes limited to Conversational and Semiformal or Informal use: *We figured they'd never think of looking there.* But it can occasionally occur even in Edited English.

FIGURE OF SPEECH is the generic term for nonliteral devices used to clarify, decorate, or otherwise improve a piece of language. Metaphors and similes are examples of *figures of speech.*

Filipino See PHILIPPINE(S).

FILLERS See VOCALIZED PAUSES AND SPEECH FORMULAS; see also EXPLETIVE (2).

final (*adj.*), when used with *conclusion, destination, outcome, resolution,* and the like, is frequently faulted as redundant. You may deliberately choose this sort of redundancy, however, for purposes of emphasis; sometimes it can improve the effectiveness of your prose rather than mar it.

final analysis See ANALYSIS (1).

finalize (*v.*), meaning "to make final," is still frequently hated for having been coined at all, probably particularly because it features the useful but often-maligned suffix *-ize.* Nevertheless *finalize* is now Standard in all but the purest of purist speech and writing and in conservative Edited English. Its chief written use is in journalism and bureaucratic and commercial prose.

fine (*adv., adj.*), **finely** (*adv.*) *Fine* is a very high frequency adjective, but it is nonetheless a very powerful one: *She is a fine singer; We were pleased that the day was fine.* The flat adverb *fine* means either "with almost no margin to spare," as in *We knew we were cutting it fine, but we did make the plane,* or "splendidly, very well, excellently," as in *The new sofa fits the space fine; I liked my blind date fine; The blue tie goes fine with the blazer.* The adverbial uses are best limited to Semiformal, Informal, or Conversational levels, however.

The adverb *finely* is not usually interchangeable with the adverb *fine,* as testing in the examples above will demonstrate. *Finely* means

"thoroughly, well-done," "precisely," or "minutely": *Sprinkle with finely chopped parsley. Her students were finely rehearsed and polished. The knives were all finely honed.* In speech, of course, you need to be certain that your listeners don't confuse *finely* and *finally.*

fine arts See ART (1).

finicky, finicking, finical (*adjs.*) These are exact synonyms meaning "over-particular, overly fastidious, fussy, meticulous, or over-meticulous": *She's a finicky eater. Finicky* is far and away the most frequently used; the other two are a bit bookish, but all are Standard. Note that only *finical* has no medial *-k-.* See SPELLING OF *-ING* AND *-ED* FORMS OF VERBS ENDING IN *-IC, -AC.*

finished (*past participle*) is Standard when used with forms of either *have* or *be,* as in *I have finished* or *I am finished,* both of which mean "I have completed whatever it was." But note that *finished* itself as participial adjective means either "completed" or "defeated, ruined," and the like: *He has finished the task. He is finished with the task. She is finished, through, and done for.* The adjective also occurs in passive structures: *He has been finished for some time now; he's all washed up.* All are Standard, although the uses with forms of *be* as auxiliaries tend toward the Conversational, Semiformal, or Informal.

FINITE AND NONFINITE VERBS *Finite verbs* are verb forms suitable for use in predicates in that they carry inflections or other formal characteristics limiting their number, person, and tense. *I walked, they walk,* and *she walks* are *finite verbs; (to) walk* is an infinitive, *nonfinite.* In *I had walked, had walked* is a *finite verb; walked,* the past participle, is a *nonfinite verb.* Some grammarians describe *finite verbs* as verbs capable of making an assertion (*he thinks*), whereas a *nonfinite verb* (sometimes also called a *verbal*) is incapable of doing so on its own (*thinking*).

fireproof, fire-resistant, fire-retardant Only *fireproof* is supposed to mean that an object cannot burn; in structures and materials, *fireproof* is very hard to document. *Fire-resistant* and *fire-retardant* are labels used to suggest documentable qualities of materials that resist catching fire, burn slowly, or tend to stifle or retard burning. See FLAMMABLE.

firm (*adv., adj., n.*) The adjective *firm* means "steady, unyielding, solid, not subject to change": *She has a firm grasp of the situation. He is very firm with the children.* Whether *firm* in *Stand firm* and *Hold firm* is an adverb is doubtful; rather it may be a predicate adjective, following two verbs that are not always linking verbs but that in this case appear to function the way *be, seem, look,* and similar linking verbs do. Note that in any case *firmly* in *Stand firmly* and *Hold firmly* is clearly adverbial, and note too that it does not mean precisely the same thing as *firm* would in the same spots. The noun *firm* means "a business enterprise of some sort" and is Standard in that use. *Firm* is a collective noun (*Our firm is doing well in this quarter*), although the British use it more often than we do with a plural verb: *The firm appear likely to survive the crash.*

first (*adv.*), in the idiomatic chestnut *When we were first married,* is not usually taken as ambiguous: it means "early in our marriage," "shortly after we married," not "during our first marriage(s)." See also FIRSTLY; FIRST TWO.

first and foremost is an alliterative cliché and a slight redundancy too, but it sometimes offers a moderately formal yet comfortable way to ease into a topic. To use it or avoid it is as much a matter of style as it is of efficiency.

first floor, ground floor (*nn.*) For Americans, the *first floor* of a building is the *ground floor*; for the British and other Europeans, the *first floor* is the one just above the *ground floor*—what Americans call the *second floor.*

firstly, first (*advs.*) Both *firstly* and *first* are adverbs, and some have argued that *firstly* (which has been around since the sixteenth century) is unnecessary and ought to be avoided. But both are Standard, even though *firstly* may seem a bit old-fashioned. Remember though that in a series of items, you should stick with the form you begin with: if *first,* then *second,* and so on; if *firstly,* then *secondly,* etc.

first name, baptismal name, Christian name, forename, given name (*nn.*) Your *first name* is the one that comes first when you give your full name, **Alexander** *Graham Bell* or **Mary** *Baker Eddy.* The rest of the terms in the list are synonyms for *first name,* although *baptismal name* and *Christian name* apply, technically at least, only to Christians or others following Christian conventions. *Given name* comes about because we are born with an automatic family name, but others then give us a *first name,* and perhaps a *middle name* or two as well.

FIRST PERSON SINGULAR AND PLU-RAL See I; ME; MY; MYSELF; OURS; PERSON; PERSONAL PRONOUNS; REFLEXIVE PRONOUNS; US; WE.

first two/two first, last three/three last These are idiomatic expressions, and commentators have sometimes objected to the second in each pair. Logically, they argue, *the first two* includes number one and number two, but *the two first* implies that there are two number ones. This logic chopping does not hold up when applied to natural language. All four expressions are still Standard, even if *the two (three) first* and *the two (three) last* sound a bit old-fashioned.

fish (*n.*) There are two plurals: the unchanging *fish* and the less frequent but regularly formed *fishes.* The second is either archaic, as in biblical use, or chiefly a form used by biologists and others distinguishing various kinds or species of fish. See RELIC PLURALS OF NOUNS.

fit 1 (*adj., n., v.*) The principal parts of the verb are *fit, fitted* or *fit, fitted* or *fit: She fitted [fit] the children with shoes. His jeans fit [fitted] him like a glove.* As past participle, *fitted* seems more frequent than *fit* in most American English dialects, but not in all. Note however that *fit* and *fitted* are not always interchangeable in all senses, particularly those of the participial adjective: *He was fit* [that is, "able to perform"] *for work again. She was fitted* [that is, "trained or prepared or adapted"] *for the task.* And note how those adjectives work in attributive positions: *He's not a fit person to handle money* means "He's not suitable, particularly ethically or morally"; in *I bought a fitted case to hold my cameras, fitted* means "the case was shaped and equipped particularly to hold cameras." And note too that the adjective meaning "in good health and physical condition" is limited to the form *fit.* The noun related to these adjectives and to the verb is also *fit,* as in *He didn't like the fit of his new jacket.*

fit 2 (*n.*) means "a seizure, an attack," either literal, as in *The baby had a kind of convulsive fit,* or figurative, as in *He was struck by a fit of depression.* It also means "a temporary burst of vigorous activity": *We had a fit of housecleaning that lasted for nearly a week.* With this noun come some idioms: *to do something by [in] fits and starts* is Standard, meaning "to do it in irregular, spasmodic bursts, not steadily." *To have a fit* and *to throw a fit* mean "to have some sort of temper tantrum, to carry on emotionally and irrationally." Both these idioms are Conversational and Informal.

fix (*n., v.*) The verb in particular is an Americanism, and we use it in many senses: "to make permanent or stable" (*The instrument is fixed in place*); "to immobilize" (*She fixed him with a* *basilisk stare*); and many others, such as *to fix* [that is, "to locate"] *one's position on the chart, to fix* [that is, "to place"] *the blame,* and all sorts of "repair," "mend," "restore," and "cure" senses, all meaning essentially "to make it whole or make it better." *Fix* also has several idiomatic uses, as in *to fix* [that is, "to get withdrawn"] *a traffic ticket* (usually slang or Conversational), in the euphemism *to fix* ("spay" or "castrate") *a pet,* and in *to fix* ("prepare") *supper*; these latter two are Standard, although not usually used in the most Formal or Oratorical contexts. Another sense, meaning "to get ready to, to be about to," as in *She was just fixing to go to the store,* is dialectal, mainly South Midland and Southern, where it is usually limited to Casual and Conversational levels.

The noun *fix* has several Standard meanings: "a position for a ship" (*He got a noon shot of the sun on which to base a fix of where we were*); "a difficult situation, a quandary" (*We're in a terrible fix*); "an assessment of a situation" (*We're trying to get a fix on the size of the deficit*). Two uses are slang or Conversational at best: "a shot of a drug," usually in the sense of "something that will temporarily restore to equilibrium an addict who has been without the drug for some time," and figuratively "a cure or temporary repair," as in *The politicians were looking for a quick fix for the revenue shortfall.*

flaccid (*adj.*) is conventionally pronounced *FLAK-sid,* but *FLA-sid* can also be heard (and is often questioned). It means "weak, limp, flabby, slack": *After weeks of inactivity my muscles felt flaccid.*

flack See FLAK.

flagrant See BLATANT.

flair (*n.*) For a time commentators thought *flair* should mean only "a sense of smell," as it does in French. But in English today it is Standard meaning "a special talent, ability" (*He has a flair for interior design*), "an aptitude or a tendency" (*She has flair for picking out good new songs*), "stylishness, an attractiveness, smartness" (*She's got real flair—she has only to enter a room to become the center of attention*). See also FLARE.

flak, flack (*nn.*) *Flak* is an acronym from the German name for antiaircraft guns (*Fliegerabwehrkanonen*); it also refers to their bursting shells and therefore to figurative shellbursts as well: *My statement earned me a lot of flak from my friends.* Such figurative senses are Informal and Conversational, but the literal sense is Standard. *Flack,* a homophone of *flak,* is a slang

word meaning "press agent": *He worked as a flack for several television personalities. Flack* has now also become a variant spelling of *flak,* but you should avoid it as needlessly confusing.

flak jacket (*n.*) is a kind of bulletproof vest worn by policemen and others who are at risk of being shot at. The term is Standard. The media sometimes spell it *flack jacket.*

flamingo (*n.*) The plural is either *flamingos* or *flamingoes.* See PLURALS OF NOUNS ENDING IN *-O.*

flammable, incombustible, inflammable, noncombustible, nonflammable (*adjs., nn.*) *Flammable* and *inflammable* are synonyms, both meaning "susceptible of or capable of catching fire and burning rapidly." *Inflammable* was the word of choice for a long time, but fire-fighting associations and insurers, apparently concerned that the *in-* prefix would be misunderstood to mean "un-" or "non-" (which in another *in-* prefix it does) decided to remove all doubt by labeling materials, gasoline trucks, and other things that can burn *flammable.* Both words are still in use, and both are Standard. *Nonflammable, incombustible,* and *noncombustible* are antonyms of *flammable* and *inflammable:* they mean "fireproof." But see FIREPROOF.

flare (*n., v.*) *Flare* and *flair* (which see) are homophones, but unrelated. *To flare* is "to break out, to burst forth, to stream forth as in the wind"—*tempers flare, candles flare, skirts can be cut to flare* [*out*] *from waist or hips*—and there are other literal and figurative senses. When it combines, the verb *flare* usually takes *up* or *out: The fire flared up. The light from the lighthouse flared out over the horizon.* The noun *flare* is "a light or fire," especially "a temporary warning light such as truckers post around their stalled vehicles or such as boaters fire into the air at night when they seek assistance."

flat (*adv., adj., n.*), **flatly** (*adv.*) The adjective poses no particular problems: *We had a flat tire. The left front tire is flat. Flat* is also a flat adverb, however, and is Standard in these uses: *She turned me down flat. My joke fell flat. We were flat broke. On the backstretch he drove flat out. She sang flat much of the time.* As noun, *flat* is Standard meaning "apartment" and Conversational, Informal, or Semiformal meaning "*flat* tire." The adverb *flatly* is not always interchangeable with the adverb *flat: I contradicted her flatly. She flatly refused to go.*

FLAT ADVERBS are old, mostly high-frequency adverbs that in Old English usually had an *-e* ending. When they lost it, they looked and sounded like adjectives, and some of them then added the -*ly* suffix of modern adverbs, often being used adverbially then in both forms. *Slow, hard, right, wrong, loud, soft, quick, late, high, low,* and several more are all *flat adverbs.* Some pairs (*loud/loudly, slow/slowly, soft/softly,* etc.) mean essentially the same thing; others have different meanings (*hard/hardly,* for example). Some adverbs, such as *fast,* have only a *flat* form.

We have many idioms involving *flat adverbs: My tooth aches something awful* has an adverbial effect in its low-level contexts; *The broker played fast and loose with our money* is Standard at all levels.

flatly See FLAT.

flaunt, flout (*vv.*) This pair is causing increasing trouble, and the mistaken use of *flaunt* for *flout* is growing, despite much criticism. *Flaunt* means "ostentatiously to show something off, deliberately to call attention to it," as in *She flaunted her expensive clothes and jewelry on all occasions. Flout* means "deliberately to break or disregard a rule or law," as in *He flouted the parking regulations almost daily, seemingly daring the police to ticket his car.* The openness and arrogance of both *flaunting* and *flouting* have probably contributed to the confusion of the two, but Edited English still insists on the two verbs being distinguished, and many Standard users consider use of *flaunt* for *flout* a first-class shibboleth.

flautist See FLUTIST.

flavor, flavour (*n., v.*) Americans spell both noun and verb *flavor,* the British, *flavour.* See SPELLING (1).

flee See FLY.

flesh, flesh tones (*nn.*), **flesh-color(ed), skin-color(ed)** (*adjs.*) Long traditional use has made many people unthinking when they refer to *flesh* as only "white, or the color of Northern Europeans' skin," but there are many more *flesh* or skin colors than that. The sensitive speaker and writer will keep that in mind in order to avoid affronting or confusing the audience (advertising has virtually dropped the word from its list of colors). The words are not taboo in the "white" sense, but they do require careful contextual control.

fleshly, fleshy (*adjs.*) *Fleshly* means "of the flesh," "carnal," "sensual," "interested in pleasures of the flesh," and hence "self-indulgent," "not spiritual": *She frequently yielded to most of the usual fleshly temptations. Fleshy*

means "fat," "full of or characterized by flesh": *He described his own fat face as "a trifle fleshy."*

flesh tones See FLESH.

fleshy See FLESHLY.

flier, flyer (*n.*) A *flier* is Standard meaning "an airplane pilot," "a train noted for keeping a fast schedule," "a daring speculation" (as in Conversational and Informal *to take a flier*), or "an advertising circular." *Flyer* is a variant spelling, somewhat favored by the British.

FLOATING ADVERB See SENTENCE ADVERB.

floor See CEILING.

floppy disk See HARD DISK.

flora See FAUNA.

flotsam, jetsam (*nn.*) *Flotsam* is floating debris made up of the wreckage of a ship and its cargo; *jetsam* is debris made up of the parts of a ship or its cargo flung overboard in the effort to lighten it and prevent its sinking. Together, *flotsam* and *jetsam* cover both kinds of marine loss. The cliché is also used figuratively to mean "odds and ends." Mnemonic device: *jetsam* is what they *jettison* in hopes of saving the ship.

flounder, founder (*vv.*) *Flounder* means "to fumble, blunder, and stumble about, especially in deep mud or water," and it is said to be a blend of *founder* and *blunder. Founder* means "to break down," "to stumble or bog down in mud," and (of a ship or boat) "to fill with water." The words are often confused, particularly in the inadvertent substitution of *flounder* for *founder* in the seagoing cliché *to founder and sink,* which is often used figuratively as well, meaning "to break down and collapse or die," said especially of institutions and enterprises. (*Founder* can also be used alone to describe a sinking or a company's failure.)

flout See FLAUNT.

flunk (*n., v.*) *Flunk* in all its uses is Conversational and Informal. As a verb it means "to fail," "to get a failing grade": *I flunked chemistry. My teacher flunked me in the course.* It combines with the preposition *out* to mean "to be obliged to leave school or college for reasons of academic failure": *At the end of my first semester I flunked out.* As a noun *flunk* means "a failing grade, an F," and "a person who receives a failing grade": *I got a flunk from Mr. Smith. She said there were four flunks in her section of the course.* Often *flunk* expresses the idea of the grossest of failures: *I didn't just fail the exam; I flunked it cold.*

fluoride, fluorine (*nn.*), **fluorescent** (*adj.*) The first syllables of these words are often misspelled as *flour-* instead of *fluor-*. *Fluorine* (pronounced *FLOR-EEN, FLOR-in, FLOOR-EEN*, or *FLOOR-in*) is a yellowish nonmetallic toxic gas, and a *fluoride* (pronounced *FLOR-EID, FLOO-or-EID, FLOO-uhr-EID*) is a chemical compound made up of fluorine and another element or compound. *Fluorescence* is the light-producing characteristic of a substance that makes it give off light when acted upon by radiation from another source.

flush See BLUSH.

flutist, flautist (*nn.*) A *flutist* (pronounced *FLOOT-ist*) is a person who plays the flute; *flautist* occurs less frequently and means the same thing, but it is pronounced so that the first syllable rhymes with either *tout* or *taut*.

fly, flee (*vv.*) One verb *fly* has these principal parts: *fly, flew, flown: We flew home from Denver. I had never flown before.* A second *fly* is a baseball verb whose principal parts are *fly, flied, flied*; it means "to hit the ball in the air to a fielder who catches it before it touches the ground," and it often combines with *out: He flied [out] to center. Flee* has these principal parts: *flee, fled, fled.* It means "to run away," "to escape," and it can take a direct object or the preposition *from: We fled the country. We fled from our pursuers.* See STRONG VERBS (2).

flyer See FLIER.

fob See FOIST.

fo'c'sle See FORECASTLE.

focus (*n.*) has two Standard plurals: *focuses* and *foci.* See FOREIGN PLURALS.

foist, fob (*vv.*) *Foist* combines with the prepositions *on, off on, upon,* and *off,* meaning "to pass off as something else, to introduce sneakily" and "to pass off as true what is false," as in *She foisted some excellent forgeries of Impressionist paintings on [off on, upon] the galleries that year. Fob off* means essentially the same thing, "to pass off something fake as genuine" (*He was trying to fob off some fool's gold as gold*), "to deceive by means of a trick" (*She succeeded in fobbing her customers off onto a much more expensive appliance than the one advertised; She succeeded in fobbing it off onto her customers*), and "to put off or avoid what is not welcome," as in *When we called again, they fobbed us off with some excuse or other.*

folio See DUODECIMO.

folk, folks (*n.*) The singular *folk* means "a people," "a nation, including its traditional values and practices," as in *These early inhabitants were an agrarian folk with a strong clan government.* Hence we can speak of *folk art* and *folk tales* as being "of the *folk*, of the people." The plural, *folks,* has two main senses, both Informal and Conversational: one means "people in general," as in *Folks around here don't much like strangers*; the other means "relatives, relations, family (especially parents)," as in *Her folks haven't met her young man yet.*

FOLK ETYMOLOGY is the name given both the processes and their results when, either deliberately or inadvertently, words or meanings are changed to match an incorrect origin. When a foreign word was hard to pronounce, for example, sometimes the English colonists changed it to something that sounded more familiar: thus the American Indian word *wuchak* (variously spelled and pronounced by the earliest colonists), for the marmot found here, became an English compound, *woodchuck.* In another example, *Welsh rabbit* became *Welsh rarebit,* perhaps in an attempt to make the name of the dish less insulting to the Welsh. *The cellar* in *salt cellar* is really a *sel-er,* from medieval French *salière,* "a salter." But perhaps the most amusing are mishearings such as the one that made *cockroach* of Spanish *cucaracha* and *Bob Ruly* (a Louisiana placename) of *bois brulé.* However erroneous these *folk etymologies* may be, many of the words so created have become Standard from long use: a *woodchuck* is really a *woodchuck* now.

folks See FOLK.

follow See AS FOLLOWS.

following (*adj., n., prep., present particip.*) *Following* is a noun (*Please note the following*), an adjective (*The following people should report to the office*), a preposition (*Following his initiation, he fell ill*), and a present participle (*Following her to the car, he asked her to have dinner with him*). The possible usage problem is in a sentence in which *following* could be either preposition or present participle, thus creating ambiguity: *Following the routine, they went next to their table:* if *following* is a preposition, then the sentence means "After the routine ended, they went next to their table"; if *following* is a participle, then the sentence means "Pursuing the routine—that is, as the routine dictated—they went next to their table." Make context prevent ambiguity.

foment See FERMENT.

fond (*adj.*), meaning "having affection for," combines with the preposition *of*: *She is fond of her roommate.* When *fond* meant only "foolish or silly," it combined with *to* plus an infinitive, but that combination is archaic at best today, or perhaps obsolete, even with *so as* or *enough*: *She is so fond as not to see his obvious flaws. He is fond enough to say witless things.* In the cliché *fond hope(s)*, meaning "vain or foolish hope(s)," the old sense still occurs, but mainly in the superlative, where, as in *It was her father's fondest hope,* most people today understand it to mean not "most foolish or silliest hope," but rather "dearest or most desired hope."

fondness (*n.*) combines frequently with the preposition *for* plus a noun or nominal (usually a gerund): *She has a great fondness for [eating] strawberries.*

foot (*n.*), in its common meanings, has two plurals: *feet,* as in *My feet are cold,* and *foot,* as in *The house and yard are enclosed in a six-foot fence. She's five feet six* and *She's five foot six* are both Standard. *Foot* also occurs as a plural when it is a clipping of the British *foot guards* or *foot soldiers,* as in *Three companies of foot straggled by. Foots* is Conversational and Informal theater jargon when the referent is *footlights,* as in *The foots blinded him so that he couldn't see the audience.* Otherwise, like *feets,* it is a Substandard babytalk plural. See RELIC PLURALS OF NOUNS.

for (*prep.*), in sentences such as *I want for you to come too* and *They said for us to come in,* usually gets unfavorable comment, especially in written use. The first is dialectal and Nonstandard; the second is Casual, Impromptu, or Informal. *I asked for help* and *We will not want for money* are both Standard. See WANT FOR.

forbear (*v.*), **forebear** (*n.*) *Forbear,* stressed on the second syllable, means "to refrain or stop doing something," "to hold back," "to abstain," as in *If you'll forbear commenting, I'll be grateful. Forebear* (like its infrequent variant spelling *forbear*) is a noun, stressed on the first syllable and meaning "ancestor," as in *My forebears lived in Scandinavia.*

forbid (*v.*) The principal parts are *forbid, forbade* (usually pronounced *for-BAD* but sometimes *for-BAID*) or *forbad* (pronounced *for-BAD*), and *forbidden* or *forbid.* When combined with a preposition, *forbid* usually takes *to* plus an infinitive, as in *They will forbid her to call him again,* occasionally *to* plus a noun or pronoun, as in *Their owner forbade the living room to the dogs,* and once in a while *from* plus either a gerund or another noun, as in *We had forbidden them from [attending] the meeting.*

forceful, forced, forcible (*adjs.*) *Forceful* is usually used figuratively, as in *His is a forceful personality,* whereas *forcible* is usually used literally, as in *It looked like a case of forcible entry. Forced* is regularly both literal and figurative; it means "something compelled, involuntary," as in *It was very clear that her compliance had been forced* and *The police concluded that entry had been forced. Forceful* humor is overwhelmingly strong—loud and determined; *forced* humor is faked, not sincere, required somehow and so put on.

forcemeat (*n.*) is finely chopped, seasoned meat or fish, either stuffed into casings or served loose as stuffing. The *force* comes from *farce,* a cooking term meaning "to stuff." Sausage is a kind of *forcemeat.*

forceps (*n.*) is a plural and works grammatically much the same way as *scissors* and *shears* do, almost always with plural verbs and plural subsequent pronouns. See RELIC PLURALS OF NOUNS.

forcible See FORCEFUL.

forebear See FORBEAR.

forecast (*n., v.*) The verb is stressed usually on the first syllable, but occasionally on the second; principal parts are *forecast, forecast* or *forecasted, forecast* or *forecasted.* The noun is stressed on the first syllable. See BROADCAST; DIVIDED USAGE.

forecastle, fo'c'sle (*n.*) *Forecastle* is the full spelling, and it may be pronounced either *FOR-KAS-ul* or in the nautical way, *FOK-sul,* the pronunciation reflected in the variant spelling, *fo'c'sle.* Both are Standard.

forego, forgo (*vv.*) The infrequent and stiffly Formal *forego* means "to go before, to precede," as in *The ceremony will forego the reception. Forgo* means "to abstain, to neglect, to overlook," as in *We'll forgo meeting until next week. Forego* is also an occasional variant spelling of *forgo,* but it's better to avoid it and the unnecessary confusion it can cause.

forehead (*n.*) The most frequent pronunciations are *FAHR-id* or *FOR-id,* but spelling pronunciations are also widely heard—either *FAHR-HED* or *FOR-HED.* All four are Standard.

foreign (*adj.*), **alien, foreigner** (*nn.*) The adjective is Standard and usually unexceptionable when applied to things: *She got some foreign object in her eye. His view is foreign to us. I* *speak one foreign language.* But when applied to people, sometimes *foreign* and certainly the nouns *foreigner* and *alien* have pejorative overtones: *She's an alien* and *He's a foreigner* will almost certainly be taken to be prejudicial statements except when used in their technical senses having to do with legal status. Even then it is usually wise to use them sensitively. See ALIEN; INTERNATIONAL.

FOREIGN   PHRASES,   FOREIGN WORDS, AND FOREIGNISMS of all sorts have their place in American English, but they require restraint of author and speaker, and they demand a careful assessment of what the reader or hearer can easily understand. Never use *foreignisms* to impress others with your erudition; use them only when nothing else will do or when they contribute the precise tone you wish to achieve, but make dead certain that any you do use are used correctly and are bound to be understood by your audience or readers. Otherwise, stick with English.

FOREIGN PLURALS English has borrowed words from nearly every language with which it has come into contact, and particularly for nouns from Latin, Greek, Hebrew, and French, it has often borrowed their foreign plurals as well. But when loan words cease to seem "foreign," and if their frequency of use in English increases, they very often drop the foreign plural in favor of a regular English *-s.* Thus at any given time we can find some loan words in divided usage, with both the foreign plural (e.g., *indices*) and the regular English plural (e.g., *indexes*) in Standard use. And occasionally we'll find a semantic distinction between the two acceptable forms, as with the awe-inspiring Hebrew *cherubim* and the chubby English *cherubs.*

Following are examples of some common loan words, together with the plurals—foreign, regular English, divided, or some other combination—now in current American English use; nearly all the forms listed below are Standard. Asterisks indicate entries elsewhere in this book.

SINGULAR	PLURAL
from Latin	
*agendum, agenda	agendums, agenda, agendas
*alumna (fem.)	alumnae (fem.) (*uh-LUM-nee, uh-LUHM-nee*)
*alumnus (masc.)	alumni (masc.) (*uh-LUM-nei, uh-LUHM-nei*)
crisis	crises (*KREI-seez*)
curriculum	curriculums, curricula
*data, datum	data
index	indexes, indices (*IN-duh-seez*)

from Greek	
*criterion	criteria, criterions
*kudos, kudo	kudos (*KOO-doz*)
stigma	stigmata, stigmas
from Hebrew	
*cherub	cherubs, cherubim, cherubims
seraph	seraphs, seraphim
from French	
bureau	bureaus, bureaux
chateau	chateaus, chateaux
sou	sous (*SOOZ*), sous (*SOO*)
from Italian	
*graffito, graffiti	graffiti, graffitis
concerto	concertos, concerti
soprano	sopranos, soprani

Confusion over the pronunciations and spellings of the plurals have made the Conversational or Informal clipping *alum* (plural *alums*), with the stress on the second syllable, a very high-frequency word in all but the highest levels and even in Semiformal writing. The masculine *alumni* is most frequently used as the generic plural of the full word when the referent is a mixed group: *The state university's alumni council meets at Homecoming.*

Words borrowed from the scholarly classical languages have tended to keep their foreign plural forms in English longer than have most other foreign borrowings, both because many of their users have studied the original languages, and because in scientific and other technical vocabularies there is more compulsion to "get it right" and so "preserve the tradition" than there is in the general lexicon. The otherwise overwhelming power of the English plural patterns is clearly apparent in what has happened to words borrowed from most other languages—especially words that developed high frequency in English and came from languages that the borrowers probably couldn't speak or write: *kamikaze(s)* (Japanese), *safari(s)* (Swahili, through Arabic), *thug(s)* (Hindi), *marimba(s)* (Bantu), *decoy(s)* (Dutch), and *renegade(s)* (Spanish) all conformed almost immediately to the English *-s* plural pattern.

FOREIGN WORDS See FOREIGN PHRASES.

forename See FIRST NAME.

foreseeable future is "that part of the future near enough to us for sensible predictions to be made about it." It is a cliché, but it is Standard. Just don't overuse it.

foreword, introduction, preface (*nn.*) Sometimes these distinctions are proposed: authors and general editors usually write *prefaces* to their own books, but they have others write *forewords*. A *preface* frequently precedes a *foreword*. Another view holds that the *foreword* introduces the author, the *preface* contains the author's opening remarks about the book, and then the author may contribute an *introduction,* an essay introductory to the full topic of the book, perhaps the first part of the book itself. In editions and anthologies, the *introduction* is often a very long and detailed essay.

Whatever you do, don't misspell *foreword* as *forward*; the *foreword* of a book is "the word that comes before."

for free, free, gratis, without charge, without cost All these synonyms are Standard, except for *for free,* which is Nonstandard slang, and all are variations on the Standard phrase *for nothing: She got her new book for nothing* [*for free, free, gratis, without charge, without cost*].

forget (*v.*) is a strong verb whose principal parts are *forget, forgot, forgotten* or *forgot. Forgotten* occurs as past participle more frequently in American English, but *forgot* is also Standard: *I had forgotten* [*forgot*] *what she looked like.*

forgetful See OBLIVIOUS.

forgo See FOREGO.

forlorn See DESPONDENT.

FORMAL AGREEMENT See NOTIONAL AGREEMENT.

FORMAL LANGUAGE See FORMAL WRITTEN ENGLISH.

formally See FORMERLY.

FORMAL WRITTEN ENGLISH, FORMAL LANGUAGE, FORMAL USAGE *Formal* is the level of written American English suitable for and typical of the most elevated conventional writing. Like Edited English, *Formal English* is the language most publishers require of their authors of serious expository and argumentative works; it is the level of language used most often in the judicial opinions of justices—ideally, at least—and in the written pronouncements of major governmental figures. It is also the level of language required in formal correspondence for either public or personal communication. Letters to people you do not know, as well as instructions and reports designed to be seen by readers of unknown constituency and tastes, are usually best couched in *Formal Written English.* It comes closer than any other level to being able to serve as a written lingua franca both for native users and for those who use English as a second language. At its best it will be restrained but not stuffy, pre-cise but not precious, clear but not simplistic. It will be correct and never overfamiliar, and it will have a natural dignity, yet it will never suggest any hint of superiority. It will serve for an essay in political theory or a letter of condolence, a declaration of independence or a preamble to a constitution, a statement of principle or an editorial on national policy. (Much of this book is written in Formal English.) It is the level of written English that is ideally the least relaxed, the most handsome, the best tailored, the most admirable, the most reputable, and the most expressive of seriousness and high purpose that we have in which to clothe our ideas. And because it is written, worthy examples of it can last. (The other levels of written English are Informal and Semiformal.) See LEVELS OF USAGE.

former, latter (*adjs., nn.*) Conservative advice is to use these words to refer to members of a group of no more than two: The *former* is the first of the pair, the *latter* the second. But even some Edited English, which usually demands *the last* for three or more, will occasionally permit *latter* to be used of the last or most recently mentioned item—and sometimes items—in a group containing more than two: *The catcher, two infielders, and the right fielder all missed the team bus, and by game time, only the latter had reached the ballpark.* In Semiformal and Conversational use, both *former* and *latter* are sometimes used to refer to members of groups containing more than two, but they frequently make a clumsy sentence: *We sat around on the terrace—Beth, Lisa, and the young cousins and I—and the former regaled us with stories about her trip. Former* as adjective—*the former secretary, a former champion*—usually means the same thing as *ex-* (which see) does when used as a prefix.

formerly, currently, formally (*advs.*) *Formally* means both "in a formal way or manner" and "according to or with regard to form": *He formally welcomed them to the meeting. The document is formally correct but substantively flawed. Formerly* means "earlier," "some time ago," as in *She formerly lived here.* Some commentators insist that *once* or *used to be* would be more explicit in this example: *She once lived* [*used to live*] *here.* Whichever you choose, make sure it fits the style you have in mind. *Currently* means "now, at present," as in *We currently reside in the country,* but many commentators consider it pretentious and overformal, preferring the simpler *now, these days,* and the like. See also PRESENTLY.

formidable (*adj.*) is more frequently pronounced with the stress on the first syllable, *FOR-mid-uh-bul*, but it can be heard in Standard English as *for-MID-uh-bul* too, although that pronunciation is sometimes criticized.

formula (*n.*) has two plurals: *formulas* (pronounced *FOR-myoo-luhz*) and *formulae* (pronounced *FOR-myoo-lee* or *FOR-myoo-lei*). See FOREIGN PLURALS.

formulate, assemble, compose, concoct (*vv.*) These are more studied, more formal verbs than are *make, make up, put together,* or *form,* and their lower frequency gives them certain semantic distinctions not available in the plainer words: just as you *compose* music or poetry with your brain and imagination, so you *assemble* the parts of something, perhaps with your hands. And you *formulate* a plan or a compound, just as you might *concoct* a new elixir. (*Concoct* also adds a touch of showmanship and perhaps even of charlatanism not in any of the others.) These words are not automatically pretentious or windy: they are just different, and they represent only the tiniest fraction of the rich resources English has to offer for the expression not merely of substance, but of nuance as well. Fit them to your purposes and your style, and be grateful.

for nothing See FOR FREE.

forte (*adv., adj., nn.*) One noun *forte,* spelled *fort* (masculine) and *forte* (feminine) in the original French, in English is always spelled *forte.* It has two Standard pronunciations, *FORT* and *FOR-tai,* although purists insist that only *FORT* will do. This *forte* means "strength, special ability," as in *The mayor's forte is putting an audience in a good humor.*

A second *forte,* an Italian cognate of the French word, is pronounced in English either *FOR-tai* or *FOR-tee.* As adjective it means "loud," as in *The forte passage is for the brass instruments.* As adverb it means "loudly": *Play it not piano but forte.* And as noun, this *forte* is simply the name of a loud passage so labeled: *Bassoons, please play the forte as marked.* See also FORTISSIMO.

forthcoming, forthright (*adjs.*) *Forthcoming* has two clusters of meaning: "approaching, oncoming," as in *the forthcoming spring vacation,* and "available," in both literal and figurative senses, the latter leading to senses of "open, cooperative, frank, candid," as applied to people: *He is a friendly, forthcoming sort of man. Forthright's* dominant senses as adjective are "unambiguous, direct, candid, unevasive": *Her comments were forthright and unequivocal.* The two words are synonymous only in the "candid" sense, and *forthright* is perhaps a bit more outspoken, more vigorous: a *forthcoming* speaker may be more open, a *forthright* one more positive.

for the simple reason (that) See SIMPLE REASON.

fortissimo (*adv., adj., n.*) The three parts of speech mean respectively "very loud," "very loudly," and "a very loud passage," and the noun has two plurals in English: the regular *fortissimos* and the Italian *fortissimi.* All are music terms, but they can be used figuratively too. See FOREIGN PLURALS; PLURALS OF NOUNS ENDING IN *-O*.

fortuitous, fortunate (*adjs.*), **fortuitously, fortunately** (*advs.*) *Fortuitous* means "by chance, accidental," but it is more often used to mean "by favorable chance," "by lucky accident," and so "fortunate": *It was certainly fortuitous that I found you in that crowd. Fortunate* means "having good luck" or "favorable": *Whoever wins that jackpot will be fortunate indeed. We'll be operating in fortunate circumstances, I believe.* The adverbs also speak of luck and chance. *Fortunately* means only "by good fortune, luckily, by happy chance": *Fortunately we both were paying attention. Fortuitously,* however, still means "by chance of whatever sort," although it can also mean "by happy chance, by good luck": *We met fortuitously at the races* could be ambiguous; only context can indicate whether the chance involved was favorable or unfavorable or neither lucky nor unlucky.

forum (*n.*) has two Standard plurals: *forums* (by far the more frequent) and *fora.* See FOREIGN PLURALS.

forward See FOREWORD.

FOSSIL SUBJUNCTIVES See RELICS AND FOSSILS.

foul (*adj., n.*), **fowl** (*n.*) The adjective *foul* means "disgusting, offensive, dirty, wicked," and other unpleasant things: *The weather and our dispositions were foul.* The nouns *foul* (meaning "an infringement of the rules," as in *He committed three fouls in the first half*) and *fowl* (meaning "a domestic or wild bird, particularly a large, edible one," as in *She bought a large fowl for stewing*) are homophones. *Fowl* has two Standard plurals: *fowls* and *fowl.* See RELIC PLURALS OF NOUNS.

found (*v.*) meaning "establish, base, begin," when it combines with prepositions, takes *on* or *upon,* as in *He founds his businesses on* [*upon*] *integrity;* occasionally *in* or *amid(st),* as in *The new government was founded in* [*amid, amidst*] *the high hopes of the people*; and, to indicate who or what did the founding, with *by,* as in *The college was founded by a local financier.*

founder See FLOUNDER.

fowl See FOUL.

fractious See FACTIOUS.

FRAGMENT, FRAGMENT SENTENCE

A *fragment sentence* is one that lacks either a predicate or both a subject and a predicate. In the terms of traditional grammar, it is not *a complete sentence. Fragments* can never stand alone but must always have clear and close relationship to a context if they are to make sense. *Fragments* are also called *incomplete* sentences, but in fact many of them are response utterances, constantly used and easily understood in the give-and-take of conversation but requiring great care in writing lest the situation utterance to which each responds not be immediately clear.

fragrance See ODOR.

franchise See DISFRANCHISE.

frangible See FACTIOUS.

Franglais is a French blend of *Français* and *Anglais,* coined by a Frenchman irritated at the constant intrusion of English words and meanings into the French vocabulary (*weekend, cowboy, hamburger, whisky,* to name just a few). The French Academy does what it can, but its strictures never do more than slow the influx a bit. There are too many English and American books, songs, films, products, and tourists circulating in France for the result to be other than what it is.

Frankenstein was the name of the inventor of the monster, not the monster itself, but semantic change has caused a *Frankenstein* today to be Standard English for any sort of man-made monster, literal or figurative. *In creating that committee, we created a Frankenstein that will eventually destroy the organization.* Purists still insist on *a Frankenstein('s) monster* in such uses.

frantically, franticly (*advs.*) *Frantically* is the usual spelling, but the variant *franticly* is also Standard, although rare.

fraught (*adj.*) means "filled, loaded, charged, especially emotionally charged" and combines frequently with the preposition *with: The situation in the office is fraught with tension. Fraught* is also Standard without a following phrase, although usually limited to Informal and Con-

versational use: *Everyone was tense; the atmosphere in the room was truly fraught.*

free (*adv., adj.*), **freely** (*adv.*) The adjective (*a free spirit; no free lunch*) poses no special problems, but the two adverbs, *free* and *freely,* are not interchangeable. *All guests will be admitted free* means "the guests won't have to pay," but *All guests will be admitted freely* means "they'll be admitted without any restrictions as to numbers, time, or anything else." *To let the prisoner go free* is "to set him permanently at liberty"; *to let him go freely* is "to let him come and go as he pleases, even though he is still technically a prisoner," or it is "to let him go without any argument on his captors' part, with no disagreement or reservation." See FOR FREE.

freedom (*n.*) can combine with several prepositions, including especially *of,* as in *freedom of the press,* but also *for, from, in,* and *to,* as in *freedom for doing what you wish, freedom from want, freedom in all speaking and writing,* and *freedom to speak and write as you wish.*

free gift is redundant and tautological, an unsolicited gift of the advertising trade. Perhaps the hyperbole has been called for because in our commercial world (where there is certainly no *free lunch*), seldom is anything truly without cost to the receiver. To use *free gift* other than jocularly is unwise: Standard users scorn its serious use. See TAUTOLOGY.

freely See FREE.

freeway See THRUWAY.

FRENCH PLURALS See FOREIGN PLURALS.

FREQUENCY Words and meanings frequently employed by speakers and writers of good reputation tend to become Standard; so it is with pronunciations, spellings, and grammatical matters too. The circumstances or contexts in which we encounter them and the frequency of those encounters are the primary determiners of appropriateness in language usage, as well as in other manners.

friable (*adj.*) is a homophone of the nonce word *fryable* ("capable of being fried"), but the Standard adjective *friable* (from the Latin *friare,* "crumble") has nothing to do with cooking: *friable soils* are "crumbly, easily pulverized soils."

fridge (*n.*) is an abbreviated slang version of *refrigerator,* having lost its first syllable to apheresis and its clipped final syllables to apocope.

friend (*n.*), when combined with a preposition, most frequently takes *of: He's a friend of the family. To* has a rather old-fashioned air but still occurs: *She is a friend to every stray animal.* *With* occurs particularly with the plural, in the phrases *be friends with* and *make friends with.* All are Standard.

friendly (*adj., adv.*), **friendlily, friendlylike** (*adv.*) Both *friendly* and *friendlily* are Standard as adverbs, with the second used the more frequently, but most people aren't very comfortable with either. The problems are that *friendly* is too strongly an adjective (*He was a friendly man*) and *friendlily* is too cumbersome and tongue-twisting an adverb. In Formal situations we often turn to a circumlocution such as *in a friendly way* or *in a friendly fashion*, and Conversationally, especially in Casual dialectal situations, we may turn to locutions such as *friendlylike*, with *-like* underscoring the adverbial function of the word.

Similar problems arise and similar solutions serve when we need to make adverbs of other adjectives that end in *-ly* (e.g., *lovely, lively, timely, lonely, kindly*).

frightened (*adj.*), when it combines with prepositions, most frequently takes *of,* as in *I'm frightened of horses,* but it can also combine with *about, at,* and *by,* as in *We were frightened about* [*at, by*] *what we learned.*

frightfully (*adv., intensifier*) This originally British intensifier (as in *frightfully bad form*) has been taken up by some Americans, often as a consciously "refined" jocular locution.

fro (*adv.*), related to Old English *fram,* meaning "from," means "back, away, backwards." It is obsolete today except in the idiom *to and fro,* meaning "forth and back": *For nearly an hour he walked the colicky baby to and fro.*

from hence, from thence, from whence have long been faulted for a redundancy said to exist because *from* is implicit in all three. The matter is academic today, except for *from whence,* which continues in somewhat Formal and Oratorical use: *From whence he came, I never learned.* In current use *hence* and *thence* are now used only separately from *from: You must go hence and inquire* is very formal, and even more elevated and perhaps more pretentious is *We hurried thence at once.*

Hence by itself means "away," as in the very stiff-sounding *Go hence, and never return*; "hereafter, thereafter, after this," as in *A few years hence it will no longer matter*; and, most frequently of all, "as a result, therefore," as in *It was dark and rainy; hence we didn't see that the bridge was out.*

frown (*v.*) most frequently takes the prepositions *on* and *upon: Her parents frowned on* [*upon*] *his constant telephoning,* although *at* also occurs in Standard use: *She frowned at the interruption.*

FROZEN FIGURES (sometimes called *dead* or *tired metaphors*) are metaphors, similes, and other figure(s) of speech whose comparisons are lost or unclear because our knowledge of at least one part of the comparison has deteriorated or vanished. For example, *mad as a hatter* makes no sense today to anyone who doesn't know that hatters once frequently displayed symptoms of St. Vitus' dance and other irrational behavior as a result of poisoning by the mercurous oxides they used in making felt hats. It's a metaphor that's nearly dead today, a *frozen figure.*

fruitful (*adj.*) combines most often with *of* and *in: This discussion group is fruitful of* [*in*] *vigorous arguments.* It can also take *to* and *for: This town has an atmosphere I find fruitful for my work* [*to work in*].

fruition (*n.*) once meant "enjoyment, the pleasure derived from possessing or using something," but that sense is rarely encountered these days. Today *fruition* is used to mean either literally "reaching the fruit-bearing stage," as in *My orchard has finally come to fruition,* or, most often of all, in a figurative sense meaning "a state of accomplishment, realization, or fulfillment of something striven for," as in *After years of planning, his dreams of success had come to fruition.*

fugitive (*adj., n.*) When the noun combines with a preposition, it usually takes *from,* as in *She is a fugitive from Lebanon.* Occasionally it takes *of,* as in *He is a fugitive of his homeland's political revolution.* The adjective means "running away, escaping," as in *Her great great grandmother was a fugitive slave*; "wandering, hard to capture or retain," as in *I had some fugitive thoughts on that subject*; and "evanescent, of only brief or temporary interest," as in *I published some of her fugitive poems, but the main collection of her work has long been in print.*

-ful (*suffix*) is typically added to nouns to turn them into adjectives: *peaceful, helpful, joyful, sinful.* It is also added to the names of containers to form nouns meaning containers full of something: *boxful, handful, cupful, spoonful.* The plural is usually formed by adding the regular *-s* plural inflection to *-ful,* as in *boxfuls, handfuls, cupfuls, spoonfuls,* but Standard English also has a variant with the *-s* inflection added to the first element of the compound, as in *boxesful, handsful, cupsful, spoonsful.* See PLURALS OF COMPOUND NOUNS.

full (*adj.*), when combined with a preposition, usually takes *of: She is full of bright ideas.* In the idiom *to have the hands full,* the preposition is *with: They had their hands full with the unexpected dinner guests, each one having a special dietary requirement.*

full dress (*n.*), **full-dress** (*adj.*) The noun refers to ceremonial clothes for official and formal occasions: *We were told to be in full dress tonight.* An evening *full-dress occasion* would normally require men to wear white tie and tails, women long dresses, and military officers *full-dress* uniforms. The adjective uses a hyphen.

full-faced, full-figured (*adjs.*), **full-face** (*adv.*) *Full-faced* and *full-figured* share one sense of *full*—"round or rounded," "ample, plump, or even heavy-set": *He was a full-faced man, with a fleshy nose and a good bit of jowl. She was an imposing woman, tall and full-figured. Full-faced* also means "with the face turned directly toward the viewer," as in *Police identification photographs usually include one side or profile view and one full-faced view.* The adverb reflects a similar meaning: *Driver's license photos are always taken full-face.* All three are Standard.

full-fashioned (*adj.*) is a specialized term from the clothing industry. It is applied to knitted clothing such as sweaters and stockings and means that the articles so labeled are made to conform to the shape of the human body. Rather than being a simple tube, a *full-fashioned* stocking is made wider at thigh and calf than at knee, ankle, and foot.

full-figured See FULL-FACED.

fulsome (*adj.*) requires caution. Currently it is pejorative in one sense, "overblown, too much," particularly as applied to praise or other verbiage: *His comments on his party's candidates were fulsome enough to please even the most immoderately partisan.* But it is also now increasingly being used to mean simply "abundant," without any pejorative overtones, and many commentators strongly object to that use. Let context help prevent confusion: is *a fulsome spread* only generous or much too much?

fun (*adj., n.*) *Fun* is clearly a noun: *We had a lot of fun.* It also clearly occurs after linking verbs where we expect either a predicate nominative or predicate adjective: *This is fun.* It is often hard to demonstrate which of those structures it is, but either way it is Standard. *Fun* is

now also an attributive adjective, but so far only in Casual and some Informal use: *This was a fun evening. Everybody thought it was a fun play.* That use is growing, however, despite a good deal of critical objection to it. Note too that in adjectival use *fun* differs semantically from *funny.*

FUNCTIONAL CONNECTIVES See SUBORDINATING CONJUNCTIONS.

FUNCTIONAL GRAMMARS were school grammars of the 1920s, 1930s, and 1940s that aimed especially at the elimination of grammatical and usage errors rather than at the teaching of the system of English grammar. Such grammars contributed to the perception that grammar and usage were the two main aspects of language to be mastered. See GRAMMAR.

FUNCTIONAL SHIFT is the grammatical process by which we change a word from one part of speech to another. It is a great expander of the English vocabulary. Consider the verb *like. Functional shift* since the early Middle Ages has given us *like* as several other parts of speech: as a noun in *I have my likes and dislikes*; as an adjective in *cars of like quality*; as an adverb in *Sometime, like enough, she'll change her mind*; as a preposition in *She sings like an angel*; as a conjunction in *He talks like he means it*; as an auxiliary in *I like to have died*; and as an interjection, intensifier, or expletive (or perhaps simply a filler or vocalized pause of sorts) in *It was, like, wow!* and *I didn't know, like, what to say.* Some of these uses of *like* are Substandard or dialectal or are in divided usage (see LIKE [1] and [2]), but all are English and all illustrate the process of *functional shift. Functional shift* can also be achieved by affixes of one sort or another—*fuse* becomes *refuse, govern* becomes *governor* and *governmental, bliss* becomes *blissful, dark* becomes *darken*— or by change of stress or pronunciation: *object,* n. (*AHB-jekt*) becomes *object,* v. (*uhb-JEKT*) and *house,* n. (*HOUS*) becomes *house,* v. (*HOUZ*).

FUNCTION WORDS, a term given currency in Fries (1952), are words such as determiners, auxiliaries, conjunctions, and prepositions. They augment syntax in English grammar, and they seem to provide more grammatical than lexical meaning: for example, *the, this,* and *a/an* perform the same grammatical work; each word introduces a noun or other nominal, but the lexical or semantic content of each differs from that of the others.

funeral director See MORTICIAN.

fungus (*n.*) has two plurals: *fungi* (pronounced either *FUHNG-GEI* or *FUHN-JEI*) and *funguses* (pronounced *FUHNG-guhs-iz*). See FOREIGN PLURALS.

funny (*adj.*), meaning "amusing, intended to amuse, or risible" (*That act was very funny*) is clearly Standard. The sense "peculiar, strange, or odd" (*There's something funny about this proposal; My soup tastes funny*) has long been labeled Colloquial by many dictionaries but seems now to be Standard for almost any use, with the possible exception of the highest level of Formal or Oratorical language, where *odd* or *peculiar* might be preferred as a bit more dignified. *Funny* meaning "tricky or deceptive" (*You'd better not try anything funny*) is probably still best limited to Conversational or Informal use.

further, furtherest, furthest See FARTHER.

FUSED PARTICIPLE See GENITIVE BEFORE A GERUND.

future 1 (*adj.*) When it modifies plans, schemes, and other terms suggesting matters not yet formed or executed, as in *We have no future plans or appointments,* the adjective *future* is sometimes criticized as redundant, but it need not automatically be ruled out on that account, so long as the emphasis the adjective adds is helpful.

future 2, in the near; in the not too distant future These idioms are clichés, the first meaning "soon," and the second, "after a while, eventually." Their wordiness may sometimes be a drawback, as may their triteness, but sometimes their length may soften a style that might otherwise be judged too terse, or their familiarity may add useful clarity to a demanding passage.

FUTURE TENSE, NOTIONAL FUTURE English forms what some grammarians call its *future tense* by combining the auxiliaries *shall* or *will* or their contractions with the infinitive form of a verb: *They will arrive tomorrow. I shall be there. Of course we'll come.* (Other grammarians argue that because there is no change of form or inflection for the verb, English really doesn't have a *future tense*.) With forms of *be* plus the present participle of a verb, English also has something usually called the *notional future,* as in *She is going next year; I am expecting to get the call soon*; the *notional future* is also apparent in *Our plane leaves at ten tonight*. See TENSE.

FUTURE PERFECT TENSE is the name some grammars give to the tense made up of the auxiliaries *shall* or *will* (or their contractions), the past tense of the auxiliary *have,* and the past participle of a verb: *I'll have seen her by then. You will certainly have heard by then.* See TENSE.

G

-g, -ge An *e* after the letter *g* at the end of a word (or at the end of an element in a compound such as *changeable*) usually reflects the pronunciation: *berg* is *BUHRG,* but *barge* is *BAHRJ,* and *change* in a compound still ends with a *j* sound, as in *CHAINJ-uh-bul.*

-g-, -gg- See CONSONANTS (2).

gabardine, gaberdine (*nn.*) *Gabardine* is a tight, hard-finished weave of wool or synthetic fibers. A *gaberdine,* a homophone of *gabardine,* was a smock or coat worn by medieval Jews, although the British use this spelling for the cloth as well. See SPELLING OF UNSTRESSED VOWELS.

gage See GAUGE.

gainfully employed is a cliché used to distinguish working for pay from working without compensation. It is sometimes argued that *employed* includes the idea of payment and that therefore *gainfully employed* is redundant, but that's not really true: you can be employed—that is, "engaged"—in all sorts of volunteer or other unpaid activity.

gainsay (*v.*), meaning "deny, dispute, oppose, or contradict," is usually used in the negative, and has a somewhat literary or archaic air, as in *None of us is in a position to gainsay him* [or *what he claims*]. *Gainsay* can take as direct object either a claim or its claimant.

gala (*adj., n.*) The adjective means "festive," and the noun means "a festive, lavish occasion." Americans pronounce both parts of speech either *GAI-luh* or *GA-luh*; *GAH-luh* is mainly but not exclusively British.

gall (*nn., v.*) There are three nouns, meaning (1) "bile" and, figuratively, "bitterness or rancor or brazen rudeness or impudence"; (2) "a skin sore caused by friction" and, figuratively, "an irritation, an exasperation"; and (3) "a swelling or lump on a plant, caused by a parasite." All these are Standard, although the "brazen rudeness" sense (*She had a lot of gall to come without being invited*) is overcautiously labeled Colloquial by one current dictionary. The verb is also Standard and means "to irritate or make sore, to chafe," either literally or figuratively.

gallant (*adj., n.*) In its senses "brave, spirited, noble, stylish," and the like, the adjective is pronounced *GAL-uhnt,* as is the noun, but when the adjective means "especially attentive to women and to amatory matters involving them," pronounce it *guh-LAHNT*.

gallows (*n.*) is singular; its plurals are *gallows* or, occasionally, *gallowses*. A *gallows* is a framework from which people are put to death by hanging, and, by extension, it is also the means of execution itself, as in *He got [was sentenced to] the gallows for killing the clerk*).

gallows humor (*n.*) is a Standard term for humor that makes light of life-and-death or other terrifying or very serious matters, as in the old line, *"Aside from that, Mrs. Lincoln, how was the play?"* See BLACK HUMOR; SICK HUMOR.

galore (*adj.*), from the Irish *go leor,* meaning "enough," is now a Standard English word meaning "aplenty," unusual only in that it always appears after the noun it modifies (*aplenty* is another of these adjectives): *There were opportunities galore*.

gambit (*n.*) is an opening move in chess, in which the player risks minor pieces in order to gain an advantage. Hence in chess, the idiomatic phrase *opening gambit* is probably tautological. But in extended and figurative uses a *gambit* is a way of beginning a conversation or of turning it to one's advantage. And even more generally, it can now be any sort of stratagem designed to give its user an advantage: *Her gambit in argument was to begin shyly and tentatively, invite her opponent's overconfidence, and then pounce.* Compare GIMMICK.

gamble, gambol (*nn., vv.*) These are homophones, pronounced *GAM-bul*. The verb *gamble* means "to wager or take risks in order to win," the noun, "a risk or the act of risk taking"; the verb *gambol* means "to frolic or skip around," the noun, "a frolic." All are Standard.

gamer (*n.*) is a sports slang term. *He's a gamer* is high praise of a player's dedication and determination.

gamut (*n.*) means "the full range," originally of the medieval musical scale, but now of anything else, as in *She was a consummate actress, able to express the gamut of emotions with ease.* See also GAUNTLET, because *Run the gantlet* [or *gauntlet*] is sometimes confused with *Run the gamut*.

gamy, gamey (*adj.*) These are variant spellings, *gamy* being somewhat more commonly encountered. It means "characteristic of the flavor of game" and through extension and semantic change has come to mean "strong and unpleasant smelling" (*The locker room had the gamy smell of sweat and damp towels*), "spirited and competitive" (*She was a gamy, spunky little player*), and "lewd, salacious, risque, or suggestive" (*His peculiar delight is to tell gamy stories in company known to dislike them*). All are Standard.

ganglion (*n.*) has two plurals: *ganglia* and *ganglions*. See FOREIGN PLURALS.

gantlet See GAUNTLET.

gaol, gaoler (*nn.*) are British spellings of *jail* and *jailer* and are similarly pronounced *JAIL* and *JAIL-uhr*. There are reports that British journalism has begun to shift to *jail* and *jailer*. The main thing is not to confuse the spellings *goal* and *gaol*. See SPELLING (1).

gap (*n.*) has recently become a cliché and vogue word in compounds such as *generation gap, gender gap, credibility gap, communication gap, information gap,* and *confidence gap,* each suggesting some unspecified hiatus or disruption between or within, say, the generations, or some break in the continuity of desired value, such as confidence or credibility. These locutions are not very explicitly informative, but they are exceedingly popular at present, especially in journalese and in the language of those who imitate it.

garage (*n., v.*) Americans say both noun and verb either *guh-RAHZH* or *guh-RAHJ*; the British say *GER-ij, GER-ahzh,* or *GA-rahzh*. Americans thus retain the stress of the French original, whereas the British anglicize it, stressing the front syllable.

garb (*n., v.*) Both noun and verb are Standard, the noun meaning "clothes" and the verb, "to clothe," especially in its past participle, *garbed: All wore servants' garb. All were garbed in a sort of livery.* Both parts of speech are useful but relatively low frequency, bookish words.

gargantuan, gigantic (*adjs.*) These Standard adjectives both mean "huge, enormous," but *gargantuan* (after Rabelais's giant, who had an insatiable appetite for food and drink) usually applies to appetites, whereas *gigantic* refers to giants and hence to anything of great physical size. Both are Standard.

garote, garrote, garrotte (*n., v.*) Americans tend to prefer the *garrote* spelling for both noun and verb, although the past tense and both present and past participles also occur with two *t*'s. Stress is usually on the second syllable, either *guh-ROT* or *guh-RAHT,* but *GER-uht* does occur. The noun refers to the collar, cord, or wire used to strangle someone, and the verb represents the action of using one of these to strangle someone.

gas (*n., v.*) has two plurals, *gases* and *gasses,* and the verb doubles the *s* in the past tense and past and present participles (*gassed, gassed, gassing*) and can double it in the third person singular present tense, *gases* or *gasses.* The noun means (1) "a substance that is neither liquid nor solid," (2) "especially such fuels as the one we call *natural gas,*" (3) "the intestinal event that causes flatulence," (4) "the fuel we call *gasoline*" (see GASOLINE), (5) "the figurative name for fatuous talk," (6) "nitrous oxide, also called *laughing gas,* used as an anesthetic," and (7) "the slang word for a delightfully entertaining and enjoyable occasion" (as in *The party was a gas*). All but the last sense are Standard. The verb means (1) "to provide with gas," (2) "to subject to poison gas," (3) "to fill the gas tank of a vehicle" (often combined with *up*), and (4) "to converse or chatter idly" (this last is slang). *Gas* also is the first element in many compounds: *gas tank, gas chamber, gas station, gaslight, gas mask, gas main, gas man,* and the like.

gaseous (*adj.*) is pronounced either *GAS-ee-uhs* or *GASH-uhs* and is Standard meaning "characteristic of (a) gas or like (a) gas" and Conversational or Informal meaning "flatulent" or "full of boastful, windy talk."

gasoline, gas, gasohol, gasolene (*nn.*) *Gasoline* is by far the most usual American spelling of the motor fuel; *gasolene* is an older and fading variant. *Gas* is the clipped form of *gasoline,* now Standard in most circumstances, although you must take care to avoid confusion with other meanings of the word *gas. Gasohol* is the blend name for the motor fuel that is a mixture of *gasoline* and *ethyl alcohol.*

gather (*v.*) is Standard, meaning "to understand, to conclude," as in *We gather that the Senate will defeat the bill.*

gaucho (*n.*) The plural of this name for a South American cowboy is *gauchos.* See PLURALS OF NOUNS ENDING IN *-O.*

gauge, gage, gouge (*nn., vv.*), **gouging** (*n.*) These words are never confused in speech, but *gouge* is sometimes misspelled *gauge,* and *gauge* is often misspelled *guage.* The noun *gauge* (pronounced *GAIJ*) is a measure or an instrument for measuring, and there are many specialized meanings, such as the *gauge* of metal or other fabrics, and the like. The verb *gauge* (pronounced *GAIJ*) means to take measurements, to estimate, and it too has some specialized meanings. *Gage* is a variant of *gauge,* but apparently in dwindling use. The other *gage* is a glove or some other item offered as a pledge, as in giving a challenge to a duel.

The noun *gouge* means "a tool" and "the mark such a tool or another instrument makes in wood or another material," and the verb means "to use such a tool or to make such a mark." Figuratively, the verb *gouge* means "to cheat" or "to overcharge," in uses that are limited to Conversational or Informal contexts. Pronounce both noun and verb *GOUJ.* The figurative use of the gerund, *gouging,* is common; it means "cheating or extorting," especially "overcharging for goods or services."

gauntlet, gantlet (*nn.*) A *gauntlet* is "a heavy glove, often armored" or "a glove with a heavy cuff covering part of the arm." *To throw down the gauntlet* is to challenge someone; *to pick up the gauntlet* is to accept someone's challenge. A *gantlet* is "a lane between two lines of people armed with staves or whips, through which someone being punished is forced to run while being clubbed or whipped by the people on either side" (*run the gantlet*) and, figuratively, "any series of trials and difficulties." To complicate matters, each is a variant spelling of the other. Compare GAMUT; GAUGE.

gay (*adj., n.*) *Gay* has meant "bright, lively, cheerful," and the like for centuries, and as early as the seventeenth century it was also used to deal with sexual matters: *a gay female* was a prostitute, *a gay male* a womanizer, and *a gay house* a whorehouse. Use of *gay* in the sense of "homosexual," especially "male homosexual," is an Americanism that began as a slang adjective in the 1930s, but within a generation its use as both noun and adjective in this sense has become Standard. Today when you intend to use the adjective (in particular) in the older generalized senses of "bright, cheerful," etc., you must take care that context makes that meaning clear: the modern specialized sense is very difficult to avoid today, especially in writing. See also HOMOSEXUAL.

gazebo (*n.*), the summerhouse from which one surveys the landscape, has two plurals: *gazebos* and *gazeboes*. See PLURALS OF NOUNS ENDING IN -*O*.

-ge See -G.

gear (*n., v.*) The noun figures in several idioms having to do with the transmissions of vehicles or other machines but also having widespread figurative use: *to shift gears*, meaning literally "to put a transmission from one gear to another" and figuratively "to change plan, method, or approach to something"; *to get it in gear* applies literally to a vehicle or other machine, but figuratively applied to people or their posteriors, it means simply "to get moving"; *in high gear* means "to be at top speed or efficiency" either literally or figuratively. The verb also combines to make idioms: *geared to* means "suited to or adapted for," as in *The plan was geared to the needs of the local people*; *to gear up* means "to prepare for," as in *The factory geared up for more production*; *to gear down* means literally "to shift the transmission into a lower gear" and figuratively "to reduce activity or scope or size of an operation, as in *Management decided to gear down all phases of production*. All the literal senses of both noun and verb are Standard; most of the figurative senses are Conversational or Informal, but *to get [it] in gear* is still slang.

gendarme (*n.*) is used literally to refer to a French police officer (more accurately, to a representative of the French national police), but it is used whimsically in a broader sense for any police officer anywhere, as in *The local gendarmes were annoyed at our celebrating*. The English pronunciation is *ZHAHN-dahrm*.

gender 1 (*n.*) was once a solely grammatical quantity (see GENDER [2]), but it is now used to replace *sex* (a biological term), particularly in discussions of feminist issues, as in *a gender problem, issues of gender, discrimination on the basis of gender*, and the like. Both terms are now Standard in both biological and sociological uses, so restricting *gender* to a grammatical sense now requires careful attention to context. See SEX.

GENDER 2, GRAMMATICAL AND NATURAL Old English, like certain modern foreign languages, had something called *gender,* a grammatical consideration that classified all nouns as belonging to either a masculine, feminine, or (sometimes) a neuter class based entirely on grammatical considerations, not on sex or the lack thereof. All nouns were referred to by pronoun declensions that also were classed according to *grammatical gender*. During the Old English period this system of *grammatical gender* began to disappear, and Modern English nouns now have only *natural gender,* the gender stipulating the sex of the referent or its lack of it. Today's English can give this grammatical information only through pronoun reference: a man is *he,* a woman, *she,* a hen, *she,* and a tree, *it*; a horse can be *he, she,* or *it,* and so can many other animals, including human babies; but a lioness can be only *she* or *it,* and a rooster, *he* or *it*. Then too there are other possible confusions, in that we can conventionally refer to ships and colleges with feminine pronouns and also use plural pronouns when we are unsure of the sex of the referent (*Someone called, but they didn't leave a message*). But see INCLUSIVE LANGUAGE; SEXIST LANGUAGE.

gender gap (*n.*) is a compound meaning "the differences between men and women in achievement, opportunity, values, and the like" or "the perceptions of such differences." As with other compounds with *gap*, this one requires careful control of context if it is to be more than a jargon expression. See GAP; SEXIST LANGUAGE.

genealogy (*n.*), the science or study of lineage, adds the -*alogy* suffix to the noun *gene*. Pronounce it either *jeen-ee-AL-uh-jee* or *jeen-ee-AHL-uh-jee*.

General, general (*n.*) The title is capitalized when it precedes the person's name or is used alone in direct address, but not when the rank is the referent: *General Smith is not yet a full general*. Compounds in which *general* is the second element are rarely hyphenated, but the plurals vary: *brigadier generals, major generals, attorneys general* or *attorney generals,* and *solicitors general* or *solicitor generals* are all Standard today, although conservative Edited English will usually still prefer *attorneys general* and *solicitors general*. See PLURALS OF COMPOUND NOUNS.

general consensus See CONSENSUS.

GENERALIZATION is the process of semantic change that extends and widens the meaning of a word to apply to or include a greater range of ideas. For example, the word *barn* is today "a place where all sorts of grain, hay, animals, and machinery may be housed," but the word originally meant "a place where barley is stored" (Old English *bern* comes from *bere,* "barley," and *aern,* "house"). The meaning of *barn* has *generalized.* See also SPE-CIALIZATION.

GENERALIZATIONS, GRAMMATICAL
See RULES AND GENERALIZATIONS.

generation gap (*n.*) is a current cliché for failures of agreement and communication between the generations. See GAP.

generic (*adj., n.*) Anything *generic* applies to a whole class; it applies generally: *Chicken soup is a generic remedy against the common cold.* The noun today refers to drugs or grocery items sold without brand names: *My physician always prescribes generics whenever they're available.*

GENERIC PRONOUNS
All the personal pronouns are *generic* (that is, they can each refer to masculine, feminine, or even neuter antecedents) except those for the third person singular: *he, him, his, she, her, hers, it, its.* Edited English still sometimes insists that *he, his,* and *him* are also generic, to be used whenever a singular referent of unspecified gender is required, but more and more publishers are now opting for inclusive language instead. See GE-NERIC THIRD PERSON MASCULINE SINGULAR PRONOUN; INCLUSIVE LANGUAGE.

GENERIC THIRD PERSON MASCU-LINE SINGULAR PRONOUN
Traditional grammars describe the masculine singular pronoun as generic and able to refer to either or both sexes or to neuter objects in sentences such as *Everybody put on his coat and hat,* even when the people referred to by *everybody* may include both males and females. Much conservative usage, especially within the older generations, still accepts this practice, but more and more Edited English seeks to use inclusive language instead. See also AGREEMENT OF INDEF-INITE PRONOUNS AND OTHER SINGULAR NOMI-NALS WITH VERBS AND OTHER PRONOUNS; IN-CLUSIVE LANGUAGE; SEXIST LANGUAGE.

GENERIC WORDS
are nouns such as *person, individual, voter, doctor, lawyer, merchant, thief, pilot, farmer, preacher, teacher,* and *senator,* none of which specifies the sex of the person referred to. *Mother, sister,* and *daughter* clearly have female referents; *father, brother,* and *son* have male referents. See IN-CLUSIVE LANGUAGE.

genetic, congenital, innate (*adjs.*) *Genetic* means "having to do with genes and origins,"

as in *His physical problems were apparently the result of a genetic disorder. Congenital* means "existing at birth" and hence "of a natural origin," as in *She had a congenital clubbed foot. Innate* also means "present at birth" and by extension "essentially a part of," "inherent," and, most recently, a distinction of the nature side of the nature-nurture argument: what is *innate* is a given, rather than the product of experience, as in *The ability to use a natural language is in some way innate in human beings* (see ACQUIRED). All are Standard.

genial See CONGENIAL.

genie, djin, djinn (*n.*) These are variant spellings of an Arabic loan word, *jinni,* meaning "demon" or "spirit," as in Aladdin's *genie of the lamp. Genie* is a homophone of *Jeanie; djin* and *djinn* are homophones of *gin.*

GENITIVE, ATTRIBUTIVE
See ABSOLUTE POSSESSIVE PRONOUNS.

GENITIVE, CLASSIFYING
See DESCRIP-TIVE GENITIVE.

GENITIVE, DESCRIPTIVE
See DESCRIP-TIVE GENITIVE.

GENITIVE, DOUBLE
See DOUBLE GENI-TIVE.

GENITIVE, INDEPENDENT
See ABSO-LUTE POSSESSIVE PRONOUNS.

GENITIVE, OBJECTIVE
See OBJECTIVE GENITIVE.

GENITIVE, PERIPHRASTIC
See PERI-PHRASTIC.

GENITIVE, SUBJECTIVE
See SUBJECTIVE GENITIVE.

GENITIVE BEFORE A GERUND
This construction, in which a noun or pronoun modifies a gerund (*I don't like his driving so fast,* rather than *I don't like him driving so fast,* or *They felt that Mary's coming in late was bad,* rather than *They felt that Mary coming in late was bad*) was long required in English classes. But for some time now either the genitive (possessive) or the objective case has also been Standard before gerunds, although Formal writing may use a bit more genitive with pronouns than it does with nouns. Native speakers can now trust their ears.

GENITIVE CASE
in English conveys the ideas of possession, source, attribution, origin, measure, and the like, and its grammatical function is indicated either by inflection (*Fred's suitcase, their father, our sisters' hats*) or by the periphrastic genitive with *of* (*the surface of the water,*

the floor of the house). See also APOSTROPHE (2); APPOSITIVE GENITIVE; CASE (1); DESCRIPTIVE GENITIVE; DOUBLE GENITIVE; GENITIVE BEFORE A GERUND; OBJECTIVE GENITIVE; PERIPHRASTIC; SUBJECTIVE GENITIVE.

GENITIVE OF ORIGIN is the name some grammarians give genitive cases that indicate by genitive inflection the originator or source of a modified noun: *Hawthorne's novels, his grades, the minister's sermon.* See CASE (1).

GENITIVE OF PURPOSE Some grammarians classify certain descriptive genitives as *genitives of purpose.* The inflected form (*women's locker room, boys' bicycles*) is matched by a periphrastic form made usually with *for* rather than the otherwise more frequent *of* (*locker rooms for women, bicycles for boys*). See also GENITIVE CASE.

genius (*n.*) has two meanings, and each has two plurals: in both its "guardian spirit" (*the genius of the fountain*) and its "great natural ability" (*a man of great genius*) senses, the plurals are *geniuses* and *genii,* the latter occurring almost solely with the "guardian spirit" use and only rarely there. *Geniuses* is almost universal as the plural in the "natural ability" sense. See FOREIGN PLURALS.

gent (*n.*) is a Conversational and Informal clipped form of *gentleman.* The plural is *gents,* and its genitive plural, *the gents',* is a somewhat dated whimsical euphemism for "men's toilet."

genteel, gentle (*adjs.*), **gentile** (*adj., n.*) *Genteel* means "showing good taste, good manners," "polite," as in *His deportment was genteel and thoughtful,* or "affectedly displaying manners and false delicacy or prudery," as in *She was cloyingly genteel in everything she said and did. Gentle* has three main clusters of meaning, "well-bred, well-mannered," "not rough or tough," and "belonging to good society." A *gentile* is any person not a Jew or, among Mormons, anyone not a Mormon. All these are Standard, and the only overlap among them is in the politeness and good breeding reflected in *genteel* and *gentle.*

GENTEELISM See EUPHEMISMS.

gentile See GENTEEL.

gentle (*v.*) The meaning "to make gentle" is now relatively rare, but the meanings "to soothe" and "to train or break an animal, such as a horse" are more frequent. All three are Standard. See also GENTEEL.

gentleman, gentlewoman (*nn.*) A *gentleman* is a man of cultivation, good manners, and some

social station. The term is usually paired with *lady.* A *gentlewoman* is even more specifically someone of gentle birth and breeding; the term is only infrequently used today, but it is still Standard.

gentrification (*n.*), **gentrify** (*v.*) Both the verb (meaning "to restore to middle-class standards and purposes a deteriorated part of a city") and the noun (the process of doing so) have achieved Standard status, though only relatively recently. Each also has a pejorative generalized use meaning "to uplift or improve status of speech, dress, or other manners."

genuine (*adj.*) is pronounced *JEN-yoo-in*; *JEN-yoo-WEIN* is either jocular or dialectal. It is sometimes used in a quaintly naive way for stress: *This is genuine* [that is, *real*] *leather,* or *These are genuine* [not *fake*] *rubies.* See AUTHENTIC.

genus (*n.*) (pronounced *JEE-nuhs*) has two plurals: *genera* (*JEN-uhr-uh*) and *genuses* (*JEE-nuhs-iz*). See FOREIGN PLURALS.

geometric progression See PROGRESSION.

geriatric (*adj.*), **geriatrics** (*n.*) The noun, the name of the medical specialty and study concerned with aging and the aged, is plural in form but takes a singular verb and succeeding pronoun: *Geriatrics* [or *geriatric medicine*] *is now a medical specialty in its own right.* They are pronounced *JER-ee-A-trik(s).*

germ (*n.*) A *germ* is a tiny bit of living matter that is the beginning stage of a larger, more complex organism. It can also be an embryonic part of a cereal grain, as in *wheat germ,* and has a Standard transferred sense, "the initial stage of anything," as in *the germ of an idea.* Another meaning is "a microorganism, especially one that can cause disease," and from this sense came the fading slang pejorative applied to a person and meaning "a tiny, unpleasant, crawling thing." See BACTERIA; BUG.

German, Germanic, Teutonic (*adjs., nn.*) The adjective and noun *German* have as their referents qualities characteristic of the language and its speakers and of the citizens of the European country called Germany, as in *Goethe was a German author; He was a German; He wrote in German. Germanic* and *Teutonic* are synonyms but broader in their referents than *German.* They refer to the *Germanic* [*Teutonic*] peoples and their languages. *Germanic* is the more frequently encountered word today, although both are Standard. See GERMANIC LANGUAGES.

GERMANIC LANGUAGES The *Germanic languages* are a large, mostly European branch of Indo-European. The main modern languages of this branch are Swedish, Danish, Norwegian, and Icelandic (the North Germanic subgroup) and German, Dutch, Afrikaans, Flemish, and English (the Western subgroup). Gothic, now dead, is the only Eastern *Germanic language* of which we have written evidence.

gerrymander (*n., v.*), pronounced *JER-ee-MAN-duhr* or occasionally *GER-ee-MAN-duhr*, is a blend of *Gerry* (last name of a Massachusetts governor) and *salamander* (the rough shape of the election district he created in order to keep political control of it). The verb means "to create such a district," and the noun is the kind of district that results.

GERUND A *gerund* is a verbal noun; it has the same form as the present participle of a verb (*walk* becomes *walking*). *Gerunds* function as do other nouns: *Swimming is my best sport. We were used to sleeping late.* See GENITIVE BEFORE A GERUND.

GERUND, GENITIVE WITH See GENITIVE BEFORE A GERUND.

GERUND, POSSESSIVE WITH See GENITIVE BEFORE A GERUND.

gesture, gesticulation (*nn.*) The two are Standard synonyms in both their specific and abstract senses: *Her gestures [gesticulations] were rapid and excited. His use of gesticulation [gesture] is extremely effective.*

get (*v.*) is Standard as a passive-making auxiliary, as in *He got elected last fall.* It is also Standard meaning "obtain" or "possess," as in *She's got the votes she needs* (although purists once frowned on this use, preferring *She has the votes . . .*). The past tense is always *got.* For past participle, British usage relies almost exclusively on *got* rather than *gotten,* whereas American usage has both forms, often with a semantic distinction (encountered usually only with perfect tenses: *She's got the votes she needs* means "She has them," and *She's gotten the votes she needs* means "She has obtained or acquired them"). The pronunciation *GIT,* often spelled *git* in eye dialect, is dialectal or even Substandard but also occurs in idiomatic expressions in Conversational and Informal use, as in *Git lost! Git outta here! To get it,* meaning "to understand or comprehend it," is slang: *He didn't get it at all.*

get hold of, get ahold of See AHOLD.

get up See RISE.

-gg- See CONSONANTS (2).

ghetto (*n.*) has two Standard plurals: *ghettos* and *ghettoes.* See BARRIO; PLURALS OF NOUNS ENDING IN *-O.*

gibe See JIBE.

gift (*v.*) has been Standard since the Renaissance, but some commentators have begun objecting to it as an unnecessary synonym of the verb *give.* Edited English still uses it. See also FREE GIFT.

gigantic See GARGANTUAN.

gild the lily, meaning "to further decorate something already beauty at its best," is a Standard idiom, even though it's not quite Shakespeare's "To gild refined gold, to paint the lily . . . / Is wasteful and ridiculous excess" (*King John* IV.ii.11ff).

gill (*n.*) has four Standard meanings, two of them frequently encountered: "part of a fish's breathing apparatus" and "a liquid measure (a quarter of a pint)." Relatively rare are the meanings "a small stream" and "a young woman or girl," a clipped form of the given name *Gillian.* All have the initial hard *g* sound of *game.*

gimmick (*n., v.*), **gimmicky** (*adj.*) A *gimmick* is a device, a gadget, or a secret trick used to perform some service or achieve some other end. Noun (*He had a gimmick he thought would work*), verb (*She had gimmicked the doorbell so it would ring if anyone even approached the door*), and adjective (*They developed a gimmicky campaign to sell worthless stock in the venture*) have all been limited until recently to Conversational or Informal use, but Edited English now has begun to use them in all but the most Formal circumstances. Compare GAMBIT.

Gipsy, gipsy See GYPSY.

girl (*n.*), used to refer to an adult woman, is taboo in most Standard use today. Use *woman* instead.

girlfriend, boyfriend (*nn.*) These once Conversational and Informal words are now Standard compounds, with stress on the first element, both in the general senses of "a friend (of the specified sex)" and in the specialized sense of "a lover (of the named sex)." The range of meanings is great: her *boyfriend* may be a woman's escort, sweetheart, steady date, or live-in lover; a man's *boyfriend* is his homosexual partner. *Girlfriend* also has a wide semantic range. Use great care, therefore, to make certain that context prevents your audience from drawing incorrect inferences. Older uses of each may be found written as either two words or hyphenated, but current spellings are as one word. See PRONUNCIATION OF COMPOUND WORDS; SPELLING OF COMPOUND WORDS.

girlish See BOYISH.

git See GET.

given name See FIRST NAME.

gladiola, gladiolus (*n.*) *Gladiola* is the Latin plural of *gladiolus* ("a small sword"). The flower is technically a *gladiolus*, but *gladiola* is its nontechnical Standard English singular, and its plurals are *gladioli, gladiolus, gladiolas,* and *gladioluses.* The term *gladiolus* also refers to a part of the human breastbone, and for that sense the Standard plural is *gladioli.* Perhaps because of its confusing singulars and plurals, the flower is regularly referred to by its clipped Conversational and Informal form, *glad* (plural: *glads*). See FOREIGN PLURALS.

glamour, glamor (*adj., n.*), **glamorize** (*v.*), **glamorous** (*adj.*) Both *glamour* and *glamor* are Standard spellings, although *glamour* is more frequent. Interestingly, *glamorize* and *glamorous* almost never use the *-our* spelling.

glance See GLIMPSE.

glean (*v.*) is Standard, meaning either "to gather painstakingly, laboriously" or simply "to gather," as in *We gleaned what we could from the local gossip. Glean* still has its historic sense, "to collect grain left behind by the reapers," although the job itself has practically disappeared from Western agriculture.

glimpse, glance (*nn., vv.*) The nouns usually combine with different prepositions: *I got a glimpse of her. I took a glance at her.* The verbs differ in that *glimpse* is usually transitive, as in *She glimpsed the mountain briefly through the clouds* (although very rare intransitive uses also occur, as in *She glimpsed at the mountain*), whereas *glance* is almost always intransitive, as in *He glanced at her as he went by; The stone glanced off the windshield.*

GLOTTAL STOP Some British English dialects and some speakers of the Metropolitan New York City regional dialect replace the usual medial *t* sound in words such as *bottle* and *water* with a *glottal stop,* which closes off the column of air briefly (to form a stop) at the *glottis,* the space between the vocal cords in the throat. The phonetic symbol for a *glottal stop* is [ʔ].

glow (*v.*) is Standard in combination with several prepositions, among them *with, from, in,* and *at: She glowed with [from, in] good health*

expresses the source of the *glow; He glowed at her praise* means "because of."

go (*v.*) Principal parts are *go, went, gone. Went* as past participle is Substandard and a shibboleth in such uses as *We had never went there before.* Similarly Substandard is the use of *gone* as a past tense, which is encountered in Vulgar English and in some Black English, as in *They gone and done it when we wasn't lookin'* (but see also GO AND). A more recent usage problem is the omnipresent slang use of *go,* meaning "say," in the Casual speech of teenagers, young adults, and their older imitators, as in *"So she goes, 'What did you tell 'im?' and I go, 'Nothing!' and she goes, 'No way!' "* Avoid this use except jocularly; it has become a cliché, the badge of gum-chewing youth.

go along with is an idiom meaning "to agree with, to concur," as in *She'll go along with our plan.*

goals and objectives is a cliché from business and other organizational or educational jargon. The terms are essentially synonymous, and the cliché is therefore redundant.

go and is an emphatic use of *go* that puts the stress on a second verb that follows, as in *She went and told her mother; He'll go and spill the beans, I'm afraid.* We also use it for the same purpose without *and: Go fly a kite!* With and without *and,* the locution occurs mostly in Conversational use or its Informal imitations. See TRY AND; UP AND.

go ape See APE.

gobbledygook, gobbledegook (*n.*) is a slang word for the obfuscatory wordiness of officialese, which may be confusing at best and meaningless much of the rest of the time. *Gobbledygook* is the usual spelling, *gobbledegook* a variant. See JARGON.

goes without saying, that (it) is a Standard English idiom, a literal translation of the French *Cela va sans dire* that has found a home among us primarily for adding emphasis, another evidence of our penchant for hyperbole.

gofer, go-fer See GOPHER.

good (*adj., n., intensifier*), **well** (*adv., adj.*) When following the linking verb *feel,* both *good* and *well* function as predicate adjectives: *I feel good [well] today,* although with careful control of context it is also possible to use *well* as an adverb after *feel* as intransitive verb, as in *The sense of touch in the blind is much sharpened: they feel well and sensitively.* Further, in Conversational contexts, *I feel good* means "I'm pleased, elated,'' whereas *I feel well* usually means "I feel physically fine." When used with the verb *do, good* is a noun and a direct object (*We want to do good with our money*), and *well* is an adverb (*She did well on the exam*). *Good* can also serve as adverb in Common and Vulgar English (*My watch runs good again*; *This job pays good*), and it is widely used in Standard Casual sporting contexts: *She hits real good to right field.* Finally, *good* is an intensifier, particularly in the spoken language, as in *There was a good deal to be done; We had a good fifty students in attendance; She saw a good many of them.* See BAD; FEEL BAD.

good and (*intensifier*) This idiom works just as *quite* and *very* do in the sentence *I'm quite [very] angry. I'm good and angry* is Standard, but mainly for Conversational and Informal use. See NICE AND.

good-bye, good-by, goodbye, goodby (*n., interj.*) The more frequent spelling is with a final -*e*, although all the spellings are Standard. The interjection is either hyphenated or spelled as one word. The noun (plural: *goodbyes*) is usually written as one word.

goodwill, good will (*nn.*) As one word, *goodwill* usually means "kindly disposition, friendly attitude" or "agreement and consent," as in *I rejoice in your evident goodwill toward me and my efforts.* As two words, *good will* can be another way of spelling *goodwill*, or it is an intangible asset in a business, as in *He sold his store—inventory, equipment, building, and good will—for a good price.*

GOOD WRITER See CAREFUL WRITER.

gopher, gofer, go-fer (*nn.*) These homophones are all variant spellings of the slang word for a person employed to do menial work, especially to run errands (such as "*go for* coffee"), but *gopher* is of course also the Standard spelling of the name of the ground squirrel, and that spelling of the errand runner is folk etymology.

go somebody (them) one better is a Standard Conversational or Informal idiom meaning "to surpass," as in *I plan to go him one better by submitting several entries.*

got See GET.

go them one better See GO SOMEBODY.

go to the bathroom See BATHROOM.

gotten See GET.

got to See HAVE GOT TO.

gouge, gouging See GAUGE.

gourmet (*n., adj.*), **gourmand** (*n.*) *Gourmet*, a French borrowing meaning "a connoisseur of food and drink, a person of discriminating palate," is much more in use in English today than its compatriot, *gourmand*, which sometimes means "a big eater and drinker," or even "a glutton," and sometimes simply "a heartier sort of *gourmet*." *Gourmet* has become a cliché for anyone with pretensions to good taste in food and drink, and the adjective today often describes any cook or any eatery thought to be better (perhaps) than indifferent. *Gourmand* is fading; *gourmet* is overused. See FOREIGN PHRASES.

government, environment (*nn.*) Both these words are often pronounced in Standard discourse without their medial -*n*-: GUHV-uhr-mint and en-VEI-uhr-mint or en-VEIR-mint, instead of GUHV-uhrn-mint and en-VEI-ruhn-mint. Like GUHV-uhr-mint, en-VEI-uhr-mint is frequently considered Substandard, however, because of the metathesis.

governor (*n.*) is one of those words rarely pronounced in connected speech to reflect its medial -*r*-; GUHV-uh-nuhr is as Standard as the GUHV-uhr-nuhr pronunciation. Compare HANDKERCHIEF.

gown (*n.*), meaning "a woman's dress," is a fairly Formal, even pretentious word, the more frequently encountered meanings being "a woman's nightdress," "an academic robe," and "the robe worn by a surgeon and others in a medical operating room." Make sure that context prevents ambiguity.

grab (*n., v.*) The verb, in the sense "affect," as in *How does that idea grab you?* is Conversational and Informal at best. The noun, in the plural idiom *up for grabs* means "available to anyone who gets to it first or who tries hardest to get it," and is also Conversational and Informal.

grab hold of See AHOLD.

graduate (*adj., n., v.*), **post-graduate** (*adj., n.*) A *graduate* has received a degree or diploma and is eligible for further study; a *post-graduate* is someone embarked on study beyond the degree or first diploma level, and in that sense the noun is synonymous with the term *graduate student*. Both words are also used as modifiers: *graduate* has become the first element in several compounds (*graduate student, graduate study, a graduate course*); *post-graduate* occurs occasionally in a compound (*a post-graduate course*). Both are Standard in these uses.

Graduate as an intransitive verb in sentences such as *I graduated from college this June* is now Standard; the once-required passive (*I was graduated from . . .*) is now old-fashioned, a bit stuffy, and obsolescent. As a transitive verb in such uses as *I graduated college this spring,* however, *graduate* is Nonstandard at best and probably Substandard.

graffiti (*n.*) is an Italian plural meaning "writing or pictures scrawled on walls, floors, and other surfaces." Although Edited English and its Oratorical equivalents usually insist on using it with plural verbs and pronouns, the less Formal and Conversational levels treat *graffiti* as a mass noun and use singular verbs and pronouns. *Graffito* is the Italian singular, and it too is used in Standard English, especially in technical contexts. See FOREIGN PLURALS.

GRAMMAR We use this important word in a number of different ways. *The grammar* of American English is the full system of the language: morphology, syntax, function words, phonology, and intonation, as well as vocabulary—its words and their meanings. The grammar of English is what a child learns to use in the first few years of its life; it is what each of us knows how to use for communication, even if we can't say precisely what it is that we know we know.

A grammar of English, on the other hand, can be any attempt to describe—sometimes with scientific or theoretical purposes, sometimes for pedagogical purposes—how the language works. Scholarly *grammars* include traditional *grammars, functional grammars,* structural *grammars,* and transformational-generative *grammars* (all of which see), to name a few of the more widely recognized kinds. Each has its purposes and its methods. Language textbooks developed for teaching the young are called *grammars* too. These are systems of rules that purport to describe how the language should be used. Frequently they are simplifications of one or another (or a combination) of the scholarly descriptions; sometimes they ignore full description and address only "troubling" aspects of *grammar*. The term *a grammar* may also mean simply "a book containing such a designedly teachable description." The rules of *grammar* of course can refer to rules derived from any of these sources, and frequently the rules are not rules at all, but generalizations. (See also USAGE [1]; RULES AND GENERALIZATIONS.)

We also use the term *grammar* to assess the acceptability of an individual's use of the language; when it fails to meet our expectations, we usually remark on the person's *grammatical* errors: *His grammar was poor; We were put off by her bad grammar.*

Finally, to compound further our difficulties with the word, we frequently talk of the *grammar* of any subject, meaning the elementary principles of that subject or a book that describes them, as in *There's a special grammar of computer use that you'll have to master.*

This guide, when talking of *grammar,* tries to make sure that you know whether it is the system, a particular description of the system, a normative view of acceptable practice, or some other sense of the word *grammar* that is before you.

GRAMMARIAN is the name applied to a scholar or expert in grammatical matters.

GRAMMATICAL AGREEMENT See all entries for AGREEMENT.

GRAMMATICAL AND NATURAL GENDER See GENDER (2).

GRAMMATICAL ERROR, BAD GRAMMAR See GRAMMAR; USAGE (1).

GRAMMATICAL SUBJECT See SUBJECT, GRAMMATICAL.

grapple (*v.*) combines most frequently with the preposition *with,* to indicate the topic or object of the grappling, as in *We grappled with the problem for days.* Occasionally *for, on, over,* or *about* also combines for similar purposes: *The wrestlers grappled for an advantage. The contestants grappled on [over, about] who should go first.*

grateful (*adj.*) combines with *to* and *for: to* indicates the someone or something that is the source or cause of the gratitude; *for* specifies the advantage or benefit received. These combinations can appear separately or together: *She was grateful to us for our contributions.*

gratis (*adv., adj.*) is from Latin ("freely") and means "free" or "freely," "without charge." It is Standard as adverb, as in *They fed us gratis that night,* or adjective, as in *Our meal was gratis.* See FOR FREE.

gratuitous (*adj.*), **gratitude, gratuity** (*nn.*) *Gratitude* and *gratuitous* derive from the same word, the Latin *gratus* ("grace"), but whereas *gratitude* means only "gratefulness, thankfulness," *gratuitous* has two meanings: "free, without charge," now fairly rare, and the much more frequent "uncalled for, unjustified, unnecessary, without good reason," as in *It was a gratuitous insult, quite undeserved.* Context must make clear which meaning you intend. A *gratuity* is a gift for service, a tip. Compare EGREGIOUS; SUPERFLUOUS.

GRAVE ACCENT This mark (`` ` ``), whose name is pronounced either *GRAHV* or *GRAIV*, is the French accent mark that indicates vowel length or quality when printed over the letters *a* or *e* in such words as *chère* or *tout à fait* or *voilà*. Some of the *à la* idioms no longer always print the *grave* accent in American English—for example, *à la mode/a la mode* and *à la carte/a la carte*. See also DIACRITICS.

graving dock See DOCK.

gray, grey (*adj., n.*) Americans spell it *gray* except when they imitate the British *grey*, which is a Standard variant. See SPELLING (1).

graze See BROWSE.

Great Britain See BRITAIN.

Grecian, Greek (*adjs., nn.*) The adjective *Grecian* refers to anything Greek, especially to ancient institutions and artifacts, although it is increasingly being used today of contemporary things. The noun *Grecian* refers to a person of that nationality, although *Greek* is much more commonly encountered as noun for both persons and the language. *Greek,* the adjective, is applied to anything associated with Greece, Greeks, or the Greek Orthodox Church. Two other senses, both Conversational or Informal, are important to Americans: (1) the idiom meaning "incomprehensible," as in *It's all Greek to me* (*Julius Caesar* I.ii.288), and (2) the American use of both noun and adjective to refer to campus fraternities and sororities with Greek names, as well as to their members: *On campus there were fewer Greeks than independents.*

greenhouse effect (*n.*) is now Standard, meaning "the warming of the planet (and resulting physical changes in life on earth) caused by increasing amounts of the so-called *greenhouse gases* (among them, carbon dioxide and carbon monoxide) that trap solar radiation within the earth's envelope."

grey See GRAY.

gridlock (*n., v.*) The noun means "the monstrous urban jam with blocked intersections halting all vehicular traffic," and the verb means "to cause, create, or undergo *gridlock.*" Both uses are Standard, although quite new, and the verb may still seem unfamiliar to some readers.

grieve (*v.*) can combine with several prepositions: *for* is most usual (*The dog grieved for his dead master*), but *about, at, concerning,* and *over* also occur in Standard use, as in *She grieved for days about* [*at, concerning, over*] *her loss.* One relatively new specialized sense of *grieve* can be either transitive or intransitive, although the transitive use is more clearly Standard than the intransitive: it means "to file or bring a grievance under a labor contract," as in *She grieved her new assignment*; *She decided to grieve about her new assignment.*

grievous (*adj.*), **grievously** (*adv.*) Pronounce *grievous* with only two syllables, *grievously* with only three (*GREE-vuhs, GREE-vuhs-lee*). Beware the Substandard *GREE-vee-uhs, GREE-vee-uhs-lee,* and don't let a misspelling reflect that mispronunciation. See also MISCHIEVOUS.

grill (*n., v.*), **grille** (*n.*) Both homophones stem from the Latin word for "a wickerwork gate," but *grill* is the usual spelling for both the noun meaning "a griddle or metal grate on which broiling or other cooking may be done" and the verb meaning "to cook in that fashion." *Grille* is the more common spelling for "the metal screen or grating for the front of a car or for a gate or the front of a fireplace," but *grill* is a Standard variant.

grimace (*n., v.*) Pronounce it either *GRIM-uhs* or *gri-MAIS*.

grinder See SUBMARINE.

grisly, gristly, grizzled (*adjs.*), **grizzly** (*adj., n.*) *Grisly* (pronounced *GRIZ-lee*) means "horrible, gruesome": *The scene of the shootout was grisly enough to satisfy the most bloodthirsty. Gristly* can be a dialectal homophone of *grisly,* but it is based on the word *gristle* and simply means "containing or characterized by *gristle,*" so that it is usually pronounced *GRIS-lee: My steak was very gristly. Grizzled* (*GRIZ-uhld*) and *grizzly* (*GRIZ-lee*) both mean "gray, graying, or partly gray," especially "gray-haired" and so by extension "old or at least more than mature," although *grizzled* is much more frequently used: *The old man's hair and beard were long and grizzly* [*grizzled*]. And so a *grizzly* bear (or *grizzly*) is so named not because it is horrible but because its coat is *grizzled* or grayish. All these are Standard.

groom, bridegroom (*nn.*) *Groom* is Standard both for the person who takes care of horses and as the clipped form of *bridegroom,* even though the latter is apparently a folk etymology from *bryd* ("bride") plus *guma* ("man") in earlier English.

grope (*n.*) can combine with the prepositions *for, after, through, in, into, to, toward,* and *towards,* as in *We groped through* [*in, into*] *the dark hall to* [*toward, towards*] *the faint light* and *We were groping after* [*for*] *some sort of explanation of the mystery.*

grotto (*n.*) has two plurals: *grottoes* and *grottos*. See PLURALS OF NOUNS ENDING IN *-O*.

ground floor See FIRST FLOOR.

ground zero (*n.*) is the Standard technical name for the point on the ground directly above which a nuclear bomb is detonated. It is also a Conversational or Informal term meaning "the beginning, the most elementary starting point."

group See BAND.

GROUP GENITIVE is the name given genitive case constructions such as *The man across the street's dog* and *The governor of New York's campaign*. These are Standard, sometimes awkward, ways to use the genitive in complicated structures; at lower levels, especially of speech, we follow almost ridiculously complicated *group genitives* without much problem: *The girl on the sofa next to the door's mother*.

groupie (*n.*) A *groupie* is a teenaged devotee, usually female, of rock bands and musicians or, more generally, any unquestioning fan of an entertainer, sports figure, or the like. The word is slang, or at best Conversational.

grow (*v.*) of course can mean "increase in size," but it can also mean simply "become," even when the becoming represents a decrease in size or amount. Both *She had grown much taller* and *She seemed to have grown much smaller since I had last seen her* are Standard.

grungy (*adj.*), pronounced *GRUHN-jee*, is a slang term meaning "dirty, disreputable, worn, or unpleasant," as in *The room looked grungy and smelled grungy too*.

gruntle (*v.*), **gruntled** (*adj.*) These are nonce words and lost positives, antonyms of the Standard *disgruntle*, meaning "to upset, to displease," and *disgruntled*, meaning "discontented, sulky."

guarantee, guaranty (*n., v.*) These are interchangeable in meaning. Dictionaries report *guarantee*, noun and verb, always with its primary stress on the final syllable, but *guaranty* with it on the first syllable. All problems are *guaranteed* to disappear if you use only the spelling *guarantee* and pronounce it only *GER-uhn-TEE*.

guerrilla, guerilla (*adj., n.*) Both spellings are Standard. Today the noun refers to an irregular soldier, one not recognized as an official representative of a government, and the adjective (in *guerrilla warfare* or *guerrilla raids* and the like) applies the idea of irregular military action to the modified noun. It is of course never to be confused with *gorilla*, which is reserved for the ape and its human imitators.

guess (*v.*), in locutions such as *I guess I'll go now* and *She guessed she didn't want to see him*, are Standard English, although probably not often employed in the most Formal or Oratorical contexts. Such uses were brought from Britain and kept alive by the new Americans, while atrophying and dying at home. Only recently is *I guess* now once again being used a bit in Britain, presumably borrowed back from the United States.

guesstimate (*n., v.*) This Americanism is a blend (of *guess* and *estimate*) serving as both noun and verb, and it is slang in both functions: *I'd say there are one hundred of them, but it's just a guesstimate. I'll guesstimate their numbers at twice that.*

guff (*n.*) is a slang word meaning "nonsense, foolish or insolent talk," as in *She won't take any more of his guff*.

gunwale, gunnel (*n.*) *Gunwale,* pronounced *GUHN-uhl*, is the Standard spelling of the noun meaning "the upper edge of the side of a boat or ship," and *gunnel* is a Standard variant, reflecting *gunwale's* usual pronunciation.

gussy, gussie (*v.*), **gussied** (*adj.*) *Gussy* (sometimes spelled *gussie*) is a slang or Conversational verb meaning "to dress or decorate in a showy way"; it usually combines with *up*, as in *They gussied up the apartment as best they could in preparation for her visit*. The participial adjective is a frequent predicate adjective (again combining mostly with *up*), as in *She was all gussied up for the dance*.

gut (*n.*) refers to the belly or belly and bowels, as in the Informal and Conversational *I have a pain in my gut*. Figuratively, in the plural, the *guts* are the seat of courage, daring, nerve, and pluck, and the slang term *sand*, as in *She has a lot of guts, and she won't back down*. In this sense the word is Conversational and Informal at best and is therefore frequently and tiresomely replaced by a euphemism and cliché, *intestinal fortitude*. Best advice: use *guts, courage, determination*, or another explicit quality and skip all tired metaphors and frozen figures.

gut feeling, gut course, gut reaction, gut response (*nn.*) Each of these locutions is a slang idiom. *Gut feeling, gut response,* and *gut reaction* describe immediate and instinctive feeling, response, and reaction, relatively uninfluenced by thought. (*Visceral* is sometimes used as a euphemistic synonym for *gut*.) A *gut course* is an academic course that requires little effort from the student.

guttural (*adj., n.*) is spelled with a *u* as the vowel of the second syllable—even though the first two syllables rhyme with *gutter*.

guy (*n., v.*) The noun is Casual as a term of direct address to a man or boy or sometimes as a plural for mixed groups (although some women don't like it) or groups of males or females: *Have you guys seen my briefcase?* The referent is also male or female in uses such as *We need to be able to tell the good guys from the bad guys* and *Are you a good guy or a bad guy?* wherein *good guys* and *bad guys* are specialized terms for heroes and villains, respectively; these uses are Conversational and Informal. The verb *guy* is somewhat literary or old-fashioned in the sense "to tease or make fun of," as in *My friends guyed me unmercifully over my blunder.*

gybe See JIBE.

gymnasium, gym (*n.*) The usual American meaning is "a building or hall equipped for athletic activities and contests," as in *We played volleyball in the gymnasium.* This sense of the word is pronounced *jim-NAI-zee-uhm,* and it is regularly clipped to *gym* (*JIM*) in all but the most Formal and Oratorical uses. The other sense of *gymnasium* is "a secondary school in many European countries," and this sense is pronounced *gim-NAI-zee-uhm* or *gim-NAH-zee-uhm* (there is no clipped English form for this sense). Both senses are Standard.

gynecology, gynaecology (*n.*) These are Standard variant spellings of the branch of medicine that deals with female reproductive matters and diseases. The more common American spelling is *gynecology,* the more usual British spelling, *gynaecology.* Pronounce it *GEI-nuh-KAHL-uh-jee,* although *JIN-uh-KAHL-uh-jee* and *JEI-nuh-KAHL-uh-jee* are also considered Standard. See DIGRAPHS; SPELLING (1).

gyp (*n., v.*) is best limited to Conversational and Informal contexts in its noun senses of "someone who cheats" and "an instance of cheating" and in its verb sense of "to cheat." If, as some dictionaries suggest, the word is a clipped form of *gypsy,* it could well be considered an ethnic slur, but in fact it seems usually not to be so taken.

Gypsy, Gipsy (*n.*), **gipsy, gypsy** (*adj.*) The more usual spelling of both the proper and common nouns is with two *y*'s. A *Gypsy* is member of a wandering people said to have originated in India who now reside in many parts of the world, some of them retaining their itinerant habits and being known as musicians, fortune tellers, tinkers, and horse traders. The common noun describes people and practices thought to reflect some aspect of Gypsy life or character, especially its reputation for wandering and for some kinds of irregular practice. *Gypsy trucker, gypsy barber,* and other adjunct uses of the term suggest unlicensed, nonunion, or itinerant practitioners. See SPELLING (2).

gypsy cab (*n.*) A *gypsy cab* is an unlicensed one permitted to take fares when summoned but not legally permitted to cruise for fares, although so named for apparently frequently doing so.

H

h- In certain regional dialects, *human* is pronounced *YOO-muhn* rather than *HYOO-muhn,* and *Hugh,* although usually pronounced *HYOO,* can also be a homophone of *you.* Even more widespread in some regional dialects is the pronunciation of words spelled with the initial letters *wh-,* which many say as an *hw* sound cluster (as in *HWICH* for *which,* as opposed to *WICH* for *witch*), with a *w* sound, so that the words in each of these pairs, *where/wear, wheel/weal,* and *whine/wine,* are pronounced alike, as *WER, WEEL,* and *WEIN,* respectively. Nearly all Americans pronounce *herb, honor,* and *heir* without the initial *h* sound (*UHRB, AHN-uhr, ER*), and in words such as *historic* the initial *h* sound usually disappears when the sound accommodates to a preceding *n,* as in *It was an historic moment* (*is-TOR-ik*). And most Americans drop the initial *h* sounds from the pronouns *him, her, his,* and *her* at Casual and Impromptu levels when they are relatively unstressed: *"I'll ask 'er." "Give it to 'im." "Tell 'im to call 'is mother."* And in a few words such as *vehement,* they frequently suppress a medial *h* sound, as in this Standard pronunciation of *vehicle: VEE-ik-ul.* See also A; HISTORIC.

haberdasher, haberdashery (*nn.*) In the United States a *haberdashery* is an upscale name for a shop that sells men's furnishings—shirts, hats, ties, and the like—while in Britain a *haberdashery* is the place to buy notions. A *haberdasher* is either the proprietor of the shop or the shop itself, often in the genitive (*I'm going to the haberdasher's*).

habitable, inhabitable (*adjs.*) These synonyms mean "livable, livable in, suitable or fit for living in": *The old homestead is no longer habitable* [*inhabitable*].

HAČEK This accent mark (ˇ) rarely appears in English; instead we usually respell with either *cz* or *ch* the Czech, Slovak, and other Slavic names that use it (*Chekov*, for example). The sound is indeed that of *ch* in English, and phoneticists frequently use the č with a *haček* over it to represent that sound, as in [čərč] for *church*. See also DIACRITICS.

had (*v., aux.*) *Had* is the past tense and past participle of *have*, as in *I had* [*have had*] *dinner at home*. It is also an auxiliary used to make past perfect tenses of verbs: *I had written*. See BE; HAD BETTER; HAD RATHER; HAVE; HAVE GOT; PLUPLUPERFECT TENSE.

had better, had best, as in *You had better* [*best*] *call your mother*, and their contractions, as in *He'd better hurry* and *She'd best mend her ways*, are Standard English idioms, the contractions being Conversational and Semiformal. *You better do your homework* is also Standard if limited to the Casual level and Informal writing, if indeed the idiom is ever written down except in imitation of speech.

had have, had of See PLUPLUPERFECT TENSE; SHOULDA.

had ought, hadn't ought These locutions— *She had ought to ask permission; You hadn't ought to be here*—are Northern (especially New England, New York, and Pennsylvania) regional dialect usages, appropriate there at the lower Conversational levels only (or in the writing that imitates such conversation) and Nonstandard elsewhere. See OUGHT.

had rather, like *had better, had best,* and *would rather,* is a Standard expression: *He had rather* [*would rather*] *she go with him. She had rather* [*would rather*] *stay home*. The contractions of *had* and *would* are of course indistinguishable. See KIND OF; QUALIFIERS.

had to See HAVE GOT TO.

haemophilia, haemorrhage See HEMOPHILIA.

hail (*n., v.*), **hale** (*adj., v.*) These are homophones; the verb *hail* means "to call out to, to welcome, to cheer, or to summon" and combined with *from,* becomes a Standard idiom, meaning "to come from, to have originated in": *We hailed the victor and the victory. She hailed a cab. He hails from Montana. Hale* has only one current sense as a verb, "to compel (someone) to go," as in *Her attorney haled him into court*. The noun *hail* is "a shout or greeting" or "frozen rain." The adjective *hale* means "vigorous, healthy": *He's a hale, well-preserved eighty-year-old.*

hain't is a dialectal contraction of *have not* or *has not,* but it is archaic even there. It is also apparently a variant of *ain't*. In any event, it is Nonstandard. See AIN'T.

hairbrained See HAREBRAINED.

hairdresser See COIFFEUR.

hale See HAIL.

hale and hearty This cliché comes in various spellings, thanks in part to possible confusions of *hail* and *hale* and even more to possible confusions of *hearty* ("full of vigor and enthusiasm") and *hardy* ("strong and durable"). Both seem to fit with the good health and stamina of *hale,* but the original figure was probably with *hearty,* because *hardy* would have been redundant.

half (*adj., n.*), when it is a subject, usually takes a singular verb unless notional agreement with the number of the object of the preposition makes a plural seem sensible: *Half the membership seems satisfied, but I'm afraid half* [*of*] *the members are not*. All these uses of *half* are Standard: *Give him a half piece* [*half a piece*], *half an apple* [*half of an apple, a half apple*]. And in use with verbs such as *cut, slice, saw, divide,* and *break,* though it's logically true that two halves result from these operations, the Standard idiom is usually *cut* [*slice,* etc.] *in half,* with *in halves* used where extra precision or self-conscious logic seems important.

half an eye, see with See SEE WITH HALF AN EYE.

half-breed See MULATTO.

half-mast, half-staff To honor someone who has died, a flag is flown at *half-staff* everywhere except on shipboard, where *half-mast* is the term, according to naval usage, at least. Nevertheless either *half-mast* or *half-staff* is Standard these days to describe any such recognition on land or sea.

hallelujah See ALLELUIA.

ham, pork (*nn.*) In most animals, including humans, the thigh or thigh and buttock may be called the *ham,* but the specialized meatmarket meaning of *ham* is "the cured (by salting, smoking, or another method) meat of the upper part of the hind leg of a hog," and *a ham* is that joint of meat. *Pork* is the generic name for the meat of the hog, usually when fresh rather than cured.

hamburg, burger, cheeseburger, hamburger (*nn.*) A folk etymology has helped us name many sandwiches made of cooked meat, cheese, fish, and the like. The first, of course, was named after the German city *Hamburg,* and ordinarily a *hamburg* (a clipping of its full name) or *hamburger* contains beef, not ham or pork. But the *-burger* clipping has caught on so thoroughly that if venison were to be available tomorrow, *venisonburgers* (or *deerburg[er]s*) would be close behind. *Hamburg* and *hamburger* are also conventional names for ground beef itself.

hamstring (*v.*) is modeled on the strong verb *string:* principal parts are *hamstring, hamstrung, hamstrung.*

hand, at; to hand If you have something *at hand,* it's nearby, within reach, where you can consult or find it easily. If you have something *to hand,* it's even closer, right here where you can lay a hand on it. But *to hand* was overused in business correspondence until it became a cliché: *Yours of the 21st to hand, and . . . .* Today the locution has a very old-fashioned air and is fast becoming archaic. *At hand* is still a current and Standard idiom, perhaps tending toward overuse itself.

handful (*n.*) has two plurals: the more frequent *handfuls* and the equally Standard *handsful.* See PLURALS OF COMPOUND NOUNS.

handicap parking This curious locution illustrates the same accommodation of sounds and spellings as has occurred in phrases such as *ice cream* (which see). *Handicap[ped] parking* is more complicated grammatically, because the parking is *for* the handicapped; it's not the *parking* that is *handicapped.* But idioms do not shrink from that sort of challenge: *handicapped parking* is Standard, and *handicap parking,* although ugly or puzzling to some, soon probably will not cause a raised eyebrow, let alone a hackle.

handicapped See CRIPPLE; DIFFERENTLY ABLED; HANDICAP PARKING; UNDERPRIVILEGED.

handkerchief (*n.*) Pronounce it *HANG-kuhr-chuhf, -chif,* or *-cheef,* although the middle syllable often becomes *-kuh-* in rapid speech and also is Standard. Spell the plural either *handker-*

chiefs or (infrequently) *handkerchieves.* See NOUNS ENDING IN *-F.*

hands, wash one's See WASH UP.

hands full See FULL.

hands-on (*adj.*) describes a situation wherein you learn by taking an active role, as in *a hands-on experience.* The adjective is Standard, but it is suffering from some overuse these days.

hang (*v.*) The principal parts are *hang, hung* or *hanged, hung* or *hanged.* For all senses the past tense and past participle are usually *hung: We hung the new painting in the foyer. I had hung about all week.* Most Edited English and some other levels still insist on *hanged* as past tense and occasionally as past participle when the meaning is "to execute by hanging," as in *They hanged him for her murder; The state has hanged three people this year.* The participial adjective in that sense is always *hanged* (*The hanged man will be buried tomorrow*).

hangar, hanger (*nn.*) A *hangar* is a shed for garaging and repairing aircraft; a *hanger* can be anything suspended, including a small sword, any sort of device from which something is to be suspended, or a wooden, plastic, or wire frame from which a coat, dress, or other article of clothing can be hung to keep it wrinkle-free on a coat rack or in a closet.

hanger-on (*n.*) is a follower or parasite, one always in someone's entourage. The plural is *hangers-on,* and the word is Standard: *All his hangers-on applauded whatever he did.* See PLURALS OF COMPOUND NOUNS.

hangout (*n.*), **hang out** (*v.*) *To hang out* is literally "to lean out, as of a window, or to display by hanging out, as of a flag" and figuratively "to loiter at or frequent," as in *We hung out at the drive-in that summer,* or simply "to do nothing, to lounge about," as in *We weren't doing anything, just hanging out.* That usage is slang, and dictionaries list many other slang and Conversational combined forms and idioms using the verb *hang.* A *hangout* is a place where groups of young people, criminals, or others *hang out.*

hang-up, hangup (*n.*) Usually spelled with a hyphen, *hang-up* is a slang word meaning "a problem" or "a personal or emotional difficulty with which one has had trouble dealing": *She has a hang-up about speaking in public.* The plural is *hang-ups* or *hangups.* See PLURALS OF COMPOUND NOUNS.

hanker (*v.*) is Standard and can take the prepositions *after* and *for,* as in *I've always hankered* *after* [*for*] *a cashmere sweater.* It can also take *to* plus an infinitive, as in *She hankers to learn Spanish.*

hanky-panky (*n.*) means "trickery," "double dealing," or "sexual dalliance" and is limited to Conversational and Informal use: *There was clearly some sort of hanky-panky going on behind that curtain.* See RHYMING COMPOUNDS.

HAPAX LEGOMENON (pronounced *HAI-peks luh-GAH-me-NAHN*) is the term applied to a word that is recorded only once in the work of an author or in the whole of a language. The plural is *hapax legomena.* See FOREIGN PLURALS.

happening (*n.*) A *happening* is an event, especially a noteworthy or dramatic one, or one staged deliberately for theatrical effect, as in *Her parties were always planned to be happenings, intended to be talked about for weeks afterwards.* The word is Standard.

hara-kiri (*n.*) The name for the Japanese ritual suicide is frequently mispronounced and misspelled: it is *HAHR-uh-KIR-ee* or *HAHR-uh-KAHR-ee.* The pronunciation *HER-ee KER-ee* is widely used, but this is Common English, not Standard.

harangue, tirade (*nn.*) Each word means "a long-winded, ranting speech," but a *harangue* need not be threatening or abusive, whereas a *tirade* always is.

harass (*v.*) means "to worry, annoy, pester, wear out." Spell it with one *r* and two *s*'s, and pronounce it either *huh-RAS* or *HER-uhs.*

hard (*adv., adj.*), **hardly** (*adv.*) *Hard* as adjective (*a hard time*) poses no problem. *Hard* is also a flat adverb, however, meaning "strenuously, with determination, strongly," as in *We tried hard.* It is not interchangeable with *hardly,* which means "scarcely": *We hardly tried.* *Hardly* can also (in British English especially) mean "severely, cruelly, harshly," and that sense can sometimes create ambiguity, as in *She was hardly used in the campaign,* meaning either "her talents were scarcely employed" or "she was harshly treated during the campaign." Note that the position of *hardly* can control—*She was used hardly* calls only for the "harshly" sense— but a shift in diction (*scarcely used, ill-used,* or *underused,* for example) can do an even surer job of avoiding ambiguity.

hardback (*n.*), **hardcover, paperback, softback, softcover** (*adjs., nn.*), **hardbacked, paperbacked** (*adjs.*) A book with board-and-cloth cover, in contrast to one with a flexible paper cover (a *paperback, softback,* or *softcover* or a *paperback*[*ed*], *softback,* or *softcover book*), is called a *hardback* or *hardcover* or a *hardbacked* or *hardcover book.* The words are Standard.

hard copy means "a copy printed on paper, as opposed to one stored in or displayed on tape, on a computer terminal, or in microform." The term is Standard. A *hard copy* is also called a *paper copy.*

hardcover See HARDBACK.

hard disk is a computer term, contrasting with *floppy disk.* Both kinds of disk are used to store information magnetically for use on a computer; *hard disks* can hold much more information than floppies. The term is perhaps still jargon, but it is close to being Standard today. See DISK.

hardly See HARD.

hardly, can't; couldn't hardly These two are always classed and punished as double negatives, even though *hardly* ("scarcely") isn't a negative at all, and the negative probably makes them less forceful than *hardly* by itself would be. Even so, both locutions are Substandard, and most Standard users consider them shibboleths.

hardly . . . when, hardly . . . than *Hardly had I fallen asleep when a crash woke me* is Standard; *Hardly had I fallen asleep than a crash woke me* is usually considered Nonstandard, not acceptable in Edited English, and at best limited to the Conversational levels. See also SCARCE.

hard-nosed (*adj.*), meaning "stubborn, hardheaded, practical, unsentimental" is Conversational: *Her father is a hard-nosed pragmatist.*

hard put, hard put to it (*adj.*) both mean "scarcely able," "pushed to the extreme," as in *We were hard put* [*to it*] *to collect enough money.* The idioms are both Standard, but the shorter form is much more frequent.

hard sell, soft sell (*nn.*) These are idioms. A *hard sell* is high-pressure salesmanship, and salespeople who work that way are often called *hard sells.* *Soft sell* is the antonym. These terms are Standard in all but Formal or Oratorical contexts.

hardy, hearty (*adjs.*) These two sound much alike and can easily be mistaken for each other in the spoken language. *Hardy* means "strong, daring, able to withstand stress" and, of plants, "able to live through the winter." *She's a hardy person, at eighty-two still caring for her own house and garden.* *Hearty* means "cordial, enthusiastic, unrestrained, vigorous,'' as in *She gave us a hearty welcome followed by an equally hearty dinner*. See HALE AND HEARTY.

harebrained, hairbrained (*adj.*) Spell it *harebrained* (with a brain like a hare's), meaning "foolish, reckless, giddy." *Hairbrained* is a frequent misspelling traceable to a folk etymology.

hark, hark back, harken back, hearken back (*vv.*) *Hark* means "listen, pay attention," as in *Hark! Was that the phone?* It has sometimes been labeled archaic and poetic, but it is still Standard in American English. *Hark back* means "return to an earlier topic of discussion," "pay attention to something discussed earlier," as in *Hark back to what we said at the outset*. *Hearken* (*harken* is a variant) means to "listen, pay attention," just as *hark* does, and *hearken back* and *harken back* mean "to revert to something said earlier and to heed it." All are in Standard use, although sometimes with a somewhat studied flavor.

has got See HAVE GOT.

hassle, hassel (*n., v.*) The usual spelling is now *hassle*. The noun means "a loud quarrel, a fight, a state of confusion, or a troublesome situation." *There was a prodigious hassle at the meeting before things calmed down.* The verb means "to argue, fight, or annoy," as in *She hasseled me all evening about my being late*. Both words are rapidly gaining status: the noun is probably Standard, although some dictionaries still label it Informal, and Edited English may still reject it in some Formal contexts; the verb is still probably slang, although some consider it Conversational at least.

have (*v., aux.*) is a full verb meaning "to possess," as in *I have my new car now*. It is also an auxiliary used to make the perfect tense of most verbs: *She has lost her keys*. See HAVE GOT; POSSESS.

have got, have gotten This is the standard distinction in American speech: *I've got some money* means "I have some money"; *I've gotten some money* means "I've obtained some money." As the contractions suggest, these locutions are primarily spoken. *Have got* and *have gotten* are appropriate in Edited English, but alternatives such as those in *I have some money* and *I have obtained some money* still are much used in Formal writing and at the Oratorical level. See GET.

have got to, got to, had to, have to *I have got to leave* and *I've got to leave* mean "I must leave," but they are more emphatic, more forceful than *I have* [*HAF*] *to leave*, particularly if *got* is heavily stressed. As the contractions suggest, *I've got to leave* and the elliptical or clipped *I got to leave*, both meaning "must," are primarily Conversational. And *I got to leave* is also ambiguous: it means either "I must leave" or "I was permitted to leave." See GET.

With *to* and *two, have* and *has* are almost always pronounced differently and are each in fact two different words: *HAF* and *HAS* with *to* are an auxiliary meaning "must"; *HAV* and *HAZ* with *two* are the verb meaning "possess." Note the possibility of ambiguity in writing.

have sex is an idiom, one of several euphemisms meaning "to engage in sexual intercourse." Like most such euphemisms, it sometimes attracts more attention with its illogical coyness than another locution might do with matter-of-factness. But manners here are under some duress. See PROFANITY; VULGAR.

have the hands full See FULL.

have to See HAVE GOT TO.

havoc See WREAK.

he, he or she, he/she, him, him or her, him/her, his, his or her, his/her, his/hers, (s)he, s/he, their, them, they These represent various schemes for dealing with the problem of generic pronouns, a problem (in sentences such as *Everybody hung up his* [*his/her, their*] *coat*[*s*]) that antedates the current concern with the use of the masculine singular as generic. See also AGREEMENT OF INDEFINITE PRONOUNS AND OTHER SINGULAR NOMINALS WITH VERBS AND OTHER PRONOUNS; AGREEMENT OF SUBJECTS AND VERBS (3); EPICENE PRONOUNS; INCLUSIVE LANGUAGE; SEXIST LANGUAGE.

head, head up (*v.*) You can *head a corporation* or you can *head up a corporation*; these days both are Standard. Some commentators, however, consider the *up* an excrescence, acceptable only (if at all) in Informal and Conversational use, and some Edited English will not allow it. Assess your readers' expectations carefully.

head over heels isn't logical for "upside down"; *heels over head* was the original, the more logical, and the more graphic expression. But the cliché is *head over heels* these days, and it's a Standard idiom.

headquarter (*v.*) is usually transitive, as in *He headquarters his company miles from the factory*, but can also be intransitive, as in *My unit headquartered in a suburb of Paris*.

headquarters (*n.*) is both singular and plural and therefore takes either a singular or a plural verb: *This headquarters is too far from the action. Our headquarters are too small for our numbers.* See AGREEMENT OF SUBJECT AND VERBS (3).

healthy, healthful (*adjs.*) *Healthy* means "having good health, traceable to good health," as in *He's a healthy boy,* and *healthful* means "salutary, conducive to good health," as in *She eats nothing but healthful foods.* Much Edited English and some conservative practice tries to maintain those distinctions, but most Standard English now accepts *healthy* as readily substitutable for *healthful,* as in *Milk is a healthy thing to drink. Healthy* also is used in the sense of "vigorous, thriving, great," as in *I learned a healthy respect for his left hook*; some argue that this sense is Colloquial, but there is considerable evidence that it is Standard.

heap (*n.*), in the expression *a heap of,* literal (*a heap of dirty laundry*) or figurative (*a heap of misery*), is singular and Standard, although the figurative is sometimes labeled Informal or Conversational. The plural *heaps* is always Casual or Informal, in expressions such as *heaps of trouble, heaps of time.* The adverbial use of *a heap,* as in *She helped us a heap last night,* sounds rural and is certainly limited to Casual level or its written imitation.

hearers See AUDIENCE.

hearken back See HARK.

heartrending, heart-rendering (*adjs.*) The real adjective is *heartrending,* meaning "heart-tearing" or "heartbreaking" and hence "grief-causing." *Heart-rendering* is a nonce word, possibly a malapropism, but more likely a deliberate jocularity.

hearty See HARDY.

heave (*v.*) The principal parts are *heave, heaved* or *hove, heaved* or *hove. Heaved* is the usual past tense and past participle meaning "to rise and fall" (*Her shoulders heaved with her sobbing*), "to throw" (*His mother had heaved out his beer can collection*), or "to vomit" (*The dog had heaved all over the rug*). *Hove* occurs in nautical uses (*They hove to until morning; We hove* [*heaved*] *him a line*), and it also occurs in the idiom meaning "came" or "appeared," as in *The ship hove into sight about noon.* All these senses are Standard, although the "vomit" sense is Conversational at best.

Hebrew (*n.*) is the name of the language, and the plural is the name of the people of Abraham and Moses, but the term for the modern Jewish person is *Jew* and for the people, *Jews.* Used to refer to a person, the term *Hebrew* may come across as a slur or as an ill-advised genteelism. See also ETHNIC SLURS AND TERMS OF ETHNIC OPPROBRIUM.

HEBREW PLURALS See FOREIGN PLURALS; YIDDISH WORDS IN AMERICAN ENGLISH.

heck (*expletive*) *Heck* is a euphemism for *hell,* and like *darn*[*ed*] for *damn*[*ed*] is considerably less frequent than it once was, now that the originals are getting wider use. But *Where the heck do you think you're going!* is still familiar and Standard Casual or Informal American English.

hectic (*adj.*) today means primarily "filled with confusion, haste, and excitement," as in *We had a very hectic few minutes until we had subdued the sail.* An older sense, originally having to do with a recurrent fever or other wasting disease that caused a red face, is archaic at best and probably obsolete except in the frozen figure of a complexion *of hectic red.* Only the figurative sense of *feverish* (as in *feverish activity*) is in *hectic's* current cluster of meanings.

height (*n.*) is spelled today without the final *-th* that analogy with words like *eighth* might lead you to expect. American English has two Standard pronunciations, however: the conventional and usual *HEIT* and a surprisingly common variant, *HEITTH,* with a *th* sound that is not reflected in the spelling at all.

heir, heiress (*nn.*) The initial *h-* is always silent: *ER, ER-es.* See H-.

heist (*n., v.*) A *heist* is a holdup, a robbery. The verb means "to perform such a holdup"; apparently it is a dialectal variant of *hoist,* in the sense of "to lift (someone's watch or wallet)." All uses of *heist* are slang.

helicopter (*n., v.*) is pronounced either *HEL-uh-KAHP-tuhr* or, occasionally, *HEEL-uh-KAHP-tuhr. HEEL-ee-o-KAHP-tuhr* is a Vulgar mispronunciation based on or leading to a surprisingly frequent misspelling, *heliocopter.* Both are shibboleths.

help See AID (2); CANNOT HELP BUT; SUCCOR.

HELPING VERBS See AUXILIARIES.

helpmate, helpmeet (*nn.*) This curious pair is really a single word: *helpmeet* is a misreading of Genesis's description of Eve as being "a help meet" for Adam—that is, "suitable for him." The phrase was mistaken in the King James version for one word, and then folk etymology tried to fix what made no sense by changing the word to *helpmate,* what a spouse should be. Both words are Standard today, even so.

hemophilia, haemophilia, haemorrhage, hemorrhage (*nn.*) The spellings beginning *hemo-* are American; the *haemo-* versions are chiefly British. The first syllables rhyme with *dream* or occasionally *stem.* See DIGRAPHS; LIGATURES.

hence See FROM HENCE.

he or she See HE.

hep See HIP.

her (*pron.*) is the possessive and objective case of the feminine singular personal pronoun. See HE; IT'S ME.

herb (*n.*), **herbaceous** (*adj.*), **herbage** (*n.*), **herbal** (*adj., n.*) Most but not all Americans pronounce the basic noun *UHRB,* with the initial *h-* silent; some Americans and most Britons pronounce it *HUHRB.* Each of the other words also has two pronunciations: some Americans pronounce the initial *h-* in *herbaceous* and *herbal,* and the variants with their silent *h* seem to have slightly lower frequencies. *Herbage,* however, is usually pronounced without the *h.* See H-.

here is, here are When a dummy subject such as *here* (which can also be an adverb) begins a sentence, the verb will agree with the real subject that follows: *Here is the key. Here are the keys.* See AGREEMENT; THERE IS.

hern See ABSOLUTE POSSESSIVE PRONOUNS.

hero See SUBMARINE.

heroic (*n.*) is relatively rare and specialized, meaning usually "a *heroic* poem"; the plural, *heroics,* however, has two meanings: *heroics* means first simply "*heroic* actions," as in *The firefighter's heroics were widely praised,* and second "showily *heroic* performance," this one clearly pejorative, as in *His heroics were carefully and thoroughly publicized by his agent.* In sports reporting, however, the term is generally used without sarcasm.

hero sandwich See SUBMARINE.

hers (*pron.*) This absolute possessive pronoun has no apostrophe.

herself See MYSELF; REFLEXIVE PRONOUNS.

he/she See HE.

hesitant (*adj.*) can combine with the prepositions *about* or *in:* *She is hesitant about applying. She is hesitant in getting involved.* It can also combine with *to* plus an infinitive, as in *We were hesitant to get involved;* better here, however, would be to shift to the verb: *We hesitated to get involved.*

heterosexual See HOMOSEXUAL.

hiccup, hiccough (*n., v.*) There are two Standard spellings but only one Standard pronunciation, *HIK-uhp.* See VARIANT SPELLINGS.

hidden agenda (*n.*) means "a concealed purpose" and suggests deviousness. It is a Standard cliché.

hierarchy, bureaucracy (*nn.*) These two words, and others that refer to groups in power, are usually Standard in those senses, although they frequently appear in contexts where, like *brass*— as in *What will be the reaction of the big brass to his outburst?*—they seem more nearly Conversational and Informal and even have a suggestion of slang. Watch your tone with both.

high (*n.*) has several Standard meanings: "an area of high atmospheric pressure" (*a high over the Ohio valley*), "a record upper level on any scale" (*a new high for the market this year*), "top gear in an automobile transmission" (*She shifted into high*), "a figurative reference to heaven" (*Her prayers must have been heard on high*). And there is a slang sense, referring to "a stimulated state, literally drug induced, but figuratively induced by excitement, success, or the like": *We were still on a high from our last win.*

high, highly (*advs.*) These two adverbs are rarely interchangeable in use. The flat adverb *high* seems most often to apply to elevation: you climb *high* but praise *highly*; you aim *high* and live *high,* but you're *highly* successful, *highly* praised, or *highly* esteemed. *Highly* modifies adjectives usually and is also used after certain verbs to express enthusiasm: *She thought highly of his work.* One spot where *high* and *highly* do seem interchangeable is before the participial adjective *priced* (*a high-priced car/a highly priced car*); one other is before *placed* (*a high-placed official/a highly placed official*), although *high-placed* is less frequent.

hijack (*n., v.*), **hijacker** (*n.*) The verb (the variant spelling *high jack* is fading fast in favor of *hijack*) means "to steal a vehicle and its contents and occupants in transit" and especially now "to seize control of an aircraft or other transport." The agentive ending gives us *hijacker,* and both that noun and the verb, which are still labeled Informal or Colloquial by some dictionaries, seem now to be Standard. The noun *hijack,* as in *The hijack took place just before the scheduled landing at Rome,* is probably still Informal; the gerund *hijacking* would be in that example Standard.

hike (*n.*, *v.*) The noun meaning "an increase, a raising or pulling up," as in *a hike in prices* or *a wage hike*, and the verb meaning "to raise or pull up," as in *They hiked prices again* and *He hiked up his trousers and strode to the next tee*, are still Conversational and Informal, but they are beginning to appear in some Edited English.

him is the objective case form of the masculine third person singular personal pronoun. See HE; IT'S ME.

him/her, him or her See HE.

himself See MYSELF; REFLEXIVE PRONOUNS.

hinder (*v.*), when it combines with prepositions, usually takes *from*, as in *My job hinders me from spending as much time outdoors as I'd like*, but can take *in* or *by*, as in *I won't let my other responsibilities hinder me in my practicing* and *She won't be hindered by the new requirements*.

hindrance, hinderance (*n.*) *Hindrance* (pronounced with only two syllables) is overwhelmingly the Standard spelling; *hinderance* (with three syllables) is becoming rare, and most desk dictionaries no longer give it as a variant. When combined with a preposition, *hindrance* usually takes *to* or *in* (*His stutter was only a mild hindrance to* [*in*] *his public speaking*), but it occasionally occurs with *of* (*No arthritic hindrance of movement was going to keep him idle*).

hint (*n.*, *v.*) The noun, in its meaning "a small bit of advice," "a tip," as in *Here are some household hints that may help you*, is a cliché, probably journalese. Curiously enough, such *hints* are overt and explicit instructions, not at all "indirect suggestions," the other sense of *hint*.

The verb can take the prepositions *at* and *of*: *She hinted at dark secrets. Her words hinted of desperate doings still to come.* Combinations also occur with *about* and *concerning*: *He had hinted about* [*concerning*] *her reputation before her joining the club.*

hip, hep (*adjs.*) This word *hip* (*hep* was an earlier and now ancient-sounding form of this slang word) means "alert, up-to-the-minute, knowing," as in *In my teens, I was really hip* and *She was hip to all the latest language fads*, is also found in the slang idiom *to get hip to*, meaning "to become aware of and knowing about," as in *You have to get hip to the latest clothes*. Most such slang can turn elderly and dated in an incredibly short time.

hippie, hippy (*n.*) is the term applied to the 1960s' flower children and their drugs, long hair, communal living, and music. Many of its details have faded, however, and you should make certain that context helps. But though the sixties are over, the term has bred many another, and new variations seem to appear weekly, now primarily as acronyms. See YUPPIE.

hippopotamus (*n.*) The plurals are *hippopotamuses* and *hippopatami*, the first having more general use, the second, more technical use. See FOREIGN PLURALS.

hippy See HIPPIE.

his (*pron.*) is the masculine third person possessive singular personal pronoun and also is an absolute possessive pronoun. See APOSTROPHE (2); CASE (1); HE.

his/her, his/hers See HE.

hisn See ABSOLUTE POSSESSIVE PRONOUNS.

his or her See HE.

Hispanic (*adj.*, *n.*), **Hispanic-American** (*adj.*, *n.*) The adjective *Hispanic* means "Spanish, Portuguese" or "referring to anything or anyone *Hispanic*": *All Hispanic languages from both hemispheres belong to the Romance language group*. The nouns apply specifically to Spanish-speaking people of Latin-American origins who now live in the United States. The terms seem to be acceptable to all.

hisself (*pron.*) *Hisself* is a Substandard form of the reflexive and emphatic pronoun *himself*. It occurs almost exclusively in speech and is used as a shibboleth against all inadvertent users except very small children. See REFLEXIVE PRONOUNS; THEIRSELVES.

historic, historical (*adjs.*) These two overlap in part, but most readers and hearers will perceive a general distinction: *historic* means generally "important in history," as in *It was a* [*an*] *historic occasion of great significance*; *historical* means "about history, relating to history," as in *Historical novels are my favorite reading*, and "in chronological order," as in *Historical linguistics traces languages over time*. But *historical* too is occasionally used to mean "important in history," so sometimes you will find both *a* [*an*] *historical occasion* and *a* [*an*] *historic occasion*. Best advice: try to maintain the distinction between *historic* and *historical*. Note too that although pronunciation of the initial *h-* in both words can lead to a choice of *a* or *an*, Edited English insists on *a*. See A and H- for an explanation of the phenomenon.

HISTORICAL PRESENT TENSE is the name given the use of the present tense in narrative to impart a sense of breathless immediacy and Conversational directness: *I get to the office* on Tuesday, and I find a note on my desk. So I reach for the phone and call Mary. Nobody answers. It is a useful device, but be careful: it can create an air of thoughtless disorganization that may not serve some purposes.

histrionics See HYSTERICS.

hit (*n., v.*) Most uses of the verb and noun are Standard, but note the limitations on these other senses of the verb: "To arrive at a place," as in *We hit Chicago about nightfall,* is Conversational, as is *My stocks hit a new low yesterday* and *Her comments really hit home. To hit the books,* meaning "to study," is slang; so is *to hit someone up for something,* meaning "to ask someone for something." Various baseball and cardplaying uses are similarly limited to particular special audiences. The noun also has several Standard senses, plus some Conversational or Informal senses too, such as "a witty or insulting remark," as in *He got home a sharp hit with that observation.* Conversational or Informal too is the use of *hit* meaning "an instant popular or box office success," used of plays, songs, books, movies, and the like. Slang uses of the noun include "a murder," as in *The mob made a hit on that storekeeper,* "a dose of a drug or of liquor," as in *She needed a hit right away.* And again there are many baseball and other gameplaying uses of the noun, all of which must be carefully attuned to audience and situation.

hither (*adv., adj.*), **thither, whither** (*advs.*) These somewhat quaint or old-fashioned adverbs mean respectively "to here, or to this place," as in *We moved hither from Chicago*; "to there or to that place," as in *We moved thither from New York*; and "to where or wherever or whatever place," as in *At Memphis, whither we had gone for a vacation, we met some friends. Hither* is also used in a cliché with *yon,* meaning "here and there," as in *We ran hither and yon but saw nothing of them.* Again, the sound is either old-fashioned or quaintly literary. *Whither* is used figuratively and in a familiar rhetorical convention as a one-word way of saying "Where will it or they go or end?" as in *Whither the commercial networks now? Hither* is also used as an adjective meaning "near," as in *The house was on the hither side of that little village,* and *thither* means "on the other, farther away side," as in *We climbed the thither face of the mountain.* All these uses are Standard.

hitherto, thitherto (*advs.*) Respectively, they mean "until now" and "until then," as in *She*

is a hitherto unknown singer; We saw her yesterday, but thitherto we had never encountered her. Both words are Standard, but although *hitherto* is quite frequently used, *thitherto* is rare and old-fashioned.

hit list, hit man (*nn.*) These compounds have until fairly recently been underworld argot but both now are Conversational and Informal: a *hit list* is a list of people or organizations to be wiped out or at least opposed and injured or, by extension, a list of proposed sources to be approached in fund raising. A *hit man* is a person hired to murder someone.

hoagie See SUBMARINE.

hoard (*n., v.*), **horde** (*n.*) Of these homophones, the noun *hoard* refers to a hidden collection of treasure or supplies, and the verb *hoard* means "to collect and hide away such a reserve of money or things." The noun *horde* means "a wandering or nomadic tribe" and more generally now "any mob or large group of people, especially one in motion." The term is pejorative: a *horde* of this sort is probably dangerous.

Hobson's choice is no choice at all. Thomas Hobson (1544?–1631), a Cambridge livery stableman, rented his horses in the order of their closeness to the door; you took the next one in line or none at all. The expression is a frozen figure.

hoi polloi is a Greek tag meaning "the common people, the rabble, the masses." One usage issue is whether you should use *the* with *hoi polloi* in English, and the answer seems to be you may if you wish. Most people no longer know Greek, and *the hoi polloi* is now simply an English cliché. Of more moment is a later development, an apparently ignorant use of *hoi polloi* to mean "the rich and highborn." Avoid that one no matter how much you hear or see it. It is a splendid evidence of the wisdom of avoiding foreign phrases you do not thoroughly understand.

hold See AHOLD.

holdup (*adj., n.*), **hold up** (*v.*) The noun, meaning "a robbery at gunpoint or the like," is a one-word compound. The verb, meaning "to conduct such a robbery," as in *He plans to hold up a bank,* is always two words and is a combined form, not a compound. The adjective, as in *the holdup man,* is another one-word compound (and also is part of a second compound with *man*).

holocaust, Holocaust (*nn.*) The word began with and may still retain a specialized meaning, "a burnt offering," and from there it has generalized and retained a second meaning, "huge destruction of life, especially but not solely by fire"; this sense is frequently employed with reference to the bombing firestorms that destroyed much of Hamburg and Dresden in World War II, as well as to the fear of *nuclear holocaust*. Finally, the word specialized again (and in this use is often capitalized and preceded by *the* in English), meaning "the genocidal killing of millions of Jews by the Nazis during World War II."

hom-, homo- (*prefixes*) The Greek prefix means "the same or similar," and English uses it in dozens of words, such as *homophone, homograph, homonym,* and *homosexual.* The Latin word meaning "man" is also used as the first element in English compounds, such as *hominoid* and *hominid,* but the Greek prefix has provided many more English words than the Latin one has.

home 1 (*adv.*) is Standard when used with verbs of motion, such as *run, go,* or *return,* as in *I ran [went, returned] home after lunch,* but it is also Standard meaning "at home," where no motion is involved, as in *She's been home all day.* Some Americans (especially at more elevated levels) and many of the British use *at home* for this purpose.

home 2, house (*nn.*) Realtors have turned *home* into a euphemism: no realtors worth their salt will sell *houses,* only warm, emotion-filled *homes.* Edgar Guest did much damage earlier in the century when he persuaded some newspaper readers that "It takes a heap o' livin' to make a house a home." Nor is this the only euphemistic entanglement the highly charged word *home* has been involved in: the terms *convalescent home, retirement home,* and *nursing home* are in such universal use that the more explicit, informative *asylum, convalescent hospital, retirement center,* or *nursing hospital* are no longer current. Much tugging and hauling is ill-concealed in this double use of the word: *We wanted to keep mother at home, but the doctor said she'd be better off in a home.*

home in on is an idiom meaning "to guide or be guided, as by radar, to a destination," as in *We finally picked up the radio signal and were able to home in on the end of the runway.* But see HONE IN ON.

homey, homely (*adjs.*) *Homey* means "home-like," with special emphasis on the familiar, unpretentious, and cozy, as in *The room was warm and homey, the furniture worn but comfortable, and the light just right. Homely* can mean "homelike" too, but the more common meanings today are "inelegant, unattractive, plain, not handsome." Both senses appear in this sentence: *She had all the homely virtues, but alas, her person was homely too.*

homo (*n.*) The Standard sense is that of the Latin word itself, the genus name for "man" (plural *homines*), and most familiar in combinations such as *homo sapiens. Homo* is also a slang term, a clipped version of *homosexual;* it is always a derogatory or contemptuous word.

homo- See HOM-.

homoerotic See HOMOSEXUAL.

homogeneous, homogenous (*adjs.*) *Homogeneous* (pronounced *ho-mo-JEEN-yuhs*) means "of the same kind or structure, of like composition": *It was a homogeneous community, its members holding remarkably similar values. Homogenous* (pronounced *ho-MAH-jen-uhs* or *huh-MAH-jen-uhs*) means "similar in makeup because similar in descent": *These animals are homogenous, as their similar physiology makes clear.* The antonyms are, respectively, *heterogeneous* and *heterogenous.*

HOMOGRAPH, HOMONYM, HOMOPHONE *Homographs* are words spelled alike but with different meanings and usually with different pronunciations (*lead,* v. [*LEED*], meaning "to conduct," and *lead,* n. [*LED*], the name of the metal). *Homophones* are words pronounced alike but different in spelling and meaning (*to, two,* and *too*). *Homonyms,* a more general term, are words spelled or pronounced alike but having different meanings: *soar* and *sore* are one sort of *homonym; gore,* meaning "the tapered piece of cloth in a skirt," and *gore,* meaning "blood," are examples of another sort. *Bow,* v., "to bend at the waist," and *bow,* n., "the front end of a boat," are *homonyms,* and some would add the differently pronounced *bow,* meaning variously "the weapon for shooting arrows," "the decorative knot used in hair ribbons and *bow* ties," "the long, slender rod strung with horsehairs used to play stringed instruments."

homosexual, gay, heterosexual, homoerotic, lesbian (*adjs., nn.*) Functional shift permits each of these adjectives to function as a noun as well. *Homosexual* describes a tendency to feel sexual desire for a member of the same sex, and a *homosexual* is a person with such a tendency. *Homoerotic* is a synonym for *homosexual. Het-*

erosexual describes the tendency to feel sexual desire for the opposite sex, and a *heterosexual* is a person with such a tendency. *Lesbian* refers to *homosexual* relations between women, and a *lesbian* is a woman so inclined. *Gay* means "homosexual," specifically "homosexual tendencies in a man"; a *gay* is a *homosexual* man. All these terms are Standard English. See also GAY.

Hon. See ABBREVIATIONS; HONORABLE.

hone in on is an erroneous version of *home in on*, attributed to George Bush among others.

honky, honkie, honkey (*n.*) These are variant spellings of the same Vulgar slang word (plural: *honkies*) meaning "a white person." It may be an alteration of the ethnic slur *hunky* (Hungarian), but its origin is still uncertain. *Honky* and its variant spellings are considered to be racist language and are therefore taboo in Standard English.

honor (*v.*), when combined with a preposition, usually takes either *by* or *with*: *They honored her by naming a park after her. They honored him with a reception.* Other prepositions occasionally appear as well: *I was honored at their remembering. She was honored for bravery. He was honored in receiving the award.* Note that *honor* in all meanings and functions (and as a component of other words) is always pronounced without the initial *h-* (see H-).

Honorable (*adj.*) Though more used in Britain than in the United States, this honorific continues to have a certain vogue among Americans, especially in political life. This last point may account for the term's frequent use ironically, sarcastically, pejoratively. Abbreviated as *Hon.*, it is usually used with *the*: *The Hon.[orable] John J. Jones.* See ABBREVIATIONS; REVEREND.

honorable, honorary, honorific (*adjs.*), **honorarium, honoree** (*nn.*) *Honorable* means "worthy of honor," "being honest"; *honorary* is applied to anything given as an honor only, such as an *honorary* degree (as distinguished from an earned one) or an *honorary* office that requires no duties; *honorific* means "showing respect" (and functional shift makes it a noun, meaning "any term or title bestowed out of respect"); an *honorarium* is a sum given in payment of whose value the professional value of whose work is not otherwise specified (its plurals are either *honorariums* or *honoraria*; see also SALARY); an *honoree* is someone being honored. All these terms are Standard. See FOREIGN PLURALS.

hoof (*n.*) Pronounce it either *HUF* or *HOOF*. Plurals are either *hoofs* (*HUFS* or *HOOFS*) or *hooves* (pronounced either *HOOVZ* or *HUVZ*). See NOUNS ENDING IN *-F*.

hooky, hookey (*n.*) is part of an idiom, to play hooky, which means "to be a truant, to *hook* [escape] school." Its plurals are *hookeys* or *hookies,* and neither is much used. *Hooky* was once slang, but it has lasted so well that it is now Standard in its idiom.

hooraw, hooray See HURRAH.

hope (*n.*), when combined with a preposition usually takes either *of* or *for*, as in *There's little hope of his passing the course; there's little hope for her, either. In, on,* and *that* clauses can also occur with *hope,* especially in the idioms *in* [*the*] *hope*[*s*] *of, with* [*the*] *hope*[*s*] *of,* and *in* [*the*] *hope*[*s*] *that,* as in *She tried again, in* [*with*] *the hope*[*s*] *of persuading them* and *She did it in* [*the*] *hope*[*s*] *that she'd succeed.*

hopefully (*adv.*) is a sentence adverb that has raised the hackles of some conservatives, but probably its overuse has made most of the trouble; it had been a perfectly good sentence adverb for generations before the recent objections were heard. Those who don't like it usually urge that *I hope that* or *It is hoped that* be used instead, but *hopefully* is in fact Standard, just as are most other sentence adverbs (which see).

horde See HOARD.

horrid, horrible (*adjs.*), **horridly, horribly** (*advs.*) These pairs are synonyms, meaning "frightful, unpleasant, very bad" and "frightfully, unpleasantly, very badly," respectively: *They had a horrid* [*horrible*] *quarrel. They quarreled horridly* [*horribly*]. The chief distinction is with the adverbs: only *horribly* is used regularly as an intensifier: *I have a horribly bad cold.*

hors d'oeuvre (*n.*) is a French name (plural: *hors d'oeuvres*) for *appetizer(s)*, such as served before or at the beginning of a meal. Pronounce it *or-DUHRV* (plural: *or-DUHRVZ*, unless you try it in French (*or-DUHVR*). See FOREIGN PHRASES; FOREIGN PLURALS.

horse opera, oater (*nn.*) are terms for *Westerns,* the romances—novels, plays, and movies—about cowboys and rustlers and the American West of the late nineteenth century. *Horse opera,* like *soap opera,* is now Standard in all but the most Oratorical and Formal contexts; *oater* remains slang and appears to be fading.

hose, hosier, hosiery (*nn.*) *Hose* were originally garments that covered the body from the waist down, like today's pantyhose or tights. The term was also applied to some other garments as well but now refers to various leg coverings, including socks, stockings, footlets, and pantyhose or tights. *Hosiery* is a generic term for these items and similar knitwear, a term used mainly by the British and by toney American retailers of such items. The British retailer is a *hosier*.

hospitable (*adj.*) has two Standard pronunciations, each in wide use: *HAHS-pit-uh-bul* and *hah-SPIT-uh-bul*.

host (*v.*), as in *to host a party,* has recently been attacked as journalese, apparently on the assumption that it is a recent functional shift from the noun. It has been Standard as a verb since the Renaissance, and the uproar was and remains pointless.

house See HOME (2).

househusband, houseperson (*nn.*) *Househusband* was made on analogy with *housewife* and is a relatively new term to describe the husband who stays at home and does the domestic work. The zeal for inclusive language has also given us *houseperson,* which is now in at least one desk dictionary. Since advertisers and food page editors now need an inclusive word for addressing the person who runs the house, *houseperson* too may prosper, at least in that kind of speech and writing.

hove See HEAVE.

how (*conj.*), meaning "that," as in *She told us how she had left home to seek her fortune* and *I see how the president is going to London,* has long been Standard, although some commentators believe it is now being limited more and more to Conversational and Informal use. See also AS HOW.

how come is a Casual or Impromptu idiom meaning "Why," "How is it that," or "How does it happen that," as in *How come you took so long?* It occurs in writing that imitates conversation but is not usual in Edited English and may be a contraction of *How does it come about that.* . . .

however (*adv., subord. conj.*) The adverb can be placed variously in the sentence, even at the beginning, although—like *moreover, furthermore, yet, also,* etc.—it is sometimes more graceful later in the sentence: *However long he wants to stay will be fine. I believe, however, that it won't do. The need, however, is here now. However did you get him to agree? This is the best we could do, however. However, he*

declined to wait. The conjunction, a subordinating one, is less frequent: *She can have it done however she wishes.* All these uses are Standard. Compare WHATEVER.

hubris (*n.*) is pronounced either *HYOO-bris* or *HOO-bris* and means "an excessive pride or arrogant overconfidence that often ends in retribution."

hugeness See ENORMITY; SYNONYM.

huh-uh, oh-oh, uh-huh, uh-oh, uh-uh These imitative spellings are used in the effort to re-create some sounds of speech. *Huh-uh* and *uh-uh* often go with a shake of the head and are conventional representations of the two-syllable negative: *Time to go? Huh-uh [uh-uh].* *Uh-huh,* often with a nod of the head, is the conventional representation of the two-syllable affirmative: *Time to go? Uh-huh.* *Uh-oh* and *oh-oh* are moderate equivalents of *oops!,* expressions of surprise, especially unpleasant surprise. In speech, the vowels in all these locutions are often somewhat nasalized.

human (*adj., n.*) *Human* is Standard both as adjective, as in *She has some very human faults,* and as noun, as in *He is not a monster; he's a human, and a very nice one at that.* Some commentators have objected to the noun, preferring the full *human being,* but either choice is Standard.

humanity, humanism, humanities (*nn.*), **humanitarian** (*adj., n.*) *Humanity* means "the human qualities" and "the human race," as in *His humanity was quite apparent* and *All humanity will rejoice at the news.* *Humanism* is any of a number of value systems based upon the central importance of human beings, as in *Humanism was one of the strongest intellectual threads in the fabric of the Renaissance.* The *humanities* are the branch of knowledge based on language and literature and including history and philosophy, as in *Everyone must take courses in the humanities as well as in the sciences.* As an adjective *humanitarian* describes values centered on the perfectibility of the human race; it also describes actions devoted to promoting the welfare of *humanity,* as in *She belongs to several humanitarian organizations;* as a noun it refers to a person devoted to promoting human welfare, as in *He has been a noted humanitarian all his life.*

humble-bee See BUMBLE-BEE.

humor (*n.*) (pronounced either *HYOO-muhr* or *YOO-muhr*) has two important clusters of meaning in current English. The most constantly before us is "something funny," "a sense of what is ludicrous, amusing, comical, silly, or funny,'' and ''writing or speech that expresses or illustrates these things.'' But also important are the older senses clustered on the four cardinal *humors* that underlay medieval ideas of health, personality, or temperament: these were blood, phlegm, choler, and melancholy. The meanings of *humor* in *I'm in a bad humor* (meaning ''mood'') and *Develop a good-humored attitude* (meaning ''a pleasant, cheerful one'') are not the same as the meaning of *a sense of humor,* which refers to a sense of the ludicrous. See also BLACK HUMOR; BURLESQUE; SATIRE; SICK HUMOR.

hung See HANG.

hunting, shooting (*nn.*) The British call it *hunting* when their targets are animals, *shooting* when their targets are birds. Most Americans call it all *hunting,* generically, and American *shooting* is generally at paper targets.

hurrah, hooraw, hooray, hurray (*n., v., interj.*) *Hurrah* and *hurray* are the most usual spellings of the interjection, which is ''a shout of joy or a cheer.'' The verb means ''to raise such a shout,'' and the noun is the name of such a shout. The four spellings reflect some of the pronunciations: *huh-RAH, huh-RAI,* and *hoo-RAI* are the most frequently encountered, but the noun occasionally is pronounced to stress the first syllable (*HOO-RAW*), as the *hooraw* spelling suggests, and this word means ''uproar, excitement, contretemps.''

hydrometer, hygrometer (*nn.*) A *hydrometer* is an instrument for measuring the specific gravity of liquids. A *hygrometer* is an instrument for measuring the amount of moisture in the air.

hyper (*adj.*) is slang meaning ''excitable, keyed up, high-strung,'' as in *The youngster was in a hyper state, unable to sit still.* See HYPERACTIVE.

hyper-, hypo- (*prefixes*) *Hyper-* means ''above, beyond, too far,'' and the like, as in *hyperacid, hyperbolic, hypertension, hyperthyroid,* and *hypercritical. Hypo-* means ''under, beneath, less than, or subordinated to,'' as in *hypoallergenic, hypodermic, hypoglycemia, hypotaxis,* and *hypothyroid.* These prefixes are usually joined to other words without use of hyphens.

hyperactive (*adj.*) *Hyperactive* is hyperbolic but Standard as a psychological term meaning ''extremely or abnormally active,'' as in *The little boy was hyperactive, and he nearly drove his parents frantic.* See HYPER.

HYPERBOLIC (*adj.*),   **HYPERBOLE** (*n.*) *Hyperbole* (*hei-PUHR-buh-lee*) is exaggeration for effect, a locution that exaggerates or makes an extravagant statement: *I'm so tired, I'm just dead. Their center must be eight feet tall—a monster.* To be *hyperbolic* (the adjective, pronounced *hei-puhr-BAHL-ik*) in speech is a characteristic frequently attributed to American enthusiasm, and it can indeed make discourse lively and interesting. But few peaks stand out in a mountain range full of peaks, and too much *hyperbole* is like shouting all your conversations. Use *hyperbole* sparingly. See also EXCLAMATION POINT; LITOTES; UNDERSTATEMENT.

HYPERCORRECTION in golf occurs when you overcorrect for your slice and so create a hook instead; in trying to avoid the pit on one side, you fall into the pit on the other. In grammar and usage, *hypercorrections* are the new mistakes we make in the effort to avoid old ones. They are probably most common in the case of pronouns, as in using *whom* where *who* was called for, as in *Whom shall I say was calling?* or when, in trying to be correct, we use a nominative in a place where an objective is expected, a morass frequently encountered in compound nominals with a pronoun as second element: *It turned out that they were looking for my wife and I.* Only those conscious of the pitfalls will *hypercorrect,* of course; it's usually a matter of trying to please, but without really knowing what is required. The best defense against *hypercorrection* usually is circumlocution: when in doubt, say it another way, and avoid stepping onto the quicksand in the first place: try saying *between the two of us* instead of risking *between you and I.*

hypercritical, hypocritical (*adjs.*) To be *hypercritical* is to be ''supercritical, too severely critical,'' as in *Her hypercritical nagging about his manners finally drove him away.* To be *hypocritical* is ''to be a hypocrite, one who pretends to virtues without justification,'' as in *His hypocritical imitation of deepest piety would never have fooled even the most naive missionary.*

HYPERFOREIGNISMS is the Merriam editors' name for our frequent bad imitations of foreign language pronunciations. The best advice is to avoid practicing in public those foreign pronunciations you haven't truly mastered. When you get them wrong, the knowing snicker. *Lingerie,* like many other French words we've borrowed as elegant names for mundane things, has become common in English, and apparently because it seems somehow classier than does *women's underwear,* we often try to keep it French-sounding, never really Americanizing it, but never really learning the French way of saying it, either. Alas, the usual two-syllable French *LANZH-REE,* with a nasalized first vowel, comes in many American variants, the most common of which is probably the three-syllable *LAWN-zhuh-RAI.* We could learn from our more sensible treatment of the equally French word *brassiere:* we rarely spell it with the grave accent in English these days, and we no longer even attempt a French pronunciation, except for keeping the stress on the final syllable: we say *bruh-ZEER,* or else we dodge the issue and clip the word to *bra,* pronounced *BRAH.* An unabashedly American pronunciation is always preferable to a fake foreign one. Avoid *hyperforeignisms.* See COUP DE GRACE.

hypermarket (*n.*) is a British name for what Americans call a *supermarket.*

HYPERURBANISMS are erroneous or inept locutions—pronunciations, word forms, syntactic structures, or word choices—that occur when we try to use language we consider more prestigious, more cultivated, more impressive, than we have full mastery of. (The term is based on the old notion that urban life is or ought to be more sophisticated than rural life.) Words such as *irregardless* are probably *hyperurbanisms,* and so are most malapropisms and all the other big words we use to impress without being sure of what they mean. Use the language you can control. See also HYPERCORRECTION.

HYPHEN This is the mark (-) English uses to link the parts of some compound words (*drug-dependent, blow-dry*), including most of those containing prepositions (*mother-in-law, top-of-the-line*); to combine single-word proper nouns such as place names (*the London-Paris flight,* although in printed matter *the New York–London flight* and *the Saint-Lambert–Montreal route,* will look slightly different, because printing uses the en dash to form compounds when one or both of the words are made up of two words or are already hyphenated); to put between some prefixes and the root words to which they're joined (*non-Christian, self-destruct, pre-Columbian*); to avoid ambiguity in compound modifiers (*blue-green enamel, a slow-moving van,* but *a slowly moving van,* because *-ly* adverbs and the adjectives they modify are not hyphenated); to use between parts of fractions as these are spelled out, especially as modifiers (*a three-fourths majority*); to mean "up to and including" when used between numbers or dates (*50–59, 1922–1930,* although here Edited En-

glish requires en dashes); to divide elements of compound two-digit numbers over twenty (*twenty-one, ninety-nine*). Note that even if you use a *hyphen* between parts of an adjective or adverb (*an eighteenth-century statesman*), you should not do so in a modifier plus a noun (*She lived in the eighteenth century*).

The *hyphen*'s other main use is to link the parts of a word divided for lack of space at the end of a line of writing; in this use the *hyphen* appears at the end of the last syllable for which there is room on that line, with the rest of the word then appearing at the beginning of the next line. Good desk dictionaries show you where words may conventionally be divided, usually with a dot or space between syllables where a *hyphen* may go. Generally editors try to avoid hyphenating any word at the end of a line when the word already has a hyphen in it. But see PUNCTUATION.

hyphenate, hyphen (*vv.*) Both verbs mean "to insert *hyphens* where needed," but Americans use *hyphenate* far more frequently. See HYPHEN.

hyphenated American (*n.*) This turn-of-the-nineteenth-century term meant recent immigrants, new Americans of recent foreign origin, such as Polish-Americans, Irish-Americans, and Italian-Americans. The term is still Standard for referring to ethnic groups of many sorts.

hypo- See HYPER-.

hypocritical See HYPERCRITICAL.

HYPOTAXIS See PARATAXIS.

hypothecate, hypothesize (*vv.*) The specialized sense of *hypothecate* is "to pledge property without actually giving up possession or title to it." In its more generalized sense it is a synonym of *hypothesize,* meaning "to make up or adopt a hypothesis." *Hypothesize* may seem a bit stiff or pretentious in some circumstances, perhaps not least because it can be something of a tongue twister; the Standard circumlocution is *to make a hypothesis.*

hypothesis (*n.*) The plural is *hypotheses,* pronounced *hei-PAHTH-uh-seez* or *hi-PAHTH-uh-seez.* Be wary: using *hypotheses* as a singular is Substandard, probably a hypercorrection by someone unsure, and it will be harshly judged by Standard speakers. See FOREIGN PLURALS.

hypothesize See HYPOTHECATE.

hysterics, histrionics (*nn.*) *Hysterics* are any of a range of uncontrolled emotional outbursts, perhaps with fits of laughing or crying. The word is usually used in the plural, but it can take either a singular or plural verb (*Hysterics is* [*are*] *hard to get under control by yourself*). The noun *histrionics* also appears usually in the plural, but it too can take either a singular or plural verb. It means "theatrical performances," usually in the singular, as in *He's made a considerable study of American histrionics,* but its far more common meaning is "theatrical outbursts, melodramatic behavior produced usually for effect," as in *When she couldn't get her way, her histrionics were something to behold.*

I

I (*pron.*) *I* is the nominative case form of the first person singular personal pronoun, a very high frequency word in English. Some commentators insist humility requires that *I* be used sparingly in Formal written English, particularly in Edited English, but the prohibition of all uses in writing is silly and should be ignored: it can lead to circumlocutory syntax and indirect, abstract, and stuffy prose. If you have an idea, acknowledge it directly with *I think;* just avoid the monotony of windy, self-centered discourse, to which constant repetition of the pronoun *I* so often contributes. See CASE (1); HYPERCORRECTION; IT'S ME; MYSELF; PERSONAL PRONOUNS; PRESENT WRITER.

ibid., ibidem *Ibid.* is the abbreviation, *ibidem* the full Latin word meaning "in the same place." The abbreviated form in particular is a convention of scholarly footnoting: when you wish to cite a work and a page for which you have just given a reference, *ibid.* does the job succinctly. Consult your publisher's stylebook for precise format and ground rules if any. See ABBREVIATIONS; FOREIGN PHRASES.

-ibility, -ability (*suffixes*) These two suffixes appear on nouns either made from adjectives or borrowed from Latin with the suffixes already in place (*visibility, risibility, predictability, laudability*). While they augment our vocabulary, they sometimes unfortunately contribute to our spelling problems: see SPELLING OF UNSTRESSED VOWELS. See also -ABLE.

-ible See -ABLE.

-ic, -ical (*suffixes*) make adjectives of other words: *hysteria* becomes *hysteric* and *hysterical; academy* becomes *academic* and *academical.* Note that in these (and many other) instances, there are often semantic and further grammatical distinctions between two adjectives made from the same noun: for example, *academic* has both a generalized sense, "pertaining to matters of the academy," which it shares with the less-frequent *academical,* and a specialized sense not shared with *academical,* "not real, but only theoretical," as in *The question is merely academic and not of practical importance.* This pair also shows how such adjectives often turn into new nouns with further specialized meanings: an *academic* is a person in that vocation, and *academics* (plural) refers to academic subjects as a group or topic in itself; *academicals* (plural) are the cap, gown, and hood that are the traditional ceremonial attire of *academics* (meaning "academic people"). Other such distinctions are frequent: compare *historic/historical; classic/classical; economic/economical; politic/political.* See also AGREEMENT OF SUBJECTS AND VERBS (3); -ICS.

ice cream, iced coffee, ice milk, ice tea, ice water These and other combinations with *ice*[*d*] display some interesting changes currently in progress: if primary stress is on the first word, then we know we have a compound; if it's on the second word, then we still have an adjective or noun adjunct modifying a noun. Older Americans (for whom *ice cream* was once only an infrequent homemade Sunday novelty) may well recall when it was spelled *iced cream,* in full recognition, through the participial adjective *iced,* of both process and chief ingredient. But younger Americans, who know only the product and may never have seen a hand-cranked freezer or, for that matter, a cow, today would find the participial spelling (and the occasional hyphen) odd indeed. And the pronunciations reflect the difference. The dental suffix on *iced* is gone from everyone's pronunciation, of course. But in some of the younger speakers the primary stress is on the first word—*EIS-KREEM* and *EIS-kreem-KON*—whereas older Americans may still say *EIS-KREEM* and *eis-KREEM-KON.* Several such compounds or near-compounds are currently in divided usage for either or both pronunciation and spelling: *EIS-TEE* (*ice tea*) is usually stressed on *tea,* but the dental suffix that once was on the end of *ice* has disappeared from both pronunciation and spelling. *Iced coffee,* on the other hand, retains the participial dental suffix both in some speech and in nearly all spelling, probably because this beverage is a much more recent development than *ice tea. Ice water* usually lacks the dental suffix today and is usually stressed on the first element. Though some uses of it may not ever have had that *d, ice[d] milk* is clearly too new to be a compound: the stress is still on *milk. Mash[ed] potatoes* and *handicap[ped] parking* are two other examples.

-ICS, NUMBER IN NOUNS ENDING IN Nouns ending in *-ics,* particularly those that are the names of topics or subjects of study, such as *acoustics, economics, ethics, politics,* and *statistics,* are treated as singular: *Economics is the dismal science.* Several of them, however, can be treated as either singular or plural: *Ethics is a subject you ought to take. His ethics are not admirable. Statistics* and a few others have also developed *s*-less singular forms as well, through the process of back-formation.

idea (*n.*) is a word that, like *business, thing, concept, matter,* and several similar terms, has many meanings, both general and specific, and its indefinite senses get particularly great use: *The idea is to help all those who need it. What's the big idea? She matches my idea of a fine teacher.* Some commentators assert that *idea* in its nonspecific senses is overused, but common sense suggests that although these fillers do get weary, they can serve us well when great precision is neither possible nor required.

ideal (*adj.*) *Ideal* is frequently listed as an absolute adjective, but some editors, especially in the news media, will let stand this sort of sentence: *She should be the most ideal candidate the party could nominate.* Others would insist that *She should be an [the] ideal candidate . . .* is the only possible way of using the term, and *She should be the most nearly ideal candidate . . .* the only acceptable qualification of it.

idealism (*n.*) has at least two clusters of meaning. The most general Standard sense is "behavior and conclusions based on a world as it should ideally be, rather than the way it really is." With this sense we get the pejorative overtones that add the taint of "impracticality." In this meaning, *idealism* is the antonym of *realism.* In the field of philosophy, *idealism* involves several theories, all of which hold essentially that only ideas are real and that material things either do not exist or are only derivative manifestations of ideas.

identical (*adj.*) combines frequently with the prepositions *with* and *to: These little brown shore birds seem identical with [to] those over there.*

identify (*v.*) is Standard combined with the preposition *with* when used intransitively or reflexively, as in *Though barely five-and-a-half feet tall, he had always identified [himself] with John Wayne.* These uses mean "to feel empathy with, to imagine oneself in the shoes of." The verb is also Standard in regular transitive use meaning "to establish the identity or ownership of": *He identified the wallet as his.*

ideology (*n.*) is pronounced either *EI-dee-AHL-uh-jee* or *ID-ee-AHL-uh-jee.*

IDIOLECT (pronounced *ID-ee-o-lekt*) is the term linguists use to designate the idiosyncratic speech of individual people—an *idiolect* is a one-person dialect, unique in pronunciation, grammar, and vocabulary.

IDIOMATIC (*adj.*), **IDIOM** (*n.*) The noun *idiom* has two specialized senses that refer particularly to language, for which a good dictionary is the best source, but the most important meaning of the term as used in this book is "a speech form, syntactic pattern, meaning, or locution that is unique in that it overrides or ignores normative language patterns and means something quite different from what its several components appear to add up to: it is more than the sum of its parts," as are *to jump start a car, a grassroots campaign,* and *a wallflower.* If a locution is *idiomatic,* it is Standard because we have all agreed that it is, logical or not. These *idiomatic* aspects of English are the most difficult for learners of English as a second language to grasp, precisely because there are few obvious or orderly explanations for them. One other problem with *idioms* is that overuse can make them clichés.

We also use the term *idiom* in a quite different and broader Standard sense, meaning "the full qualities of language use, either of an individual or a speech community," "the characteristic sound and flavor," even "the style and the words and the way they're said." It means almost what we mean by idiolect and dialect: *The idiom of Garrison Keillor is unmistakably his own. The idiom of Nantucket Islanders is very different from the speech of mainland coastal New England.*

idiosyncratic (*adj.*), **idiosyncracy, idiosyncrasy** (*n.*) *Idiosyncracy* is a very rare old variant spelling; today's Edited English overwhelmingly uses *idiosyncrasy.* The adjective is *idiosyncratic.*

idiot savant See SAVANT.

idle (*adj., n., v.*), **idol, idyll** (*nn.*) These three homophones are wholly distinctive in spelling and meaning. The adjective *idle*, as in *He's a lazy, idle person; It's been a lovely, idle afternoon*, has also undergone functional shift to noun, as in *She constantly reprimands the idle in the class*, and verb, intransitive, as in *Engines idle, wasting fuel*, or transitive, as in *Power outages idle factory workers*. Peter Sellers's rock singer being interviewed by a reporter ("What does it feel like to suddenly find yourself a teenage idol?" "Well, . . . I was idle before I was a teenager") nicely illustrates the distinction between *idol*, "an image of a god" or "an object or person the subject of adulation," and the adjective *idle*.

An *idyll* (sometimes spelled *idyl*) is either "a flawless, carefree, romantic interlude" or "a literary work describing such an interlude, especially a simple pastoral one": *Tennyson's* Idylls of the King *depicts the never-never land of Arthurian romance*.

i.e. See E.G.

-ienne See -ESS.

if (*subord. conj., n.*) Among its range of meanings, the conjunction is Standard used to express a condition, as in *If she's ready, we can go*; to describe an assumption, as in *If [Assuming that] it happened, I certainly didn't see it*; to mean "though, although," as in *She was clearly very happy, if also a bit teary*; to introduce an ejaculation of surprise or irritation, as in *If only you'd warned me!*; and to introduce an indirect question, as in *I inquired if [whether] there was any news* (many commentators insist you use *whether* here instead, but *if* is Standard).

A point that is currently much discussed is whether the conjunction *if* introducing a conditional statement must always be followed by the subjunctive. Clearly in certain circumstances this does not always happen in Standard English: *If he were to inquire, you must tell him where I am* uses the subjunctive, but *If she was to call, you would have to give her my number* does not. Both these are Standard, although Edited English uses the subjunctive more frequently than do most other levels. But see INDICATIVE.

The noun *if* is Standard in sentences in which either a determiner or a noun's inflection make clear that it is in fact a noun: *The if in the second line must be a mistake. Her proposal has far too many ifs for my taste*. A verb's inflection can turn *if* into a verb as well, although the tentative spellings tell you that this use is best restricted to Conversational levels: *She if'd [iffed] and hemmed and hawed until we got bored and left*.

if . . . , then . . . *Then* is required for the main clause of a complex sentence whose subordinate clause begins with *if* only when the subordinate clause is very long, as in *If we get there in time and the guests have not arrived, then we can ask about tomorrow's schedule*, or when you seek greater emphasis on the result, as in *If X occurs, then (and only then) will Y result*.

if and when, when and if These are essentially interchangeable clichés, and in most uses they are Standard. Chief charges against them have been redundancy and faulty parallelism. This second charge is usually unwarranted, except when *if and when* are followed by *to* plus an infinitive. In *Let's consider when and if to seek help*, for example, *Let's consider when to seek help* is fine, but *Let's consider if to seek help* is unidiomatic—the second infinitive would probably be better introduced by *whether*. Nevertheless, this *if*-plus-*to*-plus-infinitive structure will probably pass muster at most Conversational levels and in Informal written use; it just won't work in Edited English. See FAULTY PARALLELISM.

iffy (*adj.*) is slang and mainly Conversational, but it also appears at all but the most elevated levels of speech and writing, meaning "doubtful, chancy, improbable": *Our success was very iffy*. The phrase *iffy proposition* is a cliché.

if I was, if I were See INDICATIVE; IF.

if (when) worse (worst) come(s) to worst These clichés are variations of the same locution (sometimes the article *the* is added before one or both of the *worse/worsts*), each meaning essentially "If the worst that can happen actually does happen" or "If this already bad situation gets as bad as can be." All these variations are idiomatic (even though *if worst comes to worst* is probably a distortion of *if worse comes to worst*), and all are Standard, whether the verb is indicative or subjunctive, as in *If worse come[s] to worst*.

ignoramus (*n.*) (pronounced either *ig-nuh-RAI-muhs* or *ig-nuh-RA-muhs*) has a regular English plural: *ignoramuses*.

ignoring, ignorant of The present participle *ignoring* means "leaving out of account," "paying no attention to," as in *Ignoring the disturbance, he went on lecturing*. *Ignorant of* means "being unaware of," as in *Ignorant of the disturbance, he lectured on*. See OBLIVIOUS.

I guess See GUESS.

il- (*prefix*) is a form of the negative prefix *in-* that occurs before words beginning with *l-*, as in *illogical* and *illegible*. But see also IM-; IN-; IR-.

ilk (*n.*) long ago meant "like" or "same" and was used in Scotland to identify people by associating them with the place they hailed from, as in *McLeod of that ilk*, meaning "McLeod of the same (place)," or "McLeod of McLeod." But today the only Standard meaning of *ilk* in English is "kind" or "sort": *We don't socialize with people of that ilk.*

ill (*adj.*) combines with the prepositions *with*, as in *She was ill with hives*, and *of*, as in *He was ill of a fever*. Both are Standard.

ill, illness See SICK.

illegal, illegitimate, illicit (*adjs.*) These three are synonyms, but there are some useful distinctions among them. *Illegal* means "against the law, unlawful": *It was illegal to possess a weapon of that sort. Illicit* means almost the same thing, "unlawful, prohibited by law, improper," but many of its uses suggest the furtive or clandestine nature of acts so characterized: *The family had been operating an illicit still. Illegitimate* overlaps with the other two in the general sense of "unlawful," but it has other, more specialized meanings as well: "a bastard, born out of wedlock," as in *He was an illegitimate child*, and "contrary to logic," as in *Their conclusions were clearly illegitimate*, or "against the accepted usage of words," as in *She said that* **irregardless** *was an illegitimate word and so not a word at all.*

illegible, ineligible, legible, readable, unreadable (*adjs.*) *Legible* and *readable* are synonyms used to say that something is physically in such condition as to permit it to be read, but *legible* is essentially limited to that meaning, as in *The signpost was so faded as to be scarcely legible*, whereas *readable* has a more general sense of accessibility, including interest and attractiveness and the idea of ease of reading, as in *Her prose style was informal and very readable.* A piece of writing can be *illegible* if the handwriting is impossible to decipher, if the ink has faded, or the like. A piece of writing can be *unreadable* because of *illegibility* or because it is too dull, too full of hard words, too badly punctuated, or simply senseless.

A visual or tongue-twisting metathesis could conceivably cause *illegible* and *ineligible* ("not qualified, not suitable") to be interchanged accidentally. Don't let it happen.

illegitimate See ILLEGAL.

illicit See ELICIT; ILLEGAL.

illness See SICK.

ILLOGICAL COMPARISON See FALSE COMPARISON.

illusion See ALLUSION; DELUSION.

illusive, illusory See ELUSIVE.

illustrate (*v.*) is pronounced either *IL-luhs-TRAIT* or *il-LUHS-TRAIT*, and when it combines with prepositions, it can do so with *by* (*I'll illustrate by telling you a story*), with *with* (*I'll illustrate with a story*), and sometimes with *in* (*We can illustrate in several ways*). To explain where the illustrations might come from, *illustrate* can also combine with *from: She illustrated from her vast store of theatrical anecdotes.*

illy (*adv.*) is Standard still but rarely encountered because the flat adverb *ill* is also available and is much more commonly used: *She behaved illy* [*ill*] *before her grandparents. Illy* sounds very old and deserves an archaic label. See also FLAT ADVERBS.

-ily See -LY.

im- (*prefix*) is an assimilated adaptation of the prefix *in-*, one of whose meanings negates the rest of the word (*accurate* becomes *inaccurate*). Assimilation causes *in-* to become *im-* before a following bilabial consonant such as *m* (*immaterial*) or *p* (*improper*). When the prefixes *in-* and *en-* have other meanings, assimilation also takes place before a following bilabial, such as *b* (*embroil, emboss*), *m* (*immure*), and *p* (*impel, implore*). See also IL-; IN-; IR-.

image (*n.*), in its senses of "reputation" and "popular public impression," is sometimes called a vogue word: *The candidate was trying to establish an image as a virile and commanding leader.* The use has been press relations argot for some years, but it is now Standard, even in Edited English.

imaginary, imaginative (*adj.*) *Imaginary* means "not real, but imagined, found only in the imagination," as in *The child's best friend was an imaginary penguin. Imaginative* means "displaying imagination, given to using the imagination, or resulting from the use of the imagination," as in *His short stories are imaginative and scary,* and also "resourceful," as in *Her method of escaping trouble was remarkably imaginative.* Both words are Standard.

imbecile (*adj., n.*), **imbecilic** (*adj.*) *Imbecile* is Standard as both noun and adjective, although adjectival use is less frequent: *His imbecile ideas always lead to trouble.* The noun is sometimes used technically to mean "a retarded person with a mental age of three to eight years," but its more common (and hyperbolic) meaning is similar to that of both adjectives, "a foolish or stupid (person)." *Imbecilic* is a Standard adjective, usually with the generalized sense (see -IC): *Everyone thought her behavior imbecilic.*

imbibe (*v.*) is a slightly formal, perhaps pretentious verb meaning "drink," and although it can be used generically, it has a specialized sense, "to drink alcoholic beverages," as in *After several bad hangovers, he decided that hereafter he would no longer imbibe.* It is also used occasionally in the consciously literary figurative sense of "to drink in, to absorb," as in *Inhaling deeply, she imbibed the warm spring air.*

imbue, infuse, instil(l) (*vv.*) *Imbue* combines with the preposition *with* to mean "to provide or fill someone with something," as in *His patriotism imbued him with unexpected courage.* It occurs often in the passive: *She was imbued with strong family loyalty. Into* and *in* combine with *instil(l)* and *infuse,* and usually you *instil(l)* or *infuse* something *in* or *into* someone or something, as in *The stirring music infused [instilled] new determination into [in] every heart. Instil(l)* usually has two *l*'s, but *instil* is a Standard variant for the uninflected forms.

imitation See ARTIFICIAL.

IMITATIVE SPELLINGS Because speech precedes and is often more complex than writing, we frequently have to take special pains to make our written representations of spoken language clear to the eye. For example, American English has a good many conventional representations of noises that we make that are not quite speech (*uh-huh, huh-uh, shh, psst, teehee, ha-ha, kerchoo,* and the like); sometimes these are called ejaculations. Others are actual words that seem to be deliberate imitations of the sounds they represent; these we call echoic words: *honk, gag* (meaning "choke"), *swoosh,* and *whinny* are examples. See also EYE DIALECT; ONOMATOPOEIA.

immanent See EMINENT.

immature, premature (*adjs., nn.*) Both words are primarily adjectives, *immature* meaning "not yet of full growth, not adult" and *premature* meaning "born too soon, not yet ready for life." The nouns are used technically: *The gull was [an] immature, as its coloration showed; Our hospital has a special section in obstetrics to handle prematures [premature births]* (see PREEMIE). Both adjectives are also Standard in figurative use, *immature* meaning "not behaving like an adult, being childlike or even childish," as in *Her conversation was giggly, girlish, and immature,* and *premature* meaning simply "too soon, before its time," used of all sorts of ideas, propositions, and the like, as in *It was an ambitious plan, but premature.*

immediately (*subord. conj.*), meaning "as soon as," is almost exclusively British, although there is no hindrance to its use by Americans other than its unfamiliarity: *I'll give him the details immediately he returns my call.* See also DIRECT.

immigrant, immigrate, immigration See EMIGRANT.

imminent See EMINENT.

immoral See AMORAL.

immune (*v.*) combines with the prepositions *from, to,* and *against:* Typically, people are immune *from* prosecution for something, immune *to* particular diseases, and immune *against* either. *Against* is much less frequent than the other two.

immunity (*n.*), when it combines with prepositions, does so most frequently with *from, against,* and *to,* the last of these being used especially in reference to diseases: *We seek immunity from [against] government intervention. This latest inoculation program should restore the students' immunity to measles.* See also IMPUNITY.

immure (*v.*) means "to wall in," "to enclose." When it combines with a preposition, it usually takes *in,* whether the use is transitive, as in *His captors immured him in a gloomy cell in the basement;* passive, as in *She was immured in her room, campused for a week;* or as a participial adjective, as in *Immured in the castle all winter, they were pale and ill when spring came. Within, inside,* and *behind* also occur in Standard English: *The prisoners were immured inside [within] the keep. They immured him behind several feet of hewn stone. At, near,* and similar prepositions also occur when a place is to be specified by name: *The prisoners were immured at [near, beside, around, throughout, etc.] Paris.*

impact (*n., v.*), **impacted** (*adj.*) The verb, meaning "to strike" (especially in combination with *on*), and the noun have increased greatly in use, particularly figurative use meaning "to have effect (on), to change or influence." Some figurative uses are becoming clichés, but although often wearying and mechanical, they are still Standard. Best advice: try to find other ways to say what you mean.

Impacted, meaning "wedged or crowded," as in *an impacted wisdom tooth,* is a Standard participial adjective. There is also a peculiarly American use applied to regions, cities, and other population centers, meaning "an area under heavy duress because of the demands of crowding on public services such as schools, hospitals, water, sanitation, and transportation, and on the taxes and other funds that support them": *Most large Northeastern cities are seriously impacted areas.*

impanel, empanel (*v.*) *Impanel* means to put people themselves or names of people on a panel, especially on a list from which jurors are to be picked. You can also *impanel* the jury itself. *Empanel* is a variant spelling.

impassable, impassible (*adjs.*) These homophones have very different meanings and frequencies. If a route—literal or figurative—is *impassable,* you can't get through. *Impassible* is a synonym of *impassive,* which see. See also -ABLE; SPELLING OF UNSTRESSED VOWELS.

impassioned See DISPASSIONATE.

impassive (*adj.*) means "showing no emotion," "unmoved," "unfeeling." *He appeared impassive, apparently uninterested in her story.* See also IMPASSABLE.

impatient (*adj.*), when combined with a preposition, can be followed by *of, at, for, to,* or *with: She became impatient of [at, with] his excuses. We were impatient for the curtain to go up. They seemed impatient to begin.*

impeach (*v.*) means "to accuse, to lay a charge against, or to raise a question about (testimony)." It does not mean "to convict," although it is often mistakenly so used, particularly when the question of *impeaching* an elected official arises. In fact, if *impeached,* an official must be tried and convicted or found not guilty of the charges contained in the bill or writ of *impeachment.* When *impeach* combines with a preposition, it almost always does so with *for,* as in *The committee recommended that she be impeached for abuse of the privileges of office;* rarely with *on,* as in *He was impeached on charges that he had taken bribes;* and infrequently with *of* (which was long ago common in Britain), as in *The duke impeached him of high treason.*

impecunious (*adj.*) may be a bit arch or deliberately polysyllabic, but it means both "without funds" and "poor," and these are not precisely the same thing. At the other end of the spectrum is the Conversational word *broke,* which see.

impedance, impediment (*nn.*) They have the same root, but *impedance* (pronounced *im-PEED-uhns*) has specialized to mean "a kind of resistance within an alternating current in electricity and electronics," whereas an *impediment* (pronounced *im-PED-i-mint*) has a generalized meaning of "anything that prevents or interferes" and specialized but similar meanings in physiology (*She has a speech impediment*) and in law (*The lack of a valid will is an impediment to settling the estate*).

impel See COMPEL.

impenetrable (*adj.*) The preposition that most frequently follows *impenetrable* is *to: This slicker is impenetrable to rain. He is impenetrable to ideas. By* can also occur: *His reserve was impenetrable by the questions of reporters.*

IMPERATIVE This is the grammatical mode or mood of a verb, usually in the infinitive form, that gives a command or makes a request: *Run! Think. Come back. Surrender!* It has no subject (sometimes it is said that the pronoun *you* is "understood" as the subject). An *imperative* can govern most of the usual predicate structures, including the predicate adjective (*Feel better soon*), the predicate nominative (*Be a man*), the direct object following a transitive verb (*Think snow*), and the adverbial following an intransitive verb (*Drive slow*).

imperative, imperious (*adjs.*) If something is *imperative* (rhyme the stressed second syllable with *pair*), you have to do it; it is required (although if you have an *imperative* air, it may suggest merely that you're accustomed to giving orders). *Imperious* (rhyme the stressed second syllable with *peer*) applies mainly to people and their gestures or actions: *An imperious woman is impatient and determined to have her way; she will not brook restraint. Imperious* has a pejorative edge, whereas something *imperative* is not necessarily good or bad.

IMPERFECT PASSIVE See PROGRESSIVE PASSIVE.

imperious See IMPERATIVE.

impersonate See PERSONIFY.

impervious (*adj.*), when followed by a preposition, usually takes *to,* whether the meaning is literal, as in *This varnish is impervious to water,* or figurative, as in *She is impervious to his comments.* See also OBLIVIOUS.

impetus (*n.*) The plural is regular: *impetuses.*

impinge, infringe (*vv.*) To *impinge* is "to strike, to make an impression, to encroach," with the preposition *on* or *upon* usual in each sense: *Her practice times impinged on [upon] mine.* Only in the sense "to encroach" is *impinge* synonymous with the verb *infringe* (usually also with *on* or *upon*; see INFRINGE), which also means "to overlap, intrude upon, or interfere with": *Your proposal infringes on [upon] my patent.* Both are Standard in all these senses.

implement (*v.*) is Standard in the sense "to carry out": *We agreed to implement the new policies.* Be careful: in some uses it may smack of jargon or even cliché.

implicit (*adj.*) usually takes the preposition *in* or *within,* as in *Our new directions are implicit in [within] every new piece of legislation.*

IMPLICIT COMPARISON, IMPLICIT COMPARATIVES Six English adjectives (*major, minor, junior, senior, inferior, superior*) are sometimes called *implicit comparatives.* Once comparative adjectives in Latin, they already have the forms of inflected comparatives but lack positive and inflected superlative forms. They behave in English like regular positive adjectival forms, and some of them indeed can occasionally take the periphrastic comparative or superlative with *more* or *most: Fred is more senior than Tom.*

imply See INFER.

important (*adj.*), **importantly** (*adv.*), **more/ most important** (*adj.*), **more/most importantly** (*adv.*) When combined with a preposition, the adjective *important* is followed usually by *for, in,* or *to: Important to [for, in] understanding our actions is the original cause of the problem. Important* can also use *to* plus an infinitive or no preposition and a *that* clause: *It was important to see [that we see] his reasons.* Following the superlative, *important* usually combines with *of: She was the most important of all the contestants.*

Either the adjectival *more/most important* or the adverbial *more/most importantly* may serve as a sentence adverb; both are Standard in this use: *More [Most] important [importantly], we now have the right answer.*

impose (*v.*) combines frequently with *on* or *upon,* as in *We don't want to impose on [upon] your kindness;* sometimes with *by* or *from,* as in *These rules have been imposed by [from] headquarters;* and sometimes with prepositions indicating place, such as *between, around, over, against,* and the like, as in *These new difficulties were imposed between us and our goal* and *They*

imposed new controls around [over, against] our encampment. All these are Standard.

impossible (*adj.*) is usually considered an absolute adjective.

impostor, imposter (*n.*) *Impostor* is the more common spelling, but *imposter* is also acceptable. Pronounce this word, which means "someone who puts on a false identity," im-PAHS-tuhr, with just three syllables; an intrusive *i* before the final syllable is Substandard.

impotent, impudent (*adjs.*) These two may be confused in spelling by the inexperienced because their pronunciations are vaguely similar: *IM-puh-tent* and *IM-pyoo-dent. Impotent* means "weak or powerless" and (as applied to males) "unable to perform sexually, unable to have an erection." *Impudent* means "saucy, bold, or insolent" and (as once applied especially to females) "shameless."

impractical, impracticable (*adjs.*) There is some overlap: *impractical* is the antonym of *practical* in its sense of "feasible": if the scheme is *impractical,* it's not feasible; *an impractical person* lacks common sense and ordinary prudence. *Impracticable* is an older word, mostly replaced by *impractical* in the "infeasible" sense but still used to mean "unworkable, not doable." *Your plan is impractical* means it's not likely to work; *Your plan is impracticable* means it won't work, it can't be done. *Impracticable* no longer is applied to persons. Compare PRACTICABLE.

impresario (*n.*) Pronounce it either *im-pre-SAHR-ee-o* or *im-pre-SER-ee-o,* and spell it with only one *s.* The plural is *impresarios.* See PLURALS OF NOUNS ENDING IN *-O.*

impress (*v.*) can combine with these prepositions in the sense of "being compelled to notice or admire or draw some other conclusion": *on* or *upon (That we must never cheat was strongly impressed on [upon] us);* and *by, with,* or *at (I was impressed by [with, at] her good sense).* In the specialized sense of "being forced into service" (as in the *impressing* or *impressment* of seamen), *as, in, into,* or *for* can combine with *impress: His father was impressed as a deputy marshal during the riots. Many were impressed in [into] the British Navy in 1812.* Both senses can be transitive as well: *They impressed us with their skill. The military impressed all available taxicabs for transporting the troops to the front.* Out of context, the phrase *impressed by the British Navy* could be ambiguous, meaning either that one "admired it" or was "forced to serve in it."

IMPROMPTU is the level of spoken language (Gleason [1965] called it *consultative key*) in which each of you does most of your communicating with people who are not close friends or relatives. It is the face-to-face language you use speaking to the store clerk, to your child's teacher, or to strangers at the bus stop. Because it is face to face, it offers continuous opportunities for you to make certain by direct observation that you are being understood. *Impromptu* diction and syntax tend to be simple and repetitive. Its function words are usually limited to a few of each variety needed: *and* and *but* will usually be the only coordinating conjunctions used, and a very few prepositions will do most of the work. Its syntax is strung together simply, and the whole of any speech is rhetorically quite loosely structured and seemingly syntactically unplanned.

Every normal person can talk at the *Impromptu level*, just as everybody can also handle Casual and Intimate speech. But many speakers of limited social opportunity do not master any level beyond *Impromptu*. Children go to school to learn Planned patterns, but some achieve only minimal competence in using them. This means that where others—in groups or in more formal situations—might expect Planned speech, they may instead hear only Impromptu, which, although appropriate in its own situations, will, in an obviously unfamiliar context, mark the speaker as unskilled and make the speech ineffective. See LEVELS OF USAGE.

impromptu See EXTEMPORANEOUS.

improve (*v.*) When *improve* combines with a preposition, it is usually either *on* or *upon* (*His design considerably improves on* [*upon*] *the earlier model*) or, rarely, *over: This one improves our product a good deal over anything we've seen before.*

improvement (*n.*) can be followed by any of several prepositions, including *in, of, on, upon, to,* and *over: They made improvements in* [*on, upon, to*] *the brakes. Improvements of all components were being designed. It was an improvement over the original model.*

impudent See IMPOTENT.

impugn, impute (*vv.*) *Impugn* means to "challenge the truth or integrity of something," "to attack its veracity," as in *She impugned his stated reasons for resigning. Impute* means "to attribute something, particularly a crime or a fault, to someone or some cause," as in *He imputed their loss of the match to their lack of practice.* The verb *impute* is used only when the

observation made is critical or unflattering, and it often invites an inference that the observation is unfair or unreasonable.

impunity, immunity (*nn.*) *Impunity* means "exemption or freedom from punishment or other harm," as in *The aerialist seemed to believe she had been granted an impunity from the law of gravity. Immunity* means "protected from or not subject to a disease or other harm," as in *The inoculations guaranteed her an immunity to all the common childhood diseases.* The difference is that *impunity* means only that you can't be punished by whatever threatens others, whereas to have *immunity* means that you are simply not subject or susceptible to whatever unpleasantness might threaten those lacking such *immunity*. When it combines, it is followed by *to*. See also IMMUNITY.

impute See IMPUGN.

in, into (*preps.*) Purists and grammarians have often wished that *in* would mean "static location" (*She was in the house*) and *into,* "motion to or toward" (*She went into the house*), but language doesn't work that neatly, and *in* and *into* overlap. Native speakers have no problem with the distinction between *running in the yard* and *running into the yard* (although note that *I ran into the house* can be ambiguous if you weren't looking where you were going or if you were driving a car), but the nature of the verb is always important too: *to tiptoe in the hall* and *to tiptoe into the hall* obviously mean different things, but *to jump in the car* and *to jump into the car* may be only modestly different, at least for adults.

The combination of the verb *turn* with *in* plus *to* and with *into* can create a problem: *A man can turn himself in to the police, but, unless he's a magician, he can't turn himself into a rabbit.* The spelling in this instance reflects a difference in intonation, the two-word spelling being a reflection of a distinctive separation between *in* and *to* in speech. The frequent semantic differences between *in to* and *into* as combined prepositions are significant; for example, *She ran in to her father* means "She ran into the room where he was and approached him," whereas *She ran into her father* means either "She literally bumped into him" or "She accidentally or unexpectedly met him."

Into is also current slang, meaning "interested in, excited about, or knowledgeable about," as in *She's really into birdwatching.* Reserve this cliché for Casual and very Informal use at best; it's badly shopworn.

in-, non-, un- (*prefixes*) These mean "the negative of," "the opposite of," or "the antonym of," as in *intolerant, insolvent, non-Christian, nonsmoker, unpleasing, unsavory. In-* (sometimes *en-*) is also a different prefix meaning "in, toward, into, inside of," as in *intern* and *enshrine.* (See also IL-; IM-; IR-, which discuss instances where assimilation causes a change in the final consonant of the prefix.) Normally none of these prefixes uses a hyphen; for exceptions, consult a desk dictionary.

in about is often faulted as wordy—*I'll be there in about an hour; He moved away in about 1965*—but it's a perfectly good way to suggest approximation. It is Standard, although most common in Conversational and Informal contexts.

inaccessible (*adj.*), when combined with a preposition, usually takes *to: The new addition is inaccessible to the handicapped.* Spell the suffix *-ible*, not *-able.*

in addition to is a compound preposition, not a coordinating conjunction: *Milk, in addition to fruit juices, is the best drink for children.* Most often *in addition to* works much the way the preposition *besides* works: *Eating right, in addition to [besides] helping me feel stronger, also helps me control my weight.* For certain purposes of style—parallelism, for example—*in addition to* is not too wordy: *Using a good deal of patience, in addition to the requisite skill but not in place of it, you can teach almost anyone anything.* Besides, as this example shows, *in addition to* is not always interchangeable with the preposition *besides.*

in advance of This compound preposition means either "before" or "ahead of," as in *The scouts got there well in advance of the main body of troops.* Sometimes *in advance of* may appear a bit stilted or wordy, but at other times it can be the best choice.

inadvertence, inadvertency (*nn.*) The meanings are identical, but *inadvertence* is much more commonly seen and heard than *inadvertency.* Their plurals are *inadvertences* and *inadvertencies.*

inalienable, unalienable (*adjs.*) These two exact synonyms are still Standard, but *inalienable,* though a trifle younger than *unalienable* (both are seventeenth century words) is the more common today. Things *inalienable* [*unalienable*] cannot be given away, transferred, or otherwise removed.

in any case is an idiom and a cliché, but it nonetheless is a handy substitute for other idiomatic clichés such as *in any event* or *after all* or *nonetheless.* It is one of our fillers, of course, but a useful one. See CASE (2).

inapplicable See APPLICABLE.

inapt, inept, unapt (*adjs.*) *Inapt* means "lacking skill, unsuited, or inappropriate": *She studied the piano for years, but all her teachers agreed that she was a remarkably inapt pupil.* *Unapt* means "unskillful, unlikely, lacking in ability," and so it is essentially a synonym for *inapt,* except in its further sense of "inappropriate" as applied to actions, remarks, and the like, as in *His comments were singularly unapt and embarrassing. Inept* means "clumsy, awkward, unsuitable, and inefficient," as in *Our waiter was about as inept as could be, dropping things and spilling anything he tried to pour.* Here *inept* may overlap the "embarrassing" sense of *unapt.*

inasmuch as, insofar as (*subord. conjs.*) Both locutions are conventionally spelled as two words and have meanings and functions similar to *since, because,* and *as;* and to *due to the fact that, given the fact that,* and a few other clichés designed to vary these conjunctions. *Inasmuch as* and *insofar as* are occasionally criticized for being too wordy, but they are Standard and useful for variety.

inaugurate (*v.*) has a specialized sense concerned with the swearing-in of a president or other official, but it also has a more generalized sense, meaning "to begin, start, commence, initiate, introduce," and the like. Commentators have long claimed *inaugurate* is pretentious and overly formal, and journalese has frequently overused it, but you'll be all right as long as you use it appropriately: to *inaugurate* a new set of golf clubs, a new vending machine, or a newly appointed dogcatcher is certainly pretentious, but by all means *inaugurate* a new alderman or a new era of foreign policy.

in back, in back of See BACK OF.

in behalf of, in behoof of See BEHALF.

in case (*subord. conj.*), **in case of** (*subord. conj., prep.*) These are idioms and clichés, often used where *when* or *if* might serve: *I'll be there in case* [*when, if*] *you need me. In case of* [*If, When there is*] *fire, break glass.* See CASE (2).

incentive (*n.*) combines most frequently with the prepositions *to, for,* and *toward,* as in *Her forthcoming trip abroad is a great incentive to* [*for, toward*] *save* [*saving*] *money. Of* appears when the incentive itself is identified: *She has the incentive of a forthcoming trip abroad.*

incentivize (*v.*) Possibly a nonce word, but in any case formed with the much-maligned *-ize* suffix, *incentivize* means "to provide with incentive(s)": *He incentivized them for seeking to improve.* Given the fairly widespread animus against such coinages, the wiser choice would be *He gave them incentives for seeking improvement.* See -ISE.

inchoate, incoherent (*adj.*) Though not likely to be confused, these words do overlap in the meaning "unformed, amorphous." Some commentators object to *inchoate* as a synonym for *incoherent* or *amorphous,* arguing that it should be reserved for uses involving the senses of "early, beginning, or immature." But *inchoate* meaning "unformed" is Standard and since it does refer to that vague, misty, amorphous stage of early developmental geology or biology, it is appropriately used in figurative applications of those senses.

incident (*n.*) Some people argue that *incident* is overused as a euphemism for an unpleasant or dangerous occurrence: *Three incidents were reported last night.* The echoes of *incidental,* suggesting triviality or unimportance, may contribute, but *incident* meaning "an occurrence of unspecified nature, pejorative because unpleasant, dangerous, or violent, or merely potentially so" is Standard and useful; it is euphemistic (or downright dishonest) only when nervous officials try to hide behind it rather than use accurate but naked words such as *murder, rape, attack,* or *bombing.*

incidental (*adj.*), when it combines with a preposition, usually takes *to,* and the object of the preposition is a consequence or result, albeit perhaps a minor one, of the main action: *The complaints of a few should be considered only incidental to the benefits afforded the many by the compromise.*

incidentally (*adv.*) is always the spelling in Edited English. The spelling *incidently* reflects the four-syllable pronunciation most commonly heard in conversation; it does occur in print, but only rarely. Stick with *incidentally*; it is Standard as a sentence adverb.

inclose, inclosure See ENCLOSE.

include See COMPRISE.

INCLUSIVE LANGUAGE *Inclusive language* is vocabulary and a set of pronouns so chosen as to minimize or eliminate the use of words that mean or seem to mean one sex to the exclusion of the other: *flight* [or *cabin*] *attendant* is *inclusive language*; *steward* and *stewardess* are *exclusive language.* Most publishers now urge their authors to avoid any taint of sexist language (or *exclusive language*) and to use *inclusive language* wherever possible instead. But consult common sense as well, lest you sacrifice your prose to your good intentions. See also EPICENE PRONOUNS.

incoherent See INCHOATE.

incombustible See FLAMMABLE.

incoming See UPCOMING.

incomparable, irrefutable, irreparable, irrevocable (*adjs.*) Each of these words has two pronunciations in divided usage in Standard English. *Incomparable* is usually pronounced *in-KAHM-puhr-uh-bul* when it means "beyond comparison, unequaled"; *in-kuhm-PAIR-uh-bul,* when it does turn up, means "incapable of being compared, beyond comparison." *Irrefutable* normally has primary stress on the second syllable, but such stress on the third is also Standard; *irreparable* and *irrevocable* follow the same pattern. Some argue (although documentation is difficult) that there may be a slight but significant semantic difference between the two pronunciations of each of these three, analogous to that described for *incomparable,* but even if there is one, most listeners will likely ignore it in favor of the meaning they consider more obvious. See also -ABLE.

INCOMPARABLES See ABSOLUTE ADJECTIVES.

INCOMPLETE COMPARISON See ABSOLUTE COMPARATIVES; AS GOOD OR BETTER THAN; FALSE COMPARISON.

INCOMPLETE SENTENCES See FRAGMENT.

incongruous (*adj.*), when combined with a preposition, uses *about, among, in, on, to, with,* and *within: There are a few characteristics that seem to me incongruous about her. Her face looks incongruous among all those grim visages. It seems incongruous in him to hate so fiercely. The guardsman's mustache looked incongruous on his cherubic face. We appeared incongruous to the other guests. Her high spirits were incongruous with the gloomy appearance of her husband. His zeal was incongruous within the context of everyone else's lassitude.*

in connection with is a Standard compound preposition, and since brevity is not the only virtue in either speech or prose, it can sometimes serve better than *about, concerning,* or *with* to achieve the meaning and tone you seek.

inconsequential See CONSEQUENTIAL.

incorporate (*v.*) When combined with prepositions, *incorporate* normally takes *in, into, with,* and *within: We will incorporate your proposed changes in [into, with, within] the final version. In* is by far the most usual.

incredible, incredulous (*adjs.*) *Incredible* means "unbelievable": *The news you brought is incredible. Incredulous* applies to people and their attitudes and means "unable or unwilling to believe": *She was incredulous, and she found his story incredible. The claim he made was outrageous, and the expressions on their faces were uniformly incredulous.* Using *incredulous* to mean "unbelievable" was Standard until about two hundred years ago, but not today, except humorously as a malapropism. See CREDENCE.

incubus See SUCCUBUS.

inculcate (*v.*) The prepositions combining with *inculcate* are usually *in* or *into,* as in *We have tried to inculcate some of the principles of the work ethic in [into] our students. On, onto,* and *with* also combine, but very rarely: *Inculcate if you can on [onto] your classes a sense of the excitement of discovery. Inculcate your classes with a sense a pride.* When used with *with, inculcate* takes a direct object first: *We tried to inculcate a sense of pride into the team* or *We tried to inculcate into the team a sense of pride,* but *We tried to inculcate the team with a sense of pride.* This last combination is probably Standard but it is rare in Edited English, and some conservatives don't like it at any level.

incumbent (*adj.*), when it combines with a preposition, does so with *on* or *upon,* followed by the object of the preposition, as in *These duties were incumbent on [upon] their leader,* or by the prepositional phrase plus an infinitive phrase with *to: It was incumbent upon us to convene the session.* See also PRESENT INCUMBENT.

incursion (*n.*) has the generalized meaning of "an overrunning, an intrusion," as in *Every morning there was a heavy incursion of fog from the sea,* and the specialized meaning of "an invasion," as in *There were frequent incursions of rebel troops into the district. Incursion* is a literary, formal-sounding word with pejorative overtones.

indecorous See DECOROUS.

INDEFINITE PRONOUNS *Anyone, anybody, someone, somebody, none, each, either, neither, one,* and some other *pronouns* are called *indefinite* because they specify no antecedent. Each presents one or more usage problems (for details, see ANYBODY; EACH; EITHER; NEITHER; NOBODY; NONE; SOMEBODY), but all have in common the problem of agreement with following verbs and pronouns and sometimes also with certain direct objects, as in *If everybody takes his [their] coat [coats] with him [them], it will save time.* Because *everybody* specifies neither a singular nor a plural antecedent, the following verb, pronoun, and direct object each can be either singular or plural. In fact, most spoken English has long been treating the following pronoun and the direct object as plural in all but the most formal situations; only purists and Edited English have insisted on the generic singular at least for the following pronoun and object. Common and Vulgar English, however, have never followed that dictum, and much Standard English is now increasingly ignoring it, especially in view of the campaign for inclusive language, which objects to the use of the generic masculine singular pronoun as sexist language. The plural is now Standard in all speech and most writing. See THEY.

INDEFINITE *YOU,* INDEFINITE *ONE* Compare *When one has talent, one must do one's best to develop it* and *When you have talent, you must do your best to develop it. You* sounds much more direct, conversational, and concrete, and it is far more common than *one* in almost all modern American English, written and spoken. *You* also is much less likely to pose the problems with parallelism and agreement that frequently occur with *one* as the indefinite pronoun. *One ought not to jump to conclusions if he can avoid it* shows the first bit of slippage, when *one* shifts to the generic pronoun *he,* but the much more common and more harshly judged problems are the shift from singular *one* to plural *they* and the shift from singular *one* to either singular or plural *you: One ought not to jump to conclusions if they [you] can avoid it.*

Aside from occurring in speech and writing where generality is the aim, both these indefinite pronouns often substitute for *I,* particularly when a speaker is trying to avoid sounding immodest. Unfortunately, *one* is frequently more stiff-sounding and attention getting than the first person pronoun would have been. If you must be humble, *you* is your best bet: *Even if I don't [you don't, one doesn't] like what's being served, I try [you try, one tries] not to be unpleasant about it.* See YOU.

independence (*n.*) takes the prepositions *from* and *of: Her independence from (of) most petty desires is admirable.*

independent (*adj.*), when it combines, does so with the preposition *of: We are independent of our parents.*

INDEPENDENT CLAUSE A clause containing both subject and predicate is an *independent clause,* one that can stand alone as a complete sentence. It is also called a *main clause,* to which one or more dependent clauses may be attached. (An imperative can consist of a predicate only.)

INDEPENDENT GENITIVES See ABSOLUTE POSSESSIVE PRONOUNS.

in-depth (*adj.*), **in depth** (*idiom*) These are becoming clichés, so use them sparingly: *an in-depth study* is thorough and detailed; *to examine something in depth* is to examine it completely, thoroughly, fully, top to bottom.

indestructible See DESTRUCTIBLE.

indeterminately See DETERMINATELY.

index (*n.*) has two Standard plurals: *indexes* (pronounced *IN-deks-iz*) and *indices* (pronounced *IN-di-SEEZ*). See FOREIGN PLURALS.

Indian (*adj., n.*) The word has been a semantic problem ever since Europeans mistakenly assumed that the discovery of the Americas was the rediscovery of India and the Far East. The adjective means "of or pertaining to the country of India (or the Indian subcontinent)" and "of or pertaining to the original populations of North and South America." The noun refers to a member of any of these populations in this hemisphere or to a citizen of the Asian country of India. In recent years, the increased sensitivity of many Americans to the possibility of ethnic slurs has made *Indian* a somewhat troublesome word in general if not in technical use; some insist that it be replaced by *Native American(s),* partly to counter the European blunder that attached the original name and partly as a reminder of who got here first.

INDICATIVE, SUBJUNCTIVE These terms apply to the mood of verbs: an *indicative* verb is one that makes a factual or actual statement, as contrasted with a verb in the *subjunctive* mood, which makes a doubtful, conditional, or hypothetical statement or one contrary to fact or in some sense subordinate to another statement. *Fred wins both sets, so he is the champion* has two *indicative* verbs, *wins* and *is. If Fred win both sets, he will be the champion* is a rather stiffly formal example of a *subjunctive* verb, *win.* The *subjunctive* shows up much more often today with the verbs *be* and *have* than with other verbs, as in *If he be winner of both sets* or *If he have luck enough to win both sets,* but even these sound formal. Much more common today is the use of the auxiliaries *should* and *would* (*If he should win both sets . . .*), and most common of all in many conditional statements is the *indicative: If he wins* [*is the winner, has luck enough to win*]. . . . All these are Standard.

It has long been conventional to observe that the inflected *subjunctive* is fast disappearing from English, and the statement is partly true. But particularly at the upper levels of both speech and writing the *subjunctive* is regularly used in Standard English, and even at the lower levels divided usage and the replacement of the *subjunctive* by the *indicative* occur only in certain grammatical situations. In conditions contrary to fact, for example, finite verbs such as *arrive* are rarely put into the *subjunctive,* except in the most careful Formal English; you're more likely to hear *If he arrives in time* than *If he arrive in time.* But with *was* and *were* there is much more divided usage and much more argument about the appropriate usage, especially after verbs like *wish:* both *I wish that his argument were sounder* (subjunctive) and *I wish that his argument was sounder* (indicative) are heard and seen today in Standard English. Some relic or fossil *subjunctives* (*if I were you, far be it from me, if need be,* and the like) also continue to be Standard; to say or write *If I was you* is still Substandard and will be severely judged. Standard English also continues to require the subjunctive in *that* clauses following verbs such as *move, request, command, insist,* and the like: *I move that the secretary cast one ballot. We suggest that the treaty be abrogated. I urged that he consult a physician.*

One reason so much of the *subjunctive* appears to have fallen off is that only in the third person singular present tense of most finite verbs can we recognize a distinctive *subjunctive* form: *he goes* is *indicative, if he go* is *subjunctive. Be* has a couple of additional distinctive *subjunctive* forms: *be* in the present tense and *were* in first and third persons singular past tense. All others have been replaced either by the regular *indicative* forms or by the use of auxiliaries such as *should.*

indict, indite (*vv.*) The same root, meaning "to write down," gives us both words. They are homophones, both pronounced *in-DEIT,* but *indict* means "to bring formal charges, especially from a grand jury," and *indite* is a partly archaic word, or at least an old-fashioned one, meaning "to compose, to write down, to create in a literary sense." (The variant *endite* is entirely archaic.)

indifferent (*adj.*), when it takes a preposition, usually takes *to* (*She seemed indifferent to his pleas*) or *concerning, as to, in regard to,* or *about* (*They were indifferent concerning* [*as to, in regard to, about*] *the date of the trial*).

INDIRECT ADDRESS, INDIRECT DISCOURSE See DIRECT ADDRESS.

INDIRECT OBJECT The *indirect object* is the first of two contiguous nouns, pronouns, or other nominals in a predicate that contains a transitive verb and where each of the nouns has a different referent: in the sentence *Jack gave Jill the book, book* is the direct object, and *Jill* is the *indirect object,* the receiver of the thing on which the transitive verb acted. (Some grammars say that a *to* is "understood" before the first noun, as in *Jack gave* [*to*] *Jill the book,* but the explanation seems as strained as the example.) The syntax of these sentences is always the same—*indirect object* first, direct object second—unless the sentence uses a periphrastic construction with the preposition *to,* as in *Jack gave the book to Jill,* or unless the verb is one of the handful that permit an object complement.

INDIRECT QUOTATION See DIRECT ADDRESS.

indiscriminate, indiscriminating, undiscriminate, undiscriminating (*adjs.*) *Indiscriminate* and *indiscriminating* both mean "lacking distinctions," "haphazard," "careless or confused," as in *Her indiscriminate buying of clothes made her dress oddly indeed* and *Her tastes were indiscriminating.* But *indiscriminating* is used much less often than *undiscriminating,* which means "making no choices, without making any distinctions," as in *Her choice of music seemed bafflingly undiscriminating. Undiscriminating* (the synonym *undiscriminate* is rare in American English) can be pejorative, but *indiscriminate* almost always is.

indisputable (*adj.*) has two equally acceptable Standard pronunciations, *in-dis-PYOOT-uh-bul* and *in-DIS-pyuht-uh-bul.*

individual (*n.*) Commentators have fussed a good bit about *individual* used simply to mean "person," as in *He's a nicely behaved individual, but I don't know him well,* without contrasting an *individual* with a group of some sort, and they are probably justified. Mostly when we use the word we do intend to distinguish the individual from the state, or from the crowd. Just don't use it where *person* or *man* or *woman* would

serve, if you want to avoid putting purists' backs up. See also INCLUSIVE LANGUAGE; PARTY; PEOPLE; PERSON; SEXIST LANGUAGE.

INDO-EUROPEAN is the name of the large, ancient language family of which all the Germanic languages form one branch. English is one of the Germanic languages, and American English is one dialect of English.

indorse See ENDORSE.

indubitably See DOUBTLESS.

induce, deduce (*vv.*) The main contrast is between the senses applied to reasoning: *to induce* is to reach a conclusion based on an accumulation of evidence; *to deduce* is to infer from general principles to a conclusion (see also DEDUCE; DEDUCTIVE). *Induce* also has another cluster of meanings, "to persuade, to cause, to lead someone to do or conclude something," as in *She induced him to apply; The stuff she took was intended to induce sleep.*

induction, deduction (*nn.*) The distinction in logical methods is the key concern: *induction* is reasoning from particular cases and instances to a general conclusion; *deduction* is reasoning from a general proposition to a specific application and conclusion. The other senses of each word are not likely to be confused; consult a desk dictionary for them. See also DEDUCE; DEDUCTIVE.

inductive See DEDUCE; DEDUCTIVE.

indulge (*v.*) The transitive verb *indulge* combines with the prepositions *in* or *with,* as in *He frequently indulges his friends in* [*with*] *an expensive dinner at his club.* The intransitive verb combines only with *in,* as in *She indulges in too much self-pity.* A Conversational use, rather arch and euphemistic, appears in the host's question as he lingers with the bottle in hand, "*Will you indulge?*" meaning, "Will you have a(n) alcoholic) drink?" And there is the archaic sense in *A popular stereotype is that grandparents indulge their grandchildren too much,* meaning ". . . grandparents let their grandchildren have their way too often or spoil them with attention or gifts and the like." The generic sense, "Let me have my way," in *Indulge me, please, just this once* is still Standard, as is the use of *indulge* with a reflexive pronoun: *They indulged themselves with an expensive dinner.*

indulgent (*adj.*) can combine with several prepositions: *in,* as in *He is too indulgent in disciplinary matters*; *of,* as in *They are too indulgent of her crotchets*; *to,* as in *He seems indulgent to* [*toward*] *all their foibles*; and *with*, as in *We try not to be too indulgent with the children.*

-ine See -ESS.

inedible, poisonous, uneatable, unedible (*adjs.*) Something *inedible* is "unfit to be eaten," and so are things *unedible* and *uneatable*: *The bread was so maggotty as to be inedible* [*unedible, uneatable*]. (*Inedible* seems to be the term of choice.) Something *poisonous*, however, would be capable of injuring or killing. *Poisonous* is also used hyperbolically of food, simply to mean that it tastes awful, "as though it were poisoned," and it has a transferred sense used of people's behavior: *He has a poisonous disposition.*

ineffective, ineffectual, inefficacious (*adjs.*) These are synonyms meaning "not able to produce the needed result": *All the treatments proved ineffective* [*ineffectual, inefficacious*]. *Ineffective* and *ineffectual*, when applied to a person, differ somewhat: *ineffective* is a relatively matter-of-fact report on a current lack of success; *ineffectual* implies an ingrained inability to succeed, in the past and probably in the future as well. *Inefficacious* is a relatively low frequency, pretentious word that has one more syllable than *ineffective* but not much else. See EFFECTIVE.

ineligible See ELIGIBLE; ILLEGIBLE.

inept See INAPT.

in excess of is a cliché, sometimes criticized for being pretentious when *around* or *near* is available but often useful when numbers are big, round, and vague: *The deficit had grown to a number somewhere in excess of* [*around, near*] *a hundred million dollars.*

inexecrable, execrable, inexorable (*adjs.*) *Inexecrable* is obsolete, if indeed it really ever existed as an English word outside certain copies of Shakespeare's *Merchant of Venice* (IV.i.128), where it is probably a misspelling of *inexorable*. If not, then it may be a hyperbolic nonce word version of *execrable*, meaning "disgusting, detestable, wretched, cursed." *Inexorable* means "not to be moved by words" and hence "relentless," "inflexible." *She was inexorable, determined to have her way, and not to be made to change her mind.*

inexplicable (*adj.*) Both *in-EKS-plik-uh-bul* and *in-eks-PLIK-uh-bul* are Standard pronunciations, but note that the second grates on many conservative ears.

in fact See FACT.

infamous (*adj., n.*), **infamy** (*n.*) *Infamous* means "of incredibly bad repute, known to be evil" and is pronounced *IN-fuh-muhs*. The related noun *infamy* is pronounced *IN-fuh-mee*. See NOTORIOUS.

infatuated (*adj.*) combines with the preposition *with*, as in *She was infatuated with foreign travel*, and rarely *by*, as in *He was infatuated by her and was determined to win her.*

infectious (*adj.*) See CONTAGIOUS.

infer, imply (*vv.*) You *imply*—that is, "hint at or suggest (usually indirectly)"—and your readers or listeners must then *infer* from your hints what it is they understand your words to mean (which may not always be what you intend to say): *If he implies that the mayor is dishonest, you may infer from what he says that he thinks the mayor's a crook. He later said he had meant to imply nothing of the sort, but from his remarks some of us had inferred that the mayor was a crook. Imply* often has a pejorative overtone, suggesting that whatever is being *implied* is not laudable and that the speaker is hinting at wrongdoing without actually charging it: *I wasn't sure what she was implying, but it didn't sound good.* If you *imply* things about someone, what you say is generally not to that person's credit. *Infer* seems not to pose that danger; its chief usage problem is that it is frequently misused for *imply,* and for many Standard users, that's a shibboleth. Keep them straight.

inferior, superior (*adjs.*) are often called implicit comparatives, and when followed by a preposition, they always take *to* in Standard English: *This cheese is inferior* [*superior*] *to the cheddar we had last week. Than* in place of *to* is Substandard.

inferno (*n.*) The plural is *infernos.* See PLURALS OF NOUNS ENDING IN -O.

infest (*v.*), when combined with a preposition, does so most frequently with *with*, as in *The closets are infested with silverfish,* but often with *by*, as in *Our food locker was infested by insects of various kinds.*

infiltrate (*v.*) can combine with two groups of prepositions. If the locution designates the place, group, or other entity that is being *infiltrated*, the prepositions are *into* (*Our agents hope to infiltrate into their intelligence-gathering organization*) and sometimes *to* (*Our pioneer companies infiltrated to the enemy supply dumps on the other bank*). If the locution designates who or what is doing the *infiltrating*, then *with* or *by* are the prepositions: *Their intelligence agency was infiltrated at several levels with* [*by*] *our agents.* Other prepositions also occur occasionally, including *among, from, through, toward,* and *within: Our spies infiltrated among [through, within] the crowd. Our scouts were told to infiltrate from [toward] the ravine. Infiltrate* can also be transitive and take a direct object, without a preposition: *We infiltrated their perimeter line.*

infiltration (*n.*) can combine with several prepositions. *Of* and *into* are most frequent: *They planned an infiltration of [into] European labor unions. Among, in, inside,* and *within* also occur: *Infiltration among [in, inside, within] liberal groups of all sorts was part of their intelligence scheme.*

INFINITIVE 1 This is the base form of a verb in English; usually it has the same form as the first person singular present tense of the verb (e.g., *jog, walk, believe*), and it is frequently used with and marked by the function word *to*. The *to-plus-infinitive* locution can also function as a noun, as in *I like to jog*. See also SPLIT INFINITIVE; TRY AND.

INFINITIVE 2, SUBJECT OF AN When it is a personal pronoun, the *subject of an infinitive* is always in the objective case: *I want **him** to learn Spanish.* Pronouns used as subjects of finite verbs are of course always in the nominative case. See also CASE (1).

INFIX See AFFIX.

inflammable See FLAMMABLE.

INFLATED DICTION results from choosing pretentious, studied, overblown words. It's a kind of elegant variation (which see).

INFLECTION, INFLEXION (*n.*), **INFLECTED, INFLECTIONAL** (*adjs.*) In language matters, *inflection* (the American spelling; *inflexion* is British) has two meanings—the general sense "tone of voice" (*There was a doubtful inflection in his voice*) and the technical one for grammar that refers to the process of adding grammatical suffixes (the suffixes themselves are *inflections*) to nouns to specify number and case (*dog* plus -*s* becomes *dogs*; plus apostrophe plus -*s*, it becomes *dog's*, the genitive singular), to verbs to indicate tense or number (*sign* plus -*ed* becomes *signed; sign* plus -*s* becomes *signs*), and to other words for other grammatical or semantic purposes (such as the -*er* added to the end of *bright* to form the comparative of the adjective or the -*ly* tacked on to some adjectives to make them into adverbs (*brightly*, for example). See SPELLING (1).

inflict, afflict (*vv.*) Both meaning and combined prepositions keep these from being confused: You *inflict* punishment or other torments *on* [*upon*] someone, and you *afflict* someone *with* punishment or other torments. Both verbs are transitive.

influence (*n., v.*) The noun combines with several prepositions: to identify the influence, with *of: The influence of Hemingway on the narrative styles of some American writers has been considerable*; to identify where the influence is felt, with *on, in, among, within, throughout,* and the like (*The influence of American blue jeans, popular music, and television is apparent on [in, among] Russian youth. The influence of certain great musicians is widely felt within [throughout] the world of jazz). For, from,* and *with* also occur: *She is a powerful influence for good among young people. Influences from all sorts of earlier composers are evident in his music. He says he has some influence with the town council.*

There are two Standard pronunciations of both the noun and the verb: *IN-floo-ins* for most Americans, and *in-FLOO-ins* for users of Southern Regional dialect. Some commentators have wrongly assumed that the pronunciation with stress on the second syllable is Common or Vulgar; it's not—it's Southern, and it's Standard there.

INFORMAL WRITTEN ENGLISH, INFORMAL USAGE, INFORMAL In this book these terms apply to written usage at the lowest level on the scale of formality. It is the most relaxed and the least constrained written language, the language in which we write to close friends and relatives, to colleagues and others whom we know well. It uses abbreviations, contractions, and other syntactic shortcuts. It avails itself of slang and other kinds of special diction and in all respects seeks to imitate as closely as is reasonable the cadences and usages of the lower levels of speech—that is, of Intimate, Casual, and much Impromptu conversation. In this guide, locutions labeled *Informal* are perfectly acceptable Standard English so long as their use is limited to the constituencies and contexts appropriate for informality. (In some general dictionaries, *Informal* has been introduced as a usage label to replace *Colloquial*.) See LEVELS OF USAGE.

informant, informer (*nn.*) *Informant*'s general sense is "someone who provides information": *I just learned the news yesterday; my informant was my sister.* Its specialized sense is "someone working for a researcher in societal topics or in language, someone who has information or experience the researcher needs": *While he was working on the tribal dialects, he used three* *elderly female informants. Informer* is usually a pejorative term, meaning "a person paid to give information, particularly someone paid to reveal inside information about people and affairs in a group to which he or she belongs," hence "a traitor."

infrastructure (*n.*), "the underlying structure of a society or other organization," is used today particularly to designate the roads, bridges, schools, sewers, electrical installations, and other structural systems that make possible a complex urban society. The term has come close to being a cliché; use it as precisely as possible, and avoid figurative uses that may blur its distinctive qualities.

infringe (*v.*) is both transitive, as in *They promised not to infringe our rights,* and, combined with prepositions *upon* and *on,* intransitive, as in *We promised not to infringe on [upon] the privileges they've already won.* Both uses are Standard. See also IMPINGE.

infuse (*v.*) combines frequently with the preposition *with,* as in *We were infused with new energy,* and occasionally with *in* and *into* and, rarely, *by: The coach tried to infuse some optimism and renewed hope in [into] his downcast players. She was infused by a completely new willingness to work.*

-ing (*suffix*) This is the ending attached to the infinitive of a verb to form the present participle or gerund (*run* becomes *running; study* becomes *studying*). We also use this suffix to make the progressive form of verbs, as in *We are working better this week.* A great many Americans, especially at Intimate and Casual levels, pronounce *-ing* to rhyme with *in,* a practice often criticized as slovenly or careless. It is certainly much more widespread in Common and Vulgar English than it is in Standard, where, at the Casual and Impromptu levels, it nevertheless frequently occurs without eliciting notice or comment.

ingenious, ingenuous (*adjs.*), **ingenuity, in genuousness** (*nn.*) These words are rarely confused, except perhaps by the inexperienced, and even then the problem may be primarily poor spelling or proofreading. *Ingenious* (pronounced *in-JEEN-yuhs*) means "inventive, clever, imaginative, talented," as in *She's invented an ingenious little device; He is an ingenious man with several patents to his credit. Ingenuous* (pronounced *in-JEN-yoo-uhs*) means "frank, open, innocent, youthful, unsophisticated," as in *His ingenuous remarks won everyone's sympathy. Ingenuity* is "the demonstra-

tion of inventiveness," while *ingenuousness* is "the display of the innocence and candor of youth."

ingenue, ingénue (*n.*) Spelled either with or without the acute accent, this French borrowing means "a naive or innocent young woman or girl, particularly one playing such a role in a drama." Pronounce it either *AN-juh-noo, AN-zhuh-noo,* or *AHN-zhuh-noo.* See FOREIGN PHRASES.

ingenuity, ingenuous, ingenuousness See INGENIOUS.

in-group (*n.*) is hyphenated and is now a Standard word meaning "clique" or "a group of people who share common interests that bind them closely together." Anyone not in our *in-group* is clearly an *outsider.* Stress is on *in-.* See COMPOUNDS.

inhabitable See HABITABLE.

inhibit, prohibit (*vv.*) *Inhibit* means "to hold back from doing something, to restrain or repress," as in *A teacher's frowns of disapproval are often enough to inhibit conversation in the classroom. Prohibit* (which see) means "not to permit, to forbid (as though by law), to prevent from doing (something)," as in *The referee's decision prohibits his reentering the game.*

in hope(s) of, in hope(s) that See HOPE.

inhuman, nonhuman, unhuman (*adjs.*) The more frequently encountered *inhuman* has a strong moral sense; to be *inhuman* is to lack all good, redeeming, admirable human qualities, to be unfeeling, cruel, monstrous, as in *Her treatment of her employees was inhuman and barbarous. Unhuman* and *nonhuman* mean simply "not human," "other-than-human in nature or character," as in *Regardless of how they can perform, robots are after all unhuman [nonhuman]; they lack both our virtues and our vices.*

inimical, inimicable (*adjs.*) are synonyms meaning "adverse or hostile to, unfriendly." *Inimical* is much more commonly used, but either word is Standard with the preposition *to,* as in *Her opinions are inimical [inimicable] to our proposal.*

INITIALISMS are acronyms of a special kind, abbreviations made up of the initial letters of a phrase: *BTU* for *British Thermal Unit; E.R.A.* for *Equal Rights Amendment* or *Earned Run Average.* We pronounce *initialisms* only by saying the names of the letters, not as though they are words.

initials as abbreviations for names of people
A common practice in headlines and in other places where abbreviated reference is needed is the use of initials: *FDR* for *Franklin Delano Roosevelt, HST* for *Harry S. Truman, JFK* for *John Fitzgerald Kennedy, LBJ* for *Lyndon Baines Johnson,* and the like have long been Standard, with the abbreviated cluster being spoken as the names of the letters: *EL-BEE-JAI,* for example. When such names have additional capital letters, as in the names of *Archibald Mac-Leish, William McKinley,* or *Eugene O'Neill,* it is conventional to keep all the capitals as *initials: A. MacL., W. McK.,* and *E. O'N.,* although these may rarely be pronounced. The use of periods after each initial is optional; headline writers tend not to use them, and that practice has spread to other written uses. See ABBREVIATIONS.

ink, pencil (*vv.*) *Ink* is Standard in the sense meaning "to apply ink to or to fill in with ink" and often combined with *in* or *out,* as in *She inked in the foreground of the drawing; We inked out the error.* The sense meaning "to sign a contract or other document" or "to get the signature of" is Informal and Conversational at best, limited in writing mainly but not exclusively to journalese: *The team had inked its star pitcher just that morning. Pencil* is Standard when used in similar constructions with *in* meaning "to write in in pencil" and, in contrast to *ink in,* may suggest a tentative or impermanent action.

INKHORN TERMS Specifically these were the many anglicized Latin and Greek words that Renaissance scholars and pedants created out of their inkwells when it seemed to them that the English vocabulary, when compared with the classical languages, was impoverished, unattractive, and unable to cope with abstractions. Many such coinages stayed with us (*describe, education, encyclopedia, eradicate*); many others failed and disappeared (*attemptate, disaccustom, effectuous, eximious*). But the virus of unrestrained *inkhornism* lurks today, ready to damage the prose of writers who think there are no words in the language sufficiently refined to communicate their ideas and who believe that long, impressive-sounding words must represent impressive ideas. There is nothing wrong with coining words or borrowing them from other languages, but exhaust the resources of the existing English lexicon first. It's already the world's largest and fullest such resource.

in kind See SALARY.

INLAND NORTHERN REGIONAL DIALECT This regional subdialect of the Northern Regional dialect of American English is spoken mainly in New York state outside the lower Hudson valley and the metropolitan New York City area, as well as in the western parts of the states of Vermont, Massachusetts, Connecticut, and Maine. It has much in common with Great Lakes Northern, and it differs notably from the Eastern New England and Metropolitan New York City regional dialects in that it retains its medial and final *r*'s, as they do not.

-in-law (*suffix*), **in-law** (*n.*) The plurals of *mother-in-law, father-in-law, brother-in-law,* and the like, are *mothers-in-law, fathers-in-law, brothers-in law,* etc. A Common English plural, *mother-in-laws,* is rare and generally unacceptable in Edited English. All these *-in-law* words are hyphenated. The genitives are a bit unusual: *This is my mother-in-law's hat. These are our mothers-in-law's hats.*

The clipped form of the noun, used to refer to relatives by marriage (*My in-law was there*) is mainly Informal or Conversational, but it does occur in some Edited English; it is pronounced with primary stress on the *in.* Its plural is *in-laws.*

in length, in number, in shape, in size, in width, and the like can seem wordy: *It was ten feet long* and *It was ten feet in length* say the same thing. They can also be downright redundant: in the sentence *The field was circular in shape,* for example, *circular* already specifies that we're dealing with a precise shape and so removes the need for further specification.

in line See ON LINE.

in-migrant, in-migrate, in-migration See EMIGRANT.

innate (*adj.*), when it combines with a preposition, usually does so with *in,* as in *The ability to use language appears to be innate in humans,* and somewhat less frequently with *to,* as in *This characteristic seems innate to these peculiar animals.* See ACQUIRED; GENETIC.

innervate, innerve See ENERVATE.

inning See STANZA.

innocent (*adj.*), when combined with the preposition *of,* means "not containing any, without, or lacking," as in *His conversation was innocent of any trace of humor.* It is at worst a mild cliché. See also PLEAD.

innovation (*n.*), **innovative** (*adj.*) An *innovation* is something new, newly proposed, or newly created: *The product line for the spring contains* *several innovations. Innovative* can apply either to what is created—*His proposals were very innovative*—or to the creator—*She's an unusually innovative designer.* Since an *innovation* is of itself something new, *a new innovation* is tautological and Substandard.

in number See IN LENGTH.

inoculate See VACCINATE.

in one's birthday suit See BIRTHDAY SUIT.

in order that In American English, it is Standard to follow *in order that* with *may, might, can, would,* or any other auxiliary that fits the sense intended: *In order that we can have enough time, we ought to leave by noon.*

in order to Some commentators urge that to save space and time *to* alone should replace *in order to,* but sometimes that can create ambiguity: *We left our jobs to serve the war effort* could mean either "We left our jobs, which departure served the war effort" or "We left them so that we could serve the war effort instead." *In order to* removes the redundancy. In exposition, brevity is less important than clarity.

in part See IN WHOLE.

in point of fact See FACT.

input, output (*nn., vv.*), **throughput, thruput** (*nn.*) *Input* is the amount of electricity, energy, money, or (in computers) information put into a system (it also means simply "contribution" or "opinion," as in *We want your input on this*); *output* is the resultant finished work, manufactured goods, or other product(s) turned out by such a system. Both nouns are Standard. The verbs *input* and *output* are jargon, used especially in computer and electronics work but figuratively extended to describing activity in almost any system; such uses are slang or, at best, Conversational and Informal. *Throughput* (sometimes unconventionally spelled *thruput*) is usually only a noun, analogically related to *input* and *output* and referring to energy, information, and the like passed through the system in a given period of time, a way of measuring productivity in a computer system, for example. In computer jargon, functional shift has occasionally made *throughput* also a verb, but it has not so far been extended to general use elsewhere. Be wary of all these in general use; they've become clichés. See COMPOUNDS; FUNCTIONAL SHIFT; SPELLING (2).

inquire, enquire (*v.*), **enquirer, enquiry, inquirer, inquiry** (*nn.*) American English usually uses the spellings with an *i*; British English uses both forms about equally. *Inquire* occurs

with *about, after,* and *concerning,* as in *She inquired about [after, concerning] his mother's health,* and with *into, for,* and *as to,* as in *He inquires every week into [for, as to] any new developments in the case.* All these combinations specify the object of the *inquiry. Of* and *from* also combine with *inquire,* the combination specifying to whom or to what agency the *inquiry* is directed, as in *She inquired of [from] his employer.* See QUERY; SPELLING OF UNSTRESSED VOWELS.

in re (*prep.*) is a Latin tag meaning "concerning," "in regard to," as in *They have come* in re *the Cadwallader case.* It's legal and business jargon, often written in italics. Stick to English—*about* works better. See FOREIGN PHRASES.

in regard(s) to See REGARDING.

in respect to, in respect of, respecting, with respect to (*preps.*) All but *respecting* are compound prepositions, and those who value brevity above all other stylistic considerations argue that *about, concerning,* or *respecting* would be preferable. Actually, all are Standard, and all seem particularly well suited to Formal writing, which is often measured or thoughtful exposition. *In respect of* is perhaps more frequently used by the British and by American Anglophiles.

inroad (*n.*) Often used in the plural, *inroad* (pronounced IN-ROD) most often is followed by *into, in, on, upon,* as in *The guests made impressive inroads into [in, on, upon] the splendid buffet supper we had laid out.* See also COMPOUNDS.

insanitary, unsanitary (*adjs.*) These two are synonyms, meaning "unhealthful, unclean, disease-causing." *Insanitary* may occur somewhat more frequently than *unsanitary,* but both are Standard. See IN-.

insensible, insensitive (*adjs.*) *Insensible* has a wide range of meanings, among them "unable to sense or appreciate with the senses" (*She seemed insensible of the terrible noises around them*), "unconscious" (*The first punch knocked him insensible*), "unresponsive emotionally, unaware" (*She seemed insensible of anything out of the ordinary*), rarely, "trivial, imperceptible" (*The speed of the plane was unnoticed, insensible*). As the preceding examples show, when it combines with a preposition, *insensible* usually does so with *of. Insensitive* overlaps *insensible* somewhat, especially in the meaning "being unaffected by, or lacking feeling or sensitivity to," as in *She seemed insensitive to all the hostility around her.* This sense is usually strongly pejorative: to be *insensitive* is to lack humaneness. When it combines, *insensitive* does so almost exclusively with the preposition *to*. See also OBLIVIOUS.

inseparable (*adj.*), when it combines, takes the preposition *from*: *He is inseparable from his smelly old dog.*

in shape See IN LENGTH.

in short supply See SHORT SUPPLY.

inside, inside of (*preps.*) Each is Standard, although many argue that *inside of* is unnecessarily wordy. It does appear to have a somewhat more relaxed and Conversational air than does *inside* alone, but it's not wrong: *We've known them for years, but we have never been inside [of] their house.*

insight (*n.*) means "self-knowledge," especially in psychology and psychiatry, as in *He's a wise man, with a good deal of insight into his own personality,* and it also means "a sudden illumination or penetration of something hitherto not understood," as in *Suddenly I had an insight into the cause of our problem.* When it combines with prepositions, *insight* takes *into* most commonly but also *about, as to, regarding,* and *on: We shared our several insights into [about, as to, regarding, on] the reasons for the delay.*

insightful (*adj.*) is a relatively new Standard adjective, meaning "having or displaying insight," but it has become a vogue word recently and so has received some unfavorable comment. If you mean *intelligent, wise,* or *perceptive,* you might do well to use those words, at least for variety.

insignia (*n.*) The Latin singular was *insigne,* the Latin plural, *insignia,* but Standard English uses *insignia* as both singular and plural, and we also have a Standard plural on the regular English pattern, *insignias. Insigne* as a singular is rare in English and probably a bit too precious for most contexts. See FOREIGN PLURALS.

insinuate (*v.*), when it means "to work your way into, by indirect or artful means," is usually reflexive: *She insinuated herself into the family's affections.* When it means "to suggest something unpleasant or unflattering," as in *He insinuated that they had tried to buy his vote,* it frequently takes a *that* clause as direct object.

insist (*v.*), when combining with a preposition, does so with *on* or *upon: He always insists on [upon] having his own way.* As a transitive verb, *insist* takes a *that* clause as direct object: *He insisted that we stay for dinner.*

in size See IN LENGTH.

insofar as See INASMUCH AS.

insoluble, insolvable See UNSOLVABLE.

inspire (*v.*), **inspiration** (*n.*), **inspirational** (*adj.*) When it combines with a preposition, *inspire* takes *among, from, in, within, through, from, by, with, into, to,* and *toward: She inspired real zeal among [from, in, within] her followers. He was inspired through [from, by, with] the example she set. They were inspired into [to, toward] new efforts. To* plus an infinitive also follows *inspire,* as in *Your success inspired me to try.*

Inspiration and *inspirational* both have two levels of intensity, the higher suggesting a stimulus of divine or similar intensity, the lower a figurative and relaxed bit of hyperbole, suggesting almost any stimulus, however trivial. Both clusters are Standard, but the hyperbolic one is frequently overused.

inspissate (*v.*), **inspissated** (*adj.*), **inspissation** (*n.*) These are low-frequency but useful Standard words, the verb meaning "to thicken, to condense," the participial adjective meaning "thickened, or made heavier and more condensed," especially in a figurative sense, and the noun meaning "the process or result of such thickening." London fogs are excellent examples of *inspissation* of the atmosphere. Pronounce them *in-SPIS-AIT(-id)* or *IN-spis-AIT (-id)* and *IN-spi-SAI-shuhn.*

in spite of (*prep.*) Those who insist that brevity and conciseness are the highest virtues urge the use of *despite* (which see) or *although* in place of *in spite of.* All three locutions are useful and Standard, and each has its place, depending on context and style.

in spite of the fact that is a locution often criticized for being wordy, as in *We went to the meeting in spite of the fact that our attendance wouldn't do any good.* Perhaps *even though* or *although* would be more concise than *in spite of,* and *the fact that* could be faulted because *fact*'s referent here is not fact but opinion or something even less substantial. The wordiness of *in spite of the fact that* may occasionally be justified by style or rhythm, but the assertion of *fact* where none exists is unjustifiable overkill.

instance See CASE (2); EXPLETIVE (2); VOCALIZED PAUSES AND SPEECH FORMULAS.

instill, instil (*v.*) Both spellings are Standard, but *instill* is the more common in the United States. See also IMBUE.

instinctive, instinctual (*adjs.*) These are synonyms, both meaning "caused by or characterized by instinct," but *instinctive* is much more often employed; *instinctual* is rare, except in Britain.

institution (*n.*), **institutionalize** (*v.*) The noun has a number of meanings: "the establishment or instituting of something," as in *The institution of the new regulations was our first step*; "a practice," such as *the institution of veterans' memorials in Washington* or *the institution of commencement speeches*; "any organization or establishment, such as a university, a church, or a hospital"; or "an asylum." It is this last sense that gives us one of several euphemisms for places where orphans, the mentally ill, or those otherwise incapacitated are cared for; we also speak of mental institutions, orphan asylums (originally *asylums* were simply "places of safety"), homes for unwed mothers, and schools for the mentally retarded. These are Standard (and pardonable) euphemisms, so long as they do not blind us to the requirements of those we sequester there. Similarly euphemistic is the verb *institutionalize*, which means "to place someone in such an institution," the key point being that the placement is usually the decision of others, not of the person *institutionalized*. *Institutionalize* can be a euphemism for *incarcerate*, *relegate*, and similarly pejorative verbs, and it also means "to turn some informal arrangement or activity into a formal structured organization or practice"—an *institution*. See HOME (2).

instruct (*v.*), when combined with a preposition usually takes *in* (*She instructed us in penmanship*), *on* (*We were instructed on how to behave*), *as to* (*She instructed him as to which fork to use*), and *to* plus the infinitive (*They instructed us to wait outside*).

instructional, instructive (*adjs.*) Matters pertaining to instruction are *instructional: She had a desk full of instructional materials, some of them quite useless.* Matters that truly instruct or assist in instructing are *instructive: Some instructional manuals are worthless, but the best of them can be most instructive.*

instructor See PROFESSOR.

INSTRUMENTAL CASE This was the distinctive case form in (among other languages) Old English that was used normally with the prepositions *by* or *with*, as in *with* [*by*] *the sword*, wherein *sword* would be put in the instrumental case. These distinctive inflections disappeared from the language during the Old English period.

insure, assure, ensure (*vv.*) Americans frequently prefer *insure* when it comes actually to writing or buying insurance policies, whereas both *insure* and *ensure* have the generic sense of making certain of outcomes, as in *Our careful planning will insure* [*ensure*] *our success.* *Assure* often conveys that same general sense, but it can also be applied specifically to people: *Her remarks seem to assure success* is Standard, but *Her remarks seem to assure us of success* is much more commonly encountered in Standard English. See ASSURE.

insurance, assurance (*nn.*) For fire and casualty insurance, both Americans and Britons use the term *insurance,* but British firms, and some American firms in imitation of them, use the term *assurance* for "life insurance." Both are Standard. See MEANING: AMERICAN AND BRITISH DIFFERENCES.

in surgery See SURGERY.

in't See EN'T.

integral (*adj., n.*) is sometimes mispronounced and misspelled, with the *r* turning up wrongly at the end of the second syllable as a result of metathesis. Be sure to pronounce it *IN-te-gruhl* and to limit yourself to a single *r* and only in the final syllable.

integrate See DESEGREGATE.

integration See DESEGREGATION.

intend (*v.*) combines with the preposition *for* as in *His mother intended him for the church,* as well as with a direct object plus *to* plus infinitive, as in *She intends her daughter to become a doctor,* or *to* plus infinitive alone, as in *Neither child intends to obey her.* It can also be followed by a clause with or without *that: They intended* [*that*] *everyone would stay for dinner.* See also DESIGN; MEAN FOR.

intend for See MEAN FOR.

intense See INTENSIVE.

INTENSIFIERS, INTENSIVES These parts of speech are function words, usually originally and perhaps still also adverbs, used in this role to modify or *intensify* and also to help identify adjectivals and adverbials in particular: *He's too awful. She's awfully attractive. It's pretty late.* The list is fairly long, and we create new *intensifiers* frequently, especially as slang. The common *intensifiers* are *very, quite, awfully, really, pretty, too, fairly, more, rather, most, still, even, much, somewhat, not so,* and *ever so*; very high frequency in use, but Nonstandard except at the lowest levels, are *awful* and *real: I've got an awful bad cold. She was real nice to us.* Student slang *intensifiers* are a constantly renewable kind of slang. *Wicked* was a vogue word a short time ago on many campuses: *That was a wicked bad exam. Outstanding* is also being heavily overworked these days: *She has an outstanding new car.* And by the time you read this, all these will be faded and will no doubt have been superseded by new ones.

intensive, intense *(adjs.) Intensive* means "highly concentrated," as in *After the heart attack, he was in intensive care for several days; Education is a labor-intensive industry; They put her through an intensive course in spoken Spanish. Intense* means simply "strong, vigorous, unusually firm, highly emotional," as in *Competition for appointments was intense; She's a very intense sort of person with little sense of humor.*

INTENSIVES See INTENSIFIERS.

intent 1 *(adj.)* usually combines with the prepositions *on* or *upon,* as in *We were so intent on [upon] winning that we didn't notice the rain.* It can also combine with *about,* as in *She's very intent about her work,* and can be used with *in* plus a gerund, as in *She was intent in getting her message across,* and with *to* plus an infinitive, as in *He was intent to learn how the problem might be resolved.*

intent 2, intention *(nn.)* These are synonyms in some uses, especially when we speak of purpose, aim, meaning, and the like: *It is my intent [intention] to run in the next primary. Intention* is not entirely interchangeable with *intent* in the specialized reference it sometimes has to a man's and woman's plans for their sexual relationship: *Their parents insisted on knowing what their intentions were* (living together? getting married?). Sometimes jocular or ironic, this use is also a rather poignant euphemism for puzzled elders. In *An important consideration for the courts is the legislative intent behind this bill, intent* is almost interchangeable with *intention,* but the idiom is *legislative intent.*

inter *(v.)* means "to bury or entomb"; it is slightly technical, certainly formal, but not pretentious. Note that it doubles its final consonant before adding suffixes: *interred, interring.* Primary stress is on the second syllable (*in-TUHR*).

inter-, intra- *(prefixes) Inter-* means "between, among, shared among two or more," and the like: *interplanetary travel, interfaith ceremonies, intercity buses. Intra-* means "within, inside, during": *intracity school competition, intrastate transportation, intrauterine devices.* Check your dictionary for hyphenation of words beginning with these prefixes; most but not all such high-frequency words are not hyphenated.

intercede *(v.),* when it combines with prepositions, does so usually with *in* (*We will intercede in this matter*), *with* (*She asks that you intercede with her parents*), *for* (*Please intercede for me*), *against* (*They interceded against the angry neighbors*), and *between* (*She interceded between her two quarrelsome roommates*). All these uses are Standard.

interest *(n.)* has a wide range of Standard meanings, including "a share" (*an interest in the company*), "a curiosity or concern" (*an interest in their welfare*), "importance" (*of little interest to me*), and "money paid for the use of money" (*seven percent interest*).

interesting *(adj.),* **interestingly, interestingly enough** *(advs.) Interesting* in its strictest sense means "significant," as in *Her research is trivial and not really interesting,* but the far greater use of *interesting* in Standard practice is as a very non-specific word: *I don't know why I like her, but I somehow find her interesting.* When more explicit words will serve, use them, but sometimes fake precision is much worse than honest vagueness. Be careful, though, to control through context *interesting*'s possibly skeptical overtones: *When she'd finished droning on about her new life insurance policy, we all murmured, "How interesting."*

Interestingly and *interestingly enough* are both frequently and appropriately used today as sentence adverbs: *Interestingly [enough], she decided to enroll in the course.* Pronounce them either *IN-tuhr-est-ing-(lee)* or *IN-trest-ing-(lee).*

interface *(n., v.)* The noun has been Standard for more than a century, meaning "the point where two systems meet" or "the common boundary between two entities." The computer age however has recently made the noun a much higher frequency word and has also stimulated the creation of a verb through functional shift. It too is now Standard, as in *This computer network can interface with all others now in commercial production,* even though it has become a vogue word and, in the figurative sense meaning simply "to communicate," a cliché. Don't *interface* with the new committee; just meet, talk, or communicate with them. Save the word for explicit uses. Compare INPUT.

interment, internment *(nn.)* Don't confuse these somewhat similarly spelled words: *interment* is made from the verb *inter* and means "burial." *Internment* comes from the verb *intern* and means "to be confined," as in

The downed fliers' internment was in neutral Sweden.

in terms of (*prep.*) is a compound preposition that in mathematics and other objectively measurable fields expresses precise relationships and quantities: *We measured sales in terms of the number of units sold per year, rather than in dollars taken in per year.* But in general use the locution has become a cliché, and it encounters a good deal of criticism when used to speak of one ill-defined thing *in terms of* another equally vague and ill-defined. Perhaps no real relationship exists between them. *In terms of* is too often a symptom of padded prose.

international, foreign (*adjs.*) *International* is often used these days as a euphemism for *foreign*, as in *The international community in Washington was much upset over the new restrictions.* It may serve as a replacement for a time, but unless our views of the referents ameliorate, eventually it will take on the same pejorative overtones as *foreign*. When that happens, we will come up with yet another euphemism, since we will continue to require some appropriate objective way of reporting what is native and what is not. See ALIEN; FOREIGN.

INTERNATIONAL PHONETIC ALPHABET, THE (abbreviated IPA) is the set of phonetic symbols used internationally to represent the sounds human beings use in speech. Each symbol represents one sound, and every speech sound, irrespective of language, is (at least ideally) represented by only one symbol. For example: English *sinner* is [sInər], *singer* is [sIŋər] and *finger* is [fIŋgər]; English *king* is [kIŋ], and Norwegian *kong* is [kɔŋ] (rhymes with *gong*).

internecine (*adj.*), meaning "full of killing," "deadly," "mutually or internally destructive," has two chief American pronunciations, *in-tuhr-NES-in* and *in-tuhr-NEES-in*, and a final syllable *-een* is also acceptable with either of these in the United States, as is the mainly British *in-tuhr-NEE-SEIN*. The word is used mainly in its sense of mutual slaughter but is increasingly used where the internal killing may be only figurative.

internment See INTERMENT.

interpersonal (*adj.*) means "between persons," and has become something of a vogue word in referring to the way people get on with each other. *Interpersonal relations* is a cliché.

interpose (*v.*) When used with prepositions, *interpose* usually takes *between*, *in*, or *into*: *She interposed herself between the police officer and*

the boy. We interposed ourselves in [into] their heated conversation.

interpretive, interpretative (*adjs.*) These are synonyms in every respect, although *interpretive* has the higher frequency of use.

INTERROGATIVE PRONOUNS These pronouns—*who, whom, whose, which, what,* plus (sometimes) the *-ever* forms of these function words, are used for asking questions: *Who called? What did you say to him? Whomever did you ask?*

INTERROGATIVE SENTENCE See QUESTION SENTENCE.

interstate See THRUWAY.

intervene (*v.*), when followed by a preposition, is usually found with *in* and *between*, as in *I think I'd better intervene in this quarrel to prevent real harm* and *She intervened between her brothers,* although it infrequently also occurs with *with, into, concerning,* and *to* plus an infinitive.

intestinal fortitude See GUT.

in that case, in the case of See CASE (2).

in the absence of See ABSENCE OF.

in the altogether See ALL TOGETHER.

in the buff See BUFF.

in the circumstances See CIRCUMSTANCES.

in the course of See COURSE OF.

in the event that See EVENT.

in the final analysis See ANALYSIS (1).

in the hope(s) of, in the hope(s) that See HOPE.

in the last analysis See ANALYSIS (1).

in the light of, in light of These locutions mean "instructed by," or "illuminated by," as in *We changed our vote, in (the) light of the new information he brought.* Both forms are Standard Idioms.

in the near future, in the not too distant future See FUTURE (2).

in the worst way See WORST WAY.

in this day and age See DAY AND AGE.

INTIMATE LEVEL is the lowest level of speech, limited to conversation among immediate family members or equally intimate special friends. Each of us knows little about other families' *Intimate levels;* our own serves us, and we never try to take it out of its very small, tight constituency. Schools are not concerned with the *Intimate level:* they do not use it, they do not hear much of their students' use of it beyond kindergarten, and they have no need to teach it. Indeed, their chief interest in the *Intimate level* is to make sure that children learn to leave it at home. See LEVELS OF USAGE.

into See IN.

intolerant, intolerable (*adjs.*) *Intolerant* means "unwilling to tolerate, accept, or permit others' opinions, etc.," as in *She was intolerant of almost every value he held. Intolerable* means "unbearable, not tolerable in any way," as in *She considered all his values intolerable.*

INTONATION is, among other things, the technical term linguists use for the rise and fall of pitch contours at the ends of clauses and phrases as a speaker talks. Some of the patterns of American English *intonation* have grammatical force, as for example in the difference between these two otherwise identical sentences: *My mother is sick. My mother is sick.* The first example, ending with a falling *intonation* contour, is a statement; the second, ending in a rising *intonation* contour, is a question. And if the contour rises only slightly—*My mother is sick*—we understand it to mean grammatically that there is more to come in the utterance. When a sentence is already a question because of its interrogative pronoun—*What did he say?*—the normal downward *intonation* contour is exactly the same as that for the statement *My mother is sick.* But if you put a rising *intonation* contour on the sentence *What did he say?* it turns out to mean "Is this what you just asked? Am I repeating accurately what you just said?" Note that the question mark sometimes indicates the *intonation* of the spoken sentence when we put that sentence in writing, but not always.

intra- See INTER-.

INTRANSITIVE VERBS are verbs that do not take direct objects: *He behaved badly in school. She limps because of her sprained ankle.* Many verbs that are usually transitive (taking direct objects), such as *studies* is in *She studies Latin,* can also be used *intransitively: She studies assiduously.* See TRANSITIVE.

intricate (*adj.*), **intricacy** (*n.*) The primary stress is on the first syllable of each word.

intrigue (*n., v.*) The verb means (among other things) "to cheat or deceive," "to plot or scheme," and "to carry on a sexual affair," but what seems to be its most frequent current sense is "to arouse the interest of, to fascinate, to make (someone) curious," as in *Her air of mystery intrigued him.* All these senses are Standard, but you should be aware that some conservatives may object to the last, at least in Oratorical or Formal contexts, primarily on grounds

that it weakens a powerful and precise word by applying it to relatively trivial matters.

The noun means "a scheme," "a plot," and "a secret love affair" and is Standard in all these senses.

introduce (*v.*) When combined with a preposition, *introduce* usually appears with *to, into,* or *in: She introduced him to her mother. He introduced a new topic into* [*in*] *the conversation.*

introduction See FOREWORD.

intrude (*v.*) combines with the prepositions *into, in, on,* and *upon: She burst into the room, intruding abruptly into his reverie. I hate to intrude in your deliberations. He hated to intrude on* [*upon*] *her privacy.*

INTRUSION, INTRUSIVE R, INTRUSIVE SOUND OR LETTER *Intrusion* is the process of change in pronunciation wherein unanticipated sounds come into a word, usually because of their phonetic environment (the cluster of sounds around them and the transitions between them): dialectal pronunciations such as *EL-uhm* for *elm* and *ATH-uh-leet* for *athlete* illustrate Nonstandard *intrusions* of vowels. *Intrusions* such as the medial consonant *-p-* in *something* (*SUHMP-thing*) and the *-k-* in the midst of the consonant cluster at the end of *length* (*LENGKTH*) are normal Standard pronunciations at all levels. Sometimes spelling errors result when the inexperienced try to spell a word the way they incorrectly pronounce it, with three syllables—e.g., *athalete* for *athlete.*

In Eastern New England, Metropolitan New York City, and Southern regional dialects, the intrusive *r* can be heard at the ends of open syllables before vowels, as in John F. Kennedy's *KYOO-buhr* (for Cuba) and in the phrase *law and order* (pronounced *LOR uhn AW-duh*).

intrust See ENTRUST.

intuit (*v.*) (pronounced *in-TOO-it* or sometimes *IN-too-it*) is a back-formation, now more than a century old, from *intuition.* It is a Standard verb meaning "to understand or learn by means of intuition": *She correctly intuited what he would say.*

inundate (*v.*) combines in Standard English with *by, with,* and *in: Her fans inundated her in* [*with*] *letters, gifts, pictures, and other attentions. He was inundated by invitations from eager hostesses.*

inure, enure (*v.*) *Inure* (pronounced usually *in-YOOR,* but sometimes also *in-OOR*) is the more frequent of these two Standard spellings (*enure* is more often British than American). The word has two meanings: "to get used to" or "to learn to put up with something unpleasant," as in *She became inured to his constant hovering over her,* and "to become useful or advantageous, to accrue," as in *The long hours of practice ultimately inured to his benefit.* The preposition *to* is most commonly found in combination with *inure/enure,* as in the preceding examples, but in the "accrue" sense *for* may also occur: *All these hardships will eventually inure [enure] for our benefit.*

inveigh, inveigle (*vv.*) *Inveigh* (pronounced *in-VAI*) means "to complain or protest strongly," "to speak or write against," as in *She inveighed loudly against his decision to stay home. Inveigle* (pronounced either *in-VAI-gul* or *in-VEE-gul*) means "to lure or trick someone into doing something," as in *He inveigled her into attending the meeting, even though she'd sworn she wouldn't go.*

invent See DISCOVER.

inverse See OBVERSE.

inversion 1, diversion, perversion (*nn.*) An *inversion* is "a reversal, a turning upside down or over"; the noun has many specialized meanings, but the general sense is clear in *The inversion of your coffee cup tells the server you don't want coffee. Perversion* has the general sense of "anything that is wrongly or corruptly changed to a different course or purpose," as in *Their perversion of democratic principles was a shock to Americans.* But by far the most common specialized meaning of *perversion* is "sexual abnormality, deviation from the norms of sexual behavior," as in *Rumors of his perversion cost him the nomination.* See also PERVERSE.

Diversion has two clusters of meaning, literally "a turning aside," as in *The diversion of the path led him away from the lake,* plus a figurative sense that is perhaps even more frequently encountered, meaning "a distraction" or "an amusement," as in *Her diversion of his attention almost caused an accident* and *After hours of deskwork, he needed some diversion.*

INVERSION 2, SYNTACTIC *Syntactic inversions* are variant word orders that put a direct object, a complement, a verb, or even an entire predicate in front of the subject, reversing or scrambling the normal English order of subject-verb-object or subject-verb-complement: *A handsome woman she seemed to all of us* (predicate nominative precedes subject and verb). *A huge appetite for work he had* (direct object precedes subject and verb). *A huge appetite for work had he* (direct object precedes verb, which

precedes subject). *Says I, "Oh, no you don't!"* (verb precedes subject, which is followed by direct object). Some *inversions* sound a bit stilted or archaic; others seem quite familiar and acceptable. Perhaps the most common *inversions* are (1) those we accomplish by means of the passive voice, as in *The prize was awarded by the queen,* wherein *The queen awarded the prize* has been inverted to make the normal object and normal subject exchange locations and functions; and (2) the expletive plus verb, as in *There goes my last chance,* wherein the "real" sentence, *My last chance goes* [or *is going*], has been inverted so that the subject follows the verb. See also INVERSION IN QUESTIONS.

INVERSION IN QUESTIONS Early Modern English asked many of its questions by simply reversing the positions of subject and verb or subject and predicate: *Rides the King to the wars? Think you he will conquer? He will conquer, think you?* Today we still use *inversion* for many questions, but we no longer do it with most of our finite verbs; rather, we do it chiefly with forms of the auxiliaries *be, do, have, ought, dare, shall, should, will, would,* and the like. The rest of the verb appears later in the sentence, following the subject as usual, but we put the auxiliary first and make it agree with the subject: *Is your dog lost? Have they seen any change? Shall I call a cab? Dare we ask for more?*

INVERTED COMMAS is the British name for *quotation marks.*

invest (*v.*) This verb's first cluster of meaning has to do with the idea of "clothing or enfolding someone or something with or in the symbols of power and authority," which includes both the idea of "(in)vesting someone with authority," as in *The new officers were invested at a colorful ceremony,* and the somewhat less frequent idea of surrounding troops or cities so that they are cut off: *The invaders invested the capital and laid siege to it.* The second cluster means "to commit money to an enterprise in order to win a financial return": *He invested his money mainly in blue chip stocks and bonds.* Both these clusters are Standard.

in view of the fact that See FACT.

invite (*n.*) is a clipping from *invitation,* pronounced *IN-VEIT*; the word is slang, found in Casual, Impromptu, and Informal uses only. *Invitation* is the fully Standard noun.

invoke See EVOKE.

involve (*v.*) combines most frequently with the prepositions *in* and *with*: *She has been involved* with that organization for years. He's never been involved in politics before. The intransitive verb without a preposition, as in I just don't want to get involved, is also Standard, meaning "enmeshed," "engaged," or "entangled."

invulnerable (adj.) Some commentators consider invulnerable an absolute adjective, but Informal and Conversational users frequently ignore that distinction in favor of hyperbole.

in whole, in part These are clichés, formulaic ways of saying "all" and "some" and often used together (in whole or in part, in whole and in part). Wholly and partly sound slightly less stilted.

in width See IN LENGTH.

iota See SCINTILLA.

IPA is the conventional abbreviation for International Phonetic alphabet, which see.

ir- (prefix) is a form of the negative prefix in- that occurs before words beginning with r, as in irrespective and irreverent. But see also IL-; IM-; IN-.

iridescent (adj.) has only one r.

ironically (adv.) is Standard as a sentence adverb, but many literary commentators have regretted the use meaning "unusually, oddly, peculiarly, or simply strangely or unexpectedly," preferring instead that the word be restricted to occasions when genuine irony is involved.

IRONY (n.) is specifically the use of language to mean something quite opposite from what the words literally say. Irony is usually either sardonic or humorous in intent: She looked out at the rain and fog and said, "What a lovely day for a picnic!" Things ironic are not what they at first appear. Irony can be a two-edged sword: if your hearers or readers miss or misinterpret it, you're worse off than if you'd never tried it. Compare BURLESQUE; SATIRE. See also BLACK HUMOR; SICK HUMOR.

irrefutable See INCOMPARABLE.

irregardless (adv., adj.) is a word, all right, a blend probably of irrespective and regardless, but it is a Substandard one, limited to Common and Vulgar English. If a jocular use of it is taken to be an inadvertent one, the user may be judged harshly. Stick with regardless. See PRESCRIPTIVE AND DESCRIPTIVE GRAMMAR AND USAGE.

irrelevant (adj.) means "not related, not germane" and for a time was overused by those who insisted that only the relevant—as they defined it, often quite subjectively—was worth

attention. Its chief usage problems occur when the l and the v are interchanged through metathesis in either pronunciation or spelling.

irreligious, nonreligious, not religious, unreligious (adjs.) To be irreligious means "to lack religion or to be heedless of it"; it suggests, however, a deliberate posture, not an inadvertent one. Nonreligious is matter of fact, simply an opposite of religious, meaning "secular." Unreligious may be a synonym of either irreligious or nonreligious, but its overtones suggest the overtness or deliberateness we find in irreligious. In the predicate adjective position, not religious is matter of fact and closer in meaning to nonreligious. See also SACRILEGE.

irreparable See INCOMPARABLE; UNREPAIRABLE.

irrevocable See INCOMPARABLE.

irrupt, irruptive See ERUPT.

is, are See AGREEMENT; BE.

is because See BECAUSE; REASON IS BECAUSE.

-ise, -ize (suffix) is an extremely prolific word-forming suffix, and many conservatives balk at what appears to be unnecessary invention and overuse of the device to coin such originally nonce words as concretize, computerize, pauperize, and the like. Americans make more use of -ize; Britons use more of -ise, but there are many American spellings with -ise as well. See SPELLING (1).

ism (n.), **-ism** (suffix) An ism is an ideology, a theory whose name ends in -ism: communism, fascism, socialism, vegetarianism, liberalism, libertarianism, conservatism. These are all Standard, as is the word ism itself. Compare OLOGY.

isolate (v.) The prepositions that usually combine with isolate are by, from, in, and with, as in We were isolated by the unplowed roads; Her shyness isolated her from her peers; In his pride, he isolated himself in every social situation; Isolate the infected animals with separate housing, or the disease will spread.

Israeli See JEW.

issue (v.) combines with with in British English, as in The recruits were issued with ditty bags, but Americans would omit the with or choose another verb, such as provided, equipped, or something similar to use with it.

-ist (suffix) is an agentive ending, as in organist, manicurist, and violinist. The feminine versions, ending in -iste, of some words borrowed from French (e.g., *artiste*) are becoming obsolescent.

-istic (*suffix*) means "in imitation of" or "having some characteristics of," as in *modernistic*. Both *-istic* and *-esque* (which see) are sometimes partly or wholly pejorative, often meaning "a poor or cheap imitation of." See MODERN.

is when, is where See WHEN.

it is the third person singular neuter pronoun; both nominative and objective cases have the same form. It is used as a formulaic function word to begin sentences such as *It's raining* and *It's time to go*. It occasionally causes problems because of vague reference to its antecedent. See IT IS I WHO; IT'S ME; THAT (2).

Italian (*adj., n.*) Pronounce it *i-TAL-yuhn*; *EI-TAL-yuhn* is usually considered an ethnic slur. See ETHNIC SLURS AND TERMS OF ETHNIC OPPROBRIUM.

ITALIAN PLURALS See FOREIGN PLURALS.

Italian sandwich See SUBMARINE.

ITALICS American printed matter uses *italics* (the type fonts whose letters slant to the right) for the titles of literary and other artistic works (*War and Peace,* Verdi's *Requiem*); for the names of journals and newspapers (*The New York Times, Newsweek*); for words, letters, and numbers cited as words, letters, and numbers (as here with the word *italics*); for foreign words and phrases (*ars longa, vita brevis est*), although when these loan words and phrases have been fully assimilated into English, we usually cease to *italicize* them, as with *à la mode*; for the names of ships (*Queen Elizabeth II,* or *Q.E. II*); and for a number of other technical purposes such as are usually specified in a publisher's stylebook. In handwriting or typescript, underline what you wish to *italicize. Italics* are also used for emphasis and to indicate a heavier-than-normal stress on a word, particularly in Semiformal and Informal writing, although most editors discourage the practice. To achieve the effect of *italics* in the midst of a full sentence already in *italics,* put the word to be stressed in roman: *We thought she'd* never *leave!*

iterate See REITERATE.

it goes without saying See SAYING.

it is I who, it is they who These locutions preserve the nominative case pronouns in predicate nominative functions, perhaps in part because the nominative *who* follows immediately and therefore agrees with the preceding predicate nominative. Such usages are typically found at the upper levels; most Conversational and Informal uses would start out *It is me.* See AGREEMENT; CASE (1); IT'S ME.

its, it's The genitive of the pronoun *it* is *its,* without an apostrophe; the contraction of *it is* is spelled *it's,* with an apostrophe. Most errors involve using the contraction when the genitive is intended; these are usually the errors of inattention or carelessness, but they're often judged as though ignorance caused them, so inspect carefully what you write.

it's me Most speakers of English tend to put nominative case pronouns at the lefthand side of the clause, in "subjective" territory before the verb, and objective case pronouns at the righthand side of the clause, in "objective" territory after it. Apparently the pressure of this habit is so great that it overwhelms the Standard Formal pattern for the special class of verbs called linking or copulative verbs, wherein *It is she* is required, at least by rule, rather than *It's her,* or where *This is he* is needed, not *This is him.* The primary use of the objective case pronoun after linking verbs is in the first person: *It's us, It's me.* With third person, singular and plural, many Standard speakers will retain the nominative, even at lower levels of speech and in Informal uses. (And of course with second person *you,* the nominative and objective are indistinguishable.) But *It's me* and *It's us* are both Standard in all Conversational and most Informal uses, perhaps in part because they occur almost exclusively in speech anyway. Consider the way you answer the phone if the caller asks for you. To a stranger you'll respond (if you're a Standard speaker), *This is she* [*he*], not *This is me,* or you'll dodge the issue entirely and say *Speaking.* If you know the caller well, though, *It's me* will serve. In Oratorical speech and Formal writing, however, Standard English demands the nominative: *It is we who must shoulder the burden. It is us* just won't do in that sort of context.

-ix See -ESS.

-ize See -ISE.

J

jacket (*n.*) has a generalized sense, "any short coat, usually opening down the front," but it has two specialized senses as well: (1) "a suitcoat, blazer, or other tailored short coat," including the combinations *dinner jacket, mess jacket, Norfolk jacket, shooting jacket,* and *sport(s) jacket*; and (2) "any informal coatlike outerwear with a slide fastener, snap, or button closing, usually loose fitting and intended for knockabout use." Some Americans regularly describe a man's suit as having a coat or suit coat; others call it a *jacket*. Both usages are Standard.

jamb, jam (*nn.*) Of these homophones, *jamb* means "the side frame member of a door or other opening": *The lefthand door jamb was splintered. Jam* (1) is a functional shift from the verb *jam,* meaning "to squeeze or wedge or crowd together"; the noun means "a crowd or mass of people or things," as in *There was a large log jam in the river; A traffic jam blocked the intersection.* This word also has a Conversational and Informal sense meaning "a difficulty, a predicament," as in *Having lost my billfold, I was in a real jam. Jam* (2) is the confection made by boiling fruit to use as a spread for toast. All except the "predicament" sense are fully Standard.

JAP is an acronym for *Jewish-American princess,* a slur apparently used by Jews and non-Jews alike to refer to the supposedly spoiled, materialistic daughters of wealthy suburban and urban Jewish families.

Jap, Japanese (*adjs., nn.*) *Jap* is a clipped form of *Japanese,* and it is taboo both as noun and adjective because it is an ethnic slur. The appropriate ethnic designation is *Japanese: The Japanese are touring the United States in great numbers. She gave me a Japanese print.*

JARGON, CANT *Jargon* is a strongly pejorative label applied to language you can't understand; it refers to those needlessly specialized words that other people use to impress or baffle the outsider with their erudition and distinction. And *cant,* which began by meaning "a whining beggars' or thieves' speech" or "the argot peculiar to a religious sect or other group," came also to mean "hypocritical, insincere, pious talk," as well as "the speech, the special words of a particular group or trade." And *cant* too is almost always pejorative.

But *jargon* is mainly the language of the specialist: *gentrification* is likely to be a *jargon* word to one not familiar with downtown real estate, city planning, and urban sociology, but for those whose occupational or other interests are involved, it can be a useful term, saving much time and explanation. The trouble most language people find with *jargon,* however, is that much of it is needlessly obscure, and some of it is windily pretentious; its use where not really necessary is a hindrance, not a help, to communication. Nearly all commentators belabor governmental use of *jargon,* some of it euphemistic and full of doublespeak, and the worst of it inaccurate, imprecise, and confusing to the ordinary citizen. Yet when physicians and surgeons begin to discuss your case among themselves, you don't begrudge them their *jargon*; what you will object to is their unwillingness or inability to tell you what you need to know, in language you can understand. There may be good *jargon* and bad *jargon,* but if the listener or reader cannot understand it, it is all useless language or worse. See also SECRET LANGUAGES.

jawbone (*v.*) means "to try to persuade by means of appealing publicly, rather than by using one's authority or public office or the like," as in *The president tried to jawbone the union leaders into bargaining further, rather than requiring them to do so under the provisions of the Taft-Hartley Law. Jawbone* is now Standard, although conservatives might prefer not to use it in the most Formal or Oratorical of contexts. It is as graphic as the verb *to jaw,* a Standard Conversational and Informal word for "talk vigorously."

jealous, zealous (*adj.*) Once synonymous, these are now distinct in all but one sense. *Jealous* means "resentful of a rival," as in *He is jealous of her other suitors*; "envious as a result of this emotion," as in *He is subject to jealous fits*; "intolerant of competition," as in *Ours is a jealous God. Zealous* means "full of zeal for, vigorously devoted," as in *They are zealous to uphold [in upholding] the law.* Only in the sense "watchful in guarding" does *jealous* overlap with *zealous* today, as in *I'm jealous of [zealous about] my reputation; I don't want it damaged.*

Jealous combines usually with *of* (*She's jealous of her sister*), sometimes with *for* (*His mother is jealous for her son*), occasionally with *over* (*He's jealous over her slightest sign of inattention*), and sometimes with *to* plus an infinitive, as in *They're jealous to preserve their political power. Zealous* combines with *for* (*We're zealous for their success*), with *about* (*He's zealous about doing his duty*), and with *to* plus an infinitive (*You must be zealous to protect your good name.*) All these are Standard.

jeer (*v.*) combines with these prepositions: *at,* as in *She jeered at his ineptness*; *about* and *over,* as in *She jeered about [over] their cowardice*; and *to* plus an infinitive, as in *The class jeered to see him cry.*

jejune (*adj.*) means "lacking interest," "empty," "insipid," as in *She wrote jejune plays that bored audiences and critics alike*; figuratively it also means "empty" in the sense of "not nutritionally good," as in *She followed a series of jejune diets that undermined her health*; and, possibly because of a confusion with French *jeune* ("young"), it has come also to mean "childish, immature," as in *His humor was unfortunately jejune.* Standard English now uses *jejune* in all these senses, but some commentators object to the "immature" sense. Best advice: stick with the two "empty, insipid" senses.

jet lag (*n.*) is now Standard as the name for the disruption of your body's biological clock caused by your boarding a jet in one time zone, flying through many intervening time zones, and deplaning in still another.

jetsam See FLOTSAM.

jet set (*n.*) was until recently a Conversational and journalese term, but it is now Standard used to identify those people who fly about on jet aircraft, seeking expensive pleasure and diversion in each others' "beautiful" company at the world's exclusive spas and resorts.

Jew (*n.*), **Israeli** (*adj., n.*), **jew** (*v.*), **Jewish** (*adj.*) *Jew* is the Standard name for a member of the *Jewish* religion or heritage, and *Jewish* is the Standard adjective. *Jew* used as adjective, as in *that Jew mayor,* is an ethnic slur and hence taboo; use the Standard adjective, *Jewish,* instead. Also taboo, and for the same reason, are the verb *jew,* meaning "to cheat or swindle," and the combined form *to jew down,* meaning "to bargain to reduce a price." An *Israeli* is a citizen of Israel, the modern *Jewish* state at the eastern end of the Mediterranean Sea; *Israeli* is also an adjective: *The ship flies the Israeli flag.* See also HEBREW.

jewelry, jewellery (*n.*) *Jewelry* is the American spelling, *jewellery,* a British variant, but both have a three-syllable Standard pronunciation, *JOO-uhl-ree.* Also Standard is the American variant pronunciation *JOOL-ree,* but the frequently heard *JOO-luh-ree,* caused by metathesis, is Nonstandard.

Jewess (*n.*) may have been considered an ethnic slur even before it was objected to as sexist language; in any event, it is taboo today, even though there are reports that some Jewish women still use it of themselves. *Jew* is the appropriate noun for either sex. See also JEW; -ESS; NEGRESS.

jibe (*vv.*), **gibe, gybe** (*nn., vv.*) *Jibe* (1) means "to shift suddenly from one side to another" and is usually used of fore-and-aft-rigged sailboats when they turn to put the wind on the other side of their sails and thus snap those sails to the opposite side of the boat. It can also be used generally and figuratively for any sudden shift of direction. *Jibe* (2), usually combined with *with,* means "to be in agreement, to match," as in *Her version of the incident jibes with his.* The word in this sense appears now to be Standard, although at least one dictionary labels it Colloquial. *Gibe,* often with *at,* is a verb meaning "to taunt, to deride, to jeer," as in *The spectators gibed at him mercilessly when he struck out,* and the noun *gibe* means "a taunt," as in *She winced at each new gibe.* Spelling is a considerable complication in these homophones, since *jibe* is a frequent variant spelling of *gibe,* and *gybe* occasionally occurs as a variant of *gibe* and, rarely, of either *jibe.* Edited English usually sticks to *jibe* for the "shift" and "agree" senses and *gibe* for the noun and verb meaning "taunt."

job action (*n.*) is now Standard, having begun as a recent addition to American labor movement jargon. It is a specialized compound meaning "some sort of work slowdown or other organized refusal or protest short of a strike, staged by employees seeking to bring pressure on an employer in a labor dispute."

jobless (*adj., n.*) Both parts of speech are Standard; each means "unemployed," as in *She's been jobless for six months; He's one of the thousands of jobless in this state.*

john (*n.*) Two of its many slang meanings are of very widespread frequency: *john* meaning "toilet" is employed as a euphemism in Casual and

Informal contexts throughout American English, and *john* meaning "a prostitute's customer" is regularly encountered in the press and must now be considered general slang.

join (*v.*) can take any of several prepositions in Standard English: *to* or *with*, as in *Our committee was joined to* [*with*] *theirs*; *in*, as in *The whole room joined in the chorus of booing; even I joined in.* Commentators sometimes object to *join up* and *join together* as redundant, but *join up* is a Standard idiom meaning "to enlist in the armed forces," as in *He joined up as soon as the school term ended*, and *join together* is also Standard, simply emphatic, and very familiar at that, as in the traditional marriage ceremony words from Matthew 19:6, . . . *what therefore God hath joined together . . .*). See REDUNDANT.

jot See SCINTILLA.

JOURNALESE is a term used by commentators on usage, usually pejoratively, to describe the locutions they find infelicitous in the language they read in newspapers and magazines and hear from radio and television journalists. It usually signifies a greater informality than the observer is willing to permit, a freer admission of slang and other innovations to status in the language than the observer would grant, and in general a breeziness and inattention to precision and good manners that the observer finds irritating or offensive. At its best, the language of journalism may be indistinguishable from the best Edited English, and even in relaxed contexts, it will meet Semiformal standards. But at its worst it may admit both Nonstandard locutions and breaches of good language manners.

Jr. See SENIOR.

judgment, judgement (*n.*) *Judgment* is the more commonly used American spelling, but *judgement* (the usual British spelling) is a Standard American variant, even though not widely used in Edited English.

judicial, judicious (*adj.*) *Judicial* means "concerning law, judges, and the courts," as in *This dispute will require judicial handling; the court must decide*, and "characteristic of or like a judge," as in *Her appointment is doubtful; she lacks the judicial temperament. Judicious* means "showing good judgment, sensible, wise," as in *His advice was judicious and carefully phrased.* Occasionally *judicial* will be used as a synonym of *judicious* in the sense of "wise, judgelike," but Standard English usually maintains the distinctions between the two words.

judiciary Pronounce it *joo-DISH-ee-ER-ee*, never *joo-DISH-uhr-ER-ee*.

judicious See JUDICIAL.

Jugoslavia See YUGOSLAVIA.

juncture (*n.*), in the sense "this particular time or stage in the course of events," as in *At this juncture we're uncertain which would be the better choice*, is Standard, although it is sometimes criticized as pretentious or as being a cliché. Avoid its overuse, but use it where it can graphically specify where events or forces intersect.

junior See SENIOR.

junket (*n.*) derives from a Latin word for "a sweetmeat, apparently brought to market in a rush basket" (the Latin for *rush* is *juncus*); hence the modern *junket*, "a sweet milk-based custard." But semantic change has operated to make the noun also mean "a picnic" or "an excursion, still pleasant and harmless," and then "a trip or outing taken at public expense," as in *The three representatives were on some sort of junket in Las Vegas.* In that sense (and in the Conversational and Informal verb based on it) *junket* is now thoroughly pejorative.

junkie, junky (*n.*) A *junkie* (*junky* is a less-frequent variant spelling) is someone addicted to drugs, particularly heroin (*junk* is one of many slang words for heroin), but the term has been used figuratively and widely to mean anyone with a strong or indiscriminate preference for something, as in *She's a pop music junkie who will listen to any band at all.* In both uses *junkie* is slang.

junta (*n.*) is a Spanish term meaning "a ruling group or council." For pronunciation, Standard English uses the Spanish *HUN-tuh*, the fully anglicized *JUHN-tuh*, and several other variants that begin with either *h-* or *j-* sounds and with stressed vowels ranging from *OO* to *UH*. Best advice: stick to *HUN-tuh* or *JUHN-tuh*, and particularly avoid the *zh* sound of the initial consonant of the French *gendarme*, which is an ignorant hyperforeignism.

jurist, juror (*nn.*) A *jurist* is someone who knows the law—a scholar or a judge. A *juror* is a member of a jury, so named because he or she takes an oath. The term *juror* is infrequent but Standard in the meaning "anyone who takes an oath."

just (*adv.*) is at least Conversational and Informal in the following senses, which also occur frequently in Edited English, although not necessarily in the most Formal uses: "precisely" (*It's just six o'clock now*), "a short time ago"

(*We just arrived*), "scarcely, barely" (*They were just too late*), "immediately" (*It's just in the next block*), "only" (*We need just ten dollars more*), "very, remarkably" (*It's just wonderful to hear your voice*), and "perhaps, maybe" (*She just might do it for us*). *Just not* and *not just* are idioms: *just not* means "simply, unquestionably," as in *He's just not the sort to play that part*; *not just*, however, means "not only, not merely" and is sometimes paired with *but also* or *but . . . besides*, as in *She's not just weary, but she's ill besides* or *She's not just tired; she's exhausted*. Both these uses are Standard. See ONLY.

just as See THE SAME AS.

Justice (*n.*) is conventionally used in the titles of justices of the U.S. Supreme Court and occasionally for judges of other courts as well, as in *Mr. Justice Holmes*.

justify, explain, account for (*vv.*) When *justify* combines with a preposition, it frequently takes either *by* (indicating who or what did the justifying), as in *Her actions were justified by subsequent events*, or *in* (indicating the justified actions taken), as in *He was justified in calling the police*. Both are Standard, as are these less frequently used prepositions: *as*, as in *I thought it was justified as a stopgap measure*; *to* followed by either an infinitive, as in *We felt we were justified to cancel the meeting* (although *in canceling*, with a gerund, is more frequent), or a noun, as in *She tried to justify her behavior to anyone who would listen*; *because of* and *for*, as in *Our departure was justified because of* [*for*]

their obvious interference; and *on* or *upon (the) grounds of*, as in *He justified his decision on* [*upon*] [*the*] *grounds of the need for haste*.

Hierarchic organizations recognize a key distinction between *justifying* and *explaining*, in that superior officers may choose to explain orders, but ordinarily they need not persuade their people of their correctness or justice: *I will explain the directive I gave my assistants, but I need not justify it to them*. To account for the accuracy of something is either to *explain* it or, if there are suitable records, to *justify* it (that is, to prove its correctness).

juvenile (*adj., n.*) The adjective means "young, immature, childish," as in *Their giggling was juvenile and annoying*, and it also means "for young people," as in *juvenile furniture, juvenile books*. The noun has a legal sense, specifying that a person is still legally a child, of an age at which he or she is treated as a child rather than an adult: *The judge ruled that the prisoner was a juvenile and must be tried in juvenile court*. The noun also is used sometimes to refer to a book or books intended for children: *She has written several successful juveniles*. See also TEEN.

juvenilia (*n.*) is the plural noun used to refer to all sorts of things done in one's youth, especially creative works: *That closet is full of juvenilia—drawings and paintings from their school years*. It also means "books for children," as does one sense of *juveniles*. The misspelling *juvenalia* reflects a common mispronunciation. Pronounce it *joo-vuh-NIL-yuh*; the third syllable rhymes with *bill*, not *bail*.

K

kangaroo (*n.*) The plural is either *kangaroos* or *kangaroo*.

kaput (*adj.*) is pronounced either *kuh-PUT* or *kuh-POOT*, and in English it is slang meaning "broken, worn out, dead, finished, or destroyed," as in *The batteries in my flashlight are kaput*.

karat See CARAT.

kempt (*adj.*) is a back-formation from *unkempt* and means the opposite of it, "neat, well-groomed." It's a lost positive that has become Standard.

kerb (*n.*) is the British spelling of *curb*. See SPELLING (1).

kernel See SEED (2).

kerosene, coal oil, kerosine, paraffin (*nn.*) *Kerosene* is the most common American spelling of the name of the fuel, and *kerosine* is a variant. *Coal oil*, which has other meanings too, is also another name for *kerosene*, and *paraffin* is the British name for it, as well as the American name for the white, waxy material used in home canning and in candle making.

ketchup, catchup, catsup (*n.*) *Ketchup* is the most common spelling; the others are variants of the name of that thick, tomato-based sauce (sometimes called *tomato ketchup*) used with meat and other dishes. Pronounce *ketchup* and *catchup* interchangeably as *KECH-uhp* or *KACH-uhp*, and *catsup* as *KAT-suhp*; all are Standard.

key See QUAY.

kibbutz (*n.*), pronounced *ki-BOOTS* or *ki-BUTS*, is a modern Hebrew word (plural: *kibbutzim,* pronounced *ki-BOOT-seem*) meaning an Israeli collective farm or village. Members of such collectives are called *kibbutzniks* in English. See FOREIGN PLURALS.

kibosh (*n.*) pronounced either *KEI-BAHSH, KEI-BAWSH,* or *kuh-BAHSH,* is slang in the idiom *put the kibosh on,* meaning "put a stop to," "squelch," as in *Dad put the kibosh on my plan to stay for the weekend. Kibosh* has been said to be of Irish or of Yiddish origin, but the etymology is really not known.

kickback (*n.*) is Conversational and Informal meaning "any sharp reaction or objection," as in *There was no kickback from the members when the assessment was announced,* but it is slang in the sense "illegally returned money as part of a sale or contract," as in *They claim that a kickback was paid to the buyer of the property.*

kickoff (*n.*), **kick off** (*v.*) The noun means "the initial kick that begins play or resumes it after a score or at the start of a half in football or soccer." The verb describes the action of *kicking off.* Both are Standard in that use, as in *We kicked off, but the kickoff was called back because we were offside.* Both noun and verb are usually limited to Informal and Conversational contexts when used figuratively to refer to the beginning of a campaign or any other enterprise, but Edited English is beginning to contain more and more sentences of this sort, some of them labeled journalese: *They kicked off the campaign last week. The kickoff dinner was well attended.*

kid (*n.*) is Standard as the name for a young goat and for leather made of that animal's skin, but its widest use in American English is as the Conversational and Informal word for a child, a youth, or even a young adult, as in *He's just a kid, not over ten* [or *twenty,* or perhaps even *thirty*]. According to one commentator, the plural *kids* in this sense has in most Conversational use and indeed in almost all but Edited English and other Formal and Oratorical use managed to drive out or at least submerge words like *children,* particularly when older Americans refer

to their own adult offspring. This may be because other terms pose problems: *adolescents* seems clinical or sociological; *youths* may seem patronizing and too limiting in age; *teens* and *teenagers* are too explicit in age reference to be more generally useful; *young people* and *young adults* sound euphemistic and vaguely like librarians' or Sunday schoolteachers' jargon; and the terms *boys* and *girls* are suitable only for the very young, because they are likely to be judged racist or sexist or both in a good many contexts.

kill See EXECUTE.

-kill See STREAM.

kilo (*n.*), pronounced either *KEE-lo* or *KIL-o,* is the clipped form of *kilogram* (a unit of weight measurement amounting to slightly more than two pounds), as in *Get three kilos of that flour, please,* and occasionally of other words using *kilo-* as a prefix. It's Conversational and Informal.

kilo- (*prefix*) is a combining form meaning "a thousand," as in *kilocycle, kilogram, kilometer, kilowatt,* and the like, each of which means "a thousand of whatever is the second element of the compound." See KILOMETER.

kilometer (*n.*) has two standard pronunciations, either *ki-LAHM-i-tuhr* or *KIL-uh-MEE-tuhr.* Nearly every other *kilo-* compound puts the primary stress on *KIL-,* as with *kilobyte* (*KIL-uh-BEIT*) and *kilobit* (*KIL-uh-BIT*).

kilt, kilts (*nn.*) *Kilt* is the standard singular form of the name of the Scottish man's skirt, although, on analogy with *pants* and *trousers,* it is frequently heard from Americans as *kilts* even when modified by a singular *his.* One bagpiper wears *his, a,* or *the kilt,* not *kilts;* the members of a pipe band wear *kilts* (or *the kilt*). Scottish-Americans usually insist on *kilt,* not *kilts;* courtesy suggests that you do the same.

kin (*adj., n.*) *Kin* is a collective noun, meaning "relations, family," as in *All our kin come to these reunions,* but it can be used in the singular, as in *He's a kin of mine.* It also serves as a Conversational or Informal adjective, as in *She's kin, all right, but not very near.* See KITH.

kind, in See SALARY.

kind, manner, sort, style, type, way (*nn.*) These nouns, introduced by *this/that, these/those,* or *any/all* and followed by prepositional phrases introduced by *of,* present a good many usage problems. Edited American English and most conservative American commentary insist that the singular nouns *kind, manner, sort, type, style,* and *way* must be modified by singular demonstratives (*this/that kind* or *manner* or *sort* or *style* or *type* or *way*) and that normally each will be followed by an *of* phrase with a singular object (*this kind of dog, that manner of chatter, that sort of dilemma, this type of book, this way of writing*). Further, these same conservative American standards insist that when *kind, manner, sort, type, way,* and the like are plural, then the preceding demonstratives and any count nouns serving as objects of the following prepositions must also be plural: *these kinds of studies, those sorts of poems, these types of airplanes.* But when the following objects of the preposition are mass nouns, they may be singular, as in *those sorts of gravel, those types of sand, these ways of thinking.* Whatever the American Edited English standards demand, however, British English and American Conversational and Informal uses clearly display a full range of combinations of singulars and plurals, although these usages are under considerable stress at present. Best advice: for publication and Oratorical or Formal use, stay as close to the conservative patterns as possible, and at other levels be aware that you may sometimes be faulted by those who use and prefer the conservative patterns. See KIND OF; SOME KIND OF.

kindly (*adv., adj.*) As adjective *kindly* is familiar and poses no problem: *She's a sweet, kindly old grandmother.* As adverb, it has some fairly unproblematic uses, as in *He kindly offered her his seat.* When *kindly* means "please," or "would you be so kind (or so good)," however, the situation becomes a bit more complicated. In *Kindly step to the back of the bus* and *Kindly keep off the grass, kindly* means "please," but it's a very emphatic sort of "please," as the imperiousness of *Kindly keep your distance* demonstrates. And, as *Kindly permit me to pass* suggests, it is Formal and can deliberately distance the speaker from the person(s) addressed. See also FRIENDLY.

kind of, a bit, rather, somewhat, sort of These are all qualifiers suitable for various levels, and all mean essentially the same thing. *We kind of [sort of] wished they'd hurry* is Informal and Casual, as is *I was kind of [sort of] upset by her remark.* But *I was somewhat [rather, a bit] upset by her remark* is clearly Standard, suitable for any level, although possibly a bit stiff for some Casual use. See HAD RATHER; QUALIFIERS.

kind of a, sort of a These qualifiers are used with nouns, as in *What kind of a dog is that? Do you have this sort of a material?* and with adjectives, as in *I have sort of a bad back; She*

has kind of a yearning to go home. In the adverbial use with adjectives, these locutions are Conversational and Informal. In the use with nouns they are Standard, although conservative usage prefers omission of the *a*, as in *What kind of dog is that? Do you have this sort of material?* especially in Formal and Oratorical contexts.

King James See ST. JAMES.

kith (*n.*) is a word obsolete today except in the cliché *kith and kin*, wherein *kith* means something like "friends (people known to me) and fellow citizens," and *kin* means "relations." The cliché is not absolutely redundant, but it is close.

kitsch (*n.*), **kitschy** (*adj.*) The noun, meaning "cheap, tawdry, tasteless things, pretentious, junky, but popular," and the adjective, meaning "of shoddy, pretentious character or quality," are both Standard; they apply particularly to furniture, architecture, and other designs that unjustifiably pretend to artistic merit. In German and Yiddish, *kitsch* means "trash," especially "gaudy trash." American English probably borrowed the word from Yiddish rather than German. See YIDDISH WORDS IN AMERICAN ENGLISH.

kitty-corner(ed), catty-corner(ed), cater-corner(ed) (*adv., adj.*) All these are Standard variants of an idiom, based on folk etymologies developed from the French *cater (quatre)*—"four"—prefixed to *corner(ed)*; the idiom means "diagonal" or "obliquely opposite," as in *The gas station was kitty-corner(ed) [catty-corner(ed), cater-corner(ed)] from the flower stand.*

klutz (*n.*) is slang, a Yiddish word meaning "a stupid, clumsy, doltish person." See YIDDISH WORDS IN AMERICAN ENGLISH.

knee-jerk (*adj.*) is a Conversational and Informal figurative idiom, occurring frequently in the cliché *a knee-jerk reaction*, which means "an automatic, predictable response," so-called after the reflex a physician stimulates by tapping a patient just below the kneecap with a little rubber hammer: *She's a knee-jerk liberal, absolutely predictable in every opinion.*

kneel (*v.*) The Standard past tense and past participle are each in divided usage between *kneeled* and *knelt. Kneeled* displays the weak verb pattern; *knelt,* a combination of weak and strong verb patterns. See also CREEP.

knickers (*n.*) Always used as a plural, *knickers* are loose trousers fastened at and ending just below the knee. The word is a clipped version of *knickerbockers* (which is a synonym still, if archaic and whimsical), the name of Washington Irving's fictitious Dutch author of his *History of New York,* Diedrich Knickerbocker, who was said to wear those voluminous Dutch breeches. *Knickerbockers* is still a literary nickname for New Yorkers, and the *Knicks* (a clipped form of the word) are New York City's professional basketball team. One variety of *knickers* is the golfer's plus fours, now having a mild new run of popularity. In British English *knickers* are a woman's underdrawers. See PANTS; SLACKS.

knife See NOUNS ENDING IN *-F.*

knit (*v.*) The Standard past tense and past participle are each either *knit* or *knitted,* as in *She had knit [knitted] sweaters for both her nieces.* Many literal uses, involving the process of knitting, use *knitted* a bit more frequently as participial adjective, as in *This dress is knitted rather than woven,* but figurative uses seem to favor *knit* as the adjective, and when *closely* or *tightly* or *densely* (or *close-* or *tight-*) are used with it, *knit* again is the usual form: *Our family is a tightly knit [close-knit] unit.*

knock up is an idiom and an old chestnut used to illustrate the traps for unwary Britons that American slang may set: in the United States *to knock up a woman* is to make her pregnant, while in Britain *to knock someone up* is simply a Conversational expression for "to rouse or summon," as in *They knocked me up early this morning,* or, as a participial adjective, for "worn out, exhausted," as in *After that hike, I was completely knocked up.*

knot (*n.*) means "one nautical mile per hour," and so among the nautically knowing, to say *five knots per [an] hour* is a lubber's tautology. Inland, the blunder is not so serious, but Edited English, however, studiously avoids *knots per [an] hour.*

know (*v.*) The past tense is *knew,* past participle *known,* and any use of *knowed* in either function is Substandard and a Vulgar shibboleth.

Maddeningly recurrent in some speech, especially of the young, is *you know,* inserted at almost any pause or point of hesitation. It sometimes appears to be only a vocalized pause or tic, but it may also reflect the speaker's unconscious effort to ensure understanding: *Y'know, I don't believe that she, y'know, quite realizes, what she's, y'know, asking.*

know as, know that *Know as,* as in *I don't know as I like him,* is dialectal or Conversational at best; in negative statements with *know,*

think, believe, and the like, Standard English calls instead for *that,* as in *I don't know that I like him.*

know-how (*n.*) is an Americanism now appropriate for use in Edited English and all other levels, even though one or two dictionaries still label it Informal or Colloquial: *Our manufacturing know-how should help us compensate for our higher labor costs.* Some editors may still prefer the more conventional *skill, training,* or *experience* instead.

knowing, knowledgeable (*adj.*) *Knowing* means "full of information, shrewd, deliberate, conscious," as in *She gave him a knowing look; His actions reflected not inadvertence but a knowing display of disrespect. Knowledgeable* means simply "having knowledge, being intelligent or well informed," as in *She's knowledgeable about all sorts of tax matters.*

know that See KNOW AS.

kosher (*adj., n., v.*) *Kosher* (pronounced *KO-shuhr*) is a Jewish term (acquired from Hebrew through Yiddish). The adjective means "clean, prepared under proper dietary rules, fit to eat," as in *That company caters kosher meals.* As an extended sense, the adjective also means simply "in the Jewish tradition," as in *They keep a kosher table and live in the kosher way.* In generalized slang use, *kosher* means "proper, acceptable, according to rule, irrespective of Jewish referents," as in *She always did things things kosher; nothing irregular was permitted.* The noun means "food prepared according to the Jewish dietary laws," as in *They always eat kosher at their house.* The verb, often pronounced *KAH-shuhr* and sometimes spelled *kasher,* means "to make *kosher*" in the literal senses.

kowtow (*n., v.*) is of Chinese origin; the noun means "a deferential bow, touching the forehead to the ground," and the verb means "to perform such a bow" or in extended use "to show respect or deference to someone" or "to be servile and obsequious," as in *She'll never kowtow to her mother-in-law.* Pronounce it to rhyme with *how now,* with both syllables stressed, with primary stress on either syllable.

kraft paper, craft paper (*nn.*) *Kraft* is from the German word for "strength," and *kraft paper* is that heavy brown paper used for bags and wrapping paper. *Craft paper* is the wrong spelling for this kind: *craft papers* are of varied colors, weights, and textures and take their name from the *handicraft* projects for which they're used.

kudos, kudo (*n.*) *Kudos* is a word originally Greek meaning "praise, fame, glory," and it is singular: *True kudos comes only to the deserving.* When it came into English (via British university slang), it was pronounced either *KOO-daws* or *KYOO-daws*, and conservative commentators insist that only this singular mass noun use and these pronunciations are appropriate. But our fading knowledge of Greek has affected the word's pronunciation and number: it has come frequently to be pronounced *KOO-doz* and to be taken for a plural whose singular (via back-formation) is *kudo* (pronounced *KOO-do*), all of which are considered Nonstandard by conservatives. Nevertheless, journalese and other increasing Semiformal uses of *kudo/kudos* in Edited English make clear that the count noun is gaining frequency. Best advice: follow conservative practice in Formal and Oratorical contexts, and note that many written uses will not reveal whether the word is in fact singular or plural: *They presented him with well-earned kudos.*

L

-l-, -ll- See CONSONANTS (2).

lab, Lab (*nn.*) Uncapitalized, *lab* is a clipped form of the word *laboratory*; the usually capitalized *Lab* is a clipped form of *Labrador retriever,* the name of a breed of dog. Both *lab* and *Lab* are Conversational and Informal.

labor, labour (*n., v.*) The American spelling is *labor,* the British *labour.* The noun means "work" or "workers"; the verb *labor* means "to work." Both are Standard. See BELABOR; SPELLING (1).

laboratory, lavatory (*nn.*) A *laboratory* is a place for experimentation or research or for the teaching of these; Americans pronounce it *LAB-ruh-tor-ee,* the British, *luh-BOR-uh-tree.* A *lavatory* is a basin or sink for washing hands and face, a room with a toilet and sink, or (in British use) a flush toilet. The nouns derive from different roots, *laboratory* from Latin words meaning "pain, effort," and the like, *lavatory* from the Latin for "wash." Note: there is no *r* in the second syllable of *lavatory,* as there is in *laboratory:* never pronounce it *LAV-ruh-tor-ee.*

labour See LABOR.

lack (*v.*) combines frequently with the preposition *for,* especially in negative constructions: *She'll never lack for amusement.* It also can combine with *in,* especially in the present participial form: *He's lacking in credentials.* Both are Standard, as are the two slightly different meanings of the verb itself: "to have none of," as in *Our team lacked a coach,* and "not to have enough of," "to be short of," as in *We lacked enough experienced players.*

lacuna (*n.*) is a gap or omission, as in a text; its plural is either *lacunas* (pronounced *luh-K[Y]OO-nuhs*) or *lacunae* (pronounced *luh-K[Y]OO-nee* or *luh-K[Y]OO-nei*). See FOREIGN PLURALS.

lad, lass (*nn.*) Today these words for boy and girl, young man and young woman, sound rather quaint even though they are still Standard.

lade (*v.*) means "to load" or "to draw (ladle) water." Its principal parts are *lade, laded, laded* or *laden,* and the word is rare except in its present participial form, which gives us the noun *lading,* as in *a bill of lading,* which documents a load or cargo, and the past participle, which gives us the adjective *laden.*

laden (*adj.*) When this participial adjective combines with a preposition, it almost always takes *with: She was laden with her purchases.*

LADINO See YIDDISH.

lady (*adj., n.*) has undergone a number of shifts in usage in recent years. It remains the Standard polite term for a woman and is the word usually paired with *gentleman,* but many now prefer *woman* or *women* to *lady* or *ladies* in the general sense where *man* or *men* might be used for males. *Lady* continues in use meaning "the consort or the legal equal of a lord," "a woman of refinement or elevated social position," or "the mistress of a household," as in the cliché *the lady of the house.* In the idiomatic *Our Lady,* meaning "the Virgin Mary," it is still Standard, but as an adjective, as in *lady doctor,* it is (like *woman doctor*) rapidly approaching archaic status, thanks to a change in the referent of *doctor* from male only to either male or female. It has also lost ground in compounds, where inclusive terms are increasingly preferred: for example, *salesperson* has largely replaced *saleslady*, *saleswoman*, and *salesman* as a generic term for someone who works in a store or peddles goods for a living; similarly, *police officer* has outstripped *policewoman* and *policeman* in popularity. See FEMININE OCCUPATIONAL FORMS; GENTLEMAN; INCLUSIVE LANGUAGE; SEXIST LANGUAGE.

lady-in-waiting (*n.*) The plural is *ladies-in-waiting*. See PLURALS OF COMPOUND NOUNS.

lag (*v.*), when it means "to linger, loiter, or fall back," combines almost always with the preposition *behind: The favorite lagged behind the pacesetters until the far turn.*

laid-back (*adj.*) is a graphic Americanism from the 1970s, Conversational and Informal at best (some insist it is still just slang), meaning "relaxed, unflappable, easygoing," as in *He has a laid-back approach to every problem.*

lama, llama (*nn.*) A *lama* (pronounced *LAH-muh*, the plural spelled *lamas*) is a Tibetan monk or priest; a *llama* (pronounced either *LAH-muh* or *YAH-muh*, the plural spelled *llamas*) is the South American cousin of the camel.

lament (*v.*) occurs regularly and best without a following preposition, as in *She lamented her lost opportunity,* but it can combine with the prepositions *about, concerning, for,* and *over,* as in *The losers lamented about [concerning, for, over] their many mistakes.*

lamentable (*adj.*) is regularly pronounced with stress on the first syllable (*LA-ment-uh-bul*), although a second Standard pronunciation with stress on the second syllable (*luh-MENT-uh-bul*) is frequently heard and occasionally criticized.

lampoon See BURLESQUE.

landward (*adv., adj.*), **landwards** (*adv.*) In Standard English, *landward* is both adjective, as in *Look on the landward side,* and adverb, as in *The swell moved majestically landward. Landwards* is adverb only: *Landwards we sailed. Landwards we could see some other boats.*

LANGUAGE COMMUNITY See CONSTITUENCY.

LANGUAGE OF BASEBALL See BASEBALL.

LANGUAGE OF BASKETBALL See BASKETBALL.

large (*adv., adj.*), **largely** (*adv.*) *Large,* meaning "sizably," is probably a flat adverb, as in *Sizes in this dress run large,* and the adverb *largely,* meaning "freely" or "mostly" rather than "sizably," will not replace it, as it can in uses such as *She gestured large[ly].* In the phrases *bulk, loom,* and *writ large, bulk, loom,* and *writ* are linking verbs (like *be, look, seem, appear,* etc.), and *large* is a predicate adjective, but the verbs may also be described as intransitive followed by the flat adverb *large,* which could be replaced by *largely.* Either way, the phrases are grammatical and Standard clichés, though *writ large* is archaic.

largeness See ENORMITY; SYNONYM.

large-scale, small-scale (*adjs.*) are often used simply to mean "big or sweeping" (*a large-scale campaign*) and "little and compressed" (*a small-scale experiment*), wherein they are becoming clichés. For maps, however, they have very specific meanings: a *large-scale map* pictures a relatively small area, such as a township, but provides much detail; a *small-scale map* pictures a relatively large area, such as a continent, but provides relatively minimal detail.

larva (*n.*) has two Standard plurals: *larvae* and *larvas.* See FOREIGN PLURALS.

larynx (*n.*) has two Standard plurals: *larynxes* (pronounced *LER-ingks-iz*) and *larynges* (*luh-RIN-jeez*). Frequent Nonstandard pronunciations of both singular and plural are *LER-niks* (*-iz*) or *LAHR-niks*(*-iz*); avoid these as shibboleths. See FOREIGN PLURALS.

lass See LAD.

last, latest (*adjs., nn.*) Does *last* mean only "final," *latest* only "most recent"? The truth is that they are partly synonymous, that they partly overlap, and that each can in certain contexts mean either "final" or "most recent." *Her last performance* may be her most recent one, her last of the season, or, because she's now retired or dead, her final one. *Her latest performance* seems to imply that there may be more to come, but if, following it, she has died, then her most recent performance was her final one too. In either case let context make clear which sense you intend.

lastly See FIRSTLY.

last three See FIRST TWO.

late See EX-; WIDOW.

later on, later (*advs.*) These are Standard synonyms: *She's coming later [later on] this evening. Later on* may have a slightly more expansive tone than *later,* but that's hard to prove. See also EARLY ON.

latest See LAST.

LATINATE VOCABULARY VERSUS ANGLO-SAXON WORDS Our language is frequently the site of contests between using simple down-to-earth words from Old English (*herds of cows*) and using more "elevated" or "important"-sounding words from Latin, Greek, Hebrew, or another of the languages from which we have borrowed so much vocabulary (*cohorts of bovines*). Reliance on either sort to the exclusion of all others is silly, but it is equally silly to try to elevate your matter by using polysyllabic, unfamiliar words. Rejoice in and choose wisely from the wealth and variety of the full English lexicon. See INKHORN TERMS; SCIENTIFIC ENGLISH.

LATIN PLURALS See FOREIGN PLURALS.

latter See FORMER.

laudable, laudatory (*adjs.*) *Laudable* means "praiseworthy, worthy of commendation," as in *His was a laudable purpose*. *Laudatory* means "expressing or containing praise," as in *She made a laudatory speech, honoring the winners*. Though somewhat similar in sound and appearance, these two are never interchangeable.

laugh (*v.*) combines usually with *at* or *over*, whose objects indicate the cause of the laughter: *They always laugh at our silly mistakes; we can laugh over them too, but not until later*.

lavatory See BATHROOM; LABORATORY.

lawman (*n.*), which originally meant "one who declares or makes the law," now means "police officer, peace officer (sheriff, marshal, etc.)" and is Standard in its use in the American western, where its referent is always masculine.

lawyer, attorney, attorney-at-law, barrister, counsel, counselor, counselor-at-law, solicitor (*nn.*) All these refer to members of the legal profession. A *lawyer* is someone trained in the law, able to advise clients on the law and to represent them in court. An *attorney* is a lawyer empowered to represent clients' interests and to act for them; an *attorney-at-law* is a practitioner qualified to prosecute or defend in a court of law. *Counsel* is a term for a lawyer who is directing a case in court or advising or representing persons or organizations on legal matters (as in the cliché, *You should seek advice of counsel*). *Counselor* and *counselor-at-law* are other names for lawyers who advise or represent clients in court. A *barrister* is a lawyer admitted to plead and undertake trials in a British superior court. A *solicitor* is a British lawyer who advises and represents clients in the lower courts and briefs (prepares cases for) *barristers* to plead in higher courts.

lay, lie (*vv.*) These two are often confused, and failures to choose the correct form are shibboleths usually rigorously enforced in Standard English. *Lay* is a transitive verb whose principal parts are *lay, laid, laid*, as in *This hen lays* [*laid, had laid*] *an average of four eggs a week*. *Lie* is an intransitive verb (not to be confused with *lie* meaning "to tell an untruth," which derives from a different word); it has the principal parts *lie, lay, lain*, as in *That book lies* [*lay, had lain*] *there every day*. The usage problem stems in part from the fact that *lay* is the infinitive and present tense form of one verb and the past tense of the other; also troublesome is the use of the higher-frequency weak verb form—*laid*—for past tense and past participle when the intransitive verb is intended, as in *She laid in bed all morning,* a Substandard usage. Even more slippery is the relatively low frequency of the intransitive past participle form, *lain: The dog had lain by the door all day.* Many Americans who are otherwise users of Standard English err with *lie* and *lay* and as a result fearfully seek another way of saying what they have in mind. See also SET.

lay hold of See AHOLD.

lay of the land See LIE OF THE LAND.

lead (*n., v.*) These are homographs only when the verb is in the infinitive or present tense, where it rhymes with *deed*. But the verb spells its past tense and past participle *led*, which rhymes with *dead*, as in *Afterwards, she led us to the library*. The noun, the name of the metal, also rhymes with *dead*, but is always spelled *lead*. The noun meaning "a leading role" and "a leash for a pet" rhymes with *deed*.

leader (*n.*) Readers should be alert to the specialized British sense of *leader* meaning "an editorial": *The Guardian's leader attacked the government's position*.

leading edge See AVANT-GARDE; STATE OF THE ART.

leading question is a locution from the courts. A lawyer may object to an opponent's asking the witness a *leading question*, one designed to elicit precisely and only the answer the questioner hopes to get. The verb *lead* in this sense (*leading* is its present participle) is used in the objection: *Your Honor, I object; counsel is leading the witness*.

leaf (*n., v.*) spells its plural *leaves* and its genitives *leaf's* and *leaves'*, respectively. The third person singular of the verb is *leafs*. See NOUNS ENDING IN -F; PAGE.

lean (*v.*) has these principal parts: *lean, leaned* or *leant, leaned* or *leant*. Americans use *leaned* almost exclusively for past tense and past participle, the British prefer *leant* (pronounced *LENT*) for both. The combined form *lean on* (sometimes *lean upon*) is Standard meaning "depend on" or literally "rest your weight on," as in *Lean on me; I'll help you get to the car*; it is also a slang idiom meaning figuratively "to put pressure on, to intimidate or coerce," as in *They leaned hard on her to make her change her vote*. *Lean* also combines with *to, toward,* or *towards,* as in *I lean to [toward, towards] giving them some more time,* and with *in, over,* and *against,* as in *He leaned in the window [over the counter, against the wall]*.

leap (*v.*) spells its past tense and past participle in three ways: *leaped* (pronounced *LEEPT*) and *lept* or *leapt* (both pronounced *LEPT*). All are Standard. See CREEP; STRONG VERBS (1); WEAK VERBS.

learn, teach (*vv.*) Long ago, *learn* meant what *teach* means today, and in turn-of-the-century children's books the wicked stepmother always snarled, "I'll learn you," proving that she was both ill-tempered and ill-spoken, because by that time the use was clearly Substandard. Today Standard English won't have it, and it seldom poses much problem: *Teachers teach, and pupils learn*. The past tense and past participle forms of *learn* are *learned* and (infrequently in the United States but often in Britain) *learnt*. See also TEACH.

learned (*adj.*), like *alleged*, has two pronunciations and two meanings: *LUHRND* means "acquired by learning" (*His was a learned response, one he'd committed to memory*); *LUHRN-id* means "highly educated, wise in lore" (*They were an unusually learned couple*). Each is Standard in its particular sense.

leary See LEERY.

lease, rent (*nn., vv.*), **let** (*v.*) A *lease* is a contract for real estate or equipment specifying both the amount to be paid and the guaranteed period of time involved. *Rent* is the amount to be paid, either under a *lease* or per month or week for an indefinite period. To *lease* or to *rent* something is to enter into such agreements. In a related sense, to *let* is to offer or enter into an agreement to *lease* or to *rent* something: *The owner has let [leased, rented] his house to a tenant for* a year. *The tenant has let [leased, rented] the house from the owner.*

leastways, leastwise (*advs.*) These words, meaning "at least" or "anyway," occur mainly at the Conversational levels or in their written imitations, and *leastways* is generally labeled Nonstandard and dialectal.

leave, let (*vv.*), **leave (me) alone, let (me) alone** In one area where *leave* and *let* overlap they pose a usage problem: *leave me alone* and *let me alone* are both Standard, and both mean either "Stop bothering me" or "Go away; I wish to be alone." *Let* plus a pronoun plus an infinitive without *to,* as in *Let me go* and *Let them find us,* is Standard, but *leave* in that construction is Substandard, so clearly so that locutions such as *Leave me go* and *Leave them find us* are often used jocularly by Standard speakers. If the construction with *leave* includes *to* before the infinitive, however, it is Standard, although the meaning is somewhat different: *Leave me to go; Leave them to find us.*

lectern See PODIUM.

lecture See ORATION.

led See LEAD.

leery, leary (*adj.*) *Leary* is a relatively infrequent variant spelling of the adjective *leery,* meaning "wary, anxious, suspicious": *She's leery of having to meet them*. Some dictionaries label *leery* Colloquial or Informal, but others don't label it at all. Best advice: use *leery* freely in any but the most Formal writing where readership may include conservatives. When it combines with a preposition, *of* is the usual choice, as in *He's leery of returning to school,* but *about* and *as to* are also used, as in *I'm a bit leery about [as to] the wisdom of replying.*

leeward (*adj., n.*) Sailors pronounce it *LOO-(w)uhrd,* but the rest of us properly say *LEE-wuhrd* for all uses including the name of the Caribbean *Leeward Islands*.

leeway (*n.*) retains its specialized nautical meaning, "off-course drifting caused by wind or current," as in *We were making a good deal of leeway because of the missing centerboard,* but by far its most common meaning is the figurative "acceptable range for free movement," "room," as in *They set us a goal but gave us a lot of leeway in deciding how to approach it*. Both senses are Standard, although one dictionary still considers the figurative sense Colloquial.

left bank (of a river) See BANK OF A RIVER.

legend, myth (*nn.*), **legendary, mythical** (*adjs.*) A *legend* is a story handed down over time, one supposed to have some historical basis but unverifiable today. A *myth* is like a legend in being possibly historical and certainly unverifiable, but its chief distinction is that it claims to explain or account for some natural phenomenon or religious or other human convention or institution. Its characters are usually gods or heroes or both. The noun has pejorative overtones in much of its general use because *myths* are often held to be the sources of widely accepted but unproved or unfounded beliefs, as in *the myth of male superiority*. *Mythical* suggests vagueness, if not untruth. *Legendary* has two senses, one stressing the unprovable or unverifiable, as in *the legendary Robin Hood*, and the other simply hyperbole applied to real people whose reputations are the stuff of which *legends* are made, as in *the legendary Greta Garbo*.

legible See ILLEGIBLE.

legislative intent See INTENT (2).

legitimate, legitimatize, legitimize (*vv.*) All three verbs are synonyms, meaning "to make lawful or legal or legitimate," as in *His birth certificate legitimated* [*legitimatized, legitimized*] *his claim to the property*. The verb *legitimate* is pronounced *luh-JIT-i-MAIT*, whereas the adjective is pronounced *luh-JIT-i-mit*. *Legitimatize* seems to have slightly less use than the other two, but all are Standard.

leisure (*adj., n.*), **leisurely** (*adv., adj.*) Each word has the same two Standard variant pronunciations of the first syllable: *LEE-zhuhr-(lee)* or *LE-zhuhr-(lee)*. *Leisure* is both noun, as in *I have no leisure to devote to it*, and adjective, as in *She devotes all her leisure time to tennis*. *Leisurely* is both adjective, as in *We had a long leisurely walk home*, and adverb, as in *We walked leisurely home*.

lend (*v.*), **loan** (*n., v.*) *Lend* (principal parts *lend, lent, lent*) and *loan* (principal parts *loan, loaned, loaned*) are both clearly Standard in American English, although the British still object to *loan* as a verb, and as a result several American commentators reject or dislike it. *Lend* and *loan* are synonyms in their literal senses as verbs (the transitive "to give someone the use or temporary possession of something" and the intransitive "to engage in the act or practice of doing so"), but only *lend* has figurative uses: *The morning sun lends a cheery air to the usually gloomy library*. The noun *loan* is also Standard:

He made me a loan to cover my outstanding tuition bills.

length (*n.*), **lengthily** (*adv.*), **lengthy** (*adj.*) All three words share with *strength* (which see) a curious pronunciation problem: the Standard pronunciation is *LENGKTH*, although *LENTH* occurs. The noun poses no other usage problem: *The boat was about fourteen feet in length.* *Lengthy* has sometimes been criticized for being a pretentious substitute for *long,* but it has useful overtones implying not just "long," but "overlong": *The speech was lengthy and dull.* *Lengthily* may seem a bit hard to say, but it is a low-frequency Standard adverb, different in meaning and therefore not to be replaced by *lengthwise: The two of them conversed lengthily in whispers.*

lengthwise, lengthways (*advs.*) They are Standard and interchangeable in the meaning "along the length," "in the direction of length," "longitudinally," as in *He stretched out lengthwise* [*lengthways*] *on the narrow bench.*

lengthy See LENGTH.

lesbian See HOMOSEXUAL.

lèse-majesté, lese majesty is a French phrase (literally meaning "injured majesty") that is pronounced either *lez MAZH-es-TAI* or *lez MAJ-es-tee* and is spelled usually with the grave and acute accents. Today it means "an offense against a sovereign" or, more generally, any slight or insult that wounds someone's dignity. See FOREIGN PHRASES.

less, fewer (*adjs.*) Standard English still usually requires this basic pattern: use *less* with mass nouns and *fewer* with plural count nouns, as in *less employment, fewer jobs*. But Common English—and even some Standard—increasingly uses *less* with plurals, especially after *than*. Edited English still follows the basic pattern rigorously, however, except in a few idiomatic locutions, as in *in ten words or less*; in certain phrases involving money, such as *less than a thousand dollars*; and in some phrases involving plural measures of time and distance or other measures, also with *than* (*less than four days, less than ten miles, less than five cups of coffee*). Even in these, Edited English prefers *fewer*, and for many conservatives, the use of *less* where *fewer* is expected remains a strong shibboleth.

lessee, lessor (*nn.*) The *lessee* is the person to whom something is leased, and the *lessor* is the person who does the leasing. See -EE.

lesser (*adv., adj.*) is a second comparative form for the adjective *little* (*littler* is the other) and means "smaller" in almost any sense: *A lesser man would have given up.* The adverb, also Standard, means "less," as in *She was the lesser-known of the sisters.*

lessor See LESSEE.

lest (*v.*) is followed usually by a subjunctive or occasionally by a verb phrase using *should,* as in *She ran all the way, lest she miss [should miss] the train.*

let See LEASE; LEAVE.

let, don't let's, let's, let's don't, let's not
This verb, in its meaning of "permit" or "grant" (see LEAVE) is frequently followed by a pronoun in the accusative case: *Let us pray. Let's try to win.* Redundancy sometimes occurs at the Casual level, resulting from a mistaken repetition of the pronoun already present in the contraction (*Let's us be sure to be on time*), but this is Standard if limited to Casual or Informal use. *Let's you and I play them* also is acceptable at those levels (the pronouns are notional or virtual subjects), but generally the nominative case is Substandard, as in the frequent misquotation *Let he [should be him] who is without sin cast the first stone.*

There are three negative idioms: *Let's not stay, Don't let's stay,* and *Let's don't stay.* All are Standard, although *Let's don't* is more typically American than *Don't let's,* which is more typically British.

let alone is an idiom meaning "to say nothing of," "not to mention," as in *It seemed unlikely that she would ever be able to speak again, let alone resume her radio talk show.*

let (me) alone See LEAVE.

let's, let's don't, let's not See LET.

levee, levy (*nn.*) *Levee* (1) is a formal reception: *The new ambassador was introduced that afternoon at a levee at the embassy. Levee* (2) is a dike built to keep a river within its banks: *We sandbagged the weak spots in the levee.* A *levy* is either an assessment or a tax or the imposition of one, or it is a draft or conscription class of troops or the process of collecting them: *The most recent levy raised disappointingly few dollars [or troops].*

level (*adj., n., v.*) The noun *level* is now unquestionably Standard in the sense "rank or position on a scale": *She's been promoted to management level. To be on the level* is a slang use of the noun, meaning "to be honest, fair, and straightforward." The adjective, in the idiom *to do one's level best,* meaning "to do the very best one can," is Conversational and Informal.

Level as a transitive verb combines most often with *at,* meaning "to direct or aim," as in *He leveled an unpleasant stare at his waiter.* As an intransitive verb, *level* takes *with* and means "to deal honestly and truthfully," as in *He leveled with the team members about their chances;* this usage is labeled slang or Colloquial in some dictionaries, but others consider it Standard. Two other Standard combined forms with the intransitive verb are *to level off,* meaning "to make level" or, as in flight, "to return to a horizontal course," and *to level out,* which has much the same two senses.

LEVELS OF USAGE; USAGE LEVELS IN STANDARD AMERICAN ENGLISH
These phrases describe two different sorts of linguistic variation found in American English. One set of differences involves the distinctions we identify by the labels *Standard English, Common English,* and *Vulgar English,* and by the terms *Standard English, Substandard English,* and *Nonstandard English.* Each of these sets is a continuum of differences—essentially class differences—in the details of grammar, usage, and vocabulary in both spoken and written English.

Levels of usage can also be used to describe two other continuums of linguistic variation, one representing the levels of our speech, the other the levels of formality (or lack thereof) of our writing (see the figure, adapted from Gleason [1965]). These schematized five levels of speech and three levels of writing overlap in places, but the differences indicated on each scale are truly significant both in the details of

The Levels of Standard American English

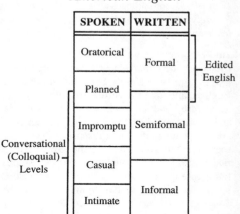

	SPOKEN	WRITTEN	
	Oratorical	Formal	Edited English
	Planned		
	Impromptu	Semiformal	
Conversational (Colloquial) Levels	Casual	Informal	
	Intimate		

language that are characteristic of each and in the values language users attach to them. In this book, the five *levels* of speech are named *Intimate, Casual, Impromptu, Planned,* and *Oratorical* and the three *levels* of writing are named *Informal, Semiformal,* and *Formal. Conversational* and *Colloquial* are useful descriptors for a particular cluster of *levels* (or parts of levels) of speech; *Edited English* describes a cluster of *levels* (or parts of *levels*) of writing. (See Joos 1952; Gleason 1965.)

levy See LEVEE.

LEXICON See VOCABULARY (2).

liable (*adj.*) has two Standard pronunciations, usually semantically distributed: *LEI-uh-bul* is the usual pronunciation for the senses in the cluster meaning "obligated, legally responsible," as in *You'll be liable for any damages caused by the accident. LEI-bul* is a variant pronunciation often encountered in the Standard cluster meaning "subject to, apt, likely," as in *You're liable to get into a lot of trouble over this. Apt, likely,* and this sense of *liable* are essentially synonyms. See APT.

liaise (*v.*) is a back-formation from the noun *liaison,* and although at least one dictionary insists that it is a British Colloquialism, the verb now appears to be Standard except perhaps in very Formal and Oratorical contexts. It means "to establish a liaison" or "to perform the work of a liaison officer": *His task was to liaise with the French combat team on our left flank.* Pronounce it *LEE-AIZ.*

liaison (*n.*), pronounced *lee-AI-zuhn, LEE-ai-ZAWN, LEE-uh-ZON,* plus a widely heard but Nonstandard *LAI-uh-zuhn,* has a generalized meaning of "an interlinking, a relationship," and three specialized senses: "an illicit sexual relationship, an affair"; "a French language practice wherein a silent final consonant is pronounced as the first sound of a following word beginning with a vowel, as in *chez elle* (*SHAI ZEL*); and "the title of the person who acts as go-between, especially between groups or organizations."

liar, lyre (*nn.*) These are homophones in some speech, but sometimes *liar* ("one who tells lies") has two syllables and *lyre* ("a small ancient form of harp") only one (*LEI-uhr* and *LEIR*).

libel See SLANDER.

liberal arts See ART (1).

LIBERALS IN LANGUAGE MATTERS favor liberal usage. They are often young, full of zeal for change, and determined to adopt the new, the modish, the different. They frequently chafe under what they consider the constraints of the dead hands of convention and tradition, and in their impatience they often try to hurry change along, with the result that they may not always be understood. See LIBERAL USAGE; compare CONSERVATIVES IN LANGUAGE MATTERS.

LIBERAL USAGE prefers and defends the new, the different. It frequently quarrels with the standards of Edited English, seeking to advance the causes of the Conversational locution and the Informal word and to win them places in untrammeled Standard English. Its speech and writing are full of the new and the daring in vocabulary, meanings, forms, and syntax. At its worst, *liberal usage* is slangy and unstable; at its best, it is bright, breezy, and full of the conversational sounds of lively American discourse. It is often quick to throw away tradition, and therefore it can date rapidly and can sometimes be less than fully comprehensible to users from older, less liberal generations. The *liberal usage* of the young is frequently what makes their conservative elders despair of the future of the language. But it often provides vigor and liveliness for that future as well. Compare CONSERVATIVE USAGE.

libertarian, libertine (*adjs., nn.*) A *libertarian* is a believer in free will or, more frequently, a supporter of absolute freedom of thought, word, and deed. A *libertine* was once a freed slave in Rome, but today a *libertine* is morally unrestrained, a profligate, dissolute person, and the word as both noun and adjective is a pejorative.

library (*n.*) is sometimes mispronounced *LEI-ber-ee* instead of Standard *LEI-brer-ee* by people who otherwise use Standard English; the error is harshly judged.

libretto (*n.*) has two plurals: *librettos* and *libretti.* See FOREIGN PLURALS; PLURALS OF NOUNS ENDING IN -O.

license, licence (*n., v.*) Americans spell both noun and verb with a final *-se*; the British spell the verb that way, but their noun ends in *-ce*.

licensed See CERTIFICATED.

licorice, liquorice (*n.*) *Licorice* (pronounced either *LIK-uhr-ish* or *LIK-uhr-is*) is the American spelling; *liquorice* is the British spelling.

lie See LAY.

lie of the land, lay of the land Both locutions are Standard, meaning "the way things are literally or figuratively positioned with respect to other things," as in *As soon as we get a look at* *the lie [lay] of the land, we'll decide what to do next.*

life (*n.*) The plural is *lives*, pronounced *LEIVZ.* See NOUNS ENDING IN -*F*; STILL LIFE.

LIGATURES In writing and printing, a *ligature* is a character composed of two letters joined together; these can occur in American English today, but very rarely: æ, œ. *Ligature* is also the name given to the line used to join two letters together, as in the character some dictionaries use to indicate the pronunciation of voiced *th* (*th*) in *thy*. See also DIGRAPHS; DIPHTHONG.

lighted, lit are both Standard past tense and past participle forms of the verb *light*. *Lit* is the only form that can be used for the slang meaning "drunk" (as a participial adjective); otherwise *lit* and *lighted* are interchangeable in all senses.

lightening (*pres. participle*), **lightning** (*adj., n., v.*) *Lightening* (three syllables) is the present participle of two different verbs: *lighten* meaning "to brighten up with light," as in *The sky was lightening perceptibly as the sunrise neared,* and *lighten* meaning "to make lighter in weight," as in *Every meal we ate was lightening the loads we had to carry. Lightning* (two syllables) is the electrical charge that comes in bolts from the sky; it is a noun, as in *Did you see the lightning?,* a verb, as in *It lightninged a moment ago,* or an adjective, as in *She moved with lightning quickness.*

light-year (*n.*) A *light-year* (the distance light can travel in a solar year) is a measure of distance (5.88 trillion miles), not time, and figuratively it means an incredibly long distance, not an incredibly long time.

likable, likeable (*adj.*) These are Standard variant spellings. *Likable* is probably somewhat more frequently encountered.

like 1 (*adv., adj., prep., subord. conj., n., v., interj.*) *Like* is a noun (*I've never seen his like before*), a verb (*I really like her*), an adjective (*In like circumstances, I think I'd quit*), an adverb (*You'll change your mind, like enough*), a preposition (*She looks like her mother*), and a subordinating conjunction (*It seemed like it would never end*). The adverbial example may be dialectal or simply Conversational, but the rest are unquestionably Standard, although Edited English frequently prefers to limit the conjunctive use to Conversational and Semiformal use.

The big usage issue since the nineteenth century has been the use of *like* as a conjunction, but the evidence is clear that we have been both speaking and writing it in Standard English even as we have been filling our handbooks with

prohibitions of the usage. The fact is that many will say *He runs like he's pulled a muscle,* even though not all will write it and relatively few will try to get it printed in Formal use.

The use of *like* as intensifier or interjection, however, is Casual at best and Substandard in its heaviest, most adolescent uses: *It was, like, three o'clock before we, like, got to the station.* See also FUNCTIONAL SHIFT.

like 2, as, as if, as though (*subord. conjs.*) Edited English and, indeed, much of Standard English still use *as, as though,* and *as if* as conjunctions, especially in those Formal or Oratorical situations where conservatives continue to be uncomfortable with *like: She runs as if* [*as though*] *she were frightened. Treat your students as you would want to be treated.* Probably as a result of hypercorrection, *as* also turns up in prepositional use where *like* would normally be expected, as in *He behaved as an old veteran.* Standard English considers such uses Nonstandard, especially when they turn out to be ambiguous.

In Edited English some conservative editors insist that you avoid using *like* to mean "such as" (*Words such as* [not *like*] *license and licorice have two Standard spellings*). See also AS (2); AS IF.

likeable See LIKABLE.

like crazy See MAD (2).

liked to See LIKE TO.

like for, as in *She'd like for you to call her tonight,* is dialectal, originally characteristic of Midland and Southern Regional dialects but now much more widespread. Best advice: limit it to Casual, Impromptu, or Informal use.

likelihood (*n.*) Note that a medial -*i*- replaces the final -*y* of *likely*.

likely (*adv.*) is equally Standard with or without a modifier such as *more, most, quite,* or *very,* despite the insistence of some commentators that it should never appear without one: *He will* (*most*) *likely remain in town for a few days.* See APT.

like mad See MAD (2).

liken (*v.*), when it combines with a preposition, does so with *to* and means "compare," as in *She likened him to a large shaggy bear.*

likes of, like of The combined form *likes of* has two meanings, one unexceptionable, as in *I was seated with the likes of two deans and a provost—VIPs all,* and one pejorative and disparaging, as in *"I won't associate with the likes of him,"* she said. *Like of* can avoid being pejorative with a singular object and not disparage at all, as in *I don't know where you'd find the like of him,* meaning "his equal"; more often, however, the idiom is *where you'd find his like.*

like to, liked to (*auxs.*) function to mean "almost," "nearly," or "came near to" in dialectal uses such as *She like to died laughing.* They also occur in the past tense, as in *They like[d] to never have seen us if we hadn't called them.* Standard English doesn't use these in this sense even at Conversational levels, although *like to* and *liked to* are Standard as verb plus infinitive preceded by *to,* as in *I like to play squash; She liked to sing.*

limit, delimit, delimitate (*vv.*) *Limit* is transitive and means "to place bounds to, to set a boundary," as in *She limited her remarks to three minutes. Delimit* and *delimitate* are also transitive and mean essentially the same thing, "to set limits to" or "to establish the boundaries of." *Delimitate* is a back-formation from the noun *delimitation* or the adjective *delimitative.* All are Standard, but *delimitate* is and should remain very rare.

lineament, liniment (*nn.*) *Lineament* (pronounced *LIN-ee-uh-ment* and usually in the plural) means "distinguishing features, especially of a face or a topography." *Liniment* (pronounced *LIN-uh-ment*) is an ointment or liquid medication to be rubbed on the skin to help ease discomfort from sprains, strains, and stiffness.

lingerie (*n.*) is a word borrowed from French in order to give women's underwear a more elegant name. It is a Standard term, but its pronunciations are of particular interest as examples of hyperforeignism (which see).

LINGUA FRANCA This term originally referred to the hybrid mixture of nearly all the Mediterranean countries' chief languages that was once spoken in their ports—a combination of at least three Romance tongues, plus Greek, Turkish, and Arabic. Today the more general meaning is the more important: a *lingua franca* is any language, pure or mixed, that serves as a means of communication for peoples whose native tongues are different. A dialect or dialects of British English serve today as the *lingua franca* of the Indian subcontinent, just as Swahili serves as a *lingua franca* for several Central and West African nations.

LINGUIST, LINGUISTICS; PHILOLOGIST, PHILOLOGY *Linguist* has two main meanings: "a person who specializes in *linguistics* (the science of language) either as applied to a single language or to language in general";

and, especially for the layperson, "a polyglot, a person who knows and can use many languages." Both senses still flourish. *Philology* originally meant "the love of learning"; it came then also to mean "the study of whatever is preserved in writing," and so *philologists* were "literary scholars" and hence "scholars who knew languages." Until the term *linguistics* became popular, *philology* also meant "the study—especially the historical study—of language, languages, and the literatures preserved in them."

LINGUISTIC CHANGE is any change that takes place over time in the phonology, morphology, syntax, or vocabulary (including semantics) of a language. Consider the following versions of Genesis 1.1: "On angynne gesceop God heofonan and eorðan" (Old English); "In the first made God of nought heuen and erth" (Middle English); "In the beginning God created the Heaven, and the Earth" (Early Modern English). See also CHANGE AND VARIATION IN LANGUAGE.

LINGUISTIC VARIATION See CHANGE AND VARIATION IN LANGUAGE.

liniment See LINEAMENT.

LINKED GENITIVES, LINKED POSSESSIVES These terms apply to the sometimes ambiguous result of having two or more possessives modifying and acting as determiners for the same noun. *Martha and Alan's father* and *Martha's and Alan's father* are not ambiguous in most contexts: both phrases refer to one father and his two children. But *John's and Elizabeth's hats* may indicate one hat per person or more than one for either or both of them, and *his and her house* seems to refer to one shared house, but *his and her houses* leaves it ambiguous whether both share two or more houses or whether each has just one. Further ambiguity is possible in *The prosecutor's and the defense attorney's motion*—it could be a motion put forward jointly—and while *The prosecutor's and the defense attorney's motions* are probably separate efforts, they could also be several motions all jointly made. When pronouns are involved, note the further possible problems: When you speak of *your and my idea* or *your idea and mine,* are you talking about one shared idea, or one idea each? And if you say *your ideas and mine,* do you mean that they are all shared, that I have several and you one or more, or that the whole package is a mélange of shared and individually created ideas? Always reword rather than permit any ambiguity, particularly in writing.

LINKING OR COPULATIVE VERBS are the special and relatively few verbs that tie a subject to a predicate complement—either a predicate nominative (*Mary is my sister*) or a predicate adjective (*Mary seems bright*). (Historically, adverbs used to appear regularly after linking verbs too.) *Be, seem,* and *become* are *linking verbs,* or *copula,* in almost all uses; *come, feel, get, go, grow, lie, look, prove, remain, sound, stay,* and *turn* can serve as linking verbs (*I grew weary*), transitive verbs (*I grew roses*), or intransitive verbs (*I grew slowly*). See LINKED GENITIVES.

lion's share as used by most speakers of Standard English means "the largest part," not "the whole thing."

liqueur, liquor (*nn.*) *Liqueur* is the French name for any of a long list of flavored and usually sweetened brandy-type drinks. Americans pronounce it either *li-KUHR* or *li-KYU(uh)r*, although the second of these grates on many Standard users' ears. *Liquor* (pronounced *LIK-uhr,* with the stress on the first syllable in the English fashion) is a generalized term meaning "any liquid," but it is much more frequently used in its specialized sense, "any distilled alcoholic beverage, such as whiskey, gin, rum, or vodka."

liquorice See LICORICE.

listeners See AUDIENCE.

lit See LIGHTED.

litany, liturgy (*nn.*) A *litany* is a prayer containing various invocations or, in its more generalized sense, any long, repetitive recitation or list, often pejorative because boring to hear, as in *The old man whined out a well-rehearsed litany of grievances against his family.* A *liturgy,* sometimes capitalized, especially in reference to the Christian Eucharist, is a religious rite or a collection of them for use in public worship.

liter, litre (*n.*) *Liter* is the American spelling, *litre* the British, of the metric measure of volume; it is the volume of one kilogram of water at a controlled temperature and pressure. See SPELLING (1).

literal (*adj., n.*), **figurative** (*adj.*) *Literal* means "exactly according to the letter" and hence "factual," as in *She made a literal transcription of the poem; His testimony was the literal truth.* A *literal* is "a typographical or orthographical error, usually of a single letter," as in *Her only mistakes were a handful of literals. Figurative* means "suggesting or using a figure or figures of speech," as in *His presentation*

used figurative language rather than facts, and hence also "representing in a figurative or emblematic way," as in *Her answers were all figurative defenses of her loyalty.*

literally, figuratively (*advs.*) *Literally* means "actually" or "virtually," as in *He was literally six feet eleven inches tall.* The chief problem is caused by our penchant for hyperbole: *She felt literally dead from fatigue* is much too much, unless she is truly dead (*figuratively* is what is meant). *Literally* is a bad intensifier, almost always overkill.

LITERARY See POETIC.

literature (*n.*) of course has long meant poems, plays, novels, essays, and the like, all of characteristic belletristic intent, but purists frequently object to another sense of the word, "anything written or printed," as in *Here's some literature on that new washing machine.* Both meanings are Standard, nonetheless. But be alert to some purists' objections to the newer, more generalized sense.

litmus test See ACID TEST.

LITOTES (pronounced *LEI-TO-teez*) is a figure of speech also called understatement; the word is both singular and plural and need not take an article. Typically *litotes* makes a positive statement indirectly by stating a contradictory proposition, as in *It was no minor matter,* meaning "It was a major matter." The same effect is achieved with certain double negatives, as in *She's not unlike her mother.* Compare HYPERBOLIC.

liturgy See LITANY.

lived (*adj.*) In hyphenated combinations there is a mild grammatical confusion caused by our inability to be certain whether *lived* is a participial adjective resulting from functional shift of the plural noun *lives* to participle (as *slippered* means "provided with slippers," so *lived,* rhyming with *strived,* can mean "provided or equipped with *life* or *lives*") or whether it is simply the participial adjective that is the past participle of the verb *live* (rhymes with *give*). The only possible semantic distinction between the two pronunciations may be that *long-lived* and *short-lived* (vowel of *strive*) are more likely to be applied to a class of organisms, as in *These roses are very long-lived,* whereas *long-* or *short-lived* (vowel of *give*) refers to an individual person or thing's living a long or short time, as in *Her reputation was long-lived and richly deserved.* But such a distinction is speculative and impossible to prove. Most dictionaries now conclude that a rhyme with *strived* is somewhat more frequent, although some conservatives argue stoutly that the rhyme should always be with *sieved,* because if *life* had been the source (rather than *to live*), the words might have been spelled and pronounced *short-lifed* and *long-lifed.* That's logical, but usage is a matter of custom, not logic.

lively See FRIENDLY.

livid (*adj.*) has a chameleonlike history of color changes: it began by meaning "purplish, bruise-colored, black and blue," then "pale and colorless," and then "red and angry-looking." This last is probably what most people would understand in *She was livid with rage;* she could be white with rage, but flushed or red seems at least equally possible. Today the figurative sense of the adjective is frequently "angry": *She was livid when she heard the news.* All these senses are Standard, although the first may be nearly archaic. If the precise color is important, make sure that context makes plain the one you intend.

living room, drawing room, lounge, parlor, sitting room These are some of the more familiar names for the room that, along with the dining room, serves as the main room for social purposes in a dwelling. Americans use *living room* most frequently, but *sitting room* and *parlor* are common older American terms, sometimes with a quaintly rural flavor. *Drawing room* (from *withdrawing room,* the room to which one goes after dinner) is a more formal term, *lounge* more modern and modish, and both are predominantly British, although American mansions may have *drawing rooms* too, and American hotels and motels may have *lounges.*

-ll- See CONSONANTS (2).

llama See LAMA.

loaf (*n., v.*) The plural of *loaf* is *loaves,* pronounced *LOVZ.* The third person singular present tense of the verb is *loafs,* pronounced *LOFS.* See NOUNS ENDING IN -F.

loan See LEND.

loaner See LONER.

LOAN WORDS are words borrowed from other languages and gradually incorporated into the vocabulary. (For example, *bouillon* and *boulevard* are two of hundreds of French *loan words* in English.) English has *loan words* from almost every language its speakers have ever come in contact with.

loath, loth (*adj.*), **loathe** (*v.*), **nothing loath** (*adv., adj.*) The adjective (pronounced to rhyme with either *both* [*BOTH*] or *loathe* [*LOTH*])

means "reluctant, unwilling," as in *She was loath to stay longer. Loth,* though mainly British, is an infrequent American variant spelling. *Nothing loath* is an idiom meaning "willing or willingly," as in *We were nothing loath to try the new game; Nothing loath, we plunged in.* The verb *loathe* ends in a voiced *th* sound and voices the final *-s* in its third person singular present tense, as in *He loathes* [pronounced *LOTHZ*] *asparagus.* See PRONUNCIATION OF WORDS ENDING IN -*TH,* -*THE.*

locate (*v.*) means "situate, place," as in *The house was located at the end of the lane;* "find," as in *Try to locate a dentist for me;* and, in American English particularly, "to settle somewhere, to begin to reside in," as in *After some hesitation, they decided to locate in Nebraska.* Commentators often point out the redundancy or at least the wordiness of locutions such as *Cheyenne is located in Wyoming; Cheyenne is in Wyoming* would be enough. "Situated" is a Standard meaning, as are all the others discussed above.

-log, -logue (*suffix*) The more common spelling has long been -*logue,* as in *catalogue, monologue,* and the many other terms that use as a second element this suffix meaning "word." The Standard variant spelling -*log* is gaining ground, however, and in Edited English, spellings such as *catalog* and *dialog* are beginning to predominate.

lonely See FRIENDLY.

loner, loaner (*nn.*) Of these homophones, a *loner* is a person who keeps to himself or herself, who prefers to be and to work alone, as in *All his classmates considered him a loner and no one's close friend.* The term is Standard. A *loaner* is either someone who loans, "a lender," or a car or other item being loaned as a replacement while the owner's is being repaired: *The garage gave me a loaner to drive while my car was being fixed.* This sense is a jargon term, particularly from the garage and machine rental businesses.

long-lived See LIVED.

LONG S, ROUND S *Long s* is one form of the letter *s* that was used in printing and writing English both here and abroad until the end of the eighteenth century. The *long s* looked like a lowercase printed *f,* but with the crossbar only on the left of the letter (∫); it was used initially and medially but never finally in a word, so *sisters* looked like this: ∫i∫ters. In contrast, the *s* we now use everywhere was then used at the ends of words and called a *round s.*

look (*v.*) is both linking verb, taking a predicate adjective, as in *He looked meticulous,* and intransitive verb, taking an adverb, as in *He looked meticulously. Look* followed by *to* and an infinitive or *be* plus a present participle plus *to* and an infinitive occurs regularly in the sense "planning or anticipating or expecting to," as in *She looked [was looking] to take a trip to Europe in October.* The participial construction occurs frequently in the negative, as in *We're not looking to set any records this year.* There is also a use of *look* followed by *to be,* with the meaning "appeared," as in *She looked to be about five feet tall.* And these two expressions occur in British English: *The new song looks like being a hit. She looks a perfect dear, don't you think?* Americans would more likely use *looks to be* or *seems (likely) to be.*

loom See LARGE.

loose, loosen, lose (*vv.*) To *loose* something is to turn or set it free: *We loosed the horses in the small pasture.* Pronounce it *LOOS.* To *loosen* something is to make it less firm, to undo it: *He loosened his collar.* Pronounce it *LOOS-en.* To *lose* (pronounce it *LOOZ*) means "to misplace or be unable to find something," as in *They always lose their mittens;* "to fail to win a contest of some sort," as in *We did lose the game;* "to be unable to save something," as in *He may lose this year's crop* or *She did lose her baby;* "to get rid of something undesirable," as in *I lost ten pounds;* or "to fail to maintain something," as in *She lost her poise* and the synonymous (but Casual or Impromptu) *She lost it.* It also can mean "to cause the loss of something," as in *We speeded up and lost our pursuers.* It can also be used figuratively, meaning "to confuse," as in *The teacher lost me after the first example.* All these except *She lost it* are Standard. And there are a number of other specialized senses as well. The chief spelling problem is the inadvertent misspelling of *lose* as *loose.* See also UNLOOSE.

loss leader (*n.*) is the name applied to an article sold very cheaply, often below cost, and advertised in order to attract customers to a store. It has long been commercial jargon, but the word is Standard now.

lost (*adj.*) means "ruined, damned, misplaced, not won, wasted, killed, destroyed," and the like, as in *The ship was lost; She was a lost woman; He was a lost soul; Lost battles are discouraging. Lost* in many of these senses is considered an absolute adjective, but for emphasis Conversational and Informal English (and occasionally even Edited English) frequently qualify it, as in *We were thoroughly lost that night.*

LOST POSITIVES are English coinages made by cutting off the negative prefixes of familiar words. Some of these clipped coinages may indeed once have existed but now may be obsolete; nevertheless, James Thurber's *gruntled,* words such as *sheveled* and *kempt,* and dozens of other such coinages continue to amuse, often as nonce words.

loth See LOATH.

lots of, a lot of Many commentators label these locutions Colloquial, but it is clear that they are both Standard and acceptable at all levels of use, although some conservatives may think *lots of* unsuited to formal contexts: *We had lots of comment on the proposal. There was a lot of good-natured dissent expressed.* See ALOT.

loud (*adv., adj.*), **loudly** (*adv.*) *Loud* can be an adjective, as in *He wore loud socks* and *She seems unnecessarily loud,* or a flat adverb, as in *Please play it loud. Loudly* is also an adverb: *The team clattered loudly into the locker room. He wore a loudly painted necktie.* All these uses are Standard.

lounge See LIVING ROOM.

love (*v.*) used to be strongly criticized when used as a hyperbolic *like,* as in *I love to play bridge* or *My wife loves zucchini,* but today such uses are Standard.

lovely See FRIENDLY.

lover (*n.*) generically means "anyone who loves," regardless of who or what the object of that love is, but the word needs careful contextual control because today it almost always means "an extra-marital sexual partner." *Lover(s)* is Standard in both these uses.

LOWER HUDSON VALLEY REGIONAL DIALECT This Northern dialect, is spoken mainly in southeastern New York State below Albany and in northeastern New Jersey. It shares some characteristics with the Metropolitan New York City dialect, but for some people its main distinction in its cultivated form lies in its having been the dialect of Franklin Delano Roosevelt, the first president of the United States whose voice (thanks to radio) became known in nearly every household in the land in the 1930s and 1940s and continues to be recognized by a great many people today, even those who were not alive when he died in office in 1945. Native speakers of the dialect, though relatively few in number, preserve a few linguistic relics (mainly in place names, such as the *-kill* in *Catskill, Peekskill,* and *Fishkill,* and the *zee* in *Tappan Zee*) of the Dutch, who were the first Europeans to colonize the Hudson Valley.

luck out, luck into (*vv.*), **push one's luck** To *luck out* is to succeed by good fortune, as in *When the assignments were drawn, I lucked out and got the one I had hoped for. Luck into* occasionally also occurs as a combined form with essentially the same meaning: "to be successful because of good luck." *To luck out* is intransitive; *to luck into* usually has an object. Limit both to Conversational and Informal use. *To push one's luck* is to take unnecessary risks when things are already going well; it means "to be greedy," and it's slang.

luggage See BAGGAGE.

lugubrious (*adj.*), **lugubriety, lugubriosity, lugubriousness** (*nn.*) The adjective *lugubrious* means "mournful, gloomy, especially affectedly, exaggeratedly so." Functional shift and various suffixes have provided English with the three nouns: *lugubriousness* and *lugubriosity* are more frequently encountered; *lugubriety* may be a nonce word. The ponderousness of each nicely matches the self-conscious gloom of its exaggerated meaning.

lunch (*adj., n., v.*), **luncheon** (*n.*) Although *lunch* is a clipped form of *luncheon,* it has long been Standard as all three parts of speech: noun, as in *We decided to have lunch early*; verb, as in *They lunched at an excellent new restaurant*; and adjective, as in *The lunch menu was disappointing. Luncheon,* as noun and adjective (it doesn't ordinarily appear as a verb), is now comparatively Formal.

luster, lustre (*n.*) *Luster* is the American spelling, *lustre,* the British. They are both pronounced *LUHS-tuhr.* See SPELLING (1).

lustful, lusty (*adjs.*) These two overlap only a trifle and mainly in archaic or low-frequency senses: *lustful* means primarily "driven by lust," as in *Susannah evoked lustful thoughts in the elders*; *lusty*'s predominant modern meaning is "vigorous, hearty, enthusiastic, full of joy for life," as in *The new baby was a lusty ten-pounder with a voice to match.* Since each word also has an older or little-used sense that is synonymous with the other's main sense, be careful to let context reinforce the primary meaning when using either.

lusty See LUSTFUL.

luxuriant, luxurious (*adjs.*) *Luxuriant* means "abundant, thick, profuse, unrestrained," as in *His hair and beard were long and luxuriant. Luxurious* means "choice and expensive, of the very best kind, full of luxury, self-indulgent," as in *They had a luxurious Manhattan penthouse where, high above all unpleasantness, they denied themselves nothing.*

-ly, -ally, -ily (*suffixes*) These three word-forming suffixes work primarily to make adjectives into adverbs: *furtive/furtively; splendid/splendidly; temporary/temporarily; primary/primarily.* But *-ly* is also used to make adjectives—for example, *lovely, heavenly, lively, timely, kindly, friendly, sickly*—which usually do not combine well with these suffixes to form adverbs, perhaps because the resulting combinations are too hard to say: *friendlily* seems unlikely at best, and *unlikelily* is even more so.

lyre See LIAR.

M

-m, -mm- See CONSONANTS (2).

M' See MAC-.

ma'am See MADAM.

Mac-, M', Mc- are forms of the Celtic word meaning "son," the *Mc* and *M'* forms being sorts of contractions, variant spellings. As parts of proper names (*MacKay, Macbeth, McKenzie, M'Donald*) they are capitalized; the second element of such names is not always capitalized. Most reference books alphabetize names beginning with *Mac-, Mc-,* and *M'* as though they

were all spelled *Mac,* which is convenient when you are unsure of the spelling of the name you seek.

macho (*adj., n.*), **machismo** (*n.*) *Macho* is a Spanish word derived from the Portuguese, *machismo* is Spanish, and both have entered English through contact with Hispanic-Americans. The adjective *macho* describes a virile, aggressive, overassertive male, and the noun refers to such a man or to such qualities. *Machismo* is the abstract noun for these qualities of exaggerated masculinity, particularly as applied to the domination of women. As used in English, these terms are usually at least partly pejorative, and it is probably accurate to say that they have not become completely assimilated into English. In print they occur both with and without italics, and although *machismo* is considered Standard, *macho* should be limited to Semiformal and Informal use in writing.

MACRON The *macron* is the diacritical mark (ˉ) used to indicate a long vowel, as in *feel* (*fēl*). See DIACRITICS.

mad 1, angry (*adjs.*) There have long been objections to *mad* being used to mean "angry" instead of being limited to its Standard, almost literary sense of "insane," but the "angry" sense has been around for centuries. It is usually Conversational and Informal, but it can turn up in Semiformal and Planned use on occasion.

Mad can combine with several prepositions: *They were mad at* [and occasionally *with*] *us* means "we were the objects of their wrath." *They were mad about it* means either "They were angry about it" or "They were wildly or insanely attracted to it" or "greatly excited about it"; the latter sense is also frequently expressed by *for*, as in *Everyone was simply mad for one of those jackets.* The British use *on* with *mad* to mean either "angry about" or "besotted on," and the slang idiom *to have a mad on* means "to be angry." All the combinations with *on* are in wide use but mainly limited to Conversational and Informal or Semiformal levels. See also ANGRY.

mad 2, like; like crazy These idioms are synonymous meaning "greatly," "overwhelmingly," and especially "very rapidly," as in *The souvenirs sold like mad* [*like crazy*]. It's interesting that the *mad* is in the "insane," not the "angry," sense. Limit them to Conversational and Informal contexts.

madam, ma'am, madame, mesdames (*nn.*) *Madam* (stress usually on first syllable, occasionally second) is a term of polite address for a woman, especially a mature woman; in direct address it is the counterpart of *sir.* Use it with or without the woman's family name. A *madam* or *madame* is also the woman in charge of a whorehouse. *Madam* has two plurals: *madams*, usually but not always the plural of the "procuress" sense, so control context carefully, and *mesdames* (pronounced *mai-DAHM* or *mai-DAM*), the polite form of address or reference for a group of women. The singular spelled with a final *-e* is usually stressed on the second syllable. *Ma'am* (pronounced *MAM*) is a polite contraction of *madam*, limited usually to direct address: *Thank you, ma'am.* See MRS.

mad as a hatter See FROZEN FIGURES.

madding (*adj.*) means "frenzied, maddened," and it always occurs in a cliché, *Far from the madding crowd's ignoble strife*, from Thomas Gray's poem, *Elegy Written in a Country Churchyard* and later from the title of one of Hardy's novels, *Far from the Madding Crowd.* Only rarely is it misused to mean, or misspelled to be, *maddening.*

maestro (*n.*) has two plurals: *maestros* and *maestri.* See FOREIGN PLURALS; PLURALS OF NOUNS ENDING IN -O.

magi (*n.*) is the plural of *magus*, an ancient Persian priest. We know it primarily in the plural, usually capitalized in writing, meaning "the three wise men who sought the newborn Jesus."

magic (*adj., n.*), **magical** (*adj.*) *Magic* is primarily an attributive adjective (*a magic box*), but both *magic* and *magical* can appear in predicate use, *magical* clearly as predicate adjective and *magic* as either that or a predicate nominative: *Her sudden appearance was magic* [*magical*]. We use both words literally (*a magic wand, a magical top hat*) and figuratively (*It was a magic moment; His hold on the audience was magical*).

Magna Carta Spell it *Magna Carta*, pronounce it *MAHG-nuh* or *MAG-nuh KAHR-tuh*, and when it's the famous document itself you are discussing, it is customary to omit the article.

magnate, magnet (*nn.*) These words differ in spelling and pronunciation. A *magnate* (pronounced *MAG-NAIT*) is "a very important person, especially someone powerful in business." A *magnet* (pronounced *MAG-nit*) is "an iron or steel piece that attracts similar materials by means of its magnetic field."

magnifico (*n.*) means "a Venetian noble" and, by extension, "a high-ranking very important person"; it is pronounced *mag-NIF-i-ko.* The plural has two spellings: *magnificos* or *magnificoes.* See PLURALS OF NOUNS ENDING IN -O.

magnitude (*n.*) is a Standard noun used in both technical and general contexts to describe size and importance. *Of the first magnitude* is a locution applied by astronomers to the relative brightness of stars, and it is now frequently applied to stars of the entertainment world and to other matters deemed important. Like any other frozen figure, it has sometimes been overused, but that is its only weakness.

magus See MAGI.

Mahomet See MOHAMMED.

MAIN CLAUSE See INDEPENDENT CLAUSE.

major (*adj.*) Commentators have argued that *major* is a comparative and that it therefore must not be used as a positive adjective meaning "important, impressive, big, or grand" but reserved for use when a real comparison is involved, as in *Of all her songs, this one is the major critical success.* But in fact using *major* as an implicit comparative is Standard.

majority, plurality (*nn.*) *Majority* regularly takes either a singular or plural verb: *The majority is* [*are*] *unchanged.* There is a good deal of objection to the use of *majority* with a mass noun: not *the majority of his argument*, but *most of his argument. The majority of those present* is Standard, but *The majority of the audience* is Informal and Casual at best; *Most of the audience* is Standard.

Majority is regularly modified by *great, large, huge,* and *overwhelming,* and so long as such combinations do not become personal clichés, they'll work fine. *Vast majority* is already a cliché; so is *bare majority,* meaning the minimum number needed to make a *majority* (100 to 99 is a *bare majority*).

A *majority* of votes is at least one more than half of them; a *plurality* is the largest number of votes given any of the contenders. Hence there must be at least three contenders if a *plurality* is not automatically a *majority* as well: If A gets ten votes, B gets five, and C gets nine, A wins with a *plurality* of one, but A would have needed thirteen votes to win a *bare majority* of the twenty-four votes cast.

majordomo (*n.*) means "the chief of the house" and hence "the butler or any chief deputy"; it has one plural: *majordomos.* See PLURALS OF NOUNS ENDING IN -O.

MALAPROPISM Named for Mrs. Malaprop, a silly woman who used big words in wrong ways in Sheridan's *The Rivals* (1775), a *malapropism* is the ludicrous substitution of a wrong word for the right one, as in *He's a deciduous* [instead of the intended *assiduous*] *worker.* Inexperienced people trying to stretch their vocabularies too fast are likely to stumble into *malapropisms,* and authors from Shakespeare on have amused us with their pedants and bumpkins who confidently confuse one long word with another. Many of us sometimes deliberately create *malapropisms* just for fun, but *inadvertent malapropisms,* as when someone writes that a potentially explosive situation has been *diffused* (rather than *defused*) or when someone confuses *entomology* (insects) with *etymology* (word history), can be serious embarrassments. See MIXED METAPHORS and entries for any of these pairs: *perpetrate/perpetuate; perquisite/prerequisite; permissible/permissive.*

male, female See EFFEMINATE; GENDER (1); GENDER (2); MANNISH.

malign, malignant See BENIGN.

man (*n.*) can mean "a human of either sex," "the human race," or "a male human being." Many consider the first sense to be exclusive language, but the word seems not likely to disappear soon in any of these senses. See -ESS; FEMININE OCCUPATIONAL FORMS; INCLUSIVE LANGUAGE; -IST; SEXIST LANGUAGE.

-man (*suffix*) There has been considerable objection to some words compounded with this suffix, particularly to occupational titles. See -ESS; FEMININE OCCUPATIONAL FORMS; INCLUSIVE LANGUAGE; -IST; SEXIST LANGUAGE.

manageable, managing (*adjs.*) *Manageable* retains the *e* of *manage; managing* does not.

maneuver, manoeuvre (*n., v.*) *Maneuver* is the usual American spelling; *manoeuvre* is a mainly British variant. See DIGRAPHS.

mango (*n.*) spells its plural either *mangoes* or *mangos.* See PLURALS OF NOUNS ENDING IN -O.

mania, phobia (*nn.*) The chief difference between these two is that a *mania* is an obsessive and irrational craze or desire for something, whereas a *phobia* is an equally obsessive and irrational fear of something. See also -PHILE.

manifesto (*n.*) spells its plural *manifestos* or *manifestoes.* See PLURALS OF NOUNS ENDING IN -O.

manifold (*adj., n.*), **manyfold** (*adj.*) The adjective *manifold* means "of many parts, varieties, kinds," as in *Our group had manifold plans for money raising.* The noun has several technical meanings. *Manyfold* means "many times," as in *We increased our original investment manyfold.*

mankind (*n.*) takes either singular or plural verbs and subsequent pronouns, but the usual pattern requires the singular: *Mankind shows its main strengths in time of trouble.* Many users of English now consider this word to be exclusionary. See INCLUSIVE LANGUAGE; SEXIST LANGUAGE.

manner, manor (*nn.*), **to the manner (manor) born** These words are homophones, *manner* meaning "a mode of behavior" (see also KIND), *manor,* "a house or mansion and its land." *To* *the manner born* is an idiom meaning "from birth accustomed to the behavior expected and therefore able to meet the standards easily," and *To the manor born* is an idiom meaning "accustomed as from birth to the ways and demands of being landed gentry." *Manner* appears to have the stronger literary sanction (see *Hamlet* I.iv.15), but both forms of the idiom are in use in Standard English.

mannish, male, manly, masculine (*adjs.*) *Manly* is applied usually to men and especially to boys; it is an elevated, flattering term. *Mannish* is applied more often to women and is pejorative in some unflattering or critical uses, although it can be noncommittal, especially when used to describe the tailoring of women's clothes, for example. *Masculine* suggests qualities thought to be typical of men, including physical strength, physical courage, and the like. It is also a grammatical term used in dealing with gender. *Male* is the sexually explicit adjective; its basic information is biological. See EFFEMINATE.

manoeuvre See MANEUVER.

man-of-war (*n.*) The plural is *men-of-war*. See PLURALS OF COMPOUND NOUNS; RELIC PLURALS OF NOUNS.

manor See MANNER.

manse (*n.*) is archaic in the sense "a large house, a mansion." Its more common meaning today is "the parsonage, especially of a (Scottish) Presbyterian minister."

mantel, mantle (*nn.*) *Mantel* means "the support over a fireplace, particularly the protruding slab, usually of stone or wood, above the fireplace"; *mantle* means "a cloak or cape" and hence "a metal gridwork cap over a gas lamp's flame," "the layer of material between the earth's crust and its core," and indeed, "anything that covers over as would a cloak," as in *The mantle of darkness obscured the view.*

many a is a locution that is followed by a singular noun, which in turn takes a singular verb: *Full many a flower is born to blush unseen . . .* (Thomas Gray, *Elegy Written in a Country Churchyard*). See AGREEMENT.

manyfold See MANIFOLD.

mar (*v.*), when combined in the passive voice with a preposition, takes either *by* or (sometimes) *with: The party was marred by [with] several noisy arguments.*

marathon (*adj.*), meaning "of extremely long (and tiring) duration," as in *We entered our fourth day of marathon collective bargaining,* is Standard. The adjective is based on the noun

marathon, the twenty-six mile footrace named after a messenger's run from Marathon to Athens to bring the news of the Greeks' victory over the Persians in 490 B.C.

margarine, margarin (*n.*) is pronounced *MAHR*-juhr-in, *MAHR*-juhr-*EEN*, or *MAHR*-juhr-*EEN*, although it can sometimes be heard with a second syllable pronounced -*guhr*. The *margarin* spelling is rare.

marginal (*adj.*) means "in or on the margin," "near the edge," "trivial," "part-time," "on the fringe," "barely qualified," and the like. All these Standard meanings tend to be pejorative, as in *Our success was marginal at best; She was only a marginal participant.*

marionette See PUPPET.

marital, martial (*adjs.*) *Marital* (pronounced *MER-i-tuhl*) means "pertaining to marriage": *They took their marital vows in her family's garden. Martial* (pronounced *MAHR-shuhl*) means "concerning war," "warlike": *He studied the martial arts.* Metathesis may occasionally cause confusion of the two spellings.

marry, Mary See MERRY.

marshal, marshall (*n.*, *v.*) These variant spellings are both Standard, but *marshal* is by far the more common in American English today.

marten, martin (*nn.*) Of these homophones, *marten* refers to the weasel-like animal and its fur, and a *martin* is any of several kinds of swallow.

martial See MARITAL.

martyr (*n.*, *v.*) The noun, when combined with a preposition, usually takes *to* or sometimes *of: She's a martyr to [of] her hay fever. For* also occurs on occasion: *He determined to be a martyr for his cause.* The verb combines almost always with *for,* to express the cause of the martyring: *She was martyred for refusing to recant.*

Mary, marry See MERRY.

masculine See MANNISH.

MASCULINE, FEMININE, NEUTER These are the grammatical genders in English, today signaled only by the gender of the third person singular pronouns that refer to them: *masculine* (*he, his, him*), *feminine* (*she, her, hers*), *neuter* (*it, its*). See GENDER (2).

mash potatoes See ICE CREAM.

massive (*adj.*), meaning "very large, ponderous, important," and the like, seems to have become a vogue word over the past few decades. Be careful not to overuse it.

MASS NOUNS, COUNT NOUNS A *mass noun* denotes something uncountable or abstract, a substance like *sugar* or *iron*, or a concept such as *integrity* or *courage*; mass nouns usually do not have plurals, and the determiners used with them are typically *some* and *any*, never *a* or *an* or numbers. A *count noun*, on the other hand, denotes something countable, such as *tree, cat,* or *ocean. Count nouns* do have plurals, and they can have *a* or *an* and numbers as determiners. Some nouns can be either *mass* or *count nouns: Grain has become very scarce. Several grains are grown in this region.*

masterful, masterly (*adjs.*) mean "skillful, adroit, expert," as in *His control of the language was masterful [masterly].* The adverb is usually *masterfully: He played the Chopin pieces masterfully.*

mastery (*n.*) can combine with *of,* as in *His mastery of computer graphics was complete,* and *over,* as in *Mastery over a cageful of lions and tigers was her claim to fame.*

material, materiel (*nn.*) *Material,* pronounced *muh-TEER-ee-uhl,* is "the stuff of which something may be made," and it has specialized senses too, including "cloth," "a performer's script or act," and "the equipment and tools needed for doing or making something." *Materiel,* pronounced either *muh-TEER-ee-EL* or as a homophone of *material,* is "the tools and equipment of an army or some other enterprise."

materialize (*v.*), meaning "to appear suddenly" or "to become solid and made of material," is Standard English.

materiel See MATERIAL.

mathematical progression See PROGRESSION.

matrix (*n.*) has two Standard plurals: *matrices* (*MAI-tri-seez*) and *matrixes* (*MAI-triks-iz*). See FOREIGN PLURALS.

mature (*adj., v.*), **maturity** (*n.*) These mean "adult" (*The immature robin's breast is spotted; the mature bird's is solid orange*), but they can also be euphemisms for "getting on in years," as in *He has a mature build, complete with potbelly,* and in the name of the journal of the American Association of Retired Persons, *Modern Maturity.* The verb means "to reach adulthood, to ripen," and (of bonds and notes) "to fall due." See SENIOR CITIZEN.

maunder (*v.*), **meander** (*n., v.*) Both mean "to wander aimlessly," but *meander* is the high-frequency word in the literal sense of walking slowly and aimlessly and to describe winding or complicated movement. The noun stands for any serpentine path but specifically names a bend in the winding watercourses typical of old streams and rivers. *Maunder* is usually used figuratively of speaking: *She maundered on and on, but we had no idea what she was talking about.*

mauve (*adj., n.*) The color is any of several light purples. Pronounce it *MOV* or *MAWV.*

maxim See APHORISM.

maximize, minimize (*vv.*) Some insist that *maximum* and *minimum* are both absolute adjectives and that therefore the verbs based on them are absolutes too and should not be qualified with adverbs. If these are conceptually absolute, there is only one *maximum,* only one *minimum*; hence *to maximize* or *minimize* (which see) is to increase or reduce something to precisely that amount or number. But in fact both verbs also mean "to tend in the specified direction, not necessarily to reach the specified goal." "To make the most (or least) of" is also a Standard use, as in *We decided to maximize as best we could our chances of winning; We tried as much as possible to minimize our chances for failure.* Compare OPTIMIZE. See SPELLING (1).

maximum (*n.*) has two Standard plurals: *maxima* and *maximums.* See FOREIGN PLURALS.

may See CAN (1).

may, might (*auxs.*) For events in the present or immediate future, use either *may* or *might (I may [might] decide to go after all),* but for past time, most Standard users still prefer only *might,* as in *Yesterday I might have decided to stay home,* not the increasingly encountered *Yesterday I may have decided to stay home.* Journalese is now peppered with *may* where until recently *might* has been solidly entrenched. See also CAN (1); COULD; SEQUENCE OF TENSES.

maybe (*adv., n.*), **may be** (*v., aux.*) *Maybe,* an adverb meaning "perhaps," is Standard (*Maybe she'll come anyway*), even though some argue that *perhaps* sounds more cultivated. *Maybe* is also a Conversational and Informal noun (*No maybes, now; you must come!*). The auxiliary and verb are always spelled as two words (*She may be on her way already*), the adverb and noun as one.

may can See DOUBLE MODAL AUXILIARIES; MIGHT COULD.

mayo (*n.*) is a Casual clipping of *mayonnaise,* part of the jargon of fast foods and fast feeding.

may of See OF (2); SHOULDA.

mayoral (*adj.*), **mayoralty** (*n.*) Pronounce the adjective *MAI-or-uhl, MAI-uhr-uhl,* or (in rapid speech) *MER-uhl,* and the noun similarly, but ending in *-tee.* Don't stress *-or-.* The adjective applies to matters concerning the officer or the office, and the noun refers to the office, the term of office, and the abstract idea of having a *mayor* or serving as one.

Mc- See MAC-.

me (*pron.*) is the accusative or objective case of the first person singular pronoun, and whether to use *I, me,* or *myself* often raises usage questions.

After *than* or *as,* as in *She is taller than me* [*I*] and *She is as old as me* [*I*], the issue is whether *than* and *as* are functioning as subordinating conjunctions or prepositions. Each can be either one: if they are conjunctions, the pronouns will be nominative case subjects of the clauses they introduce; if prepositions, the pronouns will be objective case objects of prepositions. Both uses are Standard today.

Compound subjects and direct objects (*John and I* [*not me*] *are going*; *They sent Mary and me* [*not I*]) cause trouble that single-word subjects or objects never create (*I am going; They sent me*). Standard English requires nominative forms as subjects and objective forms as objects. Never confuse the two: never say or write *Me and Fred are going* or *They asked Mary and I.*

Reserve *myself* for emphasis, as in *I myself saw her,* and for reflexive use, as in *I gave it to her myself.* Don't use *myself* as the pronoun in a compound structure such as *Give it to John and myself*; instead, make it *Give it to John and me.* See CASE (1); MYSELF; PERSONAL PRONOUNS; SYNTAX.

meager, meagre (*adj.*) Both spellings are Standard, although Americans generally use *meager,* and the British, *meagre.*

mean See MEDIAN.

meander See MAUNDER.

mean for, intend for, want for, as in *She didn't mean for* [*intend for, want for*] *you to hear,* are dialectal and even then occur primarily in speech. Outside their dialect areas (mainly Midland and Southern) these constructions are considered at least Nonstandard and perhaps Substandard, but they may be spreading into some Casual, Impromptu, and Informal contexts. *She didn't mean* [*intend, want*] *you to hear* is unquestionably Standard, as is *We will not want for company,* meaning "lack it." See also INTEND; WANT.

MEANING See SEMANTIC; SEMANTIC CHANGE; SEMANTIC DISTINCTION.

MEANING: AMERICAN AND BRITISH DIFFERENCES Nearly every American user of Standard English can give lists of differences in the vocabularies of the two countries: *truck* and *lorry, elevator* and *lift,* (*life*) *insurance* and *assurance, wrench* and *spanner, sedan* and *saloon, trunk* and *boot, hood* and *bonnet, traffic circle* and *roundabout, molasses* and *treacle,* and hundreds more are known on both sides of the Atlantic, thanks to tourism, films, television, and publications. In the proper contexts, nearly all are understandable to nearly all. Americans should usually stick to American terms, however, except for special effects.

meaningful (*adj.*) is beginning slowly to recover from prodigious overuse in the 1960s and 1970s, especially in clichés such as *a meaningful relationship, a meaningful discussion,* and *a meaningful dialogue.* Let it convalesce; use *pleasant, instructive, helpful, thought-provoking,* or one of the dozens of other, more explicit adjectives available for describing the quality or nature of an experience or a communication.

meaningless, mindless, nonsensical, senseless, silly (*adjs.*) All are loosely synonymous, sharing a sense of behavior or ideas that don't help. If it's *meaningless,* it serves no purpose and communicates no idea. *Mindless* means "thoughtless," "without intellectual content," or even "heedless or careless." *Senseless* adds "stupid, foolish, and irrational" to the senses associated with *mindless,* and *nonsensical* and *silly* suggest again the "irrational" but also "foolish" and "purposeless."

means (*n.*), meaning "wealth or ability to pay," "anything useful in attaining a goal," or "a way of doing things," is a plural noun, but it can take either a singular or a plural verb: *The means is* [*are*] *not always justified by the end.* It occurs most frequently in two Standard idioms: *means to an end,* "a way of accomplishing what one seeks," as in *It wasn't pretty, but it was a means to an end,* and *by all means,* meaning "at all costs," "in any way possible," and hence "without question": *By all means, ask him to come.*

meant See DESIGN.

meantime, meanwhile (*advs., nn.*) *Meantime* and *meanwhile* are essentially interchangeable both as nouns, as in *In the meanwhile* [*meantime*] *we rested and read,* and as adverbs, as in *Meantime* [*meanwhile*] *the others played softball.*

measles (*n.*) is a plural (a *mesel* was the Middle English name for one of the red spots) that today takes either singular or plural verbs and pronouns: *Measles is [are] dangerous; it [they] sometimes causes [cause] lasting damage.*

medal (*n.*), **meddle** (*v.*) These homophones are unlike in all other respects: a *medal* is a coinlike award or decoration, and *to meddle* is "to tamper, to interfere without the right to do so." *Meddle* combines with *with, in,* or *into,* as in *Don't meddle with [in, into] matters that are none of your concern.* See also METAL.

media See MEDIUM.

median, average, mean (*adjs., nn.*), **modal** (*adj.*), **mode** (*n.*) A *median* number is one at the numerical midpoint between the highest and lowest in a series, and, by extension, something in the middle: 7 is the *median* between 5 and 9. *Mean* means midpoint but is also an *average* of all the numbers in a series: of 5, 7, 8, 8, 9, the *median* is 7, but the *mean* or *average* is 7.4. *Mode* in statistical distributions is the number or value that occurs most frequently: in the series above, the *mode* or *modal number* is 8.

mediate (*v.*) can combine with *between,* as in *We'll mediate between the two parties,* and occasionally with *among,* as in *There are three claimants, and you'll have to mediate among them.* It can also use *for* and *on behalf of: I've been asked to mediate for [on behalf of] the committee.* And when it means "transmit" or "interpret" *mediate* can combine with *through* and *to,* probably as a vogue word, as in *She attempted to mediate the manners of the society to the immigrants through a series of playlets.* See ARBITRATE.

medieval, mediaeval (*adj.*) Both spellings are Standard, but Americans favor *medieval,* the British, *mediaeval.* See DIGRAPHS.

mediocre See ABSOLUTE ADJECTIVES.

meditate (*v.*) combines with *on* or sometimes with *upon* or *about,* as in *We meditated on [upon, about] how we should proceed.*

medium, media, mediums (*n.*) *Medium* is a singular noun meaning "a size in the middle, between large and small," as in *She wears a medium, I think,* but among its other referents it also is "a means of communication, such as the press, television, or radio." In this sense the word is both singular and plural, but its plural is always the Latin plural *media: The media is [are] going to be useful to us.* Another referent is "a person supposed to be able to communicate with the spirit world," a sense that uses the regular English plural, *mediums,* as does the size sense: *She's one of several mediums practicing here in town. These sweaters are both mediums.* See FOREIGN PLURALS.

meet with, meet up, meet up with *Meet with* is a Standard idiom (*I hope to meet with them next week*), meaning "to hold a meeting, an encounter," as distinguished from *I hope to meet them,* which could also mean "to be introduced to them." *Meet up* (*I hope you and I meet up again some day*) is Casual at best, possibly dialectal. Standard users would use only *meet* at higher levels. *Meet up with,* however, is at least Conversational, and at least one dictionary considers it Standard; it simply means "encounter," as in *I hope to meet up with her again some day.*

mega (*adj., interj.*), **mega-, meg-** (*prefixes*) These are combining prefixes that mean "large, huge" and "a million" or "millions." A *megabyte* is a million bytes, a *megadose* is a huge dose, and a *megaphone* is used to make the voice larger or louder. There are a good many nonce words that use *mega-* before consonants, as in *megastupidity,* and *meg-* before vowels, as in *megopulence,* and *mega* itself is clipped slang currently much in vogue with the young.

meld (*nn., vv.*) There are two verbs, both Standard, one from cardplaying, meaning "to declare cards for scoring, as in pinochle," and another, a blend of *melt* and *weld,* meaning "to blend or merge or combine," as in *His music melds folk and country-western themes.* Both verbs have used functional shift to create nouns: *Her meld won the game. The sauce was a meld of unidentifiable but delicious-smelling things.*

melted See MOLTEN.

memento (*n.*) is pronounced *me-MEN-to* and means "a reminder, a souvenir"; it has two plurals: *mementos* and *mementoes.* To mispronounce or misspell it with an *o* in the first syllable is to be guilty of a shibboleth, even though some dictionaries report that *momento* has been used enough to make it a variant. See PLURALS OF NOUNS ENDING IN -O.

memo (*n.*) (plural: *memos*) is a clipping of *memorandum,* Standard in all but the most Formal and Oratorical contexts. See PLURALS OF NOUNS ENDING IN -O.

memorandum (*n.*) has two plurals: *memorandums* and *memoranda.* See FOREIGN PLURALS.

mendacity, mendicity (*nn.*) *Mendacity* is lying; *mendicity* is begging.

menial (*adj., n.*) Both have to do with the household and refer first of all to housework and then to any labor or laborers held in low esteem. Both are pejorative, because no matter how they are defended, *menial* labor and *menials* themselves are considered to lack dignity.

mentality (*n.*) Even though its general sense is "mental capacity," *mentality* is usually pejorative, suggesting limitations on such capacities: *People of that mentality never really understand democratic traditions.*

mention See ALLUDE.

meretricious, meritorious (*adjs.*) *Meretricious* means "fake, flashy, tawdry, attractive but bad, like a prostitute": *His arguments seemed attractive at first, but they proved to be meretricious through and through. Meritorious* means "deserving of praise, reward, and honor": *Her citation was for meritorious service.*

merry, marry, Mary In Midland and some other regional dialects these three words are homophones pronounced *MER-ee.* In some other dialect areas (Eastern New England, Metropolitan New York, and some areas farther down the eastern seaboard), some people pronounce *marry MA-ree* and distinguish it from their pronunciation of *merry* (*MER-ee*). And some speakers in the Lower Hudson Valley, in Eastern New England, and especially in Southern dialect areas further distinguish *Mary* (pronounced *MAI-ree*) from the distinctive pronunciations of either or both *merry* and *marry.* In these dialects, the same sorts of divided pronunciations usually can be heard in *Kerry/carry* and *Perry/parry.* Some Americans have difficulty hearing the pronunciations they themselves do not use, but it doesn't matter: you may use one pronunciation for all or distinguish *Mary* or *marry* from the other two, whichever seems natural to you. All are Standard regional variations.

mesdames See MADAM.

Messrs. Today this is the plural of *Mr.*, and we pronounce it to rhyme with *dressers.* It comes from a foreign plural, the French *messieurs,* and we usually spell it as an abbreviation.

metal, mettle (*nn.*) A *metal* is a chemical element such as iron, copper, silver, or gold and various alloys made of them; *mettle* is a figurative variant of *metal,* meaning "courage, spirit, high quality of character." Listeners may have trouble distinguishing either of these words from *medal* or *meddle* in American English unless context makes clear which the speaker intends.

metamorphosis (*n.*) is a change or alteration in form, as when a tadpole turns into a frog, or a frog into a prince. The plural is *metamorphoses,* pronounced *met-uh-MOR-fuh-SEEZ.* See FOREIGN PLURALS.

METAPHORS are figures of speech that make implied comparisons between qualities of otherwise disparate or unlike things: *The rest of the week was a nightmare. Her entrance was a production.* Compare SIMILES. See FROZEN FIGURES; INFER.

METATHESIS (primary stress is on the second of the four syllables) is the transposition of sounds or letters in the speaking or writing of words. The error causes the confusion of *Calvary* with *cavalry* and often makes *revalent* of *relevant.* All such errors are Substandard, as are the metathetic pronunciations *NOO-kyoo-luhr* for *nuclear, PUHR-tee* for *pretty,* and *WAHPS* for *wasp,* as well as the spelling *ax* and the pronunciation *AKS* for *ask.* See also SPOONERISMS.

meter, metre (*nn.*) Americans spell the unit of measure, the technical word for rhythm in poetry, and the instrument for reading pressures, *meter.* The British spell the instrument *meter* but spell the other senses *metre.* See SPELLING (1).

meticulous (*adj.*), in the sense "painstaking, very careful of details," has lost its once-pejorative overtones of "overly careful," "overly finical about details." Today to be called *meticulous* in your work is to be paid a compliment.

metre See METER.

METROPOLITAN NEW YORK CITY REGIONAL DIALECT is the subdialect of Northern dialect spoken in New York City, Northern New Jersey, Long Island, and along the Connecticut shore as far east as New Haven. It is characterized by loss of *r* sounds before consonants (*PAHT* for *part*), as well as by other Hudson Valley sounds, and it also has some "foreignisms" such as the glottal stop in *bottle* (wherein instead of a *t* sound with the tip of the tongue, the air column is cut off by the soft palate; the IPA symbol is [ʔ]) and the hard *g* sound following nasals that makes *singer* rhyme with *finger* instead of with *ringer,* as in most other U.S. dialects. This is perhaps the only American English dialect whose Standard, cultivated form seems to lack prestige even among some of its own speakers.

mettle See METAL.

Mexican, Mexican-American (*nn.*) *Mexican* refers to a citizen of Mexico; when used to refer to a *Mexican-American,* it is sometimes considered taboo. *Mexican-American* refers to a member of that ethnic group who is a U.S. citizen; the term is usually hyphenated. See also CHICANO; HISPANIC.

MIDDLE ENGLISH was the stage of the language following Old English, distinguished from it by two factors. First, the Norman invasion in 1066 began a long and increasing influence of French words on the English vocabulary; second, the growing importance of London, both politically and commercially, made its Southeast Midland dialect (in which Geoffrey Chaucer wrote) the most influential of English dialects and turned it ultimately into the basis for the English we know today. *Middle English* gradually lost many of its grammatical inflections, replacing them with function words and an increasingly modern-looking syntax. We have many literary works from the *Middle English* period, some of them masterpieces. We conventionally date *Middle English* after 1066 to the appearance of printing in the late 1500s. Here is some of Genesis from a late fourteenth-century translation: compare its more familiar-looking vocabulary with that of the same passage in the Old English entry, and note the syntactic and other grammatical differences too:

> In the first made god of nought heuen and erth. The erth forsothe wæs veyn withinne and voyde, and derknesses weren vp on the face of the see. And the spirite of God was yborn vp on the waters. And God seid, "Be made light," and made is light. And God sees light that it was good and dyuidide light from derknesses. And clepide light day and derknesses night, and maad is euen and moru, o day.

The next chronological stage of the language was called Early Modern English, the language of the Renaissance.

might See MAY.

mighta See OF (2); SHOULDA.

might could, might should, might would These are double modal auxiliaries, limited to the spoken Midland and Southern regional dialects. *I might could do it* means "I might be able to do it" or "Maybe I could do it." Outside their regions these are shibboleths.

mightily See MIGHTY.

might of See OF (2); SHOULDA.

might've See OF (2); SHOULDA.

might would See MIGHT COULD.

mighty (*adj., n., intensifier*), **mightily** (*adv.*) *Mighty* is Standard as adjective and noun, as in *He's a mighty man; Even the mighty know fear,* but as intensifier, as in *She's a mighty good tennis player,* it is limited mainly to Conversational and Semiformal contexts. The adverb *mightily* is Standard: *They labored mightily to finish before nightfall.*

migrant, migrate, migration See EMIGRANT.

milieu (*n.*) is borrowed from French; it means "social setting, environment," is pronounced *MEEL-yu, mil-YOO,* or *MEEL-YOO,* and has two plurals: *milieus* and *milieux.* See FOREIGN PLURALS.

militate (*v.*) is usually combined with *against*; it means "to work, to have effect," as in *Their low tax base militates against their providing needed services.* Occasionally it is used with *in favor of* or *for,* as in *Their youth and zeal militate in favor of [for] their winning a hearing.* See MITIGATE.

millennium (*n.*), spelled with two *l*'s and two *n*'s, means "any period of a thousand years," "a time of great good fortune," or "a golden age" and has two plurals: *millenniums* and *millennia.* See FOREIGN PLURALS.

milliard (*n.*) was the original British word for "one thousand millions," but today the British frequently use *billion,* just as American English does. See BILLION; TRILLION.

mind-boggling See BOGGLE.

mindless See MEANINGLESS.

mine is the absolute possessive form of the pronoun *my.* See ABSOLUTE POSSESSIVES; CASE (1).

mine, my, in compound constructions See LINKED GENITIVES.

mineralogy (*n.*) The third syllable is stressed and pronounced either *-AHL-* or *-AL-*, and the *-AHL-* pronunciation sometimes causes a misspelling with *-ol-* instead of *-al-*. See also GENEALOGY.

minimal (*adj.*) means "least possible," as in *They fed the animals the minimal amount required to keep them alive,* "barely enough, some," as in *Our room had minimal accommodations for two people,* and "very little or very small," as in *They cleaned, but with minimal attention to polish.* All these are Standard.

minimize (*v.*) has two meanings, "to reduce or make as small as possible," as in *We decided to minimize our risk,* and "to make something look as low or small as possible," as in *He arranged the numbers to minimize the apparent size of the deficit.* See MAXIMIZE; SPELLING (1).

miniscule See MINUSCULE.

minister (*v.*) combines most frequently with the preposition *to: She ministered to the sick and helpless.* For the noun, see PRIEST.

minor (*adj.*) is an implicit comparative, already inflected for the comparative, although it can occasionally take a periphrastic comparative modifier, as in *Her injury was more minor than at first had been feared.* See IMPLICIT COMPARISON.

minority (*n.*) refers to the smaller of two groups making up a larger whole, to less than half, or simply to a splinter group. It usually takes a plural verb, but it can take a singular: *The largest minority are voting against. This small minority is voting in favor.* To use *minority* in the singular to mean "a member of a racial or ethnic minority," as in *I think the new teacher is a minority,* is Informal and Conversational at best; some commentators consider it Substandard, and some members of minority groups consider it offensive.

Minority also refers to the period prior to a person's "coming of age": *Fred's still a minor, still in his minority.*

minus (*adj., prep.*) The preposition means "without" or "less" and is Standard today in all but the most Formal use: *We've invited them to attend, but minus their scruffy hangers-on.* In arithmetic *minus* is fully Standard both as adjective (*a minus quantity*) and as preposition (*three minus two*).

minuscule, miniscule (*adj., n.*) Some consider *miniscule* a variant spelling of *minuscule*; others say it is a misspelling. Best advice: spell it *minuscule.* The noun is the name of a small ancient and medieval lowercase handwriting; the adjective refers to that writing but is used more often to mean "tiny."

minute (*adj., n.*) The noun means "one-sixtieth of an hour" and "one-sixtieth of an angular degree": in both, a *minute* consists of sixty seconds. The generalized meaning is "any short time": *She'll be down in a minute. A minute hand* on a watch or clock is the longer hand, the one that marks off the *minutes* in an hour. All these are pronounced *MIN-it(s).* The adjective *minute,* pronounced *mei-N(Y)OOT* or *mi-N(Y)OOT,* means "very tiny" and frequently "insignificant" or "minor"; it comes from a Latin participle meaning "made smaller."

minutia (*n.*) A *minutia* (*min-OO-shee-[y]uh*) is a tiny detail, but the word is used most often in the plural, *minutiae* (*min-OO-shee-[y]ei*). See FOREIGN PLURALS.

misanthrope, misogamist, misogynist (*nn.*) are haters all: a *misanthrope* hates people; a *misogamist,* marriage; and a *misogynist,* women. All are Standard; *misogamist* is rare.

mischievous (*adj.*) Note the spelling—the *i* precedes the *e*—and pronounce the word *MIS-chi-vuhs*—it doesn't rhyme with *devious.* See also GRIEVOUS.

misdemeanor, misdemeanour (*n.*) *Misdemeanor* is the American spelling, *misdemeanour,* the British. See FELONY; SPELLING (1).

mishap, accident (*nn.*) A *mishap* is generally trivial but always unfortunate; an *accident* may be trivial or important, but it may also be either fortunate or unfortunate, and it is unexpected: *Bumping into her in the hall was a lucky accident. A few mishaps may delay but not stop us.*

misinformation See DISINFORMATION.

mislead (*v.*) The principal parts are *mislead, misled, misled,* and, as with *lead* (which see), the past tense and past participle are frequently misspelled. *Mislead* is infinitive and present tense only.

misogamist, misogynist See MISANTHROPE.

MISPLACED MODIFIERS, MISRELATED MODIFIERS See DANGLING MODIFIERS.

Miss, Misses These are the singular and plural of the title traditionally used for unmarried women and girls: *Miss Mary Jane Jones, the Misses Smith.* Today some adult females prefer *Ms.* (which see), but others oppose it. *Miss* is also used in direct address where *madam* might be used for an adult or older woman, or when addressing a woman who is a paid server, waitress, or store clerk: *May I have the check, please, Miss?* Americans also use the title for winners of beauty contests: *Miss Colorado, Miss Fig Newton of 1995.* In clothing jargon, *misses'* are a set of sizes for females, along with *juniors'* and *women's* sizes. Compare MR.; MRS.

missile, missal, missive (*nn.*) A *missile* (Americans say it *MIS-uhl,* the British, *MIS-EIL*) is something thrown, fired, or projected (such as a spear, a bullet, or a rocket), as in *They fired ground-to-air missiles at the plane.* A *missal* (a homophone of the American pronunciation of *missile*) is a book containing the words for the Mass. A *missive* is a letter, a written message. Compare EPISTLE.

Missis, missis, Missus, missus See MRS.

misspell (*v.*), **misspelling** (*n.*) Both have two *s*'s.

MISSPELLING See SPELLING.

Mister, mister See MR.

mistrust, distrust (*vv.*) *Mistrust* means "to doubt, to lack confidence in," as in *I mistrust his ability to persuade her. Distrust* means much the same but adds *suspicion* to the mix: *He distrusts her because he thinks she'll cheat him.*

mistrustful (*adj.*), when it combines, takes the prepositions *of* and (occasionally) *toward: She was mistrustful of Frank's loyalty; The child was taught to be mistrustful toward strangers.*

misunderstanding See UNDERSTANDING.

mitigate (*v.*) means "to ease, to alleviate, to moderate," as in *Our awareness of her recent bereavement considerably mitigated the sting of her bitter words.* The cliché *mitigating circumstances* means circumstances that make an action less damning, less serious. *Mitigate* is frequently confused with *militate*, which see. See also AMELIORATE.

mix (*v.*), when it takes a preposition, usually takes *with*, as in *She doesn't mix much with her neighbors*; it also takes *in* and *into*, as in *I try not to mix in [into] matters I know nothing about*, but these two combinations are best limited to Conversational or Semiformal contexts.

MIXED METAPHORS are two or more contiguous metaphors that are inconsistent, often laughably so: consider *With her head in the sand and her heels dug in, she remained coolly above the fray; To take arms against a sea of troubles*; and *The hand that rocked the cradle has kicked the bucket.* In an instant this sort of inadvertence can transform a piece of serious prose into a joke. See MALAPROPISM; SYNTACTIC BLENDS.

-mm- See CONSONANTS (2).

mnemonic (*adj., n.*) The adjective means "something assisting memory": *A string tied around a finger is a mnemonic device.* The noun is a name for such devices, such as the spelling *mnemonic "I before E, except after C."* Pronounce it *ni-* or *nee-MAHN-ik.*

moat See MOTE.

mobile (*adj., n.*), **movable, moveable** (*adj.*) *Mobile* (Americans pronounce it *MO-bul, MO-bil,* or *MO-beel*; the British say it *MO-BEIL*) means "moving or movable, especially on wheels" and, figuratively, "capable of change." *We are a mobile society: most of us drive cars,* and in a generation or two many of us can move from the lowest to the highest social class and back again. A *mobile* is a piece of sculpture, its parts suspended independently by wires from the ceiling, so that it can be in constant and varied motion. *Movable* (also spelled *moveable*) describes something that can be moved from one location to another, as in *His garden was movable: all the plants were in pots,* or from one date to another, as in *Easter is a movable feast.*

mock, mock up (*vv.*), **mockup, mock-up** (*n.*) *Mock* can take a direct object (*She mocked him*), or it can sometimes be combined with the preposition *at* (*Everyone was mocking at me*). A *mock(-)up* is "a model, a facsimile," and *to mock up* means "to make a *mock(-)up.*"

modal See MEDIAN.

MODAL AUXILIARIES, MODALS are function words that accompany verbs and signal mood. They consist of a finite list of words (*can, could, may, might, must, shall, should, will, would*), and although they are sometimes called verbs, they lack the English verb's distinctive third person singular present tense forms and have no participial forms, either: *We could inquire. They may call us. She should write them a reply.* See CAN (1); COULD; MUST (2); SHALL; SHOULD. See also DOUBLE MODAL AUXILIARIES.

mode See MEDIAN.

MODE See MOOD.

modern, modernistic (*adjs.*) *Modern* means "of the present or very recent time," "current," "up to date," as in *They lived in a modern house. Modernistic* means "associated with modernism," but its more frequent meaning is "contemporary" and especially "trendy," in what is often a pejorative sense stressing the imitative or affectedly "new" in design and execution: *This modern painting has the integrity that modernistic paintings nearly always lack.*

MODERN ENGLISH is the language from the end of the seventeenth century to the present day, the successor to Early Modern English. This book describes the present state of the Standard American version of *Modern English.*

modernistic See MODERN.

MODIFIERS,   MODIFICATION, STRUCTURES OF MODIFICATION *Modifiers* are locutions that limit or describe or somehow change the meaning of the entity modified. *Modification* in English is done by adjectives and adverbs or by other structures, called adjectivals and adverbials, which function in the same way. These are the main structures of modification in English:

adjective + noun (*red barn*)

noun + adjective (*fudge royale*)

adverb + verb (*quietly go*)

verb + adverb (*go quietly*)

sentence adverb + independent clause (*Happily, he left*)

independent clause + sentence adverb (*He left, happily*)

independent clause containing verb + adverb (*He left happily*)

noun + prepositional phrase (*boy with freckles*)

verb plus prepositional phrase (*ran with abandon*)

adverbial prepositional phrase + independent clause (*In haste, he fled*)

subordinate clause + independent clause (*After we had eaten dinner, I felt ill*)

See DANGLING MODIFIERS.

Mogul, mogul, Mongol (*nn.*), **Mongoloid, mongoloid** (*adjs., nn.*) *Mogul* is a Persian name for *Mongol*, a variant name for a *Mongolian*. All these are proper names. A *mogul* (not capitalized) is any powerful autocrat or other large or powerful thing, such as a kind of large bump in a ski trail. *Mongoloid* is Standard as an anthropological term for the central Asian racial type, with its dark hair and eyes, yellow-brown skin color, and prominent cheekbones, but either capitalized or not and clipped to *Mongol* or not, both noun and adjective are offensive and taboo today when applied to Down's syndrome or those who have it.

Mohammed is a common spelling of the name of the prophet and founder of Islam (A.D. 570–632). See MUSLIM.

Mohammedan See MUSLIM.

mold, mould (*n., v.*) Americans spell both noun and verb *mold*; the British, *mould*. See SPELLING (1).

molt, moult (*n., v.*) Americans spell both verb and noun *molt*; the British, *moult*. See SPELLING (1).

molten, melted (*adjs.*) *Molten* is used primarily of liquid lava and metals liquefied by heat. *Melted* is used of snow and ice, butter and chocolate, and other common substances turned liquid by heat, and *melted* is usually the generic adjective as well. It is also used figuratively, as in *Her heart melted at the sight of the puppy.*

momentarily (*adv.*) means "for just a moment, briefly," as in *I was momentarily stunned*; "at once, instantly, now," as in *Momentarily I recognized her*; and "at any moment, soon," as in *I expect him to arrive momentarily.* Compare PRESENTLY.

momentary, momentous (*adjs.*) *Momentary* means "briefly, for a moment," as in *I had a momentary lapse of memory. Momentous* means "of great moment, of great importance or consequence," as in *These were momentous decisions.*

momento See MEMENTO.

momentous See MOMENTARY.

money (*n.*) There are two plurals used when *money* is a count noun: *moneys* and *monies*. As a mass noun *money* takes singular verbs: *Money earns interest.*

Mongol See MOGUL.

mongoose (*n.*) The plural is *mongooses*, although the force of analogy with *goose* (perhaps with the aid of jocularity) makes *mongeese* familiar, although not Standard.

monogram, monograph (*nn.*) A *monogram* is a symbol of a person's identity, usually made up of initials. A *monograph* is a treatise or detailed study of one relatively narrow topic.

monologue, dialog, dialogue, duologue, monolog (*nn.*) A *monologue* is a long speech by one person. A *duologue* is a conversation between two persons, as is a *dialogue*. But *dialogue* is a much higher frequency word, and it has generalized as well, so that it can also refer loosely to conversations with various numbers of speakers, as well as to the scripts that record actors' speeches. The *-logue* spellings are all Standard, but so are those that end in *-log,* and the use of the latter is increasing. See DIALOGUE; -LOG.

monopoly (*n.*) combines with the prepositions *of* and *on* (*a monopoly of* [*on*] *all suitable shipping*), as well as *over* (*a monopoly over most of the available timber*) and *in* (*a monopoly in wheat*). See also DUO.

MOOD, MODE *Mood* or *mode* is an attribute of verbs that suggests part of the speaker's attitude toward the action the verb specifies. If the action is a fact (*He went home*), the *mood* is indicative. If the action is conjectural or is a possibility (*If he were to go home, . . .*), the *mood* is subjunctive. And if the verb gives a command (*Go home!*), the *mood* is imperative.

English distinguishes *mood* partly through morphology; for example, third person singular present indicative verbs end in *-s* (*she goes*; *it rhymes*; *he lingers*), and third person singular present subjunctive verbs don't (*if she go; if it rhyme; if he linger*). English also indicates subjunctive *mood* by means of modal auxiliaries (*if she should go; if it might rhyme; if he could linger*). See MODAL AUXILIARIES.

moot (*adj.*) has three Standard meanings: "discussable, debatable"; "under discussion, being disputed"; and "without practical significance, academic." Thus *a moot question* may be open to discussion, in the process of being discussed, or not worth discussing at all, depending on the sense dictated by context.

moral, morale (*nn.*) A *moral* is a piece of practical wisdom, a lesson to be drawn: *The moral of the story is "Don't count your chickens before they're hatched."* The plural, *morals,* means "principles or standards of conduct, especially in sexual behavior, integrity, and other ethical concerns": *Her morals are unblemished, so far as anyone knows. Morale* is the mental or emotional condition of a person or a group of people, a spirit of confidence or enthusiasm, or the reverse: *Despite their recent defeats, the team's morale was still good; they believed in themselves.* Problems arise when *moral* is sometimes spelled *morale,* and *morale* (in senses other than "group spirit") is occasionally spelled *moral.* Best advice: try to maintain the distinctions in meaning and spelling, and pronounce *moral* with stress on the first syllable (*MOR-uhl*), *morale* with stress on the second (*mor-AL*).

moratorium (*n.*) means "a legally granted delay of payment" and "the period of such a delay": *The town council passed a six-month moratorium on the payment of the new tax.* There are two plurals: *moratoriums* and *moratoria.* See FOREIGN PLURALS.

more, most See ANOTHER; ADJECTIVES (1); MOST (1); PERIPHRASTIC.

more important, more importantly See IMPORTANT.

mores (*n.*) This Latin plural of *mor,* "custom," is an American English plural, pronounced *MOR-aiz* or *MOR-eez.* It too means "customs," as applied especially to groups, and also "folkways that have the force of law."

more than one As subject, this phrase takes a singular verb when *one* is followed by a singular noun, as in *More than one child was homesick*; but sometimes when it is followed by some plural nouns or in more complex structures, notional agreement may make a plural verb sound better, as in *More than one of these children were homesick.* See AGREEMENT.

MORPHOLOGY in English is the study of the shape, form, and structure of words and the contribution of these to the grammar of the language. The inflections for number, case, and gender in pronouns and for tense and mood in verbs are *morphological* matters; so too are compounding and some other structural contributors to functional shift. The adjective is *morphological,* the adverb, *morphologically.*

mortar See CEMENT.

mortician, funeral director, undertaker (*nn.*) Of these names for those who embalm the dead, arrange funerals, and see to burials, *undertaker* is the oldest, dating from the end of the seventeenth century. *Mortician* and *funeral director* are both late nineteenth-century euphemisms, but they have been so thoroughly adopted that most people have forgotten that they were intended to make an unpleasant topic appear less unpleasant. All three are now Standard. Best advice: use *undertaker.*

Moslem See MUSLIM.

mosquito (*n.*) The plural is either *mosquitoes* or *mosquitos.* See PLURALS OF NOUNS ENDING IN *-O.*

most 1 (*adv., adj., intensifier*) is Standard meaning "more than half": *She kept most of the money.* It is the superlative adjective, but it is frequently used of two things, instead of *more,* especially in Conversational, Informal, and Semiformal contexts: *She loves both her parents, but her mother means most to her.* See ADJECTIVES (1).

The adverb is used to form the superlative degree of adjectives and other adverbs: *Of the three houses, the second is the most spacious.* As an intensifier, *most* is sometimes a useful change from *very,* but don't overdo it: *We were most happy to see you; I have a most devastating cough.*

most 2 (*adv.*) *Most,* which was once printed *'most,* is an apheptic of the adverb *almost,* Standard in all but Formal and Oratorical contexts: *This set will please most anyone; Like most everybody else, I was shocked.* Like contractions and other clippings, this *most* form is a strong style mark of the Informal and Conversational.

most important, most importantly See IMPORTANT.

mostly (*adv.*) usually means that the adjective, verb, or sentence that it modifies is not unqualifiedly true: *The boys were mostly ready to play. We mostly walked but took the bus part of the way. Mostly, road noises drowned out the speaker's words.* These are Standard, although they seem to tend toward the Conversational and the Informal (in some uses *mainly* or *chiefly* will seem slightly more formal).

mote, moat (*nn.*) Of these homophones, a *mote* is a tiny particle of dust such as you see floating in a shaft of sunlight, and a *moat* is a defensive ditch, usually filled with water, dug around a castle or fortress.

mother-in-law (*n.*) See -IN-LAW; PLURALS OF COMPOUND NOUNS.

motif, motive (*nn.*) A *motif* (pronounced *mo-TEEF*) is a recurrent theme or design in an art work, a repeated figure: *The operas of Wagner's Ring make complex use of identifying motifs for particular characters.* A *motive* (*MO-tiv*) is a drive or impulse that causes a person to act in a certain way, as in *The profit motive drove him constantly: he undertook nothing except to make money.* When combined, *motive* can take the preposition *for,* or occasionally *of,* plus a gerund (*He had no apparent motive for wanting to interfere; The motive of her action was never clear*) or *to* plus an infinitive (*His motive to get involved was mostly curiosity*). *Motive* also can combine with the prepositions *behind, beneath,* and *underneath: We could find no motive behind [beneath, underneath] her odd behavior.*

motorway See THRUWAY.

mould See MOLD.

moult See MOLT.

moustache See MUSTACHE.

movable See MOBILE.

move, your See BALL'S IN YOUR COURT.

moveable See MOBILE.

mow (*v.*) is a weak verb whose principal parts are *mow, mowed, mowed* or *mown.* As past participle, Americans usually use *mowed (He had just mowed the lawn),* but both *mowed* and *mown* function as participial adjectives: *The smell of newly mowed [newly mown, new-mowed, new-mown] grass was in the air.*

Mr., Mister, mister *Mr.* (with or without the period) is the abbreviation used conventionally in direct address, as in *Mr. [John] Adams.* The plural is *messrs.* The lowercase word is a noun used in Common or Vulgar English, particularly with *the,* to mean "husband": *I'll have to ask the mister.* The title alone, without a following name, is used in direct address, especially by the young in accosting their elders (*Mister, is this your hat?*); well-spoken adults in such a situation would conventionally use *sir* instead.

Mrs., Missis, missis, Missus, missus *Mrs.* is the Standard abbreviation (with or without the period) of the title used in traditional direct address to a married woman or widow: *Mrs. [John] Jones,* or *Mrs. [Mary] Smith.* Today, many but by no means all women prefer *Ms.* (which see) to *Mrs. Mesdames* is used as its plural, abbreviated *Mmes.* The pronunciation of *Mrs.* (*MIS-iz*) is reflected in the dialectal *Missus* and *missis* spellings we find as eye dialect in some literary contexts. *The missus [missis] is also a Common or Vulgar English synonym for "wife": *I'll have to ask the missus [missis].* For addressing a woman whose name is unknown, *Madame, Madam,* or *Ma'am,* the counterparts of *Sir,* are Standard; in this context *Missus* or *Mrs.* would be considered Common or Vulgar. See also MISS.

ms, MS are abbreviations for *manuscript*; the plural is *mss* or *MSS.* Periods are omitted.

Ms., Ms are variants of a title (pronounced *MIZ* or *MUHZ*) used in direct address to women regardless of marital status. Like *Miss* and *Mrs,* *Ms.* is a Standard locution, especially in Formal and business correspondence. Some women insist on it; others prefer *Miss* or *Mrs.* Where you can, try to anticipate and meet individual preferences. Spell the plural either *Mss.* or *Mses.*

much (*adj.*) doesn't modify plurals in Standard English; reserve it for mass nouns in the singular (*much trouble, much coffee*), and use *many* or *most* with count nouns in the plural (*many troubles, most situations*).

muchly (*adv.*) is at best a Casual or Informal adverb, used almost solely in mildly jocular efforts to spruce up a conventional *Thank you very much,* as *Thank you muchly.*

mucous (*adj.*), **mucus** (*n.*) These are homophones, but the adjective is always spelled *mucous,* the noun, *mucus.*

mug (*nn., vv.*), **mugging** (*n.*) The heavy cup was once usually decorated with a human face, hence the noun *mug,* a slang term meaning "face," and the compound slang term *mug shot* (a police photograph designed for identification purposes). The verb *to mug,* as in acting or simply making faces, means to use exaggerated facial expressions and gestures. Both *mug shot* and this sense of *to mug* are slang. Another verb *to mug* means "to assault usually with robbery as motive," and the nouns *mugging* and *mugger* mean "such an assault" and "the individual who commits it": *On her way home she was mugged. It was a brutal mugging—besides taking his wallet, the mugger broke the victim's nose.* These are now Standard, except perhaps in the most Formal writing.

Muhammad See MOHAMMED.

Muhammadan See MUSLIM.

mulatto, half-breed, octoroon, quadroon (*nn.*) These are old terms, today encountered mainly in nineteenth- and early twentieth-century writing. All are now deemed offensive by many people. A *mulatto* would be the offspring of one black parent without white ancestry and one white parent with no black ancestry. A *quadroon* would be a person one-quarter black, with one black grandparent, the child of a *mulatto* and a white; an *octoroon* would be a person with one black great-grandparent, the child of a *quadroon* and a white. *Half-breed* is even more clearly a taboo term, being considered a racial slur and hence offensive. It was once used generically for a racial blend of any sort, but originally it meant "the offspring of a North American Indian and a European." It has not been in polite use for nearly a century. *Mulatto*'s plural is either *mulattoes* or *mulattos*. Avoid all these words. See also AFRICAN (-)AMERICAN; NATIVE AMERICAN.

multilateral See BILATERAL.

multiple negation See BLACK ENGLISH; DOUBLE NEGATIVE.

munch (*v.*) began by meaning "to chew foods that crunch, such as celery," but today it also means simply "to eat, perhaps with enthusiasm": *We were drinking cider and munching all sorts of good things.*

munchies (*n. pl.*) is usually used in the plural and means "snacks, especially crunchy ones such as potato chips and raw vegetables, usually served with drinks"; occasionally the singular *munchy* appears as a nonce word. *To get (have) the munchies* is an idiom meaning "to crave such snack foods." All forms of the word are half-whimsical and limited to Informal and especially to Casual uses.

murder See EXECUTE.

murderer See ASSASSIN.

muse (*v.*), when combined with a preposition, can take *on, upon, over, about*, as in *She was musing on [upon] what her new job would be like; He mused for several days over [about] what to do next.*

MUSLIM, MOHAMMEDAN, MOSLEM, MUHAMMADAN (*adjs., nn.*) A *Muslim* (variously pronounced, but most commonly *MUHZ-luhm, MUHZ-lim*, or *MUZ-lim*) is an adherent of Islam. *Moslem* (*MAHZ-luhm* or *MAHS-luhm*) is a variant of *Muslim*. *Muhammadan* and *Mohammedan* are based on the name of the prophet Mohammed, and both are considered offensive. *Muslim*, as both noun and adjective, seems to be the most acceptable to all concerned.

must 1 (*adj., n.*) The noun and the adjective are both best limited to Conversational, Informal, and Semiformal use: *These books are musts for my Christmas list. They're going to be must reading for a lot of people, I think.*

must 2 (*v., aux.*) is a Standard modal auxiliary that either precedes or follows an infinitive (*We must go; Go we must*) or, like the other modal auxiliaries, occurs as the sole verb rather than as part of a verb phrase, in which case it echoes or refers back to an earlier verb in the context (*Do you plan to go? I must [go]*). *Must* is a one-form word, taking its tense colorations from grammatical and contextual cues elsewhere in the passage (*Did you lose it? I must have; Will he call? He simply must*), and unlike the usual verb, it does not add an *-s* for its third-person singular uses: *I, you*, and *he/she/it must. Must* means that its subject "is required, urged, or compelled" to act as the attached infinitive indicates (*She must vote early*).

musta See OF (2); SHOULDA.

mustache, moustache (*n.*) Americans usually spell it *mustache* and pronounce it either *MUH-stash* or *muh-STASH; moustache* is a variant for some Americans and is preferred by the British, who use both pronunciations as well.

must needs See NEEDS.

must of, must've See OF (2); SHOULDA.

mute See DUMB.

mutual, common, reciprocal (*adjs.*) are synonyms in the sense "shared or equally returned," as in *We felt a mutual [reciprocal, common] dislike for each other.* But *mutual* meaning "shared" or "in common," as in *We have a mutual friend* and *My insurance is with a mutual company*, does not mean "reciprocal," and *reciprocal* has meanings that *mutual* does not: "equivalent," "interchangeable," or "complementary," as in *We negotiated a recip-*

rocal trade agreement in which they sold us electronic gear and bought equal dollar amounts of our grain. *Common* in this meaning cluster means "shared" (*a common drinking cup*), but be careful to avoid confusion with other meanings ("ordinary, omnipresent, coarse, or tawdry") of the adjective: *We used a common cup* may mean either "a shared cup" or "an ordinary cup." The prepositional phrase *with the noun* is usually unambiguous: *We used that cup in common.*

my, mine, in compound constructions See LINKED GENITIVES.

myriad (*adj., n.*) As a noun, *myriad* means "ten thousand," but its most frequent sense is "any very large, indefinite number of persons or things," as in *We could see a myriad of stars* or *We could see myriads of them.* The plural is hyperbolic but Standard. The Standard adjective *myriad* simply means "innumerable": *There were myriad stars in the sky.*

myself (*pron.*) is the first person singular reflexive (*I hurt myself*) and emphatic (*I myself washed the car; I washed the car myself*) pronoun. These uses are Standard. Avoid using *myself* as a part of a compound direct object when the subject of the sentence has a different referent; instead of *They gave a party for my wife and myself,* use the Standard *They gave a party for my wife and me.* See REFLEXIVE PRONOUNS; YOURSELF.

mysterious See EQUIVOCAL.

mystery (*n.*) has many meanings, but they cluster in two groups: (1) things unknown and apparently unknowable or inexplicable, as in religion or the supernatural (*We spoke of the mystery of an afterlife*); (2) things unknown into which we must be initiated (*She promised to introduce me into the mystery of wallpaper hanging*). This cluster also involves *mysteries* that can or ought to be solved. See ENIGMA.

myth, mythical See LEGEND.

N

-n-, -nn- See CONSONANTS (2).

'n' is an eye dialect spelling that represents the way *and* is often pronounced in Casual and other rapid Conversational situations, as in *fun 'n' games.* See APOSTROPHE (2).

nadir See ZENITH.

nag (*v.*) combines usually with *at* and *about,* as in *The animals always nag at me to feed them around two o'clock,* although it is more often transitive, with a direct object: *They nag me mercilessly until I give in.*

naif, naïf (*n.*), **naive, naïve** (*adj.*), **naivete, naiveté, naïveté, naivety, naïvety** (*n.*) Pronounce the four words *nei-EEF, nei-EEV, nei-EEV-TAI,* and *nei-EEV-i-tee,* respectively. In French, *naif* (variant *naïf*) and *naive* (variant *naïve*) are respectively masculine and feminine forms of the adjective, but in English *naive* is now the only adjective, and it is no longer gender-distinctive: *He's naive about the danger, and so is she. Naif* in English is now almost always only a noun, meaning "a naive person": *His lack of experience marks him as a real naif. Naïveté* (or *naiveté* or *naivete*) and *naivety* (or *naïvety*) are variant spellings of the

abstract noun meaning "the quality or condition of being naive." American English tends to omit the dieresis except in the abstract noun, for which *naïveté* is the most frequent spelling.

naked (*adj.*), **nude** (*adj., n.*) These are synonyms in their literal sense of "unclothed, uncovered," but they are used in somewhat different environments. *Naked* concentrates on the simple physical fact, whereas *nude* has artistic overtones: *The naked soldiers were bathing in the pond. The model posed nude for the class.* Figurative uses are also differently distributed, *nude* being used frequently as a color designation (but see FLESH), *naked* being widely employed to mean "unadorned, unvarnished," as in *the naked truth.* The noun *nude* refers to a drawing, painting, or sculpture depicting the unclothed human body.

namely (*adv.*) means "that is to say," "to wit"; it's a rather stiff, scholarly word, often preceding a restatement, a clarification, or a list. See E.G.

names of organizations See ORGANIZATIONS.

naphtha See DIPHTHERIA; -PHTH-.

napkin See SERVIETTE.

narc (*n.*) is a slang term for an antinarcotics officer.

narcissus (*n.*) has three Standard plurals: *narcissuses, narcissi,* and *narcissus.* See FOREIGN PLURALS.

narcotic (*adj., n.*) *Narcotics* is the plural of the noun, and it requires a plural verb: *All these narcotics are addictive, but only that narcotic has a deadly narcotic effect.*

nary (*adj.*) is a form of *ne'er a,* meaning "never a," as in *There was nary a soul in sight.* It is Standard in that phrasal use, but without *a* or *an* following, it is dialectal and Nonstandard. See ARY.

native (*adj., n.*) The noun, used in the plural to mean "the people, especially of nonwhite races, who are indigenous to a place," and in the singular to mean "someone born and living in a place," is now considered racially or ethnically offensive in sentences such as *The natives are restless tonight* or *A native came rushing into the compound.* In the designation Native American the adjective is still appropriate and Standard, as it is when used to identify a person's *native language,* and so also is the noun when it is used to say that someone is *a native of a place,* meaning that he or she was born there.

Native American (*n.*) has become the Standard name for the American Indian, as well as for some peoples native to the Hawaiian Islands and Alaska, although the term *Indian* is still Standard in some technical uses as well.

NATURAL LANGUAGE, ARTIFICIAL LANGUAGE A *natural language* is any of the hundreds of languages spoken (many of them also written) by human beings: Latin, English, Spanish, Japanese, Arabic, and Albanian are *natural languages.* The living ones among them—those actively in use—are constantly changing. Each has its own system of sounds and its own grammar and vocabulary too, and each is full of redundancy and variety.

Artificial languages are man-made too, but there are two quite different sorts. The *artificial languages* that are arbitrarily assembled from parts of one or more *natural languages,* such as Basic English, Esperanto, or Interlingua, try to use a simplified grammar and vocabulary and to prevent or hinder change or variation of any sort in the effort to create a new and easily learned lingua franca. None has been successful thus far. Of greater interest to us are the dozens of *artificial languages* such as mathematics, musi-

cal notation, wiring diagrams, and international road signs. *Artificial languages* of this kind are neat and efficient. They usually have only one symbol for each meaning and only one meaning per symbol, and their symbols never carry semantic overtones or social marks of favor or disfavor and almost never acquire new meanings or undergo any other sort of semantic change or functional shift. A group of musicians who know conventional musical notation can all understand that *artificial language,* even if they have no *natural language* in common. $6 + 6 = 12$ is a sentence in an *artificial language* that both Americans and Finns can easily understand.

Natural languages of course are far more troublesome, and their redundancies and other apparent inefficiencies often irritate their users. Instinctively, most of us wish the language we have taken such pains to master would change no more, would not develop new words and meanings at every turn, and would not permit its grammatical devices to atrophy or develop in new ways. Some of the most unreasonable arguments of purists and other language conservatives stem from their unrealistic desire that *natural language* behave as though it were *artificial.* But the fact is that usage always changes, and to deal with it sensibly, you must know and respect the differences between *natural* and *artificial languages.*

nature See CHARACTER.

naught, nought (*n.*) These spellings are in divided usage in the United States, but *naught* is more frequent meaning "nothing," as in *It was all for naught,* and *nought* is more frequent for the relatively infrequent meaning (in the United States, anyway) "zero," as in *It's a big number with a lot of noughts in it.* In British use, *naught* is always "nothing," *nought* always "zero."

nauseous, nauseated, nauseating (*adjs.*) The problem is whether *nauseous* can be restricted to meaning "causing nausea" and *nauseated* to meaning "feeling nausea," which orderly division is what most Edited English tries to enforce. But alas for neatness, both adjectives have both meanings, though a few dictionaries insist that *nauseous,* meaning "feeling nausea," is limited to Colloquial use. Best advice: follow the Edited English practice in speech and writing, and no one will object. In adjunct use *nauseous* and *nauseating,* meaning "causing nausea," are roughly interchangeable in both adjunct and predicate adjective use and get a great deal of Standard figurative use meaning "sickening, disgusting."

naval (*adj.*), **navel** (*adj.*, *n.*) The adjective referring to the navy is spelled *naval*; the *navel* is the small dent in the middle of the abdomen where the umbilical cord was once attached; a *navel orange* has a similar-looking feature on one end. The words are homophones, pronounced *NAI-vuhl*.

nay See NO.

near (*adv.*, *adj.*), **nearly** (*adv.*) *Near* is both adjective, as in *It was a near thing*, and flat adverb, as in *It was near a record; It was a near (-)fatal accident*. *Near* is Standard in uses where it is interchangeable with the adverb *nearly*, as in *I'm not nearly* [*near*] *ready*, as well as in those such as *Come near and see for yourself*, where *nearly* won't work.

nearby (*adv.*, *adj.*), **near by** (*adv.*) Americans use the one-word spelling for both parts of speech: *We knocked at the door of a nearby house. We went nearby to a store*. Some British editors insist that the adjective is one word, the adverb two.

nearly See NEAR.

near miss Logical quibbles insisting that this locution really means "near hit" show no sign of unseating this Standard idiom. It means "a close call" as distinguished from a miss that never truly threatened to hit at all. It's used especially of airplanes that nearly collide and of all sorts of shooting results, and you should be aware that some stylebooks now insist on *near collision* or something similar.

neat (*adj.*, *interj.*) As adjective *neat* is Standard, meaning "trim, clean, orderly," as in *She kept her room and her person neat, with nothing out of place*. But recently *neat* has had a second burst of use as a counterword meaning "good" or "pleasing," as in *What a neat party! We had a neat visit to the zoo*. (This is a use similar to one that developed and then faded away about forty years ago.) In this use *neat* is slang, cliché, and tiresome, as it also is when it functions as an interjection expressing approval. If the word has you by the throat in either of these uses, shake it off.

neaten (*v.*), meaning "to make neat, to set straight," combines often with *up*, as in *Please neaten up your desk*, and is Standard.

nebula (*n.*) has two plurals: *nebulas* and *nebulae*. See FOREIGN PLURALS.

necessary (*adj.*) combines most frequently with the preposition *to*, introducing either an infinitive or a prepositional phrase, as in *It will be necessary to stop* and *His help is necessary to our success*, and also with *in* and *for*, as in *A computer is necessary in* [*for*] *my work*.

necessity (*n.*) can combine with the prepositions *of*, *for*, and *in*, as well as with *to* plus an infinitive, as in *They saw the necessity of* [*for*, *in*] *restoring the company's credit; They saw the necessity to restore it*.

née, nee (*adj.*) appears in American English both with and without the acute accent of its original French. It is the feminine past participle of the French verb meaning "to be born" and so indicates a woman's maiden name (*Mary Smith-Jones, née Smith*). Extended use sometimes has it mean "formerly known as" and applies it to the original names of men and women whose aliases or pen or stage names are more widely known than their original ones (*Leon Trotsky, né Lev Davidovich Bronstein; Dame Margot Fonteyn, née Margaret Hookham*; it has even been stretched to include place names (*Cape of Good Hope, née Cape of Storms*). Conservative editors usually would prefer *originally*, *once*, or even *aka* to these extended uses. Pronunciation of *née* rhymes with either *say* or *see*, although the latter bothers many who know French. See FOREIGN PHRASES.

need (*n.*, *v.*, *aux.*) The noun, when it combines with a preposition, takes *of*, *for*, or *to* plus an infinitive: *There is need of* [*for*] *haste. We have a great need to hurry*. The verb means "to want, desire, or require" as in *She needs help*, and it can combine with the preposition *to* plus an infinitive or a passive infinitive, as in *She needs to see* [*to be seen by*] *a dentist*, or it can be followed by a gerund as direct object, as in *The lamp needs fixing*. The past participle in a somewhat similar construction is dialectal and Nonstandard: *This lamp needs fixed*. The auxiliary is uninflected, means "to be required to," and is followed by an infinitive without a *to*, as in *The only thing he need do is write them*. It is particularly frequent with a negative: *No one need fear reprisal. She need never learn of it. They need not attend*.

needless to say is sometimes challenged for being illogical, inasmuch as it is almost always followed by the words it said need not be spoken. But it's an idiom, Standard, and a cliché.

needs (*adv.*) occurs in the idioms *needs must* and *must needs*, which mean "must of necessity, must necessarily" and are examples of hyperbole, as in *She must needs* [*needs must*] *listen to* *him, even though she'd rather not.* The form of *needs* is unchanging in these uses.

ne'er (*adv.*) is an old-fashioned literary contraction of *never.* The spelling reflects its pronunciation as a one-syllable word rhyming with *care.* See APOSTROPHE (2); E'RE.

NEGATION See DOUBLE NEGATIVE; RAISING.

NEGATIVE See AFFIRMATIVE; DOUBLE NEGATIVE.

NEGATIVE-RAISING See DOUBLE NEGATIVE; RAISING.

neglectful See OBLIVIOUS.

negligent, negligible (*adjs.*) *Negligent* means "neglectful, careless," as in *She was a negligent worker, careless of details,* and "casually relaxed," as in *His conversational style was courteous but negligent.* When it combines with prepositions, *negligent* does so with *about, in,* or *of: He was negligent about [of, in] his dress. Negligible* means "unimportant, so trivial as to be safely disregarded," as in *The risks were negligible.*

negotiate (*v.*), meaning "to cross or travel through, over, or around," is Standard, although at least one commentator thinks it unsuitable for Formal use. But today you may *turn a corner* or *make, round,* or *negotiate a turn* or *corner* if you wish, and at any level.

Negress (*n.*) is archaic and taboo on grounds of racial and sexual objections. Like *Jewess,* it employs the *-ess* feminine ending now out of favor in nearly all uses, and *Negro,* on which it is based, is no longer the preferred name for members of the race. See AFRICAN(-)AMERICAN; RACIST LANGUAGE; SEXIST LANGUAGE.

Negro See AFRICAN(-)AMERICAN.

neither (*pron.*) is the negative counterpart of *either* and is usually considered singular (*Fred and George are coming, but neither has arrived yet*), even though it may also be treated as a plural when a plural modifier falls between it and the verb (*Mary and Fran were invited but neither of them have appeared yet*). In writing, use the singular where you can; Edited English will demand it. But in most Conversational and Informal situations, use whichever number of the verb seems natural. Note too that *neither* can be used of more than two of something: *Neither of my three classmates took the exam* is Standard in many situations, although Edited English would prefer *none* as the pronoun.

neither . . . nor (*coord. conj.*) *Neither* is paired with *nor* as *either* is with *or,* and in those uses as conjunctions they pose usage problems of agreement. Usually they will take a singular verb if both parts of the structure are singular, as in *Neither he nor his friend is ready,* and if the first element is plural but the second element remains singular, the structure may still take a singular verb, as in *Neither my friends nor my father is ready,* although a plural is also possible. But if the second element is plural, the verb will almost always be plural: *Neither my father nor his friends are ready.* Agreement between *neither/nor* and the verb is frequently a matter of notional agreement: hence Standard English in all but its most Formal and Oratorical situations will usually accept either number of the verb.

NEOLOGISM See NONCE WORD.

ne plus ultra (*n.*) is a Latin tag literally meaning "no more beyond" and used today to mean "the highest or best or farthest development or progress possible." There is nothing better than a *ne plus ultra.* Italicize it, and pronounce it either *NAI* or *NEE PLUHS* or *PLOOS UHL-truh* or *OOL-truh.* See FOREIGN PHRASES.

nerve-wracking, nerve-racking (*adj.*) These homophones are variants of the same word meaning "intensely stressful on the nerves," "trying of the patience," as in *That oral exam was a nerve-wracking [nerve-racking] ordeal.* Both spellings are Standard.

-ness, -ty (*suffixes*) are added to adjectives to bring about their functional shift to nouns: *sad* becomes *sadness; tender* becomes *tenderness; sure* becomes *surety; certain* becomes *certainty.*

NEUTER GENDER See GENDER (2).

never (*adv.*) has two meanings, both of them Standard: "not ever, at no time," as in *She has never taken French*; and "not under any condition, not in any degree," as in *They'll never be able to catch us now.*

new innovation See FREE GIFT; TAUTOLOGY.

new record See RECORD.

news (*n.*) is plural in form but is treated grammatically as a singular: *This news is bad.*

Newspeak (*n.*), Standard as either proper or common noun, was coined by George Orwell in his novel *1984*; it means "deceptive or lying language used by government to manipulate its citizens" and hence by extension "deliberately ambiguous, misleading language used by the devious to deceive the unwary into believing that the bad is really good." See DOUBLESPEAK; EUPHEMISM; EUPHEMISMS; WEASEL WORDS.

NEW YORK CITY DIALECT See METRO-
POLITAN NEW YORK CITY REGIONAL DIALECT.

next See FIRST TWO.

nice (*adj.*) has frequently been criticized as vague
and overused in its sense of "approved, mildly
pleasing, pretty good," as in *We had a nice
time* or *She was nice to the children*, but although it may be neither powerful nor fresh, it
is a useful Standard word. When moderate enthusiasm is exactly what you wish to express,
nice expresses it. Although this "pleasing,
agreeable" sense is the most frequently encountered, *nice* also has other very important senses,
among them: "coy, shy," as in *She's too nice
to object*; "finicky," as in *They're too nice to
get their hands dirty*; "exacting or punctilious,"
as in *a nice distinction* and *a nice knowledge of
horses*; "well-bred, respectable," as in *He's a
very nice little boy*; and the sarcastic "bad, inappropriate," as in *A nice mess you've made
of it*.

nice and (*intensifier*) is Standard Conversational
language, meaning *very* or *quite* or *thoroughly*,
as in *She's nice and warm in her new coat.*
Compare GOOD AND.

nicely (*adv., adj.*) As adverb *nicely* is Standard,
meaning "well, satisfactorily, acceptably, appropriately": *She was nicely dressed. He thanked
his grandmother nicely.* As adjective in predicate adjective position, *nicely* is at best dialectal: *She looks nicely.* Use *nice* instead. But compare FEEL BAD.

nicety, niceness (*nn.*) These nouns are not synonyms. *Niceness* is simply the quality of being
nice, especially in *nice*'s adjectival sense of
"satisfactory, mildly approved," as in *It was
her decency, her downright niceness that won
them over.* (But it could also reflect one or more
of *nice*'s other senses.) *Nicety*, however, means
"subtlety, detail, inner workings," as in *This
book deals with the niceties of English usage.*

nickel, nickle (*nn.*) *Nickel* is the preferred Standard spelling, *nickle* a fairly rare variant to which
many people firmly object. Use *nickel*, especially in Edited English, for both the metal and
the coin.

nickname See EKE.

nigger (*n.*) is dialectal slang, originally a spoken variant, in Southern and South Midland
dialects in particular, of *negro*, but today taboo
in Standard and most Common and Vulgar English as well. See AFRICAN(-)AMERICAN; RAC-
IST LANGUAGE.

nigh (*adv., adj.*), although it has a literary past,
is mainly a dialectal word today, as in *I'm nigh
starved; Don't go nigh him; The nigh horse is
lame.* It means "nearly, almost" or "near,"
and it is generally archaic in Standard English
except in the clichés *well-nigh* and *nigh on[to]*,
as in *We were well-nigh worn out; It was nigh
on [onto, unto] midnight.*

nights See ADVERBIAL GENITIVE.

-nik (*suffix*) is of either Yiddish or Russian origin and is an agentive ending similar to English
-er, meaning "one who does or is linked to the
action, object, or state described in the word to
which it is affixed": *beatnik, peacenik*, and
computernik are typical of these slang coinages,
and Americans continue to use *-nik* to make
nonce words.

nimbus (*n.*) has two plurals: *nimbi* and *nim-
buses*. See FOREIGN PLURALS.

nite (*n.*) is a Nonstandard but popular variant
spelling of *night*, apparently used for humor,
for attention-getting, for eye dialect in certain
kinds of literature, and possibly for brevity in
Informal writing, as in *nite light* [or *lite*] and
nite club. Today, it's neither very fresh nor very
funny.

nitty-gritty (*adj., n.*) is slang, meaning "the essential, practical details," as in *He got down to
the nitty-gritty right away; She turned then to
nitty-gritty matters of wages and hours.* See
RHYMING COMPOUNDS.

-nn- See CONSONANTS (2).

no (*adv., adj., n., interj.*) Wherever it is used, *no*
means "negative, negation." As an adverb it
can stand alone or as an introductory part of a
response utterance (*No; No, I'm not going*), or
it can modify an adjective: *We found no better
route.* As an adjective it can modify nouns: *We
have no time.* As an interjection it can loudly
deny something or express surprise, horror, or
disbelief: *No! You don't say!* And as a noun, as
in *His no was very firm*, it frequently appears in
the plural, especially as the opposite of *aye* or
*yes: The ayes were very numerous, but it was
the nos that carried the day.* (*Nay[s]* is the more
formal and literary noun, especially for pairing
with *aye[s]* or *yea[s]*.)

No is frequently one element in double negative constructions (*I don't get no respect*), which
are of course Nonstandard. In Standard uses it
can be followed by *nor*, as in *There were no
towels nor soap nor hot water*, where *neither*
would more likely be encountered; *or* also occurs in such uses. It is also Standard when used
in such series constructions as *There were no*

towels, no soap, no hot water. And *no* is Standard when used in place of *not* in the *whether or not* construction and in others similar to it: *Injured* [*injury*] *or no, she insisted on driving home.*

nobody, no one (*prons.*) These two indefinite pronouns demand singular verbs, but because of notional agreement subsequent pronouns that refer to them may be plural in Standard English, as in *Almost nobody* [*no one*] *comes to these meetings, but they always want to see the minutes.* Note, however, that most Formal Edited English will usually try to maintain the strict singular in subsequent pronouns unless clarity would be damaged thereby.

nod (the head) See SHAKE THE HEAD.

no doubt See DOUBTLESS.

no-host (*adj.*) is a jargon phrase from the world of banquets and receptions, where the specification *No-host bar* means that guests will pay for their own drinks. The phrase is not always hyphenated. Limit its use to audiences who know the jargon. *Cash bar* is jargon too, but clearer.

nohow (*adv.*) is Nonstandard, but it is used jocularly at Casual and some other Conversational levels to mean "in no way," frequently in a jocular imitation of Vulgar Speech, complete with double negative: *We ain't goin' there nohow!* See also NO WAY.

noisome, noisy (*adjs.*) These two are wholly unrelated, and mistakenly to use *noisome* in place of *noisy* is a serious blunder. *Noisome* means "unwholesome, foul-smelling," as in *The dungeon was a damp, noisome place; noisy* means "making or filled with noise," as in *She was just one more noisy child in a noisy room.*

no less than See LESS.

nom de plume (*n.*) is the French term translated by the English *pen name,* "a writer's pseudonym." Its plural is spelled *noms de plume,* and both *nom* and *noms* are pronounced *NON,* with the second *n* sound nasalized. *Pen name* is better for English use. See AKA; FOREIGN PHRASES; PSEUDONYM.

NOMINAL 1, the name of a part of speech in some grammars, is a noun, a substantive, or another structure that does the work of a noun: *I miss **my dearest friends and neighbors in that town;** **Swimming** is my hobby; **To run away** seemed sensible; **That we were surrounded** was clear.*

nominal 2 (*adj.*), in Standard phrases such as *a nominal payment* or *nominal support,* means "token," "in name only."

NOMINATIVE CASE is the grammatical case that in English dictates the forms of pronouns being used as subjects or as predicate nominatives: *We hope to be there* (*we* is subject). *It is we who will suffer* (*we* is predicate nominative, *who* is subject of an included clause modifier). *I, you, he, she, it, we, you, they,* and *who* are the *nominative case* pronouns, although *you* and *it* are not distinguished from the accusative case forms. Traditional grammars frequently speak of nouns that act as subjects or predicate nominatives as being in the *nominative case,* although they show no formal inflections or other signs of it.

non- See IN-.

NONCE WORD, NEOLOGISM A *nonce word* is one coined "for the nonce"—made up for one occasion and not likely to be encountered again. When Lewis Carroll coined it, *frabjous* was a *nonce word. Neologisms* are much the same thing, brand-new words or brand-new meanings for existing words, coined for a specific purpose. Analogy, especially with familiar words or parts of speech, often guides the coiner, and occasionally these words will enter the Standard vocabulary.

noncombustible See FLAMMABLE.

none (*pron.*) is and long has been either singular or plural. *None of this is mine* and *None of these are mine* are both Standard; notional agreement (in these examples, the number of the object of the preposition) governs.

nonetheless (*adv.*) is always spelled as one word.

none too See NOT TOO.

NONFINITE VERBS See FINITE AND NONFINITE VERBS.

nonflammable See FLAMMABLE.

nonhuman See INHUMAN.

nonreligious See IRRELIGIOUS.

NONRESTRICTIVE APPOSITIVES See APPOSITIVE.

NONRESTRICTIVE CLAUSES See RESTRICTIVE AND NONRESTRICTIVE CLAUSES.

NONRESTRICTIVE MODIFIERS See RESTRICTIVE AND NONRESTRICTIVE MODIFIERS.

NONSENSE WORD is the name some grammarians give to meaningless words they invent in order to demonstrate grammatical principles that operate even when there is no semantic indication of the word's possible function. For example, the plural of the noun and *nonsense word flern* (whatever a *flern* might be) is *flerns,* thus illustrating one aspect of the regular pattern for forming English plurals.

nonsensical See MEANINGLESS.

non sequitur, pronounced *nahn SEK-wi-tuhr,* is a Latin phrase meaning literally "it does not follow." It labels a statement as illogical, nonsensical, not following logically from what has preceded. See FOREIGN PHRASES.

nonsocial See ANTISOCIAL.

NONSTANDARD See STANDARD; SUBSTANDARD.

non-U See U.

no one See NOBODY.

noplace See ANYPLACE.

no problem is a cliché meaning every shade of agreement from "What you propose will be easy, and I'll be delighted to do it," to simple acquiescence. Although limited to the Conversational levels, its mindless overuse has made it grate on the nerves of many Standard speakers, and for some it has become a hallmark of the unthinking, if not of the Vulgar, particularly when used in response to *Thank you* instead of *You're welcome.*

nor (*coord. conj.*) Both *nor* and *or* are Standard after an initial *no* or *not,* although *or* is more frequent today: *No running nor [or] shouting is permitted in the corridors. Not wheedling nor [or] threatening could move her.* Typically *nor* is Standard after *neither,* particularly in Oratorical contexts, Edited English, and other Formal uses, as in *Neither her father nor her mother attended her recital.* But *or* can also occur there. *Nor* is also Standard in other negative statements, as in *I didn't want dessert, nor did I want coffee. Nor* meaning *than* is Nonstandard and regional at best, and many would label it Substandard instead: *She's no brighter nor I am.*

normalcy, normality (*nn.*) These synonyms are both in Standard use today, *normalcy* having at least partly lost whatever notoriety it acquired from its associations with President Warren G. Harding. Both mean "the state of being normal." See NOTORIOUS.

north, North, northerly, northern, Northern See EAST.

NORTHERN REGIONAL DIALECT is one of the major regional dialects in the United States. It is spoken in New England and New York State, in parts of New Jersey and Pennsylvania, and in most of the Great Lakes states north of a line beginning in Cleveland and stretching west

through Chicago and beyond. Coastal New England, Metropolitan New York City, Lower Hudson Valley, and several others are subdialects of *Northern.*

NORTHERN URBAN AMERICAN BLACK ENGLISH See BLACK ENGLISH.

NORTH MIDLAND REGIONAL DIALECT is spoken in a widening wedge from southern New Jersey, Delaware, and northern Maryland through southern Pennsylvania and northern West Virginia, and across the southern two-thirds of Ohio, most of Indiana and Illinois, and into much of Iowa, Missouri, Nebraska, and Kansas, plus the panhandle of Oklahoma and a bit of eastern Colorado. *New, due,* and the first syllable of *Tuesday* rhyme with *coo* rather than with *few* as they do in South Midland (which see), and like South Midland, North Midland dialect retains its *r*'s after vowels and has the voiceless *th* sound in *with* rather than the voiced *th̸*.

northward, northwards See EASTWARD.

no sooner usually is followed by *than,* as in *No sooner had I hung up than the phone rang again,* but *when* can also occur, perhaps mainly in Conversational use, as in *No sooner had we decided to compromise when suddenly the argument broke out again. Than* is best for Edited English.

nostalgia (*n.*) retains both its older meaning of "homesickness" and its newer and more generalized senses of "yearning for a past time or place, for the recovery of the world of one's youth." All are Standard.

nosy, nosey (*adj.*) may be spelled either way, although *nosy* is the more usual.

not about to, as in *She's not about to resign,* can mean simply "does not intend to" but in recent years has become a Standard idiom meaning "is determined not to." The locution is thought to be Southern or South Midland in origin, and it is still usually encountered at Conversational levels and in the writing that imitates them, although today's Edited English sometimes has it too.

not all, all . . . not Placement of *not* in written versions of a sentence can cause ambiguity that speech might avoid with the help of intonation. Compare *All players are not here* and *Not all players are here.* The first version could mean that some or all of the players are absent; the second version clearly means that some are present and some are not.

not all that See ALL THAT.

notary public (*n.*) has two Standard plurals: *notaries public* is usual in Edited English, but *notary publics* also occurs.

not as, not so See AS . . . AS.

not . . . but The use of *but* after a negative, as in *We weren't there but a few minutes,* is sometimes challenged as old-fashioned, but it seems to be Standard, if limited mainly to Conversational use. For more on *but* meaning "only," see BUT.

not hardly See HARD.

nother occurs in slang idioms such as *a whole nother thing* and *a whole nother story,* hyperbolic renderings of *another thing* and *another story,* wherein *whole* is jocularly inserted into *another* immediately after the *a,* which is treated like the article it would normally be before a consonant such as *n.* Such locutions are Casual at best.

nothing loath See LOATH.

notion (*n.*) means "a belief, concept, or opinion," as in *Their notion is that sincerity will carry the day;* "a vague thought or idea," as in *I had a notion to run away;* and—especially in the plural—"useful small items employed especially in sewing," as in *I was to buy needles, buttons, snaps, and some other notions.* All are Standard.

NOTIONAL AGREEMENT (NOTIONAL CONCORD) is the agreement or concord of verbs with their subjects and of pronouns with their antecedent nouns on the basis of meaning rather than form. If you think of *committee* as one entity, then *The committee has its agenda;* if you think of *committee* as representing several people, then *The committee have their agenda.* *Notional agreement* gives us sentences like these from British English: *The government are eager to compromise. Manchester United are ahead, three to nil.* Americans would use *is* in both sentences, having different notions of the entities *government* and *athletic team.* And these from American English also illustrate: *My admiration and love for her is without limit. Everybody has their own opinion of the proposal.* All these are usage problems because although no one is confused about what they mean, strict grammatical agreement of plurals with plural forms and singulars with singular forms doesn't occur. Edited English tries usually to avoid these last structures, and many a Standard-using reader will find fault with them whenever they notice them. If you saw that one (*reader . . . they*), then you are probably quite able to police your own writing for agreement problems; if you missed it, you must decide whether your readers will accept a particular *notional agreement* without objection or whether they will insist absolutely on full grammatical concord.

NOTIONAL FUTURE See FUTURE TENSE.

NOTIONAL PASSIVE is a name sometimes applied to structures wherein a verb in active voice works semantically to achieve a passive effect, as in *This shirt washes well,* which is notionally the same as the passive *This shirt can be washed well.*

NOTIONAL SUBJECT See LET.

not only . . . but also (*coord. conj.*) These function as correlatives, as in *They were not only willing that he go but also eager that he do so.* The *also* is frequently omitted, especially in shorter structures. Some commentators insist on complete parallelism in such locutions, but in fact the omission of the *also* is not only frequent but Standard. See ONLY.

notorious, infamous (*adjs.*), **infamy, notoriety** (*nn.*) *Notorious* and *infamous* both mean "well and unfavorably known," as in *She's the notorious [infamous] muckraking biographer.* They both are always pejorative. *Infamy,* the state of being infamous and of bad reputation, is also pejorative, but the noun *notoriety* is currently in some divided usage, with much journalese and other Informal use meaning merely "a state of being widely known, fame," as in *His splendid record as a pitcher has at last earned him notoriety and a chance for an All-Star berth.* (British English uses the plural to mean "prominent or well-known people, celebrities.") Be aware, though, that the noun retains its pejorative associations in most Edited English and other Formal use; context should make clear whether the pejorative is intended or not.

not religious See IRRELIGIOUS.

not so, not as See AS . . . AS.

not that big of a deal See OF A.

not too, as in *She's not too happy these days,* is an idiom used for understatement, irony, or variety. *I'm not too eager for the summer to end* is an understated but Standard way of saying *I would rather that summer wouldn't end just yet. I'm not too sorry to see her go* suggests ironically that *I'm really glad to see her go.* See also LITOTES.

not to worry was originally a British English idiom, meaning "don't worry," "never fear," but it's now beginning to appear in Conversational and Informal American use.

not un- See DOUBLE NEGATIVE; LITOTES.

nought See NAUGHT.

NOUN ADJUNCT A noun positioned to modify another noun is called a *noun adjunct.* Noun adjuncts form the first elements of hundreds of compound nouns in American English (*bird house, ball field, name brand,* and *fieldhouse*); others are not elements in actual compounds but simply modify another noun, as *college* does in *college dictionary* and *school* in *school principal.*

NOUN MODIFIER See NOUN ADJUNCT.

NOUN PHRASES are multiword structures that are not clauses and that are used as nouns: *Riding my exercise bike every evening is a bore.* A noun plus its modifiers is also called a *noun phrase: the tallest building in the city,* for example, is a *noun phrase* in which *building* is the noun headword.

NOUNS are parts of speech usually defined on the basis of meaning: the traditional definition is "a *noun* is the name of a person, place, or thing." Some dictionaries call them *substantives,* and some grammars include *nouns* and pronouns and other structures that behave like *nouns* in an overarching category called *nominals* (which see). *Nouns* and nominals function primarily as subjects, objects, or complements of various kinds.

NOUNS AS ADJECTIVES See ATTRIBUTIVE ADJECTIVES; FUNCTIONAL SHIFT; NOUN ADJUNCT.

NOUNS AS VERBS, VERBIFIED NOUNS These are synonymous names for nouns that have undergone functional shift to serve as verbs, as in *to host a meeting, to chair the committee,* and *to gift your hostess.* There is nothing wrong with this much-used process of functional shift, but occasionally a specific example will meet strong opposition. It is nearly impossible to predict which will pass and which will not, but if enough people persist in their objections, such uses can undergo long or even permanent proscription from Standard use.

NOUNS ENDING IN -F, -FE: SPELLING AND PRONUNCIATION OF PLURALS AND FUNCTIONAL SHIFTS TO VERBS Some of these words add *-s* to make the plural; far more replace the *-f* or *-fe* with *-ves* for the plural. All reflexive pronouns add *-ves: yourself* becomes *yourselves; myself* becomes *ourselves; himself, herself, and itself* become *themselves.*

Still other words do both, sometimes with a semantic distinction between the plurals. The spellings reflect the pronunciations of these consonants, an *f* sound for the voiceless one in, for example, *wife* (*WEIF*), a *v* sound for the voiced one in *wives* (*WEIVZ*).

Beef has two plurals, *beeves* and *beefs,* with a semantic distinction: *beefs* is slang for complaints or objections.

Calf (the animal) has two plurals, *calves* and *calfs.* The part of the leg has one plural, *calves.* The verb meaning "to give birth to a calf" is *calve,* and the participial adjective meaning "provided with calves (on the legs)" is *calved.*

Dwarf has two plurals, although *dwarfs* is much more common than *dwarves.* The verb in its past tense is always *dwarfed.*

Elf is usually *elves* in the plural, but both *elfish* and *elvish* are Standard spellings.

Handkerchief has two plural spellings, *handkerchiefs* and the less-common *handkerchieves.* The first spelling is sometimes pronounced with the *v* sound of the second.

Hoof has two plural spellings, *hoofs* and *hooves,* and the pronunciations of singular, plurals, and genitives reflect the two vowels: *HOOF* and *HUF.* The slang verb's past tense is *hoofed,* as is the adjective.

Knife has one plural, *knives,* but the past tense of the verb is *knifed,* and the third person singular present tense is *knifes.*

Leaf has a plural, *leaves,* with a participial adjective, *leaved.* But the past tense of *leaf* (turning the pages of a book) is *leafed;* the past tense of *leaf* (growing *leaves*) may be either *leafed* or *leaved.*

Life has a plural, *lives,* with the same vowel. The participial adjective (as in *long-lived*) has a *v* in place of the *f,* but the second element of the combination may have either a long vowel (rhyming with *drive*) or a short vowel (rhyming with *give*). The plural of *still life* is *still lifes.*

Loaf has the plural *loaves,* but the verb *loaf* has the past tense *loafed.*

Scarf's plural is *scarves* for the neckwear but *scarfs* for the carpenter's joints. The past participle of the verb meaning "provided with a scarf to wear" and the past tense of the carpenter's verb are both *scarfed.*

Sheaf has the plural *sheaves.* The verb is either *sheaf* or *sheave,* with past tense and participle both *sheaved.*

Shelf's plural is *shelves,* and the verb is *shelve, shelved, shelved.*

Staff's plural is *staffs*, except for the music *staves* and barrel *staves*, both pronounced to rhyme with *braves*. (The music *staff* also can have *staffs* as a plural.) The verb *staff* has a past tense and past participle *staffed*.

Turf has two plurals, *turfs* and *turves*; the verb is *turf, turfed, turfed*.

Wolf has one plural, *wolves*. The genitives are *wolf's* and *wolves'*. The verb is *wolf, wolfed, wolfed*.

NOUNS JOINED BY *AND, OR* See AGREEMENT OF COMPOUND SUBJECTS WITH THEIR VERBS AND SUBSEQUENT PRONOUNS.

nouveau riche (*n.*) is a French idiom meaning "someone newly wealthy" and pronounced *NOO-VO REESH*. The plural is spelled *nouveaux riches* and pronounced like the singular. The term is usually pejorative, suggesting that the newly rich don't know how to wear their wealth easily or unostentatiously. See FOREIGN PHRASES.

now (*adj.*) was a vogue word in the 1960s and 1970s, especially in phrases like *the now generation, the now film*, and the like, but its meaning of "contemporary" and "the very latest" is today quite dated.

no way (*n., interj.*) The adjective-noun phrase is Standard followed by *to* plus infinitive or *of* plus gerund, as in *He had no way to reach* [*of reaching*] *them* and *There is no way to avoid* [*of avoiding*] *trouble*. It is also Standard when followed by the preposition *for*, as in *That is no way for a parent to act*. And frequently it is preceded by *there is* and followed by a *that* clause, with or without the *that*: *There's no way* [*that*] *she'll marry him!* As interjection, *no way* is an idiom, meaning an emphatic negative, "under no circumstances, never," as in *Will I retire? No way! No way am I going to vote for her*. The interjection and the last use of the phrase are appropriate only in Casual, Impromptu, or Informal contexts, and the phrase is often considered slang regardless of use.

nowhere near is a Standard adverbial meaning "not nearly" or something even a bit stronger: *She's nowhere near being ready to leave;* it is frequently *She's nowhere near ready*. The emphatic or hyperbolic quality of *nowhere near* should usually be restricted to Conversational and Semiformal or Informal use. *Nowhere nearly* might serve better as intensifier at higher levels.

nowheres (*adv.*), like *anywheres* (see ANYWHERE) and *somewheres* (see SOMEWHERE), is considered Substandard by most users of Stan-

dard English, although some commentators believe that it is essentially a regional rather than a social dialectal matter and so Nonstandard instead.

nth (*adj.*) *N* is the mathematical symbol for an unspecified number, so *nth* means "some unspecified number" and by extension "the highest, the utmost." It is Standard in either sense but occurs most often in the cliché *to the nth degree* meaning "to the greatest possible degree, to the utmost degree," as in *His musicians were rehearsed to the nth degree of polish*. (Note that although the mathematical symbol is italicized, the adjective is not.)

nubile (*adj.*) is used almost exclusively of young women. It began by meaning "of marriageable age or condition" but now almost always means "sexually attractive." To convey the older sense today requires considerable assistance from context.

nuclear (*adj.*) Say it *N(Y)OO-klee-uhr*. The pronunciation *NOO-kyuh-luhr* is a shibboleth for many Standard users. Some commentators explain the much-criticized pronunciation by President Eisenhower and other prominent persons as resulting from a folk etymology, an analogy with words like *particular, vernacular, spectacular, vehicular*, and the like, because the language affords almost no other words that end in *-klee-uhr*. However it comes about, inadvertent use of that minority pronunciation is likely to make you the butt of amused or impatient comment.

nucleus (*n.*) has two Standard plurals: *nuclei* and *nucleuses*. Never pronounce it *NOO-kyuh-luhs*. See FOREIGN PLURALS.

nude See NAKED.

NUMBER 1 is a grammatical concept important in English usage because Standard English demands agreement or concord in number between pronouns and their antecedents and between nouns serving as subjects and the verbs in their predicates. *Singular number* involves one person, thing, or concept, and *plural number* involves two or more. Nouns and pronouns display number through their inflections and forms: *cat, satisfaction, I*, and *she* are singular; *cats, satisfactions, we*, and *they* are plural (see PERSONAL PRONOUNS; PLURALS OF NOUNS). Regular verbs have only one *number*-distinctive form, that for the third person singular present tense (*John swims*). (*Be* and *have* are a bit more complicated.) Inadvertent faulty agreement between subject and verb is usually a shibboleth, betraying a user of Vulgar English. But compare NOTIONAL AGREEMENT.

number 2 (*n.*) can be construed as either singular or plural, depending on the sense (when it means "several or some," it takes a plural verb; when it comments on the size of something, it takes a singular) and on whether the determiner is *a* or *the* (the usual pattern is *A number of people are going; The number of registered voters is declining*). See also AMOUNT.

Number meaning "a musical selection," as in *They played one of my favorite numbers,* meaning "characteristic pattern of behavior or motive," as in *I've got his number,* and meaning "a special item or person," as in *This is our best-selling number* or *She's a hot number this season,* is slang. In the plural, *the numbers* refers to an illegal lottery and is slang. Finally, avoid using the phrase *in number* with a cardinal number, as in *We were three in number*; except in unusual need for emphasis, the cardinal number itself is enough.

NUMBER IN NOUNS ENDING IN -*ICS* See -ICS.

numbers Should you write them in words or in numerical symbols? Your publisher's stylebook will specify the policy. In your other writing simply be consistent. One sensible general scheme is to use written words for numbers up to and including *ten* and figures for the rest, except when beginning a sentence, where the spelled version is usually more easily read. Use commas to set off the hundreds in large numbers (*5,300,000*), and never mix the spelled and symbol versions except in a contract or other

legal document where precision is paramount (*. . . three [3] feet from the boundary*).

numbers, cardinal and ordinal See ORDINAL NUMBER.

NUMBERS, THE VERBAL REPRESENTATION OF See ZERO.

numerals, Arabic See ARABIC NUMERALS.

numerals, Roman See ROMAN NUMERALS.

numerator See DENOMINATOR.

numerous (*adj., pron.*) *Numerous* is most frequently an adjective: *We found numerous errors in the text. Numerous are the pitfalls for the unwary.* It occurs only rarely as a pronoun, and most contexts will prefer *numbers* or *many* in constructions followed by a prepositional phrase with *of: Numerous* [better*: many* or *most*] *of the victims of the storm are still without shelter. Numerous* in this use is Nonstandard at best. See also VARIOUS.

nuptial (*adj.*), **nuptials** (*n. pl.*) Pronounce each of these with only two syllables, *NUP-shuhl(z)* or *NUP-chuhl(z)*; a three-syllable pronunciation is Nonstandard at best. The adjective describes something to do with marriage, as in *The nuptial arrangements required much planning.* Note that the noun, meaning "a marriage, a wedding," is used normally in the plural: *Their nuptials will be celebrated in June.*

nurse (*n.*) is now inclusive: its referent is either male or female, and either masculine or feminine pronouns will fit. *Male nurse* is now almost hopelessly ambiguous: it could be a man serving as a *nurse* or a *nurse* of either sex caring for male patients.

O

O, oh (*interjs.*) *O* is almost always a symbol: the letter itself, a zero, the chemical symbol for oxygen, and the like. When it is an *interjection* it is formal and highly rhetorical or poetic: *Hear me, O Lord!* By itself it is almost never followed by an exclamation point or a comma. *Oh* is the more commonly used interjection, an exclamation expressing surprise, agreement, distress, or some other response, as well as a way of getting attention in direct address: *Oh, John, will you come here, please?*

-o See PLURALS OF NOUNS ENDING IN -O.

oasis (*n.*) The plural is oases, pronounced *o-WAI-seez.* See FOREIGN PLURALS.

oater See HORSE OPERA.

oath (*n.*) The plural is pronounced either *OTHZ* or *OTHS*.

obedient (*adj.*), when combined with a preposition, takes *to: She will be obedient to her leaders.*

obeisance, obesity (*nn.*) *Obeisance* means "a bow or curtsy as a gesture of respect or homage," as in *She made a small obeisance before leaving her mistress's presence. Obesity* means "the state of being too fat," as in *His obesity prevented his sitting on ordinary folding chairs.*

OBJECT See DIRECT OBJECT; INDIRECT OBJECT; OBJECT COMPLEMENT; OBJECT OF A PREPOSITION.

object (*v.*), when combined with a preposition, takes *to,* which may introduce a prepositional phrase whose object may be a noun, a pronoun, or a gerund: *She objects to the dog* [*to it, to sitting still*].

OBJECT COMPLEMENT (sometimes called an objective complement) has two meanings in grammar. In general an *object complement* is a word or other construction that completes the complement, the end of the predicate part of the sentence: *She slapped him in the face* has a direct object, *him,* and an *object complement,* the prepositional phrase *in the face.*

The narrower sense of the term, more frequently used by grammarians than the general sense, describes the word *treasurer* in *The club elected me treasurer.* It is a noun or other nominal construction following a direct object and with the same referent as that direct object: in the sample sentence, both *me* and *treasurer* refer to the same person.

OBJECTIVE AND SUBJECTIVE PRONOUNS See SUBJECTIVE AND OBJECTIVE PRONOUNS.

OBJECTIVE CASE See ACCUSATIVE CASE.

OBJECTIVE GENITIVE Most of us readily recall being taught that the genitive is an older name for the possessive: *Mary's mother, my sweater, Uncle Fred's car.* Further distinctions in the purpose of the genitive attempt to suggest relationships other than that of simple possession: *objective genitive* (sometimes *object genitive*) is one of these, wherein the genitive modifies a noun from which we can infer an action worked on the genitive modifier: *Mary's engagement, your father's illness, his tormentors.* See also DESCRIPTIVE GENITIVE; GENITIVE OF ORIGIN; GENITIVE OF PURPOSE; GROUP GENITIVE; SUBJECTIVE GENITIVE.

objectives See GOALS AND OBJECTIVES.

OBJECT OF A PREPOSITION A preposition is the first word of a phrasal structure of modification very common in English; the phrase always ends with a noun, pronoun, or other nominal, which we call the *object of the preposition.* In the examples *in my pocket, through the trees, after me,* and *by tripping over the hurdle,* the words *pocket, trees, me,* and *tripping over the hurdle* are the *objects of the prepositions in, through, after,* and *by,* and *hurdle* is the *object of the preposition over* in the prepositional phrase *over the hurdle.* See PREPOSITION (2).

objet d'art, art object, object of art *Objet d'art* is a borrowed French phrase, pronounced *awb-ZHAI DAHR,* and literally meaning "object of art" or "art object"—that is, sculpture, painting, ceramics, metalwork, or the like made particularly for its beauty and artistic quality rather than for its utility. Put it all in English (*art object*) or all in French (*objet d'art*), not in the misspelled mixture that sometimes crops up, *object d'art.* See FOREIGN PHRASES.

obligated, obliged (*adjs.*), **obligate, oblige** (*vv.*) The two participial adjectives are synonyms in the sense of "being constrained or legally or morally required to do or pay something," as in *I was obligated* [*obliged*] *to repay her for the funds she had advanced me.* Both verbs can be transitive: *By loaning them the money she obligated* [*obliged*] *them to make a series of repayments. Oblige* can also be intransitive, meaning "to acquiesce": *They asked for more time, and I obliged and gave them some. Oblige* also has other senses, moral and ethical but not legal in their implications, one for the adjective, meaning "forced" (*I was obliged to leave the meeting before that item came up*), and another for the verb, meaning "yield to request or need, and so earn gratitude" (*He obliged us by relinquishing his time to the others*).

obliqueness, obliquity (*nn.*) *Obliqueness* and *obliquity* are synonymous in their literal senses, "the quality of being on a slant, at an angle," but figuratively, although both do mean "a state lacking clarity or explicitness," even "a condition of evasiveness," *obliquity* seems to be much more frequent, whereas *obliqueness* seems to occur more frequently with reference to literal angularity. Both are Standard.

oblivious, forgetful, neglectful, unaware (*adjs.*) All can combine with the preposition *of* in structures indicating what is being either not noticed or not dealt with; only *oblivious* can also combine with *to. She was oblivious of* [*to*] *the noise* can mean either "that she was *unaware of* it" or that "she was *forgetful of* it." *Neglectful of* adds still another sense: if she was *neglectful of* the noise, she knew it was there but did nothing either to correct it or accommodate to it. *Oblivious of* and *to* both need context to make clear which sense is intended; the others are clear on their own. See also IGNORING.

obnoxious (*adj.*) has two meanings, but the older one, "exposed to something bad or dangerous," as in *Sitting out in the damp air was obnoxious to her fragile health,* is infrequent when compared with the newer meaning, "very objectionable, highly offensive or unpleasant," as in *His behavior to our guests was utterly obnoxious.* Both senses are Standard.

OBSCENE 1 In English usage, the label *obscene* describes a basis for rejection of a word, meaning, or locution from Standard English. Certain four-letter words, for example, are often labeled both Vulgar and *obscene,* the first suggesting Substandard, the second the reason for that label. See VULGAR.

obscene 2 (*adj.*), **obscenity** (*n.*) *Obscene* means "offensive to feelings and current standards of decency," with the implication that anything so designated appeals (or indeed may have been intended to appeal) to base, depraved tastes. The word is sometimes given definitions under law, often being used as a basis for proscribing certain public behavior, publications, displays, or entertainments. An *obscenity* is any word, gesture, or action displaying such qualities.

observance, observation (*nn.*) *Observance* means "keeping or recognizing a rite, custom, or holiday," as in *Official observance of Washington's birthday seldom falls on the actual anniversary of his birth,* and *observation* means simply "the act of watching or putting under surveillance or scrutiny," as in *He was under observation in the hospital.* The words can also be synonymous in each sense and are Standard either way. *Observation*'s meaning "a pointing out or statement of something," however, is not shared by *observance: My observation* [not *observance*] *that I was hungry went unheeded.* Note that the verb from which each of these words comes can be used in either sense: *They don't observe Christmas. We observed these birds' behavior for some weeks.*

observant (*adj.*), when it combines with a preposition, uses *of: She is particularly observant of her friends' manners.*

observation See OBSERVANCE.

obsessed (*adj.*), when it combines with a preposition, usually does so with *with* or *by,* as in *She was obsessed with* [*by*] *her determination to be first.*

OBSOLETE 1, OBSOLESCENT These usage labels appear in many dictionaries and in this book. A word or meaning labeled *obsolete* is no longer in use and is of historical interest only; a word or meaning labeled *obsolescent* is on the way to being *obsolete.* Compare ARCHAIC.

obsolete 2 (*v., adj.*), **obsolescent** (*adj.*) The adjective *obsolete* means "no longer in use, out of fashion, discarded," as in *No one wears spats any more; they're obsolete.* The adjective *obsolescent* means "in the process of becoming obsolete, nearly obsolete," as in *Twelve-cylinder engines for passenger cars are obsolescent; you almost never hear of one these days.* The verb *obsolete* means "to make something obsolete, by replacing it with something newer or better," as in *His new mousetrap obsoletes all others.* The verb is now Standard, although some conservatives still prefer a phrasal substitute such as *makes* or *renders obsolete.* See also the preceding entry.

obtain (*v.*), as a transitive verb, means "to get, especially by dint of hard work or planning," as in *We finally managed to obtain a copy of her novel.* Intransitive *obtain* means "to prevail, to be in effect," as in *A tomblike silence always obtains in the reading room.* This use is usually considered fairly Formal.

obtrude (*v.*) means "to thrust forward," "to insert or impose one's views," or "to interfere or intrude," and it can combine with any of several prepositions: *Thoughts of her obtruded frequently in* [*into, on, upon, onto*] *his daily activities.*

obtuse, abstruse (*adjs.*) *Obtuse* in its literal sense means "blunt or dull," and an *obtuse* angle is one of more than 90 degrees but less than 180 degrees. The figurative sense of *obtuse* (which is almost always applied to people and their behavior) is "dull, imperceptive, unintelligent, unthinking": *How can he be so obtuse as not to understand us? Abstruse* means "difficult to grasp or comprehend, needlessly complex, impossible to understand" and is applied typically to arguments, propositions, and the like: *Her proposals were so abstruse as to be meaningless to us.* Using *obtuse* as a rough synonym of *abstruse* is Nonstandard, and you should avoid it.

obverse, converse, inverse, reverse (*adjs., nn.*) The *-verse* part of these words means "to turn," and the prefixes suggest the direction or nature of the turn involved. *Obverse* means "turned toward you" and hence "the front," as in *The obverse side of the coin is the heads side.* As a noun, the *obverse* is the opposite of the *reverse*, both generally used of coins and medals: *Tails is the reverse [side] of a coin. Inverse* means "opposite" or "upside down," as in *an inverse ratio.* The *inverse* of a proposition is its opposite. A *converse* proposition or theorem is one reversed in order or meaning, and the *converse* is such a reversed proposition or theorem: *Having demolished his proposition, I will now prove the converse.*

obviate (*v.*) is Standard meaning either "prevent," as in *Firing him now would obviate our having to fire him later,* or "makes unnecessary," as in *Her generous gift obviates the need to pass the hat.*

occasion (*n.*) can combine with the prepositions *for* or *of* or with *to* plus an infinitive: *Her birthday was the occasion for a great celebration. The occasion of their anniversary was also the Fourth of July. We took this occasion to inquire about his mother.* Spell *occasion* with two *c*'s but only one *s.* See CONSONANTS (2).

occupy (*v.*) can combine with the prepositions *with, by,* and *in: He was occupied with giving examinations. They occupied themselves by [in] arguing about how to pass the time.*

occur See TAKE PLACE.

occurrence (*n.*) Spell it with two *c*'s and two *r*'s. See CONSONANTS (2).

ocher, ochre The usual American spelling is *ocher*; *ochre* is a variant, favored by the British. See SPELLING (1).

octavo See DUODECIMO.

octet, octette See QUARTET.

octopus (*n.*) has two plurals: *octopuses* (pronounced *AHK-tuh-pus-iz*) and *octopi* (pronounced *AHK-tuh-pei*). *Octopod* is a relatively rare word, referring to any eight-footed mollusk, including the *octopus*; *octopod* has two plurals: *octopods* (pronounced *AHK-tuh-podz*) and *octopodes* (pronounced *ahk-TAH-puh-deez*). See FOREIGN PLURALS.

octoroon See MULATTO.

oculist See OPHTHALMIA.

(-)odd (*adj.*) The adjective *odd* means "peculiar," "odd-numbered," and "singular," as in *He was an odd, difficult sort of man; Play one of the odd ones, and leave the even ones to others; I found one odd glove and one odd mitten, but no pairs.* When the word is used as a kind of suffix, meaning "an unknown or unspecified number" (*She was forty-odd years old*), avoid ambiguity by using a hyphen.

odious, odorous (*adjs.*) *Odious* means "hateful, disgusting, offensive": *His was an odious character with no redeeming feature. Odorous* means "giving off an odor (usually unpleasant)."

odor, aroma, fragrance, odour, perfume, scent, smell, stench, stink (*nn.*) Of these occasional synonyms, *aroma, fragrance, perfume,* and *scent* have pejorated the least, and even they are not wholly free of occasional taint. *Scent* and *perfume,* for example, although they frequently suggest flowers and sweetness, have also been applied to the emanations of skunks and barnyards. And one can easily see how *fragrance* and *aroma* can degrade under observations such as *Someone had been far too liberal in applying a cloying, cheap fragrance* and *The aroma of burned toast took me by the throat when I entered the room. Smell* and *odor* (*odour* is the British spelling; see SPELLING [1]) are nominally unspecific, but you rarely use them without specifying the sort of *smell* or *odor* you have in mind; if you don't, we'll assume it's an unpleasant one—literally or figuratively—almost every time. *Stink* and *stench* have always been bad *smells.*

odorous See ODIOUS.

odour See ODOR.

-oe- See DIGRAPHS.

o'er, over (*prep., adv.*) *O'er* (rhymes with *oar*) is a poetic spelling, reflecting a poetic pronunciation of a contraction of *over.* It's one of those words that is the versifier's friend, since it can be either one or two syllables, pronounced to rhyme either with *more* or with *clover.*

oesophagus See ESOPHAGUS.

oestrogen See ESTROGEN.

of 1 (*prep.*) is Standard when used in the periphrastic of the adverbial genitive, in phrases such as *We go there often of an afternoon.*

of, **compounded** See ALONGSIDE OF; DOUBLE GENITIVE; INSIDE; OFF OF; OUTSIDE.

of 2, for '*ve* We all pronounce the contraction of *have* with a preceding *I would* or *I'd* the same way we pronounce unstressed *of,* and substituting *of* for '*ve* in writing can be an example of eye dialect, which deliberately misspells words to suggest Nonstandard or dialectal speech. But not every such misspelling is deliberate; we can all do it in haste and inadvertence. The important thing is to correct it when it isn't intentional. See also PLUPLUPERFECT TENSE.

of a occurs more and more frequently in Non-standard Common and Vulgar English in uses such as *It's not that big of a deal; She didn't give too long of a talk; How hard of a job do you think it'll be?* All these are analogous to *How much of a job will it be?,* which is clearly idiomatic and Standard, at least in the spoken language where it most frequently occurs. It is possible, therefore, that the first three could achieve idiomatic status too before long, despite the objections of many commentators. Until they do, keep them all out of your Planned and Oratorical speech and your Edited English.

When *of* is omitted in constructions such as *a couple pair of shoes,* instead of *a couple of pair[s] of shoes,* the usage is considered dialectal and Nonstandard, although Standard speakers from some dialect areas may use it at Casual and Intimate levels.

of any See ANY.

of color See AFRICAN(-)AMERICAN.

of course is a Standard idiom: it permits you to reassure (*Of course you may*), to remind people of things they already know, and to repeat the obvious without affronting someone, but be careful: it can also be quite unpleasant, when you appear to rub people's noses in something obvious to everyone but them.

off (*prep.*), when it means "from," is limited at best to Casual or Impromptu uses and is frequently faulted as Nonstandard: *I got this knife off a boy in my class.* See OFF FROM; OFF OF.

off- (*prefix*), **-off** (*suffix*) The prefix, as in *off-center, off-white,* and *off-limits,* is usually joined to the base word by a hyphen, but some uses are spelled as single words (*offbeat, offhand, offside*). The suffix may be tacked on to the base word without a hyphen, as in *payoff,* but many combinations are in divided usage, as in *blast[-]off,* and *playoff;* still others, such as *cook-off* and *face-off,* are almost always hyphenated. Both affixes—especially the suffix—are often used to make nonce words.

offense, offence (*n.*) *Offense* is the American spelling; *offence,* the British. See SPELLING (1).

offensive (*adj.*) takes *to* when it combines with a preposition: *Her remarks were offensive to me.*

OFFENSIVE EPITHETS AND DISPARAGING LABELS Most people are conscious of the offensiveness of the more obvious and publicized racial, sexual, and ethnic locutions (see ETHNIC SLURS AND TERMS OF ETHNIC OPPROBRIUM; RACIST LANGUAGE; SEXIST LAN-

GUAGE; see also OBSCENE (1); PROFANITY; and TABOO WORDS). But other terms—clearly, those of homophobia, such as *queer, fag, dyke,* and *queen,* but also others simply disparaging, such as *fatty, baldy, skinny,* and the like—can also be offensive, even though not under the same strong taboos. Here as elsewhere the best advice is to call people only what they *want* to be called. Apply sharp-pointed epithets only to yourself.

off from Juxtaposition of *off* and *from* is Standard in such sentences as *They were cut off from their base camp for weeks* but is often criticized as redundant where it seems to parallel *off* and especially *off of,* as in *I got it off from [off of] a boy in my class.* Avoid this second use.

offhand (*adv., adj.*), **offhanded** (*adj.*), **offhandedly** (*adv.*) *Offhand* and *offhanded* both serve as adjectives, but *offhand* is much more frequently used: *It was just an offhand [offhanded] remark. His manner is rather offhand. Offhand* and *offhandedly* also serve as adverbs but rarely interchangeably: *offhand* is usually a sentence adverb, as in *Offhand, I can't think of anyone. Offhandedly* is used in other adverbial positions, as in modifying adjectives: *It was an offhandedly pleasant conversation,* or verbs: *She praised him highly but offhandedly.*

office (*v.*) is a functional shift from the noun, meaning "to assign or to have or share an office": *They officed me on the top floor. I was officed with three other people.* The verb is rare in the desk dictionaries but is certainly Standard, although some would prefer to limit it to Conversational and Informal use.

officer, cop, patrolman, peace officer, policeman, police officer, policewoman (*nn.*) *Officer* and *police officer* are still and increasingly the best Standard designations for a member of a police force; sometimes *police officers* are distinguished from other officers by being called *peace officers,* especially if they're not actually police but rather are sheriffs, deputies, marshals, constables, etc. Although technically a *patrolman* is not an *officer,* the term is the only word that will work in direct address except another rank: *What's the problem, officer [sergeant]?* Unlike *policeman* and *policewoman, police officer* and *officer* are inclusive. *Cop* is still widely used and is also inclusive, but it's slang.

official See OFFICIOUS.

officiate (*v.*) The intransitive verb is Standard, as in *Her son officiates at high school basketball games.* Transitive use, as in *He officiates nearly* *fifty games a season,* continues to meet with some objections, especially in Edited English, but it too is now unquestionably Standard in all but Oratorical and the most Formal contexts.

officious, official (*adjs.*) *Officious* means "interfering, overbearing, insisting on offering help or service" and is pejorative: *The manager was fussy and officious, pestering the diners and interfering with the waiters. Official* means "with full legal authority," as in *This is an official request for information.*

offload (*v.*) means "to unload, to remove cargo from a carrier," and it is Standard both as a transitive, as in *We offloaded the freight,* and as an intransitive verb, as in *As soon as you've offloaded, you may depart.* In computerese *offload* means "delete."

off of (*prep.*) is a compound preposition that many commentators insist should be replaced by *off* alone to avoid redundancy but which is nonetheless Standard at most Casual and Impromptu levels: *Get your elbows off of the table!* Avoid it at Planned and Oratorical levels and in Semiformal and Formal writing. With *get, buy,* and some other verbs, *off of* is Substandard and a shibboleth: *He got [bought] it off of a boy in the class* is strongly condemned everywhere by Standard users. See also OFF; OFF FROM.

offspring (*n.*) is Standard as both a singular, as in *His offspring is about three and looks much like her father,* and a plural, as in *Her offspring were both present.* A regular plural form, *offsprings,* occurs occasionally but is uncommon in Standard English.

off the cuff, off-the-cuff (*adv., adj.*) are Conversational, Informal, and Semiformal idioms meaning "spontaneous, unplanned" and referring usually to a spoken response or remark or to the making of such speeches: *He gave an off-the-cuff opinion that he later regretted. She spoke hurriedly, off the cuff.*

off-the-rack (*adj.*) means "ready-made," as compared to custom-made, tailor-made, or bespoke clothing, which is made to order for the individual customer.

off the record, off-the-record (*adv., adj.*) are Standard idioms meaning "not for quotation or attribution." They suggest that no record of an occasion or remarks is to be kept.

off-the-wall See WALL.

of one's own accord See ACCORD.

often (*adv.*) The normal Standard pronunciation is *AWF-in,* but the spelling pronunciation *AWF-tin* is frequently heard and considered by some

to be an ignorant affectation. *Often* employs either inflected forms for comparison (*oftener, oftenest*) or the periphrastics (*more often, most often*), although the periphrastics have a higher frequency of use. See SPELLING PRONUNCIATIONS.

oh See O.

oh-oh See HUH-UH.

O.K., o.k., OK, ok, okay, okeh (*adv., adj., n., v.*) As adverb (*The motor's working O.K.*), adjective (*I'm OK again now*), noun (*Please get your supervisor's okay*), and verb (*Will she OK it?*), the term *okay* has very wide use, but it should be limited to Conversational, Informal, or Semiformal use. (The noun occurs frequently in print media these days.) The abbreviation is written with and without the periods but usually with both letters capitalized. *Okay* is the only current spelled-out version; *okeh* is obsolete.

Avoid letting *O.K.* overwhelm your speech, especially as a mechanical appeal for concurrence; it is a kind of tic in some speech, especially of the young, as in *"O.K., now here's what I have in mind, O.K.? We'll leave at six, O.K.? and I think you'll really enjoy it, O.K.?"* Compare LIKE (1); WELL (2).

old adage See ADAGE; APHORISM.

old cliché has been criticized as a tautology, but the problem, if any, is trivial. Technically a cliché need not be *old*; some locutions have become clichés almost overnight. Emphasis too may affect the need for a modifier: if a cliché seems really ancient, the point may need to be stressed.

olde (*adj.*) is a clichéd bit of heavy-footed marketing whimsy. See COMPLEAT; YE (2).

olden (*adj.*) means simply "old" or "extremely old, ancient, medieval," and the word is archaic today: *In (the) olden days* is clearly back beyond the days that are merely old, and the locution smacks of old poems and tales; in some contexts it's a frozen figure.

OLD ENGLISH is the name given to the earliest versions of English spoken by the mid-fifth-century invaders of Britain, the Angles, Saxons, and Jutes (hence *Anglo-Saxon,* another word for it). Our earliest written records of the language are somewhat later, but we have a fair range of materials written in it by the tenth century. The conventional dates for *Old English* are 449 to 1066. It was a highly inflected Germanic language, with a heavy stress on front or root syllables of its words. It had both weak and strong verbs, and it tended to compound its words to accommodate new meanings rather than to borrow from other languages. It also had some special letters, including the thorn (Þ) and the eth (ð) for the sounds we now spell with *th*. Here are a few verses from an *Old English* version of Genesis:

On angynne gesceop God heofonan and eorðan. Seo eorðe soðlice waes idel and aemtig, and Þeostra waeron over Þaere nywelnysse bradnysse; and Godes gast waes geferod ofer waeteru. God cwaeÞ Þa: Gewurðe leoht, and leoht wearð geworht. God geseah Þa Þaet hit god waes, and he todaelde Þaet leoht from Þam Þeostrum. And het Þaet leoht daeg and Þa Þeostru niht: Þa waes geworden aefen and morgen an daeg.

The next chronological stage of the language was called Middle English. (Be careful in speech to make context distinguish *Old English* from an old English—Chaucer's, for example, which is indeed old, but is called Middle English.)

older, oldest See ELDER.

old-fashion, old-fashioned (*adj.*) *Old-fashioned* is the conventionally formed participial adjective, and *old-fashion* is a variant, made (according to the *Oxford English Dictionary*) of the noun *fashion* rather than the verb and now obsolete. *Old-fashion* has reappeared, however, and is criticized in much the same way and for the same reason that *ice cream* once was and *handicap parking* is now.

old people See SENIOR CITIZEN.

old saw See SAW.

oldster, old-timer (*nn.*) Limit both these nouns mainly to Conversational or Informal or Semiformal use. *Oldster* was made on analogy with *youngster*; *old-timer* is a synonym for *oldster* and also has overtones *oldster* lacks, particularly in the sense of being old-fashioned, not just old.

ology (*n.*), **-ology, -alogy** (*suffixes*) The suffixes are combining forms, from Greek *logos,* and mean "the science or study of," as in *genealogy, geology, mineralogy, psychology,* and *sociology.* The plurals are *-ologies* and *-alogies.* *Ology* (there is no *alogy,* and the plural is *ologies*) is a jocular clipped form (see APHERESIS) meaning "a science, a branch of study," as in *I don't know what new ologies they're adding to today's curriculum.*

omelet, omelette (*n.*) Both spellings are Standard, *omelet* a bit more frequent in the United States, *omelette* in Britain.

OMITTED RELATIVE, CONTACT CLAUSES These two terms are used, along with others, to describe the common and perfectly acceptable practice of omitting the relative pronoun from a restrictive clause or restrictive modifier: *Here's the dress Mother brought me. There is the woman I'm going to marry.* Two centuries ago people argued that all *relatives* ought to be stated, as in *the dress that Mother brought,* or *the woman whom [that] I'm going to marry,* and a few people still insist that omitting *relatives* be limited to Informal or Semiformal writing and the Conversational levels, while others consider the omission suitable only to conversation. It is a matter of tone or style, not of correctness: sometimes omitted *relatives* can sound a bit more relaxed than the situation may require, and on other occasions including the relative pronoun may seem a bit ponderous or stiff. Standard English accepts either.

on, upon (*preps.*) Those for whom simplicity and conciseness in language use are the highest and only virtues argue that *on* should almost always replace *upon,* but this is nonsense. Both are useful words, offering variety at the very least, and occasionally *upon* offers a precision *on* lacks or can usefully provide a slightly more elevated tone. Both prepositions are Standard, and both are high-frequency words. See ONTO.

on a [. . .] basis, on a basis of See BASIS.

on account of (*prep., subord. conj.*) As a compound preposition, *on account of* meaning "because of" is in every respect Standard, although it can sometimes be clumsy: *We went there on account of the excellent hiking available.* As a subordinating conjunction, *on account of* meaning "because" is Nonstandard, probably dialectal, and frequently used to sound humorous or folksy (it occurs almost exclusively in speech or its written imitations): *I went to bed, on account of I hate late-night television.*

on balance See BALANCE (2).

on behalf of See BEHALF.

oncoming See UPCOMING.

one (*pron.*) Should *one* begin an impersonal statement with *one,* or should *you* start off with *you*? Style is the problem: *one* can sound very formal and self-consciously elevated, especially to Americans (the British use *one* much more frequently). *You* is clearly less formal and constrained, but it may sometimes seem a bit too relaxed, or at other times, too directive.

Assume *one* is the choice; should *one* continue with it or shift to *you, she, he,* or *he or she* (or one of its variants) or go to *they,* as in *If one has time, he [she, he or she, you, they] ought to make full notes?* To stick with *one* is to be consistent but also is to guarantee a stiff, impersonal tone. To shift to *you* is to achieve a more relaxed and direct tone at the cost of irritating those who believe shifting person (from third to second) in the same sentence is bad grammar. To shift to the plural *they* may be an affront to agreement but at least will not upset those opposed to the use of exclusive pronouns such as *he* or *she.* Best advice: for all but the most Formal prose, stick with *you,* and if you decide instead to begin with *one,* stay with it. The generic *he* may be acceptable in some of the most Formal prose, but many editors would rather that you use *he or she* or vary the pronoun, and some would even prefer *they* to *he.* Consistent use of any option is Standard, but switching options in midsentence is Nonstandard, clumsy, and to be avoided. See also INDEFINITE YOU; ONE OF THOSE WHO.

one another, one another's See EACH OTHER.

one fell swoop See FELL SWOOP.

one in (out of) See AGREEMENT OF SUBJECTS ONE OR MORE.

one of the See ONE OF THOSE WHO.

one of the . . . if not the The problem is that full parallelism is not possible since both a plural noun and a singular noun are demanded, yet the sentence tries to make do with only one: *That is one of the tallest, if not the very tallest, mountain[s] in this range. One of the tallest* needs to modify a plural; *if not the very tallest,* needs to modify a singular. This failure of agreement is usually taken as idiomatic in Conversational and Informal contexts, but it is not acceptable in Edited English or its spoken equivalents, which require that the sentence be recast: *That is one of the tallest, if not the very tallest, of the mountains in this range.*

one of those who, one of those things The question is one of notional agreement: Is it *She is one of those people who worries incessantly* or *She is one of those people who worry incessantly?* Is it only *one* who worries, or do all of *those people* worry? Subsequent pronouns can make the choice clear, of course: *She is one of those people who worries herself needlessly; She is one of those people who worry themselves needlessly.* But either *one* or *those* may be the antecedent for *who* or *that* or *which* and so set the grammatical tone in this structure in Standard English. Best advice for Edited English: let the verb agree with the plural substantive except

when *She is the only one of those people who worries.*

one or more See AGREEMENT OF SUBJECTS ONE OR MORE.

oneself, one's self (*pron.*) Both the one-word and the two-word spellings are Standard, but *oneself* is much more commonly used.

one's own accord, on; on one's own account See ACCORD.

ongoing (*adj.*), meaning "continuing, in progress," is Standard, although some commentators have been concerned that it is being overused.

on line, in line For now, *to stand* or *wait in line* is Standard. New Yorkers used to be the only Americans who spoke of *waiting* or *standing on line,* and then other Americans began to pick up the locution, but a completely new recent use for *on line* may bring that development to a halt: *on line* also means "directly connected to a computer," as in *My printer is now on line and ready to print.* This sense began by being jargon, but it is now Conversational at the very least, and it may shortly be fully Standard.

only (*adv.*) The location of *only* is very flexible in speech but poses problems in written use, mainly because of certain logical ambiguities: *Only he could save us* (he was the only one); *He only could save us* (ambiguous: either he was the only one who could save us, or he could save us but could do nothing else for us); *He could only save us* (he could do that but nothing more); *He could save only us* (others were lost); *He could save us only* (ambiguous: either he could save just us but had to let the others go, or he could save us but do nothing more for us). Of course when we say or read these sentences aloud, the ambiguities disappear, our meaning established by stress and intonation. See also ADVERBS (2); EVEN.

ONOMATOPOEIA is the effect created by words made to sound like or otherwise imitate what they refer to, words sometimes called echoic: *growl, titter, hiss, crash, yipe.* The related adjective is either *onomatopoeic* or *onomatopoetic.*

on one's own account See ACCORD.

on the basis of, on a basis of See BASIS.

on the part of is a Standard idiom meaning "by, among" that some people think is too long and rambling to be a good choice in prose. Actually, it is a sensible varied way of attributing and a Standard idiom: *Objections on the* *part of some commentators seem quite irrelevant, unless, of course, the only value is brevity.*

on the qui vive See QUI VIVE.

onto, on to (*prep.*) *Onto* is the usual spelling of the compound preposition: *He stepped onto the ice, lost his footing, and fell.* As two words it may suggest slightly more independence for each of its parts: a combined verb (*hung on*) and a prepositional phrase (*to his arm*) in the sentence *She hung on to his arm,* for example. There is also a slang use of *onto,* meaning "alert to," "aware of": *The police are onto this new confidence game.*

onward (*adv., adj.*), **onwards** (*adv.*) *Onward* is the adjective: *Its onward momentum crushed the car into the wall*; *onward* and *onwards* are both adverbs: *She ran onward[s] for two more blocks.* All are Standard.

opaque See TRANSLUCENT.

op. cit. is an abbreviation of the Latin phrase *opera citato,* meaning "in the work already cited." It has been much used in footnotes documenting quotations and citations.

opera (*n.*) The singular noun *opera* (pronounced *AH-puhr-uh* or *AHP-ruh*) refers to the musical drama, its works, its theaters, and the like. Its plural is *operas* and usually pronounced *AHP-uhr-uhz* or *AHP-ruhz. Opera* can also be a mass noun or a count noun. See OPUS.

operate (*v.*) When a surgeon is performing an *operation* (a surgical procedure), the idiom is *operate on: They operated on him yesterday. She was operated on this morning.*

operation See SURGERY.

ophthalmia, oculist, ophthalmology, ophthalmologist, optician, optometrist, optometry (*nn.*) *Ophthalmia* (pronounced *ahf-THAL-mee-yuh,* but see DIPHTHERIA; -PHTH-) is the medical term for an inflammation of the conjunctiva of the eye; *ophthalmology* is the medical specialty involving the physiology and function of the eye and the treatment of its diseases; an *ophthalmologist* is a physician with that specialty. *Oculist* is an older generic term for *ophthalmologist,* someone who specializes in the eye; today the term is used loosely (and rarely) to apply to an *optometrist.* An *optician* is a manufacturer or seller of optical instruments or a maker and retailer of eyeglasses. An *optometrist* is trained to describe and correct with lenses the faults and distortions caused by imperfect refraction in the eye; an *optometrist* cannot prescribe drugs or perform surgery. In effect *optometry* deals with the physics of the eye.

opine (*v.*) is Standard but seems frequently to be used jocularly, meaning "to give or formally state one's opinion": *She opined that he would lose the contest.* You can use it without humorous intent, despite what some commentators suggest, but you will need to watch context lest you sound either stiffly pretentious or deliberately jocular.

opportunity (*n.*) combines often with *to* plus an infinitive: *They gave us an opportunity to reply.* With *for, opportunity* takes a noun or other nominal: *take this opportunity for some rest* [*for resting*]. With *of,* a gerund frequently follows (*She requested the opportunity of questioning her accuser*), so also can a noun or noun phrase (*The opportunity of uninterrupted study is rare*).

opposite (*adj., n.*) The noun combines usually with *of* and occasionally with *to: His view is the opposite of mine. His beliefs are the exact opposites to mine.* Some consider the use of *to* odd and clumsy, or British-sounding. The adjective combines regularly with either *from* or *to: Her room is opposite from* [*to*] *mine.* (This use of *to* is much more often British.) But note that in this use the preposition is often unnecessary: *Her room is opposite mine.*

opposition (*n.*), when combined with a preposition, usually takes *to* or, rarely, *against: There was no opposition to* [*against*] *our idea.* With *of,* the combination identifies the opposing force(s), as in *We feared the opposition of the management.* With *between,* the combination identifies two opposing forces: *We hadn't expected the opposition between her mother and father.*

opt (*v.*) means "to choose" and combines with *to* plus an infinitive (*They opted to await the next session*), with the preposition *for* (*We opted for the second sitting*), or with *out,* meaning "decline or decide not to participate" (*When they proposed we join the movement, we opted out*). Generally *opt* is used for a fairly formal choice of options, but *opt out* and *opt* used simply as a variation on *choose* are Standard, though probably limited to Conversational and Semiformal contexts at best.

optician See OPHTHALMIA.

optimal (*adj.*), **optimum** (*adj., n.*) As adjectives, these synonyms mean "best available, most favorable, ideal," as in *We should have optimal* [*optimum*] *weather conditions early next week.* Neither the adjectives nor the noun *optimum* is always interchangeable with (*the*) *best,* which is usually an absolute. Both *optimal* and *optimum* are Standard.

optimize, maximize (*vv.*) *Optimize* is infrequent as an intransitive verb, meaning "to take an optimistic view," but it has very frequent use as a transitive verb, meaning "to make the most of," "to get the optimum value or use from," as in *Her hard work optimized the scanty resources available. Maximize* means "to increase to the maximum" and "to make the most of" and hence in this latter sense is an exact synonym of *optimize: Swift response will maximize our chances for success.* These verbs have seen considerable popularity in recent years, *maximize* in particular coming close to cliché status. But see also MAXIMIZE; SPELLING (1).

option, alternative, choice (*nn.*) An *option* is any of several: *His options were to buy, to sell, or to do nothing.* A *choice* is one among an unlimited number: *You may have your choice of these.* An *alternative* can be any of a very few options—*She chose the alternative that would take less time*—but purists are generally still adamant that *alternatives* can involve only two options. Edited English, however, is not always so insistent on that point today. See also ALTERNATE (2); CHOICE.

optometrist, optometry See OPHTHALMIA.

opus (*n.*) has two plurals: *opuses* (pronounced *O-puhs-iz*) and *opera* (pronounced *O-puhr-uh* or *AH-puhr-uh*). *Opus* means "a work or composition, especially in music." See also FOREIGN PLURALS; OPERA.

or See AGREEMENT OF COMPOUND SUBJECTS WITH THEIR VERBS AND SUBSEQUENT PRONOUNS; EITHER; NEITHER; NEITHER . . . NOR; NOR.

-or See AGENTIVE ENDINGS.

-or, -our See SPELLING (1).

oral, orally See AURAL; VERBAL.

orate (*v.*) is a back-formation from the noun *oration*, and it is Standard, if often pretentious, jocular, or suggestive of overkill. Pronounce it *or-AIT*.

oration, address, discourse, lecture, speech, talk (*nn.*) These synonyms all name kinds of public speaking. An *oration* is a particularly formal kind of address, usually on some sort of ceremonial occasion: *He gave the funeral oration.* A *discourse* is a speech imparting information on a particular subject: *Her discourse was devoted to the perils and pleasures of trailer travel.* A *lecture* is an informative talk, usually prepared in advance and given to a class or another audience: *I delivered a lecture on what is known of Chaucer's life.* An *address* is a

formal speech, usually on a formal ceremonial occasion: *We read Washington's Farewell Address and Lincoln's Gettysburg Address.* A *speech* is generic for nearly all these others, used to denote any kind of public speaking, informal or formal, on any subject and to any sort of audience: *I gave them a short speech on what they could expect of me.* A *talk* is an informal *speech,* sometimes perhaps as focused as a *discourse,* sometimes as informal as a coach addressing his players at half-time: *The coach gave them a rousing talk at the half.* All these are Standard.

ORATORICAL LEVEL is the highest, most formal level of the spoken language. It is the language of professional and polished public speakers, orators, lecturers, preachers, and others who regularly address large audiences. This speech at its best is carefully planned, rhetorically sophisticated, and deliberately varied in syntax, vocabulary, and style. At its worst it can be stuffy and overwrought. It typically has a great deal in common with Formal written English: it often makes striking use of metaphor, conspicuous parallelism, contrastive sentence length, anaphora, and other devices of formal rhetoric. None of it is unplanned, and even its rare suggestions of spontaneity are usually carefully contrived. It evokes the image of the speaker at the lectern, quite ready—and indeed hoping—to be quoted directly. See LEVELS OF USAGE.

orchestra See BAND.

orchestrate (*v.*), **orchestrator, orchestration** (*nn.*) After a composer has composed, often an arranger or an *orchestrator* will take over, arranging and parceling out how the performers will actually present this composition. Figurative uses of these words have grown prodigiously (see also SCENARIO): *His manager had carefully orchestrated the candidate's appearances and speechmaking.* Both literal and figurative uses are Standard.

order See IN ORDER THAT; IN ORDER TO.

orderly (*adv., adj., n.*) As noun and adjective, as in *The captain's orderly was in the orderly room, orderly* is Standard and in frequent use. The adverb, however, seems to be falling into disuse. Dictionaries do not yet mark it archaic, but some desk dictionaries omit it. When it does occur, it may well be almost as a nonce word: *Put your clothes away orderly, now,* meaning "in an orderly way or fashion." An adverb *orderlily* also occurs rarely and only as a nonce word, usually jocular. See FRIENDLY; -LY.

ordinal number, cardinal number (*nn.*) The *ordinal numbers* are adjectival forms, ending in -*st*, -*nd*, -*rd*, -*th*, setting the named item "in order," as in *She won the first prize; He's the third entrant; This is the one hundred sixty-eighth day of the year.* The *cardinal numbers* are those we use in counting: *one, two, three, one hundred sixty-eight.* General advice: don't intermix *ordinal* and *cardinal numbers* in speech or writing.

ordinance, ordnance (*nn.*) An *ordinance* is a directive, a law, a statute: *The council passed an ordinance prohibiting smoking in city hall.* *Ordnance* is a military term for weapons, wagons, supplies, and especially artillery: *We captured most of their field ordnance.* Both words are Standard, but note their spellings.

oregano (*n.*) is any of several mint plants whose leaves are used in cooking. Pronounce it *o-REG-uh-no* or *uh-REG-uh-no*.

organizations, names of American English frequently considers the names of organizations (*the Smith and Jones Agency, Anaconda Copper, Standard Brands, Inc., General Motors, the Republican National Committee, the House Committee on Ways and Means*) collective nouns. See also AGREEMENT OF SUBJECTS AND VERBS (3).

orient See ORIENTATE.

Oriental See ASIAN.

orientate, orient (*vv.*) Both verbs, meaning literally "to locate east and so adjust to the compass directions" and figuratively "to adjust to circumstances or situation," are Standard, but American commentators continue to object to *orientate* (used more frequently by the British), mainly because *orient* is shorter but also because the figurative use is outstripping the literal one. See DISORIENT.

originate (*v.*), when it combines with prepositions, does so most often with *in*, as in *This song originated in New Orleans*, and *from*, as in *It originated from a melody played at funerals.* Other prepositions *originate* can take include these: *This custom originated as a sacrifice for good luck. It originated at Santa Fe [on the shore, with the Navaho, beside the stream, above the tree line, inside the house, beyond the burial ground, etc.].*

or less See LESS.

or no See NO.

or not See WHETHER OR NOT.

or otherwise See OTHERWISE.

orotund (*adj.*) means "full, rounded, and deep" when used of the voice, "bombastic and pompous" when applied to a style or tone of speech or writing: *His rich bass voice was deep and orotund, and so, alas, was his lecture.* See ROTUND.

orthodox, centrist, conservative, conventional (*adjs., nn.*) All these adjectives have a relatively objective cluster of meanings vaguely related to each other but not precisely synonymous, and they all can also be used in pejorative ways to suggest the stodgy, the unventuresome. All are frequently used to characterize the majority opinion within an established group, often suggesting an unwillingness to experiment and a resistance to change. *Orthodox* means "conforming to established doctrine, whether religious, political, or some other." *Conservative* means "likely to preserve the established rather than entertain the new" (see also CONSERVATIVES IN LANGUAGE MATTERS; CONSERVATIVE USAGE). *Centrist* means "characterized by the mean, the average, rather than by the extremes of principle or policy within a group." *Conventional* means "sanctioned by custom or use" and so "adhering closely to accepted rules and customs." All are Standard.

ORTHOGRAPHY means "spelling" (see SPELLING [1]).

oscillate, osculate (*vv.*) *Oscillate* means literally "to swing back and forth" and figuratively, therefore, "to vacillate, to be indecisive": *Like a flower in the wind, he oscillated between one view and another, unable to make up his mind.* *Osculate* means "to kiss," "to touch." The "kiss" sense—a very pretentious word for a very simple physical action—is usually jocularly employed: *His chief political skill was in osculating the infants of eligible voters.*

ostensible, ostentatious (*adjs.*), **ostensibly, ostentatiously** (*advs.*) *Ostensible* means "apparent, likely," as in *His ostensible reason for calling was to see her father.* *Ostentatious* means "showy, pretentious, especially of wealth or knowledge," as in *She was ostentatious in displaying her recent reading.* *Ostensibly* means "apparently, but not necessarily actually," as in *She was ostensibly unperturbed by his call.* *Ostentatiously* means "pretentiously," "with great ceremony," as in *He ostentatiously pointed out the virtues of his new car.* All four are Standard.

other (*adv., adj., n., pron.*) *Other* is Standard serving as four parts of speech: adjective (*He gave me the other sweater*); adverb (*There was* *no option other than to resign*); noun (*I took one road; she took the other*); pronoun (*I can do no other*). *Other . . . than, other . . . but,* and *other . . . except* are Standard idiomatic constructions (*I know of no other than [except, but] the one we saw earlier*); they function similarly to compound prepositions. For the use of the idiom *any other,* see ANY.

otherwise (*adv., adj., pron.*) *Otherwise* is Standard in all three functions: as adverb it means "differently, in another manner," as in *I was otherwise engaged* and *Otherwise, she was a delightful person*; as pronoun it functions just as a noun would and means "something or anything else," as in *The experts may say that the recession is ending, but the unemployment figures indicate otherwise*; as adjective it means "different," as in *She looks happy, but she feels otherwise*.

ought (*aux.*) *Ought* poses usage problems in the negative contraction plus an infinitive; it comes in two main forms in the United States, *oughtn't* and *hadn't ought* (a double modal auxiliary); *didn't ought* is mainly British, although it occasionally occurs in Substandard American English. *Oughtn't* and *hadn't ought* are regional Conversational locutions: *You oughtn't to go* is mainly Midland or Southern; *You hadn't ought to go* is mainly Northern Conversational. Without the contraction, *ought not* is unexceptionably Standard (*You ought not to go*). In negative constructions, sometimes the *to* introducing the infinitive is omitted, as in *You ought not go,* although rarely in the negative contraction (*You oughtn't to go*) or in Edited English. See also HAD OUGHT.

ought to of See OF (2); SHOULDA.

-our See SPELLING (1).

ours, ourn (*pron.*) *Ours* is an absolute possessive pronoun, and it is spelled without an apostrophe. *Ourn* is a dialectal and Nonstandard variant.

ourselves See MYSELF.

-ous (*suffix*) makes adjectives of nouns: *adventure* becomes *adventurous*. The adjective then usually means "characterized by or having the attribute expressed by the noun (in this case, *adventure*)."

out (*adv., prep.*), **out of** (*prep.*) By itself, *out* is more frequently an adverb, as in *She's never been out with him before* or *Turn out the light, please,* than it is a preposition, as in *Throw it out the window.* It is not always interchangeable with *out of*—compare *He went out the door* with

these unique uses of the preposition *out of: He's out of the office today; She's coming out of her daydream at last; The bird flew out of sight; I'm badly out of condition; He made it out of some previously published essays; She drove him out of his mind; His brother cheated him out of his inheritance; Only three out of the four dozen cookies were left.* In addition, *out of* serves as part of several hyphenated idioms: *out-of-bounds,* meaning "outside set limits"; *out-of-date,* meaning "old-fashioned, obsolete"; *out-of-door(s),* meaning "outdoor(s)"; *out-of-hand,* meaning either "directly, at once" or "uncontrolled"; *out-of-pocket,* meaning "cost in actual cash"; *out-of-the-way,* meaning "unusual, off the beaten track," "away from here"; and, with the agentive ending, *out-of-towner,* meaning "a visitor from another town." See also OUTSIDE.

outgoing (*adj.*) means "going away" (*the outgoing mail*), "leaving, giving up a position" (*the outgoing chancellor*), and "friendly, extroverted" (*an outgoing personality*). All are Standard.

out loud is a synonym for *aloud,* as in *She unconsciously spoke her thought out loud [aloud]. Aloud* may be slightly more Formal, but *out loud* is also Standard.

out-migrant, out-migrate, out-migration See EMIGRANT.

out of See OUT.

out of (one in) See AGREEMENT OF SUBJECTS ONE OR MORE.

out of sight The idiom *out of sight* has two other uses beyond the literal "beyond the range of eyesight." Prices that are *out of sight* are so high that they cannot be "seen." This use is Conversational at best. The other use is slang, an almost meaningless expression of admiration meaning "remarkable, terrific, beyond description" and sometimes spelled *outtasight* in eye dialect.

output See INPUT.

outside (*adv., prep.*), **outside of** (*prep.*) As adverb, *outside* poses no difficulties: *Come outside.* As prepositions, *outside* and *outside of* are roughly synonymous, as in *Stay outside [of] the white line,* and commentators whose primary concern is conciseness argue that *outside of* is needlessly wordy—but brevity isn't everything. Unlike *outside, outside of* also means "besides," "in addition to," or "other than" and is Standard in these uses: *Outside of my father, no one has called today.* See INSIDE; OUT.

outstanding (*adj.*) means "prominent, standing above or beyond others," as in *That outstanding peak has a name; the lesser ones are unnamed.* This literal sense has developed into the figurative use that is so frequent in English, "distinguished, prominent, notable," as in *She's an outstanding gymnast.* It also has another sense meaning "unsettled, uncollected, unpaid," as in *There is the stack of outstanding bills.* All three senses are Standard, although, as with *splendid, wonderful,* and *great,* so *outstanding* too has been overused, and hyperbole has somewhat weakened it in recent years, to the point that some consider it a vogue word today.

There is one other usage issue: whether *outstanding* is an absolute adjective or not. Some commentators urge that it not be modified as in *more outstanding* or *most outstanding.*

outtake (*n.*), once a jargon term from motion pictures and television, is now Standard: an outtake is a scene, also called a "take," edited out of the finished production, something left "on the cutting room floor" (to use another bit of associated jargon).

over (*prep.*), in the meaning "more than," is Standard and has been so for a long time, despite many commentators' objections: *It's been over fifty years since he visited us.* See also O'ER.

over- See OVERLY.

overall (*adj.*), as in *The overall response has been favorable,* is a useful Standard word, but it has been criticized recently for overuse, so be careful not to overdo it.

overlie (*v.*), **overlay** (*n., v.*) The verbs, like *lie* and *lay* on which they are based, are frequently confused, partly because of the partial overlap in their principal parts (*overlie, overlay, overlain; overlay, overlaid, overlaid*). *Overlie* is usually but not always intransitive, *overlay* always transitive: *An impenetrable fog overlay the airport. I overlaid the map with a transparency.* Errors in their past tense and past participle forms serve all too often as shibboleths. See LAY.

The noun *overlay* is Standard, meaning "a transparency or other sheet, such as a map, to be superimposed on another map, drawing, or picture."

overlook, oversee (*vv.*) One older sense of *overlook,* now very rare, is a synonym of *oversee*'s main meaning, "to manage, supervise, watch over." But the rest of *overlook*'s many meanings give it plenty of use, even though "supervise" is now wholly reserved to *oversee: A good supervisor will oversee the work and will overlook nothing important.*

overly (*adv.*), **over-** (*prefix*) For many adjectives, either arrangement will do the trick: *He seems overly committed to this venture. He seems overcommitted to this venture.* The addition of the prefix usually does not require a hyphen. Both patterns are Standard.

oversee See OVERLOOK.

overview (*n.*) is new but Standard, meaning "a general survey," as in *She gave us an overview of the project's history.*

overwhelm (*v.*), when it combines with prepositions, usually uses *with* or *by: I'll overwhelm her with compliments. I'll overwhelm her by paying her compliments. She will be overwhelmed by [with] my compliments.*

over with is an idiom meaning "finished, completed, ended" and occurs regularly in Conversational and Informal contexts: *When the shouting is over with, we can go back to work. When the shouting is over, we can go back to work* would be fully Standard.

owing to See DUE TO.

own See POSSESS.

OXYMORON is a figure of speech in which contradictory, antonymous, or opposing ideas are combined (the Greek meant something like "particularly silly or foolish"), as in *a deafening silence, a truthful liar, a chaste prostitute.*

P

-p-, -pp- See CONSONANTS (2).

pace (*prep.*), meaning "peace to," and hence "with deference to," "with the permission of," "with due respect or regard for," or "contrary to the opinion of," is a Latin tag that can be an economical way to oppose or contradict politely, with an apology in advance: *I think, pace my opponent, that we must act now.* But it is an intellectual's term (pronounced either *PAI-see*, *PAH-kai*, or *PAH-chai*): make certain that your audience will understand it and won't think it pretentious; otherwise, use English. In writing you must italicize it to help avoid confusion with the English word *pace*. See FOREIGN PHRASES.

pachyderm (*n.*), **elephantine, pachydermatous** (*adjs.*) A *pachyderm* is not just an elephant but any thick-skinned beast; hence the hippopotamus and the rhinoceros are also *pachyderms*. Figuratively, the terms are also used of thick-skinned people, and the other traits that accompany such beasts as elephants often go along in the package. Like *elephantine, pachydermatous* suggests slow, heavy, cumbersome, and undivertable.

package (*adj., n., v.*) "A box or wrapped container" is the main meaning of the noun, but we also use it figuratively to suggest a group that must be dealt with as a unit: *He presented his ideas as a package; he wanted them adopted as a package.* Functional shift then gives us the verb, meaning "to make up into or treat as a package": *She packaged airfare, hotel, meals, and car rental for us.* In Conversational or Informal use, such an arrangement is called *a package deal.* Other adjectival uses are really parts of compound nouns, as in *package freighter, package tanker* (or *parcel tanker*), and the like. All these uses except *package deal* are fully Standard.

pact (*n.*) means "an agreement between persons, groups, or nations" and has never been limited to international treaties and agreements.

PADDED PROSE, PADDING FOR IMPORTANCE These are more names for the meandering syntax, the windy phrasing, and the pretentious diction that remind us how great a virtue economy can often be and how much it can assist clarity. Don't pad your prose; let its substance dictate its shape, and its shape reflect its content.

paean, paeon, peon (*nn.*) For the ancient Greeks a *paean* was a thanksgiving hymn to the gods, and today it is a literary name for such an outpouring of thanksgiving: *His admirers offered paeans of praise.* A *paeon,* in Greek and Latin verse, was a prosodic foot made up of one long and three short syllables; in English it is usually made up of one stressed and three unstressed syllables, occurring in any order. The word *peon* once had several specialized senses, all referring to social have-nots: a farm worker in Spanish America, usually landless; a peasant or prisoner

obliged to work off a debt; an Indian or Sri Lankan foot soldier, policeman, servant, or messenger. Today it has generalized to mean "an unskilled worker at the bottom of the socioeconomic scale." All these senses are Standard, but only the generalized meaning will be clear without contextual definition.

paed-, paedi- See PED-.

page, leaf (*nn.*) In books the generic term for the two-sided sheet is *page,* but technically in bookmaking it is a *leaf,* with two numbered sides or *pages.* See RECTO.

paid See PAY.

pair (*n.*) The problems involve number and agreement. The singular *pair* is Standard: *A pair of ice skates is lying on the closet floor.* But a *pair* can notionally take a plural verb too, as can other collective nouns: *A pair of ugly floor lamps were tipped over onto the rug.* The plural is usually *pairs* when there is no singular modifier, such as *one* or *a,* and always takes a plural verb: *Pairs of birds were flying about in the spring morning.*

Some commentators object to locutions such as *three pair of shoes,* arguing that the modifying number should force *pair* to be *pairs.* But at least in most Conversational and Informal use, *three pair* and *four pair* are appropriate.

A few purists have argued that *a pair of twins* is redundant and logically adds up to four people. But *a pair of twins* is idiomatic, adds up to two, and is Standard, in all but the most Formal English. See NOTIONAL AGREEMENT.

pajamas, pyjamas (*n.*) The American spelling is *pajamas,* the British *pyjamas,* even though some American haberdashers (the same ones who advertise men's *braces* instead of *suspenders*) may use the British spelling. See SPELLING (1).

palate, palette, pallet (*nn.*) These are homophones, all pronounced *PAL-it.* The *palate* is the roof of the mouth and its soft, fleshy pendant; figuratively it is also the sense of taste. A *palette* is the painter's board on which paints are mixed, and it is also figuratively the collection of colors with which a given painter works. A *pallet* is any of a number of specialized tools or devices, the most common of which is the rough wooden platform used for stacking boxes or for holding machinery and other large items so that they can be moved by materials-handling equipment.

paleo-, palaeo- (*prefix*) It means "old," and Americans usually spell it *paleo-,* as in *paleography,* which means "ancient writing, or the

study of it.'' The British prefer *palaeo-*. See
DIGRAPHS; LIGATURES; SPELLING (1).

palette See PALATE.

palimony (*n.*) is a relatively recent coinage, a
blend of the Conversational *pal* (for a very close
friend) and *alimony*. *Palimony* refers to the financial settlement claimed by or made to one of
two people who although unmarried have been
living together as though married and have now
separated as though divorced. The word is frequent in the media but probably should be labeled Informal until it achieves full status as a
legal term, if indeed it ever does.

palimpsest (*n.*) is a piece of writing that has
been erased one or more times and written over,
so that it is layers deep. It then provides a
metaphor for complicated reading or decipher-
ing or simply for penetrating to truth through
layers of matter overlying it. The metaphor is
not so much about mystery or age as it is about
layers of meaning.

palindrome (*n.*) is a locution that is spelled and
reads the same both forward and backward, as
do *madam, 1991,* and *Able was I ere I saw
Elba.*

pallet See PALATE.

palm off See PAWN OFF.

palpable (*adj.*), **palpably** (*adv.*) The adjective
literally means "touchable, tangible, feelable,"
and hence figuratively and by extension it means
"clear, obvious, apparent." A *palpable lie* is
"an obvious lie," and it is a cliché, as is the
use in *Hamlet:* "A hit, a very palpable hit"
(V.ii.295). But in other applications, whether
the literal sense of touch or the figurative intellectual grasp is involved, *palpable* and *palpably,* its related adverb, are useful Standard words.
See also PERCEPTIBLE.

pan- (*prefix*) means "all, common to all, em-
bracing all parts," as in *Pan-American* or *Pan-
Slavic.* It is almost always hyphenated in proper
nouns, but not in common nouns.

panacea, placebo (*nn.*) A *panacea* is a magical
cure for all diseases and hence, figuratively, a
magical solution to any and all problems. Most
uses of the word occur in denials of or questions
about a *panacea*'s worth or existence.
  Placebo is the opening of a part of the Latin
vesper service for the dead, and it also means
"something done to placate or please someone."
But its use in medicine—"a harmless, unmedi-
cated dose or pill given a patient who insists on
a treatment that the physician believes is not
needed"—is its most frequently used sense, oc-

casionally confused with *panacea*. In medical
experiments, a *placebo* is the nondrug given the
control group in order that the effectiveness of
the drug being given the other patients can be
assessed more accurately.

pandemic See ENDEMIC.

pander (*n., v.*), **panderer** (*n.*) *Pander* is a noun
made by functional shift from the verb *pander*,
meaning "to procure, to pimp for, or to assist
in satisfying the sexual or other ignoble desires
of another person." *Panderer* is a word built by
the addition of the agentive ending *-er* to the
verb. The noun *pander* has been around much,
much longer than its synonym, *panderer*, but
both are Standard.

pandit, pundit (*nn.*) These are variants of the
same Sanskrit word, meaning "wise or learned
man." In Hindi it is a title, an honorific, as in
Pandit Nehru. English uses the *pundit* spelling
(and pronunciation) half-jocularly: a *pundit* is
someone who has or claims to have expert
knowledge, perhaps even wisdom.

panic (*n., v.*) Other forms are spelled *panicked,
panicking, panicky.* See SPELLING OF -ING AND
-ED FORMS OF VERBS ENDING IN -IC, -AC.

panties (*n.*), meaning "women's underpants,"
is always treated as plural, although it can refer
to one garment—one pair—or many. The term
is Standard.

pants (*n.*) is a clipped form of the word *panta-
loons* and is used for various forms of trousers,
slacks, or underdrawers; *underpants* refers primarily to women's and children's garments but
has also been applied to men's, where *undershorts, briefs, boxer shorts,* and the like are
more usual, although *briefs* and *boxer shorts* are
used for women's and children's underdrawers
too. All these uses are Standard, and all are
plural whether the referent is one garment or
many, as in *These pants* [one pair or a rackful]
are on sale. In some compounds (a woman's
pantsuit, a *pantleg* or *pantlegs*), *pant* is used in
the singular, and tailors, clothing manufacturers, and wholesale buyers also use the singular,
as in *We have this pant in several fabrics.* This
use is argot and Conversational at best. See
SLACKS.

paparazzi (*n.*) (pronounced *PAH-pah-RAHT-
see*) is the plural of the Italian singular noun,
paparazzo, one of the freelance news photogra-
phers who make such pests of themselves taking
candid pictures of the notable or notorious. Perhaps it is because they seem to appear only in
swarms that American English journalese often
treats the Italian plural form as a singular, and

much Conversational English does the same. See FOREIGN PLURALS.

paperback, paperbacked See HARDBACK.

paper copy See HARD COPY.

papier-mâché (*adj., n.*) is still usually spelled the French way (*paper-mâché* occurs but is rare), but the pronunciation is in divided usage, with most Americans anglicizing its first element but keeping the French stress pattern: *PAI-puhr-muh-SHAI*.

parable See ALLEGORY.

paradigm (*n.*) means "a pattern or model," and it is pronounced either *PER-uh-DEIM* or *PER-uh-dim*. In grammar a *paradigm* is a pattern or an example of grammatical forms: *cat, cat's, cats, cats'; swim, swims, swam, have swum, has swum, swimming* are typical *paradigms*—full lists of the forms that the noun *cat* and the verb *swim* can take. The more general sense, "model," usually indicates the best of its kind: *The house was a paradigm of good taste.*

paraffin See KEROSENE.

PARAGRAPH A *paragraph* is a unit of prose a sentence or more in length, logically cohesive and set off in writing by its indented first line. The only limits on the length of a *paragraph* are provided by common sense: a string of choppy, very short *paragraphs* can have a breathless, disconnected quality damaging to the flow of exposition. An extremely long *paragraph*, with no relief for the eye or the mind, can be boring and cause the reader's attention to wander.

One convention to note: in presenting dialogue, let each speaker's words begin a new paragraph.

parallel (*adj., n., v.*) Spell it with two *l*'s first, then one, and don't double the final consonant when you inflect the verb (*paralleled, parallel-ing*). The adjective combines with *with* and *to: This line is parallel with [to] that one.* The noun combines with *with, to, among,* and *between: Find a parallel with [to] our present situation. There surely are parallels among [between] these situations.* And *in parallel* and *out of parallel* are idioms: *This circuit is wired in parallel, not in series. You fell because your skis got out of parallel.*

PARALLELISM is a stylistic arrangement in which similar syntactic patterns repeat, thus allowing reader or listener to rely on the grammatical repetition to echo the logical similarity of the thought and thus improving the clarity and efficiency of the passage: *The new car was too small, too brightly colored, and too expen-sive. He was tall and homely, and she was short and pretty.* See also FAULTY PARALLELISM; NOT ONLY . . . BUT ALSO.

paralysis (*n.*) The plural is *paralyses*, pronounced *puhr-AL-uh-SEEZ*. See FOREIGN PLURALS.

paralyze (*v.*) is the American spelling, *paralyse* the British variant. See SPELLING (1).

parameter, perimeter (*nn.*) Both mean "boundaries or outer limits," but even in those senses they are not interchangeable. *Parameter,* pronounced *puh-RAM-uh-tuhr,* has some specialized mathematical meanings and two very widely used general meanings—"a boundary or limit" and "a characteristic element or factor"—both usually in the plural: *We sketched in the parameters of the problem as we saw them. Perimeter,* pronounced *puhr-IM-i-tuhr,* is "the outer boundary of any mathematical plane figure," "the outer edge or boundary of an area," "the outer defense line of a military area," or "the length of any of these": *We walked the perimeter of the woodlot. Parameters* are more likely to be abstract or figurative; *perimeters* are usually literal boundaries.

paramount (*adj.*) means "superior to all others, supreme, or chief," as in *Winning the election was her paramount goal.* It is sometimes considered an absolute adjective, but hyperbole seems not to accept that limitation; hence *very* or *pretty paramount,* meaning "really important," can sometimes be Standard too, although mainly in Conversational and Informal contexts.

paranoia (*n.*), **paranoiac, paranoid** (*adjs., nn.*) *Paranoia* in psychiatry is "a mental disorder—a psychosis—in which the patient has systematic delusions, commonly of persecution." *Paranoiac* and *paranoid* are the adjectives used to describe symptoms and conditions characteristic of *paranoia,* and functional shift has made each of them a noun as well: *I think she's [a] paranoiac [paranoid]; she is suspicious of everybody.* The technical psychiatric uses continue, but all three terms, and especially the adjectives, have also generalized to mean "fearful," especially "worried about what others may be thinking or doing that could be harmful to oneself." Like so many other terms from medicine and psychiatry adopted by the general vocabulary, these too reflect in general use the hyperbole so frequent in Standard English. *Paranoid* has a higher frequency than *paranoiac,* often meaning in Conversational or Informal use little more than "anxious or worried." It combines with the prepositions *about, over,* and (very rarely) *of: She's paranoid about [over, of]* not being dressed appropriately. Best advice: use these words sparingly in all senses but the literal, and combine them only with *about* and *over*.

paranormal See SUBNORMAL.

paraphernalia (*n.*) is a Latin plural form, and in English it can be treated as either plural or singular, there being no special singular form in English: *The paraphernalia professional golfers carry in their bags is [are] considerable.* It can be either a mass noun (*Paraphernalia requires . . .*) or a count noun (*These paraphernalia require . . .*). See FOREIGN PLURALS.

PARAPHRASE *To paraphrase* means "to re-state in other words," and the noun *paraphrase* means "such a restatement." See DIRECT ADDRESS.

PARATAXIS, HYPOTAXIS *Parataxis* is a rhetorical and syntactic arrangement in which clauses are strung together in series, without subordination: *We ran, we sang, and we told jokes. Hypotaxis* is the syntactic subordination of one clause to another: *As we ran, we sang and told jokes.*

PARENS is the plural abbreviation—a clipping—of *parentheses,* used as a Conversational jargon term by those who must use the word often, as could be required in discussing the use of these marks in printed matter. In referring to either of a pair of *parens* (pronounced *PER-en* or *puh-REN*), the stream of authorial dictation or editorial talk might go like this: "The United Nations—*paren*—hereafter the U.N.—*close paren*—will convene here next week." The resulting print would look like this: *The United Nations (hereafter the U.N.) will convene here next week.*

PARENTHESES (the singular is *parenthesis*) are the punctuation marks we use to set off explanatory or other additional material not needed in the main sentence. Stylistically, *parentheses* are a way of setting off an aside in a syntactic structure. Paired dashes can do this too—they're the most vigorous of such marks— and *parentheses* are a bit stronger than paired commas for a similar purpose. Conventionally *parentheses* are also used to set off numbers, as in *(1), (2),* etc.; to repeat and confirm a number or give an abbreviation in a text, as in *There were fifteen hundred three (1,503) applicants* and *The agency was the United Nations Relief and Rehabilitation Agency (UNRRA)*; and to indicate alternative possibilities, as in forms to be filled out: *Fill in name(s) of occupant(s) of this address.*

Conventional combinations of *parentheses* and other marks of punctuation are these: a full sentence within *parentheses* but not within another sentence begins with a capital letter and ends with a period or other terminal mark, all placed within the *parentheses*; inside a sentence, the materials within *parentheses* need not be capitalized nor have end punctuation within them but may include a question mark or an exclamation point; abbreviations within *parentheses* may end with a period; within a sentence, punctuation will go not immediately before a parenthetical insertion but directly after the final parenthesis mark, as in *He gave his name (grudgingly), but he refused to give his address*; and a parenthetical remark within *parentheses* will be surrounded by square brackets, not by a second set of *parentheses* (in mathematical expressions, the reverse is true: material already containing parentheses will be enclosed by square brackets, which in turn may be enclosed by braces). See also BRACES; BRACKETS.

parenthesis (*n.*) (pronounced *puhr-EN-thuh-sis*) uses only its foreign plural, *parentheses* (pronounced *puhr-EN-thuh-SEEZ*), in English. It has two main meanings: "explanatory or additional material not necessary to the main sentence, an aside" and a mark of punctuation, used in pairs. See PARENTHESES.

parenting (*n.*) is a word only a generation old meaning "whatever skills and luck it takes to have and rear children" and "the process of being (a) parent(s)." It is unquestionably Standard, but you should be aware that some conservatives still consider it unnecessary sociological jargon (see JARGON).

par excellence is a French phrase, a cliché in English meaning literally "by way of excellence" and figuratively (the sense in which we use it most often) "the highest form of excellence," "absolutely the best." *Incomparable, splendid, superb,* or *preeminent* will substitute nicely if you're cutting down on foreign phrases.

parkway See THRUWAY.

parlay, parley (*nn., vv.*) *Parlay* is a betting term: the verb (pronounced *PAHR-lai, PAHR-lee,* or *pahr-LAI*) means specifically "to bet the winnings from one race on the next, and so on"; its generalized sense is "to exploit whatever you have into something much more valuable," as in *She parlayed a simple invention and her own promotional skills into a multinational corporation.* The noun *parlay* (stress on first syllable) is "such a string of bets" or, more generally, "the idea of continually rebetting winnings in a series of bets." The verb *parley* (pronounced *PAHR-lee*) means "to confer with an enemy, to negotiate or discuss," and the noun is "such a conference or discussion, especially to arrange a truce or an exchange of prisoners."

parlor, parlour (*n.*) *Parlor* is the American spelling, *parlour* the British. See LIVING ROOM; SPELLING (1).

parlous (*adj.*) is a word that nearly became archaic but then made a comeback, even though some commentators think it is a bit pretentious. It means "perilous, risky, clever," and the like, and it is a cliché when used with *times* and *state: These are parlous times. The economy is in a parlous state.* It is Standard, but use it carefully, for it can be taken as jocular when you don't mean it to be.

parody See BURLESQUE.

parricide, patricide (*nn.*) *Parricide* is the murder of a parent, *patricide* the murder of one's father.

parson See PRIEST.

part (*v.*) combines with the prepositions *with* and *from. Part with* means "to give up": *He hates to part with a dollar. Part from* means "to go away from, to be separated from": *The little girl didn't want to part from her mother.* Both are Standard. See also ON THE PART OF.

part, portion (*nn.*) These words partly overlap. A *part* of something is a fraction or piece of it; a *portion* of something is a share, a (measured or specified) *part* of it.

partake (*v.*) is intransitive and combines with *in* and *of.* It is rather stiff and old-fashioned, particularly when it deals with food and drink rather than general behavior, but it is Standard nonetheless: *My sprained ankle meant that I could not partake of* [*in*] *any of the outdoor activities. We partook liberally in* [*of*] *a huge buffet luncheon.*

part and parcel is old legal language, emphasizing the all-inclusiveness of the thing to which it is applied. It's a cliché, but it also has a venerable quality and is Standard. Use it for serious emphasis, however, not for trivial hyperbole.

partial (*adj.*) meaning "favoring one person or thing more than another," combines with *to* and *toward* and is usually a predicate adjective: *She's partial to chocolate in any form. Grandmother was always partial toward* [*to*] *my brother.* The other use of *partial* is regularly both an attributive adjective and a predicate adjective. It means "incomplete, involving only a part, not the whole": *We had only a partial success, not a complete one.* In a sentence such as *They offered only a partial explanation,* it's not certain whether *partial* means "biased and preferential" or "incomplete, not full." Be careful to make context prevent ambiguity.

partiality (*n.*) combines usually with *for* but sometimes with *to* or *toward: I try not to show partiality for* [*to, toward*] *either twin.*

partially, partly (*advs.*) These adverbs are largely interchangeable, although some commentators insist that *partially* means only "to a limited degree" (*My liver and bacon were only partially cooked; they were practically raw*), and *partly* means only "in part" (*My lunch was only partly cooked; the salad and vegetable were meant to be served cold*). But in fact these distinctions are doubtful: *The stream was partly polluted* and *The stream was partially polluted* mean precisely the same thing to most Americans: any distinction you establish will probably come from context, not from the choice of adverb.

participate (*v.*) combines usually with *in: He participated in several amateur tournaments.* In a different sense, *participate* also combines with *with: He participated with golfers from three other high school teams.*

PARTICIPIAL ADJECTIVES are the present or past participles of verbs, used adjectivally. *To part* is a verb, and *parting,* its present participle, is used as a *participial adjective* in the expression *a parting shot;* the past participle, *parted,* is a *participial adjective* in *a severely parted hairstyle. Participial adjectives* are another sort of functional shift.

PARTICIPIAL ADJECTIVES WITH VERY See VERY.

PARTICIPLES English verbs (e.g., *study, swim*) have present participles ending in *-ing* (*studying, swimming*), and past participles ending in *-ed* (*studied*) or, in strong verbs, in a distinctive morphological form involving either a change of vowel, the dental suffix, some combination of the two, or another distinctive form (*swum, fit, slept, driven*). *Participles* are forms of verbs that can function as nouns (present participles so functioning are called gerunds), as in *Jogging is my usual exercise,* or as adjectives, as in *He goes at a jogging pace.* The present participle is also used with auxiliaries to form the progressive aspect of the verb: *She was writing a short story.* The past participle is used with auxiliaries to form the so-called perfect tenses: *She has written several stories. We had studied one of Emerson's essays.* See also DANGLING MODIFIERS; GENITIVE BEFORE A GERUND.

PARTICLE is a term used in at least two ways in English grammar: (1) it may be either a prefix or suffix, such as those used to change a word from one part of speech to another, as in adding *en-* to *rich* to form **enrich** (adjective to verb) and *-able* to *predict* to form *predictable* (verb to adjective); or (2) it may be any of certain types of function words, such as determiners or prepositions, which usually have unchanging forms and perform functional grammatical duties such as identifying following nouns (determiners), as in **an** *age,* or identifying and governing modifiers such as prepositional phrases (prepositions), as in *seen* **by** *candlelight.*

particular (*adj.*) After *this* or *that, particular* is often judged redundant. But to distinguish *that particular hat* from several others much like it is not wasteful but helpful, and without *particular* the meaning is not the same. Overuse of *particular* occurs most frequently in Conversational and Informal language.

Particular also has other meanings, one of which is "especially or excessively interested in the correctness of details and the niceties of procedure, fussy": *She's very particular about her speech and her dress.* This sense too is Standard.

partly See PARTIALLY.

PARTS OF SPEECH Grammars generally classify words and word groups as *parts of speech* according to meaning, form, function in the sentence, or some other criterion or combination of criteria. The traditional grammar's eight *parts of speech* are noun, pronoun, verb, adjective, adverb, conjunction, preposition, and interjection. Nearly all grammatical systems describe the first five of these *parts of speech,* but some make many further distinctions, distinguishing articles or determiners from adjectives, intensives or intensifiers from adverbs, and auxiliaries from verbs, and listing several other small groups of *parts of speech* under the broad heading of "function words." One of the reasons *parts of speech* sometimes baffle the layperson is variation in terminology, but another is that English readily applies functional shift to change a word's part of speech without any change in form: *We study after supper. The study is my favorite room. My study habits are poor.*

party (*n.*), meaning "person," was at one time thought to be Common or Vulgar English, but in fact the word in this sense, singular and plural, has been in Standard use for centuries. There is a good deal of legal use (*the party of the first part and the party of the second part*) and considerable jocular use (*a really funny old party, but very sound in his views*), but it is also regularly used in serious, quasi-legal contexts as well, as in *We urged the parties to the quarrel to discuss their differences.* Just don't use it as a synonym for *person(s)* in most nontechnical contexts.

pass, pass away, pass on (*vv.*) are all euphemisms for the verb *die,* and we're quite accustomed to reading *passed away* in obituaries, perhaps especially those appearing in small-town newspapers, where almost every reader is personally acquainted with the deceased. *Pass on* is much the same; *pass,* as in *Aunt Mary passed late last night,* is probably dialectal, from Southern or South Midland. Cynics and the worldly wise sometimes ridicule those who can't bring themselves to say *died* and *dead,* but here the euphemism is harmless and prompted by a decent instinct; if *pass away* and *passed on* make the bereaved feel any less miserable, to use them need not always be judged dishonest.

passable, passible (*adjs.*) are homonyms, pronounced *PAS-uh-bul,* but they have different meanings, spellings, and frequency of use. *Passable* is a frequently used word meaning "of roads and bridges, usable or serviceable" and, more generally, "acceptable or at least minimally satisfactory": *His behavior was passable, but no more than that. Passible* is a very rare word meaning "capable of feeling or suffering": *Her nature was exceptionally passible: she empathized and sympathized with everyone and everything.*

pass away See PASS.

passé (*adj.*) is French in origin but, except for spelling and pronunciation, is now an English word. It means "old-fashioned, out-of-date" and hence "uninteresting." American English usually retains the acute accent in spelling (Edited English will still occasionally also use the feminine French form, *passée,* where appropriate, but its use is dwindling). There are three pronunciations: *pas-AI, pahs-AI,* and *PAS-ai,* the latter infrequent in the United States. Some commentators dislike it as another foreign word, but others agree that it's now Standard English.

passed (*past tense, past participle*), **past** (*adv., adj., n., prep.*) These are homophones undistinguishable in speech other than by use; in written

English *passed* is always the past tense and past participle of the verb *pass: I passed Spanish* [*another milestone, the final exam, a kidney stone*]. *Past* is a noun (*She pretends to a shady past*), an adjective (*That's all past history*), an adverb (*Two fire engines went past*), and a preposition (*We stayed past midnight*).

passel (*n.*) is a dialectal form now used Conversationally. It means "a group, a large number," as in *They brought a passel of children with them. Passel* is said to be an altered form of *parcel.*

passerby, passer-by (*n.*) has *passersby* or *passers-by* as plurals. See PLURALS OF COMPOUND NOUNS.

passible See PASSABLE.

passim (*adv.*), pronounced *PAS-im*, is a Latin word meaning "from here on, everywhere, here and there, throughout the work." It is essentially scholar's jargon, usually put in italics; make sure its use won't delay your readers.

PASSIVE VOICE See VOICE (2).

pass on See PASS.

past See PASSED.

pastel, pastille (*nn.*) A *pastel* is a kind of chalky crayon used by artists; a *pastille* is a medicated candy, such as a cough drop.

past history is sometimes called a redundancy, but it is actually a Standard Conversational idiom, hyperbolic but sometimes useful, stressing a more distant record of the past, in contrast to current history. *Past history* is not likely to be criticized except in some Edited English.

pastiche (*n.*) has three current meanings: (1) "a work of literary, musical, or visual art made up of pieces and echoes of other such works—a kind of scrapbook or quilt of recognizable bits"; (2) "an imitation, caricature, or parody of another artistic work"; and (3) as an extension of the first sense, "a hodgepodge, a mixture of this and that, a collection without order." This last meaning tends to undo the force of the first two, and it appears to be getting more and more use in Standard English. Today, if you wish to use either of the first two senses, you'll do well to make context indicate which of them you intend, especially since the third sense is pejorative.

pastie, pasties See PASTY.

pastille See PASTEL.

pastor See PRIEST.

pastoral (*adj.*), **pastorale** (*n.*) *Pastoral* applies to shepherds, sheep, and the rural life or, in its extended sense, to spiritual shepherds—pas-

tors—and their "flocks"—congregations. A *pastorale* is a musical composition suggesting idyllic pastoral or rural subjects; the term is sometimes loosely or figuratively used of literary or dramatic works in that vein.

PAST PARTICIPLE is the third principal part of an English verb. In weak verbs, the pattern is *glide, glided, **glided***; in strong verbs the pattern varies in form: it can be unchanging, as in *set, set, **set***; it can change vowels for past tense and *past participle*, as in *swim, swam, **swum***; it can change vowels and add a final -*n* or -*en* for the *past participle*, as in *fly, flew, **flown*** and *drive, drove, **driven***; or it can have various combinations of these three general patterns. The forms of strong verb *past participles* are often in divided usage (*show, showed, **showed*** or ***shown**; prove, proved, **proved** or **proven***).

PAST PERFECT TENSE (also called the *pluperfect*) is the name some grammars give to the tense made up of the past tense of the auxiliary *have* and the past participle of a verb: *I had gone to the store. They had slept badly.* It describes an action completed sometime in the past. Compare PRESENT PERFECT TENSE. See also PLUPLUPERFECT TENSE.

PAST TENSE, sometimes called the *preterit(e)*, is that form of the verb that describes events or actions that took place earlier: *She **went** to church. He **was** at home.* It is the second principal part of the English verb: a weak verb example is *parade, **paraded**, paraded*; a strong verb example is *write, **wrote**, written.*

pasty (*adj.*), **pasty, pastie, pasties** (*nn.*) The adjective comes from the noun *paste*, and its first syllable is pronounced like it, *PAIST*. It means paste-like in color or texture or both and gives us a stock description of a pale, unhealthy-looking complexion, as in *He is a pasty-faced little runt.* A *pasty* (usually pronounced *PAS-tee*, but sometimes *PAIS-tee*, possibly under influence of the noun *paste*) is a pie or tart, especially a meat pie. The pie is sometimes spelled *pastie*, and its plural is *pasties.* The same spelling gives us the noun used for the small adhesive circles stripteasers sometimes paste on their nipples; this word, however, is always pronounced *PAIS-teez.*

pâté, pate (*nn.*) In spelling the French word for a meat paste, be sure to retain the circumflex and acute accent or at least the acute accent, in order to distinguish the word from *pate*, meaning "the top of the head," as in *His bald pate glowed in the bright lights. Pâté* has two syllables (*pah-TAI*), *pate* only one (*PAIT*).

patent (*adj., n., v.*) has two pronunciations in American English, and fear of confusing them can bother inexperienced speakers. The adjectival sense illustrated in *letters patent,* which are open to public view, and *patent medicine,* is pronounced *PAT-int,* as are all senses having to do with the *patent office,* including the noun *patent* and the verb *to patent.* But the more general adjectival senses, "affording free passage, open, unobstructed" and "visible and obvious," are pronounced *PAIT-int.* The British generally use that pronunciation for the other senses and functions as well, but Americans would say that *to PAT-int* a *PAT-int* medicine and then advertise it widely is to make *PAIT-int* the fact that it's *PAT-int-id.*

pathos, pathetic See BATHOS.

patio (*n.*) The plural is *patios.* See PLURALS OF NOUNS ENDING IN *-O.*

patois (*n.*) is a local or provincial dialect, differing markedly from the Standard language of which it is an offshoot. It clearly marks its speakers as to region or class or both. Sometimes the term is also applied to jargon.

patricide See PARRICIDE.

patrolman See OFFICER.

patron See CLIENT.

patronize (*v.*) means (1) "to be a customer of," as in *I've patronized that hardware store for thirty years; I wouldn't go anywhere else;* (2) "to be a patron or supporter of," as in *We have patronized the symphony society for many years*; and (3) "to treat someone condescendingly, to be snobbish toward or to look down on," as in *She has always patronized me insufferably, every time we've met.* The problem is to prevent the third meaning from inadvertently coloring either of the others and making them into pejoratives. Be sure that your readers or listeners understand which sense you intend.

pavement (*n.*) in American English is usually "a paved surface, such as a road": *The crate of tomatoes fell from the truck to the pavement.* But in Britain and Philadelphia, the *pavement* is the sidewalk: *We were allowed to skate on the pavement but not in the street.*

pavilion (*n.*), frequently misspelled, has only one *l.* Don't spell it like *million.*

pawn off (*v.*) is a slang idiom, possibly an adaptation from *palm off,* which means "to pass off," as in *The pitchman was trying to pawn off these awful neckties as genuine silk.* Use *palm off.*

pay (*v.*) spells its past tense and past participle *paid.* The single exception occurs when sailors *pay out* rope: then the past tense and past participle are spelled *payed.*

payment in kind See SALARY.

peace See PIECE.

peaceable, peaceful (*adjs.*) They do overlap a bit, but the distinctions can be useful. *Peaceable* means "inclined toward peace, quiet, well-behaved, not quarrelsome," as in *He was a peaceable man, never ruffled and not interested in strife of any sort. Peaceful* means "quiet, undisturbed, tranquil, and the opposite of warlike or noisy," as in *It was a quiet, peaceful Sunday afternoon.* A *peaceful* person is likely to be resting; a *peaceable* one is likely to avoid unpleasantness.

peace officer See OFFICER.

peak, peek, pique (*nn., vv.*) These homophones are spelled differently and have different meanings as well. A *peak* is the top of a mountain or of something else high and pointed, and its verb means "to reach or come to the topmost point." A *peek* is a quick and perhaps furtive glance, and the verb means "to take a quick, furtive look." The noun *pique* means "resentment, offense taken," as in *She said unpleasant things in a fit of pique* (note that *fit of pique* is a cliché), and the verb means "to cause resentment or, more commonly, to rouse, excite, or stimulate," as in *Her sudden departure piqued everyone's curiosity* (*to pique someone's curiosity* is also a cliché, but still a useful one).

peal, peel (*nn., vv.*) These are homophones. The noun *peal* is the ringing of bells, a set of bells itself, and any loud, extended noise, including *peals of laughter* or *thunder.* As a verb it simply means "to ring or make such a sound": *The thunder pealed through the valley.* The verb *peel* means "to cut away the skin of a fruit, etc., to pare, or to have skin come off on its own," as in *Her sunburn peeled and itched.* The noun *peel* has three referents: "the skin of a fruit or vegetable" (*a banana peel*), "the long wooden shovel the baker uses to remove bread from the oven," and "a tower or fortified dwelling built in the Scottish border country during the sixteenth century."

peccadillo (*n.*) means "a trivial or minor sin." The plural is *peccadilloes.* See PLURALS OF NOUNS ENDING IN *-O.*

peculiar (*adj.*) means "unique," as in *The practice is peculiar to that island;* hence it also means "odd, special, or unusual" and in that sense is often pejorative: *She wears peculiar clothes.*

ped-, pedo-, paed-, paedi- *(prefixes)* The first set, *ped-, pedo-,* is a Greek prefix familiar in the words *pediatrics, pederasty, pedagogue,* and others having to do with *child* and *children.* This prefix must not be confused with the Latin prefix from *pedalis* and *pes, pedis,* meaning "foot," from which we get *pedal, pedestrian, pedestal,* and *pedicure,* among others. Don't guess wrong; consult your dictionary. See also DIGRAPHS; LIGATURES.

pedagogue, pedagog *(n.)* The preferred spelling is *pedagogue,* but *pedagog* is now also Standard. Compare CATALOG. See SPELLING (2).

pedal *(n., v.),* **pedaler, peddler** *(nn.),* **peddle** *(v.)* A *pedal* is a foot-operated lever on a bicycle, a piano, or another machine, and the verb *to pedal* means "to operate a *pedal* or *pedals.*" The addition of the agentive ending gives us *pedaler,* "one who *pedals.*" A *peddler* is the person who travels about selling small items from door to door, and the verb is a back-formation from the noun, meaning "to do such traveling and selling." Of course *peddlers* who make their rounds on bicycles are also *pedalers,* but to confuse the two in spelling is a shibboleth.

pee *(n., v.)* is a euphemism dating from the eighteenth century from the initial letter of the Middle English word *piss* when that word fell into disfavor. But *pee* has turned out not to be euphemism enough: it's usually considered Vulgar and is taboo in many venues. *Urinate* and *urine* are now the Standard terms, and there are of course many other euphemisms.

peek See PEAK.

peel See PEAL.

peer *(n., v.),* **peerage** *(n.),* **peerless** *(adj.),* **pier** *(n.)* The noun *peer* means "one of equal rank or standing" or "a member of the British nobility, the *peerage.*" Something *peerless* is "without an equal" and hence "matchless": *He was a peerless golfer, the club champion year after year.* The verb means something quite unrelated: "to look narrowly, to try to see more clearly," as in *The baby peered over the arm of the chair.* A *pier* is a heavy vertical structure supporting a part of a bridge or a part of a building, and by extension a structure supported on *piers* stretching out from a shore and over the water is also called a *pier.*

PEJORATION, PEJORATED, PEJOR-ATING, PEJORATIVE, DEGRADA-TION, DEGRADED, DEGRADING These synonymous terms stand for a kind of semantic change in which a change in association or reputation of the referent causes a word to fall in status: our word *vulgar* comes from a Latin word meaning simply "the common people," but even though we keep the word *Vulgate* to stand for a particular Bible written in the common Latin of its day, the general associations with "the common people" have dragged the English word *vulgar* down to its present meanings, "characteristic of the common people, and hence common, cheap, crude, gross," and so on, to its lowest ebb, "obscene." In its most-used meanings, the word *vulgar* has *pejorated* greatly.

pencil See INK.

pendant *(n.),* **pendent** *(adj.)* In Edited English the usual spelling of the necklace-like piece of jewelry is *pendant,* whereas the adjective *pendent* means "hanging," as in *There were huge icicles pendent from the edge of the cliff.* But (alas for simplicity), each spelling is also a rare Standard variant of the other.

penetrable *(adj.)* has four syllables, pronounced *PEN-uh-truh-bul.* It means "susceptible of penetration," and it is the only adjective you need for that meaning; *penetratable* (*PEN-uh-TRAIT-uh-bul*) is a nonce word.

Pennsylvania Dutch See DUTCH.

pensioner See SENIOR CITIZEN.

penultimate, ultimate *(adjs.)* *Penultimate* is not more *ultimate* than *ultimate: ultimate* means "last," and *penultimate* means "next-to-last." Rhyme the first syllable of *penultimate* with either *den* or *dean,* and stress the second syllable.

peon See PAEAN.

people, persons *(nn.)* There is a fair-sized history of complaint about the use of *people* as a plural with specific numbers, and some older conservatives still don't like the practice. But both *seven people* and *seven persons* are Standard, with *people* getting a good deal more use than *persons.* Any difference is stylistic; to some people, *persons* may seem a bit more formal. Note too that recently *person* has replaced *-man* as the second element of many occupational compounds: *chairperson, spokesperson, deliveryperson,* and the like turn up fairly frequently, along with even newer coinages. Some may catch on and remain in the vocabulary; others may fade quickly. See INCLUSIVE LANGUAGE; SEXIST LANGUAGE.

per (*adv., prep.*) *Per* did indeed begin as Latin, but it has long since become English and is now unquestionably Standard in all but one use. When it means "for each," as in *We paid twenty dollars per day,* and "through, or by," as in *They sent us money per postal money order,* the preposition is Standard. When it means "according to," as in *We did the work per the landlord's instructions,* and when combined with *as* in *As per the manual that came with the machine, no extra oil is required,* some people prefer limiting it to Conversational and Informal use. But these two are so heavily employed in business and governmental writing that many Standard users don't rule them out even in Formal writing.

The adverbial use, as in *He was doing about eighty per when he went into the skid,* is an abbreviated version of *eighty miles per hour,* and it should be used only in Casual or Impromptu English.

peradventure (*adv., n.*) is archaic, but the noun in particular occurs occasionally in elevated, pretentious, or whimsical use, usually with *beyond* or occasionally with *without,* in an idiomatic use with either *doubt* or *chance: Beyond any peradventure of doubt* [or *chance*], *he will win the election. Without peradventure of doubt* [or *chance*], *our leaders will prevail.* The adverb occurs even less frequently, usually as a sentence adverb meaning "perhaps" or "by chance," as in *Peradventure some good will come of all this upheaval.*

per annum, per capita, per diem are Latin tags so widely used today that their cliché status usually prevents them from sounding very foreign or very learned. They are business jargon, and people who want to avoid jargon prefer *She earns over $40,000 a year,* to *over $40,000 per annum,* which sounds pretentious. *Per capita* occurs more frequently: *The deficit works out at about $5,000 per capita,* but *per person* would work as well, and *apiece* might hit even harder. *Per diem* is more nearly unexceptional today because it has become a noun in very wide, fully Standard use, meaning "the money available for daily expenses of room, board, travel, and the like": *His per diem was too low to permit him any splendid dinners.* Rather than *She had an expense allowance of $150 per diem,* however, many would prefer a native English modifier: *She had an expense allowance of $150 a day.*

perceive (*v.*), **perceived** (*adj.*) There are two meanings for each part of speech: "to observe, see," as in *He could faintly perceive the outline of the cliffs;* and "to understand, to imagine," as in *They perceive us as unwilling allies.* The past tense form meaning "observed, literally seen," is less frequently encountered than is the past participle, especially in the passive voice figurative sense of "understood, imagined (to be)": *We are perceived as unwilling to negotiate.* That one is also regularly encountered as a participial adjective in adjunct position: *Management's perceived unwillingness to negotiate precipitated the strike.*

percent, per cent (*adv., adj., n.*) Both spellings are acceptable, but Americans increasingly prefer *percent.*

percent, percentage (*nn.*) *Percentage* is the more widely accepted noun, especially in Edited English, but Informal use of *percent* (*What percent of your time do you spend watching TV?*) seems thoroughly established. Limit *percentage,* meaning "advantage or gain," as in *There's no percentage in my taking the job,* to Conversational and Informal use.

perceptible, perceptive, percipient, perceptual, sensible, palpable, visible, tangible, audible (*adjs.*) All these words have to do with what the senses can take in. Something *perceptible* can be observed by the senses; the adjective refers especially to that moment when the thing perceived can be only faintly observed: *The outlines of the house were just perceptible in the mist.* Someone *perceptive* is able to use the senses well: *She was very perceptive—she noticed his pallor at once. Percipient* means much the same as *perceptive,* and it is also sometimes used as a noun, meaning "a person especially adept at perceiving." *Perceptual* is applied to anything related to perceiving: *Her perceptual powers are much weaker now than they were before her health began to fail.* Something *sensible* (aside from the "reasonable" meanings) is something that can be sensed: *We were sensible of something breathing in the next room.* These next four all refer to particular senses: if a thing is *palpable,* you can touch it; if it's *tangible,* you can grasp it; if it's *visible,* you can see it; and if it's *audible,* you can hear it. All are Standard in these uses.

perchance (*adv.*) means "by chance, perhaps, maybe" but is old-fashioned and literary. In most uses today it is self-consciously elevated or whimsical. Consider it archaic, and spell it as one word.

percipient See PERCEPTIBLE.

percolate (*v.*), **percolator** (*n.*) Pronounce them *PUHR-kuh-LAIT* and *PUHR-kuh-LAIT-uhr,* and avoid the common mispronunciation *PUHR-kyoo-LAIT(-uhr)*, along with the misspelling it sometimes causes: *perculate*. See also NUCLEAR.

per diem See PER ANNUM.

peremptory, perfunctory (*adjs.*) *Peremptory* (pronounced *puhr-EMPT-tuh-ree*) means "something that can't or won't be denied" and hence "something dogmatic and dictatorial," as in *She was a tyrant, peremptory in ordering us about.* A *peremptory challenge* in the courts brings about the automatic dismissal of a possible juror. *Perfunctory* (pronounced *puhr-FUHNK-tuh-ree*) means "trivial, something done without attention, routinely, carelessly," as in *His performance was perfunctory and lackluster.*

perennial See ANNUAL.

perfect (*adj.*), in its strictest meaning, is considered an absolute adjective and is not qualifiable through comparison. But much of the time we use *perfect* as an ordinary adjective, and perhaps because of our love of hyperbole, we seem constantly to find things that are *more perfect than others* or that are *the most perfect of all.* Edited English, especially Formal Edited English, and the Oratorical level usually try to hold to the absolute adjective rule for *perfect,* but otherwise Standard English merely prefers *more nearly perfect* and *most nearly perfect* when it thinks of doing so and lets many another comparison of *perfect* pass without comment at all other levels.

PERFECT INFINITIVE There is nothing wrong with the *perfect infinitive*; the problem is the sequence of tenses. *I would have liked to have met* her means that "back then I would have liked already to have met her, but today I have no preference," but in Conversation and Informal writing it frequently is intended to mean "I would (now) like to have met her (back then)," which would better be said that way, making clear the time of the initial liking. When using the *perfect infinitive,* use particular care with the time sequencing of nearby verbs.

perfectionist (*n.*) *Perfectionists* are those who seek to have everything they touch be perfect. These high standards are often too much for the rest of us, however, and the noun is in many uses a pejorative applied to those we find so finical that we'd finally prefer someone with a few flaws but more common sense.

perfectly (*adv., intensifier*) is regularly used as an intensifier at every level of Standard American English: *She was perfectly furious at his unconcern.* Don't overdo it.

PERFECT TENSES For the verb *see,* the present perfect tense is *I have seen,* the past perfect is *I had seen,* and the future perfect is *I will have seen.*

perfume (*n., v.*) The noun is usually pronounced with primary stress on the first syllable (*PUHR-FYOOM*), but occasionally *puhr-FYOOM* occurs; the verb is usually *puhr-FYOOM,* occasionally *PUHR-FYOOM.* See ODOR.

perfunctory See PEREMPTORY.

perimeter See PARAMETER.

PERIOD 1 This punctuation mark (.) is used to indicate the ends of sentences or sentence fragments that do not use question marks or exclamation points. Conventionally it occurs at the ends of some abbreviations, after numbers and letters that indicate the items in lists of outlines, and after initials in a person's name; in some stylebooks, *periods* are specified as the punctuation in act, scene, and line references (II.iii.45–48) and the like. See also ELLIPSIS (3).

period See STANZA.

period 2 (of time) has been objected to as redundant, but it isn't always so. Sometimes style and meaning are aided by a fuller locution: *For recurrent periods of three or four months she would feel strong and vigorous.* Context should control: *We stayed there a long period of time* is wordy, but *What period of time are you thinking of?* is a question about the unit of time to be specified—a month, a year, a day? The locution also can sometimes avoid confusion, since *period* does not mean only a simple measure of time—witness the name of the punctuation mark, the specialized use in compounds such as *period piece* and *period costume,* and formal rhetoric's *periodic sentence.*

PERIODIC SENTENCE is a sentence with its main clause at the end, following all subordinate clauses and other elements: *That night, in the rain and the wind, when we could see no lights in the town, we slipped away.*

peripheral (*adj., n.*) The adjective combines with the preposition *to,* as in *Their other complaints are peripheral to the one about the food service. Peripherals* are also various kinds of equipment—printers, displays, and other accessories—to be attached to or used with computers. Avoid the mispronunciation *puhr-IF-ee-uhl(s)*; it's *puhr-IF-uhr-uhl(s).*

PERIPHRASTIC (*adj., n.*), **PERIPHRASIS** (*n.*), **PERIPHRASTIC COMPARATIVE, PERIPHRASTIC GENITIVE** *Per-*

iphrastic structures apply circumlocution (which is the general meaning of *periphrasis*) to grammatical functions such as the genitive and comparison. Both these functions can be signaled by morphology—that is, by inflectional endings (*the table's finish, the handsomer actor*)—but with the *periphrastic,* English employs a function word construction instead: *the finish of the table* (with *of* and occasionally other prepositions, such as *for,* in the *periphrastic genitive; see also* GENITIVE CASE and other GENITIVE entries) and *the more handsome actor* (with *more* in the *periphrastic comparative; see also* ADJECTIVES [1]; ADVERBS [1]). *The birds did fly* is a *periphrastic* form of *The birds flew. Periphrasis* is simply the name of the process, and it offers stylistic variety.

perk (*n.*) (plural: *perks*), is the clipped form of *perquisite* (which see). It's slang, so limit it to Informal or Conversational use: *The perks of my job were worth more than the wages.*

permanence, permanency (*nn.*) These synonyms mean "a state of being permanent." *Permanence* has the higher frequency in Standard use; of the plurals, however, *permanancy's permanencies* occurs more often.

permeate (*v.*) combines with the prepositions *by* and *with: His speeches are permeated by* [*with*] *pessimism. Through* and *throughout* are also used, but *permeate* is better off without them, taking a direct object instead: *Her unflagging energy permeates* [*through, throughout*] *the organization.*

permissible, permissive (*adjs.*) "Anything allowable, anything that is permitted" is *permissible: It is permissible to repeat that course once for credit. Permissive* means "tolerant, lenient," or "over-indulgent," as in *Permissive parents rear disobedient children.* Pejoration has marked *permissive* particularly in this last sense.

PERMISSIVENESS is a loaded term used by conservatives to describe what is at best simply a view held by liberals in language matters. It tends to welcome and encourage novelty and change as bringing life and color to language use, and its champions are less deferential to convention and tradition than conservatives think wise. But the term *permissiveness* is used mostly with pejorative intent, by those who consider it a weakness, a failure of nerve or taste. Liberal usage is perhaps a more nearly objective label. See also PURISTS.

permit, admit, allow (*vv.*) These can combine with *of* in idioms, as in *The new regulations are general enough to permit* [*admit, allow*] *of a*

great deal of interpretation. The idioms mean just what the verbs mean by themselves, but the combinations often sound more Formal and stiff.

pernickety See PERSNICKETY.

perpendicular, vertical (*adjs., nn.*) Something *perpendicular* must be at a precise right angle to another line or plane but need not necessarily itself be *vertical*; something *vertical* is always at least roughly at right angles to the ground, the floor, or the horizon.

perpetrate, perpetuate (*vv.*) To *perpetrate* something is "to commit a bad act, to do something criminal or hurtful": *The enemy perpetrated several acts of sabotage.* To *perpetuate something* is "to preserve something, to make it last": *They raised a monument to perpetuate the memory of the victory.*

perquisite (*n.*), **prerequisite** (*adj., n.*) A *perquisite* is "something received over and above salary, a privilege granted to the holder of the position, a tip or an extra benefit": *One perquisite of his new post was a reserved parking place; perquisite* regularly takes *of* (*the perquisites of her new job*). (See also PERK.) A *prerequisite* is "something required prior to the thing ultimately sought": *At least one advanced degree is a prerequisite for job application in this field.* As an adjective *prerequisite* means that the referent of the word to which it is attached must be acquired first, before something else is sought, as in *The prerequisite forms must be filed at least a week before the interview. Prerequisite* combines more often with *for* and *to,* but occasionally with *of: Membership in a political party is a prerequisite for* [*to, of*] *voting in a primary election in this state.*

persevere (*v.*) combines with the prepositions *in* and *with: If you persevere with* [*in*] *your studies, you may win a scholarship.* Don't spell it *perservere.*

persistently See CONSISTENTLY.

persnickety, pernickety (*adjs.*) Both adjectives mean "over-particular, over-fussy." *Persnickety* is the American version of Scottish and British *pernickety,* though most Americans will also accept the British version.

PERSON is a grammatical concept expressed in the forms of personal pronouns (which see) and the inflections of the verbs that agree with them. In most verbs, only the third *person* present tense singular has a distinctive form to agree with its subject in number: *it runs.* All other *persons* merely *run.* And of the personal pronouns, only the third *person* singular forms agree with their antecedents in gender as well as in number.

persona (*n.*) (pronounced *puhr-SO-nuh*; the plural is either *personae*—final syllable pronounced either *-nee* or *-nei*—or *personas*) has two central meanings as a present-day English word, one based ultimately on its Latin etymon, which was "a Roman actor's mask"; today that meaning has become "the personality we show the world" and, more particularly, "the personality we consciously create to show the world": *His platform manner presents a persona urbane, witty, and cool, but at home he's impulsive, impassioned, and voluble.* The other sense most used today is that based on Jungian psychology: the soul (*anima*) is the inner self, the *persona* is the outer self, that in which the inner one is wrapped.These two meanings of *persona* overlap nicely, especially with echoes of the theater (*dramatis personae,* which we use always in the plural and translate "the [cast of] characters in the play") and the general sense of the person the actor creates: *His persona in this act shifts gradually from one driven by unhappiness to one driven by malice.* Both senses are Standard, but context will have to make clear which is to be understood by the reader.

persona grata See PERSONA NON GRATA.

personal (*adj.*), **personnel** (*n., adj.*) *Personal* is often criticized as being redundant: *That's my personal opinion* is wordier but not otherwise different from *That's my opinion.* But some other applications of this very high frequency word seem to impart useful information: *She has an entourage of some size, including her personal maid, her personal secretary, and her personal trainer.* We understand these people to be dedicated, like *personal computers,* to the requirements of this one woman; the idea of exclusivity adds to our sense of her importance, even if the use of *personal* doesn't add much other information.

Personal and *personnel* come from the same root, but they are spelled and pronounced differently (*PUHR-suhn-uhl* and *PUHR-suhn-NEL*) and have only *person-* in common: *personnel* as noun means "people, especially employees," and "the field of employee matters itself" and as adjective refers to "departments responsible for hiring and keeping records about the employees of an enterprise."

personality (*n.*), in the sense of "a celebrity, a famous person" is sometimes considered a cliché; it may not occur often in Formal or Oratorical situations but is Standard nonetheless: *She's be-*

come a television personality. Limit its use meaning "unusually engaging or attractive," as in *He's got a lot of things going for him—looks, money, and personality,* to Informal and Conversational situations, unless you modify it: *He has an engaging personality.*

personally (*adv.*) is much used in Casual speech and Informal writing to add an emphasis we fear may be lacking when we talk about ourselves: *Personally, I never eat broccoli. I personally would never have expected her to do it.* At most other levels *personally* will be thought redundant unless the emphasis it provides makes clear a semantic distinction, as in *I've seen him several times, but I don't know him personally* (meaning "I've never met him").

PERSONAL PRONOUNS have some distinctive forms for number, person, and case, and usage problems generally arise when these forms fail to match Standard English expectations. Here are the forms (those marked with asterisks are sometimes called absolute possessive pronouns):

PLURAL CASE	FIRST PERSON	SECOND PERSON	THIRD PERSON
Nominative	we	you	they
Genitive	our, ours*	your, yours*	their, theirs*
Objective	us	you	them

SINGULAR CASE	FIRST PERSON	SECOND PERSON	THIRD PERSON
Nominative	I	you	he, she, it
Genitive	my, mine*	your, yours*	his, her, hers, its
Objective	me	you	him, her, it

There are also some archaic second person pronouns, today used mainly in certain religious contexts: singular *thou, thy, thine, thee*; plural *ye, your, ye.* Quakers traditionally have used *thee* in both nominative and objective cases.

None of the genitive pronouns ending in *-s* takes an apostrophe: never spell them *her's, it's, our's, your's,* or *their's.*

persona non grata, persona grata These Latin tags come originally from the jargon of diplomacy: someone who is *persona non grata* is a foreigner officially unwelcome in another country. We use both terms in extended senses, mainly about people unwelcome or welcome in any figurative sense. *Persona grata* is much less often encountered. See FOREIGN PHRASES.

personate See PERSONIFY.

PERSONIFICATION is a figure of speech wherein an idea, an object, or some other inanimate entity is represented as though it were a person: *Then Lechery appeared, leering and making lewd gestures toward his audience.*

personify, impersonate, personate (*vv.*) *Personify* means "to represent something inanimate as though living" or "to be the living example of something inanimate," as in *I've got a new canoe, and she's a beauty* or *To me that judge personifies integrity.* To *personate* is a rather low frequency verb meaning "to play the part of, to masquerade as someone else, often with illegal intent"; it is only rarely used as a synonym for *personify. Impersonate* means "to imitate or play the role of," as in *By impersonating a police officer, she was able to gain entrance to the hall.*

personnel See PERSONAL.

persons See INCLUSIVE LANGUAGE; INDIVIDUAL; PARTY; PEOPLE; PERSON; SEXIST LANGUAGE.

perspective (*adj., n.*), **prospective** (*adj.*) The spelling and pronunciation of the first syllables, always unstressed, make all the difference: The noun *perspective* (first syllable pronounced *puhr-*) means "the representation of objects to the eye so that their relative distance and position are clear" and hence, figuratively, "a point of view, perhaps from a distance, for seeing events or ideas": *Later, when she had time to get a new perspective on what had happened, she understood.* The adjective represents a simple functional shift: *He bought a small painting, a perspective view of the harbor. Prospective* (first syllable pronounced *pro-* or *prah-*) means "occurring or likely to occur in the future" and hence "expected," as in *He's a prospective father, and he beams at the thought.*

perspicuous, perspicacious (*adjs.*), **perspicacity, perspicuity** (*nn.*) If you display *perspicacious* qualities, you appear to have good judgment; you are perceptive, and therefore you have *perspicacity.* If you display *perspicuous* qualities, you are clear of statement, lucid; you make things clear, and hence you have *perspicuity.* These relatively low frequency pairs may be hard to keep distinct, but there are those who will fault you for confusing them: look them up rather than risk using them inaccurately, or choose instead some words you understand.

perspiration (*n.*) Spell and pronounce the prefix *per-* (*puhr-*), not *pres-* (*pres-*).

persuade (*v.*) most often takes *to* plus an infinitive, as in *We persuaded her to come with us,* a *that* clause, as in *We persuaded her that she should come with us,* or any of several other prepositions, among them *of, into, by, about, with: He was finally persuaded of his error. Can you persuade her into accepting our offer? I was persuaded by her letter. I was persuaded about* [*with*] *his sincerity.* See CONVINCE.

persuasion (*n.*) is most often used to mean "the use of argument or other nonviolent means to shape opinion or influence actions," as in *We used persuasion, not force, to win them over.* It also once meant "religious preference or membership," as in *She's of the Baptist persuasion,* but it has jocularly and figuratively been used to apply to everything from membership in political, national, or racial groups to representations of one item in a collection: *She served bowls of fruits and nuts of every persuasion under the sun.* Most figurative uses these days are tiresomely arch and heavy-footed.

pertinent (*adj.*) combines most often with *to* but occasionally with *for* or *in,* all followed by a noun, as in *His remarks were particularly pertinent to* [*for, in*] *the occasion*; it will sometimes combine with *to* plus an infinitive, as in *It will be pertinent to review all the proposals now.*

peruse (*v.*), **perusal** (*n.*), **peruser** (*n.*) The verb means "to examine carefully, to read or study," but it has also come to mean "to glance through, read over, or skim," and the noun *perusal* is the doing of these things. Both verb and noun are a bit stuffy and bookish: *read, skim,* or *study,* depending on your meaning, would be simpler and in most contexts less likely to confuse (compare SCAN). *Peruser,* "one who peruses," should be similarly restricted; *perusers* are readers unless you're feeling whimsical or unusually literary.

perverse (*adj.*), **perversity, perversion** (*n.*), **pervert** (*n., v.*), **perverted** (*adj.*) To be *perverse* (to show *perversity*) is to be "contrary, stubborn, or wrong-headed," as in *He's not really opposed to our going; he's just being perverse. Pervert* (the Standard verb is *puhr-VUHRT*) is "to turn aside" and hence "to corrupt or misdirect," and the noun (*PUHR-vuhrt*) is "one who does such things, especially a sexual deviate." The "corrupt" sense is used frequently in a sexual context: *perversions* in that sense are "abnormal sexual practices or tendencies." We sometimes hear a Substandard *PREE-vuhrt* for *pervert.*

The verb *pervert* combines with *by, into,* and *to* in Standard English: *He has perverted my meaning by quoting out of context. They will pervert his decisions into* [*to*] *travesties of justice.*

pessimistic (*adj.*) is Standard whether it modifies person(s) or thing(s): *He holds pessimistic views of everything.*

pH is the term chemists use to indicate the acidity or alkalinity of a solution. Distilled water is neutral, with a *pH* of 7; a *pH* higher than 7 is alkaline, one lower than 7 is acidic. The symbol is jargon beyond the experience of a good many readers, but where you feel you must use it, the idiom is *a pH of* followed by a number. In speech, simply say the names of the letters *pee-AICH.*

phalanx (*n.*), pronounced *FAI-LANKS* and meaning "the ancient military infantry formation with overlapping shields" or "any massed group of people with a common purpose" has two plurals: *phalanxes,* made on the regular English pattern and by far the more frequently encountered, and the old Latin form, *phalanges* (*fai-LAN-jeez*), which is used always and only when the referents are the digital bones of the hand or foot. See FOREIGN PLURALS.

phantasy See FANTASY.

pharmacist See DRUGGIST.

pharmacopeia, pharmacopoeia (*n.*), the book listing drugs and other medical remedies, may be spelled either *pharmacopeia* or *pharmacopoeia,* although Americans prefer the first spelling, without the ligature (*æ*) or the digraph (oe). Pronounce it *FAHRM-uh-ko-PEE-uh.*

phase See FAZE.

phenom (*n.*), usually pronounced *FEE-nahm,* is slang, a clipped form of *phenomenon*; in print it occurs mainly in the journalese of sports and other entertainments.

phenomenon (*n.*) was the singular, *phenomena* the plural when English borrowed the word from Greek. These are still the forms required in Edited English and other Formal and Oratorical uses. But today *phenomena* is widely used (but often much decried) as a singular at most other levels, where its plural is sometimes also *phenomena* and sometimes *phenomenas.* But Standard English limits these two almost entirely to the spoken language, and unlike *data, agenda,* and other words borrowed with their foreign plurals that then changed their patterns, *phenomenon* is still in divided usage. It means "an observable event or occurrence," "something very unusual," and—an extension of the "unusual" sense—"a person of unusual capabilities

or attainments." Compare CRITERION; PHENOM.

-phile, -phobe (*suffixes*) The suffix *-phile* means "someone who likes, desires, or loves (someone or something)": *An Anglophile delights in all things English.* The suffix *-phobe* is an antonym of *-phile*; it means "someone who dislikes, fears, or hates (someone or something)": *An Anglophobe hates all things English.*

Philippine(s), Filipino (*adjs., nn.*), **Pilipino** (*n.*) The islands are the *Philippine Islands* or the *Philippines,* but *Filipino* both as adjective (*Filipino culture*) and noun for the name of a citizen (a *Filipino*) is Standard and carries no trace of ethnic denigration. *Pilipino* is one name for one of the languages spoken in the Philippines.

PHILOLOGIST, PHILOLOGY See LINGUIST.

-phobe See -PHILE.

phobia See MANIA.

Phoebe, phoebe, Phoebus, Phoenicia(n), phoenix, Phoenix These are nearly all the words whose American English spellings retain both orthographic indications of their classical origins: the initial *ph-* and the *-oe-* digraph or ligature.

phone 1 (*n., v.*), meaning the noun *telephone* and the verb *to telephone,* is an aphetic word now Standard at all levels except the Oratorical and the upper reaches of Edited English. Some dictionaries still label it Colloquial, however.

phone 2 (*n.*) means "any speech sound." See PHONETICS.

PHONEMES are the smallest clusters of varied speech sounds that speakers of a language hear as distinctive units in the sounds of that natural language. One scheme (modified from Trager and Smith 1957) for listing the American English phonemes is this: consonants /p/, /b/, /t/, /d/, /k/, /g/, /č/, /j/, /f/, /v/, /ɵ/, /ð/, /s/, /z/, /š/, /ž/, /m/, /n/, /ŋ/, /l/, /r/, /w/, /y/, /h/; vowels /i/, /e/, /æ/, /ɨ/, /ə/, /a/, /u/, /o/, /ɔ/; semivowels /y/, /w/, /H/. In this manual, sounds are generally represented by the letters that symbolize them, in italic, followed by the word *sound:* See PHONETICS.

PHONETICS, PHONEMICS, PHONOLOGY *Phonetics* is the study of the sounds of languages—how we produce them, what their waves are like in the air, and how their hearers perceive them. Conventionally, *phonetics* transcribes sounds in square brackets ([ ]), as does the International Phonetic Alphabet. *Phonemics* is the study of the phonemes, the smallest units of linguistically distinctive sound peculiar to a given language. These sounds are conventionally transcribed within virgules (/ /). *Phonology* is the overall name for the study of *phonemics*, *phonetics*, and all other aspects of speech sounds.

In the words *tip, bitten,* and *cat,* the English phoneme is /t/. But phonetically, each of these sounds is different in most people's speech: [t] as in *tip* is exploded with enough air escaping to move a tissue hung in front of the lips. The medial [t] in *bitten* is one American English rarely explodes; indeed, the British (who do explode it) usually hear the American sound as a [d]. The final [t] in *cat* is sometimes exploded, sometimes not. Phonetically these three are different sounds; they are called allophones of the phoneme /t/.

phony, phoney (*adj., n.*) *Phony* is the usual American spelling (the plural is *phonies*), *phoney* a fading variant (and the usual British spelling). This Americanism as an adjective has a present status of Standard in all but the most Formal and Oratorical uses. Most Edited English accepts an adjectival use: *They called it the phony war.* As noun *phony* is still restricted by many Standard users to Conversational or Informal use: *Most of the people in the room looked like crooks or phonies to me.*

photo, picture (*nn.*) (the plural is *photos*) is a clipping of *photograph,* and it is Standard only in Informal and Conversational use and some Semiformal writing, except in some combinations such as *photo opportunity, photo film, photo journalism,* and the like, which are mostly limited to the Edited English characteristic of our major newspapers. We have other short words we can use instead of the noun *photograph* (*snapshot, candid, snap, shot,* and *picture*), and the idiom *to take a picture* is just as Standard although not so Formal as *to take* [or *make*] *a photograph.* The verb *photograph,* both transitive and intransitive, is Standard in all uses, including the curious ambiguity of *She photographs well,* which is sometimes called a notional passive and can mean either that she is an excellent subject for photographs or that she can operate a camera well. The idiom *to take good pictures* has exactly the same possibly ambiguous meanings. A *picture,* of course, can be a photograph, a drawing, or a painting.

PHRASAL PREPOSITIONS These are also called compound prepositions; English has many of them (*in back of, on top of, on behalf of,* etc.), and American English often uses them where many conservatives would prefer a single word (*behind, atop, for,* etc.). They frequently begin in prepositional phrases that then become frozen into *phrasal prepositions.* Most frequently heard strings of this sort are Standard.

PHRASAL VERBS are combined forms (of verb plus preposition[s] or adverb) that have taken on meanings different from that of the sum of their parts: *put up with, walk through, run in, run over,* and many, many more.

PHRASE A *phrase* is a syntactic unit of two or more words that do not make up a clause. See ADJECTIVE; ADVERB; FAZE; PREPOSITION (2); VERB PHRASE.

PHRASE AND CLAUSE MODIFIERS work grammatically in the same way: *After dinner, we went for a walk. After we had had our dinner, we went for a walk.* Coming at the beginning of the sentence, each of these structures works adverbially, as a sentence modifier. If we place each after the main clause instead, it modifies the predicate (and the verb in the predicate): *We went for a walk after dinner. We went for a walk after we had had our dinner.* In *We went for an after-dinner walk,* what was the prepositional phrase turns into an adjectival modifying *walk,* a part of a larger noun-plus-modifier structure marked by the determiner *an.* Note that although the sentence is clumsy and odd, grammatically it will still work if we move the subordinate clause modifier into the same position: *We went for an after-we-had-had-our-dinner walk* turns the clause into an adjectival that works exactly as did the prepositional phrase in that position. Note too that *after* in these two constructions is two kinds of function word, depending on the following structure—a preposition if followed by a noun, a subordinating conjunction if followed by a clause.

-phth- This medial consonant cluster occurs in few English words (*diphtheria, diphthong, ophthalmology, naphtha*), and in each instance the clustered *f* and *θ* (as in **thin**) sounds, both unvoiced, are usually shortened to *p* plus *θ*, a stop plus a continuant rather than two continuants. Therefore *diphtheria* has two Standard pronunciations—*dip-THIR-ee-yuh* and *dif-THIR-ee-yuh*—and so it is with the other three words too.

physic, physics, physique (*nn.*) *Physic* is singular and in English means "a medicine, especially a laxative"; *physics* is a plural, but as an academic subject or branch of natural science it is usually treated as singular: *Physics is the most interesting of the courses I'm taking. Physic* and *physics* are pronounced *FIZ-ik(s). Physique* means "the structure, build, development" of the human body: *Proper diet and exercise can* *help maintain a good physique.* Pronounce it *fi-ZEEK.*

pianist, accompanist (*nn.*) Both these people play the piano; a *pianist* is a soloist; an *accompanist* plays an accompaniment on the piano (or some other instrument), for a singer or singers or performer(s) on other instruments. *Pianist* has three Standard pronunciations: *PEE-uh-nist, pee-AN-ist,* and *PYAN-ist*; the first is the most widely heard. *Accompanist* is this word's much-preferred Standard form; *accompanyist* exists as a very rare variant spelling, one that most editors reject. Pronounce *accompanist uh-KUHM-puhn-ist.*

piano (*n.*) The plural is *pianos.* See PLURALS OF NOUNS ENDING IN -O.

picaresque (*adj., n.*), **picturesque** (*adj.*) The adjective *picaresque* means "roguish, rascally, sharp-practicing, vagabondlike," and the noun is "a type of fiction with a *picaresque* hero, who is also called a *picaro.*" *Picturesque* means "picturelike, quaint, worth looking at." See -ESQUE.

piccolo (*n.*) The plural is *piccolos.* See PLURALS OF NOUNS ENDING IN -O.

picnic (*v.*) spells its past tense and past participle *picnicked* and its present participle *picnicking.* The agentive ending gives us *picnickers.* See SPELLING OF -ING AND -ED FORMS OF VERBS ENDING IN -IC, -AC.

picture See PHOTO.

picturesque See PICARESQUE.

pidgin, pigeon (*nn.*) These homophones have very different meanings: a *pidgin* is a special language, using some of the grammar of one language with a vocabulary mainly from one or more other languages; it is never the native language of its speakers but is used as a means of communication for people who have no other language in common. A *pigeon* is a kind of dove whose sometimes foolishly fearless behavior has given the word a figurative slang use as a name for the naive victim of a confidence trickster or other cheat.

PIDGIN ENGLISH is a pidgin used as a commercial or trade language in the ports of the Far East and the Pacific islands.

piece, peace (*nn.*) are homophones. *Piece* is a high-frequency term meaning "a part or section of something"; it has many senses, including some taboo ones. *Peace* means "freedom from war, strife, noise, or disruption"; it too is a high-frequency word, with a number of special-

ized senses. There is no overlapping of meaning between the two.

pier See PEER.

pier glass (*n.*) is a large mirror placed between *piers* or columns in the wall of a room, usually between tall windows. The term is structural, and it has nothing to do with *peering* into a mirror.

pigeon See PIDGIN.

PIG LATIN is a secret language used by schoolchildren: words are pronounced beginning with their first vowels, and the initial consonants and consonant clusters are tacked onto the ends of the words as new syllables ending with *-ay* (pronounced *-ai*). *My father spanked me* becomes *EI-mai AH-thuhr-fai ANKT-spai EE-mai,* which is written *Imay atherfay anked-spay emay.* As with most schoolyard traditions, this one can have many local variations.

pigmy See PYGMY.

pilaf (pronounced *pi-LAHF* or *PEE-lahf*) is the usual American spelling of the name of a dish, especially a Middle Eastern or Asian dish, made with rice or wheat and sometimes fish or meat. But *pilaff* is also a Standard spelling, and *pilau* and *pilaw* also turn up on menus from time to time.

Pilipino See PHILIPPINE(S).

pinch-hit (*n., v.*), **pinch hitter** (*n.*) In baseball the verb means "to bat for another player in hopes of being more successful than that player is likely to be"; the player who does so is a *pinch hitter,* and what pinch hitters hope to get are *pinch hits*—which will let them reach first base and probably advance runners already on base. The figurative use is limited to the verb, meaning "to substitute for another in an emergency, (in a pinch)," and to the noun *pinch hitter,* which is what that substitute is called: *She pinch-hit for me at the circulation desk and then had to call for another pinch hitter when the regular evening person didn't show up.* The baseball uses of these terms are the argot of the game; the figurative generalized uses are Standard Informal and Conversational.

pip See SEED.

pique See PEAK.

piqué, piquet (*nn.*) These homophones are pronounced *pee-KAI. Piqué* is spelled sometimes without its acute accent and is the name of a ribbed cotton fabric; *piquet* is a two-handed card game and has a variant pronunciation, *pee-KET.*

pistachio (*n.*) The plural is *pistachios* (see PLU-RALS OF NOUNS ENDING IN -*O*). Rhyme the second syllable with either *ash* or *gosh*.

pistil, pistol, pistole (*nn.*) *Pistil* and *pistol* are homophones, pronounced *PIS-tuhl*; a *pistil* is the seed-carrying organ of a flower, and a *pistol* is a small handgun. A *pistole,* pronounced *pis-TOL,* was a gold coin, usually but not always Spanish.

pit See SEED.

piteous, pitiable, pitiful (*adjs.*) *Piteous* (pronounced *PIT-ee-uhs*) means "capable of arousing pity or compassion": *The wretched refugees were a piteous sight. Pitiful* (pronounced *PIT-i-ful*) is only a partial synonym. (The sense of *pitiful* meaning "full of pity [for others]" is now obsolete.) *Pitiful* and *pitiable* (pronounced *PIT-ee-uh-bul*) also mean "deserving or worthy of pity," but both have an edge of "deserving scorn or contempt too": *His efforts to win promotion were inept and pitiable* [*pitiful*].

-place, -where (*suffixes*) Some commentators object strongly to locutions such as *to go someplace, to get someplace,* and the like, arguing that all such combinations should be with -*where*, not -*place*. *Anyplace* and *someplace* and the like are clearly Conversational and Informal, but they sometimes have idiomatic force, as in *I want to get someplace and be somebody,* which is almost as widely useful as *to get somewhere and be somebody. To be going places,* that is, "to be getting ahead, making a success of things," is a Standard idiom and is useful at all but the most chastely Formal levels, where *succeed* or *prosper* or *advance* (*oneself*) might seem more dignified.

placebo See PANACEA.

PLAGIARISM is the unethical quotation of another's words or the unethical use of another's ideas or data in such a way as to let the world conclude they are your own words, ideas, or data. With proper attribution, to quote another's thoughts and words is appropriate; *plagiarizing,* however, is cheating, and it may break copyright law as well. Unconscious *plagiarism* does occur, but even that not everyone will excuse.

plaid (*adj., n.*), **tartan** (*n.*) For purists the *plaid* is the right-angle-striped Scottish blanket worn over the shoulder and draped around the torso, the *tartan* a particular pattern for it. Today, for most Americans, *plaid* is the name of the pattern itself, *tartan* is the *plaid*-patterned cloth, usually a unique pattern adopted by a particular Scots clan; *tartans* are made into various garments, including *plaids*. Both senses are Standard.

plain, plane (*adjs., nn.*) A *plain* is "a broad, flat expanse of country," and so the corresponding adjective means "level," "lacking decoration," "unpretentious," and "uncluttered and obvious." Used of persons, *plain* means "homely or lacking in beauty." A *plane* is "a geometrically flat surface," "a tool for smoothing wood to make it flat," "a kind of tree," and any of a number of specialized names for surfaces of like qualities, such as the *planes* of a glider or airplane. *Plain* and *plane* are homophones, but confusion can arise when you spell the name of the specialized flat surface you have in mind: is it a *plane* or a *plain? Plain* is topographical at the outset, and *plane,* geometrical, but from there on, your dictionary should be your guide.

plaintiff (*n.*), **complaint** (*n.*), **plaintive** (*adj.*) The prefix *plaint-* is cognate with *complaint,* and all these *plaint-* words stem ultimately from *planctus,* a Latin past participle meaning "to lament," but *complaint* itself has two main meanings: "legal complaint (the bringing of a suit in a court of law)" and "grief and dissatisfaction." In the latter cluster is the malady or illness sense: *One symptom of this complaint was a racking cough.* The noun *plaintiff* is the name given the person bringing a *complaint* in a legal matter. The adjective *plaintive* means "mournful, sad, melancholy, or woeful."

plan (*n., v.*) *To make plans for the future, to do future planning,* and *to have future plans* all have been criticized as redundant, as have *advance*[*d*] *planning* and *to plan in advance* or *to plan ahead. To plan out* extends the idea in a slightly different sense. All these locutions are Standard when restricted to Conversational, Semiformal, and Informal levels. The more Formal the prose, however, the more likely editors and readers are to be sensitive to possible redundancies.

The verb *plan* combines frequently with *on* and *to,* forming Standard idioms we use constantly: *Plan on my being there by eight. Please plan to stay for dinner. We'll plan on pizza and beer after the game.*

plane See PLAIN.

PLANNED LEVEL is the kind of speech we use to address fair-sized groups of people—a classroomful, for example. Speech in such situations receives less feedback than does Impromptu, and it inevitably underscores the literal and figurative distance between speaker and hearers. It is called *planned* (Gleason [1965] called it "deliberative") because it is more prearranged and varied than the speech of lower *levels:* its syntax is more varied, its vocabulary is more extensive, and anacoluthon frequently occurs in it, as does the vocalized pause, when the speaker tests and alters what he or she is saying in order to improve it. Not every speaker of English is comfortable or even competent at the *planned level*; it has to be learned and practiced. Many people encounter so few situations in which they must face a roomful of listeners that they never learn to use it well. When schoolteachers have their pupils address the entire class, they are trying to provide some of the experience necessary to master *planned* speech. This *level* demands planning ahead of utterance, monitoring rather more complex syntactic and other grammatical structures, finding synonyms, and anticipating if possible what the listeners are hearing and understanding. It tends to be more self-conscious than Impromptu speech, but less so than Oratorical. See LEVELS OF USAGE.

plateau (*n.*) The plurals are either *plateaus* or *plateaux*, both pronounced *pla-TOZ* in English. See FOREIGN PLURALS.

plausible (*adj.*) ends with the suffix *-ible*, not *-able*. See also SPECIOUS; SPELLING OF UNSTRESSED VOWELS.

play See also WREAK.

playwright (*n.*), **playwrite** (*v.*) A *playwright*, like a *shipwright*, makes or builds something (the word *wright* comes from an Old English form of *worker* and is related to *wrought*); to write plays is to do *playwriting*, although the *playwrighting* spelling also occurs. Edited English usually insists that a maker of plays is a *playwright* and that the craft be called *playwriting*, not *playwrighting*.

plead (*v.*) The past tense is *pleaded, pled,* or *plead* (this last pronounced *PLED*), and the past participle, *pleaded, pled,* or *plead* (*PLED*). *Pleaded,* the regular weak verb form, is more frequent for both parts of speech, and the *pled* and *plead* past and past participle forms are labeled Colloquial by some dictionaries, Standard by others.

Plead not guilty and *plead guilty* are Standard idioms (*His lawyer advised him to plead not guilty* [*guilty*]), and the media almost always uses *pled* to report a defendant's actions: *The defendant pled* [*not*] *guilty.*

pleasantry, pleasantness (*nn.*) A *pleasantry* is "a bit of agreeable banter, a mild jest"; *pleasantness* is a more general term, meaning "a

manner or behavior that gives pleasure, that is pleasing and agreeable."

please (*v.*) in the passive voice can take either a *that* clause or the preposition or function word *to* plus an infinitive: *We were pleased that we got* [*to get*] *an invitation.* When followed by a direct object, *please* takes *to* plus an infinitive: *It pleased them to learn of his achievement.* The once-common *please to* plus infinitive (*Please to not make a scene*) is still found in British English but is rare in the United States.

pleasing (*adj.*) combines either with the preposition *to* plus a noun or pronoun or *to* plus an infinitive: *The news was pleasing to my family* [*to me*]; *it was most pleasing to hear.*

pled See PLEAD.

plenitude, plentitude (*nn.*) Both mean "an abundance, a great sufficiency," but *plenitude* is the word to use. *Plentitude* is a rare variant, perhaps originally an error or a misprint or else made with *plenty* in mind, rather than the Latin *plenus* "full," which gives us *plenitude*. *Plentitude* occurs so seldom that most Standard users consider it a mistake.

plenteous, plentiful (*adjs.*) These are synonyms meaning "abundant." *Plentiful* occurs more often; *plenteous* is somewhat more literary.

plentitude See PLENITUDE.

plenty (*adv., adj., n., intensifier*) Most of *plenty*'s problems are in the spoken language; in Standard writing it lives a much straitened life, mostly as a noun, which causes no trouble: *They had plenty of money. October is a season of plenty.*

As a predicate adjective, as in *Starlings surely are plenty these days, plenty* rarely occurs today in the written language, but it does occur in Conversational—especially Casual—English. As an attributive adjective, as in *We had plenty money in those days,* it looks odd and is Nonstandard in print but occurs frequently in Conversational contexts, especially at the Casual level. Right alongside it, however, and unquestionably Standard at all levels are the use of *plentiful* instead of *plenty* in predicate adjective functions (*starlings are plentiful*) and the insertion of *of* between *plenty* and the noun instead of using *plenty* as an attributive (*plenty of money*).

As an adverb, *plenty* is used most often as an intensive, as in *They were plenty angry,* and as a full adverb, as in *I've exercised plenty today.* But these uses too are limited to speech, mainly Casual and Impromptu levels. And the use of *plenty* with *more* also is for Conversational English only, where it is Standard, both when *more* behaves like a noun, as in *We got plenty more yesterday,* and when *plenty* seems to be an intensifier, as in *We got plenty more calls.*

PLEONASMS are words too many or redundancies. In *Assemble everyone all together in the dining room, all together* is superfluous unless the tone or style is helped by the extra stress on "togetherness." Otherwise, *Assemble everyone in the dining room* is enough. In good exposition, a *pleonasm* may once in a great while assist you in achieving clarity, but be sparing.

plethora (*n.*) has long meant an unfortunate, undesirable overabundance of something: *She's had a plethora of telephone calls today.* But semantic change is causing it to appear in Edited English meaning simply "a lot of something (but not too much) not necessarily bad at all, but neither good nor bad, or in some instances, downright good." If enough Standard users keep on using *plethora* in these senses, the meaning of the word will change. Meantime, make context support your pejorative use of it.

plow, plough (*n.*) Americans spell it *plow,* the British, *plough.* See also SPELLING (1).

plunge (*n., v.*) When the verb *plunge* combines with a preposition, it can take *into, in, to, toward, through* and other directional words, such as *under, over,* and the like: *She plunged into her work. The baby was plunged in the bath. He plunged to his death; She plunged through the wheat toward the overturned tractor.* The noun can combine with an equally long list of prepositions: *a plunge into [in] the pool, toward [to] the bottom, under [beside] the raft, after [before, during] work,* etc.

PLUPERFECT TENSE See PAST PERFECT TENSE.

PLUPLUPERFECT TENSE *If only we would've known, we'd've stopped them* contains a *plupluperfect* (sometimes called *superpluperfect*), a verb (*known*) with two auxiliaries, one of them redundant. Either auxiliary can be a contraction (*If only we'd have known, . . .*), and the uncontracted auxiliaries can be either *would have* or *had have.* All such locutions are Substandard, although the *plupluperfect* can occur in Standard jocular use (a measure of how certain the speaker is that Standard listeners will recognize the joke), which, when written, often uses *of* in place of the contraction *'ve; We'd of loved to see them.* Spoken or written inadvertently, the *plupluperfect* is a powerful shibboleth in Standard English.

PLURAL See NUMBER (1).

plurality See MAJORITY.

PLURALS OF COMPOUND NOUNS Words like *doghouse, ballpark,* and *icemaker* are compounds; they have primary stress on the first syllable or front element, tertiary stress on the second syllable or rear element. All form their plurals by adding *-s* to the end of the second element: *doghouses, ballparks,* and *icemakers. Mouse dropping, clothing store,* and *pit bull* exhibit the same stress pattern and form their plurals the same way. Hyphenated words like *brother-in-law, mother-in-law,* and *commander-in-chief* all add *-s* to the end of the first element to form their plurals: *brothers-in-law, mothers-in-law, commanders-in-chief.* If the *compound* ends in *-ful* (*basketful, armful, cupful*), the plurals usually add *-s* to the end of *-ful* (*basketfuls, armfuls, cupfuls*), although *basketsful, armsful,* and *cupsful* do sometimes occur. *Advocate general, attorney general,* and *mother superior* have the primary stress on the second element and so are not true compounds, despite a superficial resemblance; hence it is not surprising that they usually form their plurals by adding *-s* to the first element—the noun—to make the plural: *advocates general, attorneys general, mothers superior.* Even so, although still rare in Edited English, the plurals *advocate generals, attorney generals,* and *mother superiors* are now beginning to turn up in Standard English, limited still (but perhaps not for long) mainly to Conversational and Informal uses.

PLURALS OF LETTERS AND NUMBERS usually add *-s: two Xs, Ph.D.s, MIAs, 1990s, the '20s.* Use an apostrophe only when you need it to prevent confusion: *Mississippi has four i's. He got A's in both courses.*

PLURALS OF NOUNS, THE REGULAR PATTERNS FOR The regular *-s* plural pattern actually involves the addition of one of three endings, which sound like *-s, -z,* or *-iz,* depending on the final sound in the singular. New words such as *quark(s)* and *psion(s),* many borrowed words from languages we do not know well such as *kimono(s)* and *orangutan(s),* and nonsense words such as Lewis Carroll's *borogove(s)* and *mome rath(s)* all usually make their plurals according to these generalizations:

1. After final voiceless consonants except *s,* [č], and [š], add the sound [s], and spell accordingly: *cat* becomes *cats; cup* becomes *cups.*

2. After all voiced sounds except the sounds [z], [j], and [ž], add the sound [z], but spell with

an *-s: dog* becomes *dogs*; *sofa* becomes *sofas.*

3. After these six exceptions, add the sound [iz], and spell with a final *-es: kiss* becomes *kisses*; *church* becomes *churches; dish* becomes *dishes; buzz* becomes *buzzes; bridge* becomes *bridges; and mirage* becomes *mirages.*

Sound, not spelling, controls; the formation of regular English noun plurals is phonologically conditioned. But see also FOREIGN PLURALS; RELIC PLURALS OF NOUNS.

PLURALS OF NOUNS, UNCHANGING
See RELIC PLURALS OF NOUNS.

PLURALS OF NOUNS ENDING IN *-F*, *-FE* See NOUNS ENDING IN *-F.*

PLURALS OF NOUNS ENDING IN *-O*
sometimes retain a foreign plural (*pizzicato* becomes *pizzicati*), sometimes form their plurals by adding an *-s* (*piano* becomes *pianos*), sometimes by adding *-es* (*potato* becomes *potatoes; tomato* becomes *tomatoes*), and sometimes they may have two plurals (*contralto* becomes *contraltos* or *contralti; salvo* becomes *salvos* or *salvoes*).

plus (*adv., adj., n., prep., coord. conj.*) As preposition and conjunction, *plus* is Standard in some uses. *One plus one equals two* illustrates the Standard mathematical use meaning "and"; note that it ordinarily doesn't change the verb to plural as *and* would, which suggests that in this use *plus* is a preposition. Nor does the preposition *plus* make the verb plural in nonmathematical use: *The wind, plus several inches of rain, has caused many power outages.* But *plus* can also be a conjunction, and this shows when the verb shifts to plural: *The growing unemployment plus* [*and*] *the oil price increase have unsettled the stock market.* This use is also Standard. The conjunctive *plus* is limited mainly to Conversational and Informal uses, such as *I don't have time to go with you, plus I don't have any money either.* Uses of *plus* as a sentence adverb meaning "besides" also seem to be Conversational and Informal only: *She hates having to wait around. Plus it's raining.* As an adjective, as in *That she's got her own car is a plus factor*, and noun, as in *The short commute to my job is a plus for me, plus* is Conversational and perhaps Semiformal; it seems not to appear much in Formal writing, but it does occur in some Edited English.

plus fours (*n.*) are golfer's knickers, cut four inches longer than ordinary knickers so that they blouse more fully. Modish in the 1920s and 1930s, they are having a modest revival in golf today.

P.M. See A.M.

podium, dais, lectern, pulpit (*nn.*) A *podium* is a raised platform on which a lecturer or the conductor of an orchestra stands. Don't confuse a *podium* with a *lectern* as people often do; you stand *on* a *podium* but *behind* a *lectern*—a raised reading desk on which speakers can place books and notes comfortably within their view. A *pulpit* is a *lectern* raised usually well above the level of the congregation in a church, often with a short staircase leading up to a railed platform holding preacher and *lectern*. A *dais* (stress the first syllable, and rhyme it with *day,* not *dye*) is a platform at one end of a hall, for the high table at a banquet, or for speakers or performers.

poetess (*n.*) is a feminine form of the noun *poet*; it was old-fashioned and often thought objectionable by some even before sexist language and inclusive language became matters of discussion. Today it is obsolescent. See -ESS.

POETIC, LITERARY Locutions so labeled suggest literary or poetic contexts rather than those of everyday life. In the wrong situations they may sound arty, stiff, or pretentious.

POETRY, THE QUOTATION OF A stanza or a couplet should usually be reproduced as it looks on the original page:

> Since sorrow never comes too late,
> And happiness too swiftly flies.
> Thought would destroy their paradise.
> No more; where ignorance is bliss,
> 'Tis folly to be wise.
> —Thomas Gray, *Ode on a Distant Prospect of Eton College*, 96–100

If the passage is shorter, or if it involves parts of lines, you may print it within quotation marks in the regular lines of your paragraph, using the virgule to indicate the ends of lines in the verse, as in *Frost ends his* Fire and Ice *with this remark about the force of hate:* ". . . *that for destruction ice / Is also great / And would suffice*" (7–9).

point in time is a cliché, a bit of padded prose. It has been around for a long time, but the Watergate hearings of the 1970s made many people conscious of it and determined to root it out of their language. A single word will usually do nicely: *At this point in time* is *now*; *at that point in time* was *then*; *at some point in time* will be *sometime*.

point is, the This cliché is a kind of throat clearer, a formula for emphasis, for rounding up a scattered discourse in hopes of giving it a clarity that has thus far eluded the speaker or writer. There's nothing wrong with *the point is* except too much of it. Compare FACT.

point of fact, in See FACT.

point of view See STANDPOINT.

poison, poisonous See INEDIBLE; VENOM.

poke See BAG (2).

police officer, policeman, policewoman See OFFICER.

political, politic (*adjs.*) *Political* is the general adjective today for referring to governmental matters, politics, and political parties. It sometimes has a pejorative edge, suggesting that *political* considerations will rule rather than the merits of the issue, as in *When it appeared the decision would be political, we withdrew our support. Politic* (pronounced *PAHL-uh-tik*) means "political" only in the cliché *the body politic*; otherwise it means "shrewd, prudent, thoughtful," and sometimes "tactful": *We thought it would be politic to avoid that subject.*

politically correct (*adj.*), **P(.)C(.)** (*abbrev.*), **political correctness** (*n.*) *Politically correct,* or *PC,* is an epithet applied by those who disagree with attitudes expressed by a number of *isms* to programs their supporters insist represent the only desirable treatment of these issues. Especially in academic and liberal environments, *politically correct* terms tend to cluster around such issues as feminism, sexism, racism, and speciesism (all of which see), as well as around many other issues of the day about which all men and women of good will (as defined by the speaker) must feel as the speaker does. For usage, this vexed issue matters greatly because one of the key programs has been the effort to replace old terms with new ones, primarily euphemisms: for example, some reformers urge that the euphemisms *disabled* and *disadvantaged,* which have largely replaced *crippled,* be themselves replaced with *differently abled* or another such euphemism. And in the speed with which the first set of euphemisms lost its power to satisfy lies the clue to *PC's* pitfalls: saying does not necessarily make it so, and whitening a sepulcher does little to alter what's in it, even when everyone agrees to the paint job. In view of the absurd exaggerations of partisans on both sides of every one of these issues, lasting change in the vocabulary seems unlikely. Nevertheless, the impact of *PC* ideas, the weight of social pressures, and the truth of the linguistic force of the question of who will call the shots—Humpty Dumpty's "Who shall be master?"—are impossible to predict and should not be underestimated. *PC* itself may be a short-lived vogue word, but the forces and counterforces it represents are not likely to disappear while the language is in use.

politics (*n.*) can be either plural or singular for purposes of agreement with verb or pronoun, depending on whether you think of them as a bundle of items or it as a single topic: *His politics are liberal. Politics is a fascinating subject.*

pollute (*v.*), **pollution** (*n.*) These words are rapidly becoming overused, thanks to our growing concern over what we have done to our air, water, and earth. The literal sense of *pollute* is "to make unclean, or impure" or "to contaminate, defile, or dirty," and all these invite figurative uses applied to any and all things that disgust or anger us. The literal senses of *pollute* and *pollution* are sufficiently varied to warrant our trying to protect them from the wear and tear of figurative overuse. *Noise pollution* and *polluting the thoughts of the young* or *the processes of government* are graphic figurative uses, but they're becoming worn.

polyglot (*adj., n.*) A *polyglot collection* is one spoken or written in several languages; the noun means "a person who can speak several languages" or "a book written in several languages." *Polyglot* also has come to mean simply "a mixture of languages." *Polyglot* books or dictionaries typically present parallel texts or entries in columnar form, a different language's version in each column. See LINGUIST.

pommel (*n.*), **pummel** (*v.*) One of the two Standard variant pronunciations of *pommel* is a homophone of *pummel: PUHM-uhl.* (The other is *PAHM-uhl.*) A *pommel* is the knob at the end of the handle of a sword or dagger or the front knob (called the *horn*) on a saddle; *to pummel someone* is "to beat or pound (someone), especially with the fists."

poncho (*n.*) The plural is *ponchos.* See also PLURALS OF NOUNS ENDING IN *-O.*

ponder (*v.*) when it combines with a preposition, can take *on, upon, over,* and *about: We left him to ponder on [upon, over, about] our offer.* But *ponder* can also be transitive and take a direct object: *We left him to ponder our offer.*

poof, poofter See POUF.

poor boy See SUBMARINE.

poorly (*adv., adj.*) The adverb gives no difficulty: *I did poorly on the test.* The adjective, however, meaning "ill, indisposed, not feeling well," is considered by some to be Conversational at best, probably dialectal, and in any event old-fashioned, as in *Mother felt poorly after breakfast.* There is a British idiom, *to be taken poorly,* meaning "to become ill": *He was taken poorly in the night.*

pop See SODA.

pore, pour (*vv.*) These homophones get confused only in spelling, mainly when the relatively infrequent *pore,* meaning "to read or study carefully" and always combined with *over,* as in *He pored over his maps all evening,* is mistakenly spelled *pour,* which is how you move a liquid out of a container.

pork See HAM.

porpoise See DOLPHIN.

portentous, pretentious (*adjs.*) *Portentous* has three meanings: "forecasting evil or unpleasantness," "striking awe or amazing," and "ponderous or pompous." It is this last sense that slightly overlaps *pretentious,* which means "claiming unjustified importance or standing," "being ostentatious." The main distinction is that a *portentous* man just might be as important as he seems, but a *pretentious* one cannot be as important as he claims. *Portentious* (also sometimes *portenteous*) is Substandard, a misspelling (and mispronunciation) of *portentous.*

portfolio (*n.*) The plural is *portfolios.* See PLURALS OF NOUNS ENDING IN -O.

portico (*n.*) has two Standard plurals: *porticoes* or *porticos.* See PLURALS OF NOUNS ENDING IN -O.

portion See PART (2).

PORTMANTEAU WORDS See BLENDS.

positive attitude, positive advice, positive influence, positive thinking Each of these phrases is a cliché, and thanks to the many meanings and nuances of the adjective *positive,* each can sometimes be vague or ambiguous: *a positive attitude* might be "optimistic" or "favorable"; *positive advice* or *positive criticism* could be "affirmative," "supportive," "constructive," or "helpful"; *a positive influence* could be a "forthright," "effective," or "good" influence, and *positive thinking* is likely to be either "affirmative" or "optimistic." Limit these phrases to Conversational and Informal uses, and choose more specific language at least for higher levels.

POSITIVE DEGREE, COMPARATIVE DEGREE, SUPERLATIVE DEGREE These are the three levels of grammatical comparison in adjectives, as in *cold, colder, coldest,* and in adverbs, as in *beautifully, more beautifully, most beautifully.*

POSITIVES, LOST See LOST POSITIVES.

positivism (*n.*) is a system of philosophy, developed by Auguste Comte, that assumes that speculation is fruitless and that only empirically verified data acquired by the senses can be useful. The term *positivism* is sometimes also used loosely to mean either "the state of being positive" or "the state of being overconfident," but both these uses are too easily confused with the system of philosophy and with each other to be helpful. Nor has either anything to do with *positive thinking* (see POSITIVE ATTITUDE). Use context and definition to avoid confusion.

possess, have, own (*vv.*) are synonyms in the sense that things that you *possess, own,* or *have* are yours. But *possess* and *own* have overtones: *I have* or *I own a house,* but saying *I possess it* is too formal. *I have a cold,* but *I neither possess nor own it.* I have, own, or *possess a large collection of jazz recordings,* but the verbs get increasingly Formal and stuffy. *Own* makes better sense when the contrast is with *rent* or *lease: I don't own a car; I lease one.* But if you *have* an apartment, you may either rent, lease, or *own* it. And in the end, *possess* can sound greedy or raise the question of whether you *possess* your possessions or they you.

possessed (*participle, adj.*) *Possessed* combines with the preposition *of* in either a passive structure (meaning "had") or a reflexive structure (meaning "got hold of"): *He was possessed of a handsome writing desk. She possessed herself of her daughter's diary.* When it means "controlled by" or "under the influence of," *possessed* combines with *by* or *with: She was possessed by an urge to keep moving. He was possessed with the idea that he had to earn a great deal of money. Possessed* also refers to demonic possession, which we use both literally and figuratively: *They thought she was possessed, so they hired an exorcist. She worked like a woman possessed. Whatever possessed you to do that?*

POSSESSIVE See APOSTROPHE (2); DOUBLE GENITIVE; GENITIVE BEFORE A GERUND; GENITIVE CASE.

POSSESSIVE PRONOUNS See PERSONAL PRONOUNS.

POSSESSIVE WITH GERUND See GENITIVE BEFORE A GERUND.

possibility (*n.*) combines with *of* and *for* to mean "the likelihood or chance of (something's) occurrence," as in *There is almost no possibility of our winning the lottery* and *There is almost no possibility for us to win the lottery. Possibility* also can take a *that* clause, wherein it is important to use *will* rather than *may* as auxiliary—*There is a possibility that we will* [not *may*] *arrive on time*—because *possibility* supplies the same doubt that *may* would. Compare PROBABILITY.

possible, probable (*adjs.*) Something *possible* can conceivably occur; something *probable* very likely will occur. *Possible* is sometimes considered an absolute adjective (which see).

POSSLQ is a slang acronym that has achieved considerable status in Conversational, Semiformal, and Informal use. It stands for *persons of opposite sexes sharing living quarters* and is pronounced *PAHS-uhl-KYOO*.

posterior See ANTERIOR.

post-graduate See GRADUATE.

postscript See P.S.

potato (*n.*) The plural is *potatoes*. See PLURALS OF NOUNS ENDING IN -O.

pouf, poof, poofter, pouff, pouffe (*nn.*), **poof** (*interj.*) A *pouf* (*pouff* and *pouffe* are variant spellings) was a puff or something that looked like one: today's most usual referent is a soft, overstuffed ottoman. *Poof!* is the conventional exclamation attending a sudden appearance or disappearance, as in a magician's trick. The noun *poof* is (mainly) British slang meaning "a male homosexual," as is its cognate *poofter;* both are disparaging and therefore taboo in polite use.

pour See PORE.

-pp- See CONSONANTS (2).

practicable, practical (*adjs.*) These two overlap partly in the sense of "feasible, usable, workable," as in *His new plan seems practicable* [*practical*], but *practical* always suggests that experience has proved it so, whereas *practicable* suggests that the plan is as yet untested but seems likely to be useful. *Practicable* cannot be applied to persons, whereas *practical* can, and *practical* has of course a good many meanings in addition to those it shares with *practicable*. Compare IMPRACTICAL.

practically (*adv.*) means both "in a manner that's practical," as in *By considering the problem practically, he was able to solve it,* and "almost, virtually, nearly," as in *We're practically*

finished with our report. One dictionary labels the "virtually" sense Colloquial, and one or two others object to use of that sense in Edited English. Others rightly consider it Standard, but you should be aware that a few purists still don't like it in Formal contexts. And whichever sense you intend, place the adverb carefully to avoid ambiguity: *He thought he could practically solve the problem* is ambiguous; *He thought he could solve the problem practically* is not. *A practically solved problem* is hopelessly ambiguous.

practice (*n., v.*), **practise** (*v.*) The Americans and the British spell the noun *practice;* Americans usually spell the verb *practice* too, although occasionally we'll spell it *practise,* as the British always do. See SPELLING (1).

preacher See PRIEST.

precede, proceed (*vv.*) Be wary of the spellings of these and other words formed with -*cede*, -*ceed*, -*sede* (which see).

precedence (*n.*), **precedent(s)** (*adj., n.*) *Precedence* is a noun meaning "priority in rank, a ranking according to relative importance": *In the procession, previous winners will have precedence over this year's contestants.* Pronunciation of *precedence* is either *PRES-i-dens* or *pree-SEED-ens,* the first variant being a homophone of the plural of the noun *precedent,* which means "an earlier action that sets a model or example for later ones" and combines usually with *for,* as in *There is no precedent for such action,* and occasionally with *against* or *of: I know of no precedent against it. He set a precedent of painstaking evenhandedness in chairing the meetings.* The adjective *precedent* is pronounced *pree-SEED-ent,* and it combines usually with *to,* as in *Filing of your application must be precedent to any action by the committee,* but occasionally with *of,* as in *Circumstances precedent of* [*to*] *the final vote now call the whole matter into question.*

precip, precipitation (*nn.*) *Precipitation* is the meteorologist's generic word for rain, mist, hail, snow, drizzle, and the like, and *precip* is the TV weatherperson's clipped jargon form of it.

precipitate, precipitous (*adjs.*), **precipitately, precipitously** (*advs.*) A *precipitate* action is one done hastily, rashly, suddenly. To do something *precipitately* is to do it hastily, abruptly. A *precipitous* slope is a steep one, as is a *precipitous* fall. A bluff that falls away *precipitously* does so steeply. However, these once clear differences have for centuries been blurred at least in part, perhaps because of two hundred years of apparent overlap in *an abrupt* *action* and *an abrupt slope; precipitous* and *precipitously* regularly appear, even in Edited English, meaning "hastily, suddenly, abruptly," sometimes combining the ideas of suddenness and steepness and sometimes not involving steepness at all, just haste. This overlap of course can make *a precipitous drop in interest rates* ambiguous: did they drop suddenly or steeply or both? Best advice: make context prevent ambiguity, and consider carefully the likely expectations of your readers.

precipitation See PRECIP.

precipitous, precipitously See PRECIPITATE.

précis See ABSTRACT (2).

preclude (*v.*), when in the active voice it combines with a preposition, does so with *from: The ruling precludes all nonmembers from casting ballots.* In the passive, it can combine with *from, by,* or *to: She was precluded by her illness from joining the group. No legislative device seems precluded to a group as desperate as theirs.*

precondition, condition (*nn.*) Purists have claimed that *precondition* is redundant, and, indeed, sometimes it can be: If I set *conditions* you must meet before you may do something, then that's enough. A *precondition* would be a requirement you must meet even before you meet the *conditions,* and that's not the sort of thing intended at all. But in fact, although they are synonymous above, there are two differences between *condition* and *precondition* in some uses: (1) the *pre-* prefix adds emphasis and stresses more heavily the necessity that these requirements be satisfied first, and (2) the two words cannot always combine with the same prepositions for the same meanings. *Precondition* combines with *of, for,* and *to: A precondition to [of, for] the purchase of a new house is finding a willing lender. Condition* too combines regularly with *of* and *for,* as in *Her mother set two conditions for granting approval* and *The conditions of there being enough money and enough time were set at the outset,* but *to* doesn't force *condition* to mean "a set requirement"; instead it may turn out to be just "a circumstance" or something even less specific.

predestine (*v.*) combines with *to,* as in *They felt they were predestined to succeed,* and with *for,* as in *Their consultant feared they were predestined for failure. Destine* would mean the same, except perhaps a bit less emphatically, and *predestine* sometimes has stronger overtones of fatalism.

PREDICATE 1 (*n.*) The *predicate* of a sentence is the second of its two chief elements; the subject is the first. The *predicate* contains (and may consist solely of) a finite verb, and it may also contain direct or indirect objects, object complements, or modifiers of the verb or its complements. In the following sentences, the words in boldface type form the *predicates: She **smiled**. I **went home**. They **planned a long vacation**. They **gladly gave me the keys to the car**. She **told me that my book was overdue**.*

predicate 2 (*v.*) (pronounced *pred-i-KAIT*) can combine with *on* or *upon* when it means "to base or found on," as in *We have predicated our plans on [upon] what we learned.* When it combines with *of,* it means "to affirm or declare," "to assert that something is a quality or attribute of someone or something," as in *Such results are predicated of many philosophical schemes. Predicate* is a Formal, low-frequency word, and some commentators have worried that it may be mistaken for the much more common *predict,* but that malapropism is likely to be committed only by the youthful or inexperienced. All these uses are Standard.

PREDICATE ADJECTIVE A *predicate adjective* is an adjective appearing in the predicate of a sentence, following a linking verb and modifying the subject of the sentence: *The building is **new**. I feel **uncomfortable**.*

PREDICATE NOMINATIVE Sometimes called a predicate noun, a *predicate nominative* is a noun or pronoun that appears in the predicate of a sentence, following a linking verb and having the same referent as the subject of the sentence: *She is my **sister**. I was the **captain**.* Pronouns in this function are in the nominative case in Oratorical and Formal contexts, but Conversational levels can use objective case pronouns: *It's me* and *It was us* occur in Standard Conversational uses, alongside *This is she* and *It was we who were embarrassed.*

predominant, predominate (*adjs.*), **predominantly, predominately** (*advs.*) *Predominant* and *predominate* are exact synonyms, meaning "having authority over, superior, most noticeable, most important," but *predominant* is by far the more frequently used. Similarly, the two adverbs are synonyms, *predominantly* the much more widely used. But all are Standard.

preemie (*n.*) is a Conversational slang term, originally medical jargon, a clipped and eye dialect spelling of *premature,* a noun (also medical jargon, at least originally) meaning a baby born *prematurely,* before achieving full term in the womb: *The neonatal ward holds seven pree-mies [prematures, premature infants] at the moment.*

preempt, pre-empt (*v.*) is usually but not always spelled without a hyphen. See DIERESIS; PREFIXES.

preface (*n., v.*) The noun takes *to* most often but can also take the prepositions *of* and *for:* *The editors said the preface to [of, for] her book was too long.* The verb combines with *by, with,* and occasionally, when the verb is passive, *to:* *She prefaced her speech by [with] a long, pointless anecdote. He was unwilling to have someone else's words prefaced to his.* See also FOREWORD.

prefer (*v.*), when it combines with prepositions, does so most often with *to* and sometimes with *over: She prefers tea to coffee. He prefers swimming over jogging. To* plus an infinitive is also frequent: *They prefer to leave now rather than wait to [and] go tomorrow.* The *rather than* is sometimes omitted but usually only in Conversational or Informal situations: *He prefers to ride, not walk.* The more common use is with gerunds: *He prefers sleeping late to rising early.* The other forms of *prefer* are *preferred* and *preferring* (note the doubled *r*), both of which can combine with *to* or be followed by nouns. See CONSONANTS (2).

preferable (*adj.*) is pronounced with the stress on the first syllable and in rapid speech often drops the second syllable, as does *preference. Preferable* is often considered an absolute adjective.

preference (*n.*) combines usually with the preposition *for,* as in *She has a strong preference for Italian food.* In another idiom, the noun occurs in the phrase *in preference to,* as in *We stay at this motel in preference to the one across the street.* Other prepositions with which *preference* combines are *about, among, concerning, in,* and *regarding: He expressed no preference about [concerning, regarding] our departure time. They said they had no preferences in [among] the restaurants in town.* Pronounce it either *PREF-rens* or *PREF-uhr-ens.*

PREFIX See AFFIX.

PREFIXES, HYPHENATION OF When the prefix of a word ends with the same vowel letter that begins the following root word, the new word will sometimes—but not always—be hyphenated: *semi-independent, reengage, reenlist.* But many of these are in divided usage: *cooperate/co-operate, preempt/pre-empt.* See also DIERESIS.

pregnant (*adj.*) combines most frequently with *with,* as in *The situation was pregnant with possibilities,* occasionally with *by,* as in *She was [made] pregnant by a man she'd scarcely known,* and rarely with *in,* as in *This comedy is pregnant in laughter, much of which will be stillborn.* It's usually an absolute adjective, although hyperbole and attempts at humor can make it comparative.

prejudice (*n., v.*), **prejudiced** (*adj.*) A *prejudice* may be either a predisposition in favor of something or a predisposition opposed to it, and the verb reflects these same two diametrically opposite views; hence context must make clear which sort is meant, especially since, left unspecified, *prejudice* will usually be taken to be negative, pejorative, and against. The verb *prejudice* combines most frequently with a direct object or a reflexive pronoun followed by *against, toward(s),* or (rarely) *in favor of: His nagging prejudiced the children against [toward(s)] him. She deliberately prejudices herself against [in favor of] anything new.* The noun *prejudice* combines with these same prepositions, again only rarely with *in favor of: Her prejudices against [toward(s), in favor of] Italian cooking are well known.* The preposition *to* is Standard only in the phrase *without prejudice to: My decision is quite without prejudice to any new proposals.*

prejudicial (*adj.*) is usually followed by the preposition *to,* occasionally by *toward(s): The judge's remarks seemed likely to be prejudicial to a fair trial. Her comments were openly prejudicial toward(s) foreigners.* All overtones for *prejudicial* are pejorative and negative.

premature See IMMATURE; PREEMIE.

premier (*adj., n.*), **première, premiere** (*adj., n., v.*) Pronounce both nouns and adjectives either *pri-MIR, pri-MYIR,* or *pree-MEE-uhr* (the British say *PREM-yuhr*). The adjectives, which are variant spellings (originally the masculine and feminine versions of the French etymon) of the same word, mean "first, top-ranked," and they are absolute adjectives. The nouns have distinctive senses: a *premier* is a prime minister, a *première* is a first performance of a play, film, or musical composition or of a performer, and the verb means "to make or have such a first performance." Some older purists dislike the verb *première,* arguing that it is jargon, but it has clearly been Standard for almost a generation. American English now often omits the grave accent on all parts of speech.

premises, premise, premiss (*nn.*) A *premise* (and the British variant spelling *premiss/premisses*) is a "statement of a proposition in logic"; the plural means "two or more of these." But *premises* also has another highly specialized meaning, spelled *premises* both here and in Britain: "land, or a building, or a part of one, referred to in deeds and other documents as *the premises*" and usually treated as plural even when the referent is singular: *Sir, leave these premises! Get off this property!*

PREPOSITION 1, ENDING A SENTENCE WITH A English combines prepositions with so many of its verbs, often making them into idioms such as *to sit up, to run through,* and *to talk over,* that it's no wonder they turn up at the ends of sentences; English's subject-verb order almost invites them to. Although some conservatives still consciously avoid and dislike all terminal prepositions, only in Oratorical or Formal contexts need you ever seek to replace the more Conversational sound you get with prepositions ending your sentences, and even there let prepositions fall naturally at the end rather than say anything stuffy or awkward in trying to avoid it.

PREPOSITION 2, PREPOSITIONAL PHRASE *Prepositions* are parts of speech, single words or compounds with both grammatical and lexical meanings: *of, for, by, in, within, in spite of,* and *inside of* are examples of *prepositions*. A *preposition* is one of a nearly finite list of function words we use to head structures called *prepositional phrases*. The *preposition* introduces such a phrase and serves to (1) govern the object of the preposition and its modifiers, if any, and (2) direct the grammatical force of the entire phrase as a structure of modification, of either a word or a structure immediately preceding or of the rest of the sentence following the phrase. In *He wore a hat **with a red feather**, with* is the *preposition* introducing the phrase *with a red feather* (of which *feather* is the object) and making the entire phrase act adjectivally to modify the noun *hat*. In *In spring the flowers bloom, in* is the *preposition, spring* is the object, and since the phrase is at the beginning of the sentence, it acts adverbially as a sentence adverb modifying the entire main clause, *the flowers bloom.*

prerequisite See PERQUISITE.

prescribe, proscribe (*vv.*) *Prescribe* means "to set down a rule," "to dictate, direct, or order," and, in a specialized medical sense, "to order a treatment or medicine for a patient," as in *The doctor prescribed aspirin and rest. Proscribe* means "to banish," "to sentence to death," "to outlaw," and, in its generalized sense, "to forbid a behavior," as in *The judge firmly proscribed his driving a car.*

PRESCRIPTIVE AND DESCRIPTIVE GRAMMAR AND USAGE For the past half-century, these terms have served as useful labels for two contrasting approaches to the study of grammar and usage and especially to the teaching of these matters. They have also long served as epithets in the recurrent name-calling that quarreling over correctness, appropriateness, and permissiveness in language seems to elicit.

The terms represent polar values: (1) A *descriptive* approach to language describes in full detail precisely how we use that language. The chief values of this approach are accuracy and an unretouched picture of usage, warts and all. (2) A *prescriptive* approach insists that however many variables might be found, there are better and worse choices; it will specify at least which is most appropriate, more likely which is acceptable, or, in its most rigorous application, which is correct. Clearly, the *prescriptive* approach is easier to teach—there is always one right answer; the *descriptive* approach may offer several possible answers, each appropriate in one or another context.

This book uses both approaches. Users are seeking help, and they should find it. The problem is that a simplistic "correct" answer may seem helpful, but often when it appears to contradict users' experience, they will either shrug off the *prescription* or find themselves unable to accept it. For example: to say succinctly that *irregardless* is not a word or at least that it ought to be treated as though it were not a word, is *prescriptive*. The "rule" being promulgated is: Don't use *irregardless;* pretend it doesn't exist, because, in fact, it's not in Standard English.

But, in fact, that's not true. It *is* a word, and therefore it is in the dictionaries; many people use it, including some who in other respects speak Standard English. A *descriptive* account of the word will show who uses it and when, where, and why. *Irregardless,* it turns out, occurs regularly in Common and Vulgar English, but in Standard its only acceptable use is jocular. A *descriptive* account will end by pointing out that the inadvertent use of *irregardless* in Standard English can be a shibboleth.

The *prescriptive* commentator then impatiently inquires, Why all the fuss? Why pussyfoot about? Just tell the world not to use *irre-*

gardless—that's simple, sound, and teachable. The *descriptive* commentator will offer at least two objections: (1) The word may be Substandard now, but you can't be sure it won't change in status. In fact it may be in the process of such change even now: it may be fading to an obsolete status (in which case we can stop talking about it), or it may someday become Standard. (2) Even more important, sometimes Standard speakers *do* use *irregardless;* the issue is where and how.

Even in spelling and pronunciation, where *prescription* may seem less problematic, *description* may sometimes be more nearly accurate. *Prescription* says *judgment* is the correct spelling, but *description* accurately points out that even Edited English considers *judgement* correct too. And although the teacher may prescribe *DEK-uh-dent* as the correct way to say *decadent,* the student will discover other teachers who say (also in Standard English) *dee-KAI-dent.*

This book, as it must, uses both approaches, depending on the problem. See the entry on RULES AND GENERALIZATIONS for an account of the aptness of each approach to particular kinds of questions: Where real rules apply, *prescription* is the way to go. But much of grammar and most of usage require generalizations rather than rules, because what so often we must provide is some current best advice on a problem that is undergoing change even as we discuss it. *Description* faces up to complexity and raggedness and avoids simplistic glossing over of existing variation in pronunciations, forms, or meanings. Rigorous *prescribers* often charge *describers* with being permissive, and the countercharge of *describers* is that *prescribers* are simplistic, peddling half-truths and lies as though they were true. But in the end, a guide to usage must give advice, and so this manual *prescribes* for its users when it can. The difference is that it also explains such other experiences as users are likely to encounter and where possible explains what they mean. See also CONSERVATIVES IN LANGUAGE MATTERS; CONSERVATIVE USAGE; LIBERALS IN LANGUAGE MATTERS; LIBERAL USAGE; PURISTS.

present (*v.*) When *present* (pronounced *pree-ZENT*) combines with *to,* as in *to present X to Y,* the person or thing *presented* is X; when it combines with *with,* as in *to present X with Y,* the person or thing *presented* is Y. *Present* with a reflexive pronoun or a direct object is often followed by the prepositions *as, at,* or *for: They presented themselves at dinnertime. She pre-*

sented herself as the only member in attendance. They presented a slate for election.

present incumbent is a cliché, but it is not always redundant, as is sometimes claimed. An *incumbent* is "someone occupying a position or office," either at present or at another time; thus only when there are other clear evidences that the time of incumbency is *now,* is *present incumbent* redundant. *The present incumbents were not running that year; neither had yet been nominated* is not redundant. But *Neither of the incumbents is up for reelection next year* needs no further temporal information; *present incumbents* would be redundant here.

presently (*adv.*) means either "shortly, soon" or "now, at present." Both meanings are Standard, although there has been much objection until fairly recently to the "at present" meaning, even though it has been in steady use since the early Renaissance. The tense of the verb and other contextual evidence usually make clear which sense is in use in a given sentence. *I'll be seeing you presently* clearly means "I'll be seeing you shortly or soon." *He's presently at work on a new novel* means that he is working "at present" and would mean the same thing with *now* or nothing at all instead. See also FORMERLY.

PRESENT PARTICIPLES are the *-ing* forms of verbs that are used with auxiliaries to make the progressive aspects of verbs (*She has been running a lottery*) or to serve as attributive adjectives (*The dog has a running sore on its foot*) or predicate adjectives (*This musical is longest running*). These *-ing* forms can also function as gerunds: *Swimming is his only exercise.*

PRESENT PERFECT TENSE is the name some grammars give to the tense made up of the present tense of the auxiliary *have* plus the past participle of a verb. It expresses action completed in the present time, as in *He has promised* and *She has slept,* or still going on, as in *We have lived here for years.*

PRESENT TENSE is the tense of the verb that describes action taking place now, at the present time, as in *He seeks help,* or that describes current conditions: *We are all friends here.* But see HISTORICAL PRESENT TENSE.

present writer, present author, present commentator, present observer, and the like use the adjective *present* plus a noun as the subject of verbs such as *think, conclude,* or *believe,* thus avoiding use of the pronoun *I* and implying the objectivity of the opinion or conclusion. But overuse has made *present writer* a cliché, and the phrase can often add a ponderous stuffiness. In most contexts, the pronoun *I* is preferable.

preside (*v.*), when it combines with a preposition, usually does so with *over*, as in *She presided over the first session*, although both *at* and *in* also occur, as in *The mayor presides at [in] all town committee meetings*.

PRESTIGE DIALECT is the name for the dialect spoken by the people of most social, political, and economic power and influence in a large language community. The United States has no single *prestige dialect*. In Britain, Received Standard Southern British English is the main *prestige dialect*.

presume See ASSUME.

presumptive, presumptuous (*adjs.*) Something *presumptive* is "likely"; *a presumptive ending* is one "expected, probable." Someone who is *presumptuous* is "arrogant and forward"; *a presumptuous person* takes too much for granted and oversteps the bounds of good manners. Note the spelling of *presumptuous* and its four-syllable pronunciation: *pri-* or *pree-ZUHMP-choo-uhs*.

pretense, pretence (*n.*) Americans spell it *pretense*, the British, *pretence*. Stress on the second syllable (*pri-TENS*) is slightly more frequent, but *PREE-tens* is also Standard.

pretentious See PORTENTOUS.

PRETENTIOUS WORDS are usually not *pretentious* by nature but rather when used where they seem inappropriately stiff. *Pretentiousness* is a matter of relative frequency of use in a given situation: most of the time *unnecessary questions* are ones no one needs, but in a formal situation they might be called *superogatory inquiries*. Move that phrase to the kitchen or another informal setting, however, and it will seem *pretentious*. Match your diction to your situation and to the expectations of your audience. Ball gowns and tails are not *pretentious* at formal dances, but at clambakes on the beach they are, and silly besides.

PRETERIT(E) See PAST TENSE.

preternatural See SUPERNATURAL.

pretty (*adv., adj., n., v., intensifier*) As an adjective meaning "nice-looking, attractive," *pretty* is Standard in all uses, although its ironic use (*This is a pretty mess you've put us in!*) may need careful handling in writing. In the meaning "skillful or elegant" (*He's a pretty swordsman*), the adjective is now nearly archaic.

As an adverb, *pretty* means "fairly," "rather," or "somewhat," as in *a pretty long*

trip, two pretty miserable days*, and from that sense it has drifted into use as a qualifier simply designed to prevent anyone from taking an adjective or another adverb full-strength: *She had some pretty grim news. They'll be here pretty soon.* Grammatically it works like the intensifier *very*, although they are semantically different: compare *a very bad cold* and *a pretty bad cold.* This rather flabby use of *pretty* may have been the cause of some editors' preference for *somewhat* and *rather* as qualifiers, even though *pretty* is also Standard in this use.

Pretty as a noun, especially in the plural, is an old-fashioned word: *pretties* are nice objects or things handsome to look at, and just about everyone has heard the hateful witch in Oz sarcastically call Dorothy "My pretty."

As a verb (*She prettied up her room with flowery curtains*), *pretty*'s use is mainly Conversational. Some Americans would use *prettify* instead and often would use it ironically, stressing its pejorative overtones: to *prettify* something or *to pretty it up* is somehow fake and deceitful; such changes are cosmetic, not real.

prevail (*v.*) combines with *upon* and *on*, as in *They prevailed upon [on] her to accept the nomination.*

prevaricate, procrastinate (*vv.*) Both are pejorative: to *prevaricate* is "to mislead or lie (about something)"; to *procrastinate* is "to put (something) off," "to postpone or defer."

prevent (*v.*) is Standard in all these structures: *The darkness prevented him from finding his penknife. It prevented finding it. It prevented his finding it. It prevented him finding it.* See ADVERT; GENITIVE BEFORE A GERUND.

preventative, preventive (*adjs., nn.*) These two are synonyms, and each is Standard as both adjective and noun: *She practices preventive [preventative] medicine—if you can call eating an apple a day a preventative [preventive].*

previous to, prior to (*preps.*) These are both Standard as substitutes for *before*, just as are some other compound prepositions. *She had never held elective office previous to this year's landslide. Prior to the election he had been unemployed.* Both locutions are more self-consciously formal than *before* or another single-word preposition and may therefore sometimes be thought pretentious or stuffy, but the choice is a matter of style, not correctness.

prewar (*adv., adj.*) The adjective is Standard: *He had a funny old prewar refrigerator in the basement.* The adverb is Conversational and Informal at best, and some people consider it slang or Nonstandard: *Prewar, we spent our summers in Maine.*

priest, clergyman, curate, dominie, minister, parson, pastor, preacher, rabbi, rector, vicar (*nn.*) *Clergyman* has until recently been the most nearly generic of these names for the leaders of religious groups or congregations, but because it is compounded with *-man/-men,* it is viewed by many as a sexually exclusive term; it remains wholly useful only for reference to male clergy. Neither *clergywoman* or *clergyperson* nor any other substitute on that compound pattern has any currency at present. *Cleric(s)* and (sometimes) *clerical(s)* are used, but the latter still refers more often to clerical dress than to persons. This issue is further affected by the fact that in many Christian churches (and in nearly all the Protestant ones) all the other applicable terms for clerical titles are now, like *priest* and *minister,* inclusive, their referents having changed to reflect the fact that both women and men hold these posts. Still further confusion arises because the presence of women in the clergy is still a divisive issue in some churches and in other faiths as well. Hence usages are divided in many quarters.

Rabbi is the Hebrew term used for the title of the teacher of a Jewish congregation; all the others are or can be Christian and are inclusive in most sects. *Priest* is fairly general and is applied historically to non-Christian religions as well, but it is explicit in Roman Catholic, Eastern Orthodox, Episcopal, and some Lutheran Christian denominations. (In some of these, it refers to men only, in others to both men and women.) A *curate* is an assistant to the *vicar* or *rector* of a church. *Dominie* is a Scottish name for either a schoolmaster or a *parson;* Americans now occasionally use it whimsically to refer to the *minister* of almost any Protestant church. A *minister* is the person in charge at almost any Protestant church. *Parson* today is used to refer to an Anglican (Episcopal) *priest* in charge of a parish church, but, like *dominie,* the term is used loosely or whimsically as both title and name for the *minister* of any (usually Protestant) church. A *pastor* (Latin "shepherd") is the *priest* or *minister* in charge of the congregation ("flock"). Since one of this person's duties is to preach, he or she is often called a *preacher;* especially in some Protestant sects the title may be used in direct address. A *rector* is a parish *priest* in an Episcopal church, but the term is also used for the heads of various Roman Catholic seminaries and colleges and, in some schools and colleges, for the headmaster,

headmistress, or principal, whether a *cleric* or not. A *vicar* is a deputy: in the Roman Catholic and Episcopal churches *vicars* may be parish *priests* who are salaried and don't collect tithes, or they may be *priests* in charge of chapels or other religious foundations. The *pope* is also called the *Vicar of Christ.*

prima donna (*n.*) A *prima donna* (plural is *prima donnas*) is a principal female singer in an opera or concert group and by extension anyone—male or female—who exhibits some of the less admirable traits said to be typical of such performers: vanity, sensitivity, temperament, and willfulness. Pronounce it either *PRIM-uh DAH-nuh* or *PREE-muh DAH-nuh.* See FOREIGN PLURALS.

prima facie is a Latin phrase meaning "at first sight" and hence "on the face of it, at face value, without further examination." In its literal sense it is used mainly in the law, but its general meaning is much more widely applied. Pronounce it either *PREE-muh FAI-shuh* or *PREE-muh FAI-shee-uh.* See also FOREIGN PHRASES.

PRIMARY REFERENCE See SECONDARY REFERENCE.

PRIMARY STRESS, SECONDARY STRESS, TERTIARY STRESS, UNSTRESSED Spoken English exhibits up to four levels of relative stress, which all speakers of English can hear when necessary. All two-syllable locutions will have one *primary stress,* but the other syllable may be either a *secondary* or—in a compound—*tertiary stress* or relatively *unstressed.* Compare *deep heat, heat rash,* and *heater; my hand, handball,* and *handy:* in these words, *heat* and *hand* have *primary stresses, deep* and *my, secondary stresses, rash* and *ball, tertiary stresses,* and *-er* and *-y* are *unstressed.* Or consider the following grammatical chestnut that illustrates the four levels of *stress* possible in English: *A light housekeeper* (*uh LEIT HOUS-keep-uhr*) is "a housekeeper who does light housekeeping" or "a housekeeper who doesn't weigh much"; *house* gets the *primary stress, light* a bit less (*secondary*), *keep* still less (*tertiary*), and *a* and *-er* still less (*fourth level,* or *unstressed*). *A lighthouse keeper* (*uh LEIT-hous-KEEP-uhr*) is "a person who keeps a lighthouse"; in this *compound compound* (it could be spelled as one word), *light* has *primary stress, keep secondary, house tertiary,* and *a* and *-er* are *unstressed.*

principal (*adj., n.*), **principle** (*n.*) The spellings and meanings of these homophones differ:

the adjective is always spelled *principal* and means "first, chief, main, or most important": *She was his principal reason for being there.* Hence the person in charge of a school has this noun as title: *She is the principal of a high school. Principal* also means "a person whom an agent represents" (*the agent's principal*) and "an amount of money in an investment": *Money first invested is the principal, and it earns interest. Principle* too is a noun, with a variety of meanings such as "a law," "a source or beginning," "a basis," *We will object on principle.*

PRINCIPAL PARTS OF VERBS Conventionally these are the infinitive (without its *to* sign), the past tense, and the past participle: *run, ran, run; think, thought, thought;* and *rain, rained, rained* are the *principal parts* of the verbs *run, think,* and *rain.*

principle See PRINCIPAL.

PRINCIPLE OF PROXIMITY See AGREEMENT OF SUBJECT AND VERBS (4).

prioritize (*v.*) is a jargon word, meaning "to set or arrange in order of priority"; limit its use to situations where that jargon is at home. Edited English is usually sparing of this verb in general use. See -ISE.

prior to See PREVIOUS TO.

prise See PRIZE.

pristine (*adj.*) Americans stress it on either syllable. It has an interesting semantic history, the most recent American parts of which some British commentators dislike. The word began by meaning "belonging to the earliest or the original state, original" but then developed into meaning "unsullied, clean, inviolate, unspoiled" and most recently simply "new, untouched," with no touch of "old" or "original" at all. All three senses are still Standard, but to communicate the idea of "earliest, original," let context add "age" to the ideas of "unspoiled" and "new."

privatize (*v.*) means "to award a public service or property to a private operator": *The town voted to privatize trash collection and sell the town's garbage trucks.* The British have used the word since shortly after the end of World War II; Americans have taken it up only fairly recently, but it is Standard, although some people still consider it jargon, possibly because they dislike adding to the list of -*ize* words.

prix fixe is a French phrase meaning "a fixed price" for a whole meal. Pronounce it either *PREE FIKS* or *PREE FEEKS*.

prize, prise, pry (*vv.*) There are two verbs spelled *prize.* The first means "to value highly"; it poses no particular problems. The second *prize* means "to pry (open or up)," as in *She used the poker to prize open the locked file drawer. Prise* is this *prize's* British spelling. *To pry* is "to use a tool called a *pry* as a lever in moving, opening, or raising something": *We pried open a window on the side of the house.* In this sense *pry* and *prize* (2) are synonyms, but they are not in the intransitive figurative sense of *pry* meaning "to intrude, to seek information rudely," as in *She was always prying into matters that were none of her concern.*

pro (*adj., n.*) is a clipped form of *professional*; limit its use to Informal and Conversational situations: *After several years of amateur tennis, she turned pro. He used to play pro football.* It is also slang in the extended noun sense meaning "highly skilled," as in *She handles committee work like a real pro.*

proactive (*adj.*) A *proactive* measure is one designed to intervene in, prevent, or control something that is expected to occur. The word is more than fifty years old, but it recently has seen some much-expanded use, especially in discussions of legislative, political, and social issues: *I believe we must take a proactive stance on matters of racial discrimination.* It illustrates our penchant for hyperbole, and some criticize it as jargon.

probable See POSSIBLE.

probability (*n.*) usually takes *of: There is a low probability of success in this venture.* That plus a clause is also Standard: *There is little probability that we will win.* Compare POSSIBILITY.

probe (*n., v.*) *Probe* fits newspaper headlines much more easily than *investigation* does, and its frequent use there has caused some commentators to object to its use elsewhere. But both noun and verb are Standard in both literal and figurative senses: *Dentists use several kinds of probes to determine the extent of tooth decay. Patients usually believe dentists probe too deeply and too long. The prosecutor probed deeply into the witness's story but could not shake it.*

problem (*adj., n.*) is getting considerable use—perhaps overuse—as a generic term these days: *He has a drug [drinking, weight, wife, sleeping, communication, money,* etc.] *problem* illustrates the variety of *problem* clichés we have developed to refer to things too complex to describe fully. Note too that usage requires that you *solve* a *problem,* not *answer* it, and in the passive too, *your problem is solved,* not *answered.* See also NO PROBLEM.

proceed (*v.*), **proceeds** (*n. pl.*), **procedure, proceeding(s)** (*nn.*) The spellings are a bit tricky (*see* -CEDE; PRECEDE). The verb *proceed* is pronounced either *pro-SEED* or *pruh-SEED*; the plural noun *proceeds* is pronounced *PRO-SEEDS.* The verb has become a cliché in police reporting and the police officer's testimony: *I proceeded to the complainant's residence* would be less solemnly self-conscious as *I went [walked, drove,* etc.] *to the complainant's house.*

procrastinate See PREVARICATE.

procure (*v.*), **procurement** (*n.*) there are many words to describe acquiring things: you may *get* them, *buy* them, *obtain* them, *secure* them, or *procure* them. *Procure* may seem stuffier or more consciously elegant than the others, but there are times when that shift in tone may be useful. The word is Standard, and it is pretentious only in the wrong context, particularly because of its echoes of the *procuring* of sexual favors.

 Procurement is military and governmental jargon for purchasing—both the process and the departments charged with it.

prodigal (*adj., n.*) To be *prodigal* is to be wasteful, and a *prodigal* is a spendthrift, not a wanderer, a runaway, or someone long lost to his family. *The prodigal son* (*Luke* 15) was so called not because he left home but because he was a wastrel; however, in figurative use the full parable is usually the referent. The adjective combines most frequently with the prepositions *of* or *with* (*She has always been prodigal of* [*with*] *her money*) and occasionally with *in* or *as to* (*The audience was prodigal in* [*as to*] *its applause*). But *as to* is a poor choice.

producer, conductor, director (*nn.*) In theatrical, motion picture, and musical recording work, the *producer* is in overall charge, especially of finances, management, and coordination. The *director* is in artistic charge, supervising the actors and other performers directly involved in the creation of the play, musical, or film. In music making, the *director* is also called the *conductor.*

product, end See END PRODUCT.

productive (*adj.*) combines with the preposition *of: The meeting was productive of more heat than light.*

PROFANITY The most important meaning of *profanity* for the subject of language usage is "language that belittles or displays disrespect or contempt for sacred things." "Taking the name of the Lord in vain" or other disrespectful reference to a religion, its symbols, or its beliefs still represents that specific sense of the word. But *profanity* has also generalized to mean to many people (both those who use such expressions and those for whom they are taboo) language that is simply distasteful, debased, or improper; hence *profanity* and *obscenity* are in some senses synonyms. One of the most interesting developments in recent American English usage has been the considerable weakening of the prohibitions against *profanity* in many contexts of language use wherein it had hitherto been taboo or much restricted.

professor, instructor, teacher (*nn.*) A *professor* holds a *professorship,* and his or her title is *professor of history* or *professor of physics.* Using the title *Professor* in direct address is usually reserved for formal situations, such as introducing a speaker or the like. *Fred is a professor at the university* can be pretentious; the generic term is *teacher: He's a teacher at the university;* his rank is *professor,* but his *profession* is *teaching.* The usual academic ranks in American colleges and universities begin at the bottom with *instructor* (which is also a generic term like *teacher*) and then move upward to *assistant professor, associate professor,* and *professor*—or within academe "*full professor,*" to distinguish it from the two other professorial ranks when the rank itself is under discussion. When a teacher signs her letters she will write *Mary J. Smith, Assistant Professor of Chemistry,* but when she is introduced, or when her students use her academic title to address her, she's *Professor Smith,* regardless of which of the three professorial ranks she holds. *Prof* (pronounced *PRAHF*) is slang in continuous discourse or writing; limit the abbreviation to written addresses on letters and packages. See also DOCTOR.

proficient (*adj.*) combines most frequently with the prepositions *at* and *in: She is highly proficient at* [*in*] *solid geometry.* When the proficiency involves a musical instrument or a machine of some sort, *proficient* can combine with *on, at,* or *with: He is proficient on* [*at, with*] *the computer* [*the trombone*].

profit (*v.*), when it combines with prepositions, does so with either *from* or *by: You'll profit a good deal from* [*by*] *studying Latin.*

prognosis See DIAGNOSIS.

program (*n., v.*) Americans spell the noun and the infinitive of the verb with one *m;* other forms of the American verb are in divided usage: *programed* or *programmed, programing* or *programming.* The noun with the agentive ending is similarly divided—*programer* or *programmer*—but the adjective *programmable* always has two *m*'s, and Americans usually use the two *m*'s when the subject is *programmed instruction* or *computer programming.* The British spell the noun and verb *programme* and consistently spell the other forms of the word with two *m*'s. See CONSONANTS (2); SPELLING (1).

progression (arithmetic, geometric, mathematical) (*nn.*) An *arithmetic* (pronounced *er-ith-MET-ik*) *progression* is a sequence of numbers in which the difference between succeeding terms is the same number: *1, 4, 7, 10, 13,* etc. A *geometric progression* is a sequence of numbers in which the ratio of each number to the one it follows is the same: *1, 2, 4, 8, 16, 32, 64,* etc. A *mathematical progression* is a sequence of numbers in which each succeeding number is obtained by the action of the same rule on the preceding number; hence both *arithmetic* and *geometric progressions* are *mathematical progressions.*

PROGRESSIVE ASPECT See ASPECT (1).

PROGRESSIVE PASSIVE, also called the *imperfect passive,* was once frowned on but is now Standard English, and it's hard to imagine the language without it today. *Our carpet is being cleaned today* has a *progressive passive verb;* once we'd have said *Our carpet is cleaning today,* but no longer.

prohibit (*v.*), when it combines with a preposition, usually takes *from* plus an *-ing* form of a verb: *The rules prohibit us from leaving the room.* Prior to the mid-nineteenth century, the common construction was with *to* plus an infinitive: *The rules prohibit you to leave the room*; most editors and commentators consider that combination obsolete today. *Prohibit* can also take a direct object, either a noun or a gerund: *The rules prohibit your departure. The rules prohibit your leaving.* See INHIBIT.

project (*n., v.*) The noun is pronounced *PRAH-jekt,* the verb *pro-JEKT.*

prolegomenon (*n.*) is the singular of a noun meaning "a preliminary or prefatory essay or introductory statement or remark." It is a low-frequency learned word, and the inexperienced sometimes mistake *prolegomena* for a singular—it's the plural. See FOREIGN PLURALS; compare CRITERION; PHENOMENON.

PROLIXITY See WORDINESS.

promise (*v.*) Among its meanings is the long-standing "to assure," as in *I promise you, we'll win the game.* Don't use this sense in Formal and Oratorical contexts.

prone, prostrate, supine (*adjs.*) The literal senses of these are very explicit, but the figurative uses are much more commonly encountered: to lie *prone* is "to lie face down," but the figurative sense, "to be inclined or have a tendency toward something," is much more frequently used, as in *She is accident-prone* or *The children are prone to winter colds* (see also APT; LIKELY). To lie *supine* is "to lie face up," but the figurative sense is much more frequent: "to be slack, yielding, unresistant," as in *He was supine and irresolute from the beginning.* To *prostrate* yourself is in the literal sense "to lie face down before a deity," but the figurative uses are again much more commonly encountered: "to be knocked off your feet, to be felled, as by grief, exhaustion, or sickness," as in *She was prostrate with grief at the death of her child* and *He was prostrate for fully half an hour after the marathon.*

PRONOUN This high-frequency part of speech belongs to a relatively short, finite list of words used in place of nouns or other *pronouns.* See INDEFINITE PRONOUNS; PERSONAL PRONOUNS; REFLEXIVE PRONOUNS; RELATIVE PRONOUNS.

PRONOUN AGREEMENT See AGREEMENT; AGREEMENT OF COMPOUND SUBJECTS WITH THEIR VERBS AND SUBSEQUENT PRONOUNS; AGREEMENT OF INDEFINITE PRONOUNS AND OTHER SINGULAR NOMINALS WITH VERBS AND OTHER PRONOUNS; NUMBER (1).

pronounce (*v.*), when followed by a preposition, usually takes *on* or *upon: She's always eager to pronounce on* [*upon*] *the behavior of other people's children.* It sometimes combines with *about: He was constantly pronouncing about the need for more police.* With a reflexive pronoun *pronounce* also combines with *for, in favor of, against,* and *opposed to,* as in *They pronounced themselves for* [*in favor of, against, opposed to*] *the amendment.*

PRONOUNS, REFLEXIVE See REFLEXIVE PRONOUNS.

PRONOUN WITH POSSESSIVE ANTECEDENT *Milton's blindness forced him to dictate to an amanuensis.* Some have argued that a personal pronoun such as *him* in the example cannot have a noun in the genitive case (*Milton's*) as its antecedent; they insist that only a genitive pronoun with noun will work: *Milton's blindness forced his dictation to an aman-*

uensis. But there is nothing wrong with the example using *him:* we know that it refers to Milton, and although the logic may be imperfect the common sense of the grammar prevails. Occasionally, especially when the pronoun is *who* or *whom* instead of *whose* (*A prodigious piece of work was Johnson's dictionary, who now gets credit for a one-man effort*), the resulting sentence will be awkward regardless of whether the pronoun is genitive or something else. But otherwise you may comfortably use a noun in the genitive case as antecedent for a pronoun in any case.

pronunciation 1 (*n.*) is often mispronounced and misspelled by the inexperienced, who say and write its first two syllables as they would those in *pronounce.* Note the spelling of the second syllables of the two words, and say *pronunciation pro-NUHN-see-AI-shuhn.*

PRONUNCIATION 2: AMERICAN AND BRITISH DIFFERENCES There are several words that are pronounced differently in American and British English: *laboratory* is *LAB-uhr-uh-TOR-ee* or *LAB-ruh-TOR-ee* in American English, *luh-BOR-uh-tuhr-ee* or *luh-BOR-uh-tree* in British. *Clerk* rhymes with *murk* in the United States, but the British pronounce it to rhyme with *mark.* And what Americans call *VEIT-uh-minz* most Britons call *VIT-uh-minz.* But by far the largest number of words we think of as being peculiarly British pronunciations are pronounced much the same way in this country in one or another of our regional dialects (e.g., *tuh-MAH-to, VAHZ*).

The vowels we spell with the letters *a* and *o* have a different sound in some British uses from those in much of American English, but again, Eastern New England dialect has sounds for them that are very nearly like those of British English. And while most Americans retain their *r* coloration, those in New England, New York City, and the Southern dialect regions do not: they pronounce *car* as *KAH,* as in British English.

Americans notice the differences in stress and syllable count in words like *secretary* (*SEK-ruh-TER-ee, SEK-ruh-tree*) and *extraordinary* (*ek-STROR-din-ER-ee, ek-STRORD-nree*), and Britons are usually hard-pressed to tell the difference between American *ladder* and *latter.* And there are also differences in intonation, especially in short questions, wherein the American would say *Are you/READY?,* while the Briton would likely say it *ARE you\READY?*

All these differences are dialectal rather than signs of the development of separate American and British languages. Speakers of either Standard dialect can understand almost everything that speakers of the other say, even as each is aware of the other's different ways of talking.

PRONUNCIATION OF COMPOUND WORDS English compounds put primary stress on the first element and a slightly lower stress (secondary or tertiary but not unstressed) on the final element of the word or phrase. It is that stress pattern that tells us we have a compound: when someone mentions a *haht DAWG,* we know that the dog is panting heavily, with its tongue hanging out; if that person mentions a *HAHT-dawg,* we know that a weiner is the subject of conversation.

PRONUNCIATION OF NOUNS ENDING IN -AGE These originally French words reflect in their pronunciation some indications of their relative frequency of use and their relative length of time in English: those with a final consonant *j* sound in an unstressed final syllable (*courage, carriage, cleavage, steerage, sewage, windage*) have been relatively long in this language and have relatively high frequency of use; those with a final consonant *zh* sound in a final syllable still stressed in the heavier French manner (*barrage, mirage, badinage*) have been in English relatively briefly and have not had very heavy use; and words such as *garage* exhibit both patterns of pronunciation (*guh-RAHJ* and *guh-RAHZH*), plus the British variant pronunciation *GER-ij* (rhymes with *carriage*), all three of which suggest the word's relatively short time in English but its relatively high frequency of use.

PRONUNCIATION OF NOUNS ENDING IN -F, -FE See NOUNS ENDING IN -F.

PRONUNCIATIONS, SPELLING See SPELLING PRONUNCIATIONS.

PRONUNCIATIONS, VARIANT See VARIANT PRONUNCIATIONS.

PRONUNCIATIONS OF WORDS ENDING IN -TH, -THE Three generalizations apply to most words ending in -th and -the when they undergo functional shift to become verbs: they add a final -e in spelling, a short medial vowel becomes long, and the voiceless *th,* as in *thigh,* becomes voiced, as in *thy: breath* (*BRETH*) becomes *breathe* (*BREETH*); *sheath* (*SHEETH*) becomes *sheathe* (*SHEETH; teeth* (*TEETH*) becomes *teethe* (*TEETH*).

PROOFREADER'S MARKS These are the standardized, specialized marks used by printers' and publishers' proofreaders to indicate corrections and other changes on manuscripts and printed matter. Consult a desk dictionary for a listing.

propaganda (*n.*) is always singular and has no plural form. See DISINFORMATION.

propellant, propellent (*adj., n.*) These spellings are in divided usage in American English, but *propellant* is by far the more common spelling for both noun and adjective. British English has more instances of *propellent*.

propeller, propellor (*n.*) *Propeller* is the more frequent spelling; *propellor* is rare.

PROPER NOUNS, PROPER NAMES
Proper nouns are in fact *proper names: Cleveland, Mississippi, Frederick S. Smith, Boeing, Second Congregational Church, Palace Theater, Memorial Stadium.* These are the names of specific persons, places, organizations, and the like, and American English conventionally capitalizes the first letter of each word in a name other than conjunctions, prepositions, and articles: *the House of Representatives, the Army of the United States, the Fourth of July, the Treaty of Versailles.* In titles of works, the initial article is also capitalized: *The Toronto Globe and Mail, The Naked and the Dead, A Man for All Seasons.*

prophecy (*n.*), **prophesy** (*v.*) Although in the past the noun and the verb have been spelled both ways, today they seem quite settled, with *-cy* for the noun, *-sy* for the verb. Their different pronunciations seem not to confuse: the noun is *PRAH-fuh-see,* the verb *PRAH-fuh-SEI.* The problem is only for the poor speller.

prophesize (*v.*) is Substandard, apparently an error caused by a feeling that *prophesy* needs a suffix to be a real verb. To say or write *prophesize* is a shibboleth.

prophesy See PROPHECY.

propitious (*adj.*) can combine with the prepositions *for* and *to: This was a time propitious for [to] entering the market.*

proportion (*n.*) Some commentators have long and wrongly argued that *proportion* cannot be used to indicate size or magnitude or to mean "part" or "portion" but should be used only to express a ratio of one thing to another. Actually, it has long been Standard in all three senses: *The run on the bank quickly reached epidemic proportions* ["size"]. *A noticeable proportion* ["part"] *of the residents failed to attend the meeting. The proportion* ["ratio"] *of those vot-*ing on the resolution was about three in favor, one opposed.*

proportional, proportionable, proportionate (*adjs.*) All three words mean the same thing: "determined by proportion, in proportion to or with, relative to," or "in a proper ratio with." *Proportional* is the most frequently encountered, and *proportionate* also has a fair amount of use. *Proportionable* is at least archaic and may be obsolescent.

proposal, proposition (*nn.*) Both are suggestions or offers of some sort, as in *He made us a proposal [proposition] that I thought was very reasonable. Proposition,* like *business, affair, situation,* and *concern,* is used loosely to mean "a matter of some sort" or almost any "concern" or vague "thing": *This looks like a tough proposition* (whatever *this* may be). Each word also has a specialized meaning concerning the relationships of man and woman: a *proposal* is an offer of marriage; a *proposition* is an invitation to have sexual intercourse outside the marital bond. *Proposition* in this sense is also a verb, meaning "to make such an invitation"; the verb in that sense is possibly Standard but certainly appropriate at the Conversational, Informal, and Semiformal levels.

proprietary (*adj.*), **propriety** (*n.*) A *proprietary* right is one held by reason of a patent or a title or some other basis for a claim of ownership: *He has a proprietary interest in that publishing house. Propriety* is what is decent, fitting, and proper and conforms with accepted standards of behavior: *The propriety of his questions was never in doubt.*

prorate (*v.*), meaning "to divide, assess, or share proportionally among those eligible," is Standard English, an Americanism based on the Latin *pro rata,* meaning "according to the proportional share." Pronounce *prorate* either *pro-RAIT* or *PRO-rait*; pronounce *pro rata* either *pro-RA-tuh* or *pro-RAI-tuh,* but use it sparingly except when the jargon of finance, taxes, and other numerical work is appropriate.

prosaic, prosy (*adjs.*) *Prosaic* means "dull, commonplace, unimaginative"; *prosy* means "long-winded, garrulous and rambling." *Most people live prosaic everyday lives, and detailed descriptions of their days would very likely be unendurably prosy.*

proscribe See PRESCRIBE.

PROSE is the unrhymed, nonmetrical, everyday language we speak and write at any or all levels. We usually mean written language when we use the word *prose,* however, and we contrast *prose* with poetry or verse. Sometimes (but rarely) we contrast it with fiction, as well. But see EXPOSITORY WRITING.

proselyte, proselytize (*vv.*) These verbs are exact synonyms, the first the result of functional shift from the noun *proselyte,* the second made by adding the *-ize* suffix to the noun. Both mean "to attempt to recruit or convert someone to your group, movement, religion, or other belief." Americans seem to use *proselytize* more frequently, perhaps because the suffix makes its part-of-speech designation unmistakable.

prospective See PERSPECTIVE.

prostate (*adj., n.*), **prostrate** (*adj., v.*) To add an *r* to the second syllable of *prostate* (the gland) is to make these two words into homophones, an inadvertent Substandard blunder and malapropism that will make the knowing laugh.

prospectus (*n.*) Its plural is regular: *prospectuses.*

prosthesis, prosthetics (*nn.*), **prosthetic** (*adj.*) A *prosthesis* is a device that substitutes for all or part of a missing human limb or organ; the plural is *prostheses.* The adjective is *prosthetic: Dentures are prosthetic devices. Prosthetics* is the subject and process of designing, making, and fitting *prosthetic* devices. See FOREIGN PLURALS.

prostrate See PROSTATE.

prosy See PROSAIC.

protagonist See ANTAGONIST.

protect (*v.*), when it combines with prepositions, usually does so with *from* or *against: Protect yourself against [from] the flu by getting a flu shot. By* and *with* also occur, indicating the protection itself rather than the thing to be protected against: *She protected herself by taking her German shepherd with her on her evening walks. The mansion was protected with elaborate electronic warning devices.*

protégé(e) (*n.*) This word, borrowed from French, usually but not always retains both its acute accent marks in American use. The masculine *protégé* is sometimes used for female referents as well, although the feminine *protégée* also occurs, especially in Edited English. Pronounce both forms either *PRO-tuh-ZHAI* or *PRO-te-ZHAI.*

protest (*n., v.*) The noun is always pronounced with the primary stress on the first syllable; the verb is in divided usage, usually with primary stress on the second syllable but sometimes with it on the first. When the noun combines with a preposition, it usually does so with *against* but sometimes with *about, at,* or *over: Their protest against [about, at, over] the new tax was loud. To* and *of* also occur, but less often: *This demonstration was in protest to [of] all proposed fee increases.* The verb combines with *against, about, at,* and *over: The entire chamber protested against [about, at, over] the chair's ruling.* The verb also can appear without a preposition in both transitive (*The party protests all new taxation*) and intransitive use (*We protested vehemently*).

protractor (*n.*) has two pronunciations, usually semantically distinguished from each other: it's *PRO-TRAK-tuhr* for the mathematical instrument used for plotting angles, but *pro-TRAK-tuhr* for something or someone that protracts, delays, or extends something.

provable (*adj.*), **provably** (*adv.*), **provability** (*n.*) All three drop the final *-e* of *prove* before adding suffixes.

prove (*v.*) The principal parts are *prove, proved,* and *proved* or *proven.* Both *proved* and *proven* are used not only as past participles but also as participial adjectives, as in *a proved [proven] champion* or in *His guilt is proved [proven].* Generally, *proved* is much more frequent as participle, *proven* more frequent as attributive adjective. See also EXCEPTION PROVES THE RULE.

proverb See APHORISM.

provide (*v.*) In transitive use, *provide* combines (1) with *to* or *for* to name the recipient of whatever is being *provided,* as in *The government provided temporary housing to [for] the refugees;* (2) with *with* to indicate whatever is being *provided,* as in *The Red Cross provided the victims with food and shelter;* (3) with a *that* clause to indicate a condition or stipulation, as in *We provided that someone else would always do the driving.* In intransitive use, *provide* combines with *for* or *against: His retirement plan is supposed to provide for his declining years. Her insurance program was intended to provide against every possible contingency.*

provided, providing (*conjs.*) These two are synonyms, meaning "on condition (that)" or "if": *I will attend every session, providing [provided] that I can get transportation.* Both are Standard. *That* is often omitted in Conversational and Informal contexts.

provident, providential (*adjs.*) To be *provident* is "to be one who plans ahead, to be frugal and economical": *He was a provident husband and father*. *Providential* means "through the intervention of divine providence" and hence "fortunate, lucky," as in *The rain after the long drought was providential*. See PRUDENT.

province See AREA.

proviso (*n.*) The plural is either *provisos* or *provisoes*. See PLURALS OF NOUNS ENDING IN -O.

provoke (*v.*) has an interesting array of meanings: "to call up, stir up, or instigate": *His jokes provoked a lot of laughter from the class. Her words provoked some introspection on my part; they were thought-provoking*. But it also has a specialized cluster of senses, meaning "to stir to anger, to irritate, to annoy": *I was really provoked by her behavior. Her inconsiderateness was provoking*. All these uses are Standard, but the specialized senses are better limited to Conversational or Informal contexts.

proximity See CLOSE PROXIMITY.

PROXIMITY, THE PRINCIPLE OF See AGREEMENT OF SUBJECTS AND VERBS (4).

prudent, prudential, providential (*adjs.*) The first two are synonyms, meaning "careful, wise, shrewd, circumspect, frugal, especially in business or financial matters." Actions and policies may be either *prudential* or *prudent*, but people are always described as *prudent*, not *prudential*: *She's a prudent manager who follows prudent [prudential] practices*.

Possibly because *prudential* and *providential* turn up as parts of the names of insurance companies and certainly because to be *provident* is to be *prudent*, sometimes *prudential* is confused with *providential* in the minds of the inexperienced. Something *providential* is good fortune indeed, as though decreed by divine providence. Something *prudent*, however, is an action or policy planned by the individual, using common sense. See PROVIDENT.

pry (*v.*) means "to peer into, to inquire, to be nosey," as in *Don't pry into my affairs*. This *pry* is not the same verb as the one meaning "to raise or move, as with a lever." But see also PRIZE.

pseudo (*n., adj.*), **pseudo-** (*prefix*) The noun and "quasi-adj." (as the *OED* calls it) has been in English since the fourteenth century, a pejorative meaning "fake, false, counterfeit"; the noun's plural is either *pseudoes* or *pseudos*. The adjective has since the 1970s had a much increased use, stimulated no doubt by the growing list of standard words with *pseudo-* as prefix or combining form (*pseudo-event, pseudonym, pseudoscience*, etc.) Nonce words using *pseudo-* are coined regularly; *pseudo-* is indeed a vogue combining form these days; it is probably a cliché in that use.

Pseudo itself, however, is Conversational and Informal at best, even though it has appeared mainly as adjective, in the print media. Some Conservatives vigorously oppose its growing use, and its future is cloudy at the moment. Pronounce adjective, noun, and prefix *SOO-do;* the inexperienced pronunciation *SWAI-do* is a devastating shibboleth.

P.S., usually capitalized but not always using periods, is an abbreviation meaning "postscript," an afterthought at the end of a letter, added below the signature. If you add subsequent *postscripts*, label them *PPS*. Avoid using postscripts in other than Informal personal correspondence, however, since they suggest that the writer was careless or not interested in saving the reader's time.

pseudonym (*n.*) means "a false name" and hence "an assumed name." Consider also the actor's *stage name*, other performers' *professional names*, and the expression *AKA*, "also known as," for dealing with any of these, including criminals' aliases. See AKA; ALIAS; NOM DE PLUME.

psychoanalyze See SPELLING (1).

psychosis The plural is *psychoses*. See FOREIGN PLURALS.

publicly, publically (*advs.*) *Publicly* is the usual spelling; *publically* does occur, but rarely in Edited English.

publish (*v.*) To *publish* a book or a newspaper is "to issue it, to put it before the public," but in the technical sense it is not to write it: *The parent company published a series of these studies. A university press published her new monograph*. Loosely, however, the current Standard senses of *publish* also include the idea of being the author of a published work, though purists regret the newer sense as blurring a useful distinction: *The Columbia University Press has published many books, but so has James Michener*.

pulpit See PODIUM.

pummel See POMMEL.

punctilious, punctual (*adjs.*) A *punctilious* person is scrupulously attentive to details; a *punctual* person is always on time.

PUNCTUATION; PUNCTUATION MARKS *Punctuation* is the conventional graphic system that uses symbols—*punctuation marks*—to separate or link sentences and their parts in order to make written English grammatically clear. Some aspects of *punctuation* are meant to suggest graphically what intonation makes clear in speech; other sorts of *punctuation* are visual signals only, often conveying meanings that cannot be signaled in speech. See the entries for the individual *punctuation marks* themselves: APOSTROPHE (2); BRACKETS; COLON; COMMA (1); DASH; DOUBLE HYPHEN; ELLIPSIS (3); EXCLAMATION POINT; HYPHEN; PARENTHESES; PERIOD (1); QUESTION MARK; QUOTATION MARKS; SEMICOLON; VIRGULE.

pundit See PANDIT.

punish (*v.*) combines with *by* and *with* to indicate the nature of the punishment itself: *We were punished by being sent to bed without supper. In the fifth round he was punished with many hard blows to the head. Punish* combines with *for* to name the reason for the punishment: *She was punished for not getting her parents' permission.*

pupil, student (*nn.*) A *pupil* is usually a child in an elementary school, but the noun is also used of anyone of any age studying any subject or skill, especially under the tutelage of a teacher: *He was her piano pupil for more than ten years. Student* is the usual term for those in high school, college, and beyond, but it is also the generic word for those involved in formal education of any sort, except for the extremely young. In other uses the two words are synonyms meaning "learner," in either a formal educational sense or in the tutorial role of *tutee.*

puppet (*adj., n.*), **marionette** (*n.*) Technically a *puppet* is a kind of hollow doll that may be moved by a hand and arm thrust inside it, or by rods, or simply as a shadow on a wall or screen, and, also technically, a *marionette* is a doll with articulated joints moved from above by means of wires and strings. *Puppet* is also the generic term for all such dolls and figures, however, and the art itself is called *puppetry;* those who manipulate *puppets* of any sort are *puppeteers.* Finally, we make much extended use of *puppet* to refer as adjective or noun to people or governments not their own masters but manipulated by others: *He had the title of king, but he was the prime minister's puppet. The party formed another puppet government.* All these senses are Standard.

purchase (*n., v.*) Some commentators, urging simplicity, argue that *You purchased something* is a pretentious way of saying *You bought it. Purchase* is a lower-frequency, more studied word than *buy,* but it will also offer variety when needed and perhaps some sense of scale. As for the noun: perhaps a pair of shoes on sale is a good *buy,* but certainly *a good purchase* is an appropriate way to describe something as considerable as the *Louisiana Purchase.*

purebred See THOROUGHBRED.

purge (*v.*), when it combines with prepositions, takes *of* when it is followed by the thing(s) eliminated (*The army was purged of all the troops who revolted*), *from* to stress what it was that was cleared of the thing(s) eliminated and what was eliminated (*They purged from the army all who had been in revolt*), and *by* to specify the way the *purging* is or was done (*They intend to purge the bureaucracy by making wholesale dismissals and new appointments*).

PURISTS insist on sticking to the rules, even if sometimes the rules do not actually describe Standard practice. Their lexicons and grammars are full of absolutes that they insist are not subject to change; to *purists,* to permit deviation from the language norms they admire and wish to preserve is to be unacceptably permissive (it is not surprising that the most outspoken and unyielding of *purists* are sometimes called *absolutists*). The term *purists* is frequently pejorative, but at its least combative it can also identify linguistic conservatives (not necessarily reactionaries) who reject the fads and swift changes of vocabulary and grammar in favor of as rigorous an adherence to traditional and conventional standards as they can enforce. When they err, it is usually because they cling too long to the old, but sometimes they preserve the good middle way from the depredations of the new and modish. Compare PERMISSIVENESS.

purport (*v.*) *This publication purports to be the voice of the new party* and *This publication is purported to be the voice of the new party* differ in meaning: *purports to be* suggests that it "intends" or "pretends" or "claims" to be; *is purported to be* suggests that it "is thought to be" or "has been put forward by others as being."* Both uses are Standard.

purposefully, purposedly, purposely (*advs.*) *Purposefully* means "with determination, with a specific goal in mind": *She walked purposefully to the lectern. Purposely* has a slightly different sense—"deliberately, on purpose, intentionally": *I purposely avoided calling on him. Purposedly* is an exact synonym of *purposely,* but rare.

pursuit (*n.*) sometimes combines with the preposition *of: The pursuit of knowledge is often a rather slow chase.*

pusillanimous (*adj.*) is a high-flown word for *cowardly, fearful,* or *timid.* Don't spell it *pussilanimous.*

put down (*v.*), **putdown** (*n.*) *To put down a revolt* is "to stop it and defeat the rebels." That is Standard. *To put down the baby* is "to set or lay it down on something," and that is Standard too. But *to put someone down,* meaning "to squelch or repress or shame or silence him or her," is Conversational and Informal or Semiformal, as is the noun *putdown,* meaning "an undercutting remark," "a squelch." Related to these is the veterinary euphemism meaning "purposefully to kill an animal": *The mare has a broken leg; we'll have to put her down.*

put English on means "to put a spin on a ball (bowling, billiards, or some other) to make it follow a curved course." The idiom is not suitable for the most staid of Formal English but is common in much Conversational and Informal language. See SPIN.

put stock in See STOCK.

put your best foot forward See BEST FOOT FORWARD.

puzzle See ENIGMA.

Pygmy (*n.*), **pygmy, pigmy** (*adj., n.*) The more common spelling of the word is *pygmy,* and when the African peoples are referred to, the word is usually capitalized. The adjective also has extended meanings, applied to anything very small in comparison to more usual examples: *The dik-dik is any of several African pygmy antelopes.*

pyjamas See PAJAMAS.

Pyrrhic victory (*n.*) The term means a victory that cost too much, and it is usually capitalized, as is the name of the ancient king who won one, *Pyrrhus.* When *Pyrrhic* is used as an adjective applied to other nouns, its meaning may become more generalized and may tend toward a merely pejorative meaning—not one of explicitly "too costly" but just "not good."

Q

qua (*adv.*) is the Latin ablative singular of the pronoun *who* and means "in the character or function of," "in the role of," or "as being": *This bestseller is not art qua art as most people would define it.* It is now an English word and need not be italicized, but its modest efficiencies are only rarely worth its pretentiousness. See FOREIGN PHRASES.

quadroon See MULATTO.

QUALIFIERS are words or phrases (typically adjectives or adverbs or word groups functioning as these do) that work grammatically much as do intensifiers, but semantically they limit or modify the meanings of other words or word groups rather than emphasize or intensify them, as in *She is **nearly** always prepared; **Normally** we get there early; They served a **rather** good dinner.*

quandary (*n.*) is sometimes misspelled *quandry.*

quantum (*n.*) means "quantity, amount," and in its uses in physics its plural is *quanta.* Semantic change has made it mean "a large quantity," "a specified quantity," and in *quantum theory,* "a fixed elemental unit." The problem is that among its senses are both "large bulk" and "very small increments into which energy is subdivided" or "a very tiny subdivision of quantized physical energy." Use context carefully to make clear which sense you intend. See FOREIGN PLURALS; QUANTUM JUMP.

quantum jump, quantum leap (*nn.*) Both terms mean "a very sudden change in an energy level" and hence, by extension, "any very sudden change or improvement in something," as in *Audiology has made a quantum leap over the past few years in the miniaturization of hearing aids.* The usage issue is that in energy physics *a quantum jump* is very rapid but very small, whereas the layperson understands and uses the term to suggest a major, sudden, and very large change or improvement. But both uses are now

Standard, even though scientists often object to the lay sense, which has become a cliché. Be sure of your audience's expectations when you use the scientific sense, and avoid the cliché.

quarter See STANZA.

quartet, quartette, quintet, quintette, sextet, sextette, septet, septette, octet, octette (*nn.*) The French originals of these diminutives all ended in *-ette,* but American English usually prefers the simple *-et* ending. All these are Standard today, however.

quarto See DUODECIMO.

quasar (*n.*) is an acronym (from *quasi-stellar object*), meaning "a very distant celestial body farther away than other stars that emits much radiation." Pronounce it *KWAI-zahr* or *KWAI-sahr.*

quash (*vv.*) *Quash* (1) means "to nullify or set aside by means of judicial action": *The court order was quashed on appeal. Quash* (2) means "to destroy, shatter, or extinguish": *The army quashed the revolt almost before it began.* Both are Standard.

quasi (*adj.*),   **quasi-** (*prefix*) Pronounce them either *KWAI-ZEI, KWAI-ZEE,* or *KWAI-SEI.* The adjective means "partly resembling or in some respects like," as in *We staged a quasi oral examination so they could get some experience; it was quasi-formal, but very like the real thing.*

quay, cay, key (*nn.*) A *quay* is a landing platform beside a navigable waterway. Pronounce it *KEE* or, rarely, *KAI* or *KWAI.* A *key,* pronounced *KEE,* is a small low island, frequently part of a reef, and so is a *cay,* pronounced either *KAI* or *KEE.*

queer (*adj., n., v.*) The adjective is Standard in its generalized meaning "odd or peculiar," as in *It's a queer little house. Queer* also has several specialized senses, including "eccentric," "a bit insane," "worthless or counterfeit" (as in *queer money,* a slang term), "suspicious or questionable" (as in *There's something queer about this offer*), and "not well," "sick or ill" (as in *She woke in the morning feeling very queer in her stomach*). All these except "worthless or counterfeit," are Standard. But all have been nearly overwhelmed by another specialized sense, an insulting slang label that is taboo in most Standard use, meaning "sexually deviant," especially "homosexual," and particularly by its use as a noun meaning "a homosexual," as in *According to people who know him, he's a queer.* So strong is the effect of this

meaning of adjective and noun that you must be careful to use context to make clear and unambiguous any other sense of this word you might use.

The verb seems not to be affected by the slang and taboo "homosexual" senses of noun and adjective; it means "to stop or spoil an enterprise," as in *She queered the deal by making it public,* or "to embarrass yourself," as in *I queered myself by talking out of turn.*

query (*n., v.*),   **inquiry** (*n.*) The verb *query* means "to question" and poses no usage issue. The noun *query* means "a question" and in that sense is synonymous with *inquiry: Reporters' queries* [*inquiries*] *can be awkward. Query* also means "a doubt, a mental reservation or question," as in *Her query about our sincerity made her hesitate.* An *inquiry* can also be "a series of questions" or "an investigation," and *query* is sometimes used loosely in that sense as well, especially in journalese headlines. These and other uses are Standard, including *query* as a synonym for *question mark.*

question (*n.*) can combine with the prepositions *about, as to, concerning,* and *of,* as in *I have some questions about* [*as to, concerning*] *her punctuality; It's a question of his honesty.* Preceded by *no, little, some,* or another qualifier, *question* is frequently followed by a clause introduced by *that, what, but that,* or *but what,* as in *There's no question* [*but*] *that she has the votes; There is little question that she'll be elected. Which* and *whether* can also introduce clauses following *question: There is* [*some*] *question* [*as to*] *whether he'll accept; There can be no question* [*as to*] *which he'll choose.* All these are Standard.

One other usage item: Standard idiom is that you **answer** a question, not **solve** a question.

questionable (*adj.*),   **questioning** (*adj., n.*) Anything *questionable* is doubtful and gives you reason to raise questions about its accuracy, morality, legality, or soundness, as in *His honesty was questionable.* The adjective *questioning* describes a quizzical attitude, as in *She had a questioning look on her face,* and the noun means "the asking of questions," as in *The lawyer's questioning of the witness took an hour.*

QUESTION MARK This punctuation mark (?) appears at the end of sentences that are questions. In direct quotations, the *question mark* falls inside the final quotation mark: *"Where?" she asked.* In indirect quotations, no *question mark* is used: *She asked where he had been.* We also use *question marks* to indicate that we are unsure of a fact or opinion: *The life dates of Ethelred II (the Unready) were 968?–1016.* See QUESTION SENTENCE.

questionnaire (*n.*) The English spelling retains the French *-nn-*. Pronounce the initial consonant cluster *KW-* as in *question,* not *K-* as in *kestrel.*

QUESTION SENTENCE One of the three rhetorically defined sentence types (*statement* and *command* are the others), the *question sentence* has three main patterns in English: (1) It may begin with interrogative pronouns or other question-asking function words: *Who is your favorite player? Which bike is yours? How far is it to the drug store?* (2) It may use inversions of subject and verb (*Is he your father?*), although inversions using most full verbs (for example, *Think you he will accept?*) are archaic today, or it may use the modern inversion pattern that employs *be, have,* or another auxiliary plus a past participle or infinitive, as in *Has he been here this week? Did he do his math today? Must you go so soon?* (3) It may use the same form and syntactic order as does a statement sentence but change the intonation from a falling to a rising curve at the end to make it a *question: You're going home? He's a good student?* In written form, only the *question mark* is available, of course, to do the work of that change in spoken intonation.

quick 1 (*adj., n.*) The Standard meaning of the noun—"living beings," as in *the quick and the dead*—comes from the now archaic or obsolete sense of the adjective, "alive, not dead," and is archaic itself. The noun also has a specialized sense still much in use, meaning "very tender or sensitive flesh, especially the part under the fingernails or toenails." The cliché *to cut* (*someone*) *to the quick* uses that meaning of the noun, generalized to mean "any very sensitive spot."

quick 2, quickly (*advs.*) *Quick* is a flat adverb, but it is restricted to Conversational (especially Casual) use, as in *Quick, call your mother.* Most commonly it follows the verb, as in *Run quick; Come quick; We'd better do something pretty quick. Quickly* is the fully Standard adverb and serves nicely in place of *quick* in each of the examples and at all levels.

quick fix (*n.*) is "a temporary expedient," "an inadequate and hurried attempt at solving a problem." The term is mainly Conversational, but it does occur occasionally in Semiformal contexts and is beginning to appear even in some Edited English.

quid pro quo is a Latin tag meaning "this for that," "one item in exchange for another of equal value," and it has become a handy cliché, often the most efficient way of describing an equal exchange, a cause and effect, or a stimulus and a response. See FOREIGN PHRASES.

quiet, quieten (*vv.*) *Quiet* is the Standard American verb: *The sea quieted by morning. The teacher quieted his class.* The British also use *quieten* as both intransitive and transitive.

quilt, comfort, comforter, duvet (*nn.*) A *quilt* is a bedcover, usually made of a filling of felt, cotton, down, feathers, or something similar sandwiched between two layers of cloth. To keep it from shifting, the lining is sewn to the covers, often in intricate and decorative patterns; the process of sewing these padded layers is called *quilting* and anything so constructed is said to be *quilted.* A favorite American *quilt* is the *patchwork quilt,* wherein the cover is made of many brightly colored and oddly shaped pieces sewn together. *Comforter* and *comfort* (probably a clipped form) are two more Standard names for *quilted* bed coverings. A *duvet* is a particular sort of *quilted comforter,* usually down- or feather-filled, with a decorative slipcover to keep it clean.

quint See QUINTUPLET.

quintet, quintette See QUARTET.

quintuplet, quint (*nn.*), pronounced *kwin-TUHP-lit, kwin-T(Y)OO-plit,* or *KWIN-tuh-plit,* works grammatically as does *twin*(*s*). Just as each of a pair of *twins* is a *twin,* so each of five *quintuplets* is a *quintuplet. Quint*(*s*) is a clipped form invented by the press and welcomed by the language when the Canadian Dionne *quints* were born in 1935.

quip (*n., v.*) The noun is "a witty remark, a snappy comeback, a joke," but many commentators have pointed out that when someone is quoted, as in *"Twenty-three skidoo," she quipped,* the wit too often seems not to have traveled well. Don't label anything a *quip* or any speaking *quipping,* unless its wit is clearly apparent.

quire See CHOIR.

quisling (*n.*) is a traitor, especially one who, like Vidkun Quisling of Norway in World War II, collaborates with an invader of his or her country. See EPONYM.

quit (*v.*) The principal parts are *quit, quit* or *quitted, quit* or *quitted.* Americans rely almost entirely on *quit* as past tense and past participle, except perhaps for some uses of *quitted* in the sense "departed, left, vacated," as in *We quitted the place after the warning*. The British prefer *quitted* as past tense and past participle in all senses.

quite (*adv., intensifier*) has developed three Standard clusters of meaning, not always distinctly different. It functions as an intensifier meaning "wholly, completely," as in *I'm quite pleased with my new shoes* and *He's quite mad, you know*. As a similar intensifier it means "more than, positively," as in *She was quite beside herself with joy;* in this use it frequently modifies an absolute adjective, as in *The town was quite leveled by the tornado*. As a qualifier it can also reduce the strength of the adjective and means "rather, a bit," as in *It's getting quite cold in here* and *I'm quite tired tonight*. In Conversational idioms such as *quite a few* and *quite a bit*, the effect is moderately to strongly intensive: *She has quite a few snapshots of her family. He's quite a bit taller than his father. Quite a* and *quite the* function as intensives, as in *She's quite a musician* and *He's quite the ladies' man*. Compare RATHER.

qui vive, on the *Qui vive?* was a French sentry's challenge, meaning "Long live whom?"—in other words, "Whose side are you on?" To be *on the qui vive* (pronounced *KEE VEEV* and italicized when written or printed), therefore, is to be "alert or on the watch," either of which is a quite satisfactory way to say it in English. See FOREIGN PHRASES.

Quixote (*n.*), **quixotic** (*adj.*) *Don Quixote*, the name of the hero of Cervantes's satire, in anglicized Spanish is pronounced either *DAHN kee-HO-tee* or *-tai*, or, fully anglicized, *DAHN KWIK-suht;* the adjective, never capitalized, is pronounced *kwik-SAH-tik* or *kwik-ZAH-tik* and means "visionary, impractical, and foolishly romantic and idealistic."

quiz (*n., v.*) The verb senses "to make fun of someone" and "to look teasingly at someone" and the noun senses "an eccentric person" and "a practical joke" are obsolete, obsolescent, or archaic today. The remaining meanings, however, are now Standard: "to question closely," as in *The police quizzed the suspect for an hour*, and "a short examination or test," as in *She gives weekly quizzes in all her classes*.

quondam (*adj.*) is a word borrowed from Latin but now Standard English that means "former, one-time," as in *She is a quondam officer of the firm*. It's not italicized any longer, but it's a rather low frequency term, in some ways self-

consciously old-fashioned. See ERSTWHILE; WHILOM.

QUOTATION, DIRECT AND INDIRECT
See DIRECT ADDRESS.

quotation, quote (*nn.*) Both *quotation*, which is fully Standard, and *quote*, a clipped form of the noun that may be mainly Informal and Conversational but appears in some Edited English as well, have the same meanings: "the act of quoting," "a copy of a passage of someone's speech or writing," and the specialized sense "the current price of a stock or commodity." In addition, the plural *quotes* can mean quotation marks, as in *You've forgotten to close your quotes on page three. Direct quotes* are put inside quotation marks; *indirect quotes* are paraphrased and are not put inside *quotes*. See DIRECT ADDRESS.

QUOTATION OF POETRY See POETRY.

QUOTATION MARKS These punctuation marks (the British call them *inverted commas*) come in two forms, double and single. The *double quotation marks* (opening " and closing ") are used to enclose the words of a direct quotation: *She said, "I'll never see you again."* (They are never used in indirect quotation: *She said she'd never see him again*.) They are also used to enclose words or phrases quoted from others or words that may be slang or that are in some other way being used peculiarly: *The speaker tried to put a favorable "spin" on his denial. The "pacification plan" was in fact simply a euphemism for a bloody conquest*. But be sparing: most editors discourage the use of such quotation marks for effect rather than for a substantive reason, and overuse of these marks in any writing is affected.

Convention also calls for *double quotation marks* around the titles of short stories, short poems, short musical compositions, and the names of plays, chapters in books, and radio and television programs: Frost's "The Road Not Taken," "Eye Witness News." (Titles of longer works usually require italics instead, and sometimes the decision is arbitrary or simply conventional: books of the Bible, for example, are almost always italicized rather than placed in *quotation marks*, and the same is true of the titles of Shakespeare's plays.)

A key problem with *quotation marks* is which other marks of punctuation go inside the closing *quotation mark(s)* and which belong outside. In the United States, most stylebooks and most editors follow these rules: periods and commas belong inside, colons and semicolons outside.

Other marks—question mark, dash, and exclamation point, for example—go inside when they belong with the quoted material, outside when they belong to the main sentence. British editorial conventions differ.

When quoting a long passage of two or more paragraphs, the usual procedure in written American English is to use no *quotation marks* and instead to set off the entire passage of quoted matter by indenting it. If you decide to use *quotation marks* instead, however, the usual procedure is to begin each paragraph of the long quotation with *quotation marks* but to use a closing *quotation mark* only at the end of the final sentence in the quoted passage. In any event, use only one of these methods with any given quotation. See also POETRY.

British publishers frequently use *single quotation marks* (opening ' and closing ') where Americans use *double quotation marks*. In American writing, however, *single quotation marks* are restricted mainly to enclosing a quotation within a quotation: *The dealer said, ''I'm sorry, I thought you said 'I pass.' ''* Note that a period goes inside both final *quotation marks* when the two quotations end together.

quote See QUOTATION.

quoth is the first and third person singular past tense form of an Old English verb, *cwethan*, meaning "speak, say." The rest of the verb has long been obsolete, but the archaism *quoth* is still used fairly frequently for humor or other special effect. The syntax is also archaic, in that this verb form nearly always precedes its subject (*quoth he*).

quotient See DIVIDEND.

q.v. is an abbreviation for Latin *quod vide*, meaning "which see." It was much used in footnotes until fairly recently but is often replaced today by the English words themselves, often printed in parentheses in the body of the text. It's another of those foreign phrases (which see) to use (if you must) only with readers who know what it means.

R

-r-, -rr- See CONSONANTS (2).

rabbi (*n.*), when modified as in *Jewish rabbi*, is redundant: *rabbis* are only Jewish; *priest* (which see) is a different instance: there are Orthodox priests, Roman Catholic priests, Episcopal or Anglican priests, and various non-Christian priests as well.

rabbit (*n.*, *v.*) Several figurative senses are in considerable but restricted use, including the Conversational and Informal sports term for a footracer who agrees to set a fast pace (like the mechanical *rabbit* in dog racing) for a stronger runner seeking to set a record and the other sports term, probably slang, applied to a novice in professional golf, who is obliged to qualify for each tournament and plays his or her round very early in the day with the real *rabbits* and the dew and who is also like a *rabbit* in being timorous and unconfident. The verb usually means "to behave like a rabbit, to be timorous, to run away, to show no courage": *As soon as they heard the sirens, the prowlers rabbited away into the night.* See also WELSH RABBIT.

rabbit ears (*n.*) has two meanings: The Standard figurative sense graphically describes the indoor television antenna that sits atop the set and uses its two movable rods (which look like rabbit's ears) to improve reception. The slang use, applied especially in sports, describes players whose play is adversely affected because they are bothered by uncomplimentary remarks from spectators or other players: they are said to have *rabbit ears* or to be *rabbit ears*.

race (*adj.*, *n.*), **racial** (*adj.*) These are sensitive words today, when racism is so frequently alleged or suspected. *Race* has long been used biologically to refer to groups of plants, animals, or people, each group coming from a common stock or at least sharing some dominant characteristic usable for classification (*the white race*). It has also been used to speak of a biologically varied nationality group (*the French race*) whose common characteristic is its citizenship or, even more broadly, in the phrase *the human race,* the group to which all human beings belong. In addition, there have long been figurative uses wherein the *race* referred to is narrow and special and grouped only around an idea (*a new race of television addicts*). But *race* and *racial* also are frequently used as generalizations, and effects are attributed to *race* or *racial* characteristics over which there is strong disagreement. Hence these terms must be used with extreme care for what is claimed for or attributed to them in any context, and with considerable sensitivity to the likely opinions and prejudices of audience and readers. See also RACIST LANGUAGE.

racialism (*n.*) is a rarely used synonym for *racism.*

racism (*n.*) is a pejorative term with two chief clusters of meaning. The first is "a belief that race determines human characteristics such as intelligence, physical ability, and the like, and hence that certain races may be genetically superior to or inferior to certain others in these qualities"; this belief is without documented scientific foundation. The second meaning of the term is simply a generic label for various forms of racial discrimination, racial prejudice, racial segregation, and the like. See RACIST LANGUAGE.

RACIST LANGUAGE consists mainly of words taboo in Standard English (and often in Common and Vulgar English as well) because they are thought to be discriminatory or offensive. Avoid using language that consensus says is *racist.* Some terms—*nigger, chink, darkie,* and the like—have clearly been unacceptable for many years. But there is also rapid change in the acceptability of terms once thought proper even by the members of the particular racial group itself (see the entry for AFRICAN(-)AMERICAN for an example), and insensitive use can cost you a reader or listener or bring harsh social judgments down on you. Therefore, be attentive to change in fashions and taboos involving names for ethnic groups and races. Remember too that *any* race can be in the minority somewhere; *every* race can be offended by racial slurs. Hence everyone must be sensitive to this very serious matter of usage. It is good manners (and therefore good usage) to call people only by the names they wish to be called. See also ETHNIC SLURS AND TERMS OF ETHNIC OPPROBRIUM.

rack, wrack (*nn., vv.*) In some senses, the verbs *rack* and *wrack* are synonymous, and the two words, each as either noun or verb, are nearly interchangeable at some points. The usage problems arise over which spelling to use where there seems to be a possible or a clear overlap in meaning. Most Edited English will prefer *rack your brain, wrack and ruin, storm-wracked,* and *pain-wracked,* but other Standard written evidence, including some Edited English, will use the variant spelling for each (see NERVE-WRACKING).

The noun *rack* has a great many meanings, some of the most important being "a frame, stand, or grating," plus many figurative but specialized extended meanings, such as "a pair of antlers," "an instrument to which the victim's body is strapped prior to various forms of torture," "wreckage" (limited usually today to the cliché *rack*—more often *wrack—and ruin*), "a great cluster of clouds blown about by the wind," and "a cut of meat, particularly the *rack of lamb,* which includes spine and ribs." Many of these extended senses have related verb meanings, usually also spelled *rack:* the key one is "to put on a *rack*" or "to enclose in a *rack,* as with billiard balls." A figurative sense of the "torture" noun is the verb "to oppress (especially the poor or tenants), particularly by charging exorbitant rents." All these are currently Standard.

Wrack, the noun, stems ultimately from an Old English word meaning "misery" and has a general meaning of "destruction or wreckage," literal or figurative, plus senses including "a shipwreck" and "the uprooted marine plant life cast up on shore by the sea." The verb made from the noun *wrack* (and spelled like it) means "to suffer or to be subjected to terrible pain or suffering, literal or figurative."

racket, racquet (*nn.*) A tennis *racquet* or *racket* is Standard in either spelling, but the game *racquets,* "a four-wall game something like court tennis," is always spelled *racquets* in American English, *rackets* in British English. It is a plural form that takes a singular verb: *He thinks racquets is as interesting as tennis.* A second noun *racket* has several other meanings, including the Standard sense "noise or uproar," as in *Stop making all that racket*; a Conversational and Informal word for "any scheme for obtaining money illegally," as in *He spent most of his adult life working in the rackets*; and a related slang word meaning "a painless, effortless way to earn a living," as in *She's got a real racket and never has to do a thing.*

radiator (*n.*) is always spelled with the *-or* agentive ending, whether it's "the specific cooling device for an automotive engine" or simply "anything that radiates."

radical (*adj., n.*), **radicle** (*n.*) *Radical* is the Standard spelling for all meanings of the adjective and for all but one highly specialized botanical meaning of the noun: "a part of an embryo seedling" or "a rudimentary root."

radio (*n.*) The plural is *radios*. See PLURALS OF NOUNS ENDING IN -*O*.

radius (*n.*) has two plurals: radii (pronounced *RAI-dee-ei*) and *radiuses* (pronounced *RAI-dee-uhs-iz*). See FOREIGN PLURALS.

railing See BALUSTER.

railroad, railway (*nn.*) are mostly interchangeable in American English, except that the system is most commonly referred to as a *railroad* or *railroads*. British English seems to prefer *railway* for most uses.

rain See REIGN.

raise 1, bring up, rear (*vv.*) Today Americans *raise, rear,* or *bring up* children, even though a good many Standard-speaking Americans can still recite the old saying: *The British raise plants and animals and rear children, but Americans raise all three. Bring up* is the peculiarly American locution, but all three terms can be considered interchangeable in Standard American English. See also RAZE.

raise 2, rise (*nn., vv.*) Rise (*rose, risen*) is almost always intransitive: *The river rose overnight. Prices have risen again this month. Raise (raised, raised)* is usually transitive: *We finally raised the money. Raise* also has some intransitive use, most of it dialectal or otherwise Nonstandard, but some of it fairly widely heard, particularly in sentences that drop the reflexive pronoun, such as *She raised [herself] up on her elbow in bed to peer at the clock.* Even Standard users sometimes use *raised* this way, but only at the lower levels of speech, and other Standard users can sometimes be highly critical.

The British still call "a pay increase" a *rise* in pay, but Americans almost always call it a *raise: She gave her employees large raises last year.* See also RAZE; RISE; SALARY INCREMENT.

raise havoc See WREAK.

RAISING Contrary to what you might expect, *raising* has nothing to do with "higher" or "better" language—quite the reverse, according to some. It is the technical name for the location of the negative in this sentence: *I don't think he's very helpful.* The version some people urge as logically better is *I think he's not very helpful,* but for most of us that has a more Formal ring. There is absolutely nothing wrong with either version; the grammar of each is Standard: choose the tone you seek. *Raising* simply shifts the negative from the subordinate clause where it logically belongs to the main clause, especially when the main clause's verb is *suppose, think, believe, seem,* or the like. Those who oppose *raising* argue that statements such as *I don't think* are illogical—but so is much in Standard English. See DON'T THINK.

raison d'être is a French idiom meaning "reason for being"; its popularity in Standard English means that sometimes it is written without italics and minus its circumflex accent, but Edited English always insists on the accent and frequently requires italics as well. In anglicized French, it is usually pronounced approximately *rai-* or *re-ZAWN DET-ruh,* sometimes with the end of the second syllable of *raison* nasalized in the French fashion. See FOREIGN PHRASES.

Ralph Americans pronounce the man's given name with a spelling pronunciation, *RALF.* The British usually prefer the older pronunciation of the name, which rhymes with *safe,* as with the name of composer Ralph Vaughan Williams. The British spell the name either *Ralph* or *Rafe.*

rambunctious (*adj.*), meaning "boisterous, loud, disorderly, wild, and unruly," is Standard English: *She's a rambunctious young woman, not easily broken to the harness of office work.*

rancor, rancour (*n.*), **rancorous** (*adj.*) Americans spell the noun *rancor,* the British *rancour.* Both spell the adjective *rancorous.* See SPELLING (1).

range (*v.*) combines with many prepositions but most frequently with *from,* as in *Her interests range from scuba diving to ballroom dancing.*

rap (*n., v.*) The verb has two main Standard meanings: "to pound or tap (on something)," as in *She rapped on the table for attention,* and "to perform rap music," as in *He learned how to rap with the best of his models.* The other meanings of the verb are slang: "to criticize severely" and the aging "to talk or converse" and "to discuss seriously." The noun has two Standard senses, one related to each of the Standard verb meanings: "a tap or blow" and "a rhymed song sung or recited to a strong rhythm." It also has three related slang meanings: "sharp criticism" or "a penalty," as in *to take the rap,* and the now somewhat faded "a chat or conversation" and "a serious, deep discussion," as in *We had a good rap after supper.*

rape (*n., v.*) Nineteenth- and early twentieth-century prudishness caused both noun and verb to be almost taboo outside legal or other Formal contexts until fairly recently, but now the literal crime of "forcible sexual intercourse with an unconsenting person," the figurative or extended "sacking or seizure and destruction of a city or other place," and the verbal uses meaning "to perform one of these actions," are all Standard.

rapport (*n.*), pronounced *ra-POR, rah-POR,* or *ruh-POR,* means "a close, understanding relationship": *Their rapport had grown and developed over the years.* When it combines, the noun usually takes *with, between,* or *among: She has good rapport with her family. The sisters have great rapport between [among] themselves.*

rapt, wrapped (*adjs.*) These are homophones: *rapt* means "transported, carried away, engrossed, or completely absorbed," as in *Her rapt expression showed that she was gripped by the music. Wrapped* means "enveloped, enfolded, or surrounded," as in *We wrapped Mother's present yesterday* and *He is completely wrapped* [*up*] *in his work.*

rarebit See WELSH RABBIT.

rarefy (*v.*), **rarefied** (*adj.*) Commentators report many instances of the misspelling of both words in print, especially *rarified* for *rarefied,* apparently on analogy with words such as *identify* and *indemnify.* Remember that the Standard spelling has a medial *-e-,* not an *-i-.*

rarely ever (*adv.*) is a Standard idiom, *rarely* being an adverb turned intensifier or qualifier modifying the adverb *ever,* as in *We rarely ever see him now.*

rarify is a frequent misspelling of *rarefy* (which see).

rather See HAD RATHER; KIND OF; QUALIFIERS.

rather than is a compound function word that serves as either preposition or coordinating conjunction, as in *Rather than run for office this year, I've decided to wait* and *She decided to laugh and play rather than sit and mope.* In the construction *I am more interested in seeing her sister rather than in talking to Mary,* the *rather* is unnecessary and unidiomatic; omit it. See also PREFER.

ratio (*n.*) The plural is *ratios.* See PLURALS OF NOUNS ENDING IN -*O.*

ration (*n., v.*) has two Standard pronunciations for each part of speech: *RA-shuhn* or *RAI-shuhn.*

rattle (*v.*) is Standard in all senses, including "to confuse, fluster, or disconcert," as in *The whispering in the audience rattled her, and she forgot her lines,* although a few conservatives would limit this sense to Informal or Conversational use. Combined with *on* it means "to talk volubly, to chatter," as in *He rattled on nervously about anything that came to mind.*

ravage, ravish (*vv.*), **ravishing** (*adj.*) *Ravage* means "to ruin, destroy, plunder, or devastate": *The marauders ravaged the village. Ravish* has three related meanings: "to rape (literally or figuratively)" (*The soldiers killed the few men there and brutally ravished the women*); "to capture and carry off violently" (*The storehouse door had been broken, and all the supplies had been ravished away*); and, by extension, "to overcome emotionally, to enrapture, to transport with delight" (*Their playing of the double concerto simply ravished the audience*). This use of the verb, like most uses of the adjective *ravishing,* is figurative and hyperbolic: *She looked stunning, absolutely ravishing, when she made her entrance.*

Only in the sense "to seize or rob and carry off" are *ravage* and *ravish* synonymous, even though they both come from the Old French verb *ravir,* meaning "to carry away," and ultimately from the Latin *rapere,* from which we get English *rape* as well. Best advice to avoid confusion: limit *ravage* to destroying and devastating, and separately specify when things are carried off as well. Or use *ravish* to cover both ideas.

rave (*adj., n., v.*) Most uses, literal and figurative, are Standard: *The poor madman raved and writhed most pitiably. Everyone raved about the fine view from the terrace* is hyperbolic, however, and some dislike such figurative uses in Formal or Oratorical contexts. Only the adjective, meaning "a wildly enthusiastic review or comment," as in *He wrote a rave review,* should be limited to Conversational, Informal, or Semiformal use.

ravel, unravel (*vv.*) Both words have variant spellings when adding affixes: (*un*)*raveled* or (*un*)*ravelled,* (*un*)*raveling* or (*un*)*ravelling.* Once *ravel* meant "to entangle and so to confuse," but now it means "to come unwound, unknit, or separated into strands": *The sleeve of my sweater has begun to ravel.* But the likely confusion between tangling and untangling (even though a *raveling* or *ravelling* is "a separated single thread or strand") has been enough to give us an even more frequently used verb, *unravel,* which makes certain the undoing, the unmaking, the reducing to *ravelings* that we intend. So in Standard English your sleeve can *fray and begin to ravel,* but it is even more likely to be reported as *fraying and beginning to unravel.* Figuratively, *unravel* means "disentangle or solve," and *ravel* rarely occurs in that sense: *He thought he could unravel the mystery.* Compare LOOSE; UNLOOSE.

ravish, ravishing See RAVAGE.

raze, raise (*vv.*) These homophones are antonyms: *to raze a building* is "to unmake it," "to tear it down right to the ground"; *to raise a building* is "to make it," "to put it up."

re (*prep.*) is an abbreviated version of the Latin tag *in re*, and it is a similarly overused bit of business and legal jargon not much shorter than the prepositions (*about, concerning, as regards,* and the like) it replaces. Try *about* instead: *I must have your advice about the contract.* Sometimes *re* is no longer italicized in English print, probably a measure of its overuse. See FOREIGN PHRASES.

re- (*prefix*) The prefix, meaning "again, anew, once more," as in *review, rethink,* and *rewrite,* or "back or backward," as in *recall* or *return,* usually uses no hyphen, except when there is another word with which the new compound might be confused; for example, *recover* means "to get something back," whereas *re-cover* means "to put on another cover" or "to go over the matter again."

-re, -er See SPELLING (1).

reaction (*n.*) is another of the many scientific (in this instance, chemical) terms now in figurative and extended use in the general language. Conservatives have tried to prevent its figurative use and, when that failed, to restrict its general use to mean "response to a stimulus," rather than an unchanging "idea," "view," or "opinion": *The public's reaction to the speech was entirely favorable.* They have succeeded to some extent: the figurative use is Standard, but especially so when it indicates a response to something, not simply a report on an unchanged or unchanging position to which no stimulus has been applied.

read (*n.*) The British have long used *read* as a noun meaning "a period of time spent reading": *I spent the whole afternoon having a good read.* In popular reviews and commentary, Americans have begun wide use of another noun sense, also a functional shift from the verb, this one meaning "a book or essay as something to read," as in *Her new novel is not very deep, but it's lively and a very good read.* Both uses are considered Standard by the dictionaries, but some conservatives may balk, considering "a good read" Conversational or Semiformal at best.

readable See ILLEGIBLE.

readers See AUDIENCE.

read where See WHERE.

ready-made (*adj., n.*) is usually hyphenated and means "mass-produced and ready to be sold and worn at once." The term is the antonym of *tailor-made* or *bespoke,* which describe things made to order, fitted to the requirements of the purchaser from the moment work on them begins. *Ready-made* can be a pejorative sometimes, when critical commentators use it to belittle the fit of a jacket obviously not made solely to fit the person wearing it or to suggest that a response is not apt or genuine. But it can also have an elevated air when it is meant to imply the directness, simplicity, unaffected nature, and perhaps democratic character of the individual sporting the not-very-expensive off-the-rack coat or opinion.

real (*adv., intensifier*), **really** (*adv.*) It is quite clear that the adverbs *real* and *really* are not interchangeable: *a real good time* (simply "very good") and *a really good time* ("unquestionably good") are not the same thing. *Real* is in fact either an adjective (*a real blizzard*) or an intensifier (*a real bad cold*). As an adjective it is of course Standard, but the intensifier is Intimate or Casual at best, and most Standard users consider it Nonstandard and characteristic of Common or Vulgar English. It does however have wide Conversational use, and writers frequently adopt it as another evidence of the sound of living speech.

Really is the Standard adverb, and the difference between the intensifier and the adverb is grammatical and occasionally semantic: *He is a really distinguished man* could mean either that he is very distinguished or that his distinction is genuine, not doubtful. *He is a real distinguished man* means just that he is very distinguished; no question has been raised or answered about whether the distinction is there or not—*real* is just an effort to underscore its presence, unless intonation or punctuation make it unquestionably an adjective.

real facts See TRUE FACTS.

realistic, unrealistic (*adjs.*) *Realistic* means "facing facts, practical, considering only the possible," as in *Her view of their chances is quite realistic. Unrealistic* means "not facing facts, dreamily impractical, expecting the impossible," as in *He refused even to consider failure, although it was unrealistic to expect anything else.*

really something See SOMETHING ELSE.

realm See AREA.

realtor (*n.*) Pronounce it *REE-uhl-tor* or *REE-uhl-tuhr*, not *REE-luh-tor* or *REE-luh-tuhr*. See JEWELRY; METATHESIS.

ream 1 (*n.*) is Standard meaning either a specific number of sheets of paper (20 quires or 480 to 516 sheets) or, especially in the plural, "a great many, a lot." The hyperbolic figurative sense can be applied to both mass and count nouns: *We turned out reams of work* [*widgets*] *today.*

ream 2 (*v.*) often combines with *out* and is Standard meaning "to enlarge an opening or a tube by stretching or reshaping its inside with an instrument," just as it is in its figurative sense meaning "to clean out," as in *A pipe cleaner can ream* [*out*] *the gunk from a pipestem.* Appropriate only in Conversational and Semiformal or Informal uses are *ream*'s slang senses, "to cheat" (*That dealer really reamed us on the trade-in*) and "to scold or castigate severely" (*Coach really reamed us* [*out*] *at halftime for all our mistakes*).

rear See RAISE (1).

rear (end) See BUTTOCKS.

rear-end (*v.*) is a specific Standard verb describing a vehicle crashing into another from behind. It is usually hyphenated.

reason, cause (*nn.*) These are synonyms, but there is a difference: *There was no reason for the accident* differs from *There was no cause of the accident. Reason* implies an explanation or justification; *cause* can suggest the operation of forces beyond anyone's control. See also CAUSE.

reasonable (*adj.*), meaning "acceptable, willing to listen to reason, sensible, displaying common sense," and the like, has long been Standard in all these senses. It is also Standard in the sense "not expensive" or "not too expensive," as in *I thought their prices were reasonable when compared with the competition's.* This use can be ambiguous when the adjective modifies something that could conceivably be able to reason, as in *Chickens are reasonable this week, but I'm afraid beef is not.*

reason is because This locution has long been in use in Standard English; it has also long been criticized, the explanations for the harsh judgments varying from redundancy to bad grammar. But some reputable authors continue to write it, and some Standard users continue to say it at nearly all Conversational levels. Edited English and many of those who write for its editors, however, continue to prefer *the reason is that.* Some Standard users never say *the reason is because,* others use it even though they've been taught otherwise, and many never notice it in their speech. Best advice: avoid it at Planned, Oratorical, and Formal levels, and especially in Edited English, or risk the censure of conservatives.

reason why, the This locution is often blacklisted as redundant: the commentators who dislike it usually prefer *The reason is: The reason* [*that*] *I'm late is* [*that*] *I ran out of gas* instead of *The reason why I'm late.* . . . But some of our best authors have been writing *the reason why* for several centuries, and most of us now say it and use it Informally without even noticing. The expression is Standard, and today even Edited English seldom objects to it. Only in Formal and Oratorical—and perhaps in some very demanding Planned—contexts will a few insist on another locution.

rebel (*v.*) The verb, pronounced *ruh-BEL* or *ree-BEL,* spells its inflected forms *rebelled* and *rebelling.* See CONSONANTS (2).

rebuff, refuse, reject, repel, repulse (*vv.*) At least one and sometimes more than one of these words can serve to define each of the others, and all are at least partial synonyms. *To rebuff* is "to check or reject," "to refuse bluntly," "to snub," as in *She rebuffed his familiarity with a haughty stare*; *to repulse* is "to reject rudely," "to drive back," as in *She repulsed him with a sharp comment*; *to repel* is "to turn away or turn back," "to decline (a proposal)," or "to disgust and so drive away," as in *His proposal of marriage repelled her, so she repelled it*; *to reject* is "to say no to or spurn," "to turn back," as in *When he proposed, she rejected him out of hand*; and *to refuse* is "to decline, to say no, not to accept," as in *He refused to accept her answer as final.* See RE-.

recall See RECOLLECT.

receipt See RECIPE.

receipt (*v.*) In both transitive and intransitive uses this verb is Standard: *She receipted my bill when I paid it. We receipted for everything they transferred to us.* The letter *p* is silent: *ri-SEET.*

receptive (*adj.*), when it combines with a preposition, usually takes *to* or, less frequently, *of: She was usually receptive to* [*of*] *his constant attentions.*

recess (*n., v.*) The noun is pronounced *REE-ses* a bit more often than it is *ri-SES,* but the verb is much more commonly *ri-SES,* although *REE-ses* is Standard here too.

recession See DEPRESSION.

recipe, receipt (*nn.*) (pronounced *RES-i-pee* and *ri-SEET*, respectively) mean the same thing: originally they were the instructions and lists of ingredients for making and administering medicines, but they have long since come to mean "the instructions for preparing food and drink." *Recipe* is now much more frequently used in this sense than is *receipt*, which today has an old-fashioned sound and is probably best labeled archaic. *Recipe* also has considerable Standard figurative use today, meaning "a way of accomplishing something," as in *His recipe for success is hard work plus more hard work.*

recipient (*n.*) is a very stiff and formal synonym for *receiver* that turns up too often as an elegant variation. Save it for the rare occasions that are as Formal as the word itself: *He was the recipient of the Nobel prize for chemistry that year.*

reciprocal See MUTUAL.

recital See CONCERT.

reckon (*v.*), in its meanings of "think, suppose, and count on," is Conversational, Informal, and sometimes dialectal: *She'll be here by noon, I reckon. He reckoned that there would be objection. Reckon with* means "take into account," as in *We'll have to reckon with their hostility, I fear. Reckon without* is said to occur in the opposite sense, meaning "not to take into account, not to consider," but it is not common: *Reckon without them, and you'll regret it. Reckon on* also occurs, in the sense of "plan or count on" or "take into account": *We don't reckon on there being any trouble.* All these combined forms are Standard, as is *reckon* followed by a *that* clause: *They reckoned that we would have funds enough to finish.*

recognize See BELIEVE; FEEL; SENSE.

recollect, recall, remember (*vv.*) These synonyms all have to do with recovering information once known. *Remember* is the generic and most commonly used word, meaning "to recover something from the memory and bring it up to consciousness and usefulness," as in *Can you remember her telephone number? Recollect* means the same thing: "to recover information that once was available for use," as in *I can only faintly recollect what she looked like.* Some people insist that conscious effort is inherent in *recollect*, as well as in *recall: I'm trying to recall what day it was.* Of the three, *recollect* is perhaps the most folksy or old-fashioned: it seems to go somehow with verbs like *reckon* and *calculate* and the like. But *remember, recollect,* and *recall* are all Standard.

reconcile (*v.*) When it combines with a preposition, *reconcile* as a transitive verb uses either *with* or *to,* as in *We finally reconciled their accounts with* [*to*] *our records,* and only *with* when the verb is intransitive, as in *They finally reconciled with their parents.* In the passive, the verb takes either *with* or *to: They were reconciled with* [*to*] *their new circumstances.* All these are Standard.

record, new In sentences such as *She set a new record for that distance,* purists often label this construction redundant, since any record must be new. But it's a finical point, not worth arguing over. While it is technically true that there can be only one record at a time, each is always different from the one it supersedes and in that loose sense must also be new. The world of sports journalism distinguishes old and former records and record-holders, and new ones too. *New record* is Standard English.

recorder (*n.*) has at least three main meanings, all Standard: (1) an official who records official acts and documents, such as deeds, birth and death certificates, and the like; (2) any of several wind instruments with eight finger holes, blown like a pipe or whistle; (3) an electronic recording device, such as a tape recorder.

recourse See RESOURCE.

recrudescence (*n.*) in its literal sense means "the breaking out again of a disease, an infection, or some other medical unpleasantness," and it is Standard in such use. Figuratively it also is applied to the rebirth or reestablishment of anything unpleasant (*the recrudescence of racial hatred,* for example). It's a very low frequency word at best, and Edited English restricts it to pejorative uses; you would do well to do the same on the rare occasions when you use it.

recto, verso (*nn.*) These Latin terms are the technical names for the front and back surfaces of a page: the *recto* is the right-hand (usually odd-numbered) page in an open book, and the back of that page (which, when the page is turned, becomes the left-hand page, usually even-numbered) is the *verso.* These two may be italicized as foreign words. See PLURALS OF NOUNS ENDING IN -O.

rector See PRIEST.

recur, reoccur (*vv.*), **recurrence, reoccurrence** (*nn.*), **recurrent** (*adj.*) The usual Standard words are *recur,* meaning "to return (to)," "to come back (to)," "to occur again," as in *The trouble recurred last week for the dozenth time; recurrence,* meaning "one of several repetitions, yet another return," as in *If there's* another recurrence, we must take action; and the related adjective recurrent. Reoccur and reoccurrence are said to differ from recur and recurrence in that they suggest a first or single repetition: That odd noise reoccurred an hour later. They are rare in Edited English, and most desk dictionaries don't include them, but they appear fairly often in the speech of the inexperienced as synonyms for recur and recurrence: That odd noise reoccurred just after you'd left. Its reoccurrence made me nervous. Especially in writing, best practical advice is to stick with recur and recurrence, for one repetition or many.

redolent (adj.) means "smelling (of), giving off an odor (of)": Her clothes were redolent of moth balls and cedar closets. It can combine with of or with: The air was heavily redolent of [with] the scent of pine needles. Some argue that redolent, like so many other words having to do with smells, always has pejorative overtones, but that is clearly not so. Figurative uses are frequent, meaning "to evoke memories or images (of)," and these tend usually to be pleasant: His memories of her were redolent of warm summer evenings at the shore.

REDUNDANT, REDUNDANCY Redundant language is usually "too much, repetitive, more than necessary." Yet redundancy in language is by no means all bad. The grammar of natural languages is often redundant: that is, its sentences often contain repeated and overlapping signals giving the same grammatical information, so we can pick up the cues we need in order to understand even against considerable background noise or other distraction. And as every preacher and teacher knows, it is often pedagogically sound to "tell 'em first what you're gonna tell 'em, then tell 'em, and finally tell 'em what you've told 'em." Sometimes repetition—redundancy—is a good way to ensure effectiveness.

But we also admire the spareness of artificial languages, which say things only once, with maximum efficiency: were we to permit a redundant 2 to appear in 2 + 2 (by adding an extra +2, for example), we would quite likely get 6 as an answer. Hence many people look at wordy, repetitive prose with justifiable irritation. Say it once, clearly and correctly, they urge. And for much expository prose, they're right. In the end, however, the most helpful guide to usage in this matter is probably this: write the most effective prose you can. If you need some redundancies to be effective, use them; sometimes belt-and-suspenders constructions are safest. Repeat your message until you're

sure your reader understands it, but not one more time than necessary. When redundancies cloud your meaning or merely waste your reader's time, they'll ruin your effort. Compare BREVITY; CONCISENESS (1).

refer See ALLUDE.

refer back is a locution frequently criticized for redundancy, but there can be a difference between refer and refer back: He referred to my opening chapter and He referred back to my opening chapter are not quite the same, since the second suggests that he might have been over this ground before, that this may not be the first reference to the chapter.

referee, umpire (nn.) In sports and in the law, these persons have similar tasks. The referee in boxing or basketball interprets and enforces the rules, stops play and restarts it when necessary, and assigns penalties when these are called for under the rules. The umpire has similar responsibilities in baseball. Wherever officials bear one of these titles, we understand them to be disinterested third parties, prepared to maintain order, examine the evidence, and give judgments.

referendum (n.) There are two Standard plurals: referendums and referenda. See FOREIGN PLURALS.

REFERENT is the linguist's term for the idea, object, person, or other entity that lies behind a word or locution. Sailfish has for Americans at least two referents: that large game fish itself and the small sailboard (actually, its trademark name) that dots our lakes, rivers, and harbors in warm weather.

reflection, reflexion (n.) The American spelling is reflection, the British reflexion. See SPELLING (1).

REFLEXIVE PRONOUNS are the -self forms added to the genitive forms of the first and second person pronouns (myself, ourselves, yourself, yourselves) and to the objective forms of the third person pronouns (himself, herself, itself, themselves) used reflexively, as in He hurt himself. In reflexive use both the subject and the direct object have the same referent. The reflexive forms also occur in nonreflexive use, as emphatic pronouns. See also HISSELF; MYSELF; THEIRSELVES; YOURSELF.

refuse See REBUFF.

refute (v.) Refute has two Standard meanings: "to deny the accuracy of" and "to disprove, to demonstrate the error of." Each of these can be used of an argument or, loosely, of a person. In the sense "to deny the truth of," as in *We refuted his allegations, refute* has sometimes been criticized by commentators, but it is in regular use in that sense in Standard American English; British English still frowns on it. See CONFUTE.

regalia (*n.*) is a plural and takes a plural verb: *The college president's regalia include a cap, gown, hood, and often some sort of chain or other badge of office.* It is sometimes heard with a singular verb, but such use is still usually considered Nonstandard. See FOREIGN PLURALS.

regard (*v.*) can combine with the preposition *as* (*She regarded her supervisor as her mentor*; compare *She chose him mentor*) and is sometimes included in the brief list of transitive verbs that can take two complements, one a direct object and the second a bit like an object complement (with its referent the same as the direct object's), except that it is nearly always introduced by a particle (*She regarded him her mentor*). If *regard* is also one of these very few doubly transitive verbs, it is at best a low-frequency and odd-sounding one, and some commentators reject it entirely in favor of the version with *as*. Nevertheless, *regard* with an object complement appears to be Standard today, if primarily limited to Informal and Conversational contexts.

regarding, as regards, in regard(s) to, with regard(s) to *In* and *with regard to, regarding,* and *as regards* are all Standard, synonymous prepositions, slightly longer and more varied than but meaning much the same as *about* and *concerning: I spoke to him regarding* [*as regards, in regard to, with regard to*] *his future. With regards to* is Nonstandard and frequently functions as a shibboleth, although it can be Standard and idiomatic in complimentary closes to letters: *With* [*my*] *regards to your family*. . . . *In regards to,* however, is both Substandard and Vulgar, although it appears unfortunately often in the spoken language of some people who otherwise use Standard. It never appears in Edited English.

regardless (*adv., adj.*) is Standard; see also IRREGARDLESS.

REGIONAL DIALECT A *regional dialect* is a pattern of language use peculiar to a geographical area and its occupants. Chief American *regional dialects* are Northern, North Midland, South Midland, Southern, Southwestern, and Western, and within each of these there are distinctive smaller groupings. For example, in

the northeastern megalopolis of the United States, marked dialectal differences set off these Northern dialects from each other: Eastern (or Coastal) New England, Inland Northern, Metropolitan New York City, and Lower Hudson Valley. See DIALECT.

regret (*n.*), when it combines, does so usually with the prepositions *over* or *for,* meaning either "remorse over an event in the past," as in *my regrets over* [*for*] *my wasted youth,* or "sorrow over someone dead or absent," as in *We expressed our regrets over* [*for*] *the loss of Aunt Mary.*

regretful, regrettable (*adjs.*), **regretfully, regrettably** (*advs.*) *Regretful* means "feeling or showing regret," as in *She had a regretful frown on her face*; *regrettable* means "unfortunate" or "contributing to regret," as in *She wrote a regrettable letter, one that caused a lot of trouble.* The adverbs *regretfully* and *regrettably* reflect similar distinctions; both can serve as sentence adverbs as well as in other adverbial roles: *Regretfully, she made her apologies and left. Regrettably, he forgot to thank her for her help. She spoke regretfully and wearily. His remarks were regrettably insolent.* See also CONSONANTS (2).

REGULAR is of course an adjective whose basic meanings are "usual, customary, evenly spaced or timed, and normal," but in this book it has a specialized grammatical sense as well, "by rule or generalization": *Regular English plurals of nouns are formed by adding an* s, *a* z, *or an* iz *sound at the end of the word, as in* pots, bags, *and* judges.

REGULAR PATTERNS FOR PLURALS OF NOUNS See PLURALS OF NOUNS.

reign, rain, rein (*nn., vv.*) These homophones differ in meaning and spelling. Of the nouns, a *reign* is "a monarch's power or period of rule," a *rein* is "one of the paired leather straps (*reins*) fastened to the bit in the horse's mouth, by means of which you steer it," and *rain* is "the water that falls from the heavens." Of the verbs, to *reign* is "to rule a nation as its monarch," to *rein* is "to steer a horse or team" (and to *rein in* is "to cause the horse or team to slow or stop" and, figuratively, "to steer, slow, or stop almost anything"), and to *rain* is what the weather does on picnics.

reiterate, iterate (*vv.*) Commentators frequently argue in favor of a distinction that makes *iterate* mean "repeat" and *reiterate* mean "repeat again," but most Standard users make no such distinction. *Iterate* is the rarer word, used primarily in scholarly and technical writing, where the distinction may indeed be in effect: *The proof of the second example simply iterates the proof of the first. Reiterate* is far more frequently used, and it usually means only "repeat," whether once or many times: *When she spoke again, she simply reiterated what she'd said once* [*many times*] *before.* The one certain usage judgment: to *reiterate again* is unquestionably a tautology and must be avoided.

reject See REBUFF.

rejoice (*v.*) can combine with the prepositions *at, in,* and *over,* as in *We rejoiced at* [*in, over*] *their good fortune.*

relate (*v.*) has two main clusters of meaning: as a transitive verb it means "to tell a story" or "to demonstrate a relationship between one thing and another": *She related the story of her good fortune. I tried to relate her actions to her words.* As an intransitive verb *relate* has a set of meanings stemming from psychology and having to do with establishing relationships or understanding with one's surroundings or with people nearby, as in *He simply can't relate and doesn't understand why* or *I'm confused, and I'm having difficulty relating.* The intransitive verb can also combine with *to* and *with,* as in *I just can't relate to* [*with*] *her and her values.* The uncombined intransitive uses are jargon, probably best limited to Conversational and Informal contexts (compare COPE), and even the combined uses still sometimes draw purists' criticism when put to general use instead of being restricted to technical use in psychology. Nevertheless, some Edited English is now beginning to consider them more widely appropriate, and most dictionaries now label them Standard.

relating to See RELATIVE TO.

relation, relative (*nn.*) These are synonyms that mean "someone to whom I am related, by blood, marriage, or some other link to be specified." There's no difference between *She's a close relative* and *She's a close relation.* Generally when a family relationship is to be specified or denied, the preposition to be used is *of—She's a relative* [*relation*] *of mine*—but sometimes you may encounter the preposition *to,* especially in the negative: *She's no relation to me.* In structures like the last, *relative* and *relation* are not quite fully interchangeable in Standard English.

relationship (*n.*) has long been a Standard general term for "the condition of being related to each other, usually by blood or marriage," and for "any specifiable connection or association," such as in *The economic relationship between*

these two countries is vital to each. But in recent years a new, specialized and at first Conversational and Informal meaning has developed, meaning "a sexual tie between consenting adults, not involving marriage," as in *We've had a relationship for three years now, but we've never really discussed getting married.* This sense is still not fully Standard, but given recent changes in the manners and values affecting such matters, it is widely used and increasingly useful in nearly all but the most Oratorical and Formal contexts, including some Edited English.

relative See RELATION.

RELATIVE CLAUSES are dependent clauses introduced by relative pronouns or constructed along those lines but without the relative pronoun itself (these are called contact clauses): *He's the man* **who won the race.** *She's the student* **whom they chose.** *The swing,* **which is broken,** *was my favorite plaything in those days. The swing* **that is broken** *is the one on the end. The woman* [**that**] *I marry must be rich.* See also OMITTED RELATIVE; RELATIVE PRONOUNS; RESTRICTIVE AND NONRESTRICTIVE CLAUSES.

relatively (*adv.*) Like *comparatively, relatively* has often been criticized for being used when there is no literal comparison involved. Actually it can be used with or without a comparison, and one of the most common uses is to mean "fairly," as in *Mother's been in relatively good health this year.* Or there can be a real comparison, as in *Compared to* [*with*] *her peers, she's a relatively poised young woman.* Both uses are Standard, despite the critical noise.

RELATIVE PRONOUNS are *that, what, which, who, whom,* and *whose.* They introduce dependent clauses. See also OMITTED RELATIVE; PRONOUN; RELATIVE CLAUSES.

RELATIVE PRONOUNS, OMITTED See OMITTED RELATIVE; PRONOUN.

relative to, relating to (*preps.*) These two compound prepositions mean much the same as *concerning* and *about: We have a report relative to* [*relating to, concerning, about*] *trends in the economy.* The several commentators who object that both are vague and pretentious are right: the compound prepositions imply by their circumlocutory length that they can specify the nature of things more explicitly than *about* can, but in fact they are even less explicit: in the example, they merely *relate* the report in some wholly unspecified way to the topic, whereas *about* implies at least what the topic of the report is. Use *about* or *concerning*—either is quicker, clearer, and more accurate than *relative to* or *relating to.*

release(d) time (*n.*) *Released time* is time during which a worker is freed of ordinary duties in order to do something else, as a teacher might be relieved of teaching a class in order to devote time to committee work. *Released,* the regular participial adjective, ends in a *t* sound, and *time* begins with another, but the frequent use of the phrase caused the two sounds to coalesce into a single consonant, and the occasional occurrence in writing of *release* instead of *released* reflects that change. Some conservative Edited English still frequently insists on *released,* however, and the two spellings are in divided usage at present. See HANDICAP PARKING; ICE CREAM.

relevant (*adj.*) has long been Standard as an attributive adjective, as in *He had some relevant information,* as well as in combined use, usually with *to* or *for* plus an object of the preposition: *Figures on costs are surely relevant to [for] our study.* The recent usage issue has been the growing use of *relevant* as a predicate adjective meaning "useful, worthwhile," and the like: *We don't think the study of marketing is relevant today; it doesn't address anything we're interested in. Most of the questions sociology studies today are not relevant.* Objection to this use has died down lately, and what began as a jargon term of the campus unrest of the 1960s seems now to have become Standard and is no longer a cliché: *I hope today's voters will see this issue as relevant.*

Metathesis can sometimes be a problem with *relevant* in both spelling and pronunciation: look out for *revelant;* its inadvertent use is a shibboleth. See also IRRELEVANT.

relic, relict (*nn.*) These are partial synonyms, in the sense "something surviving from a mostly decayed or vanished past." Arrowheads and pottery shards are *relics* of past civilizations; certain plants, animals, and other natural phenomena are often labeled *relicts,* being the last remaining vestiges of older developments. *Relict* is also an archaic or at least old-fashioned and very stiffly Formal word for "widow": *She is the relict of the late governor.* Both words also can function as adjectives.

RELIC PLURALS OF NOUNS Besides the regular pattern for making plurals (see PLURALS OF NOUNS), English has kept some Old English *relic plurals,* because the words are so common, with such high frequency of use. These are the most common of the *relics:* (1) A small number of words add the sound *z* or *iz* to the stem after changing the final stem consonant sound: *house/houses; calf/calves* (and a handful of other words); *path/paths* (and a few other words). Note that of these sound changes, only the *calf/calves* shift is reflected in the spelling too. (2) A few words, mostly the names of animals, have an unchanging singular and plural form: *sheep, deer, fish* (which has a regular plural as well, *fishes*), *quail,* etc. There may be some slight semantic distinctions between the meaning of the unchanging plural and the regular one, as in the instance of *fish/fishes.* (3) In three words, the plural adds a syllable including the sound *in: child/children; ox/oxen;* and *brother/brethren* (although *brother* also has a regular plural, *brothers,* and there is a semantic distinction between the two). (4) A few Old English *relics* make their plurals through an internal vowel change: *man/men, woman/women, foot/feet, goose/geese,* and *mouse/mice.* Note that these are all closed lists of words; we do not add new ones except in jest based on analogy (*house/hice* and *mongoose/mongeese,* for example).

RELICS AND FOSSILS are terms sometimes applied to certain still current idiomatic expressions that contain subjunctives, such as *if I were you, if need be,* and the like. See also INDICATIVE; RELIC PLURALS OF NOUNS.

relict See RELIC.

relieve See AMELIORATE.

religious See IRRELIGIOUS; SACRILEGE.

relish (*n.*), when it combines with a preposition, takes *for* or, rarely, *of,* as in *She has a real relish for crossword puzzles; The entire family exhibited an insatiable relish of whodunits.*

remains (*n. pl.*) is Standard in its generalized sense, "what is left after most has been consumed" and "relics of the past," as in *The remains of a large dinner were still on the table; We found the remains of an old farmhouse crumbling away in the weeds. Remains* is also a euphemism in its specialized sense meaning "body," "corpse," as in *They shipped the soldiers' remains home by air.* See also CREMAINS.

remand (*v.*), **remand back** *Remand,* meaning "to send back or order back or order returned," applies specifically to court cases, prisoners, people under arrest or indictment, and the like: *His case was remanded to the district court. She was remanded to jail to await trial.* The usage problem arises with the locution *to remand back,* which is frequently criticized as redundant. Technically, it is redundant if the case or person is being sent back for the first time, but the fact is that, whether to reflect additional *remandings* after the first or for emphasis, clarity, or hyperbole, *remand back* turns up fairly frequently in Standard use, even though some Edited English may continue to reject it. Compare REFER BACK.

remediable, remedial (*adjs.*) If it's *remediable,* it can be remedied; it is subject to remedy. If it's *remedial,* it is intended as a remedy: *The surgeons thinks his foot problems are remediable. They propose some remedial exercise therapy first and then possibly some remedial surgery.* Pronounce them *ruh-MEE-dee-uh-bul* and *ruh-MEE-dee-uhl,* respectively.

remedy (*n.*), when it combines with a preposition, can take *against, for,* or *to,* as in *We're seeking a remedy for [against] the common cold; we want a remedy to such infections.*

remember See RECOLLECT.

remind (*v.*) is almost always transitive: *I reminded her of her promise. Your son reminds me of his father.* Intransitive use, meaning "is reminiscent of," as in *That music reminds of our visit to Bavaria,* is usually considered Nonstandard and unidiomatic.

remittance, remission (*nn.*) *Remittance* is "the sending of money" and "money so sent," as in *His remittance reached us on Thursday.* A *remittance man* is someone living abroad, being supported by *remittances* of money sent from home; the term was much used in nineteenth-century Britain. *Remission* is "a postponement," "the cancellation of a debt," "the lessening of pain or discomfort," and in the idiom *in remission,* "a period of time during which the symptoms of a disease abate or disappear," used particularly of the symptoms of certain cancers, which, as they lessen or even vanish for a time, are said to be *in remission.*

remunerate (*v.*), **remuneration** (*n.*) These are formal and technical words used for large amounts of money and for other forms of payment, as in *The president's remuneration consisted of a large salary plus stock options and several incentive clauses based on total sales volume and quarterly profits.* The error that crops up is usually the result of metathesis, which produces spelling or pronunciation mistakes such as *renumeration.*

Renaissance, renascence (*n.*), **renascent** (*adj.*) *Renaissance* (pronounced *REN-uh-SAHNS* or *-ZAHNS*) and *renascence* (pronounced *ruh-NAI-sins* or *ruh-NA-sins*) are variant spellings of the word meaning "rebirth"; Americans generally use the spelling *renaissance.* The proper noun *Renaissance* is the term used to describe that important period in Western European history,

roughly the fifteenth, sixteenth, and early seventeenth centuries, known for its intellectual and artistic accomplishments and influences. The adjective *renascent* means "showing rebirth, new life, new vigor."

render (*v.*) is Standard, although at times perhaps more stiff and formal than some other verbs that might be used to mean "to give or pay," as in *She rendered our thanks for their generosity,* "to cause to become," as in *The blow rendered him unconscious,* "to picture, paint, or translate," as in *He rendered the brief Italian lyric as an English sonnet,* and "to hand down a judgment," as in *She promised to render a decision within a month.* In the sense "to melt down, to extract by melting," as in *They rendered all the lard from the freshly slaughtered pig,* it is precise and technical for that cooking process. In some uses, such as descriptions of musical performances, as in *She rendered "O Promise Me" as an encore, render* almost always sounds pretentious, and more than one cynic has noted the suggestive similarities between the cliché *rendering music* and *rending* it (tearing it to tatters). Avoid or be very sparing of musical or other "performing" uses.

rendezvous (*n., v.*) The noun *rendezvous* (pronounced **RAHN**-*di-VOO* or **RAHN**-*dai-VOO*) is both singular and plural: *These rendezvous must be stopped.* As a verb, its other forms are *rendezvoused* (*-VOOD*), *rendezvousing* (*-VOO-ing*) and *rendezvouses* (*-VOOZ;* third person singular). See FOREIGN PLURALS.

renowned (*adj.*), **renown** (*n.*) The adjective is always spelled *renowned,* never *renown* or *reknown(ed): She is a renowned authority on cats.* Similarly the noun is always spelled *renown,* never *reknown: His renown is increasing yearly, thanks to a good press.* There are no such English words as *reknown* or *reknowned.*

rent See LEASE.

reoccur, reoccurrence See RECUR.

rep (*n.*) is a slang clipping of *representative,* as in *She's a rep for a publishing company,* and *reputation,* as in *He has a fine rep in the community.* It is also a jargon or slang clipping of *repertory theater: She's been playing [in] rep for three years now.* Capitalized, and sometimes with a period at the end, *Rep*(.) is an abbreviation for *Representative* (a member of the House of Representatives) or for *Republican* (a member of the Republican party). And finally, *rep* is also the full Standard name for a ribbed cloth fabric, often used for men's neckties: *She gave him a handsome rep tie for Christmas.*

repairable, reparable (*adjs.*) These two both mean "capable of being repaired," but *repairable* (pronounced *ruh-PER-uh-bul*) is used of material things such as chairs, lawn mowers, and church steeples, while *reparable* (pronounced *REP-(uh)-ruh-bul*) is used figuratively and of nonmaterial things. Compare *The jeweler said my watch was repairable* and *The chairman agreed that the damage to the candidate's reputation was probably reparable.* See also UNREPAIRABLE.

repast (*n.*) means "food and drink," "a meal," and although it has a somewhat literary and hyperbolic air, it is Standard: *On very short notice they served us a splendid dinner, a truly bountiful repast.*

repeat See REPLICATE.

repeat again is a locution usually criticized as a redundancy, but like *reiterate again* and *refer back,* it all depends on what you intend. If you do something twice, then the second time you are *repeating* the first action; but if you *repeat it again* (*and again*), you are performing many repetitions—a perfectly plausible set of circumstances.

repel See REBUFF.

repellent, repellant (*adj., n.*), **repulsive, revolting** (*adjs.*) *Repellent* is the usual American spelling of both the adjective, meaning "pushing back," "causing distaste or dislike, causing an aversion," and "resistant to water or other liquids" (*His manners are repellent to me; This lotion is repellent to insects; My raincoat is supposed to be repellent to water*), and the noun, meaning "something that repels," "a substance or coating that repels" (*I bought a new repellent to use against mosquitoes*). *Repellant* is a variant spelling of *repellent.*
 Repulsive means "tending to repel," or "offensive, causing strong dislike or disgust": *There was a repulsive odor in the house; She found his appearance repulsive. Revolting* can mean "rebellious," but the meanings synonymous with *repellent* and *repulsive* are "disgusting, loathsome, causing revulsion," as in *She said some shocking, revolting things about her family; His revolting table manners ruined my appetite.* All these are Standard.

repertoire, repertory (*nn.*) These are synonyms in that one meaning of *repertory* is *repertoire,* "the full list of plays, compositions, skills, abilities, or other matters that can be called on," as in *He tried every trick in his repertoire* [*repertory*] *in order to make the audience laugh.* A *repertory* is also "a repository,

a place where things may be stored," but its most frequently used senses are those involving the theater: "a company that does several plays in sequence or alternately during season," "a theater housing such a company," and "the list of plays that that group is performing," as in *She joined a repertory company whose repertory that season consisted of two Shakespeare comedies, a Shaw comedy, and Wilde's* Earnest.

REPETITION See REDUNDANT.

repetitious, repetitive (*adjs.*) *Repetitious* means "full of or characterized by repetitions" and especially "boring or tedious repetitions," as in *Her conversation was silly and repetitious. Repetitive* simply means "characterized by repetitions": *Making these wooden handles involved several repetitive procedures on the lathe.* Had the procedures also been *repetitious,* the worker would almost certainly have found them tedious; that they were *repetitive* does not insist on their tediousness.

replace (*v.*) has two meaning clusters and can be inadvertently ambiguous if context does not assist: it can mean "return to its place, put back," as in *I replaced on its shelf the dictionary I had taken down*; and it can mean "put something else in its place, substitute something for it," as in *We replaced the broken dishes with some we had bought downtown.* See also DISPLACE.

replete (*adj.*) usually means "filled to overflowing, abundantly provided with," as in *The barns, silos, and granaries were replete with the fall's harvest, which had been an unusually large one.* There may even be a suggestion of "too much," as in *fulsome.* And some dictionaries indicate that the older and at one time apparently archaic sense "complete" may still be in use.

replica, copy, reproduction (*nn.*) All these mean "an imitation," but there is some uncertainty about differences among the three. A *replica* is a copy of sorts, perhaps miniaturized, and the term is usually applied to imitations of artifacts rather than of works of art such as paintings: *He bought a metal replica of the Leaning Tower mounted on the edge of an ashtray.* A *copy* is what the art student (or a counterfeiter) seeks to make of a museum masterpiece. And a *reproduction* is sometimes photographic, usually of prints or paintings or drawings. All three terms are used both literally and figuratively, and only *copy* usually suggests that the new one will be as much as possible exactly like the original in all dimensions, colors, and textures (note, however, that *exact copy* is not usually considered a redundancy).

replicate, copy, duplicate, repeat (*vv.*) All these suggest a process of imitating, of making a copy of something. A singer may find it difficult to *replicate* a particularly brilliant performance—that is, repeat it exactly in every detail. A scientist expects to be able to *replicate* a soundly designed experiment. To *duplicate* with all our electronic devices these days seems easier than ever: we have many photographic processes for *duplicating* pictures and print and the like. And again, we can *repeat* such visible materials electronically just as we can record and *repeat* sounds. All these verbs can accumulate some pejorative edges, however, if context does not control: when they are pejorative, it is usually in deference to the primacy of any original.

reportedly (*adv.*), meaning "according to report" or "as reported," is a Standard adverb. As so often happens, a few objections have been raised to its use as a sentence adverb, as in *Reportedly the government forces have repulsed the rebel troops,* but there has never been anything wrong with that use.

repository See DEPOSITORY.

reprisal (*n.*), when combined with a preposition, can be followed by *against, on,* or *upon,* as in *They decided to make reprisals against [on, upon] the countries harboring the rebels. Reprisal* also can combine with *for, in response to,* and *because of,* to indicate the reason for the reprisal, as in *We made reprisals for [in response to, because of] their aiding the rebels.*

reproduction See REPLICA.

republican, Republican (*adjs., nn.*) The common noun and the general adjective are not capitalized, as in *These African nationalists are republicans; that is, they favor establishing a republican form of government.* Capitalized, the proper noun names a *Republican,* a member of one of the two major American political parties, the *Republican party.* Compare DEMOCRAT.

repugnance (*n.*), when it combines with prepositions, usually takes *for, to, toward,* or *towards,* as in *She feels great repugnance for [to, toward, towards] her neighbors.*

repulse See REBUFF.

repulsive See REPELLENT.

request (*n., v.*) The verb is a bit more studied than *ask.* It can be followed by *of,* as in *We requested of them a second meeting, to discuss terms of a settlement. For* is Standard almost exclusively with the noun: *She has two requests for autographs.* Analogy with *ask* may have caused the use of *for* with the verb to be denied status as a Standard idiom. In *I request [for] you to grant us a delay* or *I ask [for] you to grant us a delay,* the *for* is deemed extraneous and dialectal; Standard English omits it. See BEHEST.

require (*v.*) has several key senses: "demand," as in *She requires our attendance at every session;* "need," as in *He's so weak that he requires constant attention from nurses and orderlies;* and "want," as in *She is querulous and impatient and is constantly requiring attention she doesn't really need.* Make certain that context removes any ambiguity.

requirement (*n.*), **requisite** (*adj., n.*) *Requirements* and *requisites* are "things needed": *She has completed all the requirements and now has all the requisites to apply for the position.* As an adjective, *requisite* means "needed, required, necessary," as in *He has the requisite skills to do the work.* See PERQUISITE.

resemblance (*n.*), when it combines with prepositions, usually does so with *to* or *between,* although *among* is also possible: *There is a strong resemblance between John and his father. Her resemblance to her father is striking. I see no family resemblances whatever among their children.*

resentment (*n.*) combines with any of several prepositions, some designating those against whom the resentment is directed (*His resentment of [at, against, toward, towards] them was apparent*), others specifying its cause (*Her resentment over [for, at] what she felt was a slight kept growing*).

reside (*v.*) is a somewhat stiff and legal-sounding word for *live: She resides at 7 Oak Street.* Save it for formal and courtroom uses, and avoid flirting with pretentiousness or pomposity. Only *is domiciled* is stuffier.

resin, rosin (*nn.*) *Resin* is the generic term for all sorts of sticky fluids and gums exuded by plants. Synthetic *resins* are manufactured in imitation of these and are widely used in the making of plastics. *Rosin* is a particular natural *resin* from pine trees; in dried powder or cake form it is used by gymnasts and other athletes to prevent hands and feet from slipping and by musicians on the bows with which they play stringed instruments, to insure firmer contact between bow and strings.

resource, recourse, resort (*nn.*) The only reason for confusion among these nouns seems to be that each can be used in the sense of "a place or person to turn to for help or support'': *My father is my main resource [recourse, resort] when I'm out of funds.* In any event, the distinctions are clear: A *resource* is ''a supply of something,'' ''a source,'' or ''an ability to do something,'' as in *She's a constant resource for encouragement.* A *recourse* is ''the act of turning to someone or something for assistance'' or ''that someone or something itself'': *My only recourse was to bring charges against them. Resort* can be a synonym of *recourse,* in the sense of ''a person or place to whom or to which you turn for help,'' as in *That office is our court of last resort, our last chance to get justice. Resort* of course also means ''a gathering place for recreation and relaxation'' and hence ''a place to turn to,'' as in *They went to a seaside summer resort every year.*

respect See IN RESPECT TO.

respectable, respectful, respective (*adjs.*) A *respectable* person is worthy of respect and esteem; a *respectable* amount of something is worth consideration and probably reasonably large; a *respectable* appearance is a presentable one. *Respectful* means ''to show respect toward,'' ''deferential,'' as in *He was always respectful toward his father. Respective* means ''separate,'' ''several,'' or ''particular,'' as in *We all then left for our respective homes.*

respecting See IN RESPECT TO.

respective See RESPECTABLE.

respectively (*adv.*) means ''separately and individually'' or ''in the order specified,'' as in *We reviewed each of the three programs respectively.*

RESPONSE UTTERANCE See SITUATION UTTERANCE.

responsibility (*n.*), when it combines with prepositions, takes *for* or *to,* as in *I have responsibility to the owners for the security of their property.* You may also *have the responsibility of [about, in] keeping track of inventory* and *show responsibility toward [towards] someone or something.* All these are Standard.

restaurateur, restauranteur (*nn.*) Edited English nearly always demands the older French *restaurateur* (pronounced *RES-tuhr-ah-TUHR* or *-TOOR*), but *restauranteur* (pronounced *RES-tuhr-ahn-TUHR* or *-TOOR*), by analogy with the fully anglicized *restaurant,* is commonly heard and seen, and most dictionaries consider it a Standard variant spelling and pronunciation. *Restauranteur* can still raise conservative eyebrows, however, even in some Semiformal and

Conversational contexts, so know your audience and readers and their expectations.

restive, restless (*adjs.*) *Restive* has more than one meaning: ''stubborn or balky,'' ''restless or fidgety,'' and ''impatient.'' *Restless* of course is synonymous with the ''fidgety'' sense and also overlaps somewhat with the ''impatient'' sense. Perhaps because of this, there has been a good deal of argument over whether *restive* should be limited to use in the ''balky, stubborn'' sense, but all the evidence suggests that all three meaning clusters for *restive* are Standard.

RESTRICTIVE AND NONRESTRICTIVE CLAUSES These are *restrictive* and *nonrestrictive* modifiers in clause form: *The convertible **that had its top down** was mine* (restrictive); *The convertible, **which had its top down,** was mine* (nonrestrictive). The *restrictive clause* in the first sentence specifies which convertible is under discussion; the *nonrestrictive clause* in the second sentence merely adds interesting but not crucial detail about the only convertible under discussion. Using or omitting the commas makes a difference, reflecting as it does the differing intonation patterns the spoken language provides for restrictive and nonrestrictive modifiers. But see also THAT (4) for a discussion of the distribution of these two relative pronouns. See also RELATIVE CLAUSES.

RESTRICTIVE AND NONRESTRICTIVE MODIFIERS may be either phrases or clauses. In *The convertible **with its top down** was parked on the street,* the *restrictive modifier* specifies which convertible was parked; in *The convertible, **with its top down,** was parked on the street,* the *nonrestrictive modifier* adds some interesting but not crucial detail—it is the same convertible whether the modifier is there or not.

The sentence *My son **the brain surgeon** has a penetrating gaze* illustrates a special type of *restrictive modifier,* sometimes called a *restrictive appositive,* made so in speech by the intonation and in writing by the lack of punctuation. Without that *restrictive appositive,* the sentence will not mean what it does with it. If the speaker has only one son and doesn't need to distinguish him from any other, the sentence might be instead: *My son, **the brain surgeon,** has a penetrating gaze.* Here the intonation or the commas separate *the brain surgeon* from the rest of the sentence, from which that phrase could be omitted without destroying the meaning; hence it is a nonrestrictive appositive, a *nonrestrictive modifier.* See also RESTRICTIVE AND NONRESTRICTIVE CLAUSES.

RESTRICTIVE APPOSITIVES See APPO-
SITIVE.

result, end See END PRODUCT.

resume (*n., v.*), **résumé, resumé** (*n.*) The noun
resume may be spelled either with or without
the acute accents, but Americans usually retain
at least the final one in order to avoid confusion
of *résumé* with the verb *resume* (*ree-Z(Y)OOM*),
"to begin again." However spelled, the noun
résumé is always pronounced *RE-zoo-MAI*. Its
general meaning is "a summary," and in the
United States it also has a specialized sense,
"the statement that people applying for jobs
draw up to summarize their educational background, work experience, and other qualifications."

reticent (*adj.*), **reticence** (*n.*) The adjective has
long meant "restrained, silent, taciturn," but it
is now developing a new sense, "hesitant or
reluctant," which is slightly different and which
may not be understood everywhere. Let context
make clear whether the *reticence* you refer to is
merely "not talking" or "not talking because
of diffidence or timidity."

retiree See SENIOR CITIZEN.

retro- (*prefix*) means "backward," "back," or
"behind," and when added to another word it
usually does not use a hyphen: *retroactive, re-
trofit, retrograde.*

return back is often criticized for being a redundancy, as it may indeed be, since *return*
already means "to go back." But as with *refer
back* and *reiterate again* and similar constructions, *return back* may mean literally "to return
more than once," or it may simply be used for
emphasis, as a kind of hyperbole. Even in this
second instance, it is still Standard, at least in
Informal and Conversational contexts.

Rev. See REVEREND.

revel (*v.*), when it combines with a preposition,
takes either *in* or *at*: *She revels in her new fame.
I reveled at finally having some money.*

revelation, Revelation(s) (*nn.*) A *revelation* is
a revealing or disclosing of something; the proper
noun (usually without a final *-s*, but informally
often with one) is the name of the final book of
the New Testament.

revenge See AVENGE.

Reverend, Rev. (*adj.*) This honorific (*Rev.* is
an abbreviation) is a title for a member of the
clergy. Conservative usage specifies the forms
*The Reverend John M. Smith, The Reverend
Mr. Smith,* and in direct address, simply *Mr.*

Smith, and sometimes proscribes as Substandard
(*The*) *Reverend Smith* and in direct address,
Reverend, and in third person reference, the
noun *the reverend.* But some dictionaries now
report these same Nonstandard forms as Standard, despite the continued objections of many
conservatives.

reversal, reversion (*nn.*) A *reversal* is "a turning completely about" or "a complete and usually unfortunate about-face in one's luck," as in
*After a year of successful operation, the young
company suffered a severe reversal.* A *reversion*
is a kind of *reversal,* but particularly "a turning
back to some former condition or state," as in
the law, when a will stipulates the *reversion* of
property to an original owner, or as in *His illness caused him to undergo a reversion to a
state of innocence characteristic of children.*

reverse See OBVERSE.

reverse discrimination is a somewhat illogical
but idiomatic Standard English locution, meaning "discrimination against members of a majority, which is claimed to give unfair advantage
to members of a minority." *Reverse discrimination* can be understood only in the light of the
new, pejorative sense of *discrimination,* for
which, see DISCRIMINATE.

reversion See REVERSAL.

revert back, revert (*vv.*) Like *refer back* and
return back, revert back is often called a redundancy. *Revert* means "to go back to" or "to
return to," as in *She reverted to her old slipshod
ways; to revert back,* then, seems redundant if
there was only one return. If there was a series
of returnings, then *revert back* would be logical
and Standard, and if, as is frequently the case in
Conversational and Informal use, the effort is
simply to provide extra emphasis, then *revert
back* is also Standard, although Edited English
may reject this use.

review, revue (*nn.*) *Review* is the generic and
usual spelling, meaning "a looking back," "a
report or survey of a topic," "a reexamination,"
and the like and also having some specialized
senses, such as "a journal of topical essays"
and "a musical theatrical show of skits, dances,
and comedy, sometimes satirical." The last sense
is the meaning of *revue,* and that spelling is
Standard only in that sense.

revise (*v.*) Etymologically, *revise* meant "to look
back over something, to inspect it and change it
if necessary," so in that sense *a revised version*
might have no changes in it at all. Today, however, *revise* almost always means "to change
and try to improve," as in *She revised her first*

draft and improved it considerably with changes in diction.

revolting (*adj.*) can be ambiguous unless context assists in making clear which of its two Standard meaning clusters is intended: *Those troops are revolting* may mean either "they are rebelling, in a rebellious state" or "they are loathsome, repulsive, and disgusting." See also REPELLENT.

revue See REVIEW.

reward (*v.*) combines with the preposition *for* to indicate the purpose of the reward, as in *He was rewarded for his bravery*, with *by* or *with* to indicate what the reward was, as in *They rewarded her by paying for her trip* or *They rewarded her with a week at the beach*, and with *by* to indicate who gave the reward, as in *They were rewarded by the town council.*

RHETORIC has two meanings today: (1) It is the ancient and formal art of using words effectively, and it is the study of the devices and procedures employed in speaking and writing well. In this book are entries for some of the more important terms of formal rhetorical devices and plans; they enable you to discuss with some precision the various ways of making your expression and argument more effective. (2) It has also come to mean the use of fancy (and often empty) words and arguments. Make certain that context makes clear which *rhetoric* you intend.

rhinoceros (*n.*) This curious word has three Standard plurals: *rhinoceros, rhinoceroses, rhinoceri* (although *rhinoceri* is rare). See FOREIGN PLURALS.

RHYME, RIME (*n., v.*), **ASSONANCE, CONSONANCE** (*nn.*) Both spellings, *rhyme* and *rime*, are Standard for all uses of the word except the "frost" sense of *rime*. *Rime* is the older spelling of the verse word, and its relative simplicity still appeals to many. Edited English admits both spellings, but some publishers (including this one) insist that only *rhyme* will do. Words that *rhyme* have both *assonance* and *consonance*. To have *assonance*, words must have identical vowel sounds in their final syllables, as in *set, intend,* and *fresh* (*SET, in-TEND, FRESH*); to have consonance, words must have identical consonant sounds ending their final syllables, as in *balloon, marine,* and *tan* (*buh-LOON, muh-REEN,* and *TAN*). To have *rhyme*, the final syllables of line-ending words in two or more verses must end in both *consonance* and *assonance*, as in *spleen, tureen,* and *ob-*

scene (*SPLEEN, tuh-REEN, uhb-SEEN*). See ALLITERATION.

RHYME IN PROSE, RIME RICHE Inadvertent rhyme in prose, as in *Please clean the screen,* can often mar a passage's effectiveness, just as deliberate use of it is a favorite attention-getting device in advertising. Like excessive alliteration, deliberate rhyme in prose, especially *rime riche* (pronounced *REEM REESH*), which uses two or more words pronounced and sometimes spelled alike but with different meanings (as in *He's a fishy sort, with no more soul than a sole*), is of dubious merit except for jocular use.

RHYMING COMPOUNDS are catchy and surprisingly durable self-imitating words such as *nitty-gritty, hanky-panky, hurdy-gurdy, namby-pamby,* and *itty-bitty*. Of these, *hurdy-gurdy* is Standard; the others are slang, suitable mainly for Conversational and Informal use.

RHYMING SLANG (especially the British kind) replaces a word whose meaning is intended with a word or phrase that rhymes with it (*facts* becomes *brass tacks*; *gloves* becomes *turtle doves*; *my wife* becomes *storm and strife*).

RHYTHM IN PROSE Good prose usually avoids repetitive regular metrical patterns, just as it avoids or minimizes inadvertent *rhyme*, but that doesn't mean it lacks rhythm. Avoid insistently obvious patterns, particularly overlong stretches of text, because rocking-horse regularity can be either soporific or inadvertently funny. Seek instead the variety and effectiveness of a rhythm that reinforces meaning, provides variety, and is easy and pleasant to read, silently or aloud. Parallelism, as in *I came, I saw, I conquered,* judicious placement of adverbs, as in *Attempt the work willingly, accept its discomforts patiently, and respond to the result cheerfully,* variety in lengths and kinds of sentences, as in *We planned the attack with care, we committed our resources with restraint, and we controlled our zeal with patience; nonetheless, we failed,* and juxtapositions of grammatical and rhetorical stress, as in *with liberty and justice for all,* are all examples of ways you can vary and control the rhythm of your prose.

rich, wealthy (*adj.*) *Rich* and *wealthy* are synonyms in the sense of "possessing great amounts of money or property," but although *wealthy* can be used figuratively, *rich* is far more frequently so used, as in *rich in friends, rich in influence, rich food and drink,* etc. When *rich* takes prepositions, *in* is most frequent, as in *She is rich in friends,* but *with* also occurs, as in *My birthday cakes always are rich with chocolate.*

rid (*v.*) combines most frequently with the preposition *of,* as in *We want to get* [*be*] *rid of these books. Get rid of* and *be rid of* are Standard idioms. *Rid* has two past tense and past participle forms: *rid* or *ridded, rid* or *ridded,* as in *The piper rid* [*ridded*] *the town of rats; The piper had rid* [*ridded*] *the town of rats.*

riddle See ENIGMA.

right (*adv., adj., n., v., interj., intensifier*) *Right* is an interjection when used as an affirmative response: *"Put it here?" "Right!"* As an adverb, it has much use: *Do it right. Go right straight ahead. He's the right person* illustrates the "correct" sense of the adjective, and there is also the directional sense, *"Take the right fork in the road, not the left one."* The poet called him *"a right jolly old elf"* illustrates *right* as an intensifier, and *You have the right to ask* illustrates the noun. The verb means "to restore to proper order or position": *We righted the canoe and bailed it out.* There are also idioms, two of them slang, as in the vigorously affirmative *Right on!* and the approving interjection *All right!* (pronounced *AW REIT,* with lingering stress on the second syllable), plus a Conversational idiom, as in *I had him dead to rights.* Although the flat adverb frequently turns intensifier, it has a somewhat folksy Southern or Midland dialectal quality often used at the Casual level, perhaps only jocularly in Standard: *She's a right good dancer.* Compare WRONG; see RITE.

right bank (of a river) See BANK OF A RIVER.

rightly (*adv.*) The inflected adverb *rightly* is not interchangeable with most uses of the flat adverb *right: She rightly refused to call him.* It is used as a sentence adverb, as in *Rightly, we concluded that they weren't coming.* It also has a dialectal use meaning "exactly," which may turn up in negative jocular use in Conversational and Informal contexts in Standard English: *She said she didn't rightly know where he'd gone.*

right of way, right-of-way (*n.*) There are four Standard plurals: *rights of way, rights-of-way, right of ways,* and *right-of-ways.* See PLURALS OF COMPOUND NOUNS.

right-to-life (*adj.*), **right-to-lifer** (*n.*) The adjective is a Standard idiom applied to a person, group, or policy opposed to abortion: *Right-to-life groups promised to demonstrate against the proposal.* The noun *right-to-lifer,* made with the agentive ending, is relatively new and is still limited to Informal and Conversational use, although it has also appeared in journalese: *All the right-to-lifers were carrying signs.*

right-to-work (*adj.*), meaning "concerning laws or legislation opposing or banning unions or closed shops in labor agreements," is Standard.

rigor, rigour (*n.*), **rigorous** (*adj.*) Americans spell the noun *rigor,* and the British spell it *rigour,* but both spell the adjective *rigorous.* See SPELLING (1).

rill See STREAM.

RIME See RHYME.

RIME RICHE See RHYME IN PROSE.

ring 1 (*v.*) is a strong verb having to do with bells and chimes and the placing of telephone calls. The Standard past tense is *rang,* the past participle *rung: The alarm rang at five, just as it had rung for the last six months. Rung* as a past tense form still occurs but is considered dialectal or obsolete. Compare (and don't confuse) RING (2).

ring 2 (*v.*) is a weak verb having to do with making circles and finger rings and the like; its past tense and past participle are both *ringed: The media people ringed the winner, hoping to get interviews. She was lavishly ringed and necklaced.* Compare (and don't confuse) RING (1).

riparian See RIVERINE.

rip off (*v.*), **rip-off, ripoff** (*n.*) The verb is slang or Conversational and Informal at best and means "to cheat or rob," as in *That con man rips off old people.* The noun is spelled either with a hyphen or as a single-word compound, and it too is slang, meaning "an instance of cheating or stealing," as in *Their "free offer" is just a ripoff* [*rip-off*].

rise See RAISE (2).

rise, arise, get up (*vv.*) These three, when they mean "to get out of bed" or "to stand up after lying or sitting down," are synonymous in those senses, but *arise* and *rise* both have an elevated, slightly studied air that makes them sound most suitable in relatively Formal or Oratorical contexts: *He rose* [*arose, got up*] *to object.* The gerunds may also display similar semantic difference: *She has a habit of rising* [*arising, getting up*] *early.*

rite, right, wright (*nn.*), **write** (*v.*) These are homophones: a *rite* is a ceremony, a ritualistic practice; a *right* (which see) is, among other things, something legally or morally due, as in *She has a right to hear the charges,* or something correct or proper, as in *He's in the right* *this time*; a *wright* is a worker, especially an artisan who makes things such as wheels or ships (see also PLAYWRIGHT). The verb *write* means "to record in writing." All are Standard.

River (*n.*) Convention dictates whether *River* comes first or last in a proper noun: it's *the River Avon*, but *the Ohio River*; *the Thames* and *the Nile* can have it either way, but it's always *the Mississippi River* and *the Hudson River*.

riverine, riparian (*adj.*) *Riverine*, meaning "of or associated with a river or its banks" or "living in or on the banks of a river," is a very low frequency word: *She published a book on certain riverine animals*. *Riparian* is also low frequency, but not quite so unusual as *riverine*; it is more specifically concerned with just the banks of rivers and is applied to things living there or associated with them, as in *His holdings along the river gave him full riparian rights on both sides for nearly a quarter of a mile*.

rivulet See STREAM.

rob, steal (*vv.*) *Rob* poses a usage problem when used in the archaic sense meaning "steal," as in *The fox robbed the chickens*. Standard English today prefers *The fox robbed the henhouse* or *The fox robbed the farmer*, but *The fox stole* [not *robbed*] *the chickens* (so long as he made off with them, not just with their possessions). Although *rob* does turn up sometimes in writing as *to rob the loot*, many still consider that use Nonstandard or dialectal. Note too that some purists insist that *to rob your house*, someone would have to take the whole structure—while you watched; *to rob you*, the thief would only have to make off with something of yours, not with you yourself. Nonetheless, modern usage seems regularly to permit the loose use of the passive voice, as in *Our house was robbed last night while we were away*, in all but the most conservative Edited English. *Rob* combines almost always with the preposition *of*, as in *Indigestion robbed me of my sleep; from* is occasionally heard and seen as well, as in *Bad press relations robbed her hard-earned popularity from her*, but it's Substandard, and Edited English won't have it. See BURGLARIZE.

robbery See BURGLARY.

rock, stone (*nn.*) If there is a distinction between these two as count nouns, it is that a *rock* is usually larger than a *stone* (but not everyone makes that distinction). As mass nouns, the terms are largely interchangeable. In referring to diamonds and other precious gems, the Standard term is *stone(s)*. To call a diamond or other gemstone a *rock* is hyperbolic slang, stressing

the remarkable size of it: *He must be rich; he gave her a real rock for an engagement ring*. See also SEED (2).

rock and a hard place, between a See BETWEEN A ROCK AND A HARD PLACE.

rocks, on the This idiom has two meanings, both figurative. *Our business finally went on the rocks in December* means that it met financial disaster, bankruptcy, or some other misfortune similar to the shipwreck that is the basis of the metaphor. That use is Conversational, but another use, common in the ordering of alcoholic drinks, is Standard: the metaphor here compares ice and *rocks: bourbon on the rocks* is undiluted whiskey poured over ice.

rodeo (*n.*), either Americanized as in *RO-dee-o* or pronounced to reflect the original Spanish, as in *ro-DAI-o*, once meant "a cattle roundup" but today means "a show and contest featuring various cowboy skills, such as riding bulls and unbroken horses or roping steers." The plural is *rodeos*. See PLURALS OF NOUNS ENDING IN *-O*.

role, rôle, roll (*nn.*) A role (sometimes spelled *rôle*, with the French circumflex accent) is "a character or a part in a theatrical piece," as in *She played the role of Rhonda in the first act*, or "a pattern of behavior, a function," as in *His role was to be a good listener*. The noun *roll* has many meanings, such as "a rolling," "a kind of bread or sweet cake," "a roll of paper, including the lists of names that might be recorded on one (*the class roll*)," "a series of rapid blows on a drum," and the like. All these and other specialized senses are spelled *roll*, as are all the generalized senses about "the action of rolling." The phrase *on a roll* is Casual or Impromptu and Informal slang, meaning "achieving one success after another."

ROMAN, as in *The insert was in roman* [*roman type*], is the name (usually in lowercase) of the normal, upright body type used for most printed materials. Italics are used to contrast with *roman*.

romance (*v.*) is Standard when it means "to lie or exaggerate," but when it means "to make love to" or "to flatter," as in *He was always romancing her, trying to make her pay attention to him*, it is Conversational and Informal.

Romania, Rumania (*n.*) These are variant spellings of the name of the Eastern European country on the Black Sea; pronounce it *ro-MAIN-yuh*, *roo-MAIN-yuh*, *ro-MAIN-ee-yuh*, or *roo-MAIN-ee-yuh*.

Roman numerals contrast with the more familiar Arabic numerals. From one to ten, *Roman* numerals read I, II, III, IV, V, VI, VII, VIII, IX, and X. Forty is XL, fifty is L, one hundred is C, four hundred is CD, five hundred is D, and one thousand is M. MCMXCV is 1995. *Roman numerals* are written without commas, and numbers above 30 are unfamiliar enough to slow most readers to a crawl, if not to stop them altogether. Generally, save *Roman numerals* for places where they are conventionally familiar in either upper- or lowercase (*Act I, scene iii, Chapter IV*), and lowercased as page numbers for front matter in books (prefaces, introductions, etc.) and for buildings and gravestones, where they add formality and an additional sense of the monumental. Otherwise, stick to Arabic numerals (which see).

rondeau, rondo, round (*nn.*) A *rondeau* (pronounced *rahn-DO* or **RAHN-DO;** plural *rondeaux,* pronounced *rahn-DOZ* or **RAHN-DOZ**) is a ten-, thirteen-, or fifteen-line lyric verse type in three stanzas, with two rhymes and an unrhymed refrain; it is also a medieval French lyric or song with interwoven repetitions of two refrains or themes. A *rondo* is a musical composition with three repeated themes; it's pronounced *RAHN-do,* and its plural is *rondos* (*RAHN-doz*). A *round* can be many different things, but in music and dance it should be distinguished from *rondeau* and *rondo:* a *round* dance is one in which small groups of dancers do figures in circles; a *round* in music is a short song with two or more voices, sung so that each new voice begins the song just as the preceding voice reaches the end of the first phrase. See FOREIGN PLURALS; PLURALS OF NOUNS ENDING IN -*O.*

roof (*n.*) may be pronounced either *ROOF* or *RUF,* and its plural is *roofs* (pronounced *ROOFS* or *RUFS*).

rooftop (*n.*) is a Standard compound noun meaning "the top of a house, or its roof." Pronounce it **ROOF-TAHP** or **RUF-TAHP.**

root, rout, route (*nn., vv.*) Some of the variant pronunciations of these three are homophones. *Root,* noun and verb, is pronounced either *ROOT* or *RUT.* The noun *root* is "the lower part of a plant or tree, the part in the ground," and it has many figurative senses as well, most of them suggesting "the beginnings or basic or fundamental parts of something." The verb *root* means "to dig up, as with the snout": *Pigs root around for acorns.* They work hard at it, as does anyone who *roots* for a thing, and this in turn leads to the Conversational and Informal verb sense, "to

cheer for a team," as in *We rooted for our side, but to no avail.*

The noun *rout* is always pronounced *ROUT* and means "a mob or rabble" and by extension "a total defeat," "a disorderly retreat." The verb *rout,* pronounced *ROUT,* is a variant of the verb *root* and means "to dig or rummage for." It has combined forms that are idiomatic: *to rout out,* meaning "to force out (of bed or the house)," as in *They routed me out before breakfast,* and *to rout up,* meaning "to turn up, to find," as in *They routed up enough people for a second table of bridge.*

The noun *route* is pronounced either *ROOT* or *ROUT* (the latter especially for *paper routes* and *roads*) and means "a road or course to follow," as in *They mapped out a new route for me.* The verb, also pronounced either *ROOT* or *ROUT,* means "to schedule a trip or path for someone or something to follow," as in *They routed the packages through Chicago to save time.* All these uses are Standard, but some people object to the *ROUT* pronunciation of *route,* noun and verb, especially at the Oratorical level.

rosin See RESIN.

rostrum (*n.*) was once the beak or prow of a Roman galley, and then became a place for a Roman senator to stand to speak. Today it means "a speaker's platform," as in *He spoke from his usual spot on the rostrum.* The plural is either *rostrums* or *rostra.* See FOREIGN PLURALS; PODIUM.

rote, by See BY HEART.

rotund (*adj.*) means "round, plump, chubby," as in *Santa Claus is usually pictured as rotund.* As applied to the sound of the human voice, *rotund* means "full, orotund."

round See RONDEAU.

round, 'round See AROUND.

ROUND *S* See LONG *S.*

rouse See AROUSE.

rout, route See ROOT.

royal *we* See WE.

-rr- See CONSONANTS (2).

R's, the three is a Standard idiom, meaning "reading, writing, and arithmetic." Spelled out, the expression is commonly *readin', ritin', and 'rithmetic* to stress the alliteration.

rucksack See BACKPACK.

ruddy See BLOODY.

RULES AND GENERALIZATIONS In discussions of grammar and usage, you often hear of *rules,* but you would do well to consider *generalizations* as well and to heed the differences between them. In its generic sense, a *rule* is a law, a decree, an unchanging regulation; it should permit no exceptions, or at least none without penalty: *The rule is that no smoking is allowed in the house.* Presumably punishment or other penalty will follow breach of a rule. And in the case of a natural law or rule, breaches usually bring severe if not permanent penalties: defiance of the law of gravity, such as might occur when a child decides to fly by jumping off the barn and flapping its arms, suggests the importance of obedience to real *rules.* A *generalization,* on the other hand, describes what *usually* happens or what your *usual* expectations ought to be.

In grammar, English has certain rules that you break at your peril: for example, if you put the direct object before the indirect object without a preposition, as in *I gave the book the boy,* you will make a hash of your communication. It is a *rule* of English grammar that if it is not preceded by a preposition, the indirect object must precede the direct object. But a *generalization* simply describes expectations. For example, subjects and verbs usually agree in number, but when they do not, the penalty may be fairly severe, minor, or nonexistent: *This criteria is very important* will usually bring you trouble; *Each of us who have time are to turn in our lists today,* however, may bring no penalty in many contexts, because there are a good many qualifications of that *generalization* about agreement; and *This agenda is blurred* will bring no one any trouble at all. The *generalization* is very powerful, in that it works most of the time, but sometimes notional agreement overcomes it.

In much of English grammar, and almost always in English usage, you encounter not *rules* but *generalizations* that describe what conditions should govern your speech and writing. If the *rule* you break is truly a *rule,* you're likely

not to communicate at all; if the *generalization* you break is fairly powerful, you may bring down much criticism on your head, but rarely will you fail to communicate at all—although you may communicate some unflattering ideas about yourself.

RULES OF GRAMMAR See GRAMMAR.

Rumania See ROMANIA.

rumor, rumour (*n.*) *Rumor* is the American spelling; *rumour* is British. See SPELLING (1).

rump See BUTTOCKS.

run (*v.*) is a slightly irregular strong verb; the principal parts are *run, ran, run: I ran as I had never run before.* To use *run* as a past tense or *ran* as a past participle is glaringly Substandard and a shibboleth.

run See STREAM.

run for office See STAND FOR OFFICE.

runner-up (*n.*) The plural is *runners-up,* meaning "the ones who did not finish first." See PLURALS OF COMPOUND NOUNS.

RUN-ON SENTENCES are syntactically flawed sentences consisting of two or more independent clauses incorrectly or infelicitously merged into one. The most frequently encountered *run-on* is the one often called a comma fault, wherein a comma is used to splice together two independent clauses: *We got there late, we found they had already gone to bed.* Stylistically the term *run-on* is also sometimes attached to *paratactic* sentences, which are very long sentences with many independent clauses linked together by coordinating conjunctions; these are sentences whose ideas are strung together like beads on a string, without any effort at the subordination of one idea to another: *We went shopping, and we bought a few things, and my parents met us at the car, and we drove home, and my brother's car was in the drive.*

S

-s, -es The regular plural endings for nouns are *-s* or *-es* and pronounced *-s, -z,* or *-iz,* as in *cats, dogs,* and *churches.* The third person singular present tense endings for verbs are spelled and pronounced the same way, as in *hits, throws,* and *cashes.* See PLURALS OF NOUNS.

-'s, -s' The possessive or genitive case in nouns adds apostrophe (') plus *s* in the singular, *s* plus apostrophe in the plural. The pronunciations are not always as distinctive as the spellings: *boys, boy's bike, boys' bikes*; *dresses, this dress's skirt, these dresses' skirts.* Proper nouns already ending in *-s* vary in spelling and sound of genitives: *Mr. Jones's car* (pronounced *JONZ* or *JONZ-iz*), *the Joneses' cars* (pronounced usually *JONZ-iz*), and either *Yeats's poem* or (rarely) *Yeats' poem* (pronounced either *YAITS-iz* or *YAITS*). See also APOSTROPHE (2); PERSONAL PRONOUNS.

sabotage (*n., v.*) Use both verb and noun (pronounced *SA-bo-TAHZH*) only of "malicious, secret damage." Most dictionaries now record more generalized meanings, "destroy" and "destruction," respectively, but Edited English reserves both noun and verb for destructive work done on the sly.

sack (*n.*) Most senses of the noun are Standard. The "firing from a job" sense and the "bed or bedroll" sense, however, are slang, best limited to Conversational and Informal use, and *sack* meaning "a base in baseball" and "the tackling of a quarterback behind the line of scrimmage" are sports jargon. See BAG (2).

sacrilege (*n.*), **sacrilegious** (*adj.*) Watch the spelling of the vowels in the second and third syllables; these words are neither related to nor spelled like *religion* or *religious*. *Sacrilege*'s Latin etymon was formed of *sacer*, "sacred" and *legere*, "to gather or steal"; *sacrilege* is "the stealing of sacred things" or doing other violence to them.

sacrosanct (*adj.*) To be *sacrosanct* (pronounced *SAK-ro-SANGKT*) is to be "super-sacred," with overtones of "untouchable" or "inviolable," and sometimes also with a pejorative suggestion of too much ("just too sacred for words"). See HYPERBOLIC.

sadism (*n.*) The first syllable rhymes with either *aid* or *add*; the first pronunciation is more frequent in the United States.

Sahara Desert (*n.*) *Sahara* means "desert" in Arabic, but only the finical argue that *Sahara Desert* is tautological.

said (*adj.*) Like *the aforementioned case* and *the above instance, said dog*, as in *My client saw the defendant's dog every day, but on June 1, said dog bit my client*, is stiff, stuffy, and not really necessary for precision; instead make your syntax point out the referents of your words.

sailer, sailor (*nn.*) The meanings of these homophones differ, but they are distinguishable only in writing or from context. A boat can be *a good sailer* because it sails well; but *a good sailor* is always "a person who is expert at sailing or helping to sail a boat" or, sometimes, "someone who never gets seasick."

Saint(e), St(e). Place names (*St. Petersburg, St. Paul*) usually abbreviate *saint*, and the saints themselves frequently but not always are spelled out (*Saint Agnes* or *St. Agnes; Saint Paul* or *St. Paul*). There are many exceptions, even in place names: it's *Saint John, New Brunswick*, but *St. John's, Newfoundland;* it's *Sault Ste. Marie, Michigan*, on the *St. Mary's River*. *Sainte (Ste.)* is the French feminine form.

St. James, King James The British royal court, to which foreign diplomats are accredited, is *the Court of St. James's* (named after a palace built by Henry VIII on the site of St. James's Leper Hospital). The "authorized version" of the Bible, first published in 1611, is named after King James I (1566–1625), and is known as the King James Bible.

St. John When this is a personal or family name, the British pronounce it as though it were spelled *SIN-jin.*

sake, sakes (*nn.*) In idiomatic expressions similar to *for heavens' sake* (also *for heaven's sake* or *for heavens sake*) wherein the modifier—*goodness', mercy's, righteousness'*, or the like—ends in one of the sounds of the letter *s*, use an apostrophe or not, as you wish.

salad days It was not youth's vigor, but its inexperience and lack of judgment that Shakespeare's Cleopatra was referring to when she contrasted her present love for Antony with the days of her former love for Caesar: "My salad days, When I was green in judgement: cold in blood" (*Antony and Cleopatra*, I.v.73). But today *salad days* has changed into a metaphor rather than for unflagging, enthusiastic youth. If you want your readers to have Shakespeare's original sense of it, you must help them with context.

salary, fee, honorarium, payment in kind, wage (*nn.*) Usually a *salary* is a rounded-off dollar rate of weekly, monthly, or annual compensation; *wages* are stated in dollars and cents per hour, per day, or per piece of work; and an *honorarium* (plural: *honoraria* or *honorariums*) is a single payment, often including expenses, for a service rendered, particularly one for which taste or tradition forbid the setting of a precise rate. A *fee* is a rate charged for a service. Rural clergymen at one time often received payment *in kind*—that is, in garden produce, other foodstuffs, coal, kerosene, and clothing. See also KIND; REMUNERATE.

salary increment, bonus, COLA, raise, rise (*nn.*) A *salary increment* means "a pay raise"; sometimes there is the added inference that the increase is regular in size or timing. It is probably a euphemism, intended to add dignity to a topic felt to be grubby. A *raise* (British *rise*) in salary may be based on merit (a *merit raise*) or longevity or something else. A *COLA* (an acronym for *cost-of-living adjustment*) is an increase that keeps real wages aligned with the average rate of inflation. A *bonus* is a single lump-sum payment not part of an annual salary.

salmon, salmonella (*nn.*) Pronounce the *l* at the end of the first syllable of *salmonella* like *Sal*; pronounce the first syllable of *salmon* like *Sam*, without an *l*.

salon, saloon (*nn.*) have been pulled up and down through the years by the semantic forces of elevation and pejoration, and both words continue to be splendid examples of both euphemism and dysphemism. *Salon* has kept its original French meanings, "a large reception room in a large house" and "the collection of people likely to be present at a social affair therein": *Mme. Dumas held a salon on Thursdays.* Our American penchant for gilding anything not already obviously golden has made us try to attach the suggestion of opulence and high society to more mundane spaces: hence *beauty salons, tanning salons,* and the like.

A *saloon* was a nineteenth- and early twentieth-century tavern, and the word came to suggest to many all that was unsavory about drinking and its attendant dissolutions. In an English pub, the *saloon bar* is a bit more refined than the *public bar,* and recently some of this elevation has returned to the better *saloons* in large American cities, although generally the use is self-conscious. But like *salon, saloon* too has been added to the names of pool halls, barbershops, and muscle-building parlors in an effort to elevate what may still sound and smell like a gin mill or locker room. Also, the *saloon* on a yacht or passenger ship is a public lounge or parlor, and in Britain a *saloon* is also an automobile style (what Americans call a *sedan*).

salt, salts (*nn.*) *Salt* (sodium chloride), is a mass noun, construed as singular. *Salts* is a count noun, construed as plural. Such compound nouns as *Epsom salts, bath salts,* and *smelling salts* usually take plural verbs.

salutary (*adj.*), **salute** (*n., v.*), **salvo** (*n.*) The Latin etymon for *salutary* and *salute* is *salus,* "health," but although *salutary* has kept to that general meaning, *salute* has developed from a figurative use meaning "to wish health to, to greet." Today's *salute* is only a greeting. A *salvo* (from *salve,* "safe") fires many guns at

once and originally was also intended as a *salute,* that is, as a greeting and a compliment. It has now come to mean figuratively "any sudden burst of loud, simultaneous sound" as in *a salvo of cheering.* The plural is *salvos.* See also HEALTHY; PLURALS OF NOUNS ENDING IN -*O*.

salvable, salvageable (*adjs.*) Both mean "savable," but *salvable* is rare.

salvo See SALUTARY.

same See SAID.

same as See THE SAME AS.

same token, by the See TOKEN.

sanatorium See SANITARIUM.

sanctimonious (*adj.*), **sanctimony** (*n.*) In the mid-sixteenth century the adjective meant "holy, saintly," but by the early seventeenth century it had come to mean both "holy" and "hypocritically holy," and today it has pejorated to mean only "affectedly saintly, falsely holy."

sanction (*n., v.*) The verb means only "to give approval or permission, to support," although at one time it also meant "to punish." Today only the noun has both nearly antithetical senses: "approval" and "punishment or penalty." Both are Standard, and context must distinguish them.

sanctum, sanctum sanctorum (*nn.*) Literally, "a holy place," and "the holy of holies." These religious terms are often applied figuratively— and usually hyperbolically or ironically—to places that can be entered only by the privileged and the most privileged, respectively. *Inner sanctum* is a related cliché.

sand See GUT.

sand (*n.*) *Sand* can be either a mass noun, as in *The sand was too hot to walk on,* or a count noun, as in *Some of the sands were shiny as glass.*

sang See SING.

sanguine, sanguinary (*adjs.*) The Latin *sanguis,* "blood," is behind both of these, but their meanings differ sharply. The medieval *sanguine humor* was dominated by the blood; hence a *sanguine* person was red-cheeked, vigorous, and cheerful, and so *sanguine* came to mean "cheerful, optimistic, confident." *Sanguinary,* however, means "bloody, bloodthirsty, or bloodstained" and by extension "grim, cruel, murderous."

sanitarium, sanatorium, sanitorium (*nn.*) Some Americans try to maintain a semantic distinction between *sanatorium* (the usual British spelling; *sanitorium* is a variant common in the United States), "a kind of health resort," and *sanitarium,* "a real hospital, such as a tuberculosis (TB) hospital." But for most people these are all the same word with the same meaning, "a special sort of hospital." As TB hospitals grow fewer, that sense of the term will be less often encountered; we possibly now have a good prospect of settling not only on one meaning, but on one spelling too, probably *sanitorium.* The most common plural is *sanitoriums,* but *sanitoria* also appears. See FOREIGN PLURALS.

sank See SINK.

sans (*prep.*) This French loan word is now fully English, pronounced to rhyme with *cans* or occasionally with *cons:* it means "without" and is usually written *sans* italics.

sarcasm, sarcastic See IRONY.

sarcoma (*n.*) This originally Greek name for a cancerous tumor has two plurals: *sarcomata* is most common, especially in technical writing, but the regular English plural *sarcomas* is increasing in frequency, probably because cancer is no longer a taboo subject. See FOREIGN PLURALS.

sarcophagus The foreign plural *sarcophagi,* pronounced *sahr-KAH-fuh-gee, sahr-KAH-fuh-gei,* or (rarely) *sahr-KAH-fuh-jee,* still occurs, especially in technical use, but the regular plural, *sarcophoguses* (always with a hard *g*), is increasingly common in Standard English.

sardonic See IRONY.

sartorial (*adj.*), **sartorially** (*adv.*) English added the adjectival suffix *-ial* to the Latin *sartor,* meaning "tailor" and, perhaps humorously, "patcher." Some purists continue to object to *sartorial* as a cliché and as overconsciously elegant, but it seems to be replaceable only by longish phrases, and it is therefore useful. Once it referred only to tailoring, but today it refers to any aspect of clothing or, by extension, to a person's overall appearance. The adverb *sartorially* has similarly generalized in meaning.

sat See SET.

sated, satiated (*adjs.*) Each takes *with,* but the meanings are a bit different: *sated* suggests simply "full, having had enough"; *satiated* can also imply "too full, having had too much."

sateen See SATIN.

satellite (*adj., n.*) Some people used to object to this word's figurative use, particularly as applied to hangers-on, but although a *satellite* is still a natural or man-made object revolving around a planet in space, its meanings have also generalized and respecialized, particularly in

world political affairs. Until recently, journalism couldn't have discussed Eastern Europe without the figurative use of the word *satellite.*

satiated See SATED.

satin, sateen (*nn.*) *Satin* was the original shiny silk fabric, smooth and slippery, and it has subsequently been imitated in rayon, nylon, and other fibers. *Sateen* is usually the cotton imitation of *satin*; the word is modeled on *velveteen,* which is the cotton imitation of silk's *velvet.*

satire, satyr (*nn.*) A *satire* (pronounced *SA-TEIR*) is "a mocking attack on evil and stupidity"; a *satyr* (pronounced either *SAI-tuhr* or *SA-tuhr*) is the "oversexed classical woodland figure, part man and part goat," and its modern successor, the dirty old man. For *satire,* see also IRONY.

saturate (*v.*) is usually followed by *with: The evening air was saturated with moisture. By* and *in* occur occasionally too, but the first can sound odd to conservative ears (*The track was saturated by rain and hail*), and if people are involved, everyone is more comfortable if the reflexive *-self* form of the pronoun is also present with *in* (*He saturated himself in Mozart*).

saturnalia (*n.*) is a plural, pronounced *SAT-uhr-NAIL-yuh.* The Romans held these hectic feasts in the god Saturn's honor, and the word has generalized to mean all types of wild parties and drunken orgies. Today, however, we usually construe *saturnalia* as singular and make a new plural, so that one orgy is a *saturnalia* and two or more orgies are *saturnalias.* Both Latin and English patterns are Standard, in divided usage. See FOREIGN PLURALS.

satyr See SATIRE.

Saud, Saudi Pronounce *Saud* and the first part of *Saudi* either *sah-OOD* or as a monosyllable rhyming with *loud; Saudi* may also be pronounced *SAW-dee.*

savant, idiot savant (*nn.*) *Savant* (pronounced *suh-VAHNT* or *suh-VANT*) used to be a good, low-frequency word meaning "a scholar, a learned person," but it began to be overused, especially in the press, to apply to any nominally articulate person of prominence and has become both a cliché and a euphemism in such uses. An *idiot savant* is a mentally retarded person with one incredibly well-developed mental ability, such as doing complicated mathematics at lightning speed or memorizing complex material effortlessly.

save, save for (*preps.*) In the sense of "except" or "but," as in *We all went in save Dr. Strauss,* *save* is not yet archaic, but it occurs most often in Formal and Oratorical contexts. The compound preposition occurs more frequently and is Standard at all levels: *We were well prepared, save for our finances.*

saving See PROVIDED.

saving (*n.*) *Saving* is the singular, *savings* its plural (*Saving was too difficult*; *Now his savings are gone*), and conservative editors usually insist on this distinction. But today journalism and advertising promise *a savings of x,* and both singular and plural forms are now acceptable in most Standard English. The pattern is the same for *daylight saving time* and *daylight savings time:* most Edited English prefers the singular, but both forms are now Standard.

saving grace is literally the grace that wins salvation; applied frequently to minor virtues such as nice manners or a pleasant voice, it is hyperbole and a cliché.

savior, saviour Both are acceptable American spellings. British English uses only *saviour.* See SPELLING (1).

savvy (*adj., n., v.*) is a transitive and intransitive verb of pidgin origin meaning "understand," an adjective meaning "smart, wise," and a noun meaning "intelligence, good sense." All these senses are slang, but the noun and the adjective appear sometimes in Standard Informal and Semiformal writing, as well as at Conversational levels.

saw 1 (*v.*) The verb meaning "to cut wood" is weak, and its past tense is *sawed,* but it has two Standard past participles, *sawed* and *sawn,* the latter reflecting a strong verb pattern and usually found in British English. See also SEE.

saw 2, old (*n.*) The noun *saw,* meaning "an old saying," developed from the Old English *sagu,* "a saying." *Old saw* is a tautological cliché. See APHORISM.

say (*adv., n., v., interjs.*) is the infinitive of a hard-working verb meaning "to state, to speak." Its present tense is unusual in that its third person singular has a vowel sound different from that common to all the other five persons: *says* rhymes with *fez,* whereas *say* rhymes with *May.* Functional shift provides us with the noun *say,* as in *I've had my say* ("I've expressed my opinion"), as well as three other uses: (1) as an interjection or attention-getting function word (*Say, have you seen my book?*); (2) as an interjection indicating wonder, astonishment, or admiration (*Say!*); and (3) as an adverb, in such contexts as *Meet me at the library—say, in about*

ten minutes? All of these are Standard, the interjections and adverb limited mostly to the Conversational levels.

say the least, to This idiom is a cliché used to emphasize statements that seem insufficiently superlative or hyperbolic.

saying See APHORISM; SAW (2).

saying, that (it) goes without See GOES WITHOUT SAYING.

saying goes, as the; they say *As the saying goes* refers to some sort of familiar wisdom—an aphorism or something of the sort—and attempts to use such folk wisdom in support of a present instance: *Our goose, as the saying goes, is cooked. They say* is an idiom and cliché meaning "it is widely said (and believed)" or "it is common knowledge . . .": *They say she's going to marry him.*

scabrous, scabious, scabby (*adjs.*) *Scabrous* literally means "with a rough, scaly, prickly, or pimply surface," but its figurative senses all mean "dirty," from "dirt-covered" to "shocking and indecent." *Scabby* and *scabious* ("covered with scabs") are apparently not related to *scabrous.*

scale, large and small See LARGE-SCALE.

scallop, scollop (*n., v.*) In all senses and as either noun or verb, *scallop* is the more common spelling, and the vowel sound of its stressed first syllable is usually *AH* but sometimes *A. Scollop* is always pronounced *SKAH-luhp.*

scan (*v.*) has two nearly contradictory senses: in the fourteenth century it meant "to analyze closely the metric quantities of poetry," and it subsequently developed other, related senses that cluster around the idea of "close, intense, careful scrutiny." In the 1920s and thereafter the sense "to examine quickly," "to skim over," began to develop. Some conservatives have argued that the new senses ought not to be admitted because they differ so greatly from the original meanings, but this view has not prevailed: both clusters of meaning are Standard. Make certain that context tells your reader or listener which one you intend.

scant (*adj., v.*) The adjective means "inadequate, meager, not quite enough," and the transitive verb means "to limit, to give an inadequate amount, to treat inadequately." Both are Standard.

scapegoat (*n.*) is probably a translation through Latin of Hebrew words meaning "departing goat, or the goat who wanders" (*Lev.* 16:8). At Yom Kippur the ancient Hebrews symbolically stacked all their sins on the head of a goat that was then turned loose to wander in the wilderness, taking the sins with it. Human *scapegoats* still serve to take the rap for others' mistakes.

scarce (*adv., adj.*), **scarcely** (*adv.*) *Scarce* is an adjective (*scarce commodities*) and also a flat adverb with an archaic flavor today (Emily Dickinson's *I died for beauty, but was scarce / adjusted to the tomb*). *Scarcely* has two usage problems: (1) It sometimes contributes to double negatives, as in *I couldn't scarcely see him in that light. I could scarcely see him* is Standard (compare HARDLY). (2) The construction *scarcely . . . than* (*I had scarcely turned on the lights than the power went off*) has been called unidiomatic and unacceptable for a century or more, whereas the *scarcely . . . when* construction (*We had scarcely found our seats when the train pulled out*) is usually accepted without a murmur. Edited English still usually rejects *scarcely . . . than*, and you would do well to restrict its use to the Conversational levels.

scared (*adj.*), **scare** (*v.*) The Americanism *scared* encountered a good many objections during the first half of the twentieth century from those who preferred *afraid of*, but *scared of* and *scared* are clearly Standard today in all but the most Formal or Oratorical uses. *To scare up*, meaning "to collect or find quickly," is a Conversational idiom.

scarf (*n., v.*) The noun, meaning "neckwear," has two plurals: *scarfs* (the more common in the United States) and *scarves*, each pronounced as spelled. The verb *scarf*, meaning "to wolf down (food)," is unrelated to neckwear but comes instead from the verb *scoff*.

scarify (*vv.*) Today there are two verbs spelled this way, the older (first syllable rhymes with *scar*) meaning "to scratch or make scars on" and the newer (first syllable rhymes with *scare*) meaning "to frighten or terrify." The second began as dialect and slang but is now Standard, even though not all dictionaries list it; it probably is an instance of folk etymology (from *scare*, possibly on analogy with *terrify*).

scena (*n.*) The first syllable of this highly technical two-syllable name for "an operatic aria and recitative" is pronounced like *shay*; the plural is *scenas*.

scenario (*n.*) Pronounced *sen-ER-ee-o* or *sen-AHR-ee-o*, its plural is *scenarios*. This word began in music, spread to the theater, films, and television, and is now an overused vogue word, a cliché meaning literally "an outline of the action proposed" and figuratively a "plan or

proposed course of action" or simply "any kind of explanation of an intention." In these figurative senses, use it sparingly, if at all. See PLURALS OF NOUNS ENDING IN -O.

scene (*n.*) Like scenario and many other theatrical terms, *scene* has generalized from its literal theatrical meanings into a cant word: the once-modish wanted *to make **the** scene*, "to be where the action is." *To make **a** scene* is a different idiomatic figure, meaning "to create a fuss, to rant or quarrel loudly." To be *on (at) the scene (of an event)* is "to be present at it."

scent See ODOR.

sceptic, sceptical, scepticism See SKEPTIC.

scheme (*n., v.*), **schema** (*n.*) The verb has much the same pejorative meaning on both sides of the Atlantic: "to make a plan, but particularly to intrigue, to plot." The noun *scheme* has that same pejorative sense for Americans, but in British English it is simply "a plan." A *schema* (pronounced with a hard *c*) is a plan, outline, or preliminary draft, and it has a rather consciously intellectual air about it; the only plural is *schemata*, which is *not* a plural of *scheme*.

schism, schist, schizo (*nn.*), **schizo-** (*prefix*) all come ultimately from the same Greek root, but their pronunciations vary: *schism* is usually *SIZ-uhm*, sometimes *SKIZ-uhm*, and rarely *SHIZ-uhm*; *schist* is always pronounced *SHIST*; the Conversational or slang clipped form *schizo* and the prefix *schizo-* are either *SKITZ-o*(-) or *SKIZ-o*(-).

schlemiel, schlep, schlock, schmaltz, schmo, schmooze, schmuck, schnook, schnozzle, schtick All but *schmaltz* are slang, and all came into English from Yiddish. A *schlemiel* is "an unlucky, awkward person"; to *schlep* is to "carry or to walk slowly"; *schlock* is "something cheap, inferior"; *schmaltz* is "something sentimental"; a *schmo* is "a foolish, stupid person"; to *schmooze* is to "chat or gossip"; a *schmuck* is a "jerk" (from the word for *penis*); a *schnook* is a "stupid, gullible person"; *schnozzle* is a word for "nose, especially a big nose"; *schtick* (sometimes *shtik*) is "a talent or speciality, an entertainer's routine." Spellings sometimes vary. See YIDDISH WORDS IN AMERICAN ENGLISH.

SCHOLARLY GRAMMARS See FUNCTIONAL GRAMMARS; GRAMMAR; STRUCTURAL GRAMMARS; TRADITIONAL GRAMMARS; TRANSFORMATIONAL-GENERATIVE GRAMMAR.

SCHWA This phonetic symbol (ə) is widely used in dictionaries to represent the sound of unstressed vowels in American English: *sofa*

(*SO-fuh*) is typically transcribed "′sō-fə," and *Webster's Ninth New Collegiate Dictionary* indicates the pronunciation of *convertible* as "kən-′vərt-ə-bəl," using the *schwa* for one stressed and three unstressed vowels, a good illustration of the high frequency of unstressed vowels in English. See SPELLING OF UNSTRESSED VOWELS.

science and art See ARTS AND SCIENCES.

SCIENTIFIC ENGLISH The language of science is full of low-frequency, highly specialized terms, usually encountered only in special contexts where the parts and processes of scientific experiments and their theoretical explanations must be carefully distinguished. Laypersons are usually ill-prepared to understand a good deal of *scientific English*. But even when scientific writing is intended for other scientists, one rule ought to obtain: the more complex the subject, the simpler the diction and syntax should be. Some people—scientists and laypersons alike—unwisely try to impress by using long words and involuted syntax, on the false assumption that if the prose sounds hard or obscure it must be very learned. Nothing could be more wrong-headed. The best science writers use polysyllables and long sentences reluctantly and only when no simpler means will serve.

scintilla, iota, jot, smidgin (*nn.*) All these mean "an infinitesimally small bit," and all are clichés. *Jot* is a spelling pronunciation of a late medieval spelling of *iota* (*jota*), the name of the smallest letter in the Greek alphabet. *Smidgin* may come from a dialectal word, *smitch,* meaning "a tiny smudge" and hence "a very small bit." And *scintilla* means "a spark" in Latin; the singular is almost the only form we ever use, although it has two plurals: *scintillas* and, very rarely, *scintillae.*

scissors (*n.*) is either singular or plural: *This scissors is* or *these scissors are* can refer to a single instrument. Americans usually and the British always use the plural: a single pair or a basketful are *these scissors.* With *pair* always use the plural form, but treat the full phrase as a singular unless *pair* itself is plural: *this pair of scissors is; these pairs of scissors are. Scissor* is both a verb and a noun, although the noun is usually used attributively in compounding, as in the haircut called a *scissor-cut* (usually not *scissors-cut*); other compounds, especially those referring to an actual instrument, use the plural: *scissors grinder, nail scissors.*

scoff (*v.*) is slang, mostly British, usually takes *up,* and means "to eat or devour," both literally and figuratively: *We scoffed* [*up*] *our stew.* The

army quickly scoffed up the rebel outposts. (*Scoff* meaning "to jeer" is Standard but is another verb entirely.)

scollop See SCALLOP.

scone, Scone The shortbread is good eating but chancy pronouncing—it is said to rhyme acceptably with *stone, lawn, on,* and possibly even *stun.* But the Scottish village and the Stone of Scone that fits under the coronation chair at Westminster rhyme with either *stone* or *swoon.* These may be two of those words for Americans to say firmly and loudly at home but to say not at all in Britain.

score (*n.*) Meaning literally "the number 20," *score* is also used to refer to "an indefinite large number of people or things." It takes the regular plural form *scores* whenever it lacks a numerical modifier (*scores of people came*), but when it has a numeral modifier (*one* [or *a*] *score of bikers, fourscore years*), treat it as a singular, as you would a cardinal number. Nowadays you also may acceptably use or omit *of* in the phrase, with or without the plural *-s* on *score* (*three score*[*s*] [*of*] *birds*).

scorn (*v.*) This verb regularly takes a gerund or another noun as direct object, as in *He scorned dieting* [*diets*], but it can also take an infinitive with *to,* as in *He scorned to diet.*

scotch 1 (*v.*) means "to block or destroy": *We've scotched those rumors.* The origin may not be entirely certain, but it has nothing to do with the Scots. It appears to come from an Old French verb meaning "to cut, scratch, or notch," and there is also a sense meaning "to block a wheel." In English it began by meaning "to wound or impair," but today its only meanings are "to destroy, block, or bring to an end."

Scotch 2, Scottish, Scots (*adjs.*), **Scot, Scotchman, Scotsman, Scotswoman** (*nn.*) *Scotch whiskey* is made in Scotland (where it is called simply *whisky*) and fancied in the United States (where it is called *Scotch*). Americans and Scots alike know about *Scotch broth* (mutton, barley, and vegetable soup), *Scotch eggs* (hardboiled eggs covered with fried sausage and breadcrumbs), and other idioms using *Scotch* as the adjective. But in Scotland and here, Standard usage frequently prefers the adjective *Scottish* whenever (as in reference to the language or the people) it does not prefer the adjective *Scots.*

The four nouns are perhaps less complicated, referring as they do to the people themselves. Most *Scots* do not mind being called *Scots, Scotsmen* or *Scotswomen.* Historically, the word

Scotchman has been used by the Scots of themselves. But in the United States, especially for those of Scottish descent, the word has a pejorative overtone stemming perhaps from historic English antipathies to many things Scottish and perhaps most immediately from the stinginess said to be peculiarly Scotch: "He's such a Scotchman" usually means "He's a terrible penny-pincher, a dedicated tightwad." Many Americans therefore avoid the word Scotchman, as they do the adjective Scotch, meaning "stingy," as ethnic slurs. Curiously, however, the Scottish immigrants who settled in southern Ontario in the nineteenth century called themselves and were called, apparently without animus, "the Scotch." Nor does the term Scotch-Irish appear to be other than an acceptable ethnic descriptor.

scrip, script (nn.) Scrip and script were once the same word—"a writing." Scrip is now "a certificate or certificates issued in place of money or other financial instruments." The most common American use of scrip is as "a sort of negotiable promissory note issued to government employees in lieu of wages and salaries during hard times." Script, on the other hand, can mean "any handwriting or what's written in it," plus several specialized senses, the most common of which is "the working text of a speech or a play, from which the speaker or actors read their parts." (The scrip that was the medieval bag or satchel is a different word entirely.)

scripture, Scripture(s) (nn.) The generic word once meant "anything in writing," "any writing," and it had both singular and plural forms. But the meanings of "the Bible" or "religious writings" have overwhelmed the generic sense, which is now almost obsolete. The word is always capitalized when the referent is biblical (Scripture or Scriptures). Idiomatic use calls for the plural when an article precedes the word, the singular when there is none: The Scriptures say so; Scripture says so.

scruffy See SCURFY.

scrumptious (adj.) The dictionaries of slang still record this word (it means "splendid"), but, although the British and some American conservatives have been slow to accept it as a Standard adjective, it seems to have improved in status. It may be a bit effusive or hyperbolic, but it is now certainly appropriate at least at all Conversational levels and in the Informal writing that imitates them.

scruple (v.) The noun scruple, usually in the plural (He has no scruples when he plays cards),

poses no problem, but the verb, which occurs infrequently, is usually followed by an infinitive, mainly in Formal writing and at the higher levels of speech: He did not scruple to gossip about them. Its use with a gerund is rare but also Standard: He did not scruple gossiping about them.

scull, skull (nn., vv.) These two are homophones; in speech, only context can distinguish them. The noun scull is "an oar, usually with a slightly cupped blade." To scull is "to use one such oar over the stern of the boat, moving it back and forth in the water, or to row over the sides of the boat with pairs of sculls." The noun skull is "the bony structure of the head," and as a verb skull means "to strike a blow to the head." Both scull and skull may derive from the French escuelle, "dish," but this is uncertain.

sculp, sculpt, sculpture (vv.) Before World War II many conservatives at first objected to the functional shift of the noun sculpture to verb and then to its subsequent clipping to form sculpt and sculp, but these three verbs are all Standard today, although sculp is rare.

scurfy, scruffy (adjs.), **scurvy** (adj., n.) The adjective scurfy comes from the noun scurf (probably a Scandinavian word borrowed by Old English), meaning "the scales of flaked-off skin, dandruff, or other scale incrustation that can appear on a surface." The adjective scurvy means "low, mean, or contemptible" and is a variant of scurfy that has generalized and is now more widely used than its source. Scruffy was probably a dialectal variant of the adjective scurvy. The name of the disease scurvy, however, is a noun that comes from the French scorbut and seems to have been spelled and pronounced scorby in its early anglicized versions. The disease, as we now know, is caused by a dietary deficiency in vitamin C (ascorbic acid). This scurvy is also used as an adjunct, as in scurvy grass, and is unrelated to scurf and its derivatives. All are Standard.

scuttlebutt (n.) Like the office watercooler, the shipboard water barrel—the scuttlebutt—was a social meeting place and the center of shipboard gossip and rumor. So today, the latest scuttlebutt is figuratively "the latest rumor." The literal sense is Standard, as is its figurative sense in all but Formal and Oratorical uses.

s.d. See SINE DIE.

seamy (adj.) In expressions such as the seamy side of life, the literal meaning of this Standard cliché is almost forgotten: the beauty of most clothing shows only from the "right side." If it is *seamy side out,* all the tailoring devices, seams, untrue colors, and loose ends show.

seasonable, seasonal, unseasonable, unseasonal (*adjs.*), **seasonably, seasonally, unseasonably, unseasonally** (*advs.*) *Heat and humidity are seasonable here in summer* means "they're normal for this season of the year." *Sentimentality is seasonal at Christmas* means "it's typical or characteristic of Christmas seasons." *Seasonable* can also mean "opportune" or "in time," as in *Their arrival was seasonable, just when we hoped for it.* If people arrive *seasonably,* they are on time or possibly even a bit early; if they arrive *seasonally,* they visit annually at about the same season of the year. Never use *seasonable* for *seasonal* (the other possible confusion almost never occurs). *Unseasonable, unseasonal, unseasonably,* and *unseasonally* are precise antonyms of *seasonable, seasonal, seasonably,* and *seasonally* respectively.

second See MINUTE.

SECONDARY REFERENCE In establishing helpful context for listeners or readers, make certain that the first time you mention a name or an idea (the *primary reference*), you give it identification enough that all *secondary* and later partial references will be clear: for example, refer to *President Harry S. Truman* first, and only later to *Truman, the president,* or *HST.*

SECONDARY STRESS See PRIMARY STRESS.

secondly See FIRSTLY.

SECOND PERSON SINGULAR AND PLURAL See PERSON; PERSONAL PRONOUNS; REFLEXIVE PRONOUNS; THOU; YE; YOU; YOUR; YOURS; YOURSELF.

second to none is a cliché, a hyperbole used as a modifier meaning "best of all."

secrete (*vv.*) is actually two different Standard verbs, homonyms whose stressed second syllables rhyme with *neat.* One, meaning "to generate a fluid from a gland or other organ," is a back-formation from the noun *secretion*; the other is a functional shift from the noun and adjective *secret,* meaning "to hide something."

secretion (*n.*) The principal meaning cluster, "the process or product of glandular or other such activity," is the only one to concern yourself with. Avoid the meaning "the hiding or concealing of something"; it's rare and can be needlessly confusing. Use *secrecy* or *keeping secret,* instead.

SECRET LANGUAGES are a way of separating our group from the rest of the world. Criminal argot and the cant and jargon vocabularies of the underworld are examples, but there have been efforts at fuller *secret languages,* with their own grammars, such as the pig latin schoolchildren delight to learn. Alas, some people who ought to know better frequently adopt secret languages of arcane polysyllables wrapped in labyrinthine syntax (long words confusingly strung together). Clear speaking and clear writing put at risk only those with something to hide. *Secret languages* are for children, lovers, and spies.

secular, sectarian (*adjs.*) *Secular* matters are things of this world, not the next. *Sectarian* matters pertain to one or more religious sects or to other kinds of sects or parochial groups.

secure (*v.*) In sailors' jargon, *Secure that boathook* is the equivalent of "Make it secure," "Tie it down," or "Put it where it's supposed to be." Some people feel that using *secure* to mean "to get" or "to buy" is pretentious: compare *He secured a position* and *He got a job.* See also LATINATE VOCABULARY VERSUS ANGLO-SAXON WORDS.

-sede See -CEDE.

see (*v.*) is a strong verb, transitive in *I see the point* and intransitive in *I see better with glasses.* It has a good deal of Informal use in extended senses such as *Please see to it, She'll see you at nine,* and *I see you're confused.* Its principal parts are *see, saw, seen. Seen* and *seed* used as past tense forms, as in *I seen* [*seed*] *her yesterday,* are Substandard, Vulgar, and powerful shibboleths.

seed 1 (*adj., n., v.*) Functional shift has led to a specialized Standard sense of *seed* in sports: as a verb (*We seed the best players to be certain that they don't meet early in the tournament*); as a noun (*Fred was the second seed in the tournament*); and as a participial adjective (*He's been a seeded player for years*). All these are transferred "planting" senses and functions.

seed 2, kernel, pip, pit, stone (*nn.*) All are Standard American except *pip,* which is British English. One regional dialect may prefer *pit* where another uses *stone* (as in plums and peaches, for example); *kernel* is usually limited to corn and nuts and figuratively to the hard central core of an idea; and *seed* is the generic botanical term used by gardener and scientist alike, while also used poetically (perhaps an archaic use today) for *semen* in describing human reproduction.

seed (*v.*) See SEE.

-seed See -CEDE.

see eye to eye In *Isaiah* 52:8, "eye to eye" meant "face to face," but today in English *to see eye to eye* is a cliché for "to reach or to be in agreement," often used with *on: We see eye to eye on that issue.*

seeing, seeing as, seeing as how, seeing that The participial *Seeing* [*that*] *she wasn't ready, he sat down* is Standard. *Seeing as* and *seeing as how* are conjunctions meaning "because" and are limited to the lower levels at best; some conservatives consider both locutions—especially *seeing as how*—countrified and unacceptable at any level.

seek (*v.*) as a combined form with *after* and *for* sometimes presents usage problems not posed by the verb when it is combined with *to* plus an infinitive or with *out. We seek your help, They seek to improve their position,* and *She sought out a guide* are Standard. *I seek after guidance* has an archaic ring, probably from scriptural echoes, but the participial adjective (*a much sought-after speaker*) is unexceptionably Standard. *They are seeking for guidance* is Standard, although the *for* might be omitted without changing the sense. But a difficulty arises with the echo in *I seek for you to help me* of the dialectal *I want for you to. . . .* Here the *for* is Casual at best, the phrase is unacceptable in Edited English.

seem See DON'T THINK; LINKING OR COPULATIVE VERBS; RAISING.

seen See SEE.

see where See WHERE.

see with half an eye is a cliché, meaning "to notice something so obvious that full attention is unnecessary."

segregate See DESEGREGATE.

segregation See DESEGREGATION.

seldom ever, seldom if ever, seldom or ever, seldom or never These all seek to be emphatic, but the literal-minded can see them as ambiguous: *I seldom ever go there* might mean either "I seldom go there" or "I don't ever go there." Choose either *seldom* or *ever/never*, not both.

self (*n.*) *Self and spouse attended* is an arch stylistic device, supposedly echoing Pepys or another meticulous reporter. Use it jocularly only, and sparingly then. The more serious usage problems with *self* are with the pronoun forms

myself, himself, and the like. See MYSELF; REFLEXIVE PRONOUNS.

-self See MYSELF; REFLEXIVE PRONOUNS.

self- See HYPHEN.

self-confessed, self-addressed, self-defeating, self-deprecating, self-destruct These and several other verbs and verbals prefixed with *self-* present problems. *A self-confessed murderer* and *a confessed murderer* mean much the same thing; the *self-* is not needed. But *to self-destruct* is different from *to destruct*; we appear to need the *self* on one end or the other: either *It destructed* [or *destroyed*] *itself* or *It self-destructed* (see DESTRUCT). *Self-defeating* and *self-deprecating* seem to work much the same way. *A self-addressed envelope,* however, does not mean "an envelope that wrote out its own address"; a different *self* is meant, and the phrase makes rough common sense: the envelope has been "addressed by self to self," i.e., to the sender by the sender. It's a Standard idiom.

seltzer See SODA.

semantic (*adj.*), **semantics** (*n.*) The primary senses of both words involve "meaning": the phrase *semantic change,* for example, means "change in meaning"; the noun *semantics* (it's plural in form but may take either a singular or plural verb and may be referred to with either singular or plural pronouns) is "the study of meaning." For other senses (in philosophy or in General Semantics, for example), see an unabridged dictionary.

SEMANTIC CHANGE in the meaning of a word reflects change in the status or character of its referent. There are four main types of *semantic change: generalization, specialization, elevation* (or *amelioration*), and *pejoration* (or *degradation*), all of which see.

SEMANTIC DISTINCTION, SEMANTIC DIFFERENCE These terms mean "difference or distinction in meanings," as between the two plurals of the noun *brother:* the archaic, usually figurative flavor of *brethren* creates a *semantic distinction,* and the word is not fully interchangeable with *brothers.* Another *semantic difference* is illustrated by *sanguine* ("cheerful, optimistic") and *sanguinary* ("bloody, blood-covered, eager to shed blood"). The words are similar in origin and grammatical function, but the meanings are different. Or consider the *semantic difference* between the plurals of *cherub: cherubs* ("cute, chubby, babylike angels") and *cherubim* ("fearsome, powerful, eight-foot angels"). Even what looks and sounds like the same word can sometimes exhibit *semantic dif-*

ference: consider, for example, *sanction* ("approve" or "punish") and *secrete* ("exude" or "hide"). See HOMOGRAPH.

semi (*n.*) is a clipping of *semitrailer,* a Casual and slang term for a tractor-and-trailer combination, or a clipping of *semifinal,* meaning "the next-to-the-last stage in an elimination contest, as in tennis tournaments."

semi- (*prefix*) means "half, partly, or a bit," as in *semiformal, semi-annual, semiautomatic,* and the like. Compare DEMI-, and see BI-; HYPHEN; PREFIXES.

semiannual, semi-annual, semimonthly, semi-monthly, etc. See BIANNUAL.

SEMICOLON This punctuation mark (;) has two important uses in written English. (1) It coordinates (separates yet connects evenhandedly) two independent clauses not joined by a coordinating conjunction: *I ran to the door; no one was there.* Notice particularly its use when independent clauses are joined by conjunctive adverbs such as *however* and *furthermore.* These are not coordinating conjunctions, and therefore a comma is not enough punctuation; a *semicolon* does the job: *We were there early; nonetheless, they had already left.* With a coordinating conjunction such as *and* or *but,* a comma would serve: *We arrived early, but they had already left.* (2) The *semicolon* also serves to separate clauses or phrases in series constructions when these already contain commas (*He had a tall, black horse; a wagon, which someone had given him after the battle; and a threadbare, tattered carpetbag*) and elsewhere where there are already other commas.

Another point about the *semicolon:* the convention is that the *semicolon* always belongs outside the final quotation marks: *He said, "I hit him"; he smiled wickedly.*

SEMIFORMAL, SEMIFORMAL WRITTEN ENGLISH, SEMIFORMAL USAGE

Midway between Informal and Formal written language, the *Semiformal* level uses diction and syntax suitable for most readers in many situations (it is a level occasionally used in this book). A good deal of our magazine and newspaper prose and much of our personal correspondence is *Semiformal.* It is suited to a broad range of constituencies and a wide spectrum of purposes and contexts. In syntax and diction, it has much in common with Impromptu and some Planned levels of speech. It permits less studied or elaborated syntactic and rhetorical patterns than Formal writing requires, but it is not so relaxed as Informal writing: it is sparing of contractions,

for example. But, like Formal, it insists upon conventional spelling and punctuation. At its best it is controlled writing with a somewhat relaxed tone; it can be persuasive without stiffness. See LEVELS OF USAGE.

semi-monthly See BIANNUAL.

seminal (*adj.*) Many things may be "creative" that are not truly *seminal,* that is, "seedlike." Apply this frequently overused adjective only to things that truly "begin something new."

Semitic, anti-Semitic (*adjs.*) The *Semitic* peoples and languages include both Jews and Arabs, Hebrew and Arabic (and others), but both *Semitic* and *anti-Semitic* have specialized in much American use to refer only to Jews and anti-Jewish matters respectively. Context must therefore make it clear whenever the more generalized senses are intended. As it stands today, *anti-Semitism* cannot ordinarily include anti-Arab matters.

senile, senescent See OLDSTER; SENIOR CITIZEN.

senior, junior, Jr., Sr. (*adjs.*) The abbreviations used after the names of identically named fathers and sons are *Sr.* (for *senior*) and *Jr.* (for *junior*), with some publishers preferring not to use the periods. Convention usually capitalizes the *S* and *J* and puts a comma between the last name and the *Sr.* or *Jr.,* as in *John M. Jones, Jr.* See IMPLICIT COMPARISON.

senior citizen (*n.*) Some old people dislike this euphemism for those over 55 or older, but it's Standard now, especially in journalism. *Old people, the aged, retirees, seniors, pensioners,* and other such terms are often preferable in the eyes and ears of those among the elderly who dislike the clichés applied to them now that they are a recognized political, social, and economic force. For example, *Modern Maturity* is the euphemistic name given the journal of the American Association of Retired Persons. See also OLDSTER.

sense, feel, recognize (*vv.*) We use these and many similar sensory words when we mean "think," "believe," or "conclude," but the figurative use of sensory terms to describe the frequently inexact "thought processes" through which we all go as we come to our conclusions about what we "see" or "grasp" has long been acceptable in English. When you *can* distinguish your thoughts from your feelings or intuitions, by all means let your choice of word make clear which process you used. But your diction in Informal writing and conversation need not always be literal; figurative words can be equally graphic, familiar, effective, and Standard, even in Oratorical and Formal contexts. See BELIEVE; FEEL.

senseless See MEANINGLESS.

sensible, sensitive, susceptible (*adjs.*) The common meanings of *sensible* today include "having good sense, showing common sense, being reasonable," and "being conscious of," although this last meaning is sometimes thought to be archaic. If you're *sensitive* to something, it affects you more strongly or quickly than it might others. To be *susceptible* to something is to be unusually *sensitive* to it (*I'm very susceptible to colds*). See also PERCEPTIBLE; SUSCEPTIBLE.

sensibility, sensitiveness, sensitivity (*nn.*) In Jane Austen's time (1775–1817), all the best people had *sensibility,* some to the detriment of their common sense; that is, they had highly refined tastes and emotional responses, what we might now call *sensitivity* or *sensitiveness.* But today these two may also be physiological—the response of the senses to stimuli of all kinds: *He has great sensitivity to cold. She has no sensitiveness to what others say about her.* Today *sensibilities* are often simply "feelings": *My words wounded her sensibilities.*

sensitive See SENSIBLE.

sensitiveness, sensitivity See SENSIBILITY.

sensual, sensuous, sensory (*adjs.*) The first two are often used interchangeably, with pejorative overtones stemming from the idea that intellect should control animal urges—the senses. *Sensual* seems to be the more uninhibited word, the more carnal; it evokes images of unbridled appetites for food, drink, or sex. But all three terms can suggest the primacy of the senses and the neglect of the spiritual and intellectual, although *sensory* lacks the overtones of sin and illicit pleasure that the other two convey. Milton tried to make *sensuous* involve the *sense* but not the *sensory* lusts that *sensual* suggested, but he could not make the distinction stick. And all efforts to make *sensuous* refer just to the senses, as *sensory* truly does, have been unsuccessful.

SENTENCE In most grammars, and particularly in the written language, a sentence consists of a subject, such as *she,* and a predicate, such as *swims* or *eats apples* (except in commands, where a predicate alone suffices, and where *you* is sometimes said to be "understood" as subject: *Stop! Take off your hat!*). A *sentence* is also an independent clause. A complete *sentence,* required for most Edited English, differs from a fragment *sentence* in that the fragment lacks either subject or predicate or both. Fragments do occur in Standard prose, but only under carefully controlled circumstances (see FRAGMENT; SITUATION UTTERANCE).

SENTENCE ADJECTIVES This term is applied to the rare adjectives that function like sentence adverbs, modifying entire sentences or independent clauses. The most common *sentence adjective* is the comparative *more important,* as in *More important, the rain held off until the parade had passed.* Some grammarians describe *important* as a flat adverb here, and they note that the comparative adverb *more importantly* would work equally well in the sentence.

SENTENCE ADVERBS are adverbs that modify whole sentences or independent clauses: *Fortunately, he had already decided to enlist.* They are also called adverbial disjuncts, and they may appear in three different locations in the sentence: at the beginning, as in *Happily, they had advertised in a lot of out-of-town papers*; at the end, with a comma to set the word or phrase off from the main clause as intonation would in speech, as in *They had advertised in a lot of out-of-town papers, happily;* and medially—that is, within the independent clause—again set off by commas or other separating punctuation marks or by intonation in speech, as in *They had advertised, happily, in a lot of out-of-town papers.*

Sentence adverbs can be adverbial phrases too, as in *Amusingly enough, no one recognized this famous celebrity.* They are economical constructions, replacing longer phrasal and clausal structures such as *It is amusing to note that . . . ,* and this efficiency itself may explain some purists' objection to certain *sentence adverbs:* to some, efficiency apparently smacks of haste and compromise. See HOPEFULLY.

SENTENCE MODIFIER is another name for a sentence adverb.

SENTENCE TYPES There are two main classifications of sentences, one based on grammar (i.e., on the number and kinds of clauses they contain), the other based on rhetorical purpose or meaning. The grammatical *sentence types* are four: *simple, compound, complex,* and *compound-complex.* The meaning-based *types* are three: *statement, question,* and *command* (also called *declarative, interrogative,* and *imperative*). See COMMAND; COMPLEX SENTENCE; COMPOUND-COMPLEX SENTENCE; COMPOUND SENTENCE; QUESTION SENTENCE; STATEMENT.

sentinel, sentry (*nn.*) *Sentinel* is the broader, more general word for someone on the watch. The more common one for "the soldier on guard duty" is *sentry,* which we also use in certain compound forms such as *sentry box* and *sentry duty.*

sentient, sententious (*adjs.*) These words are unrelated but frequently confused. *Sentient* (from the Latin *sentire,* "to sense, to feel") means "to be aware." *Sententious* comes from a Ciceronian word spelled almost the same way, meaning "full of meaning." Chaucer's wise elders were "full of hye sentence"—hence the usual modern pejorative sense of *sententious:* "full of moralistic and possibly righteous wisdom" and thus "preachy."

sentry See SENTINEL.

separate (*adj., v.*), **separateness, separation** (*nn.*), **separately** (*adv.*) All these pose the same spelling problem: the first unstressed syllable is unexpectedly spelled with an *a,* not an *e.* Misspelled, these are shibboleths. See also DIFFERENT.

SEQUENCE OF TENSES Editors and schoolteachers alike have corrected hundreds of thousands of sentences for failure of the tense of the verb in the main clause to govern the tenses of the verbs in subsequent clauses: for example, *I thought yesterday that he went home to Chicago* should be *I thought yesterday that he had gone home to Chicago.* In *His secretary announced this morning that the senator was going to Chicago tomorrow,* should we leave that second verb as *was going* or instead should common sense govern the tense of that verb, so that the sentence reads *She announced this morning that the senator is going tomorrow* or *that he will go tomorrow* or *that he would go tomorrow?* Each of these handles *sequence of tense* differently from the others. Common sense is a good guide in such matters, and perhaps the key bit of advice is: don't jerk your reader about unnecessarily. Shift tenses only when it seems necessary to do so, especially when you are telling a story. Keep events in order, so that the reader knows what happened first and what happened next. And if one thing happened prior to another event in the past, make certain that those times are clear. Finally, remember that there is nothing wrong with sometimes telling your story in the historical present tense, so long as that breathless sense of immediacy is what you wish to communicate: *He swings and misses! He's the third out, and that's the ballgame!*

seraph (*n.*) Milton is the earliest citation for *seraph* in the *Oxford English Dictionary,* whose editors believe he may have coined that backformation as a singular. *Seraphim* is the Hebrew plural, and Standard English still uses it, but the King James Bible in at least one place added an English *-s* ending to it to form an English plural, *seraphims,* now obsolete or Nonstandard. Possibly slightly more frequent than *seraphim,* however, is the Standard plural *seraphs.* See FOREIGN PLURALS.

serendipity (*n.*), **serendipitous** (*adj.*) *Serendipity* means "good luck or good fortune, unearned and unexpected." It's from Walpole's *The Three Princes of Serendip*—the princes had it. But these and other self-conscious polysyllables (such as *thaumaturgical*) should be sparingly employed. As with Turkish delight, a very little is often more than enough.

serial See CEREAL.

series (*n.*) is a plural noun, but it's frequently construed as singular: *This series of books has been popular, but all three series have sold well. Serieses* is a nonce word, jocular or juvenile only.

SERIES CONSTRUCTIONS list three or more words, phrases, or clauses of roughly equal weight in syntax. In speech, intonation, and in writing, punctuation (usually a comma) links the several items in the series: *They issued us our eating utensils: a tin cup, a mess kit, a spoon, a knife, a fork, and a canteen.* Conventionally, the last two items in the series are linked with a coordinating conjunction, usually (but not always) preceded by a comma in written American English. Some American and most British stylebooks permit omission of this comma when the conjunction is there, but it is easier to include both every time.

serum (*n.*) *Serums* is the regular plural, but *sera* still occurs occasionally. See also FOREIGN PLURALS.

serve my turn Whatever will *serve my turn* will "meet my need"; "it'll do." The expression is Standard.

service (*adj., n., v.*) As three parts of speech and with many senses in each function, this word having to do with routine maintenance of equipment and, more generally, with providing assistance, is often badly overused, and some of its senses have pejorated as well. *To serve* still means "to aid or assist" and is laudable, but frequently today those senses can sound ironic and cynical instead: too often your *service representative* seems only *self-serving.* As a verb *service* is best limited to the maintaining of vehicles and the breeding of livestock; better *serve* than *service* a customer. The transitive verb is so heavily used today that experience may add irony to its meaning even when none was intended. In some uses the noun is a euphemism, a once-powerful noun that now requires adjectives in order to distinguish *good service* (once a pleonasm) from *bad service* (once an oxymoron).

serviette, napkin (*nn.*) The British have for many years considered *serviette,* for "table napkin," a non-U class mark, and many Canadians consider it Vulgar, as does the *Oxford English Dictionary.* Americans don't use the term at all. See U, NON-U.

session See CESSION.

set, sit (*vv.*) The sun *sets,* and so does concrete. Hens *set* or *sit,* but judges and the rest of us *sit.* And when we *set* something down, it just *sits* there. Standard English uses *sit* as the intransitive, *set* as the transitive verb (although we do *sit* horses—i.e., "have a certain posture in the saddle"). Substandard dialects have long confused *sit* and *set,* and many Standard users consider the fault a shibboleth that indelibly brands the Vulgar speaker. The principal parts are *sit, sat, sat* (intransitive) and *set, set, set* (transitive).

settee, settle See SOFA.

sew (*v.*) This verb is for needlework, not planting. The principal parts are *sew, sewed,* and either *sewed* or *sewn.* American English prefers *sewed* as past participle: *She had sewed the rip neatly.* The participial adjective is usually *sewn,* as in *hand-sewn dresses.* Compare SOW.

sewage, sewer, sewerage (*nn.*) *Sewers* carry *sewage,* the waste matter, liquid and solid. *Sewerage* is either "the system of sewers" or "the process of transporting sewage by that means"; it's not a suitable synonym for *sewage.*

sex, gender (*nn.*) A once-useful distinction between these two words is now blurred: *gender,* once limited to grammatical uses, has become more and more a synonym for what was once the biological term, *sex.* The *Oxford English Dictionary* labels biological uses of *gender* as "jocular," but some feminists have adopted *gender* as a preferred word for *sex,* possibly as a more general word, possibly as a euphemism, which may already have suggested itself to the overmodest. See also SEXIST LANGUAGE.

sexism (*n.*), **sexist** (*adj., n.*) *Sexism,* like *racism* and *feminism* (which see) and some other

isms too, is a much-vexed and tormented term today. Its literal senses are "belief in the superiority or supremacy of one sex over the other," "prejudice or discrimination against members of one sex," or "the fostering of stereotyping of social roles for members of a given sex." But the energy and vituperation that have controlled much of the term's use, the nature of the issues it raises, and the attitudes involved in the programs people have devised to defeat (or defend) it have encrusted it with an emotional loading—almost wholly pejorative—that makes nearly impossible any use of the term *sexism* or the noun and adjective *sexist* in rational discussions. Both are so heavily governed by ideas of what is politically correct (which see) and the heat of the issues to which they refer that they are rarely usable as other than insulting epithets. This is true both of today's overwhelming specialized senses of these words—prejudice and discrimination, etc., toward women—and of the rarer but still-encountered ideas of reverse discrimination and prejudice in these matters. Hence, except when we know we are addressing fellow believers, if we are to be able to discuss and treat the issues *sexism* raises, we must at present either control context sufficiently to neutralize these terms or give them up entirely in favor either of temporary and probably short-lived euphemistic substitutes or (a more cumbersome but probably more promising course) in favor of circumlocutory descriptions that avoid any whisper of name-calling.

SEXIST LANGUAGE is the label applied to English words and grammatical features that appear to favor one sex over another or to stress the separateness or inequality of the sexes; its current application is almost entirely to features that appear to favor men and to imply lesser roles for women (but see SEXISM). Today, Standard English seeks to avoid language that may be thought *sexist,* even though there is much evidence that not all users agree completely on the details of how best to pursue that goal. Being sensitive to the linguistic manners expected of you by those to whom you write or speak, however, is likely to serve you as well as can be hoped until such time as the values underlying our language practices change enough to cause the language to change to reflect them. Major changes in this matter of gender are now in train: the referents for *pilot* and *priest* are no longer only masculine, as once they were. Like *parent,* they may be either male or female, and so they and many occupational terms once clearly gender-distinctive now reflect a change in English treatment of gender. The only caution is that change, trivial or sweeping, cannot be cited as Standard until actual language use reflects it. The results of pressures to eliminate such language must in the end be measured on a word-by-word basis; the choices will be based upon what Standard users actually say and write in each instance, rather than on any overall policy about avoiding particular words or substituting one for another.

The aspect of the grammar of English that has received the most attention in this regard is the long-standing Standard insistence on the generic masculine third person singular pronoun, as in *Each person [Everybody] must bring his own calculator.* The fact that only the third person singular pronouns reflect gender makes this issue stand out. At least four ways of avoiding the generic masculine pronoun have been proposed: (1) deliberately to substitute feminine singular pronouns for the masculine singular pronouns in such structures (*Each person [Everybody] must bring her own calculator*); (2) to insist that both masculine and feminine pronouns be used in each instance (*Each person [Everybody] must bring his or her own calculator*); (3) to add a second example everywhere, so that one of each pair may be masculine and one feminine, like Noah's animals; or (4) to use the third person plural pronouns instead (*Each student [Everybody] must bring their own calculator*). This fourth approach appears to be the one most likely to succeed, both because it sticks with nouns and pronouns of common gender, so-called because they are gender-inclusive rather than gender-distinctive, and also because Common and Vulgar English have long used the plural pronouns in these positions.

Best advice: Standard in all but the most Formal of Edited English, and perhaps in some Oratorical circumstances is the use of the plural pronoun in such sentences: *Each person [Everybody] must bring their own calculator(s).* For Edited English, most editors will recommend shifting the entire sentence into the plural: *All persons [Everybody] must bring their own calculators,* either avoiding the impersonal pronoun *everybody* or using it and taking a chance on some conservative objection to the breach in agreement. Actually, that problem is likely to disappear with this generation, since the notional agreement of impersonal pronouns with subsequent pronouns is now widely accepted, even as these impersonal pronouns continue to require singular verbs. *Everybody* and its like are now clearly gender-inclusive.

For further aspects of this subject, see also -ESS; FEMININE OCCUPATIONAL FORMS; FEMINISM; FEMINIST VIEWS OF ENGLISH; HE; INCLUSIVE LANGUAGE; SEXISM; S/HE.

sextet, sextette, septet, septette See QUARTET.

shade, blind (*nn.*) These devices for blocking light and providing privacy at windows have different regional names in English. Some Americans call the pull-down, cloth-on-a-roller device a *shade;* some call it a *blind.* (The British stick pretty much to *blinds.*) Americans have many compound names for the various types: *roller shades, Venetian blinds, Roman shades* or *Roman blinds,* and *bamboo shades* or *bamboo blinds,* for example.

shake (*v.*) The principal parts of this strong verb are *shake, shook, shaken. Shaken* as a past tense and *shooken* as a past participle are both Vulgar, Substandard forms.

shake the head, nod (the head) These are idioms describing the head gestures most native speakers of English use to express disagreement or agreement, to communicate *no* or *yes* either without speaking or to reinforce speech. *To shake your head* is usually understood to be a side-to-side movement; it means "no" or "I won't" or "I disagree." *To nod your head* is usually an up-and-down movement; it means "yes," "I will," "I understand," or "I agree."

The usage problem is with *He shook his head yes.* Most people will take the statement to be a description of an affirmative nod, and it's not even a contradiction, since the generalized meaning of the verb *shake* is to "move rapidly in any direction or in all directions." Nevertheless, the phrase can be confusing, and it may cause you to shake your head no, regretfully.

Shakespeare (*n.*), **Shakespearean** (*adj.*) Edited English both here and abroad seems now to have fixed on these spellings of the poet's name and the adjective made from it.

shall, will (*auxs.*) Americans use *shall* and *will* (and their contraction *'ll*) almost interchangeably, except in certain questions: for example, *Shall I kick you?* meaning "Do you want me to?" and *Will I kick you?* meaning "Do you think I'm going to?" Furthermore, when Americans seek unusually polite forms of speech or writing, they seem to think *shall* a bit more elegant, respectful, or impressive.

For Standard Formal written English some people try to adhere to certain school-taught rules specifying that for the simple future, *shall* should be used with the first person, as in *We shall overcome,* and *will* with second and third persons, as in *They will find us here,* and that to express special volition, determination, and the like, these distributions should be reversed, as in *I will have my way* or *They shall do what we ask.* Alas, these rules have never really described the way Standard users speak the language at nearly all levels or the way they write it in Semiformal and Informal situations. It appears that we generally use *will* or the contraction *'ll* at all but the upper levels, reserving *shall* for certain questions and for statements whose formality or whose stress on the auxiliary seems to require variation from the more usual *will.* Our negative contractions also seem to be mainly with *will:* Americans nearly always say *won't,* and rarely use *shan't.* Native users of American English can trust their instincts on *shall* and *will.* Stress can make *You WILL do as I say* every bit as forceful as *You SHALL do as I say,* and most of us would feel it necessary to italicize or capitalize either auxiliary in writing anyway, just to make sure the reader recognizes that stress. Where there is semantic difference between *shall* and *will,* as in certain questions, native speakers do not make errors. See also FUTURE TENSE.

sham See ARTIFICIAL.

shambles (*n.*) is always plural in form but either singular or plural in construction. In Old English a *shamble* was "a bench or footstool." It developed additional senses, specializing into "a counter for displaying wares," then "a meat counter," then "a meat market," and then "a slaughterhouse." During the seventeenth century a transferred sense developed from the "slaughterhouse" meaning: "something that looks like a slaughterhouse, any blood-covered mess." And finally in the 1920s, semantic change caused the "bloody" aspect to disappear from the most widely used sense: the meaning generalized to "a scene of general disorder and devastation": *His room was a shambles: nothing was picked up or put away.* Today in that meaning the word is a hyperbole and almost a cliché.

shan't See SHALL.

share 1 (*v.*) is just now a hackneyed word when used for *tell.* Its overuse (more often spoken than written) irritates many people today, so you'll be wiser if you *tell* or *show* what you know, and *share* only when dividing tangibles such as cookies or money.

share 2 (*n.*), **stock** (*adj., n.*) Americans buy *shares of stock* and have their money *in stocks* or *in the (stock) market;* the British put their money *in shares.* See also STOCK.

shark (*n.*) The fish's name dates from the sixteenth century, but its ferocity, appetite, and reputation led subsequently to several pejorative transferred senses, particularly involving those who prey on others, as do *loan sharks, pool sharks,* and the like. But early in this century, U.S. college students began to use the noun to refer to classmates who excelled in a particular subject: *Only a math shark could ace that exam. He's a shark at history.* When you use *shark,* be sure that context makes clear whether you intend it as a compliment or an insult.

sharp (*adv., adj.*) *Sharp* is of course an adjective (*Keep a sharp lookout*), but it is also a flat adverb: *Look sharp to the right when you reach the corner.*

she (*pron.*) Some purists object to the use of feminine personal pronouns to refer to inanimate things—boats, cars, nations, universities, Mother Nature, the wind and weather, and the like. Some of these uses are jocular; others are long-established convention. In Formal language, all but the most conventional of such uses (the college as *she* reflects *alma mater*) are replaced by the neuter pronoun *it,* but at all Conversational levels and in Informal writing, most people find no problem with an inanimate referent for "She's a beauty!"

s/he, (s)he (*prons.*) These two coinages were designed by those unhappy with the generic masculine pronoun: *A student must attend classes if he hopes to pass the course.* Americans proposed *s/he,* and the British tried *(s)he,* but both are already doomed as unspeakable (they are ugly, and they cannot be read aloud with euphony); *he or she* serves conservatives who insist on literal evenhandedness, even at the expense of bulk. The fact is, however, that the plural *they* has already overwhelmed the singular *he* as generic pronoun at most levels and in all prose except some Edited English and very Formal writing. Much Edited English now avoids the singular entirely by using the plural for all parts of the sentence: *Students must attend classes if they hope to pass their courses.* See also INCLUSIVE LANGUAGE; SEXIST LANGUAGE.

sheaf (*n.*) Conservatives insist on *sheaves* as plural in both speech and writing, but the spelling *sheafs* occasionally occurs and reflects a frequently heard Standard pronunciation.

shear (*v.*) The principal parts are *shear, sheared, sheared. Shorn* is frequently the participial adjective, but it can also be the past participle when applied to haircutting or taking honors away: *His baby ringlets had been shorn. The* *senator was shorn of his chairmanship.* See also WIND SHEAR.

shears (*n.*) *Shears* is plural and takes plural verbs, but it can refer either to one or to many such tools: *These shears have [all] been sharpened. My shears have been sharpened too. This pair of shears has been sharpened.* The singular appears in compounds, as in *shear-blade.*

sheath (*n., v.*), **sheathe** (*v.*) The noun plural is either *sheathes* (with a voiced *-thz* sound for the final consonant cluster, to rhyme with *breathes*), or *sheaths* (with the final cluster a voiceless *-ths,* to rhyme with *Keith's*). The third person singular present tense of the verb has the same two pronunciations and spellings as the noun plural. The past tense and past participle of the verb are both spelled *sheathed* but pronounced with either a voiced (*-thd*) or voiceless (*-tht*).

sheer (*adv., adj., v.*) The verb means "to veer or turn away": *The destroyer sheered off to the east.* The adjective can mean "see-through or transparent" (*She wore sheer pantyhose*), "utter" or "wholly obvious, pure, clear, total, undiluted" (*His idea was sheer folly*), and "steep or perpendicular" (*There was a sheer drop from the headland to the beach*). *Sheer ice* ("pure"?) is probably a relic idiom. *Sheer* also infrequently appears as a flat adverb: *The cliff falls away sheer.* As a noun *sheer* means "a sharp turn" and "the curve of a ship's hull that makes bow and stern higher than the midship portion."

sheik, sheikh (*n.*) Both spellings and their pronunciations are Standard, but Americans usually pronounce the Arab chieftain's title to rhyme with *sleek* and spell it *sheik;* the British usually rhyme it with *shake* and spell it *sheikh.*

shelf life (*n.*) is a relatively recent but already Standard compound, meaning "the length of time a product may remain on the seller's shelf without falling below an acceptable level of freshness, potency, or quality": *The shelf life of fresh milk is a few days.*

sherbet, sherbert, sorbet (*nn.*) Now the name of a frozen dessert, the word *sherbet* appeared in English in the seventeenth century, meaning "a cold fruit drink," and developed two spellings reflecting its two pronunciations, *sherbet* (*SHUHR-bit*) and *sherbert* (*SHUHR-buhrt*). Today both spellings and both pronunciations are regularly encountered in both British and American use, to the discomfort of some purists, who argue that only *sherbet* is acceptable. Meantime, food fanciers have reborrowed this word in its French form, *sorbet,* pronounced both in the French way (*sor-BAI*) and an angli-

cized (*SOR-bet*). Standard English now uses all three forms, although Edited English usually clings to *sherbet* and continues to italicize the French *sorbet* as foreign. Australian English now uses *sherbert,* both alone and in compounds, as another name for *beer.*

sheveled See LOST POSITIVES.

SHIBBOLETH This word is Hebrew, meaning something like "stream, flood, or freshet," and the story behind its modern English senses comes from Judges 12:5–6: the Gileadites test a man they have caught near their camp; they suspect he may be an Ephraimite, an enemy:

> . . . the men of Gilead said unto him, Art thou an Ephraimite? If he said, Nay; Then said they unto him, Say now Shibboleth: and he said Sibboleth: for he could not frame to pronounce it right. Then they took him, and slew him . . . [and 42,000 others].

"To pronounce it right," of course, meant "to pronounce it as the Gileadites did."

The modern meanings of *shibboleth* are crucial to any discussion of usage: specifically, it refers to a sound or word whose pronunciation is difficult or impossible for some non-native speakers, or a test word or locution by means of which *in* persons can keep *out* persons out. By extension, a *shibboleth* is any peculiarity of language, dress, or other manners that marks people as belonging to one group or another.

shine (*v.*) This strong verb now has a full set of weak forms as well: past tense and past participle are each either *shined* or *shone.* There is some interchangeability in those forms, but there are also some semantic distinctions. It's always *He shined his shoes* (never *He shone his shoes*), but it can be *The sun shined all day,* although *The sun shone all day* is more frequent. Nor is it simply the transitive/intransitive distinction that governs choice: transitive *He shined his light into the cellar* and *He shone his light into the cellar* are both acceptable (although British English uses *shone* almost exclusively in such sentences). Intransitive sentences can use either *shined* or *shone,* but *shone* is more prevalent, especially in Edited English, unless the meaning is "to polish": *His cheeks shone with embarrassment. With wax and elbow grease we shined all day.*

ship 1 (*v.*) Because when the British *ship* something, they do it only by water, on a ship or barge, some American purists argue that we should too. We don't: *to ship* is Standard American English for "to send merchandise or other freight to its destination by water, air, rail, road, or any other means available.''

ship 2, boat (*nn.*) Distinctions between these two are largely unheeded in general use, except that *ships* are generally understood to be larger than *boats*. Naval and other nautical people usually insist on more technical distinctions, however: a *ship* carries *boats*—lifeboats, barges, and other small craft—and every specific type of vessel is classed as either *ship* or *boat*. (Among sail-driven vessels, a *ship* is ship-rigged: square-rigged on all of its three or more masts.)

shirk (*v.*) *Shirk* works like *avoid:* when, in its transitive use, it takes a direct object, that object will be either a noun, as in *He shirks responsibility,* or a gerund, as in *He shirks [his] practicing,* but not an infinitive with *to: He shirks to practice* is Nonstandard.

shoe (*v.*) The verb has two past tense forms, *shod* and *shoed,* and three past participle forms, *shod, shoed,* and, rarely, *shodden.* There may be a semantic distinction: *shoed* most frequently has to do with applying shoes to horses' hooves (or, if you prefer, *hoofs*): *He had shoed the horses recently. Shod* is the usually encountered participial adjective, meaning "equipped (with)": *She was shod in glistening boots. We were well-shod for hiking.*

shone See SHINE.

shook (up) (*adj.*) Edited English uniformly uses *shaken,* meaning "upset" or "disturbed," as the past participle and participial adjective, but Standard speakers increasingly use the Substandard *shook* and *shook up* as Casual or Impromptu slang, especially jocularly: *I was really shook [up] after the accident.*

shooting See HUNTING.

shop 1 (*v.*) The verb *shop* can be intransitive, as in *She shops tirelessly,* or transitive, as in *He always shops the department stores first.*

shop 2, bodega, boutique, shoppe, store (*nn.*) What Americans call a *store,* the British call a *shop,* but Americans now use both terms, although frequently with a semantic distinction: retail establishments that sell groceries or hardware or liquor, for example, are nearly always called *stores,* but hats and dresses are usually sold in *shops* or, if very select and expensive (or with pretensions to being so), in *boutiques* (English pronunciation *BOO-TEEKS*). And many other retail places can be any of the three. *Shoppe* is an archaic spelling of *shop,* restored to service by shopkeepers hoping to add some distinction to the names of their businesses.

Bodega (pronounced *bo-DAI-guh*) was originally the Spanish name for a wineshop or a wineshop-and-grocery combination, and Hispanic-Americans now use the term generally for their ethnically distinctive food-and-drink retail stores.

shoptalk (*n., v.*), **talk shop** (*v.*) The idiom *to talk shop,* meaning "to talk about business or professional or vocational matters," also provides an Informal or Conversational verb, *to shoptalk.* Both are based on the sense of the noun *shop* meaning "the workplace," and *shoptalk* usually bores anyone not part of the shop.

shorn See SHEAR.

short (*adv., adj.*) *Short* can be either an adjective, as in *a short haircut,* or a flat adverb, as in *I cut short my vacation.* The regular adverb *shortly* is semantically different from the flat adverb: *He'll be here shortly, unless he runs short of money.*

short-lived See LIVED.

short supply, in Commodities that are scarce are said to be *in short supply.* It's an idiom and a cliché.

should, would (*auxs.*) In most uses, *should* and *would* are interchangeable, with the following exceptions. In the first person, *should* sometimes occurs meaning "it could happen in the future," especially when the speaker may be trying for a bit of elegance (normally, it's *I would like to be there,* but sometimes, even from the same speaker, you'll hear *I should like to be there*). In other than first person, *would* is almost universally the American preference for describing something that may happen in the future. *Should* is used regularly in conditionals, as in *If he should ask for me, tell him . . . ,* and as the equivalent of *ought to,* as in *She really should write her mother tonight.*

Like *shall* and *will, should* and *would* have never really been used the way the rules have said Standard English uses them. Today Americans use *would* much more often than *should,* just as we use *will* more often than *shall.* If you are a native user of the language, you can safely choose whichever form feels right. In all but a few instances, the meanings will guide you.

shoulda, should of, coulda, could of, woulda, would of These are aberrant spellings of *should have, would have,* and *could have* or their contractions *should've, would've,* and *could've,* made to reflect actual pronunciations. The spellings with *of* are frequently inadvertent; when writing hurriedly we may spell as we pronounce, and *would've* can come out *would of.* The *of* spellings also appear in eye dialect. The spellings *shoulda, woulda,* and *coulda* are always eye dialect, locutions deliberately misspelled to suggest the way our speech sometimes sounds. See OF (2).

show (*v.*) The past tense is *showed,* the past participle either *shown* or *showed.* (Spellings *shew, shewed,* and *shewn* are now archaic.) Edited English doesn't use *show* in the sense of "appear," as in *He didn't show for the meeting,* but that sense is widely and acceptably used at all Standard Conversational levels and in Informal writing. See also SHOW UP.

shower activity (*n.*) is meteorological jargon by which the television weather commentator means to predict either rain or showers. The locution is padded prose. See also PRECIP.

show off (*v.*), **showoff** (*n.*) The verb has two Standard senses, a transitive, "to display for others' admiration," as in *He showed off his new pony,* and an intransitive, "to make a vulgar display of self," as in *She showed off so shamelessly that we all hated her.* A *showoff* (stress on *show-*) is just such an exhibitionist.

show up (*v.*) The two most commonly encountered senses, the intransitive "to appear" (*He hasn't shown* [*showed*] *up yet)* and the transitive "to expose" or "to reveal" (*The little man's challenge showed up the bully for the coward he was*), are appropriate in all but the most Formal and Oratorical English.

shrink 1 (*n.*), is a clipped form of *headshrink(er),* slang names for a *psychiatrist,* who figuratively is seen as trying to reduce the size of the patient's swollen head.

shrink 2 (*v.*) The Standard past tense is usually *shrank* but occasionally *shrunk,* and the past participle is always *shrunk,* with the participial adjective usually *shrunken: She shrank* [*shrunk*] *from telling him. The market for shrunken heads has shrunk. Shrank* as past participle, as in *This sweater has shrank,* is Vulgar and a shibboleth.

shrouded in secrecy is journalese. *To shroud* (that is, *to cover with a shroud*) is gloomy enough, but the figurative cliché *in secrecy* is even deadlier.

shy of, shy about Shy *of* means either "just short of," as in *She's not much shy of two hundred pounds* or "bashful about," as in *He's terribly shy of women. Shy about* also has the sense of "reluctant to": *I'm shy about introducing myself to strangers.*

shyster (*adj., n.*) The first syllable rhymes with *dice.* Both the noun (meaning "an unscrupulous lawyer") and the adjective (meaning "characteristic of such cheats and their unethical methods") are slang. The etymology is unclear: possibly the word comes from *Scheuster,* the name of a nineteenth-century lawyer with a bad reputation, or possibly from a figurative sense of the scatalogical German noun *scheisser,* "defecator."

sibling (*n.*) Originally a rare Middle English word meaning "kin, a relative," *sibling* became obsolete until the twentieth century, when the biological and social sciences brought it back, first as a generic term meaning "blood relative" and then as a specialized term meaning either "brother or sister," as in *She has three siblings—two brothers and a sister.* For some time it seemed to be limited to scholarly and technical use, but today its inclusiveness (see INCLUSIVE LANGUAGE) has made it handy in the law, in journalism, and in conversation. *Sibling* is related to *sib,* but the latter can mean any blood kindred group, not just brothers and sisters; *sib* is not a clipped form of *sibling,* although it is sometimes erroneously used as though it were. *Sibling* is Standard, but be wary of annoying those few conservatives who still consider it jargon.

sic (*adv.*) Americans pronounce this Latin word (meaning "thus") to rhyme with either *sick* or *seek,* and use it mainly to dissociate themselves from errors in a text they're quoting. It isn't an abbreviation, so it requires no period, and it usually appears in square brackets following a misspelling or misuse of a word, in order to show that the error is in the original. This use of *sic* may be defensive, but its overuse is offensive (nor does a following exclamation point help matters); in typographical and other truly minor matters it's usually better quietly to correct the original.

sick, ill (*adjs.*), **sickness, illness** (*nn.*) These words are interchangeable and Standard in American English. In Britain, *sick* means "nauseated" or "vomiting, throwing up," whereas *ill* is the general word for "feeling unwell." Hence *seasick* has as its second part the British sense of *sick.* Like American English *vomit,* British *sick* can also be a noun meaning "the regurgitated matter itself." There are possibly some occasional class nuances too: an American seeking to sound refined may more often use *ill* than *sick,* just as an *illness* may be thought by some to be a more elegant thing to have than a *sickness.*

sick at the stomach See SICK TO.

sick day, sick leave (*nn.*) These are Standard compounds from labor relations, referring to a day or a longer period for which an employee absent because of sickness will continue to be paid.

sick humor, sick joke (*nn.*) are abnormal, gruesome, or morbid humor and jokes. Both terms are Standard. See BLACK HUMOR; GALLOWS HUMOR.

sick in the stomach See SICK TO.

sick leave See SICK DAY.

sickness See SICK.

sick-out (*n.*) This compound noun is Standard; in labor relations it means "a planned absence by a group of workers who call in sick on short notice, in order to put pressure on the employer." The primary stress is on *sick-*.

sick to (at, in) the stomach These are American regional dialectal variants of the same locution; all mean "to be nauseated" or "to throw up." For example, most New Englanders say *sick to my stomach*, but most Midwesterners from the Great Lakes region say *sick at my stomach*. Each locution is Standard in its own region, but outside it will sound odd at all levels.

side (*n.*) The British slang use of *side,* meaning "conceit, pretentiousness, reserve, swagger," is beginning to turn up in American English, nearly always in a negative statement: *He's got no side at all* means "He's very friendly and approachable, not at all reserved or conceited."

side of the angels In the mid-nineteenth-century controversy over Darwin's theory of evolution, many people put the question simplistically: were we God's creatures, made "in His image," or were we descended from the monkeys? Disraeli declined to join the monkey side, choosing instead "the side of the angels." Since then the meaning has generalized to indicate that if you're "on the side of the angels" in any argument, you're on "the good side, the side that is morally right."

side by side, side to side These Standard idioms are not interchangeable: *side by side* describes the contiguous location of two persons or things (*We installed the washer and dryer side by side in the kitchen*); *side to side* describes motion (*Her bicycle wobbled from side to side on the road*).

sidious See LOST POSITIVES.

sight See CITE.

significant (*adj.*), **significantly** (*adv.*) Both are heavily used, and as a result their meanings have begun to generalize, so that most often they mean simply "important(ly) or large(ly)." Some argue that such loose use deprives us of the specific sense of "having a measurable or influential meaning." Not true: these words now have both their old specialized and their new generalized senses.

SIGNS OF AGGREGATION See BRACKETS; PARENTHESES.

silencer (*n.*) What the British call an automobile's *silencer* is what Americans call its *muffler*; but the British and Americans alike put *silencers* on handguns. See also VOCABULARY (1).

SILENT LETTERS See SPELLING (2); see also SPELLING PRONUNCIATIONS.

silicon, silicone (*nn.*) Distinguishing between these two becomes increasingly important as we multiply the names and numbers of compounds (called *silicones*) based on the ubiquitous element (*silicon*). Primary stress in each is on the first syllable, with a secondary stress on the third syllable, which in *silicon* rhymes with *con* and in *silicone* rhymes with *cone*.

silly See MEANINGLESS.

similar (*adj.*) *Similar* is an adjective: *We have similar neckties.* Things *similar* may be *somewhat like* or *much like* each other, but they are not *identical. Similar* as an adverb is Substandard: *He walks similar to his father.* Better: *He walks similarly to his father.* Or *His walk is similar to his father's.* Or *His walk is much the same as* [or *much like*] *his father's.*

Similiar is a frequent misspelling of *similar,* sometimes causing a mispronunciation as well, perhaps either as an erroneous spelling pronunciation or as a false analogy with *familiar.*

similar in, similar to *Similar* is used with *in* and *to* but not with *with* in Standard English: *Your shoes are similar to mine; they're similar in color.* But *These shoes are similar with those* is Nonstandard.

SIMILAR OR APPARENTLY SIMILAR WORDS, CONFUSION OF See HOMOGRAPH; MALAPROPISM; METATHESIS; SPOONERISMS.

similar to See SIMILAR IN.

SIMILES are figures of speech in which one entity is compared with another, using *like* or *as: He was as emaciated as a skeleton. Her frown was like an oncoming squall.* Compare METAPHORS.

simpatico (*adj.*) As Americans use it, *simpatico* (pronounced either *sim-PAHT-i-ko* or *sim-PAT-i-ko*) means "congenial, agreeable, or compatible," and we may have borrowed it from either Italian or Spanish or both. Until recently it has been Conversational and Informal, but it is now fully naturalized and Standard in all uses except perhaps the Oratorical and the Formal.

simple (*adj.*) means "uncomplicated," as in *This is a simple machine*; "easy," as in *Solving the problem was simple*; "undecorated, plain," as in *She wore a simple white dress*; "pure, innocent," as in *He had a simple, easy manner*; "stupid, retarded," as in *Her brother is simple—not all there*; and "unimportant, ordinary, humble," as in *They have a very simple cottage at the shore*. Context must control which of these or other senses you intend. See SIMPLICITY.

simple reason (that), for the *For the simple reason that* adds emphasis, but it may also add an impatience or insult you do not intend: it can suggest that the reason is so simple that only a dolt could fail to grasp it. Unless you intend to be unpleasant, leave out the adjective, or, even better, say *because*.

SIMPLE SENTENCE A *simple sentence,* one of the four grammatically classified sentence types, contains just one independent clause; it may be short or long, so long as it has only one subject and one predicate: *My father was a very tall man.* Commands may also be *simple sentences,* even though they lack subjects: *Call home.* See SENTENCE TYPES.

SIMPLICITY in style of speaking or writing is usually considered a virtue, first because it assists clarity and enhances conciseness, and second because it eschews decoration and other efforts to inflate or prettify. It is not the only virtue, but it is a great one. See SIMPLE.

simplistic is not a higher-powered version of *simple.* It means "unacceptably oversimple" or "oversimplified," and it's a pejorative. See MODERN.

simply Like *only, simply* is an adverb that in speech can occur at almost any place in the sentence and never be grammatically ambiguous, because stress and other intonation will usually make clear what it modifies. In writing, however, *simply* can sometimes be grammatically ambiguous, as in *He wrote simply to make others happy.* Without a comma to replace the missing intonation, we can't be sure whether he wrote in a simple style in order to make others happy (*He wrote simply, in order to . . .*), or whether he wrote solely to make others happy (*He wrote, simply to make others happy*). In your writing make certain that *simply* is grammatically unambiguous, either through its position, its punctuation, or the two combined. Otherwise, rephrase or reword the sentence.

simulate, dissimulate (*vv.*) To *simulate* is "to pretend or feign, to imitate": *We simulated an emergency.* To *dissimulate* is "to hide one's feelings," "to pretend," "to dissemble": *He dissimulated well; no one knew how miserable he felt.*

simultaneous (*adj.*), **simultaneously** (*adv.*) Using the adjective adverbially, as in *The two programs ran simultaneous,* is Nonstandard and a shibboleth. Pronounce the adjective *SEI-muhl-TAI-nee-uhs* or *SEI-muhl-TAIN-yuhs;* the British and Canadians pronounce the first syllable *SIM-*.

since (*adv., subord. conj., prep.*) As a subordinating conjunction *since* can introduce a dependent clause and mean "because": *Since no one objected, I continued.* In the same grammatical role, it can also have a temporal meaning: *I haven't talked to her since she moved away.* As a preposition it can have that same temporal sense: *It's been there since Wednesday.* And as an adverb, it can have a similar temporal sense, putting one event after another in time: *She called last week, but I haven't heard from her since.* Ambiguity can be a problem in sentences wherein the conjunction may mean either "because" or "during the period when," as in *Since I've been ill I haven't written him.* Make certain that context indicates clearly whether the conjunctive use is causal or temporal.

sincerely, faithfully, truly (*advs.*) The complimentary close of a letter often uses *sincerely* in certain formulaic ways: *sincerely yours, very sincerely yours, yours sincerely,* and *sincerely.* Americans frequently use *truly* in place of *sincerely* in all but the single word closing formula. Some Britons, and a few Americans too, may also use *faithfully* in some of these formulas. The tone or style of these is mostly a matter of convention, but the single-word versions are probably the most informal, and the three-word models the most overtly formal.

sinecure See CYNOSURE.

sine die is a Latin phrase, but one thoroughly anglicized for use in courtroom and parliamentary procedures. To adjourn *sine die* means "to adjourn indefinitely, without naming a day for reconvening." Journalists use the phrase to save space, but plain English will be clearer to more readers. Pronunciations vary, although both words always have two syllables: the first syllable of *sine* usually rhymes either with *sin* or *sign,* and the word *die* is stressed on the first syllable and pronounced either *DEI-ee* or like the names of the letters *d* and *a.* In parliamentary jargon *sine die* is sometimes abbreviated *s.d.* See FOREIGN PHRASES.

sine qua non The Latin means "without which not," so that anything so described is "a necessity." Americans have made it a cliché, perhaps in part because we love hyperbole. The phrase is so widely used that it has developed a regular English plural: *It's another of those sine qua nons; we just can't do without it.* Pronounce it *SI-ni-KWAH-NON* or *-NAHN,* with heavy stress on the last syllable. See FOREIGN PHRASES.

sing (*v.*) *Sang* is the regular past tense of *sing,* as in *Last week we sang Bach,* but *sung,* the regular past participle of this strong verb, as in *The year before we had sung Mozart,* also occurs as a past tense, as in *That Christmas they sung a cantata,* and you can find it regularly in reputable authors, especially of the eighteenth and nineteenth centuries. As a past tense today, *sung* may be archaic, and unfortunately some may wrongly judge it Nonstandard.

single, singles Several new meanings or modifications of old meanings have recently developed into slang, Conversational, or Informal uses: *singles* are (among other things these days) one-dollar bills; unmarried, unattached people (as contrasted with couples; they frequent *singles clubs* and *singles bars*); and recordings of individual songs, as in *That vocal group made several hit singles last year.*

SINGLE QUOTATION MARKS See QUOTATION MARKS.

SINGULAR (*adj., n.*) The grammatical category of number that refers to one person or thing is called the *singular,* as are the forms of nouns, pronouns, and verbs (as well as *a/an,* the number *one,* and the first in each of these pairs of determiners: *this/these, that/those*). In *A woman sings,* every word is marked for the *singular.* See also NUMBER (1).

sinister See BAR SINISTER.

sink (*v.*) The past tense of this strong verb is either *sank* or *sunk;* the past participle is *sunk* only: *I sank* [or *sunk*] *a lot of money in it. They had sunk two small ships. Have sank* is Substandard. The participial adjective is usually *sunken: Their house had a sunken living room.*

Sino- (*prefix*) *Sin* is an Arabic word for "China," borrowed by the Greeks, and *Sino-* (pronounced usually to rhyme with *rhino*) is an adjectival prefix used to link China with something else, as in the *Sino-Japanese War. Chinese-Japanese* would have been more nearly parallel, but *Sino-* was handy for American headline writers and therefore much used during the 1930s. Use it warily: today not everyone knows what it means.

Sir, Dame The British title for knight or baronet can be a trap for unwary Americans: it can't be used with just the last name. The English actor is *Sir John Gielgud,* or *Sir John,* but never *Sir Gielgud.* The same rule applies to *Sir's* female counterpart, *Dame* (which see): it's *Dame Agatha Christie,* or *Dame Agatha,* but never *Dame Christie.*

Uncapitalized, *sir* is the term used in direct address to a man whose name is unknown or to whom you intend to show respect: *Thank you, sir. Ma'am* and *madam* are the terms used for these purposes for women.

sirup See SYRUP.

sister-in-law See -IN-LAW; PLURALS OF COMPOUND NOUNS.

sit See SET.

site See CITE.

sitting room See LIVING ROOM.

situate (*adj.*) is archaic, encountered nowadays mainly in real estate titles, wills, and other legal documents: *The dwelling, situate on a knoll twenty feet from the railroad track. . . .* In normal speech and writing, use instead *situated, set,* or nothing.

situation (*n.*) We have built this generally useful word into a number of cliché phrases, such as *a conflict situation* ("a fight or quarrel") or *a no-win situation* ("one with no possible good outcome"), and we also find it an easy-to-use, nonspecific, all-purpose word, like *business, concern,* or *thing.* As a result, we now overwork *situation.* See also PROPOSAL.

SITUATION UTTERANCE, RESPONSE UTTERANCE C. C. Fries (1952) used these terms to describe the two clusters of syntax he encountered in American English speech. Essentially, *situation utterances* begin conversations, and *response utterances* continue or end them. A *situation utterance* normally requires a complete sentence, a question, statement, or command: *Is Fred home? I have your book. Call me on Thursday.* A *response utterance,* however, can be any sort of syntactic fragment, based as it is on the *situation utterance* that elicited it: *Not yet. Good. If you wish. Of course. Never. Why not?* Both kinds of syntax are Standard in speech. In expository writing, nearly all sentences are *situation* types; because you cannot see your readers, you cannot risk losing them by using a fragmentary *response* sentence, unless you carefully control it with context. And much of the time such fragments will sound too informal for Formal or Semiformal writing. In writing dialogue, you will of course use both kinds of utterances, but otherwise when writing, reserve the fragmentary *response utterance* for very special circumstances.

sizable, sizeable (*adj.*) Both spellings are acceptable, *sizable* the more common.

skeptic, sceptic, scepticism, skepticism (*nn.*), **sceptical, skeptical** (*adj.*) The *sk-* spellings are almost universal in the United States; the British still prefer *sc-*.

ski (*n., v.*) The noun plural is *skis,* and the verb's past tense and past participle are both spelled *skied.* Present participle and gerund are *skiing.* The British plural noun *ski* is archaic, as is the Norwegian-imitating pronunciation of *ski* words that makes them sound like English *she.*

skillful, skilled (*adjs.*), **skill, craft, trade** (*nn.*) You can be *skillful* (the usual American spelling, although *skilful* is an acceptable variant) at any sort of task or undertaking: you'll be "nimble, apt, effective, competent." To be *skilled,* you must have "mastered a trade or craft." *Skilled carpenters* and *skilled cabinet-makers* are in different *crafts*; each has a different *skill*; each has mastered a different *skilled trade.* See CRAFT (1).

skin-color(ed) See FLESH.

skirt (*v.*) To skirt something is "to go around it"; hence *to skirt around something* is redundant, although it is frequent in Informal and Conversational use. Some consider the redundancy inappropriate in all contexts.

skull See SCULL.

skycap (*n.*) A *skycap* (the word was formed on analogy with the railroad station's *redcap*) is "a porter who handles baggage and wheelchairs at an airport." The term is Standard.

skyjack (*v.*), **skyjacker** (*n.*) These words, built on analogy with *hijack* and *hijacker,* refer to the taking over of an airplane by threat of violence. Because they are of recent origin and hence of unsettled repute, both words are variously labeled in the dictionaries. Slang, Colloquial, and Standard are all assigned at present, but *hijack* and *hijacker* appear to be taking back ground once lost for a time to *skyjack* and *skyjacker.*

slack, slacken, slake (*vv.*) *Slack* is used most frequently with *off* or *up* and means "to ease up, slow down, or fail to do your part": *We slacked off against a weaker team and ended by being beaten.* To slacken is "to ease off, take the strain off, or slow the pace": *You must slacken your speed on the turns.* Slack and *slacken* are each both transitive and intransitive. To slake (rhymes with *lake*) *thirst* is "to satisfy it"; *to slake* (also rhymes with *lake*) *lime* is "to moisten it," but you can also *slack* (rhymes with *tack*) *lime* to achieve the same end.

slacks, knickers, pants, trousers (*nn.*) All these items of clothing have two legs, and they usually occur only in the plural: *Those are my good pants. These trousers need pressing.* There are singular forms, however, limited to the argot of tailors and clothing salesmen: *This is a fine trouser. We sell that slack in several fabrics.* See also KNICKERS; PANTIES; PANTS; PLUS FOURS.

slake See SLACK.

slander, libel, slang (*vv.*) *To slander* is "to say false unpleasantnesses about someone"; *to slang* is "to talk to or address someone abusively"; *to libel* is "to slander someone *in writing.*"

SLANG is the usage label applied to those Nonstandard, Conversational, or Informal words that are limited usually to use in Informal or Conversational circumstances within a particular constituency. Sometimes *slang* refers specifically to the jargon, cant, or argot words used by a special group, such as a trade or other occupational association. Sometimes *slang* is simply the specialized language of a sport or a hobby. And sometimes it is used and understood by most Standard speakers of the language, as is the word *egghead.* Those who use Standard English use *slang* but limit it to those situations where its use is appropriate: usually the three Conversational levels of speech and Informal and some Semiformal writing. *Slang* is evanescent: it is often coined deliberately to be colorful or funny, and many of its words burst into view like skyrockets and then vanish just as quickly. But some *slang* words eventually achieve respectability and enter the Standard vocabulary; *jinx* is an example. And once in a great while a word will remain *slang* for centuries: *booze* still carries a *slang* label in some dictionaries today, despite its eighteenth-century start. See SLANDER.

SLASH, SLASH MARK See VIRGULE.

slave of, slave to Literal meanings normally require *of,* figurative ones usually use *to:* you can be *a slave to a habit* but *the slave of a conqueror.*

slay (*v.*) The past tense is *slew,* except that *slayed* occurs in the slang sense of "to delight or overwhelm," a jocular and hyperbolic figurative use: *His comic routines just slayed me!* The Standard past participle is *slain,* also widely used as a participial adjective, which together with *slayer* has become a headline writer's cliché. See EXECUTE.

sleep (*v.*) The principal parts of this verb are *sleep, slept, slept.* See CREEP.

sleeper (*n.*) The literal sense with the agentive ending is quite regular, meaning "one who sleeps," but figurative uses are varied. In Great Britain a *sleeper* is also "a railroad tie," and in the United States the word once had wide use meaning "a railroad car with beds or staterooms—a sleeping car—and briefly, in the 1930s, an airplane similarly equipped." The newest and liveliest figurative sense, however, is the slang sense from sports, entertainment, and business, meaning "a player (or contestant, play, film, book, or company) from which little is expected at the outset but which turns out to be unexpectedly successful": *Her last play was a sleeper—it ended up running an entire year.*

sleep sound, sleep tight See SOUND (1).

sleight of hand The *sleight* is pronounced just like *slight,* and it means "manual dexterity, usually used to deceive" or "a trick produced by it."

slept See SLEEP.

slew See SLAY.

slick (*adj.*) The Standard adjective means "smooth, slippery" in the literal sense, but there are several figurative senses, both elevated and pejorative. *A slick way of solving the problem* is elevated but slang, and perhaps archaic; it expresses admiration. *A slick salesman* may be pejorative, meaning "one full of deception," or it may be admiring. The term is also applied figuratively in commentary on literary or other artistic productions, meaning "the work is glib or glittery on the surface but lacking in substance or depth."

slink (*v.*) This strong verb has *slunk* as its main past tense and past participle forms, but the weak-verb–patterned *slinked* has begun to appear in the media; most Edited English will not yet accept it, and some Standard users consider it a shibboleth. Even so, *slinked* bears watching. See SNEAK for the opposite process.

slit (*v.*) This verb has unchanging principal parts: *slit* is infinitive, past tense, and past participle.

slow, slowly (*advs.*) *Slow* is a Standard flat adverb: *Go slow. The traffic was slow-moving. My watch runs slow. Slowly* is acceptable in every situation where *slow* appears, plus a good many others where *slow* won't work, as in *He has only slowly won their approval.*

slunk See SLINK.

small businessman, small-business man These spelled versions of the phrase illustrate one of the rare instances when spelling can remove an ambiguity that is much harder to prevent in speech. The first chap is "a little man engaged in a business of unspecified size." The second, in hyphenated form, is "a man of unspecified size engaged in a small business."

small-scale See LARGE-SCALE.

smarmy (*adj.*) This British word, which some Americans have adopted, means "unctuous and insincere" and for now is best limited to Conversational levels and the Semiformal and Informal writing that imitates them.

smashing (*adj.*), meaning "beautiful" or "handsome" or "otherwise overwhelming," is so fashionable currently that its figurative senses have the effect of slang and are quickly overdone. Avoid it.

smell (*n., v.*) The American past tense and past participle are *smelled;* the British more frequently use *smelt* in both functions. The verb may be used transitively (*She smelled chocolate*) or intransitively followed by an adjective (*Whatever you're cooking smells good*) or an adverb (*The room smelled strongly of disinfectant; The mothballs smelled perceptibly*). See ODOR.

smidgin See SCINTILLA.

sneak (*v.*) *Sneaked* has long been the regular past tense and past participle of *sneak,* but today *snuck* also occurs frequently in Standard English, though it is still sometimes limited in the most Formal Edited English. Compare SLINK for the opposite process of change.

snow (*v.*), **snow job** (*n.*) Aside from its literal senses, the verb *snow* is widely used as slang meaning "to deceive, as with lies or flattery": *The dealer snowed me about the car's condition.* The compound noun *snow job* is "a deceptive attempt to persuade," apparently (as with the verb sense) a figurative use reflecting the ability of snow to conceal the true features of what it covers. In the passive especially, it means "deceived or persuaded": *She was snowed by his flattery.*

snuck See SNEAK.

so (*adv., intensifier, subord. conj.*), **so that** The Informal uses of *so* in these functions suggest conversation, and for the higher levels of speech and more Formal levels of the written language (and especially for Edited English) such uses sometimes seem too relaxed, too imprecise; nonetheless, both as adverb, as in *He's so witty!* and as conjunction, as in *I thought she looked tired, so I sent her to bed,* such uses are quite appropriate in the right contexts, although some other uses can earn censure.

So as adverb is usually an intensifier heavily used in conversation: *She was so happy! I've never been so scared in my life!* Most editors object to these exclamatory adverbial uses but will accept without question adverbial uses that have a causal relationship with a following clause, as in *I was so sleepy that I nodded off.* Standard English usually restricts the simple ejaculatory *I was so sleepy!* (often with heavy stress on *so*) to Informal and Conversational uses.

So as a conjunction is one of the most heavily used causal connectives in the language: *I came early, so we could chat,* where *so* means "in order that," and *He didn't believe me, so he fired me,* where *so* means "and for that reason" or "and therefore." The frequency of these uses is higher in spoken than in written English, and speakers of Vulgar and Common American English use it much more often than do Standard users, who have *consequently* and *therefore* and several other words to provide variety and minor sense distinctions.

The claim that *so that* is somehow better than *so,* as in *They stood up so [that] we could see them,* seems to have little merit. Both structures work; both are clear. One boasts economy, the other a bit of decoration with a slightly different rhythm, so (that) you may quite safely use *that* or not, just as you wish.

soap opera, soap (*nn.*) These serial dramas began first on radio and then became even more elaborate on television, picking up where nineteenth-century melodrama and sentimental theater left off. Some argue that the term *soap opera* is Informal or Colloquial, but though figurative (many of these serials are or once were sponsored by soap manufacturers) the term is now Standard; *the soaps* is a slang name for the same dramas. Compare HORSE OPERA.

so . . . as See AS . . . AS.

sob See WEEP.

so-called (*adj.*) Don't follow *so-called* with quotation marks around the following noun. If he's a bad actor, then write either *He's an "actor"* or *He's a so-called actor,* not *He's a so-called "actor."* One aspersion is enough.

sociable (*adj.*), **social** (*adj., n.*) *Sociable* people are "friendly people, who enjoy being with others." The adjective *social* refers to *society* and therefore has both the general adjectival sense of "pertaining to society" and the specialized sense that refers to "those groups considered elite and trend-setting among the classes of a society." *My brother is very social* means that he is much seen (and perhaps seeks visibility) among the admired and reported "somebodies" of the community. *Sociable* has an elevated meaning; *social,* in the specialized sense illustrated here, is often pejorative.

The noun *social* is a somewhat old-fashioned, quaint name for a large party, as in *a church social, an ice cream social.*

SOCIAL DIALECT, CLASS DIALECT

These are the dialects that reflect social-class origins: formal education, social position, occupation, and economic level are some of the contributors to an individual's *social dialectal* level. This book speaks of three broad *social* or *class dialects:* Standard English, Common English, and Vulgar English. Note however that language practices may be either typical or atypical of class of origin; a *social dialect* label means only that its characteristics are those typical of most of the speakers in that class. Compare REGIONAL DIALECT.

social disease (*n.*) This euphemism for any venereal disease (itself a euphemism for STD, or sexually transmitted disease) is dated and faded, its tastefully noncommittal drapery no longer required now that the once-taboo names and causes of these diseases are openly discussed and printed.

SOCIOLINGUISTICS, SOCIOLINGUIST

Sociolinguistics is the branch of linguistics that looks at the effects social and cultural forces have on the language of speech communities; a *sociolinguist* is a practitioner, a scholar in that field.

socks, sox (*n.*) *Socks* is the regular plural, but the variant spelling *sox* is also Standard, although most people prefer to limit it to proper names (*Boston Red Sox*) and Informal contexts. See STOCKING.

soda, club soda, pop, seltzer, soda pop, soft drink(s), sparkling water, tonic (*nn.*) All these are names for nonalcoholic beverages, usually carbonated so as to fizz, bubble, or "sparkle." The general terms are *soft drinks* (as distinguished from "hard" [alcoholic] drinks), *soda, pop,* and *soda pop* (although *soda* is also a clipped name for *ice cream soda,* a combination of ice cream, flavoring, and carbonated water). These beverages may have any of a variety of flavors or none at all. *Seltzer, club soda, sparkling water,* and *soda* itself in the right context (as in *whiskey* and *soda*) are all essentially effervescent water. In New England, *tonic* is both a generic term for any carbonated, nonalcoholic drink and (as it is for all the rest of the United States) a quinine-flavored sparkling drink often mixed with gin, vodka, or rum as a highball.

sofa, chesterfield, couch, davenport, day bed, settee, settle, studio bed, studio couch (*nn.*) These are the names of long pieces of furniture designed to seat three or more adults; they are also suitable for one to lie on at full length. Some—the *studio couch,* for example—open into double beds. *Sofa* and *couch* are generic; the others are special kinds, except for *davenport* and *chesterfield,* which are also regional terms. All are Standard. See also CHESTERFIELD.

so far as See AS FAR AS.

softback, softcover See HARDBACK.

soft drink(s) See SODA.

soft sell See HARD SELL.

software See HARD COPY.

soiled (*adj.*) Use *soiled* sparingly; perhaps it's only a self-consciously delicate term that should be replaced by *dirty* or *filthy* or something equally earthy (the English in particular consider *soiled* a euphemism); perhaps uneasiness about it stems from the excremental overtones it shares with *dirt, dirty,* or *nightsoil.* Or perhaps it's just that to many Americans, *soiled* is a cliché: soap and detergent advertising and journalism have accustomed us to trying to deal with *soiled* laundry and to our public figures "laundering their *soiled* linen in public." Try a synonym instead.

SOLECISM The people who lived in ancient Soloi apparently spoke a version of Attic that other Greeks thought crude, and nowadays a *solecism* is "a grammatical or other linguistic blunder and hence, by extension, any other breach of manners." Wiping your mouth on your sleeve is a *solecism,* and so is saying *She don't know any better. Solecism* is pronounced either *SAHL-uh-siz-uhm* or *SOL-uh-siz-uhm.*

solicitor See LAWYER.

SOLIDUS See VIRGULE.

solon (*n.*) Solon was a wise Athenian legislator of the sixth century B.C. whose name has come to mean "a wise man." Alas, perhaps because it fits nicely into headlines, it is now a threadbare journalese cliché likely to be applied to any legislator who displays the most trifling sign of common sense, however briefly.

so long is a stereotyped farewell. No one knows its origin, but it is Standard Conversational English.

so long as See AS LONG AS.

solution (*n.*) The prepositions *to* and *for* combine with *solution* in Standard English: *He has a solution to [for] our problem. Of* also occurs, but not always appropriately: *He has the solution of our problem* is Standard, but *He has a solution of our problem* is Nonstandard. Best advice: use *to* or *for.*

some (*adv., adj., pron.*) As an adverb *some* is used to reduce or approximate figures that might otherwise be taken as firm numbers: *He's been here some sixteen years*; it means "about." Also adverbial is the use of *some* meaning "somewhat" or "a bit": *He seems some taller than when I saw him last. The girls have practiced some, but they're still not ready.* The first example may be either Conversational or regional, but the second example is appropriate in most conversation and even in Semiformal writing. For Edited English, however, use *somewhat* or *a little* instead.

In uses such as *May I have some soup?* the adjective is a Standard workhorse, but it has also become slang or Conversational in this use: *He's some halfback!* Here *some* is always heavily stressed in speech, and its meaning is hyperbolic: "He's a wonderful halfback!" (See also SOME KIND OF.) An explicit adjective would be as effective. *He's been here for some years* has a different and Standard sense: *some* here means "several."

Some as indefinite pronoun can be either singular or plural; the key is whether its referent is a count noun or a mass noun: *Take trees—some lose their leaves early. Consider firewood: some burns quickly, and its ash is negligible.*

-some (*suffix*) makes adjectives of some nouns: *adventure* becomes *adventuresome.* It means "like or tending toward something" (in this case, *adventure*).

somebody, someone (*prons.*) *Someone* is not necessarily a more polished choice than *somebody;* use whichever word makes the most effective, rhythmically satisfying sentence. The important usage issue is subsequent reference to these indefinite pronouns: both are singular and always take singular verbs, but each increasingly is followed by plural references, even though Standard English used to be adamant (and the most Formal Edited English usually still is) that it should be *Somebody left his* [or *his or her* or *a*] *coat in the front hall* or *Your guests left their coats in the front hall*. Now, almost everyone will accept *Somebody left their coat(s) in the front hall*. See also GENERIC PRONOUNS; INCLUSIVE LANGUAGE; SEXIST LANGUAGE.

somebody else's It should always be *somebody else's*, never the Substandard *somebody's else*. See ELSE.

someday, some day See SOME TIME.

some kind of The Standard meaning, as in *That bird is some kind of* [*a*] *thrush*, poses no particular problem, although some commentators insist that the *a* is unnecessary. But the modern slang use of the phrase, employed first in sports but now more widely, needs watching: *He's some kind of hitter* means "He's a splendid hitter." *Some kind of* in this use is a modern variant of a much older slang use of *some: She's some dancer*, with heavy stress on *some* and with the meaning "She's a wonderful dancer."

some of With nouns, Standard syntax is *Some of the girls went home early* or *Some girls went home early*. With pronouns, it is *Some* [or *Some of them*] *went home early*.

someone See SOMEBODY.

someplace See ANYPLACE.

somersault, summersault (*n., v.*) *Summersault* is an acceptable variant spelling, but *somersault* appears more often. The *summer-* spelling probably came from a folk etymology involving the season, but the word has nothing to do with *summertime*, coming instead from the medieval French *sombresaut*, in turn from the Latin *super* plus *saltus:* "over" plus "jump."

something, somethin', sumpin' See -ING.

something (*adv., intensifier*), **somewhat** (*adv.*) *Something* and *somewhat* function interchangeably as adverbs, as in *Blue herons look something* [or *somewhat*] *like cranes*, except when directly modifying the verb or an adjective, when only *somewhat* will do, as in *Her choice somewhat puzzled me* and *Her choice left me somewhat puzzled*. *Something*, however, can be used at Conversational levels and in Informal writing as an intensifier: *She yelled and screamed something fierce*, in this case meaning "intensely, very fiercely," not "an unspecified fierce expression." This use is inappropriate in Edited English.

something else, really something These two idioms involving *something* are slang locutions found only at the Conversational levels and in Informal imitations of them. *She's something else!* means "She's absolutely extraordinary, remarkably different." And *She's really something* has much the same meaning, although perhaps a shade less hyperbolic: "Far from being uninteresting and unremarkable, she's truly a person to be taken into account."

some time, someday, some day, sometime, sometimes *Some time* is an adjective-plus-noun combination: *We still have some time left before dinner*. *Sometime* is both an adverb meaning "approximately," as in *He'll arrive next week sometime* [or *sometime next week*], and an adjective meaning either "former" or "occasional," as in *My mother was a sometime officeholder in our town* and *She had a passion for the theater and a sometime interest in the cinema*. In the phrase *a sometime thing*, however, the meaning seems to have drifted beyond "occasional" to a mildly pejorative sense meaning "on-again-off-again," with the implication that *sometime things* are fairly unstable.

Sometimes is unequivocally adverbial: *We sometimes go there for dinner*. Compare BACKWARD.

Some day is the normal adjective-plus-noun construction, meaning "one day, but not a particular day." *Someday* is an adverb, working much as the adverb *sometime* does: *Someday* [*Sometime*] *soon, we must have lunch together*.

someway, someways (*advs.*) Like *somewheres, nowheres, anyways*, and a number of similarly compounded adverbs that occur both with and without a final *-s, someways* is Substandard, even in the regional dialects where it usually occurs: *Someways, I'd like to help him*. *Someway, I'd like to help him* is Standard in speech, but it isn't often found in print; *I'd like to help him in some way* [or *somehow*] would be more appropriate.

somewhat See KIND OF.

somewhere, somewheres (*advs., prons.*) *Somewhere* is the Standard form; *somewheres* is widely heard in American speech, but it is inappropriate for Standard use, and in the spoken language it frequently serves as a shibboleth for identifying the uncultivated. *The paper is somewheres on the porch* is at best Common English, more probably Vulgar.

son-in-law See -IN-LAW; PLURALS OF COM-POUND NOUNS.

sophisticated (*adj.*), **sophisticate** (*n., v.*), **sophistication** (*n.*) Probably because of their etymological basis in *sophistry* and the *sophists,* these words have not always been thought to suggest wholly admirable qualities: "complex," yes, but perhaps "deviously, needlessly complex" was sometimes the implication. Today the meaning has generally elevated to "complex, elegant, polished" or (especially of persons) "experienced and worldly-wise," an antonym of *naive* and *innocent*. When you find these words in older prose, however, be alert for the pejorative senses.

soprano (*n.*) The plural is *sopranos.* See PLURALS OF NOUNS ENDING IN *-O.*

sorbet See SHERBET.

sort See KIND.

sort of See KIND OF.

sort of a See KIND OF A.

so that See SO.

sound (*adv., adj.*), **soundly** (*adv.*) *Sound* is both adjective (*a sound sleep*) and flat adverb (*sound asleep*). *Soundly* is the regular adverbial form (*Our team beat them soundly*). *To sleep sound,* like *to sleep tight,* is a Standard American idiom; *to sleep soundly* is also Standard, but *to sleep tightly* of course doesn't work—only *tight* is idiomatic there.

sound, sound off, sound out (*vv.*) Occasionally commentators claim that the *out* is unnecessary: *to sound* means literally "to test or measure the depth, to fathom" figuratively "to find out what someone thinks." But Standard American English much more frequently uses *sound out* figuratively: *I'll sound her out on the question. Sound off* is Standard as a military command, in response to which a marching unit counts cadence aloud or each person in a formation standing at attention speaks or counts off in turn. *To sound off* meaning "to boast or speak loudly or opinionatedly" is slang: *He was always sounding off about how rich his father was.*

south, South, southerly, Southern, southern See EAST.

SOUTHERN REGIONAL DIALECT What most people think of as "the Southern drawl" characteristic of natives of the lower right-hand quarter of the continental United States is actually two regional dialects, *Southern* and South Midland. They share many features of sound, word forms, syntax, and vocabulary, but each also has features that distinguish it from the other. Most noticeable to the listener from another part of the country is that *Southern,* like Eastern New England and Metropolitan New York City dialects, loses its *r*'s except before vowels, so that *swimmer* in *Southern* sounds like *swimmuh* to many Northerners. *Southern dialect* is spoken in the coastal savanna and Piedmont areas from Maryland south, in some of Florida, and in the lowlands and coastal areas of Georgia, Alabama, Mississippi, Louisiana, and eastern Texas—essentially in all the old cotton plantation country that was the first part of the South the Europeans settled.

SOUTH MIDLAND REGIONAL DIALECT This is one of the two main divisions of the regional dialect that other Americans often incorrectly believe all Southerners speak. (*Southern* is the other.) *South Midland* occurs in the high country and inland in all the southern states below the Ohio River, as well as through the lower Mississippi valley, the Ozarks, Oklahoma, and the Texas panhandle. Unlike *Southern, South Midland* retains its *r* coloration; it also has a number of vowels, diphthongs, and other features peculiarly its own (to Northern ears, South Midland *pen* sounds like *pin,* and *think* like *thank,* for example). It shares certain linguistic features with *Southern,* and it also shares many with North Midland, the dialect of the Midwest below the Great Lakes and of the states of the Central Mississippi valley.

southward, southwards See EASTWARD.

SOUTHWESTERN REGIONAL DIALECT This regional dialect of American English has as its chief distinguishing feature its many Spanish borrowings, both in vocabulary and in certain idioms. It is spoken in central and western Texas, New Mexico, Arizona, and southern California. Because most of this area has been settled by speakers of English for a relatively short time, and because the last few decades have seen huge migrations into much of this region from other parts of the country, the dialect is less well marked than are the dialects of the eastern half of the country. *Southwestern* shares a number of features with the Western dialect.

soviet (*adj., n.*) In Russian, *soviet* means "council," and, while colloquially referred to as *Russia,* the largest of the fifteen republics that until recently made up the Soviet Union, the official name of the country in English was *The Union of Soviet Socialist Republics (USSR).*

We sometimes used *the Soviet* or *the Soviet Union* as short names for the country, *Soviets* as a name for its citizens, and *soviet* (capitalized or not) as an adjective to modify many things Russian. It now appears that these terms are of historical interest only.

sow (*v.*) *Sow*—the activity performed with *seed*—pronounces its past tense *SOD* and its two past participle forms *SOD* and *SON,* exactly as does the other *sew* (the activity performed with a needle and thread); but it spells them differently—*sowed, sown.*

sox See SOCKS.

spacial See SPATIAL.

spake See SPEAK.

SPANGLISH is the blend name recently given to the Spanish-English mixture (of both vocabulary and syntax) spoken by native speakers of Mexican or other Central American and Caribbean Spanish descent who live and work in Southern California, the other states bordering Mexico, and in Florida and certain northern urban centers. This name may originally have been derisive or jocular, and it is now slang in the general language, but it is widely understood by linguists as a technical term describing some dialects, one or another of which may be for some Hispanic-Americans their native language. Some linguists and Mexican-American commentators argue that the term properly applies only to the language of some Mexican-Americans, not to Puerto Rican and other Caribbean people from Spanish-speaking nations. See also PIDGIN; PIDGIN ENGLISH.

Spaniard, Spanish (*nn.*) Both nouns are Standard English names for citizens of Spain, and there appears to be no ethnic slur or other pejorative sense attached to *Spaniard,* as has sometimes been alleged. See also HISPANIC.

sparing in, sparing of, sparing with *Sparing of* and *sparing in* are the common combinations: *He is sparing of praise for his students. They are sparing in the food they provide their guests. Sparing with* occurs only rarely and stiffly, as in *Americans are said not to be sparing with their praise of their possessions.*

sparkling water See SODA.

spat See SPIT.

spate (*n.*) It originally meant "a flood," a literal sense still much used in Britain, but Americans use it almost exclusively in its figurative sense of "a great many, a lot, a huge number or amount": *The current spate of books on sports figures illustrates a growing trend.*

spatial, spacial (*adj.*) *Spatial* is the usual spelling; *spacial* is its homophone and a rare but Standard variant.

spay (*v.*) *To spay* a female animal is to remove its ovaries; the principal parts of this transitive and intransitive verb are *spay, spayed, spayed.* The variously spelled *spade* and *spayd* (for the infinitive and present tense) and *spayded* (for the past tense and past participle) are Substandard; *spayded* represents a Substandard pronunciation as well.

speak (*v.*) This strong verb's past tense is *spoke,* its past participle *spoken.* In Renaissance writing you'll often see the now-obsolete past tense form *spake.*

speak to, speak with (*vv.*) In most uses these combinations are interchangeable: *I spoke to* [*with*] *her for only a few minutes.* In some instances, however, there may be semantic distinctions: *Speak to* sounds a bit more one-sided, perhaps, than *speak with,* which may imply more give and take. And in one sense *speak to* suggests strongly that the speech is to be both one-sided and admonitory: *I guess I must speak to him* [*about his behavior*]. *Talk* works much the same way, except that you *speak to* [*on the subject of*] *an issue* far more often than you *talk to an issue.*

special, especial (*adjs.*), **specially, especially** (*advs.*) *Special* and *especial* are adjectives, *special* much more frequently used: *She's a very special sort of person. Special* appears increasingly in stereotypical phrases such as *special agent* and *special delivery,* including a growing number of euphemisms such as *special education,* which stress the idea that something *special* is "designed or intended for a particular purpose"; hence "unusual." *Especial* is more Formal in many uses, perhaps because it occurs relatively infrequently. The adverbs *specially* and *especially* are distributed somewhat differently: uses such as *specially planned, specially constructed,* and *specially created* are very common; *especially* only rarely occurs in them. Otherwise, the adverbs are semantically interchangeable, although *especially* is a bit more formal in some contexts, where it contrasts with the aphetic *specially: We were especially pleased you'd decided to join.*

speciality, specialty (*nn.*) *Speciality* (five syllables, with heaviest stress on the third) and *specialty* (three syllables, heaviest stress on the first) have most of their meanings in common, but in contexts such as *the specialty of the house,* most Americans always use *specialty,* whereas the British prefer *speciality*. *Speciality* meaning "a distinguishing mark or characteristic feature" gets occasional American use, as in *The specialities of the quarter horse are fast starts and great speeds over short distances.*

SPECIALIZATION is the process of semantic change wherein a change in the referent makes the meaning of a word become narrower and more specific: *corn* once meant "any grain," and *meat*, "any food," but today their primary senses have *specialized*. See also GENERALIZATION.

specialty See SPECIALITY.

species, specie (*nn.*) *Species* is both singular and plural: *He thinks this plant is a different species. These species are difficult to tell apart. Specie*, a back-formation singular, has been around since the eighteenth century, but it is Nonstandard for all biological and general meanings; *species* is the Standard term. The specialized word *specie*, meaning "coin, hard currency," is a regular singular English mass noun.

speciesism, meaning "discrimination or prejudice directed against other species, resulting from a belief that the human species has primacy over all," is a current vogue word among some environmentalists and proponents of animal rights. This word, made on analogy with other *-ism* words (among them *ageism, racism,* and *sexism,* all of which see), currently requires a self-defining context if it is to communicate anything to people not already familiar with it. It may disappear as quickly as it appeared, but, in the meantime, use it with care. See POLITICALLY CORRECT.

specious (*adj.*) once meant "showy," and the like, but it has pejorated and now means "something that may *look* good but really isn't," "deceptively pleasing."

spectators See AUDIENCE.

speech See ORATION.

SPEECH COMMUNITY, LANGUAGE COMMUNITY These terms refer to any constituency whose intragroup relationships and common experiences form their speech into a dialect or subdialect. Such dialects may be regionally or socially distinctive, or both. A large metropolitan city is a *speech community* in itself, and it contains many smaller *speech communities* (even down to single families) and in turn is part of a still larger *speech community*, such as a region or a nation.

SPEECH FORMULAS See VOCALIZED PAUSES AND SPEECH FORMULAS.

spell 1 (*v.*) means "to relieve someone for a limited time": *Fred spelled me at the wheel while I ate.* Its principal parts are *spell, spelled, spelled,* and it is Standard.

spell 2 (v.) has to do with orthography and means "to arrange letters of the alphabet to form a word." Its principal parts are *spell, spelled* or *spelt, spelled* or *spelt,* Americans preferring *spelled,* the British, *spelt.*

SPELLING 1: AMERICAN AND BRITISH DIFFERENCES These lists, by no means exhaustive, illustrate the chief differences:

AMERICAN ENGLISH	BRITISH ENGLISH

1. Words ending in *-or* and *-our*. (Note, however, that not all such words differ in spelling; consider, for example: *emperor, error, mirror,* and *stupor*.)

arbor	arbour
armor	armour
behavior	behaviour
candor	candour
color	colour
demeanor	demeanour
favor	favour
flavor	flavour
glamour, glamor	glamour
harbor	harbour
honor	honour
labor	labour
neighbor	neighbour
rancor	rancour
rigor	rigour
savior, saviour	saviour
splendor	splendour
tabor, tabour	tabour
vapor	vapour

2. Words ending in *-er* or *-re*. (But, again, other examples do not differ: for example, *acre, lucre, mediocre,* and *meter* [the instrument].)

caliber	calibre
center, Centre	centre
goiter	goitre
liter	litre
maneuver	manoeuvre
meter (measure)	metre (measure)
miter	mitre
specter	spectre
theater, Theatre	theatre

3. Words ending in *-ize* or *-ise*. (But these do not differ: *circumcise, compromise, exercise, improvise,* and *surmise*.)

baptize	baptise, baptize
capsize	capsise, capsize
civilize	civilise, civilize
organize	organise, organize

realize	realise, realize
sympathize	sympathise, sympathize
visualize	visualise, visualize

4. Words ending in -se or -ce. (But *suspense* is the same for both nations.)

defense	defence, defense
offense	offence, offense
pretense	pretense, pretence

5. Words using the digraphs *ae* and *oe*.

anemic, anaemic	anaemic
aesthetic, esthetic	aesthetic
archaeology, archeology	archaeology
diarrhea	diarrhoeia
encyclopedia, encyclopaedia	encyclopaedia, encyclopedia
eon	aeon
esophagus	oesophagus
estrogen	oestrogen
hemoglobin, haemoglobin	haemoglobin
hemorrhage	haemorrhage, hemorrhage
maneuver	manoeuvre
medieval, mediaeval	mediaeval, medieval
pediatrician	paediatrician

6. Words with medial -ct- or -x-. (But *complexion* and *infection* do not differ.)

complected, complexioned	complexioned
connection	connexion
inflection	inflexion
reflection	reflexion

7. Miscellaneous differences.

aluminum	aluminium
check	cheque
curb	kerb
disk, disc	disc
draft	draught
fulfill	fulfil
gray, grey	grey, gray
Gypsy	Gipsy
inquire	enquire
jail	jail, gaol
mold	mould
mustache	moustache
omelet, omelette	omelette
pajamas	pyjamas
plow	plough
program	programme
skillful	skilful
sulfur	sulphur
tire	tyre
vise	vice
wagon	waggon, wagon

See also CONSONANTS (2).

SPELLING 2, MISSPELLING, AND SPELLING REFORM Correct spelling is a must for Americans; failure to spell words according to the conventions recorded in dictionaries is perhaps as powerful a shibboleth as Americans use on each other. As Thorstein Veblen (1899) pointed out:

English orthography satisfies all the requirements of the canons of reputability under the law of conspicuous waste. It is archaic, cumbrous, and ineffective; its acquisition consumes much time and effort; failure to acquire it is easy of detection.

Therefore it is the first and readiest test of reputability in learning, and conformity to its ritual is indispensable to a blameless scholastic life.

Almost none of us is without blemish in this matter, but fortunately poor spelling is not usually a clear indication of ethical flaws or bad work habits, any more than it is of stupidity. Nevertheless, considering the large numbers of us who spell indifferently, we are merciless in correcting others' misspellings, as though they proved the culprit indeed unethical, lazy, or stupid.

The main requirements for being an accurate speller are a combination of innate qualities and experience. If your visual imagination is good, you can envision the image of the word correctly spelled and then match that image when you write. If your imagination is not good, or if your experience includes too much exposure to a misspelled word, you will be helpless without a dictionary, brute memorization, or rhymes and other mnemonic devices.

It has long been customary to fault the English language spelling system for being a hodgepodge of contradictory rules, silent letters, and unstressed vowels variously represented. It does indeed present those difficulties, but actually, considering its history and its remarkably cosmopolitan vocabulary (with loan words from nearly every language in the world), today's English is quite reasonably spelled. The chief problem is one faced by every natural language: it changes its words, their meanings, and their pronunciations over time, as people use the language, resulting in more than one spelling for a given sound and more than one sound for a given spelling. But there are generalizations that explain some problems reasonably well: see, for example, CONSONANTS (2) and SPELLING OF -*ING* and -*ED* FORMS OF VERBS ENDING IN -*IC*, -*AC*. It's not a hodgepodge; it's a system, and the system works well.

Spelling reformers have long been unhappy over the inexact match between some of our English speech sounds and our alphabet, and every generation brings proposals for new, "improved" alphabets or parts of alphabets. But none of these alphabets can succeed, for at least two reasons: because English pronunciation keeps changing and varying (see CHANGE AND VARIATION IN LANGUAGE), to make our spelling accurately reflect its sounds would mean respelling the language every decade or two to reflect change, and also respelling it to reflect dialectal variation in various parts of the country and world. And if we respelled it that often, we would have to give up our fixed images of many, many words: we would all have several images of some words, and we would be at sea. Because so much of what we read we need only to skim, we would be horribly handicapped by not being able to read silently. Wholesale spelling reform would also cost us our investment in the conventions of English spelling—those fixed mental images of certain words to which we refer almost unconsciously as we write would be as useless as all the rules hammered into us in grammar school. To be obliged to learn a new system or perhaps a revision of the old every decade or so would be unthinkable. Even more unthinkable would be the cost of respelling all the old books in our libraries. If we respelled everything three or four times a century to reflect our changes in pronunciation, Charles Dickens's language would soon look as odd to us as Chaucer's does today. So spelling reform is piecemeal at best; a variant spelling here and there will gradually replace another, and it all happens a word or two at a time.

English spelling began to freeze during the Renaissance, soon after printing with movable type began to replace the handcopying of manuscripts. By Thomas Jefferson's time, most major spelling variations had disappeared. There were still a few eighteenth-century *-ick* spellings that Webster later reduced to *-ic* (*musick* became *music*), but few spellings in the Declaration of Independence would require a modern proofreader's red pencil. Even so British and American spelling still differ in a fair number of details (see SPELLING [1]), such as *labor/labour* and *curb/kerb*, and since we read English from all over the globe these days, our dictionaries frequently record variant spellings of that sort. And some variants exist simply because the conventional spellings of certain words have not quite settled down yet: a few years ago *programming* and *programmers* posed a problem (should they be *programing* and *programers?*),

and if you consult a good recent dictionary, you will find that both spellings of each are acceptable at present: these spellings are still in divided usage.

Given the huge numbers of foreign words this language has borrowed over the centuries, it is not at all remarkable that their English spellings reflect the cosmopolitan character of their sources. A few relatively trivial inconveniences in spelling in return for the unparalleled richness of our augmented lexicon is a great bargain.

Some have thought that with the electronic spelling checkers available on our word processors, spelling errors will be no more. Alas, *some* spelling errors may easily be rooted out by this means, but others (the language is full of homophones like *to, two,* and *too,* all good words but variously distributed) will not yield quite so easily. So, in view of the unfair but constant use of spelling as shibboleth, you must take steps to protect yourself. Consult dictionaries, stop grousing, and be grateful that yours is the richest, most varied language in the world.

SPELLING: PLURALS OF NOUNS ENDING IN *-F, -FE* See NOUNS ENDING IN *-F.*

SPELLING: PLURALS OF NOUNS ENDING IN *-O* See PLURALS OF NOUNS ENDING IN *-O.*

SPELLING OF COMPOUND WORDS is not entirely simple: the question is whether to write them as two words, as hyphenated words, or as single, uninterrupted words. Edited English permits considerable variation. Generally, compound nouns display all three possibilities: compare *side meat, sideline,* and *side-glance.* Compound verbs are usually written either as single words or hyphenated: *to downplay, to double-space.* Compound adjectives are usually hyphenated when they modify a noun (*a fierce-looking dog, a rough-textured fabric*) and left as separate words when they are really compound noun adjuncts modifying another noun (*An English department meeting, a Red Cross nurse*). The best (and simplest) advice, however, is to consult a current desk dictionary for the spelling. If the compound is not listed, do as you think best, because there is probably no consensus.

SPELLING OF *-ING* AND *-ED* FORMS OF VERBS ENDING IN *-IC, -AC* *Panic, picnic, traffic,* and other verbs whose infinitives end in *-ic* add a *k* before putting on a further inflection or suffix: *panicked, panicking, picnicked, picnicking, trafficked, trafficking,* etc.

Bivouac does the same: *bivouacking, bivouacked.*

SPELLING OF UNSTRESSED VOWELS
Spoken English is full of *unstressed vowels,* and we spell them with almost every vowel letter and combination in the alphabet. Consider the spellings of words such as the adjectives *separate, desperate,* or *indolent.* Consider too words that might end in either *-ance* or *-ence, -ibility* or *-ability.* For most bad spellers, *unstressed vowels* are the greatest single cause of error; therefore, whenever you are unsure, consult your dictionary. See also -ABLE.

SPELLING OF WORDS CONTAINING -EI- OR -IE-
These are spelled with *-ei-: conceit, conceive, deceive, either, forfeit, height, leisure, neighbor, receipt, receive, seize, seizure, sleigh, sleight, their, veil, weight, weir, weird.* And these are spelled with *-ie-: field, grief, shield, shriek, siege, wield.* There are many more examples.

SPELLING OF WORDS ENDING IN -ER, -OR
See AGENTIVE ENDINGS.

SPELLING OF WORDS ENDING IN -ER, -RE
See SPELLING (1).

SPELLING OF WORDS ENDING IN -IZE, -ISE
See SPELLING (1).

SPELLING OF WORDS ENDING IN -OR, -OUR
See SPELLING (1).

SPELLING OF WORDS ENDING IN -SE, -CE
See SPELLING (1).

SPELLING OF WORDS USING DIGRAPHS
See DIGRAPHS; SPELLING (1).

SPELLING PRONUNCIATIONS
are an oddity. The spoken language of course came first, and the written language is mostly an accommodation to it. But our literate society puts such emphasis on spelling that a good many people believe that the written form of a word is somehow truer and more basic than the spoken one. So it should not surprise us to find unwary speakers deciding that since *often* is spelled with a medial *-t-,* that hitherto silent consonant should be pronounced, as *AWF-ten.* And so too it is that although *forehead* has long been pronounced without an *h,* as *FOR-id,* many people, conscious of the spelling, say it *FOR-HED.* It is *spelling pronunciation* too that gives us the second pronunciations of *gunwale—GUHN-il* and *GUHN-WAIL—*and *forecastle—FOK-suhl* and *FOR-KAS-il.* And in at least one instance spelling pronunciation has given us both a second pronunciation and then a second spelling as well: originally *boatswain* was pronounced

something like *BOT-SWAIN,* and inexperienced landlubbers may still pronounce it that way, working as they must from the printed word. But nautical folk came to pronounce it *BOS-uhn,* and Gilbert and Sullivan were early users of the now widely current variant spelling *bosun.* See SYNCOPE.

Some *spelling pronunciations* catch on and ultimately become Standard, at least in divided usage; others remain odd and Nonstandard or disappear. In any event you'll be wise to check your dictionary when unsure.

SPELLING REFORM See SPELLING (2).

SPELLINGS, VARIANT See VARIANT SPELLINGS.

spell out (*v.*) "To detail clearly" is the phrase's figurative meaning, so the often-encountered *to spell out in detail* is redundant: use either *spell out* or *give in detail,* unless you need unusually strong emphasis.

spend (*v.*) The past tense and past participle are both *spent.*

sperm (*n.*) Originally a singular mass noun, *sperm* is a clipped form of the singular *spermatozoon,* whose plural is *spermatozoa.* Because *sperm* has had such wide use, and because even scientists appear to have welcomed its brevity when compared with the unclipped form, it has developed both a regular plural, *sperms,* and an unchanging plural form, *sperm,* as in *These sperms* [or *sperm*] *are highly susceptible to cold.* The unclipped scientific noun, *spermatozoon,* has a variant, *spermatozoan,* which has a regular English plural, *spermatozoans.* See also FOREIGN PLURALS; MASS NOUNS.

sphere See AREA.

spick-and-span, an idiom meaning "as clean and spotless as if brand new," is Standard with or without hyphens and with the first word spelled either *spic* or *spick.*

spiffy (*adj.*), meaning "bright and splendid-looking," is slang limited to Informal and Casual or Impromptu contexts.

spill (*v.*) has two past tense and past participle forms. Americans use *spilled* for both functions, as in *He spilled* [*had spilled*] *his beer*; the British prefer *spilt* for both. The American participial adjective in the cliché *crying over spilled milk* sometimes retains the British spelling and the pronunciation it reflects.

spin (*n., v.*), **spin doctor** (*n.*) The principal parts of this strong verb are *spin, spun, spun.* The noun *spin* has several specialized senses beyond its basic "the act of spinning." The clipped *spin* (from *tailspin*) is Standard, describing the aircraft's rotating, stalled dive; Standard too is the sense "a dizzied mental or emotional state" (*I'm confused—in a spin about all this*). At best Conversation and Semiformal is the sense "a short trip in or on a vehicle," as in *He took me for a spin on his motorcycle.*

A new slang and jargon sense of the noun comes from the argot of political campaigners and their spokespeople: "a new, distinctive interpretation, even a distortion, of a statement or an opinion," as in *She took his press statement's apparent blunder and put a spin on it that would be acceptable to the voters.* A person employed to do that sort of thing is what current slang calls *a spin doctor.* The figurative analogy is with bowling or billiards or another ballgame: seeking to gain an advantage, the player puts *spin* on the ball, to make it react differently from a ball without the *spin* and to make it deceive (or persuade) the receiver. See PUT ENGLISH ON.

spiral (*n., v.*) Purists used to argue that a *spiral* always goes down, not up, but in today's Standard English a *spiral* may go either way, so the word requires either context or a modifier to indicate the direction: *The plane spiraled up through the clouds. The glider made an upward spiral.*

spiritual, spiritous, spirituous (*adjs.*) All three adjectives come from the Latin *spiritus,* meaning "a breath." *Spiritual* has to do with the soul or other intangible "breaths," as in *affairs of the spirit,* whereas *spirituous* and *spiritous* are highly specialized and refer to distilled alcoholic spirits only. *He preferred spiritual pleasures to spirituous* [or *spiritous*] *ones. Spiritous* once also meant "pure," but that sense is now archaic, perhaps obsolescent.

spit (*vv.*) There are two different verbs, each with the infinitive *spit,* but with differing past tense and past participle forms. The strong verb *spit,* meaning "to expel saliva," has two Standard past tense forms, *spit* or *spat,* and the same two forms are its Standard past participle as well, with *spitten* and *spitted* Nonstandard past participles. *Spitted* is the Standard past tense and past participle form for the weak verb *spit,* meaning "to place on a spit as for roasting."

spit and image, spitten image, spittin' image, spitting image, very spit of The key to this puzzling cliché is the word *spit,* which seems to have been an early-nineteenth-century dialectal noun meaning "an exact likeness or counterpart of a person or thing," as in *He's the very*

spit of his father. The question is, how did *spit* develop that sense, dialectal or not? The *Oxford English Dictionary* concludes that it developed somehow from the noun *spit,* meaning "expectorated saliva," but no really satisfactory explanation of the semantic change involved has thus far turned up. In the late nineteenth century the full cliché developed: *He's the very spit and image of his father,* followed by the folk etymology that replaced *spit and* with *spitting* (or *spittin'* or *spitten) image.* The phrase has a rather countrified air about it, and it is not likely to be found today in either Formal writing or at the higher levels of speech.

splendiferous (*adj.*) is a word many consider typically American in its ebullience, an exuberant, hyperbolic near-synonym for *splendid.* Most dictionaries don't limit its usage at all, although some readers may consider it a trifle overenthusiastic. For an Informal bit of showy sparkle, however, there's nothing wrong with an occasional *splendiferous.*

split (*adj., n., v.*) Most of this word's uses are Standard, but two deserve comment: the sense of the verb meaning "to leave suddenly or quickly," as in *Fred and I split [the scene] and went for coffee,* is somewhat dated slang, as is the British sense meaning "to inform on, or to turn in an accomplice." But the noun meaning "a small bottle of champagne or other wine or a soft drink containing one serving" is Standard English, although a few commentators still want it limited to Conversational levels and their written imitations.

SPLIT INFINITIVE A *split infinitive* consists of the function word *to,* followed by an adverb (usually an *-ly* adverb), followed by an infinitive: *to happily conclude, to weakly demur, to needlessly suffer.* The construction got its name and ill fame many centuries after it first appeared in English (indeed, it was good English when this nation began), but during the nineteenth and early twentieth centuries great numbers of *split infinitives* appeared in print, and many complaints followed. One possibly after-the-fact reason for the objections was that since Latin and Greek infinitives were not (indeed, as single words, could not) be split, neither should English infinitives, even though they often came in two parts, *to* plus infinitive, and so were vulnerable to being split by adverbs. Or the crusade may have been launched by people seeking rules about where to put adverbs, the location of which is very flexible in the English sentence. Certainly *split infinitives* sometimes can cause very clumsy sentences, as in *We seek* to adequately and sincerely persuade you of our gratitude. Unfortunately, the rule against splitting, although simple, did not take actual usage into account. Ideally, English adverbs immediately precede the verbs they modify, as in *He stoutly defended his opinion,* or come at the end of the predicate and modify it or the whole sentence, as in *He defended his opinion stoutly,* or modify the entire sentence rather than just the verb by appearing at the beginning of the sentence, as in *Stoutly, he defended his opinion.* These generalizations also describe the placement of adverbial modifiers of infinitives; these adverbials, however, can be ambiguous in writing, where intonation is not available to assist in specifying grammatical relationships. This potential for confusion probably accounts for the popularity of the *split infinitive,* which eliminates all possibility of ambiguity. Consider these three sentences: *The driver is instructed periodically to check the oil level. The driver is instructed to periodically check the oil level. The driver is instructed to check the oil level periodically.* The first, which avoids splitting the infinitive, is possibly ambiguous, at least in writing: is the driver *instructed* periodically, or is it the *checking* that's to be done periodically? The second splits the infinitive but makes it clear that *periodically* modifies the verb *check.* The third doesn't split the infinitive, but unless it's punctuated as a sentence modifier, it could conceivably be thought to modify *instructed* rather than *to check.* It's a weak ambiguity, but readers can be notoriously obtuse sometimes.

Today, *split infinitives* continue to appear often in Standard speech and even in Edited English, especially in sentences where to avoid them would be clumsier and less effective than to use them. Conservative practice still tries to avoid them, especially at Planned, Oratorical, and Formal levels, particularly when they're not necessary for grammatical clarity, and it uses them only when they seem clear, add emphasis, and help avoid contorted syntax. Best advice: split an infinitive in speech whenever you wish, if the result sounds clear and unambiguous, but in writing follow the conservative path, especially when you're uncertain of your readers' expectations and sensitivities in this matter.

spoil (*v.*) *Spoiled* is both past tense and past participle of this weak verb, but *spoilt* also occurs, particularly as a participial adjective. British English has a much higher frequency of *spoilt* in these uses.

spokesperson See CHAIR; CHAIRMAN; INCLUSIVE LANGUAGE; PEOPLE; SEXIST LANGUAGE.

sponge (*n., v.*) *To sponge on (off) someone* is "to be a parasite, to use another's resources without paying for them"; it's Conversational and pejorative. *To be a sponge* is "to soak up drink or information or whatever there is to be absorbed." The noun is frequently not pejorative in its figurative senses: A bright youngster enthralled with a new subject can be a *sponge* and be admired for it. An idiom with the literal sense of the noun comes from prizefighting: *to throw in* (or *throw up*) *the sponge*—when a second throws into the center of the ring the sponge he's been using on his fighter between rounds, he's signaling that his fighter is beaten: "We quit." *To throw in the towel* is a variant with the same meaning. We use both today in all sorts of activities: they're colorful clichés, Conversational and Informal.

spontaneity (*n.*) Pronounce the third syllable either *-EE-* or *-AI-*.

spoof See SATIRE.

spook (*n., v.*) The noun, meaning "ghost," is slang; meaning "secret agent," it's slang or perhaps Conversational jargon. But *spook* is also an offensive slang term meaning "a black person," and that sense is taboo in Standard use. Make sure that context does not inadvertently suggest it. The verb is both transitive and intransitive and means "haunt," "scare," or "upset": *The weird music really spooked me. When the coyote howled, the cattle spooked and stampeded.* Both uses are Informal or Conversational at best.

SPOONERISMS, named after the Reverend William A. Spooner (1844–1930), an English clergyman who uttered them frequently and apparently involuntarily, are the amusing result of the transpositions of sounds in a pair of words or phrases: *I fool a little feelish.* More commonly *spoonerisms* involve transposed initial sounds: one of Spooner's most famous is said to have been *The Lord is a shoving leopard.* These verbal pratfalls are one kind of metathesis, and some of the most famous may be deliberate wit rather than inadvertent slips.

spoonful (*n.*) The plural *spoonsful* is Standard, as is *spoonfuls,* which occurs much more frequently. See -FUL.

sport (*adj., n., v.*), **sporting** (*adj.*), **sports** (*adj., n.*) Americans use both *sport* and *sports* as the first elements in idiomatic compounds, sometimes *sport* (*sport shirt, sport coat*), sometimes *sports* (*sports palace, sports reporter*), sometimes either (*sport car, sports car*). *Sporting* has a different set of meanings as adjective: *a sport-*

ing chance and related uses have to do with reasonable betting odds: a very long shot is not much of *a sporting chance,* but a reasonable gamble is. The British use *sporting* as a description of fair play or good competition or their lack, as in *His play was rough and not really sporting,* and some Americans use it in that sense too, Conversationally. Another meaning of *sporting* is probably archaic: *sporting house* is an old American euphemism for *whorehouse.* The noun *sport* in *Be a good sport* is idiomatic, and the phrase means "Enter in; play the game" and "Don't get angry when you lose."

As a verb *sport* is an overused journalese term meaning "to boast, to display, to flaunt": *The gambler sported a huge diamond tiepin.* And the chap who *sports* such a pin is probably also a *sport,* "someone game for any excitement, particularly excitement that involves gambling and women." That rather old-fashioned sense is different from still another Standard noun sense used especially in biology: "an individual showing a difference from type, usually as a result of mutation," as in *An albino robin must be some sort of sport.*

spouse (*n.*) Like *sibling, spouse* is inclusive language, an economical way to refer to either *husband* or *wife* without having to use both words, but it also has a slightly bookish air about it that may sometimes limit its use in Informal language. Indeed, the jocular Nonstandard plural *spice* (on analogy with *mouse/ mice*) is frequently heard in Conversational levels. The regular plural is *spouses,* pronounced *SPOU-siz,* not *SPOU-ziz.*

sprain See STRAIN.

spring, spring for (*vv.*) The past tense of this strong verb is either *sprang* or *sprung*; the past participle is *sprung. To spring for* is a Casual idiom, meaning "to pay for, to treat someone to," as in *He said he'd spring for lunch for all of us.*

sprite, spright (*n.*), **sprightly** (*adj.*) The elf or brownie is usually spelled *sprite,* with *spright* a rare and probably archaic variant, but the adjective is almost always spelled *sprightly,* not *spritely,* which some dictionaries consider an archaic spelling.

spurious See ARTIFICIAL.

SQUARE BRACKETS See BRACKETS.

square one (*n.*) If you're *back to* (or *back at*) *square one,* you're "back at the beginning"; you must start over. The idiom comes from board games wherein a penalty takes you back to the first numbered square. It's rather similar

to the rueful *back to the drawing board,* delivered when a design or venture has failed.

squoze is a Nonstandard dialectal form of the weak verb *squeeze,* used jocularly in Casual contexts in place of the Standard past tense or past participle form, *squeezed.* Analogy with the past tense of *freeze, froze,* probably accounts for it.

stadium (*n.*) has two plurals: the regular English *stadiums* and the Latin plural, *stadia. Stadiums* has a far higher frequency in American English, but if the ruins should be Greek or Roman, archaeologists and experienced tourists alike may well call them *stadia.* See FOREIGN PLURALS.

staff (*adj., n., v.*), **staffer** (*n.*) The usual noun plural is *staffs,* but the plural *staves* (rhymes with *graves*) occurs, particularly when the referents are the wooden pieces making up the sides of a barrel (although *barrel staves* also have a singular, *stave*) or the lines and spaces on which musical notation is written. Of the several senses of the noun *staff,* which include the pole on which you lean while hiking or the one from which you fly a flag, the most interesting and complex in usage are the senses and functions surrounding *staff* meaning "assistants, helpers, or subordinate specialists." It may originally have been a euphemism used to avoid the demeaning name of *servant,* even if the *staff member* still gets leaned on. In commerce, industry, and the military, there is an important distinction between *line officers,* who have operational responsibility, and *staff officers,* who serve *line officers* and may have considerable authority but technically no responsibility; they are typically "assistants to," advisory rather than having operational titles of their own. In this sense, *staff,* as in *She's just a staff officer,* may have a mildly pejorative quality.

Formally, *staff* in this sense can be either singular or plural: *The general's staff agree* [*agrees*] *on the new strategy.* Or, in a complex organization, you might talk about *the headquarters staffs,* meaning two or more such groups at headquarters. Functionally, *staff* can also be a verb, meaning "to provide with staff," as in *Hire more cooks, until you have staffed the kitchen fully.* And in sentences such as *Smith isn't line; he's staff,* the word may be a predicate adjective.

Normally you shouldn't use *staff* to stand for a single individual: someone is *a staff member,* not *a staff.* But reports of its occurring informally suggest that there is a need for a singular noun in this sense, and so we have *staffer.* This journalese term has wide use, and some dictionaries already give the term Standard status. Nevertheless, some conservatives insist that it is Informal at best, and you should be aware that a good many people would prefer the more Formal *staff member* or *staff person.*

stage (*v.*) Some readers dislike this term when used for other than the theater, but modern journalism finds it handy to describe heavily contrived photo opportunities and other carefully orchestrated appearances of public figures, and the transferred sense of the theatrical verb seems so apt that it has become Standard in this more generalized use.

stalactite, stalagmite (*nn.*) *Stalactites* hang down from a cave's ceiling; *stalagmites* build up from its floor. Mnemonic device: there's a *c* in *ceiling,* a *g* in *ground.*

stall (*n., v.*), meaning "to delay or put off by trick or evasion," comes from the obsolete *stale,* "a lure or one who lures." Hence *to stall for time* is "to delay by deceiving, by means of a trick." The noun in this sense is "a trick, a dodge, a delaying by deception." All such uses are Standard, as is the combined form *to stall off.*

stamen, stamina (*nn.*) The regular -*s* plural for *stamen,* "the pollen-producing part of a flower," is *stamens. Stamina,* the Latin plural of *stamen,* meaning "a thread in the warp of human life spun by the Fates," is a singular English noun, meaning "endurance." Both words are Standard, from the same etymon. See FOREIGN PLURALS.

stamp See STOMP.

stanch, staunch (*adj., v.*) Both the verb, meaning "to stop the flow of blood or another liquid," and the adjective, meaning "watertight, leakproof, sound" and, figuratively, "steadfast, strong," come from the same medieval French root, the verb *estancer* (or *estanchier*). Our English verb is usually spelled *stanch,* but *staunch* also appears frequently in Edited English; the adjective is nearly always spelled *staunch,* although *stanch* does occur. *Stanch* may be pronounced *STAHNCH, STAWNCH,* or (especially as a verb) *STANCH. Staunch* usually is said either *STAWNCH* or *STAHNCH.*

STANDARD, COMMON, AND VULGAR ENGLISH

Students of language—grammarians, dialectologists, and sociolinguists in particular—have frequently divided the users of American English into three rough categories on the basis of some combination of three factors: formal education, occupation, and economic and social position or power. Then, surveying the language practices of those in each of three groups so delineated, they have proposed that the language characteristic of the topmost group—those with the most formal education (college graduates, in most instances), whose occupations are in the professions and the top range of Bureau of Labor Statistics classifications, and who have the largest share of economic and social power (as measured perhaps by income or other relatively objective criteria)—should be considered *Standard English.* At the other extreme, those with minimal formal education (grade school at best, say), who do only unskilled work, and who have the lowest economic and social positions, must be speakers of what can properly be called *Vulgar English*—the language of the people, of the masses. Finally, the middle group comprises all that large number of Americans who fall into the educational, occupational, and economic and social categories in between the other two. The language of this group can be said to be *Common English,* sharing many characteristics of *Standard,* but not quite up to it in some respects, yet clearly not displaying the peculiar hallmarks of *Vulgar.* Taken together, the labels Standard English, Common English, and Vulgar English, when attached to usages of all sorts, permit us systematically to discuss and classify the details of linguistic variation. However, as Charles C. Fries remarked long ago (1940, 288), the most characteristic differences between *Vulgar English* and *Standard English* stem from the poverty-stricken character of the first. It typically avails itself of far fewer of the wide resources of the English language, its grammar, and its vocabulary than does Standard English. Rather than any list of the shibboleths of usage, the real hallmark of *Vulgar English* is its poverty of expression. See also SOCIAL DIALECT.

Distribution of Language Characteristics Among Standard, Common, and Vulgar English

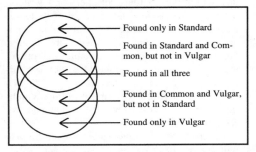

Found only in Standard

Found in Standard and Common, but not in Vulgar

Found in all three

Found in Common and Vulgar, but not in Standard

Found only in Vulgar

STANDARD ENGLISH, STANDARD

Every commentator on usage eventually comes

back to these two terms and to what is or is not *Standard,* even though, despite its many objectively measurable qualities, any definition of *Standard English* is partly subjective. Ideally, *Standard English* is the language acceptable and normative among reputable people in reputable circumstances—the prestige dialect recognized throughout the area and populations to whom the standard applies. One can argue, for example, that there are indeed grammatical constructions and senses of words that are universally accepted wherever and by whomever English is spoken. One can then say that they are *Standard English,* in that everybody who is anybody uses, accepts, and approves them. Certainly few who meet that standard will accept deviations from it by others who claim to be their social equals. And when *Standard* speakers converse, most will deliberately use locutions proscribed by *Standard English* only if they are absolutely certain that their listeners will know they know better; if there is any chance that anyone will think the usage inadvertent, few will take the risk just to get a laugh.

But obviously Standard American, Standard British, Standard Australian, and Standard Canadian English differ from each other in many particulars. And in some particulars, Boston Standard differs from that of New Orleans. This is clear to anyone who travels, goes to the movies, or listens to radio or television. It is also clear that there are differences *within* each of these regional dialects, and that the acceptability of one feature or another also may vary, depending upon who is calling the shots.

One definition of *Standard English* is that it is the language used by all the speakers of all the cultivated regional dialects of English, the one they all have in common. It permits them to communicate among themselves on all subjects. In its written forms, especially its edited, printed form, it is conservative in that it preserves as much as it can of the lexicon and the grammar that will serve all these speakers and writers, listeners and readers, and, because of its familiar ring and appearance, win immediate comprehension and approval of what are, finally, familiar and therefore comfortable and proper manners. Good language manners, you see, filter out most of the intrusive social "noise" in a communication, thus insuring it optimal conditions for its success. This is the language we seek as *Standard.*

Descriptions of *Standard American English* will always differ on details, on the acceptability of particular constructions, and on the meaning or propriety of particular locutions. The main causes for such differences are differences in judges. Are they old or young, conservative or liberal in their view of manners, current in their information? The greatest changes in a language and in what its users consider *Standard* are made over extended periods of time. It may take a century for some locutions to move from Nonstandard to *Standard* or from *Standard* to Substandard; for others—especially changes in the meaning of a word or in the acceptance or disappearance of a slang term—just a short time may be enough. (The once-dialectal and Common English past tense form *snuck* took only about thirty years to become *Standard* in divided usage along with the long-time favorite *sneaked.* But the double negative has been *Substandard* for at least two centuries now—after many earlier centuries of being quite acceptable—and shows no signs of becoming *Standard,* as its confident jocular use by *Standard* speakers demonstrates.) See also SUBSTANDARD.

STANDARD USAGE describes an acceptable locution or a pattern of acceptable locutions employed by a reputable linguistic community under a full range of circumstances. Language practices that fail to meet the community's standards usually bring disapproval, moderate if the questioned locution is tolerable, and vigorous if it is thought to be Substandard, Nonstandard, or taboo. See also LEVELS OF USAGE and the several categories of usage described in those entries. See also STANDARD; STANDARD ENGLISH.

standee See -EE.

stand for office This is the British equivalent of American English's *run for office,* meaning "to be a political candidate and seek election to office."

standpoint, point of view, viewpoint (*nn.*) When *standpoint* was a new word (early in the nineteenth century), nearly every commentator objected to it; whatever the stated reasons, the real objection was that it was new. Today *standpoint* is Standard English, as are *point of view* and *viewpoint.* See also ANGLE (1).

stanza (*n.*) In poetry, a *stanza* is a physically separate group of several lines of verse (which see), usually in a metrically regular pattern that is repeated in subsequent *stanzas.* In free verse and other nonmetrical poetry, a *stanza* is usually any paragraphlike division (sometimes called a *verse paragraph*) containing a group of lines. A transferred sense of *stanza* as a measure of time (it might well be called an attempt at elegant variation) is the sportswriters' jargon and cliché use of it as a synonym for *period, quarter, chukker, inning,* and the like.

start (*v.*) This weak verb can be combined with either a gerund or *to* plus an infinitive: *He started speaking* and *He started to speak* mean the same.

stash (*n., v.*) As a verb *stash* has long meant "to hide away, to conceal": *He stashed the jewels at the back of his closet.* Functional shift now provides us with a noun *stash,* meaning both "the thing hidden" and "the hiding place." All are Standard.

stat (*adv., n.*) *Stat* (plural: *stats*) is a clipped form of *statistic(s)*; both singular and plural are slang, typically in use in sports journalism and in talk about sports: *His batting average is .300, but his other stats aren't impressive.* The adverb is hospital jargon from the Latin *statim,* meaning "at once, immediately."

state (*v.*) *State* is a more Formal, more precise synonym of the common verb *say: State your name. He stated his position.*

STATEMENT A *statement* is a sentence type, sometimes also called a declarative sentence when classified rhetorically. *He has gone home* is a *statement.* See SENTENCE TYPES.

state of the art (*n.*), **state-of-the-art** (*adj.*) The hyphenated spelling is the adjective; without hyphens it's the noun. A technical term originally, like *on the cutting edge* this locution has come to be applied to everything from engineering to cheerleading. It means simply "up-to-date, in the forefront of originality and design." These days it's a cliché. See also AVANT-GARDE.

station See DEPOT.

stationary (*adj.*), **stationery** (*n.*) Americans pronounce these alike, with four syllables and a secondary stress on the third syllable: *STAI-shuhn-ER-ee.* The British usually give each word only three syllables, the third being unstressed: *STAI-shuhn-ree.* See STRESS.

The usage problem results from these homophones' different meanings and spellings: *stationary* is an adjective meaning "standing still, not moving"; *stationery* is a noun meaning "writing paper." The mnemonic device some people use to help them choose the right spelling is this: a *stationer* sells writing paper, and both the paper and the seller are spelled with an *e*; the other word is spelled with an *a*.

statistics, statistic (*nn.*) *Statistic* is a singular back-formation from *statistics,* which itself can be either singular or plural: *Statistics is a hard subject, but these statistics are really worth ex-* *amining.* Both forms, and both numbers for *statistics,* are Standard. See -IC; -ICS.

status (*n.*) Americans pronounce the first syllable to rhyme with either *state* or *hat*; many use both pronunciations (it is quite normal to discuss *STAIT-uhs LAI-bulz* but also to refer to someone's *immigration STAT-uhs*). The British and a good many Americans prefer on all occasions to rhyme the first syllable with *late.*

STATUS LABELS are terms such as *Standard, Nonstandard, Substandard, Common, Vulgar, slang, argot, cant, Colloquial, dialectal, Intimate, Casual, Impromptu, Planned, Oratorical, Formal, Informal, Semiformal, archaic, obsolescent,* and *obsolete* (all of which see), used in dictionaries and guides to usage to indicate to readers under what circumstances they are most likely to encounter a given word and hence where (if at all) they might properly employ it and what limitations there are to its use. That a dictionary entry (or an entry in this guide) carries no *status labels* means that editors consider that word Standard and likely to be appropriate in any and all written and spoken contexts. But if, for example, a word is labeled *Colloquial,* you know that its use should be limited to conversation or to written situations imitative of conversation.

staunch See STANCH.

stave (*v.*) The past tense and past participle can be either *staved* (*We staved off disaster*) or *stove* (*The collision stove in our bow*). In most uses other than the nautical, the past form *stove* may sound a trifle old-fashioned today.

stay, stop, stop by (*vv.*) Some British try to distinguish between *staying* (overnight) with friends, and *stopping* (briefly) to lunch with them. Americans use the terms interchangeably but use *stay* in both senses far more frequently than they use *stop* in either. For Americans, *to stop for lunch* includes a slightly different, more literal cessation of motion or interruption of activity: at the wheel of the speeding car, the American driver might ask her companion, *"Shall we stop for lunch?"* If the answer is yes, they'll *stop* at a restaurant. If, as you rise and prepare to leave his house, your English host says, *"But surely you'll stop for lunch?"* you are to understand that you are being asked *to stay for lunch.* *To stop by* means "to pay a short informal call on someone or go to a specific place": *Please stop by* [*at*] *the cleaner's to see if my suit is ready.* Americans also regularly use *stop by* and *stop in* when issuing invitations to visit.

steal (*v.*) The past tense is *stole,* the past participle *stolen. Stole* as past participle is Substandard and a shibboleth. See BURGLARIZE; ROB.

stem (*v.*) You can *stem a tide,* that is, "oppose it or hold it in check," by heading the *stem* (the front of your boat) into it and so making progress against the tide. And ideas can *stem from another source,* wherein the figurative sense comes from the literal *stemming* or formation of *stems* in plants.

stem to stern *From stem to stern* means "from the extreme front to the extreme rear of a boat or ship" and so by extension means "completely."

stench See ODOR.

stepmother, stepchild, stepfather (*nn.*) These and other *step*-prefixed words are usually not hyphenated today, but readers will encounter the hyphenated forms in nineteenth- and early-twentieth-century Edited English. See also HYPHEN; PREFIXES; SPELLING OF COMPOUND WORDS.

STEREOTYPE is a term from printing, the "one-piece metal casting of a sheet of printed matter." Its figurative sense is "a fixed and unvarying pattern, with neither change nor individual variation possible," and from that we get a further figurative development, usually pejorative: "unoriginal, hackneyed, repetitive—a cliché."

stewardess See -ESS; FEMININE OCCUPATIONAL FORMS; INCLUSIVE LANGUAGE; SEXIST LANGUAGE.

stick (*v.*) The principal parts are *stick, stuck, stuck.*

stigma (*n.*) has two plurals: the borrowed Greek *stigmata* and the regular English *stigmas.* Americans pronounce *stigmas* STIG-muhz, but we have three pronunciations for *stigmata:* STIG-muh-tuh, stig-MAH-tuh, and stig-MAT-uh; the British also have stig-MAIT-uh. Where a semantic distinction is maintained between the two plurals, *stigmata* is sometimes used for real marks or scars, visible to the eye, whereas *stigmas* may be invisible figurative marks. But these are not very powerful generalizations. *Stigmata* sounds more Formal to most audiences, and some Christians use it only in referring to Jesus's wounds. See FOREIGN PLURALS.

stiletto (*n.*) The plural is spelled either *stilettos* or *stilettoes;* see PLURALS OF NOUNS ENDING IN *-O.*

still and all is a cliché with a Conversational ring, and some conservatives argue that because less is often more, *still* by itself will better convey your meaning. But if you want to suggest the relaxed sound of conversation, there's nothing wrong with *still and all.*

still life (*n.*) When there is more than one picture of lifeless objects, the plural of this compound noun is *still lifes* (rhymes with *fifes*).

stimulant, stimulus (*nn.*) A *stimulant* is any chemical that increases the activity of an organ, plant, animal, or person to whom it is administered; *stimulus* is a more general term: *This new drug is a stimulant and may cause insomnia. Fear can be a stimulus to flight.* The Standard distinction is worth keeping, even though interchangeable use of these two is unfortunately increasing.

sting 1 (*n.*) This slang word began as criminal argot, meaning "a confidence game, a deception designed to cheat those taken in by it," but as it has come into more general slang use (thanks in part to the motion picture *The Sting*), it has developed a specialized sense meaning "a police scheme for entrapping a criminal." In this use the journalese idiom is often *a sting operation.*

sting 2 (*v.*) Both past tense and past participle of this strong verb are *stung.*

stink (*v.*) *Stank* and *stunk* are both Standard past tense forms: *The cellar stank of rot and mildew. I thought her singing stunk.* Some users prefer *stank* and avoid *stunk* as past tense in Oratorical and Formal contexts. The past participle is only *stunk: The rotting fruit had stunk for several days.* See ODOR.

stock (*n.*), **to put stock in, to take stock in, to take stock of** *To take* (or *put*) *stock in something* is an American idiom meaning "to believe in, to accept (perhaps to the point of investing in) it." *I put* (or *take*) *no stock in what you say* means "I don't believe you." *To take stock of something* is "to survey it carefully, to count the pieces, as in taking inventory of the stock on the shelves." *We must take stock of our situation* means "We must carefully examine and consider it." See also SHARE (2).

stocking, sock (*nn.*) *Stocking* is the generic name for the knitted covering for foot and leg (*a pair of stockings*). Nowadays, women sometimes wear them (when they aren't wearing *panty hose*); *silk-stocking(ed) candidate* seems no longer to be used to label wealthy amateur men running for American political office. Today both sexes wear *socks,* foot coverings that reach perhaps as high as the knees, both sometimes walk about at home *in their stocking feet,* and both may wear knitted *stocking caps* on occasion.

stoic (*adj., n.*), **stoical** (*adj.*) *Stoic* is both noun and adjective; *stoical* is also an adjective: *He is a stoic about pain. He is stoic about pain. He is stoical about pain.* Each is Standard.

stomp, stamp (*vv.*) *To stamp* may be a trifle less heavy than *to stomp:* dainty princesses *stamp* their feet when angry; professional wrestlers appear to *stomp* (*on*) their opponents. *Stomp* began as a dialectal form of *stamp,* meaning "to put the foot down hard." It now is Standard in most senses, and it has developed one specialized sense that is not interchangeable with any sense of *stamp:* "to trample or destroy by trampling," as in *The elephants stomped their keeper to death.* Some purists argue that such uses are Informal at best, and they also object to the use of *stomp* in expressions with *foot* or *feet,* presumably for fear of redundancy.

stone See ROCK; SEED (2).

stoned (*adj.*) This slang sense of the verb *stone* is a participial adjective that for many years has meant "drunk." Today we encounter it more frequently as a description of being under the influence of other drugs: *He was stoned on crack.*

stonewall (*v.*) The intransitive verb began in British cricket, meaning to play a purely defensive game; it then figuratively described certain British parliamentary tactics used to delay or prevent a vote. Americans have a more generalized sense, meaning "to refuse to cooperate," as in *He stonewalled, refusing even to give his name.* The transitive verb, mainly American, means "to refuse to respond to or cooperate with," as in *He stonewalled the Senate committee for several days.* All the American senses are Conversational, Informal, and journalese.

stood is sometimes heard as a Vulgar past tense or past participle of the verb *stay,* as in the famous *I shoulda stood in bed.*

stop, stop by See STAY.

store See SHOP (2).

story, storey (*nn.*) *Story,* with a plural *stories,* is both American English and British English for a "narrative," and it is also the American English word for "the floor of a building": *She lives in an apartment on the fourth story. She tells her grandchildren wonderful stories.* British English spells the floor level *storey,* with a plural *storeys.* A further difference: Americans call the ground-level floor of a building the *first floor,* but the British call it the *ground floor* and

call the floor above that (Americans' *second story*) the *first storey.*

straight (*adj., adv.*), **strait** (*adj., n.*) These homophones are spelled differently. *Straight* means "without curves, unbending"; *strait* means "narrow, constricted" and is archaic in most uses except the functional shift to a noun meaning "a narrow passage or channel between two larger bodies of water." The biblical gate is *strait,* and unswerving lines are *straight:* hence the cliché should be *straight and narrow,* not (as you frequently see) *strait and narrow,* which would be redundant.

Straight has figurative meanings as adjective: It means "virtuous, honest, conventional," as in *He's straight as can be: doesn't drink, smoke, or swear*; it also means "undiluted," as in *I'll take my whiskey straight* or *I'll have a straight whiskey.* As adverb it means "honestly, virtuously"(*She's given up stealing and has gone straight for more than a year*) or "truthfully, candidly, unadorned" (*She gave us the bad news straight [up]*). *Straight* is also current slang for "heterosexual." This last sense is Conversational and Semiformal or Informal.

straightened, straitened (*adjs.*) Of these homophones *straightened* means "with all curves removed": *The bulldozers left only straightened contours. Straitened* means "narrowed, constricted" and hence "deprived, ill-provided," and it occurs frequently in the cliché *in straitened circumstances.* Both are Standard, although *straitened* is a relatively low frequency word.

straightjacket, straightlaced See STRAIT-JACKET.

strain, sprain (*nn.*) The distinction between these names for damage to ankles, knees, wrists, shoulders, backs, and other parts of (especially) the human frame is that a *strain* stretches, twists, or otherwise overstresses nerve fibers, tendons, and muscles without doing serious damage; a *sprain* is more serious, a rupture or tear of a ligament that may take some time to repair itself, often with swelling and temporary loss of use. Each can be painful, but a *sprain* is likely to be worse.

strait See STRAIGHT.

straitened See STRAIGHTENED.

straitjacket, straightjacket (*nn.*), **straitlaced, straightlaced** (*adjs.*) Each of these words is properly spelled when *strait-* is the first element of the compound (see STRAIGHT). To be *straitlaced* is literally to be "tightly laced into a corset, bodice, or other garment" and figuratively (the main current meaning) to be "unbending, unyielding, and rigid, especially in manners and morals." And a *straitjacket* is so named because it prevents any movement of the arms. But folk etymologies appear to have justified the misspellings that begin with *straight-*, and conservative and liberal dictionaries alike today approve both spellings for each word, although the original spellings with *strait-* are more frequent, especially in Edited English.

strangle (*v.*) *Strangle* is both transitive and intransitive, meaning "to kill someone by strangling" and "to die by strangulation." Like drowning, *strangling* cannot be done part way, although the *strangled to death* redundancy occurs frequently in Common and other Nonstandard English, where *strangle* is apparently thought to be synonymous with *choke*. (A person may *choke* but not die or may *choke* to death; death must be specified.) Standard use of *strangle*, however, needs no such specification; death is almost always included, whether *A strangles B*, *B is strangled*, or *B strangles [to death]*.

strata, stratas See STRATUM.

strategy, tactics (*nn.*) *Strategy* is "the long-term plan for the war or the campaign," and *tactics* (either singular or plural) are "the day-to-day schemes for the battle or the skirmish." Adapted to figurative nonmilitary uses, both words generalize: the "big picture/little picture" distinction tends to fade, and common usage makes both words tend to mean "plans for action." But the distinction can be useful and, for audiences who can take it in, are well worth maintaining.

stratum (*n.*) The first syllable is always stressed, and Standard English rhymes it with *hate, hat,* or *hot*. The plural *strata* (like *data*) has come to be used as both singular and plural: *This strata is* . . . occurs more and more often in English, with the result that now we have a new variant English plural based on it: *stratas*. At the same time, however, the regular English pattern has exerted its pressures on the old Latin singular, *stratum,* to give us *stratums* as still another variant plural. Conservative practice and Edited English still prefer *stratum* as the singular and *strata* as the plural, but *strata* as both singular and plural is gaining respectability, and *stratas* and *stratums* are more and more frequently heard (and occasionally seen). See FOREIGN PLURALS.

stream, beck, brae, branch, brook, creek, crick, rill, rivulet, run (*nn.*), **-kill** (*suffix*) All these words (and others too) are names for small courses of flowing fresh water, although a *creek* can also be tidal. *Stream* is the generic and most widely used term. *Branch* and *run* are Midland and Southern, respectively; *brook* is Coastal Northeastern, *beck* and *brae* are mainly British and Scottish, *creek* and *crick* are Northern and North Midland regional variants of the same word, and *-kill* is a Hudson River Valley form, an affix of Dutch origin now found only in place names such as Peekskill and Catskill. *Rill* has a somewhat literary quality today; it is a very small *brook* or *stream*. A *rivulet* is similar but perhaps even smaller—a mere trickle.

strength, length (*nn.*) These two words present the same pronunciation problem: a fair number of Americans say them as though they were spelled *strenth* and *lenth*. Most other Americans think these are "funny" pronunciations; to some they are shibboleths, even though they are not region- or class-distinctive. Note also that the medial consonant cluster of each Standard pronunciation contains a *k* sound: *STRENGKTH, LENGKTH*.

STRESS is the relative loudness or emphasis placed on a sound or a syllable in speech. In the phrase *a new raincoat* we can hear four levels of *stress:* most heavily stressed is *rain-*, less heavily stressed is *new*, still less heavily stressed is *-coat*, and least stressed, or relatively unstressed, is *a*. If the emphasis is on *new* (in contrast to *old*), rather than on *raincoat,* the heaviest *stress* moves to *new*, next heaviest to *rain*, and so on. And depending on the meaning intended, each of the other two elements could in turn get the heavy *stress*, with the other stresses changing accordingly.

The usual names of these levels of *stress* are *primary, secondary, tertiary,* and *unstressed*. In two-syllable words we will hear two levels of *stress,* but we can still discriminate at least three levels of *stress* in a pair such as *raincoat* and *rainy*. In both words, *rain-* has the heavy or primary *stress*; *-coat* and *-y* differ, however, with *-coat* more heavily stressed than is *-y*— they are tertiary and unstressed, respectively, and the primary plus tertiary pattern indicates that *raincoat* is a compound.

Dictionaries indicate *stresses* in their pronunciations by various diacritical marks placed before or after the *stressed* syllable or over its vowel. The marks vary in order to distinguish among primary, secondary, and tertiary *stresses*. Gross errors in *stress* in polysyllabic words often serve as shibboleths.

STRESS IN COMPOUND WORDS AND PHRASES See COMPOUNDS.

strew (*v.*) This formerly strong verb has adopted the weak verb pattern for forming its second and third principal parts—past tense and past participle are both *strewed*—but it also retains the strong past participle, *strewn*, in Standard divided usage: *Wreckage was strewn [strewed] all along the beach.*

stricken See STRIKE.

stride (*v.*) The past tense is *strode*, and the past participle *stridden*, but *stridden* is so seldom encountered that people are uncomfortable enough with it to try in Conversation *strode* or the weak form *strided* instead. At present it's possible that if *stridden* is to be replaced in Standard English it might unexpectedly be with *strode*, not *strided*.

strike (*v.*) *Struck* is both past tense and one of two Standard past participle forms; *stricken* is the other past participle, much used as a participial adjective: *panic-stricken*. There is a semantic distinction between the two participles: in transitive use only *struck* is literally "hit" (*She had struck him on the cheek*); *stricken* is mostly figurative, sometimes meaning "infected, afflicted" (*Typhoid had stricken [struck] the entire village*), sometimes "crossed out, deleted" (*The agent had stricken her name from the passenger list*). The participial adjective is also much used to mean "wounded" or "hurt," as in *Her stricken look spoke volumes.*

string (*v.*) The verb has among its meanings "to provide with string(s)," as in *He strings tennis racquets for a living.* Its past tense and past participle are both *strung*, as in *She strung [or had strung] her flowers on a chain.* There is also another participial adjective form, *stringed*, applied only to guitars, violins, and other *stringed instruments* (*string instruments* is Conversational and Informal only).

strive (*v.*) means "to try very hard," and it usually has a rather Formal, bookish air when compared with *try*. It is a strong verb, its principal parts being *strive, strove* or *strived*, and *striven* or *strived*. The weak form *strived*, as past tense and past participle, is in divided usage with the strong forms but is somewhat less frequently encountered. *Strive* occurs regularly with *to* plus the infinitive: *I'll strive to please her.* It also occurs with many other prepositions and by itself: *We'll strive for total victory. We've striven [strived] against terrible odds.*

stroke (*v.*), **stroking** (*gerund*) The Standard meaning, "to caress," has specialized into what began as slang and is now an Informal and Conversational sense meaning "to flatter and deceive by flattery so as to persuade": *We stroked the mayor until he agreed to go along.* This sense is heavily used in politics and business and in the journalism that describes them. The gerund is also very widely used in the same Informal and Conversational sense: *This customer needs a lot of stroking, but he always comes around.*

STRONG VERBS 1 are those that form their past tense and past participle by a change of vowel, as does *swim* (*swam, swum*), or a combination of change of vowel and other changes such as *fly* (*flew, flown*). See also STRONG VERBS (2); WEAK VERBS.

STRONG VERBS 2, WEAK VERBS, THE ORIGIN AND MEANING OF THE TERMS Jacob Grimm (1785–1863), one of the two fairy-tale–collecting brothers from Germany who were also famous grammarians, chose the names *strong verbs* and *weak verbs* for the two dominant patterns of verbs in the Germanic languages. Those he called *strong* made their past tenses and past participles mainly by changing medial vowels, as do English *begin, began, begun* and *drive, drove, driven.* His *weak* verbs made their tense changes by adding various forms of the *dental suffix*, as in English *study, studied, studied* and *bake, baked, baked.* The irony of the terminology is that *strong* verbs, more numerous during the Old English period, have been a slowly dwindling group in English over the centuries, while the *weak* verbs have become the dominant pattern in English. Many verbs that were formerly *strong* now use the *weak* pattern, and many more, such as *weave, wove, woven*, are in the middle of change from *strong* to *weak*, currently displaying *weak* forms in divided usage with *strong* ones (*weave, weaved, weaved*). When we borrow or coin new verbs, we almost always put them in the *weak* pattern (we have recently made a new verb, *to fax*, and we did it on the *weak* pattern—*fax, faxed, faxed*—not with a vowel change for past tense and past participle), and today we have to learn the past and past participle forms of the *strong* verbs almost word by word (note how very young children first learn the dominant *weak* pattern for the past tense and say *swimmed;* only later do they correct to the strong *swam*). See also STRONG VERBS (1); WEAK VERBS.

strove See STRIVE.

struck See STRIKE.

STRUCTURAL GRAMMARS are grammars based on the spoken language. They describe the phonology and morphology of the language, attempting to work with grammatical meaning and to ignore lexical and total meaning. They are weaker on syntax than some other grammars, and they are more likely to stress generalizations rather than rules. See GRAMMAR.

STRUCTURES OF MODIFICATION See MODIFIERS.

strung See STRING.

stuck See STICK.

student See PUPIL.

studio bed, studio couch See SOFA.

stuff (*n.*) *Stuff* is a much-used and much-abused word; its primary Standard sense is "material, the matter of which something is composed." In the compound *foodstuffs*, meaning "food supplies in general," *-stuff* is Standard. It also has a specialized Standard meaning, particularly in Britain, "textile—especially woolen material." But it has a wide range of slang, Conversational, and Informal meanings as well: "personal possessions," as in *I've got to get my stuff sent home*; "nonsense," as in *I don't want to hear any more of that stuff*; and "courage, stamina, strength, and the like," as in the current cliché *the right stuff*, "the stuff of which heroes are made," presumably. This sense may owe something to the word *stuffing,* as in *He had the stuffing knocked out of him,* wherein the referent is the inner resources of strength, stamina, and courage that constitute the *stuff* of which a real man is made. And *stuff* is also a euphemism for unpleasant or disgusting and therefore unmentionable matter of all sorts: *Your puppy has left stuff all over the carpet in the corner.* Finally, we use *stuff* as an inexact term for undifferentiated items or qualities we haven't time or need to specify. Except in conversation and the Informal writing meant to sound like conversation, use this sense of *stuff* sparingly.

stung See STING (2).

stunk See STINK.

stunning (*adj.*) It was once very effective, but it's now a trifle old-fashioned, and overuse has made it a cliché. *A stunning dress* is "so beautiful it deprives the viewer of sense and judgment." *Stunning news,* good or bad, "renders the receiver all but unconscious." At best it's a Conversational and Informal hyperbole except in its literal sense, as in *She stepped on the rake, and the handle gave her a stunning blow in the face.*

sty, stye (*nn.*) *Sty* (plural: *sties* or, rarely, *styes*) is a place to keep pigs; both *sty* and *stye* (plural

is also either *sties* or *styes*) spell the name of a swollen inflammation on an eyelid.

STYLE in language use is "manner," "mode," or "the way it is done." Especially in writing, *style* is a measure of excellence, stressing in part the "fit" between the subject and the way it is being expressed. In publishing, *style* refers to a publisher's rules for punctuation, spelling, capitalization, and the like; such rules are often contained in a *stylebook.*

style See KIND.

stylus (*n.*) The plural is either *styluses* or *styli.* See FOREIGN PLURALS.

suave (*adj.*) The pronunciation sometimes traps the inexperienced: *suave* is a monosyllable, pronounced *SWAHV; SWAIV* is sometimes heard, but it's jocular for Standard users, most of whom would consider its inadvertent use a shibboleth.

sub See SUBMARINE.

subconscious, unconscious (*adjs., nn.*) Each functions as both adjective and noun, but their meanings cause them to be differently distributed. *The subconscious* is an older psychological name for the workings of the mind below the level of consciousness; *the unconscious* is another technical term, from psychoanalysis, meaning "that part of the psyche that cannot be directly observed." *A subconscious desire* is one of which you are not fully aware, but the adjective does not modify nouns referring to persons, either as adjunct or predicate adjective. For the meaning "not conscious" or "below the level of consciousness," the adjective is *unconscious: She was unconscious for several minutes. The unconscious victim of the accident was taken away.*

SUBJECT, GRAMMATICAL English sentences usually (see COMMAND) have a *subject* and a predicate; *subjects* are nouns or other nominals, and in the most typical English sentence pattern, the *subject* will precede the verb and will agree with it in number. In active voice sentences, the *subject* is the doer of the action indicated by the verb: *The boy ran away. The girl saw a fox.* In passive voice sentences, the *subject* is the receiver of the action indicated by the verb: *The fox was seen by the girl.* With linking verbs the subject is the person or thing described: *Mary is a jogger. The water is hot.* See AGREEMENT.

SUBJECTIVE AND OBJECTIVE PRONOUNS are frequently confused, especially in compound use: *Mary and I [not me] went home early. We [not Us] boys were punished. They* *gave the prizes to* **her** [*not she*] *and* **me** [*not I*]. Such confusions are heavily censured when they appear where Standard English is expected. Confusions of *who, whom* (which see) are particularly common; although less likely to be criticized in the lower levels of speech, they are usually unacceptable in Edited English. See also CASE (1); PERSONAL PRONOUNS.

SUBJECTIVE GENITIVE is a kind of *genitive* in which the thing "possessed" is a noun naming an action performed by the word in the *genitive* case: *my father's permission* (he gave it), *Mary's diary* (she wrote it), *Paul's wood carving* (he carved it). Some of these are also called *genitives of origin*.

SUBJECT OF AN INFINITIVE See INFINITIVE (2).

SUBJECT-VERB AGREEMENT See AGREEMENT.

SUBJUNCTIVE See INDICATIVE.

SUBJUNCTIVE MOOD See INDICATIVE; MOOD.

submarine, grinder, hero, hoagie, Italian sandwich, poor boy, sub, torpedo (*nn.*) All these terms are regional variants for the name of a popular sandwich made by splitting a long, torpedo-shaped roll in half lengthwise and filling it with some or all of these: cold cuts, sausage, cheese, lettuce, tomato, pickles, and other condiments. The chief interest here is that there is no apparent generic name for this sandwich—in fact, many major cities have their own names for it. Compare SODA.

submariner (*n.*) There are three Standard pronunciations: *suhb-muh-REEN-uhr*, *SUHB-muh-reen-uhr*, and *suhb-MER-i-nuhr*, roughly in that order of frequency. The last pronunciation may have arisen because some of the general public has apparently been influenced by the pronunciation of *mariners* (*MER-in-uhrz*)—which these sailors are, after all—but the sailors themselves are said to prefer to call attention to the boat, so they tack the agentive *-er* onto the regular pronunciation of the name of the vessel: *suhb-muh-REEN-uhr*.

submit (*v.*) *Submit* doubles the *t* for its present participle (*submitting*) and its past tense and past participle (*submitted*) forms (see CONSONANTS [2]). *Submit to* is usually followed by a gerund (*She will submit to having her hair cut*), but occasionally an infinitive will serve, even though many conservatives don't like it (*He won't submit to go to the dentist*). Edited English prefers the gerund.

subnormal, abnormal, paranormal, supernormal (*adjs., nn.*) *Subnormal* means "below normal, below average, below the expected." *Abnormal* means simply "different from the norm, the average, the expected"; the *abnormal* may be either above or below the normal. *Supernormal* means "above or beyond the normal," although there is also a slang meaning "more normal than normal—matchlessly normal," a dubious bit of hyperbole. *Paranormal* refers to psychic phenomena outside or beyond the normal or natural.

SUBORDINATE CLAUSE See DEPENDENT CLAUSES.

SUBORDINATING CONJUNCTIONS are also called subordinate conjunctions and are an essentially finite list of function words whose common members are *after, although, as, as if, because, before, if, lest, since, so that, than, that, though, till, unless, until,* and *whether,* plus *inasmuch as, in order that,* and (more recently, but in divided usage) *like.* (Some of them are also prepositions or adverbs.) *Subordinating conjunctions* link clauses of unequal grammatical weight in structures wherein a subordinate clause (introduced by a *subordinating conjunction*) modifies an independent clause or some element in it. Another way of describing the purpose of a *subordinating conjunction* is to say that it permits the inclusion of the clause it introduces within a larger clausal structure.

The term *functional connectives* is sometimes used to cover certain interrogative pronouns, relative pronouns, adjectives, and adverbs that do the same work as the *subordinating conjunctions:* they link *subordinate clauses* to or include them within main clauses or parts of them, although they also have another grammatical function to perform within their own dependent clause. In *I know* **whom** *you mean, whom* includes *whom you mean* in the main clause (*I know* plus the direct object), and the *whom* clause is direct object of that main clause. In its own clause, *whom* serves as direct object of the verb *mean.*

The relative and interrogative pronouns are also a finite list: *that, what, whatever, whatsoever, which, whichever, whichsoever, who, whoever, whose, whosoever, whosesoever*; the adverbs (sometimes called *conjunctive adverbs*) are *how, when, whence, where, whither, why.*

subpoena, subpena (*n., v.*) Even though modern American English has dropped most of the old *oe* and *ae* digraphs (as in the old spellings of *oeconomics* and *mediaeval*), *subpena* is not yet widely used, and Edited English still usually prefers *subpoena*. See SPELLING (1).

subsequent (*adj.*), **subsequently** (*adv.*), **subsequent to** (*prep.*) Most of the time, simpler words such as *later, later on, following, after, next,* and the like, will do very nicely and will seem less formal and self-important: *His subsequent actions betrayed him. They were subsequently seen in Rome.* Occasionally the similarities in strings of actions may add a certain semantic refinement to *a subsequent occurrence,* a sense suggesting a relationship more than just sequence in time—perhaps "an occurrence of the same sort." But seldom will these words carry that meaning without adding formality and possibly some stuffiness too. In general, save *subsequent* and its friends, if you must use them, for formal documents.

subsist, exist (*vv.*) *To exist* is the general verb, meaning "to be in being": *People, ideas, and conditions exist. To subsist* is more specialized, usually meaning "to find enough nourishment to keep alive": *In graduate school we subsisted on peanut butter.*

substance abuse, controlled substance The curious compound noun *substance abuse* is a euphemism (as is the phrase *controlled substance* on which it is based); it is also jargon, and possibly an ambiguity too. The *controlled substances* are drugs, alcohol, or tobacco, materials that can be purchased only with prescription or with proof that you are of legal age to have access to them. On analogy with *child abuse, substance abuse* means that someone is abusing the substance. But the sense of *abuse* is somewhat different in each case: the child sustains harm or injury, but the drug does not; rather, it is **misused**. *Substance abuse* is now Standard idiom, but it illustrates how illogical and obfuscatory our euphemisms can sometimes be. *Use of illegal drugs* or *misuse of controlled substances* would be clearer, and *substance misuse* would be more accurate, but for now *substance abuse* is Standard.

SUBSTANDARD, NONSTANDARD In this book Substandard usage refers to a pronunciation, spelling, word, meaning, grammatical structure, or other locution that the Standard-using language community deems typical of other than Standard English; the usage may seem typical rather of Common or even Vulgar English. Substandard means "absolutely unacceptable and inappropriate at any level of Standard English," and Nonstandard means something less absolute, perhaps that the locution may be acceptable regionally but not nationally or that it's simply not so egregious a blunder as a Substandard locution is. Substandard usages are frequently shibboleths; Nonstandard usages are usually not so damning. See also STANDARD ENGLISH.

substantial, substantive (*adjs.*) These two words both mean "having substance, real, firm, solidly constructed." But *substantial* also means "ample, enough to sustain," and "prosperous, wealthy, and considerable in importance," and *substantive* also means "independent, not subordinate," "directly bearing on the matter," and "essential, actual."

SUBSTANTIVE (*n.*) is another name for a noun or another nominal.

substitute (*v.*) Everyone agrees that *to substitute* means "to put or act or use in place of" when used with *for: We substituted skim for whole milk. She substituted for the regular teacher. Sometimes imagination can substitute for money.* But some people strongly object to the use of *substitute with* or *by* to mean "to replace, to take the place of," as in *We substituted Reynolds with Cummings at tackle.* The question is, who went in for whom? Some would argue that Reynolds came out and that Cummings replaced him. Others would insist that only Reynolds *for* Cummings is unambiguous, and that *with* or *by* creates an ambiguity. Even so, the use of *substitute* with these prepositions meaning "to replace" has long been frequent in American English, although many Standard users avoid it, and Edited English usually insists on using *substitute for.* The curious fact is that although this sense has been in use for three centuries, it still has not achieved full and unquestioned status as Standard in the eyes and ears of some lexicographers, perhaps in part because commentators have fussed so about it. The *Oxford English Dictionary* (1989) says flatly that *substitute* is used incorrectly to mean "replace," but most American dictionaries at least tacitly accept it. Be aware, then, that some people may still object: unreasonable or not, the objection has lasted long enough to suggest that it may last still longer.

For the adjective *substitute,* see ARTIFICIAL.

subway, tube, underground, underpass (*nn.*) In the United States, a railroad under a city is a *subway.* In Britain it's the *underground,* or the *tube.* In Britain a *subway* is usually what we in the USA call a pedestrian *underpass.*

succeed (*v.*) takes the preposition *in* plus a gerund, not *to* plus an infinitive: *He succeeded in* *finding his dog.* (Not *He succeeded to find his dog.*) Only crown princes and other heirs *succeed to* anything, and then it's to *thrones* or *fortunes,* not *infinitives.*

successfully, successively (*advs.*) The gymnast made her vault *successfully* means "She succeeded in making it." *She made three vaults successively* means "She made them one after another—in *succession.*"

succor, succour (*n., v.*) *Succor* is the American spelling, *succour* the British. In either spelling, and as either noun or verb, it's more inflated and Formal than *help* or *aid.* See also SPELLING (1).

succubus, incubus (*nn.*) A *succubus* (plural: *succubi* or *succubuses*) is "a female demon who has sexual intercourse with a sleeping man." Presumably the plural is rarely needed; hence the borrowed Latin plural, *succubi,* is more usual than the regular English one. An *incubus* is "a male demon who copulates with a sleeping woman." Because this word is also used figuratively for "nightmares, haunting dreams, and visions," the plural is fairly frequently encountered; hence the regular English plural, *incubuses,* is more common than the Latin form, *incubi.* See also FOREIGN PLURALS.

such (*adv., adj., pron., intensifier*) *Such* has long functioned in English as pronoun, adjective, and intensifying adverb. At various times some uses have been criticized as too Formal, too Informal, or logically incoherent, but almost all of them are still Standard English. As a pronoun, as in *Of such is the Kingdom of Heaven* and *Such is his nature that you are bound to like him,* it has a somewhat formal air, perhaps less noticeable when it is used to round out a list, as in *The zoo has many antelopes and zebras and gazelles and such.* By choosing a more ordinary pronoun, you can reduce the stiffness and formality that *such* as pronoun may create. Instead of *They wanted an engineer; one such was my father,* try *They wanted an engineer; my father was one* or *. . . , and that's what my father was.*

As an adjective, *such* has wide use: *We seek such help as is available. Such questions are discouraged.* We also use it with *a* plus a singular count noun: *It was just such a night as this.*

Some have objected to *I have never seen such a beautiful bouquet,* arguing that it should be *. . . so beautiful a bouquet* [*as this*], instead, but that's nonsense; such sentences are Standard English, suitable for most levels of formality, even if *so beautiful a bouquet* may seem a more

consciously elegant way to phrase it. The use of *such* as adverb and intensifier is now often criticized, but it is Standard still, although usually confined to Conversational levels and Informal writing. You should be aware, however, that some think it sounds "gushy."

such as See LIKE (2).

suffer (*v.*) The intransitive verb (*He suffers mostly at night*) affords no real difficulty, but an older transitive sense, meaning "permit" or "allow," as in *Suffer the little children to come unto me,* is still around, although we seem to keep it mainly in the sense of "to endure": *He will not suffer contradiction.* We also preserve something of that sense in the adjective *insufferable,* which means "unendurable," "impermissible."

Another question of usage is whether *suffer* should ever be followed by *with,* rather than the usual *from: I suffer frequently from* [*with*] *migraines.* Apparently *with* is used only in Informal and Casual situations; Edited English uses *from* almost exclusively.

suffice (*v.*) The verb *suffice* has a Formal ring, whether in a subjunctive, as in *Let this answer suffice for now* and *Suffice it to say, I can no longer assist you;* a conditional using an auxiliary, as in *Should your present medication suffice, I'll be pleased,* or a future with *will,* as in *These funds will suffice for the next few days.* When a less stilted tone would be better, try *This answer ought to serve* or *This answer should do for now.*

sufficient, enough (*adjs., nn.*), **sufficient enough** (*adj.*) Using *sufficient* instead of *enough* as a noun is clumsy and sounds old-fashioned, as in *Thank you, but I've had sufficient,* and even as an adjective *sufficient* almost always sounds stiffer and more Formal than *enough,* as in *I have sufficient information to write the article,* as does *insufficient* for a negative: compare *We don't have enough time to reach the station* with *We have insufficient time to reach the station.* In any case, use either *sufficient* or *enough,* depending on the level you seek, but don't use both together, as in *This flour is sufficient enough for today's baking. Sufficient* is sufficient. *Enough's* enough. See AMPLE ENOUGH.

sufficiently (*adv.*) When this adverb modifies an adjective, the construction is usually followed by an infinitive: *Turnout of our party's voters was sufficiently high to guarantee victory.* Some people have argued that following the construction with a *that* clause instead of an infinitive is not Standard English. If this was once true, it is true no longer: *Turnout of our party's voters* *was sufficiently high that we knew we'd win* is now Standard. Note too that, like the adjective *sufficient*, the adverb *sufficiently* may sometimes sound over-Formal: *was high enough* may be enough.

SUFFIX See AFFIX.

suffragan (*n.*) Pronounce this title (of an assistant or deputy bishop) with the stress on the first syllable and either a hard or soft *g* sound.

suffragette, suffragist (*nn.*) A *suffragette* historically was "a woman advocating women's right to vote." A *suffragist* is "anyone, male or female, who advocates the extension of the right to vote to all, but particularly to women." Some people objected to *suffragette* originally because it began as a derisive term, but the more important objection was and is that it is narrow in scope, since it can be applied only to women and not to all who might support the same political view. *Suffragette* is now archaic in the United States, both for those reasons and because women now have the vote. But in some countries the issue is very much alive, and Americans will find *suffragist* the more generic term to use in discussing the issue. See also -ESS; FEMININE OCCUPATIONAL FORMS; INCLUSIVE LANGUAGE; SEXIST LANGUAGE.

suggested, suggestive (*adjs.*) The final syllables make a world of difference: *suggested* is the past tense and participial adjective form of the verb *suggest*; it means simply "offered for consideration": *He suggested that we make a contribution. The suggested contribution was ten dollars. Suggestive* has two meanings: "thought-provoking, rich in ideas and allusions and the like," as in *His observations about the report were suggestive—that is, helpful.* But the much more frequently used meaning is "implying something indecent or improper": *He made suggestive remarks about that woman.* Note that this raised-eyebrow, fleering sense of *suggestive* is so strong that it's usually necessary, when that's not the intended sense, to use ameliorative adverbs or adjectives with it to avoid ambiguity or misunderstanding: *Her comments were suggestive and proved helpful.*

suitable (*adj.*) Either of two prepositions can follow *suitable*—*for* (almost always) and *to* (rarely): *This music will be suitable for the occasion. These lyrics are suitable to the melody.*

sulfuric, sulfureous, sulfurous, sulfury (*adjs.*) All four are adjectives made by adding adjectival endings to the noun *sulfur* (also spelled *sulphur*). All mean "of, relating to, containing, or somehow like sulfur," but *sulfuric* and *sulfur-* ous have explicit technical senses as well: *sulfuric,* as in *sulfuric acid* (H_2SO_4), refers specifically to a hexavalent sulfur, that is, an atom of sulfur capable of bonding with six atoms or molecular groups. Technically, *sulfurous* is used by the chemist only of tetravalent or bivalent sulfur, but its figurative meanings are broad and colorful, particularly in the "hellfire" cluster of senses. *Sulfury* and *sulfureous* both are very general: "sulfurlike" or "containing sulfur." All these uses (and more) are Standard.

summersault See SOMERSAULT.

summon, summons (*n., v.*) Usage problems arise only with the legal senses of the word *summons*. In the courts *a summons* is "a document requiring the receiver to appear." Its plural is *summonses*. There is also a verb *to summons,* again restricted to legal matters: *The counsel for the defense summonsed me to testify. He gave out three other summonses.* The verb *summon* is a regular weak verb meaning simply "call": *He summons birds by imitating their calls.* The usual noun made from it (other than the infinitive itself) is a gerund: *Summoning all his nerve was not enough.*

sumpin', somethin', something See -ING.

sundry (*adj.*), **sundries** (*n.*) *Sundry* is an adjective of somewhat pedantic or archaic flavor; it means "several, several kinds, various." The cliché *all and sundry,* meaning "every one or everything, the whole collection," is still in use, and the noun, especially in the plural, has wide use meaning "a hodgepodge, a miscellany, typically of small items such as might be sold in a drugstore or novelty shop," and in a specialized plural sense meaning those particular items themselves: *Try the department where sundries are sold.*

sung See SING.

sunk, sunken See SINK.

super-, supra- (*prefixes*) These prefixes are high-frequency additions to the fronts of adjectives, nouns, verbs, and even adverbs, usually added without hyphens. *Super-* means "above, over, superior in size, excessive, better, more inclusive," and the like. *Supra-* also means "above and over," but its distinctive senses include "greater than, beyond, outside, transcending," and the like. The chief semantic differences show up when you apply each prefix to a word such as *nationalistic: supernationalistic* means "nationalistic to a superlative degree," "displaying the strongest possible nationalistic qualities"; *supranationalistic* means "beyond nationalism," "above or outside all nationalistic qualities."

Both prefixes are often used to create nonce words.

supercede See SUPERSEDE.

superfluous (*adj.*) means "not needed," "more than enough," and especially "extra" and "wasteful": *She wasted most of her time on superfluous details.* Pronounce it *soo-PUHR-floo-uhs,* and note its semantic overlap with *gratuitous* and its differences from *egregious* (both of which see).

superhighway See THRUWAY.

superior See IMPLICIT COMPARISON.

SUPERLATIVE DEGREE See POSITIVE DEGREE.

SUPERLATIVE DEGREE USED OF TWO Although locutions such as *the best of the two* are unacceptable in most Edited English, American penchant for hyperbole and other forms of enthusiasm gives us many examples, in Semiformal and Informal writing and at all levels of speech except the Oratorical, of the *superlative* forms of adjectives and adverbs being used where the comparative might be required. Most Standard users would make no demur in relaxed circumstances over *Math and physics are both hard for me, but physics is hardest,* but many would want *harder* at the higher levels of speech and in any but the most Informal writing.

supernatural, preternatural, supranatural, unnatural (*adjs.*) All carry some sense of "not natural, not found in nature." Something *supernatural* is "not of this world, spooky" and suggests "nonrational, mysterious forces at work." *Supranatural* is a rarer and more technical term, meaning "transcending nature." *Unnatural* means "deviating from nature or natural laws," "outrageous, uncharacteristic of natural feelings or behavior," and hence often "perverted or evil"; it also means "artificial, contrived, strained," as in *She was wearing an unnatural smile. Preternatural* means "beyond or transcending nature and natural laws and feelings" and hence often "exceptional, extraordinary," or even "unusual."

supernormal See SUBNORMAL.

SUPERPLUPERFECT See PLUPLUPERFECT TENSE.

supersede, supercede, surpass (*vv.*) We got the word *supersede/supercede* from the Latin *supersedere,* by way of the Old French *superceder* (later *superseder*), so etymology offers arguments in favor of each spelling. *Supersede* is the overwhelming preference of Edited English, although *supercede* does occur in print. If one regulation replaces another, the new one *supersedes* the old one; if you excel or outstrip others, you *surpass* them. See also -CEDE.

supervise See SPELLING (1).

supervisor See AGENTIVE ENDINGS.

supine See PRONE.

supper See DINNER.

supplement, complement (*nn., vv.*) When you *supplement* something, you "add to it": *We'll supplement our rations with what we can scrounge.* When you *complement* something, you "complete it, fill it out": *His powerful ground game complemented her excellent volleying and net play.* A *supplement* is "something added": *The new book was a supplement to the old.* A *complement* is "something that fills out or completes," as in *Her recent essay complements the contributions of her predecessors; The arrival of the new recruits gave us a full complement of troops.* See also COMPLEMENT.

supplementary, complementary (*adjs.*) Something *supplementary* is something additional: *I was well fed, but I still watched for Mother's supplementary food packages.* Something *complementary* is something that makes up for what is missing, especially something lacking in one of a pair: *The partners' personalities were complementary; one was talkative, the other taciturn.* See also COMPLEMENTARY.

supportive (*adj.*) A perfectly acceptable term meaning "in support of" or "helpful," *supportive* has become trendy. Use the verb or a simpler adjective when you can: instead of *They were supportive of his position,* use *They supported his position*; instead of *Her supportive attitude gave him strength,* try *Her support gave him strength* or *Her help strengthened him.* See also VOGUE WORDS.

suppose (*v.*), **supposing** (*pres. participle*) These words are interchangeable when they introduce a hypothetical situation: *Suppose [Supposing] he won't agree.* Or in proposing something: *Suppose [Supposing] I offer them money.*

supposed (*adj.*) Inexperienced or hurried writers sometimes misspell *supposed,* as in *You're not suppose to take food into the library,* presumably because the final *d* sound of *supposed* coalesces with the initial *t* sound of the following *to.* In Casual and Impromptu speech you appropriately pronounce only one stop, but only Substandard writing or inadvertency spells it *suppose to.*

supposing See SUPPOSE.

supra- See SUPER-.

supranatural See SUPERNATURAL.

supreme (*adj.*) Some argue that nothing can be more supreme than *supreme*; it's considered an absolute adjective. But our penchant for hyperbole has made this a lily frequently gilded, as in *My supremest thrill has been getting the first-place medal.* Best advice: let *supreme* stand on its own.

Supreme Court See CHIEF JUSTICE.

surcease (*n., v.*) The verb (meaning "to stop or delay") is usually considered archaic, but the noun (meaning "respite, end, or a stopping or relief from") occurs quite regularly in Edited English of a Formal, literary kind. In Informal writing and at Conversational levels, it may seem affected or stiff.

sure, surely (*adj., adv., function words, intensifiers*) Purists often claim that *sure* is correctly used only as adjective (*He has sure hands*), *surely* only as adverb (*He catches the ball surely; Surely she'll call*), except in a few old idiomatic phrases wherein *sure* is still adverbial (*sure enough; as sure as*). But both words have other uses today, and these so-called exceptions are actually basic parts of the pattern. The flat adverb *sure* is widespread at Informal and Conversational levels, although some commentators insist that it is Common or even Vulgar rather than Standard: *He sure is a nice guy. They sure wanted her to visit them. Sure, I like chocolate; who doesn't?* In Edited English and at the more Formal, consciously planned levels of speech, *surely* appears as the adverb: *He surely is a splendid athlete. Surely* also occurs in Conversational circumstances where *sure* won't work semantically: *Surely you can see my problem. You don't believe her, surely?*

As function words, both *sure* and *surely* belong to the very short list of words (headed by *yes*) for the affirmative in response utterances: *Want some more coffee? Sure. Will you come again on Wednesday? Surely. Surely* is Standard in all such uses, *sure* is Standard in Informal writing and at most Conversational levels.

Sure, surely, real, really, and *truly* serve also as intensifiers, but use them sparingly, and note that although *sure* and *real* are suitable at Casual and Informal levels, conservatives usually will consider them Substandard, whereas the other words are Standard: *She sure [surely, truly] is bright. Their team is real [really, truly, sure, surely] tall.*

sure and See TRY AND.

surely See SURE.

surgery, operation, surgical procedure (*nn.*), **in surgery** Americans use *surgery* as a general term for all sorts of *surgical procedures,* from the removal of warts (*office surgery*) to appendectomies and more serious *operations.* When American surgeons are *in surgery,* they are performing *surgical operations,* or they are *operating,* or they are *operating on* patients; when a British physician is in his *surgery,* he's in what Americans call "the doctor's office," holding "office hours."

surmise See SPELLING (1).

surpass See SUPERSEDE.

surprised (*adj.*) can be combined with either *at* or *by: She was surprised at his being so intractable; He was surprised by her tears.*

surveillance, surveillant (*nn.*), **surveil** (*v.*) Americans stress the second syllables of all three words and pronounce them to rhyme with *veil.* All three come from a French verb meaning "to oversee," the same source that gives us *survey. To be under surveillance* is "to be under the watch of an observer." Most commonly the phrase is used of suspected criminals or places where crimes or criminals are anticipated. *Surveil* is a fairly recent back-formation, a verb describing what a *surveillant* ("watcher," an even more recent coinage) does. All these terms are Standard, although some might consider *surveil* and *surveillant* primarily police and spy argot.

susceptible (*adj.*) *Susceptible of* and *susceptible to* mean "capable of," as in *something susceptible of [to] proof. Susceptible to* can also mean "unable to resist" or "having low resistance to," as in *She's very susceptible to colds.* Note, however, that without specifying a stimulus, to speak of someone as being *susceptible* can be a rather tired bit of suggestive whimsy, as in *He's at a susceptible age,* meaning "He's susceptible to the charms of every female who happens by." That use is a cliché. See also SENSIBLE.

suspected (*adj.*), used in locutions such as *a suspected gambler,* is idiomatic, and almost everyone would understand this to mean "a person suspected of gambling or of being a gambler." Some finical protectors of the language, however, take pleasure in analyzing such idioms and pointing out their apparent illogic: that *suspected gambler* may indeed be a *gambler,* but is it gambling or something else that he's suspected of this time? Most readers don't see these nits; the idiomatic meanings are far stronger. Best advice, however, is not to leave such nits lying about in your Edited English prose where someone might, to your disadvantage, pick them and label them ambiguous. See also ACCUSED; ALLEGE.

suspenders (*n.*) This plural is a cause of reciprocal Anglo-American amusement. British *suspenders* are what Americans call *garters,* especially women's *garters,* the kind that hang down from a *garter* belt and fasten to the tops of stockings. But some British and American men also wear *garters,* elastic bands with fasteners, worn usually just below the knee and attached to the tops of socks. American *suspenders* are British *braces,* and both hold trousers up, just as American dialectal *galluses* do. These days tony American haberdashers often use the British term *braces* for the American *suspenders.* See VOCABULARY (1).

sustain (*v.*) means "to hold up or support," both literally, as in *The buttressed walls sustain that vaulted roof* and figuratively, as in *The hot food sustained him for another day.* It also means "to undergo, to suffer," as in *He sustained a few cracked ribs.* In each of these instances, *sustain* is a rather stiff, literary-sounding word, and most of these sentences would seem less self-consciously elevated in tone with a simpler, more common verb—perhaps *hold up, kept him going,* and *cracked a few ribs,* respectively. *To sustain an injury* is a stuffy journalese cliché to use sparingly, if at all.

swap, swop (*n., v.*) *Swap* is the American spelling, with *swop* more common in British English. Both verb and noun are Informal or Conversational; elsewhere, and especially in Edited English, *trade, exchange,* or *barter* might be better choices for either the verb or the noun.

swear (*n., v.*) **swearword** (*n.*) *Swore* is the past tense, as in *I swore I'd get even; sworn* is the past participle, as in *He had sworn at the cat. Swore* as past participle, as in *He had swore he'd be true* is Substandard. *Swear* is also a noun, a recent functional shift meaning "a swearword," from which it could be a clipping. Limited mainly to Conversational or perhaps even slang use among the young, it can be heard today in both singular and plural: *Billy said a swear. She let go with several swears when she saw her grade.*

sweat (*n., v.*) Both past tense and past participle are either *sweated* or *sweat. Sweat* was a grubby word: the saw was *Laborers sweat, gentlemen perspire, and ladies glow.* But in today's jogging, working-out, health-conscious world, it's all right for everyone to sweat. Manners have changed, and both verb and noun have elevated

as a result. The expression *don't sweat it* means "don't try too hard or make too much of it" or "don't let it upset you." *To sweat blood* means "to overwork or to suffer impatience or apprehension." Both these slang idioms should be limited to Casual and Impromptu use or to the Informal level that imitates them. The idiom *no sweat* is also slang, an interjection meaning "no trouble" or "no inconvenience." It's a response much like *no problem,* which see.

sweat equity (*n.*) This term, standing for the value of work put into a house or other property by the owner, is less than a generation old. It is still considered Informal or Conversational by some, but it is clearly a Standard technical term today, undergoing functional shift to adjectival use (*a sweat-equity plan for renovating a decayed neighborhood*) and being used in such a way that it probably needs only a field label (probably *Real Estate*), if any.

sweep (*v.*) The past tense and past participle are both *swept.*

swell 1 (*adj., n., interj.*) The adjective *swell* is slang: *We had a swell time. She's a swell golfer.* The interjection is also slang, meaning "wonderful," and often used ironically. The noun is fully Standard in only two senses, the *swell* on the surface of the ocean and the *swell* in the volume of the music produced by an organist. It is Conversational and Informal as a rather dated term for someone stylish and socially important—*a real swell.*

swell 2 (*v.*) The past tense is *swelled,* and the past participle has two forms, *swelled* and *swollen. Swelled* is used as an adjective in at least one primarily American context, *He has a swelled head,* meaning "He's conceited," from which we have the Casual and Informal compound *swellhead,* meaning "conceited person"; the British say, *He's swollen-headed.* Almost all other adjectival uses of the participle are with *swollen: His knee was badly swollen. The swollen streams and rivers caused great damage.* There is some inconclusive evidence that we choose *had swelled* or *had swollen* depending on a semantic distinction—whether the *swelling* is thought helpful or harmful: *The crowd had swelled until the hall was full (and we were delighted). The crowd had swollen until the hall was jammed (and we were worried about fire or panic).*

swift (*adv., adj.*), **swiftly** (*adv.*) *Swift* is the adjective (*a swift river*), *swiftly* the usual adverb (*a swiftly flowing river*). But *swift* is also a flat adverb (*a swift-flowing river*). All are Standard.

swim (*v.*) The principal parts of this strong verb are *swim, swam, swum.*

swine (*n.*) is both singular and plural. When we refer to the group containing boars, sows, hogs, and little pigs, we say *These are swine* or *These are pigs.* If we refer to one female pig, we may say *A sow is a female swine.* And if we use the figurative sense meaning "a gross or contemptible person," we refer to him (or rarely to her) as a *swine: That swine was rude to my sister.* *Swine* developed from the Old English word for *sow,* somewhat the same way that *kine* developed from the Old English word for *cow.* To call a person a *pig* is to criticize his or her greed or manners, but to call someone a *swine* is somehow much more insulting.

swing (*v.*), **swinger** (*n.*), **swinging** (*adj.*) The past tense and past participle are both *swung.* *Swang* as either past tense or past participle is Substandard, a shibboleth. *Swinging,* an adjective meaning "lively and uninhibited," is slang and probably fading slang at that, as is *swinger,* the agentive noun in the related slang sense.

swivel See CONSONANTS (2).

swollen See SWELL (2).

swop See SWAP.

swore, sworn See SWEAR.

swum See SWIM.

swung See SWING.

SYLLABLES are the units of speech that are next larger than single sounds. A spoken *syllable* is either a single vowel, a syllabic consonant, or a vowel preceded, followed, or enclosed by consonants or consonant clusters. Each part of the following pronunciations is one *syllable:* O (the word *oh*); *SAI* (*say*); *STAI* (*stay*); *IMP* (*imp*); *BAD* (*bad*); *SHUHRT* (*shirt*). *BAT-ul* (*battle*), wherein the final syllable is considered by some to be a syllabic consonant, is two syllables.

In written and printed words, *syllables* are the vowel-centered clusters that represent these speech units. Dictionaries put spaces, dots, or hyphens between the *syllables* of their entry words to indicate where such words are conventionally to be hyphenated when they must be divided at the ends of lines: *ob·nox·ious* can be hyphenated in either of two places, and its pronunciation has three *syllables,* separated here by hyphens: *uhb-NAHK-shuhs.* But *delirious,* although it ends in the same *-ious* spelling as *obnoxious,* has four syllables (*dee-LIR-ee-uhs*), and a dictionary might indicate those four syllables thus: *de·lir·i·ous*

syllabus The plural is either the regular English *syllabuses* or the borrowed Latin *syllabi* (the last syllable rhymes with *sky*), but the Latin is becoming stuffy sounding. See FOREIGN PLURALS.

SYLLEPSIS is a syntactic fault wherein either one word or a longer locution has two syntactic functions, only one of which fits or agrees grammatically: *My family, as well as I, am happy* (*am* goes only with *I,* not with *family*). A *syllepsis* is also a rhetorical figure, wherein a single word is used in both a literal and a figurative sense, one of which is unconventionally paired with the other: *He was driving his car carelessly and his wife crazy. He ate with gusto and his penknife.* It can sometimes be a rather contrived form of wit. The plural is *syllepses.* See also FOREIGN PLURALS.

symbol See CYMBAL.

sympathetic, sympathize, sympathy See EMPATHETIC.

symposium (*n.*) The Latin plural, *symposia,* was the higher frequency form until recently, but the regular English plural, *symposiums,* appears to have overtaken it even in Edited English. Both are Standard. See FOREIGN PLURALS.

SYNCOPE in language is the shortening of a word by cutting out a letter, a sound, or a syllable, as in *guv'nor* (for *governor*) or the British pronunciation of *secretary, SEK-ruh-tri.*

syndrome (*n.*) Like so many other technical terms from medicine and psychology, *syndrome* has been taken into nearly everybody's vocabulary, generalized, inflated, and then flattened by overuse. In medicine, a *syndrome* is a pattern of signs and symptoms characteristic of a particular disease or psychological condition. As the general public now uses it, a *syndrome* has come to be either "any pattern of behavior" or just "behavior." When young women began to wear greatly oversized sweaters, shirts, jackets, and sweatshirts, someone immediately named this fad *the big top syndrome.* Only when such new figurative senses are neither clichés nor hyperboles run wild will they be really effective. A single manifestation of human folly is not a *syndrome* of anything; it's just *foolishness.*

SYNECDOCHE is a figure of speech that makes a part stand for the whole: *He owns sixty head of cattle.* To say that the villain was accompanied by *three hired guns* is a *synecdoche,* a figurative way of saying that he had with him three men carrying and ready to use those guns.

synergy, synergism (*nn.*), **synergistic** (*adj.*) All three refer to the effects achieved by a combination of two or more entities, each of which could not achieve the result alone. These are perfectly good words, technically useful in, for example, describing the effects of combinations of drugs or other therapies in the treatment of illness. And they are also effective in figurative uses so long as the figure is fresh and new. But as with *syndrome,* so here: when the figurative uses are clichés, avoid these words in other than their technical senses.

SYNONYM, SYNONYMIES (*nn.*) *Synonyms* (pronounced *SIN-uh-nimz*) are two or more words that mean the same or nearly the same things. *Bigness, hugeness, largeness,* and *enormity* are *synonyms,* but *hugeness* may have a slightly frightening overtone, and *enormity* a suggestion of the monstrous and the grotesque that, for example, *bigness* and *largeness* do not share. Dictionaries usually contain *synonymies* (pronounced *si-NAHN-uh-meez*), brief essays that try to distinguish among the individual words in groups that seem to have roughly similar meanings. Usage problems often attend *synonyms,* as many entries in this guide attest (see, for example, SUPERNATURAL). *Synonymy* is also the name given the study of clusters of words of similar or overlapping meanings, a study that must precede the writing of *synonymies.*

synopsis (*n.*) The plural of *synopsis* ("a brief outline or abstract") is either *synopsises* or *synopses.* The second is a bit more frequent, probably because its sibilants are fewer. See also FOREIGN PLURALS.

SYNTACTIC is the adjective based on syntax.

SYNTACTIC BLENDS are blunders fairly common in speech but rare in any sort of print. The *syntactic blend* is a pushmi-pullyu sort of structure, usually inadvertent but occasionally deliberate, trying to make something ludicrous; it is usually composed of the front of one syntactic structure followed by a shift in midstride to end with another. This one was probably caused by the intrusion of parenthetical matter between the two halves: *She is not so strong (or at least it appears that way now) than her sisters.* The example combines the front of *She is not so strong as her sisters* with the end of *She*

is weaker than her sisters. In *We accepted the majority report alongside with the minority report, alongside* combines awkwardly with (*along*) *with.*

SYNTACTIC INVERSION See INVERSION (2).

SYNTAX is the term for that aspect of grammar that describes word order, the relationships among words, and the structure of phrases, clauses, and sentences.

synthesis (*n.*) The plural is *syntheses.* See FOREIGN PLURALS.

synthetic See ARTIFICIAL.

syringe (*n., v.*) Placing the stress on either syllable is Standard for both noun and verb, but stress on the second syllable is somewhat more frequent in the noun, and stress on the first syllable may be a trifle more frequent in the verb.

syrup, sirup (*n.*) *Syrup* is the usual American spelling, *sirup* an acceptable variant. There are two acceptable, regionally varied American pronunciations, one with the first, stressed syllable pronounced as in *sear,* the other with it pronounced as in *sir.*

systematic, systemic (*adjs.*), **systematically, systemically** (*advs.*) *Systematic* is the general adjective describing anything "characterized by or consisting of a system": *They made a systematic effort to destroy his reputation. Systemic* refers only to "physiological systems": *A systemic infection* may affect any or all parts of, say, the cardiovascular system. *Systemic* is also used figuratively, usually applied to organizations or institutions: *The ills of the Pentagon are systemic.* The related adverbs are respectively *systematically* and *systemically.*

systemize, systematize (*vv.*) Both verbs mean "to put into a system or to arrange systematically," but *systematize* seems to get the American call almost every time. Perhaps the choice between the two reflects the same love of polysyllables represented by our apparently growing preference for the verb *orientate* over *orient. Systemize* added the *-ize* ending to the noun *system; system* plus *-atic* produced the adjective *systematic,* and then we replaced the *-ic* with *-ize* to produce the verb *systematize.* Why we took the longer route is uncertain.

T

-t-, -tt- See CONSONANTS (2).

table (*v.*) in American parliamentary use means "to remove from consideration, and so to defer action indefinitely," as in *We voted to table the measure and hoped never to see it again.* In Britain *to table* means quite the opposite: "to put on the agenda, to submit for consideration," as in *By tabling the motion, the government hope to see it enacted shortly.*

tableau (*n.*) has two Standard plurals: *tableaux* and *tableaus,* both pronounced *TAB-LOZ.* See FOREIGN PLURALS.

table d'hôte, a French phrase meaning literally "table of the host," indicates "a full meal with all courses, offered at a set price." Distinguish it from *à la carte,* and pronounce it and the plural, *tables d'hôte,* either *TA-buhl DOT* or *TAHBL DOT.* See FOREIGN PHRASES.

tablespoonful, teaspoonful (*nn.*) The plurals are usually *tablespoonfuls* and *teaspoonfuls,* but *tablespoonsful* and *teaspoonsful* can also occur in Standard English. The insecure frequently dodge decision and specify instead *two tablespoons of X,* or *three teaspoons of Y.* See PLURALS OF COMPOUND NOUNS.

TABOO WORDS A *taboo* is a socially enforced prohibition, and in language such a prohibition forces the substitution of another word for one that is *taboo.* Sometimes *taboos* in language are inexplicable, but others can be traced to specific social attitudes. Generally only when manners have changed do old *taboos* seem silly and fall away; some Renaissance English might seem pretty explicit today, even to many liberated modern American ears. Some *taboos* enforced by Standard English at least in mixed company and in most publications earlier in the twentieth century have eased radically since the late 1960s, especially for those vulgar or obscene words involving sexual intercourse and excretion; many have much wider currency, if not full acceptance, in both speech and writing, than could have been envisioned forty or fifty years ago. On the other hand the *taboo* against words of racial and ethnic opprobrium that Standard English enforced only moderately and selectively earlier in the century is now much more rigorously enforced in both speech and writing and among nearly all users of both Standard and Common English. See also DIRTY WORDS; ETHNIC SLURS AND TERMS OF ETHNIC OPPROBRIUM; OBSCENE (1); OBSCENE (2); PROFANITY; RACIST LANGUAGE; SEXIST LANGUAGE; VULGAR.

tactics See STRATEGY.

tailor-made See BESPOKE; OFF-THE-RACK.

take (*v.*) combines with prepositions such as *on, over, up, in,* and many others: *They'll take on* [that is, *hire*] *some new employees. I wish they wouldn't take on so* [that is, *make such a fuss*]. *We'll take on* [that is, *fight or argue with*] *all comers.* The "hire" sense is Semiformal at least; the "fuss" and "fight" senses are slang or Conversational at best. *Take* also combines with other parts of speech in a wide range of idioms, some of them Standard, many more Conversational or slang. Consult a dictionary for full lists. See also BRING (3).

take aback (*v.*) has two current Standard senses: a literal nautical one meaning what happens to square sails (and to the ship that carries the sails) when the wind suddenly begins to blow on the wrong side of the sails, as in *The wind suddenly veered and took the ship aback, causing her to slow and wander off course,* and a generalized sense, "to be taken by surprise," as in *Their unreasonable anger took us both aback.*

take and is padded prose, but it occurs mainly in Casual and Impromptu contexts, where it works the way *up and, go (ahead) and,* and *try and* do: *We'll take and* [*up and, go ahead and, try and*] *call them in the morning.* Conservatives will insist that *take and* is Substandard, and they will usually consider it a sign of Vulgar English.

take exception to See EXCEPTION.

take food, take meals These uses of *take* with food and drink of all kinds are Standard idioms today: *The nurse took meals with the family. Do take some more wine.*

take hold of See AHOLD.

take it easy is a Standard Conversational and Informal idiom meaning "relax," "don't hurry so,'' or ''don't try so hard.'' *Easy* is a flat adverb.

take it under advisement See ADVISEMENT.

take meals See TAKE FOOD.

taken See TOOK.

take place, occur (*vv.*) These verbs are synonyms, despite some purists' efforts to restrict *take place* to planned events and *occur* to chance ones, as in *The accident occurred last Thursday, and the funeral took place today.* But these verbs can be and often are interchanged in Standard use.

take stock in (of) See STOCK.

take thought See THOUGHT.

talisman (*n.*) The plural is *talismans.* See PLURALS OF NOUNS.

talk See ORATION.

talk (*v.*) combines with several prepositions to make Standard idioms: *to talk around* means ''to persuade,'' as in *We talked them around to our point of view*; *to talk at someone* is ''to permit no response, to conduct a one-sided lecture''; *to talk back* is ''to answer sharply, rudely''; *to talk down* is either ''to drown the other person out, and talk him or her into silence,'' ''to assist an airplane pilot to land the plane by giving him or her instructions over the radio,'' or ''to get someone out of trouble or danger by calm instruction and reassurance''; *to talk down to someone* is ''to condescend, to insult that person's intelligence, to treat him or her as an inferior''; *to talk into* is ''to persuade''; *to talk something out* is ''to discuss it fully in order to come to an agreement''; *to talk someone out of something* is ''to persuade someone not to do something''; *to talk something over* is ''to discuss it''; and *to talk up something* or *to talk something up* is ''to praise it or try to promote it.'' *To talk to someone* can mean either ''to address that person'' or ''to admonish him or her.'' *To talk with someone* means simply ''to discuss'' or ''to give someone a message,'' as in *We talked with her about her plans.* Compare SPEAK TO.

talk shop See SHOPTALK.

tangible (*adj.*) ends in *-ible.* See PERCEPTIBLE; SPELLING OF UNSTRESSED VOWELS.

taps (*n.*), ''the nightly bugle call,'' is plural in form but nearly always takes a singular verb and subsequent pronoun: *Taps sends its mournful echo over the cemetery.*

tarry (*adj., v.*) These are homographs, two different words: the verb *tarry* rhymes with *marry* and means ''delay, loiter, wait about,'' as in *Tarry awhile here in the shade.* The adjective *tarry* rhymes with *starry* and means ''covered with tar,'' as in *His pants were all tarry from the rigging.*

tart (*adj., n.*) The adjective means ''sharp and with an acid taste,'' as in *The jelly had a tart flavor.* The noun means ''a small fruit pie or pastry.'' In Britain *tart* is also a generic word for ''pie,'' as well as a word for ''prostitute.''

tartan See PLAID.

taste (*v.*) is a linking verb, as in *The stew tastes wonderful*, a transitive verb, as in *I tasted the wine*, and an intransitive verb, as in *Here's your food; taste slowly and carefully.* The intransitive verb can also combine with *of*: *My milk tastes of garlic.* All these are Standard.

tasteful, tasteless, tasty (*adjs.*) *Tasteful* means ''giving evidence of good taste, of good judgment about appearance or design, and the like'': *The study had tasteful furnishings. Tasty* means ''flavorful, good to savor or taste on the tongue'': *She served a wonderfully tasty lunch. Tasteless* is the antonym of both *tasteful* and *tasty: The tasteless furnishings were all gifts of her family. The vegetables were boiled to a tasteless mush.* See DISTASTEFUL.

tattoo (*nn., vv.*) For both *tattoo* meaning ''designs punctured and colored beneath the skin'' and ''to make such designs'' and *tattoo* meaning ''a drummed signal or a military exercise accompanied by drums'' or ''any drumming'' and ''to beat a drum,'' the plural is *tattoos.* The past tense and past participle are *tattooed.* See PLURALS OF NOUNS ENDING IN *-O.*

taught (*past tense, past participle*), **taut** (*adj.*) These homophones have nothing but their sounds in common. *Taught* is past tense and past participle of the verb *teach*, and *taut* is an adjective meaning ''stretched tightly,'' ''under strain,'' and ''efficient'': *The rope was taut, and so was the ship's discipline.*

TAUTOLOGY A *tautology* is the unnecessary repetition of a meaning through the use of two words that mean the same thing. It has been argued that *consensus of opinion* is a *tautology*, because *consensus* itself means ''a preponderance of opinion.'' But see CONSENSUS. *Helpful assistance* is unquestionably *tautological*, as are *free gift* and *new innovation.* See PLEONASMS; REDUNDANT; WIDOW.

tax (*v.*), in the sense of ''charge, accuse,'' combines with the preposition *with*: *She taxed him with misleading her.*

teach (*v.*) The idiom *teach school*, although once criticized, is clearly Standard today, as are other combinations of *teach* with a direct object such as *class, English, twenty students, a topic,* and *a lesson. Teach* can also be intransitive: *He taught for forty years.* See LEARN.

teacher See PROFESSOR.

team (*n., v.*), **teem** (*vv.*) Of these homophones, *team* as noun is "a pair of draft animals" or "a group of people forming one side in a contest or game," and the verb *team* means "to form such a group"; frequently it combines with *up,* as in *We teamed (up) with a transfer student. Team player,* meaning "one who cooperates well with teammates," began as sports jargon but is now Standard in almost all contexts. The figurative use of *team* in commerce and other activities to suggest unity when it may be hard to achieve is becoming a cliché: *Our sales force is a winning team.*

One verb *teem* means "to bear many offspring, to abound in or swarm with," as in *That swamp teemed with mosquitoes.* A second verb *teem* means "to empty or pour out" and is much used in the cliché with the present participle *a teeming rain.*

teaspoonful See TABLESPOONFUL.

teem See TEAM.

teen, adolescent, juvenile, teenager, young adult (*nn.*) *Teen,* frequently used in the plural, refers to the years from thirteen to nineteen and to young persons of those ages: *She's in her late teens. The room was full of gangling teens. Teenager* refers to a person of that same age group. An *adolescent* is a person in the same general age group, perhaps less explicitly defined as "between childhood and adulthood." *Young adult* may be a euphemism or simply another term for someone just outgrowing *adolescence* but having only barely achieved adult status; in publishing it describes readers aged thirteen to seventeen or so. A *juvenile,* especially in the eyes of the law, is someone immature, a child, not subject to the same responsibilities an adult must meet. All these terms are Standard, although *teen(s)* as a noun meaning person(s) of that age group may be considered Semiformal at best and is less likely to occur in Formal English than the others; *teens* as a range of ages, however, is Standard.

tee shirt See T-SHIRT.

telecast, televise (*vv.*) Both verbs are Standard, *telecast* being a blend of *television* and an analogy with radio's *broadcast; televise* is a back-formation from *television* itself. See SPELLING (1).

temblor, trembler, tremblor (*nn.*) *Temblor* is the Spanish word for earthquake ("trembling of the earth" was the idiom); it was first adopted into English in the earthquake country of the American Southwest and is now Standard English. *Tremblor* and *trembler* are American folk etymologies, mispronunciations and misspellings of *temblor,* or perhaps back-formations from *tremble* or *tremor.* They're rare in print, but they do occur there.

temerity, timidity (*nn.*) *Temerity* is "reckless, rash boldness, foolish daring," and *timidity* is an antonym of it, meaning "lack of courage, boldness, self-confidence."

temperature (*n.*) means generally "the measurement of the hotness or coldness of anything," but a widely used specialized sense means "fever," any temperature above "normal" (usually 98.6 degrees Fahrenheit in a human being), as in *The doctor inquired whether you have a temperature [fever].* This is a Standard idiom.

tempo (*n.*) has two Standard plurals: *tempos* and *tempi.* See PLURALS OF NOUNS ENDING IN -*O*; FOREIGN PLURALS.

temporize See EXTEMPORIZE.

tenant, tenet (*nn.*) These two nouns pose little trouble in writing, but in speech the nasal in the unstressed second syllable of *tenant* may sometimes be hard to hear and so make *tenant,* meaning "a renter, an occupant of a house or lands," sound like *tenet,* meaning "a doctrine or principle held to be a truth by a group." Compare *He's been our tenant at the farm for years* with *Belief in some sort of afterlife is a tenet of many religions.*

tend (*vv.*) There are two verbs *tend,* both Standard in English. The first is based on a clipped Middle English version of *attend,* meaning "to look after, care for": *Tend to your own business.* The second means "to incline toward" and comes from the Latin *tendere,* "to stretch": *She tends usually toward compromise.* Both verbs combine regularly with *to,* and the second *tend* also combines with *toward.*

tendency (*n.*) combines regularly with *to, toward,* or *towards: I have a tendency to talk too much. He has a tendency to asthma. She has a tendency toward[s] gaining weight.*

tender (*n., v.*) The verb means "to offer payment, to present an offer" and is rather formal, even in clichés such as *He tendered his resig-*

nation after the meeting. The noun in one sense is both Formal and specialized, "a formal offer or bid to meet an obligation, a formal proposal for some sort of contract, and the like": *His tender for the stock should reach us this morning. Legal tender,* the money that must be accepted in a transaction, is any sort of currency or coinage that is fully guaranteed by the issuing government.

A *tender* is also (a) a fuel-and-water car attached to a steam railroad engine in order to supply it, (b) a boat or ship for supplying and servicing other ships or installations, including the small boat that plies between its yacht and the shore, running errands and fetching people and supplies, and (c) a person who *tends* or maintains and services machinery or almost anything else.

tendinitis, tendonitis (*n.*), means "inflammation of a tendon," and both spellings are Standard.

tenet See TENANT.

TENSE is one way English indicates the time of the actions specified in its verbs. English verbs have a present tense (*he walks*) and a past tense (*he walked*). Using the auxiliaries *have* and *had* plus a past participle (*walked*), English verbs also create the so-called perfect tense (*they have walked*) and the past perfect tense (*they had walked*). Some grammars describe a future tense, with *shall* or *will* plus the infinitive of the verb (*she will walk*); other grammars, concluding that the idea of the future is reflected in the infinitive rather than in any distinctive form, consider the future as represented by the present tense plus adverbial indications of time (*I go tomorrow*). See also STRONG VERBS (1).

TENSES, SEQUENCE OF See SEQUENCE OF TENSES.

TERMINAL PREPOSITION See PREPOSITION (1).

terminate (*v.*), meaning simply "end," is sometimes criticized as pretentious by those to whom brevity is the highest value, but it carries certain specialized legal senses that *end* lacks, such as "to dismiss or fire someone," as in *We had to terminate* [*the employment of*] *ten people. Terminate* is useful and Standard, but it is often pretentious and a euphemism, especially in the jargon sense from the criminal world, where it means "kill."

terms See IN TERMS OF.

terrible (*adj.*), **terribly** (*adv., intensifier*) Both words have been weakened by overuse to a point where they reflect terror less than mere disagreement or unpleasantness. Certainly, both have taken on a wider and more generalized set of meanings, but both are still Standard. *I had a terrible time getting anyone to listen* is perfectly useful in either Conversational or Edited English. The adverb *terribly* has remained an adverb (*She suffered terribly toward the end*), but it has also become an intensifier (*He seems terribly thin*), and in that use it can sound somewhat elevated, even though it risks being criticized as gushy (*Her parents were terribly pleased*). These uses too are Standard.

TERSENESS See BREVITY.

TERTIARY STRESS See PRIMARY STRESS.

tête-à-tête is a French phrase, literally "head to head," and it is very useful for indicating the character of a private conversation between two people. Americans pronounce it *TAIT-ah-TAIT* or *TET-uh-TET,* and in writing it usually retains the circumflex and grave accents. See FOREIGN PHRASES.

Teutonic See GERMAN.

textual, textural (*adjs.*) *Textual* (pronounced *TEKS-tyoo-uhl* or *TEKS-choo-uhl*) means "based on or involving a text," as in *She based her conclusions on textual evidence. Textural* (pronounced *TEKS-tyoor-uhl* or *TEKS-chuhr-uhl*) means "the feel or appearance of a surface," "characteristic of the texture of some object," as in *The textural similarity between these two upholstery fabrics is close.*

th is a two-letter spelling of two single consonant sounds, made identically except that one is voiced, as in *thy* (pronounced *THEI*), the other voiceless, as in *thigh* (pronounced *THEI*). These two can also occur medially, as in this pair: *either* (pronounced *EE-thuhr* or *EI-thuhr*) and *ether* (pronounced *EE-thuhr*). Phoneticians usually represent the voiced sound with the Old English letter called an *eth* (ð) and the voiceless sound with the Greek letter *theta* (θ). (The words *eth* and *theta* themselves contain the same voiced and voiceless sounds respectively.)

than (*subord. conj., prep.*) *Than* is both a subordinating conjunction, as in *She is wiser than I am,* and a preposition, as in *She is wiser than me.* As subject of the clause introduced by the conjunction *than,* the pronoun must be nominative, and as object of the preposition *than,* the following pronoun must be in the objective case. Since the following verb *am* is often dropped or "understood," we regularly hear *than I* and *than me.* Some commentators believe that the conjunction is currently more frequent than the preposition, but both are unquestionably Standard. The eighteenth-century effort to declare the preposition incorrect did succeed in giving trouble, not least because it called the *than whom* structure into question, but it too is again in good order: *He is a fine diplomat, than whom we would be hard-pressed to find a better*. *Than* is frequently involved in syntactic blends. See CASE (1); DIFFERENT FROM.

Than is frequently misspelled *then*, although in Edited English it is usually caught and corrected. But watch for the error.

than any, as in *He is stronger than any man living today*, has long been used at least in Conversational and Informal English, but there has been a good deal of effort to spruce up its logic to *He is stronger than any other man* [or *all other men*] *living today*. Edited English frequently prefers that sort of emendation, but in Casual or Impromptu speech and its imitation in writing, the idiomatic effect usually prevents most harm. See ANY.

thankfully (*adv.*) for a time occasioned some disapproval when used as a sentence adverb, as in *Thankfully, that nonsense is over*, although never so severely criticized as was *hopefully*. Like many sentence adverbs *thankfully* can replace a clause (in this case, *We are thankful that . . .*); it is not limited to meaning "with thanks." *Thankfully* is now Standard as sentence adverb.

thanking you in advance is a cliché long used in commercial correspondence until better judgment ruled it out. Avoid it. Say *I'm grateful you are willing to help*, or some such. Make the words sound as though they were your own.

thanks to is a Standard idiom meaning "because of" or "as a result of," and it can be used of other than good or beneficial things: *My garden is ruined, thanks to the torrential rains we've had*.

than whom See THAN.

that 1 (*adv., intensifier*) *That* as adverb occurs in sentences such as *I don't know that much about her*. As intensifier we use it very frequently, usually in Conversational and Informal situations.

that, **omitted** See OMITTED RELATIVE.

that 2, this (*prons.*) Questions have often been raised about the appropriateness of using *this* or *that* (or *these* or *those* or *it*) as a pronoun to refer to an entire sentence, paragraph, or even a whole argument preceding. Nevertheless, *that* (or *this*) is a Standard reference today, in either speech or writing: *This* [*It*] *is why we decided to*

act. Be careful, however, that the limitations of that broad antecedent are clear to the reader or hearer. See IT.

***that 3*, unnecessarily repeated** is a fairly frequent error in first drafts: *He believes that, if we ever get clearance from the government and assemble all the approvals, that we can complete the job in a few weeks*. Get rid of one or both *that*s, or else recast the sentence to do without them.

that 4, which (*prons.*) Many have thought it would be good were *that* always to be used to introduce only restrictive clause modifiers (*The big dog that is barking is a nuisance*) and *which*, only nonrestrictive ones (*The big dog, which is barking, is mine*). This neat dichotomy has been much recommended, and some conservative watchdogs of our Edited English do follow it pretty generally. But—especially in Conversational or Informal contexts—most of us use *which* almost interchangeably with *that* in restrictive modifiers and rarely but sometimes use *that* to introduce nonrestrictive modifiers. Then too we often omit any relative at all, as in *the car I want to own*, rather than *the car that I want to own* or *the car, which I keep in the garage*. (See OMITTED RELATIVE.) Best advice: use *that* or *which* or nothing, depending on what your ear tells you. Then, when writing for certain publications, know that you may have to replace a good many *which*es with *that*s, and perhaps a *that* or two with a *which*, to conform to the "rule" almost no one follows perfectly in other than Edited English and few can follow perfectly even there. See RELATIVE CLAUSES; RELATIVE PRONOUNS; RESTRICTIVE AND NONRESTRICTIVE CLAUSES; RESTRICTIVE AND NONRESTRICTIVE MODIFIERS; RULES AND GENERALIZATIONS.

that 5, which, who, whom (*prons.*) *That* can be used to refer to persons or things: *the woman that I met; the city that was bombed*. *Who* and *whom* refer mainly to persons: *the visitor who is coming; the cook whom I hired*. *Which* usually refers to things, but can also refer to people: *the last soda, which I suspect you took*; *We were both late, but which was the later doesn't matter*.

that big of a deal, (not) See OF A.

that goes without saying See GOES WITHOUT SAYING.

that there, this here These are Vulgar English and Substandard demonstrative pronouns, and Standard English has long considered them shibboleths. It's *this book here*, or simply *this* *book,* but never *this here book*; *that dog there,* or *that dog,* but never *that there dog.*

the (*determiner*) This word in unstressed positions before a consonant, as in *Give me the book,* is pronounced *thuh.* In an unstressed position before a vowel, as in *Give me the apple,* it is pronounced *thi* or even *thee.* If the thing referred to is the greatest, the only, or the sought-after book or apple, then *the* will be stressed, and regardless of the following sound, it will be pronounced *THEE,* as it will also in an interrupted spoken sentence wherein you break off temporarily after *the,* pausing before naming the noun that *the* modifies: *This is the* [often with an intervening vocalized pause such as *uh*] one *I've chosen.*

theater, theatre (*n.*) Americans spell it *theater* except sometimes in proper names, where, in imitation of the British spelling, *theatre* can occur. See SPELLING (1).

thee See THOU.

the fact is, the fact of the matter is, the fact that See FACT.

their (*pron.*), **there** (*adv., expletive*), **they're** (*contr.*) *Their* (possessive plural personal pronoun; see HE; THEY), *there* (adverb and expletive), and *they're* (contraction) are occasionally confused in spelling, usually because of inattention rather than ignorance. But readers will judge them harshly just the same, so be on guard.

theirn is a Substandard form of *theirs,* formed on analogy with *mine* and heard only in Vulgar English speech and its imitations.

theirs (*pron.*), is the absolute possessive or absolute genitive form of the third person plural personal pronoun: *These are their books; these books are theirs.* Important: there's no apostrophe in *theirs.*

theirselves, themself These are Substandard reflexive pronouns, made on analogy with *myself, yourself, herself, itself, ourselves,* and *themselves. Theirselves* and *themself* for *themselves* are limited to Vulgar English speech or imitations of it; both are shibboleths. *Themself* can also occur as an unfortunate result of trying to avoid using a gender-explicit reflexive pronoun by using a blend of the plural *them* with the singular *self.* The choices are *themselves* or *himself* or *herself* or both the last two: *Everyone must take responsibility for themselves* [or *himself or herself*]. See REFLEXIVE PRONOUNS; HISSELF.

them 1 (*pron.*) is the objective case plural personal pronoun. See CASE (1); HE; IT'S ME; THEY.

them 2 (*pron.*) as a demonstrative pronoun is Substandard, limited in use to Vulgar speech and its written imitations, as in *Them boys are back.* Inadvertent use of *them* in this way is a shibboleth: use *these* or *those* instead.

themself See THEIRSELVES.

themselves See REFLEXIVE PRONOUNS; THEIRSELVES.

then (*adj.*) is Standard, is occasionally but not usually hyphenated with the word it modifies, and works as an attributive adjective: *He married the then*[-]*publisher of the paper.*

then See THAN; IF . . . , THEN . . . .

thence See FROM HENCE.

theorize (*v.*), when it combines with a preposition, can take *about, on,* and *concerning: In his talk he theorized about* [*on, concerning*] *economic recovery.*

there (*adv., expletive*) Both functions are illustrated in this sentence: *There there is some snow. There is some snow there on the lawn.* At the front of the sentence, when two *theres* appear together, the first is always the adverb, the second the expletive. When the *theres* are not contiguous, as in the second example, the first one, close to its verb, is always the expletive and the one tagging along anywhere after the verb is always the adverb. See DUMMY SUBJECTS; THEIR; THERE IS.

thereabouts, thereafter, thereat, thereby, therefrom, therein, thereof, thereon, thereto, thereupon, therewith (*advs.*) These adverbs all have a fairly formal air about them, some of them sounding rather legal and very precise, if not pretentious. All are Standard: *thereabouts* means "near or close to that place, time, number, etc."; *thereafter* means "subsequently, from then on"; *thereat* means "at that place or time"; *thereby* means "in that way, connected with that" and is in the cliché *Thereby hangs a tale; therefrom* means "from this, that, or there"; *therein* means "in that place, in that matter"; *thereof* means "of that, from that cause, therefrom"; *thereon* means "on that"; *thereto* means "to that place, besides"; *thereupon* means "at once, right after or because of that, therefore"; and *therewith* means "together with that, in that way, thereupon."

there are See THERE IS.

the reason why See REASON WHY.

therefor, therefore (*advs.*) *Therefor* is by far the rarer word and means "for or in return for that, for it," as in *I'll explain what we must do* *and the causes therefor. Therefore* means "consequently, hence, for that reason," as in *I don't have a key; therefore, I'll have to ring the bell.*

therefrom, therein See THEREABOUTS.

there is, there are The expletive takes either a singular or plural form of *be,* depending on the number of the real subject deferred by use of the expletive: *There is time to spare. There are several minutes to wait.* See DUMMY SUBJECTS.

thereof, thereon, thereto, thereupon, therewith See THEREABOUTS.

the same as, just as (*advs.*) These idioms are Standard: *She looks the same as she did a year ago. She looks just as she did a year ago.* The second is perhaps a trifle more staid.

these kind of, these sort of American English insists that all levels of the written language and nearly all levels of the spoken except Casual and Intimate use *this* or *that* with singular *kind* or *sort* and follow them with *of* plus a singular noun; all levels also use *these* or *those* only with plural *kinds* or *sorts* and follow them with *of* plus a plural noun: *this kind* [*sort*] *of dog; those kinds* [*sorts*] *of dogs.* Common English is much less worried about mixing the numbers of the three variables in these constructions, and British English is too. But for many Standard-using Americans, failures on these structures are powerful shibboleths. See KIND.

thesis See DISSERTATION.

the three R's See R'S.

the way is an idiom in which *way* is a noun but the phrase itself functions like an adverbial or a conjunction much of the time. All such uses as these are Standard in American English: *Where did she learn to walk the way she does? She knits the way her mother did. They look funny the way they wear their hats. This is the way it's going to be.*

they, their, them (*prons.*) *They* is the nominative case plural personal pronoun; *their* is the possessive or genitive plural; *them* is the objective or accusative plural. See AGREEMENT OF INDEFINITE PRONOUNS AND OTHER SINGULAR NOMINALS WITH VERBS AND OTHER PRONOUNS; GENERIC PRONOUNS; GENERIC THIRD PERSON MASCULINE SINGULAR PRONOUN; HE; INCLUSIVE LANGUAGE; PERSONAL PRONOUNS; SEXIST LANGUAGE; THEIRS.

they're See THEIR.

they say See SAYING GOES.

thief (*n.*) The plural is *thieves* (pronounced *THEEVZ*). See NOUNS ENDING IN -F.

thine See THOU.

thing (*n.*) Should you always replace *thing* with a more specific word? *Thing* is indeed an all-purpose word, and it is heavily used in Conversational and Informal contexts precisely because it has a relaxed, broad-spectrum quality: *This proposal may be the thing we've been looking for.* Use it where it fits, but shun it should it seem likely to become a tic in your speech or prose. Don't let the *thing* become a *thing* with you, either way.

think (*n., v.*) The verb *think* combines with *to* plus an infinitive, particularly but not only in the negative, as in *I didn't think to ask* and *I thought to speak to her about it, but I forgot.* In such uses the meaning is "remember, expect, or intend to" and is Standard. Also Standard is *He didn't think she'd mind,* just as is *He thought she wouldn't mind.* The noun *think* is a result of functional shift and is Conversational and Informal: *I'll give it a good think tonight.* See BELIEVE; RAISING.

third, thirdly See FIRSTLY.

THIRD PERSON SINGULAR AND PLURAL See HE; HERS; HIS; HISSELF; ITS; MYSELF; PERSON; PERSONAL PRONOUNS; REFLEXIVE PRONOUNS; SHE; S/HE; THEIR; THEIRN; THEIRS; THEIRSELVES; THEM (1); THEM (2); THEY.

this, that See THAT (2); THAT THERE.

this here See THAT THERE.

thither See HITHER.

thitherto See HITHERTO.

tho, tho' (*adv., conj.*) *Tho* is a variant spelling of *though*; it has been in use for centuries, and it is frequently used in poetry and in Informal correspondence to suggest the informality of Conversational language. It occasionally still has an apostrophe to indicate the omitted letters. See SPELLING (2).

thorn See OLD ENGLISH.

thoroughbred, purebred (*adjs., nn.*) Both words mean "carefully bred through a long genetic line," but *thoroughbred* is usually used of horses, *purebred* of dogs, other animals, and plants. In horsebreeding a *thoroughbred* is one of a particular line of horses, stemming from Arabian stallions and English mares. *Thoroughbred* is also used figuratively as noun and adjective to indicate excellent qualities of breeding, stamina, beauty, performance, and the like: *They were both real thoroughbreds: they had brains,* *looks, and manners, and the stamina and drive to use them well to achieve their goals.*

those kind of, those sort of See THESE KIND OF; KIND.

thou, thee, thine, thy (*prons.*) These archaic forms are second person singular personal pronouns. *Thou* is nominative, *thee*, objective, and *thy* and *thine* are genitive and absolute genitive. Our familiarity with them comes mainly from the King James Bible, Shakespeare's plays, and other Renaissance literature. *You, your,* and *yours,* once only plural, have now taken over the second person singular function, although some Quakers still use *thee* as both nominative and objective.

though See ALTHO; ALTHOUGH; THO.

thought, to take This idiom, meaning "to think, to ponder, to consult one's thoughts," has an old-fashioned air: *He advised me to take thought before replying.*

THOUGHTFUL WRITER See CAREFUL WRITER.

thoughtless See UNTHINKABLE.

three last See FIRST TWO.

three R's, the See R's.

thrill (*v.*), **thrilled** (*adj.*) The verb *thrill* is both transitive, as in *The news thrilled us,* and intransitive, when it combines with the prepositions *at* or *to: We thrilled at the news. I thrilled to the sound of the band.* The participial adjective combines with *by, at,* and *with,* as in *We were thrilled by* [*at, with*] *his announcement,* and with *to* plus an infinitive, as in *She was thrilled to learn that she had won.*

thrive (*v.*) The principal parts are *thrive, throve* or *thrived, thriven* or *thrived*; all are Standard. See STRONG VERBS (1).

throng (*v.*), **thronged** (*adj.*) The verb is both transitive, as in *The students thronged the square,* and intransitive, when it frequently combines with the prepositions *to* or *toward(s),* as in *The bystanders thronged to* [*toward(s)*] *the bandstand.* In the passive voice, *thronged* combines with *by* and *with* to indicate who did the thronging, as in *The streets were thronged by* [*with*] *demonstrators.*

through (*adj.*), meaning "finished," was once labeled Colloquial, but today it is unquestionably Standard: *He says he's through with tournament tennis.* Compare DONE; FINISHED.

throughput See INPUT.

throughway See THRUWAY.

throw in the towel See SPONGE.

thru (*adv., adj., prep.*) is a variant spelling of *through,* widely written but relatively seldom printed; it was formally proposed by spelling reformers in the late nineteenth century as a simplification, and like *tho* has rarely been questioned seriously in Informal use. See SPELLING (1).

thruput See INPUT.

thrust (*n.*) This Standard noun, besides its literal senses (the thrust of a jet engine), has shown a much-increased use in figurative senses (*the thrust of his argument*), to which many conservatives object because they are jargon, because they are overused, or because sexual inferences may be drawn from them. Nonetheless, *thrust* is Standard in these figurative uses.

thruway, expressway, freeway, interstate, motorway, parkway, throughway (*nn.*) *Thruway* is the Standard spelling of the word meaning "a high-speed, limited access, multiple-lane highway." It is a blend of *through* and *highway. Throughway* is a variant. Also called an *expressway* (the British call it a *motorway*), a *thruway* that is part of the federal system is often called an *interstate* or a *freeway.* A *parkway* is a specially landscaped divided highway limited to passenger cars.

thusly, thus (*advs.*) Prefer *thus,* or use circumlocutions such as *as follows* or *in this way* if you have any doubts about *thusly*'s reception; to some people it is still jocular at best. *Thusly* apparently began in the nineteenth century as a humorous "ignorant" substitute for *thus,* but it has now come into much wider use, often for serious purpose, particularly in introducing an example. Most dictionaries label it Colloquial or Informal at best, although at least one considers it Standard at nearly all levels. It is frequently but not always interchangeable with *thus,* but *thus* is the better choice.

thy See THOU.

thyself See REFLEXIVE PRONOUNS.

-tiate, -tiation See -CIATE.

tight (*adv., adj.*), **tightly** (*adv.*) *Tight* is Standard as both adjective (*He runs a tight ship*) and flat adverb usually appearing immediately following verbs such as *close, fasten, hold, shut, sleep, sit, stick,* and the like (*Hold tight to my hand*). *Tightly,* the *-ly* adverb, can appear in adverbial positions where *tight* is seldom or never encountered (*a tightly woven fabric, tightly to argue the case, to tightly argue the case, to argue the case tightly*).

'til See TILL.

TILDE See ACCENT (2); DIACRITICS.

till, 'til, until (*preps.*) *Till* is not a clipped version of *until:* both are Standard words. *Until* may be considered a trifle more Formal, but both occur at all levels. *'Til* is a variant spelling used by those who think (incorrectly) that *till* is a clipped form. At best it looks old-fashioned and self-conscious. Use *till* instead.

timber, timbre (*nn.*) *Timber* (pronounced *TIM-buhr*) is "wood or lumber" in its generic mass noun use, and as a count noun it is "a very large piece of wood of a size for use in heavy construction." *Timbre* (usually pronounced *TAM-buhr* or *TAMBR,* but occasionally *TIM-buhr*) is the name for the difference in sound that makes a note played on one instrument—say, a clarinet—sound different from the same note played on another—say, a trumpet.

timely See FRIENDLY.

time period Many object to this idiom as a redundancy. It is true that *time* or *period* will frequently suffice for exposition, but it is also true that sometimes emphasis or other stylistic purpose may make *repetition* useful. See also PERIOD (2); POINT IN TIME.

times more, times less are both idiomatic and hence need not be restrained by mathematical logic, which sometimes argues that *two times more* is possible but *two times less* is not. Both are possible in natural language, and both are Standard in American English. So too is the formulaic use of either a singular or a plural verb with multiplication: *Six times two is [are] twelve.* The singular seems more common in mathematical writing generally, but laypeople seem to use either, perhaps relying most on the form of the second number in the statement: *Six times one is six. Six ones are six.* See also TWO PLUS TWO.

timidity See TEMERITY.

tin See CAN (2).

tinker (*v.*), when combined with a preposition, usually takes *with,* as in *I was tinkering with the alarm clock,* or sometimes *at,* as in *He tinkered at all sorts of odd inventions.*

tip, tipster (*nn.*) *Tip,* meaning "a bit of expert information," "a hint or a piece of inside information" is Standard, but *tipster,* meaning "a person who gives such information, especially betting information at a race track," is Conversational and Informal.

tirade See HARANGUE.

tired (*adj.*) combines with the preposition *of* plus a noun or a gerund, as in *She's tired of school* [*studying*], or occasionally with *with* or *from* followed by a noun, as in *She became tired with* [*from*] *too much study and extracurricular activity.*

TIRED METAPHORS See FROZEN FIGURES.

tits See BREAST(S).

to 1 (*prep.*), in *She was to her aunt's yesterday,* is dialectal at best, but it is also frequently considered Substandard; *at* is Standard. *To* is Standard, though, in *She went to her aunt's yesterday.*

to 2, too, two These words are sometimes inadvertently misspelled in hurried writing, but inspection should always catch and correct the error, which frequently is the use of *to* for *too.*

to a degree See DEGREE.

to all intents and purposes is a Standard idiom; it is sometimes criticized for wordiness, but it works, as long as it is not overworked.

to-do (*n.*), usually hyphenated, means "bustle, excitement, fuss," as in *There was a lot of to-do as the time to leave drew near.* It is probably still best limited to Conversational or Informal use, but it does occasionally occur in Edited English.

together 1 (*adv.*), when used with verbs such as *join, collect, assemble,* and the like, is sometimes criticized for redundancy. It can on occasion be effectively used with them, however, for emphasis.

together 2 (*adj.*), meaning "self-possessed, poised, well-organized," as in *She's a really together person,* is slang, although its use in Conversational and Informal contexts is growing. *To get (put) it all together* is also slang meaning "to organize or arrange all matters effectively."

togetherness (*n.*), meaning "harmony in a group," "a unity of purpose," "the combining in social and other activities, as in a close-knit family" is Standard: *Their togetherness will see them through these difficulties.*

together with in a sentence such as the following raises questions about agreement: *The dog, together with his young master, brings a lot of mud and dirt into the house.* Is *together with* the equivalent of the conjunction *and?* If so, the verb must be plural to agree with the compound subject. But if *together with* introduces a parenthetical phrase (as some conservatives insist it must always do), then the sentence in the example is correct as is, with the singular subject *dog* taking a singular verb, *brings*. The choice can depend either on strict agreement or on notional agreement, and either singular or plural verbs can appear in Standard English.

to hand See HAND.

token, by the same is a Standard idiom, meaning "in the same way," "following the same reasoning," "according to the same or similar logic," or something of that sort. Since *token* is merely a loose figure, make certain that the "way," the "reasoning," or the "logic" is clear to the reader.

tolerant (*adj.*), **tolerance** (*n.*) The noun *tolerance* combines with several prepositions: *Her tolerance of his grouchiness is remarkable. She has little tolerance to sunlight. He has no tolerance for criticism. He shows little tolerance toward any critic.* The adjective *tolerant* combines with *of,* as in *She is tolerant of his foibles,* and rarely with *to,* as in *His skin disease is tolerant to only the mildest of soaps.*

tomato (*n.*) Pronounce it either *tuh-MAI-to* or *tuh-MAH-to,* and spell the plural *tomatoes.* See PLURALS OF NOUNS ENDING IN -*O.*

tome (*n.*), in its most common use today, is "a large, heavy book," and its ponderous overtones usually refer as much to the contents as to the physical size of the thing itself. The word is sometimes pretentious and often hyperbolic too.

tonic See SODA.

too (*adv., intensifier*) As an intensifier, *too* can modify adjectives (*The shoes were too big for him*) and adverbs (*He was too deeply involved*) and can be used, with *much,* with verbs (*She eats too much*). In modifying past participles, *too* raises the same sort of problem as does *very* (which see). *Too* also appears sometimes as a sentence adverb, although it is rather stiff when compared with *besides, moreover, also,* and the like: *Too, there would not be time to change our plans. Not too,* meaning "not very," is Standard: *I hope we're not too late.* See also TO (2).

took, taken *Took* is the past tense, and *taken* the past participle of the strong verb *take.* Each is Substandard used for the other: *We taken and called the police. She has took great care of her car.* Both usages are shibboleths.

toothsome, toothy (*adjs.*) *Toothsome* means "good-tasting" and, by extension, "attractive, especially sexually, appetizing": *A cart full of toothsome desserts was wheeled up. The bride was a toothsome confection in white satin and lace.* Both senses are Standard. *Toothy* means "full of or showing lots of teeth," as in *His smile was unnaturally toothy.*

top 1 (*n.*) in the plural is slang, meaning "the very best," "top of the heap," as in *You're tops with me.* The singular noun also occurs in several idiomatic locutions: *Take it from the top* is a jargon expression from rehearsing music and other performances, meaning "Start from the beginning"; it may be becoming more generally Conversational. *To blow your top* is slang for "to lose your temper" or "to go mad." *To talk off the top of your head* is "to speak without thinking or planning your remarks"; it's Conversational and Informal. *Off the top* is a jargon expression from haircutting, in which the barber is told *to take a little off the top,* meaning "to shorten the hair on top of the head," transferred to finances, where *to take your money off the top* is also jargon, meaning "to take it before taxes or other expenses have been subtracted." *On top of* is Standard in the sense "on or at the top of," but in the sense "in control," as in *I'm on top of the situation now,* it's Conversational and Informal. *The top of the hour* and *the bottom of the hour* are broadcasting and possibly advertising jargon for the beginning and end of an hour or half hour of broadcasting time; they also mean "on the hour" and "on or at the half hour." *Top of the morning* (*to you*) is a somewhat dated greeting, Casual or Impromptu slang meaning "Wishing you the best or the choicest part of the morning."

top 2 (*adj., v.*) The adjective, meaning "at the top, uppermost, chief, best," as in *He's in top management* or *She's our top negotiator,* is breezy but Standard in those senses, although some commentators declare that it is much overused. *Top* is Standard both as a transitive verb, as in *He topped every joke I told* and *She topped the ball* (golf jargon), and as an intransitive verb, as in *We were cutting trees, and I was topping them* (logging jargon, meaning "to cut off the top branches before felling a tree"). *To top off* is "to put the finishing touches on or to fill to the top (a glass or container)"; *to top out* is from the jargon of building tall structures and means "to complete the framework to the very top," and its figurative sense is "to reach the highest point," as in *The stock topped out at twenty-five and a half. To top up* means "to fill (a fuel tank or another container) to the top."

All but *to top out* are Standard, although even that sense now occurs at some Planned and Semiformal levels.

topless (*adj.*) means "having no top" and specifically refers to female costumes lacking tops and so exposing the breasts. From that come *topless bars,* with their *topless dancers.* And then there is the sense of "exceedingly high," as in "*the topless towers of Ilium.*" All senses are Standard.

tormented (*adj.*) combines frequently with the preposition *by,* as in *He is tormented by his recollection of the blunder,* and sometimes with *with,* as in *She was tormented with fears of failure.*

tornado (*n.*) The plural is either *tornadoes* or *tornados.* See PLURALS OF NOUNS ENDING IN -*O*.

torpedo (*n.*) The plural is *torpedoes.* See PLURALS OF NOUNS ENDING IN -*O*; SUBMARINE.

torso (*n.*) The plural is either *torsos* or (less often) *torsi.* See PLURALS OF NOUNS ENDING IN -*O*; FOREIGN PLURALS.

tortuous, torturous (*adjs.*) These two can be confused, and for good reason. *Tortuous* (pronounced *TOR-choo-uhs*) means "winding and twisted," as in *His thought processes were incredibly tortuous. Torturous* (pronounced *TOR-chuhr-uhs*) means "causing pain and torture," as in *Their cruel comments were torturous to her.* Both words come from the same root, the Latin *tortus,* meaning "twisted," and in some uses it is impossible without contextual assistance to know which is intended, particularly when you are describing roads or paths, which can be twisty or painful to travel or both.

to say the least See SAY THE LEAST.

total (*adj., v.*), **totally** (*adv.*) The adjective and adverb, like *complete* and *completely,* are often considered absolutes or incomparables and therefore redundant or tautological when used with words like *destruction* (*total destruction*) and *destroyed* (*totally destroyed*). But again, sometimes emphasis or another stylistic consideration may make the overkill useful. Make your choice deliberately. Note too that the adverb is beginning to develop a use as an intensifier and cliché, especially among adolescents and young adults. The verb (*I totaled my car*) means "to damage beyond repair." It is slang.

totality (*n.*), when it means "all," is usually a pretentious word.

to the manner (manor) born See MANNER.

to the nth degree See DEGREE.

toward, towards (*preps.*) *Toward* and *towards* (pronounce them either *TORD*[Z] or *tuh-WORD*[Z]) are Standard and interchangeable in meaning. American English uses both, but *toward* more often; British English uses *towards* more.

towel, throw in the See SPONGE.

to wit means "namely" or "that is to say" and is a stuffy-sounding word in most other than legal or other Formal or Oratorical contexts.

track, tract (*nn.*) These words are sometimes confused, because the voiceless consonants at the ends are sometimes hard to distinguish in continuous speech, and the error is carried over into writing. A *track* is a literal or figurative route or path or marked road; a *tract* is a pamphlet, particularly a political or religious one, or an extent of space, as in *a tract of land,* or an archaic word for an extent of time, as in *this tract of years.*

trade See SKILLFUL.

TRADE NAMES When generic terms are available, use them, especially when you write for publication: *tissue,* not *Kleenex*; *copier,* not *Xerox.* Generic terms are less likely to confuse readers unfamiliar with a particular trade name you might use, and they will also eliminate possible problems of copyright infringement. When you must use *trade names* in print, be sure to reproduce the original spelling and capitalization exactly.

TRADITIONAL GRAMMARS There are a good many traditions of grammatical inquiry, but the usual referents for the term *traditional grammars* are the scholarly English grammars done by Jespersen (1909–1949), Poutsma (1914–1929), Kruisinga (1925), Zandwort (1957), and in this country, Curme (1931, 1935). They are all meaning-based, in that they consider not just grammatical indicators, but the total semantic content of the sentences they examine, and they study in great detail the sentence and sentence types, the parts of speech, inflections and syntax, all by means of the analysis of huge masses of written examples. All concentrate on the written language almost exclusively, define their parts of speech both notionally (i.e., a *noun* is the name of a person, place, or thing; it's a noun because that's what it means) and functionally (i.e., a *pronoun* is a word that can replace a noun or another pronoun; it's a pronoun because that's what it does), and their terminology and descriptive analyses have affected nearly all grammars of whatever sort done subsequently by others. See GRAMMAR.

traffic (*v.*) Spell the past tense and past participle *trafficked,* the present participle *trafficking,* and the agentive *trafficker.* See SPELLING OF -*ING* AND -*ED* FORMS OF VERBS ENDING IN -*C.*

tragedy (*n.*) Except in literary and dramatic criticism, rarely do you expect to find a classical definition of *tragedy* strictly adhered to—as, for example, an event in which a strong central character's flawed strength brings him or her to disaster. The word has generalized a great deal in use and is now regularly applied to accident, disaster, death, and suffering, especially on a large scale; moreover, thanks to our penchant for hyperbole, even spilled milk is a tragedy in some eyes. Both journalese and Conversational contexts employ the word loosely and too much; strain it no further than you must: remember the boy who cried "Wolf!''

tragic, tragical (*adjs.*) *Tragic* is the adjective most frequently used. *Tragical* is useful primarily in describing events or actions that display or attempt to exhibit characteristics of tragedy, although the distinction requires considerable contextual help: *She tore her hair and screamed in a manner apparently deemed tragical. Tragic* seems to describe the event itself, *tragical,* the portrayal of it.

transcendent, transcendental (*adjs.*), **transcendentalism, Transcendentalist** (*nn.*) *Transcendent* means "extraordinary, surpassing, beyond human experience" and is used frequently for hyperbole: *Hers is a transcendent beauty. Transcendental* deals with the philosophic, the metaphysical; it means "supernatural, otherworldly," as in *He became interested in transcendental meditation.* Rarely, *transcendental* is also used to mean *transcendent,* a use that is no help to anyone; avoid it. *Transcendentalism* is a philosophical view that insists on the primacy of the spiritual over the material. Ralph Waldo Emerson was probably the most prominent of the nineteenth-century American *Transcendentalists.*

TRANSFORMATIONAL-GENERATIVE GRAMMAR is a theoretical grammar designed to explain the process and the rules that enable us to "know" how to generate an infinite number of grammatical sentences (and how to avoid truly ungrammatical ones), even though we cannot consciously describe what scheme it is we're following. *Generative grammar* had its beginning particularly in the work of Zellig Harris and his student Noam Chomsky (especially Chomsky's *Syntactic Structures* [1957]). It assumes that all sentences begin with deep structures of brief syntactic patterns of a sort that may be common to all languages. *Transformational grammar* then states the strings of rules that transform phrase structures into finished *surface structures*—sentences either spoken or written. The following example omits many intervening stages but roughly illustrates the process: *Dogs bite people* and *Dogs bark* are deep structures that underlie the finished sentence *People are never bitten by barking dogs. Dogs bark* can be transformed by rule into *Barking dogs,* which can then be included in the other deep structure to give us *Barking dogs bite people.* Applying a negative *transformation* adds a negative at the proper place in the string—*Barking dogs never bite people*—and finally the rules for the syntactic reordering and morphological changes required for a *passive transformation* produce the surface structure, *People are never bitten by barking dogs.* See GRAMMAR.

transient, transitory (*adjs.*) Something *transient* is temporary, just passing through, impermanent, and when applied to people it means "staying just a short time," as in *The hotel's guests were transient; none was a permanent resident. Transitory* is a synonym of *transient* in its meaning "temporary," but it also means "fleeting or ephemeral," as in *She saw her days of happiness as transitory and not to be counted upon.*

TRANSITIVE, INTRANSITIVE VERBS *Transitive verbs* are verbs that take direct objects: *He hates spinach. Intransitive verbs* do not have direct objects: *She hates passionately.* Many English verbs, like *hate,* can be either *transitive* or *intransitive.*

transitory See TRANSIENT.

translate, transliterate (*vv.*) To *translate* is to put the idea in the words of another language; to *transliterate* is to record it in the letters of a different alphabet, as when we record a Greek word in the letters of our own alphabet.

translucent, opaque, transparent (*adjs.*) If a pane is *translucent,* light passes through it but is diffused so that one cannot see clearly the details of whatever is on the other side. If a pane is *transparent,* light passes through it nearly or wholly undiffused, so that one can see clearly the details of whatever is on the other side. An ordinary glass window is *transparent,* a frosted glass window is *translucent.* A panel that permits no light to pass through it, such as a piece of plywood, is *opaque*; you can see nothing through it at all.

transmute (*v.*) combines usually with *into* or *to* and means "to transform, to convert into another form or kind," as in *The Russians' effort now was to transmute their old economy into* [*to*] *a market economy.*

transparent See TRANSLUCENT.

transpire (*v.*) means "to pass vapor through the pores of the skin or the surfaces of leaves," "to become apparent," or "to happen, to come to pass." This last sense, like the other two, has long been Standard, despite some objection to its generalization: *It transpired that we were invited after all.* ·

traumatic (*adj.*), **trauma** (*n.*) *Trauma,* which means "an injury or shock" in medical use and, in psychiatry, "a painful emotional jolt of lasting effect," is a singular noun. It has two plurals: *traumas* and *traumata* (see FOREIGN PLURALS). The adjective *traumatic* has a considerably wider and more general use than the noun: it means everything from "literally wounding, injuring, or scarring" to "upsetting." Again, hyperbolic uses have tended slightly to weaken its meanings. Best advice: use it seriously or not at all.

travesty See BURLESQUE.

tread (*v.*) The principal parts are *tread, trod* or *treaded, trodden* or *trod.* The past tense of the idiom *to tread water* is usually *treaded,* but *trod* is more frequent in other senses: *We trod the path as quietly as we could.* See STRONG VERBS (1).

treat (*v.*) combines with *of* to mean "to discuss, to deal with a particular matter": *In his opening remarks he treated of the past relations between our two groups.* It combines with *with,* and occasionally with *for, on, about,* or *concerning,* to mean "to negotiate, to discuss with an eye to reaching agreement": *Our delegation was to treat with theirs on* [*for, about, concerning*] *a cease-fire.* All these uses are Standard.

treble See TRIPLE.

trek (*n., v.*) Since both noun and verb dealt originally with long, difficult overland trips such as migrations or explorations, there has always been objection by some to either jocular or hyperbolic use of either to refer to shorter, less arduous trips, especially those that don't involve pioneering in some sense. Keep those objections in mind. The television serial "Star Trek" and its fans, who came to be called *trekkies,* have given *trek* a new popularity, and it may be that its frequency in general use has increased somewhat as a result.

trembler, tremblor See TEMBLOR.

tribute (*n.*), in the phrase *a tribute to,* meaning "an evidence, proof, or demonstration of" or "a reward for" is Standard, as in *The popularity of his work is a tribute to his unerring sense of what the public likes.*

triceps See BICEPS.

trillion (*n.*) A *trillion* has two meanings in American English: "1,000,000,000,000" and hyperbolically "any very large number," as in *I have a trillion letters to write.* The British *trillion* also means a thousand billion. See BILLION; MILLIARD.

triple, treble (*adjs., nn., vv.*) Semantically these verbs and adjectives are interchangeable, but Americans usually prefer *triple* as verb and adjective for most general uses: *We hope to triple our enrollments by next fall. He's a triple threat performer in this kind of work. Treble* turns up in *Treble your returns* and *They're asking for treble damages.* The noun *triple* of course lives a separate life in baseball, as the noun and adjective *treble* do in music: *I hit two triples in today's game. The treble* [*treble part*] *is sung by a countertenor.*

triumphal, triumphant (*adjs.*) *Triumphal* means "in honor of a triumph," "like a triumph," as in *We had a triumphal celebration. Triumphant* means "victorious," "elated over a success," as in *She was wearing a triumphant smile.*

trivia (*n.*) is plural but takes either a singular or a plural verb and subsequent pronouns. See FOREIGN PLURALS.

trod See TREAD.

trooper, trouper (*nn.*) These are homophones. A *trooper* is a mounted soldier or police officer and, in the United States, a state police officer; a *trouper* is a member of an acting company, especially an experienced, steady, dependable actor. The term is extended in that elevated sense: any solid performer (not just an actor) is a *trouper.*

TROPE is a technical name for any figure of speech; any use of a word in a figurative way or sense is a *trope* (pronounced *TROP*).

trouper See TROOPER.

trousers See PANTS; SLACKS.

truculent (*adj.*) (pronounced *TRUHK-yoo-lint*) began by meaning "savage" but has come now mainly to mean "belligerent," as in *He was truculent and spoiling for a fight.*

true (*adj.*) When combined with *to, true* means "loyal or faithful," as in *She was true to her promise.* With *of* or *for, true* means that the statement is accurate as applied to the object of the preposition: *What we learned about ourselves turns out to be true of [for] them as well.*

true facts In a world where all *facts* really are true, *true facts* is a redundancy, but, alas, in our world many things alleged to be *facts* turn out not to be factual after all, so sometimes a distinction and an additional emphasis may be required to help sort out the true ones from the false ones.

truly See SINCERELY.

trust (*n., v.*) The verb *trust,* when combined with a preposition, takes either *in* or *to: We must trust in our preparations. They trusted us to cover the back of the house.* The noun usually takes *in: Place your trust in your common sense.* See ENTRUST.

trustee, trusty (*nn.*) A *trustee* (pronounced *truhs-TEE*) is someone appointed to manage the property of others or a member of a board charged with such a task. A *trusty* (pronounced *TRUHS-tee* or *truhs-TEE*) is a convict given special privileges and duties because he or she is considered trustworthy.

try See ENDEAVOR.

try and For generations, commentators have criticized *try and,* as in *I'll try and see her tomorrow,* preferring *try to* in such constructions. Both have been in constant use throughout the period, however, and the main difference is that *try and* is almost always limited to Casual and Impromptu levels and their written imitations, whereas *try to* is Standard, appropriate at all levels.

T-shirt, tee shirt (*n.*) This now unisex knit undershirt or shirt is so named because when laid flat its shape resembles the capital letter *T.* Both spellings are Standard.

-tt- See CONSONANTS (2).

tube See SUBWAY.

tubercular, tuberculous (*adjs.*) *Tubercular* is an adjective with two senses, a general one applying to anything having or characterized by *tubercules,* and a specific one applying to anyone having the disease *tuberculosis,* as in *His mother was tubercular, you know. Tuberculous* is simply a synonym of *tubercular.* Both have had relatively low frequency of use since the disease has become scarcer, but the recent increase in drug-resistant strains of *tuberculosis*

probably means that both words will remain active in the general vocabulary.

tummy (*n.*) is a clipped bit of babytalk or whimsy based on and meaning "stomach." It's Conversational and Informal at best.

turbid, turgid (*adjs.*) These adjectives look and sound a good bit alike, and since they are both used literally of abnormal conditions of flowing water, they are easy to confuse unless context guides fully. *Turbid waters* are "full of sediment, muddy, and dark," whereas *turgid waters* are "swollen." Applied figuratively, the words are perhaps a bit easier to keep separate: *turgid prose* is a fairly common application; it is pompous and overblown, windy and pretentious; *turbid prose* (a much less common application) is dark and muddy, hard to fathom.

turnpike See THRUWAY.

tweeny See BETWEEN-MAID.

twelvemo, 12mo See DUODECIMO.

two See TO (2).

two and two See TWO PLUS TWO.

two-faced See DUPLICATE.

two first See FIRST TWO.

two plus two, two and two The question of agreement, whether grammatical or notional, in describing the mathematical process of addition is interesting, as is that for multiplication (see also TIMES MORE). Writers about mathematics generally use the singular, viewing each number as a singular entity when *plus* is the connective (*sixteen plus sixteen is thirty-two*); when the connective is *and,* however, then a plural verb is likely (*sixteen and sixteen are thirty-two*). Laypeople use either: *Two and two make* [or *makes*] *four.* Sometimes, as in multiplication, the grammatical number of the second number in the statement will control, as in *nine and one is ten,* but *one and nine are ten.*

-ty See -NESS.

tycoon (*n.*) achieved its Standard status in the sense "a powerful magnate, a financier" only quite recently, but it is now unquestionably accepted.

type (*adj., n.*), **-type** (*suffix*) Until about a generation ago, the unquestioned Standard form was to use *type* as a noun followed by a prepositional phrase: *I don't care for that type of house.* But it then began to turn up in Common speech in the adjunct position: *This is a good type engine. She's a nice type singer.* Its adjectival use remains Conversational and Informal at best, although it sometimes occurs in print in hyphenated form: *a company-type picnic, an adult-type bookstore*. In Edited English, however, it is

usually unwelcome, and most conservatives don't like it much at any level. See KIND.

U

U, non-U (*adjs.*) *U* is a British Conversational and Informal adjective meaning "characteristic or typical of the upper class"; it's applied to manners and customs of all sorts, including language, as in *His speech was quite naturally and unselfconsciously U. Non-U* is its opposite, "manners never to be associated with the upper class," as in *Her dress and her speech boldly declared her non-U origins*. Both terms were modish in the United States when first borrowed in the 1950s, but they are much less frequently encountered here today.

uglies, uglify See UGLY.

uglily (*adv.*) is a Standard adverb but rare in speech. Pronouncing a second *-ly* suffix is awkward, and so we elect instead a circumlocution: rather than *He frowned uglily*, we'll say *He frowned in an ugly manner* [*way, fashion*]. See FRIENDLY.

ugly (*adj.*), **uglies** (*n. pl.*), **uglify** (*v.*) The adjective is Standard both in its literal "homely, unpleasant-looking, unattractive" senses, as in *She had as ugly a dog as I'd ever seen*, and in its figurative "offensive, nasty, vile" senses, as in *The situation suddenly turned ugly*. The plural noun is Conversational and Informal at best and is a name given anything overwhelmingly distasteful or unpleasant, as in *I woke with a bad case of the uglies*. The verb *uglify* is Standard, meaning "to make ugly," as in *His makeup uglified him shockingly*.

uh (*interj.*) is the conventional imitative spelling of the vocalized pause we utter while fumbling for a word or thinking about what to say next: *I'm—uh—afraid I don't remember—uh—your name*.

uh-huh, uh-oh, uh-uh See HUH-UH.

U.K. See BRITAIN.

ultimate (*adj., n.*), **ultimately** (*adv.*) The adjective means "the farthest or most remote," as in *at the ultimate edge of the solar system*, "final or conclusive," as in *the ultimate resolution*, and "the greatest possible, utmost," as in *the ultimate effort*; the noun means "something displaying any of these characteristics,"

as in *Their computer network was the ultimate in modern office equipment*. The adverb *ultimately* means "finally, in the end," as in *Ultimately you'll agree with me*. All these uses are Standard. See also PENULTIMATE.

ultimatum (*n.*) has two plurals: *ultimatums* and the much less frequent *ultimata*. The third syllable of each may be pronounced either *-MAI-* or *-MAH-*. See FOREIGN PLURALS.

ultra (*adj., n.*) The adjective means "extreme or excessive," as in *Her clothes are always ultra*, and the noun means "an extremist," as in *He's always been an ultra when it comes to music*. Both are Standard.

ultra- (*prefix*) means "extreme, beyond, excessive," as in *She is ultraconservative in her dress*. It's a Standard prefix, generally used without a hyphen, but it's close to being a cliché, probably because of our penchant for hyperbole.

umlaut See ACCENT (2); DIACRITICS.

umpire See REFEREE.

un- See IN-.

unabridged See ABRIDGE.

unalienable See INALIENABLE.

unapt See INAPT.

UNATTACHED PARTICIPLES See DANGLING MODIFIERS.

unaware (*adv., adj.*), **unawares** (*adv.*) The adjective means "not aware, unconscious": *She was unaware of our concern*. *Unawares* is the usual Standard adverb: *Their request caught the committee unawares*. Rare instances of *unaware* as adverb occur, but they may actually be predicate adjectives: compare *We were caught unaware* and *We were unaware*. See OBLIVIOUS.

unbeknown,   unbeknownst (*adjs.*) Although sometimes questioned as dialectal or otherwise Nonstandard, both words are in fact Standard, meaning "unknown, without knowledge of." *To* is almost always the following preposition: *Their decision was unbeknown* [*unbeknownst*] *to the rest of the membership. Unbeknownst to me, they had left early.*

unbend (*v.*), **unbending** (*adj.*) *Unbend* means "to straighten," as in *Robin unbent his bow and fitted a new string,* and "to relax," as in *After the tense debate, the delegates began to unbend and chat easily in the lobby.* But the prefix *un-* also provides a different sort of negation or opposition, as in the adjective *unbending,* meaning "unyielding, unchanging," and hence "stiff, inflexible": *Her father was unbending: she was not allowed to go.*

UNCHANGING PLURALS OF NOUNS
See RELIC PLURALS OF NOUNS.

uncomfortable, uncomfortably See DISCOMFIT.

UNCOMPARABLE ADJECTIVES See
ABSOLUTE ADJECTIVES.

unconscious See SUBCONSCIOUS.

under- (*prefix*) means "small" (*undersized*), "beneath" (*undercurrent*), "of lower rank" (*underclassman*), "below normal" (*undereducated*), and "insufficient" or "too little" (*underpowered, undercooked, undersubscribed*). It is usually prefixed without a hyphen.

underground See SUBWAY.

underhanded, underhand (*advs., adjs.*), **underhandedly** (*adv.*) *Underhanded* as an adjective, meaning "deceitful, sly," as in *He played an underhanded trick on his parents,* and "deceitfully, slyly" as an adverb, as in *He did it underhanded,* is Standard in both uses. *Underhanded* is a flat adverb, and *underhandedly* is an exact synonym, also Standard: *He did it underhandedly.*

Underhand is also both adjective and flat adverb, but although it can mean "deceitful," its more frequent meaning is a literal description of a throwing motion made with the arm always below the shoulder and contrasting with an overhand throwing motion: *She made an underhand throw. She threw underhand to first. Underhanded* is also Standard in these throwing senses, as both adjective and flat adverb, but it is somewhat more common meaning "deceitful" or "cheating": *It was a dirty, underhanded trick she played.*

underlay, underlie (*vv.*) These verbs contrast and pose usage problems exactly as do *lay* and *lie* (which see). The principal parts are *underlay, underlaid, underlaid* for the transitive *underlay* (*We underlaid the siding with an insulating board*), and *underlie, underlay, underlain* for the intransitive *underlie* (*It is supposed efficiently to underlie any sort of siding*).

underpants See PANTIES; PANTS.

underpass See SUBWAY.

underprivileged (*adj., n.*) has sometimes been challenged as illogical, since privileges are presumably not so widely available as *entitlements.* But the adjective *underprivileged* is nonetheless Standard in the sense "less fortunate than the average citizen." The noun frequently means "the poor," and it is also often used as a euphemism synonymous with *the disadvantaged, the handicapped, the disabled,* and like terms, although it is not necessarily limited to lack of material things or physical abilities alone.

undershirt See T-SHIRT; VEST (1).

understanding, misunderstanding (*nn.*) *Understanding* is Standard in most of its literal senses but is sometimes considered a bit old-fashioned in the sense of "an oral agreement not made public, especially one between a man and a woman or between two parties in any other sort of negotiation": *Although we were not formally engaged, we had an understanding before I enlisted. We hadn't yet signed the papers, it's true, but I thought the owner and I had reached an understanding that I would buy the car at the figure named.* This last example also illustrates the use of *understanding* as what has been called "a sinister euphemism," to gloss over or ignore a failure of agreement. *Misunderstanding* is also sometimes strained in order to play down and make little of a disagreement: *We were not quarreling; it was just a misunderstanding.* Some such uses suggest that there was no real disagreement, even though the literal sense of the word makes it clear that there was.

UNDERSTATEMENT Rhetorically the opposite of hyperbole, *understatement* provides less information than might be warranted; it is an intentional lack of force in expression. It has therefore an air of modesty and self-effacement, yet it frequently stems from confidence: those secure in their views need not bluster or shout. See also DOUBLE NEGATIVE; HYPERBOLIC; LITOTES.

UNDERSTOOD Some grammars, especially those intended for pedagogical use, make considerable use of the concept of words and other grammatical entities that are unexpressed but "*understood.*" For example, the words in brackets are omitted and therefore said to be *understood* in sentences such as these: *She is the woman [that, whom] I love. He's much taller than I [am]. [Have you] Been to Boston this week? Yes, [I've been there] twice.* Some grammarians belittle the concept of "*understood* words." For other grammatical explanations of

these structures, see CASUAL SPEECH; FRAG-
MENT; OMITTED RELATIVE; SITUATION UTTER-
ANCE; THAN.

undertaker See MORTICIAN.

under the circumstances See CIRCUMSTAN-
CES.

under way, underway, under weigh A ship
has *way* on it when it is in motion, and thus the
idiom *to get under way* [or *underway*] means
"to begin to move," just as the idiom *to be
under way* [or *underway*] is "to be moving,"
regardless of whether what's moving or beginning to move is a ship, a car, or a fund-raising
campaign. The idea of *weigh*, as with an anchor, is an error in either use, although in the
past many reputable authors have chosen that
form. *Under way* and *underway* are both now
Standard spellings of both adverbial and adjectival uses.

underwhelm (*v.*) began as a nonce word, and a
witty one at that (there are several suggested
originators), but it has caught on as nonce words
occasionally do and is now Standard, an antonym of *overwhelm*, heavily ironic and amusing:
*Her acting thoroughly underwhelmed all the
critics.*

undiscriminate, undiscriminating See INDIS-
CRIMINATE.

undoubtedly See DOUBTLESS.

undue (*adj.*), **unduly** (*adv.*) *Undue* means either
"not required, unnecessary," as in *Her haste
was wholly undue and unwarranted,* or "excessive, improper," as in *His undue influence over
the boy caused much suffering. Unduly* means
"unnecessarily or excessively," as in *The family were unduly alarmed at his absence.* Despite
some purist suggestions that *not to feel undue
alarm* and *not to be unduly alarmed* may be
redundancies, they appear instead to be emphatic, hyperbolic, and Standard.

uneatable See EATABLE.

uneconomic, uneconomical (*adjs.*) are synonyms, each meaning "wasteful, costly." *They
lived in a lavish style, uneconomic* [*uneconomical*] *and prodigal.*

unedible See INEDIBLE.

unequal (*adj.*) can combine with the preposition
to, usually followed by a noun or gerund: *He
was unequal to the task she set him. She seems
unequal to completing her assignments on time.*

unequivocally, unequivocably (*advs.*) *Unequivocally* is the Standard adverb, meaning
"plainly, unquestionably, clearly," as in *We*

*were unequivocally correct in our judgment.
Unequivocably* does occur occasionally, but it
is Nonstandard and should not be used.

unexceptionable,   unexceptional (*adjs.*)
Unexceptionable means "correct, without
blemish or flaw," as in *His manners were unexceptionable, and not a fault could be found with
his behavior*; sometimes it also means "merely
correct," as in *The dinner was unexceptionable,
but not very interesting. Unexceptional* has that
same rather dull meaning, "ordinary, not worth
comment," as in *His term of office was unexceptional; nothing unusual set it apart.* The distinction between *unexceptionable* as "without
blemish" and *unexceptional* as "wholly unremarkable" is worth keeping. See EXCEPTIONA-
BLE.

unflappable (*adj.*) means "imperturbable, calm,
not easily upset," as in *She was an unflappable
entertainer, despite all the problems backstage.*
The word is now Standard, although some commentators still label it Colloquial or Informal.

unhealthful, unhealthy (*adjs.*) The distinctions, such as they are, mirror the current status
of the pair *healthy, healthful* (which see).

unhuman See INHUMAN.

unilateral See BILATERAL.

uninterest See DISINTEREST.

uninterested See DISINTERESTED.

unique See ABSOLUTE ADJECTIVES.

unisex (*adj.*) Anything unisex—clothes, hair-
styles, and even manners—serves and suits both
sexes: *Their unisex haircuts, sweatshirts, jeans,
and sneakers made it hard to tell the schoolboys
from the schoolgirls.*

United Kingdom See BRITAIN.

United States (*n.*) Usually our country's name
takes a singular verb: *The United States is in a
bad recession,* and agreement requires as well a
singular pronoun when the country is dealt with
as a nation: *It's a great country.* Occasionally
we'll hear or read about *these United States,*
with plural verb and subsequent pronouns, but
this is a conscious stylistic shift designed perhaps to stress the diversity of the country's
makeup, but more probably to embellish a flowery discourse. In all other circumstances, *the
United States* [*of America*] is usually singular.

unless and until is essentially an oral filler, a
cliché used often for emphasis, but it should
seldom appear in Edited English, and then only
when the two conditions the locution specifies
both apply literally.

unlike (*prep., conj.*) The preposition frequently raises usage questions because it can so often lead to faulty parallelism: parallelism is present in *Unlike my sister, I can't swim,* but it's marred in *Unlike in this country, the British drive on the left.* Edited English frequently requires a subordinate clause beginning with *as* or *whereas* to establish the parallelism: *As the Swedes no longer do, the British still drive on the left* or *Whereas we do not, the British drive on the left.* Conjunctive *unlike,* as in *Unlike the way things are in our town, Smithfield has parking meters,* occurs frequently and appropriately in Conversational and Informal contexts, but is inappropriate in most Oratorical and Formal use. See FALSE COMPARISON; LIKE (2).

unloose, unloosen (*vv.*) These Standard weak verbs (principal parts: *unloose, unloosed, unloosed; unloosen, unloosened, unloosened*) are synonyms meaning "to set loose, release, make less tight, or undo," as in *He unloosed [unloosened] his tie.* See LOOSE.

unmoral See AMORAL.

unnatural See SUPERNATURAL.

unprecedented (*adj.*) means "without precedent"; avoid using it as a hyperbole meaning simply "unusual."

unqualified, disqualified (*adjs.*) *Unqualified* means "lacking the necessary qualifications": *She's an unqualified applicant, because she lacks a chauffeur's license. Disqualified* means "ineligible, having rights or privileges taken away": *The disqualified players had all broken the team's curfew rule.*

unquestionably See DOUBTLESS.

unravel See RAVEL.

unreadable See ILLEGIBLE.

unrealistic See REALISTIC.

unreligious See IRRELIGIOUS.

unrepairable, irreparable (*adjs.*) Both are Standard meaning "not repairable," but *irreparable* (pronounced *ir-REP-uhr-uh-bul*) is much the more frequently used. Note its spelling: *irrepairable* is a misspelling. *Unrepairable* is pronounced *uhn-ree-PER-uh-bul.* See also INCOMPARABLE.

unsanitary See INSANITARY.

unsatisfied See DISSATISFIED.

unsavory (*adj.*) means literally "lacking taste," "smelling or tasting bad," but its figurative use, applied to personal appearance, character, or reputation, has reached cliché status.

unseasonable, unseasonably, unseasonal, unseasonally See SEASONABLE.

unsociable, unsocial See ANTISOCIAL.

unsolvable, insoluble, insolvable (*adjs.*) *Unsolvable* and *insolvable* are synonyms; both mean "not susceptible of being solved": *It was one of those unsolvable [insolvable] problems. Insoluble* has two meanings: "cannot be dissolved," as in *These crystals are insoluble in water,* and "not susceptible of solving," so that *an unsolvable* or *insolvable problem* can also be *an insoluble problem.* All three are Standard in this meaning, as is *insoluble* in its first sense.

UNSTRESSED See STRESS.

UNSTRESSED VOWELS, SPELLING OF See SPELLING OF UNSTRESSED VOWELS.

unstructured (*adj.*) means "informally organized, free, lacking a structure." It can be either pejorative or elevated: an *unstructured* course may be either stimulatingly free or maddeningly disorganized. The word is much used currently in its elevated sense. In tailoring, an *unstructured* jacket is a loose-fitting one that lacks interfacing and other internal support.

unthinkable, thoughtless, unthinking (*adjs.*) Anything *unthinkable* is "inconceivable, impossible, too much": *That we wouldn't attend was unthinkable. Unthinking* means "without thought," but more often it is a synonym of *thoughtless,* meaning "heedless or inconsiderate," as in *His unthinking [thoughtless] remarks hurt her feelings.* All three words are Standard in these uses.

until See TILL; UNLESS AND UNTIL.

untimely (*adv., adj.*) The adjective means "unexpected, premature," as in *His was an untimely death,* and "unwelcome or inopportune," as in *Her arrival was awkwardly untimely.* The adverb has similar meanings, as in *She died untimely,* and *He entered the room untimely, and everyone was embarrassed.* All these uses are Standard. See FRIENDLY.

unto (*prep.*) means *to* but is archaic in most uses today, carrying with it the scriptural flavor of *Render unto Caesar . . . ,* and *. . . unto the third and fourth generations . . . ,* except in uses such as references to self: *She has become a law unto herself,* where it is Standard.

untoward (*adj.*) is pronounced *uhn-TO-uhrd, uhn-TORD,* or *uhn-tuh-WORD* and means "difficult, unfortunate, troubled, or unlucky": *These were untoward circumstances, and they exacted their price.*

unwonted, unwanted (*adjs.*) *Unwonted* has three Standard pronunciations, at least one of which is a homophone of *unwanted: unwonted*'s stressed middle syllable can rhyme with *want, gaunt,* or *won't,* and it means "rare, uncommon, not customary": *His unwonted enthusiasm was embarrassing. Unwanted* means "not needed, undesirable, unwished for": *Her interference was both unwonted and unwanted.*

up (*adv., prep., v.*) The adverb and preposition regularly combine with verbs, and *up* is usually not extraneous or redundant in such use: *to walk up* is different from *to walk, to run up a bill* or *a set of table napkins* or *a hill* is different from *to run* such things, and *to sign* and *to sign up* differ semantically too. Nearly all such uses are Standard, although occasionally one will be thought inappropriate in Edited English. *Up* distributes itself differently in relation to direct objects: you may *add up the bill* or *add the bill up,* but you must always *add it up.* Consult the entries for particular verbs for other Standard combinations with the preposition and adverb *up.*

The verb *up* is Conversational and Informal when used to mean "to increase or raise," as in *They decided to up my wages;* it is likely to be inappropriate in most Edited English and in all other Formal and Oratorical contexts.

up against the wall, up the wall See WALL.

up and is a locution much like *go and* and *try and* (which see) and is slang, limited to Casual, dialectal, and Informal use, as in *He up[ped] and punched me in the nose.*

upcoming, incoming, oncoming (*adjs.*) Functional shift has reversed the order of these verbs plus a preposition and turned the combinations into adjectives. *Upcoming* (from *coming up*) means "forthcoming, coming soon," as in *There is a carnival upcoming in July; The upcoming meetings will be important. Oncoming* also means "approaching," as in *We watched the oncoming train,* and *incoming* means "coming in, arriving," as in *Here is the incoming mail.* All three are Standard, as are others of a similar pattern. See ONGOING; OUTGOING.

upon See ON.

upper See DOWNER.

UP STYLE, DOWN STYLE An *up style* of capitalization (and to some minds punctuation as well) tends to use a good deal of each; a *down style* uses as little of each as possible. In an *up style,* both *Elm* and *Street* are capitalized: *Elm Street;* a *down style* capitalizes only *Elm: Elm street.* An *up style* punctuates a series thus: *a dog, a cat, and a duck;* a *down style* does it: *a dog, a cat and a duck.* If your words are intended for print, find out which style your publisher prefers and adhere to it.

up the pipe is a slang locution meaning "lost, wasted, irretrievable," as is smoke that has vanished up the chimney: *All our efforts were wasted, up the pipe.* Compare DOWN THE DRAIN.

uptight (*adj.*) is probably a slang term, but at least one dictionary considers it Standard; it means "angry, nervous, unbendingly conventional, tense, irritable," as in *She was uptight when the contest began, but she's always been an uptight sort of person.* Best advice: don't use *uptight* in Oratorical or Formal contexts.

up until is a compound preposition that means the same as *until,* as in *We can stay until [up until] Thursday.* Limit it to Conversational and Informal and Semiformal use, and let context make clear the relation (if any) to bedtime; *until* by itself is more appropriate in most Edited English.

upward (*adv., adj.*), **upwards** (*adv.*) *Upward* is the adjective, as in *He took an upward swing with the bat. Upwards* is the more common adverb, but *upward* too is an adverb, as in *We climbed upwards [upward] along the ridge.* All three are Standard.

Uranus, the planet, is pronounced either *YOOR-uh-nuhs* or *yoo-RAI-nus.*

urban, urbane (*adjs.*) *Urban* refers generally to cities and their characteristics, as in *The environment was urban rather than rural or suburban,* but it also has a specialized American sense, designating any place of fifty thousand or more inhabitants, as in *It's not a large town, but it classifies as urban in the census. Urbane* means "courteous, polished, refined" and is used to describe a person's manners: *He was an impressive, urbane sort of man.*

URBAN DIALECTS as topics for investigation are a development of sociolinguistics, and they seem to be a relatively more complicated issue in today's American English than they have been considered heretofore. The point is that each of our very large cities—Boston, New York, Philadelphia, Baltimore, Washington, Charleston, Atlanta, Miami, New Orleans, Chicago, Los Angeles, and San Francisco—and probably others as well, has come increasingly to display an urban dialect that is more than simply an amalgam of the regional dialect(s) surrounding it. For one thing, one aspect of the very large urban population is its lack of regional homogeneity of origin; in some cities it sometimes seems that almost everyone is originally from somewhere else. But in another way, large portions of the urban population are tied by poverty, race, ethnicity, or other constraints into inner cities and ghettolike enclaves wherein the linguistic homogeneity is far greater than would be encountered in the surrounding regional dialect areas. And most important of all, these same constraints also mean a wider divergence among the characteristics of the social class dialects concentrated within the relatively few square miles of—say—Boston or Philadelphia. Some scholars now conclude that urban dialects, particularly the lower-class dialects, especially those that also represent a racial or ethnic homogeneity, are diverging more and more from the norms of the prevailing Standard, Common, and Vulgar regional dialects spoken elsewhere in those same large metropolitan centers (Labov, as quoted in Stevens 1985a, A14).

urbane See URBAN.

U.S., U.S.A. See UNITED STATES.

U.S. AND BRITISH DIFFERENCES IN MEANING, PRONUNCIATION, SPELLING, AND VOCABULARY See MEANING; PRONUNCIATION (2); SPELLING (1); VOCABULARY (2).

us (*pron.*) As with *me, him, her,* and *them, us,* the first person plural objective case personal pronoun quite frequently occurs as a predicate nominative after the linking verb *be* in Standard Conversational language: *Don't be alarmed; it's just us. Us* also turns up in Casual and some Informal contexts as an emphatic addition to a noun as subject: *Us daddies and mommies will have to work together on this.* At other levels, however, *us* is normally replaced by the more conventional nominative: *We parents must work together.* See CASE (1); IT'S ME; PRONOUN.

USA See UNITED STATES.

USAGE 1, when applied specifically to language, is "a word, phrase, grammatical feature, or language practice actually employed within a language community or constituency." *Usage* can change over time (during the past thousand years, for example, English nouns have lost all inflectional case endings except those for the genitive case), and it may vary at any given time to reflect language practices peculiar to different regions, social classes, and contexts, including variation in level of formality or in adapting to either speech or writing. See also LEVELS OF USAGE and the categories of *usage* named in that entry.

usage 2 (*n.*) The noun *usage* can replace the noun *use* in most generic senses, although it may sometimes be thought a bit pretentious: *This equipment has had heavy usage* [*use*]. It can also mean "an accepted practice, procedure, or custom," as in *Local usage demanded a jacket and tie.*

USAGE LEVELS See LEVELS OF USAGE.

use (*v.*) is pronounced *YOOZ* when it means "employ": *I use number two pencils. I used the last paper towel.* But when the past tense or past participle is combined with *to* plus an infinitive to mean idiomatically "once did," "formerly," or "once was accustomed to," as in *She used to swim the crawl* and *She was used to playing doubles, used to* is pronounced *YOOS too* or *YOOS tuh.* These pronunciations are Standard, but the spelling *use to* is Substandard, even though it accurately represents the usual speech sounds.

In the negative idiom with the auxiliary *did*— *She didn't use to visit us*—the infinitive seems to be the appropriate form, and without the negation but with *did* still in place, again the infinitive (pronounced of course *YOOS*) is Standard: *She did use to like him, I think,* as is *She used to like him, I think.* See SUPPOSED.

used to (*adv.*) This idiom has been a dialectal adverb meaning "once" or "some time ago" in sentences such as *Used to, I could do fifty pushups,* but it's Substandard today.

used to could is a Nonstandard Southern dialect phrase, an idiom meaning "once could" or "formerly could," as in *She used to could whistle, but now she can't.*

useful (*adj.*) can combine with *to, for,* or *in,* as in *This letter may be useful to* [*for*] *you; He is most useful in* [*for*] *answering questions.*

user- (*prefix*), as in *user-friendly, user-oriented,* and similar coinages, is often heard and seen today, perhaps in vogue words riding the crest of the popularity of all things *consumer-friendly.* These words are Standard and occur in Edited English, but some conservatives might prefer not to find them in the most Formal of contexts because they are so relatively new.

usherette (*n.*) is an obsolescent word from a fast-dwindling list of feminine occupational forms. *Usher* is today's word, and *ushers* may be either male or female. See -ESS; FEMININE OCCUPATIONAL FORMS; INCLUSIVE LANGUAGE; SEXIST LANGUAGE.

utilize (*v.*) is a synonym (and often a pretentious euphemism) for the verb *use*; it can represent an effort at elevating mundane matters. Sometimes *utilize* will indeed give variety, but make certain that you really need it before you use (*make use of, employ, utilize*) *utilize*. It's become a cliché of governmental, academic, and commercial pomposity, and for some sensitive Standard users, it's a shibboleth. See -ISE.

V

vacant, vacuous (*adjs.*) *Vacant* means "empty, unoccupied," as in *The house is vacant*. It can be used figuratively to mean exactly what *vacuous* means: "empty of substance, lacking ideas, stupid, without purpose," as in *The vacuous [vacant] expression on his face suggested a lack of intelligence behind it*.

vaccinate, inoculate (*vv.*) *To inoculate* is the general term, meaning "to inject a substance into a living organism," and it has come specifically to mean "to inject a preventive serum, a vaccine." Figuratively, it also means "to introduce an idea or concept into the mind," as in *During his stay abroad he was inoculated with radical social ideas*. *To vaccinate* originally meant "to *inoculate* with a *vaccine*, a preparation of killed cowpox virus, to prevent infection by smallpox," but now also means generally "to *inoculate* against any of a number of diseases." It seems not to have picked up much figurative use as yet.

vacuity, vacuousness (*nn.*) These Standard nouns are synonyms for the condition of being *vacuous*; they mean "emptiness, dullness, stupidity, purposelessness": *The vacuity [vacuousness] of her conversation drives people wild*.

vacuous See VACANT.

vacuousness See VACUITY.

vacuum (*n., v.*) The noun has two plurals: *vacuums*, always used of carpet-cleaning machines and frequently of other kinds of *vacuums*, and *vacua*, restricted mainly to abstract or literal states of emptiness. Standard pronunciations of *vacuum: VAK-yoom, VAK-yum, VAK-yoo-uhm*.

vade mecum (*n.*) is a Latin tag (pronounced either *VAID-ee-MEE-kuhm* or *VAHD-ee-MAI-kuhm*) literally meaning "go with me," which in English means "a handy portable reference book or other bit of pocket equipment." Since most Americans today don't know the expression, its undefined use may do your discourse or prose more harm than good. See FOREIGN PHRASES.

vagary (*n.*) means "caprice, unpredictable behavior, wild notion," as in *Her vagary keeps him constantly off balance*. Pronounce it either *vuh-GAIR-ee* or *VAIG-uhr-ee*. The plural is *vagaries*.

vain (*adj.*), **vane, vein** (*nn.*) These homophones are distinctive in meaning and spelling. The adjective *vain* means "excessively proud, full of vanity": *He's vain about his looks*. A *vane* is "a blade or other surface designed to be moved by the wind or by a fluid," as in a *weathervane* or the *vanes* of a fan or turbine. A *vein* is literally "a blood vessel or a streak or band of material different from its surroundings" (*a vein of silver in the rock*) and figuratively "a quality or streak of something" (*A vein of pessimism runs through all his plays*).

valance, valence (*nn.*) A *valance* (pronounced either *VAL-uhns* or *VAIL-uhns*) is a short curtain or drapery or a wooden imitation of one, hanging from a table or other piece of furniture or, especially, stretched across the top of a window above the curtains or blinds. *Valence* (pronounced only *VAIL-uhns*) is a chemical term; every chemical element has a *valence*, a numerical representation of its ability to combine with other elements into molecules.

vale 1 (*interj.*) Pronounced *VAH-LAI* or *WAH-LAI*, this Latin word means "farewell" and has a Formal poetic air. See FOREIGN PHRASES.

vale 2, veil (*nn.*) These are homophones: *vale* is a poetic word for *valley*, and it is used often to refer to this world ("this vale of sorrow," "this vale of tears"). A *veil* is a light gauze fabric worn especially by women to conceal or partly conceal the face and head; the figurative *to take the veil* means "to become a nun."

valence See VALANCE.

valet (*adj., n., v.*) The noun and verb are pronounced either *VAL-it, VA-lai,* or *va-LAI*. The noun refers to a man's personal servant, who is charged with dressing him and caring for his clothes; by extension, it's also a kind of rack for men's clothing. The verb means "to provide such services": *I'll valet grandfather until he can dress himself again.* The adjective has moved into other kinds of service as well: *valet service* may include cleaning and pressing of clothes in a hotel, parking customers' cars at a hotel or restaurant, or a special parking and delivery service, called *valet parking,* available at large airports and other heavily trafficked installations. All these uses are Standard.

value-added *(adj.),* **value-added tax** *(n.)* The adjective refers to the estimated worth added to a commodity or an article at the various stages of its manufacture and distribution. *A value-added tax* is one added to a product at each stage of its manufacture and distribution. Its proponents argue that it is fairer than a sales tax, which is assessed only at the final sale. Both words are Standard.

van 1 *(n.)* is a clipped form of *vanguard,* meaning "the group in front," especially "the leading military element." To be *in the van* is to be among the leaders, and *van* in this sense is now Standard and general: *We are in the van on this issue.* See AVANT-GARDE.

van 2 *(n.)* was created by apheresis from *caravan,* and now has several vehicular meanings: "an enclosed, small boxy truck," "a similar vehicle made to accommodate passengers," "a large one for moving furniture," etc. In Britain a *van* is also "a railroad box car."

van 3, von *(preps.)* *Van* (pronounced *vahn*) means "of" or "from" when used in Dutch family names *(Vanbrugh, Van Gogh),* as does *von* (pronounced *fuhn*) in German *(Von Braun, von Hindenburg).* These names, like their Romance language counterparts spelled *d', de, di, du* (which see), are variously spaced and capitalized, and in American English the pronunciations are usually *van* for *van,* and *vahn* for *von,* both usually unstressed.

vane See VAIN.

vanguard See AVANT-GARDE; VAN (1).

vantage See ADVANTAGE.

variance, at The Standard idiom, meaning "differs from," is *at variance with* (usually not *from*), as in *Her statement is at variance with his in a number of particulars.*

VARIANT PRONUNCIATIONS are common in English, as with *pianist,* which has two Standard *variant pronunciations, PEE-uh-nist* and *pee-(Y)AN-ist,* plus a third that most recognize as Standard, *PYAN-ist.* Some variants are regional only.

VARIANT SPELLINGS Most words have a single conventionally accepted spelling, but English also has quite a few words with *variant spellings,* alternative spellings that are acceptable either regionally (American English *civilization, honor*; British English *civilisation, honour*) or generally *(judgment, judgement; fulfill, fulfil).* Some are relatively recent borrowings from a foreign language and have both a foreign spelling and an Americanized one in acceptable circulation *(cigarette* and *cigaret).* Others are coinages whose settled spelling has not yet been decided *(programer, programmer).* And then there are all the possible variations that involve hyphens or no hyphens, compounding, accent marks, and the like. Dictionaries usually record side by side (the more frequently encountered one first) those *variants* their editors consider Standard, adding the less frequently found *variants* either as run-ons *(margarine, "also margarin")* or giving them separate entries *("cauldron, n., variant spelling of caldron").* For writers who will publish their work, the publisher's stylebook, often in conjunction with a specified dictionary, will serve as guide. But remember that even though these *variants* will usually in the end settle down to one accepted form, the rates of change in *variant spellings* are most uneven. Some will evolve into a single form in a relatively few years; others will still be *variants* for generations. See SPELLING (2).

VARIATION, ELEGANT See ELEGANT VARIATION.

VARIATION, LINGUISTIC See CHANGE AND VARIATION IN LANGUAGE.

VARIETIES OF LANGUAGE See CHANGE AND VARIATION IN LANGUAGE.

various *(adj., pron.) Various* is Standard as an adjective, as in *Various irregularities are alleged,* but as a pronoun it is Substandard, as in *Various of my friends plan to attend. Several, some,* or *many* would be better.

various and sundry is a cliché.

various different is not redundant; it means "a variety of different things," and it is Standard. *(Various things* and *different things* are not quite the same, either.) But be aware that some commentators still object, even if unreasonably, to *various different* anythings.

vary *(v.)* can combine with the prepositions *in, from, with, between,* or *among: in* suggests the character of the variation, as in *These shirts vary in collar styles; from* and *with* stipulate what something varies from, as in *My opinion varies from* [*with*] *theirs; between* and *among* indicate two or more variants, as in *My views vary between firm and hesitant* and *My views vary among affirmative, negative, and vacillating*. All are Standard.

vase (*n.*) Most Americans pronounce it *VAIS,* but a few (and most Britons) pronounce it *VAHZ.*

vastly (*adv.*) has been objected to as a hyperbolic way of saying "much," or "very much," or even "prodigiously," as in *He has been vastly overrated as a singer.* Nevertheless, the word is Standard in such uses, nor is it always a poor choice.

vast majority See MAJORITY.

've is a contraction of *have* in locutions such as *I've* and *they've,* and it should of course be limited mainly to Conversational and Informal or Semiformal contexts. See OF (2).

veggie (*n.*) is a slang diminutive of *vegetable* and occasionally of *vegetarian.* Resist it.

vehement, vehicular (*adjs.*), **vehemence, vehicle** (*nn.*) Pronounce *vehement* and *vehemence, VEE-uh-mint* and *VEE-uh-mins; VEE-huh-mint* and *VEE-huh-mins* are also Standard, but some Standard speakers object to them, even so. The medial *-h-* in *vehicle* affords a similar problem. Say it *VEE-ik-ul* rather than *VEE-HIK-ul,* although the latter is usually considered Standard too. But note that *vehicular* is always *vee-HIK-yoo-luhr.* See also H-.

veil See VALE (2).

vein See VAIN.

venal, venial (*adjs.*) *Venal* is a strongly pejorative adjective that means "purchasable through corrupt means," "associated with bribery," as in *He was a venal judge in a venal system of courts. Venial* is not so damning; it means "forgivable, excusable, not really serious," as in *Her sins were venial; she was not a wholly bad woman.*

vengeance See AVENGE.

venial See VENAL.

venison (*n.*) is pronounced either *VEN-i-suhn* or *VEN-i-zuhn.*

venom, poison (*nn.*), **poisonous, venomous** (*adjs.*) *Poison* means "any substance that can cause illness, infection, or death when ingested or brought into contact with the skin or bloodstream of an animal or human being." *Venom* is the *poison* secreted by certain reptiles and insects and injected by means of a bite or sting. Hence such creatures are accurately referred to as *venomous,* rather than by the more generic *poisonous. Venom* also is occasionally (though

rarely) used as a synonym of the more generic *poison,* so to use both nouns and adjectives interchangeably is not wrong, but to use *poisonous* of snakes and insects is seen as sloppy by some Standard users, as it is to use *venomous* for plant secretions and other substances. Snakes can be *venomous;* plants can be *poisonous:* it's *poison ivy,* not *venom(ous) ivy.*

venture See ADVENTURE.

venue (*n.*) was formerly used only in legal senses, such as "the place where a crime was committed or where a legal action begins," "the place where a jury is formed and a trial held." Today the word has generalized to mean "the place where an event or action of any kind takes place," as in *the several venues for the events of these Olympic games.* All these senses are now Standard.

verbal, oral (*adjs.*), **orally, verbally** (*advs.*) Technically *verbal* means "in words," so it is sometimes argued that *I gave him verbal approval* is ambiguous. But it clearly is not: its chief meaning is *I gave him spoken* [*oral*] *approval.* If you mean *I gave him written approval,* you'll say *written* or *in writing.* In Standard English *to inform verbally* is to inform either in speech or possibly in writing; *to inform orally* is to inform in speech only. Even so, best advice: be accurate to avoid the scorn of purists. See also AURAL.

VERBALIZATION OF NUMBERS See ZERO.

VERBAL NOUN See GERUND.

VERBALS are nonfinite verbs, the participle or *verbal* adjective, the gerund or *verbal* noun, and the infinitive, usually used with the function word *to,* the sign of the infinitive; it can also be a *verbal* noun. See also FINITE AND NONFINITE VERBS.

verbiage (*n.*) has two meanings: an older pejorative one meaning "too many words, wordiness," as in *Her ideas were lost in her verbiage,* and a newer, more general one meaning "words or wording," as in *His verbiage was usually well chosen.* Both senses are Standard, but the latter use is still largely overwhelmed by the former. *Words* would be better.

VERBIFIED NOUNS See NOUNS AS VERBS.

verbose (*adj.*), **verbosely** (*adv.*), **verbosity** (*n.*) All three carry the message "too many words, too wordy." To be *verbose* is to be long-winded; to talk *verbosely* is to do so wordily; *verbosity* is excessive wordiness.

VERB PHRASE is the conventional name for a full verb, including any auxiliaries used with it: *is sleeping, has been seen, will be tried, go running,* and *has had to leave* are *verb phrases.* Some grammarians also include its objects and adverbs in the full *verb phrase.*

VERBS are parts of speech that present an action, a state, or an occurrence. They may be finite or nonfinite, transitive, intransitive, or linking, and they show active or passive voice. *Verbs* take various kinds of complements. They can show tense and mood, number and person, by means of their morphology, and using similar devices they can also show agreement with their subjects. Many grammars consider the auxiliaries to be special kinds of *verbs;* others consider them a distinctive part of speech. With *verb* plus adverb or preposition combinations, the English vocabulary greatly augments itself: for example, *run* plus one of these words in combination gives us *run on, run in, run out, run off, run through, run over, run by, run into, run up, run down,* and many more, all with meanings that are idiomatic, and some with more than one such meaning. See also COMPLEMENTS; FINITE AND NONFINITE VERBS; INTRANSITIVE VERBS; LINKING OR COPULATIVE VERBS; STRONG VERBS (1); STRONG VERBS (2); TRANSITIVE; VOICE (2); WEAK VERBS.

VERBS, PRINCIPAL PARTS OF See PRINCIPAL PARTS OF VERBS.

veritable (*adj.*) means "true, real, actual" and is frequently a cliché used for emphasis and hyperbole: *She was a veritable tower of strength during her husband's illness.* It can come close to causing the kind of problem that *literally* and *literal* can sometimes create. Don't overuse it.

vermin (*n.*) is most commonly used in the plural, as in *These vermin are pests and are to be exterminated,* but it occurs also in the singular, especially when applied figuratively: *He's behaved loathsomely; he's a vermin, and he's on my list.*

VERNACULAR English is a prestige language; like Latin before it, it has become a language of commerce, literature, and government for many non-native users as well as for those who learned it as their first language. But its greatest power probably comes from the fact that it is in fact the vernacular—the native language, commonly spoken by all the people of a nation or region—of many millions of people on several continents. See VULGAR ENGLISH.

verse, stanza (*nn.*) *Verse* has a generic sense, "metrical composition, poetry," as in *She writes verse,* but it is also Standard in two partly contradictory specialized meanings. A *verse* is "a line of poetry or a single line or sentence from the Bible": *This verse rhymes with the one that precedes it. She can quote chapter and verse from Scripture.* But in songs and especially in hymns we speak of *verses* as being "a series of lines," so that a typical hymn might have several *verses,* each sometimes followed by a chorus or choral refrain. *Stanza* is at least partly synonymous with that second sense of *verse,* meaning "an organized group of verses or lines of poetry, usually in a metrically regular pattern likely to be used in subsequent *stanzas* in the same work." In free *verse* and other nonmetrical poetry, a *stanza* is usually any paragraphlike division containing a group of lines: *The song leader said we would sing just the first and last verses* [*stanzas*]. The sportswriter's use of *stanza* as a jargon word for *period, quarter, chukker,* or *inning* is slang, cliché, and elephantine elegant variation.

verso See RECTO.

vertex, vortex (*nn.*) A *vertex* is a highest point, a zenith, and the word has several specialized senses in geometry and other sciences as well. The plural is either *vertexes* (*VUHR-teks-iz*) or *vertices* (*VUHR-ti-SEEZ*). A *vortex* is the hole in the midst of a whirlpool of liquid or air, and the word is much used figuratively to mean any similar violent or powerful whirlpool-like force. The plural is either *vortexes* (*VOR-teks-iz*) or *vortices* (*VOR-ti-SEEZ*). See FOREIGN PLURALS.

vertical See PERPENDICULAR.

very (*intensifier*) is Standard modifying some participial adjectives but not others. One test says that *very* should be used only with participial adjectives that can be employed attributively: *He had a very surprised expression on his face.* A second test says simply that participial adjectives that are absolute adjectives, as in *His dart game appeared perfected,* should not take *very.* And a third test asks, does *very* sound familiar and comfortable when used to modify a given participial adjective or not? If not, don't use it. Purists tend to limit severely the lists of participial adjectives appropriately modifiable by *very,* so be aware of your readers' and listeners' expectations on this point. When in doubt, use *very much* or another qualifier, as in *very much astonished* (not *very astonished*) and *very thoroughly chastised* (not *very chastised*).

One other point: Americans are frequently accused of overusing *very* and other intensifiers.

Repeated hyperboles can damage your credibility.

very spit of See SPIT AND IMAGE.

vest 1 (*n.*) is an American "waistcoat" but a British "sleeveless undershirt." See VOCABULARY (1); WAISTCOAT.

vest 2 (*v.*) combines with *in* and *with: The power to sign contracts is vested in the company's officers. The company's officers are vested with the power to sign contracts.*

vet (*nn., v.*) The nouns are clipped forms of *veterinarian* and *veteran,* Standard in all but Formal and Oratorical contexts. The verb is Standard both literally, meaning "to practice as a veterinarian," and figuratively, meaning to "check over for condition, accuracy, authenticity," as in *The curator vetted that painting thoroughly before declaring it authentic.*

veto (*n., v.*) The plural of the noun and the third person singular present tense of the verb are both spelled *vetoes.* The past tense and past participle are spelled *vetoed,* and the present participle is *vetoing.*

via (*prep.*) We borrowed the ablative case form of the Latin word for "way, road" and turned it into a preposition meaning "by way of, by means of," as in *She arrived via helicopter; I found out via the office grapevine.* It is Standard applied to actual movement in space and to any more general "way" and need no longer be italicized as foreign. Pronounce it *VEI-uh* or *VEE-uh.*

viable (*adj.*) is Standard both in its literal sense, "capable of living," as in *These seedlings look viable,* and in the more recent generalization meaning "practical, workable," as in *We don't yet have a viable plan,* but the latter use is much criticized today as a vogue word and cliché. Try *useful, workable, practical, sensible,* and the like, instead, and especially avoid *viable alternative* and *viable option* as threadbare and worn.

vial, viol (*nn.*) These homophones are differently spelled: a *vial* is a bottle or container for liquids; a *viol* is any of several stringed instruments played with a bow, including today's *bass viol.*

vicar See PRIEST.

vice, vise (*nn.*) American English orthographically distinguishes a *vice* (a moral flaw) from a *vise* (a clamping tool), whereas British English spells both homophones (pronounced *VEIS*) *vice.*

vice versa is a Latin tag that is now thoroughly English, meaning "in reverse order from what was originally stated, conversely," and pronounced either *VEIS VUHR-suh* or *VEIS-uh VUHR-suh.* It need no longer be italicized. See FOREIGN PHRASES.

vicious, viscous (*adjs.*) These two look a bit alike but are unrelated: *vicious* (pronounced *VISH-uhs*) means "given to vice, depraved, bad," as in *She's a vicious liar; viscous* (pronounced *VIS-kuhs*) refers to *viscosity,* a thickened state of a fluid, as in *Molasses is a highly viscous liquid.*

victual (*n., v.*), **vittles** (*n.*) *Victual* is pronounced *VIT-ul;* be sure to avoid the naive spelling pronunciation error, *VIK-choo-(w)uhls.* Middle English borrowed the French *vitaille,* and Standard English never has pronounced the *c* that the Renaissance spelling reformers put into it in imitation of its ultimate Latin source. The *vittles* spelling is a variant not used in Edited English except for special effect as eye dialect to suggest the old-fashioned and rural. The noun is almost always plural, as in *We made large inroads on the generous supply of victuals provided.* The verb is always spelled *victual* and is a homophone of the noun, as in *We victualed* [pronounced *VIT-uhld*] *the yacht when we reached St. Thomas.*

vie (*v.*), meaning "to contest, to compete," can combine with the prepositions *with, against,* and *for,* as in *My brother and I vied for that little girl's attention, We vied with each other,* or rarely; *We vied against each other.*

view (*n.*), in the phrase *with a view,* combines with the prepositions *to, toward,* and *of,* as in *We joined with a view to* [*toward, of*] *making some new friends.* In the phrase, *with the view, of* occurs more commonly, as in *We resigned regretfully, with the view of rejoining next year.* Both phrases mean "with the intention of" and can also be used literally of scenery with these and some other prepositions, as in *From his balcony she had a* [*the*] *view toward* [*to, of, over, through, across*] *the mountains.*

viewers See AUDIENCE.

viewpoint See STANDPOINT.

view with alarm is generally considered a cliché; its spoken occurrences today are often self-conscious or jocular.

vigilant (*adj.*) combines with several prepositions, including *about, against, for* (*We must be vigilant about* [*against, for*] *tramps and vagrants*), *in,* usually followed by a gerund, and *to,* usually followed by an infinitive (*You must* *be especially vigilant in patrolling [to patrol] the boundaries*).

villain, villein (*nn.*) These are homophones: a *villain* is "a criminal, a scoundrel," and in a drama, "the evildoer"; a *villein* in feudalism was a serf who had the privileges of a freedman except in his relationship to his lord.

viol See VIAL.

viola (*nn.*) These homographs have different meanings and sometimes different pronunciations: a *viola* (pronounced usually *vee-O-luh*) is the stringed instrument with a voice higher than a cello's, lower than a violin's. The plural is *violas. Viola* is also the spelling of the name of the flower developed from the pansy; it's pronounced either *VEI-uh-luh, vei-O-luh,* or *vee-O-luh,* and its plural is also spelled *violas.*

violation See FELONY.

violoncello See CELLO.

VIP, either with or without periods after each letter, is an abbreviation for *very important person*—a celebrity to be given special treatment. It is an initialism, pronounced as the names of the three letters; the plural, *VIPs,* is pronounced *VEE-EI-PEEZ.* It's Conversational and Informal.

VIRGULE A *virgule* (also called a *diagonal, slash, slash mark,* or *solidus*) is a slanted line (/) used between two words to suggest that they are alternatives (*and/or*), between the parts of a fraction (1/2), or for other typographical purposes, such as indicating line endings when verse is quoted without indentation, within a regular prose paragraph. Slanted in the other direction (\), these marks are sometimes used to enclose phonemes, and in computer applications, where they are called *back slashes* or *backslashes,* they are used in certain commands. See also BRACKETS.

virile (*adj.*), **virilism** (*n.*) Americans usually pronounce *virile VEER-uhl,* the British either *VEER-EIL* or *VEI-REIL.* Its meanings are "manly, having masculine strength, sexually strong and active," and it is therefore applied accurately almost exclusively to men. *Virilism* is the word used to describe the occurrence of secondary male characteristics in a female. See also MANNISH.

VIRTUAL SUBJECT See LET.

virtuoso (*n.*) has two plurals: *virtuosos* and *virtuosi.* See FOREIGN PLURALS.

virus (*n.*) is technically Standard English for an organism that attacks cells and causes disease, but it is also used more loosely at some levels of Standard English to mean "the disease caused by the virus," particularly in Conversational and Informal contexts, as in *He's got some sort of virus, I hear.*

vis-à-vis (*n., prep.*) Both preposition and noun usually retain in English the grave accent over the *a.* The preposition was borrowed from the French expression literally meaning "face to face" and is used in that sense in English, as in *I was stuck in that little room for two hours, vis-à-vis that most unpleasant woman.* It also means "in comparison with" or "in relation to," as in *Our responsibility vis-à-vis the new government is unclear,* and occasionally (and with some conservative objection still) it is used to mean "concerning," "with regard to," as in *We had no real convictions vis-à-vis these new proposals.* The noun means "your opposite number," "someone face to face with you." Pronounce the preposition and noun singular *VEEZ-uh-VEE* or *VEES-uh-VEE,* the noun plural, spelled the same as the singular, either *VEEZ-uh-VEEZ* or *VEEZ-uh-VEE.*

visceral See GUT FEELING.

viscous See VICIOUS.

vise See VICE.

visible See PERCEPTIBLE; VISUAL.

visionary (*adj., n.*) The adjective is usually pejorative, meaning "not practical, unrealistic"; *imaginative, forward-looking,* or *idealistic* would be more flattering if you intend no detriment. The noun *visionary* refers to a person wedded to idealistic or impractical values and schemes; it too is frequently taken to be pejorative.

visit, visit with (*vv.*) are not exact synonyms. *To visit* is "to pay a visit or to pay a call on someone." *To visit with* is also an idiom meaning "to converse with," "to chat with," as in *I visited with her mother for nearly an hour.*

visitation, visit (*nn.*) These do not mean the same thing: a *visit* is simply "a call on someone or a trip to a place," whereas a *visitation* is an official *visit* of some sort, as in the legal term in *He had rights of visitation to see his children* or the religious implications of a *visitation* by a deity, as a punishment or other intervention.

visual, visible (*adjs.*) *Visible* means "seeable," as in *The lighthouse was barely visible in the fog,* and *visual* normally means "related to sight or seeing," as in *Her visual faculties were unusually good. Visual* is occasionally used in Standard English to mean "seeable," as in *They sought some visual evidence of the change,* but most people would prefer *visible evidence*, and you would do well to avoid using *visual* in this sense.

vitamin (*n.*) Americans pronounce it *VEIT-uh-min*, the British, *VIT-uh-min*. See PRONUNCIATION (2).

vittles See VICTUAL.

viva voce (*adv., n.*) *Viva voce* (pronounced *VEE-vuh-VO-see* and usually italicized in print) is literally "with living voice" and hence "orally, by word of mouth," as in *I learned the news viva voce at a meeting this morning.* As a noun it is the British term for an oral examination. See FOREIGN PHRASES; HYPERFOREIGNISMS.

viz, viz. is short for the Latin *videlicet,* meaning "namely." (When you read it aloud or speak it, say *namely,* not *VIZ.*) It is usually followed by an explicit list detailing something mentioned as a whole just before it: *this committee, viz Gatta, Jambeck, Moynihan, and Stern.* The abbreviation resulted from the manuscript abbreviation of the Latin *et cetera,* which looked a bit like a letter *z;* the first two letters of *videlicet,* added to this odd-looking *etc.,* gave us *viz.*

Viz. and *i.e.,* are sometimes used interchangeably, but Edited English and most commentators prefer that any distinction between "namely" and "that is" be kept. See E.G.; FOREIGN PHRASES.

VOCABULARY 1: AMERICAN AND BRITISH DIFFERENCES

Every American who watches British motion pictures and television programs, who reads British books, and who hears British talk knows that we and the British call a good many things by different names. This list sometimes seems dauntingly long, whether it's food items (*french fries/chips, potato chips/crisps, molasses/treacle, crackers* and *cookies/biscuits, dessert/sweet* or *pudding*), automotive terms (*trunk/boot, fender/wing, hood/bonnet, truck/lorry, traffic circle/roundabout* or *circus*), or clothes (*derby/bowler, vest/waistcoat, undershirt/vest, sweater/pullover* or *jumper*). But the interesting point to be made is that both we and the British know hundreds of these pairs of terms: few speakers of Standard American English will hesitate a moment over a *spanner* or a *lift,* and neither American nor British *suspenders* and *braces* are likely to puzzle cultivated speakers of the other dialect. The different names of the parts of our lives seem not to dwindle in number; rather, both American and British English vocabularies seem to grow to include at least the recognition of many of the other dialect's differing names for those parts.

VOCABULARY 2, LEXICON (*nn.*)

A *lexicon* is either a *dictionary* or a theoretically complete list of all the words and meanings in a language—its *vocabulary*. None of us is master of any great portion of the *vocabulary*, and no *dictionary* is ever quite able to get every word and every sense into its pages, because change operates rapidly and constantly in *vocabulary* and its *lexicon*, as long as the language is in use.

VOCABULARY 3: SIZE

How many words are there in all of American English? How large is the average person's vocabulary? There are no simple, easy answers to these questions. Even if you could stop time long enough to prevent today's new words from swelling yesterday's total, just to decide what to count as a *word* is more complex than you might at first suspect. Are the noun *sleep* and the verb *sleep* one word or two? Should *sleeps* count as two more words or as part of *sleep? Sleeping? Slept?* And since *sleeping pill* is a compound, is that a separate word? Then too, should we include in the count all the obsolete words that scholars and others recognize only because Chaucer or Ben Franklin once used them? Or, if we only recognize but do not use them today, are they no longer part of American English?

What most people do in trying to estimate the size of the language's lexicon is to count the entries in a dictionary. But many functionally shifted forms are not given separate entries (for example, *Webster's Ninth New Collegiate Dictionary* defines *whistle* and *whistle-blower* in separate entries but lists *whistleable* only as a run-on in the entry for *whistle*). Merriam's unabridged *Third New International Dictionary* (1961) claimed "more than 450,000 entries," and the Random House unabridged second edition (1987) claimed "more than 315,000." And because many of the Random House entries are encyclopedic—proper names of people and places—but the Merriam book excludes most proper names, the difference is probably considerably understated. And that's just one discrepancy of who knows how many.

Estimating the size of an individual's vocabulary is at least as difficult as estimating the number of words in the language. Most commentators agree that you have one relatively small vocabulary that you use for most of your speaking and writing; they also agree that you have a relatively much larger vocabulary that includes all of these plus many, many more words and meanings that you recognize when you see or hear them but are not likely to use yourself. There may well be a third, middle kind of vocabulary, whose words will come to mind only if you are given the right clues and cues from context. Further, if you count as words in your active vocabulary only those that you can correctly define, your word stock will be relatively smaller. Besides, is it fair to say you know a word if you know only some of its several meanings? In the end, the size of your vocabulary is much less important than your ability to accurately use the words you have to communicate your ideas and express your feelings clearly. In the end, experience—with life and with dealing with it in words—is the best vocabulary builder.

vocal chords, vocal cords See CHORD.

VOCALIZED PAUSES AND SPEECH FORMULAS These are the *um*s, *uh*s, and *ah*s, the spoken equivalents of throat clearing and false starts, that we are especially conscious of in others' speech, particularly at the Planned or Oratorical level. Here also are some of the "starters" we use in beginning many response utterances. Fries (1952) included them as one group of what he called function words: *well, oh, now,* and *why* or *why-uh* (pronounced like the name of the letter *y,* even in dialects wherein the question-asking function word *why* is pronounced *HWEI*). *Yes* and *no* also appear in response utterances, and in situation utterances we have the starters *say, listen, look.* Add to these the formula *please* and the request expressed as *let's, let us,* and even the Nonstandard *let's us.* And then there are the expletive formulas, *there is, there are,* and *it is.* Some of these *vocalized pauses* and *speech formulas* may be a bit odd when considered as words, but they are in fact a part of the spoken usage of American English.

vocation See AVOCATION.

VOGUE WORDS are perfectly good Standard English words that suddenly become modish, so that for a time we hear them being used everywhere, by everyone, until we are utterly sick of them. Their voguishness is usually fleeting: they get stretched all out of shape from overuse, and they frequently fade back into the vocabulary or disappear entirely, often just as quickly as they came into *vogue.* The borrowed Russian words *glasnost* and *perestroika* were *vogue words* a short time ago, and *infrastructure, ecosystem, caring, share,* and *senior citizen* are *vogue words* today. Any part of speech may become a *vogue word.* Sometimes it seems almost impossible to avoid using them, but try, in both speech and writing. They can soon come to mean very little.

voice 1 (*v.*) is Standard meaning "to express publicly or openly," as in *She never hesitated to voice her opinions.*

VOICE 2: ACTIVE, PASSIVE *Voice* is a grammatical feature of English verbs, which expresses a particular relationship between the subject of the sentence and its direct object, if any. In *John caught the ball,* the verb *caught* is in the *active voice: John* did to the object *ball* what the verb *caught* expresses. In *The ball was caught by John,* the verb *was caught* is in the *passive voice:* the subject of this sentence is *ball,* and the action of the verb *was caught* indicates what happened to it but requires a prepositional phrase, *by John,* to let us know who did it. *Active voice* makes subjects do something (to something); *passive voice* permits subjects to have something done to them (by someone or something). Some argue that *active voice* is more muscular, direct, and succinct, *passive voice* flabbier, more indirect, and wordier. If you want your words to seem impersonal, indirect, and noncommittal, *passive* is the choice, but otherwise, *active voice* is almost invariably likely to prove more effective.

VOICED AND VOICELESS SPEECH SOUNDS *Voiced* sounds are those made while the vocal cords are vibrating: all vowels and some consonants (*b, d,* and *g,* for example) are *voiced. Voiceless* sounds (also called *unvoiced* sounds) are those made when the vocal cords are not vibrating (consonants *p, t,* and *k,* for example, are *voiceless*). Put a finger on your Adam's apple, and say *cut* (*KUHT*) and *gut* (*GUHT*); you'll feel the *voiced* vibrations of the *g,* but no vibrations from the *voiceless k.*

void (*adj.*) combines with the preposition *of,* as in *His mind was void of ideas.*

von See VAN (3).

vortex See VERTEX.

VOWELS, THE AMERICAN ENGLISH The English *vowel letters* are *a, e, i, o, u,* and sometimes *y,* but the *vowel sounds* are more numerous. They are characterized by the continuous sounds they make as the main part of any syllable. Certain *vowel sounds* appear only in one or more regional dialects, but the following, represented here with the pronunciations used in this book, are the *vowel sounds* most usually encountered in Standard American English:

The *A* in *fat*
The *AH* in *father*

The *AI* in *fate*
The *AW* in *fawn*
The *E* in *fen*
The *EE* in *feet*
The *EI* in *fight*
The *I* in *fizz*
The *O* in *foe*
The *OI* in *foil*
The *OO* in *fool*
The *OU* in *found*
The *U* in *foot*
The *UH* in *flood*
The *UHR* in *fur*
The unstressed *uh* in *sofa*

H, w, and *y* are sometimes called *semivowels,* and they, like *r,* modify or change the sound of an immediately preceding *vowel sound.*

VULGAR (*adj.*), **VULGARITY** (*n.*) The adjective *vulgar* began by referring to "the people, the masses and their characteristics," and inevitably, therefore, it pejorated into additional meanings, beginning with "lacking in taste or cultivation," then to "coarse," to "morally bad or depraved," to "gross," to "earthy," to "offensive," to "indecent," and finally to "obscene." The word still retains all these senses. A *vulgar* word or phrase—a *vulgarity*—considered indecent or obscene is usually taboo in Standard English, particularly if it is the kind of obscenity that most people consider disgusting, repulsive, or offensive to decency; the use of such language can bring harsh social judgments. *Vulgarity* is also used generally to refer to characteristics peculiar to the masses and to their lack of taste, discrimination, and good manners as judged by those who consider themselves above such people. In language use, *vulgarity* is one kind of Substandard language—coarse, crude, and ill-mannered at best, and obscene and taboo at worst. Dictionaries use *obscene*

and *vulgar* as labels to guide the inexperienced: words or senses so labeled are either taboo or extremely limited in Standard use. See also OBSCENE (1); OBSCENE (2); PROFANITY; TABOO WORDS.

VULGAR ENGLISH, VULGATE has three important meanings. (1) Historically it is the name of the language of the common people (as opposed to the language of art, literature, or the monarch); other and more frequently used terms for this sense are the *Vulgate* or *Vulgar* tongue, the vernacular, or the people's English (Jerome's Vulgate Latin Bible was written in fourth-century common Latin dialect, which was then the people's dialect in parts of Europe). (2) *Vulgar English* is the language of the lowest social and economic class in the society (see STANDARD). (3) *Vulgar English* has also pejorated severely from its meaning "of the people" to take on several increasingly degraded senses (see VULGAR), including "crude," "boorish," "tasteless," and "indecent or obscene." It's a very busy term whose meaning must always be made clear by context.

vulnerable (*adj.*) literally means "susceptible to being injured," and it still occasionally has that sense, as in *The puppy had a timid and vulnerable look that made everybody want to protect it.* But it has much greater use in various figurative senses, such as "easily hurt by criticism," "susceptible to bad influences," "open to attack of any sort," and a specialized sense in bridge, wherein partners who have won a game are said to be *vulnerable* and hence are able to benefit from much-increased bonuses but are also subject to much-increased penalties should they fail. *Vulnerable,* when it combines with a preposition, almost always takes *to: He appeared vulnerable to any of several sorts of attack.*

W

waffle (*v.*) means "to vacillate," "to speak or write foolishly, vaguely, indecisively," as in *He waffled and managed to say nothing at great length.* The term is Standard.

wage See SALARY.

waist, waste (*nn.*) These are homophones. *Waist* is the part of the body between ribs and hips, the middle and (ideally) the narrowest part of

the torso. There is also a transferred sense referring to the parts of clothing that fit or cover the waist, as well as an archaic sense meaning "a child's or woman's blouse." And there are many transferred senses that refer to the midsections of ships and airplane fuselages and the like. *Waste* is a noun meaning "uninhabited lands," "useless materials left over from another activity," "excreted body liquids or solids," or "a bunch of absorbent fibers, used to wipe oil and grease from machinery." *Waste* is also a verb, meaning "to dispose of something carelessly," "to use up materials without reason," "to make feeble," as in *The disease had wasted him terribly,* and a slang sense, "to kill, murder," as in *The mobsters threatened to waste him if he didn't pay.*

waistcoat, weskit (*n.*) These are variant spellings of the British English word for what Americans more often call a *vest. Waistcoat* can be pronounced either to reflect both parts of the compound, as *WAIST-KOT,* which is a spelling pronunciation, or *WES-kit,* which is the way *waistcoat* was originally pronounced, and still is pronounced by a good many people both in this hemisphere and abroad. In the nineteenth century the *WES-kit* pronunciation was turned into an eye dialect spelling, *weskit.* Both spellings are now Standard, as are both pronunciations.

wait, await (*vv.*) *Wait* is intransitive, as in *Wait here; await* is transitive, as in *Await instructions. Wait* combined with *for* is synonymous with *await,* but *await* is more stilted or literary in tone: *Await [Wait for] your mother.* But see also WAIT ON.

wait on, wait upon (*vv.*) These two combinations are idioms with a range of meanings in which *on* and *upon* are essentially interchangeable: "to serve, especially with food," as in *They waited on [upon] us at dinner;* "to call upon or to pay one's respects to," as in *He waited on [upon] the prince that afternoon;* "to serve in any capacity," as in *The manager waited upon [on] his customers personally;* "to result from," as in *Our next move waited upon [on] her recovery from her illness;* and "to wait for, to await," as in *I'm not going to wait on [upon] you any longer.* This final sense is limited to Casual, Impromptu, and Informal use and is probably heard mainly in Midland and Southern regional dialect areas; Standard English prefers *wait for* instead. The other senses are Standard.

waive, wave (*vv.*) These verbs are homophones, *waive* meaning "to give up, to relinquish," as in *She waived her rights to the property,* and *wave* meaning "to make a wavelike motion," as in *He waved goodbye to the children.*

waiver, waver (*nn.*) These nouns are homophones: a *waiver* is the act or document that relinquishes a right, a privilege, or a claim (*She*

signed a waiver of her right to sue for damages*); a *waver* is someone who waves.

wake, waken (*vv.*) The principal parts of *wake,* one set strong, the other weak, are in divided usage in Standard English. For the past tense the strong verb form *woke* is a bit more frequent than the weak *waked: Yesterday I woke [waked] early;* for past participle the strong *woken* is a bit more frequent than the weak *waked: She had always woken [waked] before six.* But see also AWAKE.

wall, (up) against the, with one's back to the wall, go to the wall for, off the wall, to drive (someone) up the wall The first three of these idioms are Standard and are based on the practice of standing prisoners with their backs to a wall so that they may be executed by a firing squad. All three can be used literally, but their figurative applications are much more frequent, describing as they do the extremely bleak prospects of the person at the wall: to be (*up*) *against the wall* (or simply *up against it*) is to be in desperate straits, and if *one's back is against [to] the wall,* one is similarly about to be executed; *to go to the wall for someone* is to endure another's punishment in his or her stead. A person or an action that is *off-the-wall* is "wild, irrational, unexpected, or unpredictable," the figurative sense suggested probably by the unexpected courses of objects ricocheting off a wall. *To be driven up the wall* means "to be maddened, irritated, or thoroughly upset by something." These last two idioms are slang.

wane (*v.*) means "to grow smaller," and it is typically applied to the dwindling of the moon, as in *The moon waned toward the end of the month, and the nights became darker.* Standard English frequently uses *wane* figuratively, as in *After Christmas, my interest in food waned perceptibly.* See WAX.

wangle, wrangle (*vv.*) are sometimes confused, probably because they look and sound somewhat alike, and *wrangle* is sometimes used to mean "to gain by argument," a sense synonymous with *wangle.* But *wangle* means "to obtain or to win or succeed despite difficulties by devious means or by means of hard work, contrivance, persuasion, or other insistent effort," as in *She wangled an invitation for herself when everyone else was being turned down,* whereas *to wrangle* is "to quarrel or argue (but not necessarily to win)," as in *They wrangled constantly during the first year of their marriage.* Best advice: don't use *wrangle* to mean "obtain," and note that, although it is Standard, some conservatives insist that *wangle* be limited to Conversational use. Note too the specialized meaning of *wrangle*, a Standard back-formation from the specialized noun *wrangler*, a horseherd on a ranch in the western United States: "to perform the duties of a *wrangler*."

want (*v.*) has three main meaning clusters: "to wish or desire," as in *Do you want a second helping?* (see DESIRE); "to lack," as in *This deck of cards wants a nine of clubs;* and "ought (to)" or "should," as in *You want to be careful on icy steps.* The first two uses are unquestionably Standard; the "ought (to)" meaning is usually limited to conversation and the Informal and Semiformal writing that imitates it.

want down, want in, want into, want off, want out, want up These idioms are dialectal and Casual at best, but more likely Nonstandard: *Could you hold on a moment? The kid wants down* [*up*]. *The cat's at the back door and wants in* [*out*]. *I want into that deal—it looks like a winner. He accepted the appointment just last month, but now he wants out. She wants off at the next stop.* Standard English prefers *to* plus an infinitive plus the preposition in place of the *down, in, into, off, out,* or *up* alone (*wants to come in, wants to get down, into, out, off, up*), but some of its speakers regularly use these idiomatic phrases at the Casual level.

want for See MEAN FOR.

want in, want into, want off, want out See WANT DOWN.

want that followed by a clause, as in *She wants that you should come upstairs,* is Nonstandard; *to* plus an infinitive is the Standard construction: *She wants you to come upstairs.*

want up See WANT DOWN.

-ward, -wards (*suffixes*) The suffix without an *-s*, when added to *up, back,* or *down,* creates some common adjectives (*There was upward movement; He was backward as a child; There was no forward motion*) and adverbs (*We walked upward; The machine moved backward and downward*). The *-wards* suffix creates Standard adverbs too, although there is some limitation: *Step forward* works, and *Step forwards* doesn't, but *Move backward* [*downward, upward*] and *Move backwards* [*downwards, upwards*] are both unquestionably Standard in American English. Nevertheless, Edited English often prefers the *s*-less words.

warm (*adj.*), **warmly** (*adv.*) When used with *feel*, these two are in divided usage, just as are *feel bad, feel badly* (which see), and raise similar issues of meaning.

warn (*v.*) is Standard whether transitive, as in *I warned her of the consequences,* or intransitive, as in *Those grinding noises warn of transmission troubles ahead.* Warn combines usually with *of, about, against, concerning, over,* and the like: *We have warned* [*them*] *of* [*about, against, concerning, over*] *the dangers of driving too fast.*

warp, web, weft, woof (*nn.*) are terms from weaving: the threads or yarns that run lengthwise on the loom are called the *warp*; the crosswise threads or yarns are called the *woof* or *weft.* The *web* is the name given the completed woven fabric, and it also has wide figurative use: *What a tangled web of circumstance you've woven.* All these are Standard.

wary (*adj.*), when combined with prepositions, usually takes *of* but can also take *about* or *in*: *Be wary of* [*about, in*] *accepting substitutes.*

was, were are the past tense forms of *be,* and their agreement in number with their subjects is important. *Was* is first and third person singular (*I was, she was*) and *were* is second person singular and all persons plural (*you were, we were, you were, they were*). Most failures of agreement are Substandard, and they are powerful shibboleths. See INDICATIVE.

wash up (*v.*), **washed up** (*adj., v.*), **wash one's hands** These combinations are really all idioms. *To wash up* is "to clean" and especially "to do the dishes," as in *I washed up after you left. I want to wash up* is also a euphemism for *I want to use the toilet.* The participial adjective is identical in form with the past tense, but has a different meaning, usually considered Conversational and Informal, "to be out of contention, no longer able to compete, and in that sense to be finished," as in *He was washed up as a player at age thirty.* The idiom *to wash one's hands* is a euphemism for "to use a toilet" and also means "to deny responsibility," as in *I wash my hands of the whole affair.*

waste See WAIST.

watch (*n.*) has among its meanings "the period of time on which a sailor has duty," as in *It happened on my watch; I had the watch then.* See BELLS.

watershed (*n.*) has three Standard meanings. It is "the dividing line between an area drained by a river running in one direction and one drained by another river running in an opposite direction": *The Continental Divide is a major wa-*

tershed. A *watershed* is also "an area drained by a river or river system": *The watershed of the Connecticut River covers parts of four New England states*. The figurative sense, "a turning point," as in *The decision marked a watershed in criminal legal theory*, is sometimes overused, especially in journalese. A handful of purists still insist that only the first meaning is acceptable, but they're out of touch: all three meanings are firmly established in American English.

wave See WAIVE.

waver See WAIVER.

wax (*v.*) means "to grow larger," as in *The moon was waxing that week, growing brighter each night*. Figurative use for other kinds of growing seems always to require a following adjective, not an adverb, and *wax*'s use today is frequently jocular or consciously pretentious: *She waxed furious at his words*. See also WANE; WRATH.

way 1 (*n.*) meaning "the manner or method or means" is Standard in uses such as *This is the way we do it here*. It also functions almost as a kind of conjunction, meaning "like" or "as," as in *Do it the way she showed you*, or "how," as in *That's the way it's going to be*. Sometimes there can be ambiguity between these and the other senses of *way*, as illustrated by the old comic routine wherein a mincing floorwalker, headwaiter, or restaurant hostess says to the customer, "*Walk this way, please*," and then sways off in a manner the customer can imitate only clumsily or declines to attempt at all. See also KIND.

way 2 (*adv., intensifier*) is an apheetic form of *away*; it used to be printed '*way*, with an apostrophe, but is rarely so today. It means "a great distance" or "all the way," as in *We were way off the mark* and *We went way to the end of the trolley line*. Some dictionaries consider this adverbial *way* Colloquial, and indeed it often has a Conversational or Informal tone, but others consider it appropriate for use at all levels except the most Formal or Oratorical. It also frequently functions conversationally as an intensifier, as in *She was way underprepared for the assignment* and the student slang exclamations *Way out!, Way cool!*, and the like. See also AWAY.

way, no See NO WAY.

way, under; under weigh See UNDER WAY.

ways (*n.*) is the plural of *way*, and in many noun uses it is perfectly unexceptionable: *There were three ways to get home. In some ways she seemed very poised and mature*. Used instead of the singular, however, in phrases such as *a little ways down the street*, and as a suffix added to *any*, as in *Anyways, I was too late, ways* is Nonstandard, and many Standard users consider it a shibboleth inappropriate for any Standard use. See ANYWAY.

we (*pron.*) *We* is the first person nominative plural personal pronoun (*She and I arrived at noon, and we ate a good lunch*). Use it in all instances where it performs as subject (including this appositive: *We boys ran quickly home*) and in all instances of use as predicate nominative (*In the end it was we who paid the price*), except the idiomatic *The enemy is us*. Avoid misuse of *we* in direct object function, as in *They gave advice to we* [should be *us*] *boys*. The appositive can be especially tricky.

The editorial *we*, used by journals, newspapers, and other media to express the opinion of the editors, as in *We recommend a vote in favor of Proposition Three on the ballot*, is Standard and conventional. So are uses wherein an author or speaker includes the reader in a statement, as in *Next we will consider the opposition's views*, and uses wherein *we* is used as an indefinite pronoun to mean "all of us," "most people," or "people in general," as in *We are none of us in favor of war*. All these uses are effective in both speaking and writing. Rarer but equally conventional is the royal *we*, wherein a monarch expresses the crown's personal views, as in the remark attributed to Queen Victoria, after she had seen a member of her household mimicking her: *We are not amused*. The royal *we* is very formal and may be nearly archaic today, except in ritualistic circumstances.

The use of *we* instead of a singular *you*, as in the nurse's cloying *How are we feeling this morning?* or the schoolteacher's condescending question to a child, *Are we having trouble with our fractions today?* is a cliché that every Standard user should deplore in other than satiric use. (The other first person plural pronouns—*us, our*, and *ours*—are also sometimes abused in this saccharine fashion. Avoid it.)

weak (*adj.*), **week** (*n.*) These are homophones: the adjective *weak* means "lacking strength," and the noun *week* means "a period of seven days."

WEAK VERBS are those that add the dental suffix (which see) to the stem to form the past tense and the past participle, as in *study* (*studied, studied*), *preach* (*preached, preached*), and *grade* (*graded, graded*). The *weak verb* pattern dominates when we create new English verbs: consider this nonce (and nonsense) verb, *stou-*

ple, whose other principal parts will almost surely be *stoupled, stoupled*. See also STRONG VERBS (1); STRONG VERBS (2).

wealthy See RICH.

wean (*v.*) now has three Standard meanings: (1) the literal "to accustom mammalian infants to foods other than breast milk, especially to solid foods" (*She was weaned early because of her mother's ill health and inability to nurse her*); (2) the figurative "to accustom anyone to leaving an old set of circumstances or conditions" (*Parents are trying to wean their children [away] from television*); and (3) the relatively new and curiously changed sense now in wide use "to be raised and nourished on" (*I was weaned on books of every sort*). In this last example, the implication is that the speaker went straight from mother's milk to books; it's a hyperbole, but Standard, although some conservatives object to it.

WEASEL WORDS are sly, cunning, and sneaky; they lack integrity, and they conceal the truth. In the end they say one thing but mean something quite different. The world of advertising, the fine print in warranties, the political campaign lexicon—all these can be full of *weasel words*. From the direct mail materials that masquerade under eagles and "official" labels to the "You may already have won $1,000,000!" pitch, our society exhibits a remarkable concentration of efforts to fool, entrap, or cheat through language that misleads. From carefully misworded claims for cancer-curing, cholesterol-defeating cereals, to the gentility of the *preowned* automobile, many Standard users are accustomed to *weasel words* these days, yet the con artist and the snake oil merchant continue to prosper. Don't be deceived by the *weasel words* of the free lunch and the big lie. See AMBIGUOUS; DOUBLESPEAK; EUPHEMISM; EUPHEMISMS.

weather (*n.*), **whether** (*conj.*) In some regional dialects these are homophones, pronounced *WETH-uhr*, but in other regions the conjunction is pronounced *HWETH-uhr*. Both are Standard, of course. See WH-.

weave (*n., v.*) The principal parts of the verb are in divided usage: *weave, wove* or *weaved, woven* or *weaved*. The strong verb forms for the past tense and past participle (*wove, woven*) are more often used for the clothmaking senses, but the weak verb forms (*weaved, weaved*) are the more usual choices for past and past participle when the figurative "moving back and forth" sense is intended, as in *The car weaved erratically*

through the traffic. The noun means "a pattern or process of fabric making": *This coarse weave will make attractive upholstery*. See also WARP.

web See WARP.

wed (*v.*) is less frequently used today in its literal senses (except in headlines, thanks to its brevity) than *marry*, but it has the same two meanings, "to get married," as in *The next summer she wedded him at her parents' home*, and "to perform a marriage," as in *The ship's captain wedded them*. The past tense and past participle are either *wedded* or *wed: My parents were wedded [wed] just fifty years ago*. The participial adjective is a cliché in the phrase so often used jocularly, *wedded bliss*. Figuratively, *wed* is Standard in its high-frequency uses meaning "to combine, join, blend, or unite" and the like, as in *This band's music neatly weds jazz and gospel sounds*.

week See WEAK.

weep, cry, sob (*vv.*) All mean "to shed tears," with *cry* (which has other meanings as well) usually being the most frequent and general, with *weep* meaning particularly "to express grief or sorrow or even joy by shedding tears," and with *sob* meaning especially "to weep aloud, with noticeable catching of breath." *Cry* and *sob* are both regular weak verbs, but *weep*'s past tense and past participle are both *wept: The children wept uncontrollably that night*. *Weeped* is Nonstandard at best, but more probably Substandard.

weft See WARP.

weird (*adj.*) The *e* precedes the *i*. See SPELLING OF WORDS CONTAINING -*EI*- OR -*IE*-.

welch, welcher See WELSH.

well See GOOD.

well (*interj.*) is frequently used in speech as a starter, as in *Well, I guess it's time to go*; as an ejaculatory expression of surprise, as in *Well, I never expected that!*; as a signal of grammatical hiatus and anacoluthon, as in *I was so angry I—well, I don't know what I was going to do*; and as an indication of fumbling for a word, as in *She looked angry and—well, flustered—when she got here*. All these are Standard at the Conversational levels and in the Informal or Semiformal writing that imitates them.

well-nigh (*adv.*) means "nearly, almost" and is Standard English; in some uses it has a somewhat literary air: *The troops were well-nigh exhausted after the climb*.

welsh, welch, Welsh (*adjs., nn.*), **welch, welsh** (*v.*), **welcher, welsher** (*n.*) The *Welsh* are the people who live in Wales, and *Welsh* is their language; pronounce it *WELSH*. *Welch* is an occasional variant spelling of both proper noun and adjective and reflects a variant pronunciation, *WELCH*. The lowercase spellings of the adjective usually refer indirectly to the people (attributing *welsh or Welsh rabbit* to them, for example), but the verb (usually combined with *on*) means "to fail to pay back a debt," "to break one's word," as in *She welched on her promise* or *That nation has welched on its war debt*. Pronounce it either *WELCH* or *WELSH*. Possibly (but by no means certainly—the dictionaries say "origin unknown" or "uncertain") the verb, which appeared first in the mid-nineteenth century, takes its meaning from an unflattering English characterization of the Welsh people, with whom the English were long at war and at odds. A *welcher* or *welsher* is someone who evades debts or doesn't keep promises. The *Welsh* and people of *Welsh* extraction could take offense but curiously enough none of the dictionaries marks the word as an ethnic slur. Even the most recent dictionary considers this sense of the verb and noun to be Standard. See ETHNIC SLURS AND TERMS OF ETHNIC OPPROBRIUM.

Welsh rabbit, Welsh rarebit (*nn.*) *Welsh rabbit* and *Welsh rarebit* are both Standard English names for a dish of melted cheese and beer served on toast or crackers, presumably so-called as an insult to the impoverished or uncivilized Welsh, who were said to eat it instead of the rabbit meat they lacked; hence *Welsh rabbit* is almost certainly an ethnic slur. *Welsh rarebit* is a folk etymology apparently either contrived to avoid offending the Welsh or caused by a misunderstanding of the intended noun, since perhaps some couldn't see a connection between cheese and rabbits.

were See BE; INDICATIVE; WAS.

weskit See WAISTCOAT.

west, West, westerly, western, Western See EAST.

western (*n.*) is the Standard name for a romance in the cowboy vein—one of the many novels, motion pictures, and the like about the American West of the late nineteenth century. See HORSE OPERA.

WESTERN REGIONAL DIALECT, the youngest and least distinctive of our Northern dialects, is spoken in an area settled mainly after the California Gold Rush and the Civil War. Its subdialects include those of the Pacific Northwest, central and northern California, the Rocky Mountain states, and the somewhat more clearly marked Southwestern Regional Dialect (which see). Western has many features in common with other r-retaining Northern dialects, plus a few Midland and Southern sounds and locutions, each reflecting Western's relatively brief history.

westward, westwards See EASTWARD.

wet (*adj., n., v.*) The past tense and past participle are either *wet* or *wetted*. Americans generally use *wet*, as in *Last night our son wet his bed*, but *wetted* still occurs. The participial adjective is either *wetted* or *wet*, as in *a wetted surface*, one to which a liquid has been recently applied, as opposed to *a wet surface*, which simply is in that state when encountered. The noun is Standard meaning literal "dampness" (*Come in out of the wet*), but the word is slang and is now out-of-date if not archaic in the figurative sense "someone or a jurisdiction permitting the sale and consumption of alcoholic drinks" (during contests over prohibition, those who favored alcohol were called "the wets"). Although you do not often hear about a *wet* county, you still regularly hear and see references to *dry* counties, counties in which liquor cannot legally be sold. The adjective, in the idioms *wet behind the ears*, meaning "unlicked, immature, lacking experience," and *all wet*, meaning "wrong, misguided," should be limited to Conversational use; the British still use the adjective to mean "weak, boring, ineffectual," as in *Our mayor is a wet sort of person*, and that use, also Conversational, is occasionally still heard in the United States.

wh- Words spelled beginning with *wh-* are pronounced with an initial *hw* sound in some regional dialects, and with an initial *w* sound in some others. Hence the pairs *which* and *witch*, *wheel* and *weal*, and many others are differently pronounced in some regions but are homophones, pronounced *WICH* and *WEEL*, respectively, in others. Both pronunciations are Standard.

wharf (*n.*) The plural is either *wharfs* or *wharves*, which spellings reflect the two Standard pronunciations of the plural. See DOCK; NOUNS ENDING IN -F.

what (*pron.*) is Standard Conversational and Informal in the idiom *but what: I don't know but what it's going to rain*. As a relative pronoun in utterances such as *It's the basket what has the red ribbon on it*, *what* is Vulgar, countrified, and Nonstandard at best. Any Standard use must be intended and perceived to be consciously jocular; otherwise, use *that* instead.

what clauses See AGREEMENT OF SUBJECTS AND VERBS (1).

whatever (*adj., pron.*) The pronoun occurs in Standard utterances such as *Do whatever you wish,* and in series constructions such as *He can play piano, clarinet, drums, or whatever,* meaning "any other unspecified thing of the sort." *Whatever did you do that for?* is Standard too but limited essentially to Conversational use. The adjective is also Standard, meaning "any," "no matter what kind," "of any kind," as in *Play whatever music you like* or *We'll have no trouble whatever,* but note that utterances such as *We will adopt whatever proposals that he makes* are no longer idiomatic; omit the *that.* Recently there has been a growing vogue word use of *whatever* in speech as a halfhearted affirmative response to a question: it means *Take it any way you like, Do as you wish, If I must, then I will,* or *I don't care,* as in response to "Will you take your little sister with you, please?" "*Whatever.*" It's Casual only and is a kind of slang cliché.

whatsoever (*adj., pron.*) is stiff and old-fashioned, an emphatic word with echoes of biblical style; both pronoun and adjective are best limited to Oratorical or Formal contexts when used at the beginnings of clauses or as adjuncts preceding nouns: *Whatsoever you seek you shall find. Whatsoever reward you wish you shall have.* Especially at the ends of structures, as modifiers following nouns, however, there is nothing stuffy about it; it is merely emphatic: *There is nothing whatsoever we can do; The bank was no help whatsoever.*

when, where, in the phrases *is when* and *is where,* are Standard at all but the Oratorical and Formal levels and in Edited English: *Frustration is when you can't find the car keys.* But in formal definitions, especially of abstractions, *is where* and *is when* are usually frowned on; most commentators insist on a single noun as the predicate nominative in definitions: *Hysteria is an emotion that* . . . , not *Hysteria is when* [*where*] *your emotions.* . . . See REASON IS BECAUSE; WHERE.

when and if See IF AND WHEN.

whence (*adv., subord. conj., pron.*) The adverb means "from what place or source," as in *She went back to her books, whence she always got her inspiration.* The conjunction means "from which fact," as in *I found no one there, whence*

I concluded they had left without me. These uses are Standard. For the pronoun, see FROM HENCE.

whenever (*adv., subord. conj.*) As an adverb, as in *Whenever will we learn the truth?* and as a subordinating conjunction, as in *Tell me whenever you're ready, whenever* is Standard, although some commentators would prefer to limit the adverbial use to Conversational levels. See also WHATEVER.

when worse (worst) comes to worst See IF (WHEN) WORSE (WORST) COME(S) TO WORST.

where (*subord. conj.*) Using *where* in sentences such as *I see where the market is up* or *I read where the legislature wants to raise taxes* is appropriate only in Conversational and Informal use. Edited English and other Formal and Oratorical contexts prefer *that* in such sentences: *I see that the market is up. I read that the legislature wants to raise taxes.* Using *where* to introduce adverbial or adjectival clauses is fully Standard, however: *They took us where we could get lunch. This is one of those shops where no one ever waits on you. I finally got to the point where I could speak a little French.*

where, when See WHEN.

-where See -PLACE.

whereabouts (*adv., n.*) The noun *whereabouts* is Standard with either a singular or a plural verb, even though its ending causes it to resemble a plural noun: *His whereabouts is [are] unknown.* The *-s* ending on *whereabouts* can also signal that the word is an adverb, as in *backwards, towards,* and the like. It means essentially what *where* means (*Whereabouts do you think you left your hat?*) and is Standard English too.

where . . . at, where . . . to *Where* means "in the place at (to) which," so *at* and *to* are redundant in sentences such as *Where is your brother at?* and *Where are you going to?* Both locutions are Nonstandard in written English and in most spoken English as well, although they are frequent in Common and Vulgar English, especially in some regional dialects.

whereas (*subord. conj.*) means (rather formally) "in view of the fact that." It is much used in setting forth the conditions to be met by a formal resolution or other document: *Whereas this is true, whereas that is true, and whereas the other is true, we conclude that we must do such-and-such.* A bit less stiffly, *whereas* also means "on the other hand," as in *He is brown-eyed, whereas she and all the children are blue-eyed.* Lovers of brevity sometimes urge the use of *while* or even *although* instead of *whereas,* but sometimes *while* can be ambiguous, meaning "during the time that," instead of the intended "on the other hand."

whereat, whereupon (*subord. conjs.*) These are synonyms, although *whereat* may be stiffer or more pretentious than *whereupon.* Both are Standard and Formal or Oratorical in tone and mean "following upon, as a result of, in consequence of": *This was the incident whereat the opposition took offense. He shouted something unpleasant, whereupon the others began to jeer at him.*

whereby (*subord. conj.*) means "by means of which" and is Standard but slightly Formal and legal sounding: *These are the achievements whereby the electors will be persuaded.*

wherefore (*adv., n., conj.*) The conjunction means "for that reason" or "therefore" but has a stiffly Formal ring, as in *The fog was thick, wherefore the captain declined to try to land.* As an adverb *wherefore* is archaic, meaning "why, for what reason": *Wherefore frowns the king?* The noun is part of an idiom in the plural that means simply "the reason(s) for": *They explained the whys and wherefores of their decision.* Both adverb and noun are Standard.

wherein (*adv., subord. conj.*) The adverb means "in what way," as in *Wherein did we fail?* The subordinating conjunction means "where," as in *This is the school wherein they placed me;* "the time during which," as in *Those were the years wherein my love of reading grew;* and "how," as in *Show me wherein I did wrong.* All these uses are Standard, and all suggest formality or even a slight pretentiousness that *where* avoids.

whereof (*subord. conj.*) means "of what," "of which," or "of whom," as in *From experience we know whereof we speak.* This is Formal and Oratorical in tone, and it is also close to being a cliché. At the Conversational level one would say *We know what we're talking about.*

whereon (*adv., subord. conj.*) Both functions are becoming old-fashioned, although the conjunction still occurs occasionally in Formal writing and at the more elevated levels; it means "on which or on whom": *This is the evidence whereon I base my conclusions.* The adverb is even stuffier: *Whereon shall we make our stand?*

where . . . to See WHERE . . . AT.

whereupon See WHEREAT.

wherever (*adv., subord. conj.*) Like *whatever* and *whenever,* the adverb should be limited to Conversational and Informal or Semiformal uses: *Wherever does she think she's going? We can meet here or at the office, or wherever.* The conjunction is Standard and often interchangeable with *everywhere* or *anywhere: He followed her wherever* [*everywhere, anywhere*] *she went.*

wherewithal (*n.*) is Standard meaning "the resources, especially but not exclusively financial resources, needed to accomplish something": *She lacked the wherewithal to pay her tuition bill.* It's Standard.

whether See IF; WEATHER; WH-.

whether or not, whether or no *Whether or not* and *whether or no* are semantically interchangeable Standard idioms; the only difference is that *whether or no* has a somewhat more literary ring. The *or not* can be omitted when the idiom introduces a clause working as a nominal—subject, object, or object of a preposition—*We inquired whether she planned to attend.* When the clause is adverbial rather than nominal in function, the *or not* must be kept: *We will attend, whether or not she does* [*whether she does or not*].

which (*pron.*) is Standard when used to refer either to explicit antecedents, as in *That's my book, which I left in your car,* or to general ones, as in *I asked whether I could see the patient, which turned out to be quite all right with the nurse.* Conversational English uses a great deal of the general reference, avoiding ambiguity by means of context and intonation. In writing, however, make certain that *which* is not ambiguous as to antecedent. See THAT (2) for additional comment on the use of pronouns to refer to whole ideas or collections of ideas, rather than to single-word antecedents.

A sentence such as *They had sold the last copy of the text, which I wouldn't have wanted it, except that it's required for my class* is a kind of anacoluthon (which see). The referent for *which* is a bit ambiguous (is it the selling or the textbook?), and as a result the speaker forgets that *which* is the direct object and absently supplies another, *it.* Keep track of your syntax.

See also THAT (4) and THAT (5) for the distinction on which some editors still insist: that *that* introduces restrictive and *which* nonrestrictive modifiers.

which, and See AND WHICH.

while (*subord. conj.*) means either "during the time that," as in *While she was shopping, we waited in the car,* or "although," "on the other hand," as in *While I'm eager to see her, I just can't be here on that date; My parents are ar-*

dent baseball fans, while I've never even seen a professional game. While can be ambiguous: consider *She's learning French, while I'm studying Spanish*—is it "during the time that" or "although"? Context (or perhaps syntax alone) must prevent ambiguity. See WHEREAS; WHILST.

whilom (*adv., adj.*) The adjective means "former, at one time," as in *When I returned, I met many of my whilom colleagues.* It's a very arch, stuffy use, but Standard. The adverb is now archaic and pretentiously jocular, meaning "formerly," as in *I was whilom a traveler in kitchenware.* See also ERSTWHILE; QUONDAM.

whilst (*conj.*), meaning "while," is mainly British, although some Americans use it too; pronounce it either *HWEILST* or *WEILST*, not with the short vowel of *will.*

whiskey, whisky (*n.*) Americans and the Irish prefer the *whiskey* spelling (the plural is either *whiskeys* or *whiskies*); the British and Canadians prefer *whisky* (plural: *whiskies*). The British always mean either *malt whisky* or a blend of several—what Americans call *Scotch*—when they ask for *whisky.* Americans have to specify *Scotch, Irish, bourbon, Canadian, rye, a blend,* or some other, when they ask for *whiskey.* See SPELLING (1).

white-collar See BLUE-COLLAR.

white paper (*n.*) is any official paper or report, often the result of an inquiry or a policy study, issued by a government or another organization or agency. It's a Standard term.

whither See HITHER.

who, whom (*prons.*) *Who* is the nominative case form of this interrogative and relative pronoun, *whom* the objective form: *Who called? Whom were you calling? She's the one who called. She's the one whom I took to dinner.* Only in Oratorical and Edited English and other Formal uses are these cases always distributed according to those rules. Conservative practice adheres to them in all levels as well, and such use is always appropriate, though not required: English has long given us Conversational, Informal, Semiformal, and occasionally even Formal uses where, at the beginnings of clauses where *whom* is called for, *who* occurs instead, and at the ends of utterances where *who* is called for, *whom* occurs instead. Thus, at the lower levels of usage, such diametrically opposite uses as these are Standard: *Who was the lady I saw you with? You asked* **who** *to go with you?* The one exception to the frequent occurrence of *who* toward the fronts and *whom* toward the ends of sentences: the closer a preposition is to its object

pronoun, the more likely we are to use objective case: *Who did you go with?* but *With whom did you go? I saw who you were talking to* but *I saw to whom you were talking.* Unfortunately, this sort of divided usage has led to much hypercorrection, which see. See also CASE (1).

whodunit (*n.*) (rarely *whodunnit*), meaning "a detective or mystery narrative," is now Standard except in the highest Oratorical and Formal contexts.

who else's See ELSE.

whoever, whomever (*prons.*) The case of these pronouns is distributed just the way it is in *who* and *whom:* in Formal, Oratorical, and Edited English, *whoever* is used where nominative case forms are called for (*Whoever said you could sing was mistaken*); *whomever* is used where objective case forms are called for (*Bring whomever you can find*). But in Semiformal, Informal, and Conversational use, *whoever* tends in Standard English to turn up frequently in places where we'd expect an objective form, *whomever* in places where we'd expect a nominative: *Send whoever you wish to send. I want to thank whomever brought these umbrellas.* And, again as with *who* and *whom,* if the object of a preposition is immediately after the preposition, *whomever* will usually appear, but if they're widely separated, *whoever* will usually get the call: *Give the invitation to whomever you wish. Whoever you wish to give the invitation to is welcome to it.*

whole new ball game is a slang idiom; *whole* like *brand* in *brand-new,* is an intensifier. *A new ball game* implies a clean slate, a fresh start, and hence a new opportunity, and *a whole new ball game* does so even more emphatically. But alas, the phrase itself is a cliché, and its own novelty much faded.

wholly See COMPLETE.

whom See WHO.

whomever See WHOEVER.

whopping (*adv., adj., intensifier*), **whopper** (*n.*) All have to do with great size: *a whopping baby* is a large one, *a whopping big lie* is an exceptionally monstrous one (here *whopping* functions as either adverb or intensifier and is usually slang), and a *whopper* is a huge example of something—frequently of a lie, as in *She tells terrible whoppers all the time.* At least one dictionary classes all three words as Colloquial; others consider them Standard, but you would do well to avoid using them in Formal or Oratorical situations, as well as in most Edited English.

who's, whose These are homophones, but the spelling of each is distinctive, and misspellings are costly (and frequently considered shibboleths), though easy to make: *who's* is a contraction of *who is, who has,* and perhaps rarely *who was: Who's that? Who's got the car keys? Whose,* the genitive case form of *who,* means "of whom" or "of which," and it's Standard when used of things, as in *It's an idea whose time has come,* as well as of persons, as in *We need a leader whose reputation is secure.* See also WHO'S.

why (*adv., n., subord. conj., interj.*) All but the interjection may be pronounced either *HWEI* or *WEI,* depending on the regional dialect; the interjection is always pronounced *WEI.* The adverb means "for what reason" (*Why are you late?*), the subordinating conjunction means "the cause or reason for something" (*Please explain why you are late*), and the noun, usually plural, means "the reasons or causes," especially in the idiomatic cliché, *the whys and wherefores* (see WHEREFORE). The interjection is a curious starter word that expresses hesitation, surprise, or doubt; it is particularly frequent at the beginning of a spoken response utterance: *Why, I don't know. Why, I guess I've always thought so.* In *Why, why not?,* the first *why* is the interjection, the second the adverb or question-asking function word. See SITUATION UTTERANCE. Compare WELL.

whys and wherefores See WHEREFORE; WHY.

widow, widower (*nn.*) When a husband dies, his wife becomes a *widow;* when a wife dies, her husband becomes a *widower,* although for reasons unknown this term seems to be reserved only for identification of a man's marital status at points other than the death of his wife or shortly thereafter. That is, in reporting the death of a man, obituaries usually describe the surviving spouse as either his *wife* or his *widow* (usually as his *wife*), but when the wife dies first, her husband is always described as her *husband,* never as her *widower.* Note too that *the wife of the late Mr. Smith* is appropriate, as is *the widow of Mr. Smith,* but that *the widow of the late Mr. Smith* is a tautology to be avoided. Neither *widow* nor *widower* is properly applied to people who have remarried.

wife (*n.*) The plural is *wives;* the genitive singular is *wife's,* and the genitive plural is *wives'.* All three genitive spellings reflect their pronunciations, the plurals having voiced final consonant clusters. *Wife* has two meanings: the most frequent is "a married woman," but in its older sense of "a woman," it occurs in compounds like *housewife* and *fishwife,* neither of which has anything to do with marriage. See NOUNS ENDING IN *-F.*

wilful See WILLFUL.

will See SHALL.

willful, wilful (*adj.*) means "intentional, done deliberately," "obstinately self-willed," as in *He appeared to have done willful damage to the painting.* The usual American spelling is *willful; wilful* is an occasional American variant and the preferred British spelling.

win (*n.*) is a functional shift from the verb *win,* apparently in response to a need for a more informal (and shorter for headline writers) synonym of *victory,* especially for use in sports and sports reporting. It now occurs regularly in Edited English on subjects other than sports—politics, particularly—and it is Standard, although at least one dictionary still labels it Colloquial. Conversational and Informal certainly seem to apply, but journalese might be a more accurate label.

wind (*vv.*) is really three different verbs: (1) *wind* (rhymes with *sinned* and has for principal parts *wind, winded, winded*), meaning "to make short of breath," as in *The climb to the top winded me badly;* (2) *wind* (rhymes with *mind* and has principal parts *wind, wound* [rhymes with *mound*], *wound*), meaning "to twist and turn," as in *The road winds down the valley,* or "to curl or tighten like a spring," as in *She wound the clocks,* and (3) *wind* (rhymes with either *mind* or *sinned* and has for principal parts *wind, wound* [rhymes with *ground*] or *winded* [rhymes with *rescinded* or *minded*], *wound* or *winded*), meaning "to blow a horn," as in *The huntsman should wind his horn in a special way at the kill.* All are Standard, with (3) archaic.

wind shear (*n.*) is a compound technical term for the forces acting on an object in an area where winds of various directions and speeds come together. It is now also Standard in the general vocabulary as a result of wide discussion of its likely role as a cause of airplane crashes especially during takeoffs or landings under turbulent wind conditions.

windward (*adv., adj., n.*) means "the direction from which the wind is coming" or "that side of the ship," as in *Cross over to the windward side, Sail windward,* or *Sail to the windward.* None of the three ends in *-s.* See LEEWARD.

wink (*v.*) means "rapidly to shut and open one or both eyes," but the locution *wink at* means both "to shut and quickly open one eye as a signal or suggestion," as in *He winked at his granddaughter to make her laugh,* and also "to shut the eyes to" and hence figuratively "to pretend not to see, to connive at," as in *The police officer apparently winked at her being double-parked.* Both are Standard.

winner (*n.*) is Standard in its literal sense of "the victor": *She was the winner in the first heat.* It also has wide use in an extended Conversational and Informal sense, "someone or something that appears headed for success or a triumph of some sort": *This book looks like a winner.*

-wise (*suffix*) is old and Standard in many familiar words (*lengthwise, crosswise, otherwise*), but of late it has been overused in some nonce words: *Scholarshipwise, the school has little to offer. Behaviorwise, her kids are awful.* Using the suffix in this way is a sloppy and justly criticized shortcut, much-hated by conservatives, particularly when it occurs in writing. Restrict unfamiliar compounds with *-wise* as you would restrict slang, to Conversational levels and Informal and some Semiformal writing at best.

wish, wish for (*vv.*) *Wish,* meaning "hope to achieve or obtain," is more natural (and less pretentious) when followed by an infinitive rather than a regular noun: *I wish to have wine with dinner,* rather than *I wish wine with dinner. Wish for* means something else, a separate act of specifically yearning or seeking after something; it requires belief in good luck or fairy godmothers or the like. See DESIRE.

with (*prep.*) *With* (pronounced either *with* or *wiƚh*) can sometimes pose a problem when it follows a singular subject; the object of the preposition then seems to suggest that the whole subject might be compound, so that the verb should be plural, as in *The conductor, with the soloists, are to take a curtain call,* rather than what Standard English requires: *The conductor, with the soloists, is.* . . . The literal subject establishes the number, regardless of the number of the phrasal object that follows: compare *The soloists, with the conductor, are.* . . . See AGREEMENT OF COMPOUND SUBJECTS WITH THEIR VERBS AND SUBSEQUENT PRONOUNS; ALONG.

withal (*adv.*) means "in addition, besides," as in *She was young and personable and popular,* *and withal unusually intelligent.* The word sounds old-fashioned today.

with a view, with the view See VIEW.

within (*adv., n., prep.*) is Standard in all three functions: *Inquire within. The fifth column undermined from within. Finish within the hour.* See IN; INSIDE.

with one's back to the wall See WALL.

without (*adv., n., subord. conj., prep.*) The subordinating conjunction *without,* meaning "unless," is now dialectal and Nonstandard at best: *She won't sing without somebody begs and begs her to.* Stick with *unless. Without* is also a preposition, as in *She can walk without pain,* and a noun, as in *The noise came from without.* The adverb *without* has two meanings: "outside," as in *Please await us without*; and "lacking, absent, not provided," as in *She'll just have to do without.* All these are Standard, although the noun sense and the first adverb sense are rather stiff and old-fashioned, not likely to occur much in current Conversational uses.

without charge, without cost See FOR FREE.

without doubt See DOUBTLESS.

without hardly *Without hardly,* like *couldn't hardly,* is sometimes called a double negative and is always Substandard, since *without* suggests something missing, and *hardly* (like *scarcely*) suggests something almost or truly falling short. But see HARDLY.

with regard(s) to See REGARDING.

with respect to See IN RESPECT TO.

with the company (corporation, firm) This idiom, which combines with the verb *to be,* as in *She's with Appleby and Schwartz,* suggests that she's in a position of more than minimal consequence; janitors, stock clerks, and secretaries are *employed by* the company, but our Mary Jane is *with* it.

with the exception of is a longish synonym for *except* and *except for: Everyone was present with the exception of the lawyer.* It's a stiffer locution, but it is unquestionably Standard and appropriate in the right situation: *All the guests had arrived and were gathered in the hall, with the exception of the most important guest of all—the guest of honor.* See EXCEPTION.

with the hope of, with the hope that See HOPE.

witness (*v.*) is Standard meaning "see" when the direct object is an act, a scene, or an event, but it is not used when the direct object is a person or an inanimate object: you can't *witness* a baby's rattle or a ballpark, but you can *witness* a baby's first steps or a ball game.

wizen (*v.*), **wizened** (*adj.*) *Wizen* means "to shrivel or dry up" and is pronounced *WIZ-uhn; wizened* means "withered or shriveled" and is pronounced *WIZ-uhnd*.

wolf (*n.*, *v.*) The third person singular verb is pronounced *WULFS* and spelled *wolfs* (*He always wolfs his food*); the genitive case singular of the noun *wolf* is pronounced *WULFS* too, but spelled *wolf's*. The plural of the noun, however, is pronounced *WULVZ* and spelled *wolves*. See NOUNS ENDING IN *-F*.

woman See LADY.

womanly See EFFEMINATE.

wonder (*v.*), as in *I wonder why she's late*, produces a statement, not a question, and therefore is written to end with a period, not a question mark. But compare *I wondered, "Why is she late?"* See PUNCTUATION.

wonk (*n.*) is a very recent slang coinage, one of those scornful but envious terms the newsmagazines delight in as a label for those in the know or in power or promising, like *pundit* and British *boffin* (both of which see). Its' origin is uncertain (*know* spelled backward) and its future doubtful.

wont (*adj.*, *n.*, *v.*) is Standard when pronounced to rhyme with *gaunt* or *don't* or even with *want* or *grunt*. The adjective means "inclined or accustomed" and when used as a predicate adjective is always followed by an infinitive: *He was wont to sing in the shower*. The noun means "custom or habit": *Singing in the shower had long been his wont*. The verb occurs most often as a participial adjective: *Her wonted calm suddenly vanished*. In speaking make context control where the multiple pronunciations could otherwise confuse; in writing be careful not to put an apostrophe in *wont* as if it were *won't*.

won't is the Standard English contraction for *will not*, appropriate wherever other negative contractions are appropriate. Spell it always with an apostrophe, although you'll find a few earlier-twentieth-century writers of consequence who omit it.

wood, woods (*nn.*) *Wood* in the sense of "a bit of forest" has a literary quality: Red Riding-hood's grandmother surely lived in a *wood*. American grandmothers more often live in *the woods*. *Woods* in this sense usually takes a plural verb, but it can be encountered in Standard use with a singular: *A woods has grown up in what used to be a meadow* or *The woods have grown*. . . . All these are Standard.

woof See WARP.

wop (*adj.*, *n.*) is an ethnic slur applied disparagingly to Italians. It's taboo.

WORD CHOICE *She secured a position* and *She got a job* are different in style, but they're both Standard. Mixed choices (*She played the concerto brilliantly; it was a real gas* or *His argument impressed the jury and thoroughly convinced them; he really bamboozled them*) are sometimes amusing because they call attention to themselves, but for most expository purposes, they are distracting, and you should avoid them.

WORDINESS, PROLIXITY These terms remind us how often and how justifiably our teachers, critics, and editors hound us for being long-winded, for using too many words, for letting our syntax tangle around itself, and for writing and talking ramblingly rather than crisply and concisely. A staccato, laconic style is of course not the only kind of good speech or prose, regardless of how much people urge conciseness, but all the talk about *wordiness* does suggest that most of us tend to err in that direction, filling our sentences with passive voices, involuted syntax, deadwood clichés, and polysyllabic vogue words, unless we are very conscious of style; and too few of us realize that ideas can smother under the weight of useless verbiage. Best advice: be clear, be specific, and when your idea is complex keep your diction and your syntax as simple as possible. That's the way to speak, and that's the way to write. See also ABSTRACTITIS; JARGON; REDUNDANT; SCIENTIFIC ENGLISH.

WORD ORDER See SYNTAX.

WORDS AS WORDS When writing or printing words you are discussing as words ("Define the meaning of the word *anomalous*"), it is conventional to put them in italics, small capital letters, or some other visually distinctive form or even within quotation marks, in order that readers will not lose them in the normal flow of the sentence.

WORDY See WORDINESS.

work (*v.*) The principal parts are *work, worked* or *wrought, worked* or *wrought*. There is some semantic variation in the past tense and past participle forms: *He worked wonders* differs only in tone from *He wrought wonders*, but *worked* has far more generalized meanings, "to do a job," "to labor," and the like, in addition to having the same specialized senses that *wrought* has, meaning "to shape or form something": *She worked [wrought] in silver*. The participial adjective *wrought* occurs frequently, as in *wrought iron.* As a past participle, *wrought* usually has an old-fashioned air, as in *What hath God wrought?* except in the combined *wrought up,* meaning "emotionally aroused," as in *The whole family was all wrought up [worked up] over the news.* This use is usually limited to Conversational and Informal contexts. See also WREAK.

worldly (*adj.*) means "attentive to concerns of this world, not of the next," and hence "pragmatic, knowing about practical, human things rather than about ideal or higher things"; it can also mean "sophisticated, experienced, knowing." *Worldly* is sometimes carelessly written *wordly* or *worldy.*

worse comes to worst, if (when) See IF (WHEN) WORSE (WORST) COME(S) TO WORST.

worser (*adj.*) is Nonstandard, a double comparison involving *worse,* which already functions as the comparative of *bad. Worser* is typically a small child's mistake.

worst comes to worst, if (when) See IF (WHEN) WORSE (WORST) COME(S) TO WORST.

worst way, in the This hyperbolic Standard idiom means "very much," as in *He wants a new car in the worst way,* but its hyperbole suggests irrational, uncontrollable desire—he'll stop at nothing to get that car.

worthwhile (*adj.*) is a one-word version of the phrase, *worth your while,* meaning "worth your time or effort." Something *worthwhile* has value (although unspecified). Both the word (once two words, then hyphenated, but now always one word) and the phrase are Standard.

would See SHOULD.

woulda See OF (2); SHOULDA.

would have *Would have,* in place of *had* alone as auxiliary, as in *if they would have known,* instead of the Standard *if they had known,* is frequent in Common English, especially in speech. This "extra" auxiliary is never appropriate in Standard written English, however, and most Standard speakers object to it at all levels as well. See also PLUPLUPERFECT TENSE, of which this *if I would have known* usage could be considered an example.

would of See OF (2); SHOULDA.

would rather See HAD RATHER.

wrack See RACK.

wrangle See WANGLE.

wrapped See RAPT.

wrath (*n.*), **wrathful, wroth** (*adjs.*) The noun rhymes usually with *math,* but occasionally the vowel is that of the stressed syllable in *father,* or in the British version, that of *moth. Wrath* is "fierce anger or fury," and to be *wrathful,* or more literally, to be *wroth,* is to be full of such emotion. *Wroth* rhymes with *moth* or occasionally with *both.*

wreak,   wreck (*vv.*)   *Wreak* once meant "avenge," but today its most frequent use is in the still-useful cliché *wreak havoc,* meaning "cause destruction, devastate." *Wreak* is pronounced to rhyme either with *reek* or *wreck,* hence the occasional confusion of spelling *wreak* as *wreck,* abetted by *wreck*'s somewhat similar meaning and their probably shared Indo-European etymon. Other verbs regularly used with *havoc* include *raise, play, create,* and *work,* this last sometimes raising questions about a possible confusion of *wrought* and *wreaked.* Best advice: stick with *wreak* (rhymed with *reek*), *raise, play,* and *create havoc,* and use these clichés sparingly.

wreath (*n.*), **wreathe** (*v.*) The noun *wreath* rhymes with *teeth,* and its plural is pronounced *REETHS,* with a voiceless final consonant cluster. The verb *wreathe* rhymes with *breathe,* with a voiced final consonant cluster. See PRONUNCIATIONS OF WORDS ENDING IN -*TH.*

wreck See WREAK.

wright See PLAYWRIGHT; RITE.

writ See LARGE.

write (*v.*) The principal parts of this strong verb are *write, wrote, written.* Use of *wrote* as past participle, as in *She had already wrote home,* is Substandard and a shibboleth; *She had already written home* is Standard. See also PLAYWRIGHT; RITE.

write-up (*n.*) is Standard, except in Formal prose. Some dictionaries label it Colloquial, and it is much used in journalism.

wrong (*adv., adj., n., v.*), **wrongly** (*adv.*) *Wrong* can be four different parts of speech: an adjective (*We took a wrong turn; The answer was wrong*); a flat adverb (*We went wrong somehow*); a noun (*She did him a shameful wrong*); and a verb (*They cruelly wronged her*). All are Standard. *Wrongly* is also an adverb, in some uses not interchangeable with the flat adverb: *They wrongly accused her of lying.*

wroth See WRATH.

wrought See WORK; WREAK.

X

X 1 Initially the letter is usually pronounced with a *z* sound, as in *xylophone.* Medially and finally, it is usually pronounced *KS,* as in *box,* or *KSH,* as in *complexion.* And the name of the letter itself is pronounced *EKS,* with a plural of *EKS-iz,* as in *Xs* or *X's.* When we retain a French plural spelling, such as *chateaux,* we use either of two pronunciations for that French spelling, the original French (*sha-TO*) or that appropriate for an English plural (*sha-TOZ*), just the way we say *chateaus.*

X 2 (*n., v.*) The noun, which is the name of the alphabetical letter, is a Standard high-frequency symbol for a mathematical unknown (now much generalized, so that it can stand for anything unknown—even the signature of an illiterate). The *x-axis* is the horizontal axis of a graph (the vertical is the *y-axis*). We use *X* as a map or other diagraming locator (*X marks the spot*), to mark ballots, to symbolize a kiss or kisses visually in personal correspondence, to choose answers in multiple-choice examinations, to indicate in grading tests that an answer is wrong, and as a verb to describe our crossing out written matter with it, as in *I x-ed out that whole paragraph.* It's also Standard in groups of one to four to indicate the fineness of sugar and flour, and it's the Roman numeral ten, and in clusters it is Roman twenty (XX), thirty (XXX), etc. It is also sometimes used as an Informal abbreviation for *cross,* as in *x-road* and *RR x-ing.*

Xanadu (*n.*) is the literary and mythical name Coleridge gave Kubla Khan's luxurious and beautiful summer palace and that we now sometimes use for modern palaces, real or imagined.

xenophobia, xenophobe (*nn.*), **xenophobic** (*adj.*), **xenophile** (*n.*) There are four Standard pronunciations of *xenophobia:* *ZEN-o-FO-bee-(y)uh, ZEEN-o-FO-bee-(y)uh, ZEN-uh-FO-bee-(y)uh,* or *ZEEN-uh-FO-bee-(y)uh. Xenophobia* is hatred or fear of strangers or of anything foreign or strange, and a *xenophobe* is a person who has that hatred or fear. A *xenophile* (pronounced *ZEEN-o-FEIL*) is a lover of anything foreign or strange.

xerography (*n.*) is the generic name for a dry copying process that electrically charges on portions of treated paper exact images that correspond to whatever is on an original and then inks in the charged spots to produce the copy. It's a Standard term and is not capitalized.

Xerox (*n.*), **xerox** (*n., v.*) *Xerox* is the trade name of a company and of the copying machines it makes that use xerography to make copies. The lowercase noun and verb are, respectively, a *xerographic* copy, as in *Get me a xerox of this letter, please,* and the act of copying with such a machine, as in *Please xerox this document for me.* Edited English usually prefers the more generic terms (*photo*)*copy,* (*photo*)*copying machine,* (*photo*)*copier,* and (*photo*)*copy.* See TRADE NAMES.

-xion, -ction See -ECTION.

Xmas (*n.*) is an abbreviation for *Christmas* (*X* is also sometimes used as an abbreviation for *Christ* in abbreviations such as *Xian,* for *Christian*). *Xmas* occurs mainly in advertising headlines and other Informal contexts where space is short, and it is pronounced either *KRIS-muhs* or *EKS-muhs,* the latter often jocular and usually at the lower Conversational levels. Best advice: avoid the abbreviation in Edited English, and please yourself and your correspondents in your notes and letters, as you do in conversation. Some Christians take strong exception to both the spelled and pronounced abbreviations.

X-rated (*adj.*) is the unofficial label attached to motion pictures deemed unsuitable for those under seventeen and likely to be offensive to others, because of sexual, violent, and other explicit content, including *X-rated* (that is, obscene) language. The term is Standard in its literal sense, but figuratively used it is not suitable for most Oratorical or Formal contexts.

X ray, x ray (*n.*), **X-ray, x-ray** (*adj., n., v.*) The noun *X ray* is so named because the ray was an unknown quantity—rendered in mathematics as *X*—at the time of its discovery. The noun stands for the ray itself, for the process of taking this kind of image, and for the image itself, once developed. All these senses are Standard, as are those of the adjective and of the verb (both of which can also be spelled with a capital letter and hyphenated or not), meaning ''to take such an image with an *X-ray* machine.''

***x* years young** See YOUNG AS YOU FEEL.

Y

-y (*suffix*) The *-y* suffix added to many nouns, especially monosyllabic nouns, will turn them into adjectives: *dirt* becomes *dirty*; *hair* becomes *hairy*; *rain* becomes *rainy*; *snow* becomes *snowy*.

Yahoo (*n.*) Because the *Yahoos* in Swift's *Gulliver's Travels* were ugly, brutish, degraded creatures who looked like humans and had all the human vices, the term *Yahoo* has come to mean any person disgustingly crude, grubbily materialistic, and grossly unrefined and unintelligent. A *Yahoo* is the lowest form of human life.

y'all See YOU-ALL.

yang See YIN.

yay, yea (*adv., demonstrative, intensifier*) There really is no Standard spelling for this word (pronounced to rhyme with *say*), since it occurs only in the lower levels of the spoken language, accompanied by hand gestures to indicate size, as in *That fish was yay big, I'll swear.* It functions as a kind of substitute for *this*, but carries stress and emphasis as an intensifier or demonstrative can.

yclept, y-clept (*adj.*) are two spellings of the past participle of the Old English verb *clepian*, meaning "called" or "named." The *y* is a later spelling of the unstressed *ge-* prefix of the Old English past participle; it was pronounced *yuh* in Old English and later, in Middle English, *ee*. Later poets, especially Spenser and Milton, restored *clip* and *cleppe* and especially *yclept* to literary use. Today this archaic word is used only in a self-conscious effort to make one's words sound humorous or ancient: *My elderly sedan is yclept Gwendolyn.* Pronounce it *ee-KLEPT*.

ye 1 (*pron.*) was in Old English (spelled *ge*) and Middle English (spelled with *y*) the nominative case second person plural personal pronoun, familiar to speakers of Modern English through the language of the King James Bible and its successors. In later centuries *ye* became the second person singular nominative pronoun as well, and finally in some dialects it filled the second person functions for both singular and plural,

nominative and accusative (just as *you* does today). *Ye* is now archaic.

ye 2 (*art.*) *Ye*, as in *Ye Olde Coffee Shoppe*, is a misspelled spelling pronunciation. In late Middle English book hands (the handwriting used by professional scribes), *the* was usually spelled with the *thorn:* (þ), one of the letters later represented by *th*; the letter *y* looked much the same. So *þe Olde Inne* on ancient signs came to be misread by the nineteenth- and twentieth-century uninitiated as *Ye Olde Inne*, rather than *The Olde Inne.* Never underestimate the staying power of folk etymology and other ignorant errors.

yea See YAY.

yeah, yup, yeh (*adv.*) are some of the conventional spellings for these Conversational substitutes for *yes*, each reflecting a pronunciation. *Yeah* is the most widely used spelling, just as *YA* and *YA-uh* are the most widely heard pronunciations. The word occurs only in relatively relaxed speech—Casual and Impromptu levels, typically—and in written imitations of it.

yearn (*v.*) can be combined with the prepositions *for, after, over,* and *toward(s)*, as in *Boys his age yearn for [after, over, toward(s)] pimple-free complexions. Yearn* also can be followed by *to* plus an infinitive, as in *She yearned to take flying lessons.*

years young See YOUNG AS YOU FEEL.

yeh See YEAH.

yeoman (*adj., n.*) The spelling is odd: the first syllable seems not to match its pronunciation, which rhymes with *snow.* The plural is *yeomen.*

yet (*adv.*) raises many conservative hackles at all levels when it's used with a past tense of the auxiliary *do*, as in *Did she return my call yet?* instead of *Has she returned my call yet?* or simply *Did she return my call?* The locution occurs frequently in the lower Conversational levels, but the usage is clearly Nonstandard in all writing other than Informal contexts.

YIDDISH is a Germanic language spoken by Jews from eastern Europe. It is written in the Hebrew alphabet, and its vocabulary contains words from German, Russian, Hebrew, Polish, and English, among others. The name itself comes from the German word *jüdisch,* which means "Jewish." *Ladino* is a Romance language with Hebrew borrowings that the Sephardic Jews use, especially in the Balkans. It's sometimes called *Judeo-Spanish,* but it has not had the impact in the United States that Yiddish has had.

YIDDISH WORDS IN AMERICAN EN-GLISH were once limited mainly to the Metropolitan New York City regional dialect, but vaudeville, the Yiddish theater, the movies, radio, television, and the borscht-circuit comedians who earned their spurs in the Catskill resorts have spread a good many colorful bits of the Yiddish vocabulary into Standard English or at least into its slang. Standard speakers will recognize most of these, all of which are slang except *schmaltz,* which is now Conversational and Informal: *chutzpah, dreck, kibbitz, klutz, schlemiel, schlep, schlock, schmaltz, schmo, schmooze, schmuck, schnook, schnozzle, shtik.* And there are many more.

yin, yang (*nn.*) In Chinese philosophy, these terms represent the two complementary forces in the universe that together form the basis of everything: *yin* is female, passive, dark, cold or wet, and negative; *yang* is masculine, active, bright or light, warm or dry, and positive.

yolk, yoke (*nn.*), **yoke** (*v.*) These are homophones rhyming with *smoke.* A *yolk* is the yellow part of an egg; a *yoke* is a heavy wooden frame or oxbow used to harness a team of oxen, and it has many specialized and figurative meanings as well, most of them suggested by the shape or purpose of the *ox yoke.* The verb *yoke* is very likely a functional shift from the noun *yoke* (both are Old English words); it means "to place in a yoke, to link together," as in harnessing animals or getting married.

yon (*adv., adj.*) The adjective means "yonder" or "that" (as a kind of demonstrative); it's archaic and therefore usually jocular today, as in *Yon roast chicken attracts me mightily.* The adverb also means "yonder" or "over there," and it's rare and obsolescent except in the usually jocular or self-consciously poetic cliché, *hither and yon,* as in *We looked hither and yon but found nothing.*

yore (*adv., n.*) Today the noun is limited to poetic or other deliberately elevated use in its sense of "in the days of long ago," as in *In days of yore, giants and dragons roamed the world.* The adverb, which meant "long ago," is now obsolete.

you (*pron.*) is the second person singular and plural pronoun, and it is both nominative, as in *You look tired,* and objective, as in *I'll invite you.* Note too that as a singular subject it takes a plural verb: *You are my sunshine. You walk too fast for me.* A clearly marked singular verb in such circumstances, as in *You was late for the meeting* or *You looks tired,* is blatantly Substandard and a shibboleth. Indefinite *you,* used when you're addressing nobody in particular, as in *When you hike in the woods, you take a risk of encountering ticks,* used to be criticized by teachers as a misuse of the pronoun, but it is clearly Standard in all but the most Formal or Oratorical uses. See ONE.

you-all, y'all This Southern regional dialect pronoun is almost always plural, and it is Standard in that dialect. Only ill-advised speakers of other regional dialects will attempt to imitate it in front of native speakers of Southern, who can spot fakes almost unerringly. The spellings both reflect the pronunciations.

you know is a perfectly Standard subject and verb combination when used either to wring the full meaning out of the verb, as in *Of course you know her; you met her last month,* or as a relaxed, informal way to assume agreement in a conversation, as in *You know, I really enjoyed tonight's concert.* The problem with *you know* arises only in the spoken language, when the phrase becomes a filler, cropping up several times in even short bits of conversation. It smacks of chewing gum, empty-headedness, and teen-aged callowness and inexperience, but far too many adults have let it become a kind of tic in their speech too. If you're infected, cure yourself quickly. It's hard to take seriously anything delivered against a refrain of *you knows.*

young adult (*n.*) is an idiomatic phrase that may have originated in the jargon of librarians, booksellers, and publishers. It refers to writing (and perhaps other forms of art or entertainment) aimed at people of that age group, from the mid- to late teens. See also TEEN.

young as you feel, *x* **years young** are both made on analogy with similar sayings built on old (*You're only as old as you feel; He's x years old*). These cheerful clichés often sound rather strained, perhaps because the voices that utter them are usually quavery.

youngster (*n.*) has as referent a young person in an age range from child to the relative "younger than I am," as in the oldster's remark, *Why, he's only seventy—a mere youngster.* This Standard term may have a rather old-fashioned air about it today; *the kids* seems to have replaced *the youngsters* as many parents' way of referring to their children, whatever their ages. See KID.

your (*pron., determiner*), **you're** (*contr.*) *Your* is the possessive pronoun: *Your umbrella is in my car. You're* is a contraction of *you are: You're sitting on my hat.* Even good spellers can mix them up inadvertently (see ITS), but sharp-eyed readers are quick to spot such mistakes. Proofread.

Your used as a determiner without real possessive force, as in *Now take your average politician,* is folksy stuff, possibly amusing in the right context—at the Casual level or in Informal imitation of it—but clearly out of place almost everywhere else.

your move See BALL'S IN YOUR COURT.

yourn See ABSOLUTE POSSESSIVE PRONOUNS.

yours (*pron.*) is an absolute possessive pronoun in the genitive case: *This book must be yours.* Remember that unlike nouns, possessive pronouns that already end in -*s* do not add an apostrophe. See HE; HERS.

yourself, yourselves (*prons.*) *Yourself* is singular, *yourselves* plural, and the number of each is clear from its form, as is no longer true of the pronoun *you,* which is now both singular and plural. Although *myself* in other than use as a reflexive or emphatic pronoun is Substandard, the same strictures are rarely applied to *yourself* and *yourselves,* perhaps because we find an extra usefulness in these number-distinctive forms. The reflexive use is Standard, as in *You shouldn't blame yourself [yourselves] for this mistake;* so are emphatic uses, as in *You yourself [yourselves] are to blame.* And at the Conversational levels and in Semiformal and Informal contexts, some nonreflexive uses are appropriate too, as

in *Let's keep this a secret between yourself and me* and *I'd like to recruit some better fielders, like yourselves and Fred.* Only in the most conservative Oratorical or Edited English are such uses likely to be deemed inappropriate.

youth (*n.*) meaning "boy," as in *The youth who broke his arm is my grandson,* and *youths* meaning "boys" or "young persons," as in *Those youths are noisy and ill-mannered,* are both rather stiff, old-fashioned terms. When *youth* is used collectively to refer to several persons of either sex, the pronoun reference will be plural (or neuter) and therefore nondistinctive: *The youth of America will insist on their [its] being heard. Those youths are likely to get themselves arrested. Youth* as an abstract noun, as in *She mourns her vanished youth,* is unexceptionable in any Standard use.

you was See YOU.

Yugoslavia, Jugoslavia (*n.*) The usual English spelling is with the initial *Y-,* which reflects the pronunciation, *YOO-go-SLAH-vee-(y)uh.*

yup See YEAH.

yuppie, yuppy (*n.*) is perhaps the most frequently used of several similar acronyms that label various segments of urban society, especially during the 1980s: *young urban professional(s)* provides the first syllable; the second is a familiar diminutive. The word is Standard but fading a bit, and it probably should not be used in Oratorical and very Formal contexts. Although many later and imitative coinages (without the diminutive) have remained as slang, such as *dinks,* "a married couple who both are employed and who have no children," from *double income, no kids,* still other such acronyms have advanced little further than the nonce word stage. See POSSLQ.

Z

-z-, -zz- See CONSONANTS (2).

zeal (*n.*) combines with the prepositions *for* or (rarely) *in,* followed either by a noun or a gerund, or it can take *to,* followed by an infinitive: *She has a zeal for [in] insurance [for selling insurance, in selling insurance] [to sell insurance].*

zealous See JEALOUS.

zenith, nadir (*nn.*) *Zenith* means "the highest point in the heavens, the point directly overhead"; it has also generalized to mean "the peak or topmost point," as in *He's at the zenith of his professional career.* Pronounce it ZEE-nith. *Nadir* is the exact antonym of *zenith:* it means "the lowest point in the universe, directly below the observer," and it has generalized to mean simply "the lowest point," as in *This last defeat marked the nadir of our season.* Pronounce it either *NAI-duhr* or *NAI-DEER.*

zero (*n.*) The plural is either *zeros* or *zeroes,* and the word is pronounced either *ZEE-ro* or *ZI-ro.* Most single-digit numbers have one and only one verbal representation: *one, two, three, four,* etc. (Numbers of more than one digit can be turned into more than one verbalization: *twenty-five, two five; one hundred sixty-seven, one sixty-seven, one six seven; two thousand three hundred* [*and*] *five, twenty-three hundred* (*and*) *five,* etc.) *Zero* is different: when we recite our social security, credit card, ZIP code, or telephone numbers, we say *zero, oh* (the name of the letter *o,* pronounced *O*), *naught* or *nought* (which means both "zero" and "nothing"; both variants are pronounced to rhyme with *fought*), *aught* or *ought* (an erroneous but now Standard separation of the words *a naught* or *nought* into *an aught* or *ought*). And there are also some words of much lower frequency, such as *cipher* (meaning both "zero": and "nothing") and, especially in reporting the scores of games, the word *nothing* or the slang word *zip: The Red Sox lost, three* [*to*] *nothing,* or *three* [*to*] *zip.* An even lower frequency way of saying *zero* (or *nothing*) is the noun *null,* most often heard in the cliché *null and void.* And the British make much use of *nil,* which they use in giving game scores orally and in other mathematical verbalizing. All these (except *zip*) are fully Standard.

ZERO PLURALS is a term used by some grammarians for nouns such as *deer* and *sheep* that have an unchanging form for both singular and plural. See RELIC PLURALS OF NOUNS.

ZEUGMA (pronounced *Z*[*Y*]*OOG-muh*) is a figure of speech wherein one word is used twice in the same sentence but in different syntactic and semantic relationships: *I explained, "I'm really trying," and she seemed to agree, saying, "I find you extremely trying."* See SYLLEPSIS.

zip See ZERO.

ZIP code (*n.*) *ZIP* is a consciously created acronym from *Zone Improvement Program,* used to describe the codes of originally five and now nine digits that the U.S. Postal Service uses to identify postal zones. The first two digits identify the state, and the last three the post office in that state. The additional four digits following a hyphen can specify individual postal customers or substations.

zoology (*n.*) The Standard pronunciation is *zo-AHL-uh-jee* or, in rapid speech, *zuh-WAHL-uh-jee.* The pronunciation *zoo-AHL-uh-jee*—formerly discouraged by the diaresis English once used to make clear the first two syllables—is Nonstandard and possibly even a Substandard shibboleth among some Standard speakers.

zoom (*n., v.*) is an onomatopoeia, an echoic word meaning "to move rapidly with a humming or buzzing sound." For airplanes it nearly always means "to climb rapidly," but otherwise it is Standard to indicate rapid motion in a level direction, or up or down, or (as with a zoom lens) out and in, far away or in close. Interesting point: in many such uses the buzzing sound of speed seems to have disappeared.

The combined form with the verb, *to zoom in on,* is an idiom meaning "to magnify the focus (literal or figurative), to concentrate attention on a particular rather than a general view." This use too seems to have lost any vestige of the original sound of speed in the word.

zoom lens (*n.*) This term, from motion picture camera and projector jargon first but then adapted to still cameras and binoculars, has now become Standard, at least in its literal technical senses: a *zoom lens* is one whose focal length is continuously and rapidly adjustable so that it can magnify continuously, enlarging the image without losing focus.

zydeco (*adj., n.*) is the name of the popular music of the Louisiana bayou country that owes much to both the Louisiana Black and Cajun traditions. It is a Standard term, although it may seem unfamiliar to some people not acquainted with popular music.

-zz- See CONSONANTS (2).

BIBLIOGRAPHY

Adams, Robert M. *Bad Mouth*. Berkeley: University of California Press, 1977.

Algeo, John. *Problems in the Origins and Development of the English Language*. 3d ed. New York: Harcourt Brace Jovanovich, 1982.

——. "Vogue Words Through Five Decades." *English Today* 7, no. 1 (1990): 44–46.

——. "A Meditation on the Varieties of English." *English Today* 7, no. 3 (1991): 3–6.

Allen, Harold B. and Michael D. Linn. *Readings in Applied English Linguistics*. 3d ed. New York: Knopf, 1982.

Allen, Irving Lewis. *The Language of Ethnic Conflict*. New York: Columbia University Press, 1983.

The American Heritage Dictionary of the English Language. William Morris, ed. Boston: Houghton Mifflin, 1969.

The American Heritage Dictionary of the English Language. 2d college ed. Boston: Houghton Mifflin, 1982.

The American Heritage Dictionary of the English Language. 3d ed. Boston: Houghton Mifflin. 1992.

The American Heritage Illustrated Encyclopedic Dictionary. Boston: Houghton Mifflin, 1987.

Bagnall, Nicholas. *A Defence of Clichés*. London: Constable, 1985.

Bailey, Richard W. "Dialects of Canadian English." *English Today* 7, no. 3 (1991): 20–25.

Baker, Sheridan. *The Practical Stylist*. 6th ed. New York: Harper and Row, 1985.

Barnhart, Clarence L., Sol Steinmetz, and Robert K. Barnhart. *The Barnhart Dictionary of New English Since 1963*. Bronxville, N.Y.: Barnhart–Harper and Row, 1973.

——. *The Second Barnhart Dictionary of New English*. Bronxville, N.Y.: Barnhart Books, 1980.

——. *Third Barnhart Dictionary of New English*. N.p.: H. W. Wilson, 1990.

Baron, Dennis E. *Grammar and Good Taste*. New Haven: Yale University Press, 1982.

Barzun, Jacques. *A Word or Two Before You Go. . . .* Middletown, Conn.: Wesleyan University Press, 1986.

Baugh, Albert C. and Thomas Cable. *A History of the English Language*. 3d ed. Englewood Cliffs, N.J.: Prentice-Hall, 1978.

Beard, Henry and Christopher Cerf. *The Official Politically Correct Handbook and Dictionary*. New York: Villard Books, 1992.

Bernstein, Theodore M. *Watch Your Language*. Great Neck, N.Y.: Channel Press, 1958.

——. *The Careful Writer*. New York: Atheneum, 1965.

——. *Dos, Don'ts, and Maybes of English Usage*. New York: Times Books, 1977.

Bolinger, Dwight L. "Truth Is a Linguistic Question." *Language* 49 (1973): 539–783.

——. *Language: The Loaded Weapon*. New York: Longman, 1980.

——. "Usage and Acceptability in Language/For the Affirmative." In *The American Heritage Dictionary*, 2d college ed., pp. 30–32. Boston: Houghton Mifflin, 1982.

Bremner, John B. *Words on Words*. New York: Columbia University Press, 1980.

Brown, Ivor. *A Word in Your Ear and Just Another Word*. New York: Dutton, 1963.

Bryant, Margaret M. *Current American Usage*. New York: Funk and Wagnalls, 1962.

Bryson, Bill. *The Mother Tongue*. New York: Morrow, 1990.

Buckley, William F., Jr. "Usage and Acceptability in Language/For the Negative." In *The American Heritage Dictionary*, 2d college ed., pp. 32–33. Boston: Houghton Mifflin, 1982.

Burchfield, Robert. *Unlocking the English Language*. New York: Hill and Wang, 1991.

Carver, Craig M. *A History of English in Its Own Words*. New York: Harper Collins, 1991.

Cassidy, Frederic G. *The Dictionary of American Regional English*. Vol. 1. Cambridge: Harvard University Press, 1985.

Cassidy, Frederic G. and Joan Houston Hall. *The Dictionary of American Regional English*. Vol. 2. Cambridge: Harvard University Press, 1991.

Chambers English Dictionary. Catherine Schwarz, George Davidson, Anne Seaton, and Virginia Tebbit, eds. Cambridge: Chambers and Cambridge University Press, 1988.

Chapman, Robert L., ed. *New Dictionary of American Slang*. New York: Harper and Row, 1986.

Chomsky, Noam. *Syntactic Structures*. Janua Linguarum 4. 'S-Gravenhage, The Netherlands: Mouton, 1957.

Claiborne, Robert. *Our Marvelous Native Tongue*. New York: Times Books, 1983.

——. *Saying What You Mean: A Commonsense Guide to American Usage*. New York: Norton, 1986.

Clark, John O. E. *Word Perfect: A Dictionary of Current English Usage*. New York: Holt, 1987.

Clark, Virginia P., Paul A. Eschholz, and Alfred F. Rosa. *Language: Introductory Readings*. 3d ed. New York: St. Martin's Press, 1981.

The Compact Edition of the Oxford English Dictionary. 2 vols. Oxford: Oxford University Press, 1971.

The Compact Edition of the Oxford English Dictionary. Vol. 3 (supps.). R. W. Burchfield, ed. Oxford: Clarendon Press, 1987.

The Concise Oxford Dictionary of Current English. 8th ed. R. E. Allen, ed. Oxford: Clarendon Press, 1990.

Copperud, Roy H. *American Usage and Style: The Consensus*. New York: Van Nostrand Reinhold, 1980.

Craigie, Sir William A. and James R. Hulbert, eds. *A Dictionary of American English on Historical Principles*. Chicago: University of Chicago Press, 1938–44.

Crystal, David. *The Cambridge Encyclopedia of Language*. Cambridge: Cambridge University Press, 1987.

Curme, George O. *Syntax*. Vol. 3 of *A Grammar of the English Language in Three Volumes*. Boston: Heath, 1931.

——. *Parts of Speech and Accidence*. Vol. 2 of *A Grammar of the English Language in Three Volumes*. Boston: Heath, 1935.

Cutts, Martin. "Clear Writing for Lawyers." *English Today* 7, no. 1 (1990): 40–43.

Dean, Leonard F., Walker Gibson, and Kenneth G. Wilson. *The Play of Language*. New York: Oxford University Press, 1971.

Evans, Bergen and Cornelia Evans. *A Dictionary of Contemporary American Usage*. New York: Random House, 1957.

Evans, Ivor H. *Brewer's Dictionary of Phrase and Fable*. Centenary ed., rev. New York: Harper and Row, 1981.

Flexner, Stuart Berg. *Listening to America.* New York: Simon and Schuster, 1982.

Foley, Stephen Merriam and Joseph Wayne Gordon. *Conventions and Choices: A Brief Book of Style and Usage.* Lexington, Mass.: Heath, 1986.

Follett, Wilson. *Modern American Usage.* Jacques Barzun, Carlos Baker, Frederick W. Dupee, Dudley Fitts, James D. Hart, Phyllis McGinley, and Lionel Trilling, eds. New York: Grosset and Dunlap, 1970.

Fowler, H. W. *A Dictionary of Modern English Usage.* Oxford: Oxford University Press, 1926.

——. *A Dictionary of Modern English Usage.* 2d ed. Sir Ernest Gowers, ed. Oxford: Clarendon Press, 1965.

Francis, W. Nelson. "Revolution in Grammar." *Quarterly Journal of Speech* 40 (1954): 299–312.

——. *The Structure of American English.* New York: Ronald Press, 1958.

Frank, Francine Wattman and Paul A. Treichler. *Language, Gender, and Professional Writing: Theoretical Approaches and Guidelines for Nonsexist Usage.* New York: Commission on the Status of Women in the Profession, The Modern Language Association of America, 1989.

Freeman, Morton S. *The Story Behind the Word.* Philadelphia: iSi Press, 1985.

French, Christopher W. *The Associated Press Stylebook and Libel Manual.* New York: Addison-Wesley, 1987.

Fries, Charles Carpenter. *American English Grammar.* New York: Appleton-Century-Crofts, 1940.

——. *The Structure of English.* New York: Harcourt, Brace, 1952.

——. *Linguistics and Reading.* New York: Holt, 1963.

Gleason, H. A., Jr. *An Introduction to Descriptive Linguistics.* Rev. ed. New York: Holt, 1961.

——. *Linguistics and English Grammar.* New York: Holt, 1965.

Gowers, Sir Ernest. *The Complete Plain Words.* Sidney Greenbaum and Janet Whitcut, eds. Boston: Godine, 1988.

Greenbaum, Sidney and Janet Whitcut. *Longman Guide to English Usage.* London: Longman, 1988.

Guidelines on Sexism. N.p.: Prentice-Hall, 1979.

Harris, Zellig S. *Structural Linguistics.* Phoenix Books ed. Chicago: University of Chicago Press, 1951.

Hendrickson, Robert. *The Facts on File Encyclopedia of Word and Phrase Origins.* New York: Facts on File, 1987.

Henley, Nancy and Barrie Thorne. "Sex Differences in Language, Speech, and Nonverbal Communication: An Annotated Bibliography." *Language and Sex: Dominance and Difference.* Rowley, Mass.: Newbury House, 1975.

Howard, Philip. *The State of the Language.* New York: Oxford University Press, 1985.

Hughes, Geoffrey. *Words in Time: A Social History of the English Vocabulary.* New York: Basil Blackwell, 1988.

Jespersen, J. O. H. *A Modern English Grammar on Historical Principles.* Copenhagen: Ejnar Munksgaard, 1909–49.

Joos, Martin. *The Five Clocks.* Bloomington: Indiana University Press, 1962.

——. *The Five Clocks.* New York: Harcourt Brace Jovanovich, 1967.

Key, Mary Ritchie. *Male/Female Language.* Metuchen, N.J.: Scarecrow Press, 1974.

——. "Linguistic Behavior of Male and Female." In Harold B. Allen and Michael D. Linn, eds., *Readings in Applied Linguistics,* 3d ed., pp. 281–93. New York: Knopf, 1982.

Krusinga, Etsko. *A Handbook of Present-Day English.* 4th ed. Utrecht: Kemink en Zoon, 1925.

Lamberts, J. J. *A Short Introduction to English Usage.* New York: McGraw-Hill, 1972.

Lightfoot, David. *The Language Lottery: Toward a Biology of Grammars.* Cambridge: MIT Press, 1982.

Lipton, James. *An Exaltation of Larks; or, The Venereal Game*. New York: Grossman, 1968.

———. *An Exaltation of Larks: The Ultimate Edition*. New York: Viking, 1991.

Los Angeles Times Stylebook: A Manual for Writers, Editors, Journalists, and Students. Frederick S. Holley, ed. New York: New American Library, 1981.

Lutz, William. *Doublespeak*. New York: Harper Collins, 1989.

McCrum, Robert, William Cran, and Robert MacNeil. *The Story of English*. New York: Viking, Elizabeth Sifton Books, 1986.

McDavid, Raven I., Jr. "The Dialects of American English." In W. Nelson Francis, ed. *The Structure of American English*, pp. 480–543. New York: Ronald Press Company, 1958.

McMannus, E. Leo. "A Coordinated President." *English Today* 6, no. 4 (1990): 3–6.

Marckwardt, Albert H. *American English*. 2d ed. J. L. Dillard, ed. New York: Oxford University Press, 1980.

Mathews, Mitford M. *Dictionary of Americanisms on Historical Principles*. 2 vols. Chicago: University of Chicago Press, 1951.

Mellinkoff, David. *The Language of the Law*. Boston: Little, Brown, 1963.

Mencken, H. L. *The American Language*. 4th. ed. New York: Knopf, 1945.

———. *The American Language*. Supp. 1. New York: Knopf, 1945.

———. *The American Language*. Supp. 2. New York: Knopf, 1948.

———. *The American Language*. 4th ed., with 2 supps. Raven I. McDavid, Jr., ed. New York: Knopf, 1963.

———. *The American Language*. 4th ed., with 2 supps. Raven I. McDavid, Jr., ed. New York: Knopf, 1980.

Michaels, Leonard and Christopher Ricks. *The State of the Language*. Berkeley: University of California Press, 1980.

Miller, Casey and Kate Swift. *The Handbook of Nonsexist Writing*. New York: Lippincott and Crowell, 1980.

———. *The Handbook of Nonsexist Writing*. 2d. ed. New York: Harper and Row, 1988.

Montague, Ashley. *The Anatomy of Swearing*. New York: Macmillan, 1967.

Morris, William and Mary Morris. *Dictionary of Word and Phrase Origins*. New York: Harper and Row, 1964.

———. *Harper Dictionary of Contemporary Usage*. 2d ed. New York: Harper and Row, 1985.

Moss, Norman. *British/American Language Dictionary*. Lincolnwood, Ill.: Passport Books, 1984.

Nicholson, Margaret. *A Dictionary of American-English Usage*. New York: Oxford University Press, 1957.

Nilsen, Don L. F. and Alleen Pace Nilsen. *Language Play: An Introduction to Linguistics*. Rowley, Mass.: Newbury House, 1978.

Ogden, C. K. *The System of Basic English*. New York: Harcourt, Brace, 1934.

Orwell, George. *Animal Farm*. New York: Harcourt Brace Jovanovich, 1946.

Oxford American Dictionary. Eugene Ehrlich, Stuart Berg Flexner, Gorton Carruth, and Joyce M. Hawkins, eds. New York: Oxford University Press, 1980.

An Oxford Anthology of English Poetry. Howard Foster Lowry and Willard Thorp, eds. New York: Oxford University Press, 1935.

The Oxford English Dictionary. 2d ed. 20 vols. J. A. Simpson and E. S. C. Weiner, eds. Oxford: Clarendon Press, 1989.

The Oxford Guide to the English Language. New York: Oxford University Press, 1984.

Partridge, Eric. *A Dictionary of Clichés*. New York: Dutton [1947], 1963.

———. *Usage and Abusage*. Harmondsworth, Middlesex: Penguin Reference Books, 1963.

———. *A Dictionary of Slang and Unconventional English*. 8th ed. Paul Beale, ed. New York: Macmillan, 1984.

Pence, R. W. and D. W. Emery. *A Grammar of Present-Day English.* 2d ed. New York: Macmillan, 1963.

Pooley, Robert C. *The Teaching of English Usage.* 2d ed. Urbana, Ill.: National Council of Teachers of English, 1974.

Poutsma, Hendrik. *A Grammar of Late Modern English.* 2d ed. Groningen: Nordhoff, 1914–29.

Pyles, Thomas and John Algeo. *The Origins and Development of the English Language.* 3d ed. New York: Harcourt Brace Jovanovich, 1982.

Randall, Bernice. *Webster's New World Guide to Current American Usage.* New York: Webster's New World, 1988.

The Random House College Dictionary. Rev. ed. Jess Stein, ed. New York: Random House, 1980.

The Random House Dictionary of the English Language. Jess Stein, ed. New York: Random House, 1966.

The Random House Dictionary of the English Language. 2d ed. Stuart Berg Flexner, ed. New York: Random House, 1987.

Random House Webster's College Dictionary. New York: Random House, 1991.

Rawson, Hugh. *Wicked Words.* New York: Crown, 1989.

Reader's Digest. *Success with Words.* Peter Davies, ed. Pleasantville, N.Y.: Reader's Digest Association, 1983.

Redfern, Walter. *Clichés and Coinages.* Oxford: Basil Blackwell, 1989.

Richards, I. A. *Basic English and Its Uses.* London: Kegan, Paul, Trench, Trubner, 1943.

Roget's International Thesaurus. 5th ed. Robert L. Chapman, ed. New York: Harper Collins, 1992.

Roget's II: The New Thesaurus. Expanded ed. Boston: Houghton Mifflin, 1988.

Safire, William. *On Language.* New York: Times Books, 1980.

——. *What's the Good Word?* New York: Times Books, 1982.

——. *Fumblerules.* New York: Doubleday, 1990.

Shakespeare, William. *The Works of William Shakespeare.* Vol. 2. William Aldis Wright, ed. New York: AMS Press, 1968.

Sledd, James. *A Short Introduction to English Grammar.* Chicago: Scott, Foresman, 1959.

Sledd, James and Wilma R. Ebbitt. *Dictionaries and THAT Dictionary.* Chicago: Scott, Foresman, 1962.

Sperling, Susan Kelz. *Poplollies and Bellibones: A Celebration of Lost Words.* New York: Penguin, 1977.

Stevens, William K. "Study Finds Blacks' English Increasingly Different." *New York Times,* March 15, 1985, A14.

——. "Stronger Urban Accents in Northeast Are Called Sign of Evolving Language." *New York Times,* July 21, 1985, A36.

Stookey, Lawrence Hull. *The Use of Inclusive Language in the Worship of the Church.* Washington, D.C.: Wesley Theological Seminary, 1982.

Strunk, William, Jr. *The Elements of Style.* 3d ed., rev. E. B. White, ed. New York: Macmillan, 1979.

Todd, Loreto and Ian Hancock. *International English Usage.* New York: New York University Press, 1987.

Trager, George L. and Henry Lee Smith, Jr. *An Outline of English Structure.* Washington: American Council of Learned Societies, 1957.

Urdang, Laurence. *The Oxford Thesaurus.* U.S. ed. New York: Oxford University Press, 1992.

Veblen, Thorstein. *The Theory of the Leisure Class.* New York: B. W. Huebsch [1899], 1922.

VIGILANS [pseud.]. *Chamber of Horrors.* New York: British Book Centre, 1952.

Watt, William W. *A Short Guide to English Usage*. Cleveland: World Publishing, 1967.

Webster's Dictionary of English Usage. Springfield, Mass.: Merriam-Webster, 1989.

Webster's New Dictionary of Synonyms. Springfield, Mass.: Merriam-Webster, 1978.

Webster's New World Dictionary of American English. Victoria Neufeldt and David B. Guralnik, eds. 3d college ed. New York: Simon and Schuster, 1988.

Webster's Ninth New Collegiate Dictionary. Frederick C. Mish, ed. Springfield, Mass.: Merriam-Webster, 1983.

Webster's Third New International Dictionary of the English Language Unabridged. Philip B. Gove, ed. Springfield, Mass.: Merriam-Webster, 1961.

Whitney, William Dwight. *The Century Dictionary and Cyclopedia*. 10 vols. New York: Century Company, 1902.

Wilson, Kenneth G. "The History of the English Language." In Albert H. Marckwardt, ed., *Linguistics in School Programs: The Sixty-Ninth Yearbook of the National Society for the Study of Education*, Part 2, pp. 109–32. Chicago: National Society for the Study of Education, 1970.

——. "English Grammars and the Grammar of English." In Leonard F. Dean, Walker Gibson, and Kenneth G. Wilson, eds., *The Play of Language*, pp. 102–25. New York: Oxford University Press, 1971.

——. *Van Winkle's Return: Change in American English, 1966–1986*. Hanover, N.H.: University Presses of New England for the University of Connecticut, 1987.

Wilson, Kenneth G., R. H. Hendrickson, and Peter Alan Taylor. *Harbrace Guide to Dictionaries*. New York: Harcourt, Brace and World, 1963.

Zandvoort, R. W. *A Handbook of English Grammar*. London: Longmans, 1957.